WOMEN IN ENGLISH SOCIAL HISTORY
1800–1914
A Guide to Research

Barbara Kanner

in three volumes
Volume II

GARLAND PUBLISHING, INC. • NEW YORK & LONDON
1988

Library of Congress Cataloging-in-Publication Data
(Revised for vol. 2)

Kanner, Barbara
Women in English social history, 1800-1914.

(Garland reference library of social science; vol. 409)
Includes indexes.
Contents: —v. 2. [without special title]—
v. 3. Autobiographical writings.
1. Women—England—History—19th century—Sources—
Bibliography. 2. Women—England—Diaries—Bibliography.
3. Autobiography—Women authors—Bibliography.
I. Title. II. Series:Garland reference library of
social science; v. 409.

Z7964.G7K36 1987 016.3054'0942 82–49189
[HQ1593] ISBN 0–8240–9168–X (v. 3 : alk. paper)

Cover design by Alison Lew

Printed on acid-free, 250-year-life paper
Manufactured in the United States of America

Volume II
CONTENTS

IX. CRIME AND DEVIANCE

X. SEXUAL ISSUES

Women in English Social History
1800–1914

Volume II

VII. THE EXPANSION OF EMPLOYMENT

*INTRODUCTION**

The historiography of women's employment in nineteenth- and early twentieth-century England is represented by an enormous quantity and variety of literature written from the late eighteenth century. Before the Victorian era introduced official commissions of inquiry philanthropists, journalists, government investigators, local administrators, politicians, their agents, and others "toured" heavily populated districts to study and report on the social impact of economic change said to be consequent upon industrialization. Their initial interest was the factory system. Mining areas drew their subsequent attention. The reports were published as books for general readership, and at least some aspects were incorporated into government documents. Both kinds of texts brought vivid scenes of working life and social conditions to an audience that included reformers. The facts were of course colored by the attitudes and motivations of the investigators whose writings influenced social attitudes, public policy, national prejudice and governmental legislation. The early Factory Acts of 1802, 1819, 1825, 1831, 1833 and 1844 regulated hours of work for women and children and attempted to legislate against unhealthy, unsanitary and exploitive working conditions. The unconventional activity of numerous factory women, far from home, struck a number of the reporters as immoral and unnatural. In their comparisons with patterns of the past they tended to rely upon the notion of a pre-industrial golden age dominated by a stable domestic and family economy. Thus, descriptions of social change often ignored practical, provable contexts of older local traditions and popular customs, many of which were actually continuing. The reports found their way into parliamentary Blue-books as well as into popular writings. These included portrayals of the new industrial system as negatively affecting the life, the work and the character of working women. The characterizations of factory women threatened contemporary feminine ideology by either associating female wage earners with promiscuity or showing them at death's door from overwork. Thus Victorian attitudes toward the employment of women had been negatively encoded early in the industrial era. For valuable discussions of this question see, for example:

7.1int
Neff, Wanda F., **VICTORIAN WORKING WOMEN: AN HISTORICAL AND LITERARY STUDY OF WOMEN IN BRITISH INDUSTRIES AND PROFESSIONS, 1832-1850**. New York, 1929; 1969. Neff employs books of the social investigators, government documents and contemporary fiction.

7.2int
McKendrick, Neil, "Home Demand and Economic Growth: A New View of the

Role of Women and Children in the Industrial Revolution" in **HISTORICAL PERSPECTIVES: STUDIES IN ENGLISH THOUGHT AND SOCIETY.** ed. by Neil McKendrick. 1974. See especially pp. 162-170. McKendrick also discusses the financial contributions of the women and children to family income related to increasing consumerism, a neglected consideration in economic history.

7.3int
Rule, John, "The Family" in **THE LABOURING CLASSES IN EARLY INDUS-TRIAL ENGLAND, 1750-1850.** 1986. Rule is particularly interested in the reportage of Peter Gaskell. The chapter is a useful synthesis.

7.4int
NINETEENTH CENTURY FICTION: Kovacevic, I. and Kanner, B., *"Blue Book into Novel: the Forgotten Industrial Fiction of Charlotte Elizabeth Tonna,"* 25 (1970) 152-173. Tonna's didactic tales portray the "evils" of industrialization mainly through female characters who are overworked and underpayed often to the point of starvation. Families are either destroyed or demoralized. The stories were serialized in CHRISTIAN LADY'S MAGAZINE during the late 1830s and early 1840s. They assisted, as propaganda, for the factory reform movement led by Lord Ashley (later Shaftesbury).

The reports of late eighteenth- and early nineteenth-century investigative writers, then, are valuable sources in any reconstruction of the social and laboring life of the period. Among the most noteworthy investigators were:

7.5int
Eden, Frederic Morton, **THE STATE OF THE POOR; OR, A HISTORY OF THE LABOURING CLASSES IN ENGLAND.** 3 vols. 1797; ed. by A.G.L. Rogers, 1928; 1966; 1969. In his multidimensional survey of socioeconomic life, Eden pauses to criticize spendthrift tendencies of poor workers and their indulgence in unnecessary "luxuries" and "fripperies."

7.6int
Kay, James Phillip (later Kay-Shuttleworth), **THE MORAL AND PHYSICAL CONDITION OF THE WORKING CLASSES EMPLOYED IN THE COTTON MANUFACTURE IN MANCHESTER.** 1832. A known moralist, Kay perceives factory women as responsible for the degeneration of living standards in their districts and criticizes their ignorance of household skills.

7.7int
Gaskell, Peter, **THE MANUFACTURING POPULATION OF ENGLAND.** 1833; **ARTISANS AND MACHINERY: THE MORAL AND PHYSICAL CONDITION OF THE MANUFACTURING POPULATION.** 1836; 1968. Describes unsanitary conditions at factories and renders scenes of sleeping-rooms used indiscriminately for both sexes (chapter 5). He writes scornfully of a general looseness in morals which is confirmed, he says, by the number of illegitimate children found in the mills. Gaskell ignores existing evidence of contemporary trends to illegitimacy.

7.8int
Ure, Andrew, **THE PHILOSOPHY OF MANUFACTURES.** 2 vols. 1835. Alarmed at finding that in some factories women workers outnumbered the men, Ure explains how the introduction of machinery allowed unskilled women and children to replace the more qualified masculine workforce. Ure seems to relish that women's wages were less than half of what had been paid the men. He seems to suggest that the low female wage scale was in retribution for having "abandoned"

their children at home (p. 475).

7.9int
Engels, Frederick, **CONDITION OF THE WORKING CLASS IN ENGLAND.** 1844;
1969. On the question of morals, Engels concludes that three-fourths of the factory
hands between fourteen and twenty years old were "unchaste." He writes of the
damage to pride of male breadwinners as wives and children "destroyed" their status
as providers. Engels remarks that it "unsexes the man and takes from the woman all
womanliness... [and] degrades, in the most shameful way, both sexes, and through
them, Humanity is the last result of our much-praised civilization" (p. 172 in 1969
ed.).

Historians have found great value in these sources not only because of their factual
detail but because they mirror the thought and social context of the period in ᵥhich
they were written. Making full use of them for her classic reconstruction of female
work experience is:

7.10int
Pinchbeck, Ivy, **WOMEN WORKERS AND THE INDUSTRIAL REVOLUTION,
1750-1850.** 1930; 1929; 1966; rpt. with introduction by Kerry Hamilton. 1981.

Pinchbeck's study is unequaled for the scope of design, the range of evidence and
the methodology. She also stands unrivaled for the extent of the sources she
employed. Besides books of contemporary investigators and government documents,
Pinchbeck consulted countless publications: local newspapers, pamphlets, periodicals
and their advertisements. She explored and compared the relevant social histories,
reports of societies, and handbooks of various trades. Local archives yielded court
records and reports of administrators and officials. Guild records are included.
Personal papers, journals and overseers' accounts are not neglected. And
Pinchbeck's vantage point is that of the workers themselves as they responded to
new conditions as well as personal and family imperatives. Pinchbeck weighed new
industrial occupations for women against the work they continued from the past.
Her research reveals that women wage earners existed in larger numbers before the
industrial revolution than had been generally supposed. Incredible pressures from
constantly changing circumstances tended to alter domestic life as well as work.
These unfolded differently in the various districts where industrial experimentation
was brought to bear on the local culture and social patterns. Not the least of the
disrupting changes in some regions was the separation of home and workplace, and
the necessity for many women to be productive in both. Pinchbeck has been
criticized by some historians for her optimistic long-run appraisal that women
ultimately gained back more than they lost when industrialization turned them into
either dependent wage earners or isolated and dependent housewives. But the study
itself has proven mainly reliable and worth emulating.

Taking a more pessimistic view of the long-run impact of industrialization on the
position of women is another work of extraordinary scholarship,

7.11int
Clark, Alice, **WORKING LIFE OF WOMEN IN THE SEVENTEENTH CENTURY.**
1919; 1968; rpt. with introduction by Miranda Chaytor and Jane Lewis. 1982.

Clark develops evidence that women were more active in industry in the
seventeenth century than in the first decade of the twentieth. Family and domestic
industry had allowed them richer lives, more spiritual satisfaction, and better

welfare of their children. "Though now it is taken for granted that domestic work will be done by women," says Clark, "a considerable proportion of it in former days fell to the share of men" which made for more equitable relationships (p. 5). Clark also insists that the dual identity as mother and producer offered greater rewards than work away from home for wages (p. 304 in 1982 ed.). Besides, when women undertook waged employment in crafts and trades, they worked in jobs that were subordinated to those of men who were also given a much higher rate of pay. As for the early professions—nursing, medicine and midwifery—Clark concludes that "women's position in the arts of teaching and healing [was] lost as these arts became professional" (p. 237, 1982 ed.). The loss of productivity, economic standing, and occupational status under the industrial system progressed through the next century.

Clark's view of the effect of industrialization on the lives and employment of English women workers has provided a model of social development that is still debated by historians. In simplified outline her thesis conveys that industrialization separated home and workplace wherein the household lost its function as the basic productive unit for trade or market. In a factory, mill or workshop distant from home the sexual division of labor hardened along lines of gender as compared with home industry. The work of men became identified with securing the family income, so that wife and children became dependents. The old duality of married women's work—industrial partner and wife/mother—gave way to the primacy of the domestic role. If circumstances brought her into industry, (and perhaps her children as well), she experienced low status and low pay. Single women who entered waged employment were also regarded as unskilled and marginal. It was anticipated that they would work temporarily—until marriage. Unprotected by the home environment, working women's morals were suspect. The notion of a division between private and public spheres developed in contrast to the traditionally blurred or interchangeable vision of home and workplace. Men's productive work became increasingly identified with the public sphere while women became associated with the private. This restricted women's social position *vis-a-vis* society and the state. Men's higher public status enhanced their patriarchal authority at home. This development provided precedent for the patterns and beliefs so closely associated with the Victorian age.

A very useful discussion of how historians have dealt with the paradigm of the split between home and work and its effect on English women's roles and social position is:

7.12int
INTERNATIONAL JOURNAL OF WOMEN'S STUDIES: Cohen, M., *"Changing Perceptions of the Impact of the Industrial Revolution on Female Labour,"* 7 (1984) 291-305. Besides the theses of Clark and Pinchbeck, Cohen discusses the arguments of:

7.13int
Engels, Frederick, **ORIGINS OF THE FAMILY, PRIVATE PROPERTY AND THE STATE.** 1884; subsequent eds. Engels sees industrialization in terms of drastic changes in family relationships, reduction of moral standards, and as turning private domestic labor into public industry. He observes that women as wage earners gained opportunities for "emancipation" from dependence upon family, but he is critical because this posed threats to male prerogatives.

7.14int
Tilly, Louise A. and Scott, Joan W., **WOMEN, WORK AND FAMILY.** New York,

1978. Tilly and Scott challenge the thesis of radical change in family structure and in women's labor because of industrialization. They posit considerable *continuity* from the past in women's work. It was the *pattern* of women's employment that changed: where it could take place and under what conditions. As previously, women's work remained subservient to that of men's, and industrialization not only perpetuated the sexual division of labor, it intensified it. Tilly and Scott posit a U-shaped pattern for women's productive activity which reached a high level in pre-industrial domestic economy, then declined with the industrial system, rising again well into the twentieth century.

7.15int
SOCIAL HISTORY: Medick, H., *"The Proto-Industrial Family Economy: The Structural Function of Household and Family During the Transition from Peasant Society to Industrial Capitalism,"* no. 3 (1976) 291-315. Medick finds an early point in the industrialization process where important changes in the division of labor by sex were instituted domestically in an effort to retain the family type of economy. This included enhancement of the importance of women's work.

7.16int
Rowbotham, Sheila, **HIDDEN FROM HISTORY: 300 YEARS OF WOMEN'S OPPRESSION AND THE FIGHT AGAINST IT.** 1977. Rowbotham considers the emergence of "middle-class" women who were deprived of their previous economic functions and had to become increasingly dependent upon male support. Working-class women were not necessarily an advantaged group, however, because they had to perform both domestic and employment responsibilities.

7.17int
Oakley, Ann, **WOMEN'S WORK. THE HOUSEWIFE PAST AND PRESENT.** 1976. Oakley follows Clark's view rather closely, but gives closer attention to married women who were restricted from performing their traditional work outside the home. The belief in women's "natural domesticity" gained popularity and it became a very significant thought product of industrialization, says Oakley. This in effect institutionalized in the concept of "housewife."

7.18int
Alexander, Sally, **WOMEN'S WORK IN NINETEENTH-CENTURY LONDON: A STUDY OF THE YEARS 1820-1850.** 1982; *rpt. from:* **THE RIGHTS AND WRONGS OF WOMEN.** ed. by Juliet Mitchell and Ann Oakley. 1976. Alexander produces evidence that, at least in the city of London in the nineteenth century, the U-shaped pattern of female industrial employment cannot be made to apply. For example, the trades of London continued to admit married women. These women worked on many bases, and not always steadily. They were very difficult to count among the employed so that the Census Returns often omitted them.

The Victorians conventionalized the sexual division of labor in working life just as they continued to uphold a public-private split in the personal sphere. By the mid-nineteenth and early twentieth centuries categories of employment were prescribed according to sex and class, and also horizontally within classes. By the 1850s journalists and investigators of social questions could assume that their readers understood the nuances of "ranks" among the wage-earning population. For example, there is the valuable survey analyzing women's status in relation to available and potential employment:

7.19int

Milne, John Duguid, **INDUSTRIAL EMPLOYMENT OF WOMEN IN THE MIDDLE AND LOWER RANKS.** 1857; rev. ed., 1870; rpt., New York, 1984. Milne demonstrates the importance of comprehending how the different occupations were suitable according to differential social standing:

> We have drawn a contrast in several particulars between the position of women in the better grades of the working classes, and the position of women in the middle classes;.... [We now turn to] the industrial position of women in the working classes [and] an analysis of the branches of industry to which women in these ranks have been admitted——pointing out shortly the leading circumstances affecting each occupation; and thereafter we will notice specially the more formidable agencies that in the working ranks depress the condition of the female sex——competition with the valueless time of women in the middle ranks——and restriction, within the working ranks themselves, to the menial and worst paid occupations (p. 166).

Milne gives official population figures for categories of employment which he identifies as appropriate to the different social strata. He provides supplementary statistical tables derived from the 1851 census, and offers explanations of the social gradations of female wage earners. For example, in the section on commercial undertakings, Milne advises, "The people comprised in this table stand midway between the middle ranks and the working ranks; and the list will be largely swelled when the time comes for a larger admission to industry of women of the middle ranks" (p. 176). On other data about the wives of male entrepreneurs, he explains that the census compilers had been made sensitive to the view that in lower commercial classes the connotation of wives of tradesmen "means that 'wife' takes... an active part in the business of her husband——a supposition inconsistent, on the one hand, with the present arrangements of the middle classes, where a wife takes no part whatever in the business-affairs of her husband, and on the other hand showing that women of [the lower rank]... have... some preparation enabling them on the loss of their husbands to carry on business on their own account" (p. 177).

The first edition of Milne's book was warmly welcomed in reviews, especially that of Harriet Martineau who discusses it in conjunction with other publications that focused on the broad question of women's employment:

7.20int

EDINBURGH REVIEW: Martineau, H., *"Female Industry,"* 109 (1859) 293-336. Martineau, journalist, feminist and author on political economy, works her own ideas into her discussion of ten recent publications, including Milne's. First she deals with Edward Cheshire, **THE RESULTS OF THE CENSUS OF GREAT BRITAIN IN 1851.** 1853. She responds to the "hard facts" about "the conditions of female life," especially that "a very large proportion of the women of England earn their own bread." Therefore it is "false," she says, "that every woman is supported (as the law supposes her to be represented) by her father, her brother, or her husband" (pp. 296-297). Martineau surveys the specific occupations mentioned by the authors under review in a tone that borders on exhortation: women of all classes should consider the employments for themselves, or to give assistance to others. But Martineau anticipates resistance to feminine ambition. She envisions it in the form of "difficulties created by the jealousy of men in regard to the industrial independence of women.... The same jealousy [that] cost many lives in the late war, by delaying the reception of the nurses into the hospitals in the East" (pp. 329-330). More women are at work and more need work than is generally known, says Martineau. According to official reports, "more than one third, more than two millions, are independent in their industry, are self-supporting, like men" (p. 335). Many others "appeal to us to aid them in obtaining free scope for their industry.... Old obstructions must be removed; and the aim must be set before us... to provide for the free development and full use of the powers of every member of the community" (p. 336).

Also involved with promoting the expansion of women's employment was the newly-founded feminist journal that regularly published articles evaluating women's status, enumerated its pressing problems, and published the following exemplary articles:

7.21int
ENGLISH WOMAN'S JOURNAL: *"Statistics as to the Employment of the Female Population of Great Britain,"* 5 (1860) 1-6. Calls attention to "an important controversy [that] has recently been raised... respecting the industrial employment of females." The topical question pertains to married working women:

> The opposing party in the controversy assert that.... [females] are subject to a natural disqualification for industrial labor, inasmuch as their proper and peculiar business, trade, and profession are——to get married and manage a house and family; all who fail in this enterprise being in the position of bankrupt traders who fail in their respective pursuits. It is therefore urged that all married females should confine themselves to the domestic duties.... Existing practice, then, is not in accordance with the theory... [for] a great portion of our married female population find it consistent, or make it compatible... to devote a considerable portion of their time to remunerative employment in the various trades and manufactures. The actual number of wives returned as employed in 1851, was in round numbers, 780,000 out of 3,460,000 wives; and that no doubt was an under-statement (p. 2).

7.22int
ENGLISH WOMAN'S JOURNAL: *"What Are Women Doing?"* 7 (1861) 51-53.

On employed middle-class women:

> For our present purpose, we may be allowed to include under one general heading all who, though varying in degree, are by education and position in a sphere above that from which our domestic servants are taken. This large section embraces in its ranks authors and able editors, actresses, professional singers, painters, sculptors; milliners, dressmakers, hairdressers and artists of hair; law-copyists, telegraph clerks, postmistresses; lodging-house keepers, innkeepers, shopkeepers of various kinds, and saleswomen; last, but not the least, the great army of teachers, from the ragged-school mistress up to the highly-educated and accomplished governess. This class also includes a very few managers of manufactories (p. 52).

Regarding "the lowest grade, and here the variety of work is greater than in any other class":

> There is one notable fact which ought not to be overlooked; namely, that whatever mill, yard, factory or workshop you enter, you will find the women in the lowest, the dirtiest, and the unhealthiest departments. The reason is simple. The manager of a business naturally asks who will do the inferior work at the lowest rate, and as women's labor is the cheapest, it falls as a matter of course to their share. It is an undeniable fact that in this

country a very large proportion of the hard labor is done by women....
Marriage and domestic service are not a sufficient outlet for the whole of
the female portion of the poorer classes; and there seems little reason to
expect that there will be any material alteration in this respect.... [Those]
who do not belong to what are called the working classes... are willing, but
the narrowness of the field of industry open to them not only lowers the
market value of their work, but in many cases obliges them to employ
themselves in modes of occupation unsuited to their particular tastes and
abilities.... It cannot be right that the higher kinds of work... should be
exclusively appropriated by men (p. 53).

The poor conditions that attended most employments of working-class women were
well known. When the difficulties facing middle-class women were exposed, the
revelations were said to be "startling." For, despite the picture of opportunity
suggested by the ENGLISH WOMAN'S JOURNAL, many middle-class women were
working in "unsuitable trades" but not reporting it out of fear of losing social status
or acceptance. Others were impoverished and seeking assistance. That many or most
middle-class women were ill-prepared by education or training for remunerative
occupations was becoming a topical subject. In any event, the number of
successfully employed middle-class single women constituted a comparatively small
minority until perhaps the turn of the century. Some probably carved out their own
occupational niche, but the phenomenon is largely unrecorded. On the plight of
impoverished, single, middle-class, independent women, social reformer Boyd-
Kinnear wrote a lengthy appeal: Victorians should change the predominant attitudes
against the employment of middle-class ladies. The needs of these women were very
real: "The movement and stir among women is not gratuitous, but is urged by the
iron law of necessity" (p. 336). See the important paper,

7.23int
Boyd-Kinnear, John, "The Social Position of Women in the Present Age" in
WOMEN'S WORK AND WOMEN'S CULTURE. ed. by Josephine Butler. 1869.

The most detailed account of middle-class women's employment to date is:

7.24int
Holcombe, Lee, **VICTORIAN LADIES AT WORK: MIDDLE-CLASS WORKING
WOMEN IN ENGLAND AND WALES**. Hamden, Conn., 1973. Taking each
occupation in turn, Holcombe traces the development of teaching, nursing,
distributive trades, clerical occupations and the civil service. She concludes that "in
the mid-nineteenth century ladies who had to work for their living were a surplus
and depressed minority, who were pitied and who pitied themselves. By 1914
middle-class working women, a respected and self-respecting group, were an
essential part of the country's labour force" (p. 20).

Economic historian Eric Richards studies the underemployment of Victorian
women, concluding, "It is a curious thing that the unfettered capitalist economy—
in the full flood of industrialism in the mid-19th century——should have utilized a
principal supply of labor [women] in so modest a fashion" (p. 338). This is:

7.25int
HISTORY: Richards, E., *"Women in the British Economy Since About 1700: An
Interpretation,"* 59 (1974) 337-357; *rpt. in:* **THE WOMAN QUESTION**. ed. by Mary

Evans. 1982. Richards says that, in seeking the determinants of women's economic roles and the transformations in the functions of women in the economy it is important to study the "framework of occupations," the "changes in the structure of the economy" and the "social mores [which] have powerfully reinforced trends." Still important are the factors of "the impact of government policy" and "feminist agitation" (p. 356). "The behavior of the female labor market is complex, and warrants special modes of analysis. The economic history of women is a neglected field... much more research is indispensable" (p. 356).

Considering women's employment in numerical terms, the figures gathered from 1851-1911 Census data indicate the following picture: In 1851 the number of occupied females of all ages in Great Britain was (in thousands) 2,832 out of a total female population of 9,146. In 1881, 3,887 were occupied out of 13,335. In 1911, 5,413 were occupied out of 18,625. The highest rates of concentration were in the occupational categories: Domestic Offices and Personal Services (Domestic Service), Textiles, and Clothing. These and other data are tabulated from the official Census Returns and evaluated for their possible inaccuracy by

7.26int
John, Angela V., ed., **UNEQUAL OPPORTUNITIES: WOMEN'S EMPLOYMENT IN ENGLAND, 1800-1918.** 1985. pp. 36-41.

Along with other historians studying women's occupational activity in the period 1800-1970, John is convinced that much of women's employment escaped the census-taking process:

> Census returns severely under-represent the number of 'occupied' females over ten during the period just as the 'unoccupied' category (5,192,000 in 1851 and 11,432,000 by 1911) camouflages the actuality and fluctuations of work. For example, many women did seasonal jobs such as helping in the grain harvest. As the Census was usually taken in March or April this work would have been missed.... Many women worked in family businesses yet were not recorded as being in active employment.... It is even possible that as many as one-third of all women workers were not counted in occupational categories (pp. 36-37).

7.27int
Lewis, Jane, **WOMEN IN ENGLAND, 1870-1950: SEXUAL DIVISIONS AND SOCIAL CHANGE.** 1984.

> A literally incalculable number of wives, ex-wives, widows and children were also engaged in casual work which is not recorded by the census.... A substantial number of women in the late nineteenth and early twentieth centuries were homeworkers engaged in a wide variety of tasks, including the making of matchboxes, shirts, artificial flowers, umbrellas, brushes, carding buttons, furpulling, bending safety pins and covering tennis balls.... The 1908 Select Committee did not, however, include a discussion of these workers in its report on homework (p. 55).

Perhaps an even greater handicap in dealing with data is that the categories of types of employment were revised from census to census. For a very useful discussion of this problem, (one that has plagued social investigators since the last century), see:

7.28int

SOCIOLOGICAL REVIEW: Hakim, C., *"Census Reports as Documentary Evidence: The Census Commentaries, 1801-1951,"* 28 (1980) 551-580.

Social historians repeatedly note that the separation of home and workplace that came about with the industrial revolution led to the exclusion of women from the formal labor market. This process of social change is reflected both in the way census information was compiled, and in the resulting statistics.... Until recently, little attention has been paid to the way that changes in definition and classification reflect changing perceptions and organization of work.... The 1841 Census recorded the occupations of individuals, and showed a large difference between the economic activity rates of men and women.... [It] accounts for the large number of women aged over 20, without any occupation as being unmarried women living with parents, and [it records] wives... living on the earnings but not considered as carrying on the occupations of their husbands. Thus some family labor was excluded and some family workers... were included in the count of the working population. The decision to exclude unpaid family workers was reversed in the 1851 Census, and women engaged in domestic duties were recorded in the Fifth Class of occupations rather than among the inactive, as in 1841.... The Census of 1861... states... that 'the occupation of wife and mother and housewife is the most important in the country'.... and [they] were returned as occupied.... By the 1881 Census unpaid household work was excluded from the definition of economic activity (pp. 555-556).

These changes in the organization of the census data represent but a few of many possible examples of the complicated process of recording, reporting and interpreting. Contemporary critiques of the statistics that are enlightening about these and other census difficulties are:

7.29int

JOURNAL OF THE ROYAL STATISTICAL SOCIETY: Collet, Clara E., *"The Collection and Utilization of Official Statistics Bearing on the Extent and Effects of the Industrial Employment of Women,"* 61 (1898) 219-260. Extremely valuable article; not only for the data, but for Collet's comments on the types of occupations women pursued and how these fared with changes in the economy. One such category is women as employers, not only in inherited businesses, but also in the "really most important section"—that of "dressmaking, millinery, mantle and corset making trades." These needle trades, which are represented in factories, workshops, sweated and home industries as well as in shops and services, all have employers. To identify the women there is a need for a clearer definition of "employed" as well as "employer" (p. 227).

7.30int

Mackeson, Charles, "Occupations and Vital Statistics of England and Wales" in **THE BRITISH ALMANAC AND COMPANION.** 1875. Very useful commentary.

7.31int

JOURNAL OF THE STATISTICAL SOCIETY: Booth, C., *"Occupations of the People of the United Kingdom, 1801-1881,"* 49 (1886) 314-435. (Later, JOURNAL OF THE ROYAL STATISTICAL SOCIETY.) Booth begins with a discussion, "General Review of Occupation Censuses,"which concerns the general principles of organization from 1811. His explanations of the statistical tables include indications of trends in comparative contexts. It is clear that any meaningful statistical survey of women's occupational status and its change over time must be studied in comparison with similar data for men, and for the population as a whole. Supplementing Booth's article is a section, "Discussion of Mr. Booth's Paper." This raises questions and also stimulates thinking about additional ramifications.

The questions raised about this numerical record cast considerable doubt upon the accuracy of what has been the conventional wisdom about Victorian and Edwardian women's productivity——at least as it has been derived from the nineteenth-century census data. The question of how a revision of the statistics upward might change the history of women in the English economy has not been treated by historians.

There are a great many writings that explain that there was a surplus of women applicants for employment as compared with the amount of work available, and how this surplus reflects the "overplus" of the female population to the male in general. This situation helped to keep up high competition for work and wages, as well as to keep conditions of labor disastrously low. The anxiety about staying employed played a large role in inhibiting working women from agitating for improvements in their situation and from organizing to pressure employers for better terms. Thus the population of female workers comprised a source of "cheap labor," an entity which, especially in the early and middle years of the nineteenth century, combined with other prejudices against women in the labor market to alienate the majority of working-class men. Particular anathema against married working women developed, for example, when Victorian values toward family and eugenicist ideas about race improvement of children through better motherhood were embraced by the working classes.

These questions and many more brought social reformers into fields of private and official inquiry and pressure-group activity on behalf of women. The National Association for the Promotion of Social Science, founded in 1857 to promote investigation and legislation for social problems, is an example of a group that addressed issues pertaining to working women. It included educated middle-class women among its membership and thereby provided a base and a valid organizational identity for the unpaid participation of these veritable social workers. Aside from charitable societies, these women formed leagues and associations for assistance to women waged workers. The publications by and about these groups brought attention to the range of their activity, and also provided legitimacy for their enterprises among the public. Despite considerable source material about these groups, memberships, and leadership there is surprisingly little in-depth modern scholarship about their work. Whatever the ultimate evaluation of their accomplishment may be in terms of social and economic change, there is little doubt about their impact upon a considerable number of Victorian and Edwardian women. A fine beginning toward filling the scholarly gap is the work of:

7.32int
Mappen, Ellen, "Women Workers and Unemployment Policy in Late Victorian and Edwardian London," Ph.D. diss., Rutgers Univ., 1977. Particularly Chapter 2, "Interest in and Investigation Into Women's Work in the Late Nineteenth Century." Mappen discusses the investigations of the women engaged by Charles Booth in his massive inquiries, and also the work of the first women appointed to official commissions and inspectorates by the government.

7.33int
Mappen, Ellen, "New Introduction" to **MARRIED WOMEN'S WORK** rpt. of the 1915 edition, ed. by Clementina Black. 1983. Black was a founding member and later President of the Women's Industrial Council and Vice-President of the Anti-

Sweating League in addition to following a prolific writing career and other activities. Mappen identifies Black within a wide-ranging network of women committed to ameliorating women's position in society, and who maintained that women had a role in public life even if they did not have the parliamentary vote. Black claimed that women could and should create and implement public policy, particularly as it affects other women and their families. Connecting social reform with obtaining women's rights, says Mappen, these women may be called "social feminists" (p. ii). Among the organizations they formed are: Women's Industrial Council; Women's Cooperative Guild; Women's Labour League; and the Fabian Women's Group.

7.34int
Mappen, Ellen, "Introduction" to **HELPING WOMEN AT WORK: THE WOMEN'S INDUSTRIAL COUNCIL, 1889-1914.** 1985. "The WIC became a center for social feminist commitment during the Edwardian years... Its members formed a pressure group to influence public opinion and to overcome what was later called 'masculine indifference to women's interests' through social reform methods" (p. 12).

7.35int
Mappen, Ellen, "Strategists for Change: Social Feminist Approaches to the Problems of Women's Work" in **UNEQUAL OPPORTUNITIES: WOMEN'S EMPLOYMENT IN ENGLAND, 1800-1918.** 1986. "While some of the leaders were, or had been, active in forming trade unions for women, the consensus was that trade unionism alone could not ameliorate working and living conditions" (p. 235).

For a recent survey of inter-class organizational activity for reform of working women's conditions, unionization and protective legislation see:

7.36int
Rubinstein, David, **BEFORE THE SUFFRAGETTES: WOMEN'S EMANCIPATION IN THE 1890S.** 1986. In "Women in Industry" Rubinstein provocatively observes, "The barriers between women of different social classes inhibited the development of gender solidarity, despite the sympathetic contribution to trade unionism and the amelioration of working conditions made by a not inconsiderable number of middle-class women" (p. 94). This is a theme that might well be explored parallel to Mappen's.

There are few modern biographies of the committed women reformers, investigators and officials who participated in nineteenth- and early twentieth-century women's labor movements. Some of the older books yield valuable insights without scholarly analysis and socioeconomic-historical framework. A few will serve as examples:

7.37int
Markham, Violet, **MAY TENNANT: A PORTRAIT.** 1949. As May Abraham, she became an early member of the Women's Protective and Provident League (later the Women's Trade Union League) under Emma Paterson and then met Emilia Strong Pattison (later Lady Dilke) and became her secretary. She joined in friendship and worked also with Gertrude Tuckwell with whom she participated in the Trade Union Movement. In 1892 "May Abraham's position in industrial matters was such that it was obvious that she should be included among the four women assistant commissioners who were appointed to undertake field enquiries for the Commission" (p. 19). The other women were Eliza Orme, Clara Collet and Margaret Irwin.

7.38int
Hamilton, Mary Agnes, **MARGARET BONDFIELD**. 1924. Considering Bondfield's enormous contributions to union organization and labor politics——always with women's interests foremost among her considerations——it is surprising that this simple, straightforward biography should stand without replacement. Bondfield's own autobiography, **A LIFE'S WORK** (1949), makes up for the gap in our knowledge of her contribution to some degree, but this woman, who was first of her sex to become a Cabinet member as Minister of Labour, deserves scholarly biographical treatment.

7.39int
Goldman, Harold, **EMMA PATERSON: SHE LED WOMAN INTO A MAN'S WORLD**. 1974. The Webbs referred to Paterson as "the real pioneer of modern women's trade unions" (Webb, Sidney and Beatrice, **HISTORY OF TRADE UNIONISM**. 1950) and G.D.H. Cole described her as "the only early feminist who had any knowledge of trade union problems" (Goldman p. 9). Goldman's is an interesting narrative, but it would seem that an in-depth biography is overdue.

7.40int
Anderson, Adelaide Mary, **WOMEN IN THE FACTORY: AN ADMINISTRATIVE ADVENTURE, 1893-1921**. Discusses many reformers and offers details of the official work of the "Lady Commissioners." Anderson herself was His Majesty's Principal Secretary of State for the Home Department. A full scholarly work on her life and times would certainly enhance knowledge of her own participation, but also the context of her (and her colleagues') activities.

7.41int
Pratt, Edwin A., **A WOMAN'S WORK FOR WOMEN: BEING THE AIMS, EFFORTS, AND ASPIRATIONS OF "L.M.H." (MISS LOUISA M. HUBBARD)**. 1898. Outlines Hubbard's life and work as "an authority on the 'gentlewoman' phase of the movement, and her position as such became still more pronounced when, on the suggestion of Sir James Kay-Shuttleworth... and others, she brought forward a scheme for establishing a new training college for ladies" (p. 17). Hubbard's career in practical efforts on behalf of middle-class women's employment is easily matched——or surpassed——by her publication of **HANDBOOK OF WOMEN'S WORK**, 1875, which she put out annually until 1880, and which was superseded by her **ENGLISHWOMAN'S YEAR BOOK**. 1880-1898. Also in 1875 she started **THE WOMAN'S GAZETTE** (afterwards named **WORK AND LEISURE**). Like the feminist periodical, **THE ENGLISHWOMAN'S REVIEW** (1866-) which Hubbard claimed to have inspired (and helped) her, Hubbard's publications are a treasure-house of material for reconstructing the employments and activities of Victorian women.

Several women investigators, reporters and organizers for female employment are represented with short biographical sketches in

7.42int
DICTIONARY OF LABOUR BIOGRAPHY. 7 vols. and continuing publication. ed. by Joyce M. Bellamy and John Saville. 1971-1984.

Conducting research on women's employment from the late eighteenth century through World War I is an extremely complex and challenging enterprise that has been pursued with vigor, but without any definitive answers to the questions thus far explored by scholars. Certainly working women's history must be established within the mainstream of the economic history of the nation and empire. The record of women's employment that is hidden from or is concealed within the Census Returns must be brought to light. The close details of working women's experiences must continue to be discovered and analyzed. But an old and perhaps tired question remains stubbornly unsatisfied. It is stated rather succinctly by

7.43int
Wainwright, Hilary, "Women and the Division of Labour" in WORK, URBANISM AND INEQUALITY. ed. by Philip Abrams. 1978:

> What precisely were the *processes* which in the course of industrial development laid the foundations of the present occupational division of labour by both squeezing women completely out of particular trades and by relegating them to unskilled work through which it was [and is?] impossible to earn sufficient for an independent life? (p. 199).

*NOTE: For additional entries on the social investigation of women's employment, see section 2 in Chapter 8, "Philanthropy, Social Service and Social Welfare." On child labor and legislation for the workplace, see section 6 in Chapter 4, "Law and the Amendment of the Law." For women employed as teachers, headmistresses and governesses, see Chapter 6, "Education." For women in the medical profession, see Chapter 3, "Sickness and Health Care." For more information regarding women in domestic service, see section 10 in Chapter 2, "Marriage and the Family." Also, section 7 of the same chapter includes entries on the employment of wives and mothers.

* * *

1. A SURVEY OF WRITINGS ON WOMEN AND WORK

7.1
Wakefield, Priscilla, REFLECTIONS ON THE PRESENT CONDITION OF THE FEMALE SEX, WITH SUGGESTIONS FOR ITS IMPROVEMENT. 1798; 1817; New York, 1974; 1978. Working girls need the help of middle-class women in order to obtain the necessary training and guidance for respectable employment.

7.2
Radcliffe, Mary Ann, MEMOIRS OF MARY ANN RADCLIFFE AND FAMILIAR LETTERS TO HER FEMALE FRIEND. 1799; 1810. See especially: "The Female Advocate: Part First, The Fatal Consequences of Men Traders Engrossing on Women's Occupations."

7.3
EXTRACTS FROM AN ACCOUNT OF THE LADIES SOCIETY FOR THE EDUCATION AND EMPLOYMENT OF THE FEMALE POOR. 1804.

7.4
Wade, John, HISTORY OF THE MIDDLE AND WORKING CLASS. 1833; 1835; rev. ed., 1842; rpt., New York, 1966.

7.5
MONTHLY REPOSITORY: Martineau, H., *"On Female Education and Occupation,"* 7 (1833) 489-498.

7.6
NEW MONTHLY MAGAZINE: [Bulwer, E.L.], *"Position of Independent Labours Under the Operation of the Poor Laws in England,"* 37 (1833) 277-284.

7.7
WESTMINSTER REVIEW: *"Occupations of the People,"* 48 (1848) 183-194. Provides data on the age and sex of agricultural and urban workers and their dependents; *"Work and Women,"* 131 (1889) 270-279; McMillan, M., *"The Women's Labour Day,"* 136 (1891) 517-526. Co-operation, instead of competition will grant woman "the economic conditions necessary to the full development of her powers" (p. 526); *"Professions Accessible to Women,"* 139 (1893) 381-385; Lee, A.L., *"The 'Impasse' of Women,"* 141 (1894) 566-568. The two major occupations open to women twenty years previously were teaching and nursing. Examines the phenomena of trends which allow new opportunities for women to be doctors, artists, architects, and secretaries. Feels it is best for parents to prepare their daughters for employment since this will maintain their independence instead of rushing them into an unsuitable marriage for financial stability; Baylee, J.T., *"The Minimum Wage and the Poor Law,"* 152 (1899) 628-640; Greenwood, M., *"Freedom of Contract for the Unrepresented,"* 151 (1899) 554-557; Ward, F.W.O., *"Woman as a Factor in the Labour World,"* 173 (1910) 167-174. "Woman brings into the arena [of business] not idle emotional or sentimental influences, as the common garden-wall critic supposes, but a higher standard and a purer code of honour" (p. 169).

7.8
Simmons, G., "Social Condition of the Working Classes" in THE WORKING CLASSES; THEIR MORAL, SOCIAL AND INTELLECTUAL CONDITION; WITH PRACTICAL SUGGESTIONS FOR THEIR IMPROVEMENT. by G. Simmons. 1849. Surveys various occupations such as female domestic work and dressmaking. Includes prostitutes and thieves under the classification of "fallen workers."

7.9
HOME CIRCLE: Crosland, Mrs. N., *"Working Gentlewomen,"* 1 (1849) 41-42.

7.10
ELIZA COOK'S JOURNAL: *"The Vocations of Women,"* no. 56 (1850) 59-63.

7.11
FRASER'S MAGAZINE: Ludlow, J.M., *"Labour and the Poor,"* 41 (1850) 1-18; *"Female Labour,"* 61 (1860) 359-371. Supports employment for women and delineates class differentiation of occupations between middle and working-class women.

7.12
CHRISTIAN SOCIALIST: *"Female Labour in Birmingham,"* 2 (1851) 235-236. Argues against married women working.

7.13
HOUSEHOLD WORDS: *"More Work for the Ladies,"* 6 (1852) 18-22.

7.14
Brewster, Margaret M., **WORK: OR, PLENTY TO DO AND HOW TO DO IT.**
Edinburgh, 1853.

7.15
Cobden, John C., "General Slavery Proceeding from the Existence of the British
Aristocracy" in **THE WHITE SLAVES OF ENGLAND.** by John C. Cobden. 1853;
1860; rpt., Shannon, 1971. "The subjection of the majority of a nation to an
involuntary, hopeless, exhausting, and demoralizing servitude, for the benefit of an
idle and luxurious few of the same nation, is slavery in its most appalling form.
Such a system of slavery, we assert, exists in Great Britain" (pp. 13-14). Material
throughout this book on women.

7.16
CHAMBERS'S EDINBURGH JOURNAL: *"Employments of Women,"* 20 (1853) 156-
159; *"Women's Work,"* 25 (1856) 257-259; Gray, M., *"Women's Work and Wages,"* 80
(1902) 582-584.

7.17
Davis, James Edward, **PRIZE ESSAY ON THE LAWS FOR THE PROTECTION
OF WOMEN.** 1854.

7.18
Allen, Archdeacon, "On the Everyday Work of Ladies" in **LECTURES TO LADIES
ON PRACTICAL SUBJECTS.** ed. by Frederick Denison Morrison. Cambridge,
1855. Collection of lectures delivered at the Working Men's College.

7.19
Hale, Sarah Josepha, **WOMAN'S RECORD.** 1855.

7.20
GENTLEMAN'S MAGAZINE AND HISTORICAL REVIEW: *"The Employment of
Women,"* 43 (1855) 488-491.

7.21
Bodichon, Barbara Leigh Smith, **WOMEN AND WORK.** 1856; 1857; New York,
1859. ——*see also:* Herstein, Sheila R., **A MID-VICTORIAN FEMINIST,
BARBARA LEIGH SMITH BODICHON.** New Haven, 1985; Lacey, Candida Ann,
ed., **BARBARA LEIGH SMITH BODICHON AND THE LANGHAM PLACE
GROUP.** 1987. Reprints writings of Bodichon and those of her colleagues Bessie
Raynor Parkes, Jessie Boucherett, Emily Faithfull, Isa Craig, Maria Susan Rye,
Frances Power Cobbe, Emily Davies, Elizabeth Garrett and Elizabeth Blackwell.
Some of the selections represent the work of the Society for the Promotion of the
Employment of Women which these women established in 1859. Most of the articles
originally appeared in the ENGLISH WOMAN'S JOURNAL and the
ENGLISHWOMAN'S REVIEW. This same group founded both periodicals.

7.22
Jameson, Anna Brownell, **THE COMMUNION OF LABOUR: A LECTURE ON
THE SOCIAL EMPLOYMENTS OF WOMEN.** 1856; Boston, 1857; *reviewed in:*
ECONOMIST: n.v. (1856) n.p.

7.23
Milne, John D., **INDUSTRIAL AND SOCIAL POSITION OF WOMEN IN THE MIDDLE AND LOWER RANKS.** 1857; rpt., New York, 1984; *also titled:* **INDUSTRIAL EMPLOYMENT OF WOMEN...** 1870. Intelligent and comprehensive survey; *reviewed in:* **ATHENAEUM:** no. 1552 (1857) 942. Milne points out the danger of regarding the census as a reliable index. "It seems to have been constructed at different times, upon different principles, so that the same persons do not always, even though their circumstances are unaltered, represent the same classes" (p. 942).

7.24
NORTH BRITISH REVIEW: Kaye, J.W., *"The Employment of Women,"* 26 (1857) 291-338.

7.25
Balfour, Clara Lucas, **WOMEN IN ENGLAND.** 1856. Discusses the lives of working women.

7.26
Landels, William, **WOMAN'S SPHERE AND WORK, CONSIDERED IN THE LIGHT OF SCRIPTURE.** 1859.

7.27
EDINBURGH REVIEW: Martineau, H., *"Female Industry,"* 109 (1859) 293-336. "Sooner or later it must come to be known, in a more practical way than by the figures of the census returns, that a very large proportion of the women of England earn their own bread; and there is no saying how much good may be done, and how much misery may be saved, by a timely recognition of this simple truth" (p. 294). States that half of all women in England "are industrial in their mode of life" and that more than a third "are independent in their industry, are self-supporting, like men" (p. 335).

7.28
Parkes, Bessie Rayner, **THE MARKET FOR EDUCATED FEMALE LABOUR.** 1859; **ESSAYS ON WOMAN'S WORK.** 1865. Argues, with evidence, against the charge that advising women to follow "new paths" away from the home implies "unsexing" them. "A mighty and all-pervading power——the power of trade——tenders the workman's home empty to the housemother's presence for ten hours a day, and teaches English women the advantage of being out on strike... it is clear that, since modern society will have it, so women must work" (pp. 23-24); *reviewed in:* **SATURDAY REVIEW:** 20 (1865) 459-460; *also reviewed in:* **WESTMINSTER REVIEW:** Newman, F.W., *"Capacities of Women,"* 84 (1865) 352-380; *and in:* **VICTORIA MAGAZINE:** 5 (1865) 173.

7.29
ENGLISH WOMAN'S JOURNAL: Parkes, B.R., *"On the Adoption of Professional Life for Women,"* 2 (1858) 1-10; *"How to Utilize the Powers of Women,"* 3 (1859) 34-47; *"Some of the Work in Which Women Are Deficient,"* 3 (1859) 190-196. Recommends work and activity as a cure for the ennui of the well-to-do woman; Parkes, B.R., *"Essays on Women's Work,"* 4 (1859) 98-99; Parkes, B.R., *"The Market for Educated Female Labour,"* 4 (1859) 145-152; *"Letters on the Employment of Women,"* 4 (1859) 270-282; Boucherett, J., *"On the Obstacles to the Employment of Women,"* 4 (1860) 361-375; *"Statistics as to the Employment of the Female Population of Great Britain,"* 5 (1860) 1-6. Presents census data, examining the female work force in terms of the number of women who are married, single,

widowed, etc.; Dall, C.W., *"Woman's Right to Labor; or Low Wages and Hard Work,"* 5 (1860) 127-133; L., A.R., *"Tuition or Trade,"* 5 (1860) 173-184. Refutes an article in FRASER'S MAGAZINE objecting to women's employment in industrial occupations; Parkes, B.R., *"A Year's Experience in Women's Work,"* 6 (1860) 112-119; *"What Are Women Doing?"* 7 (1861) 51-53; Parkes, B.R., *"The Balance of Opinion in Regard to Woman's Work,"* 9 (1862) 340-344; Jellicoe, Mrs., *"Women's Supervision of Women's Industry,"* 10 (1862) 114-119; Boucherett, J., *"Statistics as to the Employment of Women,"* 12 (1864) 400-408; Boucherett, J., *"Adelaide Ann Proctor,"* 13 (1864) 17-20. On the founding of the Society for the Promotion of Employment for Women; Boucherett, J., *"Report on the Employment of Women, By the Lady Assistant Commissioners,"* 25 (1894) 1-9, 75-79, 149-156; Boucherett, J., *"The Fall in Women's Wages,"* 29 (1898) 73-86. Claims that restrictions on the number of hours a woman is permitted to work, coupled with "an artificial cause of depression... introduced about 20 years ago into the industrial world of women" are the two major factors responsible for declining salaries (p. 77). Includes table comparing women's wages in 1892 and 1897.

7.30
ONCE A WEEK: *"Work of Women,"* 1 (1859) 517-519; 2 (1860) 372-374; 4 (1860-1861) 124; 241; 298; Martineau, H., *"Woman's Battlefield,"* 1 (1859) 474-479.

7.31
SATURDAY REVIEW: *"Queen Bees or Working Bees?"* 8 (1859) 575-576; *"What is Woman's Work?"* 25 (1868) 197-198; *"Women's Work,"* 37 (1874) 362-363; *"Work for Women,"* 39 (1875) 440-441; *"Women and Work,"* 89 (1900) 741-742. Argues that marriage should not affect the status of the working woman and her capabilities for working.

7.32
Boucherett, Jessie, **REMARKS ON THE OBSTACLES TO THE MORE GENERAL EMPLOYMENT OF WOMEN AND ON THE MEANS OF REMOVING THEM.** 1860. "Another obstacle is the impression that women are so intellectually inferior to men, that they would be incapable of performing their duties" (p. 5); **EMPLOYMENT OF WOMEN.** 1869; "How to Provide for Superfluous Women" in WOMAN'S WORK AND WOMAN'S CULTURE. ed. by Josephine Butler. 1869.

7.33
Dall, Caroline Wells, **"WOMAN'S RIGHT TO LABOR"; OR LOW WAGES AND HARD WORK: IN THREE LECTURES, DELIVERED IN BOSTON. NOVEMBER 1859.** Boston, 1860; **THE COLLEGE, THE MARKET, AND THE COURT, OR, WOMAN'S RELATION TO EDUCATION, LABOR AND LAW.** Boston, 1867. This discussion of women's employment in the U.S. parallels the issue in England.

7.34
Evans, Charles, **THE EVILS OF FEMALE LABOUR.** 1860.

7.35
CHURCH OF ENGLAND QUARTERLY REVIEW: *"Employment of Women: Reports of the Social Sciences Meetings, 1859-1860,"* 9 (1860) 294-302.

7.36
TAIT'S EDINBURGH REVIEW: *"Employment of Females,"* 27 (1860) 517-522. "Great caution should be manifested in the substitution of womankind for mankind in various branches of labour, such changes must be effected gradually" (p. 517).

7.37
TRANSACTIONS OF THE NATIONAL ASSOCIATION FOR THE PROMOTION OF SOCIAL SCIENCE: Bayley, Mrs., *"On the Employment of Women,"* (1861) 686; Faithfull, E., *"On Some of the Drawbacks Connected with the Present Employment of Women,"* (1862) 810; Faithfull, E., *"Unfit Employments in Which Women are Engaged,"* (1863) 767; Hodgson, W.B., *"On the Pressures for Employment Among Women of the Middle Class,"* (1866) 420.

7.38
Faithfull, Emily, ON SOME OF THE DRAWBACKS CONNECTED WITH THE PRESENT EMPLOYMENT OF WOMEN. 1862. Paper read before the National Association for the Promotion of Social Science; WOMAN'S WORK. 1871. Paper read before the Society of Arts.

7.39
Leno, John Bedford, FEMALE LABOUR. 1863.

7.40
Penny, Virginia, THE EMPLOYMENTS OF WOMEN: A CYCLOPAEDIA OF WOMAN'S WORK. Boston, 1863. Directs female labour from already overcrowded traditional "women's work" to other areas where they are needed. See especially: "Unusual Employments in England." "The most laborious and disagreeable work is left for women, and what is still worse, they are paid only from one third to one half as much as men, doing the same kind of work" (n.p.). Presents lengthy list of "odd" occupations for women listed in the 1851 census: anchor smiths, barge women, bell hangers, bill stickers, brick makers, chimney sweepers, coke burners, gun makers, oil refiners, rivet makers, undertakers, vermin destroyers, wine manufacturers, etc. (p. 479); FIVE HUNDRED EMPLOYMENTS ADAPTED TO WOMEN: WITH THE AVERAGE RATE OF PAY IN EACH. Philadelphia, 1868; rpt., New York, 1971; THINK AND ACT: A SERIES OF ARTICLES PERTAINING TO MEN AND WOMEN, WORK AND WAGES. Philadelphia, 1869; rpt., New York, 1971.

7.41
Hodgson, William B., "On the Pressure for Employment Among Women of The Upper Classes, Educationally Considered" in EDUCATION OF GIRLS AND THE EMPLOYMENT OF WOMEN OF THE UPPER CLASSES EDUCATIONALLY CONSIDERED: TWO LECTURES. by William B. Hodgson. 1864; 1866; 2nd ed., 1869.

7.42
VICTORIA MAGAZINE: Faithfull, E., *"The Unfit Employments in Which Women are Engaged,"* 2 (1863-1864) 65-73. Protests the treatment of women as mere machines; *"The Queen's Institution for the Training and Employment of Educated Women,"* 3 (1864) n.p.; *"Earnings of Women,"* 10 (1867-1868) 385; *"Work of Women"* 9 (1867) 403; Butler, J.E., *"Work and Culture of Women,"* 13 (1869) 463-566; *"Profitable Work of Women,"* 15 (1870) 555; Downing, Miss, *"Work a Necessity for Women,"* 18 (1871-1872) 221; *"Employment of Women,"* 23 (1874) 191; Le Geyt, A.B., *"Employments of Women,"* 25 (1875) 585.

7.43
JOURNAL OF SOCIAL SCIENCE: Cooke-Taylor, W., *"Employment for Women,"* (1865-1866) 299-303; 698-706. The process of natural selection provides an individual with employment for which s/he is best adapted. Instead of men deciding women's occupations, advocates opening up opportunities to women to see

which work they are best suited for.

7.44

Hadland, Miss, **OCCUPATIONS OF WOMEN OTHER THAN TEACHING.** [1866]. Claims that poor women are being cheated by paying for training in occupations which falsely promise higher wages. Discusses job opportunities available to women and the salaries related to such employment; *reviewed in:* JOURNAL OF EDUCATION: 18 (1866) 357.

7.45

Ludlow, John Malcolm and Lloyd, Jones, **THE PROGRESS OF THE WORKING CLASS.** 1867.

7.46

ENGLISHWOMAN'S REVIEW: *"Photography as an Employment of Women,"* n.v. (1867) 219-233; *"Employment for Women,"* 5 (1873) 65-70. Recommends work in the lace industries, pharmacy work, and as telegraph girls; *"Wages at Home and Abroad,"* 5 (1873) 184-190. "We must affirm that there is a terribly large class of women whom it is almost impossible to help, because they can do nothing well. The fault is partly chargeable on their parents, who, when they were young girls, preferred them to lead an idle, or at least a dependent life, which has unfitted them for ever for regular employment. Partly, too, the fault lies with society, which till very lately declared it to be undignified for a girl to earn money if she could find anybody willing to earn it for her.... Further, women, as a rule, lack the energy or enterprise to strike out a fresh path for themselves; they would rather go into a crowded and ill paid profession such as dressmaking, than work for something in which a fair chance of success could be secured, but which is odd and unusual" (p. 190); Boucherett, J., *"Occupations of Women,"* 5 (1874) 85-90; *"Events of the Quarter... The General Election; Education; Restrictions of Women's Labour,"* 5 (1874) 115-131; *"Occupations of Women,"* 5 (1874) 85-90. Relates findings from the Census Report for 1871; *"The Influence of Parents on Women's Work,"* 5 (1874) 90-96. An upper-class woman may do a day's work, but never receive a day's pay for it. Where there is only one woman in a family, she is expected to keep her husband's or her father's house, from a sense of gratitude and in return for her support; Blackburn, H., *"Pursuits of Women,"* 5 (1874) 237-246; *"Year-Book of Women's Work,"* 5 (1874) 263-265; Paterson, E.A., *"The Position of Women Engaged in Handicrafts and Other Industrial Pursuits,"* 6 (1875) 1-12. Describes job opportunities for middle- and working-class women and the differentiation of occupations for men and women. Calls for trade unionism; *"Employment for Women,"* 6 (1875) 83; *"Salary No Object,"* 9 (1878) 107; Justitia, *"Criticisms on Women's Work,"* 9 (1878) 285-287; Laye, E.P.R., *"Women and Careers,"* 9 (1878) 193-201; *"Social Science,"* 10 (1879) 433-443. Report of a Social Science Congress Conference that addressed the issues of employment, education, and the rights of women; F., E., *"Women as Manufacturers,"* 20 (1889) 348-352. "It has lately been the fashion to attribute the depreciation of the needlewomen's wages in some art to the fact that well-to-do women work in fancy workshops at low wages... fancy work for money [is] only another instance of the instinctive love of manufacturing which... may be inherent in women, remembering that by nature she is intended to be the manufacturer of humanity itself" (pp. 350-351); *"The Employment Department of 'Work and Leisure',"* 20 (1889) 540-542. Discusses the work of a prominent agency which aids women of the higher classes in finding work; *"Employment,"* 5 (1894) 281-287; Stopes, C.C., *"Some Women's Trades in Olden Times,"* 29 (1898) 247-248. Discusses 17th century occupations which women were involved in in order to give weight to arguments in favor of female employment; *"Enquirers Into Women's Work,"* 30 (1899) 14.

7.47
Butler, Josephine Elizabeth, THE EDUCATION AND EMPLOYMENT OF WOMEN.
1868; (as editor), WOMAN'S WORK AND WOMAN'S CULTURE. 1869; *reviewed in:*
SATURDAY REVIEW: 28 (1869) 159-161; LEGISLATIVE RESTRICTIONS ON
THE INDUSTRY OF WOMEN, CONSIDERED FROM THE WOMEN'S POINT OF
VIEW. 1874.

7.48
Cooper, Anthony Ashley (Earl of Shaftesbury), SPEECHES UPON SUBJECTS
HAVING RELATION CHIEFLY TO THE CLAIMS AND INTERESTS OF THE
WORKING CLASSES. 1868.

7.49
CONTEMPORARY REVIEW: Mayor, J.B., *"The Cry of the Women,"*11 (1869) 196-
215. The disproportion of the sexes affects the middle and upper classes more than
the lower classes. Because of this unequal distribution, working-class women can
find careers in domestic capacities, for example, while educated and unmarried
middle-class women suffer from "the want of a fitting career" (p. 198). Suggests
that women carve out their own niche; Hyndman, H.M., *"The English Workers as
They Are,"* 52 (1887); Black, C., *"Labour and Life in London,"* 60 (1891) 207-219;
Aldis, M.S., *"Thou Art the Women [Women in Trades],"* 63 (1893) 387-393; Collet,
C., *"The Age Limit for Women,"* 76 (1899) 868-877. Age limitation for work is
dependent upon mental training while young. If a woman's mental power is not
fully developed, atrophy sets in and therefore old age. The aristocracy and upper
middle classes are less likely to atrophy, while members of the middle-class are
more likely to deteriorate because of limited incomes which negate the possibilities
of a developed education; Zimmern, A., *"Ladies' Dwellings,"* 77 (1900) 96-104.
Discusses middle-class women working in London who have difficulty finding
suitable housing; Fawcett, M.G., *"Equal Pay for Equal Value,"* 114 (1918) 387-390.

7.50
MACMILLAN'S MAGAZINE: Fearon, D.R., *"The Ladies Cry, Nothing to Do!"* 19
(1869) 451-454; Bourne, H.C., *"The Unemployed,"* 67 (1892) 81-90; Butler, W.F., *"A
Plea for the Peasant,"* 38 (1878) 27-37.

7.51
Thackeray, Anne Isabella, "Toilers and Spinsters" in THE WRITINGS OF ANNE
ISABELLA THACKERAY. by Anne Isabella Thackeray. 1870. Examines attitudes
toward single women and the possibilities of their employment. Quotes from ads
placed by women wanting work to the Society for Promoting the Employment of
Women: "'Miss B., aged 30. Father speculated, and ruined the family, which is now
dependent on her. He is now old, and she has a sister dying; Miss C., aged 50.
Willing to do *any* thing; Miss F., husband in America, appears to have deserted her.
Wants immediate employment" (p. 393).

7.52
Barlee, Ellen, SKETCHES OF WORKING WOMEN. 1871.

7.53
LABOUR NEWS, PUBLIC WORKS AND BUILDING TRADES WEEKLY: 1871; no.
1; *continued as:* LABOUR NEWS AND EMPLOYMENT ADVERTISER: 1905 to
1927.

7.54

Kinnear, John Boyd, **THE RIGHT OF WOMEN TO LABOUR**. 1873; *rpt. from:* **WOMAN'S WORK AND WOMAN'S CULTURE**. ed. by Josephine Butler. 1869.

7.55

Phillipps, Lucy F. March, **ENGLISH MATRONS AND THEIR PROFESSION; WITH SOME CONSIDERATIONS AS TO THEIR VARIOUS OFFICES, THEIR NATIONAL IMPORTANCE, AND THE EDUCATION THEY REQUIRE**. 1873. Stresses the need for education of the housewife in the following skills: needlework and clothing arts, cleanliness and ventilation, the physical and moral management of children, primary instruction, nursing, household economy, cooking and accounting.

7.56

WOMEN'S SUFFRAGE JOURNAL: Becker, L.E., *"Employment of Women,"* 4 (1873) 51; Becker, L.E., *"Married Women and Their Employers,"* 6 (1875) 108; Becker, L.E., *"Work and Prospects for the New Year,"* 6 (1875) 1-2; *"Careers for Unmarried Women,"* 6 (1875) 133-134.

7.57

Cusack, Mary F., **WOMAN'S WORK IN MODERN SOCIETY**. 1874. Writing from a feminist perspective, Cusack calls for reform in education that is suitable to the needs of each class and occupation. As an example, the lower classes don't need lessons in chemistry but should focus more on physical labor. Advocates improving the standard of living for the poor by raising their wages.

7.58

Reaney, Mrs. G.S., **WAKING AND WORKING**. 1874.

7.59

Thorold, Anthony W., ed., **HINTS FOR LADY WORKERS**. 1874.

7.60

LAW JOURNAL: *"Separate Trading by Married Women,"* 9 (1874) 19-20; 35-36.

7.61

LEISURE HOUR: Mackeson, C., *"Curiosities of the Census,"* no. 1158 (1874) 205-207. Comparison of 1831, 1861, and 1871 returns. In proportion to population, teaching was found to be an attractive field for women while domestic service increased as a female occupation; Mackeson, C., *"Curiosities of the Census. IV.— Occupations of Women, and Matrimonial Statistics,"* no. 1181 (1874) 541-544. Notes that there are 3,000 women working in government offices, "many of whom serve, like the male clerk, to a good old age, there being more than two hundred between sixty-five and seventy-five, and nearly a hundred over seventy-five" (p. 541).

7.62

WOMEN AND WORK: A WEEKLY INDUSTRIAL: June 1874 to Feb. 1876.

7.63

WOMAN'S WORK: A WOMAN'S THOUGHTS ON WOMEN'S RIGHTS. 1875.

7.64

ALL THE YEAR ROUND: *"Employments of Women,"* 15 (1875) 187-188; *"Idle Women,"* 22 (1879) 274-277.

7.65
THE EARNINGS OF MARRIED WOMEN. 1876; *rpt. from:* WOMEN'S SUFFRAGE JOURNAL: n.v. (1876) n.p.

7.66
Caplin, Roxey Anne, "Occupation of the Women of Great Britain With a Table of the Census Returns of 1861 and 1871" in WOMEN IN THE REIGN OF QUEEN VICTORIA. by Roxey Anne Caplin. 1876.

7.67
Hubbard, Louisa M., ed., HAND-BOOK OF WOMEN'S WORK. 1876; THE ENGLISHWOMAN'S YEAR BOOK TOGETHER WITH A DIRECTORY TO ALL INSTITUTIONS (FROM 1875) OF BENEFIT TO WOMEN AND CHILDREN. 2nd ed., 1881; THE YEAR BOOK OF WOMEN'S WORK AND GUIDE TO REMUNERATIVE EMPLOYMENT. 1875; *continued as:* THE ENGLISHWOMAN'S YEAR BOOK FOR 1881(-1916). 1880-1916. From 1899 to 1908 ed. by E. Jones; THE WOMAN'S GAZETTE OR NEWS ABOUT WORK. vols. 1-18, 1875-1880; *title changed to:* WORK AND LEISURE: THE ENGLISHWOMAN'S ADVERTISER, REPORTER, AND GAZETTE. A MAGAZINE DEVOTED TO WOMEN'S INTERESTS. 1880-1893. vols. 16 and 17 ed. by Emily Faithfull; "Statistics of Women's Work" in WOMAN'S MISSION. ed. by Angela Georgina Burdett-Coutts. 1893. Provides statistics concerned with paid and volunteer female philanthropic workers. Includes valuable tables which break down occupations and the number of women involved in each classification.

7.68
GOOD WORDS AND SUNDAY MAGAZINE: Mayo, I.F., *"Forlorn Females v. Working Women,"* 18 (1877) 45-48. "When the subject of women's work was first discussed, it was often objected that they would take employment from men.... One hears less of that objection now" (p. 47).

7.69
Adams, W.H. Davenport, WOMAN'S WORK AND WORTH IN GIRLHOOD, MAIDENHOOD, AND WIFE-HOOD. 1880.

7.70
GIRL'S OWN PAPER: Caulfield, S.F.A., *"On Earning One's Living,"* 1 (1880) 74-76; King, A., *"What Our Girls May Do,"* 1 (1880) 462-463; Medicus, *"Work Versus Idleness,"* 5 (1884) 622-623; *"Economy: What to do with Your Savings: A Paper for Working Girls,"* 13 (1892) 823; Stables, W.G., *"Some Healthful Employments for Girls,"* 21 (1900) 762-763.

7.71
QUARTERLY REVIEW: *"Private Reports from Official Sources on the Employment of Women,"* 151 (1881) 181-200.

7.72
Huth, Alfred Henry, ON THE EMPLOYMENT OF WOMEN. 1882.

7.73
KNOWLEDGE: Russell, P., *"Occupations of the British People in 1881,"* 4 (1883) 330-331. Divides the employment of women into professional, commercial, agricultural, and industrial classifications.

7.74
NATIONAL REVIEW: Brabazon, R., "*A Woman's Work,*" 4 (1884) 86-90; Twining, L., "*Fifty Years of Women's Work,*" 9 (1887) 659-667; Bremner, C., "*Women in the Labour Market,*" 11 (1888) 458-470.

7.75
Mackeson, Charles, "The Occupations of the English People" in THE BRITISH ALMANAC. 1885. Compares the 1871 and 1881 census, finding that "the growth of 'female industry' in its various forms from the more intellectual employment down to the humble and even mechanical vocations, may be said to be the striking feature in the Census of 1881.... In some cases the women are evidently jostling the men, and in a few instances where the men were in a majority in 1871 the tables have been turned, not only metaphorically but literally, and the ladies are at the head of affairs" (n.p.).

7.76
ANNUAL REGISTER: 1885 to 1914.

7.77
Booth, Charles, OCCUPATION OF THE PEOPLE: ENGLAND, SCOTLAND, IRELAND 1841: BEING A RESTATEMENT OF THE FIGURES GIVEN IN THE CENSUS RETURNS. 1886; rpt. in: JOURNAL OF THE ROYAL STATISTICAL SOCIETY: 49 (1886) 314-435; LIFE AND LABOR OF THE PEOPLE OF LONDON. New York, 1902-1904. The work covers the period from 1890-1900. Volume 6 contains the indices to all volumes in this series which is divided into 3 parts: Poverty (4 vols.), Industry (5 vols.), and Religious Influences (7 vols.). Important work.

7.78
Richardson, Benjamin Ward, WOMAN'S WORK IN CREATION. [1886].

7.79
CHARITY ORGANISATION REVIEW: Q., Q., "*Married Women as Breadwinners,*" 2 (1886) 398-399; MacDonald, M.E., "*Wage-Earning Women,*" 1 (1911) 34-40. Concerned mostly with American women but makes some comparisons to their English sisters.

7.80
JOURNAL OF THE ROYAL STATISTICAL SOCIETY: Booth, C., "*On Occupations of the People of the United Kingdom,*" 47 (1886) 314-435. Detailed analysis of tables which utilize census data on many occupations. Provides exhaustive information of women's employment and changes that ensued. Many appendices are included; Booth, C., "*The Inhabitants of Tower Hamlets (School Board Division), Their Condition and Occupations,*" 50 (1887) 326-401; Bateman, A.E., "*Discussion of A.L. Bowley's Paper 'Changes in Average Wages (Nominal and Real) in the United Kingdom Between 1860-1890,'*" 58 (1895) 283; Hutchins, B.L., "*A Note on the Distribution of Women in Occupations,*" 67 (1904) 479-490. "I shall try to show what occupations include the largest number of women, with the increase or decrease in recent years, and the distribution in occupations according to age and condition. The work of women and girls is evidently indicated by the phrase 'cheap and docile labor'; it will be interesting, therefore, to consider in which occupations the proportion of women to men is high, and whether these appear to be expanding more rapidly than others in which it is low" (p. 479); Hutchins, B.L., "*Statistics of Women's Life and Employment,*" 72 (1909) 205-237. Tables break down percent of employed women according to age and marital status. "The majority of young

working women marry and leave work at marriage.... Girls' work is for the most part a 'meanwhile employment.' It is often stated by social investigators that the prospect of marriage makes working girls slack about organization and indifferent about training" (p. 216); Gales, K.E. and Marks, P.H., *"Twentieth Century Trends in the Work of Women in England and Wales,"* 137 (1974) 60-74.

7.81
Twining, Louisa, **WOMEN'S WORK, OFFICIAL AND UNOFFICIAL.** 1887; *rpt. from:* NATIONAL REVIEW: n.v. (1887) n.p.

7.82
FORTNIGHTLY REVIEW: Robinson, F.M., *"Our Working Women and Their Earnings,"* 48 (1887) 50-63; Dilke, E.F.S., *"Women and the Royal Commission,"* 56 (1891) 535-538; March-Phillipps, E., *"The Working Lady in London,"* 58 (1892) 193-203; Bulley, A.A., *"The Employment of Women: The Lady Assistant Commissioners' Report,"* 61 (1894) 39-48. A summary of the investigations of various industries, from the northern textile mills to London service industries. The inquiries range from wage differences among men and women to the effects of female employment on the home and family. Concludes that "if the wives and daughters of manufacturers were as familiar with the factories and their inmates as their husbands and fathers, it is probable that many of the discomforts and dangers to health which now exist would gradually disappear. It may be impossible to raise wages but it should not be impossible to secure healthy, decent, and comfortable surroundings for the workers" (p. 48); *"The Economic Value of Woman,"* 77 (1905) 705-710. "So far in the professions men hold their own, as they have always held their own in the arts and sciences. Where women do seem to be driving men out of the field is in the lower walks of business, and here, I am afraid, a large part of a woman's economic value is her undoubted cheapness" (p. 706); Tuckwell, G., *"Women's Opportunity,"* 89 (1906) 546-556; Robins, E., *"Shall Women Work,"* 87 (1910) 889-911.

7.83
Pfeiffer, Emily Jane, **WOMEN AND WORK.** 1888.

7.84
NINETEENTH CENTURY: Black, C., *"A Working Woman's Speech,"* 25 (1889) 667-671; Hill, O., *"A Few Words to Fresh Workers,"* 26 (1889) 452-461; Wilkins, W.H., *"How Long, Oh Lord, How Long (Women's Working Conditions),"* 34 (1893) 329-336; Gordon, A.M., *"The After-Careers of University Educated Women,"* 37 (1895) 955-960; Low, F.H., *"How Poor Ladies Live,"* 41 (1897) 405-417. Addresses the problem of employment for middle-aged ladies and their survival; Orme, E., *"How Poor Ladies Live. A Reply,"* 41 (1897) 613-619; Shaw, E.M., *"How Poor Ladies Might Live: An Answer from the Workhouse,"* 41 (1897) 620-627; Low, F.H., *"How Poor Ladies Live. A Rejoinder and a 'Jubilee' Suggestion,"* 42 (1897) 161-168; Hobert-Hampden, A., *"The Working Girl of Today,"* 43 (1898) 724-730; Hobhouse, E., *"Women Workers: How They Wish to Live,"* 47 (1900) 471-484; Creighton, L., *"The Employment of Educated Women,"* 50 (1901) 806-811; Markham, V.R., *"The True Foundations of Empire: The Home and the Workshop,"* 58 (1905) 570-582. Opposes mothers working in factories, calling it exploitation of female labor which degrades working-class motherhood; Courtney, J., *"The Prospects of Women as Brain Workers,"* 74 (1913) 1284-1293.

7.85
LANCET: *"The Influence of Female Employment Upon Marriages, Births and Deaths,"* 2 (1890) 627-628.

7.86
Stephens, Amy (pseud. for Veva Karsland), **WOMEN AND THEIR WORK.** 1891.

7.87
ECONOMIC JOURNAL: Collet, C., *"Women's Work in Leeds,"* 1 (1891) 460-473; Webb, S., *"The Alleged Differences in the Wages Paid to Men and Women for Similar Work,"* 1 (1891) 635-662. In comparison to men "The women earn less... not only because they produce less, but also because what they produce is usually valued in the market at a lower rate" (p. 660). Recommends changes to upgrade women's work through education and better training which would increase productivity and in turn increase wages; Fawcett, M.G., *"Mr. Sidney Webb's Article on Women's Wages,"* 2 (1892) 173-176; Bigg, A.H., *"The Wife's Contribution to Family Income,"* 4 (1894) 51-58; Marshall, M.P., *"Conference of Women Workers,"* 6 (1896) 107-109; Collet, C., *"The Expenditure of Middle Class Working Women,"* 8 (1898) 543-553; Bosanquet, H., *"A Study in Women's Wages,"* 12 (1902) 42-49; Tawney, J., *"Women and Unemployment,"* 21 (1911) 131-139; Collet, C., *"Professional Employment of Women,"* 25 (1915) 627-30.

7.88
NEW REVIEW: Simon, J., *"Women and Work, I,"* 5 (1891) 202-212; Black, C., *"Women and Work II,"* 5 (1891) 213-221.

7.89
Smart, William, **WOMEN'S WAGES: A PAPER READ BEFORE THE PHILOSOPHICAL SOCIETY OF GLASGOW, 9TH DECEMBER 1891.** Glasgow, 1892; *reviewed in:* **ECONOMIC REVIEW:** 3 (1893) 607; **STUDIES IN ECONOMICS.** 1895. See especially: "Women's Wages."

7.90
Ford, Isabella O., **WOMEN'S WAGES AND THE CONDITIONS UNDER WHICH THEY ARE EARNED.** 1893.

7.91
Jeune, Susan Elizabeth Mary (Lady) and St. Helier, Baroness, eds., **LADIES AT WORK: PAPERS ON PAID EMPLOYMENTS FOR LADIES BY EXPERTS IN THE SEVERAL BRANCHES.** 1893; *reviewed in:* **ECONOMIC JOURNAL:** Marshall, M.P., 3 (1893) 679-680.

7.92
Lady Assistant Commissioners to the Royal Commission, **CONDITIONS OF WORK IN VARIOUS INDUSTRIES IN ENGLAND, WALES, SCOTLAND AND IRELAND.** 1893.

7.93
Mallet, Mrs. C. (Louisa T.), **DANGEROUS TRADES FOR WOMEN.** 1893.

7.94
National Council of Women of Great Britain, **WOMEN WORKERS.** 1893; **WOMEN WORKERS: THE PAPERS READ AT THE CONFERENCE IN HULL OCTOBER 6TH TO 10TH, 1913.** 1913.

7.95
MONIST: Ferrero, G., *"The Problem of Woman, From a Bio-Sociological Point of View,"* 4 (1893-1894) 261-274. "Woman-labor is not required by the necessity of an

increased production. It only tends to lower the marketable value of male labor.... This shows that even from a sociological point of view, female labor is a pathological phenomenon; for it does not result in the common labor of the two sexes, in itself a bearable evil, but it leads to the enforced idleness of men and the merciless toil of women, entirely overthrowing the relation that nature has established in all orders of life below us" (pp. 267-268).

7.96
SPECTATOR: *"Women Workers,"* 70 (1893) 426-427; *"Ladies at Work,"* 71 (1893) 635-636; *"The Right of Women to Work,"* 71 (1893) 330-331; *"Women Workers,"* 74 (1895) 713-714; *"Money-making Women,"* 77 (1896) 852-853; *"Women's Employment,"* 98 (1907) 81-82; Baden-Powell, A., *"Our Workingirls,"* 106 (1911) 922-923.

7.97
Barnett, Edith A., **TRAINING OF GIRLS FOR WORK. AN EXPRESSION OF OPINIONS.** 1894.

7.98
Davidson, J.E., **WHAT OUR DAUGHTERS CAN DO FOR THEMSELVES: A HANDBOOK OF WOMEN'S EMPLOYMENTS.** 1894.

7.99
Bulley, Agnes Amy and Whitley, Margaret, **WOMEN'S WORK.** preface by Lady Emilia Dilke. 1894; 1896. See especially: "Preface." Dilke straddles the fence between supporting the activities of militant feminist reformers and condemning them for promoting rivalry between the sexes and endangering the family. Her proposed solution is to have women consider the interests of labor before considering men as rivals. "The highest interests of women in every sphere of life are bound up with those of men, and any attempt to deal with either separately is fraught with danger to the State and to the nation.... This principle lies at the bottom of all reasoned Trades Unionism, which, insofar as it is concerned with the organisation of women's work, has for its ultimate object the restoration of as many as possible to their post of honour as queens of the hearth" (p. xiii).

7.100
Collet, Clara, **REPORT BY MISS COLLET ON THE STATISTICS OF EMPLOYMENT OF WOMEN AND GIRLS.** 1894. Compares and analyzes the 1881 and 1891 census statistics. Examines indicated changes in employment trends, connections between wages and married women workers. Explores all categories of female work and includes tables and comparisons to male labour. Discusses the decline and advances made by women in various fields of occupation. Important work; "Women's Work" in **LIFE AND LABOUR OF THE PEOPLE OF LONDON.** ed. by Charles Booth. 1902. See vol. 4, series 1; **EDUCATED WORKING WOMEN: ESSAYS ON THE ECONOMIC POSITION OF WOMEN WORKERS IN MIDDLE CLASSES.** 1902. Collection of six essays reprinted from other journals; *reviewed in:* **ECONOMIC REVIEW:** 12 (1902) 372-373.

7.101
ECONOMIC REVIEW: Robertson, C.G., *"Women's Work,"* 5 (1895) 167-190. "In the interest of the whole nation it is unreasonable to allow one large section of women to be vitally crippled for we can never forget that it is on a healthy vigorous womanhood that national welfare depends. If, says one of the inspectors, eight hours can be properly considered the time for adult males to work, how can it be right to allow females to be employed for fourteen hours? And, if we may add, it

is right to prevent women in factories working more than fifty-six hours per week, how can it be reasonable to refuse a similar privilege to their sisters in the shops? We are told that, if their hours are restricted, they will be hampered as compared with men. But that, surely, is an argument for regulating the labour of the male worker, not for refusing to restrict the hours of women" (p. 184); Bowley, A.L. and Hopkins, A., *"Bibliography of Wage Statistics in the United Kingdom in the Nineteenth Century,"* 8 (1898) 504-520; Fyfe, W.H., *"Remuneration of Women's Work,"* 18 (1908) 135-145; Stocks, H., *"Women and State Insurance,"* 21 (1911) 439-445; Lavery, R., *"Why Women are Crowding the Labour Markets of the World,"* 24 (1914) 74-78; Morley, E.J., *"The Economic Position of Women,"* 24 (1914) 388-397. "The ordinary conditions of domestic toil among working-class wives are detestable, and press even more severly on women than the hardships of the labour-market. The mass of married women doing unpaid domestic work are an evil case, and no remedy is possible until the prevailing confusion between sex relations and economic relations comes to an end" (p. 393).

7.102
Boucherett, Jessie and Blackburn, Helen, **THE CONDITION OF WORKING WOMEN**. 1896.

7.103
Bliss, William D.P., et al., eds., **THE ENCYCLOPEDIA OF SOCIAL REFORM**. 1897.

7.104
Greville, Frances Evelyn (Countess of Warwick), ed., **PROGRESS IN WOMEN'S EDUCATION IN THE BRITISH EMPIRE. BEING THE REPORT OF THE EDUCATION SECTION, VICTORIAN ERA EXHIBITION**. 1897. Includes chapters on training of women for agriculture, business, and factory and sanitary inspection. Especially noteworthy is the chapter "Indexing: A Profession for Women." See index for sections on such employments as bee-keeping, bookkeeping, daffodil-growing, dairy work, dressmaking, poultry-keeping and laundry work; **PROGRESS IN WOMEN'S EDUCATION IN THE BRITISH EMPIRE: PT. 2, SOME PROFESSIONS OPEN TO WOMEN**. 1898.

7.105
Pratt, Edwin A., **PIONEER WOMEN IN VICTORIA'S REIGN. SHORT HISTORIES OF GREAT MOVEMENTS**. 1897; **A WOMAN'S WORK FOR WOMEN, BEING THE AIMS, EFFORTS, AND ASPIRATIONS OF "L.M.H." (MISS LOUISA M. HUBBARD)**. 1898. Hubbard started publication of guides for working gentlewomen in 1869 with THE ENGLISHWOMAN'S YEARBOOK, a catalog of 82 organizations, "all the institutions and Societies existing for the benefit of women and children." Her main object in continuing to publish guides, handbooks and periodicals was to encourage women to seek careers as alternatives to marriage. She aimed "to overcome... the old-fashioned idea that it was 'unladylike' for any person above the recognised working class of women to earn a living for herself otherwise than by teaching or by her needle" (p. 130). She helped to create "the change, comparing present with past [that] may be seen by any one who will stand at the exit from one of the London railway termini... between half-past light and nine in the morning and observe the large proportion that ladies form of the crowd of 'business people' who come regularly to the City from their suburban homes to earn their daily bread" (p. 131).

7.106
Gomme, G. Laurence, "The Industries" in **LONDON IN THE REIGN OF**

VICTORIA. by G. Laurence Gomme. 1898. Delineates the various trades and professions. See especially: "Appendix III——Occupations of Males and Females from the Census of 1851" and "Appendix IV——Occupations of Males and Females from the Census of 1891."

7.107
Phillips, Leonora, A DICTIONARY OF EMPLOYMENTS OPEN TO WOMEN. WITH DETAILS OF WAGES, HOURS OF WORK AND OTHER INFORMATION. 1898.

7.108
Webb, Sidney and Webb, Beatrice, PROBLEMS OF MODERN INDUSTRY. 1898; 1902.

7.109
SOUTH PLACE ETHICAL SOCIETY DISCOURSES: Collet, C., *"The Economic Position of Educated Working Women,"* 25 (1890) 205-216.

7.110
Marot, Helen, A HANDBOOK OF LABOR LITERATURE: A CLASSIFIED AND ANNOTATED LIST OF THE MORE IMPORTANT BOOKS AND PAMPHLETS IN THE ENGLISH LANGUAGE. Philadelphia, 1899; "A Selected List of Books and Pamphlets in the English Language on Women in Industry" in THE ECONOMIC POSITION OF WOMEN. compiled by Carola Woerishoffer. New York, 1910.

7.111
Bowley, Arthur L., WAGES IN THE UNITED KINGDOM IN THE NINETEENTH CENTURY. Cambridge, 1900.

7.112
Candee, Helen Churchill, HOW WOMEN MAY EARN A LIVING. New York, 1900.

7.113
Coumbe, Edward Holton, WHAT SHALL I BE? A GUIDE TO OCCUPATIONS FOR MEN AND WOMEN... 1900.

7.114
International Congress of Women, Professional Section, WOMEN IN PROFESSIONS. vols. 3-4, 1900. See especially: "The Effect Upon Domestic Life of the Admission of Women to the Professions."

7.115
Hutchins, B. Leigh, STATISTICS OF WOMEN'S LIFE AND EMPLOYMENT. 1901; 1909. WOMEN'S WAGES IN ENGLAND IN THE NINETEENTH CENTURY. 1908; WORKING WOMEN AND THE POOR LAW. 1909. Refers to provisions made for distressed working women who come on the rates through sickness, widowhood, desertion or unemployment of their husbands or of themselves. Concludes that the state should sustain a standard of living and that women with children should be supported first; THE WORKING LIFE OF WOMEN. 1911; CONFLICTING IDEALS: TWO SIDES OF THE WOMAN QUESTION. 1913. CONFLICTING IDEALS OF WOMAN'S WORK. 1916. Presents conflicting views and attempts to clear the ground on whether or not it is desirable for women to work. ——*see also:* JOURNAL OF THE ROYAL STATISTICAL SOCIETY: *"Discussion on Miss B.L. Hutchins's Paper,"* 72 (1909) 238-247. Examines interpretation of statistics in WORKING WOMEN AND THE POOR LAW (see above entry), citing Hutchins'

use of material from the census returns instead of the statistics from the Factory Department. References are made to the correlation of infant mortality with women's employment.

7.116
Lyttleton, Mary Kathleen (Mrs. Arthur), WOMEN AND THEIR WORK. 1901.

7.117
Webb, Beatrice Potter, "The Diary of an Investigator" in PROBLEMS OF MODERN INDUSTRY. by Sidney Webb and Beatrice Webb. rev. ed., 1902; *rpt. from:* NINETEENTH CENTURY: Potter, B., *"Pages From a Work-Girl's Diary,"* 24 (1888) 301-314. An optimistic, rose-colored view of the lower class of needleworkers. Potter investigated their situation by adopting the appearance of a needlewoman. Of her co-workers she writes: "Among the younger hands... [conversation] chiefly concerns the attraction of the rival music-halls, or the still more important question of the... attentions of their different 'blokes'. For monotonous work and bad food have not depressed the physical energies of these young women. With warm hearts, with overflowing good nature, with intellects keenly alive to the varied sights of East London, these genuine daughters of the people brim over with the frank enjoyment of low life" (p. 311); THE WAGES OF MEN AND WOMEN: SHOULD THEY BE EQUAL? 1919;

7.118
Mackenna, Ethel, ed., THE WOMAN'S LIBRARY. 3 vols. 1903. Handbooks for self-instruction in various occupations.

7.119
Burns, John, AN ADDRESS DELIVERED AT THE NATIONAL CONFERENCE ON INFANT MORTALITY... ON EMPLOYMENT OF MARRIED WOMEN. 1906.

7.120
Cadbury, Edward, Matheson, M. Cecile, and Shann, George, WOMEN'S WORK AND WAGES: A PHASE OF LIFE IN AN INDUSTRIAL CITY. 1906; 1909; rpt., New York, 1980. Survey conducted in Birmingham, based on over 6,000 interviews of employed females. Analyzes in detail, occupational conditions, home life, and specific problems and hazards encountered by working women. Cadbury and Matheson were involved in the managerial aspects of factory and educational reform; Shann was a Glasgow factory worker who became a social worker; *reviewed in:* ECONOMIC REVIEW: Heath, J. St. G., 7 (1907) 378-381.

7.121
Central Bureau For the Employment of Women, THE FINGERPOST: A GUIDE TO THE PROFESSIONS AND OCCUPATIONS OF EDUCATED WOMEN. 1906; 1910; 4th ed., 1913.

7.122
Gore-Booth, Eva, WOMEN'S WAGES AND THE FRANCHISE. 1906; WOMEN'S RIGHT TO WORK. Manchester, [1908-1909]. Author may also be cataloged as Booth, Eva Gore.

7.123
Tuckwell, Gertrude M., WOMEN'S OPPORTUNITY. 1906; (et al., eds.), WOMAN IN INDUSTRY FROM SEVEN POINTS OF VIEW. 1908. Intended for the general public interested in the question of woman's position in industry; *reviewed in:* ECONOMIC JOURNAL: 19 (1909) 228-233.

7.124
Women's Industrial Council, **WOMEN'S WAGES IN THE NINETEENTH CENTURY**. 1906.

7.125
Bell, Florence Eveleen Eleanore (Lady), **AT THE WORKS: A STUDY OF A MANUFACTURING TOWN**. 1907; rpt., 1969; rpt. with introduction by Angela V. John. 1985. See especially: "Wives and Daughters of the Ironworkers." Includes statistics relevant to female employment and descriptions of working conditions.

7.126
JOURNAL OF POLITICAL ECONOMY: Abbott, E., *"Municipal Employment of Unemployed Women in London,"* 15 (1907) 513-530.

7.127
WOMAN WORKER: Sept. 1907; no. 1; June 1908 to Dec. 1908; nos. 1-31; Jan. 1909 to Jan. 1910; vols. 3-4; Jan. 1916 to July 1921; nos. 1-64. Publication of the London National Federation of Women Workers.

7.128
Charity Organisation Society, **SPECIAL COMMITTEE ON UNSKILLED LABOUR. REPORT AND MINUTES OF EVIDENCE, JUNE 1908**. 1908.

7.129
London County Council, **WOMEN'S TRADES**. 1908.

7.130
McMahon, Theresa Schmid, "Women and Economic Evolution or the Effects of Industrial Changes Upon the Status of Women," Ph.D. diss., Univ. of Wisconsin, 1908.

7.131
TREASURY: Ransom, M., *"Unemployment Among Women and its Causes,"* 10 (1908) 468-472; 11 (1908) 163-167.

7.132
WORK FOR WOMEN. A GUIDE AND INSPIRATION TO PROFITABLE OCCUPATIONS. 1909.

7.133
Abbott, Edith, **WOMEN IN INDUSTRY**. 1909.

7.134
Apprenticeship and Skilled Employment Association, compiler, **TRADES FOR LONDON GIRLS AND HOW TO ENTER THEM: A COMPANION BOOK TO TRADES FOR LONDON BOYS**. 1909. Describes apprenticeship and indenture, how to find an opening, and types of wages. Includes sections on trade schools. Describes the various trades in terms of conditions of entry, curriculum of work, possible openings, and organizations concerned.

7.135
Berry, Thomas William, **PROFESSIONS FOR GIRLS**. 1909.

7.136
Taylor, F. Isabel, **A BIBLIOGRAPHY OF UNEMPLOYMENT AND THE UNEMPLOYED.** 1909.

7.137
Webb, Beatrice and Hutchins, B. Leigh, **SOCIALISM AND THE NATIONAL MINIMUM.** 1909.

7.138
WOMEN'S TRADE UNION REVIEW: Hutchins, B.L., *"Some Aspects of Women's Life and Work,"* 74 (1909) 6-12; Brooke, J.R., *"Unemployment,"* 75 (1909) 10-16.

7.139
Fabian Society, London, compiler, **FABIAN WOMEN'S GROUP, SUMMARY OF EIGHT PAPERS AND DISCUSSIONS UPON THE DISABILITIES OF MOTHERS AS WORKERS.** 1910. See especially: "The Effect Upon Little Children of the Mother Undertaking Work Outside the Home" by Mrs. Stanbury; **THE WORKING LIFE OF WOMEN.** 1911.

7.140
Whitmore, Clara Helen, **WOMAN'S WORK IN ENGLISH FICTION.** New York, 1910.

7.141
Wood, George Henry, **HISTORY OF WAGES.** 1910; **THE WOMAN WAGE EARNER.** 1910.

7.142
Bird, M. Mostyn, **WOMAN AT WORK: A STUDY OF THE DIFFERENT WAYS OF EARNING A LIVING OPEN TO WOMEN.** 1911. Divided into several parts that include "Manufacture," "Service," "The Professors," "The Arts," and "Philanthropy." The differences between women's and men's occupations and wages are due to the seriousness with which men take their jobs. Women do not take their jobs seriously because they will no longer work when they marry.

7.143
MacDonald, Margaret Ethel, **WAGE EARNING MOTHERS.** 1911.

7.144
Martin, Anna, **THE MARRIED WORKING WOMAN: A STUDY.** 1911; 1913; *rpt. from:* **NINETEENTH CENTURY:** Part I, 68 (1910) 1102-1118; Part II, 69 (1911) 108-122. Describes day-to-day existence of married working women and reminds the reader not to judge by middle-class standards. Includes some oral history. Argues that if women were granted the right to vote they would facilitate legislation for a "living wage" which would return their husbands to being the primary bread winner in the family; the working woman could therefore be at home to care for her children, thus arresting the problems of physical and moral defectiveness and national degeneracy.

7.145
Player, Mrs. and MacDonald, Mrs. J.R., **WAGE EARNING MOTHERS.** 1911.

7.146
Rowntree, Benjamin Seebohm and Lasker, Bruno, **UNEMPLOYMENT: A SOCIAL STUDY.** 1911. Discusses the problem of casual laborers and includes a chapter on

women.

7.147
Stewart, Jean, THREE HUNDRED AND ONE THINGS A BRIGHT GIRL CAN
DO. 1911.

7.148
Tweedie, Mrs. Alec, WOMEN AND WORK. 1911.

7.149
ENGLISHWOMAN: Haslam, J., *"Women Workers and the Census,"* 10 (1911) 18-23;
Macrosty, E.J., *"The Numerical Growth of Women in Paid Employment,"* 10 (1911)
139-146; Tawney, J., *"Some Characteristics of Women's Unemployment,"* 12 (1911)
269-277.

7.150
Beneridge, William H., UNEMPLOYMENT: A PROBLEM OF INDUSTRY. 1912.
Beneridge was involved with the administration of the Poor Law. Calls for "state
intervention to encourage individual initiative" by advocating national labor
exchanges. See index for subjects related to women.

7.151
Engel, Sigmund, "Women's Labour and Child Labour" in ELEMENTS OF CHILD
PROTECTION. by Sigmund Engel; trans. by Eden Paul. New York, 1912. "With the
development of commerce, manufacturing industry, and town life, as a sequel of
the modern economico-technical changes resulting from the evolution of capitalism,
which rendered home industry more difficult, women's work entered upon a new
phase. Women gradually adopted work for wages, completely divorced from the
home its labours... women's work had not to be conducted in accordance with a
prescribed code of rules, and the products were for consumption by unknown
persons.... It is widely maintained that this change was referable to the development
of the movement for women's emancipation, to the desire of women for
independence, but this view is erroneous.... The change just mentioned, far from
contributing to the emancipation of women, has tended rather to fix the yoke more
firmly on their shoulders" (p. 160).

7.152
Pott, Adelaide, AUTOBIOGRAPHY OF A WORKING WOMAN. ed. by James
McDonald. 1912.

7.153
Snowden, Phillip, "Some Objections and Difficulties" in THE LIVING WAGE. by
Phillip Snowden. 1912. "Women... are encroaching on trades and professions which
have hitherto been regarded as the close preserves of men... women have come to
stay in the industrial world, and if... they will enter in ever increasing numbers.... If
the legal living wage was the same for men as for women, the competition between
men and women would be not of the lowest wage, but of the most efficient worker.
That would really not work out eventually to the injury of either men or women.
The men would gravitate to the work they could best do, and so would the women"
(p. 159).

7.154
Zimmern, Dorothy M., WOMEN'S WAGES: WITH SUMMARY TABLES. 1912.

7.155
MANCHESTER DAILY DISPATCH: West, R., *"The Woman as Workmate,"* (November 26, 1912) n.p.

7.156
WOMEN WORKERS: Matheson, M.C., *"Opportunities for Training for Personal Service,"* 22 no. 3 (1912) 69-74.

7.157
ACCOUNTS OF EXPENDITURE OF WAGE-EARNING WOMEN AND GIRLS. 1913.

7.158
NEW STATESMAN: Gilman, C.P., *"The Arrested Development of Woman,"* Special Supplement, (Nov. 1, 1913) 5-6; Hutchins, B.L., *"The Capitalist Versus the Home,"* Special Supplement, (Nov. 1, 1913) n.p. On the restricted field of women's employment; Webb, B., *"Introduction,"* Special Supplement, 2 (1914) 1-2; Hubback, Mrs. F.W., *"Women's Wages,"* Special Supplement, 2 (Feb. 21, 1914) 2-6; Hutchins, B.L., *"Women in Trade Unionism,"* Special Supplement, 2 (Feb. 21, 1914) 6-9; Mallon, J.J., *"The Legal Minimum Wage at Work,"* Special Supplement, 2 (Feb. 21, 1914) 10-12; Pember-Reeves, Mrs. and Wilson, Mrs. C.M., *"A Policy for Women Workers,"* Special Supplement, 2 (Feb. 21, 1914) 12-14; *"A Select List of Works Dealing with Women in Industry,"* Special Supplement, 2 (Feb. 21, 1914) 14-15; Webb, B., *"The Rights of the Women to Free Entry Into all Occupations,"* 3 (1914) 525-527.

7.159
Low, Barbara, **SOME CONSIDERATIONS CONCERNING WOMEN IN THE LABOUR MARKET.** 1914.

7.160
Mackirdy, Olive Christian (Malvery), **THE SOUL MARKET.** 1914. On the employment of poor women.

7.161
Morley, Edith J., ed., **WOMEN WORKERS IN SEVEN PROFESSIONS: A SURVEY OF THEIR ECONOMIC CONDITIONS AND PROSPECTS.** 1914.

7.162
Papworth, Lucy Wyatt and Zimmern, Dorothy M., **THE OCCUPATIONS OF WOMEN ACCORDING TO THE CENSUS OF ENGLAND AND WALES 1911. SUMMARY TABLES.** 1914. The tables show percentage of men and women occupied amongst different categories of work, the marriage state of occupied women, occupations of women by age group, former occupations of retired females, and proportions of women in certain occupations for six census years, 1861-1911.

7.163
FRIEND: McK., B., *"Working Women at College,"* 54 (1914) 670-671.

7.164
Black, Clementina, ed., **MARRIED WOMEN'S WORK. BEING THE REPORT OF AN ENQUIRY UNDERTAKEN BY THE WOMEN'S INDUSTRIAL COUNCIL.** 1915; rpt. with introduction by Ellen Mappen. 1983. "The great mass of married women of the working class now present themselves to me in four groups: (a) Those who, although the family income is inadequate, do not earn. (b) Those who, because

the family income is inadequate whether from lowness of pay, irregularity of work or failure in some way, such as sickness, idleness, drink or desertion on the part of the husband——do earn. (c) Those who, the family income being reasonably adequate, do not earn. (d) Those who, although the family income is adequate for the supply of necessities, yet earn" (pp. 1-2). Concludes that married women's work is not detrimental to family life. Findings are based on questionnaires distributed to workers in London and other industrial areas. ——*see also:* Glage, Liselotte, **CLEMENTINA BLACK: A STUDY IN SOCIAL HISTORY AND LITERATURE.** Heidelberg, 1981.

7.165
Green, John Little, **VILLAGE INDUSTRIES: A NATIONAL OBLIGATION.** 1915.

7.166
Normanton, Helena, **SEX DIFFERENTIATION IN SALARY.** [1915].

7.167
Papworth, Lucy and Zimmern, Dorothy, **WOMEN IN INDUSTRY: A BIBLIOGRAPHY.** 1915. Excellent comprehensive bibliography of the employment of women in industry to 1914.

7.168
Smith, Ellen, **WAGE-EARNING WOMEN AND THEIR DEPENDENTS.** 1915.

7.169
WOMEN'S INDUSTRIAL NEWS: Haynes, D., *"A Comparative Study of the Occupations of Men and Women with Special Reference to Their Mutual Displacement from the Census Returns 1861-1911,"* 9 (1915) 365-414. Twenty-eight pages of charts and tables. Concludes that there was a decline in domestic work and a redistribution of women into other occupations. Includes a bibliography on displacement by Irene Hernaman.

7.170
NEW CAREERS FOR WOMEN: THE BEST POSITIONS AND HOW TO OBTAIN THEM. 1917.

7.171
Drysdale, Charles Vickery, "Birth-Control and the Wage-Earners" in **POPULATION AND BIRTH CONTROL: A SYMPOSIUM.** ed. by Cedar Paul and Eden Paul. New York, 1917.

7.172
Rathbone, Eleanor F., "The Remunerations of Women's Services" in **THE MAKING OF WOMEN: OXFORD ESSAYS IN FEMINISM.** ed. by Victor Gollancz. 1917.

7.173
Stone, Gilbert, ed., **WOMEN WAR WORKERS: ACCOUNTS CONTRIBUTED BY REPRESENTATIVE WORKERS OF THE WORK DONE BY WOMEN IN THE MORE IMPORTANT BRANCHES OF WAR EMPLOYMENT.** 1917.

7.174
Fraser, Helen, **WOMEN AND WAR WORK.** New York, 1918.

7.175
Elias, Agnes M., **WHEN WOMEN KNOW HOW.** 1919.

7.176
Fay, Charles Ryle, **LIFE AND LABOUR IN THE NINETEENTH CENTURY.** Cambridge, 1920. Although not expressly on women, the book gives an excellent background on the growth of industry and its effects on society. Includes an appendix, "The Localisation of Industry in Northern England" and a map depicting the same. The preface serves as a research guide to labor studies in England.

7.177
Knowles, Lilian, **INDUSTRIAL AND COMMERCIAL REVOLUTIONS IN GREAT BRITAIN IN THE NINETEENTH CENTURY.** 1921.

7.178
Rowntree, Benjamin Seebohm and Stuart, Frank, **THE RESPONSIBILITY OF WOMEN WORKERS FOR DEPENDENTS.** Oxford, 1921. "In fixing minimum wages for women, should any allowance be made for dependents, and if so, for how many?" (p. 6). Investigates, with supportive statistics, to provide a criterion for determining minimum wages for women.

7.179
Tickner, Frederick Windham, **WOMEN IN ENGLISH ECONOMIC HISTORY.** 1923.

7.180
LABOUR MAGAZINE: Bondfield, M., *"Women and Unemployment,"* 9 (1923) 399-400.

7.181
Bondfield, Margaret, "Women Workers in British Industry" in **BRITISH LABOUR SPEAKS.** ed. by Richard W. Hough. New York and Liveright, 1924; **UNEMPLOY-MENT.** 1930.

7.182
Brittain, Vera, **WOMEN'S WORK IN MODERN ENGLAND.** 1928. The first chapter deals with women's work from 1900-1914, while the remainder deals with the situation up to 1928. "Opportunities for promotion are not, of course, limited only by the attitude of male employers and organised male workers; they are necessarily impeded by the tradition which, in the majority of occupations, has hitherto dictated that a woman shall give up her employment on marriage. So close is the relation between the temporary nature of the average woman's work and her relegation to the lowest grades of any given occupation, that the Women's Employment Committee [1919] placed on record their opinion 'that the conditions of employment should be so improved that a woman can if necessary pursue an industrial calling throughout her life with some maintenance of interest and keenness'" (p. 5).

7.183
Neff, Wanda, **VICTORIAN WORKING WOMEN: AN HISTORICAL AND LITERARY STUDY OF WOMEN IN BRITISH INDUSTRIES AND PROFESSIONS 1832-1850.** 1929; rpt., 1966; New York, 1967. Chapters include "The Textile Worker," "The Non-Textile Worker," "The Dressmaker," "The Governess," and "The Idle Woman."

7.184
Pinchbeck, Ivy, **WOMEN WORKERS AND THE INDUSTRIAL REVOLUTION 1750-1850.** 1930; rpt., 1969. Detailed bibliography of manuscript sources and

official publications, reports of societies and of contemporary literature; *reviewed in:* BULLETIN OF THE SOCIETY FOR THE STUDY OF LABOUR HISTORY: 19 (1969) 51.

7.185
Davies, Margaret Llewelyn, ed., LIFE AS WE HAVE KNOWN IT BY COOPERATIVE WORKING WOMEN: WORKING WOMEN DESCRIBE THEIR JOBS, FAMILIES, AND POLITICAL AWAKENING IN EARLY TWENTIETH-CENTURY ENGLAND. 1931; 1975. Introduction by Virginia Woolf. Vivid personal accounts by Women's Co-operative Guild members describing family life, work and efforts of the Guild.

7.186
Anthony, Sylvia, WOMEN'S PLACE IN INDUSTRY AND THE HOME. 1932.

7.187
Clapham, J.H., AN ECONOMIC HISTORY OF MODERN BRITAIN, 1820-1929. 3 vols. Cambridge, 1932-1938; 1952. Refers to women workers in each volume.

7.188
Jermy, Louise, MEMORIES OF A WORKING WOMAN. Norwich, 1934.

7.189
Strachey, Ray (pseud. for Rachel Costelloe), CAREERS AND OPENINGS FOR WOMEN: A SURVEY OF WOMEN'S EMPLOYMENT AND A GUIDE FOR THOSE SEEKING WORK. 1935.

7.190
McCarthy, Margaret (pseud. for Margaret McKay), GENERATION IN REVOLT. 1953.

7.191
POPULATION STUDIES: Leser, C.E.V., *"The Supply of Women for Gainful Work in Britain, 1881-1951,"* 9 (1955) 142-158. Census figures during the 70-year period show a constant proportion of women employed. Study concentrates mainly on the period after 1911.

7.192
Davidoff, Leonore, "The Employment of Married Women in England and Wales, 1850-1950," M.A. thesis, Univ. of London, 1956; "The Separation of Home and Work? Landladies and Lodgers in Nineteenth and Twentieth Century England" in FIT WORK FOR WOMEN. ed. by Sandra Burman. New York, 1979. Examines the large, varied group of women who contributed to the family income by earning their living as landladies while remaining in the home. Highlights the effects of this practice on different segments of society and the domestic ideal, which stressed the sanctity and noncommercial nature of the home.

7.193
Douglas, David C., ENGLISH HISTORICAL DOCUMENTS 1833-1874. VOLUME XII(1). 1956; 1964. Includes occupation census for 1841, 1851, 1861, and 1871 on pp. 205-215.

7.194
Abramovitz, Moses and Eliasberg, Vera F., THE GROWTH OF PUBLIC EMPLOYMENT IN GREAT BRITAIN. Princeton, 1957.

7.195

Hewitt, Margaret, **WIVES AND MOTHERS IN VICTORIAN INDUSTRY**. 1958. On working-class women and how industrialization affected home life.

7.196

Lockwood, David, **THE BLACK-COATED WORKER**. 1958. "The counting house was exclusively a male concern. But as early as 1870 this exclusiveness was being broken down by women who were establishing themselves in the civil service and, to a lesser extent, in commercial firms.... By the turn of the century women were firmly entrenched in certain types of clerical work. In telephonic and telegraphic offices they formed 45 percent of all employees, in local government 29 percent, and in civil service 25 percent. In commerce they were still a small minority, and in banking, insurance and law there was strong resistance to their employment. But the first inroads had been made, and in the years immediately before the First World War the white-blouse invasion of blackcoated work was well under way" (p. 122).

7.197

Pollard, Sidney, **A HISTORY OF LABOUR IN SHEFFIELD**. Liverpool, 1959.

7.198

ECONOMIC HISTORY REVIEW: Musgrove, F., *"Middle-Class Education and Employment in the 19th Century,"* 12 (1959) 99-111; Perkin, H.J., *"Middle-Class Education and Employment in the Nineteenth Century: A Critical Note,"* 14 (1961) 122-130; Roberts, E., *"Working Class Standards of Living in Barrow and Lancaster 1890-1912,"* 30 (1977) n.p. Discusses the importance of woman's work in working-class families; Hopkins, E., *"Working Hours and Conditions During the Industrial Revolution. A Reappraisal,"* 35 (1982) 52-66. Concludes that industrialization in Birmingham and the Black Country did not change work habits. "In the two major industries of the Black Country [ironworks and coal], there are no signs of any new work disciplines resulting from intensifying industrialization. As for other industries, the restrictions imposed on women's hours by the Factory Acts now applied to workshops and other workplaces.... In other industries which employed women, the 10-1/2 hour limitation served to keep the hours down for all... life was better for women in the workshops and factories subject to inspection than in the domestic workshops which remained" (pp. 64-65).

7.199

Cole, G.D.H. and Postgate, Raymond, **THE BRITISH COMMON PEOPLE 1746-1947**. 1961. "The middle-class ladies running the ENGLISH WOMAN'S JOURNAL were immensely ignorant of all trades outside those of the needlewomen and governesses whom they chiefly had to protect, and of clerking and serving in shops, into which they hoped to introduce more and more women. They had no connection whatever with the women textile workers, nor much more with chainmakers, pithead women, and other trades.... So little were they aware of realities that they induced Henry Fawcett to attempt repeatedly to repeal the Ten Hours Act on the ground that its provisions were an infringement of women's liberties" (p. 431). See index for other material relevant to women.

7.200

Mitchell, Brian R. and Deane, Phyliss, **ABSTRACT OF BRITISH HISTORICAL STATISTICS**. Cambridge, 1962. Includes information on employed women for the years 1901 and 1911.

7.201
George, M. Dorothy, "The People and the Trades of London" in LONDON LIFE IN THE EIGHTEENTH CENTURY. by M. Dorothy George. New York, 1965. "It was an age of minute social distinctions. Lines were drawn between the artisan and the labourer, the master and the journeyman, as they were drawn between the lodger and the housekeeper.... Below the journey men or artisans in skilled trades came the unskilled labourers, and a mass of street-sellers (often the women-folk of the labourers) and casual workers" (pp. 156-157).

7.202
Klein, Viola, "Industrialization and the Changing Role of Women" in BRITAIN'S MARRIED WOMEN WORKERS. by Viola Klein. 1965; rpt. from: CURRENT SOCIOLOGY: 12 (1963) 24-34. "In Britain, women formed, up to the 1950's——with minor variations——slightly less than one-third of the working population; but, with the exception of the war periods, the proportion of married women who went out to work declined" from 25 percent in 1851 to 13 percent at the turn of the century (p. 31).

7.203
Mitchell, David J., MONSTROUS REGIMENT: THE STORY OF THE WOMEN OF THE FIRST WORLD WAR. New York, 1965.

7.204
Routh, Guy, OCCUPATION AND PAY IN BRITAIN 1906-1960. Cambridge, 1965.

7.205
Kamm, Josephine, RAPIERS AND BATTLEAXES. 1966. See index for subjects relative to women's employment.

7.206
CHAMBERS'S ENCYCLOPEDIA: Klein, V., "Employment of Women," 14 (1967) 617-619. Discusses effects of the Industrial Revolution in Great Britain and resulting patterns of employment.

7.207
Hobsbawm, Eric J., "Industrialization: The Second Phase" in INDUSTRY AND EMPIRE. by Eric J. Hobsbawm. Harmondsworth, 1968. "By 1871, Britain contained 170,000 'persons' of rank and property without visible occupation——almost all of them women or rather 'ladies'; a surprising number of them unmarried ladies. Stocks and shares, including shares in family firms formed into 'private companies' for this purpose, were a convenient way of providing for widows, daughters, and other relatives who could not——and no longer needed to be——associated with the management of property and enterprise.... The era of railway, iron, and foreign investment also provided the economic base for the Victorian spinster" (p. 119).

7.208
Hogg, Sallie, "The Employment of Women in Great Britain, 1819-1921," Ph.D. diss., Oxford Univ., 1968.

7.209
Briggs, Asa, "Work" in HOW THEY LIVED. by Asa Briggs. Oxford, 1969.

7.210
Morgan, D.H.J., "Theoretical and Conceptual Problems in the Study of Social Relations at Work: An Analysis of Differing Definitions of Women's Roles in a

Northern Factory," Ph.D. diss., University of Manchester, 1969.

7.211
Brooks, D.C., "Exploitation" and "Improvement" in **THE EMANCIPATION OF WOMEN.** by D.C. Brooks. 1970. "In 1851, there were 8,155,000 females aged ten or more (compared to 7,600,000 males): nearly one-third of them were in paid employment outside their own homes. The biggest occupation for women was domestic service (more than a million servants in private houses, farms, hotels, etc.). Half a million women worked in textile mills and 340,000 in the dress trades; 100,000 worked in agriculture, 54,000 in lace manufacture based in Nottingham and 30,000 in hosiery manufacture based in Leicester" (p. 46). Includes extracts from testimonies made to Parliamentary committees by women and photographs. The chapter on "Improvement" briefly discusses reforms pioneered for working-class women and the new occupations that opened to women as demand for workers in fields such as typing and telephone operators increased.

7.212
Crow, Duncan, "The Newly Discovered Regions" in **THE VICTORIAN WOMAN.** by Duncan Crow. 1971.

7.213
McCrone, Kathleen Eleanor, "The Economic Position of Women" and "The Economic Advancement of Women" in "The Advancement of Women During the Age of Reform 1832-1870," Ph.D. diss., New York Univ., 1971. Examines Victorian attitudes towards working women, arguments against their employment, and efforts made to expand occupational opportunities.

7.214
Sheppard, Francis, **LONDON 1808-1870: THE INFERNAL WEN.** 1971. See especially: "Appendix: the Distribution of Occupations and Social Classes in London in 1851."

7.215
LABOUR HISTORY: McCalman, J., *"The Impact of the First World War on Female Employment in England,"* no. 21 (1971) 36-47. "The Great War essentially did little to emancipate British women. Although the average female wage had risen above subsistence level, effective trade unionism had begun to grow, and due to changes in the economy, women enjoyed a wider job choice——their status as workers has not significantly risen" (p. 47); Hammerton, A.J., *"New Trends in the History of Working Women in Britain,"* no. 31 (1976) 53-60. Discusses attitudes and recent writings on the history of working women.

7.216
Bellamy, Joyce M. and Saville, John, **DICTIONARY OF LABOUR BIOGRAPHY.** 5 vols. 1972-1979.

7.217
Best, Geoffrey, "The Making of Livings" in **MID-VICTORIAN BRITAIN 1851-1875.** by Geoffrey Best. New York, 1972. See especially: pp. 99-110 on women at work. "Wherever there was improvement in the conditions and hours of labour, as for example in textile factories and mines... women shared its benefits equally with the men.... The number of working women thus affected was however small compared with the mass of them, the style of whose occupations remained just as bearable or unbearable as it had been earlier on... the scores of sentimental writers who enthused about The Home and about woman's place within it must not be

understood to have been describing a domestic state that was anything like normal for most of the working classes" (p. 100).

7.218
Black, Eugene C., "Social Organization" in VICTORIAN CULTURE AND SOCIETY. ed. by Eugene C. Black. New York, 1973.

7.219
Scott, Joan W. and Tilly, Louise A., "Woman's Work and the Family in Nineteenth Century Europe" in THE FAMILY IN HISTORY. ed. by Charles E. Rosenberg. Pittsburg, 1975. A comparative study of France and England from 1700 to 1950. The differing rates of industrialization of the two countries are used to analyze the impact on women's work; *rpt. from:* COMPARATIVE STUDIES IN SOCIETY AND HISTORY: 17 (1975) 36-64. "Great numbers of women worked outside the home during most of the nineteenth century, long before they enjoyed civil and political rights.... Rather than a steady increase in the size of the female labor force, the pattern was one of increase followed by decline.... The women who worked in great numbers... were overwhelmingly members of the working and peasant classes. Most held jobs in domestic service, garment making or the textile industry. The kinds of jobs available to women were not only limited in number and kind; they also were segregated——that is, they were held almost exclusively by women. The women who held these jobs were usually young and single" (pp. 37-39); WOMEN, WORK, AND FAMILY. New York, 1978.

7.220
BULLETIN OF THE SOCIETY FOR THE STUDY OF LABOUR HISTORY: Bridge, Mrs. E., *"Conference Report: Women's Employment: Problems of Research,"* 26 (1973) 5-22. Refers to the difficulty in interpreting the census data from 1851-1881 for women's employment. Claims that the major reason is that many part-time workers and those women who worked informally in the family business without benefit of formal wages were unaccounted for.

7.221
SOCIAL POLICY: Harris, A.K. and Silverman, B., *"Women in Advanced Capitalism,"* 4 (1973) 16-22.

7.222
Burnett, John, ed., USEFUL TOIL: AUTOBIOGRAPHIES OF WORKING PEOPLE FROM THE 1820'S TO THE 1920'S. 1974; *also published as:* THE ANNALS OF LABOUR: AUTOBIOGRAPHIES OF BRITISH WORKING-CLASS PEOPLE 1820-1920. Bloomington, 1974.

7.223
McKendrick, N., "Home Demand and Economic Growth: A New View of the Role of Women and Children in the Industrial Revolution" in HISTORICAL PERSPECT-IVES. ed. by N. McKendrick. 1974. "It was consumer demand which attracted the attention of the textile entrepreneurs and made the fortunes of the manufacturers of mass consumer goods. And it was the despised labour of women and children which helped to finance that new consumer demand" (p. 209).

7.224
HISTORY: Richards, E., *"Women in the British Economy Since About 1700: An Interpretation,"* 59 (1974) 337-357. Compares women's economic roles during the period between pre-industrialization and the Industrial Revolution, showing that the rise of industry restricted women instead of expanding their opportunities; Hollis,

P., *"Working Women,"* 62 (1977) 439-445. Review of the current literature.

7.225

Auchmuty, Rosemary, "Spinsters and Trade Unions in Victorian Britain" in WOMEN AT WORK. ed. by Susan Eade, Peter Spearitt, and Ann Curthoys. Canberra, 1975. "The leaders of the movement to extend female employment... soon realized that simply giving women the right to work was no guarantee of their right to do so on fair terms. Permitting the competition of men and women in the labour market probably helped to emancipate the middle-class elite from whose ranks the feminists were drawn, but it [brought]... to the poor... increasing poverty, and, in some instances... slavery" (pp. 109-110).

7.226

Davies, Ross, WOMEN AND WORK. 1975. See chapters 2 through 5: "Pre-Industrial Woman," "The Industrial Revolution," "Trade Unions: Men Only" and "The Professions Close Ranks."

7.227

Kovacevic, Ivanka, FACT INTO FICTION. ENGLISH LITERATURE AND THE INDUSTRIAL SCENE 1750-1850. Leicester, 1975. Traces "the development of the industrial theme in English imaginative writing.... Such a survey enables one to see much more clearly how the so-called social novel came into being, and to observe the gradual growth of the social conscience which inspired the reformist zeal of Charles Dickens and his contemporaries. Yet another gain is a better understanding of the reasons for the bias shown in fictionalized accounts of social problems——a bias against working-class organizations and their actions" (p. 13). Includes excerpts from these accounts.

7.228

Stearns, Peter, "Working-Class Women in Britain, 1890-1914" in SUFFER AND BE STILL: WOMEN IN THE VICTORIAN AGE. ed. by Martha Vicinus. Bloomington, 1973. Shows that, although the standard of living improved in basic economic terms, by the 1890s, traditions of poverty kept poor women from improving standards of housekeeping or of life in general. Demonstrates the effects of women on industry in capacities other than employment; LIVES OF LABOR. WORK IN A MATURING INDUSTRIAL SOCIETY. New York, 1975. A social history covering the period 1890-1914; *reviewed in:* JOURNAL OF SOCIAL HISTORY: Kindleberger, C.P., 10 (1977) 360-361. It was "a time of shorter hours, piece rates, and speed-up to maintain output of industry on the one hand, and incomes of workers on the other. Shorter hours made possible greater separation of work from family life" (p. 360).

7.229

JOURNAL OF SOCIAL HISTORY: Branca, P., *"A New Perspective on Women's Work: A Comparative Typology,"* 9 (1975) 129-153; Pleck, E., *"Two Worlds in One: Work and Family,"* 10 (1976) n.p. Critiques the idea of dissolution of the home as workplace; Dyhouse, C., *"Working-Class Mothers and Infant Mortality in England, 1895-1914,"* 12 (1978) 248-267. Describes the opposition to women's work outside the home that was expressed through the movement to save infant life. The Infants' Health Society was eventually "forced to recognise that the artifically-fed babies of working mothers whose wage bought a slightly better standard of living for their families showed a better rate of survival than did the breastfed babies of mothers in similar social circumstances who stayed at home" (p. 257); *rpt. in:* BIOLOGY, MEDICINE AND SOCIETY 1840-1940. ed. by Charles Webster. 1981.

7.230
NEW LEFT REVIEW: Coulson, M., Magas, B. and Wainwright, H., *"'The Housewife and her Labour Under Capitalism'——A Critique,"* no. 89 (1975) 59-71. Argues "that the central feature of women's position under capitalism is not their role simply as domestic workers, but rather the fact that they are both domestic and wage labourers" (p. 60); Gardiner, J., *"Women's Domestic Labour,"* no. 89 (1975) 47-58. Examines housework as domestic labor under capitalism.

7.231
NEW SOCIETY: Land, H., *"The Myth of the Male Breadwinner,"* 34 (1975) 71-73.

7.232
WORKING LIVES: A PEOPLE'S AUTOBIOGRAPHY OF HACKNEY. 1976.

7.233
Barker, Diana Leonard and Allen, Sheila, eds., **DEPENDENCE AND EXPLOIT-ATION IN WORK AND MARRIAGE.** 1976.

7.234
Coffrey, Kate, **THE 1900'S LADY.** 1976. See page 168 for women's occupations. Also includes census returns for 1901 and 1911.

7.235
Dawes, F.A., **A WOMAN'S PLACE——WOMEN AT WORK FROM 1830 TO THE PRESENT.** 1976.

7.236
Sachs, Albie and Wilson, Joan Hoff, **SEXISM AND THE LAW: A STUDY OF MALE BELIEFS AND LEGAL BIAS IN BRITAIN AND THE UNITED STATES.** New York, 1978. See especially: "Britain: Are Women 'Persons'?" Discusses women's entrance into medical schools, county councils, and the law profession. "The English common law, which had so often been extolled as being the embodiment of human freedom, had in fact provided the main intellectual justification for the avowed and formal subordination of women" (pp. 40-41).

7.237
SIGNS: Hartman, H., *"Capitalism, Patriarchy and Job Segregation by Sex (Part Two),"* 1 (1976) 137-170.

7.238
THEORY AND SOCIETY: Shorter, E., *"Women's Work: What Difference did Capitalism Make?"* 3 (1976) 513-527.

7.239
Harrison, Royden, **THE WARWICK GUIDE TO BRITISH LABOUR PERIODI-CALS 1790-1970.** 1977.

7.240
Mappen, Ellen Frank, "Women Workers and Unemployment Policy in Late Victorian and Edwardian London," Ph.D. diss., Rutgers Univ., 1977. Examines the development of women's place in industrialized society and the concern expressed by reformers over the problem of their unemployment. This concern did reflect a changing ideology that began to accept women as more than wives and mothers; however, the reform movement was still circumscribed by traditional views; "New Introduction" in **MARRIED WOMEN'S WORK.** rpt. of 1915 edition, ed. by

Clementina Black. 1983; "Strategists for Change: Social Feminist Approaches to the Problems of Women's Work" in **UNEQUAL OPPORTUNITIES.** 1986.

7.241

Marwick, Arthur, **WOMEN AT WAR, 1914-1918.** 1977; *reviewed in:* **TIMES LITERARY SUPPLEMENT:** Stephenson, J., (July 29, 1977) n.p. Marwick uses a "fascinating collection of contemporary photographs" detailing women's work in industry, public services, medical services and as army auxiliaries from all parts of Britain. He evokes the "herculean struggle of the miner's wife against unrelenting coal dust, the rivalry between upper-class leaders of women's auxiliary organizations, the increasingly beleaguered fortress of unmitigated male chauvinism, and above all the perpetual preoccupation with sexual morals" (n.p.).

7.242

McBride, Theresa M., "The Long Road Home: Women's Work and Industrialization" in **BECOMING VISIBLE: WOMEN IN EUROPEAN HISTORY.** ed. by Renate Bridenthal and Claudia Koonz. Boston, 1977. "Women have always worked. The Industrial Revolution did not usher in a new phase in the employment of women in that sense. But the nineteenth century did 'discover' the woman worker as an object of pity, and the Victorian social conscience was aroused as never before by the plight of working women and children" (p. 282). Also discusses the split between home and work, and the supplementation of household income by wifely earnings.

7.243

Finnegan, Frances, **POVERTY AND PROSTITUTION: A STUDY OF VICTORIAN PROSTITUTES IN YORK.** 1979. Finnegan views prostitution as a "hazardous occupation" (p. 18) to which impoverished, disadvantaged and outcast women resorted for income. The book explodes "Victorian myths," dealing in great detail with the working life of various types of prostitutes. "Poverty in some form or another was the major reason for girls initially taking to the streets... and having done so, few were afforded more than a temporary relief.... Few contemporary observers, with the exception of Refuge Committee members... placed due emphasis on the basic poverty of that class of women.... The evidence of this study suggests that fundamentally it was poverty which was the most powerful inducement to their becoming prostitutes.... [and that] low-class prostitution was not a rewarding profession" (pp. 213-214).

7.244

ORAL HISTORY: Taylor, S., *"The Effect of Marriage on Job Possibilities for Women and the Ideology of the Home: Nottingham 1890-1930,"* 5 (1977) 46-61. Examines how the ideology of women's innate inferiority operated in their family role and in their work in the lower-paid sectors of the lace and hosiery industries. Married women automatically lost their jobs and "several of those interviewed suggested in a conspiratorial sense, the existence of an employer's federation with a deliberate policy against female employment" while "other interviewees blamed male trade unionists who feared the loss of their jobs because of the cheapness of female labour" (n.p.).

7.245

Burman, Sandra, ed., **FIT WORK FOR WOMEN.** 1979. An enormously helpful anthology of essays on questions such as the origins of the domestic ideal and its effect on wage work as well as activities related to work but not defined as employment. Includes chapters on women's philanthropic work, landladies and lodgers, women cotton workers, and militancy amongst women workers.

7.246
Evans, Mary and Morgan, David, "Women and Paid Work" in **WORK ON WOMEN: A GUIDE TO THE LITERATURE.** 1979. Bibliographical listing.

7.247
Hiley, Michael, **VICTORIAN WORKING WOMEN: PORTRAITS FROM LIFE.** 1979. This book follows working women through the eyes of Arthur Munby, using excerpts from this observer's diary, and is richly illustrated with many photographs. Munby married beneath his station, choosing Hannah Cullwick, a maid-of-all-work. His diaries are full of verbal portraits of working women, who fascinated him by the colorful contrast they provided against staid society life.

7.248
Morgan, Carol Edyth, "Working-Class Women and Labor and Social Movements of Mid-Nineteenth Century England," Ph.D. diss., Univ. of Iowa, 1979. See chapter 3, "Women and the Ten Hours Movement." Discusses the enormous amount of labor agitation and organization in the 1830s, the increasingly complex position of women within industry, the role of machinery in requiring more, not less, labor, the early general protest *against* shorter hours, for fear of threats to livelihood, and women's later participation in the factory movement.

7.249
Purcell, Kate, "Military Acquiescence Amongst Women Workers" in **FIT WORK FOR WOMEN.** ed. by Sandra Burman. 1979.

7.250
HISTORY WORKSHOP JOURNAL: Hobsbawm, E., *"Man and Woman in Socialist Iconography,"* 6 (1979) 121-138; Alexander, S., Davin, A., and Hostettler, E., *"Labouring Women: A Reply to Eric Hobsbawm,"* 8 (1979) 174-182; Rose, S.O., *"'Gender at Work': Sex, Class and Industrial Capitalism,"* 21 (1986) 113-133.

7.251
LOCAL POPULATION STUDIES: Saito, O., *"Who Worked When: Life-Time Profiles of Labour Force Participation in Cardington and Corfe Castle in the Late Eighteenth and Mid-Nineteenth Centuries,"* no. 22 (1979) 14-29. Study of the labor participation of men and women by age group in two rural towns, and the effects of cottage industry on women and children in the family. Differential economic conditions in the towns resulted in variable employment opportunities for females in such industries as lacemaking and spinning, such that married women in Cardington did not stop working whereas those in Corfe Castle dropped out of the labor force.

7.252
Deem, Rose Mary, **SCHOOLING FOR WOMEN'S WORK.** 1980.

7.253
Land, Hilary, **THE FAMILY WAGE.** Liverpool, 1980. On the effect upon women's status and independence of a policy that institutes male financial power.

7.254
White, Jerry, "Work" in **ROTHSCHILD BUILDINGS: LIFE IN AN EAST END TENEMENT BLOCK 1887-1920.** by Jerry White. 1980. Discusses work of Jewish immigrants in the context of urban life in tenements which struck the author as "so oppressive, so starkly repulsive, so much without one redeeming feature" (p. xii). Presents much material on women in tailoring, cap-making, millinery, cigarette-

making, and home work, from both documented sources and firsthand accounts. Working conditions are described in detail, and wages contrasted with company profits.

7.255
Ferguson, Neal, "Women in Twentieth-Century England" in **THE WOMEN OF ENGLAND FROM ANGLO-SAXON TIMES TO THE PRESENT: INTERPRETIVE BIBLIOGRAPHICAL ESSAYS.** 1980. ——*see also:* **ALBION:** Ferguson, N., *"Employment Opportunities and Economic Roles,"* 7 (1975) 55-68.

7.256
SOCIAL HISTORY SOCIETY NEWSLETTER: Rushton, P., *"Women and Industrialization——A Critical View,"* 5 (1980) 5. Regional study of Lancashire and County Durham with an emphasis on class conflict and unionization.

7.257
Adams, Carol, "Earning a Living" in **ORDINARY LIVES: A HUNDRED YEARS AGO.** by Carol Adams. 1982. Informative overview of the kinds of work women performed. Includes middle- and working-class occupations in addition to rural labor and mining.

7.258
Cambridge Women's Studies Group, **WOMEN IN SOCIETY: INTERDISCIPLINARY ESSAYS.** 1981. See the five articles in Section one: "Women, the Family, and Wage Labour Under Capitalism."

7.259
Evans, Mary, ed., **THE WOMAN QUESTION: READINGS ON THE SUBORDINATION OF WOMEN.** 1982. See especially: "Some Notes on Female Wage Labour in Capitalist Production" by Veronica Beechey and "Women in the British Economy Since About 1700: An Interpretation" by Eric Richards.

7.260
Whitelegg, Elizabeth, et al., eds., **THE CHANGING EXPERIENCE OF WOMEN.** Oxford, 1982. Part 1, "The Historical Separation of Home and Workplace" contains several valuable articles on women's work and the family: "The Butcher, the Baker, the Candlestickmaker: the Shop and the Family in the Industrial Revolution" and "The Home Turned Upside Down? The Working-Class Family in Cotton Textiles 1780-1850" by Catherine Hall; "Women's Work in Nineteenth-Century London: A Study of the Years 1820-50" by Sally Alexander; "Women's Work and the Family in Nineteenth-Century Europe" by Joan Scott and Louise Tilly; and "The 'Family Wage'" by Michele Barrett and Mary McIntosh.

7.261
Alexander, Sally, **WOMEN'S WORK IN NINETEENTH-CENTURY LONDON: A STUDY OF THE YEARS 1820-50.** 1983; *rpt. from:* **THE RIGHTS AND WRONGS OF WOMEN.** ed. by Juliet Mitchell and Ann Oakley. 1976. According to the Census of 1851, 57 percent of all London women over twenty were without occupation. The author sets out to fill this gap in knowledge about women's unrecorded means of subsistence. She finds that London offered a wide variety of marginal occupations in contrast to the unitary opportunities of the northern textile towns; that women's employment in their husbands' trades hid them from statistical sight; and that much of their work was intermittent and casual, not fitting into the census categories and hence overlooked. A hierarchy of women's employment is impossible to construct "since most women's work is lumped at the bottom of the social and

economic scale" (p. 33). Skilled occupations ranged from dressmaking and millinery, pearl-stringing and haberdashery, outworking embroidery and fine shirt making, tailoring, bookbinding, hatting, fur-pulling, and quilling. Unskilled and casual work often began as a child and included domestic service, washing and charring, mangling, street-selling, and shopkeeping.

7.262
Benson, John, **THE PENNY CAPITALISTS: A STUDY OF NINETEENTH-CENTURY WORKING-CLASS ENTREPRENEURS.** Dublin, 1983. Working-class wives rarely extended their businesses into full-time occupations. When their businesses became successful, husbands, who appear to have been more interested in earning money for its own sake, generally took over.

7.263
Lewis, Jane, "Patterns of Employment" and "Characteristics of Women's Work" in **WOMEN IN ENGLAND 1870-1950: SEXUAL DIVISIONS AND SOCIAL CHANGE.** by Jane Lewis. 1984. Discusses the impact of industrialization. Offers many tables showing changes over time in demographics and occupational distribution of female workers. "The shift to white-blouse work was the major feature of the change in the occupational distribution of women during the period. While the number of women engaged in such work (mainly teaching, retailing, office work and nursing) increased by 161 per cent between 1881 and 1911, the number working in manufacturing industry and domestic service increased by only 24 per cent" (p. 158).

7.264
Roberts, Elizabeth, "Working Wives and Their Families" in **POPULATION AND SOCIETY IN BRITAIN 1850-1980.** ed. by Theo Barker and Michael Drake. 1982. A study of three towns in northern England between 1890 and 1940 using census data and oral history. Approximately 40-50 percent of all working wives held some form of part-time employment. Observes that oral histories can correct misleading census statistics, which do not always count women working part-time as "employed"; **A WOMAN'S PLACE: AN ORAL HISTORY OF WORKING-CLASS WOMEN, 1890-1940.** Oxford and New York, 1984. The subjects are from Lancashire. See index for sections on married women's work, specific occupations, skilled and unskilled work, working conditions, attitudes of parents to daughters' work, etc; "Women's Strategies, 1890-1940" in **LABOUR AND LOVE: WOMEN'S EXPERIENCE OF HOME AND FAMILY, 1850-1940.** ed. by Jane Lewis. 1986. Details poor women's "strategies" for augmenting and stretching their husbands' salaries for the family good, based upon oral evidence. Gives a full account of the part-time work of married women, which could include childminding, in-home "retailing" of food or notions, cleaning, and taking in washing, lodgers or sewing.

7.265
Lindsay, Charles and Duffin, Lorna, eds., **WOMEN AND WORK IN PRE-INDUSTRIAL BRITAIN.** 1985. See especially, "Introduction" by Charles Lindsay.

7.266
John, Angela V., ed., **UNEQUAL OPPORTUNITIES: WOMEN'S EMPLOYMENT IN ENGLAND 1800-1918.** Oxford, 1985. Examines sex and status in the hosiery, bookbinding and tailoring trades, and the development of opportunities in domestic science, clerical work and tin mining. Also discusses women's involvement in trade organizations and political movements.

7.267
Pennybacker, Susan, "The Labour Question and the London County Council, 1889-1919," Ph.D. diss., Cambridge Univ., 1985.

7.268
Bradley, Harriet, **MEN'S WORK, WOMEN'S WORK: A HISTORY OF THE SEX-TYPING OF JOBS IN BRITAIN.** 1986. Study of sex discrimination in employment covers from the Industrial Revolution to present and makes comparisons with America and Australia.

7.269
Lewis, Jane, ed., **LABOUR AND LOVE: WOMEN'S EXPERIENCE OF HOME AND FAMILY, 1850-1940.** Oxford, 1986. Includes "Women's Strategies, 1890-1940" by Elizabeth Roberts and "Marital Status, Work and Kinship, 1850-1930" by Diana Gittins. The entire volume provides contexts for understanding relationships between domestic life and work, and waged employment.

7.270
Lown, Judy, **WITH FREE AND GRACEFUL STEP?: WOMEN AND INDUSTRIALIZATION IN NINETEENTH-CENTURY ENGLAND.** 1986. Study of textile employment showing how paternalistic practices were perpetuated by capitalist industrialization and forced women into restricted areas of labor. Discusses implications for family life and includes contemporary feminists' challenges to this pattern; "Not So Much a Factory, More a Form of Patriarchy: Gender and Class During Industrialisation" in **GENDER, CLASS, AND WORK.** ed. by Eva Gamarnikow, David H.J. Morgan, June Purvis and Daphne E. Taylorson. 1983. Distinguishes and realigns the terms "patriarchy" and "paternalism," explaining how each is manifested in employers' and male workers' attitudes toward working women. Their "philanthropy" focused on "improving the welfare" of women and girls, and on starting evening schools. "Other attempts at paternalistic enterprises included the setting up of a boarding house, called Factory Home, in 1849 to provide lodgings for girls who came from the surrounding villages and to attract them away from lodging with 'a class of women particularly adverse to morality' who 'positively helped to instruct and encourage them in abandoned courses'" (p. 39). —*see also:* Lown, Judy, "Gender and Class During Industrialization: A Study of the Halstead Silk Industry in Essex, 1815-1900," Ph.D. diss., Univ. of Essex, 1982.

7.271
Walby, Sylvia, **PATRIARCHY AT WORK: PATRIARCHAL AND CAPITALIST RELATIONS IN EMPLOYMENT 1800-1984.** 1986. Explores gender relations in three contrasting areas of employment: cotton textiles, factory and clerical work. Walby diverges from previous analyses of patriarchy and capitalism as mutually accommodating by demonstrating inherent tension and conflict in maintenance of capitalist relations. Draws on sociological, economic and geographical materials.

7.272
Davidoff, Leonore and Westover, Belinda, **OUR WORK, OUR LIVES, OUR WORDS: WOMEN'S HISTORY AND WOMEN'S WORK.** Totowa, New Jersey, 1986. Chapters include research on women domestic laborers, tailoresses, textile workers and their Union, elementary teachers, typists, civil servant clerks and WAACs from the period 1880-1939.

7.273
Frader, Laura Levine, "Women in the Industrial Capitalist Economy" in **BECOMING**

VISIBLE: WOMEN IN EUROPEAN HISTORY. 2nd ed., ed. by Renata Bridenthal, Claudia Koonz and Susan Stuard. Boston, 1987.

* * *

2. FACTORIES, MILLS AND WORKSHOPS

7.273a
Baines, Edward, **OBSERVATION ON THE WOOLEN MACHINERY.** Leeds, 1803; **THE SOCIAL, EDUCATIONAL, AND RELIGIOUS STATE OF THE MANUFACTURING DISTRICTS; HISTORY OF THE COTTON MANUFACTURE IN GREAT BRITAIN.** [1835].

7.274
Radcliffe, William, **ORIGIN OF THE NEW SYSTEM OF MANUFACTURE COMMONLY CALLED 'POWER-LOOM WEAVING.'** Stockport, 1828. Illustrates the social changes that were consequent upon the development and introduction of machinery.

7.275
Cropper, Jeremy, **THE FACTORY SYSTEM.** Leeds, 1831.

7.276
Kay-Shuttleworth, James Phillip, **THE MORAL AND PHYSICAL CONDITION OF THE WORKING CLASSES EMPLOYED IN THE COTTON MANUFACTURE IN MANCHESTER.** 2nd ed., 1832; rpt., 1970. Author may also be cataloged as Shuttleworth, James Phillip Kay.

7.277
Royle, Vernon, **THE FACTORY SYSTEM DEFENDED.** Manchester, 1833.

7.278
Sadler, Michael T., **PROTEST AGAINST THE SECRET PROCEEDINGS OF THE FACTORY COMMISSION.** Leeds, 1833; **FACTORY STATISTICS, THE OFFICIAL TABLES APPENDED TO THE REPORT OF THE SELECT COMMITTEE, VINDICATED IN A SERIES OF LETTERS TO J.E. DRINKWATER.** 1836.

7.279
BLACKWOODS EDINBURGH MAGAZINE: Wilson, J., *"The Factory System,"* 33 (1833) 419-450.

7.280
Scrope, George P., **POLITICAL ECONOMY, VERSUS, THE HAND LOOM WEAVERS. THE LETTER OF GEORGE POULETT SCROPE... TO THE CHAIRMAN OF THE CENTRAL COMMITTEE OF THE HAND WORSTED WEAVERS, OF WEST RIDING OF YORK: WITH THEIR ANSWER TO THE SAME...** Bradford, 1835.

7.281
Norton, Caroline, **A VOICE FROM THE FACTORIES: IN SERIOUS VERSE.** 1838.

7.282
Greg, Robert Hyde, **THE FACTORY QUESTION IN RELATION TO ITS EFFECT ON THE HEALTH AND MORALS OF THOSE EMPLOYED IN FACTORIES, AND THE TEN-HOUR BILL.** 1837.

7.283
Head, George, **A HOME TOUR THROUGH VARIOUS PARTS OF THE UNITED KINGDOM. BEING A CONTINUATION OF THE "HOME TOUR THROUGH THE MANUFACTURING DISTRICTS." ALSO, MEMOIRS OF AN ASSISTANT COMMISSARY GENERAL.** 1837.

7.284
Wing, Charles, **EVILS OF THE FACTORY SYSTEM, DEMONSTRATED BY PARLIAMENTARY EVIDENCE.** 1837; rpt., 1967.

7.285
DISTRESS OF THE MANUFACTURING CLASSES OF ENGLAND. 1842.

7.286
OBSERVATIONS ON THE DISTRESSED STATE OF OUR MANUFACTURING POPULATION WITH PROPOSALS OF AN IMMEDIATE AND EXTENSIVE REMEDY. 1842.

7.287
Adshead, Joseph, **EVIDENCE OF THE STATE OF THE LABORING CLASSES IN 1840-1842.** 1842.

7.288
Cooke-Taylor, William, **NOTES OF A TOUR IN THE MANUFACTURING DISTRICTS OF LANCASHIRE.** 1842; **FACTORIES AND THE FACTORY SYSTEM.** 1844.

7.289
Kenworthy, William, **INVENTIONS AND HOURS OF LABOR.** 1842.

7.290
Dodd, George, **DAYS AT THE FACTORIES; OR, THE MANUFACTURING INDUSTRY OF GREAT BRITAIN DESCRIBED.** 1843; rpt., New York, 1967. Among the 22 trades covered, Dodd mentions women in two: bookbinding and hatmaking. He states in the introduction: "In what manner female labour is bestowed in making articles of dress is too well known to need recital... in the large bulk of female employments, as directed to dress, there is a singular uniformity of working apparatus, of posture, and of general procedure" (pp. 5-6). In reference to needlework, "It is a fortunate circumstance, considering the very limited number of employments for females in this country, that there are several departments of bookbinding within the scope of their ability" (pp. 370-371).

7.291
Nunns, Thomas, **A LETTER TO LORD ASHLEY ON THE CONDITION OF THE WORKING CLASSES IN BIRMINGHAM.** 1843.

7.292
Shaw, Charles, **MANUFACTURING DISTRICTS: REPLIES TO LORD ASHLEY.** 1843.

7.293
Hirst, William, HISTORY OF THE WOOLEN TRADE DURING THE LAST SIXTY YEARS. Leeds, 1844.

7.294
STUBBORN FACTS FROM THE FACTORIES, BY A MANCHESTER OPERATIVE. 1844.

7.295
Tonna, Charlotte Elizabeth, THE WORKS OF CHARLOTTE ELIZABETH. 3 vols. New York, 1844-1845; seven subsequent editions. Includes her fictionalized observations of women at work in factories and mills. Tonna claims to have based her stories on parliamentary reports; *first published in:* CHRISTIAN LADY'S MAGAZINE: (1839-1844). Includes the serialized novelettes, *"Helen Fleetwood," "The Forsaken Home," "The Little Pin-Headers,"* and *"The Lace-Runners"*; PERSONAL RECOLLECTIONS. 4th ed., 1854. ——*see also:* NINETEENTH CENTURY FICTION: Kovacevic, I. and Kanner, S.B., *"Blue Book into Novel: The Forgotten Industrial Fiction of Charlotte Elizabeth Tonna,"* 25 (1970/1971) 152-173; *rpt. with addendum by S.B. Kanner in:* DER ENGLISCHE SOZIALE ROMAN IM 19 JAHRHUNDERT. ed. by Konrad Gross. Darmstadt, 1977; Kovacevic, Ivanka, FACT INTO FICTION. Leicester, 1975; VICTORIAN PERIODICALS REVIEW: Fryckstedt, M.C., *"Charlotte Elizabeth Tonna and the Christian Lady's Magazine,"* 14 (1981) 43-51.

7.296
YOUNG WOMEN OF THE FACTORY. 1845.

7.297
ECONOMIST: *"The Needle Women of London. What Cannot be Done for Them, and What Can?"* (1849) 1437-1439; *"But What Can be Done for the Masses?"* 7 (1849) 1440-1441. Delineates the conditions of needlewomen and the efforts of Sidney Herbert on their behalf.

7.298
Kingsley, Charles, CHEAP CLOTHES AND NASTY. 1850. A dramatic rendering of the sweated sewing trades that was popular and effective propaganda for reform.

7.299
CHAMBERS'S EDINBURGH JOURNAL: *"Curiosities of Industry Among the Ladies,"* 66 (1855) 209-212; *"Female Nail Makers,"* 624 (1875) 799-800.

7.300
Parkes, Bessie Rayner, REMARKS ON THE EDUCATION OF GIRLS, WITH REFERENCES TO THE SOCIAL, LEGAL, AND INDUSTRIAL POSITION OF WOMEN IN THE PRESENT DAY. 2nd ed., 1856.

7.301
Bray, Charles, THE INDUSTRIAL EMPLOYMENT OF WOMEN. [1857].

7.302
James, John, HISTORY OF THE WORSTED MANUFACTURE IN ENGLAND. 1857.

7.303
Kydd, Samuel Alfred, THE HISTORY OF THE FACTORY MOVEMENT. 1857.

7.304
Milne, John Duguid, INDUSTRIAL AND SOCIAL POSITION OF WOMEN, IN THE MIDDLE AND LOWER RANKS. 1857; rpt., New York, 1984; *reviewed in:* ENGLISHWOMAN'S REVIEW: 4 (1870) 269-271. Milne's thesis is that industrial occupation of women is necessary not only for economic reasons but because it strengthens the female character and bridges the gap between men and women. Thus women's feminine influence can contribute positively in the realm of politics and society.

7.305
SATURDAY REVIEW: *"Industrial Occupations of Women,"* 4 (1857) 63-64.

7.306
TRANSACTIONS OF THE NATIONAL ASSOCIATION FOR THE PROMOTION OF SOCIAL SCIENCE: Hastings, G.W., et al., *"Remarks on the Industrial Employment of Women,"* (1857) 531-548; Bray, C., *"The Industrial Employment of Women,"* (1857) 545; Wright, T.S., *"On the Employment of Women in Factories in Birmingham,"* (1858) 538-544; Hertz, F., *"Mechanics' Institutes for Working Women, with Special Reference to the Manufacturing Districts of Yorkshire,"* (1860) 347-355; *"Female Factory Workers and Homes for Female Factory Workers,"* (1860) 723-724; Boucherett, J., *"On the Industrial Employment of Women,"* (1860) 728-729; Parkes, B.R., *"Industrial Employment of Women: A Year's Experience in Woman's Work,"* (1860) 811-819. Paper concerns educated women. The semi-mechanical arts such as telegraph worker, printing, law copying and managing sewing machines are best suited to young women living at home and for single women who aren't highly educated. The other major area equally suitable is "moral superintendence over women, and physical care of the sick and infirm of both sexes." She also supports women emigrating to the colonies; Parkes, B.R., *"Industrial Employment of Women: The Condition of Working Women in England and France,"* (1861) 632-640. Calls for efforts by middle-class "earnest and intellectual women" to improve the moral and physical life of young female laborers; McBurnie, D., *"On the Moral Tendency of Factory Labour,"* (1860) 724; Baker, R.S., *"Social Results of Employment of Girls and Women in Manufactories and Workshops,"* (1868) 537-548; Cooke-Taylor, R.W., *"On State Interference in the Industrial Employment of Women,"* (1876) 734-736; Burton, M., *"Should the Labour of Women in the Factories be Regulated?"* (1877) 246; Watherston, E.J., *"The Industrial Employment of Women in France Compared with England,"* (1878) 618-628. Discusses the disproportion between the sexes and its constant increase "as shown by every succeeding census, and with this increase there comes naturally an ever-rising difficulty in the employment of female labor. Nowhere is this difficulty more felt than in England because here the excess of females over males is greater than in any other state of Europe" (p. 618).

7.307
ENGLISH WOMAN'S JOURNAL: *"Special Meetings at Glasgow and Edinburgh with Reference to the Industrial Employment of Women,"* 6 (1860) 145-159; *"Passing Events——Social and Industrial... Employment of Women: Emigration, Orphans...; Social Science Assoc.; Population of Marylebone,"* 7 (1861) 286-287; *"Woman's Work in the World's Clothing,"* 8 (1863) 243-251. Delineates the history of English textile manufacture; describes cottage industry conditions.

7.308
Houston, Arthur, THE EMANCIPATION OF WOMEN FROM EXISTING

INDUSTRIAL DISABILITIES: CONSIDERED IN ITS ECONOMIC ASPECT. 1862. Houston, a political economist, traces "the effect on the production and distribution of wealth of the removal of the industrial restraints under which women labour" (p. 45). Declares his support of women entering the labor market in terms of its personal as well as social benefits. As for the popular view that women's nature dictates her subordination to the needs of others, "that any one portion of humanity should be called on more particularly than another to perform this self-immolation, is, it seems to me, a most absurd and abominable doctrine" (p. 11).

7.309
Merryweather, Mary, EXPERIENCE OF FACTORY LIFE: BEING A RECORD OF FOURTEEN YEARS WORK AT MR. COURAULD'S SILK MILL AT HALSTEAD IN ESSEX. 3rd ed., 1862.

7.310
ONCE A WEEK: *"An Industrial Chance for Gentlewomen,"* 9 (1863) 290-294.

7.311
Felkin, William, A HISTORY OF THE MACHINE-WROUGHT HOSIERY AND LACE MANUFACTURERS. Cambridge, 1867; rpt., Newton Abbot, 1967. See pp. 516-517 for statistics on women and girl laborers, average wages, and occupations. Includes illustrations of lace patterns and types of machines.

7.312
Christian Knowledge Society, A LETTER FROM A LADY TO WOMEN AND GIRLS WHO WORK IN THE FACTORIES. 1868.

7.313
Faithfull, Emily, WOMAN'S WORK WITH SPECIAL REFERENCE TO INDUSTRIAL EMPLOYMENT. 1871.

7.314
VICTORIA MAGAZINE: Faithfull, E., *"Work of Women in Industrial Employments,"* 17 (1871) 308; *"Women's Work, with Special Reference to Industrial Employment,"* 17 (1871) 312; *"Industrial Employment of Women in London,"* 28 (1876-77) 348.

7.315
Cooke-Taylor, Richard Whately, "The Employment of Married Women in Manufacture" in TRANSACTIONS OF THE NATIONAL ASSOCIATION FOR THE PROMOTION OF SOCIAL SCIENCE NORWICH MEETING, 1873. ed. by C.W. Ryalls and L.L.B. Cantab. 1874; INTRODUCTION TO A HISTORY OF THE FACTORY SYSTEM. 1886; THE MODERN FACTORY SYSTEM. 1891; THE FACTORY SYSTEM AND THE FACTORY ACTS, 1894. 1912.

7.316
WOMEN'S SUFFRAGE JOURNAL: Becker, L.E., *"The Women Carpet Weavers at Kidderminister,"* 5 (1874) 145-146; *"The Labour of Married Women in Factories,"* 5 (1875) 135-136. "It might be advisable before forbidding a fellow-creature to earn money for herself and family that some means of supporting her and them should first be devised.... I would like to state that it has never yet been proved that factory labour of mothers is more injurious to unborn children than standing over a washtub all day, or 'charing,' or indulgence in drinking habits" (p. 136); Becker, L.E., *"The Royal Commission on the Factory Acts,"* 6 (1875) 91-92. Argues that the Factory Acts were responsible for shutting women out of many occupations, that

they prevented a rise in wages and that women resent restrictions on their hours of work; Becker, L.E., *"The Industrial Condition of Women,"* 6 (1875) 130-131; Becker, L.E., *"Men's and Women's Work at Kidderminister,"* 6 (1875) 15; Becker, L.E., *"The Women Weavers of Dewsbury,"* 6 (1875) 39-40.

7.317
WOMEN'S UNION JOURNAL: *"The Factories and Workshops,"* 2 (1877) 17-18.

7.318
ENGLISHWOMAN'S REVIEW: *"The Night Cometh When No 'Woman' Can Work,"* 59 (1878) 97-102. Protests enactment of the Factory Acts on the grounds that it restricts women's right to work; *"Industrial Training for Girls,"* 10 (1879) 4-13. Compares industrial employment of women in France and England. Calls for independence of women and early training as opposed to an idle life; *"A Visit to the Royal Army Clothing Factory,"* 10 (1879) 537-544. Describes the working conditions in this particular clothing factory. "The employed in this establishment... are for the most part the wives or widows of soldiers... [who are] provided with employment at shirt making for the army in garrison towns, where they receive eightpence half-penny for shirt, calico or flannel, out of which sum they must find their own thread" (p. 541). Finds this wage fair, and above that made by women in the sweated industries; *"Factory Inspectors and Their Work in 1896,"* 29 (1898) 6-11. Discusses the work of five female factory inspectors, their findings, reports, and the changes they facilitated.

7.319
FRASER'S MAGAZINE: Simcox, E., *"The Industrial Employment of Women,"* 99 (1879) 246-255.

7.320
GOOD WORDS AND SUNDAY MAGAZINE: Watherston, E.J., *"Industrial Employment of Women and French Silk Manufactures,"* 20 (1879) 105-111. "Shall we repeat the old saying, 'They manage things better in France...?' What is wanted is to give woman a better education, and to complete it by technical education directed to a definite pursuit" (p. 111).

7.321
WOMAN'S GAZETTE: *"The Industrial Employment of Women in England and France Compared,"* 4 (1879) 26-27; 42-43; 75-77.

7.322
CONTEMPORARY REVIEW: Jevons, W.S., *"Married Women in Factories,"* 41 (1882) 37-53; Cooke-Taylor, R.W., *"Married Women in Factories,"* 42 (1882) 428-441.

7.323
Cole, Alan S., **REPORT TO THE HOUSE OF COMMONS ON THE PRESENT CONDITIONS OF THE HONITON LACE INDUSTRY.** 1887; **REPORT ON THE BEDFORDSHIRE, BUCKINGHAMSHIRE AND NORTHAMPTONSHIRE LACE INDUSTRIES.** 1891.

7.324
Bartlett, Elisha, **VINDICATION OF THE CHARACTER OF FEMALES IN... THE LOWELL MILLS.** 1891. On the system of housing factory girls in a company community in Massachusetts, written for an English audience.

7.325
Hobson, John Atkinson, **PROBLEMS OF POVERTY: AN INQUIRY INTO THE INDUSTRIAL CONDITION OF THE POOR.** 1891; subsequent eds. to 1921.

7.326
ECONOMIC JOURNAL: Collet, C.E. and Hutchins, B.L., *"Women's Work in Leeds,"* 1 (1891) 460-473. In 1832, the introduction of the first cloth power loom from Leeds created a demand for skilled women workers. Delineates the process which followed the mechanization of this labor and discusses the trend of men being employed at a higher wage, replaced by the "cheaper" female labor; Firth, J.B., *"Weavers of Bradford: Their Work and Wages,"* 2 (1892) 543-549.

7.327
Royal Commission on Labour, **THE EMPLOYMENT OF WOMEN: REPORTS ON THE CONDITIONS OF WORK IN VARIOUS INDUSTRIES.** 1893.

7.328
FORTNIGHTLY REVIEW: Dilke, E.F.S., *"The Industrial Position of Women,"* 60 (1893) 499-508. "We may say that the secret of England's industrial greatness is in her command of a practically unlimited supply of the cheap labour of her women and girls" (n.p.); March-Phillipps, E., *"The New Factory Bill: As It Affects Women,"* 61 (1894) 738-748. Discusses the relative merits of the bill in light of existing work conditions and workers' preferences; March-Phillipps, E., *"Factory Legislation for Women,"* 63 (1895) 733-744. In favor of legislation. Describes conditions in many industries; Tennant, M., *"The Women's Factory Department,"* 70 (1898) 148-156.

7.329
HUMANITARIAN: Holyoake, E.A., *"The Industrial Position of Women,"* n.v. (1893) 267-274.

7.330
Hill, Georgiana, "The Factory Hand" in **WOMEN IN ENGLISH LIFE.** by Georgiana Hill. 1894.

7.331
Bosanquet, Helen (Dendy), "The Position of Women in Industry" in **ASPECTS OF THE SOCIAL PROBLEM.** by Helen Dendy. 1895; *rpt. from:* **NATIONAL REVIEW:** 23 (1894) 806-814.

7.332
Boucherett, Jessie, Blackburn, Helen, et al., **THE CONDITION OF WORKING WOMEN AND THE FACTORY ACTS.** 1896. Contents include "On Working Overtime," "The Condition of Working Women," "Report to the Society for the Employment of Women," and "Trades-Unions and Clubs for Women." Against special legislation for women.

7.333
ECONOMIC REVIEW: Robertson, C.G., *"Women's Work,"* 5 (1895) 167-190. "One of the largest demands for the employment of women comes from the textile industries... cognate to these trades are printing and its subsidary branches, the metal and chemical works (including match-making), food manufactories, and lastly sack-making and rope-making and rag-picking" (p. 168). Also discusses shop assistants, dressmakers, milliners, and "waitresses of all kinds." Delineates working conditions, wages, and legislation; Harrison, A., *"The Inspection of Women's Workshops in London: A Study in Factory Legislation,"* 11 (1901) 32-46.

7.334
de Rousiers, Paul, **THE LABOUR QUESTION IN BRITAIN**. English translation, 1896. Discusses women and girl textile workers.

7.335
Webb, Beatrice (Mrs. Sidney), **WOMEN AND THE FACTORY ACTS**. 1896. "The ladies who resist further legal regulation of women's labor usually declare that their objection is to special legislation applying only to women.... Any such restriction, they assert, results in the lowering of women's wages, and in diminishing the aggregate demand for women's work" (p. 3). Webb counters objections to the Acts.

7.336
Sherard, Robert, **THE WHITE SLAVES OF ENGLAND**. 1897. Delineates the working conditions of women in factories.

7.337
Shrimpton, William, compiler, **NOTES ON A DECAYED NEEDLELAND, WITH A HISTORY OF THE NEEDLE**. Redditch, 1897.

7.338
Brooke, Emma Frances, **A TABULATION OF THE FACTORY LAWS OF EUROPEAN COUNTRIES IN SO FAR AS THEY RELATE TO THE HOURS OF LABOUR, AND TO SPECIAL LEGISLATION FOR WOMEN, YOUNG PERSONS, AND CHILDREN**. 1898.

7.339
Collet, Clara Elizabeth, **REPORT BY MISS COLLET ON CHANGES IN THE EMPLOYMENT OF WOMEN AND GIRLS IN INDUSTRY**. 1898; "The Factory Girl as She Really Is" in **LIFE AND LABOUR OF THE PEOPLE OF LONDON**. ed. by Charles Booth. 1902-1903; *rpt. in:* **HUMAN DOCUMENTS OF THE AGE OF THE FORSYTES**. ed. by E. Royston Pike. 1969. "These girls, outside their homes, lead a healthy, active life. They do not over-exert themselves at the factory.... They are rough, boisterous, out-spoken, warm-hearted, honest working girls. Their standard of morality is very low.... Their great enemy is drink.... They are nearly all destined to be mothers, and they are almost entirely ignorant of any domestic accomplishments" (pp. 322-326); **WOMEN IN INDUSTRY**. 1911.

7.340
Webb, Sidney and Webb, Beatrice, **PROBLEMS OF MODERN INDUSTRY**. 1898. Includes chapters on "Women's Wages," "Women and the Factory Acts," and "How to do Away with the Sweating System"; **INDUSTRIAL DEMOCRACY**. 1902.

7.341
JOURNAL OF THE ROYAL STATISTICAL SOCIETY: Collet, C.E., *"The Collection and Utilisation of Official Statistics on the Extent and Effects of the Industrial Employment of Women,"* 61 (1898) 219-270.

7.342
Besant, Walter, "The Factory Girl" in **EAST LONDON**. by Walter Besant. 1899; 1900; 1901.

7.343
Wilson, Mona, **OUR INDUSTRIAL LAWS: WORKING WOMEN IN FACTORIES, SHOPS AND INDUSTRIES, AND HOW TO HELP THEM**. 1899. Differentiates

between factory and workshop and explains the different classes of workshop.

7.344

WESTMINSTER REVIEW: Moulder, P.E., *"The Industrial Position of Women,"* 151 (1899) 318-323; Chesser, E.S., *"Women and Girls in the Factory,"* 173 (1910) 516-519. "Recent statisticians quote the number of women employed in textile industries as 867,000 and over 300,000 of these are workers in the Lancashire and Cheshire cotton mills. To see these women at work in the factories is a somewhat depressing spectacle. Most of them are languid, expressionless, anaemic; many are mere children, 'half-timers' of from 12 to 14, or 'young persons' of from 14 to 17 years of age" (p. 516).

7.345

Oliver, Thomas, **DANGEROUS TRADES: THE HISTORICAL, SOCIAL AND LEGAL ASPECTS OF INDUSTRIAL OCCUPATIONS AS AFFECTING HEALTH...** 1902.

7.346

Van Vorst, Bessie (McGinnis) and Van Vorst, Marie, **THE WOMAN WHO TOILS.** New York, 1903.

7.347

Chapman, Sydney J., **THE LANCASHIRE COTTON INDUSTRY: A STUDY IN ECONOMIC DEVELOPMENT.** Manchester, 1904. Valuable work which examines male and female roles utilizing statistical data.

7.348

Harrison, Amy (afterwards Spencer), **WOMEN'S INDUSTRIES IN LIVERPOOL.** Liverpool, 1904.

7.349

Hutchins, B. Leigh, **EMPLOYMENT OF WOMEN IN PAPER MILLS.** 1904; **WOMEN IN MODERN INDUSTRY.** 1915; rpt., with introduction by Linda Perks. East Ardsley, 1978. With a chapter contributed by J.J. Mallon. General survey of women's working conditions. Calls for trade unionism; *reviewed in:* **SOCIETY FOR THE STUDY OF LABOUR HISTORY BULLETIN:** Hurt, B., 39 (1979) 90-94; **WOMEN IN INDUSTRY AFTER THE WAR.** 1917; **THE GIRL IN INDUSTRY.** 1918.

7.350

NINETEENTH CENTURY: Markham, V.R., *"The True Foundations of Empire: The Home and the Workshop,"* 58 (1905) 570-582. Discusses the reasons why girls become factory workers and the negative effects of poor factory conditions on prospective mothers. "The employment of married women in factories in any considerable numbers is hostile to the health, morality, and sobriety of the district" (p. 576).

7.351

Clapham, John Harold, **WOOLEN AND WORSTED INDUSTRIES.** 1907. See especially: "Labour in the Industries." Provides statistics relevant to the wages and occupations of women and children.

7.352

Moody, A. Penderel, **DEVON PILLOW LACE.** 1907.

7.353
SOCIOLOGICAL REVIEW: Hutchins, B.L., *"Women's Industrial Career,"* 2 (1909) 338-348.

7.354
Knight, G. Kerschener, **THE WHITE SLAVES OF ENGLAND.** Denham, 1910.

7.355
Wood, George H., **THE HISTORY OF WAGES IN THE COTTON TRADE DURING THE PAST HUNDRED YEARS.** 1910.

7.356
LANCET: *"The Industrial Employment of Females and Young Persons,"* 2 (1910) 1520.

7.357
Hammond, J.L. and Hammond, Barbara, **THE VILLAGE LABOURER.** 1911.

7.358
Papworth, Lucy Wyatt and Zimmern, Dorothy M., **CLOTHING AND TEXTILE TRADES.** 1912; **WOMEN IN INDUSTRY: A BIBLIOGRAPHY.** 1915.

7.359
Chesser, Elizabeth Sloan, "The Factory Mother" in **WOMEN, MARRIAGE AND MOTHERHOOD.** by Elizabeth Sloan Chesser. 1913.

7.360
Clarke, Allen, **THE EFFECTS OF THE FACTORY SYSTEM.** 1913.

7.361
Bondfield, Margaret, "The Future of Women in Industry" in **LABOUR YEAR BOOK.** no author or editor listed. 1916; "Women Workers in British Industry" in **BRITISH LABOUR SPEAKS.** ed. by R.W. Houghe. New York, 1924.

7.362
Collier, Dorothy Josephine, **THE GIRL IN INDUSTRY.** 1918.

7.363
Matthias, Emily, "The Young Factory Girl" in **THE YOUNG WAGE EARNER.** ed. by J.J. Findlay. 1918. "The long hours worked in the factory, the necessarily unskilled character of the work, make for a monotony which is soul-killing.... The active, curious, straying mind of the adolescent girl must be fed——If we provide good meat for her she will take it with avidity" (p. 84).

7.364
Daniels, George W., **THE EARLY ENGLISH COTTON INDUSTRY.** 1920.

7.365
Heaton, Herbert, **THE YORKSHIRE WOOLEN AND WORSTED INDUSTRIES.** Oxford, 1920. See p. 116 for wage rates. The yarn for weaving was usually prepared by women and children.

7.366
Lipson, Ephraim, **HISTORY OF THE WOOLEN AND WORSTED INDUSTRIES.** 1921.

7.367
Levine, Louis, **THE WOMEN GARMENT WORKERS**. New York, 1924.

7.368
Bowden, Witt, "The Industrial Workers" in **INDUSTRIAL SOCIETY IN ENGLAND TOWARDS THE END OF THE EIGHTEENTH CENTURY**. by Witt Bowden. 1925.

7.369
Phillips, M. and Tomkinson, W.S., "Women's Industry in the Home and the Factory" in **ENGLISH WOMEN IN LIFE AND LETTERS**. by M. Phillips and W.S. Tomkinson. Oxford, 1926.

7.370
AMERICAN FEDERATIONIST: Bondfield, M., *"Women in Industry in Great Britain,"* 34 (1927) 567-570; Bondfield, M., *"Public Opinion; Women in Industry,"* 34 (1927) 836-838.

7.371
Brittain, Vera, "Women in Industry" in **WOMEN'S WORK IN MODERN ENGLAND**. by Vera Brittain. 1928.

7.372
Fang, Hsien-T'ing, **THE TRIUMPH OF THE FACTORY SYSTEM IN ENGLAND**. 1930. "To the [cotton factory] employer, the inexpensiveness in terms of money wages was a powerful motive for the employment of child and woman labor, despite the fact that cheap labor might not always be synonymous with efficient labor" (p. 39). See index for female workers in the flax, hemp, hosiery, nail, pottery, screw, silk, woolen and worsted factories.

7.373
ECONOMIC HISTORY REVIEW: Collier, F., *"An Early Factory Community,"* 2 (1930) 117-124. Describes a cotton factory established by Samuel Greg in the small village of Styal, in Cheshire, during the last part of the eighteenth century. Discusses the employment of women and girls; Taylor, A.J., *"Concentration and Specialization in the Lancashire Cotton Industry 1820-1850,"* 1 (1949) 114-122.

7.374
Dony, John G., **A HISTORY OF THE STRAW HAT INDUSTRY**. Luton, 1942.

7.375
Smelser, Neil J., **SOCIAL CHANGE IN THE INDUSTRIAL REVOLUTION: AN APPLICATION OF THEORY TO THE LANCASHIRE COTTON INDUSTRY 1770-1840**. Chicago, 1959. Detailed bibliography.

7.376
BUSINESS HISTORY REVIEW: Lindsay, J., *"An Early Industrial Community,"* 34 (1960) 3.

7.377
Collier, Frances, **THE FAMILY ECONOMY OF THE WORKING CLASSES IN THE COTTON INDUSTRY, 1784-1833**. ed. by R.S. Fitton. Manchester, 1965. Covers three main periods divided by the following classifications: pre-machine, water-power, and steam power. Examines changes in social relations following the changing types of labor demanded at each stage. The earliest stage of the factory

system, where apprentices were separated from their families, had the greatest impact. By the end of the third stage, "Machinery had reversed the occupations of the sexes——women had attained the pre-dominance they still have in the weaving, and men in the spinning branch of the [cotton] industry" (p. 3). Gives an account of working and living conditions and workers' social and economic position.

7.378
FOLK LIFE: Buck, A., *"The Teaching of Lace Making in the East Midlands,"* 4 (1966) 39-50. Originally established as schools, by 1862, these "instructional institutions" were considered workshops. Discusses conditions and wages paid to girls.

7.379
Bythell, Duncan, **THE HANDLOOM WEAVERS.** 1969.

7.380
Elovitz, P.H., "Airy and Salubrious Factories or Dark Satanic Mills?" Ph.D. diss., Rutgers State Univ., 1969.

7.381
Pike, E. Royston, ed., "Dangerous Trades" in **HUMAN DOCUMENTS OF THE AGE OF THE FORSYTES.** ed. by E. Royston Pike. 1969. Compilation of primary source material, testifying to the unhealthy and inhumane conditions and practices in various types of factories and mills. Many of the accounts are by young women. Photographs included.

7.382
Boyson, Rhodes, **THE ASHWORTH COTTON ENTERPRISE.** Oxford, 1970. See especially: "Henry Ashworth's Philosophy as an Employer of Labour and the Conditions of his Operatives."

7.383
Crow, Duncan, "All The Fault of the Factories" in **THE VICTORIAN WOMAN.** by Duncan Crow. New York, 1972. "The spread of the factory system had... provided many more jobs for women——for instance in 1818 there were 57,323 of both sexes employed in cotton-mills; by 1839 the number of women and girls alone had increased to 146,331... this increase was not confined to married women... [who] formed between a quarter and a third of all women working in factories" (p. 98). Examines Victorian-era myths and realities concerning the female factory worker, attitudes of social investigators and their findings, infant mortality in families whose mothers worked, and the initiation of the Factory Acts.

7.384
Huggett, Frank Edward, **A DAY IN THE LIFE OF A VICTORIAN FACTORY WORKER.** [1973]; **THE PAST, PRESENT AND FUTURE OF FACTORY LIFE AND WORK.** [1973].

7.385
Pearsall, Ronald, "Industrial Cruelty" in **NIGHT'S BLACK ANGELS: THE MANY FACES OF VICTORIAN CRUELTY.** by Ronald Pearsall. New York, 1975.

7.386
ARCHIV. FUR SOZIALGESCHICHTE (WEST GERMANY): Henderson, W.O., *"The Labour Force in the Textile Industries,"* 16 (1976) 283-324. Discusses the standard of living during the Industrial Revolution and the cotton factory family.

7.387
INTERNATIONAL REVIEW OF SOCIAL HISTORY: Hopkins, E., *"The Decline of the Family Work Unit in Black Country Nailing,"* 22 (1977) 184-197. Using the 1851 census data, this article examines the disintegration of the family work team of nailers in Stourbridge, and the subsequent changes in familial roles. "Unlike the wife of a man working outside the home, the wife of a nailer would be expected to share her husband's work... she was mother, housekeeper and industrial worker all in one, and her subordinate position in the family economy was emphasised by her being sent to deliver nails on Saturdays and to collect nail rod on Mondays" (p. 191).

7.388
Longmate, Norman, **THE HUNGRY MILLS**. 1978. Quotes a female visitor on the effects of cotton mill life on the children of the family: "'The children are, I was repeatedly told, "banged about" until they get about thirteen or fourteen.... Then the cupidity of the parent is roused. For the sake of the earnings of the children, they will make much of them, but, they seldom succeed in inducing them to remain at home. Girls of fourteen and fifteen leave their homes, pay sixpence per week for a lodging, and take their own course'" (p. 49). One Factory Commissioner believed that those who started as children were healthier than those starting in their teens. Plentiful work in the cotton towns allowed early marriage; 172 wives under sixteen were recorded in the census of 1861.

7.389
Joyce, Patrick, **WORK, SOCIETY AND POLITICS: THE CULTURE OF THE FACTORY IN LATER VICTORIAN ENGLAND**. Brighton, 1980. Study of class and political relationships in Lancashire. Contends that loyalty to the politics of the employer was culture bound rather than related to any kind of political consciousness; *reviewed in:* **HISTORY WORKSHOP JOURNAL:** McClelland, K., no. 11 (1981) 169-173. "The reconstruction of the family economy within the factory was accompanied by the acceptance, by women, of a subordinate role within work and the home. Though much of the discussion remains at the level of suggestion, it does at least point to some of the ways in which the nexus of class and patriarchal relations was constructed and lived, and as such might help to restore a missing dimension to the historiography" (p. 172).

7.390
Eveira, Alan, "Factory Hands" in **THE PEOPLE'S ENGLAND**. by Alan Eveira. 1981.

7.391
FEMINIST REVIEW: Gittins, D., *"Inside and Outside Marriage,"* no. 14 (1983) 22-34. A parallel study of women in the labor market and the marriage market in Devon. "The weakening of working-class women's position in the marriage market and the increased demand for them in the labour market gave many families a means to survive the effects of proletarianization. It was undoubtedly women who suffered most as a result of these changes: [they were] exploited by parents *and* by capitalists in the labour market, increasingly cut off from any chance of owning their own property, and in a weaker and more vulnerable position in the marriage market" (p. 32); Sarsby, J., *"Sexual Segregation in the Pottery Industry,"* no. 2 (1985) n.p.

7.392
SOCIETY FOR THE SOCIAL HISTORY OF MEDICINE BULLETIN: Ineson, A.,

"*Women's Work and Women's Health in the Munitions Industry in World War I,*" no. 36 (1985) 44-47. Over-fatigue was the most frequent causation of ill-health, of concern to the industry primarily because it meant inability to work.

7.393
Osterud, Nancy Grey, "Gender Division and the Organization of Work in the Leicester Hosiery Industry" in **UNEQUAL OPPORTUNITIES: WOMEN'S EMPLOYMENT IN ENGLAND 1800-1918.** ed. by Angela V. John. Oxford, 1986.

* * *

3. HOME WORK AND SWEATED INDUSTRIES

7.394
Shaw, William, **AN AFFECTIONATE PLEADING FOR ENGLAND'S OPPRESSED FEMALE WORKERS.** 1850. On needlewomen.

7.395
Mayhew, Henry, "Home is Home, Be It Ever So Homely" in **MELIORA: OR, BETTER TIMES TO COME: BEING THE CONTRIBUTIONS OF MANY MEN TOUCHING THE PRESENT STATE AND PROSPECTS OF SOCIETY.** ed. by Charles John C. Talbot (Viscount Ingestre). 1852. On sweatshops.

7.396
Cobden, John C., "Slavery in the British Workshops" in **THE WHITE SLAVES OF ENGLAND.** by John C. Cobden. 1853. "It may be asserted... that in proportion to the numbers employed, there are no occupations in which so much disease is produced as in dress-making. The report of a sub-commissioner states that it is a 'serious aggravation of this evil, that the unkindness of the employer very frequently causes these young persons, when they become unwell, to conceal their illness, from the fear of being sent out of the house; and in this manner the disease often becomes increased in severity, or is even rendered incurable. Some of the principals are so cruel, as to object to the young women seeking medical assistance'" (pp. 177-178). Includes detailed accounts of abuses suffered by neddle workers, dressmakers, assistants, seamstresses, etc.

7.397
HOUSEHOLD WORDS: Dodd, G., "*Bouquets,*" 8 (1853) 230-233. Discusses the values of artificial flower-making as a trade.

7.398
Hopley, Thomas, **WRONGS WHICH CRY FOR REDRESS.** 1859. Examines the conditions in sweat shops.

7.399
ENGLISH WOMAN'S JOURNAL: "*Warehouse Seamstresses By One Who Has Worked With Them,*" 3 (1859) 164-171; "*Woman's Work in the World's Clothing,*" 12 (1863-1864) 30-36; 92-98; 151-160; 243-250; 325-335; 377-386.

7.400
Salamon, N., **THE HISTORY OF THE SEWING MACHINE FROM 1750...** 1863.

7.401
VICTORIA MAGAZINE: *"Needleworkers v. Society,"* 1 (1863) 348-360. Presents testimony of a physician who witnessed the "very serious injury to health" sustained by milliners and dressmakers and efforts to improve conditions; Faithfull, E., *"Manufacture of Clothing by Women,"* 4 (1864-65) 350; *"Employment of Women in Cigar-Making,"* 14 (1869-70) 254; *"Cigar Women versus Needlewomen,"* 19 (1872) 464; Faithfull, E., *"Women as Watchmakers,"* 21 (1873) 504.

7.402
NINETEENTH CENTURY: Simcox, E., *"Eight Years of Co-operative Shirtmaking,"* 15 (1884) 1037-1054; Potter, B., *"Pages From a Work-Girl's Diary,"* 24 (1888) 301-314; Heather-Bigg, A., *"Women and the Glove Trade,"* 30 (1891) 939-950. Estimates that eighty-five percent of workers in the glove trade are women, who carry out much of the work at home. Describes earnings, introduction of machinery and its effect on working conditions, and the health and homes of glovers; Wilkins, W.H., *"'How Long, O Lord, How Long?'"* 34 (1893) 329-336. Refers to the deterioration of working conditions for East-End needlewomen; Heather-Bigg, A., *"The Cry Against Home Work,"* 36 (1894) 970-986; Hogg, E.F., *"The Fur-Pullers of South London,"* 42 (1897) 734-743; Knightley, L.M., *"Women as Home Workers,"* 50 (1901) 287-292. Asserts that working-class mothers need work no matter how badly paid; Phelps, S.K., *"The Home Workers of London,"* 67 (1910) 524-533. Describes the products of homeworkers and their conditions, illustrated by several case studies.

7.403
SATURDAY REVIEW: *"Needlewomen,"* 59 (1885) 614-615.

7.404
FORTNIGHTLY REVIEW: Heather-Bigg, A., *"Female Labour in the Nail Trade,"* 45 (1886) 829-838.

7.405
Harkness, Margaret Elise (pseud. John Law), **A MANCHESTER SHIRTMAKER: A REALISTIC STORY OF TO-DAY.** 1890.

7.406
McLaren, Mrs. C., **THE SWEATING SYSTEM: A SUMMARY OF THE EVIDENCE GIVEN BEFORE THE COMMISSION OF THE HOUSE OF LORDS.** [1890].

7.407
Potter, Beatrice, (later Webb), **HOW BEST TO DO AWAY WITH THE SWEATING SYSTEM.** Manchester, 1892; *rpt. in:* **PROBLEMS OF MODERN INDUSTRY.** by Sidney Webb and Beatrice Webb. 1898; 1902. Calls for reform through legislation; **NINETEENTH CENTURY:** *"East London Labour,"* 24 (1888) 161-183. Delineates sweated industries in East-End London, with a focus on the clothing trades. Claims that women who are home-workers decrease the standard of living by their cheap labor; *"Pages from a Workgirl's Diary,"* 24 (1888) 301-314; *rpt. in:* **PROBLEMS OF MODERN INDUSTRY.** by Sidney Webb and Beatrice Webb. 1898; 1902; *also rpt. in:* **HUMAN DOCUMENTS OF THE AGE OF THE FORSYTES.** ed. by E. Royston Pike. 1969. Detailed and thorough account of Webb's compassionate investigation into the sweated clothing trades. She masqueraded as a working-class sewer in order to collect evidence of abuse, which she later presented to the Select Committee of the House of Lords on the Sweating System.

7.408
Macrosty, Henry W., **SWEATING: ITS CAUSE AND REMEDY.** 1895.

7.409
CONTEMPORARY REVIEW: *"Women's Home Industries,"* 72 (1897) 880-886.

7.410
Phillipps, Lucy F. March, **EVILS OF HOME WORK FOR WOMEN.** 1898. Women's Cooperative Guild Investigation Paper no. 3.

7.411
ENGLISHWOMAN'S REVIEW: *"Home Industries,"* 29 (1898) 1-6. Responds to those who wish to abolish homework, arguing that "the mother could not leave her babes, and home work was one alternative to the workhouse starvation" (p. 2); *"Home and Home-Workers,"* 29 (1898) 244-246. Includes a list in which the adjectives employed to describe the conditions of homeworkers are tabulated and reported; *"The Question of Homework,"* 30 (1899) 10-13. "Pathetic pictures have been often drawn of the comfortless, thriftless homes when the women go to work in the factories, of the neglected children, and the wasted wages. Now the tables are turned, and we are presented with pathetic pictures of the dirt, disorder of the abodes where women work at home, while the children are pressed into the work, cheated of education, play and sleep" (p. 10).

7.412
GIRL'S OWN PAPER: Bateson, M., *"Breadwinning at Home,"* 21 (1899-1900) 60-61; 219-220; 376-378; 452-453; 538-539.

7.413
ECONOMIC JOURNAL: Oakeshott, G., *"Women in the Cigar Trade in London,"* 10 (1900) 562-572; Oakeshott, G., *"Artificial Flower Making: An Account of the Trade and a Plea for Municipal Training,"* 13 (1903) 123-131.

7.414
Kingsley, Charles, "Cheap Clothes and Nasty" in **ALTON LOCKE; TAILOR AND POET. AUTOBIOGRAPHY.** by Charles Kingsley. 1902. First-hand account of a sweated industry. Compares honorable and dishonorable shops, wages, and lodging conditions.

7.415
Irwin, Margaret H., **THE PROBLEM OF HOME WORK.** Glasgow, 1903.

7.416
MacDonald, Margaret (Mrs. Ramsay), **REPORT ON HOME WORK.** 1906. Presented to the Geneva Conference of International Association for Labor Legislation. — *see also:* **VICTORIANS INSTITUTE JOURNAL:** Vines, A.G., *"Margaret MacDonald: A Socialist Pilgrimage,"* 6 (1977) 31-41. MacDonald, a member of the Women's Industrial Council, was especially outspoken against the horrors of homework. "One of the employers [she] severely criticized was the government army supply department.... One official who agreed with the women's criticisms thought that 'The whole of the sweating business has been carried out almost under the protection of the War Office'" (p. 37).

7.417
Mudie-Smith, Richard, compiler, **SWEATED INDUSTRIES: BEING A HAND-BOOK OF THE "DAILY NEWS" EXHIBITION**. 1906; rpt., 1980. Catalog of the exhibition demonstrating 34 categories of the sweated industries. Essays by Clemintina Black, L.G. Chiozza Money and B.L. Hutchins are included. Compiler may also be cataloged as Smith, Richard Mudie.

7.418
Nash, R., **SWEATED INDUSTRIES**. 1906.

7.419
Women's Industrial Council, **HOME INDUSTRIES OF WOMEN IN LONDON, 1906. INTERIM REPORT OF AN INQUIRY BY THE INVESTIGATION COMMITTEE OF THE WOMEN'S INDUSTRIAL COUNCIL, ETC**. 1906; **HOME INDUSTRIES OF WOMEN IN LONDON**. 1908; **THE CASE FOR AND AGAINST A LEGAL MINIMUM WAGE FOR SWEATED WORKERS**. 1909.

7.420
WESTMINSTER REVIEW: Berens, L.H., *"Sweating and Race Suicide: The Price of Privilege,"* 165 (1906) 595-601. General essay on how the few gain privileges from the many. Concludes that this "extortion" leads to the disintegration of family life.

7.421
Black, Clementina, **SWEATED INDUSTRY AND THE MINIMUM WAGE**. Duck-worth, 1907.

7.422
Hutchins, B. Leigh, **HOMEWORK AND SWEATING: THE CAUSES AND REMEDIES**. 1907. "Sweating is no new thing. It occurs usually as a symptom of one of two kinds of industrial change: either as the decay of a handicraft or as an extension or offshoot of the factory system.... Out-workers are mostly very poor people, scattered about in their little homes.... They are often women who sorely need a few shillings to supplement the more or less irregular earnings of the head of the house" (pp. 4-5). Contends that since sweated workers are uneducated, isolated from each other, and lack organization, they are exploited.

7.423
Malvery, Olive Christian (later MacKirdy), "In the Sweating Dens of West and East London" and "Women Who Work and Babes Who Weep——What 'Home Industries' Mean" in **THE SOUL MARKET**. by Olive Christian (MacKirdy) Malvery. 1907. Describes the women who are employed in these industries and the conditions under which they work.

7.424
SPECTATOR: *"Minimum Wage for Home Workers,"* 101 (1908) 155-156.

7.425
Liverpool Women's Industrial Council, **HOME WORK IN LIVERPOOL**. Liverpool, 1909.

7.426
Meyer, Adele L. (Mrs. Carl) and Black, Clementina, **MAKERS OF OUR CLOTHES: A CASE FOR TRADE BOARDS: BEING THE RESULTS OF A YEAR'S INVESTIGATION INTO THE WORK OF WOMEN IN LONDON IN THE TAILORING, DRESSMAKING AND UNDERCLOTHING TRADES**. 1909. Presents

case studies of women working in the tailoring and dressmaking industries. "The large majority of the women whom we have visited are good citizens who deserve well of their country, and who mostly receive, in return for prolonged and patient labour, a very small share in the joys, the comforts or the beauties of life. To go among them is to be at the same time gratified by a deepening sense of human worth and oppressed by the intolerable weight of human burdens" (p. 11).

7.427

SOCIALIST REVIEW: Willmott, H., *"Sweating in the Textile Trades,"* 3 (1909) 364-380. Analyzes reports conducted by the Board of Trade on earnings and hours of labour in the textile trades. Compares the wages of men and women. Valuable article; Willmott, H., *"Sweating in the Clothing Trades,"* 4 (1909) 281-288. Compares the earnings of men and women. Includes statistical tables; Willmott, H., *"Sweating and the Minimum Wage,"* 4 (1910) 436-446. Reviews the findings in the report by Miss Constance Williams and Mr. Thomas Jones on the effect of outdoor relief on wages and the conditions of employment. "Out-relief is almost entirely confined to women, particularly out-relief to able-bodied adults" (p. 437). Correlates findings such as this to those related to employment of paupers in sweated industries.

7.428

British Federation for the Emancipation of Sweated Women, **FIRST (ETC.) ANNUAL REPORT AND FINANCIAL STATEMENT FOR THE YEAR...** [1913].

7.429

Chesser, Elizabeth Sloan, "The Sweated Mother in the Home" in **WOMEN, MARRIAGE AND MOTHERHOOD.** by Elizabeth Sloan Chesser. 1913.

7.430

Wright, Ted, **SWEATED LABOUR AND THE TRADE BOARDS ACT.** 1913.

7.431

Green, Jesse L., **VILLAGE INDUSTRIES. A NATIONAL OBLIGATION.** 1915.

7.432

Vesselitsky, V., **THE HOMEWORKER AND THE OUTLOOK: A DESCRIPTIVE STUDY OF TAILORESSES AND BOXMAKERS.** 1916.

7.433

Phillips, M. and Tomkinson, W.S., "Women's Industry in the Home and the Factory" in **ENGLISH WOMEN IN LIFE AND LETTERS.** by M. Phillips and W.S. Tomkinson. Oxford, 1926.

7.434

Hartley, Marle, **THE OLD HAND-KNITTERS OF THE DALES.** Clapham, 1951.

7.435

Gartner, Lloyd, P., "Old Trades in A New Setting" in **THE JEWISH IMMIGRANT IN ENGLAND, 1870-1914.** by Lloyd P. Gartner. 1960; 2nd ed., 1973. Describes workshop conditions and sweated labor, citing to primary sources. Examines women's roles, restrictions, and wages. Includes a table, on page 97, comparing rates of pay for males and females.

7.436

Pike, E. Royston, ed., "Sweated Labour" in **HUMAN DOCUMENTS OF THE AGE OF THE FORSYTES.** ed. by E. Royston Pike. 1969. Collection of primary source material, mainly testimonies made to the Select Committee of the House of Lords on the Sweating System, 1888-1890. Includes accounts of conditions in sweaters' dens; descriptions of workshops in the fur and clothing trades; wages of women in the various sweated industries; chain and nail makers; sanitation; and the problems of organization to remedy poor conditions.

7.437

SOCIETY FOR THE SOCIAL HISTORY OF MEDICINE BULLETIN: Cuthbert, J., *"Women in the Sweated Industries,"* 16 (1975) 8-10.

7.438

HISTORY WORKSHOP JOURNAL: Samuel, R., *"The Workshop of the World,"* 3 (1977) 6-72; Osterud, N., *"The Sexual Division of Labour,"* 4 (1977) 242-243. Response to preceding article by Samuels. Osterud complains that Samuels should include the differentiation of work according to sex in his analysis. A reply by Samuels is appended.

7.439

Bythell, Duncan, **THE SWEATED TRADES: OUTWORK IN NINETEENTH CENTURY BRITAIN**. New York, 1979. Asserts that while outwork may not be wholly performed in domestic surroundings it is nonetheless differentiated from factory work. Explains that outwork can be performed in small workshops as well as in the home. Some of the products include hardware (nails), shoes, boots, clothing and lace. These activities were called "the sweated trades" because of the extremely unfavorable conditions under which the worker labored; *reviewed in:* **JOURNAL OF SOCIAL HISTORY:** McBride, T.M., 13 (1980) 660-661. "The essential question involved in the history of the domestic industry is why it lasted so long, especially in textiles, garment-making, and the shoe industry. Bythell's study is an ambitious attempt to blend the complex variety of outwork industries into a unified interpretation of the transformation" (p. 661).

7.440

Walkley, Christina, **THE GHOST IN THE LOOKING GLASS: THE VICTORIAN SEAMSTRESS**. 1981; *reviewed in:* **VICTORIAN STUDIES:** Malcolmson, P.E., 27 (1983-84) 124-145. Seamstresses received much of the public attention to workers' injustices. "Pale, wan, frail, and soft-skinned, the distressed needlewoman was much easier for bourgeois Victorians to empathize with than most working women" (p. 124).

7.441

Morris, Jennifer, "The 'Sweated' Trades, Women Workers and the Trade Boards Acts of 1909: An Exercise in Social Control," Ph.D. diss., London School of Economics, 1982; "The Characteristics of Sweating: The Late Nineteenth-Century London and Leeds Tailoring Trade" in **UNEQUAL OPPORTUNITIES: WOMEN'S EMPLOYMENT IN ENGLAND 1800-1918**. ed. by Angela V. John. Oxford, 1986.

7.442

Schmiechen, James A., **SWEATED INDUSTRIES AND SWEATED LABOR: THE LONDON CLOTHING TRADES, 1860-1914**. Chicago, 1984. Examines the symbiotic relationship between sweated work and factory production, and social fragmentation that ensued with industrialization. "Sweated work was largely women's work... and... promoted racism and sexism and pitted women and Jewish immigrants against white English males in a vicious labor competition. The end result was that women and the immigrants found it difficult to rise above intraclass struggles" (pp. 3-4); *reviewed in:* **ALBION:** Hudson, P., 16 (1984) 312-314.

* * *

4. SHOPS AND SERVICE INDUSTRIES

7.443
Jerrold, Douglas, "The Dress Maker" in **HEADS OF THE PEOPLE: BEING A PORTRAIT OF THE ENGLISH.** ed. by Kenny Meadows. 1840; 1841. Melodramatic essay which traces the plight of a dressmaker from her teens to old age. Also includes an account of a middle-class girl.

7.444
FRASER'S MAGAZINE: *"Milliner's Apprentices,"* 33 (1846) 308-16.

7.445
SLOP SHOP AND SLOP WORKERS. 2nd ed., 1850.

7.446
Ralph, James, **OPPRESSIVE SHOP LABOUR.** 1851.

7.447
Norton, Caroline, **OPPRESSED CONDITION OF THE DRESSMAKERS' AND MILLINERS' ASSISTANTS.** 1856.

7.448
HOUSEHOLD WORDS: *"Day-Workers at Home,"* 13 (1856) 77-78. Recommends a home established for working girls to provide comfort and protection in a homelike atmosphere with dormitory-style accommodations and reasonable rent.

7.449
Landels, William, **THE UNPROTECTED, OR FACTS IN DRESSMAKING LIFE BY A DRESSMAKER.** 1857.

7.450
ENGLISH WOMAN'S JOURNAL: *"The Dressmaker's Life,"* 1 (1858) 319-325; *"To the Editor of English Woman's Journal,"* 3 (1859) 68. Discusses hairdressers; *"Male vs. Female Hairdressers Letter,"* 3 (1859) 140. Response to previous letter.

7.451
ONCE A WEEK: S.S., *"Women's Work: Designing Patterns,"* 4 (1860-61) 124-125; S.S., *"Women's Work: Designing Patterns II,"* 4 (1860-61) 241-242; S.S., *"Women's Work: Designing Patterns III,"* 4 (1860-61) 298-336.

7.452
VICTORIA MAGAZINE: *"Social Science: Address to the Committee of the Ladies' Sanitary Association on the Working Conditions of Dressmakers,"* 1 (1863) 571-573; Hughes, T., *"An Afternoon in Whitechapel,"* 2 (1863-1864) 288-297. Describes female cooks and waitresses at a "cooking depot"; *"Female Blacksmiths,"* 19 (1872) 90; *"Women Hair-Dressers,"* 14 (1870) 366.

7.453
WOMEN'S SUFFRAGE JOURNAL: Becker, L.E., *"Women Employed at Chatham Dockyard,"* 6 (1875) 143.

7.454
MACMILLAN'S MAGAZINE: Palmer, S.M., *"Soap Suds [On Laundresses],"* 44 (1881) 298-304.

7.455
Sutherst, Thomas, **DEATH AND DISEASE BEHIND THE COUNTER.** 1884.

7.456
SATURDAY REVIEW: *"Shop Girls,"* 58 (1884) 134-135.

7.457
Brabazon, Reginald (Earl of Meath), **SOCIAL ARROWS.** 2nd ed., 1887. Refers to The Shop Hours League and The Early Closing Movement.

7.458
GIRL'S OWN PAPER: Beale, A., *"The Emancipation of Seamstresses,"* 12 (1890) 20-21; 199; 12 (1891) 410-411; 622; *"Dressmaking as a Trade in Life,"* 13 (1892) 315-316; *"Millinery as a Career in Life,"* 13 (1892) 218-220; Crane, J., *"Lady Laundresses,"* 13 (1892) 750-751.

7.459
Wilkins, W.H., **THE BITTER CRY OF THE VOTELESS TOILERS WITH SPECIAL REFERENCE TO THE SEAMSTRESSES IN EAST LONDON.** 1893.

7.460
Thatcher, T., **HEALTH AND HIGH PRESSURE IN BUSINESS WITH A FEW WORDS ON THE PROPOSED COMPULSORY EARLY CLOSING OF SHOPS.** Bristol, 1894.

7.461
OUTLOOK: Rowe, O.M.E., *"London Shop Girls,"* 53 (1896) 397.

7.462
Fabian Society, **SHOP LIFE AND ITS REFORM.** 1897; **LIFE IN THE LAUNDRY.** 1902. Of 47,362 laundry workers (women and girls), 10,408 were homeworkers and 16,223 of the women were under the age of 20. "The chief evils connected with the present state of the laundry industry are (1) insanitary conditions, (2) excessive, and irregular hours of labor and (3) exemption of institution laundries, and laundries in which not more than two persons dwelling elsewhere are employed" (p. 11). Valuable study.

7.463
NINETEENTH CENTURY: Cavendish, L.C., *"Laundries in Religious Houses,"* 41 (1897) 232-235. Calls for State inspection of religious penitentiaries to ensure "wholesome conditions of labour." Warns that such institutions are sometimes run by "well-meaning despots" who abuse their power through religious enthusiasm.

7.464
WESTMINSTER REVIEW: Greenwood, M., *"Small Laundries,"* 147 (1897) 698-701. Women oppose the Factory Acts because of its restriction on their labor.

7.465
ECONOMIC JOURNAL: Hobhouse, E., *"Dust-Women,"* 10 (1900) 411-420. "To be employed in the vestry yards is what each dust-woman strives for; the chances however are few, and usually reserved for widows who must earn a livelihood. It is difficult to compare the yards, because of the variations of work in each. In some all the work is done by hand. In others a machine sifts and the women only sort [through the refuse]" (p. 416); Black, C., *"London's Tailoress,"* 14 (1904) 555-567.

7.466
MacDonald, J. Ramsay, ed., **WOMEN IN THE PRINTING TRADES: A SOCIOLOGICAL STUDY.** 1904. Compares the competition between male and female workers, discusses the replacement of skilled workers by technological advancements, and competition between married and unmarried women workers.

7.467
Southwark, Bishop of, **WOMEN AS BARMAIDS.** King, 1906.

7.468
WOMEN'S INDUSTRIAL NEWS: MacDonald, M.E., *"Report on Enquiry into Conditions of Work in Laundries,"* 8 (1907) 629-642; *"The Shop Assistant,"* 69 (1915) 321-344. Detailed description of sweated conditions for drapers' and other shop assistants. Argues against the supposed benefits of living-in.

7.469
WORLD'S WORK: Chesser, E.S., *"Life Behind the Counter,"* 9 (1907) 528-34.

7.470
Hallsworth, Joseph and Rhys, J. Davies, **THE WORKING LIFE OF SHOP ASSISTANTS: A STUDY OF CONDITIONS OF LABOUR IN THE DISTRI-BUTIVE TRADES.** Manchester, 1910. "Many thousands of shop assistant worked as many as ninety hours a week" (p. 12).

7.471
Bondfield, Margaret G., **THE SHOP WORKER AND THE VOTE.** 1911.

7.472
Paine, William, **SHOP SLAVERY AND EMANCIPATION: A REVOLUTIONARY APPEAL TO THE EDUCATED YOUNG MEN OF THE MIDDLE CLASS.** introduction by H.G. Wells. 1912.

7.473
Levy, Hermann, **THE SHOPS OF BRITAIN: A STUDY OF RETAIL DISTRIBU-TION.** 1948.

7.474
Hoffman, Philip Christopher, **THEY ALSO SERVE: THE STORY OF THE SHOP WORKER.** 1949.

7.475
Whitaker, Wilfred Barnett, **VICTORIAN AND EDWARDIAN SHOPWORKERS: THE STRUGGLE TO OBTAIN BETTER CONDITIONS AND A HALF-HOLIDAY.** Newton Abbot, 1973. See especially: "Shop Conditions" describing the often appalling situations of live-in female shop assistants. Margaret Bondfield reported one shop where the beds were infested with bugs and another where a defective water supply was the cause of an outbreak of typhoid fever from which six women

died.

7.476
LONDON JOURNAL: Malcolmson, P.E., *"Getting a Living in the Slums of Victorian Kensington,"* 1 (1975) 28-51. "Laundry work was by far the commonest employment for women. This trade was so dominant that in all areas in 1871 more than half of the female heads of households were laundry workers" (p. 44).

7.477
Wechsler, Robert Steven, "The Jewish Garment Trade in East London 1875-1914: A Study of Conditions and Responses," Ph.D. diss., Columbia Univ., 1979.

7.478
FEMINIST STUDIES: Taylor, B., *"The Men Are as Bad as Their Masters... Socialism, Feminism, and Sexual Antagonism in the London Tailoring Trade in the Early 1830's,"* 5 (1979) 7-40.

7.479
VICTORIAN STUDIES: Edelstein, T.J., *"They Sang 'The Song of the Shirt': The Visual Iconology of the Seamstress,"* 23 (1980) 183-210; Malcolmson, P.E., *"Laundresses and the Laundry Trade in Victorian England,"* 24 (1981) 439-462. "A largely unskilled, ill-paid, poorly organized, highly seasonal, and often physically isolated occupation, laundry work remains remarkably elusive" (p. 441).

7.480
Walkley, Christina, **THE GHOST IN THE LOOKING GLASS: THE VICTORIAN SEAMSTRESS.** 1981; *reviewed in:* **COUNTRY LIFE:** Laski, M., 170 (1981) 1243-1244.

7.481
Winstanley, Michael J., **THE SHOPKEEPER'S WORLD 1830-1914.** Manchester, 1983. See especially: pp. 66-73 on women and children who worked in shops and whose jobs were increasingly de-skilled toward the turn of the century. Argues there was a plethora of shop girls to choose from, partly because of a lack of alternative occupations requiring little training. "But shopwork was also sought after as a respectable occupation, superior to factory work or general skivvying. In addition it was still possible to obtain board and lodging in establishments in some parts of the country" (p. 69).

7.482
Malcolmson, Patricia E., **ENGLISH LAUNDRESSES: A SOCIAL HISTORY, 1850-1930.** Champaign, Ill., 1986.

* * *

5. DOMESTIC SERVICE

7.483

Blackstone, William, "Of Master and Servant" in **COMMENTARIES ON THE LAWS OF ENGLAND.** ed. by Edward Christian. vol. 1, 1800. There exist three kinds of servants: menial, apprentice, and servants "pro tempore," such as stewards, factors, and bailiffs. Under the master's service the master is responsible for any crimes the servant commits.

7.484

Provisional Protection Society, **PROVISIONAL PROTECTION SOCIETY.** 1818. The society assisted unemployed female servants or those working under adverse conditions. Supplied lodging and, in some cases, money.

7.485

HOME AND REGISTRY FOR FEMALE SERVANTS. 1834.

7.486

SERVANT'S INSTITUTION PROSPECTUS. 1835.

7.487

Female Servants' Home Society, **THE FEMALE SERVANTS' HOME SOCIETY.** 1836. Originally established in 1813, the Society provided lodging and religious instruction for unemployed female servants. It also offered a registry service.

7.488

Servants' Benevolent Institution, **TRACTS.** 1844-1856; **REPORT.** 1846.

7.489

THE SERVANT'S PROVIDENT AND BENEVOLENT SOCIETY. 1847. Provided annuities, a registry, and in 1849 merged with the servant's institution.

7.490

THE CHRISTIAN FEMALE SERVANT'S REGISTER. 1849. Offered instruction on being a good servant, and assistance when needed.

7.491

ENGLISH WOMAN'S JOURNAL: *"Domestic Life,"* 2 (1858) 73-83. Discusses educated women and household work; Alban, *"Training Schools for Female Servants,"* 3 (1859) 2-6; 3 (1859) 145-151; *"Factory Women and Servants,"* 62 (1863) 73-80.

7.492

VICTORIA MAGAZINE: *"The Difficulties of Domestic Service,"* 2 (1863-1864) 241-246. Encourages needlewomen and other underpaid working women to become servants. Acknowledges that servants must ease their personal liberties and are subject to the caprices of their employers. Makes analogies to Southern American slaveholders, concluding that imperfect employers get imperfect servants.

7.493

Crawshay, Rose Mary, **DOMESTIC SERVICE FOR GENTLEWOMEN: A RECORD**

OF EXPERIENCE AND SUCCESS. 1874.

7.494
Female Servants' Home Society, **ANNUAL REPORTS.** 1874; 1876-1878; 1881; 1882; 1884-1886.

7.495
TRANSACTIONS OF THE NATIONAL ASSOCIATION FOR THE PROMOTION OF SOCIAL SCIENCE: *"Domestic Service for Ladies,"* (1874) 947-949.

7.496
THE SERVANT'S REGISTER. 1878.

7.497
THE SERVANTS' PRACTICAL GUIDE. 1880; *excerpts rpt. in:* **HUMAN DOCUMENTS OF THE AGE OF THE FORSYTES.** ed. by E. Royston Pike. 1969. Describes the duties of housemaids, parlourmaids, ladies' maids, and cooks. Includes a table of wages.

7.498
JOURNAL OF THE ROYAL STATISTICAL SOCIETY: Booth, C., *"The Inhabitants of Tower Hamlets,"* 50 (1887) 326-329; Layton, W.T., *"Changes in Wages of Domestic Servants During Fifty Years,"* 71 (1908) 515-24.

7.499
NEWBURY HOUSE MAGAZINE: Brabrook, E.W., *"The Census,"* 4 (1891) 460.

7.500
NORTH AMERICAN REVIEW: Faithfull, E., *"Domestic Service,"* 153 (1891) 23.

7.501
FEMALE SERVANTS' UNION NEWS: 1892; vol. 1.

7.502
Calder, Fanny L., "Growth and Development of Domestic Service" in **WOMAN'S MISSION.** ed. by Angela Georgina Burdett-Coutts. 1893.

7.503
NINETEENTH CENTURY: Black, C., *"The Dislike to Domestic Service,"* 33 (1893) 454-456.

7.504
Hill, Georgiana, "The Domestic Servant" in **WOMEN IN ENGLISH LIFE.** by Georgiana Hill. 1894.

7.505
Rayner, John, **EMPLOYERS AND THEIR FEMALE DOMESTICS.** Exmouth, 1895.

7.506
Baylis, T. Henry, **THE RIGHTS, DUTIES, AND RELATIONS (LEGAL AND SOCIAL) OF DOMESTIC SERVANTS AND THEIR MASTERS AND MISTRESSES.** 1896.

7.507
Booth, Charles and Argyle, Jesse, "Domestic Household Service" in **LIFE AND**

LABOUR OF THE PEOPLE OF LONDON. ed. by Charles Booth. 1896.

7.508
James, Emily, ed., **ENGLISHWOMAN'S YEARBOOK AND DIRECTORY, 1899-1900.** 1900. Valuable section on domestic service.

7.509
SERVANT'S ADVERTISER AND REGISTER: 1900 to 1901.

7.510
Salmon, Lucy Maynard, **DOMESTIC SERVICE.** 1901. Mainly American, but contains data on Europe.

7.511
GIRL'S OWN PAPER: D., F.S., *"Lady Cooks and Their Training,"* 21 (1900) 443-445.

7.512
Bulley, Agnes Amy and Whitley, Margaret, **WOMEN'S WORK.** 1906.

7.513
Central Employment Bureau for Women, **LADY SERVANTS FOR AND AGAINST.** 1906.

7.514
Apprenticeship and Skilled Employment Association, compiler, "Domestic Service" in **TRADES FOR LONDON GIRLS AND HOW TO ENTER THEM: A COMPANION BOOK TO TRADES FOR LONDON BOYS.** 1909. Considers domestic service as an ideal employment for girls. Gives advice on how to look for situations, and discusses the wages one might expect.

7.515
Nicoll, Catherine (Pollard), **WOMAN'S SPHERE; OR THE DIGNITY OF DOMESTIC WORK.** 1913. Argues that domestic service for girls is preferable to shop or office work, and that dignity would be restored to the occupation if a certificate of competency, as a result of definite training, were required. Claims that a woman's fulfillment comes from the proper management of a domestic arrangement. Extolls the virtues of the home.

7.516
Butler, Christina Violet, **DOMESTIC SERVICE: AN ENQUIRY BY THE WOMEN'S INDUSTRIAL COUNCIL.** 1916; rpt., New York, 1980. Includes occupation differentiations. Also contains a useful bibliography of books and journals pertinent to the subject. Based on questionnaires distributed to servants and their employers.

7.517
Bondfield, Margaret, "Women as Domestic Workers" in **WOMEN AND THE LABOUR PARTY.** ed. by M. Phillips. 1918.

7.518
Schluter, Auguste, **A LADY'S MAID IN DOWNING STREET.** ed. by Mabel Duncan. 1922. Discusses her domestic service to the Gladstone family from 1877 to 1890.

7.519
MINISTRY OF LABOUR REPORT OF THE COMMITTEE APPOINTED TO INQUIRE INTO THE PRESENT CONDITIONS AS TO THE SUPPLY OF FEMALE DOMESTIC SERVANTS. 1923.

7.520
Lewis, Rosina, **THE QUEEN OF COOKS—AND SOME KINGS. (THE STORY OF ROSA LEWIS).** 1925. Describes her advancement from general servant and scullery-maid to becoming cook and friend of the royalty.

7.521
Jermy, Louise, **MEMORIES OF A WORKING WOMAN.** Norwich, 1934. Jermy was a ladies' maid.

7.522
White, Florence, **A FIRE IN THE KITCHEN: THE AUTOBIOGRAPHY OF A COOK.** 1937; 1938. "One of the objects I have in writing this autobiography is to present a correct impression of a woman's opportunities for earning a living in those days. It might be thought today that girls had no way of earning their living in the nineteenth century, except as governesses, and that that was a very poor life. This was not always the case; much depended on oneself. My father's sisters carried on the Red Lion Hotel in Fareham from 1855 to 1881, and remained gentlewomen to the end" (p. 93).

7.523
Burton, Elaine Francis (Baroness of Coventry), **DOMESTIC WORK: BRITAIN'S LARGEST INDUSTRY.** [1944].

7.524
Marshall, Dorothy, **THE ENGLISH DOMESTIC SERVANT IN HISTORY.** 1949.

7.525
Rennie, J., **EVERY OTHER SUNDAY: THE AUTOBIOGRAPHY OF A KITCHEN MAID.** 1955.

7.526
Hecht, J. Jean, **THE DOMESTIC SERVANT CLASS IN EIGHTEENTH CENTURY ENGLAND.** 1956.

7.527
AGRICULTURAL HISTORY REVIEW: Sheppard, J.A., *"East Yorkshire's Agricultural Labor Force in the Mid-Nineteenth Century,"* 9 (1961) 43-54. Concentrating on boy workers, the author contends that girls in East Riding entered domestic service between the ages of twelve and fourteen, while boys became ploughboys and waggoners.

7.528
Turner, E.S., **WHAT THE BUTLER SAW: TWO HUNDRED AND FIFTY YEARS OF THE SERVANT PROBLEM.** 1962.

7.529
Richardson, Sheila J., "The Servant Question: A Study of the Domestic Labor Market, 1851-1911," Ph.D. diss., Univ. of London, 1967.

7.530
BULLETIN FOR THE SOCIETY FOR THE STUDY OF LABOUR HISTORY:
Davidoff, L., *"Domestic Service and the Working Class Life Cycle,"* 26 (1973) 10-
12. Examines the division of labor between male and female servants. By 1880
domestic service was a field dominated by women who were often exploited and in
which "all girls left without family status were automatically expected to go" (p. 11);
Gardiner, J., Himmelweit, S., and Mackintosh, M., *"Women's Domestic Labour,"* 4
(1975) 1-11.

7.531
Burnett, John, ed., "Domestic Servants" in **USEFUL TOIL: AUTOBIOGRAPHIES
OF WORKING PEOPLE FROM THE 1820'S TO THE 1920'S.** ed. by John Burnett.
1974. Although domestic service was a major source of employment until World
War I, "no Royal Commission investigated it or suggested legislative protection... no
outburst of trade union activity called attention to the lot of the servants....
Immured in their basements and attic bedrooms, shut away from private gaze and
public conscience, the domestic servants remained mute and forgotten until, in the
end, only their growing scarcity aroused interest in 'the servant problem'" (p. 135).

7.532
Horn, Pamela, **THE RISE AND FALL OF THE VICTORIAN SERVANT.** Dublin
and New York, 1975. "Since the vast majority of working-class girls in Victorian
England went into service at an early age, the attention of a mother and her
daughter began to turn to the question of getting a place as soon as the girl had
reached about twelve or thirteen" (p. 32). Valuable study which examines all aspects
of domestic service. Provides information on the historical development of the field
and includes appendices which deal with wages and duties.

7.533
Perry, Ronald Dennis, "History of Domestic Servants in London 1850-1900," Ph.D.
diss., Univ. of Washington, 1975. Explores the claims that servants had few rights
and were easily exploited. Demonstrates that, while servant unions and organizations
were established to improve working conditions and servant-master relationships,
these organizations proved to be unsuccessful. Since servants were usually recruited
from rural areas, had limited education, and lacked skills, they usually remained in
service all their lives.

7.534
NORTHHAMPTONSHIRE PAST AND PRESENT: Horn, P., *"Domestic Service in
Northhamptonshire 1830-1914,"* 5 (1975) 267-275.

7.535
Adam, Ruth, **A WOMAN'S PLACE, 1910-1975.** 1976.

7.536
Ebery, Mark and Preston, Brian, **DOMESTIC SERVICE IN LATE VICTORIAN
AND EDWARDIAN ENGLAND, 1871-1914.** 1976. "The first section reviews the
broad structural features of domestic service in England and Wales,... examines the
changes which took place in the domestic service sector, and highlights various
aspects of the domestic service class in seventeen large towns. Chapter 3, using
household samples drawn from the 1871 census enumeration books, compares the
characteristics of domestic service in twenty areas of England.... The final chapter
discusses the life-style of the domestic servant (recruitment, accommodation, wages,
hours of work, duties, problems and prospects), and concludes with a look at
contemporary attitudes towards service from the standpoint of the social

investigator, legislator, master and servant" (p. i).

7.537
McBride, Theresa M., **THE DOMESTIC REVOLUTION: THE MODERNIZATION OF HOUSEHOLD SERVICE IN ENGLAND AND FRANCE, 1820-1920**. New York, 1976.

7.538
Kussmaul, Ann Strum, "Servants in Husbandry in Early-Modern England," Ph.D. diss., Univ. of Toronto, 1978; **SERVANTS IN HUSBANDRY, 1500-1800**. Cambridge, 1981.

7.539
Higgs, Edward J., "Domestic Servants and Households in Rochdale, 1851-1871," Ph.D. diss., Oxford Univ., 1979; "Domestic Service and Household Production" in **UNEQUAL OPPORTUNITIES: WOMEN'S EMPLOYMENT IN ENGLAND 1800-1918**. ed. by Angela V. John. Oxford, 1986.

7.540
Berk, Sarah Fenstermaker, **WOMEN AND HOUSEHOLD LABOUR**. 1980.

7.541
Snell, K.D.M., "The Standard of Living, Social Relations, the Family and Labour Mobility in South-Eastern and Western Counties, c. 1700-1860," Ph.D. diss., Cambridge Univ., 1980. Contains information on apprenticing women to servant positions.

7.542
ECONOMIC HISTORY REVIEW: Snell, K.D.M., *"Agricultural Change, Seasonal Unemployment, the Standard of Living and Women's Work in the South and East, 1690-1860,"* 2 (1981) 407-437.

* * *

6. RURAL WORK, AGRICULTURAL WORK AND MINING

7.543
Aikin, John, **A DESCRIPTION OF THE COUNTRY FROM THIRTY TO FORTY MILES ROUND MANCHESTER**. 1795.

7.544
Putteney-Bart, William, "Singular Mode of Cultivation" in **THE LABOURERS' FRIEND: A SELECTION FROM THE PUBLICATIONS OF THE LABOURERS' FRIEND SOCIETY, SHOWING THE UTILITY AND NATIONAL ADVANTAGE OF ALLOTTING LAND FOR COTTAGE HUSBANDRY**. No author or editor listed. 1835. Depicts a lady farmer and her eventual independence from relying on her neighbors.

7.545
REPORTS OF SPECIAL ASSISTANT POOR LAW COMMISSIONERS ON THE

EMPLOYMENT OF WOMEN AND CHILDREN IN AGRICULTURE. 1843.

7.546

Burke, John French, **FARMING FOR LADIES: OR, A GUIDE TO THE POULTRY-YARD, THE DAIRY AND PIGGERY.** 1844.

7.547

Stephens, Henry, **THE BOOK OF THE FARM.** 3 vols. Edinburgh, 1844; 1851; 1871; 5th ed., 1908. Illustrated handbook for the prospective farmer that depicts the sexual division of labor on the contemporary farm. ——*see also:* **HISTORY WORKSHOP JOURNAL:** Hostettler, E., *"Gourlay Steell and the Sexual Division of Labour,"* no. 4 (1977) 95-101. Steell illustrated Stephens' book, a work self-consciously concerned with the sexual division of labor, "purely because of the relative cheapness of the woman field-worker and the ease with which her labour could be hired and dispensed with.... Stephens and Steell took for granted the large numbers of women who worked not only at harvest but in every phase of the farming year, from threshing and muck-spreading to hoeing turnips and loading hay carts. All these tasks and others are depicted... in the first three editions... providing a dramatic visual reinforcement of the written evidence on the importance of the woman field-worker in nineteenth-century agriculture" (p. 99). In each successive edition, women are gradually omitted from the illustrations and text.

7.548

ELIZA COOK'S JOURNAL: *"Treatment of Women,"* 5 (1851) 225-227. "At Saelford we observed a number of young women employed in clearing weeds from a field.... Judge what was our astonishment when we actually saw the man beat one of the girls for neglect of work and that so severely, that the poor creature fairly winced under this affliction" (p. 225).

7.549

Cobden, John C., "Slavery in the British Mines" in **THE WHITE SLAVES OF ENGLAND.** by John C. Cobden. 1853. "In great numbers of the pits visited, the men were working in a state of entire nakedness, and were assisted by females of all ages, from girls of six years old to women of twenty-one——these females being themselves quite naked down to the waist" (p. 43). Includes many testimonies by women and girls.

7.550

ONCE A WEEK: Plummer, J., *"A Real Social Evil: Employment of Women in Mines,"* 11 (1864) 278-280.

7.551

Wallace, George, **A PAPER ON THE EMPLOYMENT OF WOMEN AND CHILDREN IN AGRICULTURE, AND THE EDUCATION OF LABORER'S CHILDREN READ BEFORE THE FARMERS CLUB, AT NEWBURY, JUNE 6, 1867.** Canterbury, 1867.

7.552

SATURDAY REVIEW: *"The Employment of Women and Children in Agriculture,"* 27 (1869) 78-80; *"Report on the Employment of Children and Women in Agriculture,"* 27 (1869) 212-213.

7.553

Kebbel, Thomas Edward, **THE AGRICULTURAL LABOURER: A SHORT**

SUMMARY OF HIS POSITION. 1870; rev. ed., 1893. Shows that the standard of living for the agricultural laborer is rising. Provides wage statistics for female workers.

7.554
WOMEN'S SUFFRAGE JOURNAL: Becker, L.E., *"Women's Labour in the Black Country,"* 6 (1875) 144-145.

7.555
ENGLISHWOMAN'S REVIEW: Boucherett, J., *"Agriculture as an Employment for Women,"* 10 (1879) 481-484. "Women are objectionable as tenants on two grounds, first because they have no vote with which to defend agricultural interests, and secondly because landlords are afraid that a woman would not understand the business of farming and would consequently be unable to pay her rent" (p. 481); *"Fruit-Farming,"* 20 (1898) 391-394. Encourages women to enter this field; gives advice on planning, growing, harvesting and selling produce. "Fruit-farming is an occupation that could be successfully carried on by women who possess a little money, good intelligence, and an ordinary amount of health and strength" (p. 391).

7.556
SPECTATOR: *"The 'Pit-Girls' of the Black District,"* 59 (1886) 416-417; Grosvenor, C., *"Question of Women in Agriculture,"* 114 (1915) 809-810.

7.557
Jeffries, Richard, **FIELD AND HEDGEROW**. 1889; **THE TOILERS OF THE FIELD**. 1892; rpt., 1981. See especially: "Field-Faring Women." "The farmers who form the guardians know well the history of the poor of their parishes, and remembering the long years of hard work, always allow as liberal a relief as they can to these women. Out of all their many children and grandchildren, it may happen that one has got on fairly well in life, has a business as a blacksmith, or tinker, or carpenter, and gives her a shilling or so a week; and a shilling goes a long way with a woman who lives upon tea and sops. In their latter days these women resemble the pollard oaks, which linger on year after year, and finally fall from sheer decay" (p. 106).

7.558
MACMILLAN'S MAGAZINE: Taylor, E.C., *"Work Among the Country Poor,"* 61 (1890) 423-432.

7.559
Hasbach, Dr. William, **A HISTORY OF THE ENGLISH AGRICULTURAL LABOURER**. trans. by Ruth Kenyon. Leipzig, 1894; 2nd English ed., 1920. Claims that while women forced men into competition, they were better suited for certain jobs such as hops picking. See index for extensive listing of various issues pertinent to the occupations of the female rural worker. Also includes discussion of children, often in connection to women, comparing the value of these two types of workers.

7.560
CONTEMPORARY REVIEW: Crawford, V.M., *"English Women and Agriculture,"* 74 (1898) 426-435; Pedder, D.C., *"Service and Farm Service,"* 83 (1903) 269-277. Explores employment opportunities for girls brought up on farms and in villages.

7.561
Women's Farm and Garden Association, **BIENNIAL [I.E. SEMI-ANNUAL] BULLETIN**. [1900-1904]; **HINTS ON TRAINING FOR WOMEN IN**

AGRICULTURE AND HORTICULTURE. 1913; Westminster, 1916; **ANNUAL REPORT, 1915-1916.** 1919-1920; **REPORT AND JOURNAL, ETC.** 1920/21-1939/40. [1921-1940]; **REPORT AND BALANCE SHEET, 1940-41.** [1946-1947]. [1941-1947]; **YEARBOOK, 1951.** [1951]; **QUARTERLY LEAFLET [OF THE WOMEN'S FARM AND GARDEN ASSOCIATION]:** *continued as:* **MONTHLY CIRCULAR [OF THE WOMEN'S FARM AND GARDEN ASSOCIATION]:** 1902 to 1909; nos. 1-27; 29-49; 51-58; 60-72; *continued as:* **MONTHLY LEAFLET:** 1909 to 1919; nos. 1-120; *continued as:* **MONTHLY JOURNAL:** 1919 to 1921; nos. 121-141. Edited by Mrs. T. Chamberlain.

7.562
SOCIALIST REVIEW: Higgs, R., *"Woman and Agriculture,"* 1 (1908) 202-206. Compares town life to country life "from the women's point of view," finding that although "the agricultural life is the ideal domestic life," the city woman enjoys the benefits of modern urban comforts like gas, running water, good entertainment and other similar conveniences; Dodds, S.J.V., *"Discussion: I. Women and Agriculture,"* 2 (1908) 787-792. Response to R. Higgs' previous article, writing that "small farming affords full scope for a woman's mind. It forms the larger household.... None of the work could degrade her; she rises with it" (p. 788).

7.563
Davies, Maud Frances, **LIFE IN AN ENGLISH VILLAGE: AN ECONOMIC AND HISTORICAL SURVEY OF THE PARISH OF CORSLEY IN WILTSHIRE.** 1909.

7.564
International Congress of Women, compiler, **REPORT OF THE 1909 CONGRESS.** Toronto, 1910. See especially: vol. 2, "The Women's Agricultural and Horticultural Union" by Emma S. Howard.

7.565
Hammond, John Lawrence Le Breton and Hammond, Lucy Barbara, **THE VILLAGE LABOURER, 1760-1832.** 1911.

7.566
Heath, Francis George, **BRITISH RURAL LIFE AND LABOUR.** 1911. "The employment of women in agriculture in the open fields is dying out... but those who still follow this occupation are, as a rule, unmarried women, and these are engaged by the half-year or the year, and are lodged as well as boarded in the farmhouses... women's work on the farm takes its proper course, and is concerned with such labour as a woman can properly perform——work in and about the farmhouse and sheds——feeding pigs, calves, cows, poultry, milking, and inside cooking, and domestic work of different kinds. They, however, join in with others in assisting at the usually urgent work of harvest——both hay and corn ingathering" (p. 76).

7.567
Blakeborough, J. Fairfax, **LIFE IN A YORKSHIRE VILLAGE.** Stockton-on-Tees, 1912. Refers to women farm laborers: "The woman folk assisted not a little towards the upkeep of the cottage, and claimed equal wages when they went out shearing. I have heard old Cleveland women boast of their powers with the scythe" (p. 36).

7.568
Webb, Sidney and Freeman, Arnold, eds., **SEASONAL TRADES.** 1912.

7.569
Aglionby, Mary A., **WOMEN'S WORK ON THE LAND AND ITS POSSIBILITIES.**

1915.

7.570
Greig, G.A., **WOMEN'S WORK ON THE LAND**. 1916. Asserts that since "food is a munition of war," women's value as an agricultural labourer is heightened. "Dairy work is woman's special sphere, in which she has long ago established her success" (p. 19). Includes appendices which deal with National Health Insurance, Women's County Committees, and Organising Officers in the Labour Exchange.

7.571
Simeral, Isabel, "The Emancipation of Women and Girls from Labor in the Mines and Collieries of the British Isles, and Restrictions in the Employment of Boys" in "Reform Movements in Behalf of Children in England of the Early Nineteenth Century, and Agents of Those Reforms," Ph.D. diss., Columbia Univ., 1916.

7.572
Powell-Owen, William, **POULTRY FARMING AS A CAREER FOR WOMEN**. 1918.

7.573
Lethaby, William Richard, **HOME AND COUNTRY ARTS**. 1923.

7.574
Jekyll, Gertrude, **OLD ENGLISH HOUSEHOLD LIFE: SOME ACCOUNT OF COTTAGE OBJECTS AND COUNTRY FOLK**. 1925; 1933; 1939.

7.575
Fitzrandolf, H. and Hay, M.D., **THE RURAL INDUSTRIES OF ENGLAND AND WALES**. Oxford, 1927.

7.576
Courtney, Janet E., "Women in Agriculture" in **COUNTRYWOMEN IN COUNCIL**. by Janet E. Courtney. 1933.

7.577
Springall, Lillie Marion, **LABOURING LIFE IN NORFOLK VILLAGES 1834-1914**. 1936.

7.578
Mitford, Mary Russell, "A Farmeress" and "A Dairy Woman" in **MANNERS MAKYTH MAN**. ed. by R. Brimley Johnson. [1941]. Examines the advantages of becoming a dairywoman.

7.579
Martin, E.W., **THE SECRET PEOPLE: ENGLISH VILLAGE LIFE AFTER 1750: BEING AN ACCOUNT OF ENGLISH VILLAGE PEOPLE, THEIR LIVES, WORK AND DEVELOPMENT, THROUGH A PERIOD OF TWO HUNDRED YEARS**. 1954. See especially: "Rural Industries and Crafts" which accounts for the transition from rural life to town life employment and "Women and the Village." "Before the revolution in agriculture women were much more evident as active partners in the outdoor work of the farm and as the chief supporters of the innumerable cottage industries. Their withdrawal into kitchen and parlour and their loss of home employments can be cited among the several principal causes of village degeneration. It is true that the Agricultural Revolution drastically curtailed the woman's field of endeavour. Farmers' wives, labourers' wives and female craft-

workers were the powers behind English village industries, and when those industries—such as weaving, spinning, straw-plaiting, gloving and lace-making—began to decline, the women were without employments. When manufacture and agriculture did finally separate, the losses experienced by country women were immeasurable" (p. 237).

7.580
Dennis, Norman, Henriques, Fernando and Slaughler, Clifford, **COAL IS OUR LIFE: AN ANALYSIS OF A YORKSHIRE MINING COMMUNITY**. 1956; 1969.

7.581
AGRICULTURAL HISTORY REVIEW: Sheppard, J.A., *"East Yorkshire Agricultural Labour Force in the Mid-Nineteenth Century,"* 9 (1961) 43-54.

7.582
Huggett, Frank Edward, **A DAY IN THE LIFE OF A VICTORIAN FARM WORKER**. 1972. "This book reconstructs one day in the life of... Samuel Strudwick... [and] his wife, Mary, glove-maker; and their children" (p. 11). Intended for younger readers; includes photographs.

7.583
Perry, P.J., ed., **BRITISH AGRICULTURE 1875-1914**. 1973. Collection of essays which provides a general analysis of the impact industrialization had on agricultural laborers and rural economy. While not specifically focused on women, the essays reveal valuable background information about the period and its economic structure.

7.584
Black, Eugene C., "Exploitation: Women and Children in the Mines" in **VICTORIAN CULTURE AND SOCIETY**. ed. by Eugene C. Black. 1974. Excerpts from The Shaftesbury Commission's "First Report of the Children's Employment Commission, Mines" of 1842.

7.585
Perry, George and Mason, Nicholas, eds., "The Rural Scene" in **RULE BRITANNIA: THE VICTORIAN WORLD**. ed. by George Perry and Nicholas Mason. 1974. "Women toiled in the fields as much as men" (p. 243). Valuable photodocumentary.

7.586
Kitteringham, Jennie, "Country Girls in Nineteenth Century England" in **VILLAGE LIFE AND LABOUR**. ed. by Raphael Samuel. 1975. Discusses the occupations open to girls upon leaving school.

7.587
Horn, Pamela, **LABOURING LIFE IN THE VICTORIAN COUNTRYSIDE**. 1975. General historical overview with much attention paid to women working in various capacities. See Appendix F: "The Bondagers are always women: there seems to be no such thing as a male bondager. And they are all young, and unwed" (p. 256). Discusses tasks, hiring and wages, numbers, dress, and education of bondagers. Includes photographs; **THE RURAL WORLD 1780-1850: SOCIAL CHANGE IN THE ENGLISH COUNTRYSIDE**. 1980. "[A] factor influencing wage rates was the emergence of labour shortages in some districts, thanks partly to the effect of migration but also to the labour-intensive tillage methods in vogue among improving farmers and landowners" (p. 243); *reviewed in:* **ENGLISH HISTORICAL REVIEW:** Olney, R., 96 (1981) 877-880; *also reviewed in:* **HISTORY TODAY:** Hawkins, A., 58 (1981) n.p.

7.588
SOCIETY FOR THE STUDY OF LABOUR HISTORY BULLETIN: Hostettler, E., *"Women's Work in the Nineteenth Century Countryside,"* 33 (1976) 9-11. "Apart from the women whose paid or unpaid labour contributed to agricultural production, there was a range of other jobs open to country women which any study of village life should take into account. These included dressmaking and plain sewing, nursing the sick and elderly, washing and cleaning for farmers and gentry; in villages large enough to support shops and hotels, there were barmaids, chambermaids and shop assistants, or women who ran their own shops; most villages had a midwife who also laid out the dead" (p. 10).

7.589
Samuel, Raphael, ed., **MINERS, QUARRYMEN AND SALTWORKERS.** 1977. Discusses the employment of girls and women in each chapter. Includes photographs. Examines organization among these various workers, as well as class distinctions determined by the three trades.

7.590
INDUSTRIAL ARCHAEOLOGICAL REVIEW: Griffin, C.P., *"Three Generations of Miners' Housing at Maoira, Leicestershire, 1811-1934,"* 1 (1977) 276-282.

7.591
JOURNAL OF INTERDISCIPLINARY HISTORY: Haines, M.R., *"Fertility, Nuptiality and Occupation: A Study of Coal Mining Populations and Regions in England and Wales in the Mid-Nineteenth Century,"* 8 (1977) 245-280. Discusses "the comparative absence of female employment outside the home.... Female and child labor underground was forbidden after Lord Shaftesbury's Act of 1842.... For England in the early 20th century, the high fertility of mining districts relative to textile districts has been attributed to differential employment opportunities" (pp. 263-264).

7.592
Winstanley, Michael J., **LIFE IN KENT: AT THE TURN OF THE CENTURY.** Kent, 1978. Oral histories of the occupations and day to day living of the people in Kent from 1901 to 1911. Includes chapters which examine seasonal work for women and children including middle- and upper-class women who picked for charity, and data on the female workforce and their occupations.

7.593
HISTORY WORKSHOP JOURNAL: Roberts, M., *"Sickles and Scythes: Women's Work and Men's Work at Harvest Time,"* no. 7 (1979) 3-28. Traces the changes in women's work in agriculture from as early as the Roman times to the nineteenth century.

7.594
John, Angela V., **BY THE SWEAT OF THEIR BROW: WOMEN WORKERS AT VICTORIAN COAL MINES.** 1980. "'Pit brow lasses'... sorted coal and performed a variety of jobs above ground at British coal mines.... Studying the efforts to prohibit their employment provides a useful means of exploring how Victorians perceived the problems of women's work. The pit brow debate encapsulates the ambivalence of nineteenth-century attitudes towards working-class female employment and it highlights the dichotomy between the fashionable ideal of womanhood and the necessity and reality of female manual labour" (p. 11).

7.595
INTERNATIONAL REVIEW OF SOCIAL HISTORY: Heesom, A.J., *"The Northern Coal-Owners and the Opposition to the Coal Mines Act of 1842,"* 25 (1980) 236-271. Coal mine owners supported women and children (under 13) working the pits since this was the only viable alternative employment they could utilize to maintain their capital.

7.596
Kriedte, Peter, **INDUSTRIALIZATION BEFORE INDUSTRIALIZATION: RURAL INDUSTRY IN THE GENESIS OF CAPITALISM.** Cambridge, 1981.

7.597
ECONOMIC HISTORY REVIEW: Snell, K.D., *"Agricultural Seasonal Unemployment, the Standard of Living, and Women's Work in the South and East, 1690-1860,"* 34 (1981) 407-437. Examines male and female patterns of seasonal unemployment in agriculture. Valuable article which includes statistics and tables.

7.598
Morgan, David Hoseason, **HARVESTERS AND HARVESTING 1846-1900: A STUDY OF THE RURAL PROLETARIAT.** 1982. Contends that a larger proportion of the population was involved in harvesting between 1840 and 1900 than at any time before or since in the English southern counties. "Piece work was the only method of payment where rates were not related to the sex or age of workers; indeed, paid individually, skilled women reapers using the light reaping hook, though not recorded statistically, could be of great help to the family economy" (p. 110).

7.599
Thirsk, Joan, **THE RURAL ECONOMY OF ENGLAND.** 1983.

7.600
Thompson, Paul with Wailey, Tony and Lummis, Trevor, **LIVING THE FISHING.** 1983. See especially: "Women in the Fishing." "Women... have almost everywhere made a central contribution to fishing economies through their roles in fish processing and distribution, and in preparing for the fishery; and in some few districts have actively participated in the fishing itself. Both need emphasizing, just because the conventional image of fishing as a male occupation grossly undervalues the real——and potential——part played by women in the industry" (p. 175).

7.601
Horn, Pamela, **THE CHANGING COUNTRYSIDE IN VICTORIAN AND EDWARDIAN ENGLAND AND WALES.** 1984; "Women and Girls on the Land" in **RURAL LIFE IN ENGLAND IN THE FIRST WORLD WAR.** by Pamela Horn. New York, 1984.

7.602
Burke, Gill, "The Decline of the Independent Bal Maiden: The Impact of Change in the Cornish Mining Industry" in **UNEQUAL OPPORTUNITIES: WOMEN'S EMPLOYMENT IN ENGLAND 1800-1918.** ed. by Angela V. John. Oxford, 1986.

*　　*　　*

7. ORGANIZATIONS FOR WORKING WOMEN

7.603
CRISIS AND NATIONAL CO-OPERATIVE TRADES UNION GAZETTE: April 1832 to August 1834; vols. 1-4. Numerous articles on the position of women.

7.604
Tufnell, Edward Carleton, **CHARACTER, OBJECTS, AND EFFECTS OF TRADE UNIONS.** 1834; rpt., 1972.

7.605
North London Needlewomen's Association, **NORTH LONDON NEEDLEWOMEN'S ASSOCIATION [A PLAN FOR ITS ESTABLISHMENT].** 1850.

7.606
ENGLISH WOMAN'S JOURNAL: *"Ladies Institute,"* 3 (1859) 51-53. Discusses a training home for single women; *"Association for Promoting the Employment of Women,"* 4 (1859) 54-60; *"Society for Promoting the Employment of Women in Connection with the National Association for the Promotion of Social Science,"* 5 (1860) 388-396; N., L., *"Institution for the Employment of Needlewomen,"* 5 (1860) 255-259; *"Report of the Society for Promoting the Employment of Women,"* 8 (1861) 73; C., S.D., *"The Factory Homes' Association,"* 9 (1862) 172-175; *"Report of the Society for Promoting the Employment of Women, for the Year Ending June 24, 1862,"* 9 (1862) 377-379; Boucherett, J., *"Adelaide Ann Proctor,"* 13 (1864) 17-21. Gives an account of the formation of the Society for Promoting Employment of Women.

7.607
FRIEND OF THE PEOPLE: A JOURNAL OF SOCIAL SCIENCE AND OF CHARITABLE INSTITUTIONS: *"Society for Promoting the Employment of Women,"* 1 (1860) 702-703.

7.608
TRANSACTIONS OF THE NATIONAL ASSOCIATION FOR THE PROMOTION OF SOCIAL SCIENCE: Parkes, B.R., *"Society for Promoting the Employment of Women,"* (1860) 18-20; Crowe, J., *"Report of the Society for Promoting the Employment of Women,"* (1861) 685.

7.609
VICTORIA MAGAZINE: *"Social Science: A Plea for Working Girls,"* 2 (1863-1864) 281-283. Discusses women's clubs where working women can enjoy an evening of relaxation and companionship.

7.610
Institution for the Employment of Needlewomen, **REPORT OF THE INSTITUTION FOR THE EMPLOYMENT OF NEEDLEWOMEN... MAY 1, 1863-64.** 1864.

7.611
Society for Promoting the Employment of Women, **EIGHTH [ETC.] ANNUAL REPORT... 1867, etc.; THE TWENTY-THIRD ANNUAL REPORT OF THE**

SOCIETY, ETC. 1882; **THE TWENTY-FOURTH ANNUAL REPORT OF THE SOCIETY, ETC.** 1883.

7.612
CONTEMPORARY REVIEW: Winkworth, S., *"The Alice Ladies' Society of Darmstadt,"* 21 (1872) 138-158.

7.613
ENGLISHWOMAN'S REVIEW: *"Events of the Quarter: Employment,"* 5 (1874) 281-287. Update on Trades Unions for women and the opening of a working women's club; *"Society for the Employment of Women,"* 6 (1875) 171; *"Employment,"* 5 (1875) 281-286. In reference to establishing trade unions for women; *"Women's Protective and Provident League For the Formation of Benefit and Protective Societies Among Women Earning Their Own Livelihood,"* 6 (1875) 84-89. "The objects of such societies are the raising of wages, the shortening of working hours, and the affording mutual help in times of sickness and of want of work, and information as to where work might be had" (p. 84); *"Society for the Employment of Women,"* 6 (1875) 171-172; *"Women's Protective and Provident League,"* 6 (1875) 176-178. Report of a meeting; *"First Annual Report of the Women's Protective and Provident League,"* 6 (1875) 359-365; *"Record of Events. Trades Union Congress,"* 9 (1878) 465-471; *"The Twentieth Anniversary of the Foundation of the Society for the Employment of Women,"* 10 (1879) 289-297. Traces the history of this organization from its foundation, in 1859. Reports on the limited occupations available to women in 1859 and the ever-increasing positions now open to female workers; *"The Protective and Provident League,"* 10 (1879) 103-109; *"A Housekeepers' Association,"* 10 (1879) n.p.; *"Milliners' and Dressmakers' Provident Institution,"* 10 (1879) 134; *"The Organization of Women's Industry,"* 10 (1879) 171-173. Report of the third conference of the committee of clergy formed to consider the relation of the Church to trades unions; *"Admission of Women as Members of the Pharmaceutical Society,"* 10 (1879) 453-457. "The opposition of the Council was based... mainly from the considerations that some portions of the pharmacist's duty might be unfit for women, and that their election into the body would be taken to be an undesirable encouragement to them to enter the business" (p. 453); *"The Women's Printing Society,"* 28 (1897) 181-182. Brief history and description of the society, established in 1876 by Emma Pattison; *"The National Union of Typists,"* 28 (1897) 183-185. Report of the annual conference. Such topics as wages, teaching of typing, and union policies were discussed; *"Society for Promoting the Employment of Women,"* 28 (1897) 187. Extracts from a report on the annual meeting; *"Society for the Employment of Women,"* 29 (1898) 181-184. Reports on the thirty-ninth annual meeting. The organization promotes the technical training of women for industrial employment.

7.614
Women's Trades Union League, **ANNUAL REPORTS.** 1875-1921. Argues limiting hours of work for women curtails their opportunities; **QUARTERLY REPORT AND REVIEW.** no. 1; April, 1891; **ENGLISH WOMEN IN THE LABOR AND CO-OPERATIVE MOVEMENTS: THREE SPEECHES DELIVERED BEFORE THE SEVENTH BIENNIAL CONVENTION OF THE NATIONAL WOMEN'S TRADES UNION LEAGUE, PHILADELPHIA, JUNE 2-7, 1919.** Chicago, [1919-1920]. — *see also:* Goldman, Harold, **EMMA PATERSON: SHE LED WOMEN INTO A MAN'S WORLD.** 1974. See especially: Appendix: "The Position of Working Women and How to Improve it." Emma Paterson was once an editor of the WOMEN'S UNION JOURNAL, as well as founder and president of the Women's Trades Union League. Among her accomplishments were "a group of trade unions founded... a league office serving a few hundred women and girls as an oasis of rest and dignity

in a world of harassment and humility; a printing business entirely run by women; the introduction of women into a man-run trades union congress" (p. 114). Goldman suggests that Paterson's greatest accomplishment was that of "a teacher of women in a belief in themselves, a sense of their right to equality rather than to a few privileges kindly bestowed upon them or even wrung from a man's world" (p. 114); **INTERNATIONAL JOURNAL OF WOMEN'S STUDIES:** Kennedy, S.E., *"'The Want Satisfied Demonstrates the Need of It': A Study of Life and Labour of the Women's Trades Union League,"* 3 (1980) 391-406.

7.615
SATURDAY REVIEW: *"Working-Women's Clubs,"* 41 (1876) 76-77; *"The Women's Trades Union Conference,"* 78 (1894) 593-594.

7.616
WOMEN'S UNION JOURNAL: Feb. 1876 to Dec. 1890; vols. 1-15; *continued as:* **QUARTERLY REPORT AND REVIEW:** 1891; *continued as:* **WOMEN'S TRADES UNION REVIEW:** 1891 to 1919. Publication of the Women's Trades Union League.

7.617
Working Ladies Guild, **EXPLANATORY REPORT OF THE WORKING LADIES' GUILD TO AUGUST 15TH, 1877.** 1877; **REPORT... TO CHRISTMAS 1878, ETC.** 1879-1887; **THE WORKING LADIES' GUILD, WHICH ASSISTS... GENTLE-WOMEN IN NEED OF EMPLOYMENT, ETC.** 1885; **LIST OF ASSOCIATES OF, AND DONORS...; EASTER, 1880.** 1880.

7.618
ENGLISH WOMAN'S GAZETTE: *"Society for Promoting the Employment of Women: Work for Women,"* 2 (1877) 218.

7.619
Genna, E. (pseud.), **IRRESPONSIBLE PHILANTHROPISTS: BEING SOME CHAPTERS ON THE EMPLOYMENT OF GENTLEWOMEN.** 1881. On Work Societies, the Ladies' Dressmaking and Embroidery Association, the Ladies' Industrial Society, and suggested reforms.

7.620
FORTNIGHTLY REVIEW: Verney, F., *"The Women's Protective and Provident League,"* 48 (1887) 155-156. In the absence of trade unions, gives assistance to poor working women. This letter is an appeal for contributions. "The object of the League was to organize 'protective' and 'provident' trade societies among working women: 'protective,' in the sense of doing all that can be done to secure the highest wages for women's work that the market will offer; and 'provident,'... [meaning] the collection of small sums weekly, from which members may draw out 'benefit' when they are sick or out of work" (p. 155); Dilke, E.F.S., *"Benefit Societies and Trade Unions for Women,"* 51 (1889) 852-856; Black, C., *"The Organization of Working Women,"* 52 (1889) 695-704; Black, C., *"The Chocolate Makers Strike,"* 54 (1890) 305-314; Routledge, F. and Dilke, E., *"Trades Unionism Among Women,"* 55 (1891) 741-746; 746-750; March-Phillipps, E., *"The Progress of Women's Trade Unions,"* 60 (1893) 92-104; Bondfield, M., *"Industrial Welfare in My Life,"* 162 (1944) 378-383. Delineates the progress of trade unionism. Discusses the Sweated Industries Bill of 1898, the campaign for old age pensions, and the Education Act of 1893 which limited children's employment. Stresses the lead which voluntary organizations have taken in these controversial movements, emphasizing that increased responsibility should be taken by national and local authorities.

7.621
NINETEENTH CENTURY: Black, C., *"A Working Woman's Speech,"* 25 (1889) 667-671. Relates a speech made by a female cigar-maker at a meeting to form a trade union. She recounts a struggle made against reduction of wages at her shop; Currie, E.H., *"The Working of the People's Place (Clubs for Low Income Groups),"* 27 (1890) 344-356; Webb, C., *"An Unpopular Industry,"* 53 (1903) 939-1001.

7.622
Besant, Annie, **THE TRADES UNION MOVEMENT.** 1890.

7.623
Federation of Working Girls' Clubs (Factory Helpers Union), **CLUBS FOR WORKING GIRLS.** 1890; **IN PERILS IN THE CITY. PUBLISHED UNDER THE DIRECTION OF THE FEDERATION OF WORKING GIRLS' CLUBS, OTHERWISE KNOWN AS FACTORY HELPERS' UNION.** 1909; **29TH [ETC.] YEAR ANNUAL REPORT.** 1914; **HANDBOOKS ON CLUB WORK.** 1917; **A HANDBOOK ON CLUB WORK. [A REVISED EDITION OF THE SERIES OF HANDBOOKS ON CLUB WORK].** 1921.

7.624
National Council of Women of Great Britain and Ireland, **WOMEN WORKERS; PAPERS READ AT THE CONFERENCES.** 1890-1905; **OFFICIAL REPORT OF THE CENTRAL CONFERENCE OF WOMEN WORKERS, 1893.** Leeds, [1893]; 1894; **APPENDIX TO REPORT OF THE CENTRAL CONFERENCE OF WOMEN WORKERS: MEETING OF RESCUE WORKERS... 1892 (1893).** Bristol, 1893; 1894.

7.625
Women Public Health Officers' Association, London, **OFFICERS AND EXECUTIVE COMMITTEE AND ANNUAL REPORT.** [189?].

7.626
MACMILLAN'S MAGAZINE: Wylde, E.P., *"Can Women Combine?"* 62 (1890) 121-129. Explains why "the establishment of Trades Unions among the poorer female workers would fail to accomplish the desired end" (p. 129).

7.627
NEW REVIEW: Dilke, E.F.S., *"Trades Unionism for Women,"* 2 (1890) 43-53. Reviews the successes garnered by union activists, despite initial reticence by workers, and calls for the support by more fortunate women for their working-class sisters; Dilke, E.F.S., *"The Seamy Side of Trades Unionism for Women,"* 2 (1890) 418-422. Refers to incapable leadership that results in "disastrous betrayal of common interests from sheer ignorance... the great stumbling-block in the way of our work" (pp. 420-421).

7.628
Dilke, Emilia Frances Strong (later Pattison), **WOMEN AND THE ROYAL COMMISSION.** 1891; *rpt. from:* **FORTNIGHTLY REVIEW:** n.v. (1891) n.p. Argues that women should testify on labor conditions before the Royal Commission. — *see also:* Jenkins, R.H., **SIR CHARLES DILKE: A VICTORIAN TRAGEDY.** 1958; Askwith, B.E., **LADY DILKE: A BIOGRAPHY.** 1969; **DICTIONARY OF LABOUR BIOGRAPHY:** Hutton, S. and Neil, B., *"Dilke, Emily (Emilia) Francis Strong, Lady (1840-1904) Trade Unionist and Art Historian,"* 3 (1974) 63-67. Includes bibliography of her writings.

7.629
Female Lace Worker's Union, **RULES AND REGULATIONS FOR THE WOMEN WORKING IN THE LACE TRADE**. Nottingham, [1891].

7.630
Liverpool Upholstresses' Union, **RULES OF THE LIVERPOOL UPHOLSTRESSES' UNION**. Liverpool, 1891.

7.631
Townsend, Mary Elizabeth, **ASSOCIATIONS AND OTHER PAPERS**. 1891.

7.632
NORTH AMERICAN REVIEW: Dilke, E.F.S., *"Trades-Unions for Women,"* 153 (1891) 227-239. Argues for trade unions on the basis that they would promote family cohesion since wages and employment conditions for men depend on the regulation of women's work.

7.633
A THREEFOLD CORD; A MAGAZINE FOR THOUGHTFUL WOMEN: Started in 1891, modified in 1893 to be the organ of the Women Workers' Union; *continued as:* **AN OCCASIONAL PAPER OF THE NATIONAL UNION OF WOMEN WORKERS**: 1896. Edited by Miss Janes.

7.634
WOMEN WORKERS: 1891. Quarterly magazine of the Birmingham Ladies' Union of Workers Amongst Women and Girls.

7.635
Liverpool Ladies' Union of Workers Among Women and Girls, **WOMEN WORKERS. PAPERS READ AT A CONFERENCE... CONVENED BY THE LIVERPOOL LADIES' UNION OF WORKERS AMONG WOMEN IN NOVEMBER 1891**. Liverpool, 1892.

7.636
FEMALE SERVANT UNION NEWS: [1892]; vol. 1. Edited by Mrs. M.J. Sales. Publication of the Female Servants Union.

7.637
WESTMINSTER REVIEW: Browne, H.M., *"A New Union for Women,"* 138 (1892) 528-535; Holyoake, E.A., *"Capacity of Women for Industrial Union,"* 139 (1893) 164-168.

7.638
Hubbard, Louisa, "The Organization of Women Workers" in **WOMAN'S MISSION**. ed. by Angela Georgina Burdett-Coutts. 1893.

7.639
Liverpool Tailoresses' and Machinists' Benefit Society, **RULES OF THE LIVERPOOL TAILORESSES' AND MACHINISTS' BENEFIT SOCIETY**. Liverpool, 1893.

7.640
Sala, Mrs. G.A., "Working Guilds and Work Societies" in **WOMAN'S MISSION**. ed. by Angela Georgina Burdett-Coutts. 1893.

7.641

Bleachers, Dyers and Finishers' Association, Bolton Amalgamation, Female Section, **RULES AND REGULATIONS OF THE OPERATIVE BLEACHERS, DYERS AND FINISHERS' ASSOCIATION (BOLTON AMALGAMATION) FEMALE SECTION.** Bolton, 1894.

7.642

Webb, Catherine, **SHOULD CO-OPERATIVE EMPLOYEES UNDERSTAND THE PRINCIPLES OF THE MOVEMENT AND IF SO, HOW ARE THEY TO BE TAUGHT.** Manchester, 1894; **CO-OPERATION AND DOMESTIC LIFE.** 1895; **THE MACHINERY OF THE CO-OP MOVEMENT.** 1896; **HIGH DIVIDENDS: WHAT THEY MEAN.** 1897; Manchester, 1927. —*see also:* **DICTIONARY OF LABOUR BIOGRAPHY:** Bellamy, J. and Bing, H.F., *"Webb, Catherine (1859-1947) Co-operator and Author,"* 2 (1974) 396-398. Webb was one of the earliest members of the Guild. She called for women to act as public speakers in opposition to Mrs. Alice Acland.

7.643

Webb, Sidney and Webb, Beatrice, **THE HISTORY OF TRADE UNIONISM.** 1894; rev. ed., 1920; rpt., 1950; **INDUSTRIAL DEMOCRACY.** 1897.

7.644

HUMANITARIAN: Brooke, S.A., *"The Story of the Women's Trades Union League,"* 3 (1894) 114-121.

7.645

National Union of Women Workers, **WOMEN WORKERS, THE OFFICIAL REPORT OF THE CONFERENCE HELD AT NOTTINGHAM... 1895.** 1895; **ANNUAL MEETING OF THE GENERAL COMMITTEE OF THE NATIONAL UNION OF WOMEN WORKERS.** 1895; **WOMEN WORKERS. THE OFFICIAL REPORT OF THE CONFERENCE HELD... 1894 ETC. ARRANGED BY THE CENTRAL CONFERENCE COUNCIL OF THE NATIONAL UNION OF WOMEN WORKERS, ETC.** Glasgow, 1895-1911; **TRACTS.** nos. 1-6, 1898-1905.

7.646

Women's Cooperative Guild, **ANNUAL REPORT.** nos. 13-17. Manchester, 1895-1900; **INVESTIGATIONS INTO CONDITIONS OF WOMEN'S WORK, OUTSIDE TEXTILE TRADES.** 1896; **[PUBLICATIONS]... INCLUDING INVESTIGATION PAPERS.** 1-4. Manchester, 1896-1900; **REPORT OF INVESTIGATIONS INTO THE CONDITIONS OF WOMEN'S WORK, 1895-1896.** 1896; **PUBLIC HEALTH PAPERS.** nos. 1, 3, and 4, Manchester, 1897; *continued as:* **PUBLIC HEALTH LAWS.** nos. 5-7, Manchester, 1897; **WOMEN'S CO-OPERATIVE GUILD: PUBLIC PAPERS.** Manchester, 1897; **WHY WORKING WOMEN NEED THE VOTE.** 1899; **NINETEENTH [ETC.] ANNUAL REPORT...** Manchester, 1902, etc.; **THE COOPERATIVE WHOLESALE SOCIETY FROM THE STANDPOINT OF THE WOMEN'S COOPERATIVE GUILD.** 1903; **THE WOMEN'S CO-OPERATIVE GUILD: NOTES ON ITS HISTORY ORGANIZATION AND WORK.** 1920. —*see also:* Webb, Catherine, **GUILD DIVIDENDS.** 1877. Delineates the activities of the Guild, a working-class organization composed exclusively of women, almost all of whom were married. The purpose of the Guild was to spread industrial cooperation. Wives and daughters of members of co-operative societies were admitted to this sex- and class-conscious organization; Davies, Margaret L., **THE WOMEN'S CO-OPERATIVE GUILD, 1883-1904.** 1904; Worley, J.J., **THE WOMEN'S CO-OPERATIVE GUILD AND THE CO-PARTNERSHIP MOVEMENT.** [1911]; Webb, Catherine, **THE WOMEN'S GUILD AND THE CO-OPERATIVE UNION.** 1915;

Webb, Catherine, **THE WOMAN WITH A BASKET: THE HISTORY OF THE WOMEN'S CO-OPERATIVE GUILD, 1883-1927.** Manchester, 1927; Davies, Margaret L., ed., **LIFE AS WE HAVE KNOWN IT, BY CO-OPERATIVE WORKING WOMEN.** 1931. Includes an introductory letter by Virginia Woolf; Gaffin, Jean and Thoms, David, **CARING AND SHARING: THE CENTENARY HISTORY OF THE CO-OPERATIVE WOMEN'S GUILD.** Manchester, 1983. See especially: "Foundation and First Steps: 1883-1889," "Margaret Llewelyn Davies and the Drive to Maturity: 1889-1921" and "Issues and Campaigns: 1883-1918."

7.647
Women's Industrial Council, **ANNUAL REPORTS.** 1895/1896-1912/1913; 1915-1916; **TECHNICAL EDUCATION FOR GIRLS IN ENGLAND AND ELSEWHERE.** 1897; **LONDON BOROUGH COUNCILS AND THE WELFARE OF WOMEN WORKERS.** 1903; **MEMORANDUM ADDRESSED TO THE CENTRAL COMMITTEE AND LOCAL DISTRESS COMMITTEES APPOINTED TO DEAL WITH UNEMPLOYMENT IN LONDON.** 1905; **SEVENTH ANNUAL REPORT AND BALANCE SHEET [1904-5].** 1905; **INDUSTRIES OF WOMEN IN LONDON, 1906.** [1906]; **REPORT.** 1907; **WHAT THE COUNCIL IS AND DOES.** 1911. —*see also:* **WOMEN'S INDUSTRIAL NEWS:** 1895 to 1919; Wyatt-Papworth, L., *"The Women's Industrial Council: A Survey,"* 18 (1914) 204-211. Delineates the origin and purpose of the Women's Industrial Council which grew out of the Women's Trades Union Association in 1894. The council's main objective "was the welfare of all women engaged in trades and whose duty was to watch over all industrial matters concerning women" (p. 204). Lists their committees, accomplishments, their future aims and also lists other organizations concerned with workers.

7.648
WOMAN'S SIGNAL: Hicks, A.J., *"Women and the Labour Movement,"* 28 (1895) n.p.

7.649
WOMEN'S INDUSTRIAL NEWS: 1895 to 1919.

7.650
Boucherett, Jessie, Blackburn, Helen, et al., **THE CONDITION OF WORKING WOMEN AND THE FACTORY ACTS.** 1896. See especially: "Trade Unions and Clubs for Women."

7.651
Bliss, William D.P., et al., eds., **THE ENCYCLOPEDIA OF SOCIAL REFORM.** 1897. See especially: "England and Social Reform." "Half a million members joined [Robert] Owen's Grand National Consolidated Trade-Union, including tens of thousands of farm labourers and women. The object was to put an end to all competition" (p. 560).

7.652
Women's Institute, London, **AUTUMN PROGRAMME OF LECTURES AND CLASSES.** 1897; **[PROSPECTUS].** 1897; **TRANSACTIONS.** no. 1, 1897.

7.653
Nash, R., **REDUCTION OF HOURS OF WORK FOR WOMEN.** 1898.

7.654
Davies, Margaret L., **CO-OPERATION IN POOR NEIGHBORHOODS.** 1899; **THE TRAINING OF CO-OPERATORS.** 1902; **THE EDUCATION OF GUILDSWOMEN.** 1913. —*see also:* **DICTIONARY OF LABOUR BIOGRAPHY:** Bellamy, J., Bing,

H.F. and Saville, J., *"Margaret Llewelyn Davies,"* 1 (1974) 96-99.

7.655
International Council of Women, **HANDBOOK OF THE INTERNATIONAL CONGRESS.** 1899. Furnishes an agenda of meetings on women and paid labor.

7.656
National Council of Women of Great Britain, **HANDBOOK.** 1899-1923; 1926-1929.
——*see also:* Adam, H. Pearl, ed., **WOMEN IN COUNCIL: THE JUBILEE BOOK OF THE NATIONAL COUNCIL OF WOMEN OF GREAT BRITAIN.** 1945. "Women who wanted to engage in useful work found themselves most obliged to concern themselves with seduction, rape, prostitution, illegitimacy, abortion, and all their attendant squalors" (p. 6).

7.657
FRIENDS' QUARTERLY EXAMINER: Ford, I.O., *"Industrial Women and How to Help Them,"* 34 (1900) 171-184. "Certainly trade unions will never flourish amongst women until, on election days the female trade union voice can make itself heard alongside of the male trade union voice, and some legal result of trade unionism can come to women, won by their own efforts... the parliamentary franchise [is] even more important for working women than for any other class of women" (p. 181).

7.658
Creighton, Louise, **A PURPOSE IN LIFE: A PAPER READ AT THE BRIGHTON CONFERENCE OF THE NATIONAL UNION OF WOMEN WORKERS...** 1901.

7.659
Association for the Promotion of Work in Elementary Schools as a Career for High School Girls, **REPORTS.** 1902-1905.

7.660
CHARITY ORGANISATION REVIEW: Papworth, L.W., *"The Association of Trained Charwomen,"* 14 (1903) 156-158.

7.661
ECONOMIC REVIEW: Hutchins, B.L., *"The Association of Shorthand Writers and Typists,"* 14 (1904) 339-340.

7.662
Women's Labour League, **LABOUR LEAGUE LEAFLETS.** [1905]; **PAMPHLETS.** [1905-1916]; **REPORT... WITH REPORT OF PROCEEDINGS.** 1-10. 1906-1916; **WOMEN AND THE UNEMPLOYED PROBLEM.** 1906; **ANNUAL REPORT FOR THE YEAR 1911 (1914 AND 1915).** [1912, 1916].

7.663
National Anti-Sweating League, **REPORT OF CONFERENCE ON A MINIMUM WAGE, HELD AT THE GUILDHALL, LONDON, ON OCTOBER 24TH, 25TH AND 26TH, 1906.** 1907. The League was organized in behalf of sweated laborers, advocating a minimum wage. The League utilized propaganda, investigation, and legislation to achieve its ends; **ANNUAL REPORT, ETC.** 1908.

7.664
National Union of Women Workers of Great Britain and Ireland, **WOMEN WORKERS. THE PAPERS READ AT THE CONFERENCE HELD AT**

MANCHESTER... 1907. 1907; HANDBOOK AND REPORT, 1910/11-1949/50. 1911-1950; ABRIDGED REPORT CONTAINING OFFICERS FOR 1913-14, REVISED CONSTITUTION, 18TH ANNUAL REPORT, ETC. 1913; THE LONDON HEAD TEACHERS ASSOCIATION, 1888-1938. 1938.

7.665
Right to Work National Council, REPORT ON THE CONFERENCE ON UNEMPLOYMENT. 1908.

7.666
Smith, Constance, THE CASE FOR WAGES BOARDS. [1908]. Argues for state intervention to aid in procuring a minimum wage for sweated workers. Contends that a minimum wage would upgrade the standard of living for the worker, especially for female employees. If this minimum is not obtained, "we foresee in the continued degradation of a large class of the community an inevitable lowering of both the physique and the morale of our people which will presently amount... to a national danger" (pp. v-vi).

7.667
Tuckwell, Gertrude M. and Smith, Constance, THE WORKER'S HANDBOOK. 1908; 1911. Informs working women and men of existing agencies, societies, and laws which protect laborers, including brief sketches of those agencies and laws.

7.668
Central Employment Bureau for Women, ANNUAL REPORT. 1909.

7.669
Meyer, Adele L. (Mrs. Carl) and Black, Clementina, MAKERS OF OUR CLOTHES: A CASE FOR TRADE BOARDS: BEING THE RESULTS OF A YEAR'S INVESTIGATION INTO THE WORK OF WOMEN IN LONDON IN THE TAILORING, DRESSMAKING AND UNDERCLOTHING TRADES. 1909. "If there is any immediate means by which legislation might diminish the evil of underpayment, it is the highest time that legislation should intervene in aid of a law abiding, industrious and greatly oppressed class of citizens" (p. 18).

7.670
CONSERVATIVE AND UNIONIST WOMEN'S FRANCHISE REVIEW: Nov. 1909 to June 1916; vols. 1-27. Publication of the Conservative and Unionist Women's Franchise Association (Conservative Women's Reform Association); MONTHLY NEWS: Feb. 1914 to April 1918; *continued as:* MONTHLY NEWS OF THE CONSERVATIVE WOMEN'S REFORM ASSOCIATION: Jan. 1919 to Dec. 1924.

7.671
BULLETIN OF THE BUREAU OF LABOR: Busbey, K.G., *"The Women's Trade Union Movement in Great Britain,"* 19 (1909) 1-65. A useful and informative account on the growth of women's trades unions in Great Britain.

7.672
GIRLS' CLUB JOURNAL: 1909 to 1916. Edited by Grace A. Tong. Organ of the Federation of Working Girls' Clubs.

7.673
SOCIALIST REVIEW: MacDonald, M.E., *"The Appeal of the Labour Party to Women,"* 4 (1909) 182-188. "The Labour Party... will organise industry so that every man has work by which he can support his family, or where there is not a male

breadwinner available, it will give the woman maintenance out of public funds in return for her work in the home, regarding this as the most useful service she can render from the point of view of the community" (p. 185).

7.674
Women Sanitary Inspectors' Association (Great Britain), "Woman's Place in Sanitary Administration," paper read by T.O. Dudfield. November 25, 1904. Includes report of the discussion following; **PRESENT POSITION OF WOMEN IN THE PUBLIC HEALTH SERVICE**. 1911.

7.675
Rogers, Frederick, **LABOUR, LIFE AND LITERATURE: SOME MEMORIES OF SIXTY YEARS**. 1913. Discusses his work with women's trade unions, his friend Emma Paterson, and labor movements.

7.676
NEW STATESMAN: *"List of the Principal Trade Unions Admitting Women,"* 2 (1914) 15; *"List of Some Organisations Dealing with Women in Industry,"* 2 (1914) 15.

7.677
Fletcher, Margaret, "Women in Industrial Legislation" in **CHRISTIAN FEMINISM: A CHARTER OF RIGHTS AND DUTIES**. 1915. Monograph in a series edited by the Catholic Social Guild. Differs with the views of the Women's Rights advocates, who objected to legislation restricting hours of work for women. Defines the Catholic attitude toward married women's work: "The family is a divinely instituted society, and it is instituted for the rearing of children.... For the perfect fulfillment of this task... the constant supervision of the mother is needful" (p. 68).

7.678
Henry, Alice, **THE TRADE UNION WOMEN**. [1915].

7.679
WOMAN WORKER: 1916 to 1921; vols. 1-64.

7.680
Phillips, Marion, ed., **WOMEN AND THE LABOUR PARTY**. 1918. A collection of essays including "The Claims of Mothers and Children" by Margaret Llewelyn Davies; "The Nursery of To-Morrow" by Margaret McMillan; "The End of the Poor Law" by Beatrice Webb; "Women as Brainworkers" by Rebecca West; "Women as Domestic Workers" by Margaret G. Bondfield; "The Labour Woman's Battle With Dirt" by Katharine Bruce Glasier; and "The Woman Wage Earner" by A. Susan Lawrence.

7.681
MacArthur, Mary, "The Women Trade Unionists' Point of View" in **WOMEN AND THE LABOUR PARTY**. ed. by Marion Phillips. 1918. "Women should be employed (a) at wages sufficient to ensure their maintenance in health and comfort, (b) at wages equal to those paid to men for equal work, (c) at approximate wages for approximate work, (d) under conditions which will promote and not retard their physical and mental development" (pp. 20-21). ——*see also:* **DICTIONARY OF LABOUR BIOGRAPHY:** Martin, D.E., *"MacArthur, Mary (1880-1921) Trade Union Organiser,"* 2 (1974) 225-260; Hamilton, Mary Agnes, **MARY MACARTHUR: A BIOGRAPHICAL SKETCH**. 1925; 1926; 1929; rpt., Westport, 1976.

7.682
Selley, Ernest, **VILLAGE TRADE UNIONS IN TWO CENTURIES.** 1919. "In districts where the men had migrated to the North, the women attended the meetings in place of their husbands.... Certainly, the issue at stake affected women quite as much as men.... The mother was the first to feel the pinch of starvation. In the distribution of the scanty fare she was the last to be served, and almost invariably hers was the smallest share.... The Union brought joy and hope to women" (pp. 82-83).

7.683
Drake, Barbara, **WOMEN IN TRADE UNIONS.** 1920; rpt., 1984. With a new introduction by Noreen Branson.

7.684
MacDonald, J. Ramsay, **MARGARET ETHEL MACDONALD.** 1920. Details, beyond biography, the various strands of women's political and social activities, including organizations designed to improve women's working and political status.

7.685
Bondfield, Margaret, "Women's Trade Unions" in **THE WOMAN'S YEAR BOOK 1923-1924.** ed. by G.E. Gates. 1923; **A LIFE'S WORK.** 1948. In this autobiographical work, Bondfield, who was the first Minister of Labour from 1929 to 1931, discusses her trade union activism. She also expresses her views on marriage. — *see also:* Hamilton, Mary Agnes (Adamson), **MARGARET BONDFIELD.** [1924]; **DICTIONARY OF LABOUR BIOGRAPHY:** Miliband, M., *"Bondfield, Margaret Grace (1873-1953) Trade Unionist, Feminist and First Woman Cabinet Minister,"* 2 (1974) 39-45.

7.686
Scott, J.W. Robertson, **THE STORY OF THE WOMEN'S INSTITUTE MOVEMENT IN ENGLAND AND WALES AND SCOTLAND.** Idbury, 1925. "A Woman's Institute is the village unit of a very human, democratic, non-party, non-sectarian organization, which... improve[s] the conditions of rural life and... provide[s] opportunities for mutual help and intercourse" (p. v).

7.687
Barton, Eleanor, **THROUGH TRADE TO THE COOPERATIVE COMMONWEALTH.** 1927. ——*see also:* **DICTIONARY OF LABOUR BIOGRAPHY:** Bellamy, J. and Bing, H.F., *"Barton, Eleanor (1872-1960) Co-operator and Labour Party Worker,"* 1 (1972) 38-40. Barton also worked for the Women's Co-operative Guild.

7.688
AMERICAN FEDERATIONIST: Bondfield, M., *"Women Within the Trade Union,"* 34 (1927) 1340-1342.

7.689
Wagner, Donald O., "Bos Loquitor" in **THE CHURCH OF ENGLAND AND SOCIAL REFORM SINCE 1845.** by Donald O. Wagner. New York, 1930. Examines the relationship between the church and trade unions.

7.690
Mansbridge, A., **MARGARET MCMILLAN, PROPHET AND PIONEER.** 1932.

7.691
Courtney, Janet Elizabeth, "The Labour Women" in **THE WOMEN OF MY TIME.** by Janet Elizabeth Courtney. 1934. Discusses the contributions to the labor movement of Emma Paterson, Emilia Dilke, Gertrude Tuckwell, Mary Macarthur and Margaret Bondfield.

7.692
Citrine, Walter, "How Women Played Their Part" in **SEVENTY YEARS OF TRADE UNIONISM, 1868-1938.** compiled by H.H. Elvin, Walter Citrine and W.J. Bolten. 1938. Interviews by Citrine with union leaders Gertrude Tuckwell, Florence Hancock, Julia Varley, Mary Carlin, and Anne Loughlin. Included is a "Register of Affiliated Trade Unions 1938."

7.693
Hamilton, Mary Agnes (Adamson), **WOMEN AT WORK: A BRIEF INTRODUCTION TO TRADE UNIONISM FOR WOMEN.** 1941. Based on the premise that work is the common lot for women as well as men, Hamilton also considers married women as unpaid workers that are difficult to organize because of their dual employment status. Delineates union history and the fight for trade boards.

7.694
Boone, Gladys, **THE WOMEN'S TRADE UNION LEAGUES IN GREAT BRITAIN AND THE UNITED STATES OF AMERICA.** New York, 1942.

7.695
Green, Charles H., **THE HEADWEAR WORKERS: A CENTURY OF TRADE UNIONISM.** New York, 1944.

7.696
Cole, Margaret, **MAKERS OF THE LABOUR MOVEMENT.** 1948.

7.697
Markham, Violet R., **MAY TENNANT: A PORTRAIT.** 1949. Tennant was the first woman factory inspector, secretary to Emilia Dilke, and active in the Women's Trades Union League.

7.698
Turner-Samuels, Moss, "Women in Trade Unions" in **BRITISH TRADE UNIONS.** by Moss Turner-Samuels. 1949. Delineates the history of the organization of women workers. Offers an interesting anecdote on the origin of the word "spinster": it derives from the age-old occupation of spinning that has been associated with single women (p. 186).

7.699
Wood, Ethel M., "Women and Organization" in **THE PILGRIMAGE OF PERSEVERANCE.** by Ethel M. Wood. 1949. Examines the historical evolution of Guilds and Unions created to protect working women as well as to advance female status and participation in the labor movement.

7.700
Hughes, Fred, **BY HAND AND BRAIN: THE STORY OF THE CLERICAL ADMINISTRATIVE WORKERS' UNION.** 1953.

7.701
Jenkins, Inez, **THE HISTORY OF THE WOMEN'S INSTITUTE MOVEMENT OF**

ENGLAND AND WALES. Oxford, 1953. See especially: "The Prelude and the Beginning" which sets the background for the movement's inception in England in 1915. The movement was an outgrowth of the British Agricultural Organization Society formed for the cooperation of small farmers. The Women's Institutes were conceived to educate country women, and it represented a recognition of their importance in agriculture.

7.702
Trades Union Congress, **WOMEN IN THE TRADE UNION MOVEMENT**. 1955. Provides a history of women that were involved in trade unions and strikes, and gives an overall view of the history of wage-earning women. Occupations discussed include agriculture, mining, and child labor.

7.703
Humphreys, Betty V., **CLERICAL UNIONS IN THE CIVIL SERVICE**. Oxford, 1958.

7.704
Bundock, Clement James, **THE NATIONAL UNION OF PRINTING, BOOK-BINDING AND PAPERWORKS**. Oxford, 1959.

7.705
Cuthbert, Norman H., **THE LACE MAKERS' SOCIETY: A STUDY OF TRADE UNIONISM IN THE BRITISH LACE INDUSTRY 1760-1960**. 1960.

7.706
Stafford, Ann, **A MATCH TO FIRE THE FLAMES**. 1961. Study of the Match Girls' Strike of 1888 and the Dockers' Strike of 1889. Documentary study which makes a conscious attempt to see the strikes as the workers saw them.

7.707
ECONOMIC HISTORY REVIEW: Duffy, A.E.P., *"New Unionism in Britain in 1889-1890: A Reappraisal,"* 14 (1961) 306-319. Disputes the assessment that Trade Union activities increased as a direct result from the Dock Strike.

7.708
Turner, Herbert Arthur, **TRADE UNION GROWTH, STRUCTURE AND POLICY: A COMPARATIVE STUDY OF THE COTTON UNIONS IN ENGLAND**. Toronto, 1962.

7.709
Clegg, Hugh, Fox, Alan and Thompson, A.F., **A HISTORY OF BRITISH TRADE UNIONS SINCE 1889**. 1964. Includes figures on women who belonged to trade unions on page 270. Mostly deals with men.

7.710
Steart, Margaret and Hunter, Leslie, **THE NEEDLE IS THREADED: THE HISTORY OF AN INDUSTRY**. 1964. History of the National Union of Tailors and Garment Worker's Union. Sets the account against the backdrop of the general union struggle, showing how the tailors' role was vital in raising wages and eliminating exploitative practices.

7.711
LABOUR HISTORY: Davis, A.F., *"The Women's Trades Union League: Origins and Organisation,"* 5 (1964) 3-17.

7.712

Kamm, Josephine, **RAPIERS AND BATTLEAXES**. 1966. See index for various unions, guilds, and organizations.

7.713

Ramelson, Marian, "Women in Revolt: (A) Working-Class Women; (B) Upper- and Middle-Class Women" in **THE PETTICOAT REBELLION: A CENTURY OF STRUGGLE FOR WOMEN'S RIGHTS**. by Marian Ramelson. 1967.

7.714

MARXISM TODAY: Frow, E. and Frow, R., *"Women in the Early Radical and Labour Movement,"* 12 (1968) 105-112.

7.715

Pike, E. Royston, ed., "The Strike of the Match Girls" in **HUMAN DOCUMENTS OF THE AGE OF THE FORSYTES**. ed. by E. Royston Pike. 1969. Reproduction of five articles by Annie Besant, originally published in THE LINK (July 1888) which delineate the inhumane treatment which led to the strike of the matchgirls. Also describes the events of the strike itself.

7.716

Thompson, Laurence, **THE ENTHUSIASTS. A BIOGRAPHY OF JOHN AND KATHARINE BRUCE GLASIER**. 1971.

7.717

Neale, R.S., **CLASS AND IDEOLOGY IN THE NINETEENTH CENTURY**. 1972. See especially: "Trade Unions and Women's Suffrage," in Chap. 7. "In every other industry the initiative for the little that was done to organize women in trade unions came from middle-class women. The channel along which it flowed, in the first instance, ran from the women's suffrage movement into trade unionism and not the other way" (p. 151).

7.718

DICTIONARY OF LABOUR BIOGRAPHY: Bellamy, J. and Bing, H.F., *"Acland, Alice Sophia (1849-1935) Founder and First Secretary of Women's Co-operative Guild,"* 1 (1974) 5-6; Bing, H.F., *"Enfield, Alice Honora (1882-1935) Co-operator,"* 1 (1974) 112-113. Succeeded Margaret Llewelyn Davies as general secretary of the Women's Co-operative Guild; Cole, M., *"Pease, Mary Gammell (Marjory) (1861-1950) Fabian Socialist and Labour Councillor,"* 2 (1974) 297-298; Bellamy, J. and Schmiechen, J.A., *"Hicks, Amelia (Amie) Jane (1839/40-1917) Socialist and Trade Unionist,"* 4 (1974) 89-92. Hicks was a member of the executive committee of the Social Democratic Federation. She worked for free, compulsory, secular and technical education, and for free school meals, and helped to found the Women's Trade Union Association as well as the Women's Industrial Council. She was a well known speaker on many subjects related to women.

7.719

Auchmuty, Rosemary, "Spinsters and Trade Unions in Victorian Britain" in **WOMEN AT WORK**. ed. by Susan Eade and Peter Spearritt. Canberra, 1975.

7.720

Jacoby, Robin Miller, "Feminism and Class Consciousness in the British and American Women's Trade Union Leagues, 1890-1925" in **LIBERATING WOMEN'S HISTORY: THEORETICAL AND CRITICAL ESSAYS**. ed. by Berenice A. Carroll.

Chicago, 1976. "Despite feminist ideology and rhetoric about sisterhood, it was extremely difficult for barriers of class not to come between women... when women choose to focus their activities within sexually mixed groups of their own class, they must have feminist consciousness to struggle for their rights within that group" (pp. 154-155).

7.721
LONDON JOURNAL: Olcott, T., *"Dead Centre: The Women's Trade Union Movement in London, 1874-1914,"* 2 (1976) 33-50. "From its early failures, the League learned that women workers shared the industrial needs of men, but they also required special protection of legislation, endless exertion by women organizers, and adequate recognition of their family roles in order to become effective union members" (p. 48).

7.722
Beer, Reg, **MATCHGIRL'S STRIKE 1888: THE STRUGGLE AGAINST SWEATED LABOUR IN LONDON'S EAST END.** 1977.

7.723
Lewenhak, Sheila, **WOMEN AND TRADE UNIONS: AN OUTLINE HISTORY OF WOMEN IN THE BRITISH TRADE UNION MOVEMENT.** New York, 1977. "Seeks to show why trade unionism has been less developed among women than men... trac[ing] the fluctuations in the strength of women's trade unionism and the reasons for these" (p. ix); *reviewed in:* **AMERICAN HISTORICAL REVIEW:** Oren, L., 83 (1978) 1016-1017; *also reviewed in:* **HISTORICAL REVIEW OF NEW BOOKS:** Francois, M.E., 6 .(1978) 133-134; *also reviewed in:* **JOURNAL OF ECONOMIC HISTORY:** Vatter, B.B. 38 (1978) 580-581; *also reviewed in:* **BULLETIN OF THE SOCIETY FOR THE STUDY OF LABOUR HISTORY:** Drucker, J., 37 (1978) 89-92.

7.724
Mackie, Lindsay and Patullo, Polly, **WOMEN AT WORK.** 1977. English text book. See especially: "Trade Unions: It Started With the Match Girls."

7.725
Middleton, Lucy, ed., **WOMEN IN THE LABOUR MOVEMENT: THE BRITISH EXPERIENCE.** Totowa, 1977. See especially: Part I, "The Early Years." Essays include "Women in Labour Politics" by Lucy Middleton, "Early Years in the Trade Unions" by Anne Wodwin, and "Women and Cooperation" by Jean Gaffin. In 1900, "it has been estimated that the number of working women over 15 years old was approximately 4 million, which was well over one third of the total female population" (p. 16); *reviewed in:* **AMERICAN HISTORICAL REVIEW:** Kanner, S.B., n.v. (1978) 440-441.

7.726
ORAL HISTORY REVIEW: Bomat, J., *"Home and Work: A New Context for Trade Union History,"* 5 (1977) 101-123. Based upon interviews with 23 workers from West Yorkshire.

7.727
VICTORIANS INSTITUTE JOURNAL: 1976 to 1981; Vines, A.G., *"Margaret MacDonald: A Socialist Pilgrimage,"* 6 (1977) 31-41.

7.728
Bythell, Duncan, "The Politics of Outwork: Trade Unionism..." in **THE SWEATED**

TRADES: OUTWORK IN THE NINETEENTH CENTURY BRITAIN. by Duncan Bythell. New York, 1978.

7.729

Soldon, Norbert C., **WOMEN IN BRITISH TRADE UNIONS, 1874-1976.** Dublin and Totowa, 1978. Since the main source of employment next to domestic service was the textile industry, organizing women in the textile industries was an early development, which began in 1747. In the period from 1800 to 1874, when an "attempt to encourage the growth of a women's trade union took place, five major factors should be noted: (1) the difficulty of organising women, (2) their position in the work force, (3) their relation with male trade unionists, (4) their relation with employers and (5) the impact of the women's rights movement" (p. 3); *reviewed in:* **BULLETIN OF THE SOCIETY FOR THE STUDY OF LABOUR HISTORY:** Drucker, J., 37 (1978) 89-92; "British Women and Trade Unionism: Opportunities Made and Missed" in **THE WORLD OF WOMEN'S TRADE UNIONISM.** ed. by Norbert C. Soldon. 1985.

7.730

BULLETIN FOR THE SOCIETY FOR THE STUDY OF LABOUR HISTORY: Lewenhak, S., *"The Lesser Trade Union Organisation of Women Than of Men,"* 26 (1973) 19-21; Drucker, J., *"Women's History and Trade Union Records,"* 36 (1978) 28-35.

7.731

HISTORY WORKSHOP JOURNAL: Morris, J., *"The Gertrude Tuckwell Collection,"* no. 5 (1978) 155-162. Tuckwell was the president of the Women's Trades Union League. Describes the history and holdings of the Women's Trade Union; Gibbs, C., *"The National Museum of Labour History,"* no. 10 (1980) 191-193. Some of the exhibits describe the match girl strikes in 1888 and the strike of women in Bryant.

7.732

Morgan, Carol Edyth, "Women, Cooperation, and Trade Unionism" in "Working-Class Women and Labor and Social Movements of Mid-Nineteenth Century England," Ph.D. diss., Univ. of Iowa, 1979.

7.733

ATLANTIS: McDougall, M.L., *"Women's Work in Industrializing Britain and France,"* 4 (1979) 143-151. Discusses those works on nineteenth-century women and labor published in the 1970s.

7.734

Boston, Sarah, **WOMEN WORKERS AND THE TRADE UNION MOVEMENT.** 1980. "The fact that women were paid about half the male rate for the job meant that they, as cheap labour, were seen by men as a potential, or actual, threat to men's jobs, but, with very few exceptions, men did not challenge the wage rate paid for the job; they challenged the women's rights to the job. This attitude arose from the unquestioning acceptance by trade unionists of the dominant ideology of Victorian society which saw women as second-class citizens in every sense. However, by accepting the social and economic position of women, trade unionists created a trap for themselves, from which they were only to emerge when they could see women as workers and not as a separate group——women" (p. 16).

7.735

SOCIAL SCIENCE JOURNAL: Smith, H., *"The Making of the Modern Woman: Women Workers, the Family, and Trade Unionism in Modern Europe,"* 17 (1980) 103-

106.

7.736
Davin, Anna, "Feminism and Labour History" in **PEOPLE'S HISTORY AND SOCIALIST THEORY.** ed. by Raphael Samuel. 1981. "The subject matter... of labour history in the enlarged definition which it should have, and the approach of feminist history, raising central questions about sexual division, class formation, consciousness, culture and economy, are not only not incompatible: they are indispensible to each other if historians are to further our understanding of the past and the present of class society" (p. 180).

7.737
SIGNS: Tilly, L.A., *"Paths of Proletarianization: Organization of Production, Sexual Division of Labour, and Women's Collective Actions,"* 7 (1981) 400-417.

7.738
Brown, Kenneth D., **THE ENGLISH LABOUR MOVEMENT 1700-1951.** New York, 1982. See p. 139 on the organization of women in trade unions.

7.739
Thomis, Malcolm I. and Grimmett, Jennifer, "Women's Work and Women's Protest, 1800-1850" and "Women in Industrial Protest" in **WOMEN IN PROTEST 1800-1850.** by Malcolm I. Thomis and Jennifer Grimmett. 1982. "It could no longer be supposed that women first became industrial workers when the Industrial Revolution brought them into the cotton and woollen mills, for it was long ago demonstrated that they were already then a vital part of the economy in both primary producing and manufacturing sectors. The extent of their pre-industrial involvement has, indeed, prompted the speculation that the coming of industrialisation, far from extending their employment opportunities, did in fact reduce them" (p. 17).

7.740
FEMINIST REVIEW: Rowan, C., *"Women in the Labour Party, 1906-1920,"* no. 12 (1982) 74-91. In part reference to working women and the debates on working women within the Labour Party.

7.741
VICTORIAN STUDIES: Satre, L.J., *"After the Match Girls' Strike: Bryant and Mary in the 1890's,"* 26 (1982) 7-31. Shows "the general ineffectiveness of government inspection in gaining compliance with factory labor laws" (p. 8).

7.742
WOMEN, POLITICS AND INDUSTRY, 1906-1918. MINUTES AND RECORDS OF THE WOMEN'S LABOUR LEAGUE. Brighton, 1983. Microform series from Harvester Press.

7.743
Mappen, Ellen F., **HELPING WOMEN AT WORK: THE WOMEN'S INDUSTRIAL COUNCIL, 1889-1914.** 1985. Includes selections from primary source material, including writings of Clementina Black, founder of the WIC; *reviewed in:* **ALBION:** Kanner, S.B., (Spring 1986) n.p. The work focuses on "the phenomenon of middle-class women contacting working-class women and girls to develop a movement for the welfare of industrial workers" and the commitment of the WIC to social feminism (n.p.); "Strategists for Change: Social Feminist Approaches to the Problems of Women's Work" in **UNEQUAL OPPORTUNITIES: WOMEN'S EMPLOYMENT**

IN ENGLAND 1800-1918. ed. by Angela V. John. Oxford, 1986.

7.744

Samuel, Raphael, MacColl, Ewan and Cosgrove, Stuart, **THEATRES OF THE LEFT 1880-1935: WORKERS' THEATRE MOVEMENTS IN BRITAIN AND AMERICA.** 1985. Unique study of the importance of theatrical performance in workers' campaigns. "The new trade unions, like their mid-Victorian predecessors, used musical, comic and dramatic entertainments as a way of raising strike funds: during the great Dublin transport workers strike of 1913 Delia Larkin, sister to the strike leader, set up a Workers Dramatic Company which went on tour to mobilize funds and support" (p. 13).

7.745

Bomat, Joanna, "Lost Leaders: Women, Trade Unionism and the Case of the General Union of Textile Workers, 1875-1914" in **UNEQUAL OPPORTUNITIES: WOMEN'S EMPLOYMENT IN ENGLAND 1800-1918.** ed. by Angela V. John. Oxford, 1986.

7.746

Thom, Deborah, "The Bundle of Sticks: Women, Trade Unionists and Collective Organization Before 1918" in **UNEQUAL OPPORTUNITIES: WOMEN'S EMPLOYMENT IN ENGLAND 1800-1918.** ed. by Angela V. John. Oxford, 1986.

* * *

8. CHILD LABOR

7.747

Percival, Dr., **RESOLUTIONS IN FAVOR OF LEGISLATION TO PROTECT CHILDREN EMPLOYED IN FACTORIES. DRAWN UP FOR THE MANCHESTER BOARD OF HEALTH.** 1796.

7.748

Owen, Robert, "On the Employment of Children in Manufactories..." and "To the British Master Manufacturers on the Employment of Children in Manufactories" in **OBSERVATIONS ON THE MANUFACTURING SYSTEM.** by Robert Owen. 1815; 3rd ed., 1818; rpt., 1966. Describes general working conditions of children. Appeals for reform in employment practices. Condones children's work in factories as long as there are age limits established.

7.749

REPORT OF THE SELECT COMMITTEE ON THE STATE OF CHILDREN EMPLOYED IN THE MANUFACTORIES OF THE UNITED KINGDOM. 1816.

7.750

EXPOSITION OF THE FACTORY QUESTION. Manchester, 1832. Expounds the advantages to children of factory work.

7.751

Condy, George, **AN ARGUMENT FOR PLACING FACTORY CHILDREN WITHIN**

THE PALE OF THE LAW. 1833.

7.752
THE COMMISSION FOR PERPETUATING FACTORY INFANTICIDE. 1833; *rpt. from:* FRASER'S MAGAZINE: n.v. (June 1833) n.p.

7.753
Horner, Leonard, ON THE EMPLOYMENT OF CHILDREN IN FACTORIES: AND OTHER WORKS IN THE UNITED KINGDOM AND IN SOME FOREIGN COUNTRIES. 1840; Ireland, 1971; *reviewed in:* QUARTERLY REVIEW: 67 (1840-1841) 171-181.

7.754
Jerrold, Douglas, "The Factory Child" in HEADS OF THE PEOPLE: OR, PORTRAITS OF THE ENGLISH. ed. by Kenny Meadows. 1840; 1841. A dramatic account of the life of a factory girl.

7.755
Barlee, Ellen, PANTOMIME WAIFS; OR, A PLEA FOR OUR CITY CHILDREN. 1884.

7.756
Dodd, William, THE FACTORY SYSTEM ILLUSTRATED IN A SERIES OF LETTERS TO LORD ASHLEY. 1842. Presents an account of the terrible physical abuses suffered by children working in factories, from data collected on a tour through the manufacturing district.

7.757
PHYSICAL AND MORAL CONDITION OF THE CHILDREN AND YOUNG PEOPLE EMPLOYED IN MINES AND MANUFACTURES. 1843.

7.758
REPORT OF THE CHILDREN'S EMPLOYMENT COMMISSION. 1843; 1845.

7.759
EDINBURGH REVIEW: Greg, W.R., *"Juvenile and Female Labor."* 79 (1844) 130-156.

7.760
Cobden, John C., "Slavery in the British Factories" in THE WHITE SLAVES IN ENGLAND. by John C. Cobden. 1853. Detailed accounts compiled from official documents, of the abuses and hazards experienced by workers in factories. Mostly concentrated on the physical abuses suffered by children, many of the testimonies presented here are by young girls.

7.761
Kydd, Samuel, THE HISTORY OF THE FACTORY MOVEMENT. 1857.

7.762
ENGLISH WOMAN'S JOURNAL: *"Infant Seamstresses,"* 4 (1859) 25-35.

7.763
TRANSACTIONS OF THE NATIONAL ASSOCIATION FOR THE PROMOTION OF SOCIAL SCIENCE: Norris, J.P., *"On Girls' Industrial Training,"* (1860) 366-377.

7.764

REPORT OF THE COMMISSIONERS ON THE EMPLOYMENT OF CHILDREN. FIRST REPORT. 1863.

7.765

QUARTERLY REVIEW: *"Report of the Commissioners Appointed to Enquire into the Employment of Children and Young Persons in Trade and Manufactures not Already Regulated by Law, 1863, 1864, 1865 and 1866,"* 119 (1866) 364-393.

7.766

Wallace, George, **A PAPER ON THE EMPLOYMENT OF WOMEN AND CHILDREN IN AGRICULTURE, AND THE EDUCATION OF LABORERS' CHILDREN.** Canterbury, 1867.

7.767

SATURDAY REVIEW: *"The Employment of Women and Children in Agriculture,"* 27 (1869) 78-80; *"Report on the Employment of Children and Women in Agriculture,"* 27 (1869) 212-213.

7.768

Richardson, John, **EMPLOYMENT OF FEMALES AND CHILDREN IN FACTORIES AND WORKSHOPS.** 1881.

7.769

CONTEMPORARY REVIEW: Waugh, B., *"Street Children,"* 53 (1888) 825-835. "The majority of street children maintain their parents, partly or wholly, as well as themselves. Many only indirectly maintain the father, relieving him of rent and wife-keep. His wage he spends on himself" (p. 825); Fawcett, M.G., *"The Employment of Children in Theatres,"* 56 (1889) 822-829; Burke, T., *"Street-Trading Children of Liverpool,"* 78 (1900) 720-726. A member of the Watch Committee tells the results of an experiment in which street-sellers are required to be licensed and are forbidden to trade after seven in the evening or within public-houses. It was found that the majority came from very poor homes where alcoholism was rampant. Author feels there should be "no street trading for girls, for whom such a life is a veritable hell. No better training for unfitness, not merely for domestic service, but for the management of a workingman's house in the future, can be imagined" (p. 725).

7.770

GIRL'S OWN PAPER: *"Economy: What to Do with Your Savings. A Paper for Working Girls,"* 13 (1892) 823.

7.771

"Child Labor, England" in **THE ENCYCLOPEDIA OF SOCIAL REFORM.** ed. by William Bliss, et al. 1897. "We commence with England, as no other country has had so. long or so carefully recorded an experience with child labor, or with efforts and legislation for its cure.... Children of all ages, down to 3 and 4, were found in the most painful labor, while babes of 6 were commonly found in large numbers in many factories" (p. 234).

7.772

NINETEENTH CENTURY: Hogg, E.F., *"School Children as Wage Earners,"* 42 (1897) 235-244. Emphasizes that when children are overworked, their education suffers. Describes the work as being demoralizing and low-paying. Calls for regulation in the employment of school children.

7.773
Hird, Frank, **THE CRY OF THE CHILDREN: AN EXPOSURE OF CERTAIN BRITISH INDUSTRIES IN WHICH CHILDREN ARE INIQUITOUSLY EMPLOYED.** 1898.

7.774
CHAUTAUQUAN: *"Woman Labor and Child Labor,"* 31 (1900) 463-464. A bibliography.

7.775
Tennant, May, "Infant Mortality and Factory Labour" in **DANGEROUS TRADES.** ed. by Thomas Oliver. 1902.

7.776
Bosanquet, Helen (Dendy), "The Children" in **THE STRENGTH OF THE PEOPLE.** by Helen Bosanquet. 1903. "The Poor Law Guardians themselves who were amongst the chief sinners thought that they were doing their duty to the children under their care, when they sent them in boat-loads and wagon-loads from London to the northern counties to be legally bound apprentices from the age of five or six to twenty-one, to masters from whom they had practically no appeal" (pp. 214-215).

7.777
FORTNIGHTLY REVIEW: Adler, N., *"Children as Wage-Earners,"* 73 (1903) 918-927. Cites employment of girls as street-sellers, domestic workers and laundry workers. Intimates that girl street-sellers easily drift into prostitution. Deplores the working conditions especially of domestic workers and relates "the general consensus of opinion that girls who are employed in small laundries deteriorate both in character and manners" (p. 922).

7.778
Sherard, Robert Harborough, **THE CHILD-SLAVES OF BRITAIN.** 1905. "As to this street-hawking, it is not a pleasant thing to think that, in pursuit of this occupation, many little girls wander at nighttime from one public-house to another" (p. 81). Many accounts of working children and the conditions of their employment.

7.779
Malvery, Olive Christian (later MacKirdy), **BABY TOILERS.** 1907.

7.780
Dale, Mrs. Hylton, **CHILD LABOR UNDER CAPITALISM.** 1908. Covers the kinds of work children did and the various acts to reform child labor.

7.781
Smith, Constance Isabella Stuart, **CHILDREN AS WAGE-EARNERS.** 1908; **REPORT ON THE EMPLOYMENT OF CHILDREN IN THE UNITED KINGDOM.** 1909.

7.782
Adler, Henrietta and Tawney, Jeanette H., **BOY AND GIRL LABOUR.** 1909.

7.783
Knowles, G.W., **JUNIOR LABOUR EXCHANGES: A PLEA FOR CLOSER CO-OPERATION BETWEEN LABOUR EXCHANGES AND EDUCATIONAL AUTHORITIES.** 1910.

7.784
Dunlop, O. Jocelyn and Denman, Richard, "Working Women and the Girl Employee," "Child Labour Under the Searchlight of the Nineteenth-Century Reports," and "The Conditions of Life and Work of the Industrial Child" in **ENGLISH APPRENTICESHIP AND CHILD LABOR: A HISTORY**. by O. Jocelyn Dunlop and Richard Denman. New York, 1912. "The new industrial conditions gave juvenile labour a commercial value which it had not possessed in the old days, before the extensive use of machinery had created new fields of work for children, and when the insistence upon apprenticeship had prevented parents and employers from exploiting child labor" (p. 263).

7.785
Engel, Sigmund, "Women's Labour and Child Labour" in **THE ELEMENTS OF CHILD PROTECTION**. by Sigmund Engel. trans. by M. Eden Paul. New York, 1912. Analyzes the causes and effects of women and child labor. Claims that, in England "towards the end of the eighteenth century... conditions as regards child-labour were at their worst. The factory owners hired children from the workhouses and orphan asylums. These latter institutions were far from the factories, and for this reason no official supervision of the children was possible, and their care was left entirely in the hands of the factory owners.... They were tormented with the utmost refinement of cruelty; chained, flogged, starved to emaciation and driven to suicide" (pp. 155-156).

7.786
Keeling, Frederic, **CHILD LABOUR IN THE UNITED KINGDOM: A STUDY OF THE DEVELOPMENT AND ADMINISTRATION OF THE LAW RELATING TO THE EMPLOYMENT OF CHILDREN**. 1914; *reviewed in:* **ECONOMIC REVIEW:** Green, H.L., 24 (1914) 346-348.

7.787
Papworth, Lucy Wyatt and Zimmern, Dorothy M., **THE OCCUPATIONS OF WOMEN ACCORDING TO THE CENSUS OF ENGLAND AND WALES, 1911**. 1914. Includes information concerning children.

7.788
WOMEN'S INDUSTRIAL NEWS: Drake, B., *"The Girl-Worker and the Opportunity of the Juvenile Advisory Committee,"* 18 (1914) 277-285. Those women who enter the work force at the ages of 17 or 18 are less protected from exploitation than adults and children. Argues for a law to "protect the property of minors... until the age of twenty-one" (p. 285).

7.789
Simeral, Isabel, "Reform Movements in Behalf of Children in England of the Early Nineteenth Century, and Agents of Those Reforms," Ph.D. diss., Columbia Univ., 1916. See especially: "Chimney Sweeps in England, 1788-1875," "Factory Legislation in Behalf of Children, 1800-1853," and "The Emancipation of Women and Girls from Labor in the Mines and Collieries of the British Isles, and Restrictions in the Employment of Boys."

7.790
Collier, D.J., **THE GIRL IN INDUSTRY**. 1918. In 1911, 40 percent of the total female population between the ages of 10 and 21 years were employed. Includes valuable tables which break down occupations by age.

7.791

Thomas, Maurice Walton, **YOUNG PEOPLE IN INDUSTRY, 1750-1945**. 1945; **THE EARLY FACTORY LEGISLATION: A STUDY IN LEGISLATIVE AND ADMINISTRATIVE EVOLUTION**. Essex, 1948; rpt., Westport, 1970. See especially: "The Free Children." "No disinterested observer could have denied that young people were being grossly over-worked, but it was considered impossible to limit their hours without either limiting the hours of the adults in like measure, or throwing the whole industry out of gear... it was customary to work extremely long hours, adults and children being often confined to the mills for thirteen, and even fifteen hours a day, with only short periods of intermission for meals" (pp. 16-17).

7.792

Petherwick, Miss F.R., "The Movement for the Abolition of Child Labor in the Mines of England," Ph.D. diss., Boston Univ., 1954.

7.793

VICTORIAN STUDIES: Chaloner, W.H., *"Mrs. Trollope and the Early Factory System,"* 4 (1960-61) 159-166.

7.794

Carpenter, Kenneth E., ed., **RICHARD OASTLER: KING OF FACTORY CHILDREN. SIX PAMPHLETS 1835-1861**. New York, 1972. Compilation of facsimile reproductions of letters and pamphlets on factory work, with an emphasis on the dangers posed to children. Includes a biographical sketch of Oastler by George Stringer Bull.

7.795

Pinchbeck, Ivy and Hewitt, Margaret, **CHILDREN IN ENGLISH SOCIETY FROM THE EIGHTEENTH CENTURY TO THE CHILDREN ACT 1948**. 1973.

7.796

Black, Eugene C., "Exploitation: Women and Children in the Mines" in **VICTORIAN CULTURE AND SOCIETY**. ed. by Eugene C. Black. 1974. Excerpts from The Shaftesbury Commission's "First Report of the Children's Employment Commission, Mines" of 1842.

7.797

McKendrick, Neil, "Home Demand and Economic Growth: A New View of the Role of Women and Children in the Industrial Revolution" in **HISTORICAL PERSPECTIVES: STUDIES IN ENGLISH THOUGHT AND SOCIETY**. ed. by Neil McKendrick. 1974.

7.798

HISTORICAL JOURNAL: Horn, P., *"Child Workers in the Pillow Lace and Straw Plait Trades of Victorian Buckinghamshire and Bedfordshire,"* 17 (1974) 779-796. Examines hours and conditions of work, health, and education. Based on data from census reports, articles, Parliamentary papers. Includes maps and tables.

7.799

Johnston, Johanna, **THE LIFE, MANNERS, AND TRAVELS OF FANNY TROLLOPE: A BIOGRAPHY**. New York, 1978. See the chapter on how Trollope exposed child labor in her novel MICHAEL ARMSTRONG. Describes the horrors of the mill and the exploitative industrial system's effect on boys and girls.

7.800
COMPARATIVE STUDIES IN SOCIETY AND HISTORY: Minge-Kalman, W., *"The Industrial Revolution and the European Family: The Institutionalization of 'Childhood' as a Market for Family Labor,"* 20 (1978) 454-468. "Industrialization has not brought about the demise of 'home-based' family labor... [it can be shown that industrialization]... rendered the family non-competitive with larger, mechanized production groups, [and] it also created a new market for a new kind of family production" (p. 454).

7.801
MIDLAND HISTORY: Horn, P., *"The Employment of Children in Victorian Oxfordshire,"* 4 (1978) 61-74.

7.802
Parr, Joy, **LABOURING CHILDREN: BRITISH IMMIGRANT APPRENTICES TO CANADA, 1869-1924.** 1980. Discusses the 80,000 English children sent to Canada as indentured servants under the auspices of religiously affiliated workers.

7.803
Sommerville, John C., "The High and Low Point in the History of Childhood" in **THE RISE AND FALL OF CHILDHOOD.** Beverly Hills, 1982. Describes child labor during the Victorian era.

* * *

9. A SURVEY OF MIDDLE-CLASS WOMEN'S OCCUPATIONS

7.804
TAIT'S EDINBURGH MAGAZINE: *"Women of Business,"* (1834) 596-597. "Women are, in fact, capable of almost any act of heroism, any act of virtue, any degree of endurance, any sacrifice, any exertion. But they are not capable of that self-abstraction,——that concentration of the powers of the mind,——that calm deliberate sobriety of contemplativeness indispensable to statesmanship" (p. 597).

7.805
Prendergast, Paul, "The Lodging-House Keeper" in **HEADS OF THE PEOPLE: OR, PORTRAITS OF THE ENGLISH.** ed. by Kenny Meadows. 1840; 1841. Author feels that this occupation is best suited for women because of the domestic duties entailed in running a lodging home. Calls for legislation of lodging-house keepers to improve their conduct so men "will then, happy in the enjoyment of domestic quiet and cleanliness regard his lodgings as a home; and, existing really in a state of single blessedness, be no longer tempted to exchange it for one discountenanced by the laws of his country, and justly punishable in the workhouse" (p. 100).

7.806
HOME CIRCLE: Crosland, Mrs. N., *"Working Gentlewomen,"* 1 (1849) 41-42.

7.807
PUNCH: *"The Model Lodging Housekeeper,"* 14 (1850) 55; Beckett, G.A., *"Female Barristers,"* 19 (1850) 144; Jerrold, D., *"Ladies at the Bar,"* 28 (1855) 74; *"Work for*

Women," 39 (1860) 20. Satirizes women entering the occupations. For example, law-copying would be a useful deterrence from the usual drivel women love to write, and knitting caps naturally progresses to printing "caps" in a printing office.

7.808
WESTMINSTER REVIEW: *"The Lady Novelists,"* 2 (1852) 129-142; Martyn, E., *"Women in Public Life,"* 132 (1889) 278-285; Elmy, E.C.W., *"The Part of Women in Local Administration: England and Wales, Part I,"* 150 (1898) 32-46; Elmy, E.C.W., *"The Part of Women in Local Administration in England and Wales, Part II,"* 150 (1898) 248-260; Elmy, E.C.W., *"The Part of Women in Local Administration in England and Wales, Part III,"* 150 (1898) 377-389; Elmy, E.C.W., *"The Part of Women in Local Administration in Wales and England, Part IV,"* 151 (1899) 159-171.

7.809
HOUSEHOLD WORDS: Parr, H., *"The Post-Mistress,"* 12 (1855) 305-309.

7.810
ENGLISH WOMAN'S JOURNAL: Parkes, B.R., *"Life Insurance Agency as an Employment for Females,"* 3 (1859) 120-123; *"A Ramble with Mrs. Grundy,"* 5 (1860) 269-272; *"Women Compositors,"* 8 (1861) 37-61. A paper read at a meeting of the Association for the Promotion of Social Science; Howson, J.S., *"The Official Employment of Women in Works of Charity,"* 9 (1862) 361-364; Jellicoe, Mrs., *"Women's Supervision of Women's Industry,"* 10 (1862) 114-119; Boucherett, J., *"Remunerative Work for Gentlewomen,"* 10 (1862) 183-189; Boucherett, J., *"On Choice of a Business,"* 10 (1862) 145-153.

7.811
TRANSACTIONS OF THE NATIONAL ASSOCIATION FOR THE PROMOTION OF SOCIAL SCIENCE: Parkes, B.R., *"Industrial Employment of Women. A Year's Experience in Women's Work,"* (1860) 811-819. Discusses employment for women in benevolent work and the difficulties of obtaining education or training for the relevant occupations; Faithfull, E., *"The Victoria Press,"* (1860) 819-822; *"Female Compositors,"* (1861) 685; Overend, Mrs. A., *"Remunerative Employment for Educated Women,"* (1861) 686; Howson, J.S., *"The Official Employment of Women in Works of Charity,"* (1862) 780; Jellicoe, A., *"Woman's Supervision of Woman's Industry,"* (1862) 812; Menzies, L.L., *"The Callings Suitable to Women of the Middle Class,"* (1866) 795; Merryweather, M., *"The Training of Educated Women for Superintendents,"* (1868) n.p.; Newsome, Miss, *"Women as Inspectors of Schools,"* (1870) 554-555; Hubbard, L.M., *"The Duties of Women as Managers of Elementary Schools,"* (1878) 439-442; *also published in:* **WOMAN'S GAZETTE:** n.v. (1878) n.p.; Taylor, W.C., *"The Duties of Women as Managers of Elementary Schools,"* (1878) 439-442; Biggs, C.A., *"Duties of Women as Poor Law Guardians,"* (1878) 655-656; Harland, S., *"Educated Women as Technical Workers,"* (1884) n.p.

7.812
Twining, Louisa, **NURSES FOR THE SICK. WITH A LETTER TO YOUNG WOMEN.** 1861. Concerned with upgrading the profession of nursing by replacing "ignorant and untrained" nurses with a higher class of practitioner. "Now there is one calling and profession that is far from being over-stocked. It is a noble, honourable, and remunerative one,——one essentially belonging to *women*, and yet I believe it is little known or thought of by the class of persons who might fill it so advantageously" (p. 5).

7.813
Barber, Mary Ann Serrett, **BREAD WINNING; OR, THE LEDGER AND THE**

LUTE. AN AUTOBIOGRAPHY. [1865].

7.814
CORNHILL MAGAZINE: *"Nurses Wanted,"* 11 (1865) 409-433.

7.815
MELIORA: *"Employments for Educated Women,"* 9 (1866) 44. Certain occupations, such as law-copying, telegraph work and compositing, are unsuitable for educated women and are best left to those who have little more than elementary instruction. One occupation recommended for educated women is the preparation of slides for microscope reading.

7.816
VICTORIA MAGAZINE: *"Employment of Women in the Public Service,"* 12 (1868-1869) 438-446. Argues for the employment of women as civil service clerks, debating on male displacement caused by females serving in this capacity; *"Women in the Legal Profession,"* 28 (1876-1877) 219.

7.817
Savage, Marmion W., THE WOMAN OF BUSINESS: OR, THE LADY AND THE LAWYER. 3 vols. 1870; *originally serialized in:* FORTNIGHTLY REVIEW: 11 (1869) 156-177; 12 (1869) 82-102; 13 (1870) 108-125.

7.818
ENGLISHWOMAN'S MAGAZINE: *"Woman's Work at the Postal Telegraph,"* 12 (1872) 23-25. Praises women workers who "cannot fail to be most encouraging to those who are rightly anxious for the advancement of women in every legitimate and appropriate sphere of action" (p. 23). Compares male and female operators.

7.819
March-Phillipps, Lucy F., ENGLISH MATRONS AND THEIR PROFESSIONS: WITH SOME CONSIDERATIONS AS TO THEIR VARIOUS OFFICES, THEIR NATIONAL IMPORTANCE AND THE EDUCATION THEY REQUIRE. 1873; *reviewed in:* ENGLISHWOMAN'S REVIEW: 5 (1874) 25-30. The book was written without a "political object, political questions are now too closely involved with women's welfare to be altogether passed by" (p. 30). Author may also be cataloged under Phillipps, Lucy F. March.

7.820
JOURNAL OF MENTAL SCIENCE: *"Correspondence——to the Editor: Matrons in Lunatic Asylums,"* 19 (1874) 646-647.

7.821
ENGLISHWOMAN'S REVIEW: *"Women as Pharmacists,"* 5 (1873) 228-229. While women were registered as chemists and druggists, and examiners tested them, the Pharmaceutical Society declined to consider their admission to membership; *"Correspondence: Dentistry as a Profession for Women,"* 5 (1873) 300-301; *"Female Clerkships in the Post Office,"* 6 (1875) 174-175. Delineates the subjects of the civil service examinations, qualifications, and pay rates; *"Women as Poor Law Guardians,"* 6 (1875) 157-159. Asserts that the "special attributes" of women qualify them as efficient administrators and investigators; *"Women as Dentists,"* 6 (1875) 385-386; *"Silk Culture as Employment for Women,"* 6 (1875) 406-408. This occupation should be attempted more by English women since it's been successful abroad; *"Women in the Civil Service,"* 6 (1875) 195-202; 243-248; 297-301. Report of the Civil Service Inquiry Commission. In summary, the commission presents evidence "that women

are well qualified for clerical work of a less important character, and are satisfied with a lower rate of pay than is expected by men similarly employed. We, therefore, see no reason why the employment of female clerks should not be extended to other departments where the circumstances will admit of it" (p. 195); *"Law and Ladies,"* 9 (1878) 151-156. Discusses the founding of a society called Legal Education of Women. The purposes of the society were to educate women in the matters of law and to help them pursue the study of law as a profession; *"Record of Events. Female Clerks; Matrimonial Causes Act; Suffrage,"* 9 (1878) 367-371; Blackburn, H., *"Female Clerks,"* 9 (1878) 367-368; E.W., *"Woman's Work: The Lady Dentist,"* 9 (1878) 556-558. Account of the author's surprise encounter with a female dentist; *"Record of Events. A Lady Surveyor of Roads; Other Appointments of Women; Society for the Employment of Women; The Organization of Women's Industry; Medical Society of the College of Physicians,"* 10 (1879) 168-174; Hoggan, F.E., *"On the Microscope as Affording Employment and Recreation to Women: With Hints for Beginners How to Set to Work,"* 10 (1879) 193-198. Contradicting the "theory that young women of means have no other vocation than to look and be attractive and pleasant," the author asks ladies to "consider for a moment the claims of the microscope, as a refuge from listlessness and ennui"; Drew, C., *"Women as Journalists,"* 25 (1894) 245; *"Young Women in Business,"* 28 (1897) 77-84. Examines the business and social-related activities of, as well as the problems experienced by, shop assistants. Concerned mainly with housing and food accommodations offered to these women; Biggs, M.A., *"Women As Public Librarians,"* 29 (1898) 154-157. Discusses library skill training institutions open to women in the United States as proof of the need for such British institutions; M.B., *"Ladies as Laundry Proprietors,"* 29 (1898) 17-19. Written by a woman who once owned a laundry; gives advice as to how to treat employees and customers; A.S., *"Laundry Experience,"* 29 (1898) 19-21. Advises women thinking of purchasing a small laundry as a business; *"The Public Responsibilities of Women,"* 30 (1899) 1-9; *"Women in Libraries,"* 30 (1899) 240-244. Comparison between England and America on reasons for hiring female librarians. The point in agreement is that they are best suited in the children's department.

7.822
FRASER'S MAGAZINE: A Government Official, *"Ladies as Clerks,"* 92 (1875) 335-340.

7.823
CHAMBERS'S EDINBURGH JOURNAL: *"Clerks, By One of Them,"* n.v. (1877) 573; *"Female Professionals,"* n.v. (1877) 65-67; *"Women in the Post Office,"* 2 (1898-1899) 60-63; Martin, M., *"A Neglected Branch of Woman's Work,"* 9 (1905-1906) 506-508. "Some of our most highly educated women have also be skilled embroideresses.... Harriet Martineau supported herself by the work of her fingers and needle long before she sold her first book... it surely does seem a pity that a little more time in a girl's education is not devoted to what is most essentially a woman's occupation" (p. 508); Hutchins, B.L., *"An Enquiry into the Salaries and Hours of Work of Typists and Shorthand Writers,"* 16 (1906) 447-448.

7.824
GOOD WORDS AND SUNDAY MAGAZINE: Trollope, A., *"The Young Women at the Telegraph Office,"* 18 (1877) 377-384. "Eight hundred young women at work, all in one room... earning fair wages at easy work... with a kitchen at hand and a hot dinner in the middle of the day, with leave of absence without stoppage of pay... with female superintendents and the chance of rising to be a superintendent open to each girl" (p. 377); Pendleton, J., *"The Newspaper Woman,"* 43 (1902) 57-60. "Editorial prejudice is often the slave of circumstance, and she may brush it aside

with the offer of exclusive news, or of articles he thinks indispensable; but to succeed in journalism the 'newspaper woman' must be diplomatic and indomitable. She should also be able to specialize and the subject she selects need not necessarily be the tedious one, to the male editor, of dress and fashion" (p. 60).

7.825
WOMAN'S GAZETTE: *"Women Dentists,"* 2 (1877) 138. Discusses two women practicing in London. One of them, Mrs. Harding, specializes in artificial teeth. Her services are within the income of servants and others; Cobbe, F.P., *"Gardening as an Employment for Women,"* 2 (1877) 61; 109.

7.826
THE CITY CLERKS: THE DIFFICULTY OF THEIR POSITION, AND ITS CAUSES, WITH SOME SUGGESTIONS HOW TO REMOVE THEM. BY ONE OF THEM. 1878.

7.827
JOURNAL OF THE WOMEN'S EDUCATION UNION: *"Female Inspectors [of Schools],"* 6 (1878) 107-110.

7.828
MACMILLAN'S MAGAZINE: Chesney, J., *"A New Vocation for Women,"* 40 (1879) 341-346. Refers to horticulture. "Hybridising, grafting, budding, disbudding, who could accomplish them better?" (p. 342).

7.829
B., H.G., WOMEN COMPOSITORS; A GUIDE TO THE COMPOSING ROOM BY H.G.B. 1880.

7.830
GIRL'S OWN PAPER: *"Female Clerks and Bookkeepers,"* 1 (1880) 309-18; *"Work for All Careers for Women in Teaching, Medicine, Nursing, Dispensing, Art, Music, Clerks, Bookkeeping, Misc.,"* 5 (1883-84) 25-27; 119-120; 179-181; 347-348; 518-519; 662-663; Caulfield, S.A., *"New Employments for Girls,"* 13 (1891) 20-21; P., G.H., *"Women as Journalists,"* 12 (1891) 395-396; Schofield, A.T., *"A New Career for Ladies,"* 12 (1891) 809-810; Caulfield, S.A., *"New Employments for Girls,"* 13 (1892) 229-231; 332-334; 362-363.

7.831
Genna, E. (pseud.), **IRRESPONSIBLE PHILANTHROPISTS; BEING SOME CHAPTERS ON THE EMPLOYMENT OF GENTLEWOMEN.** 1881.

7.832
QUARTERLY REVIEW: Manners, J., *"Employment of Women in the Public Service,"* 151 (1881) 181-200. Examines discrepencies in salaries between men and women as well as class problems in the workplace; Lockhead, M., *"Miss Rigby and the Quarterly Review: Pioneer Women Journalists,"* n.v. (1960) 59-69. On Lady Elizabeth (Rigby) Eastlake.

7.833
NINETEENTH CENTURY: Harkness, M.E., *"Women as Civil Servants,"* 10 (1881) 369-381. Suggests de-emphasizing class differences in favor of "a bond of mutual helpfulness, binding together all women irrespective of class to meet the obstacles incident to changing social conditions of life" (p. 381); Twining, L., *"Women as Public Servants,"* 28 (1890) 950-958; Twining, L., *"Women as Official Inspectors,"*

35 (1894) 489-494; Courtney, J.E., *"The Prospect of Women as Brain Workers,"* 74 (1913) 1284-1293. Suggests that women would be productive businesspersons because of their knack of knowing, and satisfying, the unconscious needs of the consumer, as they do their families at home.

7.834
SPECTATOR: *"Women in Business,"* 55 (1882) 1076-1077. Advocating the employment of women, refers to female clerks who can be hired at a cheaper wage than men; *"Women as Journalists,"* 70 (1893) 800-801; *"Women and Science,"* 82 (1899) 409-410; *"Women and the Bar,"* 91 (1903) 1016-1017; *"The Professional Woman,"* 96 (1906) 250-251; *"Women's Work in Colonisation,"* 98 (1907) 6-7.

7.835
Rayne, Martha Louise, **WHAT CAN A WOMAN DO: OR, HER POSITION IN THE BUSINESS AND LITERARY WORLD.** Detroit, 1884; 1885; 1887; New York, 1893.

7.836
Langford, Laura Holloway (Carter), "Woman in Journalism" in **INTERNATIONAL COUNCIL OF WOMEN, 1888. REPORT...** no editor listed. [1888].

7.837
McBride, Marion A., "Women in Journalism" in **INTERNATIONAL COUNCIL OF WOMEN, 1888. REPORT...** no editor listed. [1888].

7.838
ECONOMIC REVIEW: Webb, S., *"Women Compositors,"* 2 (1892) 42-45. "Women compositors... introduced in Lancashire forty years ago, are now to be found in various parts of the United Kingdom... they are said to receive less than half the Trade Union rate.... They receive from only one-third to one-half of the men's piece-work rates and have 'completely revolutionized the trade' in [Edinburgh]" (pp. 42-43); Linnet, A., *"Women Compositors in London,"* 2 (1892) 45-49. "Women compositors are as much to be depended upon and more easily controlled than the men" (p. 48). Delineates the reasons why certain firms do not employ women, discusses the limitations imposed by the Factory Acts on women in this trade, and provides wage rates.

7.839
YOUNG WOMAN: 1892 to 1911; 1-19; *"What it Means to Be a Lady Journalist,"* 8 (1899-1900) n.p.; *"What it Means to Be a Legal Typist,"* 8 (1899-1900) n.p.; *"House Decorating as an Occupation for Women,"* 9 (1900-1901) n.p.

7.840
Burdett-Coutts, Angela Georgina (Baroness), "Miss Ormerod's Work in Agricultural Entomology" in **WOMAN'S MISSION.** ed. by Angela Georgina Burdett-Coutts. 1893. "Although the protection of our crops from devastation is unlike the benevolent work recorded elsewhere in these pages; it is benevolent work of the highest moment. Its immediate consequence is to secure the fruits of labour and to enhance the production of food; which is to cheapen it" (p. 323). Examines Ormerod's work as an observer and recorder of various insects which endanger crops. Provides biographical background. Author may also be cataloged as Coutts, Angela Georgina Burdett.

7.841
BLACKWOOD'S MAGAZINE: Eccles, C.O., *"The Experiences of a Woman Journalist,"* 153 (1893) 830-838.

7.842

CONTEMPORARY REVIEW: Crawford, E., *"Journalism as a Profession for Women,"* 64 (1893) 362-371; Knight, H., *"Women and the Legal Profession,"* 103 (1913) 689-696. "Why should one sex be debarred from exercising this right [of admission into the profession] in an age when the legal needs of women require continual representation? The exclusion of duly qualified women... is absolutely indefensible in reason and social justice" (p. 696).

7.843

LAW TIMES: *"Women as Fellows of Scientific Societies,"* 95 (1893) 152.

7.844

NEW REVIEW: Knightley, Lady M., *"New Employments for Educated Women,"* 9 (1893) 577-582.

7.845

Davidson, J.E., **WHAT OUR DAUGHTERS CAN DO FOR THEMSELVES; A HANDBOOK OF WOMEN'S EMPLOYMENTS.** 1894. Catalogue of acceptable options for single middle-class women to support themselves. Encourages women to realistically assess their talents and abilities. Chapters on the theater and emigration are of special interest.

7.846

Hill, Georgiana, "The Gentlewomen in Trade" and "The Modern Woman of Business" in **WOMEN IN ENGLISH LIFE.** by Georgiana Hill. 1894.

7.847

LIBRARY: Richardson, Miss, *"Librarianship as a Profession for Women,"* 6 (1894) 137-142. "Labelling [and] repairing... of books... will in all probability be done more quickly and neatly by a girl than a boy; and as regards the issuing of books, there is an advantage in having at least one female assistant, as many of the lady borrowers prefer to be attended to by one of their own sex. In those libraries which have separate reading-rooms for studies, it is also essential that a female assistant should look after the room and attend to the renewal of the papers and periodicals placed there" (p. 137); *rpt. in:* **THE ROLE OF WOMEN IN LIBRARIANSHIP 1876-1976: THE ENTRY, ADVANCEMENT, AND STRUGGLE FOR EQUALIZATION IN ONE PROFESSION.** compiled by Kathleen Weibel, et al. 1979; Fredeman, W.E., *"Emily Faithfull and the Victoria Press. An Experiment in Sociological Bibliography,"* 29 (1974) 139-164. Short biography and history of the Press which was a fruitful source of employment for women. "The terms of employment at the Victoria Press were well in advance of their time. Apprentices worked an eight-hour day... and were paid on an hourly basis according to productivity and the stage of their training" (p. 149). Includes a listing of Victoria Press publications; Stone, J.S., *"More Light on Emily Faithfull and the Victoria Press,"* 33 (1978) 63-67.

7.848

Bateson, Margaret, **PROFESSIONAL WOMEN UPON THEIR PROFESSIONS.** 1895; 1897.

7.849

LADY'S REALM: Wimble, W., *"Incomes for Ladies,"* 1 (1896-97) 331-332. Discusses gardening, book-binding, and the designing and modelling of frames.

7.850
SATURDAY REVIEW: Grew, M.S., *"Women Factory Inspectors,"* 84 (1897) 136-137.

7.851
Bennett, Arnold, **JOURNALISM FOR WOMEN: A PRACTICAL GUIDE.** 1898.

7.852
Ford, Isabella Ormston, **WOMEN AS FACTORY INSPECTORS AND CERTIFYING SURGEONS.** 1898.

7.853
Guild of Women Bookbinders, **BOOKBINDING BY WOMEN.** 1898; **CATALOGUE OF BINDINGS BY THE GUILD OF WOMEN BINDERS.** 1900; **THE BINDERY THAT JILL BUILT.** 1901; **THE BINDINGS OF TOMORROW: A RECORD OF THE WORK OF THE GUILD OF WOMEN BINDERS AND THE HAMPSTEAD BINDERY.** 1902.

7.854
HUMANITARIAN: Tooley, S.A., *"Women in Journalism; An Interview with Mrs. Meynell, President of the Society of Women Journalists,"* n.v. (1898) 229-235; Middleton, J.A., *"Women Journalists of the Past,"* n.v. (1899) 193-196; Quentin, C., *"Women as Barristers,"* 17 (1899) 203-205.

7.855
Bergman Osterberg, Martina, **MADAME BERGMAN OSTERBERG ON PHYSICAL TRAINING AS A PROFESSION.** Blackheath, 1899.

7.856
ECONOMIC JOURNAL: Bradbury, L.B. and Black, A., *"Notes and Memoranda, Women Compositors and the Factory Acts,"* 9 (1899) 261-266. Includes a brief historical sketch of female involvement in the printing trade; Garland, C.H., *"Women as Telegraphists,"* 11 (1901) 251-61. Compares women working in this field in different countries, mainly focused on English telegraphists. Examines the reasons for "women's cheapness" as employees and provides data comparing their wages to those of men. "Women possess the ability to perform the routine duties of telegraphy when carried on at low even pressure, as efficiently as men... a broader worldly education gives them the judgement and ability necessary to perform duties of a higher character. In addition, they are attractive to employers because they can be obtained considerably cheaper than men. They possess too, the sovereign advantage of docility. There are not lacking signs, however, that this docility will decrease as women become more conscious of their economic value and responsibilities" (p. 260).

7.857
Harper, Ida (Husted), "The Training of Women Journalists" in **WOMEN IN SOCIAL LIFE. THE TRANSACTIONS OF THE SOCIAL SECTION OF THE INTERNA-TIONAL CONGRESS OF WOMEN, LONDON, 1899.** ed. by Ishbel Aberdeen. [1900].

7.858
Collet, Clara Elizabeth, **EDUCATED WORKING WOMEN; ESSAYS ON THE ECONOMIC POSITION OF WOMEN WORKERS IN THE MIDDLE CLASSES.** 1902.

7.859
Banks, Elizabeth, **THE AUTOBIOGRAPHY OF A NEWSPAPER GIRL**. 1902.

7.860
King, Jessie Margaret, **WOMEN AND PUBLIC WORK. THEIR OPPORTUNITIES AND LEGAL STATUS IN ENGLAND, SCOTLAND, AND IRELAND COMPARED.** 1902.

7.861
National Council of Women of Great Britain, **WOMEN AS SANITARY INSPECTORS**. 1902.

7.862
LIBRARY WORLD: Chennell, F., *"Lady Assistants in Public Libraries,"* 4 (1902) 245-248. Discusses the rise to senior positions made by female assistants, the impact of such promotions, and the effect on male employees; Pierce, K.E., *"Women in Public Libraries,"* 4 (1902) 286-288. Responds to above article by Chennell, arguing that his information was ill-perceived and that women working in libraries are as competent and responsible as men; Gilbert, M., *"The Position of Women in Public Libraries,"* 18 (1915) 100-105. "Women were first employed as public library assistants in England at Manchester in 1811. The salaries given were twenty-six pounds and eighty pounds per year, according to the ability of the assistant; eighty pounds was the salary paid to women branch librarians" (p. 100).

7.863
Mackenna, E., ed., **THE WOMAN'S LIBRARY SERIES**. 3 vols. 1903. Volume 1 treats the subject of education and the professions; Volume 2 deals with work in embroidery, dressmaking, millinery, knitting, and crocheting; Volume 3 covers nursing and childcare.

7.864
LAW JOURNAL: *"Women and the Bar,"* 38 (1903) 620.

7.865
Dudfield, T. Orme, **WOMAN'S PLACE IN SANITARY ADMINISTRATION: PAPER READ BEFORE THE WOMAN SANITARY INSPECTOR'S ASSOCIATION.** 1904.

7.866
Bache, Rene, **WOMEN AS INVENTORS.** 1906.

7.867
McKenna, Ethel M.M., ed., **EDUCATION AND PROFESSIONS. THE WOMAN'S LIBRARY.** 1908. Volume 1 in a series, "The Woman's Library," covering preparation for numerous occupations and details of employment in such fields as teaching, journalism, art, theater, medicine, and public work as factory and sanitary inspectors.

7.868
Wolseley, Frances, **GARDENING FOR WOMEN**. 1908. Recommends gardening as a paid occupation for women. "The profession of gardening offers a considerable amount of freedom, the refining influence of poetry and beauty, contact with intelligent interesting people, and health and happiness to body and mind. These, to an active, out-of-door, young woman are very good advantages" (p. 5). Other chapters discuss required training, landscaping, floral decoration, the teaching of

nature-study, dress, medical aspects, Italian Pot Gardens, reasons why employers hesitate to employ women, colleges and schools in England, on the continent, in America, Canada and Australia, market gardening. Includes an appendix, "Useful Information for Lady Gardeners."

7.869
IMPERIAL COLONIST: *"Horticulture as a Career for Women,"* 6 (1908) 7-10.

7.870
JOURNAL OF EDUCATION: Matheson, M.C., *"Training for Social Work, New University Course at Birmingham,"* 40 (1908) 640-641. "As a girl passes out of school or college.... there is a far larger choice of professions... than existed twenty years ago.... Women need to have a human interest in their life work——an interest that shall appeal to heart and imagination as well as to intellect and business capacity.... the innate interest... leads so many women to teaching and nursing.... But it seems to be unknown... that there is a small but increasing group of posts for educated workers.... termed 'the social service,' with its central salaried posts in various philanthropic undertakings" (p. 640).

7.871
Howard, Emma Shafter, **THE WOMEN'S AGRICULTURAL AND HORTICUL-TURAL UNION.** Toronto, 1909.

7.872
BOOK OF THE HOME: *"II. Occupations for Women,"* 6 (1909) 27-39. Describes and discusses the availability of positions open to women as accountants, art teachers, book-keepers, children's nurses, clerks, civil service clerks, dispensers, inspectors, journalists, librarians, matrons in institutions and schools, doctors, musicians, needleworkers, nurses, photographers, teachers of physical education, plan tracers for engineers and architects, private teachers, and typists.

7.873
SOCIALIST REVIEW: Langley, H.H., *"The Typist's Sex War,"* 3 (1909) 308-312. Writes of the difficulty experienced by trained male shorthand-typists in finding employment in a field dominated by women; A Member of the Association of Shorthand Writers and Typists, *"Discussion I. The Outlook for Typists,"* 3 (1909) 391-395. Responds to Langley, arguing that it is not the fault of women typists that male workers have trouble finding positions in the field. Both articles are valuable.

7.874
WOMAN JOURNALIST: WITH WHICH IS INCORPORATED THE BUREAU CIRCULAR, THE BI-MONTHLY ORGAN OF THE SOCIETY OF WOMEN JOURNALISTS: Dec. 1910 to Jan. 1920; nos. 1-50; Jan. 1923. Not published between 1920 and 1923.

7.875
WOMEN'S EMPLOYMENT: *"The Demand for Women Gardeners,"* 10 (1910) n.p.

7.876
Dicsee, Lawrence R. and Blain, Herbert E., **OFFICE ORGANIZATION AND MANAGEMENT, INCLUDING SECRETARIAL WORK.** 1911.

7.877
Morley, Edith J., ed., **WOMEN WORKERS IN SEVEN PROFESSIONS: A SURVEY OF THEIR ECONOMIC CONDITIONS AND PROSPECTS.** 1911; 1914. Thoughtful

examination of female professionals.

7.878
Walton, John K., **THE BLACKPOOL LANDLADY: A SOCIAL HISTORY.** Manchester, 1911; 1978; *reviewed in:* **NEW SOCIETY:** Walvin, J., 46 (1978) 650; *also reviewed in:* **ORAL HISTORY:** Lowerson, J., 8 (1980) 65-66.

7.879
Hemmeon, J.C., **THE STORY OF THE BRITISH POST OFFICE.** Cambridge, Mass., 1912.

7.880
Reynard, Helene, **BUSINESS METHODS AND SECRETARIAL WORK FOR GIRLS AND WOMEN.** 1912.

7.881
Spencer, Mary G., **OPENINGS FOR UNIVERSITY WOMEN OTHER THAN TEACHING.** 1912.

7.882
Central Employment Bureau for Women and Students' Careers Association, **WOMEN AS INSPECTORS.** [1913].

7.883
Davis, Annie E., **THE JUNIOR WOMAN SECRETARY: A GUIDE TO THE SECRETARIAL PROFESSION FOR GIRLS AND YOUNG WOMEN.** 1913.

7.884
Drake, Barbara, **THE TEA-SHOP GIRL.** 1913; **WOMEN IN THE ENGINEERING TRADES.** 1918. Covers WWI and the future of women in engineering after the war.

7.885
Mozans, H.J., **WOMAN IN SCIENCE: WITH AN INTRODUCTORY CHAPTER ON WOMAN'S LONG STRUGGLE FOR THINGS OF THE WORLD.** 1913; 1940; rpt., Cambridge, 1974. Recognizes and encourages the inevitability of women entering the professions.

7.886
Zahm, John Augustine, **WOMEN IN SCIENCE.** 1913.

7.887
ENGLISHWOMAN: Costelloe, K., *"Women in the Legal Profession,"* n.v. (1913) 38-42.

7.888
NEW STATESMAN: Courtney, W.L., *"New Types of Subordinate Women Brain-Workers,"* Special Supplement, 2 (1913) 17-19; Anderson, A., *"Women in Public Administration,"* Special Supplement, 2 (1913) 19-22. Presents arguments for female administrators, tracing the historical aspect of women pioneers in public administration.

7.889
FRIEND: Bigland, E.H.A., *"Women Police,"* 44 (1914) 519-521. Advocates police work for women, citing Germany and the U.S. as positive examples. Suggests that women's nurturing skills help bring people to seek their advice and protection and

that female officers have a stabilizing effect on the community.

7.890
Forster, Emily L.B., **HOW TO BECOME A DISPENSER: THE NEW PROFESSION FOR WOMEN.** 1917.

7.891
Barton, Edith M., **EVE IN KHAKI: THE STORY OF THE WOMEN'S ARMY AT HOME AND ABROAD.** 1918. Part 1 discusses women in England.

7.892
Sphinx, (A.) *pseud.* **JOURNALISM AS A CAREER FOR WOMEN.** 1918. Discusses the position of women journalists.

7.893
WOMAN ENGINEER: 1919+; Publication of the Women's Engineering Society.

7.894
George, Gertrude A., **EIGHT MONTHS WITH THE WOMEN'S ROYAL AIR FORCE.** 1921.

7.895
Anderson, Adelaide, **WOMEN IN THE FACTORY: AN ADMINISTRATIVE ADVENTURE 1893-1921.** 1922. Story of the Woman Inspectors of Factories and Workshops from its beginning in 1893, when the first women inspectors (Miss May Abraham and Miss Emma Paterson) took their first assignments. By 1921 there were thirty female inspectors.

7.896
Association of Women Clerks and Secretaries, **THE COST OF LIVING FOR WOMEN CLERICAL WORKERS.** 1922.

7.897
Boothroyd, H.E., **A HISTORY OF THE INSPECTORATE: BEING A SHORT ACCOUNT OF THE ORIGIN AND DEVELOPMENT OF THE INSPECTING SERVICE OF THE BOARD OF EDUCATION.** 1923.

7.898
Johnson, Edith, **TO WOMEN OF THE BUSINESS WORLD.** 1923.

7.899
OUTLOOK: Brainerd, E.W., *"Women Police as England Sees Them,"* Sept. (1924) 55-57.

7.900
Allen, Mary Sophia, **THE PIONEER POLICEWOMAN.** ed. by Julie Helen Heyneman. 1925. Margaret Damer Dawson organized the Women Police Volunteers, a corps of trained professionals. "Many of the women attracted by the idea of women police had been prominent workers for Woman's Suffrage in the militant days before the War. Their efforts... had brought some of them into close, sometimes painful touch with the police, teaching them how very unpleasant it is for an alleged woman culprit to be handled by men" (p. 13); **WOMEN POLICE.** 1925. Discusses early difficulties within the profession.

7.901
Macadam, Elizabeth, **THE EQUIPMENT OF THE SOCIAL WORKER.** 1925.

7.902
WOMAN CITIZEN: De Zouche, E.H., *"England's Pioneer Woman Barrister,"* 9 (1925) 14; 25. "In the case of her admission to the Bar, she had to wait three years" (p. 14).

7.903
Sharp, Evelyn, **HERTHA AYRTON 1854-1923: A MEMOIR.** 1926. Ayrton distinguished herself as a scientist and was elected a member of the Institute of Electrical Engineers in 1899.

7.904
Squire, Rose E., **THIRTY YEARS IN THE PUBLIC SERVICE: AN INDUSTRIAL RETROSPECT.** 1927. Squire was first a sanitary inspector, then a factory inspector, then a special investigator, and finally the Director of the Women's Training Department.

7.905
Brittain, Vera, "Women in Business," "Women in Professions," and "Women in the National Services" in **WOMEN'S WORK IN MODERN ENGLAND.** by Vera Brittain. 1928.

7.906
Pankhurst, Sylvia, "The Munition Workers——Government Appeal to Women" in **THE HOME FRONT.** by Sylvia Pankhurst. 1932.

7.907
Carr-Saunders, Alexander M. and Wilson, Paul A., **THE PROFESSIONS.** Oxford, 1933; 1937; rpt., 1964.

7.908
Courtney, Janet Elizabeth, "The Early Civil Servants" in **THE WOMEN OF MY TIME.** by Janet Elizabeth Courtney. 1934. Discusses Marianne Mason, May Abraham, Adelaide Anderson, Clara Collet, Maude Lawrence, Mona Wilson, Hermia Durham, and Meriel Talbot.

7.909
Evans, Dorothy E., **WOMEN AND THE CIVIL SERVICE: A HISTORY OF THE DEVELOPMENT OF THE EMPLOYMENT OF WOMEN IN THE CIVIL SERVICE, AND A GUIDE TO PRESENT DAY OPPORTUNITIES.** 1934.

7.910
Interallied Veterans' Federation, **FEMINA PATRIAE DEFENSOR: WOMAN IN THE SERVICE OF HER COUNTRY.** 1934.

7.911
Klingender, Francis Donald, **THE CONDITION OF CLERICAL LABOUR IN BRITAIN.** 1935.

7.912
Lambert, R.S., **THE UNIVERSAL PROVIDER.** 1938. Biography of William Whiteley and his role in the rise of the London department store. Includes bibliography.

7.913
Martindale, Hilda, **WOMEN SERVANTS OF THE STATE 1870-1938: A HISTORY OF WOMEN IN THE CIVIL SERVICE.** 1938. "By 1874 women were well established in the Telegraph Clearing Office and the Returned Letter Office. The next stronghold was the Savings Bank, and this was stormed in 1875, when some forty 'young ladies' were taken on, and were set to work on the newly introduced Daily Balance Section of the office" (p. 24). Valuable work; "A Single-Minded Servant of the State. Isabel Taylor" and "An Unforgettable Personality. Adelaide Anderson" in **SOME VICTORIAN PORTRAITS AND OTHERS.** by Hilda Martindale. New York, 1948; 1970. On two female inspectors.

7.914
Cohen, Emmeline, **THE GROWTH OF THE BRITISH CIVIL SERVICE 1780-1939.** 1941.

7.915
Gwynne-Vaughan, Helen, **SERVICE WITH THE ARMY.** Hutchinson, 1942.

7.916
FORTNIGHTLY REVIEW: Bondfield, M., *"Welfare in Distribution and Domestic Work,"* 163 (1945) 112-119. Discusses the evolution of organization among shop assistants, difficulties encountered, and achievements. "Perhaps the most difficult obstacle to overcome was the snobbishness of assistants; they were paid per annum, they were not work people, and the majority called each other ladies and gentlemen!" (p. 115).

7.917
Robinson, Howard, **THE BRITISH POST OFFICE: A HISTORY.** 1948.

7.918
Wood, Ethel M., "Women in Professional Life" in **THE PILGRIMAGE OF PERSEVERANCE.** by Ethel M. Wood. 1949. Discusses female participation in medicine, education, and law.

7.919
Tancred, Edith, **WOMEN POLICE 1914-1950.** 1951.

7.920
BULLETIN OF THE HISTORY OF MEDICINE: Edwards, R.W., *"The First Woman Dentist—Lucy Hobbs Taylor, DDS, 1883-1910,"* 25 (1951) n.p.

7.921
Dunbar, Janet, "Women Writers" in **THE EARLY VICTORIAN WOMAN.** by Janet Dunbar. 1953.

7.922
Hughes, Fred, **BY HAND AND BRAIN: THE STORY OF THE CLERICAL AND ADMINISTRATIVE WORKERS' UNION.** 1953.

7.923
ILLUSTRATED LONDON NEWS: *"Obituary of Helena Florence Normanton 1883-1957,"* 231 (1957) 704. Normanton was the first woman to be admitted to the Bar in England in 1922. She wrote books on law and sociology.

7.924
Humphreys, B.V., **CLERICAL UNIONS IN THE CIVIL SERVICE**. 1958.

7.925
Lockwood, David, **THE BLACKCOATED WORKER: A STUDY IN CLASS CONSCIOUSNESS**. 1958. Considers factors that affect the clerical worker's sense of identification with (or alienation from) the working class, and with the trade-union movement from the 1870s. Involved is the question of machine operation or automation as it affects division of labor along sex lines. For example, in civil service, introduction of machinery was accompanied by an increase in the number of women so employed. "Female clerks derive almost equally from the working and lower middle classes." The smaller proportion came from families whose head (fathers) were minor professionals or shop assistants. As for the women's marital status the tendency was for them to "marry up" rather than down in the social scale. The gradual increase in the proportion of women in clerical work affected the status of that job classification. There was talk of the "white blouse invasion of blackcoated work" immediately before the First World War——a steady feminization of the clerical labor force. The idea that clerical work was "unmanly" was reinforced. This feminization, says Lockwood, played a role in holding back blackcoated unionism (p. 151).

7.926
Kaye, Barrington, **THE DEVELOPMENT OF THE ARCHITECTURAL PROFESSIONAL IN BRITAIN**. 1960.

7.927
Bell, E.M., **THE STORY OF HOSPITAL ALMONERS: THE BIRTH OF A PROFESSION**. 1961.

7.928
Coxhead, Eileen Elizabeth, **WOMEN IN THE PROFESSIONS**. 1961.

7.929
McKenzie, S.A., **EDITH SIMCOX AND GEORGE ELIOT**. 1961. Discusses these two female writers' careers in journalism.

7.930
Fielding, Daphne, **THE DUCHESS OF JERMYN STREET: THE LIFE AND GOOD TIMES OF ROSA LEWIS OF THE CAVENDISH HOTEL**. 1964. ——*see also:* Masters, Anthony, **ROSA LEWIS: AN EXCEPTIONAL EDWARDIAN**. 1977. Biography of a woman from a lower middle-class family who began her career as a domestic servant and then became cook and owner of the Cavendish Hotel.

7.931
Jones, Kathleen, **THE TEACHING OF SOCIAL STUDIES IN BRITISH UNIVERSITIES**. 1964. Preparation for the field of social work.

7.932
Franz, Nellie Alden, **ENGLISH WOMEN ENTER THE PROFESSIONS**. Cincinnati, 1965. Sections relevant to the Victorian/Edwardian period are Teaching, Medicine, Civil Service and Architecture. Discusses the early pioneers in each field. The first women to be accepted in the professional association of architects were Ethel Mary Charles (1898) and Bessie Ada Charles.

7.933
Smith, Marjorie J., **PROFESSIONAL EDUCATION FOR SOCIAL WORK IN BRITAIN: AN HISTORICAL ACCOUNT.** 1965.

7.934
Spoor, Alec, **WHITE COLLAR UNION: 60 YEARS OF NALGO.** 1967.

7.935
White, Cynthia L., **WOMEN'S MAGAZINES 1693-1968.** 1970. Surveys the growth of the woman's periodical, the origins of the female press, and the impact of both on modern publications for women. Details various employment opportunities.

7.936
Critchley, T.A., **A HISTORY OF POLICE IN ENGLAND AND WALES.** New Jersey, 1972. In 1919 policewomen were considered an "unnecessarily extravagant luxury. Many who conceded that women were better qualified than men to undertake social and moral welfare work among women and young people, nevertheless preferred to see them enrolled in voluntary organisations rather than in police forces, an attitude reinforced by concern for economy. Few chief constables saw much value in policewomen, some suspected of feminism" (p. 215).

7.937
Holcombe, Lee, **VICTORIAN LADIES AT WORK: MIDDLE-CLASS WORKING WOMEN IN ENGLAND AND WALES, 1850-1914.** Hamden, 1973; *reviewed in:* **JOURNAL OF SOCIAL HISTORY:** Branca, P., 8 (1975) 143-146; *also reviewed in:* **SOCIAL HISTORY:** Davidoff, L., 3 (1976) 385-387.

7.938
Thomson, Dorothy Lampen, **ADAM SMITH'S DAUGHTERS: SIX DISTINGUISHED WOMEN ECONOMISTS FROM THE 18TH CENTURY TO THE PRESENT.** Jericho, New York, 1973. Discusses Jane Marcet, Harriet Martineau, Millicent G. Fawcett, Rosa Luxemborg, Beatrice Webb and Joan Robinson.

7.939
HISTORY TODAY: Jones, D., *"Lady Charlotte Guest: Victorian Businesswoman,"* 23 (1973) 38-46. Biography of a woman active in the management of the Dowlais Iron Company.

7.940
SOCIETY FOR THE STUDY OF LABOUR HISTORY BULLETIN: Davin, A., *"Telegraphists and Clerks,"* 26 (1973) 7-9. Mostly from the middle classes, female telegraphists and clerks soon dominated an originally male occupation. Contends that economics (cheaper labor) was the motivation to open the field to women; Carrier, J., *"The Control of Women by Women: the Women Police,"* 26 (1973) 16-19. Provides a contemporary account circa 1916. Asserts that women were used to enforce "norms of sexual morality."

7.941
GEOGRAPHICAL REVIEW: Sanderson, M., *"Mary Somerville: Her Work in Physical Geography,"* 64 (1974) 410-420. Without any formal education, Mary Somerville wrote the first textbook on physical geography in the English language.

7.942
PROCEEDINGS OF THE AMERICAN PHILOSOPHICAL SOCIETY: Patterson, E.C., *"The Case of Mary Somerville: An Aspect of Nineteenth-Century Science,"* 118

(1974) 268-275. Besides her works in physical geography, Somerville authored books on mathematics and astronomy; Mild, W., *"Susanna Highmore's Literary Reputation,"* 122 (1978) 377-384.

7.943
Walton, Ronald G., **WOMEN IN SOCIAL WORK.** 1975. Discusses both voluntary and paid employment for women in charitable institutions, social service agencies, and governmental welfare bureaucracy from 1860 to 1971. Walton emphasizes the subordinate status and salaries women have received as compared with men.

7.944
ANNALS OF SCIENCE: Olgivie, M.B., *"Caroline Herschel's Contributions to Astronomy,"* 32 (1975) 149-161. A woman accurate in her observations, Herschel was barred "from the ranks of creative astronomers" due to her lack of interest and inability to apply abstract concepts to the field of astronomy; Love, R., *"Alice In Eugenics Land: Feminism and Eugenics in the Scientific Careers of Alice Lee and Ethel Elderton,"* 36 (1979) 145-158. Examines the careers of these two prominent scientists and their work in the Biometric Laboratory and the Galton Eugenics Laboratory.

7.945
Anderson, Gregory, **VICTORIAN CLERKS.** Manchester, 1976. "Women were... increasingly employed in commercial occupations, the number rising from 2000 in 1861 to 26,000 in 1891 and to 157,000 in 1911. In the second half of the nineteenth century the social barriers against respectable female employment were weakening and the range of suitable jobs was widening. Women were increasingly employed as low-status clerks, typists and telephonists, particularly in large-scale offices which grew alongside, though did not replace, the small counting houses of mid-Victorian commerce" (p. 2).

7.946
Maison, Margaret, **JOHN OLIVER HOBBES. HER LIFE AND WORK.** 1976. Biography of Pearl Mary Teresa Craigie (1867-1906), novelist and President of the Society of Women Journalists in 1895. "She was never very happy about committees and societies run exlusively by women for women" (p. 21) and was against colleges, clubs, and suffrage for women.

7.947
BUSINESS HISTORY REVIEW: Silverstone, R., *"Office Work for Women: An Historical Review,"* 1 (1976) 98-110. Examines women's entry into and increase in clerical occupations.

7.948
Davidoff, Leonore, "The Separation of Home and Work? Landladies and Lodgers in Nineteenth- and Twentieth-Century England" in **FIT WORK FOR WOMEN.** ed. by Sandra Burman. 1979.

7.949
Weibel, Kathleen, Heim, Kathleen M., Ellsworth, Dianne J. and Cross, Mary, compilers, **THE ROLE OF WOMEN IN LIBRARIANSHIP 1866-1976: THE ENTRY, ADVANCEMENT, AND STRUGGLE FOR EQUALIZATION IN ONE PROFESSION.** 1979. See especially: "1876-1900. Emergence of an Organized Profession" and "1901-1921. The Move Toward Suffrage." These two parts of the book contain fifteen articles reprinted from various Victorian periodicals. Valuable primary source material.

7.950
HISTORY OF EDUCATION JOURNAL: MacLeod, R. and Moseley, R., *"Fathers and Daughters: Reflections on Women, Science and Victorian Cambridge,"* 8 (1979) 321-333. Explores opportunities available to women during the late nineteenth century with emphasis on those who read for the National Science Tripos.

7.951
VICTORIAN PERIODICALS REVIEW: Bratton, J.S., *"Hesba Stretton's Journalism,"* 12 (1979) 60-70. Stretton, also known as Sara Smith, had "taken to writing both in order to contribute to the family income, as her father approached retirement and for the sake of improving her status, which as an unmarried woman at home, was not otherwise much to be envied" (p. 61); Nestor, P., *"A New Departure in Women's Publishing: The English Woman's Journal and The Victoria Magazine,"* 15 (1982) 93-106. Traces the development of magazines for women from the seventeenth century, when men undertook the production, to the nineteenth century, when women covered all operations. "A feminist strain was traceable from the earliest years of women's periodical publishing" (p. 94).

7.952
SIGNS: Tuchman, G. and Fortin, N., *"Edging Women Out: Some Suggestions About the Structure of Opportunities and the Victorian Novel,"* 2 (1980) 308-325. Examines the submission of fiction manuscripts by women writers to MacMillan and Company between 1866 and 1887. Explores reasons why women encountered difficulties in pursuing literary careers, despite a rise in educational provisions.

7.953
Ross, Samuel, "Feminization of Clerical Labor in Great Britain. A Contrast of Two Large Clerical Employers: 1857-1937," Ph.D. diss., Univ. of Michigan, 1981. Examines the hiring practices of the General Post Office and the Great Western Railway, clerical sex ratios, and female participation in clerical unions.

7.954
McFeely, Mary Drake, **WOMEN'S WORK IN BRITAIN AND AMERICA FROM THE NINETIES TO WORLD WAR I: AN ANNOTATED BIBLIOGRAPHY.** Boston, 1982.

7.955
Schweber, Claudine and Flynn, Edith Elizabeth, "Women as Practitioners and Professionals" in **JUDGE, LAWYER, VICTIM, THIEF: WOMEN, GENDER ROLES AND CRIMINAL JUSTICE.** ed. by Nicole Hahn Rafter and Elizabeth Anne Stanko. 1982. Not English but applicable for purposes of analysis. "Women entering criminal justices used their feminine qualities" (p. 7).

7.956
Robertson, Priscilla, "Englishwomen in the Professions" in **AN EXPERIENCE OF WOMEN. PATTERN AND CHANGE IN NINETEENTH CENTURY EUROPE.** by Priscilla Robertson. Philadelphia, 1982.

7.957
Winstanley, Michael J., **THE SHOPKEEPER'S WORLD 1830-1914.** Manchester, 1983.

7.958
Sheir, Ann B., "Linnaeus's Daughters: Women and British Botany" in **WOMEN AND**

THE STRUCTURE OF SOCIETY: SELECTED RESEARCH FROM THE FIFTH BERKSHIRE CONFERENCE ON THE HISTORY OF WOMEN. ed. by Barbara J. Harris and Jo Ann McNamara. Durham, 1984. Reveals elaborate kinship networks amongst women within the botanical community.

7.959
Pennybacker, Susan, "The 'Labour Question' and the London County Council, 1889-1919," Ph.D. diss., Cambridge Univ., 1985. Chapter one deals with the L.C.C. Clerks Department and includes a discussion of female labor with reference to the typewriting staff. Chapter five discusses female L.C.C. wartime employment and white collar unionization.

7.960
DARK LANTERN: Nooger, D., *"Anna Katharine Green and Her Daughters,"* 2 (1985) 1-7. Green, who "is generally credited with being the mother of the detective novel," was the daughter of a criminal lawyer in New York. Also writing detective stories were Lillie Thomasina Meade (1899) and Baroness Orczy (1910), who created sleuth Lady Molly of Scotland Yard.

7.961
Hunt, Felicity, "Opportunities Lost and Gained: Mechanization and Women's Work in the London Bookbinding and Printing Trades" in **UNEQUAL OPPORTUNITIES: WOMEN'S EMPLOYMENT IN ENGLAND 1800-1918.** ed. by Angela V. John. Oxford, 1986.

7.962
Zimmeck, Meta, "Jobs For the Girls: The Expansion of Clerical Work for Women, 1850-1914" in **UNEQUAL OPPORTUNITIES: WOMEN'S EMPLOYMENT IN ENGLAND 1800-1918.** ed. by Angela V. John. Oxford, 1986.

* * *

10. ARTISTS AND CRAFTSWOMEN

Note: Where artists' dates are included, and the birth and death dates are unknown, the abbreviation "fl." denotes the period during which the artist flourished.

7.963
EUROPEAN MAGAZINE: Moser, J., *"[Obituary of Angelica Kauffman],"* 55 (1809) 259. In the late eighteenth century, Kauffman and her friend, Mary Moser, gained entrance into the Royal Academy. However, they were still not allowed to attend classes where nude models were used.

7.964
Jameson, Anna, **DIARY OF AN ENNUYEE.** 1826. Fictionalized account of Jameson's first trip abroad, in 1821, when she was a governess for the Rowles family. She reports extensively on art works viewed in various museums and galleries; **VISITS AND SKETCHES AT HOME AND ABROAD.** 2 vols. 1834; *also published as:* **SKETCHES OF ART, LITERATURE, AND CHARACTER.** Boston and New York, 1890. Well known in her own day as an authority on art, Jameson

has been called "the mother" of art criticism and history. Jameson was a visible advocate of women's right to employment and education, although she clearly distinguished between male and female talent, relegating women to the task of treating subjects "proper" to their sex; **MEMOIRS AND ESSAYS ILLUSTRATIVE OF ART, LITERATURE, AND SOCIAL MORALS.** 1846; **THE POETRY OF SACRED AND LEGENDARY ART.** 6 vols. 1848; 3rd ed. of vols. 1 and 2 titled: **SACRED AND LEGENDARY ART.** 1857. "I hope it will be clearly understood that I have taken throughout the aesthetic and not the religious view of those productions of art which, in as far as they are informed with the true and earnest feeling, and steeped in that beauty which emanates from genius inspired by faith, may cease to be Religion, but cannot cease to be poetry; and as poetry only I have considered them" (Preface). The first two volumes contain etchings and woodcuts by Jameson and her neice. The last volume was completed by Lady Elizabeth Eastlake, one of Jameson's friends; **A COMMONPLACE BOOK OF THOUGHTS, MEMORIES AND FANCIES.** 1854. See pp. 326-371 for a list of female historical/mythical subjects that Jameson considered appropriate for women to sculpt; **HANDBOOK OF THE COURTS OF MODERN SCULPTURE.** 1854; **MEMOIRS OF EARLY ITALIAN PAINTERS.** 1854. ——*see also:* MacPherson, Geraldine, **LIFE OF ANNA JAMESON.** Boston, 1878; Erskine, Mrs. Stuart, **ANNA JAMESON: LETTERS AND FRIENDSHIPS, 1812-1860.** 1915; Needler, Gerald H., **LETTERS OF ANNA JAMESON TO OTTILIE VON GOETHE.** 1939; Thomas, Clara, **LOVE AND WORK ENOUGH: THE LIFE OF ANNA JAMESON.** Toronto, 1967; **WOMAN'S ART JOURNAL:** Thomas, C., *"Anna Jameson: Art Historian and Critic,"* 1 (1980) 20-22. "Jameson harbored a strong personal preference for the ideally beautiful over the realistic and a preoccupation with the idealized representation of the human figure as the peak of an artist's achievement" (p. 21); Waller, S., *"The Artist, The Writer and the Queen: Hosmer, Jameson, and Zenobia,"* 4 (1983) 21-28. Mainly an account of the genesis, execution, and reception of American-born Harriet Hosmer's sculpture, "Zenobia in Chains," this essay also details Jameson's influence on the project. Includes generous excerpts from their correspondence; Holcomb, Adele H., "Anna Jameson, 1794-1860: Sacred Art and Social Vision" in **WOMEN AS INTERPRETERS OF THE VISUAL ARTS.** ed. by Claire Richter Sherman. Westport, 1981.

7.965
ART JOURNAL: Feb. 1839 to Feb 1912; vols. 1-74; *"Mrs Wells,"* 23 (1861) 273. Obituary of Joanna Mary Boyce Wells, artist, who died at age thirty during childbirth; Purnell, T., *"Woman and Art,"* 22 (1862) 107-108; Dafforne, J., *"British Artists: Their Style and Character. No. LXVV. Emily Mary Osborn,"* 3 (1864) 261-263. A member of the Society of Lady Artists, Osborn painted genre scenes and several historical canvases. She exhibited at the Royal Academy for the first time in 1851. Includes three black and white reproductions; *"Selected Pictures,"* 7 (1868) 148-149. Reproduction of Emily Mary Osborne's "God's Acre"; *"Art Work for Women, I.,"* 33 (1872) 65-66; *"Art Work for Women, II.,"* 33 (1872) 102-103; *"Art Work for Women, III.,"* 33 (1872) 129-131; Meynell, A., *"Laura Alma-Tadema,"* 22 (1883) 345-347. Written when the painter was thirty-one, this article is a good source of biographical information. Illustrations included.

7.966
JOURNAL OF DESIGN: March 1849 to Feb. 1852.

7.967
HOUSEHOLD WORDS: Horne, R.H., *"The Female School of Design in the Capitol of the World,"* 2 (1851) 577-581. Describes a school where women are taught to draw and paint for the production of commercial products. Calls for reforms to

alleviate overcrowding and dirtiness while also calling for more schools of this kind.

7.968
Art Union of London, ALMANAC. 1852.

7.969
ENGLISH WOMAN'S JOURNAL: *"The Society of Female Artists,"* 1 (1858) 205-209. Remarks on the improvement shown in ladies' art exhibitions and the problems faced by the female artist; *"Oppressed Female Potterers,"* 3 (1859) 211-212; R., M.S., *"Female Engravers from the 16th to the 19th Century,"* 3 (1859) 259-270.

7.970
ENGLISHWOMAN'S DOMESTIC MAGAZINE: *"The Society of Female Artists,"* 6 (1857) 90-93. Reviews a show coordinated by the Society. Explains that poor quality found among these works is due to lack of proper training and/or limited facilities for exhibition. Many artists are mentioned.

7.971
Ellet, Elizabeth Fries, WOMEN ARTISTS IN ALL AGES AND COUNTRIES. 1859. Rare book; *reviewed in:* WOMAN'S ART JOURNAL: Langer, S.L., 1 (1981) 55-58. "As a biographer and historian, Mrs. Ellet had her prejudices; her work was not intended for art historians, nor was she interested in writing a scholarly and critical history of women in art. It was her intention to compile a much needed popular text dealing with the lives and art of women" (p. 58).

7.972
ATHENAEUM: Jameson, A., *"The Royal Academy,"* n.v. (1859) 581.

7.973
TRANSACTIONS OF THE NATIONAL ASSOCIATION FOR THE PROMOTION OF SOCIAL SCIENCE: Stewart, J., *"Art Decoration A Suitable Employment for Women,"* (1860) 729.

7.974
JOURNAL OF THE SOCIETY OF ARTS (AND OF THE INSTITUTES IN UNION): 1863 to 1892. Publication of the Royal Society for the Encouragement of Arts, Manufactures and Commerce; Sparkes, J., *"On the Further Development of the Fine Art Section of the Lambeth Pottery,"* 12 (1880) 350.

7.975
MACMILLAN'S MAGAZINE: Palgrave, F.T., *"Women and the Fine Arts (Part I),"* 12 (1865) 118-127. Contends that women's lack of success in the fine arts is due to unequal opportunities in training; Palgrave, F.T., *"A Few Words on E.V.B. (Eleanor V. Boyle) and Female Artists,"* 15 (1867) 327-330. Asserts that since women artists work for their own pleasure, they are less restricted in content and expression; *"A Suggestion,"* 20 (1896) 365-366. Suggests that female amateur artists display their work where working men congregate in order to brighten up their lives; Sparay, W., *"Art and the Woman,"* 83 (1900) 29-34.

7.976
Redgrave, Richard and Redgrave, Samuel, A CENTURY OF PAINTERS OF THE ENGLISH SCHOOL. 1866. See pp. 176-178 on Angelica Kauffman, who is criticized and degraded.

7.977

ENGLISHWOMAN'S REVIEW: *"Exhibition of the Society of Female Artists, 9 Conduit Street,"* 2 (1867) 136-138. Praises the works shown; lists some of the artists and their paintings; Corlett, A.B., *"Art and Literature,"* 5 (1874) 293-294. Refers to a Miss Thompson, "the artistic heroine of the day"; Paterson, E.A., *"The Position of Women Engaged in Handicrafts and Other Industrial Pursuits,"* 21 (1875) 1-12. Contends that as women workers increase in number, their social position also gains value; *"Royal School of Art Needlework,"* 26 (1875) 334-336. "If the desire which had been created, and which is increasing, for more beautiful and artistic needlework should obtain even a larger influence over the wealthy classes of this rich country than at present, there is no saying how much good may not result from it to the great mass of unemployed women in England" (p. 335); *"Fancy Work,"* 9 (1878) 148-150. "Careful training and technical education are as much needed for accomplishing successful fancy work as for other things" (p. 149); *"The Female School of Art,"* 10 (1879) 36-37; *"An Hour with the Lady Artists,"* 10 (1879) 156-159. Describes the paintings at this exhibit; *"Manchester Society of Women Artists,"* 10 (1879) 469-470. Delineates courses of instruction offered in connection with the Society, and the women who formed the society; *"Wood Engraving for Women,"* 10 (1879) 450-451. Announcement of classes in wood engraving, considered especially suitable for women because of their dexterity and also because it does not require a great deal of physical strength; *"Lady Artists at the Royal Institute of Painters in Water Colours,"* 20 (1889) 181. Announcement of several of the works exhibited; Greenwell, A., *"More About Arts and Crafts Exhibition. To the Editors of the Englishwoman's Review,"* 20 (1889) 546-549. "The work executed by women is as valued and numerous as that of the designers" (p. 148); Greenwell, A., *"Women's Exhibition of Arts and Industries,"* 20 (1889) 549-550. "The Arts and Crafts Exhibitions have given valuable evidence of the desire and capability of women to do good work" (p. 549); *"Arts and Crafts Exhibition,"* 20 (1889) 446-448. "It is worthy of record that much of the beautiful needlework exhibited is not only executed by female hands, but designed by female heads" (p. 447); *"Brighton Exhibition of Women's Arts and Industries,"* 20 (1889) 182-183; H.H.R., *"Art Amongst Women in the Victorian Era,"* 28 (1897) 209-217. Discusses many female painters; *"Bookbinding by Women,"* 29 (1898) 50-52. "It is a pity that the binding as well as the ornament is not the work of women, but it is said that this defect will be remedied in the future" (p. 51).

7.978

Rossetti, W.M., **ENGLISH PAINTERS OF THE PRESENT DAY.** 1871. Mentions Maria Spartali Stillman (1844-1927), a pre-Raphaelite painter and also one of Dante Gabriel Rossetti's models. She exhibited her works at many of the major British galleries.

7.979

Hare, A.J.C., **THE STORY OF TWO NOBLE LIVES.** 1872. The Viscountess Charlotte Canning (1817-1861) is discussed, an amateur flower and landscape watercolourist who was a Lady of the Bedchamber to Queen Victoria from 1842 to 1855. Louisa Waterford, considered one of the most talented female amateurs of the period is also discussed.

7.980

FURNITURE GAZETTE: Oct. 1872 to Dec. 1893.

7.981

VICTORIA MAGAZINE: *"Women in Art,"* 19 (1872) 320; Hughes, J., *"Photography as an Occupation for Women,"* 21 (1873) 1.

7.982
Smith, Walter, **ART EDUCATION**. Boston, 1873.

7.983
Ruskin, John, **ACADEMY NOTES. 1855-1859.** 1875. The Academy Notes were critiques of the exhibits held at the Royal Academy. Among the women mentioned (some of them patronized by Ruskin) are Anna E. Blunden (1830-1915), a figure and landscape painter praised by Ruskin, A.W. Hunt, Holman Hunt, and David Roberts. Blunden exhibited at the Royal Academy from 1854 to 1872 and more frequently at the Society of British Artists, Suffolk Street. Also examines the work of Helen Allingham, a water color painter of gardens, rural scenes, and children and member of the Royal Watercolour Society. She exhibited, almost exclusively, 221 pictures at the Old Watercolour Society; Annie Feray Mutrie (1826-1893), a flower and fruit painter; Eliza Turck (b. 1834; fl. 1854-1886), an oil and watercolour painter; Martha Mutrie; Joanna Boyce; Jane Benham Hay; Helen Allingham; Louise Rayner; Elizabeth Butler; E.L. Seeley; and A. Acland; **ART OF ENGLAND.** 1884. Discusses Helen Allingham. —*see also:* Surtees, Mrs. V., ed., **SUBLIME AND INSTRUCTIVE—LETTERS FROM JOHN RUSKIN...** 1972. Contains information on Anna E. Blunden and Louisa Waterford; **WOMAN'S ART JOURNAL:** Nunn, P.G., *"Ruskin's Patronage of Women Artists,"* 2 (1982) 8-13. "Perhaps Ruskin's rejection of public exposure for the women he patronized had roots in his disdain for popular taste and judgement. But his attitude probably also reflected his stereotypical ideas about women's role and nature which made it fitting for the attractive, aristocratic Lady Waterford to be a glorious amateur, and for the plain and impoverished Anna Blunden to send her drawings to Ruskin while she painted portraits for a living" (p. 11).

7.984
WORK AND LEISURE. A MAGAZINE DEVOTED TO THE INTERESTS OF WOMEN: 1875 to 1893; vols. 1-18; vols. 1-4 titled: **WOMAN'S GAZETTE; OR NEWS ABOUT WORK:** Ridley, A.E., *"Art Work for Women,"* 2 (1877) n.p.; *"The Society of Lady Artists,"* 2 (1877) 76. Delineates the activities of this professional organization. The members are elected from among the associates and the prospective member must have exhibited at the Gallery for two or more successive years. Non-members may submit their works but usually must pay a fee.

7.985
Garrett, Rhoda and Garrett, Agnes, **SUGGESTIONS FOR HOUSE DECORATION IN PAINTING, WOODWORK AND FURNITURE.** 1876. —*see also:* Bolton, Sarah K., "A New Work for Women" in **SOCIAL STUDIES IN ENGLAND.** by Sarah K. Bolton. Boston, 1886. "Rhoda and Agnes Garrett, of London, were the first to establish the business of house decoration by women.... Women of delicacy and education seem naturally fitted for this business, and yet they have never taken it up" (p. 74). Discusses why "gentlewomen" should be employed instead of remaining idle and gives an account of the interior designs fabricated by the Garretts and their students.

7.986
McLaughlin, Louise M., **CHINA PAINTING.** Cincinnati, 1877; **POTTERY PAINTING UNDER THE GLAZE.** Cincinnati, 1880; **SUGGESTIONS TO CHINA PAINTERS.** Cincinnati, 1884.

7.987
MAGAZINE OF ART: May 1878 to July 1904; Day, L.F., *"The Woman's Part in*

Domestic Decoration," 4 (1881) 457-463.

7.988
Greenaway, Kate, **UNDER THE WINDOW**. [1879]. Greenaway was a member of the Royal Watercolour Society and the Royal Institute of Painters in Watercolours. She exhibited at the Society of British Artists, Suffolk Street from 1870 to 1876 and at the Royal Academy from 1877 to 1895. This book was her first attempt at illustrating her own text and was very successful. Greenaway was renowned in her own time for her children's books and she executed designs for the magazines PUNCH and LADIES' HOME JOURNAL. For works illustrated by her, see the Card Catalogue at the Victoria and Albert Museum; **A APPLE PIE**. 1886. **MARIGOLD GARDEN, PICTURES AND RHYMES** n.d. —*see also:* Foster, Myles B., **A DAY IN A CHILD'S LIFE**. 1881. Songbook illustrated by Greenaway; Taylor, Jane and Taylor, Ann, **LITTLE ANN AND OTHER POEMS**. 1883. Illustrations by Greenaway; Mavor, William Fordyce, **THE ENGLISH SPELLING BOOK**. 1885. Drawings by Greenaway; Bryan, Michael, **DICTIONARY OF PAINTERS AND ENGRAVERS**. ed. by George Williams. 5 vols. New York, 1903. See pp. 275-276 in vol. 2 which lists books that Greenaway published with Edmund Evans; Clement, Clara Erskine (Waters), **WOMEN IN THE FINE ARTS: FROM THE SEVENTH CENTURY B.C. TO THE TWENTIETH CENTURY A.D.** Cambridge, 1904; rpt., New York, 1974. See pp. 150-151 in volume 2 for a short biographical essay; Spielmann, Marion Harry and Layard, George Somes, **KATE GREENAWAY**. 1905. Biography that includes photographs of the artist and reproductions of her illustrations; Dobson, Austin, **DE LIBRIS, PROSE AND VERSE**. New York, 1908. See pp. 91-107 for a discussion of the artist and her work; APOLLO: Paul, F., *"A Collection of Children's Books Illustrated by Walter Crane, Kate Greenaway and Randolph Caldecott,"* 43 (1946) 141-143; Moir, Percival Horace, "The Importance of Pictures" in **ENGLISH CHILDREN'S BOOKS 1600-1900**. by Percival Horace Moir. 1954; Pressler, M.J., **A VERIE BRIEF HISTORIE OF THE LIVES AND WORKS OF FIVE ILLUSTRATORS OF BOOKS FOR LITTLE MASTERS AND MISSES...** Chicago, [c. 1965]; Ernest, Edward, ed., **THE KATE GREENAWAY TREASURY: AN ANTHOLOGY OF THE ILLUSTRATIONS AND WRITINGS OF KATE GREENAWAY**. Cleveland, 1967; Hardie, M., **WATERCOLOUR PAINTING IN BRITAIN**. 3 vols. 1967-1969; Maas, J., **VICTORIAN PAINTERS**. 1969; Engen, Rodney, **KATE GREENAWAY: A BIOGRAPHY**. 1981.

7.989
Merritt, Henry, **ART CRITICISM AND ROMANCE**. 1879. Discusses Anna Lea Merritt (1844-1940), portrait and genre painter married to the author. Her painting, "Love Locked Out" was ridiculed during the Victorian era. It demonstrates a trend among female painters of the period to utilize child models as adult nude models were forbidden to women. Often, the nude child was transformed in a picture to portray an allegorical reference, such as "love" in Merritt's painting.

7.990
Adams, W.H. Davenport, **WOMAN'S WORK AND WORTH IN GIRLHOOD, MAIDENHOOD, AND WIFEHOOD**. 1880. See especially: Chaps. 5 and 8 on art and employment for educated women.

7.991
Thomas, Margaret, **A HERO OF THE WORKSHOP**. 1880. Thomas (fl. from 1868; d. 1929) was a portrait painter, writer, and sculptor. She grew up in Australia, studied in England, lived in Rome for several years and won a silver medal from the Royal Academy school. She travelled extensively and was a prolific artist who exhibited at the major British galleries; **HOW TO JUDGE PICTURES**. 1906; A

PAINTER'S PASTIME. 1908; HOW TO UNDERSTAND SCULPTURE. 1911. —
see also: Clayton, Ellen C., ENGLISH FEMALE ARTISTS. 1876. See vol. II, p. 259
on Thomas; Ormond, R., EARLY VICTORIAN PORTRAITS. 2 vols. 1973.

7.992
Cunningham, Allan, THE LIVES OF THE MOST EMINENT BRITISH PAINTERS.
3 vols. 2nd ed., annotated and continued by Mrs. Charles Heaton, 1880. See
especially: vol. 2, pp. 347-357 on Maria Cosway.

7.993
NINETEENTH CENTURY: Alford, M., *"Art Needlework I,"* 9 (1881) 439-449.
Discusses the Royal School of Art Needlework and how it has aided women in
finding employment. Also discusses needlework as an art form, patterns used, and
the historical utilization of stitchery; Watts, G.F., *"Art Needlework II,"* 9 (1881) 450-
454. Responds to Alford article, above, stating what forms and designs are
preferable in decorative needlework.

7.994
Lewis, Florence E., CHINA PAINTING. 1883.

7.995
Alford, Marianna Margaret (Compton) Cust, (Lady Marian Alford), NEEDLEWORK
AS ART. 1886. Discusses the history of needlework and embroidery. ——*see also:*
Higgin, L., HANDBOOK OF EMBROIDERY. ed. by Lady Marian Alford. 1880.

7.996
Bolton, Sarah K., "Needlework and Cookery" in SOCIAL STUDIES IN ENGLAND.
by Sarah K. Bolton. Boston, 1886. Discusses the South Kensington Royal School of
Art Needlework. "An average worker earns six dollars and twenty-five cents per
week, and a good one, ten dollars or more.... Materials are purchased at the rooms
and work can be obtained with a portion commenced, or ladies' own materials are
prepared for work. All designs are copyrighted and designs on paper are not given"
(p. 68); "Other Work for Women" in SOCIAL STUDIES, ETC. 1886. Discusses
various opportunities in the arts such as wood engraving, wood carving, printing,
and music; "Women in the Art Schools" in SOCIAL STUDIES, ETC. 1886.
Delineates various programs available to women to study art and to train as art
teachers. Briefly discusses several contemporary female artists and illustrators.

7.997
Propert, J.L., A HISTORY OF MINIATURE ART. 1887.

7.998
ALL THE YEAR ROUND: *"Artistic Professions for Women,"* 43 (1888) 296-300. In
reference to male-female competition in the arts, the author submits that the
strongest and the best will win, not necessarily meaning the men.

7.999
Prideaux, Sarah Treverbian, EXHIBITION OF BOOKBINDINGS, WITH
INTRODUCTORY REMARKS ON THE HISTORY OF BOOKBINDING. 1891; AN
HISTORICAL SKETCH OF BOOKBINDING. 1893; A CATALOGUE OF BOOKS
BOUND BY S.T. PRIDEAUX BETWEEN 1890 AND 1900, WITH 26
ILLUSTRATIONS, PRINTED BY SARAH T. PRIDEAUX AND KATHERINE
ADAMS. 1900; BOOKBINDERS AND THEIR CRAFT. 1903; MODERN
BOOKBINDINGS: THEIR DESIGN AND DECORATION. 1906.

7.1000
Roget, J.L., **HISTORY OF THE OLD WATERCOLOUR SOCIETY**. 1891. See vol. II, pp. 247-248 on Mrs. Valentine Bartholomew (1800-1862), also known as Annie Charlotte Fayermann, a miniaturist, portrait, genre, and still-life painter. She exhibited at leading galleries, was a member of the Society of Female Artists, and also wrote poetry and plays; vol. II, pp. 337-339 on Mary Ann Alabaster Criddle (1805-1880), a figure and portrait painter who studied under Hayter and won several medals. In 1849, she became a member of the Old Watercolour Society. The Baroness Angela Georgina Burdett-Coutts purchased several of her pictures; vol. I, pp. 547-548 and vol. II, pp. 206-207 on Charlotte, Eliza, Louisa, and Mary Anne Sharpe, all miniaturists.

7.1001
North, Georgina, **RECOLLECTIONS OF A HAPPY LIFE**. ed. by Mrs. John Addington Symonds. 1892. North (a distant cousin to the botanical illustrator Marianne North) was an illustrator who, among other projects, created graphic renditions of the sylphs from Pope's RAPE OF THE LOCK.

7.1002
Royal Academy of Arts, **ROYAL ACADEMY PICTURES 1890**. 1892-1895. Includes Margaret Isabel Dicksee, historical and domestic painter; **ROYAL ACADEMY PICTURES 1893-1896**. 1906. Includes Edith Edinborough Corbet (fl. 1891-1903), figure and Italian scene painter; Fannie Moody King; Mary F. Raphael (fl. 1889-1902), portrait, landscape, and genre painter; **ROYAL ACADEMY PICTURES 1915**. [1915]. Includes Isobel Lilian Groag (1865-1917), a portrait and literary/classical genre painter.

7.1003
Stuart, C., **SHORT SKETCH OF THE LIFE OF LOUISA WATERFORD**. 1892. Waterford was an amateur painter who was friendly with Ruskin, Burne-Jones, and Watts.

7.1004
Elliott, Maud Howe, ed., **ILLUSTRATED ART AND CRAFT IN THE WOMAN'S BUILDING OF THE COLUMBIAN EXPOSITION, CHICAGO**. Paris and New York, 1893.

7.1005
Gerard, Frances A., **ANGELICA KAUFFMAN: A BIOGRAPHY**. 1893.

7.1006
Moore, George, **MODERN PAINTING**. 1893. "Women astonish us as much by their want of originality as they do by their extraordinary power of assimilation. I am thinking now of the ladies who marry painters, and who, after a few years of married life, exhibit work identical with that of their illustrious husbands——Mrs. E.M Ward, Madame Fantin-Latour, Mrs. Swan, Mrs. Alma-Tadema" (pp. 266-267).

7.1007
Morris, May, **DECORATIVE NEEDLEWORK**. 1893. "Written for... those who, without much previous knowledge of the art of embroidery, have a love for it and a wish to devote a little time and patience to its practice" (Dedicatory Note). Delineates the history of decorative needlework and illustrates the use and execution of various stitches.

7.1008

Hill, Georgiana, "Art as a Profession" in **WOMEN IN ENGLISH LIFE.** by Georgiana Hill. 1894.

7.1009

FORTNIGHTLY REVIEW: Gordon, A.M., *"Women as Students in Design,"* 61 (1894) 521-524. Critical of the patterns of cheaply produced textiles. Sees women as having good artistic instincts. Suggests that a school for training women in textile design would offer "a decent living for [woman]... and her children and an opportunity for her to display her talents" (p. 524).

7.1010

Makenzie, Tessa, **ART SCHOOLS OF LONDON, 1895.** 1895.

7.1011

Pennell, Joseph, **MODERN ILLUSTRATION.** 1895.

7.1012

Wood, Esther, **DANTE ROSSETTI AND THE PRE-RAPHAELITE MOVEMENT.** 1895. See pp. 99-103 and 159-161 on Elizabeth Eleanor Siddal Rossetti.

7.1013

STUDIO: S., E.B., *"Some Aspects of the Work of Mary L. Newill,"* 5 (1895) 56-63; Wood, E., *"Home Arts and Industries Association,"* 23 (1901) 106; Watson, W.R., *"Miss Jessie M. King and Her Work,"* 26 (1902) 177-178; Quigley, J., *"The Art of Jessie Bayes, Painter and Craftswoman,"* 61 (1914) 261-270.

7.1014

ARCHITECTURAL REVIEW: July 1896 to Aug. 1896; vol. 1.

7.1015

Neville, H.M., **UNDER A BORDER TOWER.** 1896. Louisa Waterford is mentioned.

7.1016

LADY'S REALM: *"Maternity,"* 1 (1896) 270. A drawing by Emily J. Harding; A., F.S., *"In A London Art School,"* 13 (1903) 575-582. Describes some female students, their work, and their levels of seriousness toward art studies; Dixon, M.H., *"Miss Lucy Kemp-Welch,"* 13 (1903) 575-582. Includes reproductions; Leslie, M., *"Women's Work at the Victorian Era Exhibition,"* 2 (1897) 58-65. Mentions several of the artists exhibiting their works; Chetwynd, Mrs. H., *"What to Do with Our Daughters,"* 2 (1897) 105-106. Discourages art as a profession for girls and suggests the career of domestic economy (the budgeting and directing of the home) instead.

7.1017

SECOND EXHIBITION OF ARTISTIC BOOKBINDINGS BY WOMEN. [1899].

7.1018

Bate, Percy H., **THE ENGLISH PRE-RAPHAELITE PAINTERS: THEIR ASSOCIATES AND SUCCESSORS.** 1899; 1901. See pp. 23-30 on Lucy Madox Brown; 115 on Evelyn de Morgan; 112 for reproductions of two paintings by Maria Spartali Stillman. Mary Ethel Hunter (1878-1936), a flower and portrait painter, is mentioned.

7.1019

Corporation of Leicester, **PERMANENT ART GALLERY CATALOGUE. NO. 96.**

1899. Includes Kate Mary Whitley (fl. 1884-1893; d. 1920), still-life and flower painter.

7.1020
BOOKS AND BINDINGS FROM THE GUILD OF WOMEN BINDERS AND THE HAMPSTEAD BINDERY... AGENTS FOR THE GUILD. 1900.

7.1021
British Museum, **CATALOGUE OF DRAWINGS II.** 1900. Includes Margaret Gillies; **CATALOGUE OF ENGRAVED BRITISH PORTRAITS II.** 1910. See p. 670 on Margaret Gillies; **CATALOGUE OF ENGRAVED BRITISH PORTRAITS III.** 1912. Margaret Gillies and Jessica Landseer are included; **CATALOGUE OF ENGRAVED BRITISH PORTRAITS IV.** 1914. Margaret Gillies, Elizabeth Gulland, and Dorothy Tennant (Lady Stanley) included.

7.1022
Jackson, Emily Nevill (Mrs. F.), **A HISTORY OF HAND-MADE LACE.** 1900.

7.1023
Poynter, G.J., ed., **THE NATIONAL GALLERY.** 1900. Includes information on Lucy Kemp-Welch, animal painter, and on Dorothy Tennant (fl. 1879-1909; d. 1926), illustrator and genre painter.

7.1024
Woman's International Exhibition, **LIST OF EXHIBITORS IN THE BRITISH AND IRISH SILK INDUSTRY SECTION, ETC.** 1900.

7.1025
Palliser, Mrs. Fanny Bury, **HISTORY OF LACE.** rev. ed., 1902.

7.1026
ART WORKER'S QUARTERLY: A PORTFOLIO FOR DECORATIVE AND APPLIED ART: Jan. 1902 to Nov. 1906; 6 vols.

7.1027
Bryan, Michael, **DICTIONARY OF PAINTERS AND ENGRAVERS.** ed. by George Williams. 5 vols. New York, 1903. See vol. 1, pp. 337-388 on Maria Cosway; vol. 3, p. 124 on Angelica Kauffman; vol. 3, p. 374 on Mary Moser; vol. 3, p. 313 on Anne Foldstone Mee; vol. 5, p. 354 on Joanna Wells; and vol. 1, p. 102 on Diana Beauclerk. Other women are entered in this dictionary.

7.1028
Butler, Elizabeth Southerden Thompson (Lady), **LETTERS FROM THE HOLY LAND.** 1903. Butler specialized in military painting, and though renowned and essentially accepted by the art world, was denied entrance to the Royal Academy by two votes. This book describes her travels in Palestine and includes color illustrations by Butler; **FROM SKETCHBOOK AND DIARY.** 1909. Describes her travels through Africa, Ireland, and Italy; **AN AUTOBIOGRAPHY.** 1923. ——*see also:* Benjamin, S.G.W., **CONTEMPORARY ART IN EUROPE.** New York, 1877. See pp. 37-39 on Butler; **MAGAZINE OF ART:** Oldcastle, J., *"Elizabeth Butler,"* 2 (1879) 257-262; **ART ANNALS:** Meynell, W., *"The Life and Work of Lady Butler,"* 18 (1898) n.p.; Clement, Clara Erskine (Waters), **WOMEN IN THE FINE ARTS: FROM THE SEVENTH CENTURY B.C. TO THE TWENTIETH CENTURY A.D.** Cambridge, 1904; rpt., New York, 1974. See pp. 68-70 in vol. II for short biographical essay; Meynell, Viola, **ALICE MEYNELL.** 1929. Biography of the

contemporary poet and essayist, who was Butler's sister; CONNOISSEUR: "*Lady Butler*," 92 (1933) 341; Wood, C., DICTIONARY OF VICTORIAN PAINTERS. Woodbridge, 1971. See p. 20 on Butler; CONNOISSEUR: Ash, R., "*English Paintings of 1874*," 185 (1974) 33-40. Contains a black and white reproduction of "Calling the Role After an Engagement," a painting purchased by the Queen; WOMAN'S ART JOURNAL: Lalumia, M., "*Elizabeth Thompson Butler in the 1870s*," 4 (1983) 9-14. Critiques and analyzes Butler's military paintings.

7.1029
Erskine, Beatrice Caroline Strong (Mrs. Stuart), LADY DIANA BEAUCLERK: HER LIFE AND WORK. 1903.

7.1030
Huish, H.B., HAPPY ENGLAND AS PAINTED BY H.A. WITH MEMOIR. 1903. The work of Helen Paterson Allingham is discussed.

7.1031
BURLINGTON MAGAZINE: Rossetti, W.M., "*Dante Rossetti and Elizabeth Siddal*," 1 (1903) 273-295. Biographical account with drawings of Siddal executed by Rossetti. Lists her works.

7.1032
CONNOISSEUR: Erskine, B.C.S., "*Lady Di's Scrapbook*," 7 (1903) 32-37. Illustrations included; "*[Obituary of Clara Montalba]*," 84 (1919) 263. Montalba (1842-1929) was a prolific landscape, marine and topographical painter. A member of the Royal Watercolour Society, she exhibited at all the leading British galleries and painted mainly in Venice. Her sisters, Hilda and Ellen, were also artists; "*[Obituary of Marianne Preindlsberger Stokes]*," 79 (1927) 127. Born in Southern Austria, Stokes (1855-1927) was a genre, portrait, and biblical subject painter who studied in Munich, worked in France, and settled in England with her husband, Adrian Stokes. She exhibited works at the leading British galleries; "*[Obituary of Mrs. Charles Edward Perugini]*," 84 (1929) 60. The daughter of Charles Dickens, Kate Perugini was a genre and portrait painter who exhibited in the main galleries; Sparrow, W.S., "*Angelica Kauffman's Amazing Marriage*," 92 (1933) 242-248; Long, B.S., "*Mrs. Mee, Miniature Painter*," 95 (1935) 218-221. Biographical essay on Anne Foldstone Mee (1771?-1851) who was patronized by Horace Walpole and King George IV. She exhibited at the Royal Academy between 1804 and 1837; "*A Roman Portrait by Angelica Kauffman*," 135 (1955) 190-191; "*Richard Arkwright's Cabinet*," 136 (1956) 356-357. Reproduction, in color, of a cabinet whose doors are attributed to Kauffman; "*['Sweet Dreams']*," 158 (1965) 15. Reproduction of a painting by Sophie Anderson; Wood, C., "*The Artistic Family Hayllar. Part II. Jessica, Edith, Mary, Kate*," 186 (1974) 2-10. All four sisters exhibited at the Royal Academy. Edith (1860-1948) was a still-life and genre painter; Jessica (1858-1940) painted flowers and figure subjects; Kate (fl. 1883-1898) painted still-lifes and in 1900 gave up painting to become a nurse; and Mary (fl. 1880-1885) was a flower, figure, and landscape painter who abandoned painting to raise her children.

7.1033
Clement, Clara Erskine (Waters), WOMEN IN THE FINE ARTS: FROM THE SEVENTH CENTURY B.C. TO THE TWENTIETH CENTURY A.D. 2 vols. Cambridge, 1904; rpt., New York, 1974. In vol. 1, see pp. 89-91 on Maria Cosway; 96-100 on Anne Damer; 179-190 on Angelica Kauffman; 244 on Mary Moser; 339-340 on Maria Varelst; in vol. 2, see pp. 9-10 on Laura Alma Tadema. Short biographical essays and descriptions of major works.

7.1034
Williamson, G.C., **HISTORY OF BRITISH PORTRAIT MINIATURES.** 1904. See vol. II, p. 35 on Anna Maria Kenwell Charretie, who took up painting after her husband died in order to support herself. She exhibited at several of the major galleries and was a member of the Society of Lady Artists.

7.1035
CHARITY ORGANISATION REVIEW: Sutherland, Duchess of, *"The Work of the Potteries Cripples' Guild,"* 16 (1904) 81-85; Tancred, Miss, *"Fine Needlework for Invalid Women and Girls,"* 16 (1904) 93-96.

7.1036
EMPORIUM: Vitale, Z., *"Eleanor Siddal Rossetti,"* 19 (1904) 430-437.

7.1037
INTERNATIONAL STUDIO: Holland, C., *"Lady Art Students' Life in Paris,"* no. 21 (1904) 225-231; Willis, E., *"The First Woman Painter in America,"* no. 87 (1927) 13-20. On Henrietta Johnson, an English or Irish pastellist who was active during the eighteenth century and worked in America.

7.1038
Graves, Algernon, **THE ROYAL ACADEMY OF ARTS.** 1905. See vol. 1, p. 33 on Sophie Anderson.

7.1039
Holme, Charles, ed., **THE OLD WATERCOLOUR SOCIETY 1804-1904.** 1905. Information on Alice Macallan Swan (1864-1939), a flower, landscape, and figurative subject painter.

7.1040
Sparrow, Walter Shaw, ed., **WOMEN PAINTERS OF THE WORLD, FROM THE TIME OF CATERINA VIGRI, 1413-1463 TO ROSA BONHEUR AND THE PRESENT DAY.** 1905; New York, 1909; rpt., New York, 1976. See especially: "Early British Women Painters" by Walter Shaw Sparrow and "Modern British Women Painters" by Ralph Peacock. Sparrow believed that women possessed a "nursery nature."

7.1041
Birch, L., **STANHOPE A. FORBES AND ELIZABETH S. FORBES.** 1906. Forbes (nee Armstrong) was a genre painter. She exhibited at all the major galleries and in 1899, founded the Newlyn Art School with her husband.

7.1042
Fish, Arthur, **HENRIETTA RAE.** 1906. Rae (later Mrs. Ernest Normand), was a portrait, genre, and classical/literary subject painter who lived from 1859 to 1928. She began her studies at thirteen and was a medallist at the Paris and Chicago Universal Exhibitions. A prolific painter, she showed her pictures in many of the major British galleries.

7.1043
Ashbee, Charles, **CRAFTSMANSHIP IN COMPETITIVE INDUSTRY.** 1908.

7.1044
Baily, James Thomas Herbert, ed., **CATALOGUE OF THE DAILY MAIL EXHIBITION OF BRITISH LACE.** 1908.

7.1045
Caw, J.L., **SCOTTISH PAINTING 1620-1908**. 1908. Information on Bessie MacNichol Frew (1869-1904), portrait, genre and landscape painter; Emily Murray Paterson (1855-1934), flower and landscape painter; Louisa E. Perman (d. 1921), flower painter, and Flora Reid (fl. 1879-c. 1929), a genre painter.

7.1046
Cundall, H.M., **HISTORY OF BRITISH WATERCOLOUR PAINTING**. 1908; 1929. Discusses Helen Paterson Allingham, Margaret Gillies, Mary Margetts, and Louisa Waterford.

7.1047
Chivers, Cedric, **BOOKS IN BEAUTIFUL BINDINGS**. Bath, ca. 1910. Information on Jesse Marion King (later Taylor), a Scottish illustrator who produced drawings for many books.

7.1048
Lawrence, W.J., **THE PORTRAITS OF ELIZABETH FARREN, COUNTESS OF DERBY**. 1911.

7.1049
Smith, A. Croxton, **THE POWER OF THE DOG**. 1911; **MY DOG FRIENDS. PICTURES IN COLOUR FROM PAINTINGS BY MAUD EARL**. 1913; **WHOSE DOG ART THOU? 9 PHOTOGRAVURES AFTER PAINTINGS BY MAUD EARL**. 1913. Maud Earl specialized in painting animals and was patronized by Queen Victoria to paint the royal pets.

7.1050
Rees, T.M., **WELSH PAINTERS**. 1912. Discusses Louis Johnson Jones (b. 1856; fl. c. 1880-1910), an animal painter and Buddig Anwylini Pughe (b. 1857), a landscape and portrait painter and miniaturist.

7.1051
Rochdale Art Gallery, **CATALOGUE OF THE 10TH SPRING EXHIBITION OF MODERN PICTURES**. 1913. Includes Eleanor Stuart Wood (fl. 1876-1893), a fruit, flower and portrait painter who was a member of the Society of Lady Artists.

7.1052
Strickland, W.G., **A DICTIONARY OF IRISH ARTISTS**. 1913; rpt., 1971. Includes Adelaide Agnes Maguire (1852-1876) a figurative and country subject painter; Helena J. Maguire (1860-1909), a watercolorist and Helen Mabel Trevor (1879-1900), a figurative subject painter.

7.1053
Fortescue-Brickdale, Eleanor, **ELEANOR FORTESCUE-BRICKDALE'S GOLDEN BOOK OF FAMOUS WOMEN**. 1919. An illustrator of books and painter of historical and genre subjects, Fortescue-Brickdale first exhibited at the Royal Academy in 1896. A member of the Royal Society of Painters in Watercolours, she also designed stained glass windows for Bristol Cathedral, Brixham. When she was twenty-five, she won a L40 prize for a decorative lunette, "Spring," one of the lunettes in the Royal Academy Dining Room. Among the books she illustrated are: POEMS BY TENNYSON (1905); Browning's MEN AND WOMEN (1908), DRAMATIS PERSONAE (1909), and ROMANCES AND LYRICS (1909); Tennyson's IDYLLS OF THE KING (1911); W.M. Canton's STORY OF

ELIZABETH OF HUNGARY (1912); BOOK OF OLD ENGLISH SONGS AND BALLADS (1915); THE SWEET AND TOUCHING TALE OF FLEURE AND BLANCHEFLEURE (1922); CAROLS (1925); Palgrave's GOLDEN TREASURY OF SONGS AND LYRICS (1925); and Calthorp's A DIARY OF AN EIGHTEENTH CENTURY GARDEN (1926). ——*see also:* Sparrow, Walter Shaw, WOMEN PAINTERS OF THE WORLD. 1905. See page 73; STUDIO: Sparrow, W.S., *"On Some Water-colour Pictures by Eleanor Fortescue-Brickdale,"* 23 (1901) 31-44.

7.1054
Jackson, Charles, ENGLISH GOLDSMITHS AND THEIR MARKS. 1921. Discusses many women silversmiths who worked during the eighteenth century.

7.1055
Stirling, Mrs. A.M.W., WILLIAM DE MORGAN AND HIS WIFE. 1922. De Morgan was a painter and designer of stained glass. His wife, Evelyn Pickering (1855-1919), was a pre-Raphaelite painter who exhibited mostly at the Grosvenor Gallery and the National Gallery.

7.1056
Manners, Victoria and Williamson, G.C., ANGELICA KAUFFMANN, [sic] R.A., HER LIFE AND WORKS. 1924; rpt., New York, 1976.

7.1057
Ward, Mrs. E.M., MEMORIES OF NINETY YEARS. ed. by Isobel G. McAllister. 1924; 2nd ed., New York, 1925. See especially: Chap. 4, where the author, a painter, reminisces about her decision to paint instead of devoting all her time to domestic activities and where she describes her first Royal Academy exhibits and the paintings shown there. In Chaps. 13, 23, and 28, she discusses painting and painters she knew. Chap. 17 discusses her school at 6 William Street, London. — *see also:* O'Donnell, Elliott, ed., MRS. E.M. WARD'S REMINISCENCES. 1911; CONNOISSEUR: *"[Obituary of Mrs. E.M. Ward],"* 70 (1924) 57.

7.1058
Jopling, Louise, TWENTY YEARS OF MY LIFE. 1925. Jopling was a portrait, genre and landscape painter who studied in Paris, exhibited at the Salon and the major British galleries. She was the first woman to be elected a member to the Royal Society of British Artists. ——*see also:* Clayton, Ellen C., ENGLISH FEMALE ARTISTS. 1876. See vol. II, p. 107, for a list of Jopling's best-known pictures; Sparrow, Walter Shaw, WOMEN PAINTERS. 1905. Jopling is mentioned.

7.1059
Walker Art Gallery, Liverpool, CATALOGUE OF PERMANENT COLLECTION. 1927. See p. 123 for Jessie MacGregor (fl. 1872-1904; d. 1919), a genre and historical painter.

7.1060
Fry, Roger and Woolf, Virginia, VICTORIAN PHOTOGRAPHS OF FAMOUS MEN AND FAIR WOMEN BY JULIA MARGARET CAMERON. New York, 1928. Cameron lived on the Isle of Wight and was politically active. Julia Duckworth, Virgina Woolf's mother, and Stella Duckworth, Woolf's step-sister, were Cameron's niece and great niece, respectively. She made many portraits of them. She illustrated Tennyson's IDYLLS OF THE KING in 1874.

7.1061
Waugh, Evelyn, ROSSETTI: HIS LIFE AND WORKS. 1928. See pp. 54-58; 70-75;

87-92; and 107-111 on Elizabeth Eleanor Siddal (later Rossetti's wife).

7.1062
Witherby, Kirsten Lilja, SIXTY YEARS OF A WANDERING LIFE. 1928. Witherby (1848-1932) was a Swedish landscape and flower painter who studied in Paris, exhibited in the London galleries and later settled in Ireland.

7.1063
ANTIQUARIAN: Willis, E., *"Henrietta Johnson, South Carolina Pastellist,"* 11 (1928) 46-47.

7.1064
VIRGINIA QUARTERLY REVIEW: Kimball, M., *"Jefferson's Farewell to Romance,"* 4 (1928) 402-419. Describes Thomas Jefferson's relationship with Maria Cosway, an English painter; includes letters between the two.

7.1065
Grimwood, Herbert H., THE SCHOOL OF WOOD-CARVING. 1929. Grimwood was a Fellow of the University of London College of Handicraft.

7.1066
ANTIQUES: Keyes, H.E., *"Coincidence and Henrietta Johnson,"* 16 (1929) 490-494. Keyes provides some sparse biographical information on Johnson, who worked for a time in South Carolina; Keyes, H.E., *"Hester Bateman, Silversmith,"* 20 (1931) 367-368; Gillingham, H.E., *"Concerning Hester Bateman,"* 39 (1941) 76-77. Biographical essay. Contains illustrations of Bateman's work; Wenham, E., *"Women Silversmiths,"* 46 (1944) 200-202. Mentions Hester Bateman; Ruttledge, A.W., *"Who Was Henrietta Johnson?"* 51 (1947) 183-185. Contends that Johnson came from Irish lineage and was a widow when she arrived in America; Walter, W., *"New Light on Hester Bateman,"* 63 (1953) 36-39. Compares Bateman's silversmithing to that of her children.

7.1067
City of Birmingham Art Gallery, CATALOGUE OF THE PERMANENT COLLECTION OF PAINTINGS ETC. 1930; supplements to 1950. Includes Kate Elizabeth Bunce (1858-1927), a decorative painter who studied at the Birmingham Art School and who exhibited from 1887 to 1901 at the Royal Academy. In 1888, she was elected an associate of the Royal Birmingham Society of Artists. Her later works were mostly altar pieces and church murals.

7.1068
Victoria and Albert Museum, THE SILK WEAVERS OF SPITALFIELDS AND BETHNAL GREEN; WITH A CATALOGUE AND ILLUSTRATION OF SPITALFIELDS SILKS BY A.K. SABIN. 1931; CATALOGUE OF WATER-COLOUR PAINTINGS. 1927; with supplement, 1951. The work of Helen Allingham, Margaret Gillies, Edith Augusta James, Elizabeth Heaphy Murray, Sarah Setchel, Sophy Warren, and Louisa Waterford is included.

7.1069
Hunt, Violet, THE WIFE OF ROSSETTI. 1932. Elizabeth Eleanor Siddal began as Dante Gabriel Rossetti's favorite model. She became his mistress, and later his wife. It is said that he taught and encouraged her to paint. Ruskin admired her work and agreed to buy all of it. In 1862, Elizabeth died of an overdose of laudanum, at the age of twenty-eight.

7.1070
Massey, Gertrude, **KINGS, COMMONERS AND ME**. 1934. Massey, an artist, describes the policies at Leigh's School of Art concerning female students and nude models in this autobiographical work.

7.1071
Masse, Henri J.L.J., **THE ART WORKERS' GUILD 1884-1934**. Oxford, 1935.

7.1072
Tate Gallery, London, **AN EXHIBITION OF PAINTING BY JOANNA MARY BOYCE. JUNE 14-JULY 27 1935**. [1935]. Between 1853 and 1857, Boyce exhibited at the Royal Academy; biographical sketch and reproductions included.

7.1073
Canziani, Estella, **ROUND ABOUT THREE PALACE GREEN**. [1936]. Contains an account of her connections with an international circle of artists and of how she became one herself. "During the war of 1914, members of nine nations, including Germans, met in friendliness for tea in my studio. The barriers were forgotten in mutual admiration of one another's work" (p. 4).

7.1074
Vulliamy, C.E., **ASPASIA: THE LIFE AND LETTERS OF MRS. DELANEY**. 1937. Mary Granville Delaney executed her art in many media: pastels, copies, quilt-making, embroidery, designs with shells, playing-cards, paper mosaic, etc.

7.1075
Plant, Marjorie, **THE ENGLISH BOOK TRADE: AN ECONOMIC HISTORY OF THE MAKING AND SALE OF BOOKS**. 1939; 2nd ed., 1965. "Women had entered [bookbinding] in full force by the middle of the century, and certain tasks regularly fell to their lot without opposition from the men" (p. 397).

7.1076
Knight, Laura, **OIL PAINT AND GREASE PAINT**. 3 vols. New York, 1941.

7.1077
Strasser, Alex, **VICTORIAN PHOTOGRAPHY**. New York, 1942. See pp. 113-114 for reproductions of several of Julia Margaret Cameron's photographs.

7.1078
Benezit, Emmanuel, **DICTIONNAIRE CRITIQUE ET DOCUMENTAIRE DES PEINTRES, SCULPTEURS, DESSINATEURS ET GRAVEURS**. 8 vols. 1948-1955. Numerous references to women in painting, sculpture, design, and engraving.

7.1079
Burton, Hester, **BARBARA BODICHON**. 1949. Among her accomplishments as an educator, suffragette and social reformer, Barbara Leigh Smith Bodichon was an accomplished landscape painter and watercolorist. She exhibited at the Royal Academy from 1869 to 1872. Dante Gabriel Rossetti was her friend, and she was acquainted with many of the other pre-Raphaelites.

7.1080
Scott, Edith Agnes (Baroness Kennet Young), **SELF-PORTRAIT OF AN ARTIST FROM THE DIARIES AND MEMOIRS OF LADY KENNET**. 1949.

7.1081
Gernsheim, Helmut, **JULIA MARGARET CAMERON: HER LIFE AND PHOTOGRAPHY**. New York, 1950; **MASTERPIECES OF VICTORIAN PHOTOGRAPHY**. 1951. See pp. 98-99 on Cameron, including six reproductions of her work; (with Gernsheim, Allison), **HISTORY OF PHOTOGRAPHY. FROM THE CAMERA OBSCURA TO THE BEGINNING OF THE MODERN ERA**. New York, 1969. See pp. 250-251; 304-306 for a discussion of Cameron.

7.1082
du Maurier, Daphne, **THE YOUNG GEORGE DU MAURIER**. 1951. See index for Rebecca Solomon (1832-1886), an historical genre painter.

7.1083
CORNHILL MAGAZINE: Proctor, I., *"Elizabeth Siddal: The Ghost of an Idea,"* 165 (1951-1952) 368-386.

7.1084
Reynolds, G., **PAINTERS OF THE VICTORIAN SCENE**. 1953. See p. 85, pl. 64, for a reproduction of a painting by Jane Maria Bowkett, painter of domestic scenes and coastal landscapes; **VICTORIAN PAINTING**. 1966. See p. 113 on Sophie Anderson; the cover of this book is a reproduction of Anderson's most famous picture, "No Walk Today." See pp. 16 and 156 on Maria Spartali Stillman.

7.1085
Short, Ernest, **A HISTORY OF BRITISH PAINTING**. 1953.

7.1086
Hartcup, Adeline, **ANGELICA, THE PORTRAIT OF AN EIGHTEENTH CENTURY ARTIST**. 1954. Illustrated.

7.1087
Newhall, Beaumont and Newhall, Nancy, **MASTERS OF PHOTOGRAPHY**. New York, 1958. See pp. 46-53 on Julia Margaret Cameron.

7.1088
Shure, David, **HESTER BATEMAN: QUEEN OF ENGLISH SILVERSMITHS**. Garden City, 1959. Biographical account with illustrations of Bateman's work.

7.1089
Holman-Hunt, Diana, **MY GRANDMOTHERS AND I**. 1960; **MY GRANDFATHER, HIS WIVES AND LOVES**. 1969. See p. 247 on Fannie Moody King (b. 1861; fl. 1885-1897), an animal painter.

7.1090
Pevsner, Nikolaus, **PIONEERS OF MODERN DESIGN**. Harmondsworth, 1960.

7.1091
Morris, Barbara J., **VICTORIAN EMBROIDERY**. 1962.

7.1092
Paviere, S.H., **A DICTIONARY OF FLOWER, FRUIT AND STILL LIFE PAINTERS**. 1962-1964. See vol. 3 for a reproduction of a painting by Mary E. Butler (fl. 1867-1909) who exhibited at many of the major galleries.

7.1093

Bell, Quentin, THE SCHOOLS OF DESIGN. 1963; VICTORIAN ARTISTS. Cambridge, 1967. See pp. 58-59 for a brief discussion of Julia Margaret Cameron's photography. Contains four reproductions of her pictures. Also briefly mentions Laura Knight and Henrietta Rae, with two black and white plates of their respective works.

7.1094

APOLLO: Godden, G.A., *"Hannah B. Barlow,"* 66 (1956) 22-23. Barlow was an artist at Doulton who worked in pottery decoration; Busiri, V.A., *"Angelica Kauffman and the Bariatinskis,"* 77 (1963) 201-208; Reynolds, G., *"The Pre-Raphaelites and Their Circle,"* 93 (1971) 494-501. Contains a reproduction of a drawing by Elizabeth Eleanor Siddal; Clark, A.M., *"Neo-Classicism and the Roman Eighteenth-Century Portrait,"* 78 (1973) 358-359. Briefly mentions Kauffman's portrait of Cardinal Rezzonico with a black and white reproduction; Crabbe, J., *"An Artist Divided: The Forgotten Talent of Barbara Bodichon, A Very Remarkable Victorian,"* 113 (1981) 311-313. Biographical article discussing Barbara Bodichon, her prolific career as a painter, and the public response she generated with her work.

7.1095

WARBURG AND COURTAULD INSTITUTE JOURNAL: Boase, T.S.R., *"Macklin and Bowyer,"* 26 (1963) 150; 165-166 and 177. Discusses the work that Angelica Kauffman produced for the two British publishers.

7.1096

Chamot, Mary, Farr, Dennis and Butlin, Martin, THE MODERN BRITISH PAINTINGS, DRAWINGS AND SCULPTURE. 2 vols. 1964. Catalogue of the Tate Gallery, London.

7.1097

Croft-Murray, Edward, DECORATIVE PAINTING IN ENGLAND, 1537-1837. 1964-1970. Kauffman's interior designs are discussed on pp. 227-229.

7.1098

Newhall, Beaumont, THE HISTORY OF PHOTOGRAPHY FROM 1839 TO THE PRESENT DAY. New York, 1964. See pp. 64-65 on Julia Margaret Cameron.

7.1099

Birkenhead, Sheila, "Mary 1852-1857" and "Mr. Newton 1858-1861" in ILLUSTRIOUS FRIENDS. THE STORY OF JOSEPH SEVERN AND HIS SON ARTHUR. by Sheila Birkenhead. 1965. On Ann Mary Severn, later Mrs. Newton, a painter of landscapes, portraits and antiquities. Discusses some of her portrait commissions.

7.1100

Fredeman, William, PRE-RAPHAELITISM, A BIBLIOCRITICAL STUDY. 1965. See index for information on Lucy Madox Brown Rossetti, Elizabeth Eleanor Siddal, and Maria Spartali Stillman.

7.1101

BULLETIN OF THE CLEVELAND MUSEUM OF ART: Hinson, T., *"Photography: Recent Acquisitions,"* 62 (1965) 36-46. Discusses the photography of Julia Margaret Cameron.

7.1102
Potter, Beatrix, **THE JOURNAL OF BEATRIX POTTER, 1881-1897**. transcribed by Leslie Cinder. 1966. ——*see also:* Quinby, Jane, **BEATRIX POTTER: A BIBLIOGRAPHICAL CHECK LIST**. New York, 1954; Moore, Anne Carroll, **THE ART OF BEATRIX POTTER**. 1955; Lane, Margaret, **THE TALE OF BEATRIX POTTER: A BIOGRAPHY**. 1968; National Book League, **THE LINDEN COLLECTION OF THE WORKS AND DRAWINGS OF BEATRIX POTTER**. 1971.

7.1103
Middleton, Margaret Simmons, **HENRIETTA JOHNSON, AMERICA'S FIRST PASTELLIST**. Columbia, 1966. Johnson arrived in America from somewhere in the British isles and quickly established herself as an artist.

7.1104
Hardie, M., **WATERCOLOUR PAINTING IN BRITAIN**. 3 vols. 1967-1969. See vol. 3, pp. 112-113 on Helen Paterson Allingham; vol. 3, p. 199 for a reproduction of a work by Margaret Gillies. Adelaide Agnes Maguire is discussed in vol. 3.

7.1105
Lutyens, Mary, **MILLAIS AND THE RUSKINS**. 1967. See p. 113 on Mrs. Hugh Blackburn (fl. 1850-1875), also known as Jemima Wedderburn, an animal painter whose works Ruskin praised.

7.1106
ART BULLETIN: Walch, P.S., *"Charles Rollin and Early Neo-Classicism,"* 49 (1967) 124-125. Angelica Kauffman is mentioned; Walch, P.S., *"Angelica Kauffman and her Contemporaries,"* 51 (1969) 83-85. Review of the exhibit at Vienna and Bregenz in 1968.

7.1107
Bergenz, Volalberger Ladsmuseum, **ANGELICA KAUFFMAN UND IHRE ZEITGENOSSEN**. 1968. Catalogue of an exhibition organized by Dr. Oscar Sander.

7.1108
Fildes, L.V., **LUKE FILDES: A VICTORIAN PAINTER**. 1968.

7.1109
Museum of Modern Art, New York, **VICTORIAN PHOTOGRAPHERS**. 1968.

7.1110
Peck, Herbert, **THE BOOK OF ROCKWOOD POTTERY**. New York, 1968.

7.1111
Wardle, Patricia, **VICTORIAN LACE**. 1968.

7.1112
CAMERA: Gernsheim, H., *"Sun Artists: Victorian Photography,"* 47 (1968) 13-14. Discusses Julia Margaret Cameron's photographic technique.

7.1113
Day, H.A.E., **EAST ANGLICAN PAINTERS, III**. 1969. See pp. 223-233 on Emily Coppin Stannard, a still-life painter who worked in a traditional Dutch style.

7.1114
Dickes, W.F., **THE NORWICH SCHOOL OF PAINTING, III**. 1969. See pp. 207-

221 on Eloise Harriet Stannard (fl. 1852-1893), a still-life painter who exhibited at the Royal Academy, the Society of British Artists, Suffolk Street, and other London galleries. A member of the Society of Lady Artists, Stannard's work was admired by the painter George Lance.

7.1115
Franklin, Colin, **THE PRIVATE PRESSES**. Chester Springs, 1969.

7.1116
Maas, Jeremy, **VICTORIAN PAINTERS**. New York, 1969. See p. 121 on Emily Osborn; p. 231 on Helen Paterson Allingham; pp. 145-146 on Maria Spartali Stillman.

7.1117
Post, Chandler, **A HISTORY OF EUROPEAN AND AMERICAN SCULPTURE**. New York, 1969. See vol. 2, p. 57 on Anne Seymour Damer, an eighteenth-century neoclassic sculptor.

7.1118
Vienna, Austrian Museum Fur Angewandte Kunst, **ANGELIKA KAUFFMAN UND IHRE ZEITGENOSSEN**. 1969. Exhibition catalog with color and black and white reproductions and essays on her painting.

7.1119
Walch, Peter S., "Angelica Kauffman," Ph.D. diss., Princeton Univ., 1969.

7.1120
Hartnoll and Eyre Gallery, London, **CATALOGUE OF EVELYN DE MORGAN DRAWINGS**. 1970.

7.1121
Sonstroem, D., **ROSSETTI AND THE FAIR LADY**. 1970. On Elizabeth Eleanor Siddal, Rossetti's model and fellow artist whom he later married.

7.1122
CATALOGUE OF AN EXHIBITION OF DOULTON STONEWARE AND TERRACOTTA, 1870-1925. 1971; **CATALOGUE OF AN EXHIBITION OF DOULTON POTTERY FROM THE LAMBETH AND BURSLEM STUDIOS**. 1975.

7.1123
JESSIE M. KING, 1875-1949. 1971-1972. Catalogue of an exhibition sponsored by the Arts Council of Great Britain, London.

7.1124
Naylor, Gillian, **THE ARTS AND CRAFTS MOVEMENT**. 1971.

7.1125
MacDonald, Stuart, **THE HISTORY AND PHILOSOPHY OF ART EDUCATION**. 1972.

7.1126
Mayer, Dorothy Moulton, **ANGELICA KAUFFMAN, R.A., 1741-1807**. Gerrards Cross, 1972. Includes black and white and color reproductions.

7.1127
TEXTILE HISTORY: Horn, P., *"Pillow Lacemaking in Victorian England,"* 3 (1972) 104-105.

7.1128
Ashmolean Museum, Oxford, **CENTENARY EXHIBITION OF WORKS BY ELEANOR FORTESCUE-BRICKDALE, 1872-1945, ASHMOLEAN MUSEUM, OXFORD, DECEMBER 1972-JANUARY 1973.** [1973].

7.1129
Hall, Marshall, **THE ARTISTS OF NORTHUMBRIA.** 1973. Includes Isabella Errington (fl. 1846-1850), a landscape, portrait, and coastal scene painter; Isa Jobling (fl. 1892; d. 1926), a landscape and portrait painter; Harriet F.S. Mackreth (1828-1842), a portrait painter; Elizabeth Cameron Mawson (1849-1939), a flower painter; Agnes Pringle (fl. 1884-1893), a figurative subject painter; and Lady Pauline Jermyn Trevelyan (1816-1866).

7.1130
Ormond, R., **EARLY VICTORIAN PORTRAITS.** 2 vols. 1973. Many women are mentioned.

7.1131
Staley, A., **THE PRE-RAPHAELITE LANDSCAPE.** 1973. See p. 175 on Anna E. Blunden; pp. 128 and 151 on Rosa Brett (fl. 1858-1881), a landscape, animal and still-life painter.

7.1132
Szarkowski, J., **LOOKING AT PHOTOGRAPHS: 100 PICTURES FROM THE COLLECTION OF THE MUSEUM OF MODERN ART.** New York, 1973. Julia Margaret Cameron is included.

7.1133
VICTORIAN STUDIES: Spenceley, G., *"The Lace Associations: Philanthropic Movements to Preserve the Production of Hand-Made Lace in Late Victorian and Edwardian England,"* 16 (1973) 433-452.

7.1134
Brook-Hart, D., **BRITISH 19TH CENTURY MARINE PAINTING.** 1974. Discusses Vivian C. Alger, Sarah Sophia Beale, Barbara Bodichon, Kate MaCaulay, and Mrs. Henry Harwood Robinson.

7.1135
Kamerick, Maureen, **THE WOMAN ARTIST IN THE EIGHTEENTH CENTURY: ANGELICA KAUFFMAN AND ELIZABETH VIGEE-LEBRUN.** New Research on Women at the University of Michigan, 1974.

7.1136
ART NEWS: Winteresgill, D., *"Mrs. Cameron's Hobby,"* 73 (1974) 88.

7.1137
Beaton, Cecil and Nicolson, Gail Buckland, **THE MAGIC IMAGE: THE GENIUS OF PHOTOGRAPHY FROM 1839 TO THE PRESENT DAY.** 1975. See pp. 62-67 for a biographical sketch of Julia Cameron. Illustrations included.

7.1138
Eyles, Desmond, **THE DOULTON LAMBETH WARES**. 1975.

7.1139
Forbes, Christopher, **THE ROYAL ACADEMY (1837-1901) REVISITED: VICTORIAN PAINTING FROM THE FORBES MAGAZINE COLLECTION**. New York, 1975. Includes the biographies, exhibition listings, plates and references to some Victorian women painters including Sophie Anderson, Edith Hayllar, and Jessica Hayllar.

7.1140
Irwin, D. and Irwin, F., **SCOTTISH PAINTERS**. 1975. Mentions Mrs. Ferguson of Raith, a watercolorist; Frances MacDonald (1874-1921) a portrait and figurative subject painter; and Jane Nasmyth (b. 1788; fl. to 1866), a landscape painter.

7.1141
Ovenden, Graham, ed., **A VICTORIAN ALBUM: JULIA MARGARET CAMERON AND HER CIRCLE**. New York, 1975. In 1863, Cameron's daughter "presented her [mother] with a camera. It turned out to be the most important event in Mrs. Cameron's life" (p. 3). Collection of beautiful reproductions of the works of Cameron, and some other photographers.

7.1142
Reynolds, Jan, **THE WILLIAMS FAMILY OF PAINTERS**. 1975. Kate Gilbert Hughes and Caroline Fanny Williams are discussed.

7.1143
Surtees, V., **CHARLOTTE CANNING**. 1975. Biography of the Viscountess who was an amateur artist.

7.1144
Troyen, Aimee B., "The Life and Art of Eleanor Siddal," Senior Essay, Yale Univ., 1975. On Elizabeth Eleanor Siddal Rossetti.

7.1145
ARTS: Nochlin, L., *"Some Women Realists,"* 48 (1975) 46-51. Brief discussion of Emily Mary Osborn's paintings.

7.1146
SPARE RIB: Parker, R., *"The Word for Embroidery was WORK,"* 36 (1975) 41-45.

7.1147
Harris, Ann Sutherland and Nochlin, Linda, **WOMEN ARTISTS 1550-1950**. New York, 1976. This is a catalog for an exhibit of paintings by female artists. Osborn, Siddal, Butler and Edith Hayllar are the Victorian English painters represented. Angelica Kauffman is also included. "In England, women artists participated in imposing and increasing numbers in the public exhibitions of the nineteenth century, despite the fact that they were denied membership in the Royal Academy and often had an extremely difficult time getting serious instruction... by 1859, women art students started to storm... the Royal Academy... [but] by the end of 1863 or the beginning of 1864, a group of female art students from the South Kensington and other art schools was again protesting the Royal Academy's exclusionary policies" (pp. 50-51). Excellent source with color plates and black and white reproductions.

7.1148
Campbell, Lennie, **LANDSEER. THE VICTORIAN PARAGON.** 1976. Sir Edwin Henry Landseer was a famous sporting, animal and portrait painter and sculptor who overshadowed his talented sister, Jessica, a painter, etcher and miniaturist who exhibited at the Royal Academy and other prominent galleries. Jessica also manufactured engravings of her brother's work.

7.1149
Messum, David, **THE LIFE AND WORK OF LUCY KEMP-WELCH.** Suffolk, 1976. A frequent exhibitor at the Academy, Kemp-Welch's specialty was animal painting, with a particular emphasis on horses. Kemp-Welch also bought H. Herkomer's famous art school where she and her sister Edith received instruction. Many excellent color and black and white reproductions.

7.1150
Peterson, Karen and Wilson, J.J., **WOMEN ARTISTS: RECOGNITION AND REAPPRAISAL FROM THE EARLY MIDDLE AGES TO THE TWENTIETH CENTURY.** 1976. Surveys the major female artists. The text is mainly comprised of short biographies. Many black and white reproductions. See index for various English artists.

7.1151
Wood, Christopher, **VICTORIAN PANORAMA—PAINTINGS OF VICTORIAN LIFE.** 1976. Many women are included; **THE DICTIONARY OF VICTORIAN PAINTERS** 2nd ed., 1978. Contains over 11,000 entries, with many women entered. Reproductions represent the work of Helen Paterson Allingham, Laura Alma-Tadema, Sophie Anderson, Jane Maria Bowkett, Eleanor Fortescue-Brickdale, Emma Brownlow, Elizabeth Southerden Butler, Ellen Conolly, Evelyn de Morgan, Maud Earl, Mrs. Alexander Farmer, Elizabeth Stanhope Forbes, Jessica Hayllar, Edith Hayllar, Mary Evelina Kindon, Georgina Lara, Anna Lea Merritt, Annie Feray Mutrie, Emily Mary Osborn, Mrs. (Henrietta Rae) Ernest Normand, Eloise Harriet Stannard, and Maria Spartali Stillman. Very valuable book.

7.1152
FEMINIST ART JOURNAL: Scheerer, C., *"Maria Cosway: Larger-than-Life Miniaturist,"* 5 (1976) 10-13.

7.1153
Norman, Geraldine, **NINETEENTH CENTURY PAINTERS AND PAINTING: A DICTIONARY.** 1977.

7.1154
Anscombe, Isabelle and Gere, Charlotte, **ARTS AND CRAFTS IN BRITAIN AND AMERICA.** 1978; 1983. Provides a short biographical entry on May Morris (1862-1938), a British designer, embroideress, and craft jeweler, and Anne Macbeth (1875-1948), a designer, embroidress, and teacher who executed a number of ecclesiastical commissions.

7.1155
Bachmann, Donna G. and Piland, Sherry, **WOMEN ARTISTS: AN HISTORICAL, CONTEMPORARY AND FEMINIST BIBLIOGRAPHY.** Metuchen, 1978. Provides brief biographical sketches of each individual listed.

7.1156
Fine, Elsa Honig, **WOMEN AND ART. A HISTORY OF WOMEN PAINTERS AND**

SCULPTORS FROM THE RENAISSANCE TO THE TWENTIETH CENTURY.
Montclair, 1978. See "The English School: Portraiture" for brief biographical
sketches of Angelica Kauffman, Mary Moser, Anne Damer, Maria Cosway,
Margaret Carpenter, Barbara Bodichon, Frances Reynolds, Lucy Madox Brown
Rossetti, and Elizabeth Thompson Butler. Black and white illustrations of their
work are included. After Kauffman and Moser's membership, "It was not until 1922
that another woman was elected to [Royal] Academy membership.... The first
woman invited to attend the Academy's school was Laura Hereford (1831-1870),
who began her studies in 1861/62. No woman was allowed to draw from the nude
until after 1893, when the partially draped figure was introduced into female life
classes. The Society of Female Artists was founded in the 1850s and flourished
under the guidance of Mary Atkinson" (p. 67).

7.1157
Gillett, Paula, "The Profession of Painting in England 1859-1890," Ph.D. diss.,
Univ.of California, Berkeley, 1978. Women were usually confined to seek out and
produce art as an accomplishment for their own pleasure. Those who seriously
pursued art as a profession had to contend with male prejudice and the
discriminating practices of the Royal Academy.

7.1158
Houfe, Simon, **THE DICTIONARY OF BRITISH BOOK ILLUSTRATORS AND
CARICATURISTS, 1800-1914.** 1978.

7.1159
Trevelyan, R., **A PRE-RAPHAELITE CIRCLE.** 1978. Includes information on Lady
Pauline Jermyn Trevelyan (1816-1866), an amateur artist.

7.1160
Atterbury, Paul and Irvine, Louise, **THE DOULTON STORY. A SOUVENIR
BOOKLET PRODUCED ORIGINALLY FOR THE EXHIBITION HELD AT THE
VICTORIA AND ALBERT MUSEUM, LONDON 30 MAY-12 AUGUST 1979.**
[1979]. Women were not only employed as assistants at Doulton; they also had
positions as designers. Illustrated.

7.1161
Callen, Anthea, **WOMEN ARTISTS OF THE ARTS AND CRAFTS MOVEMENT,
1870-1914.** New York, 1979; *also titled:* **ANGEL IN THE STUDIO: WOMEN IN
THE ARTS AND CRAFTS MOVEMENT, 1870-1914.** 1979. Examines both fine arts
and crafts as sources of suitable employment for working-class women and destitute
middle-class women. Includes photographs and illustrations portraying artists at
work, the schools they attended, and their work. Discusses guilds. Very valuable;
reviewed in: **NEW SOCIETY:** Rowbotham, S., *"Pretty Things,"* 48 (1979) 589-590.
"By examining the institutions and the organisation of production Callen concludes
that the radical implications of the movement were contradicted by the blindness to
the oppressive sexual division of labour within the movement" (p. 589); *also
reviewed in:* **VICTORIAN STUDIES:** Boris, E., 24 (1981) 382-384.

7.1162
Engen, Rodney K., **DICTIONARY OF VICTORIAN ENGRAVERS, PRINT
PUBLISHERS AND THEIR WORKS.** Cambridge and Teaneck, 1979.

7.1163
Greer, Germaine, **THE OBSTACLE RACE. THE FORTUNES OF WOMEN
PAINTERS AND THEIR WORK.** New York, 1979. In this invaluable and detailed

study, Greer traces the careers of many renowned painters, as well as the many "minor" and less-documented artists. Many black and white and color reproductions are included. "More and more women were finding that what they had learned in the way of genteel accomplishment and pleasant pastime was having to become their livelihood. Industrial and applied art had long been considered proper fields of female employment for women of the lower classes: now women of a higher class were seeking art education of a more pretentious kind. At the same time, few of them believed that the practice of art was in itself superior to a life of wedded bliss. Most of them tried to keep their options open, as more serious students of art often angrily testified" (p. 310).

7.1164

Hunt, Felicity, "Women in the 19th Century Bookbinding and Printing Trades (1790-1914): With Special Reference to London," M.A. thesis, Univ. of Essex, 1979.

7.1165

Pankhurst, Richard K.P., SYLVIA PANKHURST. ARTIST AND CRUSADER. AN INTIMATE PORTRAIT. 1979. Includes reproductions of paintings and drawings which depict female industrial and agricultural workers; banners and badges for the suffrage movement; several prison sketches, and portraits of Keir Hardie.

7.1166

Hedges, Elaine and Wendt, Ingrid, IN HER OWN IMAGE: WOMEN WORKING IN THE ARTS. Old Westbury, 1980. See especially: "The Artist in the Character of Design" on Angelica Kauffman.

7.1167

ATLANTIS: Sydie, R., *"Women Painters in Britain: 1768-1848,"* 5 (1980) 144-175. Delineates art education available to women, the policies of the Royal Academy, the number of women exhibiting in major galleries as compared with the number of men, and the subjects painted by women.

7.1168

Parker, Rozsika, OLD MISTRESSES: WOMEN, ART AND IDEOLOGY. New York, 1981. Offers more than information about women artists. Written from a feminist perspective, attempts to answer "why women's art has been misrepresented." Shows that the history of art is practiced with ideologies that work against women artists, past and present; THE SUBVERSIVE STITCH: EMBROIDERY AND THE MAKING OF THE FEMININE. 1984.

7.1169

Casteras, Susan, THE SUBSTANCE OR THE SHADOW: IMAGES OF VICTORIAN WOMANHOOD. [New Haven], 1982. Discusses the pre-Raphaelites and their circle.

7.1170

COUNTRY LIFE: Cornforth, J., *"An Anticipation of Victoriana: The Drawings of Mary Ellen Best,"* 173 (1983) 1549-1552.

7.1171

WOMEN'S ART JOURNAL: Lalumia, M., *"Lady Elizabeth Thompson Butler in the 1870's,"* 4 (1983) 9-14; Callen, A., *"Sexual Division of Labor in the Arts and Crafts Movement,"* 5 (1984) 1-6.

7.1172

WOMEN'S STUDIES INTERNATIONAL FORUM: Hunt, F., *"The London Trade in the Printing and Binding of Books; An Experience in Exclusion, Dilution and De-Skilling for Women Workers,"* 6 (1983) 517-524. "By the nineteenth century... women performed a vital role in the bookbinding process as folders and sewers. But they had always been considered marginal within the trades... and the growth of unions provided new arenas for industrial antagonism between male and female workers. By the end of this period women were established in low paid, low status work in spite of their historic inclusion as skilled workers in certain sectors" (p. 517).

7.1173
Anscombe, Isabelle, A WOMAN'S TOUCH: WOMEN IN DESIGN FROM 1860 TO THE PRESENT DAY. 1984; *reviewed in:* NEW SOCIETY: Carter, A., 70 (1984) 470-471. "There were enterprising, occasionally notorious women [in design]. A pioneer, Elsie de Wolfe, around 1912 'took a test case to court, refusing to pay income tax because she did not have the vote.' Syrie Maugham, of the famed, all-white interiors, used her homemaking talents to lure her reluctant husband, Somerset, back to her. Sybil Colefax peddled English country-house style to other people after she lost the ability to keep up with it herself when her fortune vanished in the Wall Street crash of 1929" (p. 470).

7.1174
Shteir, Ann B., "Linnaeus's Daughters: Women and British Botany" in WOMEN AND STRUCTURE OF SOCIETY: SELECTED RESEARCH FROM THE FIFTH BERKSHIRE CONFERENCE ON THE HISTORY OF WOMEN. ed. by Barbara J. Harris and Jo Ann McNamara. Durham, 1984. "William Curtis founded the BOTANICAL MAGAZINE in 1787, and it was the main journal during the 19th century to feature the work by female [botanical] illustrators" (pp. 66-67).

7.1175
NEW SOCIETY: Marsh, J., *"Pre-Raphaelite Women,"* 67 (1984) 279-282. "The social progress of these women is a tribute to their talents, and as well as middle class marriage they gained fame and status as 'Pre-Raphaelite women,' rather like early Hollywood actresses. In general they lived up to their role, wearing loose Pre-Raphaelite gowns, dressing their hair in loose Pre-Raphaelite style and behaving in an 'unconventional' Pre-Raphaelite manner. As models, they have received little credit for their contribution to Pre-Raphaelite art. This is hard to quantify but should be registered, for without them the paintings could not exist" (p. 281).

7.1176
Yeldham, Charlotte, WOMEN ARTISTS IN NINETEENTH-CENTURY FRANCE AND ENGLAND: THEIR ART EDUCATION, EXHIBITION OPPORTUNITIES AND MEMBERSHIP OF EXHIBITING SOCIETIES AND ACADEMIES, WITH AN ASSESSMENT OF THE SUBJECT MATTER OF THEIR WORK AND SUMMARY BIOGRAPHIES. New York, 1985. Detailed study that places women's art in a social context.

* * *

11. ACTRESSES AND MUSICIANS

7.1177
THEATRICAL BIOGRAPHY: OR, MEMOIRS OF THE PRINCIPAL PERFORM-
ERS OF THE THREE THEATRES ROYAL. 1772.

7.1178
Bellamy, George Anne, AN APOLOGY FOR THE LIFE OF GEORGE ANNE
BELLAMY, LATE OF COVENT GARDEN THEATRE. WRITTEN BY HERSELF.
1785. This English actress lived from 1731 to 1788. ——*see also:* Fitzgerald, Percy
Hetherington, THE ROMANCE OF THE ENGLISH STAGE. 2 vols. 1874. See vol.
1, pp. 104-205 on Bellamy.

7.1179
Haslewood, Joseph, THE SECRET HISTORY OF THE GREEN-ROOM:
CONTAINING AUTHENTIC AND ENTERTAINING MEMOIRS OF THE ACTORS
AND ACTRESSES IN THE 3 THEATRES ROYAL. NEW EDITION WITH
IMPROVEMENTS TO WHICH IS PREFIXED A SKETCH OF THE HISTORY OF
THE ENGLISH STAGE. 1790-1795.

7.1180
Jones, Charles Inigo, MEMOIRS OF MISS O'NEILL; CONTAINING HER PUBLIC
CHARACTER, PRIVATE LIFE, AND DRAMATIC PROGRESS, FROM HER
ENTRANCE UPON THE STAGE; WITH A FULL CRITICISM OF HER
DIFFERENT CHARACTERS, APPROPRIATE SELECTIONS FROM THEM, AND
SOME ACCOUNT OF THE PLAYS SHE HAS PREFFERED FROM HER
REPRESENTATIONS. 1816.

7.1181
Beverley, Elizabeth, THE ACTRESS'S WAYS AND MEANS, TO INDUSTRIOUS-
LY RAISE THE WIND! CONTAINING THE MORAL AND ENTERTAINING
POETICAL EFFUSIONS OF MRS. R. BEVERLEY. [1818].

7.1182
THE BIOGRAPHY OF THE BRITISH STAGE; BEING CORRECT NARRATIVES
OF THE LIVES OF ALL PRINCIPAL ACTORS AND ACTRESSES AT DRURY
LANE, COVENT GARDEN AND THE HAYMARKET! TO WHICH IS ADDED A
COMIC POEM ENTITLED "THE ACTRESES." 1824.

7.1183
[Inchbald, Mrs. Elizabeth], (1753-1821), MEMOIRS OF MRS. INCHBALD.
INCLUDING HER FAMILIAR CORRESPONDENCE WITH THE MOST
DISTINGUISHED PERSONS OF HER TIME. TO WHICH ARE ADDED 'THE
MASSACRE' AND 'A CASE OF CONSCIENCE.' 1833. Novelist, dramatist, and
actress. Edited THE BRITISH THEATER from 1806-1809.

7.1184
Rede, Leman, THE ROAD TO THE STAGE. 1836.

7.1185
Peake, Richard Brinsley, MEMOIRS OF THE COLMAN FAMILY. 1841. The

memoir of this London stage family includes a discussion of the theatrical appearances of Sarah Siddons.

7.1186
Royal Society of Female Musicians, **HER MAJESTY'S CONCERT ROOMS, HANOVER SQUARE... A GRAND MISCELLANEOUS CONCERT, FRIDAY EVENING, APRIL 23, 1841, ETC.** [1841]; **PROGRAMME WITH WORDS OF A CONCERT GIVEN AT HER MAJESTY'S CONCERT ROOMS, HANOVER SQUARE, 5 JUNE, 1850, WITH A LIST OF SUBSCRIBERS, ETC.** [1850]; **ROYAL SOCIETY OF FEMALE MUSICIANS' CONCERT... JUNE 13, 1856.** [A PROGRAMME]. [1856].

7.1187
Wilson, Margaret Baron, **OUR ACTRESSES; OR, GLANCES AT STAGE FAVOURITES, PAST AND PRESENT.** 2 vols. 1844.

7.1188
Marshall, Thomas, **LIVES OF THE MOST CELEBRATED ACTORS AND ACTRESSES.** 1847. Includes biographical notations of Eliza Mathews (b. 1797) who was famous in the 1820s as manager of one of the Drury Lane theatres. Margaret Somerville (later Bunn), a contemporary of Mathews, Mrs. Hartley (b. 1751), a "minor" actress, and Mrs. Cibber are also discussed.

7.1189
THE SINGER'S COMPANION. 1854; 1857.

7.1190
Cazalet, William Wahab, **THE HISTORY OF THE ROYAL ACADEMY OF MUSIC COMPOSITION FROM AUTHENTIC SOURCES.** 1854. See especially: pp. 279-326 for biographical sketches of young female musicians at the academy.

7.1191
Sala, George Augustus, **TWICE ROUND THE CLOCK; OR THE HOURS OF THE DAY AND NIGHT IN LONDON.** [1859]. Presents a perspective of the London scene including theatre at 7:00 p.m.

7.1192
ENGLISH WOMAN'S JOURNAL: S., *"A Few Words About Actresses and the Profession of the Stage,"* 2 (1859) 385-398. Discusses the problems faced by actresses, correcting the erroneous assumption that their lives are easy.

7.1193
TEMPLE BAR: Inchbald, E., *"Daughters of Eve,"* 1 (1861) 483-495. "The mingling in the public and garish work of the world implied in such avocations is not for the most part favorable to the development of a truly womanly woman——generally the reverse" (p. 483).

7.1194
Clayton, Ellen Creathorne, **QUEENS OF SONG: BEING MEMOIRS OF SOME OF THE MOST CELEBRATED FEMALE VOCALISTS WHO HAVE PERFORMED ON THE LYRIC STAGE FROM THE EARLIEST DAYS OF OPERA TO THE PRESENT TIME...** New York, 1865. "Every 'Queen of Song' is the central figure in a group of all that is great, and noble, and gay——and too often, unhappily, dissolute——in the society in which she moves. Her story is often of touching and romantic interest, and her fate points an impressive moral lesson... the young

debutante, emerging from the severe labor of her musical studies, enters at once on the dazzling but dangerous scene of her future triumphs, imbued with sensibility of no ordinary kind, refined by the cultivation of her voice and ear, often with the strong and wayward impulses of genius" (p. ix). Includes chapters on Clara Anastasia Novello, Catherine Hayes, and Louisa Pyne.

7.1195
Morley, H., JOURNAL OF A LONDON PLAYGOER, 1851-1866. 1866; DIARY OF A LONDON PLAYGOER. 1891.

7.1196
VICTORIA MAGAZINE: Ritter, F.R., *"Women as Musicians,"* 28 (1876-77) 195.

7.1197
Hodson, Henrietta, A LETTER FROM MISS HENRIETTA HODSON, AN ACTRESS, TO THE MEMBERS OF THE DRAMATIC PROFESSION: BEING A RELATION OF THE PERSECUTIONS WHICH SHE HAS SUFFERED FROM MR. WILLIAM SCHWENCK GILBERT. 1877. Covers the dispute between Hodson and Gilbert.

7.1198
THEATER: A MONTHLY REVIEW AND MAGAZINE: 1877 to 1878; vols. 1-3; 1878 to 1911; vols. 1-39.

7.1199
Baker, Henry Barton, OUR OLD ACTORS. 1878. Chapters include portraits of Fanny Kemble and Sarah Siddons. Also discusses Miss O'Neill, Mrs. Davinson, Miss Smith, Mrs. Bunn, and Helen Faucit.

7.1200
Kemble, Frances Anne, RECORDS OF A GIRLHOOD. 3 vols. 1879; RECORD OF LATER DAYS. 3 vols. 1882; New York, 1884. Famous stage performer, Fanny Kemble, presents a compilation of her letters. "It is a curious sensation to have a certain consciousness of power (which I have, though perhaps it is a mistaken notion), and at the same time of absolute helplessness. It seems to me as if I had some sort of strength, and yet I feel totally incapable of coping with small difficulties of circumstance under which it is oppressed; it's like a sort of wide-awake nightmare. I suppose it's because I am a woman that I am so idiotic and incompetent to help myself" (p. 623); FURTHER RECORDS. 2 vols. 1890; ON THE STAGE. New York, 1926. ——see also: Fitzgerald, Percy, THE KEMBLES. 2 vols. 1871; Bobbe, Dorothie, FANNY KEMBLE. 1932. "My physical power of voice and delivery is not diminished, which is good for tragedy; my self-possession increased, which ought to be good for comedy; and I do trust I may succeed, at least sufficiently to be able, by going from one place to another, and returning to America when I have worn out my public favour here——say, in two years——to make what will enable me to live independently, though probably upon very small means" (p. 216); Driver, Leota, FANNY KEMBLE. 1933; Armstrong, Mary, FANNY KEMBLE: A PASSIONATE VICTORIAN. New York, 1938; Gibbs, Henry, AFFECTIONATELY YOURS, FANNY: FANNY KEMBLE AND THE THEATRE. 1945. "I have attempted to see her not so much as an actress without reference to time as an actress in relation to a particular period in theatrical history" (p. 7); Marshall, Dorothy, FANNY KEMBLE. 1977. Presents Kemble's historical and philosophical perspectives on her times; Furnas, J.C., FANNY KEMBLE: LEADING LADY OF THE NINETEENTH CENTURY STAGE: A BIOGRAPHY. New York, 1982.

7.1201
Pascoe, Charles Eyre, **OUR ACTORS AND ACTRESSES; THE DRAMATIC LIST: A RECORD OF THE PERFORMANCES OF LIVING ACTORS AND ACTRESSES OF THE BRITISH STAGE.** 2nd ed., 1880.

7.1202
Cook, Dutton, **HOURS WITH THE PLAYERS.** 1881.

7.1203
Davidson, Peter, **THE VIOLIN: ITS CONSTRUCTION THEORETICALLY AND PRACTICALLY TREATED; INCLUDING AN EPITOME OF THE LIVES OF THE MOST EMINENT ARTISTS, A DICTIONARY OF VIOLIN MAKERS AND LISTS OF VIOLIN SALES.** 1881. "We have now numerous very talented lady-artists, so it may be safely said the instrument is now beginning to be fully appreciated by the fair sex, and very justly so, knowing how susceptible the violin is, so fascinating, so tender, and yet so free, so marvelously varied and bewitching" (p. 155).

7.1204
De Leine, M.A., **LILIAN ADELAIDE NEILSON. A MEMORIAL SKETCH, PERSONAL AND CRITICAL.** 1881.

7.1205
Jephson, Richard Mounteney, Murray, E.C. Grenville and Clarke, H. Savile, "Nice Girls. VI. The Young Actress" in **THE SOCIAL ZOO. BEING SATIRICAL, SOCIAL, AND HUMOROUS SKETCHES OF OUR GILDED YOUTH, NICE GIRLS, NOBLE LORDS, FLIRTS...** 1884. Tells the story of a respectable middle-class girl who succeeds in becoming a successful actress. Her uncle, an old retired major-general, yells "fire" in the middle of her performance to thwart her career in such an "undignified" profession.

7.1206
Charrington, Frederick N., **THE BATTLE OF THE MUSIC HALLS.** 1885. Argues that music halls are dens of evil and immorality. Tells the story of a friend whose wife discovers him entering the theater with a girl on his arm.

7.1207
Ellerslie, Alma, **THE DIARY OF AN ACTRESS; OR, REALITIES OF STAGE LIFE.** ed. by H.C. Schuttleworth. 1885.

7.1208
Holloway, Laura C., **ADELAIDE NEILSON: A SOUVENIR.** 1885. Neilson was an actress.

7.1209
Murray, E.C. Grenville, **SIDE LIGHTS ON ENGLISH SOCIETY SKETCHES FROM LIFE, SOCIAL AND SATIRICAL.** 1885. "Yet she could sing those pure old English ballads of love and faithful troth and homely joys with such accents as drew tears from the most hardened among the gilded crew who heard her; and on the stage she was most successful in enacting the characters of girls who are loveable for all the virtues of fidelity which she herself did not possess" (p. 166).

7.1210
Smith, E.M., **WOMAN IN SACRED SONG: A LIBRARY OF HYMNS, SACRED POEMS AND MUSIC BY WOMEN.** Boston, 1885.

7.1211
Brown, James, **BIOGRAPHICAL DICTIONARY OF MUSICIANS WITH A BIBLIOGRAPHY OF ENGLISH WRITINGS ON MUSIC**. Birmingham, 1886. The dictionary focuses primarily on male musicians; however, there are scatterings of reference to English women such as Lucy Anderson and Dora Schirmacker; (and Stratton, Stephen S.), **BRITISH MUSICAL BIOGRAPHY: A DICTIONARY OF MUSICAL ARTISTS, AUTHORS AND COMPOSERS, BORN IN BRITAIN AND ITS COLONIES**. About 150 of the entries are women, all of whom were acknowledged as professional artists. A sample of 20 of these reflects the range of accomplishment: Anderson, Lucy Philpot (1790-1878), pianist. First female pianist to perform at the Philharmonic Society in London, April 29, 1882. Also taught Queen Victoria and other members of the royal family; Armitt, Mary Louisa (b. 1851), researcher and writer on music. Wrote musical sketches and was music critic for several journals; Berry, Sarah (debut 1888), contralto vocalist. Born in Bamfield and worked as a weaver in a mill before embarking on her musical studies, for which she received a scholarship; Bisset, Elizabeth Anne (b. 1800), harpist and composer; Bright, Dora Estella (b. 1863), pianist and composer. Member of the Royal Academy of Musicians. Wrote the first orchestral work by a woman to be admitted to the programme of the Philharmonic Concerts Society; Buckley, Olivia Dussek (1799-1847), pianist, organist and composer. Taught by her mother, she made public appearances at the age of eight; Burns, Georgina (Mrs. Leslie Crotty) (b. 1860), opera performer. She and her husband established a light-opera company; Cardigan, Cora (Mrs. Louis Honig), flutist. Taught by her father; Dufferin, Helen Selina (Lady) (b. 1807), composer of songs. Sister of Caroline Norton; Glover, Sarah Ann (1785-1867), musician and teacher. Invented the Tonic Sol-fa system of musical notation and wrote manuals; Harrop, Sarah (Mrs. Joah Bates) (d. 1811), soprano. Was originally a factory worker; Lawrence, Emily M. (b. 1854), pianist and composer. Taught by her mother, Elizabeth S. Lawrence, who was conductor of the Ladies Choral Society at Rugby; Millar, Marian, pianist and writer. Millar was the first woman to obtain the degree of Music Bac. at Victoria Univ., Manchester in 1894; Shinner, Emily (b. 1862), violinist. Studied in Germany and made her debut in England in 1882. In 1887 she organized the Shinner Quartet, a string quartet of ladies; Smyth, Ethel, composer. Best known for composing the suffragist anthem; Stirling, Elizabeth (Mrs. F.A. Bridge) (b. 1819), organist and composer. First woman to pass the exam for Music Bac. at Oxford in 1856, but did not receive the degree as it was not open to women; Thomas, Adelaide Louisa, pianist. Passed the exam for Music Bac. at Oxford in 1892.

7.1212
Matthews, Brander and Hutton, Lawrence, **ACTORS AND ACTRESSES OF GREAT BRITAIN AND THE UNITED STATES FROM THE DAY OF DAVID GARRICK TO THE PRESENT TIME**. 5 vols. New York, 1886. Includes chapters on Frances Abington, Helen Faucit, Matilda Heron, and Adelaide Neilson.

7.1213
Porter, Henry C., **THE HISTORY OF THE THEATRES OF BRIGHTON FROM 1774 TO 1885**. 1886.

7.1214
AN ACCOUNT OF THE LIFE OF THAT CELEBRATED ACTRESS, MRS. SUSANNAH MARIA CIBBER. 1887. Cibber lived from 1714 to 1776. *——see also:* Nash, Mary, **THE PROVOKED WIFE. THE LIFE AND TIMES OF SUSANNAH CIBBER**. 1977.

7.1215
Barron-Wilson, Mrs. Cornwell, **MEMOIRS OF MISS MELLON.** 2 vols. 1887.
Examines the life of actress Harriot Mellon, her involvement with the London
stage, and the relationship to her patron, Edmund Kean.

7.1216
**THE LIFE OF MRS. ABINGTON (FORMERLY MISS BARTON) CELEBRATED
COMIC ACTRESS, WITH FULL ACCOUNTS OF HER VARIOUS PERFORM-
ANCES IN THE THEATRES OF LONDON AND DUBLIN. BY THE EDITOR OF
'THE LIFE OF QUIN.'** 1888. Detailed account of the life and career of Frances
Barton who was "the first comic actress of her time" (p. 6).

7.1217
Marston, Westland, **OUR RECENT ACTORS, VOL. II.** 1888.

7.1218
Kendal, Margaret, **DRAMATIC OPINIONS.** Boston, 1890. Actress Kendal (1849–
1935) discusses her acting; **DAME MADGE KENDAL. BY HERSELF.** 1933.
Autobiography. Kendal's parents were both actors and Kendal made her debut as a
child in "Uncle Tom's Cabin" at the Bristol Theatre. ——*see also:* Pemberton, Edgar
T., **THE KENDALS: A BIOGRAPHY.** 1900.

7.1219
Moore, George, **IMPRESSIONS AND OPINIONS.** 1891. Admonishes actresses who
strive to portray themselves as asexual, maternal women.

7.1220
NEW REVIEW: Terry, E., *"Stray Memories,"* n.v. (1891) 332-341; 444-449; 499-
507.

7.1221
MUSIC: Sawyer, F.E., *"For Musical Girls,"* 5 (1893) 101-103.

7.1222
Manchester Guardian, **THE MANCHESTER STAGE 1880-1900; CRITICISM
REPRINTED FROM "THE MANCHESTER GUARDIAN."** 1900. Discusses the
development of theater in Manchester. Provides reviews of memorable performances
on the Manchester stage.

7.1223
Robins, Edward, **ECHOES OF THE PLAYHOUSE REMINISCENCES OF SOME
PAST GLORIES OF THE ENGLISH STAGE.** New York, 1895; **TWELVE GREAT
ACTRESSES.** New York, 1900. Discusses Anne Bracegirdle; Ann Oldfield; Margaret
Woofington; Frances Abington; Sarah Siddons; Dorothy Jordan; Mary Robinson;
Frances Anne Kemble; Elisa Rachel Felix, Charlotte Saunders Cushman; Adelaide
Neilson; and Adelaide Ristori.

7.1224
Stuart, Charles Dougles, **THE VARIETY STAGE; A HISTORY OF THE MUSIC
HALLS FROM THE EARLIEST PERIOD TO THE PRESENT.** 1895. "Within recent
years several lady artistes have tested their powers in [ventriloquism]... Miss Collie
Conway, Miss Cissie Loftus... Miss Millie Lindon and Miss Maries Dainton" (p.
221). "Lady variety entertainers are represented by a very large and talented
contingent, and to attempt to enumerate... the many serio-comics, sisters, dancers,
male impersonators, and ballad and character vocalists would be well nigh

impossible" (p. 222). Lists many popular artists.

7.1225
Sutro, Florence, **WOMEN IN MUSIC AND LAW.** 1895.

7.1226
Bull, Sara Chapman (Thorp), (Mrs. Ole Bull), **OLE BULL, A MEMOIR BY SARA BULL; WITH OLE BULL'S "VIOLIN NOTES," AND DR. A.B. CROSBY'S "ANATOMY OF A VIOLINIST."** Boston, 1897.

7.1227
Soldene, Emily, **MY THEATRICAL AND MUSICAL RECOLLECTIONS.** 1897. Reminiscences of music hall performer Emily Soldene (1840-1912). Discusses the lives of many performers of the Victorian period and recalls memorable performances at London's top houses.

7.1228
MUSICIAN: Towers, J., *"Woman in Music,"* 11 (1897) n.p. "Women, will, ere long, in my humble opinion, fully prove to the world, that the boasted superiority of man over woman in the creative field of musical activity, is just one of those nebulous myths" (p. 97). Lists several English women composers including the following: Ann Bartholomew, Anna Bray, Mary Cowden Clarke, and Harriet Abram.

7.1229
Calvert, Walter, **SIR HENRY IRVING AND MISS ELLEN TERRY, A RECORD OF OVER TWENTY YEARS AT THE LYCEUM THEATRE.** 1897.

7.1230
Filon, Augustin, **THE ENGLISH STAGE.** 1897.

7.1231
THEATRE: [1898 to 1914]; vols. 1-17.

7.1232
Drew, Mrs. John (Louisa), **AUTOBIOGRAPHICAL SKETCH.** New York, 1899. A child actor, Drew reminisces about the Kembles and her own theatrical family.

7.1233
Lahee, Henry C., **FAMOUS VIOLINISTS OF TODAY AND YESTERDAY.** Boston, 1899. See especially: "Women as Violinists." Features biographical sketches of violinists Lady Charles Halle and Emily Shinner; **THE GRAND OPERA SINGERS OF TODAY.** Boston, 1912; 1922. "One of the noteworthy singers imported in 1902 was Madame Kirby-Lunn, an English contralto. She made her debut at the Metropolitan Opera-House in 'Lohengrin'" (p. 12).

7.1234
Leslie, Amy, **SOME PLAYERS: PERSONAL SKETCHES.** Chicago and New York, 1899. Contains a romanticized portrait of Ellen Terry. "Woman is created to bear," propounded Terry, "not only children, but woes, annoyances, gentlemen and fashions, don't you know" (p. 53).

7.1235
Upton, George Putnam, **WOMEN IN MUSIC.** 6th ed., Chicago, 1899.

7.1236
Martin, Theodore, **HELENA FAUCIT (LADY MARTIN).** 2nd ed., 1900.

7.1237
Scotson-Clark, George Frederick, **THE "HALLS" PICTURED BY G.F. SCOTSON CLARK.** [190?].

7.1238
ECONOMIC REVIEW: Russell, C.E.B. and Campagnac, E.T., *"Poor People's Music Halls,"* 10 (1900) 287-308. "A working lad or girl... has the opportunity sometimes of getting on the stage.... It is possible to see an actor or actress who has performed at one of the richer halls give the same performance at one of the cheaper places" (p. 305).

7.1239
Gilbert, Anne (Hartley), **THE STAGE REMINISCENCES OF MRS. GILBERT.** New York, 1901.

7.1240
Ebel, Otto, **WOMEN COMPOSERS. A BIOGRAPHICAL HANDBOOK OF WOMAN'S WORK IN MUSIC.** New York, 1902; 1913. Provides biographical excerpts on the following English women composers: Lady Ramsay, Kate Paige, May Ostlere, Georgeanne Hubi Newcombe, Emma Mundella, Marie Moody, Marian Millar, Florence May, Sarah A. Glover, Alice Borton, Emma Barrett, Florence Aylward, and Harriet Abrams.

7.1241
Strang, Lewis C., **PLAYERS AND PLAYS OF THE LAST QUARTER CENTURY, VOLUME I.** Boston, 1902. "The class of women players who inspire this heroine worship habitually manifest their tragic powers in the type of characterisation of which Juliet is the loftiest example; and in addition to this especial quality of tragic portrayal, they possess a decided capacity for mingled humour and pathos, which makes potently delightful their comedy as set forth in their Rosalinds and their Violas" (p. 184). Briefly sketches the careers of the following actresses: Eliza O'Neill (1791-1872), "the embodiment of appealing loveliness and pathetic tenderness" (p. 185); Mrs. Mary Ann Duff (1794-1857), "the first tragic actress of our stage" (p. 187); Mrs. Fanny Kemble (1809-1893) who detested the theatre yet who had remarkable success as Juliet, whom she played more than 120 times; Ellen Tree (1805-1880) who, "although she could not act Juliet... was a Romeo worthy of consideration... [whose] long, lithe legs and square shoulders gave her quite a masculine appearance in the part" (p. 200); Helen Faucit (1820-1898) who first acted, at age twelve, the role of Juliet and who wrote a book, some of Shakespeare's female characters; Adelaide Neilson (1848-1880) called by critics a "true dramatic genius." Other women are discussed in this book.

7.1242
WOMAN'S LIBRARY: Kendal, M., *"Some Pros and Cons of Theatric Life,"* 1 (1903) 253.

7.1243
MUSICAL COURIER: Haddon, C., *"Women and Music,"* 47 (1903) 34; King, Mrs. A.T., *"Women as Composers,"* n.v. (1919) 8-9.

7.1244
Adams, William Davenport, **A DICTIONARY OF THE DRAMA: A GUIDE TO**

THE PLAYS, PLAYWRIGHTS, AND PLAYHOUSES OF THE UNITED KINGDOM AND AMERICA FROM EARLIEST TIMES TO THE PRESENT. 1904.

7.1245

Gilman, Lawrence, "Women and Modern Music" in **PHASES OF MODERN MUSIC.** by Lawrence Gilman. New York, 1904. "Women did not begin to compete with men in the field of composition, to any extent, until music had ceased to be merely decorative or religious, as it was, predominantly, before Beethoven's time, and had begun to serve as a medium for emotional expression; therefore there was little opportunity for the development of a female Bach or Hayden" (p. 99).

7.1246

Morris, William Meredith, **BRITISH VIOLIN MAKERS; A BIOGRAPHICAL DICTIONARY OF BRITISH MAKERS OF STRINGED INSTRUMENTS AND BOWS AND A CRITICAL DESCRIPTION OF THEIR WORK, WITH INTRODUCTORY CHAPTERS AND NUMEROUS PORTRAITS AND ILLUSTRA-TIONS.** 1904; 1920.

7.1247

ENGLISHWOMAN'S REVIEW: *"Report of the Annual Meeting of the Theatrical Ladies Guild,"* n.v. (1904) 48.

7.1248

OCCASIONAL PAPERS: Oct. 1904 to March 1905. Edited by T. Beechy Newman. Includes articles on pantomime history and technique.

7.1249

Tweedie, Ethel Brilliana (Harley), (Mrs. Alec Tweedie), **BEHIND THE FOOTLIGHTS.** New York, 1904. The author discusses, in journalistic style, what the London theatre was like, including her own short career. Tweedie asserts that women enter the acting profession because men fail to provide for them; **MY TABLE CLOTHS; A FEW REMINISCENCES BY MRS. ALEC TWEEDIE.** New York, 1917. "Stageland is naturally a woman's realm. The basic desire of the audience is to be pleased.... Hence Stageland is eminently woman's world. In it her natural qualities and abilities, exercised with care, lead to success" (p. 101). The author (d. 1940) also wrote prolifically of her travels in Mexico, Iceland, Sicily and America.

7.1250

Fyvie, John, **COMEDY QUEENS OF THE GEORGIAN ERA.** 1906. Consists of "biographical sketches of some of the most prominent comedy actresses of the Georgian period" (Preface). Includes Catherine Clive, Frances Abington, Charlotte Charke, and nine others.

7.1251

Wyndham, Henry Saxe, **THE ANNALS OF COVENT GARDEN THEATRE FROM 1732 TO 1897.** vols. 1 and 2, 1906. Discusses the careers of several Covent Garden Theatre singers including Mary Ann Coward (b. 1805). "She was endowed with a pure soprano voice of remarkable compass" (p. 39).

7.1252

Crosby, Fanny (afterwards Frances Jane Van Alstyne), **FANNY J. CROSBY. MEMORIES OF EIGHTY YEARS. HER OWN STORY OF HER LIFE AND HYMNS.** 1907. Includes portraits of this blind hymn-writer and songstress. ——*see also:* Crosby, Fanny, **BELLS AT EVENING...** 1897. Poems by Crosby, with a biographical sketch by Robert Lowry; Jackson, Samuel T., **FANNY CROSBY'S STORY OF NINETY-FOUR YEARS.** 1915; Hawthorn, John, **FANNY CROSBY, THE SIGHTLESS SONGSTRESS.** 1931; Casswell, John R., **FANNY CROSBY, THE SIGHTLESS SONGSTRESS.** 1939; Rees, Jean A., **SINGING THE STORY: FANNY CROSBY AND HER HYMNS.** 1958.

7.1253
Darbyshire, Alfred, **THE ART OF THE VICTORIAN STAGE: NOTES AND RECOLLECTIONS.** 1907.

7.1254
Terry, Ellen, **THE STORY OF MY LIFE.** New York, 1908. Dame Ellen Terry lived from 1848 to 1928. —*see also:* Hiatt, Charles, **ELLEN TERRY AND HER IMPERSONATIONS.** 1898. "The present volume pretends to be neither a personal biography nor an essay in criticism. Its sole aim is to give an accurate account of the theatrical career of Miss Ellen Terry" (p. v); Scott, Clement, **ELLEN TERRY.** New York, 1900. "She was a poem that lived and breathed, and suggested to us the girl heroines that we most adored in poetry and the fine arts generally" (pp. 17-18); Pemberton, Edgar T., **ELLEN TERRY AND HER SISTERS.** New York, 1902. Traces the acting careers of Ellen Terry and her sisters, Kate, Marion, and Minnie; St. John, Christopher, **ELLEN TERRY.** 1907; St. John, Christopher, **ELLEN TERRY AND BERNARD SHAW: A CORRESPONDENCE.** 1931; Craig, Edward Gordon, **ELLEN TERRY AND HER SECRET SELF.** New York, 1932. Reveals the actress' personal life; Woolf, Virginia, **THE MOMENT, AND OTHER ESSAYS.** New York, 1948. On Ellen Terry; LISTENER: *"Memories of Henry Irving and Ellen Terry,"* n.v. (1958) 645-646; Steen, Margaret, **A PRIDE OF TERRYS.** 1962; Manvell, Roger, **ELLEN TERRY.** 1968. Includes extracts from Ellen Terry's unpublished letters; Prideaux, Tom, **LOVE OR NOTHING: THE LIFE AND TIMES OF ELLEN TERRY.** New York, 1975. "A phenomenon in her own times, Ellen was also a portent of the future when movie stars and other popular entertainers would attract an immense following among all the classes.... In Ellen's time, at last, the actor's status was rising, a process wherein she figured both as a contributor and beneficiary" (pp. 2-3); Longford, Elizabeth, "Ellen Terry" in **EMINENT VICTORIAN WOMEN.** by Elizabeth Longford. New York, 1981.

7.1255
Galloway, William Johnson, **MUSICAL ENGLAND.** 1910. Women were trained in music first to be accomplished as ladies and later for employment.

7.1256
Calvert, Adelaide Helen, **SIXTY-EIGHT YEARS ON THE STAGE.** 1911. Calvert (1837-1921) reminisces on theatre in Manchester.

7.1257
Archer, Frank, **AN ACTOR'S NOTEBOOK.** 1912. An actor recounts his experiences on the London stage and the success of such actresses as Charolette Corday and Mary Andersen.

7.1258
THE CONFESSIONS OF A DANCING GIRL. BY HERSELF. 1913.

7.1259
Jerrold, Clare, **THE STORY OF DOROTHY JORDAN.** 1914.

7.1260
Morley, Edith J., "Acting as a Profession for Women" in **WOMEN WORKERS IN SEVEN PROFESSIONS**. by Edith J. Morley. 1914.

7.1261
Pearce, Charles E., **THE JOLLY DUCHESS. HARRIOT MELLON, AFTERWARDS MRS. COUTTS AND THE DUCHESS OF ST. ALBANS**. 1915. Fanny Kemble stated, "'As Miss Mellon she was one of my mother's stage contemporaries; a kindhearted, good-humoured, buxom, rather coarse actress, with good looks, and good spirits of a somewhat unrefined sort'" (p. 307). She is described as being unpopular with her own sex. The book is a valuable record of popular tastes and interest in actresses.

7.1262
CONTEMPORARY REVIEW: Cowen, J., *"Music Halls and Morals,"* 110 (1916) 611-620. "Love, as between the sexes, on the music-hall stage frequently becomes lust. The natural and proper trend of youth toward maidenhood, which has always and everywhere provided the poet and novelist with their most congenial theme, is readily transformed into the designing overtures of the seducer, here portrayed as a subject of banter and fun. Peaceful domesticity becomes the butt of cynical jest, and while harlotry is condoned, honest matrimony is represented as a thing full of pitfalls, delusions, troubles and tricks" (p. 615).

7.1263
Ladd, George Trumbull, "Why Women Cannot Compose Music" in **YALE REVIEW**. ed. by Wilbur L. Cross. New Haven, 1917. "In architecture, sculpture, and the pictorial arts, the inferiority of woman as tested by inability to reach the more exalted, if not supremely high creations of the imagination, is almost if not quite as conspicuous and indisputable as it is in the art of musical composition" (p. 795).

7.1264
MUSICAL OBSERVER: Moller, H., *"Can Women Compose?,"* 15 (1917) 9-12.

7.1265
Elson, Louis C., **WOMEN IN MUSIC**. New York, 1918. A background of women's influence in musical circles. Some attention to English women composers including Alice Mary Smith (1839-1884).

7.1266
Smyth, Ethel, **IMPRESSIONS THAT REMAINED**. 1919. Smyth was a prolific composer. In addition, she was a suffragette, and many of her compositions served this cause; **STREAKS OF LIFE**. 1924; **A THREE-LEGGED TOUR IN GREECE**. 1927; (with Lord Berners, Harold Nicolson, and others), **LITTLE INNOCENTS; CHILDHOOD REMINISCENCES**. 1932; **FEMALE PIPINGS IN EDEN**. 1934; **BEECHAM AND PHARAOH**. 1935; **AS TIME WENT ON**. 1936. "However repulsive snobbishness in its grosser manifestations may be, it is of its essence imaginativeness shot through with a strain of religiosity; the emotion of a race that is naturally reverent" (p. 52); **WHAT HAPPENED NEXT**. 1940; **IMPRESSIONS THAT REMAINED: MEMOIRS UP TO 1892**. introduction by Ernest Newman. New York, 1946; **MASS IN D: FOR SOLI, CHORUS, AND ORCHESTRA**. introduction by Jane A. Bernstein. New York, 1980. ——*see also:* **MUSIC AND LETTERS**: Dale, K., *"Dame Ethel Smyth,"* 25 (1944) 191-194; *"Ethel Smyth's Prentice Work,"* 30 (1949) 329-336; St. John, Christopher Marie, **ETHEL SMYTH: A BIOGRAPHY**. 1959. In 1924, George Bernard Shaw writes to Ethel Smyth: "You are totally and diametrically wrong in imagining that you have suffered from a prejudice against

feminine music. On the contrary you have been almost extinguished by the dread of masculine music. It was your music that cured me for ever of the old delusion that women could not do men's work in art and other things.... But for you I might not have been able to tackle St. Joan, who has floored every previous playwright. Your music is more masculine than Handel's" (p. 185); Isbrecht, Nancy, "An Examination of the Operatic Movement in which Ethel Smyth Composed and Its Effect upon Her Career," Ph.D. diss., Univ. of Southern California, 1980.

7.1267
Brower, Harriette Moore, **VOCAL MASTERY; TALKS WITH MASTER SINGERS AND TEACHERS, COMPRISING INTERVIEWS WITH CARUSO, FARRAR, MAUREL, LEHMANN, AND OTHERS**. New York, 1920.

7.1268
Campbell, Beatrice (Cornwallis-West), **MY LIFE AND SOME LETTERS**. [1920]. Describes her experiences as a fashionable Victorian actress. Her husband attempts to earn them both a living in South Africa and fails, but apparently is proud of his wife's success in theatre.

7.1269
Lehmann, Liza, **THE LIFE OF LIZA LEHMANN**. New York, 1920; 1980.

7.1270
MUSICAL STANDARD: Bond, C.J., *"Music Composition as a Field for Women,"* n.v. (1920) n.p.

7.1271
Allen, Percy, **THE STAGE LIFE OF MRS. STIRLING: WITH SOME SKETCHES OF THE NINETEENTH CENTURY THEATRE**. introduction by Frank R. Benson. New York, 1922. Mary Anne Stirling (1813-1895) had a long and successful stage career. In a letter of 1868 she writes: "I must begin to interest myself about others, and throw myself thoro'ly into my work, or leave it altogether. I waver as to which is best. I look back and see what a lost life mine has been! How if I'd thrown myself into my art as I ought to have done, how it would have repaid me in every way. There ought to be no family——no ties——to anything but a sort of priesthood of art" (p. 177).

7.1272
Ashwell, Lena, **MODERN TROUBADOURS**. 1922; **REFLECTIONS FROM SHAKESPEARE; A SERIES OF LECTURES**. ed. by Roger Pocock. 1926; **THE STAGE**. 1929; **MYSELF A PLAYER**. 1936. Ashwell (b. 1870) managed the Kingsway theater and was also a suffragist.

7.1273
Corder, Frederick, **A HISTORY OF THE ROYAL ACADEMY OF MUSIC, FROM 1822 TO 1922**. 1922. Lists women students.

7.1274
Moore, Eva, **EXITS AND ENTRANCES**. 1923.

7.1275
Wagnalls, Mabel, **OPERA AND ITS STARS; A DESCRIPTION OF THE MUSIC AND STORIES OF THE ENDURING OPERAS, AND A SERIES OF INTERVIEWS WITH THE WORLD'S FAMOUS SOPRANOS**. 1924.

7.1276
Bachmann, Alberto Abraham, **AN ENCYCLOPEDIA OF THE VIOLIN**. trans. by Frederick H. Martens. ed. by Albert E. Wier. introduction by Eugene Ysaye. 1925. Provides short-paragraph biographies on English violinists Sarah Fennings, Mary Harrison, and Emily Shinner.

7.1277
Calthrop, Dion Clayton, **MUSIC HALL NIGHTS**. 1925. "No nonsense about our Marie [Lloyd] I tell you straight.... She makes no pretence at character study but is just herself, her own plump, rollicking self.... She is the height of vulgarity with a great heart" (pp. 81-82).

7.1278
Langtry, Lillie, (Emily Charlotte DeBathe), (1859-1929), **THE DAYS I KNEW**. 1925. Born in Jersey, Langtry married twice and became a famous society beauty. She was presented at court after her first marriage through the sponsorship of the Marchioness of Conyngham. She became an actress to support herself and her daughter after her first husband became an alcoholic.

7.1279
Benson, Constance (Samwell), **MAINLY A PLAYER: BENSONIAN MEMORIES**. 1926. Autobiography. Benson (b. 1865) was both an actress and a manager of her own theatre.

7.1280
Hamilton, Cicely Mary and Baylis, Lilian, **THE OLD VIC**. 1926. On philanthropist Emma Cons, founder of the Vic.

7.1281
Russell, Charles Edward, **JULIA MARLOWE: HER LIFE AND ART**. 1926. A Shakespearean actress, English-born Marlowe (b. 1865; pseud. for Sarah Frances Frost) spent forty years on the stage, mostly in America.

7.1282
Walbrook, H.M., **A PLAYGOERS WANDERINGS**. 1926.

7.1283
Albanesi, Effie Adelaide Maria, **MEGGIE ALBANESI. BY HER MOTHER**. 1928. Traces the life and stage career of Meggie Albanesi (1899-1923). "She had a various and unique faculty of emotional truth. I never saw her (and I watched her through some sixty rehearsals) fumble, blur or falsify an emotional effect" (p. 8).

7.1284
Newton, Henry Chance, **IDOLS OF THE MUSIC "HALLS," BEING MY MUSIC HALL MEMORIES**. 1928.

7.1285
Terriss, Ellaline, **ELLALINE TERRISS, BY HERSELF AND WITH OTHERS**. 1928. Actress Terriss (1871-1971) reminisces on her life; **JUST A LITTLE BIT OF SPRING**. 1955.

7.1286
Collier, Constance, **HARLEQUINADE: THE STORY OF MY LIFE**. preface by Noel Coward. [1929].

7.1287
Lewis, Benjamin, **MORE STAGE FAVOURITES OF THE 18TH CENTURY.** 1929.
Includes Sarah Siddons, Fanny Kemble, Dorothy Jordan and Mary J. Robinson.

7.1288
Thorndike, Russell, **SYBIL THORNDIKE.** 1929.

7.1289
Bond, Jessie and MacGeorge, Ethel, **THE LIFE AND REMINISCENCES OF JESSIE BOND: THE OLD SAVOYARD.** 1930. "For twenty years without a break I played in Gilbert and Sullivan's delightful operas——longer than any of my fellow artists——and now I sit down to write about it all, the only woman of our company who has attempted the task" (p. 16). Bond's stage career flourished from 1878 to 1897.

7.1290
Elson, Arthur and Truette, Everett E., **WOMAN'S WORK IN MUSIC; BEING AN ACCOUNT OF HER INFLUENCE ON THE ART, IN ANCIENT AS WELL AS IN MODERN TIMES; A SUMMARY OF HER MUSICAL COMPOSITIONS IN THE DIFFERENT COUNTRIES OF THE CIVILIZED WORLD; AND AN ESTIMATE OF THEIR RANK IN COMPARISON WITH THOSE OF MEN.** Boston, 1931. See especially: "England" by Arthur Elson, which discusses the contributions of Marie Parke, Mary Linwood, Elizabeth Anne Bisset, Hannah Binfield, Ellen Dickson, Mrs. Buckley, Marian Millar, and others.

7.1291
Alltree, George W., **FOOTLIGHT MEMORIES; RECOLLECTIONS OF MUSIC HALL AND STAGE LIFE.** 1932.

7.1292
McCarthy, Lillah, **MYSELF AND MY FRIENDS.** with an aside by Bernard Shaw. 1933. "The horrible artificiality of that impudent sham the Victorian womanly woman, a sham manufactured by men for men, and duly provided by the same for the same with a bulbously overclothed 'modesty' more lascivious than any frank sensuality, had become more and more irksome to the best of the actresses who had to lend their bodies and souls to it.... I had so little taste for the Victorian womanly woman that in my first play I made my heroine throttle the chambermaid" (p. 8, Shaw). McCarthy was best known for her roles in Shaw plays. Her father supported her theatrical career.

7.1293
Waitzkin, Leo, **THE WITCH OF WYCH STREET. A STUDY OF THE THEATRICAL REFORMS OF MADAME VESTRIS.** Cambridge, 1933.

7.1294
Tilley, Vesta, **RECOLLECTIONS OF VESTA TILLEY.** 1934.

7.1295
Haddon, Archibald, **THE STORY OF THE MUSIC HALL. FROM CAVE OF HARMONY TO CABARET.** 1935. Discusses many women dancers, singers, and actors.

7.1296
Jacob, Naomi Ellington, **OUR MARIE: MARIE LLOYD. A BIOGRAPHY.** 1936; Bath, 1972. Presents the career and life of Marie Lloyd (Matilda Alice Victoria

Wood), a music hall performer.

7.1297
ETUDE: THE MUSIC MAGAZINE: Wurm, M., *"Women's Struggle for Recognition in Music,"* 54 (1936) 687, 746. The author, an English pianist, discusses some of the reasons women have had such difficulty coming to the forefront in music. In the renaissance, it was only cloistered nuns who sometimes had the opportunity to develop their art, although the composer Pasquino did teach several ladies, one of whom conducted the performances of a women's convent orchestra. Women's desire to play music has historically been interpreted as vanity. However, "in the nineteenth century women wrote symphonies, and chamber music of all kinds. Almost every type of composition was attempted—operas, operettas, oratorios" (p. 687). Wurm also mentions a dictionary of women composers she authored that includes their biographies and lists their works.

7.1298
Bodeen, De Witt, **LADIES OF THE FOOTLIGHTS.** Pasadena, 1937. Provides general biographical information on Lillie Langtry, Fanny Davenport, and Ellen Terry.

7.1299
Bolitho, Hector, **MARIE TEMPEST: HER BIOGRAPHY.** Philadelphia, 1937.

7.1300
Gill, Maud, **SEE THE PLAYERS.** foreword by Sir Cedric Hardwicke. 1938; 1948. "I am a comparatively unknown actress.... Although my public is, for the most part, in ignorance of my very existence, although it shows no interest in my hobbies, my complexion, or my opinion on current topics, it has enabled me to earn my living, in almost every type of theatrical entertainment, from my eighteenth birthday to the present time, and in spite of my obscurity I do not regret having entered the profession" (p. 13).

7.1301
Short, Ernest Henry and Richett, Arthur Compton, **RING UP THE CURTAIN.** 1938; rpt., 1970. See especially: "Enter the Gaiety Girls" and "The Ladies—God Bless 'Em! Jenny Hill to Gracie Fields"; **FIFTY YEARS OF VAUDEVILLE.** 1946. See especially: "The Girls of the Gaiety, 1893 to 1914. Coming of Musical Comedy" and "The Ladies of Vaudeville, From Vesta Tilley to Bea Lillie."

7.1302
Vanbrugh, Irene, "Irene Vanbrugh" in **MYSELF WHEN YOUNG. BY FAMOUS WOMEN OF TODAY.** ed. by Margot (Emma Alice Margaret) Asquith. 1938. Began her acting career at fifteen. Left her first employer at sixteen and received the following reaction from a potential employer: "He also managed to suggest to me that I was being ungrateful, but by this time I had gained a little more courage and did not feel so crestfallen" (p. 390).

7.1303
Foster, George, **THE SPICE OF LIFE: SIXTY-FIVE YEARS IN THE GLAMOUR WORLD.** 1939. Discusses many female personages of the music hall and theatre.

7.1304
Ormsbee, Helen, **BACKSTAGE WITH ACTORS.** New York, 1939; rpt., 1969. In the discussion of Ellen Terry, Ormsbee writes that "sympathy was so strong in [her]... that she cried too easily on the stage; she had to learn to hold back her emotion. If

this readiness of response made acting easy for her, it complicated her life" (p. 182).

7.1305
MUSIC EDUCATION LIBRARY: Seahore, C.E., *"Why No Great Women Composers?,"* 26 (1939) 21-88.

7.1306
Robins, Elizabeth, BOTH SIDES OF THE CURTAIN. 1940. ——*see also:* Bell, Florence Eveleen Eleanore (Cliffe), LANDMARKS. 1929. See pp. 107-113 on Robins; LISTENER: Thorndike, S., *"Elizabeth Robins as I Knew Her,"* n.v. (1952) 108-109.

7.1307
Disher, Maurice Willson, FAIRS, CIRCUSES AND MUSIC HALLS. 1942. A chronological history; PLEASURES OF LONDON. 1950. Discusses the theatre scene in London. Includes the histories of various London theatres; VICTORIAN SONG. FROM DIVE TO DRAWING ROOM. 1955. Presents an extensive history of nineteenth century music.

7.1308
Siddons, Sarah Kemble, THE REMINISCENCES OF SARAH KEMBLE SIDDONS. ed. with a foreword by William Van Lennep. 1942. ——*see also:* Boaden, James, MEMOIRS OF MRS. SIDDONS INTERSPERSED WITH ANECDOTES OF AUTHORS AND ACTORS. 1827; MONTHLY MAGAZINE: *"Mrs. Siddons,"* n.v. (1831) 337-339; Campbell, Thomas, LIFE OF MRS. SIDDONS. 1834; Kennard, N.H., MRS. SIDDONS. 1887; Parsons, Mrs. Clement, THE INCOMPARABLE SIDDONS. 1909. A chronological retrospective of her life and work; Jenkin, Fleeming, MRS. SIDDONS AS LADY MACBETH AND AS QUEEN KATHERINE. New York, 1915; Smith, Naomi Royde, PORTRAIT OF MRS. SIDDONS. New York, 1933. Discusses the acting career and private life of Siddons; French, Yvonne, MRS. SIDDONS: TRAGIC ACTRESS. 1936; LISTENER: Macqueen-Pope, W., *"Queen of the Tragic Theatre,"* n.v. (1955) 68-69.

7.1309
DICKENSIAN: Staples, L.C., *"Fanny Kelly,"* 38 (1942) 153-58. Discusses her life and emphasizes her friendship with Dickens.

7.1310
Nicoll, Allardyce, A HISTORY OF LATE NINETEENTH CENTURY DRAMA 1850-1900. Cambridge, 1946.

7.1311
Scott, Harold, THE EARLY DOORS. ORIGINS OF THE MUSIC HALL. 1946. "Another popular specialization was that of the female duettists, usually presented under the title of "sisters." The practice owed much to the vogue created by genuine instances of relationship, such as the Vohe and the Vaughan families. A host of these sprang up from the seventies onwards, the most memorable of whom were perhaps the Bilton sisters" (p. 195).

7.1312
Macqueen-Pope, Walter J., CARRIAGES AT ELEVEN. THE STORY OF EDWARDIAN THEATRE. 1947. See especially: "The Gaiety and the Girls" which discusses female performers in musical comedy; THE MELODIES LINGER ON; THE STORY OF MUSIC HALL. 1950. Includes profiles of Bessie Bellwood, who died in 1896 at the age of 36; male impersonator Vesta Tilley, whose last

performance was in 1920; Ella Shields, and others; **LADIES FIRST; THE STORY OF WOMEN'S CONQUEST OF THE BRITISH STAGE.** 1952; **SHIRTFRONTS AND SABLES, ETC.** 1953. On the theatre during the Victorian and Edwardian eras; **NIGHTS OF GLADNESS.** 1956. See especially: "The Lady Who Led the Way" which discusses the contributions of Madame Vestris, the first woman theatre owner in London, and her role in the development of musical comedy theatre. In November of 1832, Vestris introduced the box set to the Western stage for the first time. This innovation enhanced and coincided with the development of realism in the plays of dramatists such as Ibsen and Checkov; **QUEEN OF THE MUSIC HALLS: BEING THE DRAMATIZED STORY OF MARIE LLOYD.** 1957. Pope dates the beginning of Music Hall at 1854. The entertainment was directed to an audience of workingmen who ate and drank during the performances. Lloyd came from a working-class family and desired from childhood to work in the music halls in her province. She started at the age of fifteen in 1885 and quickly became a sensation; **THE CURTAIN RISES.** Edinburgh, 1961. A chapter on Victorian and Edwardian pantomime reveals the contribution of Mrs. Sarah Lane who continued to play "principal boys when she was nearing seventy years of age" (p. 131).

7.1313

Scholes, Percy A., **THE MIRROR OF MUSIC, 1844-1944.** vols. 1 and 2, 1947. Presents an excellent overview of the musical scene between 1844 and 1944. See especially: "The Procession of British Composers" for writings on Ethel Smyth and Elizabeth Maconchy. In addition, the chapter, "The Woman Chorister Agitation of the 1890's," is of interest.

7.1314

Drinker, Sophie Lewis (Hutchinson), **MUSIC AND WOMEN. THE STORY OF WOMEN IN THEIR RELATION TO MUSIC.** New York, 1948; Washington, 1977. Examines the role of women in music throughout history. "Persons of discernment never fail to realize that the women composers of the eighteenth, nineteenth, and twentieth centuries possess talent, sometimes to a marked degree.... Not being in the class or group from which music was expected, the women of our era had neither the emotional nor the intellectual foundation to enable them to assert freely their own conception of music" (p. 278).

7.1315

Craig, Edith, **EDY. RECOLLECTIONS OF EDITH CRAIG.** ed. by Eleanor Adlard. 1949. Biographical note by Christopher St. John. Edith Craig (1869-1947), the daughter of Ellen Terry, became a celebrated actress in her own right.

7.1316

Francis, Basil, **FANNY KELLY OF DRURY LANE.** 1950. London actress Frances Maria Kelly (1790-1882) "was one of the most popular actresses of her time and, in her own way, made an important contribution to theatrical art. When Tree founded the Royal Academy of the Dramatic Arts in 1904, he completed an edifice whose stout foundations were laid by such as Miss Kelly in her dramatic school seventy years previously" (p. viii).

7.1317

Aspinall, A., ed., **MRS. JORDAN AND HER FAMILY: THE UNPUBLISHED CORRESPONDENCE OF MRS. JORDAN AND THE DUKE OF CLARENCE, LATE WILLIAM IV.** 1951. Early Victorian actress Mrs. Jordan (Dorothy Bland) discusses her career through these correspondences.

7.1318
Hudson, Lynton, **THE ENGLISH STAGE 1850-1950**. 1951. "It was women who assured the success of 'Richard of Bordeaux,' of 'The Constant Nymph' and 'Escape Me Never,' of 'Autumn Crocus' and 'Quiet Wedding.' These were all written by women playwrights" (p. 197).

7.1319
White, Eric Walter, **THE RISE OF THE ENGLISH OPERA**. 1951. See especially: "The Foundations are Laid." "The modern career of the Old Vic dates back to 1880, when Miss Emma Cons obtained a lease of the Victoria Theatre (as it was then called) and reopened it as the Royal Victoria Coffee Music Hall. Her prime interest was that of social reformer fighting by every means to counteract the temptation of the poor to indulge in strong drink: and on her committee of philanthropists music was represented by Benedict, Carl Rosa and Sullivan" (p. 157).

7.1320
Pogson, Rex, **MISS HORNIMAN AND THE GAIETY THEATRE, MANCHESTER.** foreword by St. John Ervine. 1952. Annie Horniman, born in London in 1860, became involved in the Irish Theatre movement. "In my soul," she afterwards wrote, "I felt I was doing something in Ireland that had to be done by an outsider, by someone with no axe of her own to grind, something far wider than any artistic effort" (p. 11). Horniman bought the Abbey Theatre and allowed the Irish Players free use of it. Ervine remarks that Horniman was a rebellious woman, particularly in regards to restrictions on women in society; (and Hodgkinson, J.L.), **THE EARLY MANCHESTER THEATRE**. 1960.

7.1321
Pulling, Christopher, **THEY WERE SINGING; AND WHAT THEY SANG ABOUT**. 1952. "Mrs. Chant was Mrs. Ormiston Chant, who made herself prominent in the nineties by her campaign to get the Empire promenade closed. She and her associates gained the nickname 'Prudes on Patrol'" (p. 116).

7.1322
Shaw, George Bernard, **BERNARD SHAW AND MRS. PATRICK CAMPBELL, THEIR CORRESPONDENCE**. ed. by Alan Dent. 1952. Mrs. Campbell, a famous Victorian actress, corresponded with Shaw.

7.1323
Courtneidge, Cicely, **CICELY**. 1953. In her autobiography, late Victorian music hall performer Cicely Courtneidge recalls her first male impersonation: "I was in uniform. A man's uniform. I had never done a male impersonation before, but I swaggered and sang, and burlesqued.... The audience loved it.... And I knew then that I had found my place in the Theatre" (p. 72).

7.1324
MONTHLY MUSICAL RECORD: Godman, S., *"Bach's Music in England,"* 83 (1953) 37. Elizabeth Stirling gained recognition as one of the best Bach organists of her period. She gave her first Bach recital at the age of 18 at St. Katharine's in 1837.

7.1325
Loesser, Arthur, **MEN, WOMEN, AND PIANOS: A SOCIAL HISTORY**. New York, 1954. Discusses the role of women in music in the salons of the late 18th and 19th centuries.

7.1326
Reeve, Ada, **TAKE IT FOR A FACT**. 1954. Reeve (1874-1966) was a Jewish actress whose career spanned 75 years, beginning when she was five years old. Her real name was Adelaide Mary Issacs.

7.1327
Trewin, J.C., **SYBIL THORNDIKE**. 1955. Presents a study of Thorndike's work for stage and screen.

7.1328
Guest, Ivor, **VICTORIAN BALLET-GIRL AND THE TRAGIC STORY OF CLARA WEBSTER**. 1957.

7.1329
Mitchell, Yvonne, **ACTRESS**. 1957.

7.1330
Laye, Evelyn, **BOO, TO MY FRIENDS**. 1958. Late Victorian actress Laye reminisces on her career on the London stage.

7.1331
THEATRE ARTS: Beaton, C., *"A Portrait of Mrs. Pat (Mrs. Patrick Campbell),"* July (1961) 64-65; 78-80.

7.1332
MUSICAL TIMES: Henderson, R., *"Elisabeth Lutyens,"* n.v. (1963) 551-555. "What strikes one immediately on hearing a new work by Elisabeth Lutyens for the first time is the extraordinary 'rightness' of the sound as sound. Everything is in its precisely ordered place, fulfilling its own natural function, a function clearly defined by an alert, acutely sensitive ear. Such an assured, subtly balanced aural imagination must be based on a thorough knowledge of instrumental technique; what instruments can or cannot do, how they can be employed most effectively to reveal not only their own distinctive colour and character, but also the intention of the composer in any given situation" (p. 551).

7.1333
Mackerness, Eric David, **A SOCIAL HISTORY OF ENGLISH MUSIC**. 1964. "Miss Maria Hackett, the noted advocate of the rights of choristers, complained bitterly about the nonchalance with which organist and choirmasters employed the choir boys to sing at soirees and concerts" (p. 192).

7.1334
Rose, Clarkson, **RED PLUSH AND GREASEPAINT. A MEMORY OF THE MUSIC-HALL AND LIFE AND TIMES FROM THE NINETIES TO THE SIXTIES.** foreword by John Betjeman. introduction by Val Parnell. 1964. Discusses the development of the music halls in England. "The woman who became a star had to be exceptionally accomplished and able to stand up to the many varied and excellent male performers in the program" (p. 21).

7.1335
Mander, Raymond and Murchenson, Joe, **BRITISH MUSIC HALLS**. 1965. Comprised mainly of photographs with short captions, this book presents a good pictorial history of the music hall and its celebrities, many of them women; **LOST THEATRES OF LONDON**. 1968; 1976; **VICTORIAN AND EDWARDIAN ENTERTAINMENT FROM OLD PHOTOGRAPHS**. 1978.

7.1336
Tisdall, E.E.P., **MRS. 'PIMPERNEL' ATKYNS: THE STRANGE STORY OF A DRURY LANE ACTRESS WHO WAS THE ONLY HEROINE OF THE FRENCH REVOLUTION**. 1965. On Charlotte (Walpole) Atkyns, who became resident at the court of Versailles in 1785, and her subsequent involvement in the French Revolution.

7.1337
Wagenknect, Edward, **SEVEN DAUGHTERS OF THE THEATER**. Norman, 1965. Contains a short didactic piece on Ellen Terry.

7.1338
Mellor, Geoffrey James, **POM-POMS AND RUFFLES; THE STORY OF NORTHERN SEASIDE ENTERTAINMENT**. 1966; **THE NORTHERN MUSIC HALL: A CENTURY OF POPULAR ENTERTAINMENT**. foreword by George Wood. introduction by Ken Dodd. Newcastle upon Tyne, 1970. See especially: "Gracie and Charlie," on music hall star Gracie Stansfield, born in England in 1898. She became known as the "Queen of Song" and appeared in many early films.

7.1339
Pleasants, Henry, **THE GREAT SINGERS FROM THE DAWN OF OPERA TO OUR OWN TIME**. New York, 1966; 1981. "The singular girlish sweetness and purity that characterized the voices of the great nineteenth-century coloratura sopranos may be attributable to the fact that so many of them started so young.... Throughout the nineteenth century they insured a delirium of enthusiasm never accorded any other type of singer.... Called nightingales by their worshipers, and warblers by more moderate admirers, they had beautiful voices that were lighter, more girlish, more virginal—even childlike—than the type of voice fashionable among sopranos today and a special communicative quality suggesting a kind of sublimated and eternally youthful femininity" (p. 190).

7.1340
Gilbert, W.S., **GILBERT BEFORE SULLIVAN. SIX COMIC PLAYS**. ed. with an introduction by Jane W. Stedman. Chicago, 1967.

7.1341
Shiotz, Aksel, **THE SINGER AND HIS ART**. New York, 1969; 1970.

7.1342
Howard, Diana, **LONDON THEATRES AND MUSIC HALLS**. 1970.

7.1343
Gammond, Peter, **YOUR OWN, YOUR VERY OWN: A MUSIC HALL SCRAP-BOOK**. 1971.

7.1344
Farson, Daniel, **MARIE LLOYD AND MUSIC HALL**. 1972.

7.1345
HIGH FIDELITY/MUSICAL AMERICA: Roger, J. and Robson, G.R., *"Why Haven't Women Become Great Composers?,"* 23 (1973) 46-52. Discusses and evaluates the musical talents of Ethel Smyth and other well-known composers. "Of all the women who study music, even at length, many will go into other activities and use it little or not at all. Of the more devoted, most will choose marriage and motherhood....

Despite this, should an eminent female composer some day appear on the scene, a composite portrait will show her naturally possessed of marked musical talent, aptitudes for abstract and quantitative thinking, tenacity in the face of deep discouragement, patience in developing skills until the talent flows free and masterpieces have time to evolve, a conviction that composition is the primary purpose of her existence" (p. 50).

7.1346
Appleton, William W., **MADAME VESTRIS AND THE LONDON STAGE**. 1974.

7.1347
Cheshire, D.F., **MUSIC HALL IN BRITAIN**. Newton Abbot, 1974. Chronicles the history of the music hall in England. A biographical sketch of performer Marie Lloyd is also presented. "For she above all others is seen as the epitome of the real spirit of British music hall of the pre-1914 period. As far as her posthumous reputation is concerned, she had the good fortune to be the subject of a famous essay by T.S. Eliot, in itself an important landmark in the intellectual consideration of popular entertainment from a sociological and political angle" (p. 73).

7.1348
Johns, Eric, **DAMES OF THE THEATRE**. 1974. "The title [Dame] chosen to bestow upon ladies who had rendered valuable service to the state... applies essentially to distinguished actresses remarkable for their discipline, dedication, and domination" (Introduction). Discusses May Whitty, Sybil Thorndike, Peggy Asbendt, Flora Robson, etc.

7.1349
Mander, Raymond, **BRITISH MUSIC HALL**. 1974; 1975. A comprehensive guide to the development of the British Music Hall. Discusses several English women performers including Jenny Hill, Marie Lloyd, and Harriet Vernon. Biographical and career information is provided on these women performers including photographs.

7.1350
Findlater, Richard, **LILIAN BAYLIS: THE LADY OF THE OLD VIC**. 1975. Baylis (1874-1937) managed the Vic and turned it into a famous theatre during WWI. "She was concerned with good works in the service of God and people rather than good theatre in the service of art" (p. 21); **THE PLAYER QUEENS**. 1976. "This book is about some of the most remarkable of those women who have led the legitimate stage in Britain since 1660, when the first professional actresses appeared in London" (p. 4).

7.1351
Hixon, Donald L., **WOMEN IN MUSIC: A BIBLIOGRAPHY** Metuchen, N.J., 1975. Serves as an index to the biographies of women musicians from all countries and periods. It's primarily a "brief identification type of biographical dictionary." Classical women musicians are the focus; popular musicians and performers are omitted. Includes the following English women composers and performers: Sophie Dulken, Gladys Davenport Goertz, Clara Davies, Edith Kate Clegg, Beatrice Harraden, Evelyn Howard-Jones, Henrietta Midgley, and many others.

7.1352
Johnson, Josephine, **FLORENCE FARR: BERNARD SHAW'S 'NEW WOMAN.'** 1975. Critical biography of a Victorian actress who performed in many of Shaw's plays.

7.1353
Speaight, George, **BAWDY SONGS OF THE EARLY MUSIC HALL.** selected and with introduction by George Speaight. Newton Abbot, 1975.

7.1354
Neuls-Bates, Carol, **THE STATUS OF WOMEN IN COLLEGE MUSIC: PRELIMINARY STUDIES.** 1976. Includes an annotated bibliography on women musicians and composers. Also lists women composers who performed at the Philharmonic Society of New York from 1842 to 1971; (as editor), **WOMEN IN MUSIC: AN ANTHOLOGY OF SOURCE READINGS FROM THE MIDDLE AGES TO THE PRESENT.** New York, 1982.

7.1355
FEMINIST ART JOURNAL: Neuls-Bates, C., *"Five Women Composers, 1587-1875,"* 5 (1976) n.p.

7.1356
Kent, Christopher, "Image and Reality: The Actress and Society" in **A WIDENING SPHERE: CHANGING ROLES OF VICTORIAN WOMEN.** ed. by Martha Vicinus. 1977; 1980. "To Victorians the profession of actress, like that of governess, had a symbolic importance as an occupation for women.... It offered striking opportunities for independence, fame and fortune... for those outside it the stage incarnated fantasies, providing vicarious release in the notion that here was an area of special dispensation from the normal categories, moral and social, that defined woman's place" (p. 94).

7.1357
Morley, Sheridan, **SYBIL THORNDIKE. A LIFE IN THE THEATRE.** 1977. "'Acting,' said John Casson, 'was for my mother a sort of evangelical banner under which to unite the rich, the poor, the educated, the ignorant, the long, the short and the tall'.... When she was not on stage, Thorndike was at political rallies, Indian independence conferences, suffragette meetings and pacifist demonstrations the world over" (pp. 14-15).

7.1358
Pool, Jeannie G., **WOMEN IN MUSIC HISTORY: A RESEARCH GUIDE.** New York, 1977. Pool emphasizes the need for more research into the contributions of women in music. Her bibliography includes general books and articles, articles on individual women musicians, approaches to women's music history, and lists of women composers. In this pamphlet, Pool has compiled a valuable list of international women composers before the 1900s and their country of origin and genre of composition. This list includes the following Enlgish women composers: Emma Barnett, Olivia Dussek Buckley, Edith Chamberlayne, Hannah R. Binfield, Alice Barton, Ethel Barns, Rosalind Frances Ellicott, Amina Beatrice Goodwin, Louisa Gray (Mrs. Abingdon Compton), Jeanne M. Guest, Caroline (Reinagle) Orger, Elizabeth Mounsey, and many others.

7.1359
NINETEENTH CENTURY THEATRE RESEARCH: Kent, C., *"Helen Taylor's 'Experimental Life' on the Stage: 1856-58,"* 5 (1977) 45-54. The daughter of Harriet Taylor Mill and stepdaughter of John Stuart Mill aspired to be an "intellectual actress" because of a desire for personal independence. "No career more strikingly embodied the idea of independence than that of an actress" (p. 45); Carlisle, C.J., *"The Other Miss Faucit,"* 6 (1978) 71-88. Provides a biographical sketch and

delineates the stage appearances of Harriet Faucit, the sister of the more famous Helen Faucit. "Although she never knew the hand-to-mouth existence of a stroller, never acted in makeshift productions at one of the poorer provincial houses, she was involved... in almost every other kind of theatrical experience" (p. 86).

7.1360
SIGNS: Kagan, S., *"Camilla Urso: A Nineteenth Century Violinist's View,"* 2 (1977) 727-734. Camilla Urso (1842-1902) was one of the great violin virtuosi of the nineteenth century. She became outspoken in her defense of the rights of women musicians. "In a letter to a leading music journal referring to a concert she had attended given by the Women's String Orchestra, she stated, 'I spent two hours in perfect enjoyment, listening to the rendition of a well chosen program, reflecting credit on Mr. Lachmund and the thirty-five pretty girls under his conductorship. The excellent shading and time, skillful technique, perfect intonation and graceful style of this organization goes far to confirm my demands of years ago for women's admission as violinists to theatrical and other orchestras as a means of livelihood and on an equal footing with men. Let my sisters agitate this question and assert their rights" (p. 731).

7.1361
Camner, James, ed., **THE GREAT OPERA STARS IN HISTORIC PHOTO-GRAPHS: 343 PORTRAITS FROM THE 1850'S TO THE 1940'S.** New York, 1978. Includes photographs of the following English women opera stars: Euphrosyne Parepa-Rosa (1836-1874), Dame Eva Turner (b. 1892), Dame Maggie Teyte (Margaret Tate, 1889-1976), Florence Easton (1884-1955), and Louise Kirkby-Lunn (1873-1930).

7.1362
Crow, Duncan, "The Countess of Gaiety" in **THE EDWARDIAN WOMAN.** by Duncan Crow. 1978. Discusses actresses and dancers.

7.1363
Laurence, Anya, **WOMEN OF NOTES: 1,000 WOMEN COMPOSERS BORN BEFORE 1900.** New York, 1978. This excellent biographical bibliography provides interesting facts about the lives of women composers which exceeds a brief identification. The composers' biographies are arranged alphabetically under their country of origin. Many Victorian English women are listed including Llewella Davies, Teresa Del Riego, Rosalind Frances Ellicott, Emma Mundella, and Maud Valerie White.

7.1364
Stern, Susan, **WOMEN COMPOSERS: A HANDBOOK.** New Jersey, 1978. This handbook includes a list of sources, the names of women composers arranged alphabetically and the types of music they composed. Includes the following English women: Katherine Emily Eggar, Dorothy Howell, Adelaide Kemble, Marie Moody, Marian Millar, and hundreds of others.

7.1365
Wearing, J.P., **AMERICAN AND BRITISH THEATRICAL BIOGRAPHY: A DIRECTORY.** 1979. Encompasses opera, music, circus and music-hall in addition to traditional theater.

7.1366
AMERICAN ORGANIST: Hettrick, J.S., *"She Drew an Angel Down: the Role of Women in the History of the Organ, 300 B.C. to 1900 A.D.,"* 13 (1979) 39-45.

Discusses the following Victorian English organists: Olivia Dussek, organist of the Temple Church in London, Elizabeth Mounsey, Anne Mounsey, and Elizabeth Stirling. "The distinguished careers of people like Elizabeth Stirling and the Mounsey sisters indicate that by the middle-nineteenth century the musical world and professional organ circles in England had accepted to a certain extent the prescence of women organists" (p. 45).

7.1367
THEATRE SURVEY: *"Marie Wilton [Lady Bancroft] As an Actress,"* 20 (1979) 43-74.

7.1368
Bingham, Madeline, **EARLS AND GIRLS: DRAMAS ON HIGH SOCIETY**. 1980. Discusses actresses and upward mobility into the peerage class.

7.1369
Forbes, Bryan, **THE DESPICABLE RACE: A HISTORY OF THE BRITISH ACTING TRADITION**. 1980. A popular historical account of acting. See especially: "To Drury Lane... And the Ladies."

7.1370
Gielgud, Kate Terry, **A VICTORIAN PLAYGOER**. with forewords by John Gielgud, Val Gielgud, and Eleanor Gielgud. ed. by Muriel St. Clare Byrne. 1980. Critiques the performances of Janet Achurch, Lena Ashwell, Dorthea Baird, Marion, Kate and Ellen Terry, Elizabeth Robins, Peggy Ashcroft, and Lilian Braithwaite.

7.1371
Kennedy, Michael, **THE CONCISE OXFORD DICTIONARY OF MUSIC**. 3rd. ed., 1980. Based on the original publication by Percy Sholes. Provides entries of musicians and performers which include their date and place of birth and death, field of musical specialization, education, and a brief chronology of their career. Note the following English women: Marie Brema, Dora Bright, and Marie Gossens.

7.1372
Royal, Samuel J., **SISTERS OF SACRED SONG: A SELECTED LISTING OF WOMEN HYMNODISTS IN GREAT BRITAIN AND AMERICA**. New York, 1980. Arranges entries on English women by author's last name, dates of birth and death, country of origin, denominational identity and hymnal titles with dates. Includes the following English women: Eva Barnard, Amy Baker, Frances Power Cobbe, Dorothy Greenwell, Sarah Geraldine Stock, Charlotte Saint Streatfield, and several others.

7.1373
Holledge, Julie, **INNOCENT FLOWERS. WOMEN IN THE EDWARDIAN THEATRE**. 1981. "The actress's position in any society that is dominated by men is an ambiguous one. She is successful in so far as she can recreate male images of women. Yet she may be rewarded for this knack of pleasing with the freedom to reject and challenge these very fantasies. Her private life will be exposed in newspapers and magazines to shock and thrill her audience and her political views will be published, even if they attempt to subvert the society she serves. In the late nineteenth and early twentieth centuries a group of actresses used this political and sexual influence to further the cause of women's emancipation" (introduction).

7.1374
Meggett, Joan M., **KEYBOARD MUSIC BY WOMEN COMPOSERS: A CATALOG**

AND BIBLIOGRAPHY. foreword by Nancy Fierro. Westport, 1981. Catalogs the works of 290 women composers for the keyboard. This catalog includes the following data for each composer: biographical information such as the composers full name, date and place of birth and death, field of composition, principal teachers, locations of their music (all the titles of their keyboard music which can be obtained are listed), available writings by the composer, and a bibliography emphasizing the books and articles of the individuals. The following English women are listed: Dora Bright, Hannah Binfield, Olivia Dussek, Florence May, Ann Mounsey, Elizabeth Mounsey, Caroline Reinagle, Ethel Smyth, Elizabeth Sterling, Kate Westrop, and Mary J.A. Wurm.

7.1375
Robertson, W. Graham, **TIME WAS. THE REMINISCENCES OF W. GRAHAM ROBERTSON.** with a foreword by Sir John Gielgud. 1981. See especially: "Actresses, Aunts and the Steam Hammer," "Of Ellen Terry," and "Of Nellie Farren."

7.1376
Senelick, Laurence, Cheshire, David, and Schneider, Urlich, **BRITISH MUSIC-HALL 1840-1923: A BIBLIOGRAPHY AND GUIDE TO SOURCES WITH A SUPPLEMENT ON EUROPEAN MUSIC HALL.** Hamden, 1981. Presents bibliographic references to entries on specific British music halls and regions, municipal licensing and parliamentary legislation. English individual towns, and music hall performers. Several English women are listed under performers. They include Maud Allen, Kate Carney, Maggie Dugan, Marie Lloyd, Marie Loftus, Ada Reeve and many more.

7.1377
Raby, Peter, **FAIR OPHELIA: A LIFE OF HARRIET SMITHSON BERLIOZ.** Cambridge, 1982. Smithson acted from 1821. Biographical account of her career and marriage to Hector Berlioz.

7.1378
Rasponi, Lanfranco, **THE LAST PRIMA DONNAS.** New York, 1982. Includes a chapter on singer Dame Eva Turner, who was born in England in 1892. Her first appearance in the London Opera was in 1917. She also sang in Germany and Italy.

7.1379
Johnson, Claudia D. and Johnson, Vernon E., compilers, **NINETEENTH CENTURY THEATRICAL MEMOIRS.** 1982. Annotated bibliography of autobiographical works. Also contains a useful bibliography of reference materials—dictionaries, indexes and histories of theater genres and stage performers.

7.1380
Mullin, Donald, ed., **VICTORIAN ACTORS AND ACTRESSES IN REVIEW: A DICTIONARY OF CONTEMPORARY VIEWS OF REPRESENTATIVE BRITISH AND AMERICAN ACTORS AND ACTRESSES 1837-1901.** Westport, Conn., 1983. Lists the names, dates, and selected reviews of various English actresses including Ada Cavendish, Mrs. Patrick Campbell, Lena Ashwell, and Rose Leclercq.

7.1381
Claghorn, Gene, **WOMEN COMPOSERS AND HYMNISTS: A CONCISE BIO-GRAPHICAL DICTIONARY.** 1984.

7.1382
Peters, Margot, **MRS. PAT, THE LIFE OF MRS. PATRICK CAMPBELL.** New

York, 1984. A success at the age of twenty-eight in the hit "The Second Mrs. Tanqueray."

7.1383
WORKING PAPERS ON WOMEN IN MUSIC: THE JOURNAL OF THE INTERNATIONAL CONGRESS OF WOMEN IN MUSIC: June 1985; no. 1. Published by the International Congress of Women in Music. An excellent source for those interested in approaches to research and methodology on women in music, in which specialists in musicology publish their recent findings, bibliographies and outlines of work to be completed in the field.

7.1384
Pennybacker, Susan, "'It Was Not What She Said, But the Way in Which She Said It': The London County Council and the Music Halls" in **VICTORIAN MUSIC HALL: THE BUSINESS OF PLEASURE.** ed. by Peter Bailey. 1986.

VIII. PHILANTHROPY, SOCIAL SERVICE, AND SOCIAL REFORM

INTRODUCTION

So great have been the changes and conditions in the life and work of the people of England during the last seventy years, that the new forms and channels almost seem to justify the common impression that care for the poor and suffering springs from new impulses of the present century. But the idea cannot be held with justice to those who have gone before us.... [They are] but the continuation and development of a benevolence that deserves to be called historical (p. xiv).... It is easy to trace the origin of many a great work of charity in the ordinary domestic habitude of the eighteenth century manor-house.... These houses filled many of the charitable duties which are often as not called [City] Missions in our own day. Standing in the midst of properties which in pre-railway times were more often like distinct settlements, moved by a conscious sense of responsibility... they formed centers of thought and consideration for all within a certain area about them.... The ladies who presided over these homes lived under the influence of traditional duties (p. xv).

Thus wrote Angela Burdett-Coutts, Victorian England's most well-known, most prolific philanthropist, raised to the peerage by the Queen in 1871 in recognition of her contributions of social service and reform. She set a historical context for her book on the philanthropic work of Victorian women, employing the theme of continuity in the midst of change. This sets her own active career, and that of each contributor, into the mold of English tradition, while conveying the dynamic character of their endeavors. It also implies their consistent application of a traditional social philosophy founded in social responsibility.

8.1
Burdett-Coutts, Angela Georgina (Baroness), "Preface" in WOMAN'S MISSION: A SERIES OF CONGRESS PAPERS ON THE PHILANTHROPIC WORK OF WOMEN BY EMINENT WRITERS. arranged and edited with preface and notes by Baroness Burdett-Coutts. 1893.

By selecting the title, WOMAN'S MISSION, Burdett-Coutts illustrated the longevity of the idea that femininity is synonymous with charity. Scripture may have provided her with primary sources, but so did the social teachings of the English Church. At least from the eighteenth century, they idealized local districts as communities in which a hierarchical order of classes accepted a prescribed set of personal responsibilities and duties largely identified in terms of sex roles. For women, domestic and social responsibilities were closely related in the definition of moral duty and in the anatomy of philanthropic commitment. In identifying with long-standing Church ideals, and in applying a cautious evangelical enthusiasm to her philanthropic work from the 1840s, Burdett-Coutts was not unique among charitable Victorians. For a fine discussion of the community ideal and its social application, see:

8.2
Clark, George Kitson, **THE ENGLISH INHERITANCE.** 1950.

8.3
For analysis and details of the philanthropic career of Burdett-Coutts in reformatory work, education, teacher-training, housing and female emigration in the context of her background, training, thought and social milieu, see Kanner, S. Barbara, "Victorian Institutional Patronage: Angela Burdett-Coutts, Charles Dickens, and Urania Cottage, 1846-1858," Ph.D. diss., Univ. of California, Los Angeles, 1972. ——*see also:* Orton, Diana, **MADE OF GOLD: A BIOGRAPHY OF ANGELA BURDETT-COUTTS.** 1980; and Healey, Edna, **LADY UNKNOWN: THE LIFE OF ANGELA BURDETT-COUTTS.** 1978.

Regarding the veritable "cult of benevolence" integrated into alternative religious patterns of either stern righteousness or romantic——sometimes self-sacrificing—tender-heartedness, there is

8.4
Houghton, Walter E., **THE VICTORIAN FRAME OF MIND 1830-1870.** New Haven, Conn., 1957; 1964. See especially pp. 275-282.

For an excellent discussion of religious influences on the charitable efforts of women in nineteenth-century England, see

8.5
Prochaska, F.K., **WOMEN AND PHILANTHROPY IN NINETEENTH CENTURY ENGLAND.** Oxford, 1980.

From the late eighteenth century, literate middle-class women were encouraged in specific works of charity and in efforts to improve the moral tone of society. Taking leadership in this endeavor, the influential Evangelical philanthropist and social reformer, Hannah More, advised the readers of her books and religious tracts on the current philanthropic imperatives and how to attend to them. She was primarily concerned with involving more women. In one of her works, in the form of didactic fiction, her character says: "I have often heard it regretted that ladies have no stated employment, no profession. It is a mistake: Charity is the calling of a lady; the care of the poor is her profession." This is in

8.6
More, Hannah, **COELEBS IN SEARCH OF A WIFE: COMPREHENDING OBSERVATIONS ON DOMESTIC HABITS AND MANNERS, RELIGION AND MORALS.** 1808; *published in:* **THE COMPLETE WORKS OF HANNAH MORE.** vol. 2, New York, 1856. See p. 372.

More's influence survived well into the nineteenth century as her pronouncements on female responsibility for the social and moral improvement of the poor became incorporated into early Victorian philanthropic tradition. For an informative discussion of the larger background of More's thinking there is

8.7
PAST AND PRESENT: Kiernan, V., *"Evangelicalism and the French Revolution,"* no. 1 (1952) 44-56.

More argued that women who were actively engaged in philanthropy obtained considerable power and that they should become more conscious of their power to reform and improve society through roles in education, didactic literature and social service. On More's writings along these lines, see:

8.8
Myers, Mitzi, "Hannah More's Tracts for the Times: Social Fiction and Female Ideology" in **FETTER'D OR FREE? BRITISH WOMEN NOVELISTS, 1670-1815.** ed. by Mary Anne Schofield and Cecilia Macheski. Athens, Ohio, 1986. "Hers is peculiarly a woman's answer, a domestic endurance derived from women's moral traditions... an answer that takes account of economic and material conditions" (p. 274). Myers conveys the impact of More's prescriptions to middle- and upper-class philanthropists on how to assist the poor in changing their religious and moral outlook, and their practical behavior. A related act of charity was to teach poor women and their daughters efficient methods of domestic economy.

The nineteenth-century work of Burdett-Coutts suggests the modeling of More in a number of ways, and exemplifies the tenacity of her influence. The curriculum that Burdett-Coutts developed for the teacher-training institute she financed and controlled bears a striking resemblance to More's teachings on ways to bring poor women into the movement for social improvement. There were other women who subscribed to similar philosophies about women's social commitment and who chose the medium of popular didactic writings to offer prescriptions for fulfilling their high-minded "mission." For example,

8.9
Sandford, Elizabeth, **WOMAN AND HER SOCIAL AND DOMESTIC CHARACTER.** 1831.

8.10
Lewis, Sarah, **WOMAN'S MISSION.** 1839.

8.11
Ellis, Sarah Stickney, **THE WOMEN OF ENGLAND: THEIR SOCIAL DUTIES AND DOMESTIC HABITS.** 1839.

By the mid-nineteenth century, "woman's mission" was a household phrase, and the idea that women's social service had emerged from religious and domestic inclinations permeated not only social expectations and many women's self-image, but also the content of feminine discourse. Even as society experienced great economic, demographic and intellectual changes, the dialogue associated with "woman's mission" so deeply encoded feminine expressions of social purpose that it may have been difficult to establish a positive feminine image without it.

The discourse of Josephine Butler, feminist champion of women's higher education, wider employment, suffrage, and abolition of the Contagious Diseases Acts, always included references to "home influences" and religious teachings. She was surely sincere in praising both religion and female virtues, but she also knew the usefulness of the language of "woman's mission" in drawing the Victorian establishment to her causes. Butler revealed her consciousness of feminine rhetoric when she wrote in 1869:

> Women writers are peculiarly liable to subject expression of their convictions to the promptings of a cowardly reference to the opinion of the public who will read them. For, indeed, in order to obtain a hearing at all, we are all but driven to degrading considerations of what will sell, and what will please or displease this or that class of thinkers who in turn hold rule over the literary market (p. liii).

8.12
This is in Josephine Butler's introduction to **WOMAN'S WORK AND WOMAN'S CULTURE**. ed. by Josephine Butler. 1869.

How shall we interpret the discourse of women philanthropists of the last century? Does it represent their own deepest convictions? Or do at least some of the writers always manage to include conventional ideas to secure public approval? If the latter is the case it may be possible to find greater diversity in the private attitudes and motives of even the most articulate subscribers to the "woman's mission" idea. In any event, by transposing the ideals of domesticity and notions of the godliness of women's motives to the arena of social service, women reformers and philanthropists largely succeeded in maintaining acceptance of their public activity.

This is not to say that the ambition to extend their conventional sphere was the primary motive of the majority of women who streamed into the field of charity work from the late eighteenth century. Women's motives, like men's, can be reasonably attributed to a concern and fear about cruelty, drunkenness, unsanitary conditions, immorality, criminality, illiteracy, and other social questions which appeared to threaten the health and safety of their communities. Women had held places among the patrons and charitable donors of earlier centuries, but from the eighteenth they were drawn into societies that Ford K. Brown has called the "Ten Thousand Compassions and Charities" in

8.13
Brown, Ford K., **FATHERS OF THE VICTORIANS: THE AGE OF WILBER-FORCE.** 1961. "There were societies to improve, to enforce, to reform, to benefit, to prevent, to relieve, to educate, to reclaim, to encourage, to propagate, to maintain, to promote, to provide for, to support, to effect, to better, to instruct, to protect, to supersede, to employ, to civilize, to visit, to preserve, to convert, to mitigate, to abolish, to investigate, to publish, to aid, to extinguish. Above all there were societies to suppress." Brown lists many organizations founded in the eighteenth century and discusses some of them. His major interest is the influence of the various expressions of evangelicalism.

When industrial, urban and demographic expansion accelerated its pace in the next century, charitable effort increased in an attempt to match the challenge of the consequent social and economic dislocations. Women's contributions were even more ardently solicited. Some volunteered in established societies. Other women, like Burdett-Coutts——but not on her grand scale——established their own philanthropies. These women exercised considerable social power, at least in their own communities and coteries. Although she is hardly a typical example, it is noteworthy that Burdett-Coutts not only supervised her charitable enterprises personally, but that she commanded a committee of men to assist her with investigations and management— always reserving final decisions for herself.

Writing on the more conventional pattern of women's philanthropic involvement, Pat Thane observes that nineteenth-century social service organizations counted upon the "existence of a population of underemployed middle- and upper-class women for whom unpaid charitable work was one of the very few socially acceptable occupations. They supplied a willing and almost endless supply of volunteers for such activity——such as has been available at no other period of British history" (p. 27). See

8.14
Thane, Pat, **FOUNDATIONS OF THE WELFARE STATE.** 1982.

Of course, a kind of "conspicuous charity" was also practiced. Perhaps this served as much to augment the status of donors and to display personal success as to serve the poor. Philanthropy also came into "fashion," thus motivating donations and activity that was largely connected with social gatherings. Some women went through motions in a lifestyle that only superficially mirrored serious social service. It is no wonder that women who worked directly with the needy were often obscured by dabblers in the philanthropic milieu. The latter gave the the impression that, perhaps for the most part, female philanthropic workers were all idle ladies who had nothing to do with their time but duplicate each other's charitable gestures. An often cited critique held that indiscriminate almsgiving was increasing pauperism. An article in a leading periodical complained,

> A hundred different agencies for relief of distress are at work over the same ground without concert or cooperation or the slightest information as to each others' exertions. Nine tenths of the visitors to the poor are women, and the bulk are silly and ignorant. Meanwhile, employers and landlords exploit the poor, ignoring their responsibilities as a hundred different agencies try to relieve distress (p. 811).

8.15
This is in **SATURDAY REVIEW:** Green, J.R., *"Pauperism in the East of London,"* 24 (1867) 810-811.

Green's point on the inefficiency of redundant voluntary service to meet the basic social questions was well taken. So were his remarks that pauperism could not be cured by current measures. But his complaints about women's competency in charitable enterprise were uninformed. A more reasonable observation is that of Anne Summers:

> The voluntary visiting of the poor by leisured women of the last century was not just a dilettante fashion of passing free time, but an engagement of

the self which involved the sacrifice of leisure and the development of expertise. The work of visiting, because it *was* work and not a pastime for so many women, in time created an informal interest group among them, which exercised significant political and social pressure on the direction and administration of official policies toward the poor (p. 33).

8.16
Summers, Anne, "A Home From Home—Women's Philanthropic Work in the Nineteenth Century" in **FIT WORK FOR WOMEN**. ed. by Sandra Burman. 1979.

Directories of philanthropic organizations and societies that were published from the mid-nineteenth century give a more precise indication as to why their members were accused of virtually limitless benevolence and of discouraging self-help among the poor. They also give substance to the bare but nevertheless impressive statistics for 1861 estimating 640 charitable institutions for London alone, nearly half of which had been established in the first half of the century and about 144 in the decade 1850-60. The annual income of these societies, estimated at two and a half million pounds, exceeded the expenditure of the Poor Law authorities in London. A detailed article with statistics is

8.17
Lascelles, E., "Charity" in **EARLY VICTORIAN ENGLAND, 1830-1865** ed. by G.M. Young. vol. 2, 1934.

In his valuable book, WOMEN AND PHILANTHROPY IN NINETEENTH CENTURY ENGLAND (1980), Frank Prochaska provides a more analytical survey of women's contributions through subscriptions and practical work in numerous charitable organizations and discusses contemporary attitudes toward female philanthropy.

It is the formation of the Charity Organization Society (C.O.S.) in 1869 that is generally considered to be the most significant response to wide criticism of the haphazard growth of charitable organizations. The central C.O.S. office in London established the principle that philanthropic societies should join in a cooperative relationship; that only deserving applicants should be helped; that charity was to be limited and rationalized in scope and technique; and that the assistance given should be the kind that would promote regeneration and self-help. By "the deserving" was meant those who had made every effort on their own behalf. The C.O.S. developed and systematized its methodology by replacing indiscriminate practices of Christian benevolence with structures for rational decision-making and by instituting a new, "scientific" casework method for evaluating applicants. A good number of its "visitors"—the case workers—were women. Gradually some of them became salaried. The C.O.S. placed its primary emphasis on efficiency and organization in pursuit of fulfilling its principles. Its aspirations included professionalization, and this involved the training of its visitor-interviewers. Some leaders within the C.O.S., notably Octavia Hill, had a dual perspective about the training of the staff. On the one hand, the volunteers were expected to follow the ideal of giving personalized, individual assistance to the poor. Formalized training might interfere with spontaneous interaction with applicants. On the other hand, it was essential to rationalize and organize the executive functions that were performed by trained administrators. For example, in

8.18
MACMILLAN'S MAGAZINE: Hill, O., *"The Work of Volunteers in the Organization of Charity,"* 26 (1872) 441-449. Writing on the flow of information from the interviewers of applicants and the decision-making Committee:

> I must... say something further as to the importance of the appointment of some lady or gentleman acting as *Referee*; that is, as a centre for all the volunteers working as visitors.... The referee in the district here described was appointed in the first instance by the District Committee of the... Society; she was subsequently asked to attend the Relief Committee, and has since been recognized by the guardians and the sub-committee of the School Board as the representative of all the visitors throughout the district: the guardians send to her... notes of every decision arrived at as to applications (p. 446).

This one example of expectations of female referees in the numerous districts of the C.O.S. indicates what a serious mistake it is to assume, as so many authors do, that women involved in charitable organizations filled only subservient and domestically-oriented roles. Two modern studies of the C.O.S. that are set in the context of the general development of social services in the nineteenth century are:

8.19
Woodroofe, Kathleen, **FROM CHARITY TO SOCIAL WORK IN ENGLAND AND THE UNITED STATES.** 1962; rpt. several editions to 1974.

8.20
Young, Agnes Freda and Ashton, Elwyn Thomas, "Family Case Work" in **BRITISH SOCIAL WORK IN THE NINETEENTH CENTURY.** 1956; rpt. Westport, Conn., 1984.

Both Woodroofe and Young and Ashton frequently refer to the case workers of the C.O.S. and elsewhere as "she." Woodroofe writes:

> The nineteenth century social worker evolved many principles which still form an essential part of the modern theory and practice of social casework.... She was more concerned [however] with the economic problems of her clients, and much of her 'treatment' consisted of supplying financial and material assistance... in her aim to help individuals to attain strength to meet their problems.... Octavia Hill stressed the necessity for 'knowledge of character' and divided her clients into 'deserving' and 'undeserving.' But the idea of developing a healthier, happier personality and of using the worker-client relationship to stimulate the client to want to change is common to both generations (p. 52).

Victorian female philanthropy has been conventionally identified as personal and individual. In their writings, female social service and reform leaders defended the principle of individual attention to individual beneficiaries. This placed the C.O.S. and other female, face-to-face charity workers (for example, rent collecting and hospital almoning) in the unique position of establishing and trying to understand relationships with other social classes. On this question there is the important article

8.21
TRANSACTIONS OF THE ROYAL HISTORICAL SOCIETY: McKibbin, R.I.,

"Social Class and Social Observation in Edwardian England," 28 (1978) 175-199.
McKibbin observes: "Although their subject was 'the poor' they never believed that
the poor could be understood in isolation, but only *through* their relationship with
other social classes; always an intermittent, ambiguous and sensitive one, but
probably never more so than at this period" (p. 197). The subjects of this article are
Helen Bosanquet, Margaret Loane and Florence (Lady) Bell.

We know of difficulties in overcoming distrust of middle-class visitors from the
female organizers of "domestic missions" who resorted to hiring working-class
women to sell their bibles in the homes of slum dwellers. District nurse Margaret
Loane wrote after years of experience:

> Class barriers are firmly erected and closely guarded by the poor. Any
> working man's wife would more readily confide her private affairs to the
> neighbors with whom she has had bitter, year-long quarrels, than she would
> to the kindest and most discreet of nurses or district visitors (p. 79).

8.22
Loane, Margaret, **THE NEXT STREET BUT ONE.** 1907.

The great American philanthropist, Jane Addams, wrote an excellent article on
problems of communication and understanding between middle-class social service
visitor-interviewers and poor or working-class clients:

8.23
Addams, Jane, "Charitable Effort" in **DEMOCRACY AND SOCIAL ETHICS.** by
Jane Addams. New York, 1902. Addams writes:

> [There is] a consciousness in the mind of the visitor of a genuine
> misunderstanding of her motives by the recipients of her charity and by
> their neighbors. Let us take a neighborhood of poor people, and test their
> ethical standards by those of the charity visitor who comes with the best
> desire in the world to help them out of their distress. A most striking
> incongruity, at once apparent, is the difference between the emotional
> kindness with which relief is given by one poor neighbor to another poor
> neighbor, and the guarded care with which relief is given by a charity
> visitor to a charity recipient. The neighborhood mind is at once confronted
> not only by the difference of method, but by an absolute clashing of two
> ethical standards (p. 19).

No doubt the women volunteer visitors of the C.O.S. and other societies had their
interpersonal and managerial skills tested and sharpened with every contact. At least
some of them may also have altered their perspective on questions about the cause
and treatment of poverty. It was at the time of her work for the C.O.S. in the early
1880s that Beatrice Webb began to embrace new ideas about social causation and
how to investigate it. A biographer of Webb writes:

> Beatrice frequently commented on the differences between her motives in
> becoming involved in social work and those of her sister Kate. For Kate, it
> was a combination of disgust with Society life and a charitable impulse
> towards the poor which led her to the C.O.S. For Beatrice, it was primarily
> the desire to understand the structural and economic basis of social problems

which led first to the C.O.S. and then to her own social investigation (p. 30).

8.24

HISTORY WORKSHOP JOURNAL: Caine, B., *"Beatrice Webb and the 'Woman Question,'"* no. 14 (1982) 23-43.

8.25

In her autobiography, **MY APPRENTICESHIP.** 1926, Beatrice Webb synthesizes the social philosophy, methodology and results of the C.O.S. as she found them in the 1880s. She criticizes its business-like approach and its rejection of comparatively open-handed Christian charity, although she did not claim that the latter could be a solution to current social problems of capitalist society. She praises the "well-to-do men and women of goodwill [in the C.O.S.] who had gone out to offer personal service and friendship to the dwellers in the slums [and] found themselves transformed into a body of amateur detectives" (p. 196). She virtually condemns how the Society turned their findings into remedies. Despite the intention of the C.O.S. to organize the multifarious charities of the Metropolis, she wrote, neither the Churches nor the hospitals, neither the orphanages nor the agencies for providing the destitute with food, clothing or shelter would have anything to do with a society employing its methods. The C.O.S. was thoroughly *laissez-faire* in its antagonism to provision of social services by the state, yet it turned innumerable cases over to the Poor Law authorities. Webb marks the rejection of C.O.S. methods by Canon Samuel and Henrietta Barnett, leaders in the Settlement Movement, as the point at which she and others looked in a "new" direction for solutions to poverty. "[The Barnetts] had discovered for themselves that there was a deeper and more continuous evil than unrestricted and unregulated charity, namely, unrestricted and unregulated capitalism and landlordism" (p. 200). The Barnetts were not Socialists. They were pointing to inequities in social arrangements and economic structures as the causes of poverty rather than to the failings of individuals. From this time forward, Webb reports, her desire was to find out these circumstances from scientific methods "of observation, reasoning and verification [and to apply the knowledge] to the problem of poverty in the midst of riches" (p. 209). She became the "industrious apprentice" of the social investigator, Charles Booth.

There were other women who chose investigation and experimentation rather than the work of visitation for a philanthropic society. From mid-century many joined the National Association for the Promotion of Social Science (NAPSS), a union of reform groups adhering to the conviction that for every analyzed social question, an ameliorating solution or statutory measure could be scientifically devised. The process began with investigation and discussion. Then the Association brought it before the public and if appropriate, prepared a proposed bill for legislation. It organized annual conferences from 1857 to 1884 where members and invited experts presented papers and drafted proposals for submission to the government. For analyses and historical criticisms of the Association and close details of its impressive membership, history, philosophy, operation and results, consult

8.26

Abrams, Philip, **THE ORIGINS OF BRITISH SOCIOLOGY.** Chicago, 1968. See especially pp. 38-54.

8.27

Ritt, Lawrence, "The Victorian Conscience in Action: The National Association for the Promotion of Social Science, 1857-1886," Ph.D. diss., Columbia Univ., 1959.

[There was] a preoccupation with efficiency rather than considerations of sentiment.... Like the Benthamite bureaucrat, Edwin Chadwick, [they] regarded themselves as administrative technicians and social engineers.... They were convinced... that the subjects with which they dealt were susceptible of scientific treatment, and that their deliberations would be the means of discovering a science of society.... As a pressure group it [NAPSS] influenced legislation on public health, education, law reform, housing, prison administration, and the legal position of women (quoted from author's abstract).

8.28

MANCHESTER SCHOOL OF ECONOMICS AND SOCIAL STUDIES: Rodgers, B., *"The Social Science Association 1857-1886,"* 20 (1952) 283-310. Surveys the record of the NAPSS in terms of the issues it explored and publicized in its TRANSACTIONS; the interest groups that its investigations spawned; and the proposed legislation for which it took responsibility. The issues included several that were of primary concern to women: married women's property and the opening of higher education to women. "[But] few of the papers show signs of interest in Comte's search for a really scientific 'science of society'" (p. 300).

Members of the NAPSS included women who were or were to become well-known reformers. Some of them were leaders of the women's movement: Lydia Becker; Dorothea Beale; Helen Blackburn; Jessie Boucherett; Mary Carpenter; Frances Power Cobbe; Jane Crowe; Emily Davies; Emily Faithfull; Elizabeth Garrett (Anderson); Rhoda Garrett; Maria Grey; Florence and Rosamond Hill; Octavia Hill; Florence Nightingale; Bessie Rayner Parkes (Belloc); Maria Rye; Emily Shirreff; Barbara Leigh Smith (Bodichon); Louisa Twining; Elizabeth Wolstenholme (Elmy) and others.

8.29

MACMILLAN'S MAGAZINE: Cobbe, F.P., *"Social Science Congresses, and Women's Part in Them,"* 5 (1861) 80-94. Cobbe describes and praises the work of the Social Science Association in general and specifies the contributions of women members. She also describes the satirical and otherwise negative reactions being then expressed toward women's participation. She ends on a positive appraisal:

Whether by public reading... or merely writing papers on philanthropic subjects, the extreme usefulness of women has been demonstrated beyond dispute by the Social Science Association.... Lord Brougham announced in 1859 that the most important papers hitherto presented had been those of Florence Nightingale.... Mary Carpenter has led in one of the noblest departments of Social Science——the reformation of juvenile criminals and the education of vagrants and paupers.... Lord Shaftesbury said... 'Not a little is due to the share which women have taken... in the business of this society.... Men may do what must be done on a large scale; but, the instant the work becomes individual and personal, the instant it requires tact and feeling, from that instant it passes into the hands of women (p. 94).

In several sections of the article, Cobbe's own discourse on women's "special gifts" is not much different from Shaftesbury's.

With all respect to claims made by Victorian reformers and philanthropists, the actual extent of poverty and its relation to processes affecting social distress were not "scientifically" understood. By 1880, traditional ideas on the fixity of the structure of society and the causes of poverty could not be supported by evidence that confronted educated, philanthropic "settlers" in the slums. And it was only after publication of the formal, statistically-oriented investigations of Charles Booth and Seebohm Rowntree that hard "scientific" data and new theories of social causation began to appear. From that point, governmental interference beyond the Poor Law became admissible to all but the die-hards of *laissez-faire* ideology. As to voluntary social service, the dimensions of the social problem revealed by statistical investigation indicated need for more rigorously trained personnel.

Educated women volunteers were among the first recruits for curricula in Social Studies that began to be established in connection with some of the universities. Discussing this development Kathleen Woodroofe (cited above) writes:

> In 1877 speculation was rife about 'the injury which... lady-brigades from the West End would do the East'.... Another asked severely whether this was 'the only field of human action in which... good intentions take the place of training'.... As a result of this agitation, the C.O.S. in 1896 instituted for its visitors and social workers a scheme of training through lectures and practical work.... [As Octavia Hill saw it], the problem was 'how to unite the fresh, loving, spontaneous individual sympathy with the quiet, grave, sustained and instructed spirit of the trained worker.' At the same time, Margaret Sewell, Warden of the Women's University Settlement in Southwark, began teaching her voluntary workers through the medium of group instruction in lectures and classes. In 1890, the two schemes joined hands and volunteers as well as paid workers were trained (pp. 53-54).

8.30
On opening doors of opportunity to women's professional training there is the very helpful work by Simey, Margaret Bayne, **CHARITABLE EFFORT IN LIVERPOOL IN THE NINETEENTH CENTURY.** Liverpool, 1951.

> Out of the desperate need of the poor, and the anxiety of the middle classes to do something about them, developed simultaneously a demand and a scope for the services of women far in excess of anything previously experienced. However much men might dominate the administration of charitable societies, the individual act of charity was still regarded as essentially women's work, and women were therefore able to grasp this opportunity without incurring such opposition as had greeted their endeavours to train as nurses or to secure advanced education.... Personal service was the one thing at their disposal which was really their own to give.... The voluntary nature of charitable work automatically overcame the opposition of those who disapproved of women earning a living, and eased the guilty conscience of women themselves in regard to their revolt (p. 126).... Many secured for themselves experience of considerable realism under cover of a suitably feminine object (p. 128).

Regarding the first formal training, see

8.31
JOURNAL OF EDUCATION: Matheson, M.C., *"Training for Social Work: New*

University Course in Birmingham," 40 (1908) 640-641. On the current qualifications for the trained social service worker:

> She must understand the laws which control municipal and industrial life, and she must know where to turn for help.... This means that she must understand both the principles and methods of relief, whether administered by the State or by public or private charity, and that she must know the aims and the rules of the various societies that exist for the alleviation of different kinds of suffering. She must be able to concentrate her attention on the possibilities of the individual case, but she must do more than this: she must never forget that the individual is a member of the State, and personal sympathies must not swamp a wider and more philosophic outlook (p. 640).

8.32

Macadam, Elizabeth, **THE EQUIPMENT OF THE SOCIAL WORKER.** 1925. Macadam writes of the rapid stream of social service legislation at the turn of the century. Workers were required in increased numbers as salaried organizers for the new forms of public and voluntary effort. However, the newly formed schools of "Social Study" were under-enrolled. For "the most part the number of students was small and consisted mainly of women attracted to voluntary social work" (p. 35). The Liverpool school was a pioneer in 1903. At a conference in 1918, it was reported that 269 students had qualified for diplomas in six university departments. Of these, only thirty-one were men (p. 36).

8.33

Smith, Marjorie J., **PROFESSIONAL EDUCATION FOR SOCIAL WORK IN BRITAIN.** 1952. Smith describes the first professional school of social work, the School of Sociology, founded in 1903. She traces volunteer training from Octavia Hill, the University Women's Settlements, and the Charity Organisation Society. Women were prominent among both the lecturers and trainees. The teachers were academic and theoretical, while the practice of casework was left entirely to volunteers. The School was not considered successful probably because of its emphasis on theory. Until about 1919, social work practitioners were certified through agency training, especially the Charity Organisation Society. This book includes a "Proposed Two Years' Course" for trainees of the Social Education Committee of the C.O.S., submitted 1903.

8.34

Jones, Kathleen, **THE TEACHING OF SOCIAL STUDIES IN BRITISH UNIV-ERSITIES.** 1964. Discusses the background and shows relationship to twentieth-century developments in social work education.

The most comprehensive survey of women's training and activity in voluntary and paid social work from the 1860s to the 1970s is

8.35

Walton, Ronald G., **WOMEN IN SOCIAL WORK.** 1975.

Walton traces the progress women have made in social service since the nineteenth century. He discusses some of the outstanding philanthropists and social reformers and the organizations with which they were connected. Walton is interested in singling out distinctly female interests and innovations as compared with those of male workers. He comments briefly on some of these women's connections to social reform movements including that for women's suffrage. The C.O.S. emerges as the predominant touchstone for discussing the activity and earliest training of these women for voluntary and paid social service before World War I. He shows that although these women performed important services, and were appointed to senior posts, they were not given advanced managerial responsibilities. Walton's analysis centers on a few major points: 1) Women's participation in the social service field was most often perceived as a transference of roles from the domestic to public sphere, and the work they initiated or were assigned can be identified with female family functions; 2) Victorian propriety prevailed in policies providing that women attend females and children, while men work philanthropically with men. Women therefore did not compete with men; 3) "The availability of women with independent means hampered the development of paid work which has always been an important part in the development of a sphere of professional work." Citing Thorstein Veblen from **THE THEORY OF THE LEISURE CLASS** (1934), Walton paints the picture of "a large class of the population not involved in economic activities, fighting to give expression to pent-up religious and social feelings.... The perpetuation of domestic roles in economic life as shown by the employment of women in teaching, nursing, and social work was also a consequence of long established family roles and of the impulse of many men to keep women in a servile role" (p. 87).

Walton's paradigm, unmistakably associated with the "woman's mission" motif of the early nineteenth century, foreshadows his historical interpretation of why female social workers did not achieve managerial status and remuneration proportionate to the extent and value of their work.

Reinforcing the association of social work with domestic roles and expectations fulfills the prophesy that women regard themselves, and are regarded as, subordinate to male authority. This generalized characterization of the female social worker, volunteer or paid, has been repeated so often as to have deterred closer questioning. But *have* domestic roles been transferred by *all* women indiscriminately? Or are there significant exceptions? As to the field of social work itself, are there perhaps intrinsically "domestic" qualities in the nature of the services and the processes of providing assistance so that what seems to be transference from the home to the workplace may be simply coincidence? What aspects of the practical side of social work of the nineteenth and early twentieth centuries prevented it from identification as a profession? Was it regarded as different, for example, from teaching and nursing and journalism? Why wasn't the practice of social service integrated into conceptualizations of social policy and the making of social welfare provisions? Did the women's own discourse predispose administrators to reticence about putting these women in authoritative, predominant and ultimately responsible positions?

Most modern scholarship on the development of the English Welfare State pays little attention to women philanthropists and social workers of the nineteenth and early twentieth centuries. The reason may be found in the tendency of these historians to focus on signposts in the course of the "evolution" that foreshadowed statutory welfare statism. For example, changes in ideas, experiences and economic theory that made poverty rather than pauperism the social question; developments in social theory that displaced traditional and fixed beliefs that had no modern scientific basis; discoveries about human psychology and behavior that outmoded the old prejudices against the character of the poor; alterations in social and cultural values that afforded new dignity to individuals and social groups. Concerning the advent, power and interrelationships of these intellectual developments see

8.36
Soffer, Reba N., **ETHICS AND SOCIETY IN ENGLAND: THE REVOLUTION IN THE SOCIAL SCIENCES, 1870-1914**. 1978. The modern social sciences, says Soffer, were shaped in form and content

> from the late 1860s within a small, closely knit, homogenous community of energetic, thinking people centered mostly in the universities.... convinced that it bore the responsibility for discovering and carrying out a program of individual and social reform.... These middle-class idealists were filtered through an educational system designed to supply the personnel that governed English institutions.... The crises of confidence that began in the 1870s produced only momentary confusion and dismay within the reforming community.... The new social scientists adopted an empirical and piecemeal arrangement of problems in a hierarchy of importance governed by the state of knowledge and the amount of data available. Emphasizing dynamic change, individuation, and probability, the new social sciences, and especially the revolutionary fields, provided reformers with working theories and practical techniques.... translated into effective social remedies in the hands of educators, county councillors, civil servants and business men (pp. 5-10).

The vast majority of the women committed to social service had no access to the universities and other groups to which Soffer refers, except, perhaps, as family and friends in the circles they formed. The latter have not been investigated as contributors to the new social sciences and ultimately to the new philanthropy.

As late nineteenth century politics advanced along more democratic lines, however, remedies for poverty and social distress increasingly occupied local and central government. Traditional voluntary services remained as supplemental agencies. There are valuable analyses of these new political and administrative responses to poverty and economic crises. Among them,

8.37
Fraser, Derek, **EVOLUTION OF THE BRITISH WELFARE STATE**. 1973.

> Growing public awareness of poverty was accompanied by important political developments which would in the long term ensure that the relief of poverty became a crucial political question. Parliamentary democracy had been brought appreciably nearer by the enfranchisement of urban workers in 1867 and of the rural workers in 1884, and by the redistribution of seats [in Parliament] in 1885.... At last the population was gaining the political influence previously reserved for property——numbers [of voters] were beginning to count.... Housing was an issue dear to the hearts of the new electorate (p. 128).

Statutory social service followed upon demands of an expanded electorate. New social policy and welfare legislation by the State aimed to placate voting constituencies that were male. Women remained unenfranchised and consequently beyond the pale of new governmental decision-making. Although qualified women held the municipal franchise and therefore had votes to be solicited in their localities, woman were barred from holding local office when the new statutory services caused reorganization and administrative reform of these bodies. Is it not possible that women's relatively low status in the social service schema may have related more to their political status than to the association of their work with domestic tasks?

8.38

Gilbert, Bentley B., **THE EVOLUTION OF NATIONAL INSURANCE IN GREAT BRITAIN: THE ORIGINS OF THE WELFARE STATE.** 1966. This valuable work in part traces and distinguishes statutory social services and social legislation from evangelical humanitarianism. Gilbert shows how the nineteenth-century apparatus of parochial relief and private charity either had to be abandoned or their position modified "lest it taint the new reform measures" (p. 22).

What roles *could* women have taken in this process of modification up to the period of World War I, and even after? There is an insightful discussion in Simey, Margaret B., "End and Beginning" in CHARITABLE EFFORT IN LIVERPOOL, ETC. (cited above).

> [The Royal Commission on the Poor Laws in 1909] proposed not only important modifications of the Poor Law and its administration, but also a revision of the methods of voluntary assistance (p. 140).... The publication of the Report undoubtedly marks the turning point in the history of charitable effort. From now on, the state was to take over in a series of legislative acts, the responsibility for class after class of people whose welfare had till then depended largely on... charity (p. 142).... Social work [before 1914, had rewarded women] with valuable experience and with human contacts of a very real kind: in short, the community needed them and they felt that they could not do enough to respond to this need.... Women can indeed claim to have kept alive the social conscience at a time when charity had been debased by its confusion with material relief. Nevertheless they did so at the cost of making social work a feminine prerogative, a process not without penalties.... No one seemed to know what charity stood for.... The complexity of social problems seemed to put them beyond the capacity of the amateur, and many baffled people saw no alternative to handing over to the professional worker, and to the state, many of the charitable duties... Voluntary relief... stood condemned, but.... The Commission took it for granted that personal service would continue (p. 143).

"Personal service," still largely thought of in terms of "woman's mission," did continue within the Welfare State. As a result of the tenacious associations with stereotyped female roles, women were not awarded, and perhaps they did not in significant enough numbers apply for, positions of authority and responsibility in the impersonalized state system. Walton could still write only hopefully in 1975 that the profession "now has the possibility of a creative blending of the qualities brought by men and women. In the past these qualities have often been blended into separate streams by social conventions. One of the greatest challenges facing social work is whether consciously some of these conventions can be broken down, leading to a new and vital fusion of male and female qualities in the service of those in need" (p. 263).

Have these alleged "qualities" disassociated women's work from such a vital sequence of events as the evolution of the Welfare State? Or, has women's social work been accorded low value by historians and others? One of the most respected of all historians of English welfare has appraised the nineteenth- and early twentieth-century contribution of the field in which women dominated without reference to their participation:

8.39
Owen, David, **ENGLISH PHILANTHROPY, 1660-1960.** Cambridge, Mass., 1960.

> The growth of the public welfare system has not only left ample room for voluntary helpfulness, organized as well as individual, but in some respects it has even broadened the opportunities for men to serve their fellows (p. 553).

As for the whole field of charitable effort in the past, Owen concludes: "Very likely Victorian public authorities accomplished more toward creating a basis for civilized living than did all of the voluntary services" (p. 596).

Owen's judgment that Victorian and Edwardian social services represent failed philanthropy is widely shared among modern historians. And it is with the more personal, individualized services of these periods that women have been traditionally associated. It is therefore not surprising that women are hardly mentioned in recent scholarship on the developing Welfare State. But is this a judgment that can be upheld with justice? It would seem that answering this question requires, first of all, a re-investigation of the full spectrum of the social work that women *actually* performed. It also calls for a re-evaluation of the interdependence of private and statutory assistance, employing criteria that include the non-materialistic values that are involved in "creating a basis for civilized living."

* * *

1. A SURVEY OF WRITINGS ON THE RELIEF OF SOCIAL CONDITIONS IN ENGLAND

8.40
Trimmer, Sarah, **THE OECONOMY OF CHARITY; OR, AN ADDRESS TO LADIES, ADAPTED TO THE PRESENT STATE OF CHARITABLE INSTITUTIONS IN ENGLAND: WITH A PARTICULAR VIEW TO THE CULTIVATION OF RELIGIOUS PRINCIPLES AMONG THE LOWER ORDERS.** 2 vols. 1787; rev. ed., 1801; **SOME ACCOUNT OF THE LIFE AND WRITINGS OF SARAH TRIMMER WITH ORIGINAL LETTERS, AND MEDITATIONS AND PRAYERS.** 2 vols. 1814. ——*see also:* Balfour, Clara, **A SKETCH OF MRS. TRIMMER.** 1854; Rodgers, Betsy, "Schools of Industry: Mrs. Trimmer" in **CLOAK OF CHARITY: STUDIES IN EIGHTEENTH CENTURY PHILANTHROPY.** 1949.

8.41

Dyer, George, **THE COMPLAINTS OF THE POOR PEOPLE OF ENGLAND.** 1793; **A DISSERTATION ON THE THEORY AND PRACTICE OF BENEVOLENCE.** 1795.

8.42

More, Hannah, **CHEAP REPOSITORY TRACTS.** 1795-1798. Pamphlets calling for behavioral and institutional reform and advocating charity. Includes anti-slavery propaganda; **STORIES FOR THE MIDDLE RANKS OF SOCIETY, AND TALES FOR THE COMMON PEOPLE.** 2 vols. 1818. Didactic fiction on reforming morals, manners and social attitudes. Advocates charity. —*see also:* Roberts, William, ed., **MEMOIRS OF THE LIFE AND CORRESPONDENCE OF MRS. HANNAH MORE.** 4 vols. 1834; Roberts, Arthur, ed., **MENDIP ANNALS... THE CHARITABLE LABOURS OF HANNAH AND MARTHA MORE IN THEIR NEIGHBORHOOD, BEING THE JOURNAL OF MARTHA MORE...** 1859. Known as "Patty," Hannah's sister also worked for moral reform, the relief of poverty, and the elimination of illiteracy; Yonge, Charlotte M., **HANNAH MORE.** 1888; Jones, M.G., **HANNAH MORE.** New York, 1968. A very good biography based upon More's correspondence and set in the context of relevant social movements. The discussion of More's social-religious thought and philanthropy shows her significance in the history of the period. Jones' conclusion that More's work and style were either ignored or neglected by nineteenth-century philanthropists is erroneous.

8.43

Sabatier, W., **A TREATISE ON POVERTY, ITS CONSEQUENCES, AND THE REMEDY.** 1797.

8.44

Wakefield, Priscilla, **REFLECTIONS ON THE PRESENT CONDITION OF THE FEMALE SEX; WITH SUGGESTIONS FOR ITS IMPROVEMENT.** 1798; 1817.

8.45

Cappe, Catherine, **OBSERVATIONS ON CHARITY SCHOOLS, FEMALE FRIENDLY SOCIETIES AND OTHER SUBJECTS CONNECTED WITH THE VIEWS OF THE LADIES COMMITTEE.** York, 1805. States that philanthropic work is the best area for single women to dispel the prejudices waged against them by men. "By uniting... in District Committees, for the purposes of usefulness and benevolence, single Ladies may... be the protectors and friends of the deserted Orphan, and the 'deliverers of those who have no helper.' Were their leisure thus employed, happier as they would be themselves, in the more constant exercise, cultivation and improvement of the benevolent affections; approved of God, useful to others, and respectable in the eyes of all" (p. x); **MEMOIRS OF THE LIFE OF THE LATE MRS. CATHERINE CAPPE, WRITTEN BY HERSELF.** ed. by Mary Cappe. 1822; 3rd ed., 1826; **AN ACCOUNT OF TWO CHARITY SCHOOLS.** York, 1880. Asserts that the primary aim for lower-class women is to protect and elevate their own sex.

8.46

PHILANTHROPIST: OR, REPOSITORY FOR HINTS AND SUGGESTIONS CALCULATED TO PROMOTE THE COMFORT AND HAPPINESS OF MAN: 1811 to 1819; vols. 1-7. Edited by W. Allen; *continued as:* **PHILANTHROPIC MAGAZINE:** Jan. 1835 to July 1842.

8.47

Owen, Robert, **A NEW VIEW OF SOCIETY; OR, ESSAYS ON THE PRINCIPLE**

OF THE FORMATION OF THE HUMAN CHARACTER, AND THE APPLICATION OF THE PRINCIPLE TO PRACTICE. 1813; 1816. "Under the existing laws, the unemployed working classes are maintained by, and consume part of, the property and produce of the wealthy and industrious, while their powers of body and mind remain unproductive.... They amalgamate with the regular poor, and become a nuisance to society" (p. 159). ——*see also:* **EDINBURGH REVIEW:** *"Mr. Owen's Plans for Relieving National Distress,"* 32 (1819) 453-477.

8.48
Nicoll, S.W., A VIEW OF THE PRINCIPLES ON WHICH THE WELL-BEING OF THE LABOURING CLASS DEPENDS: TOGETHER WITH OBSERVATIONS ON THE DIRECTION OF CHARITY. York, 1819. Advises postponement of marriage until the husband's income is sufficient enough to provide for a family.

8.49
Davis, William, HINTS TO PHILANTHROPISTS; OR, A COLLECTIVE VIEW OF PRACTICAL MEANS FOR IMPROVING THE CONDITIONS OF THE POOR AND LABOURING CLASSES OF SOCIETY. Bath, 1821; rpt., 1971. Advises that the poor be treated as rational beings and educated according to their condition in life.

8.50
Barbauld, Anna Laetitia, WORKS OF MRS. BARBAULD. 2 vols. 1825. "There is certainly at present a great deal of zeal in almost every persuasion.... Bible Societies, missionary schemes, lectures, schools for the poor are set afoot and spread, not so much from a sense of duty as being the real taste of the times" (vol. 2, p. 107).

8.51
QUARTERLY REVIEW: Palgrave, F., *"The Poor Laws,"* 33 (1826) 429-455; *"Causes and Remedies of Pauperism in the U.K.,"* 43 (1830) 242-277.

8.52
Carlisle, Nicholas, AN HISTORICAL ACCOUNT OF THE ORIGIN OF THE COMMISSION, APPOINTED TO INQUIRE CONCERNING CHARITIES IN ENGLAND AND WALES; AND, AN ILLUSTRATION OF SEVERAL OLD CUSTOMS AND WORDS, WHICH OCCUR IN THE REPORTS. 1828.

8.53
Wilmot-Horton, Robert J.B., AN ENQUIRY INTO THE CAUSES AND REMEDIES OF PAUPERISM. 1830.

8.54
Talbot, Charles John Chetwynd, (Lord Ingestre, Earl of Shrewsbury), SUGGESTIONS FOR THE IMPROVEMENT OF THE CONDITION OF THE LABOURING POOR. 1831; (as editor), MELIORA; OR BETTER TIME TO COME; BEING THE CONTRIBUTIONS OF MANY MEN TOUCHING THE PRESENT STATE AND PROSPECTS OF SOCIETY. 2nd ed., 1853; rpt., 1971. "It is the duty of the middle and upper classes... to convince the working classes that they are their friends and well-wishers instead of their oppressors" (p. viii).

8.55
Martineau, Harriet, ILLUSTRATIONS OF POLITICAL ECONOMY. 1832-1834. Collection of tracts and stories to explain changing economic conditions to the poor and working classes. Exhorts them to conform to the demands of the times and to extend charity at home to parents, neighbors, and children; POOR LAWS AND

PAUPERS ILLUSTRATED. 1833-1834. ——*see also*: Webb, R.K., **HARRIET MARTINEAU: A RADICAL VICTORIAN.** New York, 1960. An acute, critical analysis of Martineau's thought; Pichanick, Valerie Kossew, **HARRIET MARTINEAU, THE WOMAN AND HER WORK.** Ann Arbor, 1980. Pichanick aims for understanding the woman, the motivations behind her work and behavior, and the value of her efforts for reform and women's causes. Useful bibliography; Myers, Mitzi, "Unmothered Daughter and Radical Reformer: Harriet Martineau's Career" in **THE LOST TRADITION: MOTHERS AND DAUGHTERS IN LITERATURE.** ed. by Cathy N. Davidson and E.M. Boner. New York, 1980.

8.56
[Chadwick, Edwin], **THE POOR LAW REPORT OF 1834.** ed. by S.G. Checklands and O.A. Checklands. [1834]; rpt., Harmondsworth, 1974. ——*see also:* Brundage, Anthony, **THE MAKING OF THE NEW POOR LAW: THE POLITICS OF INQUIRY, ENACTMENT, AND IMPLEMENTATION 1832-1839.** New Brunswick, New Jersey, 1978. Provides an understanding of the circumstances surrounding the legislation and its opposition.

8.57
Loudon, Jane (Webb), **PHILANTHROPIC ECONOMY; OR, THE PHILOSOPHY OF HAPPINESS, PRACTICALLY APPLIED TO THE SOCIAL, POLITICAL, AND COMMERCIAL RELATIONS OF GREAT BRITAIN.** 1835.

8.58
NEW MONTHLY MAGAZINE: Poole, J., *"Charity,"* 50 (1837) 519-526.

8.59
QUARTERLY JOURNAL OF THE STATISTICAL SOCIETY OF LONDON: *"Progress of the Public Rescue."* 1 (1838) 154-167; *"Report to the Council of the Statistical Society from a Committee of its Fellows Appointed to Make an Investigation Into the State of the Poorer Classes in St. George's in the East."* 11 (1848) 193-249. "All those specified as unfortunate females appear, with only a few exceptions, to be persons of respectable outward manners and conduct, for the houses of prostitution were expressly excepted from inquiry" (p. 203). Includes tables which show different categories of employment, average earnings, rents of dwellings, number of beds per family, religious orientation, number of children, health statistics, and types of dwellings inhabited by those investigated.

8.60
Slaney, Robert Aglionby, **REPORTS OF THE HOUSE OF COMMONS ON EDUCATION AND ON HEALTH OF THE POORER CLASSES.** 1841.

8.61
Tonna, Charlotte Elizabeth, **COLLECTED WORKS.** New York, 1844-1845. These are novelettes and stories previously published serially in CHRISTIAN LADY'S MAGAZINE, which Tonna edited. In the guise of fiction, Charlotte Elizabeth (her pen name) wrote on the exploitation of female labor, basing her details on facts she gleaned from parliamentary Blue Books. ——*see also:* **NINETEENTH CENTURY FICTION:** Kanner, S.B. and Kovacevic, I., *"Blue Book into Novel: The Forgotten Industrial Fiction of Charlotte Elizabeth Tonna."* 25 (1970) 152-173.

8.62
HOGG'S WEEKLY INSTRUCTOR: *"Public Charity."* 1 (1848) 369-371. Advocates cultivation of resources for expansion of employment rather than short-term relief. "A system which supports only destitution, while it opens no path to improvement,

may be justly suspected of materially assisting in the perpetuation of poverty" (p. 369).

8.63

Simmons, G., **THE WORKING CLASSES; THEIR MORAL, SOCIAL, AND INTELLECTUAL CONDITION; WITH PRACTICAL SUGGESTIONS FOR THEIR IMPROVEMENT.** 1849. Chapters 5, 6, and 7 examine charitable institutions, Missionary Societies, Temperance and Total Abstinence Movements, Sunday, Charity, and Ragged Schools, Sick Societies, Free Chapels, Free and Country Lectures, Cheap Libraries, and Friendly Visiting. "To the churches, first, we must look for the preparing of the way for a thorough emancipation of the poor from their present degrading habits and practices" (p. 281). Calls for middle-class provision of these means of "improvement."

8.64

HOW CAN THE YOUNG-LADY-HOOD OF ENGLAND ASSIST IN IMPROVING THE CONDITION OF THE WORKING CLASSES? BY ONE OF THE ORDER. 1853.

8.65

Pashley, Robert, **PAUPERISM AND POOR LAWS.** 1855. Surveys the condition of poor families in rural areas, their attraction to work in towns, and the difficulties of providing aid to them in their new settlements when they are unemployed. Critical of the New Poor Law of 1834 and its aftermath.

8.66

MELIORA: A QUARTERLY REVIEW OF SOCIAL SERVICE IN ITS ETHICAL, ECONOMICAL AND POLITICAL AND AMELIORATIVE ASPECTS: 1858 to 1869; Publication of the National Association for the Promotion of Social Science; *"Helping the Poor,"* 7 (1864) 237-246.

8.67

ENGLISH WOMAN'S JOURNAL: Parkes, B.R., *"Charity as a Portion of the Public Vocation of Women,"* 3 (1859) 193-196; *"My Life and What Shall I Do with It: A Question for Young Gentlewomen,"* 6 (1860) 272-275. Discusses how leisured ladies can benefit the less fortunate; Howson, J.S., *"The Official Employment of Women in Works of Charity,"* 9 (1862) 361-364; Low, L.F.M.S. and Co., *"English Matrons and their Professions,"* 5 (1874) 25-30. Presents divisions for work: (1) work which women have to do in spreading sounder notions of household economy among the poorer classes, in training capable servants, in reducing the wasteful expenditure of the incomes of all classes, (2) the work which educated women should take in national education including the teaching of all children to 11 years old, and the organization and inspection of all those portions of national education which belong exclusively to women, and (3) the skilled care of the sick, and the supervision of the work houses, or at least of such a portion of them as are devoted to women. Three subjects are obligatory to study: household management and economy, the management of children and their primary instruction, and the laws of health and the nursing of the sick.

8.68

HEBREW REVIEW AND MAGAZINE FOR JEWISH LITERATURE: *"Charitable Movements,"* 1 (1859) 27-29; 44-45. Gives a background of attitudes and states the importance of aid to the poor; *"Increasing Munificence in Our Community,"* 1 (1860) 465. Asserts that more attention should be paid to possible donations from the middle classes rather than from "millionaires," in the effort to involve more people in charitable movements.

8.69
Barlee, Ellen, **OUR HOMELESS POOR**. 1860.

8.70
Hill, Matthew Davenport, ed., **OUR EXEMPLARS, POOR AND RICH: OR, BIOGRAPHICAL SKETCHES OF MEN AND WOMEN WHO HAVE, BY AN EXTRAORDINARY USE OF THEIR OPPORTUNITIES BENEFITED THEIR FELLOW CREATURES.** [1860]; 1861; rev. ed., 1880.

8.71
Reid, William, **WOMAN'S WORK FOR WOMAN'S WEAL**. Glasgow, 1860. By an Edinburgh minister.

8.72
TRANSACTIONS OF THE NATIONAL ASSOCIATION FOR THE PROMOTION OF SOCIAL SCIENCE: Carpenter, M., *"On the Connexion of Voluntary Effort with Government Aid."* (1861) 440.

8.73
FRASER'S MAGAZINE: Cobbe, F.P., *"Female Charity: Lay and Monastic,"* 66 (1862) 774-788.

8.74
Sewell, Mrs. (Margaret), **'THY POOR BROTHER': LETTERS TO A FRIEND ON HELPING THE POOR.** 1863.

8.75
Davies, Emily, **THE HIGHER EDUCATION OF WOMEN**. 1866. "Unpaid work, such as the management of hospitals, workhouses, prisons, reformatories, and charitable societies, naturally devolves upon the leisurely classes and offers a field in which cultivated women may fitly labour.... the problem of how to deal with pauperism——the very same difficulty which has hitherto baffled the wisest statesmen——meets them at the threshold of their work" (pp. 77-78). Davies also discusses paid positions in charitable institutions, but cautions that in these, women are employed in capacities subordinate to men.

8.76
JOURNAL OF SOCIAL SCIENCE: Nov. 1865 to Oct. 1866.

8.77
Rathbone, William, **SOCIAL DUTIES. CONSIDERED WITH REFERENCE TO THE ORGANIZATION OF EFFORT IN WORKS OF BENEVOLENCE AND PUBLIC UTILITY. BY A MAN OF BUSINESS.** 1867. "A careful enquiry into the charities of a single town or district would reveal not merely defects and omissions, but errors on the other side——errors of waste, extravagance, and superfluous machinery and expenditure: two societies undertaking the same work; two or more individuals residing in the same quarters, and giving twice over the relief which may or may not have been originally needed; various benevolent organizations, wholly unconnected, devoting their funds and energies to offices of kindness at every point intersecting and overlapping each other... the principle reason is that charity... has been an affair of sentiment rather than of principle" (pp. 64-65).

8.78
Bosanquet, Charles B.P., **LONDON: SOME ACCOUNT OF ITS GROWTH, CHARITABLE AGENCIES, AND WANTS... WITH A CLUE MAP.** 1868.

8.79
Cooper, Anthony Ashley (Lord Shaftesbury), **SPEECHES UPON SUBJECTS HAVING RELATION CHIEFLY TO THE CLAIMS AND INTERESTS OF THE WORKING CLASSES.** 1868. —*see also:* Hodder, Edwin, **THE LIFE AND WORK OF THE SEVENTH EARL OF SHAFTESBURY.** 1888. Shaftesbury was an eminent Victorian philanthropist and reformer who took a special interest in the conditions of poor and working-class women.

8.80
Fawcett, Henry, **PAUPERISM, ITS CAUSES AND REMEDIES.** 1871; "Pauperism, Charity, and the Poor Law" in **ESSAYS AND LECTURES ON SOCIAL AND POLITICAL SUBJECTS.** by Henry Fawcett and Millicent Garrett Fawcett. 1872. Diminishing pauperism rests upon the following measures: "The curtailment and gradual abolition of out-door relief; the introduction of a complete system of national education; the re-organisation of charitable bequests, and an improvement in the industrial position of women" (p. 106).

8.81
Loch, Charles Stewart, **HOW TO HELP CASES OF DISTRESS. A HANDY REFERENCE BOOK FOR ALMONERS AND OTHERS.** 1883; 5th ed., 1895; many subsequent eds. "Charity unwisely administered is capable of doing incalculable harm to its recipients. Almsgiving or charity is... the rendering of service to another out of love or pity.... The individual should provide against hunger, nakedness, and want of shelter; the father against these things both for himself and his wife and family" (pp. iv-v); *also published as:* **THE HANDBOOK OF SOCIAL CASE WORK, VOLUNTARY AND OFFICIAL (THE PREVENTION AND RELIEF OF DISTRESS. A YEAR BOOK OF INFORMATION AND STATISTICS.)** 35th ed., 1936; **AN EXAMINATION OF "GENERAL" BOOTH'S SOCIAL SCHEME.** 1890; **OLD AGE PENSIONS AND PAUPERISM.** 1892; **OLD AGE PENSIONS, THE CASE AGAINST OLD AGE PENSIONS SCHEMES.** 1903; (as editor), **METHODS OF SOCIAL ADVANCE; SHORT STUDIES IN SOCIAL PRACTICE BY VARIOUS AUTHORS.** 1904; **CHARITY AND SOCIAL LIFE. A SHORT STUDY OF RELIGIOUS AND SOCIAL THOUGHT IN RELATION TO CHARITABLE METHODS AND INSTITUTIONS.** 1910. Surveys charitable movements historically and also discusses charitable thought found in the Bible. See especially: "Charitable Movements After 1601," "The Organization of Charity," and "Particular Questions of Charitable Administration"; **A GREAT IDEAL AND ITS CHAMPION: PAPERS AND ADDRESSES BY THE LATE SIR CHARLES STEWART LOCH.** ed. by Arthur Clay. 1923. Compilation of the Charity Organization Society papers, speeches, abstracts, and correspondence by Loch.

8.82
Cobbe, Frances Power, "Woman as a Citizen of the State" in **THE DUTIES OF WOMEN: A COURSE OF LECTURES.** by Frances Power Cobbe. 7th ed., 1884.

8.83
NINETEENTH CENTURY: Cowper, K., *"Some Experiences of Work in an East-End District,"* 18 (1885) 783-793. Cowper contends that the greatest difficulty in the slums is overcrowding and that pulling down old rookeries will do nothing to discourage this tendency of the poor, who "will crowd into any other, third-, fourth-, or fifth-rate houses they can find, and there form again more rookeries

and slums" (p. 787); Stuart-Wortley, J., *"The East End as Represented by Mr. Besant,"* 22 (1887) 361-375. Critiques the view of the East End as portrayed in Besant's novels for the "systematic suppression of all the efforts made on behalf of the poor by any religious body, or from any acknowledged religious motive. Not being himself in sympathy with these influences he despises them and ignores their results" (p. 363); Hunter, R., *"The Future of the City Charities,"* 27 (1890) 72-88; *"Women as Public Servants,"* 28 (1890) 950-958; Sellers, E., *"How to Organize a People's Kitchen in London,"* 37 (1895) 409-420. Contends that a well fed man prevents misery, drunkenness and crime. The organizational structure calls for a lady superintendent; Loch, C.S., *"Manufacturing a New Pauperism,"* 37 (1895) 697-708; Jersey, M.E., *"Charity a Hundred Years Ago,"* 57 (1905) 655-670. Discusses the efforts made by The Society for Bettering the Condition and Increasing the Comforts of the Poor, founded in 1796.

8.84

Brabazon, Reginald (Earl of Meath), **SOCIAL ARROWS.** 1886; 2nd ed., 1887. See especially: "Benefit Associations" and "Social Wants of London."

8.85

Swanwick, Anna, **AN UTOPIAN DREAM (I.E., THE IMPROVEMENT OF THE CONDITION OF THE LOWER CLASSES IN LONDON) AND HOW IT MAY BE REALIZED.** 1888.

8.86

NATIONAL REVIEW: Foster, F.M., *"Women as Social Reformers,"* 13 (1889) 220.

8.87

WESTMINSTER REVIEW: Ellis, E.G., *"The Fetish of Charity,"* 135 (1891) 300-310, 373-384.

8.88

[Wright, Thomas], **THE PINCH OF POVERTY: SUFFERINGS AND HEROISM OF THE LONDON POOR.** 1892.

8.89

PHILANTHROPY AND SOCIAL PROGRESS. SEVEN ESSAYS BY MISS JANE ADDAMS, ROBERT A. WOODS, FATHER J.O.S. HUNTINGTON, PROFESSOR FRANKLIN H. GIDDINGS, AND BERNARD BOSANQUET. New York, [1893]; *reviewed in:* **INTERNATIONAL JOURNAL OF ETHICS:** Coit, S., 4 (1894) 241-246. "Above all other teachings of this volume the idea of the Social Settlement stands out" (p. 246).

8.90

Barnett, Henrietta O., "What Girls Can Do to Hush the 'Bitter Cry'"; "The Poverty of the Poor"; "Passionless Reformers"; "The Young Women in Our Workhouses"; "What Has the Charity Organisation Society to Do with Social Reform?" in **PRACTICABLE SOCIALISM: ESSAYS ON SOCIAL REFORM.** by Samuel A. Barnett and Henrietta O. Barnett. 2nd ed., 1894.

8.91

Hill, Georgiana, "The Modern Humanitarian Movement" and "The Philanthropists" in **WOMEN IN ENGLISH LIFE.** by Georgiana Hill. 1894.

8.92

Bosanquet, Bernard, et al., eds., **ASPECTS OF THE SOCIAL PROBLEM BY**

VARIOUS WRITERS. 1895. The contributors attempt to combine "trained observation in the social field with reasonable theory" developed from their experience in welfare work. Bosanquet asserts that, while external socio-economic conditions may account for the problematic circumstances of the needy, "circumstance is modifiable by character [and in] social reform, character is the condition of conditions" (p. vi). The social service worker selects for assistance the deserving poor.

8.93
Hobson, John, **PROBLEMS OF POVERTY: AN INQUIRY INTO THE INDUSTRIAL CONDITION OF THE POOR.** 1895.

8.94
Allen, W.O.B. and McClure, Edmund, **TWO HUNDRED YEARS: THE HISTORY OF THE SOCIETY FOR THE PROMOTION OF CHRISTIAN KNOWLEDGE, 1698-1898.** 1898. Represented charity aimed at taming "profanity" and "immorality." The English poor were regarded as suffering from irreligion as a result of undisciplined youth. Children were to be trained, through charitable effort, in habits of industry, morality and Protestant religion. Provisions included schools, books and pamphlets.

8.95
Bosanquet, Helen (Dendy), **RICH AND POOR.** 1896; **THE ADMINISTRATION OF CHARITABLE RELIEF.** 1898; **THE STANDARD OF LIFE AND OTHER STUDIES.** 1898; 1906. See especially: "Marriage in East London" and "The Industrial Training of Women"; "Treatment of the Destitute Classes in England" in **WOMEN IN SOCIAL LIFE. THE TRANSACTIONS OF THE SOCIAL SECTION OF THE INTERNATIONAL CONGRESS OF WOMEN. LONDON, JULY 1899.** ed. by Ishbel Aberdeen. 1900. Examines the differences between the Poor Law method of administering relief and those methods utilized by charitable enterprises; **THE STRENGTH OF THE PEOPLE.** 1902; 2nd ed., 1903. An attempt towards "the systematic study of social difficulties and their remedies" (n.p.); **THE FAMILY.** 1906; New York, 1923; **THE POOR LAW REPORT OF 1909: A SUMMARY EXPLAINING THE DEFECTS OF THE PRESENT SYSTEM AND THE PRINCIPAL RECOMMENDATIONS OF THE COMMISSION, SO FAR AS RELATES TO ENGLAND AND WALES.** 1909. "The problem of public assistance presents itself as the problem of offering help in such a way as to diminish rather than to increase the number of those requiring it" (p. 5). Claims that the failure of the Poor Law is in its administration, not the law itself; **SOCIAL CONDITIONS IN PROVINCIAL TOWNS.** 1912; **SOCIAL WORK IN LONDON. A HISTORY OF THE CHARITY ORGANISATION SOCIETY.** 1914.

8.96
CONTEMPORARY REVIEW: Hobson, J.A., *"The Social Philosophy of Charity Organisation,"* 70 (1896) 710-727.

8.97
Bliss, William D.P., et al., eds., **THE ENCYCLOPEDIA OF SOCIAL REFORM. INCLUDING POLITICAL ECONOMY, POLITICAL SCIENCE, SOCIOLOGY, AND STATISTICS, COVERING ANARCHISM, CHARITIES, CIVIL SERVICE, CURRENCY, LAND AND LEGISLATION REFORM, PENOLOGY, SOCIALISM, SOCIAL PURITY, TRADES UNIONS, WOMAN SUFFRAGE, ETC.** 1897. Short article entries cover subjects on the entire range of philanthropic and social reform issues. Includes biographies of social reformers and information on women's activities. See especially: "England and Social Reform."

8.98

Woods, Robert Archey, **ENGLISH SOCIAL MOVEMENTS**. 3rd ed., New York, 1897. See especially: "Charity and Philanthropy."

8.99

ENGLISHWOMAN'S REVIEW: *"Notes and Incidents of the Quarter. Artificial Causes of Poverty,"* 28 (1897) 32-35. Report on an address "delivered by Mr. Egmont Hake, at the request of the women's work committee" (p. 32). Hake maintains that the tax rates produced poverty and that "the device of taxing the rich above the level of the poor... meant that the rich must curtail their expenditure and loss of work be entailed on the workers——loss of ten or even a hundred-fold the value of the rates" (p. 33); *"Poor Law and Local Government Work,"* 30 (1899) 223-224; 285-286.

8.100

Chance, William, **OUR TREATMENT OF THE POOR**. 1899. Argues for the restriction of state interference in relieving the poor. The State's function should be "the relief of destitution only" (p. 10).

8.101

Mauriceau, Madame, **WOMEN AND PUBLIC CHARITY**. 1899.

8.102

Pigou, A.C., "Some Aspects of the Problem of Charity" in **THE HEART OF THE EMPIRE: DISCUSSIONS OF PROBLEMS OF MODERN CITY LIFE IN ENGLAND**. ed. by C.F.G. Masterman. 1901; rpt., New York, 1973.

8.103

Ellwood, Charles A., **PUBLIC RELIEF AND PRIVATE CHARITY IN ENGLAND**. Columbia, Mo. 1903.

8.104

Ditchfield, Peter Hampson, **THE CITY COMPANIES OF LONDON AND THEIR GOOD WORKS: A RECORD OF THEIR HISTORY, CHARITY AND TREASURE**. 1904.

8.105

Gray, B. Kirkman, **A HISTORY OF ENGLISH PHILANTHROPY. FROM THE DISSOLUTION OF THE MONASTERIES TO THE TAKING OF THE FIRST CENSUS**. 1905. See page 160 for a brief description of "the utility of women in charitable work"; **PHILANTHROPY AND THE STATE, OR SOCIAL POLITICS**. 1908. "Private corporations could not adequately deal with difficulties which result not from personal but from public causes.... It was left to experience to demonstrate that a State which assists cannot refrain from exercising control" (p. ix). See index for women's involvement as guardians, inspectors, nurses, visitors, etc.; **A MODERN HUMANIST: MISCELLANEOUS PAPERS OF B. KIRKMAN GRAY**. ed. by Henry Bryan Binns. 1910. See especially: "Two Tramps," "On Slum Theology," and "The Social Value of Hooligans."

8.106

Jebb, Eglantyne, **CAMBRIDGE. A BRIEF STUDY IN SOCIAL QUESTIONS**. Cambridge, 1906. Collection of essays which examine issues such as unemployment, housing problems, better education for mothers in domestic management, temperance societies in operation, the benefits of thrift, girls' clubs in Cambridge, and the types of charitable and religious societies available to administer relief.

8.107
Money, L.C. Chiozza, **RICHES AND POVERTY**. 1906. Concerns the unequal distribution of wealth. Discusses solutions for improvement of the conditions of poor people via state intervention.

8.108
Strachey, J. St. Loe, **THE MANUFACTURE OF PAUPERS. A PROTEST AND A POLICY**. 1906. Compilation of essays originally published in THE SPECTATOR. "The unemployed... are not a natural, but largely an artificial, product.... It is the object of the present volume to show how in various ways the State is engaged in their production; and how, if we do not stay our hand, we shall sap the strength of the people, and produce for future generations a race of paupers" (p. 2).

8.109
Conybeare, William, **CHARITY OF POOR TO POOR, FACTS COLLECTED IN SOUTH LONDON AT THE SUGGESTION OF THE BISHOP OF SOUTHWARK**. 1908.

8.110
Barnett, Canon and Barnett, Mrs. S.A. (Henrietta O.), **TOWARDS SOCIAL REFORM**. 1909. The tone is anti-state intervention except in matters of education. Asserts that the poor should be taught to help themselves and that outdated Poor Laws hinder instead of help them. However, contends that behavior is shaped by the environment instead of by inherited characteristics. Calls for social reforms to meet this train of thought. ——*see also:* Barnett, Henrietta O., **CANON BARNETT: HIS LIFE, WORK AND FRIENDS**. 2 vols. 1918. Barnett was a warden of Toynbee Hall who advocated "practical socialism"——the public initiative to provide housing, education, medical treatment and old-age pensions; Abel, Emily, "Canon Barnett and the First Thirty Years of Toynbee Hall," Ph.D. diss., London Univ., 1969. The work, attitudes and ideas of Samuel A. and Henrietta O. Barnett. Abel portrays their partnership in the settlement and other philanthropies. She offers rare details of the personality, activities and accomplishments of Henrietta. The Barnetts' early beliefs about assisting the poor by close personal service coincided with those identified with the Charity Organisation Society. However, they reformulated their ideas in accordance with contemporary social needs and conditions and recognized the need for social change. The Barnetts' eventual positive consideration of State intervention drew them away from basic tenets of the C.O.S.; Young, Agnes Freda and Ashton, Elwyn Thomas, **BRITISH SOCIAL WORK IN THE NINETEENTH CENTURY**. 1956. Quotes Samuel Barnett on his opposition to the C.O.S.: They had become "'idolaters of former dogmas,' out of sympathy 'with the forces that are shaping our times'" (p. 112).

8.111
Webb, Sidney and Webb, Beatrice, **ENGLISH POOR LAW POLICY**. 1910; 1913; **THE PREVENTION OF DESTITUTION**. 1911. See especially: "Destitution as a Disease of Society," "Destitution and Eugenics" and "The Enlarged Sphere of Voluntary Agencies in the Prevention of Destitution"; **ENGLISH POOR LAW HISTORY IN THE LAST HUNDRED YEARS**. 2 vols. 1929; rpt., 1963. Extremely valuable work for the context and treatment of poverty.

8.112
Haldane, J.B., **THE SOCIAL WORKER'S GUIDE: A HANDBOOK OF INFORMATION AND COUNSEL FOR ALL WHO ARE INTERESTED IN PUBLIC**

WELFARE. [1911]. Gives scope of social services during the period. Includes information on laws, organizations, agencies, schools, occupations for boys and girls and the sex differentiations therein.

8.113
Pearson, Edith, "Spiritual Motherhood and Philanthropic Service" in THE POSITION OF WOMAN: ACTUAL AND IDEAL. ed. by Louisa Lumsden. 1911. Finds the entrance of women in public life acceptable, if motivated as "true mothers." In this manner, women would not be outside their "sphere" and would therefore complement the male, "bringing into the life of the nation and of the race the best features and amenities of a happy home" (p. 146).

8.114
Kerr, Helen L., THE PATH OF SOCIAL PROGRESS; A DISCUSSION OF OLD AND NEW IDEAS IN SOCIAL REFORM. 1912.

8.115
Attlee, Clement Richard, THE SOCIAL WORKER. 1920.

8.116
Brittain, Vera, "Voluntary Work" in WOMEN'S WORK IN MODERN ENGLAND. by Vera Brittain. 1928.

8.117
Slater, Gilbert, POVERTY AND THE STATE. 1930. Nineteen chapters on aid to children, the aged, unemployed, poorly housed, etc. "The effect of the entry of women on the Boards was great and important.... The great majority of the women guardians were keen on the detail of work; they raised the standard of efficiency, of humanity, of courtesy, and of financial probity" (p. 165).

8.118
Woolf, Virginia, "Introductory Letter to Margaret Llewelyn Davies" in LIFE AS WE HAVE KNOWN IT. BY COOPERATIVE WORKING WOMEN. ed. by Margaret Llewelyn Davies. 1931; New York, 1975.

8.119
Macadam, Elizabeth, THE NEW PHILANTHROPY: A STUDY OF RELATIONS BETWEEN THE STATUTORY AND VOLUNTARY SOCIAL SERVICES. 1934. Analysis of the growing interdependence of statutory and voluntary services. "This partnership which I have called the new philanthropy [has come to stay]" (p. 287). Macadam appeals to voluntary agencies to cooperate with the trend. "In the sphere of voluntary social work, Charles Loch, Octavia Hill, Bernard and Helen Bosanquet during the last twenty years of the nineteenth and the early years of the present century, not only evolved methods of charity organization, but formulated principles and ideas of social progress which have left a more permanent stamp on social thought than is generally realized" (p. 21); THE SOCIAL SERVANT IN THE MAKING. foreword by S.W. Harris. 1945. See: "The Training Movement, 1890-1944." Discusses the connections among the Settlement movement, the Charity Organisation Society, the National Union of Women Workers (later National Council of Women) and the London School of Sociology and Economics and the universities' schools of social science.

8.120
Wickwar, William Hardy and Wickwar, Margaret, THE SOCIAL SERVICES: AN HISTORICAL SURVEY. 1936; rev. ed., 1949. Discusses social assistance, education,

public health and other related issues.

8.121
Williams, Gertrude, **THE STATE AND THE STANDARD OF LIVING.** 1936. Surveys the extent of poverty revealed by studies during the late nineteenth century and the subsequent governmental policy changes that occurred in the social services.

8.122
Simey, Thomas Spensley, **PRINCIPLES OF SOCIAL ADMINISTRATION.** 1937. "The history of the last two or three centuries shows that it is the rate of expansion of the social services that is new, and not the services themselves" (p. 1). See especially: "The Historical Background, 1834-1900." Briefly surveys reforms made in Poor Law administration, education and penal policies.

8.123
Lewis, William Sheldon and Williams, Ralph M., **PRIVATE CHARITY IN ENGLAND, 1747-1757.** New Haven, 1938. Emphasizes that a strong philanthropic spirit existed before the mid-eighteenth century. Individuals and organizations tended to stipulate the beneficiaries of their philanthropic efforts. Discusses motives and impulses behind private charity, isolating three: self-interest, humanitarianism, and spiritual motivation.

8.124
SOCIAL SCIENCE REVIEW: Treudley, M.B., *"The Benevolent Fair: A Study of Chairtable Organization Among American Women in the First Third of the Nineteenth Century,"* 14 (1940) 509-522. Raises questions that could be applied to the English scene.

8.125
de Schweinitz, Karl, **ENGLAND'S ROAD TO SOCIAL SECURITY, 1349-1942.** 1943. Examines the principles on which charitable organizations were founded and considers legal matters. Specific issues related to women are discussed.

8.126
Bourdillon, Anne Francis Claudine, ed., **VOLUNTARY SOCIAL SERVICES: THEIR PLACE IN THE MODERN STATE.** 1945. Important anthology with historical perspective. "Voluntary social service organizations have developed from two main sources, philanthropy and mutual aid. Up to and through the nineteenth century the vast majority... worked on a purely philanthropic basis. Service was rendered... by one group to another group, and there was no overlapping.... The privileged gave and the underprivileged received, and the condition of the people and the width of the gap between the 'Two Nations' made any other arrangement virtually impossible. At the same time... there developed also a tradition of voluntary organizations based on mutual aid" (pp. 5-6). See especially the valuable chapters by G.D.H. Cole, "A Retrospect of the History of Voluntary Service," and "Mutual Aid Movements in Their Relation to Voluntary Social Service."

8.127
Ferrill, E.W., "The Background of Old Age Pension Legislation in England, 1878-1908," Ph.D. diss., Univ. of Illinois, 1946.

8.128
Cohen, Emmeline W., **ENGLISH SOCIAL SERVICES: METHODS AND GROWTH.** 1949. See especially: "Provisions at the Opening of the Nineteenth Century." Useful summary of the history of social legislation.

8.129
Rodgers, Betsy, **CLOAK OF CHARITY: STUDIES IN EIGHTEENTH-CENTURY PHILANTHROPY.** 1949. Surveys social conditions which impelled charitable attention and analyzes more personal motivations of eighteenth-century philanthropists, such as "to escape from punishment in the next world," enhance self-esteem, gain "pleasure from giving," check fear of decrease in the population of labor, reduce crime and restore "order," allay fear of revolution, and indulge religion and emotion. "The conception of charity as a religious exercise necessary to salvation remained" (p. 7). Rodgers illustrates the motivations in philanthropic activity involving poor relief, homeless children, prison reform, Sunday schools and schools of industry, and anti-slave-trade campaigns.

8.130
Wood, Ethel M., "Women and Social Service" in **THE PILGRIMAGE OF PERSEVERANCE.** by Ethel M. Wood. 1949. Discusses woman's role in philanthropy and charitable work: Hannah More, Octavia Hill, Elizabeth Fry, Josephine Butler, and Elizabeth Garrett Anderson.

8.131
AMERICAN HISTORICAL REVIEW: Mowat, C.L., *"The Approach to the Welfare State in Great Britain,"* 58 (1952-1953) 55-63.

8.132
Bottomore, Thomas, "Social Stratification in Voluntary Organizations" in **SOCIAL MOBILITY IN BRITAIN.** ed. by D.V. Glass. 1954. Discusses methodology for studying voluntary organization, including the variables of geographical location, population by sex and age, environment, history and traditions. The organizations themselves are analyzed in terms of function, membership by sex and age, occupational status of members, etc.

8.133
Morris, Mary, **VOLUNTARY ORGANIZATIONS AND SOCIAL PROGRESS.** 1955. Delineates the role of voluntary bodies as "independent of statutory authority" and their powers as compared with public agencies.

8.134
Ross, Elizabeth M., "Women and Poor Law Administration 1857-1910," M.A. thesis, London Univ., 1956.

8.135
Mencher, Samuel, "The Relationship of Voluntary and Statutory Welfare Services in England," Ph.D. diss., Columbia Univ., 1957; **POOR LAW TO POVERTY PROGRAM: ECONOMIC SECURITY POLICY IN BRITAIN AND THE UNITED STATES.** Pittsburgh, 1967.

8.136
Rooff, Madeline, **VOLUNTARY SOCIETIES AND SOCIAL POLICY.** 1957. See especially: "Influences Affecting Social Policy and Voluntary Action," "New Forms of Partnership," and "The Maternity and Child Welfare Movement." "The emancipation of women was, in fact, one of the important influences in the advance of social welfare... middle-class women, in particular, had an opening for their talents at a time when the changing family structure and the new pattern of society had taken from them the older household responsibilities.... As the century advanced, women were playing an increasing part in public life as members of

Boards of Guardians, while others were offering help to medical officers of health as they built up a service of infant welfare" (pp. 14-15).

8.137
Jordan, W.K., **PHILANTHROPY IN ENGLAND 1480-1660: A STUDY OF THE CHANGING PATTERN OF ENGLISH SOCIAL ASPIRATIONS.** 1959. Discusses the charitable contributions of women over the period.

8.138
Roberts, David, **VICTORIAN ORIGINS OF THE WELFARE STATE.** New Haven, 1960. Important work on state intervention in social reforms: regulation of factory work, prisons, education, and public health.

8.139
Semmel, Bernard, **IMPERIALISM AND SOCIAL REFORM: ENGLISH SOCIAL-IMPERIAL THOUGHT 1895-1914.** 1960.

8.140
ARCHIVES OF EUROPEAN SOCIOLOGY: Briggs, A., *"The Welfare State in Historical Perspective,"* 11 (1961) 221-258.

8.141
Heasman, Kathleen, **EVANGELICALS IN ACTION: AN APPRAISAL OF THEIR SOCIAL WORK IN THE VICTORIAN ERA.** 1962. "There was also a deepening sense of guilt at the inequality of wealth and the appalling conditions of living of an appreciable proportion of the population.... A less worthy motive, though typical of the materialism of the Victorian era, was the desire for publicity and power. Many of the voluntary societies were what was known as 'voting charities.' It was the large subscriber who was elected to honorary office.... Beneficiaries were chosen by the vote of donors (p. 10).... The unequal proportion of men to women... left many women unmarried and large numbers of these found some compensation for the lack of a home of their own in living and working among the poor" (p. 11).

8.142
YALE LAW JOURNAL: Woodard, C., *"Reality and Reform: The Transition from Laissez-Faire to the Welfare State,"* 72 (1962) 286-328. Reveals that early Victorian philanthropists gravely misconceived the nature of poverty and underestimated its dimensions. Argues that a really powerful attack on poverty had to wait until the transition from an agricultural to an industrial society was more fully accomplished.

8.143
Hargrove, B., "The Reform of the Law and Administration of Charities in the Nineteenth Century," Ph.D. diss., Univ. of London, 1963.

8.144
HISTORICAL JOURNAL: Roberts, D., *"How Cruel Was the Victorian Poor Law?"* 6 (1963) 97-106; Crowther, M.A., *"Family Responsibility and State Responsibility in Britain Before the Welfare State,"* 25 (1982) 131-145. Good background discussion. "The Poor Law had two definitions of the family: one for legal purposes, the other an informal definition which equated the household with the family when outdoor relief was assessed.... The inconsistency of the system, in a time of mass unemployment, when the virtue of regional migration was constantly paraded, is remarkable" (pp. 144-145); Morris, R.J., *"Voluntary Societies and British Urban Elites, 1780-1850: An Analysis,"* 26 (1983) 95-118. "Voluntary societies... were the

basis for the formation of a middle-class identity across the wide status ranges, and the fragmented political members of that class. They enabled the elite to assert their economic and cultural authority within that middle class" (p. 96); Thane, P., *"The Working Class and State 'Welfare' in Britain, 1880-1914,"* 27 (1984) 877-900. Explores evidence that the mass of working people were hostile or indifferent to state welfare at least *after* measures such as old age pensions and national insurance were introduced. On compulsory education: "In London in the 1890s poorer families resented compulsory attendance.... [It] had placed poorer parents in a real dilemma... 'decent folk... didn't want to keep their children ignorant, but sometimes there were no books, sometimes there was a baby to feed, sometimes there was no food'" (p. 893, quoting Annie Besant).

8.145
Burn, W.L., "Getting and Spending" in THE AGE OF EQUIPOISE: A STUDY OF THE MID-VICTORIAN GENERATION. 1964. "Private organizations such as the District Visiting Societies, the Strangers Friend Society with 400 unpaid visitors, the Female and Domestic Bible Mission with 230 paid agents.... could not hope to render the basic remedy of poor-relief unnecessary: what they could hope to do was to create a parallel system, more flexible and intelligent and with somewhat different aims (p. 126).... [The] claim was made that, given time, solution was possible by a system in which voluntary effort played a major part" (p. 127).

8.146
Younghusband, Eileen, SOCIAL WORK AND SOCIAL CHANGE. 1964. For the period to 1914 see: "The Social Services and Social Work." Acknowledges a great debt to the Charity Organisation Society for discovering "the importance of organizing charity," for developing some of the main methods of casework, and for initiating social work education (1903). Younghusband also acknowledges the shift to American leadership in the earlier twentieth century when the English social work profession, with the exception of the psychiatric field (p. 20), suffered a "blight" and remained almost "static" (p. 18). There is no analysis of the reasons for this, and it may be worth researching.

8.147
Bruce, Maurice, THE COMING OF THE WELFARE STATE. 1961; rpt. 1965; rev. ed. with a comparative essay on American and English Welfare, New York, 1968. See especially: Part II, "Background and Beginnings," Part III, "Forty Years on The Impact of the Industrial Revolution," and Part IV, "The Victorian Poor Law"; (as editor), THE RISE OF THE WELFARE STATE: ENGLISH SOCIAL POLICY, 1601-1971. 1973. Selection of documents intended to show the stages by which the Welfare State came into existence.

8.148
Jeffreys, Margot, AN ANATOMY OF SOCIAL WELFARE SERVICES: A SURVEY OF SOCIAL WELFARE STAFF AND THEIR CLIENTS IN THE COUNTY OF BUCKINGHAMSHIRE. 1965. Shows the place of voluntary and professional social work in the administration of local government.

8.149
Lubove, Roy, THE PROFESSIONAL ALTRUIST: THE EMERGENCE OF SOCIAL WORK AS A CAREER 1880-1930. Cambridge, 1965. See especially: "Charity Organization and the New Gospel of Benevolence." The book refers to American social work, but this chapter shows the influence of English charitable organizations upon those in the United States; (as editor), SOCIAL WELFARE IN TRANSITION. SELECTED ENGLISH DOCUMENTS, 1834-1909. Pittsburgh, 1966. Valuable

collection of legislation, regulations, and reports that treat issues such as slum clearance, boards of health, medical relief and inspection, regulation of town growth, sanitary conditions, poor law administration, etc. Analytical/contextual introductions and text are provided.

8.150
Victorian Society, **THE VICTORIAN POOR: FOURTH CONFERENCE REPORT.** 1966. Compilation of papers by E.P. Thompson, J.D. Burnett, A. Armstrong, H.J. Dyos, J. Tobias, and Helen Meller on various aspects of nineteenth-century poverty.

8.151
VICTORIAN STUDIES: Harrison, B., *"Philanthropy and the Victorian,"* 9 (1966) 353-374; Gerard, J., *"Lady Bountiful: Women of the Landed Classes and Rural Philanthropy,"* 30 (1987) 183-209.

8.152
Deacon, Alan, "The Social Position of the Unmarried Woman in the Mid-Victorian Period and its Relationship to the Development of Philanthropy," B.A. honors thesis, London Univ., 1967.

8.153
SOUTH ATLANTIC QUARTERLY: O'Neill, J.E., *"The Victorian Background to the British Welfare State,"* 66 (1967) 204-217.

8.154
Pelling, Henry, "The Working Class and the Origins of the Welfare State" in **POPULAR POLITICS AND SOCIETY IN LATE VICTORIAN BRITAIN.** by Henry Pelling. 1968.

8.155
Brasnett, Margaret, **VOLUNTARY SOCIAL ACTION: A HISTORY OF THE NATIONAL COUNCIL OF SOCIAL SERVICE 1919-1969.** 1969.

8.156
Poynter, J.R., **SOCIETY AND PAUPERISM: ENGLISH IDEAS ON POOR RELIEF, 1795-1834.** 1969. "In many parishes little distinction was made between relief under the law and private charity, magistrates, overseers, philanthropists and employers co-operating in arrangements which called on both public and private financial resources. Nevertheless, wherever private charity was extensive and systematic there was always a potential conflict between its aims and ideals and traditional patterns of public relief and the charitable were likely to become outspoken critics of the Poor Law" (p. 85).

8.157
Rodgers, Brian, **THE BATTLE AGAINST POVERTY.** 2 vols. 1969. See pp. 43-48 for a discussion of "The Charity Organization Society and its Influence" and "The Beginnings of Change" which examines the work of Joseph Chamberlain. Chapters 6 and 7 discuss the Poor Law Report and Social Insurance.

8.158
Halmos, Paul, **THE PERSONAL SERVICE SOCIETY.** 1970. Argues that social work is a moral force gradually superseding that of religion. It is a section of the service professions such as nursing, medicine and teaching as contrasted with impersonal service professions like law, accountancy and insurance. Data show that women predominate in personal service, but Halmos does not analyze this gender

factor.

8.159
Stocks, Mary, **MY COMMONPLACE BOOK**. 1970. Tells how the women students in university social work training and who earned a diploma in Social Studies were known as "Professor Urwick's Harem." They were looked down upon by the Bachelor of Science students at London School of Economics.

8.160
Best, Geoffrey F.A., "Philanthropy and Poor Relief" in **MID-VICTORIAN ENGLAND 1854-1875**. by Geoffrey Best. 1971.

8.161
Jones, Gareth Stedman, **OUTCAST LONDON: A STUDY IN THE RELATIONSHIP BETWEEN CLASSES IN VICTORIAN SOCIETY**. 1971. Discusses the impact of economic developments on the pattern of change in London, and analyzes middle-class efforts to assist the poor and working classes to accommodate these changes and to adopt middle-class values.

8.162
McCrone, Kathleen Eleanor, "Female Philanthropy and Social Welfare" in "The Advancement of Women During the Age of Reform, 1832-1870," Ph.D. diss., New York Univ., 1971. Examines women's roles in charitable endeavors and participation in developing more modern social services.

8.163
Rose, Michael E., ed., **THE ENGLISH POOR LAW, 1780-1930**. 1971. Compilation of documents published on poor relief with commentary; **THE RELIEF OF POVERTY 1834-1914**. 1972. "Poverty has been regarded by many writers as a necessary element in society since only by feeling its pinch could the laboring poor be inspired to work. Thus it was not poverty but pauperism or destitution which was regarded as a social problem" (p. 7).

8.164
Searle, G.R., **THE QUEST FOR NATIONAL EFFICIENCY: A STUDY IN BRITISH POLITICS AND POLITICAL THOUGHT 1899-1914**. Berkeley, 1971.

8.165
Welsh, Alexander, "Charity" in **THE CITY OF DICKENS**. by Alexander Welsh. Oxford, 1971. "The Victorian attitude toward charity is the logical correlative of the doctrine of work. The attitude is chiefly distinguished by its emphasis on the character of the recipient of charity, an emphasis that inverts the long tradition of Christian charity as a practice contributing to the salvation of the charitable" (p. 86).

8.166
Gosden, P.H.J.H., **SELF-HELP. VOLUNTARY ASSOCIATIONS IN NINETEENTH-CENTURY BRITAIN**. 1973; New York, 1974. "Some of what are usually described as the earliest savings banks in this country were really charitable institutions. As part of her social work Mrs. Priscilla Wakefield founded a benefit society for women and children at Tottenham in 1798. Honorary members paid subscriptions which helped to meet the cost of benefits. In 1801 a loans fund was added and so was a savings bank which offered five per cent interest on deposits" (p. 210); *reviewed in:* **HISTORY**: Read, D., 60 (1975) 314-315.

8.167
Seed, Philip, **THE EXPANSION OF SOCIAL WORK IN BRITAIN.** 1973.

8.168
JOURNAL OF SOCIAL HISTORY: Lees, L.H., *"The Study of Cities and the Study of Social Processes: Two Directions in Recent Urban History,"* 7 (1973-1974) 330-337. A review essay covering recent studies by Gordon Jackson, Robert Roberts, Francis Sheppard, Gareth Stedman Jones, and Francois Vigier.

8.169
Harrison, Brian, "State Intervention and Moral Reform in Nineteenth-Century England" in **PRESSURE FROM WITHOUT IN EARLY VICTORIAN ENGLAND.** ed. by Patricia Hollis. 1974. "Moral reformers, like social reformers, were never organized into a co-ordinated movement; but they shared many personalities, attitudes, and techniques.... [One] concern... was to raise the social status of women.... Temperance organizations saw themselves as championing female dignity against male selfishness, but unlike puritan and humanitarian organizations they did not allow their feminism to affect the composition of their own hierarchies. The links between feminism and moral reform are doubly confirmed, however, in the RSPCA, the Victorian Street Society (VSS), the purity organizations and the campaign against State-regulated prostitution, for these all sympathized with women and were partly managed by them.... One further common concern of the moral reformers was to uphold the dignity of the individual in an industrial and urban context. They all championed the rights of neglected groups——of women, drunkards, prostitutes, even animals" (pp. 290-291); "A Genealogy of Reform in Modern Britain" in **ANTI-SLAVERY, RELIGION AND REFORM.** ed. by Christine Bolt and Seymour Drescher. 1980. Analysis of how an involvement in one cause could lead to commitment to others. "Women's participation helped co-ordinate all these reforming causes. Opponents of slavery and the corn laws had to face complaints that they were encouraging women into public affairs; women's prominence should almost be seen as a branch of the feminist movement itself. The Victorian reforming movement was a major forcing-ground for British feminism" (p. 142); "The Rhetoric of Reform in Modern Britain: 1780-1918" and "Philanthropy and the Victorians" in **PEACEABLE KINGDOM: STABILITY AND CHANGE IN MODERN BRITAIN.** by Brian Harrison. 1982. "Individual philanthropists naturally gravitated into social reform on seeing that personal altruism was not enough.... it was partly disappointment at the slow progress of voluntary rescue work that led Josephine Butler to campaign against state-regulated prostitution after 1869" (p. 223).

8.170
Hollis, Patricia, "Pressure From Without: An Introduction" in **PRESSURE FROM WITHOUT IN EARLY VICTORIAN ENGLAND.** ed. by Patricia Hollis. 1974. "Pressure from without... in areas of parliamentary reform, free trade, Church reform, offered a platform with a guaranteed grassroots appeal, which parties could adopt and co-opt as they saw fit. But although parties came to carry more and more 'causes,' nonetheless there were wide tracts of social policy, such as intervention in public health, factories and mines, in which party divisions did not operate" (p. 25).

8.171
Longmate, Norman, **THE WORKHOUSE.** 1974. "The policy adopted in 1834 of refusing out-relief to unsupported women soon resulted in them forming the second largest group, outnumbered only by the old, in nearly every workhouse. Some had been abandoned by their husbands; some were domestic servants between jobs; some were widows struggling to bring up a family. But a high proportion from the first

were women of, in the eyes of the authorities, low moral character.... To remind them that they were moral outcasts, many unions put their unmarried mothers into a distinctive yellow uniform, the colour of a ship's plague flag, the wearers being nicknamed 'canary wards,' but the practice was banned in 1839 as distinguishing between paupers on moral grounds" (pp. 156-157). Describes case histories and includes photographs.

8.172
Steiner, Miriam, "Philanthropic Activity and Organization in the Manchester Jewish Community, 1867-1914," M.A. thesis, Univ. of Manchester, 1974.

8.173
DICTIONARY OF LABOUR BIOGRAPHY: Bellamy, J. and Saville, J., *"Byron, Anne Isabella, Lady Noel (1792-1860) Philanthropist and Social Reformer,"* 2 (1974) 76-78. "Lady Byron's encouragement and support to individual reformers and to reforming movements is still insufficiently documented.... In the 1850s, mainly through a close friendship with Mary Carpenter, she became especially interested in the problems of juvenile delinquency" (p. 77).

8.174
INTERNATIONAL REVIEW OF SOCIAL HISTORY: Prochaska, F.K., *"Women in English Philanthropy, 1790-1830,"* 19 (1974) 4226-445. "There is no reason to suppose that women were more often inactive than their male counterparts.... Leisured women were the backbone of the expanding system of district visiting, and it might be argued that the system would have been unworkable without them.... In the early decades of the nineteenth century women worked all over England in lying-in charities, asylums for the deaf, blind, destitute, and insane" (p. 431); Evans, N., *"Urbanisation, Elite Attitudes and Philanthropy: Cardiff, 1850-1914,"* 27 (1982) 290-323. Cardiff is chosen as a case exemplifying the distinctive social climate of the nineteenth century that induced middle-class charity. Examines the response to philanthropic appeals against the background of social transformation.

8.175
Adams, B.K., "Charity, Voluntary Work and Professionalization in Late Victorian and Edwardian England, With Special Reference to the C.O.S. and Guilds of Help," M.A. thesis, Univ. of Sussex, 1976.

8.176
Fraser, Derek, ed., **THE NEW POOR LAW IN THE NINETEENTH CENTURY.** 1976. Compilation of essays which examine various aspects and issues of the Poor Law of 1834; *reviewed in:* **SOCIAL HISTORY:** Hennock, E.P., no. 6 (1977) 827-829.

8.177
McCord, Norman, "The Poor Law and Philanthropy" in **THE NEW POOR LAW IN THE 19TH CENTURY.** ed. by Derek Fraser. 1976.

8.178
Meller, Helen, **LEISURE AND THE CHANGING CITY, 1870-1914.** 1976. Discusses the rise of voluntary societies in towns after 1870 and the intensity of their "reforming," and "improving" activity. Evaluates the loss of confidence in voluntarism after the 1890s. Portrays an urban elite as undertaking a "civilized" mission to the poor.

8.179
Yeo, Stephen, **RELIGION AND VOLUNTARY ORGANIZATIONS IN CRISIS.**
1976.

8.180
SOCIAL HISTORY: Hennock, E.P., *"Poverty and Social Theory in England: The
Experience of the Eighteen-Nineties,"* 1 (1976) 67-91. The establishment of
organizations to rehabilitate down-and-outs "depended on publicity and succeeded
in obtaining it, and thereby contributed towards that preoccupation with the
meaning of poverty in the midst of plenty which both contemporaries and historians
have seen as characteristic of the 1880s" (p. 68).

8.181
Ferguson, Sheila, "Labour Women and the Social Services" in **WOMEN IN THE
LABOUR MOVEMENT.** ed. by Lucy Middleton. 1977. Especially concerned with
the work of the Women's Labour League.

8.182
Wilson, Elizabeth, "Ideology and Welfare" in **WOMEN AND THE WELFARE
STATE.** by Elizabeth Wilson. 1977.

8.183
JOURNAL OF BRITISH STUDIES: Moore, M.J., *"Social Work and Social Welfare:
The Organization of Philanthropic Resources in Britain, 1900-1914,"* 16 (1977) 85-
104. "It was the Guilds of Help that encouraged the development of responsible and
professional social work outside London; it was the Guilds that began enrolling
members of the working class in a systematic effort to aid and comfort their poorer
brethren; it was the Guilds, which made no moral distinction between public and
private welfare, that provided a foundation for cooperation between agencies
representing both spheres; and it was the Guilds that made state sponsored social
welfare palatable within the philanthropic community of Edwardian England" (p.
86).

8.184
Cook, Chris and Weeks, Jeffrey, compilers, **SOURCES IN BRITISH POLITICAL
HISTORY 1900-1951. VOLUME 5: A GUIDE TO THE PRIVATE PAPERS OF
SELECTED WRITERS, INTELLECTUALS, AND PUBLICISTS.** 1978. Includes
philanthropists, social workers, and social reformers.

8.185
Digby, Anne, **PAUPER PALACES.** 1978. Local study of the Poor Law in Norfolk.
The aim of the book is "to demythologize the Poor Law by attempting to
differentiate image from reality and theory from practice" (p. ix).

8.186
Evans, Eric J., **SOCIAL POLICY 1830-1914: INDIVIDUALISM, COLLECTIVISM
AND THE ORIGINS OF THE WELFARE STATE.** 1978. "I believe that there was
an 'age of *laissez-faire*' in the middle of the nineteenth century. I also believe that,
even in its heyday, *laissez-faire* was being 'tempered' by revelations of the seamier
side of industrial Britain and by philosophers and writers who drew certain
conclusions about these revelations (p. 2).... If 'an age of *laissez-faire*' is accepted
to the period c. 1830-c. 1870, it is necessary to inquire how governments came to
accept an increasingly interventionist position at the end of the nineteenth century.
There is no tidy answer to the question (p. 10).... By the beginning of the 1870s... a
decisive breach in the dyke of individual self-reliance and local self-government

had been made (p. 11).... Developments took place which involved an extension of State responsibilities which would have been inconceivable in the mid-twentieth century (p. 12).... The revelation that *laissez-faire* was no automatic guarantee of economic prosperity had implications for the role of the State" (p. 13). Evans follows his analytical introductory essay with a study of a wide range of social reforms that were developed to answer social problems. He illustrates, in an anthology of documents, the predominating reform agitations, ideas, private measures and government legislation that transpired 1830-1914.

8.187
Hay, James Ray, **THE DEVELOPMENT OF THE BRITISH WELFARE STATE, 1880-1975.** 1978. "Despite this reality [of unstable economic fluctuations], members of the working class held widely differing views on how best to tackle the causes of poverty. By the early 1900s many were clear as to the potential benefits and dangers of state intervention.... [Some] working-class members are often regarded as having identified themselves fully with the individualist self-help ethic of the Victorian middle class" (p. 2). Excellent introductory overview. Includes documents.

8.188
Pope, Norris, **DICKENS AND CHARITY.** 1978. "The female contribution to charitable work was utterly indispensable. Not only did a great many voluntary workers come from such groups as spinsters, widows, unmarried daughters, and middle- and upper-class women with few domestic responsibilities, but also the female role was originally unique" (p. 140).

8.189
Roach, John, **SOCIAL REFORM IN ENGLAND, 1780-1880.** 1978. Outlines the development of the political and social climate that paved the way for nineteenth-century social reform. Asserts that "reform did not begin in 1830. It has been shown that many of the main lines had been laid down in the preceding half-century. Secondly there was a strong moralistic note among men of all schools which laid a heavy emphasis on an authoritarian approach to social policy. Much more stress was laid on coercion than on persuasion" (p. 226).

8.190
Thane, Pat, ed., **THE ORIGINS OF BRITISH SOCIAL POLICY.** 1978. A collection of essays contributing valuable new material on the beginnings of the welfare state; *reviewed in:* **NEW SOCIETY:** Taylor, R., *"Welfare Myths,"* 44 (1978) 674-675.

8.191
HISTORY WORKSHOP JOURNAL: Thane, P., *"Women and the Poor Law in Victorian and Edwardian England,"* no. 6 (1978) 29-51. Contends that the English Poor Laws did not help destitute women, who were the neediest of the poor.

8.192
Bauer, Carol and Ritt, Lawrence, eds., **FREE AND ENNOBLED: SOURCE READINGS IN THE DEVELOPMENT OF VICTORIAN FEMINISM.** 1979. See especially: "Feminists and the Victorian Social Conscience." Excerpts from articles by Louisa Twining, Mary Carpenter, Octavia Hill, Bessie Rayner Parkes and Frances Power Cobbe on reform and philanthropy.

8.193
Havighurst, Alfred F., **THE BRITISH WELFARE STATE.** 1979. Short overview of social policy from the 1600s to 1978.

8.194
Henriques, Ursula R.Q., **BEFORE THE WELFARE STATE: SOCIAL ADMINISTRATION IN EARLY BRITAIN.** 1979. "Private charity for the deserving poor increased in the 19th century with the evangelization of the middle classes and some of the gentry.... Neither charity nor unchecked private enterprise was able to deal effectively with problems.... Nor was the existing public provision.... Something on a larger scale had to be done" (pp. 3-4). Surveys the public administration of reform in all areas.

8.195
McIntosh, Mary, "The Welfare and the Needs of the Dependent Family" in **FIT WORK FOR WOMEN.** ed. by Sandra Burman. 1979.

8.196
Thompson, Richard, **THE CHARITY COMMISSION AND THE AGE OF REFORM.** 1979. The Commission was created in 1818 "to examine the educational charities of England and Wales" and continued for 20 years (p. 1). Questions the assumption that reform was generally endorsed by "public opinion," which Tompson defines as more properly "elite" opinion, and discusses the rhetoric of heroism employed in reform campaigns.

8.197
Horn, Pamela, "The Relief of the Poor" in **THE RURAL WORLD, 1780-1850: SOCIAL CHANGE IN THE ENGLISH COUNTRYSIDE.** by Pamela Horn. 1980.

8.198
Humphreys, H.A., "Charity Administration and the Poor in Northwest Kent, 1870-1914," M.A. thesis, Univ. of Kent, 1980.

8.199
Prochaska, F.K., **WOMEN AND PHILANTHROPY IN NINETEENTH CENTURY ENGLAND.** Oxford, 1980. The number of women active in philanthropy in 1893 exceeded the number in any other occupation but domestic service, a statistic that makes dubious the idea of the idle Victorian woman. "Their work for the suffrage societies went hand in hand with their work as moral reformers, institutional visitors, or whatever. They dreamed of the day when men and women would work together as equals in the cause of moral and social reform, dreams nourished by the memory of their predecessors in countless charitable societies who had dealt, often unconsciously, small blow after small blow to the idea of male supremacy. The battle of the sexes in nineteenth-century England was played out in such small arenas" (p. 230); *reviewed in:* **CANADIAN JOURNAL OF HISTORY:** McCrone, K.E., 16 (1981) 503-505; *also reviewed in:* **HISTORICAL JOURNAL:** Hilden, P., *"Women's History: The Second Wave,"* 25 (1982) 501-512. Prochaska declines to portray the stereotype of female philanthropy as an extension of the housewifely role. "Instead, philanthropy provided women with a meaningful profession, one which, in Prochaska's words, 'did more than any other to enlarge the horizon of women in nineteenth-century England'" (p. 506).

8.200
BULLETIN OF THE JOHN RYLANDS UNIVERSITY LIBRARY OF MANCHESTER: Tyrell, A., *"Woman's Mission and Pressure Group Politics in Britain (1825-1860),"* 63 (1980) 194-230.

8.201
Crowther, Margaret Anne, **THE WORKHOUSE SYSTEM 1834-1929: THE**

HISTORY OF AN ENGLISH SOCIAL INSTITUTION. Athens, 1981. Explores the function of the workhouse as a refuge for the poor developed under the Poor Law. It was the last resort when other means of relief were exhausted and was looked upon as an institution for the "deserving" poor. "Anyone who accepted relief in the repellent workhouse must be lacking the moral determination to survive outside it" (p. 3); *reviewed in:* ECONOMIC HISTORY REVIEW: Fraser, D., 36 (1983) 148-149; *also reviewed in:* VICTORIAN STUDIES: Dunkley, P., 27 (1983) 118-120.

8.202
Johnson, Norman, VOLUNTARY SOCIAL SERVICES. 1981. Includes historical developments and typologies of social service agencies.

8.203
Mommsen, W.J., ed., THE EMERGENCE OF THE WELFARE STATE IN BRITAIN AND GERMANY 1850-1950. 1981.

8.204
Williams, Karel, FROM PAUPERISM TO POVERTY. 1981. Combines "three essays on the configuration of the English and Welsh poor law between 1800 and 1914, and four essays on texts of social investigation written by Mayhew, Engels, Booth, and Rowntree between the 1840s and 1940s.... The essays... develop an alternative informally semiotic mode of analysis" (p. 1).

8.205
RICE UNIVERSITY STUDIES: Roberts, D., *"Dealing with the Poor in Victorian England,"* 67 (1981) 57-74. Examines "what pervasive feelings, what widely popular attitudes, and what commonly held assumptions defined the outlooks of the many thousands who in poor law unions and philanthropies dealt with poverty.... The two [dominant attitudes] are a human concern that no one suffer extreme destitution and a strong wish that taxes be as low as possible" (p. 58). Delineates attitudes towards and conditions in workhouses and explores the work of poor law guardians. Asserts that "the desire to extend social control is an important theme, but it is one that can be exaggerated. The Victorians' desire to control and reform the poor had its limits, and their efforts to achieve both control and reform fell far short of their hopes" (p. 67).

8.206
Quadagno, Jill S., AGING IN EARLY INDUSTRIAL SOCIETY: WORK, FAMILY AND SOCIAL POLICY IN NINETEENTH CENTURY ENGLAND. New York, 1982. Includes discussions of Poor Law policy related to old age pauperism and the effects of state intervention on relationships between poor aged mothers and their grown children. The institution of welfare policies are shown to affect the life cycle patterns of work for women, particularly with regard to domestic service.

8.207
Royle, Edward and Walvin, James, ENGLISH RADICALS AND REFORMERS, 1760-1848. Lexington, 1982. "Middle-class women were more prominent than working-class women as reformers.... Campaigns challenged through the agency of churches and chapels were given a legitimacy which made them especially suitable for female participation and even leadership. The anti-slavery movement is a prime example of this, with women's groups actively spreading propaganda and petitioning on the behalf of poor blacks overseas.... The poor had their own reasons for hating the Poor Law and for wanting a restriction on the working hours of women in factories, but propaganda which exploited middle-class sensibilities about the sacredness of the family and the proper place of women undoubtedly helped win

additional support" (pp. 185-186).

8.208
Lewis, Jane, "Dealing with Dependency: State Practices and Social Realities, 1870-1945" in WOMEN'S WELFARE/WOMEN'S RIGHTS. ed. by Jane Lewis. 1983; "The Working-Class Wife and Mother and State Intervention, 1870-1918" in LABOUR AND LOVE: WOMEN'S EXPERIENCE OF HOME AND FAMILY, 1850-1940. ed. by Jane Lewis. Oxford, 1986. "Growing state concerns with motherhood as a 'social function' led to a series of interventions" (p. 109).

8.209
Barker, Paul, ed., FOUNDERS OF THE WELFARE STATE. 1984. Includes: "Towards the Welfare State" by Asa Briggs; "Josephine Butler" by Pat Thane; "Octavia Hill" by Peter Malpass; "The Webbs" by Jose Harris; and "Eleanor Rathbone" by Jane Lewis.

8.210
Himmelfarb, Gertrude, THE IDEA OF POVERTY. New York, 1984. An important work in intellectual history to fill the void in scholarly writings on the idea of poverty underlying reform, and amelioration of the conditions of the poor. Focuses on the period 1750-1850.

8.211
Darvill, Giles and Munday, Brian, eds., VOLUNTEERS IN THE PERSONAL SOCIAL SERVICES. 1984. Acknowledges developments from the past.

8.212
JOURNAL OF AMERICAN HISTORY: Boylan, Q.M., *"Women in Groups: An Analysis of Women's Benevolent Organizations in New York and Boston, 1797-1840,"* 71 (1984) 497-523. A comparative study of philanthropic and social service organizations that might be emulated for England. Boylan examines assumptions that have been made to find common denominators underlying the development of the groups involved. She concludes that there was no uniform pattern in their programs, "nor did they build on each other's experiences (p. 500).... There was not one women's organizational tradition... but several" (p. 514).

8.213
SOCIAL HISTORY SOCIETY NEWSLETTER: Perkin, H., *"Report of the Proceedings of the Conference, 'Roots of Welfare,' 21 December 1983,"* n.v. (1984) 12-14.

* * *

2. SOCIAL EXPLORATION AND INVESTIGATION

8.214
Scott, John, OBSERVATION ON THE PRESENT STATE OF THE PAROCHIAL AND VAGRANT POOR. 1773.

8.215
Eden, Fredric Morton, THE STATE OF THE POOR; OR, A HISTORY OF THE

LABOURING CLASSES IN ENGLAND. 3 vols. 1797; abridged and ed. by A.G.L. Rogers. 1928; 1966; 1969. A political economist and social critic, Eden argues that in economic life, individuals should be free to follow "their own interests." He opposes state intervention on the grounds that it would undermine "individual exertion," encourage idleness and promote charity. He differentiates the poor from the labouring classes. His survey is a valuable and pioneering work.

8.216
Colquhoun, Patrick, THE STATE OF INDIGENCE, AND THE SITUATION OF THE CASUAL POOR IN THE METROPOLIS EXPLAINED. 1799; A TREATISE ON INDIGENCE: EXHIBITING A GENERAL VIEW OF THE NATIONAL RESOURCES FOR PRODUCTIVE LABOUR; WITH PROPOSITIONS FOR AMELIORATING THE CONDITION OF THE POOR. 1806; INDIGENCE AND POVERTY. 1806. Argues that "indigence" and "poverty" should be considered separately, defining indigence as the inability to work for subsistence and poverty as indifference to work.

8.217
Owen, Robert, OBSERVATIONS ON THE MANUFACTURING SYSTEM. 1815; 3rd ed., 1818; rpt., 1966. Explores the effects of industry on society and discusses solutions to remedy its adverse effects on the working poor.

8.218
Egan, Pierce, LIFE IN LONDON. 1821.

8.219
Badcock, John, A LIVING PICTURE OF LONDON FOR 1828. 1828.

8.220
Greg, William Rathbone, AN ENQUIRY INTO THE STATE OF THE MANUFACTURING POPULATION, AND THE CAUSES AND CURES OF THE EVILS THEREIN EXISTING. 1831.

8.221
Kay-Shuttleworth, James Phillip, THE MORAL AND PHYSICAL CONDITION OF THE WORKING CLASSES EMPLOYED IN THE COTTON MANUFACTURE IN MANCHESTER. 2nd ed., 1832; [1892]; rpt., 1970. Author may also be cataloged as Shuttleworth, James Phillip Kay.

8.222
NEW MONTHLY MAGAZINE: Bacon, R.M., *"On the State of the Rural Population,"* 34 (1832) 209-224; *"The State of the Poor in a Manufacturing Town [Manchester],"* 35 (1832) 53-57; *"Letters on the Condition of the Working Classes in Various Parts of England,"* 38 (1833) 46-56.

8.223
QUARTERLY REVIEW: Fullarton, J., *"Condition of the Labouring Classes,"* 46 (1832) 349-389.

8.224
Gaskell, Peter, MANUFACTURING POPULATION OF ENGLAND. 1833; ARTISANS AND MACHINERY. 1836. —*see also:* Rule, John, THE LABOURING CLASSES IN EARLY INDUSTRIAL ENGLAND 1750-1850. 1986. See chapter 7, "The Family" pp. 168-169.

8.225
Kidd, William, **LONDON AND ITS DANGERS.** [1835].

8.226
Wade, John, **HISTORY OF THE MIDDLE AND WORKING CLASSES, WITH A POPULAR EXPOSITION OF THE ECONOMICAL AND POLITICAL PRINCIPLES... CRIMES, SCHOOLS, EDUCATION, OCCUPATION...** 1835; rpt., New York, 1966.

8.227
Grant, James, **THE GREAT METROPOLIS.** 2 series, 2 vols. 1836; 1837; Contrasts upper-class frivolity with lower-class immorality and condones the industrious and moral lifestyle of the middle classes; **SKETCHES IN LONDON.** 1838; 1840; 1850; 1861; **TRAVELS IN TOWN.** 1839; **LIGHTS AND SHADOWS OF LONDON LIFE.** 2 vols. 1842; **PICTURES OF LIFE: THE DWELLINGS OF THE POOR.** 1855.

8.228
Head, George, **A HOME TOUR THROUGH THE MANUFACTURING DISTRICTS OF ENGLAND IN THE SUMMER OF 1835.** 1836; rpt., 1968. Chapters designated according to districts visited. Journal-style account.

8.229
Hogg, John, **LONDON AS IT IS: BEING A SERIES OF OBSERVATIONS ON THE HEALTH, HABITS, AND AMUSEMENTS OF THE PEOPLE.** 1838. A physician writes about the dangers haunting the urban poor such as filthy streets, polluted water and the temptation of drink.

8.230
Howitt, William, **THE RURAL LIFE OF ENGLAND.** 2nd rev. ed., 1840.

8.231
Slaney, Robert A., **REPORTS OF THE HOUSE OF COMMONS ON THE EDUCATION (1838) AND ON THE HEALTH (1840) OF THE POORER CLASSES IN LARGE TOWNS, WITH SOME SUGGESTIONS FOR THEIR IMPROVEMENT.** 1840. Concerned with the social problems caused by urbanization; **A PLEA TO POWER AND PARLIAMENT FOR THE WORKING CLASS.** 1847. Advocates government intervention in providing sanitation, clean water, and public parks.

8.232
Tristan, Flora, "St. Giles Parish" in **THE LONDON JOURNAL OF FLORA TRISTAN.** by Flora Tristan. Paris, 1840; 1842; trans. by Jean Hawkes. 1982. "I saw children without a stitch of clothing, barefoot girls and women with babies at their breast, wearing nothing but a torn shirt that revealed almost the whole of their bodies" (p. 157). Tristan was a Frenchwoman who made repeated trips to London, recording the details of her investigations in her diaries. This is the first translation into English of the popular 1842 edition.

8.233
Parkinson, Richard, **THE PRESENT CONDITION OF THE LABOURING POOR IN MANCHESTER, WITH HINTS FOR IMPROVING IT.** Manchester, 1841; *rpt. in:* **FOCAL ASPECTS OF THE INDUSTRIAL REVOLUTION 1825-1842: FIVE PAMPHLETS.** Shannon, 1971. A plea for the cooperation of employers in the struggle to elevate the conditions of the working poor.

8.234
Adshead, Joseph, DISTRESS IN MANCHESTER. EVIDENCE... OF THE STATE OF THE LABOURING CLASSES IN 1840-42. 1842.

8.235
Cooke-Taylor, William, NOTES OF A TOUR IN THE MANUFACTURING DISTRICTS OF LANCASHIRE IN A SERIES OF LETTERS TO HIS GRACE ARCHBISHOP OF DUBLIN. 1842. Accounts of sanitary conditions, attitudes of the poor towards receiving monetary relief and brief portraits of "distressed operatives." "Miss Eccroyd, whose praise was literally in all the houses in the neighborhood.... has devoted her moderate income and all the energies of her life to elevating the condition of the poor; not merely relieving their physical necessities, but remedying their moral wants by affectionate instruction and kind remonstrance" (p. 77).

8.236
Baines, Edward, THE SOCIAL, EDUCATIONAL, AND RELIGIOUS STATE OF THE MANUFACTURING DISTRICTS. 1843; rpt., New York, 1969; reviewed in: HISTORY OF EDUCATION QUARTERLY: Harrison, J.F.C., 10 (1970) 478.

8.237
Shaw, Charles, MANUFACTURING DISTRICTS. REPLIES TO LORD ASHLEY REGARDING THE EDUCATION, AND MORAL AND PHYSICAL CONDITIONS OF THE LABOURING CLASSES. 1843. Examines charity, women in factories, and education.

8.238
Engels, Friedrich, THE CONDITION OF THE WORKING CLASSES IN ENGLAND. 1844; rpt., with critical introduction by W.O. Henderson and W.H. Chaloner. Oxford, 1958; rpt., with supportive introduction by Eric Hobsbawm, 1969. This well-known study includes observations of women's working and social conditions.

8.239
JOURNAL OF THE STATISTICAL SOCIETY OF LONDON: Hallam, H., "Report to the Council of the Statistical Society of London From a Committee of Its Fellows Appointed to Make an Investigation Into the State of the Poorer Classes in St. George's in the East...," 11 (1848) 193-249. Provides statistical tables concerning house size, number of beds, furnishings, cleanliness, rents, and employments of men and women.

8.240
Beames, Thomas, THE ROOKERIES OF LONDON: PAST, PRESENT AND PROSPECTIVE. 1850; 2nd ed., 1852; rpt., 1970.

8.241
Green, Samuel G., THE WORKING CLASSES OF GREAT BRITAIN: THEIR PRESENT CONDITION, AND THE MEANING OF THEIR IMPROVEMENT AND ELEVATION. 1850.

8.242
Kay, Joseph, THE SOCIAL CONDITION AND EDUCATION OF THE PEOPLE OF ENGLAND AND EUROPE, SHOWING THE RESULTS OF THE PRIMARY SCHOOLS, AND OF THE DIVISION OF LANDED PROPERTY, IN FOREIGN COUNTRIES. 2 vols. 1850. Comparative study. Chap. 2 discusses the English poor and condemns the level of rural education.

8.243
HOUSEHOLD WORDS: Dickens, C., *"A Walk in a Workhouse,"* 1 (1850) 204-207.
Discusses female crime and the poor; Dickens, C. and Wells, W.H., *"The Old Lady
in Threadneedle St.,"* 1 (1850) 337-360; Jerrold, W.B. and Wells, W.H., *"The
Subscription List,"* 2 (1850) 4-10; Dickens, C., *"A Nightly Scene in London,"* 8
(1856) 25-27. Portrays the shelterless and hungry; Morley, H., *"The Quiet Poor,"* 9
(1854) 201-206. Discusses the condition of the poor in Bethnal Green; Sala, G.A.,
"Houseless and Hungry," 8 (1856) 121-126. Presents scenes of destitution.

8.244
"Christopheros," CONDITION OF THE LABOURING POOR. 1851.

8.245
CHRISTIAN SOCIALIST: C., F., *"A Lady's Visit to the East End,"* 2 (1851) 316-
317; 327-328.

8.246
WESTMINSTER REVIEW: *"Tendencies of England,"* 2 (1852) 110-127.

8.247
Smith, Charles Manby, CURIOSITIES OF LONDON LIFE. 1853. "Children, young
girls and women above the age of forty excite charitable interest. They are sent
forth with a broom to pick up a few halfpence to assist in the daily provision for
one family" (pp. 55-56).

8.248
Godwin, George, LONDON SHADOWS: A GLANCE AT THE "HOMES" OF THE
THOUSANDS. 1854. Reports on the dirty and dilapidated hovels inhabited by the
poor, their wages and rents, and endemic disease in their neighborhoods; TOWN
SWAMPS AND SOCIAL BRIDGES. 1859.

8.249
Ritchie, James Ewing, THE NIGHT SIDE OF LONDON. 1857; HERE AND
THERE IN LONDON. 1859; ABOUT LONDON. 1860; DAYS AND NIGHTS IN
LONDON; OR, STUDIES IN BLACK AND GRAY. 1880.

8.250
Hume, Abraham, CONDITIONS OF LIVERPOOL, RELIGIOUS AND SOCIAL;
INCLUDING NOTICES OF THE STATE OF EDUCATION, MORALS,
PAUPERISM, AND CRIME. Liverpool, 1858.

8.251
Mayhew, Augustus Septimus, PAVED WITH GOLD: OR, THE ROMANCE AND
REALITY OF THE LONDON STREETS. AN UNFASHIONABLE NOVEL. 1858;
rpt., 1971.

8.252
Meyrick, Fredrick, THE OUTCAST AND THE POOR OF LONDON. [1858].

8.253
Denton, William, OBSERVATIONS ON THE DISPLACEMENT OF THE POOR BY
METROPOLITAN RAILWAYS AND OTHER PUBLIC IMPROVEMENTS. 1861.

8.254
Hollingshead, John, **RAGGED LONDON IN 1861**. 1861. Portrays the lifestyle of dock laborers and streetsellers; **UNDERGROUND LONDON**. 1862.

8.255
Mayhew, Henry, **LONDON LABOUR AND THE LONDON POOR**. 1861-1862; rpt. with introduction by John L. Bradley. 4 vols. 1965. Articles were originally printed in **MORNING CHRONICLE**: 1849 to 1850. Statistical charts and tables with data relating to women are included; "The Great World of London" in **THE CRIMINAL PRISONS OF LONDON AND SCENES OF PRISON LIFE**. ed. by Henry Mayhew and John Binney. 1862; rpt., 1968. Explores aspects of city life; **LONDON CHARACTERS**. 1870; 1874; 1881; **LONDON'S UNDERWORLD: BEING SELECTIONS FROM 'THOSE THAT WILL NOT WORK'**. ed. by Peter Quenell. 1950; **THE UNKNOWN MAYHEW. SELECTIONS FROM THE MORNING CHRONICLE 1849-1850**. ed. by E.P. Thompson and Eileen Yeo. 1971. Presents a collection of articles, reprinted for the first time, which reveal Mayhew's aptitude as a social investigator. Two excellent biographical chapters are included; *reviewed in:* **SOCIETY FOR THE STUDY OF LABOUR HISTORY BULLETIN**: Samuel, R., 26 (1973) 47-52; **THE MORNING CHRONICLE SURVEY OF LABOUR AND THE POOR: THE METROPOLITAN DISTRICTS**. with introduction by Peter Razell. 6 vols. Sussex, 1980-1982. "Poverty... was the result of structural changes in society, a theme which became Mayhew's over-riding concern in his MORNING CHRONICLE letters. He analyzed the poverty from changes in organization of trades, and began to generalize this into an indictment of the whole of capitalist society" (I, p. 9). ——*see also:* **VICTORIAN STUDIES**: Thompson, E.P., *"The Political Education of Henry Mayhew,"* 11 (1967) 41-64. "Mayhew's LONDON LABOUR AND THE LONDON POOR... contains the fullest and most vivid documentation of the economic and social problems, the customs, habits, grievances, and individual life experiences of the labouring people of the world's greatest city of the mid-nineteenth century" (p. 42). Thompson examines the circumstances in which LONDON LABOUR was written; Humphreys, Ann, "Henry Mayhew and the London Poor," Ph.D. diss., Columbia Univ., 1969; Humphreys, Anne, **TRAVELS INTO THE POOR MAN'S COUNTRY: THE WORK OF HENRY MAYHEW**. Athens, 1971; 1980; **VICTORIAN STUDIES**: Himmelfarb, G., *"Mayhew's Poor: A Problem of Identity,"* 14 (1971) 307-20. "Mayhew was, in fact, less influential than symptomatic. If he did not create a novel image of the poor, he did reflect, perpetuate, and reinforce an image that was fairly common at the time" (p. 318); Razell, P.E. and Wainwright, R.W., **THE VICTORIAN WORKING CLASS**. 1973. Selections from the MORNING CHRONICLE by Mayhew are included; **HORIZON**: Hibbert, C.H., *"Henry Mayhew's Other London,"* 42 (1975) 48-57; **JOURNAL OF BRITISH STUDIES**: Maxwell, R., *"Henry Mayhew and the Life of the Streets,"* 17 (1978) 87-105. "One attraction of the street people [that Mayhew investigated and described] was that they were an undiscovered population; a second attraction was that they were in a state of economic crisis.... Social and economic pressures of a new intensity were threatening the street-folk. The people Mayhew interviewed often mention that they had made more money ten or twenty years previously" (p. 91); Himmelfarb, Gertrude, "Henry Mayhew: Discoverer of the 'Poor'" and "The 'Moral Physiognomy' of the Street Folk" in **THE IDEA OF POVERTY**. by Gertrude Himmelfarb. 1984.

8.256
Shimmin, Hugh, **THE COURTS AND ALLEYS OF LIVERPOOL, DESCRIBED FROM PERSONAL INSPECTION**. 1864. An advocate of public health reform describes appalling conditions in the overcrowded slums.

8.257
Archer, Thomas, **THE PAUPER, THE THIEF, AND THE CONVICT: SKETCHES OF SOME OF THEIR HOMES, HAUNTS, AND HABITS.** 1865. Archer sympathized with those he met and worked toward improvement by active participation of the poor; **THE TERRIBLE SIGHTS OF LONDON AND LABOURS OF LOVE IN THE MIDST OF THEM.** 1870.

8.258
Smith, Theophilus Ahijah, **SHEFFIELD AND ITS NEIGHBORHOOD.** 1865. Smith was secretary of the Midnight Mission.

8.259
Greenwood, James, **A NIGHT IN A WORKHOUSE.** 1866; **THE SEVEN CURSES OF LONDON.** 1869. Among the seven curses are neglected children, fallen women, drunkenness and thievery; **IN STRANGE COMPANY: BEING THE EXPERIENCES OF A ROVING CORRESPONDENT.** 1873; **THE WILDS OF LONDON.** 1874. Greenwood was a sympathetic journalist who visited the haunts of the poor and criticized the treatment of paupers by Poor Law officers; **JOURNEYS THROUGH LONDON: OR, BYWAYS OF MODERN BABYLON.** 1875; **LOW LIFE DEEPS; AN ACCOUNT OF THE STRANGE FISH TO BE FOUND THERE.** 1876; **UNDERCURRENTS OF LONDON LIFE.** 1880; **ODD PEOPLE AND ODD PLACES: OR, THE GREAT RESIDUUM.** 1883.

8.260
CONTEMPORARY REVIEW: Shaw, B., *"Is There Room for Works of Mercy in a Busy London Life?"* 3 (1866) 1-20; Shaw, E.M., *"The Workhouse From the Inside,"* 76 (1899) 564-572. Delineates a view of the workhouse from a paid official in response to the prevailing thought that Poor-law officials mistreated the workhouse inmates; Bosanquet, H., *"Physical Degeneration and the Poverty Line,"* 85 (1904) 65-75; Loane, M.E., *"Husband and Wife Among the Poor,"* 87 (1905) 222-230. Observations on domestic violence among the poor.

8.261
Stallard, J.H., **LONDON PAUPERISM AMONG THE JEWS AND CHRISTIANS.** 1867.

8.262
Waugh, Edwin, **HOME-LIFE OF THE LANCASHIRE FACTORY FOLK DURING THE COTTON FAMINE.** 1867.

8.263
Bosanquet, Charles Bertie Pulleine, **LONDON: SOME ACCOUNT OF ITS GROWTH, CHARITABLE AGENCIES, AND WANTS... WITH A CLUE MAP.** 1868. "In some places the poor are over attended to, whilst in others they are allowed to starve in soul and body. There is no significant understanding between the different agencies, and consequently there is a want of system, and thoroughness, in the way the work is done" (p. 87).

8.264
Wright, Thomas, **THE GREAT UNWASHED.** 1868.

8.265
Kirwan, Daniel Joseph, **PALACE AND HOVEL: OR, PHASES OF LONDON LIFE...** 1870; 1963, ed. by A. Allen. See especially: "Legion of the Lost" and "Scarlet Women." Sketches the haunts of vice, misery and crime, presenting London to the

American people.

8.266

Dore, Gustave and Jerrold, Blanchard, **LONDON: A PILGRIMAGE.** 1872. Illustrated by Gustave Dore. Offers graphic proof to Londoners of the West End and the poverty and torment that lay at their doorstep.

8.267

FRASER'S MAGAZINE: Davis, G.J., *"Peasantry in the South of England,"* 87 (1873) 542-558; 679-692.

8.268

Jones, Harry, **EAST AND WEST LONDON: BEING THE NOTES OF COMMON LIFE AND PASTORAL WORK IN SAINT JAMES WESTMINSTER, AND SAINT GEORGES IN THE EAST.** 1875.

8.269

Smith, Adolphe, **STREET LIFE IN LONDON.** 1877; rpt., 1969. Includes photographs by John Thompson. Follows the line of Mayhew.

8.270

Twining, Elizabeth, **LEAVES FROM THE NOTEBOOK OF ELIZABETH TWINING, LADY VISITOR AMONG THE POOR IN LONDON.** 1877. "The chief cause of all the troubles of the poor——their weak health, their insufficient food and clothing and their dullness and hardness in seeking spiritual instruction— is the drink" (p. iv). Cites forty-five cases illustrating this point.

8.271

Rowe, Richard, **PICKED UP IN THE STREETS: OR, STRUGGLES FOR LIFE AMONGST THE LONDON POOR.** 1880; **LIFE IN THE LONDON STREETS: OR, STRUGGLES FOR DAILY BREAD.** 1881.

8.272

Sims, George R., **THE SOCIAL KALEIDOSCOPE.** 1881; **HOW THE POOR LIVE, AND HORRIBLE LONDON.** 1883; 1889. Two essays published in one volume. Sims describes his visits to the slums of London in detailed anecdotal style and he specifically examines how women managed under these conditions. He contends that overpopulation and low wages are the two conditions perpetuating impoverishment, not drinking, which is rather a symptom of poverty; **LIVING LONDON.** 1906; **OFF THE TRACK IN LONDON.** 1911.

8.273

Mearns, Andrew, **THE BITTER CRY OF OUTCAST LONDON: AN ENQUIRY INTO THE CONDITION OF THE ABJECT POOR.** 1883; rpt., ed. by Anthony Wohl. Leicester, 1970. Mearns was an East End Congressional minister who wrote this tract to remind the well-to-do of their responsibility to the poor.

8.274

Preston, W.C., **THE BITTER CRY OF OUTCAST LONDON.** 1883. Aroused the social conscience of the churches during the 1880s and inspired many male and female charity workers.

8.275

NATIONAL REVIEW: Hoare, H.E., *"Homes of the Criminal Classes,"* 1 (1883) 224-239; 824-840. "I had long wished to become acquainted with that section of the community from which the criminals of the violent unskilled kind come;... who never go to church, who do not put their money in savings banks, or join provident clubs,... do not go to museums, take no interest in politics... have no homes" (p. 225).

8.276
Cantlie, James, **DEGENERATION AMONGST LONDONERS**. 1885. Argues that environmental pollution is creating an underdeveloped race and advocates decentralization.

8.277
Garland, Thomas Charles, **EAST END PICTURES: BEING MORE LEAVES FROM MY LOG**. 1885; **LIGHT AND SHADE: PICTURES OF LONDON LIFE**. 1885; **SNAPSHOTS OF MY LIFE WORK**. 1910.

8.278
AFTERNOONS IN MANCHESTER SLUMS. BY A LADY. 1887.

8.279
Booth, Charles, **CONDITION AND OCCUPATIONS OF THE PEOPLE OF TOWER HAMLETS, 1886-1887**. 1887; **LIFE AND LABOUR OF THE PEOPLE OF LONDON**. 17 vols. 1892-1903. The first professionally systematic and comprehensive study of the poor. Four volumes are devoted to poverty; **PAUPERISM: A PICTURE AND THE ENDOWMENT OF OLD AGE: AN ARGUMENT**. 1892. Surveys various areas and suggests some solutions to help alleviate pauperism of the elderly; **THE AGED POOR IN ENGLAND AND WALES**. 1894. Presents arguments in favor of an old-age pension system; **THE GOOD POOR IN ENGLAND AND WALES**. 1924. ——*see also:* London School of Economics and Political Science, **THE NEW SURVEY OF LONDON LIFE AND LABOUR...** 9 vols. 1930-1935. This survey was made with special reference to the changes since the publication of Charles Booth's LIFE AND LABOUR; Simey, T.S. and Simey, M.B., **CHARLES BOOTH, SOCIAL SCIENTIST**. Oxford, 1960. "Attempts to describe and to explain how a Victorian man of business, a merchant, shipowner and manufacturer, came to make outstanding contributions to British sociology and social policy" (p. 1); Pfautz, Harold W., ed., **CHARLES BOOTH ON THE CITY: PHYSICAL PATTERN AND SOCIAL STRUCTURE**. Chicago, 1967; Fried, Albert and Elman, Richard M., eds., **CHARLES BOOTH'S LONDON. A PORTRAIT OF THE POOR AT THE TURN OF THE CENTURY DRAWN FROM HIS "LIFE AND LABOUR OF THE PEOPLE OF LONDON."** 1968; 1971; Norman-Butler, Belinda, **VICTORIAN ASPIRATIONS: THE LIFE AND LABOR OF CHARLES AND MARY BOOTH**. 1972. Seriously treats Mary Booth's contributions to her husband's work; SOCIAL HISTORY: Hennock, E.P., *"Poverty and Social Theory in England: the Experience of the Eighteen-Eighties,"* 1 (1976) 67-91. An examination of the theoretical framework of LIFE AND LABOUR OF THE PEOPLE OF LONDON and its reception at the time.

8.280
Green, J.R., **STRAY STUDIES IN PAUPERISM IN THE EAST OF LONDON**. 1887.

8.281
Fothergill, J. Milner, **THE TOWN DWELLER: HIS NEEDS AND WANTS**. 1889. Describes urban life and its deleterious effects on city dwellers.

8.282

Booth, William, **IN DARKEST ENGLAND AND THE WAY OUT.** 1890.

8.283

Hobson, John Atkinson, **PROBLEMS OF POVERTY: AN INQUIRY INTO THE INDUSTRIAL CONDITION OF THE POOR.** 1891; subsequent eds. to 1921.

8.284

Webb, Beatrice Potter, **THE CO-OPERATIVE MOVEMENT IN GREAT BRITAIN.** 1891; "The Diary of an Investigator" in **PROBLEMS OF MODERN INDUSTRY.** by Sidney Webb and Beatrice Webb. rev. ed., 1902; **HEALTH OF WORKING GIRLS: A HANDBOOK FOR WELFARE SUPERVISORS AND OTHERS.** 1917; **MY APPRENTICESHIP.** 1926; 1938; 1946; 1950; 1971. Autobiography; **OUR PARTNERSHIP.** ed. by Barbara Drake and Margaret I. Cole. 1948; rpt., New York, 1975. Account of the Webbs' relationship, personal and professional; **BEATRICE WEBB'S DIARIES 1912-1924.** ed. by Margaret I. Cole. 1952; **BEATRICE WEBB'S DIARIES 1924-1932.** ed. by Margaret I. Cole. 1956; **THE DIARY OF BEATRICE WEBB 1873-1943.** Cambridge, 1978. Manuscript diary and typed transcript on microfiche with printed index to the diary containing introductory essays by Geoffrey Allen, Margaret Cole and Norman MacKenzie. Index and essays also printed separately. —*see also:* Cole, Margaret I., **BEATRICE WEBB.** 1945; **BRITISH JOURNAL OF SOCIOLOGY:** Cole, M., *"The Webbs and Social Theory,"* 12 (1961) 93-105; Muggeridge, Kitty and Adam, Ruth, **BEATRICE WEBB: A LIFE 1858-1943.** 1967; New York, 1968. "Beatrice's job [as an investigator with the C.O.S.] was to examine applicants in their homes in Soho.... All her research had done was to uncover the social workers' fundamental ignorance, her own included. She realised that she had not even got a standard by which to measure the lives of the down-and-outs, because normal working-class life... was a closed book to her. And whereas a 'lady' doing charitable work had a vested right to walk into a slum tenement and cross-question its occupant about his most private concerns, members of the respectable working class... were unlikely to be so poor-spirited" (p. 103); Brennan, E.J.T., **WONDERS OF THE WEBBS.** 1975; *reviewed in:* **NEW SOCIETY:** Harrison, R., 33 (1975) 260-61; **HISTORY WORKSHOP JOURNAL:** Caine, B., *"Beatrice Webb and the 'Woman Question,'"* no. 14 (1982) 23-43; Nord, Deborah Epstein, **THE APPRENTICESHIP OF BEATRICE WEBB.** Amherst, 1985. See especially: "Social Investigation." Shows how Webb's views of the causes of poverty developed and transformed through her investigations; Himmelfarb, Gertrude, "The Webbs: The Religion of Socialism" in **MARRIAGE AND MORALS AMONG THE VICTORIANS.** New York, 1986. Webb's deeply religious nature manifested in her later adherence to "Comtism," or science as a religion. "At that time, it was Comte's 'Religion of Humanity' that demanded renunciation, asceticism being a corollary of altruism" (p. 204). The Webbs were parodied in H.G. Wells' **THE NEW MACHIAVELLI,** the title reflecting the "manipulation, machination, and downright deception" in Beatrice Webb's political tactics.

8.285

Zangwill, Israel, **CHILDREN OF THE GHETTO: A STUDY OF A PECULIAR PEOPLE.** New York, 1892; 1895; 1926.

8.286

Williams, Montagu, **ROUND LONDON DOWN EAST AND UP WEST.** 1893.

8.287

Dolling, Robert R., **TEN YEARS IN A PORTSMOUTH SLUM.** 1896.

8.288
Morrison, Arthur, **A CHILD OF THE JAGO**. 1896. Fictionalized account of life in the very worst slum areas of London. Vivid verisimilitude.

8.289
Woods, Robert A., et al., **THE POOR IN GREAT CITIES: THEIR PROBLEMS AND WHAT IS BEING DONE TO SOLVE THEM**. 1896.

8.290
Sherwell, Arthur, **LIFE IN WEST LONDON: A STUDY AND A CONTRAST**. 1897; 3rd rev. ed., 1901.

8.291
Traill, Henry D., ed., **SOCIAL ENGLAND, A RECORD OF THE PROGRESS OF THE PEOPLE IN RELIGION, LAWS, LEARNING, ARTS, INDUSTRY, SCIENCE, LITERATURE AND MANNERS**. 1897. See vol. 6 for the years 1815-1885.

8.292
Besant, Walter, **EAST LONDON**. 1899; 1900; 1901; 1980; **LONDON IN THE NINETEENTH CENTURY**. 1909. A classic of English urban history that examines the impact of growing industry and bureaucracy.

8.293
Rowntree, Benjamin Seebohm, **POVERTY: A STUDY OF TOWN LIFE**. 1901; 2nd ed., 1922. Concerned with labor relations and poverty, this work was influenced by Charles Booth's LIFE AND LABOUR and pioneered new methods of social investigation. At the beginning of the 20th century, one-third of the population was living in conditions that would not support life at the lowest level. The causes are divided into the categories of low wages and irresponsible behavior; (and Lasker, Bruno), **UNEMPLOYMENT: A SOCIAL STUDY**. 1911. Discusses the problem of casual laborers and includes a chapter on women; **HOW THE LABOURER LIVES**. 1913; 1918. See especially: "The Labourer's Outlook." "Supplementary earnings are least available when they are most needed... in the child-bearing period" (p. 334); (and Kendall, May), **HOW THE LABOURER LIVES: RURAL LABOUR QUESTIONS**. 1913; LECTURES ON HOUSING. Manchester, 1914; **POVERTY AND PROGRESS: A SECOND SOCIAL SURVEY OF YORK**. 1941; (and Lavers, George Russell), **POVERTY AND THE WELFARE STATE: A THIRD SOCIAL SURVEY OF YORK DEALING ONLY WITH ECONOMIC QUESTIONS**. 1951. — *see also:* Briggs, Asa, **SOCIAL THOUGHT AND SOCIAL ACTION: STUDY OF THE WORK OF SEEBOHM ROWNTREE, 1871-1954**. 1961.

8.294
Sherard, Robert, **THE CRY OF THE POOR**. 1901.

8.295
Haggard, H.R., **RURAL ENGLAND; BEING AN ACCOUNT OF AGRICULTURAL AND SOCIAL RESEARCHES CARRIED OUT IN THE YEARS 1901 AND 1902**. 1902; 1906.

8.296
Masterman, Charles Frederick Gurney, **THE HEART OF THE EMPIRE: DISCUSSIONS OF PROBLEMS OF MODERN CITY LIFE IN ENGLAND. WITH AN ESSAY ON IMPERIALISM**. 1902; rpt., ed. by Bently Gilbert. Brighton and New York, 1973. "THE HEART OF THE EMPIRE found the connection between British business interests and the Boer war of particular significance. For them as

well as for the population at large the war was a symbol. But instead of being a vindication of British power and rectitude it represented all that was corrupt in British life. It debauched the masses and it showed that the government had been delivered into the hands of men of wealth. War abroad and poverty at home was an equation. Power at the perimeter of the empire meant decay at its center. Of this decay, and of its meaning for the future of the British race, Masterman and his colleagues wrote" (pp. xi-xxi); **FROM THE ABYSS. OF ITS INHABITANTS BY ONE OF THEM.** 1903. While at Cambridge, Masterman became interested in social work and the settlement movement. He lived in a tenement and from that experience wrote FROM THE ABYSS which describes an "unknown London" to the South and East of the West End. Masterman believed that a revolutionary movement could develop which would threaten the foundations of the empire. In this work he correlates London's decay to its expansion and growth; **THE CONDITION OF ENGLAND.** 1909; 1911; 1960. Details the paradoxes of human society. ——*see also:* Masterman, Lucy, **C.F.G. MASTERMAN: A BIOGRAPHY.** 1939.

8.297
Women's Cooperative Guild, **THE OPEN DOOR.** [1902]. Investigations revealed a picture of profound squalor and ill-health. The Guild responded by developing a program of cooperative relief in poor neighborhoods.

8.298
London, Jack, **PEOPLE OF THE ABYSS.** [1903]; rpt., New York, 1963. Originally sent to South Africa by the American Press Association to cover the Boer War, London arrived in England first. When his assignment was cancelled, he agreed with a New York publisher to pursue another project, an examination of slum life. He remained in the East End for seven weeks, researching and writing this book which was originally serialized in WILSHIRE'S MAGAZINE.

8.299
Metcalfe, Ethel E., **MEMOIR OF ROSAMOND DAVENPORT-HILL.** 1904. Biography of a social explorer who also did work with industrial schools.

8.300
Higgs, Mary, **THREE NIGHTS IN WOMEN'S LODGING HOUSES.** 1905; *rpt. as a chapter in:* **INTO UNKNOWN ENGLAND. 1866-1913. SELECTIONS FROM THE SOCIAL EXPLORERS.** ed. by Peter Keating. Glasgow, 1976; 1978. Higgs worked with many religious and philanthropic organizations; she organized a home for destitute women and became a recognized authority on tramps and lodging-houses. This piece details the women of lodging houses. Very valuable document; **GLIMPSES INTO THE ABYSS.** 1906. Higgs "reflected that exploration was the method of science and became... an explorer of 'Darkest England'" (p. vii). Includes, in appendix 4, "Extract from Report of Vagrancy Committee," a valuable document which details the treatment of women in casual wards, the number of female vagrants and suggestions to alleviate unsatisfactory treatment of women tramps and vagrants. ——*see also:* Higgs, M.K., **MARY HIGGS OF OLDHAM.** 1954.

8.301
Loane, Margaret E., **THE QUEEN'S POOR: LIFE AS THEY FIND IT IN TOWN AND COUNTRY.** 1905; **FROM THEIR POINT OF VIEW.** 1908; 1980. Describes family life and food costs. Attempts to understand how workers perceive their life; **THE NEXT STREET BUT ONE.** 1908. Loane, who was a district nurse, describes working-class urban life in this work; **AN ENGLISHMAN'S CASTLE.** 1909. See especially: "The Position of the Wife in the Working-Class Home." "The capable woman, especially if the wife of a man earning less than forty shillings a week,

generally has the entire management of all the wages except the husband's pocket-money, which is usually calculated at a rate to cover the cost of his boots and Sunday clothes and the subscription to his Friendly Society. In cases where the wages are less than twenty-five shillings this is the almost invariable rule. However ill they were, even to the very day of their death I found that women patients kept the purse under their pillow and regulated the expenditure of the household. Men are so well aware that they cannot 'make the money go round' that they would hand their wages over to a sixteen-year-old daughter 'who knows what to do,' rather than make the attempt" (p. 183); **NEIGHBORS AND FRIENDS.** 1910. "That one great cause of the existence, perpetuation, and increase of pauperism is that voluntary and state aid compete with one another instead of dividing out their respective territories and establishing a firm and uniform system within these boundaries (p. 1).... If we would solve even the simplest of problems, we must be willing to learn from the working classes, as well as to teach" (p. 57); **THE COMMON GROWTH.** 1911. Includes examination of the lives of working-class widows, the choice of occupations, and family socialism.

8.302
Malvery, Olive C., **THE SOUL MARKET.** 1906.

8.303
Bell, Florence Eveleen Eleanor Oliffe (Lady Bell), **AT THE WORKS: A STUDY OF A MANUFACTURING TOWN (MIDDLESBOROUGH)** 1907; 2nd ed., 1911; rpt. with introduction by Frederick Alderson. Newton Abbot, 1969. A particularly valuable study of domestic and cultural life among working-class people.

8.304
Howarth, Edward G. and Wilson, Mona, **WEST HAM: A STUDY IN SOCIAL AND INDUSTRIAL PROBLEMS.** 1907. Investigation of housing, workforce, and government in West Ham outside of London.

8.305
Davies, Maude, **LIFE IN AN ENGLISH VILLAGE.** 1909. The Webbs encouraged Davies, a London School of Economics student, to conduct this study of a rural community in 1905. Very useful work.

8.306
Northrop, W.B., **WEALTH AND WANT. A STUDY IN LIVING CONTRASTS AND SOCIAL PROBLEMS.** 1909. Compares the conspicuous consumption of the wealthy to the impoverished conditions of the poor. Examines the "evils" of working mothers who must leave their children at home or bring them to work. Includes many photographs.

8.307
Rathbone, Eleanor, **HOW THE CASUAL LABOURER LIVES.** 1909; **THE CONDITIONS OF WIDOWS UNDER THE POOR LAW IN LIVERPOOL.** Liverpool, 1913.

8.308
Acorn, George, **ONE OF THE MULTITUDE. AN AUTOBIOGRAPHY BY A RESIDENT OF BETHNAL GREEN.** 1911. Conveys his experiences in the slums in the style of imaginary fiction. Examines life-style, work, and culture with a sensitive but middle-class perspective reflecting the values of the dominant culture.

8.309
Paterson, Alexander, **ACROSS THE BRIDGES: OR, LIFE BY THE SOUTH LONDON RIVER-SIDE.** 1911. Paterson lived for a time in the South London working-class district; writes from a middle-class point of view.

8.310
Bosanquet, Helen (Dendy), **SOCIAL CONDITIONS IN PROVINCIAL TOWNS.** 1912. A compilation of papers from the CHARITY ORGANISATION REVIEW on the population and economy of seven towns and local efforts in social reform.

8.311
Pember-Reeves, Magdalene Stuart, **FAMILY LIFE ON A POUND A WEEK.** 1912; 1914. Describes the crippling resources of London working men and their families when the wages range between 18s and 24s a week. Urges a national minimum wage, free and compulsory education for children, school feeding and medical clinics for babies; **ROUND ABOUT A POUND A WEEK.** 1913. A survey conducted by the Fabian Society's Women's Group on the lives of the inhabitants of Lambeth and Kennington. Pember-Reeves was an active journalist and feminist.

8.312
Russell, C.E.B., **SOCIAL PROBLEMS OF THE NORTH, LONDON, AND OXFORD.** 1913. Contends that problems in cities in northern England need the kind of attention being given to London. Gives valuable data on housing, health, education, etc. Makes a plea for establishing settlement houses.

8.313
Tressell, Robert Noonan, **THE RAGGED TROUSERED PHILANTHROPIST.** 1914; rpt., 1955; 1956; 1959. Fictionalized depiction. "It is the first account in English of the lives and opinions of a group of working men, written with realism and passion... by 'one of themselves'" (p. 5). Considered factually accurate. ——*see also:* Mitchell, Jack, **ROBERT TRESSELL AND THE RAGGED TROUSERED PHILANTHROPIST.** 1969; HISTORY WORKSHOP JOURNAL: Nettleton, J., *"Robert Tressell and the Liverpool Connection,"* no. 12 (1981) 163-171. "What Noonan did was to portray the entire social system, and the secret of his and the book's success is that he invented nothing. The hell he described was the world he saw, and as Robert Noonan he was hopelessly trapped" (p. 164).

8.314
Bowley, Arthur Lyon and Burnett-Hurst, Alexander Robert, **LIVELIHOOD AND POVERTY: A STUDY IN THE ECONOMIC CONDITIONS OF WORKING-CLASS HOUSEHOLDS IN NORTHAMPTON, WARRINGTON, STANLEY, AND READING.** 1915; rpt., 1980. A comparison of living conditions and poverty between four towns with different manufacturing or industrial livelihoods.

8.315
Adderley, James Granville, **IN SLUMS AND SOCIETY.** 1916.

8.316
Nevinson, Margaret Wynne, **WORKHOUSE CHARACTERS, AND OTHER SKETCHES OF THE LIFE OF THE POOR.** 1918; **LIFE'S FITFUL FEVER, A VOLUME OF MEMORIES.** 1926.

8.317
Ashton, T.S., **ECONOMIC AND SOCIAL INVESTIGATIONS IN MANCHESTER, 1833-1933: A CENTENARY HISTORY OF THE MANCHESTER STATISTICAL**

SOCIETY. Manchester, 1934.

8.318
Jones, David Caradog, **SOCIAL SURVEYS**. 1949. A text that indicates how Booth and Rowntree conducted their studies.

8.319
Pike, E. Royston, ed., **HARD TIMES: DOCUMENTS OF THE INDUSTRIAL REVOLUTION IN BRITAIN**. 1966. Includes excerpts from social explorers and government investigation reports; **HUMAN DOCUMENTS OF THE AGE OF THE FORSYTES**. 1969; 1970. Includes many primary source materials documenting the conditions in the slums; **HUMAN DOCUMENTS OF THE LLOYD GEORGE ERA**. New York, 1972.

8.320
Yeo, Eileen M., "Social Science and Social Change: A Social History of Some Aspects of Social Science and Social Investigation in Britain 1830-1890," Ph.D. diss., Univ. of Essex, 1972.

8.321
Keating, Peter, ed., **INTO UNKNOWN ENGLAND 1866-1913. SELECTIONS FROM THE SOCIAL EXPLORERS**. Manchester, 1976. Valuable collection of Victorian-era essays which document, in detail, the conditions experienced by the poor.

8.322
Hay, James Roy, "Welfare and the Experts: the Role of Social Investigators, Social Workers and Civil Servants" in **THE DEVELOPMENT OF THE WELFARE STATE**. by James Roy Hay. 1978. Surveys and quotes the leading social investigators from the 1880s, including Mayhew, Marshall, Booth, Rowntree, and Webb.

8.323
Coles, Nicholas J.H., "The Making of a Monster: The Working Class in the Industrial Novels and Social Investigations of 1830-1855," Ph.D. diss., State Univ. of New York, Buffalo, 1981. "The geographical focus of this study is Manchester and the Lancashire Cotton towns around it.... The highest rate of growth came in the years 1821-1831, when Manchester's population increased 45 percent.... Manchester had no civic administration worth mentioning to cope with this phenomenal influx.... The result was that in the midst of the technological marvels which generated spectacular wealth for their owners, the working class lived in a state of squalor of unprecedented scale" (pp. 2-3).

8.324
Williams, Karel, **FROM PAUPERISM TO POVERTY**. 1981. Combines "three essays on the configuration of the English and Welsh poor law between 1800 and 1914, and four essays on social investigation texts by Mayhew, Engels, Booth, and Rowntree between the 1840s and 1940s.... The essays... develop an alternative informally semiotic mode of analysis" (p. 1).

8.325
Harrison, Brian, "Finding Out How the Other Half Live: Social Research and British Government Since 1780" in **PEACEABLE KINGDOM: STABILITY AND CHANGE IN MODERN BRITAIN**. by Brian Harrison. Oxford, 1982.

8.326
ECONOMIC AND SOCIAL INVESTIGATIONS IN ENGLAND SINCE 1833. TRANSACTIONS OF THE MANCHESTER STATISTICAL SOCIETY. Brighton, 1983. A microform series from Harvester Press.

* * *

3. SOCIAL SERVICE AND REFORM: MISCELLANEOUS ORGANIZATIONS AND ACTIVITIES

8.327
Society for the Relief of Widows and Orphans of Medical Men, **PROPOSALS FROM THE SOCIETY... 1788.**

8.328
United Society for the Relief of Widows and Children of Seamen, Soldiers, etc., **A LIST OF SUBSCRIBERS TO THE UNITED SOCIETY... TOGETHER WITH THE RESOLUTIONS AND RULES OF THE SOCIETY, ETC. 1794.**

8.329
Society for Bettering the Condition and Increasing the Comforts of the Poor, **REPORTS OF THE SOCIETY FOR BETTERING THE CONDITIONS AND INCREASING THE COMFORTS OF THE POOR. 1796; [PROSPECTUS]. 1797; FIRST REPORT. 1797; REPORTS OF THE SOCIETY, ETC. 5 vols. 1798-1808; EXTRACTS FROM THE REPORTS OF THE ENGLISH SOCIETY FOR BETTERING THE CONDITION OF THE POOR, AND FROM OTHER PAPERS ON THE SAME SUBJECT, ETC. Dublin, 1799; THIRTEENTH (-SIXTEENTH) REPORT OF THE SOCIETY, ETC. 1801; EXTRACT FROM AN ACCOUNT OF THE LADIES' SOCIETY FOR THE EDUCATION AND EMPLOYMENT OF THE FEMALE POOR. 1804; THIRTY-NINTH REPORT. 1816.**

8.330
Society of Women at the School-House, Battersea, **RULES TO BE OBSERVED BY A SOCIETY, ETC. BEGUN 1ST JANUARY, 1798. 1798.**

8.331
REPORT OF THE STATE AND PROGRESS OF THE INSTITUTION FOR THE RELIEF OF THE POOR OF THE CITY OF LONDON AND PARIS ADJACENT. 1800.

8.332
Friendly Female Society, **FRIENDLY FEMALE SOCIETY. INSTITUTED JAN. 20, 1802, ETC.** 1803; **[REPORT, ETC. FOR 1837].** 1838; **[REPORT, ETC. FOR 1868].** 1868.

8.333
Ladies' Society for the Education and Employment of the Female Poor, **EXTRACTS FROM AN ACCOUNT OF THE LADIES' SOCIETY FOR THE EDUCATION AND EMPLOYMENT OF THE FEMALE POOR.** 1804.

8.334
Philanthropic Society, **AN ACCOUNT OF THE NATURE AND PRESENT STATE
OF THE PHILANTHROPIC SOCIETY.** 1804; 1814; 1816; 1823; 1824; **A LIST OF
MEMBERS AND SUBSCRIBERS OF THE PHILANTHROPIC SOCIETY.** 1827.

8.335
Society for Encouraging and Aiding the Industrious Sick and Aged Poor of
Camberwell, **REPORT OF THE COMMITTEE.** 1804.

8.336
Blackheath Friendly Society for Women, **RULES, ORDERS AND REGULATIONS,
ETC.** Greenwich, 1805.

8.337
Society for Bettering the Condition of the Poor at Clapham, **RULES AND
REGULATIONS OF THE SOCIETY, ETC.** 2nd ed., 1805.

8.338
Refuge for the Destitute, Cuper's Bridge, Lambeth, **A SHORT ACCOUNT OF THE
INSTITUTION CALLED THE REFUGE FOR THE DESTITUTE, CUPER'S-
BRIDGE, LAMBETH; CONTAINING THE NATURE AND VIEWS OF THE
INSTITUTION, WITH THE RULES AND REGULATIONS FOR THE
GOVERNMENT OF THE SAME, ETC.** 1806; 1807; **SHORT ACCOUNT OF THE
REFUGE FOR THE DESTITUTE... WITH THE RULES AND REGULATIONS...
AND A LIST OF SUBSCRIBERS.** 1808; **THE ANNUAL REPORT OF THE
REFUGE FOR THE DESTITUTE FOR THE YEAR 1832 TO WHICH IS
PREFIXED A SHORT ACCOUNT OF THE INSTITUTION.** 1833; **ANNUAL
REPORT, 1849.** 1849; **THE ANNUAL REPORT OF THE COMMITTEE OF THE
CORPORATION OF THE REFUGE FOR THE DESTITUTE, MANOR HOUSE,
DALSTON, LATE HACKNEY ROAD AND HOXTON, FOR... 1849.** Hackney,
[1850].

8.339
New Ordnance Society, **PLAN OF THE SOCIETY FOR THE BENEFIT OF
WIDOWS OF PERSONS LATE BELONGING TO THE CIVIL ESTABLISHMENT
OF THE OFFICE OF ORDNANCE.** 1807.

8.340
[Whitford, Helena], **THOUGHTS AND REMARKS ON ESTABLISHING AN
INSTITUTION FOR THE SUPPORT AND EDUCATION OF... RESPECTABLE
FEMALES.** 1809.

8.341
Highmore, Anthony, **PIETAS LONDINENSIS: THE HISTORY, DESIGN AND
PRESENT STATE OF THE VARIOUS PUBLIC CHARITIES IN AND NEAR
LONDON.** 2 vols. 1810. A compilation of "the several principal charities of our
metropolis and its vicinity" classified into the following categories: hospitals,
medical charities, colleges, alms-houses, school-charities, and miscellaneous. See
especially: pp. 237-253 on the London Female Penitentiary; **PHILANTHROPIA
METROPOLITANA: A VIEW OF THE CHARITABLE INSTITUTIONS ESTAB-
LISHED IN AND NEAR LONDON CHIEFLY DURING THE LAST TWELVE
YEARS.** 1822. Includes sections on "The Guardian Society and Asylum, For the
Preservation of Public Morals," "City of London Lying-In Institution for Providing
Poor Married Women With Midwives and Medicines at Their Own Houses,"
"Southwark Female Society," "The Ladies' Royal Benevolent Society, For Visiting,

Relieving, and Investigating the Condition of the Poor at Their Own Habitations," "The Medical Benevolent Society," "The Law Association For the Benefit of Widows and Families of Professional Men," "The Female Friendly Union Society," and others.

8.342
Ladies' Benevolent Society, Liverpool, THE FIFTH ANNUAL REPORT OF THE LADIES' BENEVOLENT SOCIETY, LIVERPOOL. Liverpool, 1815.

8.343
Refuge for the Destitute, Hackney Road, A SHORT ACCOUNT OF THE REFUGE... CONTAINING THE NATURE AND VIEWS OF THE INSTITUTION... 1818; A SHORT ACCOUNT OF THE REFUGE, ETC. 1831.

8.344
Society for the Suppression of Mendicity, SOCIETY FOR THE SUPPRESSION OF MENDICITY. 1818; THE PRACTICE OF THE MENDICITY SOCIETY. BY "ONE WHO KNOWS IT WELL" [C.R. LUSHINGTON]. 1847. —*see also:* QUARTERLY REVIEW: *"Reports of the Society for the Suppression of Mendicity,"* 64 (1839) 341-369. The society makes contributions to raise the recipient from destitution to financial independence. Claims this prevents good citizens from becoming felons.

8.345
Royal Humane Society, ANNUAL REPORT. 1820; FIFTY-THIRD ANNUAL REPORT. 1827.

8.346
Naval Charitable Society, GENERAL STATE OF THE NAVAL CHARITABLE SOCIETY, 31ST, DECEMBER, 1821. 1822.

8.347
A Lady, THE COTTAGER'S ASSISTANT; OR, THE WEDDING PRESENT. 1824.

8.348
British Ladies' Society for Promoting the Reformation of Female Prisoners, SKETCH OF THE ORIGIN AND RESULTS OF LADIES' PRISON ASSOCIATIONS, WITH HINTS FOR THE FORMATION OF LOCAL ASSOCIATIONS. 1827; A CONCISE VIEW OF THE ORIGIN AND PROGRESSION OF THE BRITISH LADIES SOCIETY FOR PROMOTING THE REFORMATION OF FEMALE PRISONERS. [1840]. The society was established by Elizabeth Fry in 1821.

8.349
Southwark Female Society for the Relief of Sickness and Extreme Want, THE FOURTEENTH ANNUAL REPORT OF THE SOUTHWARK FEMALE SOCIETY, ETC. 1827. Founded in 1813, women constituted more than a third of the membership.

8.350
Wade, John, AN ACCOUNT OF PUBLIC CHARITIES IN ENGLAND AND WALES, ABRIDGED FROM THE REPORTS OF HIS MAJESTY'S COMMISSIONERS ON CHARITABLE FOUNDATIONS, WITH NOTES AND COMMENTS. 1828.

8.351
Pratt, J. Tidd, **THE LAW RELATING TO FRIENDLY SOCIETIES, ETC.** 1829; 1834; 1838; **THE HISTORY OF SAVINGS BANKS IN ENGLAND, WALES AND IRELAND.** 1830; **A SUMMARY OF SAVINGS BANKS IN ENGLAND, SCOTLAND, WALES AND IRELAND, ETC.** 1846. Women were involved in forming savings banks which accommodated the poor and the working classes.

8.352
Society for the Relief of Distressed Widows, **THE SIXTH ANNUAL REPORT OF THE SOCIETY FOR THE RELIEF OF DISTRESSED WIDOWS, APPLYING WITHIN THE FIRST MONTH OF THEIR WIDOWHOOD.** 1830.

8.353
Adult Orphan Institution, **AN ACCOUNT OF THE ADULT ORPHAN INSTITUTION.** 1831.

8.354
Liverpool District Provident Society, **THE FIRST ANNUAL REPORT OF THE LIVERPOOL DISTRICT PROVIDENT SOCIETY FOR THE YEAR 1830.** Liverpool, [1831].

8.355
Night Asylum for the Homeless Poor, **NIGHT ASYLUM FOR THE HOMELESS POOR TO THE LIVERPOOL PUBLIC: A DESCRIPTION OF THE ASYLUM.** Liverpool, 1832.

8.356
Society for the Suppression of Juvenile Vagrancy, **REPORT OF THE HACKNEY-WICK SCHOOL SUB-COMMITTEE.** 1833.

8.357
Mogridge, George, **LONDON IN MAY: OR ANTHONY HOSKINS' ACCOUNT OF THE PRINCIPAL AND BENEVOLENT INSTITUTIONS IN LONDON.** 1835.

8.358
Servant's Institution, **THE SERVANT'S INSTITUTION, NO. 42, GREAT MARY-LE-BONE STREET, PORTLAND PLACE. ESTABLISHED 1834. [A PROSPEC-TUS].** 1835.

8.359
ESSAYS ON THE PRINCIPLES OF CHARITABLE INSTITUTIONS: BEING AN ATTEMPT TO ASCERTAIN WHAT ARE THE PLANS BEST ADAPTED TO IMPROVE THE PHYSICAL AND MORAL CONDITION OF THE LOWER ORDERS IN ENGLAND. 1836. "The researches which have led politicians to execrate pauperism, mendicity, and crime, as the elements of social disorder, have not always taught them that the pauper, the vagrant, and the uneducated criminal are the objects rather of pity than of indignation.... Every human being who, by the misfortune of his birth and position in society... has a claim not only to commiseration, but active assistance, on the part of his more favoured brethren" (p. 21).

8.360
Brownlow, John, **A POCKET GUIDE TO THE CHARITIES OF LONDON.** 1836; **REPORT ON THE CHARITIES OF LONDON SUBMITTED TO THE TREASURER OF THE FOUNDLING HOSPITAL.** 1840.

8.361
NEW MONTHLY MAGAZINE: Hewett, J.T.J., *"The Widows Almshouse,"* 67 (1843) 83-96; 212-226; 363-377; 507-521; and 68 (1843) 66-80; 226-241; 358-374; 507-522; and 69 (1843) 91-106; 225-240; 379-393; 530-545.

8.362
Association for Promoting the Relief of Destitution in the Metropolis, FIRST (FOURTH, SEVENTH, THIRTEENTH) ANNUAL REPORT OF THE COMMITTEE. 1844-1857.

8.363
Female Servants' Home Society, for the Encouragement of Faithful Servants, London, ADDRESS OF THE COMMITTEE... WITH RULES FOR THE MANAGEMENT OF THE INSTITUTION. 1844; REPORT FOR THE YEAR ENDING MARCH 31, 1874. (1876-78, 1881, 1882, 1884-86). 1874-1886.

8.364
Governess' Benevolent Institution, REPORT OF THE BOARD OF MANAGEMENT FOR 1851 (1852, ETC.). 1844+.

8.365
Low, Sampson, THE METROPOLITAN CHARITIES. 1844; THE CHARITIES OF LONDON, COMPREHENDING THE BENEVOLENT, EDUCATIONAL AND RELIGIOUS INSTITUTIONS, THEIR ORIGIN AND DESIGN, PROGRESS AND PRESENT POSITION. 1850; 1852. Includes organizations and institutions assisting female emigration; *reviewed in:* WESTMINSTER REVIEW: *"Charities, Noxious and Beneficient,"* 59 (1853) 32-46. "We find from Mr. Sampson Low's book... that the charitable institutions of London are 491 in number and that their annual income amounts to not less than L1,765,000, of which L742,006 is derived from endowments, and L1,023,000 from voluntary contributions" (p. 34); THE CHARITIES OF LONDON IN 1861. COMPRISING AN ACCOUNT OF THE OPERATIONS, RESOURCES, AND GENERAL CONDITION OF THE CHARITABLE, EDUCATIONAL, AND RELIGIOUS INSTITUTIONS OF LONDON. 1862; A HANDBOOK TO THE CHARITIES OF LONDON. 1870; *continued as:* LOW'S HANDBOOK TO THE CHARITIES OF LONDON... 1872; SAMPSON LOW'S ANNUAL. 1895.

8.366
Servant's Benevolent Institution, FIRST REPORT. 1846; A PROSPECTUS. 1850.

8.367
FEMALE'S FRIEND: 1846; vols. 1-4. Published by the Associate Insitution for Improving and Enforcing the Laws for the Protection of Women.

8.368
Royal Asylum for Destitute Females, Manor Hall, Little Chelsea, 25TH REPORT, ETC. 1847.

8.369
Farr, William, REMARKS ON A PROPOSAL SCHEME... FOR THE SUPPORT OF WIDOWS AND ORPHANS OF CIVIL SERVANTS OF THE CROWN. 1849.

8.370
FRASER'S MAGAZINE: *"The Unseen Charities of London,"* 39 (1849) 639-647. Brief history of the Sisters of Charity; discusses the alms-house called St. Anne's House and the asylum at London Wall and those housed in these various charitable institutions.

8.371
East-End Needlewomen's Home and Workshop, [PROSPECTUS]. WITH A CIRCULAR ASKING FOR SUPPORT. [1850]; [1852].

8.372
London Female Dormitory, FIFTH ANNUAL REPORT... CARRIED ON IN CONNECTION WITH THE LONDON BY MOONLIGHT MISSION. 1850.

8.373
HOGG'S WEEKLY INSTRUCTOR: *"Indigent Gentlewomen's Fund,"* 4 (1850) 18-20. Describes some of the women who obtained relief through the fund and suggests a plan for bursaries to aid unmarried women 50 years and older; *"Provision for Aged Females,"* 7 (1851) 310-312. "The unmarried females of England and Scotland have claims upon the active portions of society—upon families, upon their kindred, and even upon religion and virtue.... Taking them as a class, they are foremost in every good work... whilst their personal privations in old age... are incredibly great" (p. 311). Outlines a general plan for a scheme to provide "for females in old age, by the payment of a small annual sum, thus placing it within the reach of all classes of society to provide for declining years" (p. 312).

8.374
Hardwick, C., FRIENDLY SOCIETIES, THEIR HISTORY, PROGRESS, PROSPECTS AND UTILITY. 1851.

8.375
Statham, Richard Jervis, SUGGESTIONS FOR THE ESTABLISHMENT OF AN INDUSTRIAL ASSOCIATION, IN CONNECTION WITH NATIONAL SCHOOLS, AS A PREVENTIVE OF CRIME, VAGRANCY, AND PAUPERISM... 1851.

8.376
Female Temporary Home, LONDON BY MOONLIGHT; OR, MISSIONARY LABOURS FOR THE FEMALE TEMPORARY HOME [PAMPHLETS, FOR THE MOST PART BY JOHN BLACKMORE]. [1853-1854]; nos. 1-15; ser.2, no. 1. The home worked with prostitutes as well as vagrants.

8.377
Brightwell, Cecilia Lucy, MEMORIALS OF THE LIFE OF AMELIA OPIE. Norwich, 1854. Opie was a novelist and poet involved in philanthropic movements.

8.378
Society for Improving the Condition of the Insane, RULES AND LIST OF THE PRESENT MEMBERS OF THE SOCIETY, ETC.; AND A PRIZE ESSAY ENTITLED, THE PROGRESSIVE CHANGES WHICH HAVE TAKEN PLACE SINCE THE TIME OF PINEL IN THE MORAL MANAGEMENT OF THE INSANE... BY D.H. TUKE, M.D... TOGETHER WITH A SHORT ABSTRACT... OF CASES CONTRIBUTED BY SIR A. MORISON, M.D. 1854.

8.379
Central Association in Aid of Soldiers' Wives and Families, FIRST ANNIVERSARY

MEETING, ETC. [1855].

8.380
Hume, Abraham, ANALYSIS OF THE SUBSCRIBERS TO THE VARIOUS LIVERPOOL CHARITIES. Liverpool, 1855.

8.381
QUARTERLY REVIEW: Cheney, R.H., *"The Charities and Poor of London,"* 97 (1855) 407-450; *"The Missing Link and the London Poor,"* 108 (1860) 1-34.

8.382
Balfour, Clara Lucas, WORKING WOMEN OF THE LAST HALF CENTURY: THE LESSON OF THEIR LIVES. 1856. Biographies of various women who were active in reform movements.

8.383
Society for Improving the Condition of the Labouring Classes, PROSPECTUS OF THE SOCIETY... TOGETHER WITH PLANS AND DESCRIPTIONS OF THEIR MODEL DWELLINGS IN LONDON. [1857]; A SURVEY, 1830-1939. 1939.

8.384
Marsh, Catherine, ENGLISH HEARTS AND ENGLISH HANDS; OR THE RAILWAY AND THE TRENCHES. ed. by F. Chalmers. 1858. Very popular book that describes her work among the navvies. —*see also:* O'Rorke, L.E., THE LIFE AND FRIENDSHIPS OF CATHERINE MARSH. 1917.

8.385
ENGLISH WOMAN'S JOURNAL: E.M., *"Charities for Women,"* 2 (1858) 217-231; *"National Association for the Promotion of Social Science,"* 4 (1859) 124-128; *"Notice of Books... Transactions of the National Association for the Promotion of Social Science Edited by G.W. Hastings, Esq.,"* 5 (1860) 341; *"Friendly Societies,"* 6 (1860) 107-112; 265-272. Discusses mutual assistance leagues for women and the problems of such societies. Recommends the employment of matrons, describes the operations of Friendly societies and suggest them for aiding women.

8.386
Association for the Sale of Work by Ladies of Limited Means, SECOND ANNUAL REPORT. [1859].

8.387
Bayly, Ada Ellen, RAGGED HOMES AND HOW TO MEND THEM. 1859. Suggests ways in which women philanthropists can help the poor make the best of being poor while inculcating middle-class values; (as editor), THE MINISTRY OF WOMAN, AND THE LONDON POOR. BY "A.V.L." 1870; THE LIFE AND LETTERS OF MRS. SEWELL. 3rd ed., 1889; 1890; 1899. Sewell was engaged in a wide variety of charity works, including aid to children, servants and illiterate adults. Her motivations were religious.

8.388
Robinson, Sarah, LIGHT IN DARKNESS. 1859; THE DARKNESS PAST. 1861; THE SOLDIER'S FRIEND: A PIONEER'S RECORD. 1913. Robinson was a social reformer who visited the poor and soldiers. —*see also:* Tomkinson, E.M., THE WORLD'S WORKERS: SARAH ROBINSON, AGNES WESTON, MRS. MEREDITH. 1894.

8.389
Woman's Mission to Women (afterwards Female Mission to the Fallen), **FEMALE MISSION IN CONNEXION WITH THE REFORMATORY AND REFUGE UNION. REPORT OF THE SUB-COMMITTEE.** [1859]; **SECOND (THIRD) REPORT OF THE FEMALE MISSION, ETC.** 1860; **THE FEMALE MISSION TO THE FALLEN.** 1863-75; **FORTY-FIRST (-FIFTY-FIFTH) ANNUAL REPORT OF THE FEMALE MISSION TO THE FALLEN... THE SIXTY-THIRD (-SEVENTY-SEVENTH) REPORT OF THE FEMALE AID SOCIETY.** 1899-1913. Founded in 1858 as Female Mission, later Female Mission to the Fallen, a subsidiary of the Reformatory and Refuge Union. Amalgamated with the Female Aid Society in 1882.

8.390
Johnson, Joseph, **HEROINES OF OUR TIME: BEING SKETCHES OF THE LIVES OF EMINENT WOMEN, WITH EXAMPLES OF THEIR BENEVOLENT WORKS, TRUTHFUL LIVES, AND NOBLE DEEDS.** 1860.

8.391
Pennefather, William, **COPY OF A LETTER ADDRESSED TO A FRIEND ON THE OPENING OF AN INDUSTRIAL HOME FOR WOMEN AT BARNET.** Barnet, [1860].

8.392
SATURDAY REVIEW: *"Toasting the Ladies,"* 10 (1860) 418-419. Critical of the condescending attitude toward women at the Social Science Association banquet; *"The Social Science Association,"* 13 (1862) 668; Twining, L., *"The Official Work of Women,"* 30 (1899) 81-85.

8.393
Cobbe, Frances Power, **FRIENDLESS GIRLS AND HOW TO HELP THEM; BEING AN ACCOUNT OF THE PREVENTIVE MISSION AT BRISTOL.** 1861. **THE WORKHOUSE AS A HOSPITAL.** 1861; **ESSAYS ON THE PURSUITS OF WOMEN.** 1863; "The Final Cause of Women" in **WOMAN'S WORK AND WOMAN'S CULTURE.** ed. by Josephine Butler. 1869; **WOMEN. A COURSE OF LECTURES.** Boston, 8th ed., 1884.

8.394
MACMILLAN'S MAGAZINE: Cobbe, F.P., *"Social Science Congresses and Women's Part in Them,"* 5 (1861) 81-94. Outlines the "first beginning of the Social Science Congresses" as an outgrowth of reformatory movements; Collins, C.A., *"Beggars,"* 5 (1862) 210-218; Weigall, R., *"Friends in the Village,"* 20 (1864) 519-527; Hill, O., *"Organized Work Among the Poor,"* 20 (1869) 219-226; Clarke, C.B., *"The Existing Poor Law in England,"* 23 (1870-1871) 45-52; Hill, J., *"Workhouse Girls: What They Are and How to Help Them,"* 28 (1873) 132-139; Hill, O., *"A More Excellent Way of Charity,"* 35 (1876) 126-131; H.G., *"Endowed Charities and Pauperism,"* 41 (1880) 242-251; Williams, A.J., *"City Parochial Charities,"* 41 (1880) 469-475; Martin, F., *"The Other Side of the Question,"* 43 (1881) 461-464. Discusses the training of girls to work for the poor.

8.395
TRANSACTIONS OF THE NATIONAL ASSOCIATION FOR THE PROMOTION OF SOCIAL SCIENCE: Dale, J., *"The House of Shelter for Females,"* (1861) 560-566; Howson, J.S., *"The Official Employment of Women in Works of Charity,"* (1862) 780; Williams, C.E., *"Protective and Provident Movement Among Women,"* (1874) 945; (1876) 729-734.

8.396
Twining, Elizabeth, **A FEW WORDS ON SOCIAL SCIENCE TO WORKING PEOPLE.** 1862. Discusses the foundation of the National Association for the Promotion of Social Science by Lord Brougham, an organization "to gather together wise and good men and women from various places to speak, face to face, on subjects concerning the social welfare of all mankind; more especially on what belongs to the middle and working classes. We speak of the different classes because they surely exist, and ever will; but we know as what is for the well-being of one class is also for all" (p. 2).

8.397
Fry, Herbert, **THE SHILLING GUIDE TO THE LONDON CHARITIES FOR 1863 (1864, 1865-1866) SHOWING IN ALPHABETICAL ORDER THE NAME, DATE OF FOUNDATION, ADDRESS, OBJECTS... OF EVERY CHARITY IN LONDON.** 1863-1866; *continued as:* **THE ROYAL GUIDE TO THE LONDON CHARITIES FOR 1866-1867 (1884-1885).** 1866-1885; *continued as:* **HERBERT FRY'S ROYAL GUIDE TO LONDON CHARITIES FOR 1885-1886. (1886-1942).** 1885-1942.

8.398
ALL THE YEAR ROUND: *"A Lesson Well Learnt,"* 2 (1864) 328-331. Discusses the women who assisted soldiers and their families during the Crimean war. Florence Nightingale's work is considered a model.

8.399
Society for the Abolition of Capital Punishment, **REPORT OF THE SOCIETY FOR THE ABOLITION OF CAPITAL PUNISHMENT.** 1865.

8.400
LEISURE HOUR: *"Sewing Machines for the Poor,"* no. 14 (1865) 808. On successful efforts to teach blind women to be self-supporting through sewing work.

8.401
National Association for the Promotion of Social Science, **JOURNAL OF SOCIAL SCIENCE.** 1866. Contains papers read to the Association on matters of law, education, political economy and health.

8.402
VICTORIA MAGAZINE: *"Report on Social Science Congress,"* 3 (1866) 47-64.

8.403
Society for Promoting the Employment of Women, **EIGHTH (ETC.) ANNUAL REPORT... 1867 (ETC.).** [1867-]; **TWENTY-THIRD ANNUAL REPORT.** [1882]; **TWENTY-FOURTH ANNUAL REPORT** [1883].

8.404
THE PEOPLE'S DIRECTORY TO THE CHARITIES OF LONDON, AND GUIDE TO RELIEF FOR MORE THAN EIGHT HUNDRED BENEVOLENT INSTITUTIONS. [1868].

8.405
TINSLEY'S MAGAZINE: *"Liverpool Charities,"* 3 (1868) 189-199. Responds to criticisms of charity works by citing the "liberality and good management of... [Liverpool] charities" (pp. 192-193). As evidence, describes the benevolent activities of a nurse who "did such nursing as was possible, advised the lady what

nourishment or appliances might be needed, and instructed the family of the sufferer what to do in her absence. Her services went beyond this mere routine; here she would wean the husband of a sick wife from the public house by rendering his home comfortable, and showing him how he could really contribute to the patient's ease and recovery; here she would wash the children and send them to school; here even clean the room, open the window and teach the inmates how to admit a sufficiency of fresh air without——which is their superstitious horror— giving the patients or themselves a cold" (p. 195).

8.406
Hawksley, Thomas, THE CHARITIES OF LONDON AND SOME ERRORS OF THEIR ADMINISTRATION. 1869.

8.407
Charity Organisation Society (afterwards Family Welfare Association), REPORT OF THE COMMITTEE ON NIGHT REFUGES APPOINTED AT THE CONFERENCE HELD AT THE ROOMS OF THE SOCIETY... 1870. The purpose of the organization was to reconcile the divisions of society, to remove poverty and produce a happy, self-reliant community. Its operating belief was that the most serious aspect of poverty was the degradation of character of the poor man or woman; REPORT OF THE ST. GEORGE'S (HANOVER SQUARE) AND WESTMINSTER COMMITTEE... 1870; EMPLOYMENT. REPORT OF THE SUB-COMMITTEE APPOINTED BY THE COUNCIL OF THE CHARITY ORGANISATION SOCIETY... 1871; HOUSE-TO-HOUSE VISITATION. REPORT OF A SUB-COMMITTEE OF THE SOCIETY. 1871; REPORT UPON... SOUP-KITCHENS AND DINNER TABLES: WITH A DIGEST OF REPORTS... BY THE COUNCIL OF THE SOCIETY. 1871; REPORTS OF THE DISTRICT COMMITTEES AND OF THE COUNCIL. 1872; VOTING CHARITIES. PROCEEDINGS OF THE COUNCIL OF THE CHARITY ORGANISATION SOCIETY ON THE SYSTEM OF PERIODICAL CONTESTED ELECTIONS BY THE WHOLE BODY OF THE SUBSCRIBERS IN ITS APPLICATION TO HOSPITALS AND ORPHANAGES. [1872]; THE CHARITY ORGANISATION SOCIETY; ITS OBJECTS AND MODE OF OPERATION. 3rd ed., 1875; ORGANISATION OF CHARITY: REPORTS OF THE COUNCIL OF THE LONDON CHARITY ORGANISATION SOCIETY, ALSO OF SEVEN OF THE ASSOCIATIONS AFFILIATED TO IT, AND EIGHT OTHER CHARITABLE SOCIETIES. 13 vols. [1875-1891]; TRAINING OF THE BLIND. REPORT OF SPECIAL COMMITTEE OF THE CHARITY ORGANISATION SOCIETY, PRESENTED TO THE COUNCIL, FEBRUARY 21, 1876. [1876]; EDUCATION AND CARE OF IDIOTS, IMBECILES, AND HARMLESS LUNATICS. REPORT OF A SPECIAL COMMITTEE OF THE CHARITY ORGANISATION SOCIETY... PRESENTED JANUARY 15, 1877. [1877]; THE CHARITY ORGANISATION SOCIETY AND THE REYNOLDS-BARNARDO ARBITRATION. 1878; MODEL RULES FOR PROVIDENT DISPENSARIES. JUNE 1878. BY THE MEDICAL COMMITTEE OF THE CHARITY ORGANISATION SOCIETY. 1878; CO-OPERATION OF DISTRICT COMMITTEES OF THE CHARITY ORGANISATION SOCIETY WITH BOARDS OF GUARDIANS. RELIEF OF CASES OF TEMPORARY DISTRESS. 1879; GUIDE TO SCHOOLS, HOMES, AND REFUGES IN ENGLAND FOR THE BENEFIT OF GIRLS AND WOMEN. 1888; REGISTER OF CHARITY ORGANISATION AND RELIEF SOCIETIES IN CORRESPON-DENCE WITH THE LONDON CHARITY ORGANISATION SOCIETY. 1893; REGISTER OF CHARITY ORGANISATION AND RELIEF SOCIETIES IN CORRESPONDENCE WITH THE LONDON CHARITY ORGANISATION SOCIETY. 1896. ——*see also:* Bosanquet, Charles Bertie Pulleine, THE HISTORY AND MODE OF OPERATION OF THE CHARITY ORGANISATION SOCIETY.

1874; Hawksley, Thomas, **OBJECTIONS TO 'THE HISTORY' OF THE (CHARITY ORGANISATION) SOCIETY.** 1874; **LEISURE HOUR:** Forester, M.C., *"Charity Organisation Society,"* no. 1180 (1874) 512. "This Society is not in opposition to other societies which are not connected with it, as has often been thought by some. It is an organisation by which they can ascertain whether those persons they help are really in need of assistance or not.... During the past year 14,891 cases have been investigated, of which a little under 5,000 have been dismissed as either unworthy or not fit for relief, upwards of 4,000 have been put in the way of relief by being referred to other agencies to relieve, and close upon 6,000 have been assisted by the Society itself. Of the dismissed cases, 1,108 have been dismissed as not requiring relief, and I think it is very reasonable to suppose that a large proportion of those cases would have got help from private individuals if it had not been for the society, and that would have done more harm than good. 941 have been dismissed as not deserving, and 252 as giving false addresses. The Society has been the means of recommending 1,148 cases to the Poor-law Guardians" (p. 512); Hicks, W.N., **A CONTRIBUTION TOWARDS THE HISTORY OF THE ORIGIN OF THE C.O.S.** 1875; **MACMILLAN'S MAGAZINE:** Stephen, C.E., *"The Charity Organisation Society,"* 40 (1879) 24-31. Outlines the objectives of the organization and briefly describes procedures in dealing with "distress" cases. Calls for women with space in their homes to receive "at their own houses carefully selected poor persons either for an occasional dinner, or as guests for two or three weeks or a month at a time" (p. 27); Barnett, Henrietta O., **WHAT HAS THE CHARITY ORGANISATION SOCIETY TO DO WITH SOCIAL REFORM?** [1884]; Morris, E.E., **CHARITY ORGANISATION SOCIETIES IN ENGLAND AND THE UNITED STATES.** 1890; Townshend, Emily, **THE CASE AGAINST THE CHARITY ORGANISATION SOCIETY.** 1911; Bosanquet, Helen, **SOCIAL WORK IN LONDON 1869 TO 1912. A HISTORY OF THE CHARITY ORGANISATION SOCIETY.** 1914. "Trace[s] how the present network of agencies, voluntary and official, has been evolved. The first part of the record has been devoted to chronicling the origin and internal development of the Society itself" (pp. v-vi); **ECONOMIC REVIEW:** Nunn, T.H., *"Voluntary Workers at Newcastle,"* 24 (1914) 273-282; Bailward, William A., **THE CHARITY ORGANISATION SOCIETY. AN HISTORICAL SKETCH, 1869-1906;** 1935; Young, Agnes Freda and Ashton, Elwyn Thomas, "Family Case Work III: The Charity Organisation Society, 1869" in **BRITISH SOCIAL WORK IN THE NINETEENTH CENTURY.** by Agnes Freda Young and Elwyn Thomas Ashton. 1956; Mowat, Charles Loch, **THE CHARITY ORGANISATION SOCIETY, 1869-1913: ITS IDEAS AND WORK.** 1961; Woodard, Calvin, "The Charity Organisation Society and the Rise of the Welfare State," Ph.D. diss., Cambridge Univ., 1961; Owen, David, "'Scientific Charity': The Charity Organisation Society" in **ENGLISH PHILANTHROPY 1660-1960.** by David Owen. Cambridge, 1964; Rooff, Madeline, **A HUNDRED YEARS OF FAMILY WELFARE: A STUDY OF THE FAMILY WELFARE ASSOCIATION (FORMERLY THE CHARITY ORGANISATION SOCIETY) 1869-1969.** 1972. "To assist... upward progress the pioneers of the Charity Organisation Society saw two urgent needs: that self-respecting families who were struggling to keep themselves from destitution should be helped and encouraged, and that charities should be organised and co-ordinated so that the best use could be made of available resources" (p. 25); Fido, Judith, "The Charity Organisation Society and Social Casework in London 1869-1900" in **SOCIAL CONTROL IN NINETEENTH CENTURY BRITAIN.** ed. by A.P. Donajgrodzki. 1977. Examines the paradox inherent in the C.O.S. in terms of "the uneasy relationship between social work and social control" (p. 207). Delineates the method utilized in casework by voluntary workers and visitors; **VICTORIAN STUDIES:** Vincent, A.W., *"The Poor Law Reports of 1909 and the Social Theory of the Charity Organization Society,"* 27 (1984) 343-363. Re-evaluates the COS and critical views of its work by contemporary and modern writers. "The COS had...

been circling the problem [of the environmental factor in poverty] throughout the 1890s and the 1900s. The central question at issue for it was how far should an individual be allowed to decline before the State or some official body intervened, and how far was this intervention compatible with the individual's self-development, character, and freedom" (p. 362).

8.408
L., A.V., **THE MINISTRY OF WOMAN, AND THE LONDON POOR.** ed. and with introduction by Ada Ellen Bayly. 1870.

8.409
Loewe, Louis L., **DIARIES OF SIR MOSES AND LADY MONTEFIORE, COMPRISING THEIR LIFE AND WORK AS RECORDED IN THEIR DIARIES FROM 1812-1883.** 2 vols. 1870; 1890. Moses Haim and Judith (Cohen) Montefiore engaged in philanthropic work.

8.410
Fremantle, William Henry, **ST. MARY'S BRYANSTON SQUARE: PASTORAL ADDRESS AND REPORT OF THE CHARITIES OF THE YEAR 1870.** [1871].

8.411
Society for Organising Charitable Relief, **SOCIETY FOR ORGANISING CHARITABLE RELIEF... MANUAL CONTAINING ITS OBJECTS AND MODE OF OPERATION... FIFTY-SECOND THOUSAND.** 1872; **GUIDE TO SCHOOLS, HOMES, AND REFUGES IN ENGLAND FOR THE BENEFIT OF GIRLS AND WOMEN.** 1888.

8.412
Society for the Rescue of Young Women and Children, **18TH ANNUAL REPORT.** 2 parts, 1872-1873; **A MORE EXCELLENT WAY; OR, VOLUNTARY HOSPITALS VERSUS STATE HOSPITALS AND REGULATION OF VICE. BEING AN EXTRACT FROM THE ANNUAL REPORT OF THE SOCIETY...** 1877.

8.413
CHARITY ORGANISATION REPORTER: [1872 to 1884]; vols. 1-13. Publication of the Charity Organisation Society.

8.414
CORNHILL MAGAZINE: Lathbury, D.C., *"Women and Charitable Work,"* 30 (1874) 417-427.

8.415
ENGLISHWOMAN'S REVIEW: *"Events of the Quarter: Gentlewomen's Self-Help Institute,"* 5 (1874) 225; *"First Annual Meeting of the Women's Protective and Provident League (July 9, 1875),"* 6 (1875) 359-365; *"Social Science at Brighton,"* 6 (1875) 483-490. Discusses papers given on endowments to female education, nursing of the sick poor, and the Poor Law System; *"In Memorium,"* 8 (1877) 158-167. On Caroline Chisholm and her work in family emigration, and Jane Elizabeth Senior, who was the first State-employed Inspector; *"Social Science Congress,"* 11 (1880) 461-466. Report on the Social Science Congress held at Edinburgh on October 2; discusses women's role in philanthropic work; *"The Debt Women Owe to the Social Science Association,"* 17 (1886) 193-195. Discusses the dissolution of the Social Science Association.

8.416
Hubbard, Louisa M., ed., **THE YEAR-BOOK OF WOMEN'S WORK**. 1875; A
**GUIDE TO ALL INSTITUTIONS EXISTING FOR THE BENEFIT OF WOMEN
AND CHILDREN**. 1878; 1888; "Benevolent Associations for Befriending Women" in
THE ENGLISHWOMAN'S YEAR-BOOK OF 1882. 1882. Descriptive listings of
philanthropic and mutual benefit organizations. Includes informative advertisements;
"Association for the Benefit of Girls and Young Women Engaged in Domestic
Service and in Trade" in **THE ENGLISHWOMAN'S YEAR-BOOK OF 1882**. 1882.
A wide variety of organizations, institutions and lodgings are listed and described.
Important work for this subject; "Statistics of Women's Work" in **WOMEN'S
MISSION: A SERIES OF CONGRESS PAPERS ON THE PHILANTHROPIC
WORK OF WOMEN BY EMINENT WRITERS**. ed. by Angela Burdett Coutts. 1893.
Estimates that in 1905, churches, chapels, missions and charities in London had
7,500 volunteers and 900 salaried visitors. School care committees of the London
County Council enlisted 10,000 voluntary workers. *—see also:* Pratt, Edwin A., A
**WOMAN'S WORK FOR WOMEN: BEING THE AIMS, EFFORTS AND
ASPIRATIONS OF 'LMH', MISS LOUISA HUBBARD**. 1898. Treats the concerns
that Hubbard, a leading feminist, had for educational reforms and women's
employment.

8.417
Pennefather, Dora M., **THE REFORMERS. THEIR HOMES, HAUNTS AND
WORK**. 1875.

8.418
Howe, William Frederick, **FIRST (THIRTY-SEVENTH) ANNUAL EDITION OF
THE CLASSIFIED DIRECTORY TO THE METROPOLITAN CHARITIES FOR
1876 (-1912)...** 1876-1912. The 24th edition lists 970 charities and gives figures for
736 of them as having an income of L6,207,291; *continued as:* **THIRTY-EIGHTH
(—FORTY-FOURTH) ANNUAL EDITION OF HOWE'S CLASSIFIED
DIRECTORY TO THE METROPOLITAN CHARITIES FOR 1913 (-1919)**. 1913-
1919.

8.419
Yeames, James, **LIFE IN LONDON ALLEYS WITH REMINISCENCES OF MARY
McCARTHY AND HER WORK**. 1877. McCarthy was a Methodist who conducted
meetings for poor converts in the slums. She distributed tracts amongst the people
of Chequer Alley and collected funds for the support of this work while performing
a wide range of practical "good works." She lived among the poor by choice. Her
story informs understanding of life in poorest neighborhoods.

8.420
Daniell, Louise, **ALDERSHOT: A RECORD OF MRS. DANIELL'S WORK
AMONGST SOLDIERS, AND ITS SEQUEL**. 1879.

8.421
Society for the Relief of Distress, **MEMOIRS OF AN UNAPPRECIATED
CHARITY [THE SOCIETY FOR THE RELIEF OF DISTRESS], ETC.** 1879;
**THIRTY-SEVENTH ANNUAL REPORT OF THE SOCIETY FOR THE RELIEF
OF DISTRESS FOR THE YEAR 1897**. 1897.

8.422
Adams, William Henry Davenport, **WOMAN'S WORK AND WORTH IN
GIRLHOOD, MAIDENHOOD AND WIFEHOOD. ILLUSTRATIONS OF WOMAN'S
CHARACTER, DUTIES, REPLETE POSITION, INFLUENCE, RESPONSIBILI-**

TIES AND OPPORTUNITIES. WITH HINTS ON SELF-CULTURE AND
CHAPTERS ON THE HIGHER EDUCATION AND EMPLOYMENT OF WOMEN.
1880. See analytical table of contents for subjects treating issues connected to social
service.

8.423
Meredith, Susanna, SAVED RAHAB! AN AUTOBIOGRAPHY. 1881. Meredith gave
distinguished service in the work of prison visiting and assisting discharged women
prisoners. ——*see also:* Tomkinson, E.M., THE WORLD'S WORKERS: SARAH
ROBINSON, AGNES WESTON, MRS. MEREDITH. 1894; Lloyd, M.A., SUSANNA
MEREDITH: A RECORD OF A VIGOROUS LIFE. 1903.

8.424
LONDON QUARTERLY AND HOLBORN REVIEW: *"A Group of Female
Philanthropists,"* 57 (1881) 49-81. Review of LIFE AND WORK OF MARY
CARPENTER by J.E. Carpenter; SISTER DORA by M. Lonsdale; and
MEMORIALS OF FRANCES RIDLEY HAVERGAL by M.V.G. Havergal.

8.425
THE CHARITIES REGISTER AND DIGEST... 1882; 1884; 1890; 1895; *continued
as:* THE ANNUAL CHARITIES REGISTER AND DIGEST... 1897.

8.426
Lowe, Clara M.S., GOD'S ANSWERS: A RECORD OF MISS ANNIE
MACPHERSON'S WORK AT THE HOME OF INDUSTRY, SPITALFIELDS,
LONDON, AND IN CANADA. 1882. MacPherson, her family and helpers worked
out of the Home of Industry, established in 1869. Emigration, rescue work,
visitations to the poor and industrial training were among the philanthropies under
MacPherson's guidance.

8.427
TRAVELLER'S AID SOCIETY. 1885.

8.428
Garnett, Elizabeth, OUR NAVVIES: A DOZEN YEARS AGO AND TO-DAY. 1885.

8.429
CHARITY ORGANISATION REVIEW: 1885 to 1896; 12 vols.; 1897 to 1921; 49
vols; N.N., *"Matrons' Aid Society and Midwives' Institute,"* 1 (1885) 431-432;
Johnson, Mrs., *"Benefit Societies For Women,"* 2 (1886) 203-207; 225-227; Wayland,
H.L., *"The Old Charity and the New,"* 2 (1886) 161-164; Humphry, A.M., *"How to
Help Widows,"* 7 (1900) 291-299; *"The Relief of Widows,"* 19 (1906) 20-49; Y., C.F.,
"An Early Victorian Philanthropist," 19 (1906) 247-252. A biography of Harriet
Grote; Loch, M., *"The Order of United Sisters: A Benefit Society for Women,"* 20
(1906) 294-297; Costa, F., *"Jewish Charities,"* 37 (1915) 133-144.

8.430
Bolton, Sarah K., "Several London Charities" in SOCIAL STUDIES IN ENGLAND.
by Sarah K. Bolton. Boston, 1886. "There are over one hundred and thirty
almshouses and asylums for old people, the same number of hospitals and about one
hundred and fifty homes for girls and boys" (p. 126). Discusses, briefly, many
institutions for girls and women; "Mrs. Agnes Weston" in SOCIAL STUDIES, ETC.
Biographical sketch of a woman who did philanthropic work among English sailors;
"Mrs. Spurgeon, and Others" in SOCIAL STUDIES, ETC. Discusses Mrs. Spurgeon,
who began the Book Fund so that poor and working-class people could have books

available to them; Mrs. Meredith who aided discharged female prisoners at the Nine Elms Mission; Mrs. Daniell who provided Bible-readings for soldiers at Aldershot; Mrs. Margaret Lucas of the British Women's Temperance Union; and Mrs. William Hind Smith of the Young Abstainer's Union.

8.431
Browne, Phyllis (pseud. for Sarah Sharp Heaton Hamer), **MRS. SOMERVILLE AND MARY CARPENTER.** 1887. Carpenter devoted her life to the welfare of the poor, establishing ragged schools and reformatories for the destitute and for criminal girls. She also worked toward creating female normal schools and reformatories, and was a temperance advocate.

8.432
Hoare, E.A., **NOTABLE WORKERS IN HUMBLE LIFE.** 1887.

8.433
Martin, Frances, **ELIZABETH GILBERT AND HER WORK WITH THE BLIND.** 1887; 1891.

8.434
Metropolitan Association for Befriending Young Servants, **REPORT, 1875-1886.** 1887. The association worked to prevent young women from drifting into the workhouse "where if they do not learn evils of other kinds from bad associates, they will assuredly learn to depend far too readily on the rates and will become confirmed paupers" (p. 6); **REPORT OF THE METROPOLITAN ASSOCIATION FOR BEFRIENDING YOUNG SERVANTS FOR 1901.** 1902. "In 1898, 7,024 girls were being befriended and 1,034 ladies were befriending them" (p. 5); **THE WORK OF THE LADY VISITORS. WRITTEN FOR THE COUNCIL OF METROPOLITAN ASSOCIATION FOR BEFRIENDING YOUNG SERVANTS.** by Henrietta Octavia (Rowland) Barnett. n.d.

8.435
Spurgeon, Mrs. C.H., **TEN YEARS OF MY LIFE IN THE BOOK FUND.** 1887.

8.436
Wesley, Samuel, **MEMORIALS OF ELIZABETH ANN WESLEY, THE SOLDIERS' FRIEND.** 1887.

8.437
HELP: A JOURNAL OF SOCIAL SERVICE: 1891; vol. 1, nos. 1-5.

8.438
Burdett-Coutts, Angela Georgina (Baroness), compiler, **WOMAN'S MISSION: A SERIES OF CONGRESS PAPERS ON THE PHILANTHROPIC WORK OF WOMEN BY EMINENT WRITERS.** 1893. Valuable collection of essays on various aspects of social work and social reform including work for children, working girls, ragged schools, navvy missions and nursing. Coutts' article, "Amelioration of the Condition of the Working Classes," fervently addresses the inadequate recognition of women's accomplishments in philanthropy and offers her view that "to enable those who would otherwise by destitute to help themselves is more truly generous than to give alms. In the one case those in distress are made self-reliant, independent, and useful members of the community; in the other degradation and demoralisation are too often the result" (p. 258). An appendix describes contemporary work dealing with chariable organizations and philanthropic women in England, Ireland and abroad. Sixty-two organizations are listed for England alone; *reviewed in:*

SPECTATOR: 71 (1893) 490-492. ──*see also:* Adelaide, Mary (Duchess of Teck), **SKETCH OF BARONESS BURDETT-COUTTS.** 1893; Osborne, Charles C., ed., **LETTERS OF CHARLES DICKENS TO THE BARONESS BURDETT-COUTTS.** 1931; Patterson, Clara Burdett, **ANGELA BURDETT-COUTTS AND THE VICTORIANS.** 1953; Kanner, S. Barbara, "Victorian Institutional Patronage: Angela Burdett-Coutts, Charles Dickens, and Urania Cottage, 1846-1858," Ph.D. diss., Univ. of California, Los Angeles, 1972; Healey, Edna, **LADY UNKNOWN: THE LIFE OF ANGELA BURDETT-COUTTS.** 1978. Readable, comprehensive, and laudatory popular biography; Orton, Diana, **MADE OF GOLD: A BIOGRAPHY OF ANGELA BURDETT-COUTTS.** 1980. Well-researched biography; *reviewed in:* **VICTORIAN STUDIES:** Kanner, B., 24 (1981) 520-521.

8.439

Osborne, Charles C., ed., **LETTERS OF CHARLES DICKENS TO THE BARONESS BURDETT-COUTTS.** 1931; Patterson, Clara Burdett, **ANGELA BURDETT-COUTTS AND THE VICTORIANS.** 1953; Kanner, S. Barbara, "Victorian Institutional Patronage: Angela Burdett-Coutts, Charles Dickens, and Urania Cottage, 1846-1858," Ph.D. diss., Univ. of California, Los Angeles, 1972; Healey, Edna, **LADY UNKNOWN: THE LIFE OF ANGELA BURDETT-COUTTS.** 1978. Readable, comprehensive, and laudatory popular biography; Orton, Diana, **MADE OF GOLD: A BIOGRAPHY OF ANGELA BURDETT-COUTTS.** 1980. Well-researched biography; *reviewed in:* **VICTORIAN STUDIES:** Kanner, B., 24 (1981) 520-521.

8.440

Tomkinson, E.M., **THE WORLD'S WORKERS: SARAH ROBINSON, AGNES WESTON, MRS. MEREDITH.** 1894. Robinson was known as the "Soldier's Friend," Weston as the "Sailor's Friend," and Meredith as the "Prisoner's Friend."

8.441

Blackburn, Helen, **A HANDBOOK FOR WOMEN ENGAGED IN SOCIAL AND POLITICAL WORK.** 2nd ed., 1895.

8.442

Women's National Cooperative Self-Help Society, **PROGRAMME OF THE SOCIETY.** [1895].

8.443

CONTEMPORARY REVIEW: Hobson, J.A., *"The Social Philosophy of Charity Organisation,"* 70 (1896) 710-727. Critiques the philosophy of the C.O.S. that hand-outs encourage further idleness. "By trying to stop the free flow of charity, while refusing to recognise the social economic forces which cause poverty, Charity Organisation thinkers assume that dangerous position which is known as 'sitting on the safety-valve'" (p. 717).

8.444

NATIONAL REVIEW: Haldane, E.S., *"Registered Friendly Societies for Women,"* 28 (1896-1897) 559-566.

8.445

Pratt, Edwin A., **PIONEER WOMEN IN VICTORIA'S REIGN: BEING SHORT HISTORIES OF GREAT MOVEMENTS.** 1897. Biographical sketches and details of deeds performed by leading female philanthropists; **CATHERINE GLADSTONE: LIFE, GOOD WORKS, AND POLITICAL EFFORTS.** 1898. Gladstone was active in such philanthropic enterprises as the House of Charity for Distressed Persons,

Newport Market Refuge, convalescent homes, and relief during the cholera epidemic of 1866.

8.446
Andrew, Elizabeth W., **THE QUEEN'S DAUGHTER IN INDIA.** 1898. Discusses English female charity workers abroad.

8.447
Chappell, Jennie, **FOUR NOBLE WOMEN AND THEIR WORK: SKETCHES OF THE LIFE-WORK OF FRANCES WILLARD, AGNES WESTON, SISTER DORA AND CATHERINE BOOTH.** 1898; **WOMEN OF WORTH: SKETCHES OF THE LIVES OF CARMEN SILVA, ISABELLA BIRD BISHOP, FRANCES POWER COBBE AND MRS. BRAMWELL BOOTH.** 1908.

8.448
FORTNIGHTLY REVIEW: Wilkinson, J.F., *"Friendly Societies For Women,"* 69 (1898) 655-663.

8.449
International Congress of Women (International Council of Women), **PORTRAIT ALBUM OF WHO'S WHO AT THE INTERNATIONAL CONGRESS OF WOMEN, HELD IN LONDON... 1899.** [1899]; **REPORT OF TRANSACTIONS OF THE SECOND QUINQUENNIAL MEETING HELD IN LONDON... 1899, ETC.** 1900. Includes transactions of the International Congress of Women which convened in connection with the Council; **TOWARDS PERMANENT PEACE. A RECORD OF THE WOMEN'S INTERNATIONAL CONGRESS HELD AT THE HAGUE... 1915.** 1915; **TOWARDS PEACE AND FREEDOM. [AN OCCASIONAL PAPER CONTAINING AN ACCOUNT OF THE INTERNATIONAL CONGRESS OF WOMEN, ZURICH, 1919].** 1919. Subsequent congress reports are listed under Women's International League for Peace and Freedom.

8.450
ECONOMIC JOURNAL: Crawford, V.M., *"Philanthropy and Wage-Paying,"* 11 (1901) 96-105. Discusses methods of paying inmates in charitable homes, institutions, and convents for their work. Examines controversial attitudes towards such practices and endorses supervised programs of wage distribution.

8.451
Friendly Society for Women, Warrington, England, **RULES AND ORDERS FOR THE GOVERNMENT OF A FRIENDLY SOCIETY FOR WOMEN, ASSOCIATED TOGETHER IN WARRINGTON... INSTITUTED JANUARY 2, 1901, FOR RAISING AND SUPPORTING A BOX, OR FUND OF MONEY, FOR THE PURPOSE OF RELIEVING AND ASSISTING EACH OTHER ON JUST AND PROPER OCCASIONS.** Warrington, 1902.

8.452
Lloyd, Mary Anne, **SUSANNA MEREDITH.** 1903. Involved in a variety of philanthropic work, Meredith also aided the "feeble-minded."

8.453
Women's Industrial Council, **BOROUGH COUNCILS AND THE WELFARE OF WOMEN WORKERS.** [1903]; **MEMORANDUM ADDRESSED TO THE CENTRAL COMMITTEE AND LOCAL DISTRESS COMMITTEES APPOINTED TO DEAL WITH UNEMPLOYMENT IN LONDON.** 1905; **EDUCATION OF WOMEN AND GIRLS AT HOME AND ABROAD.** [1905].

8.454
Zimmern, Alice, **UNPAID PROFESSIONS FOR WOMEN**. 1906. Includes voluntary philanthropic works.

8.455
WESTMINSTER REVIEW: Pike, G.H., *"Why Prisoners' Wives are Helped,"* 166 (1906) 101-105. On aid given by a Mr. Wheatley on Brooke St. to women left without resources to feed their families.

8.456
National Association of Guilds of Help, **REPORT OF PROCEEDINGS**. 1908. Guild of Help was founded in 1905 in Bradford.

8.457
Weston, Agnes Elizabeth, **MY LIFE AMONG THE BLUEJACKETS**. 1909. —*see also:* Wintz, Sophia G., **OUR BLUE JACKETS: MISS WESTON'S LIFE AND WORK AMONG OUR SAILORS**. 1890; "Agnes Weston, The Sailor's Friend" in **THE WORLD'S WORKERS: SARAH ROBINSON, AGNES WESTON, MRS. MEREDITH**. by E.M. Tomkinson. 1894. Weston established Sailors Rests for the religious instruction and wholesome entertainment of sailors, and did temperance work among them as well.

8.458
Moor, Lucy M., **GIRLS OF YESTERDAY AND TODAY: THE ROMANCE OF THE Y.W.C.A.** [1910]. See especially: chapter 6, "Social Service—Departments: II," describing the YWCA's work in abstinence, thrift, emigration, employment, the blind and deaf, travellers' aid, educational libraries, etc.

8.459
Society for Visiting Hospitals, **ADDRESSES BY HENRY SEBASTIAN BOWDEN**. [1912].

8.460
Steer, Mary H., **OPALS FROM SAND, A STORY OF THE EARLY DAYS AT THE BRIDGE OF HOPE**. 1912.

8.461
Rathbone, Eleanor F., **REPORT ON THE CONDITION OF WIDOWS UNDER THE POOR LAW IN LIVERPOOL**. Liverpool, 1913. —*see also:* Stocks, Mary, **ELEANOR RATHBONE. A BIOGRAPHY**. 1949. Rathbone was a feminist social reformer.

8.462
ENGLISH WOMAN: Hutchinson, Mrs. E., *"Women in the Police Courts,"* 20 (Oct. 1913) 25-30.

8.463
Women's Emergency Corps, London, **HALF-YEARLY REPORT. 1914/15**. 1915.

8.464
Knightley, Louisa Mary (Bowater), **THE JOURNALS OF LADY KNIGHTLEY OF FAWSLEY, 1856-1884**. ed. by Julia Cartwright Ady. 1915. Knightley was the first president of the Conservative and Unionist Association for the Franchise of Women, and founder of the Girls' Friendly Society and Working Ladies' Club. She

was also active in emigration, women's education, hospitals and ambulance work.

8.465
Women's Cooperative Guild, **MATERNITY: LETTERS FROM WORKING WOMEN.** 1915. ——*see also:* Webb, Catherine, **A SHORT HISTORY OF THE WOMEN'S COOPERATIVE GUILD.** 1895; Davies, Margaret Llewelyn, **THE WOMEN'S CO-OPERATIVE GUILD.** 1904; Webb, Catherine, **THE WOMAN WITH THE BASKET: THE HISTORY OF THE WOMEN'S CO-OPERATIVE GUILD 1883-1927.** foreword by Margaret Llewelyn Davies. Manchester, 1927. The Guild was an organization of married working women for whom "the nation felt no responsibility.... Without money of her own, with no right even to her housekeeping savings, without adequate protection against a husband's possible cruelty, with no legal position as a mother, with the conditions of maternity totally neglected, married women in the home had existed apart, voiceless and unseen" (p. 11). The woman with the basket represents women's power as consumers in a growing capitalist nation. The Guild also worked in alliance with women's Trades Unions; **DICTIONARY OF LABOUR BIOGRAPHY:** Bellamy, J., Bing, H.F. and Saville, J., *"Davies, Margaret Llewelyn (1861-1944), Co-Operator and Social Reformer,"* 1 (1974) 96-99. "Margaret Davies was largely responsible for developing the Women's Cooperative Guild not only into a social and educational activity for working-class women in their own areas, but as a pressure group of considerable influence for women's rights" (p. 97); Gaffin, Jean and Thoms, David, **CARING AND SHARING: THE CENTENARY HISTORY OF THE COOPERATIVE WOMEN'S GUILD.** 1983.

8.466
Women's Institute, **SEVENTEENTH-TWENTY-NINTH ANNUAL REPORTS.** 1915-1927. ——*see also:* Robertson-Scott, J.W., **THE STORY OF THE WOMEN'S INSTITUTE MOVEMENT IN ENGLAND AND WALES AND SCOTLAND.** 1925. The object of these organizations is "to improve the conditions of rural life [for women] and to provide opportunities for mutual help and intercourse" (p. v); McCall, Cicely, **WOMEN'S INSTITUTES...** 1943; Inez, Jenkins, **THE HISTORY OF THE WOMEN'S INSTITUTE MOVEMENT OF ENGLAND AND WALES.** Oxford, 1953.

8.467
Battersea, Constance (Lady de Rothschild), **LADY DE ROTHSCHILD AND HER DAUGHTERS' REMINISCENCES.** 1922. "From childhood both my sister and I had been taught to look upon work for others, in many a good cause, as a privilege and not as a hardship nor as anything meritorious in itself" (p. 409). ——*see also:* Cohen, Lucy, **LADY ROTHSCHILD AND HER DAUGHTERS.** 1935. Mother and daughters desired to bring Jewish services, ceremonies and texts in line with Anglican aesthetic and religious traditions. Their social philanthropy also reflected this attitude.

8.468
Hamilton, Mary Agnes, **MARY MACARTHUR.** 1925. On MacArthur's work regarding women's economic rights and health care.

8.469
Tabor, Margaret E., **PIONEER WOMEN.** 1925-1930. A series of biographical sketches that include women involved in philanthropic work such as Elizabeth Fry, Elizabeth Blackwell, Florence Nightingale, Mary Slessor, Hannah More, Mary Carpenter, Octavia Hill and others.

8.470

Baylis, Lilian, "Emma Cons, The Founder of the Vic" in **THE OLD VIC.** by Lilian Baylis and Cicely Hamilton. 1926. Cons was a philanthropist, rent collector, improver of the Old Vic Theatre, activist in women's suffrage, and one of three women members of the first London County Council. She organized a hostel for girls in Drury Lane and founded creches and clinics for her tenants, and was a prime mover at a Horticultural College.

8.471

Greville, Beatrice (Baroness), **VIGNETTES OF MEMORY.** 1927. See especially: "Slumming," in which the author discusses her experiences with philanthropic work.

8.472

Montefiore, Dora B., **FROM A VICTORIAN TO A MODERN.** 1927. Discusses her charity work in the Jewish community.

8.473

Squire, Rose, **THIRTY YEARS IN THE PUBLIC SERVICE.** 1927.

8.474

Hobhouse, Emily, **EMILY HOBHOUSE, A MEMOIR.** compiled by A. Ruth Fry. 1929. ——*see also:* Fisher, John, **THAT MISS HOBHOUSE.** 1971. Chronicles the efforts of Emily Hobhouse to reform prisoner of war concentration camps during the Boer War; Kaminski, Diane C., "The Radicalization of a Ministering Angel: A Biography of Emily Hobhouse, 1860-1926," Ph.D. diss., Univ. of Connecticut, 1978.

8.475

Clephane, Irene, "Good Works and Sweet Charity" in **OUR MOTHERS. A CAVALCADE IN PICTURES: QUOTATION AND DESCRIPTION OF LATE VICTORIAN WOMEN 1870-1900.** ed. by Alan Bott. 1932; 1969. Among the spectrum of causes, some were "truly Christian" and others merely "exercises in self-flattery." "To be born within the circle of the upper ten thousand, or near it, was to be endowed by Providence with a superiority of soul which enabled one, oneself untaught, to teach others.... [In the 1880s,] doing good became positively fashionable" (p. 173).

8.476

Courtney, Janet Elizabeth (Hogarth), **COUNTRYWOMEN IN COUNCIL: THE ENGLISH AND SCOTTISH WOMEN'S INSTITUTES WITH CHAPTERS ON THE MOVEMENT IN THE DOMINIONS AND ON TOWNSWOMEN'S GUILDS.** 1933. Surveys "that many-sided effort towards rural betterment" (p. vi); "The New Philanthropy" in **THE WOMEN OF MY TIME.** by Janet Elizabeth Courtney. 1934. Discusses the social reform work of Octavia Hill, Samuel Barnett, Henrietta Barnett, Arnold Toynbee, Emma Cons, Beatrice Webb, and Sidney Webb.

8.477

Lonsdale, Sophia, "Work for the C.O.S." and "A Poor Law Guardian" in **RECOLLECTIONS OF SOPHIA LONSDALE.** compiled by Violet Martineau. 1936. Includes discussion of the work of Emma Cons, rent collector for South London and other subsidized working-class dwellings. Cons was also the manager of a music hall when it was converted into an entertainment center and lecture hall for "decent" gatherings for the public. It was Cons who sent Lonsdale to work for the C.O.S. in Lichfield.

8.478
Meyerand, Gladys, "On Women's Organizations" in **ENCYCLOPEDIA OF THE SOCIAL SCIENCES.** vol. 15, 1937.

8.479
ENCYCLOPEDIA OF THE SOCIAL SCIENCES: Meyerand, G., *"Women's Organizations,"* 15 (1937) 460-465. Discusses women's increasing participation in voluntary service organizations from the era of industrialization to 1937, in both the United States and England. Emphasizes the diversity of their achievements.

8.480
Ireland, Ivy A., **MARGARET BEAVAN OF LIVERPOOL: HER CHARACTER AND WORK.** Liverpool, 1938. Beavan headed the Invalid Children's Association.

8.481
National Council of Women of Great Britain, **WOMEN IN COUNCIL: THE JUBILEE BOOK OF THE NATIONAL COUNCIL OF WOMEN OF GREAT BRITAIN.** ed. by H. Pearl Adam. 1945. The council, established in 1895, represented a wide range of social welfare work throughout England. "Women who wanted to engage in useful work found themselves almost obliged to concern themselves with seduction, rape, prostitution, illegitimacy, abortion, and all their attendant squalors. When they spoke of these things in public——already displaying courage by speaking in public at all——at conferences and meetings, they used the circumlocutions forced upon them by the current code; they could not say a woman was going to have a baby... they were forced into what seems to us the hideous vulgarity of saying that she was 'in an interesting condition'" (pp. 6-7).

8.482
Martindale, Hilda, "A Social Worker of the Last Generation: Charlotte Spicer" in **SOME VICTORIAN PORTRAITS AND OTHERS.** by Hilda Martindale. New York, 1948; 1970.

8.483
Hobhouse, Rosa, **MARY HUGHES, HER LIFE FOR THE DISPOSSESSED.** 1949. "In her youth she spent her holidays with rich God-fearing friends and watched, and took part in, their work on behalf of the poor and the unfortunate... [but] she didn't want to visit the poor. She wanted to be with the poor and be poor herself. To do this she took herself to the East End of London and lived as an East-Ender would do" (pp. v-vi).

8.484
Dunbar, Janet, "Outstanding Women" in **THE EARLY VICTORIAN WOMAN.** by Janet Dunbar. 1953.

8.485
Galway, Marie Carola, "Charity and Philanthropy" in **THE PAST REVISITED: PEOPLE AND HAPPENINGS.** by Marie Carola Galway. 1953. Galway reminisces about her work during the Boer War aiding the wives of soldiers.

8.486
Grant, I., **NATIONAL COUNCIL OF WOMEN OF GREAT BRITAIN: THE FIRST SIXTY YEARS 1895-1955.** 1956.

8.487
Lipman, Vivian, "The Jewish Association for the Protection of Girls, Women and

Children, 1885 to 1946" in **A CENTURY OF SOCIAL SERVICES, 1859-1959.** by Vivian Lipman. 1959.

8.488
Poole, H.R., **THE LIVERPOOL COUNCIL OF SOCIAL SERVICE, 1909-1959.** 1959.

8.489
Wragge, Muriel, **THE LONDON I LOVED: REMINISCENCES OF FIFTY YEARS WORK IN THE DISTRICT OF HOXTON.** 1960.

8.490
Keeling, Dorothy C., **THE CROWDED STAIRS: RECOLLECTIONS OF SOCIAL WORK IN LIVERPOOL.** 1961. Keeling joined the staff of the Bradford City Guild of Help in 1907 and became responsible for training student interns from the Leeds University School of Social Work. She later started the Personal Service Society in Liverpool.

8.491
VICTORIAN STUDIES: Spring, D., *"The Clapham Sect: Some Social and Political Aspects,"* 5 (1961) 35-48.

8.492
Blunt, Wilfrid, "Society and Social Service" in **LADY MURIEL PAGET, HER HUSBAND, AND HER PHILANTHROPIC WORK IN CENTRAL AND EASTERN EUROPE.** by Wilfred Blunt. 1962. Paget reorganized the Invalid Kitchens of London and coordinated several charity balls.

8.493
Kamm, Josephine, "The Philanthropists" in **RAPIERS AND BATTLEAXES.** by Josephine Kamm. 1966. "Charitable work when it began was a haphazard affair, but it was gradually transformed into organized philanthropy. There was an immense amount to do, and where the need was greatest women pressed forward to fill it. They were conspicuous for their patient, courageous work in the most trying conditions and above all, perhaps, for their total lack of self-consciousness" (p. 31). Discusses the work of Mary Carpenter, Louisa Twining, Angela Burdett-Coutts and Anna Jameson.

8.494
Premble, R.J., "The National Association for the Promotion of Social Science (1857-1885)," M.A. thesis, Nottingham Univ., 1967.

8.495
Morris, R.J., "Organization and Aims of the Principal Secular Voluntary Organizations of the Leeds Middle Class, 1830-51," Ph.D. diss., Oxford Univ., 1971.

8.496
GUILDHALL STUDIES IN LONDON HISTORY: Garrett, K.I., *"Selections from the Papers of Maria Hackett,"* 2 (1975) 23-30. Hackett was a promoter of church choristers.

8.497
Minor, Iris, "Social Intervention in the Working-Class Family, 1870-1914," Ph.D. diss., Univ. of Hull, 1976. Examines the social philosophy of the C.O.S.; observations of social workers; working-class attitudes towards poverty and state

intervention; and the realities of working-class family life.

8.498
Pope, Barbara Corrado, "Angels in the Devil's Workshop: Leisured and Charitable Women in Nineteenth Century England and France" in BECOMING VISIBLE: WOMEN IN EUROPEAN HISTORY. ed. by Renate Bridenthal and Claudia Koonz. New York, 1977. Discusses changing roles and occupations of women in the context of industrialization. Involvement in philanthropy and social reform gained increasingly wide acceptance.

8.499
JOURNAL OF BRITISH STUDIES: Prochaska, F.K., *"Charity Bazaars in Nineteenth Century England,"* 16 (1977) 62-84. Fund-raisers for political and philanthropic causes were operated largely by women. After 1820, these "ladies' fairs" became widespread.

8.500
Cunnington, Phillis and Lucas, Catherine, CHARITY COSTUMES OF CHILDREN, SCHOLARS, ALMSFOLK, PENSIONERS. 1978. "Trace[s] the history in England of clothing provided for poor people of all sorts by charity; that is to say clothing given in kind by a wide range of benevolent individuals" (p. ix). Includes many photographs and illustrations.

8.501
Weeks, Jeffrey, "A Survey of Primary Sources and Archives for the History of Early Twentieth-Century English Women" in THE WOMEN OF ENGLAND FROM ANGLO-SAXON TIMES TO THE PRESENT: INTERPRETIVE BIBLIOGRAPH- ICAL ESSAYS. ed. by Barbara Kanner. Hamden, 1979. Includes three appendices on individuals, archives, and organizations together with locations of papers and other manuscript sources in England.

8.502
Prochaska, F.K., "Little Vessels" in WOMEN AND PHILANTHROPY IN 19TH CENTURY ENGLAND. by F.K. Prochaska. Oxford, 1980. Discusses children involved in philanthropic work. "Christian mothers helped to ensure that the habits of authority and benevolence passed... from generation to generation" (p. 94).

8.503
Braybon, Gail, "Biology as Destiny: Women, Motherhood and Welfare" in WOMEN WORKERS IN THE FIRST WORLD WAR. by Gail Braybon. 1981. "Welfare supervision [of workers in factories] was primarily designed for women and box workers, and involved a mixture of physical and moral guardianship. Welfare supervisors were supposed to oversee employment and dismissal, watch out for health hazards, organize canteens and recreational facilities; they were also supposed to ensure that women behaved in a discreet way with male workers, and that they lived in respectable lodgings" (p. 141).

8.504
BULLETIN OF THE INSTITUTE OF HISTORICAL RESEARCH: Prochaska, F.K., *"Female Philanthropy and Domestic Service in Victorian England,"* 54 (1981) 79-85. Discusses the charitable organization as a training institute for servants.

8.505
Boyd, Nancy, JOSEPHINE BUTLER, OCTAVIA HILL, FLORENCE NIGHT- INGALE: THREE VICTORIAN WOMEN WHO CHANGED THEIR WORLD. 1982.

All three reformers were motivated by their high valuation of the woman as mother in society. "Butler believed that social reform is only possible when it is based on the female instinct for caring for people as individuals.... Hill attributed much of her practicality, her ability to deal with the daily life of her tenants, to her maternal nature," and Nightingale's conception of her life's work "was to extend the maternal talent for caring, nursing, and healing to the uncared for, the sick and the unloved" (p. 246).

8.506
Murray, Janet Horowitz, "Public Work" in **STRONG-MINDED WOMEN AND OTHER LOST VOICES FROM NINETEENTH-CENTURY ENGLAND.** by Janet Horowitz Murray. New York, 1982. Excellent anthology of selections from contemporary writings by women.

8.507
Stuart, Denis, **DEAR DUCHESS: MILLICENT, DUCHESS OF SUTHERLAND.** 1982. The duchess was involved with social service societies and established Red Cross hospitals during World War I.

8.508
Trustram, Myna, "Philanthropy" in **WOMEN OF THE REGIMENT: MARRIAGE AND THE VICTORIAN ARMY.** Cambridge, 1984. "There was a considerable amount and variety of philanthropy available for wives, widows, and children of soldiers. This ranged from national organizations to small groups of women in garrison towns running bazaars, or individual acts of an officer's wife" (p. 163); *reviewed in:* **AMERICAN HISTORICAL JOURNAL:** Kanner, B., 91 (1986) 394-395.

* * *

4. SOCIAL SERVICE AND REFORM THROUGH RELIGIOUS INSTITUTIONS

8.509
RULES AND REGULATIONS FOR THE MANAGEMENT OF THE JEWS' HOSPITAL, MILES END. 1808.

8.510
Nichols, James, **A REPORT OF THE PRINCIPAL SPEECHES DELIVERED ON THE SIXTH DAY OF OCTOBER, 1813, AT THE FORMATION OF THE METHODIST MISSIONARY SOCIETY, FOR THE LEEDS DISTRICT.** 1813.

8.511
BIBLE SOCIETY MONTHLY REPORTER: 1817 to 1904; *superseded by:* **BIBLE IN THE WORLD:** 1905. Published by the British and Foreign Bible Society. The Society distributed Bibles among the poor in England and abroad.

8.512
HOME MISSIONARY MAGAZINE: OR RECORD OF THE TRANSACTIONS OF THE HOME MISSIONARY SOCIETY: 1820 to 1835; vols. 1-16; 1836 to 1840; vols. 1-5; 1841 to 1846; vols. 1-6.

8.513
CHRISTIAN PATRIOTISM AND HOME MISSIONS INSEPARABLE. [1821].

8.514
Port of London Society for Promoting Religion Among Seamen, **PROCEEDINGS OF THE THIRD ANNIVERSARY OF THE PORT OF LONDON SOCIETY FOR PROMOTING RELIGION AMONG SEAMEN.** 1821.

8.515
CLOTHING SOCIETY FOR THE BENEFIT OF POOR PIOUS CLERGYMEN OF THE ESTABLISHED CHURCH AND THEIR FAMILIES. 1832.

8.516
THE CHURCH, THE "NURSING MOTHER" OF THE PEOPLE. 1835.

8.517
LONDON CITY MISSION MAGAZINE: 1835 to 1860; vols. 1-26.

8.518
THE ASSOCIATED CATHOLIC CHARITIES FOR EDUCATING, CLOTHING AND APPRENTICING THE CHILDREN OF POOR CATHOLICS, AND PROVIDING FOR DESTITUTE ORPHANS. 1836.

8.519
Ansom, P.F., **THE BENEDICTINES OF CALDEY.** 1840. Discusses the work of sisterhoods in the parish.

8.520
Committee of the London Female Mission, **THE FEMALES' ADVOCATE.** vol. 3, 1840. Contains numerous articles on poor relief and the reform of fallen women. Dedicated to the "advocacy of the claims of the ignorant, the neglected, and the oppressed female."

8.521
London City Mission, **ANNUAL REPORTS.** 1843-1903. The mission's purpose was to extend knowledge of the gospel to London citizens, without reference to denominational distinctions or peculiarities of church government. Missionaries regularly visited the poor and conducted religious services. —*see also:* Weyland, John Matthias, **ROUND THE TOWER: OR THE STORY OF THE LONDON CITY MISSION.** 1875; **THESE FIFTY YEARS.** 1884. Memoirs of a mission worker; Hunt, John, **PIONEER WORK IN THE GREAT CITY. THE AUTOBIOGRAPHY OF A LONDON CITY MISSIONARY.** 1895.

8.522
CHRISTIAN LADY'S MAGAZINE: *"The Indigent Refuge for Females of Good Character,"* 19 (1843) 1-3. The institution's purpose was to "provide a refuge for the needy and distressed, but virtuous female" (p. 3). The refuge provided food and religious instruction.

8.523
London Domestic Mission Society, **NINTH ANNUAL REPORT.** 1844; **THIRTEENTH ANNUAL REPORT.** 1865.

8.524
Forbes, Alexander (Bishop of Brechin), **A PLEA FOR SISTERHOODS.** 1849. Advo-

cates the revival of sisterhoods as a force of trained visitors to schools and hospitals.

8.525
Church of England Self-Supporting Village for Promoting the Religious, Moral and General Improvement of the Working Classes, **PROSPECTUS.** 1850. This institution intended to form self-sufficient villages of 300 families on the land; **REPORT OF A PUBLIC MEETING OF... JULY 9, 1850.** 1850.

8.526
Church of England, Friend of the Clergy Corporation, **THE FRIEND OF THE CLERGY FOR ALLOWING PERMANENT PENSIONS NOT EXCEEDING L40 PER ANNUM TO WIDOWS AND ORPHAN UNMARRIED DAUGHTERS OF THE CLERGY.** 1851.

8.527
Vanderkiste, R.W., **NOTES AND NARRATIVES OF A SIX YEARS' MISSION PRINCIPALLY AMONG THE DENS OF LONDON.** 1852; 1854. Vanderkiste worked for the London City Mission, whose aim was the propagation of Christianity through "visitation and religious instruction of the poor in their own dwellings" (p. xi). The Mission also extended itself to criminal reform.

8.528
Church of England, Corporation of the Sons of the Clergy, **REPORT OF THE GOVERNORS OF THE CHARITY FOR THE RELIEF OF POOR WIDOWS AND CHILDREN OF THE CLERGYMEN... FOR... 1852.** 1853.

8.529
Garrett, Samuel, **MOTIVES FOR MISSIONS.** 1853. See especially: "The Irish in London."

8.530
Garwood, John, **THE MILLION-PEOPLED CITY: OR, ONE-HALF OF THE PEOPLE OF LONDON MADE KNOWN TO THE OTHER HALF.** 1853. Garwood was a social reformer with a Protestant evangelical mission to entice the uncivilized lower classes from vice, ignorance and Popery.

8.531
Home Missionary Society, **THE THIRTY-FOURTH ANNUAL REPORT OF THE HOME MISSIONARY SOCIETY.** 1853.

8.532
Stanley, Mary, **HOSPITALS AND SISTERHOODS.** 1853. Protestant sisterhoods could fulfill the need in English hospitals for nurses and occupy "surplus women."

8.533
Bolton, James, **MISSIONARY STICK GATHERERS: AN ADDRESS TO THE MEMBERS OF JUVENILE MISSIONARY ASSOCIATIONS.** 1854.

8.534
Jameson, Anna B., **SISTERS OF CHARITY. CATHOLIC AND PROTESTANT, ABROAD AND AT HOME.** 1855. Discusses the work of "the Sisters of Charity, not merely as the designation of a particular order of religious women, belonging to a particular church, but also in a far more comprehensive sense as indicating the vocation of a large number of women, in every country, class and creed" (p. 1). Also explores historical contributions of these women to the sick, war casualties,

pauper children, etc.

8.535
CHURCH OF ENGLAND QUARTERLY REVIEW: *"The British Jews, Part II,"* 38 (1855) 53-73. Demographic data and a list of Jewish metropolitan charities, including several which benefit women and children.

8.536
BOOK AND ITS MISSIONS, PAST AND PRESENT: 1856 to 1864; vols. 1-9. Organ of Ellen Ranyard's Bible Mission. Edited by Ranyard; *"A Ladies Bible Committee in London,"* 1 (1857) 137-144; *"The London Heathen and their Missionaries,"* 2 pts., 1 (1857) 121-126; 2 (1857) 169-178; *"A Female Bible Mission to the Women who Sift the Dust-Heaps at Paddington,"* 3 (1858) 88-96; *"A Leaf from 'Esther's' Journal,"* 3 (1858) 216; *"Accounts of Female Bible Missions,"* 3 (1858) 297-300. A report to subscribers; *"Bible Tea Party in St. Giles's,"* 3 (1858) 184-189; *"The Bible-Woman in Paddington,"* 3 (1858) 260-263; *"Clerkenwell and the Bible Women,"* 3 (1858) 135-142; *"Female Bible Mission in Clerkenwell [and] Bibleselling in Spitalfields,"* 3 (1858) 282-288; *"'Marian,' 'Sarah,' 'Lydia' and 'Esther',"* 3 (1858) 161-168. Discusses the work of four Biblewomen; *"'Martha' of Paddington,"* 3 (1858) 181-184. Biblewoman; *"More Female Missions,"* 3 (1858) 115-119; *"The Water-Cress Girls' Dormitory at St. Giles,"* 3 (1858) 134-135; *"The Bible Woman in Islington"* and *"'Rebecca' in Shoreditch,"* 4 (1859) 89-96; *"The Cottage Among the Dust-Heaps"* and *"Our Moral Wastes and their Matrons,"* 4 (1859) 62-72; *"Friends in Council Concerning Female Bible Missions"* and *"Seeds Sown in Waste Places,"* 4 (1859) 108-150; *"Report on Limehouse"* and *"What is the Chief End of of Female Missions,"* 4 (1859) 281-283; *"Ruth's Mission Room at St. Giles,"* 4 (1859) 163; *"Limehouse Fields, Stepney,"* n.v. (1859) 168; *"Experiences of a Yorkshire Coleporteur,"* 5 (1860) 71; *"The Handmaids of the Lord,"* 5 (1860) 70; *"Marian's Tea Party in St. Giles,"* 5 (1860) 237; *"A Mission for Christian Ladies,"* 5 (1860) 232; *"Ready to Perish,"* 6 (1861) 249-250; *"Take One Street At a Time,"* 6 (1861) 299; *"Don't Take Her Away,"* n.v. (1862) 334-335; *"More Female Bible Missions,"* 7 (1862) 117; *"Walks in Drury Lane on New Year's Day,"* 7 (1862) 32.

8.537
Exeter Hall, EXETER HALL SERMONS FOR THE WORKING CLASSES. 1857. —*see also:* RANDOM RECOLLECTIONS OF EXETER HALL 1834-1837 BY ONE OF THE PROTESTANT PARTY. 1838; Holmes, Frederick Morell, EXETER HALL AND ITS ASSOCIATIONS. 1881. Opened "for the purpose of accommodating the members of the religious, benevolent and Scientific Societies and Institutions connected with the Metropolis" (p. 31). Three to four thousand attended the first meeting.

8.538
Jones, Elizabeth, A LETTER RELATIVE TO THE RISE AND PROGRESS OF THE LADIES'S CHRISTIAN ASSOCIATION. 1857.

8.539
Ragged Church and Chapel Union, THE FOURTH ANNUAL REPORT. 1857.

8.540
Ranyard, Ellen, THE MISSING LINK, OR BIBLE-WOMEN IN THE HOMES OF THE LONDON POOR. 1859; LIFE WORK; OR THE LINK AND THE RIVET. 1861. An appeal, especially to upper classes, for money and workers by the founder of the first Biblewoman mission; THE TRUE INSTITUTION OF SISTERHOOD: OR A MESSAGE AND ITS MESSENGERS. 1862. Ranyard based her theories of

recruitment and supervision of biblewomen on the work of foreign missions. "A good poor woman, chosen from among the classes she wished explored, would probably be the most welcome visitor; while as a paid agent she could be kindly and firmly——tho perhaps invisibly-directed as circumstances might require" (p. 4); **LONDON AND TEN YEARS WORK IN IT.** 1868. Contains tables and charts listing receipts and expenditures of the Bible Women missions as well as geographic and demographic data showing where Biblewomen were located; **GOD'S MESSAGE TO LOW LONDON.** 1871; **NURSES FOR THE NEEDY OR BIBLE-WOMEN NURSES IN THE HOMES OF THE LONDON POOR.** 1875. Appeal to potential participants and subscribers, emphasizing the Biblewomen's ability to help the poor help themselves; **STONES CRYING OUT AND ROCK WITNESS TO THE NARRATIVES OF THE BIBLE; CONCERNING THE TIMES OF THE JEWS. THE EVIDENCE OF THE LAST TEN YEARS.** 1955. ——*see also:* Selfe, Rose Emily, **LIGHT AMID LONDON SHADOWS.** 1906. Contains the only known biography of Ranyard; Platt, Elspeth, **THE STORY OF THE RANYARD MISSION, 1857-1937.** 1937. Ranyard originally intended her Biblewomen to be evangelical workers only. However, the women discovered that she "would set out in the morning to visit her district and before she returned home she had probably been welfare worker, instructor in cookery and hygiene, minor ailment nurse and above all best friend to many a weary woman" (p. 36). "No lady could venture into many of these courts, but a woman of their own class who could... understand their difficulties... only transformed by her faith and her Christianity——such a woman could be a true missionary to them" (p. 12).

8.541
Society for Supplying Home Teachers and Books, **THIRD REPORT OF THE SOCIETY... IN MOON'S TYPE, TO ENABLE THE BLIND TO READ THE SCRIPTURES.** 1859.

8.542
Unitarian Home Missionary Board, **THE FOURTH [AND SEVENTH] ANNUAL REPORT OF...** Manchester, 1859; 1862.

8.543
HOME MISSION FIELD OF THE CHURCH OF ENGLAND: 1859 to 1888; vols. 1-30; 1889 to 1935; nos. 1-154. Published jointly by the Society for Promoting Additional Curates in Populous Places and the Women's Home Mission Association.

8.544
QUARTERLY REVIEW: [Cheney, R.H.], *"The Missing Link and the London Poor,"* 108 (1860) 1-34. Contains description of biblewomen's work. Supports the institution because it augments the efforts of the church to reach the lower classes.

8.545
Howson, John Saul (Dean of Chester), **DEACONESSES; OR THE OFFICIAL HELP OF WOMEN IN PAROCHIAL WORK AND IN CHARITABLE INSTITUTIONS.** 1862. Expanded version of an 1860 article printed in QUARTERLY REVIEW.

8.546
EVANGELICAL MAGAZINE AND MISSIONARY CHRONICLE: *"Bible Women in London,"* 4 (1862) 117-118. Provides data on Bibles sold by the British Foreign Bible Society to find out the results of the sale.

8.547
North London Deaconesses Institution, **SECOND ANNUAL REPORT AND**

BALANCE SHEET, ETC. 1863. Founded on the Kaiserworth model. The deaconesses took no vows but pursued a career without family obligations. A nursing home was a primary feature of the institution. "Deaconesses, protected by their dress and office, have been able to penetrate localities which, under ordinary circumstances, could scarcely have been assigned to district visitors" (p. 5); SEVENTH ANNUAL REPORT, ETC. 1868.

8.548
VICTORIA MAGAZINE: "*A Poor Woman's Work,*" 3 (1864) 396-399. Biblewomen are an important extension of the church into city slums. "Her work is no isolated and irregular effort, wasting some of its strength in an attempt to gain and hold an independent footing; it is linked to the whole power of the church" (p. 398).

8.549
Jewish Association for the Diffusion of Religious Knowledge, FIFTH ANNUAL REPORT. 1865.

8.550
LONDON QUARTERLY REVIEW: "*The Female Agency in the Church,*" 25 (1865) 163-188. Discusses deaconesses as a cheap source of labor for the church.

8.551
MISSING LINK MAGAZINE; OR, BIBLE WORK AT HOME AND ABROAD: 1865 to 1883; vols. 1-19; *continued as:* BIBLE WORK AT HOME AND ABROAD: 1884 to 1888; vols. 1-5; *continued as:* BIBLEWOMEN AND NURSES: 1889 to 1915; vols. 6-32; *continued as:* LONDON BIBLEWOMEN AND NURSES MISSION: 1916; vol. 33; *continued as:* RANYARD MISSION NEWS: 1939 to 1953. Originally edited by Ellen Ranyard. Intended to break down prejudice among Protestants against women's religious voluntarism and charity work. Details the development of the Biblewomen mission in London. A large portion of contents reprinted from the journal BOOK AND ITS MISSIONS.

8.552
All Saint's Church, THE MANUAL OF CONFRATERNITY OF ALL SAINTS FOR GIRLS AND YOUNG WOMEN. 1866.

8.553
Briggs, Frederick W., CHEQUER ALLEY: A STORY OF SUCCESSFUL CHRISTIAN WORK. 1866. Features the work of Mary McCarthy, describing how she found entrance into the community and gathered a congregation for local preachers.

8.554
Cotton, George Edward Lynch, THE EMPLOYMENT OF WOMEN IN RELIGIOUS AND CHARITABLE WORKS: A LECTURE DELIVERED BEFORE THE BETHUNE SOCIETY. 1866.

8.555
Lowder, Charles Fuge, TEN YEARS IN ST. GEORGE'S MISSION. 1867. The sisters of the mission "devote their whole lives to God's service... they desired to aid the Parochial and Missionary clergy in all works of mercy and charity to the bodies and souls of God's people" (pp. 91-92); TWENTY-ONE YEARS IN ST. GEORGE'S MISSION. AN ACCOUNT OF ITS ORIGIN, PROGRESS AND WORKS OF CHARITY. 1877. The mission was intended for women with domestic ties who still wanted to spend time every year in a sisterhood. They visited workhouses, taught

children, gave simple nursing advice and counselling, and operated a hostel for the aged.

8.556
FRIENDS' QUARTERLY EXAMINER: Thursfield, R., *"Female Workers: Home Mission Association of Women Friends,"* 1 (1867) 74-78. Concludes that female Friends occupy a distinct place in the Christian church and perform a special duty through their work.

8.557
Board of Guardians for the Relief of the Jewish Poor, **TENTH REPORT.** 1868. Mentions female participants in the work planned by the Board, e.g., the lady superintendant of the workroom for "training Jewish girls as needlewomen" to encourage them to seek their own financial support; **26TH ANNUAL REPORT.** 1886. On conditions in the East End; **37TH ANNUAL REPORT.** 1895. Notes that the Board still had no female officers. However, women were workroom superintendants and matrons of the nursing staff. ——*see also:* Magnus, Laurie, **THE JEWISH BOARD OF GUARDIANS (1859-1909).** 1909.

8.558
EAST LONDON EVANGELIST... ORGAN OF THE EAST LONDON CHRISTIAN MISSION: 1868 to 1869; vol. 1. Edited by William Booth; *superseded by:* **CHRISTIAN MISSION MAGAZINE... ORGAN OF THE CHRISTIAN MISSION:** 1869 to 1878; vols. 1-9; *continued as:* **SALVATIONIST... BEING AN ORGAN OF THE SALVATION ARMY:** 1879; vol. 1.

8.559
Nihill, Henry Daniel, **THE SISTERS OF THE POOR AT ST. MICHAELS, SHOREDITCH AND THEIR WORK.** 1870. "I don't suppose the poor of Shoreditch have reason to complain if some ladies live among them who otherwise would be spending their money in the country or at the West End of London, and choose to do their own hard work that they may have more to spend on the sick and starving of the neighborhood" (n.p.); **THE SISTERS OF ST. MARY OF THE CROSS. SISTERS OF THE POOR AND THEIR WORK.** 1887. Documents the constrained manners of the first nineteenth-century Anglican sisters, who were uncertain of their role in the world outside the convent.

8.560
PRACTICAL THOUGHTS AND SUGGESTIONS FOR SISTERS OF CHARITY... COMPILED FROM VARIOUS SOURCES. 1871.

8.561
Girls' Friendly Society, **A SPECIAL SERVICE ARRANGED FOR THE FESTIVALS OF THE GIRLS' FRIENDLY SOCIETY.** 1875; **A WORD ABOUT THE GIRLS' FRIENDLY SOCIETY.** 1875; Connected with the Church of England, the G.F.S was among the largest of the organizations devoted to the welfare of working women and girls. No one could remain a member of the Society if she had a "blemish" on her character or was guilty of an indiscretion before she joined. Eventually this regulation had to be discarded in order to reach more working girls. In 1880, the G.F.S. established its own emigration society; **BRANCH ASSOCIATIONS (OF THE GIRLS' FRIENDLY SOCIETY) AND HOW TO ORGANIZE THEM.** 1875; **PROSPECTUS.** 1877; **THE GIRLS' FRIENDLY SOCIETY: A SKETCH OF ITS ORGANIZATION, ETC.** 1879; **SPECIAL REPORT.** 1879; **THE CENTRAL RULES AND CONSTITUTION OF THE GIRLS' FRIENDLY SOCIETY.** 1880; **SCRIPTURE RULES FOR LIFE. COUNSELS FOR**

DAILY LIFE. 1880; THE G.F.S. LONDON DIOCESAN REPORT AND MINUTES OF COUNCIL MEETING. 1881-1882; AN APPEAL TO THE MISTRESSES OF ELEMENTARY SCHOOLS FROM THE GIRLS' FRIENDLY SOCIETY. 1882; G.F.S. LONDON DIOCESAN REPORT. 1883; THE NEED FOR THE G.F.S. 1883; ADDRESSES DELIVERED ON THE AIMS AND OBJECTS OF THE GIRLS' FRIENDLY SOCIETY. 1884; FRIENDLY COUNSEL TO MEMBERS OF THE GIRLS' FRIENDLY SOCIETY. 1886; A MANUAL OF HELP AND PRAYER FOR THE USE OF G.F.S. ASSOCIATES. 1886; G.F.S. REPORT OF CONFERENCE OF THE DEPARTMENT FOR MEMBERS IN THE PROFESSIONS. 1887; SUGGESTIONS FOR THE G.F.S. BRANCH ORGANIZATION. 1887; BIBLE READINGS FOR 1889 (-1929). 1889-1929; HONORARY ASSOCIATES: THEIR PLACE IN THE GIRLS' FRIENDLY SOCIETY. 1890; G.F.S. HANDBOOK OF ELDER MEMBERS' WORK. 1892; FORM OF ADMISSION OF WORKING AND HONORARY ASSOCIATES AND MEMBERS. 1893; OUR GIFT TO THE QUEEN. 1897; ELEMENTARY READING UNION. 1901. Teaching plan; OUR LETTER FOR G.F.S. CANDIDATES ALL OVER THE WORLD. 1902; BIBLICAL TEXTS, HYMNS, ETC., [ON CARDS]. 1906; THE EMPIRE AND BEYOND. 1913. —*see also:* Townsend, Mary Elizabeth, ASSOCIATIONS AND OTHER PAPERS. [1874]. The G.F.S recruited girls from ages 8 to 12. It sought to raise men's sense of chivalry toward women by showing them the true ideal of gentle, honest womanhood; REPORT OF THE WORK AND PROGRESS OF THE GIRLS FRIENDLY SOCIETY. 1878; 1881; 1882; 1884; 1888; 1891-1920; A FRIENDLY LETTER TO FATHERS AND MOTHERS ABOUT THE GIRLS' FRIENDLY SOCIETY. 1883; ENGLISHWOMAN'S REVIEW: *"The Girls' Friendly Society,"* 73 (1879) 198-206. Delineates the work of the G.F.S in aiding unemployed working girls by providing temporary shelter, sick care, and moral support from fellow members; FRIENDLY LETTERS TO YOUNG WOMEN IN BUSINESS. 1883; Rochester, Bishop of, REPORT OF THE G.F.S. ANNIVERSARY OF 1880. 1880; Gray, Lady B.C., LETTER TO WORKING ASSOCIATES RESPECTING MEMBERS IN SERVICE. 1883; Hawksley, C.J., G.F.S. WHAT DOES IT MEAN? 1883; Knightley, Lady Louisa M., THE WORK OF G.F.S. IN COUNTRY PARISHES. 1883; LETTER TO CANDIDATES ABOUT THE G.F.S. 1888; Hill, Joanna M., PRACTICAL SUGGESTIONS FOR THE USE OF ASSOCIATES FOR THE DEPARTMENT FOR G.F.S. CANDIDATES FROM WORKHOUSES AND ORPHANAGES. 1884; Parker, N., FRIENDLY LETTERS TO G.F.S. MEMBERS IN THE MILLS. 1884; Benson, M., SPIRITUAL WORK IN THE G.F.S. 1885; NINETEENTH CENTURY: Shrewsbury, T., *"Prevention,"* 18 (1885) 957-964; Brabazon, Mary J., Countess of Meath, HOW TO WORK THE DEPARTMENT FOR SICK MEMBERS. 1887; Hill, S.M., OUR WORK AND ITS FAME. 1891; Money, Agnes Louisa, HISTORY OF THE GIRLS' FRIENDLY SOCIETY. 1897; Money, Agnes E., THE HISTORY OF THE GIRLS' FRIENDLY SOCIETY. 1905; Trebeck, M., TRY THIS: USEFUL HOUSEHOLD HINTS. 1909; IMPERIAL COLONIST: Joyce, E., *"Thirty Years of G.F.S. Imperial Work,"* 10 (1912) 138-141; Carpenter, Minnie, MIRIAM BOOTH, A SKETCH. 1918. Describes the work of a child of Catherine and William Booth in the Salvation Army; Heath-Stubbs, Mary, FRIENDSHIP'S HIGHWAY: BEING THE HISTORY OF THE GIRLS' FRIENDLY SOCIETY 1875-1925. 1926; PAST AND PRESENT: Harrison, B., *"For Church, Queen and Family: The Girls' Friendly Society, 1874-1920,"* no. 61 (1973) 107-138. Reveals that the conservatism of the G.F.S. prevented it from adapting to changing social conditions after 1918. Thus it brought about its own demise.

8.562
Society for the Relief of Necessitous Widows and Children of Protestant Dissenting Ministers, THE HUNDRED AND FORTY-SECOND (HUNDRED AND FORTY-NINTH, HUNDRED AND FIFTY-FIRST) REPORT OF THE SOCIETY. 1875-

1884.

8.563
GIRLS' FRIENDLY SOCIETY REPORTER: 1875 to 1876; nos. 1-2. Published by the Girls' Friendly Society.

8.564
FRIENDLY LEAVES: 1876 to 1917; vols. 1-42. Published by the Girls' Friendly Society.

8.565
Hill, Octavia, **OUR COMMON LAND.** 1877. A Biblewoman should be "a careful conscientious woman of business with a clear head and very methodical ways" (p. 33).

8.566
National Sunday League, **ANNUAL REPORT.** 1877.

8.567
Saint George's and Saint James' Dispensary, **SIXTIETH (-SIXTY-FIFTH) ANNUAL REPORT.** 1877 (-1882).

8.568
Board of Guardians for the Relief of the Poor of the Spanish and Portuguese Jews' Congregation, **REPORT.** 1878.

8.569
Salvation Army, **HEATHEN ENGLAND.** 1879; **WAR CRY.** 1879; **SOWING AND REAPING: BEING A REVIEW OF THE SALVATION ARMY IN 1897.** 1898; **TALKS WITH RESCUERS: BEING A GENERAL REVIEW OF THE WORK DURING 1898 INCLUDING A SPECIAL REPORT OF THE CARDIFF BRANCH.** 1898; **WOUNDED IN THE WARFARE OF LIFE. BEING A REPORT OF THE ANNUAL MEETING INCLUDING A SPECIAL REPORT OF THE CARDIFF BRANCH.** 1898; **WOUNDED IN THE WARFARE OF LIFE. BEING A REPORT OF THE ANNUAL MEETING OF THE WOMEN'S SOCIAL WORK OF THE SALVATION ARMY...** 1900, **WITH A STATEMENT OF ACCOUNTS.** 1900; **A DAY WITH THE SALVATION ARMY.** 1904; **BETSY BOBBET... BEING THE ANNUAL REPORT OF THE WOMEN'S SOCIETY AND RESCUE WORK OF THE SALVATION ARMY.** 1905; **THE SURPLUS.** 1909. Describes work with emigrants; **REPORTS OF THE SOCIAL WORK OF THE SALVATION ARMY DURING THE YEARS 1908/1909, 1909/1910, 1912/1913, 1915/1916, 1917/1918.** 5 vols. 1918. Each volume has a separate title; **AN OUTLINE OF SALVATION ARMY HISTORY.** 1927; 1932; **THEN AND NOW. BEING STORIES OF CONTRASTS IN SALVATION ARMY SOCIAL WORK.** 1929. ——*see also:* Hume, H.S., **THE "TEMPERANCE MOVEMENT" AND THE "SALVATION ARMY." A DISCOURSE.** 1882; Butler, Josephine, **THE SALVATION ARMY IN SWITZERLAND.** 1883; Harkness, Margaret, **CAPTAIN LOBE: A STORY OF THE SALVATION ARMY.** 1889; Railton, George, **WOMEN'S SOCIAL WORK. TALKS WITH RESCUERS.** 1898; Manson, John, **THE SALVATION ARMY AND THE PUBLIC: A RELIGIOUS, SOCIAL AND FINANCIAL STUDY.** 1906; Sims, George R., et al., **SKETCHES OF THE SALVATION ARMY SOCIAL WORK.** 1906; White, Arnold, **THE GREAT IDEA: NOTES BY AN EYEWITNESS ON SOME OF THE SOCIAL WORK OF THE SALVATION ARMY.** 1909-1910. Presents results of the investigations of the Salvation Army's Anti-Suicide Bureau in 1907; Haggard, H. Rider, **REGENERATION: BEING AN ACCOUNT OF THE SOCIAL WORK OF**

THE SALVATION ARMY IN GREAT BRITAIN. 1910. See chap. 8 for a discussion of the work of the Army's Anti-Suicide Bureau; Sandall, Robert, et al., **THE HISTORY OF THE SALVATION ARMY.** 6 vols. 1947-1973. See especially: Your Daughters Shall Prophecy," "More Women Pioneers" and "Catherine Booth's Part"; Gauntlett, S. Carvasso, **SOCIAL EVILS THE ARMY HAS CHALLENGED.** 1954. Chronicles the Army's crusades and its influence on social legislation; Search, Pamela, **HAPPY WARRIORS. THE STORY OF THE SOCIAL WORK OF THE SALVATION ARMY.** 1956. Describes Catherine Booth's involvement with the Army. Contains anecdotal information about Army's work for unwed and abandoned mothers and prostitutes in foreign countries; **SALVATION CENTURY, 1864-1964.** 1964; Watson, Bernard, **A HUNDRED YEARS WAR: THE SALVATION ARMY 1865-1965.** 1964. See especially: "The Regiment of Women"; Robertson, R., "The Salvation Army: the Persistence of Sectarianism" in **PATTERNS OF SECTARIANISM.** ed. by Brian R. Wilson. 1967. Argues that from 1900 onward, membership in the Army was comprised of lower-and middle-class people; **A UNIQUE SOCIETY: A HISTORY OF THE SALVATION ARMY ASSURANCE SOCIETY LIMITED.** 1968; Parkin, Christine, "The Salvation Army and Social Questions of the Day" in **A SOCIOLOGICAL YEARBOOK OF RELIGION IN BRITAIN.** ed. by Michael Hill and Alan Deacon. 1972. Emphasizes that the Army's best feature was its concern for contemporary social problems rather than visions of a future utopia; Pearson, Michael, **THE AGE OF CONSENT: VICTORIAN PROSTITUTION AND ITS ENEMIES.** 1972. Discusses the work of the Salvation Army.

8.570
Booth, Catherine, **PAPERS ON PRACTICAL RELIGION.** 1878; **AGGRESSIVE CHRISTIANITY.** 1880. Married to William Booth and co-founder of the Salvation Army, Booth was largely responsible for the equal status of men and women within the organization. She joined Josephine Butler in the campaign against the Contagious Disease Acts; **POPULAR CHRISTIANITY.** 1887; **CHURCH AND STATE.** 1890; **GODLINESS.** 1890; **LIFE AND DEATH.** 1890. ——*see also:* Booth-Tucker, Frederick St.G., **THE LIFE OF CATHERINE BOOTH.** 2 vols. 1893; Most comprehensive account of her life; Booth, Bramwell, **ON THE BANKS OF THE RIVER OR MRS. BOOTH'S LAST DAYS.** 1894; 1900; 1911; Strahan, James, **THE MARECHALE.** New York, 1921. Biography; Powell, Cyril H., **CATHERINE BOOTH.** 1951; Bramwell-Booth, Catherine, **CATHERINE BOOTH: THE STORY OF HER LOVES.** 1970. Biography by her eldest grandchild, daughter of Bramwell Booth.

8.571
GOOD WORDS AND SUNDAY MAGAZINE: Gilbert, W., *"An Anglican Sisterhood,"* 22 (1881) 833-837. Reports that the Sisters of Bethany at Clerkenwell provide coal, groceries, hot food, and trained nursing care to the poor and sick in the district. Sisters also train orphan girls to work as domestics.

8.572
Christian Women's Union, **SISTERS IN COUNCIL. THIRD ANNUAL REPORT OF THE CHRISTIAN WOMEN'S UNION BRIGHTON CONFERENCE, 1882.** 1882.

8.573
Pitman, Emma Raymond, **LIFE'S DAILY MINISTRY: A STORY OF EVERYDAY SERVICE FOR OTHERS, ETC.** 1883; 2nd ed., 1898.

8.574
FRIENDLY WORK: 1883 to 1894; no. 1-143; *superseded by:* **GIRLS' QUARTERLY:**

A PAPER FOR WORKERS. WITH WHICH IS INCORPORATED "FRIENDLY WORK": 1894 to 1901; no. 1-28; *continued as:* FRIENDLY WORK FOR FRIENDLY WORKERS: 1902 to 1917; vols. 1-16.

8.575
NINETEENTH CENTURY: Hamilton, M.C., *"Mission Women,"* 16 (1884) 984. On the Society of Parochial Mission Women; Cowper, K., *"Some Experiences of Work in an East-End District,"* 18 (1885) 783-793. Cowper discusses her experiences as an administrator for the Parochial Mission Women's Society, and her contact with the people in her district.

8.576
OUR WAIFS AND STRAYS: THE MONTHLY PAPER OF THE CHURCH OF ENGLAND CENTRAL SOCIETY FOR PROVIDING HOMES FOR WAIFS AND STRAYS: 1884 to 1946; nos. 1-680.

8.577
Brinckman, Arthur, NOTES ON RESCUE WORK. 1885. Details the work of the Church Mission to the Fallen and the London Mission. Describes their methods of establishing a shelter in Mayfair and the division of London into districts. Female workers performed most of the rescue work.

8.578
Collier, Mrs. (of Birmingham), A BIBLE WOMAN'S STORY. BEING THE AUTOBIOGRAPHY OF MRS. COLLIER... 1885.

8.579
Booth, William, ORDERS AND REGULATIONS FOR FIELD OFFICERS OF THE SALVATION ARMY. 1886; 1925; 1927. Booth became a Methodist in 1834 and started a revivalist movement with his wife, Catherine, in 1861 which developed into the Salvation Army; IN DARKEST ENGLAND AND THE WAY OUT. 1890. Booth's plan was to alleviate poverty in England through work colonies. —*see also:* Huxley, T.H., SOCIAL DISEASES AND WORSE REMEDIES, LETTERS TO THE "TIMES" ON MR. BOOTH'S SCHEME WITH A PREFACE AND (REPRINTED) INTRODUCTORY ESSAY. 1891. "Mr. Booth's system appears to me... to be mere autocratic socialism, masked by its theological exterior" (p. 7). Viewed Booth as an irresponsible despot; THE LIFE OF GENERAL WILLIAM BOOTH: FOUNDER OF THE SALVATION ARMY. 2 vols. New York, 1920. Describes how the Salvation Army became a Booth family project. Also discusses their efforts to end prostitution and provide care for prostitutes; Collier, Richard, THE GENERAL NEXT TO GOD: THE STORY OF WILLIAM BOOTH AND THE SALVATION ARMY. 1965. In part an account of the Army's work with prostitutes.

8.580
Brabazon, Reginald, Earl of Meath, "Associations for the Benefit of Young Men, Women and Children" in SOCIAL ARROWS. by Reginald Brabazon. 1887. Girls' Friendly Society, Y.M.C.A., Ministering Children's League.

8.581
Grubb, Edward, PROBLEM OF POVERTY AND THE WORK OF THE CHRISTIAN CHURCH. 1887; SOCIAL DUTIES OF THE CHRISTIAN CITIZEN. 1889.

8.582
CHURCH OF ENGLAND HIGH SCHOOL MAGAZINE: 1888 to 1905; vols. 1-45.

Published by the Church of England High School for Girls, afterwards Francis Holland Church of England School, Clarence Gate.

8.583
MOTHERS' UNION JOURNAL: 1888 to 1925; nos. 1-49. Published by the Church of England, Mothers' Union.

8.584
OFFICIAL YEARBOOK OF THE CHURCH OF ENGLAND. 1889. Gives 47,112 as the number of district visitors in 80 percent of England and Wales. The majority were women.

8.585
MacGill, J.W. and Weigall, Mrs. A., **SEEKING AND SAVING: BEING THE RELIEF WORK OF THE MANCHESTER CITY MISSION**. 1889.

8.586
HOME MISSION FIELD OF THE CHURCH OF ENGLAND: 1889+. Published jointly by the Additional Curates Society and the Women's Home Mission Association; *also published as:* **A.C.S. NEWS**.

8.587
BROTHERS AND SISTERS. A QUARTERLY PAPER FOR CHILDREN: 1890. Edited by Helen Milman. Published by the Central Society for Providing Homes for Waifs and Strays of the Church of England.

8.588
CHARITY ORGANISATION REVIEW: Loch, C.S., *"The Charities of Church and Chapel,"* 8 no. 89 (1892) 168.

8.589
WORKER'S PAPER: 1892; 1894; no. 1-4. Published by the Young Women's Self Help Society of the Church of England.

8.590
Carpenter, Mrs. Boyd, "Women's Work in Connection with the Church of England" in **WOMAN'S MISSION**. ed. by Angela Georgina Burdett-Coutts. 1893.

8.591
Church of England, Central Society for Providing Homes for Waifs and Strays, **THIRTEENTH ANNUAL REPORT FOR....** 1893; **HANDBOOK FOR WORKERS**. 1895; **THE FIRST FORTY YEARS. A CHRONICLE OF THE CHURCH OF ENGLAND WAIFS AND STRAYS SOCIETY 1881-1920**. 1922.

8.592
Janes, Emily, "On the Associated Work of Women in Religion and Philanthropy" in **WOMAN'S MISSION**. ed. by Angela Burdett-Coutts. 1893. Surveys the spectrum of religious philanthropy.

8.593
HANDBOOK OF CATHOLIC CHARITIES ASSOCIATIONS ETC., IN GREAT BRITAIN. 1894.

8.594
HEALTH AND WEALTH. THE ORGAN OF THE CHURCH SANITARY

ASSOCIATION: 1894 to 1895; vols. 1-2. Published by the Church of England Society for the Promotion of Kindness to Animals.

8.595
Catholic Women's League, **REPORT OF A LECTURE ON THE DUTIES OF CARE COMMITTEES GIVEN BY MISS MORTON.** 1896; **SECOND REPORT OF THE... FOR 1909.** 1910; **NINTH ANNUAL REPORT.** 1916.

8.596
Walker, Henry, **EAST LONDON. SKETCHES OF CHRISTIAN WORK AND WORKERS.** 1896.

8.597
Women's Protestant Union, **OUR SIXTH [SEVENTH] YEAR 1897 [1898].** West Croyden, 1897; [1898].

8.598
ANCILLA DOMINI: A Novice of Genteel Background, *"My Experience,"* 38 (1897) 291-294. Example of the duties of a novice during her training period. Often performed tasks that she had never had to do at home, such as supervising the preparation of dinner for an institute for factory girls operated by her deaconess institution.

8.599
Stoddart, Anna M., **ELIZABETH PEASE NICHOL.** 1899. Nichol was a social reformer for the Society of Friends.

8.600
Young People's Society of Christian Endeavor, **CHURCH OF ENGLAND SECTION [A PROSPECTUS].** 1900.

8.601
Creighton, Louise, **A PURPOSE IN LIFE.** 1901; **WOMEN'S WORK IN THE CHURCH AND THE STATE.** 1907; **"PREFACE" TO REPORT OF THE WOMEN'S MEETING IN CONNECTION WITH THE PAN-ANGLICAN CONGRESS OF 1908.** 1908.

8.602
Freeman, Flora Lucy, **RELIGIOUS SOCIAL WORK AMONGST GIRLS.** 1901.

8.603
REPORTS OF THE CONFERENCE OF JEWISH WOMEN, MAY 13 AND 14, 1902. 1902.

8.604
Church of England, Mothers' Union, **HANDBOOK AND CENTRAL REPORT.** 1903. The main goal of the Union was to promulgate the idea that mothers are responsible to preserve "purity and holiness of life" in the family; **PAMPHLETS AND LEAFLETS.** 1909; **LITTLE BOOK OF PRAYERS.** 1914. —*see also:* Sumner, Mary Elizabeth, **AN EARNEST APPEAL TO MOTHERS.** 1886. "It is mothers, above all, that can work the reformation of family life in this country.... I firmly believe that the mothers neglect the religious and moral training of their children" (p. 4); Sumner, Mary Elizabeth, **TO MOTHERS OF THE HIGHER CLASSES.** Winchester, 1888. Entreaty to upper-class mothers to join the Mothers' Union; Hallet, [C.M.], **HOW TO OBTAIN THE INTEREST AND HELP OF THE**

MOTHERS OF THE HIGHER CLASSES IN THE MOTHERS' UNION. READ AT A MOTHERS' CONFERENCE. Winchester, 1889; Sumner, Mary Elizabeth, HOME LIFE: ADDRESSES TO MEMBERS OF THE MOTHERS' UNION. 1895; MacDougall, Lady E.M., MOTHERS IN COUNCIL TALKS IN MOTHERS MEETINGS. 1908; Palmer, M., MOTHERS' UNION WORK. 1910; Darlington, Lilian, MOTHERS' UNION GUIDE. WITH SPECIAL HYMNS AND PRAYERS. 1911; Lancaster, Violet, A SHORT HISTORY OF THE MOTHERS' UNION. 1958; Pownall, Margaret, THE MOTHERS' UNION, CHESTER DIOCESE, DIAMOND JUBILEE, 1898-1958. Chester, 1959; Coombs, Joyce, GEORGE AND MARY SUMNER, THEIR LIFE AND TIMES. 1965. Includes history of Mothers' Union; Parker, Olive, FOR THE FAMILY'S SAKE: A HISTORY OF THE MOTHERS' UNION 1876-1976. Folkstone, 1976. "As for talk of motherhood being a profession for which training was needed this was unheard of among women of her [Mary Sumner's] sort. They did not consider themselves concerned in any way with the professions. Training children was left to governesses and maids. The ladies considered themselves true amateurs in all things" (p. 5).

8.605
[Warburton, Mother Kate], MEMOIRS OF A SISTER OF ST. SAVIOUR'S PRIORY. 1903; OLD SOHO DAYS. 1906. Enthusiastic description of relief work in a London slum as a Sister.

8.606
WOMEN'S HELP TIDINGS: 1904; nos. 1-4. Published by the Young Women's Self-Help Society of the Church of England.

8.607
HANDBOOK OF CATHOLIC CHARITABLE AND SOCIAL WORKS. 1905.

8.608
Ladies Guild of Francis St. Alban, REPORTS OF MEETINGS. 1905 to 1913; nos. 1-23.

8.609
Church Education Corporation, THE YEARBOOK OF THE... FOR 1900 TO 1905. [1906].

8.610
Selfe, Rose Emily, LIGHT AMID LONDON SHADOWS. preface by G.H.S. Walpole. 1906. Records observations of the London Biblewomen and Nurses Mission. Selfe refers to the workers as "daughters of Consolation" and as "God's servants" with a "special vocation and ministry." She adds biographical knowledge of the founder, Ellen White Ranyard.

8.611
Richardson, Mrs. Jerusha Davidson (Hunting), WOMEN OF THE CHURCH OF ENGLAND. 1907. See especially: "Initiators of Reform, Founders of Institutes, Leaders of Social Movements, Philanthropists." Discusses Josephine Butler, Angela Burdett-Coutts, Maude Stanley.

8.612
Church of England, Scripture Readers Association, Pension and Widows Fund, SEVENTH [ETC.] ANNUAL REPORT FOR 1907 [ETC.]. 1908, etc.

8.613
Gilmore, Isabella, "Deaconesses: Their Qualifications and Status" in **THE CHURCH AND ITS MINISTRY.** 1908. ——*see also:* Robinson, Elizabeth, **DEACONESS GILMORE: MEMORIES.** 1924. Gilmore (1847-1923) was the sister of William Morris and a wealthy widow when began her career as a nursing sister at Guy's Hospital in 1886. She later became head of the Rochester Deaconess Institution. She took a professional attitude toward her work, and her Institution varied considerably from the family-type setting of the Kaiserworth model. It was to be "only a house of rest and refreshment" rather than a residence for deaconesses (p. 173). She developed great affection for the poor of the Battersea parishes with whom she worked, though she referred to them as "heathen" beyond the reach of the Education and Sanitary Laws.

8.614
Rountree, Joshua, **SOCIAL SERVICE: ITS PLACE IN THE SOCIETY OF FRIENDS.** 1913.

8.615
WORKERS' PAPER: 1914. Published by the Mother's Union of the Church of England.

8.616
Union of Jewish Women, **ANNUAL REPORT.** 1915.

8.617
ADVANCE: 1917 to 1918. Published by the YWCA for pre-teen girls.

8.618
LINKS: 1917 to 1920. Published by the YWCA for nurses.

8.619
DIRECTORY OF RELIGIOUS COMMUNITIES OF MEN AND WOMEN, AND OF DEACONESSES. 1920.

8.620
UNITARIAN SOCIAL REFORMERS. 1920-1923. Series of biographical tracts.

8.621
Kinnaird, Emily, **REMINISCENCES.** 1925. Contains author's memories of the work of Ellen Ranyard, Catherine Marsh, her mother, Mary Jane Kinnaird, and herself, all Christian institutional reformers.

8.622
Tabor, Margaret, "Agnes Jones" in **PIONEER WOMEN.** by Margaret Tabor. 1927. Jones worked in a Bible Mission before she engaged in her vocation as a nurse.

8.623
Potter, John Hasloch, **INASMUCH: THE STORY OF THE POLICE COURT MISSION, 1876-1926.** 1927. See especially: "Girls" and "Women's Work." The Mission was operated by the Church of England Temperance Society.

8.624
Wagner, Donald Owen, **THE CHURCH OF ENGLAND AND SOCIAL REFORM SINCE 1854.** New York, 1930. Introduction gives an overview of the social position and attitude of the Church towards societal changes of the nineteenth century and

reviews the variety of its social action in and attitudes towards education, state intervention, trade unionism, friendly societies, the cooperative movement, and Christian socialism. Includes bibliography.

8.625
Jorns, Auguste, **THE QUAKERS AS PIONEERS IN SOCIAL WORK.** trans. by Thomas Kite Brown, Jr. New York, 1931. Discusses Quaker activity in poor relief, education, alcoholism, care of the insane, prison reform, and abolition of slavery.

8.626
Church of England, Church Schools Company, **THE CHURCH SCHOOLS COMPANY, 1833-1933.** Cowley, 1934. Includes plates and portraits.

8.627
YOUNG WOMEN'S CHRISTIAN ASSOCIATION, OUR EIGHTY YEARS: HISTORICAL SKETCHES. 1935; The Young Women's Christian Association of Great Britain, the first institution with the name "YWCA," was founded in 1855. The national organization was established in 1877. ──*see also:* Moor, Lucy M., **GIRLS OF YESTERDAY AND TODAY: THE ROMANCE OF THE Y.W.C.A.** 1910. History with prefatory note by Emily Kinnaird. Early leaflets and correspondence between YWCA's major founders and patrons.

8.628
Pringle, John Christian, **SOCIAL WORK OF THE LONDON CHURCHES, BEING SOME ACCOUNT OF THE METROPOLITAN VISITING AND RELIEF ASSOCIATION 1843-1937. PREPARED UNDER THE DIRECTION OF THE EXECUTIVE COMMITTEE OF THE ASSOCIATION AND IN CO-OPERATION WITH THE LONDON ASSOCIATION OF VOLUNTARY SCHOOL CARE COMMITTEE WORKERS.** 1937. Demonstrates that C.O.S. methodology was preceded by organizations operating in the 1840s and 1850s.

8.629
Davies, Rosina, **THE STORY OF MY LIFE.** Llandyssul, 1942. Records sixty years' service in the Salvation Army.

8.630
Brackwell, C., "The Church of England and Social Reform, 1830-1850," M.A. thesis, Univ. of Birmingham, 1949.

8.631
Holt, R.V., **THE UNITARIAN CONTRIBUTION TO SOCIAL PROGRESS.** 1952.

8.632
National Free Church Women's Council, **FIFTY YEARS: A SURVEY OF THE WORK OF THE NATIONAL FREE CHURCH WOMEN'S COUNCIL 1907-1957.** 1957.

8.633
Clarke, W.K. Louther, **A HISTORY OF THE SOCIETY FOR THE PROMOTION OF CHRISTIAN KNOWLEDGE.** 1959.

8.634
Lipman, Vivian David, **A CENTURY OF SOCIAL SERVICE, 1859-1959: THE JEWISH BOARD OF GUARDIANS.** 1959. See especially: "The Jewish Association for the Protection of Women, Girls and Children, 1885-1946."

8.635
McGee, E.W., "The Anglican Church and Social Reform, 1830-1850," Ph.D. diss., Univ. of Kentucky. 1960.

8.636
Chadwick, Owen, **THE VICTORIAN CHURCH.** 1961. See especially: "The Church of England 1853-60: Charities."

8.637
Heasman, Kathleen, **EVANGELICALS IN ACTION. AN APPRAISAL OF THEIR SOCIAL WORK IN THE VICTORIAN ERA.** 1962. See especially: "Social Work in the 19th Century," "The Evangelicals and their Part in Such Work," "The Reform of the Prostitute," and "These Evangelical Charities." Most of the work of evangelical societies was done by middle-class "ladies" whose horizons were widened by contact with an element of society unmentionable in polite circles.

8.638
JOURNAL OF BRITISH STUDIES: Owen, D., *"The City Parochial Charities,"* 1 (1962) 115-135.

8.639
Inglis, K.S., **CHURCHES AND THE WORKING CLASSES IN VICTORIAN ENGLAND.** 1963. See especially: "The Churches and Social Reform." Discusses changing attitudes toward charity and reform among religious sects. "For most of the nineteenth century, Englishmen looked at poverty and found it morally tolerable because their eyes were trained by evangelical religion and political economy" (pp. 250-251).

8.640
Hall, M. Penelope and Howes, Ismene V., **THE CHURCH IN SOCIAL WORK: A STUDY OF MORAL WELFARE WORK UNDERTAKEN BY THE CHURCH OF ENGLAND.** 1965. "Moral welfare work is essentially social work undertaken in the name and on behalf of the Church" (p. 3). See especially: "Rescue and Reform" which discusses maintenance of illegitimate children under the Poor Law and refuges for prostitutes. "The cold ruthlessness and lack of any kind of imaginative understanding of, or sympathy with, the unmarried mother which characterised the report of the Poor Law Commissioners was, to a large extent, a reflection of attitudes and assumptions held at that time by devout Christians as well as by the callous and indifferent" (p. 18).

8.641
PAST AND PRESENT: Harrison, B., *"Religion and Recreation in Nineteenth Century England,"* no. 38 (1967) 98-125. Penetrating and detailed investigation of the efforts of religious reform organizations against Sabbath-breaking, intemperance and animal cruelty. Discusses opposition by secularists who were otherwise in favor of these reforms, but who objected to religious proselytism.

8.642
Isichei, Elizabeth, **VICTORIAN QUAKERS.** Oxford, 1970. Gives background on reasons for the extensive Quaker involvement in social reform and the field it provided for women's activism.

8.643
Stroud, John, **THIRTEEN PENNY STAMPS: THE STORY OF ENGLAND'S**

CHILDREN'S SOCIETY FROM 1881-1970'S. 1971.

8.644
Hill, Michael, "A Select Bibliography of Works on Nineteenth Century Anglican Orders" in THE RELIGIOUS ORDER. by Michael Hill. 1973.

8.645
Martin, R.H., "The Pan-Evangelical Impulse in Britain 1795-1830, with Special Reference to Four London Societies," Ph.D. diss., Univ. of Oxford, 1974.

8.646
Yeo, Stephen, RELIGION AND VOLUNTARY ORGANIZATIONS IN CRISES. 1976. Identifies two stages in religious voluntarism in Reading. The first stage is characterized by the elite expectation that voluntary action would create a universal consensus. Capitalism, poverty, and geographic segregation of socio-economic classes thwarted goals of charitable organizations and led to the second stage: a crisis of conviction; *reviewed in:* BRITISH JOURNAL OF SOCIOLOGY: Martin, D., 30 (1979) 143-146; HISTORICAL JOURNAL: Thompson, D., 22 (1979) 477-491.

8.647
JOURNAL OF IMPERIAL AND COMMONWEALTH HISTORY: Prochaska, F.K., *"Little Vessels: Children in the 19th Century English Missionary Movement,"* 6 (1978) 103-108. Examines the role of children in missionary work and the influence of parents on the children to join such movements. Children's missionary societies occurred simultaneously and in relation to women's auxiliary missionary organizations.

8.648
Summers, Anne, "A Home from Home——Women's Philanthropic Work in the 19th Century" in FIT WORK FOR WOMEN. ed. by Sandra Burman. Canberra, 1979. "The organization of a corps of Biblewomen, or 'native reformers' as Mrs. Ranyard interestingly referred to them, in London and many provincial towns, did not by any means sound the death knell of middle-class visiting" (p. 45).

8.649
HISTORICAL MAGAZINE OF THE PROTESTANT EPISCOPAL CHURCH: Holladay, J.D., *"Nineteenth Century Evangelical Activisim: From Private Charity to State Intervention,"* 51 (1982) 53-79. "While it is generally assumed that the primary stress among Evangelicals was upon the eternal, their actual treatment was, in fact, for more humanitarian than other cold and statistical responses to poverty in this period" (p. 61).

8.650
Ducrocq, Francoise, "The London Biblewomen and Nurses Mission, 1857-1880: Class Relations/Women's Relations" in WOMEN AND THE STRUCTURE OF SOCIETY. ed. by Barbara J. Harris and Jo Ann McNamara. Durham, 1984. "Both groups of social actors [Biblewomen and their middle-class patrons] were allowed to alleviate——within very distinct limits——their specific oppression... they were given an opportunity to go beyond their restricted spheres, to voice hitherto undefined requests and needs, and to create networks of friendship and sympathy" (p. 107).

8.651
Higginbotham, Ann R., "Respectable Sinners: Salvation Army Rescue Work with Unmarried Mothers, 1884-1914" in RELIGION IN THE LIVES OF ENGLISH

WOMEN, 1760-1930. ed. by Gail Malmgreen. 1986. Credits Florence Booth with establishing the Army's entrance into "maternity" work. Most of the cases were women of marriageable age in the servant class who had experienced failed courtships with men of the working classes. These statistics contradict the portrayed image of unwed mothers as orphan girls seduced by aristocratic men.

*   *   *

5. VISITORS TO THE POOR AND THE WORKHOUSE

8.652
THE LADIES' COMPANION FOR VISITING THE POOR. 1813. Instructions and suggestions.

8.653
Cappe, Catherine, **THOUGHTS ON THE DESIRABLENESS AND UTILITY OF LADIES VISITING THE FEMALE WARDS OF HOSPITALS AND LUNATIC ASYLUMS.** 1813.

8.654
An Old Visitor, **BENEFICIENT VISITS IN THE METROPOLIS.** 1817.

8.655
Ladies' Royal Benevolent Society, **THE LADIES' ROYAL BENEVOLENT SOCIETY... FOR VISITING, RELIEVING, AND INVESTIGATING THE CONDITION OF THE POOR AT THEIR OWN HABITATIONS.** 1818.

8.656
Gurney, Joseph John, **NOTES ON A VISIT MADE TO SOME OF THE PRISONS IN SCOTLAND AND THE NORTH OF ENGLAND, IN COMPANY WITH ELIZABETH FRY.** 1819. Contains Fry's instructions to prison visitors: "They will take their turns in visiting the prison daily; they will read the Scriptures with the prisoners; they will instruct the ignorant and will find employment for the idle... they will make themselves intimately acquainted with the disposition and circumstances of every prisoner; and they will endeavor to procure for him such establishment in life as will afford him an opportunity of maintenance, respectable for himself and unoffensive to his neighbor" (p. 172). ——*see also:* Rose, June, **ELIZABETH FRY.** 1980. "Although her standing as a Quaker minister gave her the authority to follow her calling, strict Quakers at that time disapproved of the involvement with worldly affairs that Elizabeth Fry's public life demanded" (prologue).

8.657
General Society for Promoting District Visiting, **FOURTH ANNUAL REPORT.** 1832. "The dirty hovels have... been made perfectly clean... some of the visitors have gone in and found two or three together reading the tracts. Several other beneficial results might be mentioned, but these are sufficient to prove that the

system works well" (p. 25).

8.658
DISTRICT VISITOR'S RECORD: 1832 to 1838.

8.659
THE DISTRICT VISITOR'S MANUAL: A COMPENDIUM OF PRACTICAL INFORMATION AND FACTS, FOR THE USE OF DISTRICT VISITORS. 1840.

8.660
Martin, Sarah, **A BRIEF SKETCH OF THE LIFE OF THE LATE MISS SARAH MARTIN.** No editor listed. Yarmouth, 1844. Martin was a prison visitor who conducted religious services for male and female inmates and worked for penal reform in the late eighteenth and early nineteenth centuries.

8.661
Charlesworth, Maria, (pseud. "A Clergyman's Daughter") **THE FEMALE VISITOR TO THE POOR; OR, RECORDS OF FEMALE PAROCHIAL VISITING.** 1846.

8.662
Brewer, J.S., "Workhouse Visiting" in **LECTURES TO LADIES ON PRACTICAL SUBJECTS.** ed. by Frederick Denison Morrison. 3rd rev. ed., 1857. "The parochial clergyman has found that the support and assistance of the ladies of his parish [are] indispensable for the improvement of the people" (p. 286).

8.663
[Sheppard, Mrs. Emma], **EXPERIENCES OF A WORKHOUSE VISITOR.** 1857; **SUNSHINE IN THE WORKHOUSE.** 1858; **AN OUTSTRETCHED HAND TO THE FALLEN.** [1860].

8.664
Hessey, Francis, **HINTS TO DISTRICT VISITORS.** 1858.

8.665
Twining, Louisa, **A PAPER ON THE CONDITIONS OF WORKHOUSES.** 1858. Twining pioneered the movement for reform of workhouse administration and conditions. She promoted the appointment of women as workhouse guardians. Her memoirs and books reveal her contributions as a social reformer, her personal life and thought, as well as the conditions under which she worked; **WORKHOUSES AND WOMEN'S WORK.** 1858; **ON THE TRAINING AND SUPERVISION OF WORKHOUSE GIRLS.** 1860. Pamphlet; *also printed in:* **DEACONESSES FOR THE CHURCH OF ENGLAND.** by Louisa Twining. 1860; **OUR POOR LAWS AND OUR WORKHOUSES.** 1862; **READINGS FOR VISITORS TO WORKHOUSES AND HOSPITALS.** 1865. Manual for lady visitors; **RECOLLECTIONS OF WORKHOUSE VISITING AND MANAGEMENT DURING TWENTY-FIVE YEARS.** 1880. Presents the argument that work for the improvement of institutions aiding the poor is not "entirely successful and satisfactory," and is only partially completed; **STATE ORGANISATION AND VOLUNTARY AID.** [1882]; *rpt. from:* **CHARITY ORGANISATION REPORTER:** n.v. (June 1882) n.p. Discusses reliance on American experience and organization; **WOMEN'S WORK, OFFICIAL AND UNOFFICIAL.** [1887]; "The History of Workhouse Reform" in **WOMAN'S MISSION.** ed. by Angela Georgina Burdett-Coutts. 1893; **RECOLLECTIONS OF LIFE AND WORK: BEING THE AUTOBIOGRAPHY OF LOUISA TWINING.**

1893; SUGGESTIONS FOR WOMEN GUARDIANS. Westminster, 1893; WORKHOUSES AND PAUPERISM AND WOMEN'S WORK IN THE ADMINISTRATION OF THE POOR LAW; 1898. Besides discussing general principles, Twining details the work and personnel of the Workhouse Visiting Society which was managed by both men and women. She indicates the participation of Emma Sheppard, Anna Jameson, Lady Shaftesbury, Mrs. Herbert, and others; *also published in:* SOCIAL QUESTIONS OF TO-DAY. ed. by Henry DeBettgens Gibbins. 1898. —*see also:* CANADIAN ASSOCIATION HISTORICAL PAPERS: McCrone, K.E., *"Feminism and Philanthropy in Victorian England: The Case of Louisa Twining,"* (1976) 123-139. Twining made an important contribution to feminism through her philanthropic activities and promotion of suffrage.

8.666

ENGLISH WOMAN'S JOURNAL: Twining, L., *"A Paper Read at a Meeting of the Workhouse Visiting Society,"* 4 (1859) 185-187. Discusses ways of promoting workhouse visiting societies.

8.667

JOURNAL OF THE WORKHOUSE VISITING SOCIETY: Jan. 1859 to Jan. 1865; nos. 1-32.

8.668

TRANSACTIONS OF THE NATIONAL ASSOCIATION FOR THE PROMOTION OF SOCIAL SCIENCE: Twining, L., *"On the Training and Supervision of Workhouse Girls,"* (1859) 696-702; Twining, L., *"Workhouse Inmates,"* (1860) 830-836; Elliot, M. and Cobbe, F.P., *"Destitute Incurables in Workhouses,"* (1860) 836-843.

8.669

Workhouse Visiting Society, REPORT OF THE WORKHOUSE VISITING SOCIETY UPON A PROPOSED INDUSTRIAL HOME FOR YOUNG WOMEN, AND THE CORRESPONDENCE WITH THE POOR LAW BOARD. 1860; FIFTH REPORT OF THE INDUSTRIAL HOME FOR GIRLS [AND THE] HOME FOR INCURABLE AND INFIRM WOMEN, ST. LUKE'S HOME. 1866; Purpose of the society was to "promote moral and spiritual improvement of workhouse inmates" (n.p.). The inmates included destitute and orphaned children and people who were sick, ignorant or depraved; JOURNAL OF THE WORKHOUSE VISITING SOCIETY: Jan. 1859 to Jan. 1865; nos. 1-32. —*see also:* TRANSACTIONS OF THE NATIONAL ASSOCIATION FOR THE PROMOTION OF SOCIAL SCIENCE: *"Workhouse Visiting Society,"* (1859) 185-187.

8.670

WESLEYAN METHODIST MAGAZINE: *"Christian Ladies Among the London Poor,"* n.v. (1860) 689-695. Describes efforts of female philanthropists to reform London slums by establishing self-help organizations for the poor.

8.671

MACMILLAN'S MAGAZINE: Cobbe, F.P., *"Workhouse Sketches,"* 3 (1861) 448-461; Stanley, M., *"Flowers for the Poor,"* 27 (1873) 525. Advises visitors to the poor to bring fresh flowers because of their "softening influence"; Barnett, H.O., *"The Young Women in Our Workhouses,"* 40 (1879) 133-139. Women enter such houses "first, in order to seek shelter when about to become mothers; secondly, because they are driven thither by the results of profligacy; thirdly, because having failed in life they choose to enter there rather than to sin or to starve" (p. 133); Poole, S.L., *"Workhouse Infirmaries,"* 44 (1881) 219-226; Barnett, S.A., *"Philanthropy and the Poor Law,"* 65 (1891) 76-80; Sellers, E., *"A Humane Poor Law,"* 67 (1893) 277-283.

8.672
Stallard, Joshua Harrison, **WORKHOUSE HOSPITALS**. 1865; **THE FEMALE CASUAL AND HER LODGING WITH A COMPLETE SCHEME FOR THE REGULATION OF WORKHOUSE INFIRMARIES**. 1866. Physician Stallard worked to appeal or reform the Poor Laws. His indirect investigations to prove the "horrors" of workhouses included hiring a "pauper widow" to enter the female ward in disguise and report her observations to him. "We have legalized a demoralizing institution.... We can only wonder that in Bethnal Green an honest woman should prefer to spend a cold December night in the public water closet rather than enter one of these dens of infamy and filth" (p. 5); **LONDON PAUPERISM AMONGST JEWS AND CHRISTIANS: AN INQUIRY INTO THE PRINCIPLE AND PRACTICE OF OUTDOOR RELIEF IN THE METROPOLIS, AND THE RESULT UPON THE MORAL AND PHYSICAL CONDITION OF THE PAUPER CLASS**. 1867. English charity relief system (Poor Law) and Jewish System (Board of Guardians) are compared and contrasted; **PAUPERISM, CHARITY, AND POOR LAWS. BEING AN INQUIRY INTO THE PRESENT STATE OF THE POORER CLASSES IN THE METROPOLIS, THE RESOURCES AND EFFECTS OF CHARITY... READ BEFORE THE SOCIAL SCIENCE ASSOCIATION, FEB. 17, OCT. 1, AND DEC. 21, 1868**. [1868].

8.673
THE DISTRICT VISITOR'S NOTE ARRANGED BY AN ALMONER OF THE SOCIETY FOR THE RELIEF OF DISTRESS... 1867.

8.674
Lois (pseud.), **PLEAS FOR THOSE WHO GREATLY NEED THEM. THREE LETTERS ON HELPING AND VISITING THE POOR ADDRESSED TO A LADY**. 1869. Notes that the poor can not be neat, clean, orderly, or odorless because mere survival consumes all of their energies. She suggests that visitors respect poor people and their privacy.

8.675
Trevelyan, Charles, **ADDRESS ON THE SYSTEMATIC VISITATION OF THE POOR IN THEIR OWN HOMES AN INDISPENSABLE BASIS OF AN EFFECTIVE SYSTEM OF CHARITY**. 1870.

8.676
Hill, Octavia, **EMPLOYMENT OR ALMS-GIVING: BEING AN ACCOUNT OF THE PLAN OF RELIEF NOW ADOPTED IN A DISTRICT OF MARYLEBONE**. 1871; **LETTER ACCOMPANYING THE ACCOUNT OF DONATIONS RECEIVED FOR WORK AMONGST THE POOR DURING 1872**. 1873; "A Few Words to the Volunteer Visitors Among the Poor" in **OUR COMMON LAND**. by Octavia Hill. 1877. Emphasizes the importance of training volunteer visitors who should encourage the poor to help themselves. "She does not think of them as people but as poor people" (p. 49); **DISTRICT VISITING**. 1877. Important work. "It seems incongruous to carry tracts in one hand and coal tickets in another" (p. 1); **LETTER TO MY FELLOW WORKERS, TO WHICH ARE ADDED ACCOUNTS OF DONATIONS RECEIVED FOR WORK AMONG THE POOR DURING 1894**. 1895.
——*see also:* Maurice, C. Edmund, **LIFE OF OCTAVIA HILL AS TOLD IN HER**

LETTERS. 1913.

8.677
FAITHFUL RECORDS: NARRATIVES OF VISITS TO THE SICK AND SUFFERING. BY A LADY. 1873.

8.678
Bosanquet, Charles Bertie Pulleine, A HANDY-BOOK FOR VISITORS OF THE POOR IN LONDON. 1874. Discusses the Poor Law, the Sanitary Law and charities.

8.679
ENGLISHWOMAN'S REVIEW: T., M., *"Homes for Working Girls,"* 5 (1874) 251-252; *"Women as Poor Law Guardians,"* 6 (1875) 157-159. Maintains that, on the subject of workhouse reform, a woman's experience is necessary for efficient administration; De Morgan, S.E., *"Recollections of a London Workhouse, Forty Years Ago,"* 20 (1889) 49-58. Describes the past conditions of St. Pancras, one of the largest workhouses in London, in order to illustrate the need for female influence in their management; *"Are More Women Guardians Needed?"* 20 (1889) 97-102. "If ladies are needed in our crowded towns, where the workhouses and infirmaries overflow with poverty in its most depressing and hopeless forms, they are no less needed in the country unions, where the busy farmers and shopkeepers who make the bulk of the Board attend less frequently than in London, and where cases of neglect or mismanagement occur with sad frequency" (p. 99); *"Women Poor Law Guardians,"* 20 (1889) 168-181. Report of incoming returns indicating the election of female poor law guardians in various districts; Greatheed, M.M., *"Workhouses, Past and Present,"* 20 (1889) 253-256. Recollections of a female workhouse visitor. Describes inmates and insanitary conditions.

8.680
HINTS ON DISTRICT VISITING. 1877.

8.681
Stanley, Maude, WORK ABOUT THE FIVE DIALS. 1878. Presents advice on reaching and helping the poor. "The best of all ways in my opinion... is that of being a district visitor under the sanction of the clergyman of the parish.... Experience has taught me that this is by far the best method of really reaching the homes and the hearts of working people" (p. 3). Surveys specific problems.

8.682
USEFUL HINTS; GATHERED FROM THE EXPERIENCE OF A LIFETIME. 1880. Visiting manual.

8.683
Barnett, Henrietta O., THE WORK OF LADY VISITORS. WRITTEN FOR THE COUNCIL OF THE METROPOLITAN ASSOCIATION FOR BEFRIENDING YOUNG SERVANTS. 1880; "Women as Philanthropists" in THE WOMAN QUESTION IN EUROPE. ed. by Theodore Stanton. New York, 1884; rpt., 1970.

8.684
WESTMINSTER REVIEW: Muller, F.H., *"The Work of Women as Poor Law Guardians,"* 123 (1885) 386-395; J., J.C., *"The London Poor: Suggestions How to Help Them,"* 133 (1890) 265-276. The time, effort and money spent on private philanthropy is a "futile diversion of the public charity" (p. 271). Suggests that

public charities should be unified in and rationalized by one organization; Blake, M.M., *"Women as Poor Law Guardians,"* 139 (1892) 12-21.

8.685
CHARITY ORGANISATION REVIEW: M., F.J., *"Notes of a Workhouse Visitor,"* 2 (1886) 428-431.

8.686
NINETEENTH CENTURY: Twining, L., *"Workhouse Cruelties,"* 20 (1886) 709-714; Hill, O., "A Few Words to Fresh Workers," 26 (1889) 452-461; Hill, O., *"Our Dealings with the Poor,"* 30 (1891) 161-170. Outlines a detailed scheme for district visitors so that their work might be more effective; Hill, O., *"Trained Workers for the Poor,"* 33 (1893) 36-43; Twining, L., *"Women as Official Inspectors,"* 35 (1894) 489-494. Argues that "women should be allowed to take a greater part in the management of workhouses, and in the inspection of them" in order to facilitate better conditions amongst the women confined there (p. 489); states, as an example, that nurses would be better able to confide in a female inspector and that this form of more open communication is crucial to instituting reforms.

8.687
Downwright, Dora, **WHY I AM A GUARDIAN.** Manchester, 1888. Reminiscences of a Poor Law guardian.

8.688
Rogers, Joseph, **REMINISCENCES OF A WORKHOUSE MEDICAL OFFICER.** 1889.

8.689
Society for Promoting the Return of Women as Poor Law Guardians, **ANNUAL REPORT.** 1889/1890-1899/1900; **WOMEN POOR LAW GUARDIANS.** Westminster, 1898; **THE WORK THAT LADIES CAN DO AS POOR LAW GUARDIANS.** Westminster, 1900. Attempts to rouse public interest in women's election to these posts, as they are "peculiarly fitted" for this work. The first woman guardian was elected in 1875. Part of their tasks were to interview poor applicants for aid.

8.690
A Parson, **MY DISTRICT VISITORS.** 1891.

8.691
Lidgett, Elizabeth S., **WOMEN AS GUARDIANS OR AS WORKHOUSE VISITORS.** Manchester, 1893.

8.692
Sewell, Margaret A., **DISTRICT VISITING.** 1893.

8.693
Bosanquet, Helen (Dendy), "Origin and History of the English Poor Law" in **ASPECTS OF THE SOCIAL PROBLEM.** ed. by Bernard Bosanquet, Helen Dendy, et al. 1895; 1898.

8.694
Lubbock, Gertrude, **SOME POOR RELIEF PROBLEMS. WITH THE ARGUMENTS ON BOTH SIDES TOGETHER WITH THE SUMMARY OF THE**

REPORT OF THE ROYAL COMMISSION ON THE AGED POOR, AND
EXTRACTS FROM THE EVIDENCE TAKEN BEFORE THAT COMMISSION. A
MANUAL FOR WORKERS. 1895. Considers charitable relief, old age pensions, and
provision of meals to the needy.

8.695
Emmott, Elizabeth Braithwaite, LOVING SERVICE. A RECORD OF THE LIFE
OF MARTHA BRAITHWAITE BY HER LOVING DAUGHTER... 1896. See
especially: "Visits to the Fallen Women and to Some Lodging Houses and Beerhouses
in Banbury, 8th Month, 1849."

8.696
Mitchell, Elizabeth Harcourt, LAY HELP IN DISTRICT VISITING. 1899.

8.697
Hutchins, B. Leigh, WORKING WOMEN AND THE POOR LAW. 1909.

8.698
Nevinson, Margaret Wynne, IN THE WORKHOUSE. 1911. Observes women's
experiences in workhouse living.

8.699
JOURNAL OF BRITISH STUDIES: Wohl, A., *"Octavia Hill and the Homes of the
London Poor,"* 10 (1971) 105-131.

8.700
Prochaska, F.K., "In the Homes of the Poor" in WOMAN AND PHILANTHROPY
IN NINETEENTH CENTURY ENGLAND. by F.K. Prochaska. Oxford, 1980.

8.701
Lewis, Jane, "The Working-Class Wife and Mother and State Intervention" in
LABOUR AND LOVE: WOMEN'S EXPERIENCE OF HOME AND FAMILY 1850-
1940. ed. by Jane Lewis. Oxford, 1986. "From [the 1870s] on there is what might be
called an invasion of the working-class family, still chiefly through the agency of
voluntary visitors, although increasingly by locally employed state officials such as
the school attendance officer and, by the early twentieth century, the health visitor"
(p. 101); "Reconstructing Women's Experience of Home and Family" in LABOUR
AND LOVE, ETC. Oxford, 1986.

*   *   *

6. SANITARY WELFARE

8.702
Chadwick, Edwin, **GENERAL REPORT OF THE SANITARY CONDITION OF THE LABOURING POPULATION OF GREAT BRITAIN**. 1842; rpt., Edinburgh, 1965. ed. by M.W. Flinn. ——*see also:* Finer, S.E. **THE LIFE AND TIMES OF SIR EDWIN CHADWICK**. 1952; 1970. On the life and work of this highly influential administrator.

8.703
Association for Promoting Cleanliness Among the Poor, **FIRST ANNUAL REPORT**. 1846. Discusses the establishment of bath/wash-houses.

8.704
Gavin, Hector, **UNHEALTHINESS OF LONDON AND THE NECESSITY OF REMEDIAL MEASURES**. 1847. Written to arouse public awareness of the insufficient sanitation in cities and its relationship with sickness and mortality; **SANITARY RAMBLINGS——BEING SKETCHES AND ILLUSTRATIONS OF BETHNAL GREEN, A TYPE OF THE CONDITION OF THE METROPOLIS**. 1848; **THE HABITATIONS OF THE INDUSTRIAL CLASSES: THEIR INFLUENCE ON THE PHYSICAL AND ON THE MORAL CONDITION OF THOSE CLASSES: SHOWING THE NECESSITY FOR LEGISLATIVE ENACTMENTS**. 1851. Published by the Society for Improving the Condition of the Labouring Classes, this work criticizes the government allowance of inadequate and overcrowded dwellings and poor sanitation.

8.705
Ladies' Sanitary Association, [TRACTS]. 1859-1872; **THE REPORT OF THE LADIES' SANITARY ASSOCIATION TO THE SEVENTH INTERNATIONAL CONGRESS OF HYGIENE AND DEMOGRAPHY**. 1891; **ANNUAL REPORTS, FIRST THROUGH THIRTY-EIGHTH 1857-1894**. 1894. ——*see also:* **ENGLISH WOMAN'S JOURNAL**: *"The Ladies' Sanitary Association,"* 3 (1859) 73-85. Discusses the rise of sanitary measures; Griffiths, E.S., **SKETCH OF THE WORK OF THE LADIES' SANITARY ASSOCIATION FROM ITS COMMENCEMENT IN OCTOBER 1857 TO DECEMBER 1865**. 1865; **TRANSACTIONS OF THE NATIONAL ASSOCIATION FOR THE PROMOTION OF SOCIAL SCIENCE**: Adams, R., *"The Ladies' Sanitary Association,"* (1874) 748-750; Dowling, William Charles, "The Ladies' Sanitary Association and the Origins of the Health Visiting Service," M.A. thesis, Univ. of London, 1963.

8.706
ENGLISH WOMAN'S JOURNAL: *"The Details of Woman's Work in Sanitary Reform,"* 3 (1859) 217-227; 316-324; *"Second Annual Report of the Ladies National Association For the Diffusion of Sanitary Knowledge,"* 3 (1859) 380-388. Contends that women are best suited to conduct work leading to sanitary reforms. Valuable article which lists objectives reached by the Association; *"On the Best Means of Forming Local Sanitary Associations,"* 4 (1859) 115-119.

8.707
TRANSACTIONS OF THE NATIONAL ASSOCIATION FOR THE PROMOTION OF SOCIAL SCIENCE: Baines, M.A., *"The Ladies National Association For the Diffusion of Sanitary Knowledge,"* (1859) 531-532.

8.708
Powers, Susan R., **REMARKS ON WOMAN'S WORK IN SANITARY REFORM.** [1862].

8.709
VICTORIA MAGAZINE: *"Social Science,"* 1 (1863) 570-573. Reports on the activities of the Social Science Congress and includes an address by the Ladies' Sanitary Association.

8.710
ENGLISHWOMAN'S REVIEW: *"Women and Sanitary Knowledge,"* n.v. (1880) 441-445. The special object of the Ladies' Sanitary Association is to diffuse knowledge among the poor. This is the focus of an address on "Woman as Sanitary Reformer," reprinted in full in this article.

8.711
FRASER'S MAGAZINE: Richardson, B.W., *"Woman as a Sanitary Reformer,"* 102 (1880) 667-83. "I press this office for the prevention of disease on womankind, not simply because women can carry it out... but because it is an office which man alone never can carry out... the man is abroad, the disease threatens the home, and the woman is at the threatened spot" (p. 671).

8.712
NINETEENTH CENTURY: Marryat, R., *"Sanitary Aid,"* 15 (1884) 840-848.

8.713
London Society For the Compulsory Vaccination, **SIXTH ANNUAL MEETING.** 1886; **ELEVENTH-THIRTEENTH ANNUAL REPORT.** 1891-1893.

8.714
Wilson, Hector Maclean, **COTTAGE SANITATION IN RURAL DISTRICTS.** 1896.

8.715
Women's Co-operative Guild, **PUBLIC HEALTH PAPERS.** nos. 1-3, 1897.

8.716
Gomme, G. Laurence, "Appendix I: Insanitary Condition of London" in **LONDON IN THE REIGN OF VICTORIA.** by G. Laurence Gomme. 1898. Contains an extract of a testimony by the Earl of Shaftesbury to the Royal Commissioners on the Housing of the Working Classes in 1884.

8.717
Kilgour, Mary Stuart, **WOMEN AS MEMBERS OF LOCAL SANITARY AUTHORITIES.** 1900.

8.718
National Council of Women of Great Britain, **WOMEN AS SANITARY INSPECTORS.** 1902.

8.719
Women Sanitary Inspectors' Association, **WOMAN'S PLACE IN SANITARY ADMINISTRATION.** 1904.

8.720
Loane, Margaret E., **SIMPLE SANITATION: THE PRACTICAL APPLICATION OF THE LAWS OF HEALTH TO SMALL DWELLINGS.** [1905]. Manual for home use.

8.721
Royden, Agnes Maude, **THE DUTY OF KNOWLEDGE: A CONSIDERATION OF THE REPORT OF THE ROYAL COMMISSION ON VENEREAL DISEASES, ESPECIALLY FOR THE USE OF SOCIAL WORKERS.** 1917.

8.722
Buer, Mabel Craven, **HEALTH, WEALTH AND POPULATION IN THE EARLY DAYS OF THE INDUSTRIAL REVOLUTION.** 1926; 1968. See especially: "The 18th Century Doctor and the British Pioneers of Public Health," "The Anti-Typhus Campaign and the Fever Hospital Movement," and "The Period 1815-1848" on public health reform.

8.723
Macadam, Elizabeth, "The New Health Services, Public and Voluntary Work" in **THE NEW PHILANTHROPY. A STUDY OF THE RELATIONS BETWEEN THE STATUTORY AND VOLUNTARY SOCIAL SERVICES.** by Elizabeth Macadam. 1934. Briefly discusses historical contributions by women to this area of social reform.

8.724
Frazer, William Mowell, **A HISTORY OF ENGLISH PUBLIC HEALTH 1834-1939.** 1950. "The main provisions of the Poor Law Amendment Act, 1834, were:— (i) the creation of Poor Law Unions under boards of guardians, (ii) the building of workhouses into which paupers were admitted under a rigid system of classification which separated husbands from wives and parents from children, and (iii) the discontinuance of outdoor relief either by way of money or food. Boards of guardians were democratically elected but worked under the constant inspection of the officers employed by the Poor Law Commission which maintained common standards throughout the country" (p. 13). See p. 92 for a description of the occupational hazards suffered by women working in domestic manufacture. Also discusses various legislation aimed at increasing the level of public health, occupational health, housing and nutrition, and reformers in the public health movement.

8.725
HISTORY TODAY: Hayter, A., *"The Sanitary Idea and a Victorian Novelist,"* 19 (1969) 840-847. Examines the content of Charlotte Yonge's novels which described "the growth of towns and the social, economic and medical problems that it caused" (p. 840).

8.726
Sheppard, Francis, "Public Health" in **LONDON 1808-1870: THE INFERNAL WAR.** by Francis Sheppard. Berkeley, 1971. Overview of sanitary reform.

8.727
HISTORICAL STUDIES: Mayne, A.J.C., *"The Question of the Poor' in the Nineteenth Century City,"* 20 (1983) 557-573. Analyzes the sanitary reforms instigated in Sydney as a case study parallel with similar growing urban environments of the 19th century. Emphasizes the middle-class perspective on urban poverty. "The conclusions drawn about health, and the Protestant-influenced assumptions concerning deviancy, were both in turn shaped heavily by class" (p. 558).

* * *

7. HEALTH SERVICES

8.728
Lying-In Charity (afterwards Royal Maternity Charity), **A PLAIN ACCOUNT OF THE ADVANTAGES OF THE LYING-IN CHARITY FOR DELIVERING POOR MARRIED WOMEN AT THEIR OWN HABITATIONS.** 1767; **ACCOUNTS.** 1791; 1798; 1817; 1818; 1820; 1833.

8.729
Benevolent Institution for Delivering Poor Married Women at Their Own Habitations, **AN ACCOUNT OF THE BENEVOLENT INSTITUTION, ETC.** 1806.

8.730
Ladies Charity, or Institution for the Relief of Poor Married Women in Childbed, Liverpool, **ELEVENTH REPORT.** Liverpool, 1807.

8.731
Cappe, Catharine, **THOUGHTS ON THE DESIRABLENESS AND UTILITY OF LADIES VISITING FEMALE WARDS OF HOSPITALS AND LUNATIC ASYLUMS.** 1816; *first printed in:* **PAMPHLETEER:** 8 (1813) n.p.

8.732
Society for Relief of the Destitute Sick, **REPORT OF THE SOCIETY FOR RELIEF OF THE DESTITUTE SICK.** 1817.

8.733
Society for Visiting and Relieving the Sick Poor, **SECOND REPORT OF THE SOCIETY FOR VISITING AND RELIEVING THE SICK POOR.** Liverpool, [1820].

8.734
Female Society for the Relief of Poor Women in Childbirth, **REPORT OF THE PROCEEDINGS OF THE FEMALE SOCIETY... OF WHICH LADY SARAH MAITLAND IS PATRONESS.** 1825.

8.735
HOUSEHOLD WORDS: Morley, H., *"Medical Practice Among the Poor,"* 10 (1854)

217-221.

8.736
[Taylor, Fanny], **EASTERN HOSPITALS AND ENGLISH NURSES; THE NARRATIVE OF TWELVE MONTHS EXPERIENCE IN THE HOSPITALS OF KOULALI AND SCUTARI, BY A LADY VOLUNTEER.** 1856.

8.737
A WOMAN'S SECRET, WOMAN'S WORK: OR, HOW SHE CAN HELP THE SICK. 1860; 1862.

8.738
ONCE A WEEK: Scott, I., *"Representative Women. The Free Nurse. Catherine Mompesson, Mary Pickard, Florence Nightingale,"* 2 (1860) 258-262; 577-581. "By the Free Nurse I mean to indicate the Sister of Charity who devotes herself to the sick for their own sake, and from a natural impulse of benevolence, without being bound by any vow or pledge, or having any regard to her own interests in connexion with her office" (p. 258).

8.739
Tompkinson, R.C., **JEHOVAH JIREH. THE MINE EXPLORED, A PLEA FOR THE CRIPPLES' HOME AND FEMALE REFUGE, NORTHUMBERLAND HOUSE.** 1863.

8.740
[Rathbone, William], **ORGANIZATION OF NURSING BY A MEMBER OF THE COMMITTEE OF THE HOME AND TRAINING SCHOOL.** 1865. The organization of paid trained nurses was patronized by women; **THE HISTORY AND PROGRESS OF DISTRICT NURSING.** 1890.

8.741
Association for the Improvement of London Workhouse Infirmaries, **REPORT OF A PUBLIC MEETING OF THE ASSOCIATION, HELD AT WILLIS' ROOMS, ST. JAMES, MARCH 3, 1866.** 1866; **THE MANAGEMENT OF THE INFIRMARIES OF STRAND UNION, THE ROTHERHITHE AND THE PADDINGTON WORKHOUSES, ETC.** 1867.

8.742
MACMILLAN'S MAGAZINE: Garrett, E., *"Volunteer Hospital Nursing,"* 15 (1867) 494-499.

8.743
Gordon, Margaret Maria, **THE DOUBLE CURE: OR, WHAT IS MEDICAL MISSION?** 1869.

8.744
Jones, J., **MEMORIALS OF AGNES ELIZABETH JONES.** 1871. Jones trained pauper nurses at the Liverpool Infirmary. Includes extracts from her nursing diary from April 1853 to June 1867 concerning asylums and hospitals for poor women.

8.745
Clayton, Louisa, **THE LONDON MEDICAL MISSION: WHAT IS IT DOING?** 1873.

8.746
QUARTERLY REVIEW: Clarke, W.F., *"The Medical Charities of London,"* 136 (1874) 371-394.

8.747
Ranyard, Ellen White, **NURSES FOR THE NEEDY: OR, BIBLEWOMEN NURSES IN THE HOMES OF THE LONDON POOR.** 1875.

8.748
Hopkins, Jane Ellice, **OCCUPATION FOR THE SICK: OR, PRACTICAL SUGGESTIONS TO INVALIDS AND THOSE WHO CARE FOR THEM.** 1879.

8.749
Charity Organisation Society, **CONVALESCENT HOMES.** 1880.

8.750
Female Humane Society of Cambridge, for the Relief of Indigent Sick Females and Others, **RULES AND REGULATIONS.** [1880].

8.751
GIRL'S OWN PAPER: *"Hospital Work and Hospital Workers,"* 5 (1883) 8-10. "Much can be done in a ward, almost unconsciously, to preserve a good moral tone.... If sister and nurses teach the patients by example, they will very seldom have occasion to resort to precept" (p. 8). Describes patients and nurses at St. Bartholomew's Hospital in London.

8.752
NINETEENTH CENTURY: Craven, F., *"Servants of the Sick Poor,"* 13 (1883) 667-678; rpt. as a pamphlet, 1885; Loch, C.S., *"The Confusion in Medical Charities,"* 32 (1892) 298-310. "Medical charity has three aims: the treatment or relief of the sickness of the poor, the education of the medical profession, and the scientific study of medicine and surgery" (p. 300). Discusses the antognism between private physicians and charity hospitals created by the competition for patients. Recommends the establishment of a board of representatives of medical charities.

8.753
Martin, Frances, **ELIZABETH GILBERT AND HER WORK FOR THE BLIND.** rev. ed., 1891. "So far back as 1863 [Gilbert]... had been in communication with Mr. Lonsdale, of the National Society, inquiring as to the state aid given to industrial schools, and the conditions under which schools for the blind could be certified so as to secure the benefit of the Acts" (p. 200).

8.754
Rentoul, Robert Reid, **THE REFORM OF OUR VOLUNTARY MEDICAL CHARITIES: SOME SERIOUS CONSIDERATIONS FOR THE PHILANTHROPIC.** 1891. Preface discusses abuses of medical charities by those who are not destitute and by doctors who have made it a trade. "No movement has been established by which the working classes might, by self-help, provide themselves with medical aid, without Medical Charity managers doing their utmost to destroy it" (p. x). Includes statistical tables for Liverpool 1888. Opposes specialty hospitals such as those run by women doctors and suggests replacing midwives with nurses at lying-in institutions in order to combat high infant mortality.

8.755
SUNDAY MAGAZINE: Bowditch, A.M., *"The Employment of Cripples,"* 22 (1893) 686-687.

8.756
Bradbrook, E.W., **PROVIDENT SOCIETIES AND INDUSTRIAL WELFARE.** 1898.

8.757
MEDICAL RECORD: *"Manufacture of Cripples,"* 54 (1898) 899.

8.758
Ramsay, Ebba D., **GUIDED STEP BY STEP.** [1899].

8.759
CHARITIES REVIEW: Brace, C.L., *"Day School for Crippled Children,"* 10 (1900) 79-83; *"English Schools for Crippled Children,"* 9 (1902) 230-234.

8.760
CHARITY ORGANISATION REVIEW: *"Difficulties in Dealing With Certain Cases of Invalid Children,"* 15 (1904) 125-135; *"Guildhall Conference on Invalid Children. Account of the Proceedings,"* 16 (1904) 61-66; Sutherland, Duchess of, *"The Work of the Potteries Cripples' Guild,"* 16 (1904) 81-85; Tancred, Miss, *"Fine Needlework Association for Invalid Women and Girls,"* 16 (1904) 93-96.

8.761
LANCET: *"Crippled Children's Christmas Hampers,"* 2 (1904) 1230; *"Work Among the Cripples,"* 2 (1904) 1251; 2 (1906) 966; 889; *"Belfast Cripples' Home. (Report of Bazaar),"* 1 (1905) 195; *"Crippled Children's League,"* 2 (1905) 1582; *"School for Crippled Children (Manchester, Swinton House),"* 1 (1906) 122-123; *"Education of Crippled and Mentally Defective Children. (Report to the Manchester Education Committee),"* 1 (1906) 980; *"Crippled Children's Union and the Adult Cripples' Guild, (Birmingham),"* 1 (1906) 1139-1140; *"Birmingham and District Crippled Children's Union,"* 1 (1906) 1858; *"Crutches to Help Crippled Children,"* 1 (1907) 1657; *"Crippled Children's Union (Birmingham),"* 1 (1907) 1675; 1 (1908) 1657; *"Work of the Liverpool Country Hospital in the Curative and Educational Treatment of Crippled Children,"* 2 (1907) 397; *"Eastpark Home for Cripples (Glasgow),"* 2 (1907) 1198; *"Christmas Hampers for Crippled Children,"* 2 (1908) 1315; *"Amalgamation of Societies for the Relief of Cripples. (Merger of Two Societies in Birmingham),"* 1 (1909) 1078; *"Admission of Cripples to Sir William Trealoar's Institution,"* 1 (1909) 1149; *"Care of Cripples. (Note on the Congress for Orthopedic Surgery),"* 1 (1909) 1425; *"Cripples' Home and College, Alton,"* 2 (1909) 1235; *"Crippled Children of Liverpool: Medical and Surgical Relief. (Work of the Invalid Children's Aid Association),"* 1 (1910) 466-467; *"Christmas Hampers and Clothing for Little Cripples,"* 2 (1910) 1257; *"Causes of Crippling. Report of the Sub-Committee on the Physically Defective of the Birmingham Education Committee,"* 2 (1911) 1435; *"Convalescent Hospital For Crippled Children (Birmingham-Woodlands),"* 2 (1911) 1711.

8.762
BRITISH MEDICAL JOURNAL: *"Crippled Children's Help Society (Manchester),"* 1 (1907) 110; 1 (1910) 1198; *"Crippled Children,"* 1 (1908) 165. Discusses quackery in treatment of children at Trealoar Institution; *"Cripples' Institute, Belfast,"* 1 (1909) n.p.; Gauvin, H.J., *"Conservative Treatment of Tuberculous Cripples,"* 2

(1910) 1124-1126.

8.763
TRANSACTIONS, SECOND INTERNATIONAL CONGRESS OF SCHOOL HYGIENE: Kimmins, Mrs. C.W., *"The Cripple Colony at Chailey in Connection with the Guild of Brave Poor Things,"* 2 (1907) 753-757.

8.764
OUTLOOK: Smith, N.A., *"Guilds of Play of Brave Poor Things,"* 40 (1908) 78-82.

8.765
WESTMINSTER REVIEW: Smith, L.C., *"The Swinton School for Cripples,"* 170 (1908) 223-227.

8.766
Elmslie, Reginald C., **THE CARE OF INVALID AND CRIPPLED CHILDREN IN SCHOOL.** 1909.

8.767
CHARITY RECORD: *"Cripples' Home for Girls (London),"* n.v. (1909) n.p.

8.768
INTERNATIONAL HOSPITAL RECORD: Irwin, C., *"What the Infirm, Crippled and Blind Can Do,"* 13 (1909) 9-10.

8.769
Hutchins, Elizabeth L., **WHAT A HEALTH COMMITTEE CAN DO.** 1910.

8.770
CHILD: *"Crippled Children,"* 1 (1910) 475-476; Trealoar, W.P. and Gauvin, H.J., *"The Treatment of Cripples at Alton,"* 1 (1910) 178-187; Haward, W., *"Invalid Children's Aid Association (London),"* 1 (1910) 195-196; Kimmins, Mrs. C.W., *"Craft for Cripples,"* 1 (1910) 277-283; Johnson, S., *"The Hospital for Sick Children, Great Ormond Street, London,"* 1 (1911) 813-819. Delineates the history of childrens' hospitals; Telford, E.D., *"The Residential School for Crippled Children,"* 2 (1911) 121-126.

8.771
HOSPITAL: *"Christmas for the London Cripples,"* 51 (1911) 169.

8.772
Phillips, Sydney, of St. Thomas Hospital, **SOCIAL WORK IN HOSPITALS: THE SAMARITAN. WITH A TABLE SHOWING THE WORK DONE IN LONDON.** 1912.

8.773
Women's Co-operative Guild, **MATERNITY: LETTERS FROM WORKING-WOMEN, COLLECTED BY THE WOMEN'S CO-OPERATIVE GUILD.** 1915. Provides an intimate portrait of the difficulties and agonies facing women of the poorer classes during maternity. Plea to the community for provision of medical aid. The letters were used as evidence for a proposed scheme of assistance to mothers.

8.774
Brend, W.A., **HEALTH AND STATE**. 1917.

8.775
Webb, Beatrice Potter, **HEALTH OF WORKING GIRLS: A HANDBOOK FOR WELFARE SUPERVISORS AND OTHERS**. 1917.

8.776
ENCYCLOPEDIA OF THE SOCIAL SCIENCES: Breckinridge, S.P., *"Maternity Welfare,"* 10 (1933) 221-227.

8.777
Hunt, Agnes, **REMINISCENCES**. 1935. The author worked with handicapped children.

8.778
Evans, J.D., "Voluntary Organizations for the Welfare of the Deaf" in **VOLUNTARY SOCIAL SERVICES: THEIR PLACE IN THE MODERN STATE**. ed. by Anne Francis Claudine Bourdillon. 1945.

8.779
Wilson, J.F., "Voluntary Organizations for the Welfare of the Blind" in **VOLUNTARY SOCIAL SERVICES**. ed. by Anne Francis Claudine Bourdillon. 1945.

8.780
Frazer, William M., "Medicine and Voluntary Effort" in **A HISTORY OF ENGLISH PUBLIC HEALTH, 1834-1939**. by William M. Frazer. 1950. District Nursing Associations, 1859; The Sanitary Institute, 1876, and other voluntary societies supported local government programs.

8.781
Young, G.M. and Handcock, W.D., "Public Health" in **ENGLISH HISTORICAL DOCUMENTS, 1833-1874**. by G.M. Young and W.D. Handcock. vol. 12, 1956; 1964. Debates the need for improved health conditions and regulations.

8.782
Jones, Kathleen, **MENTAL HEALTH AND SOCIAL POLICY, 1845-1959**. 1960. History of the transaction of attitudes toward mental health. "The social problems with which small rural communities had dealt casually, but on the whole effectively, became acute in the towns, where families crowded together in conditions of dirt and disease and despair; but industrialization, if it intensified social distress, also provided the means of dealing with it" (p. i).

8.783
Stocks, Mary, **A HUNDRED YEARS OF DISTRICT NURSING**. 1960.

8.784
Bell, Enid Moberly, **THE STORY OF HOSPITAL ALMONERS: THE BIRTH OF A PROFESSION**. 1961. Hospital almoners are "lady medical social workers" who interview charity out-patients with the object of preventing the abuse of services by those who were actually able to pay. Trained by the Charity Organisation Society, these women eventually formed a professional organization for mutual education and support. Bell traces the beginnings of the profession in 1895 to the

post-World War II period.

8.785
Dowling, W.C., "The Ladies Sanitary Association and the Origins of the Health Visiting Service," M.A. thesis, London Univ., 1963.

8.786
Brand, Jeanne L., "Voluntary Effort in Medical Care at the Beginning of the Twentieth Century" in **DOCTORS AND THE STATE: THE BRITISH MEDICAL PROFESSION AND GOVERNMENT ACTION IN PUBLIC HEALTH 1870-1912.** Baltimore, 1965. "The free medical treatment available at the voluntary hospitals of London and other large English cities was supported by private philanthropy and such regular charitable institutions as the 'Hospital Saturday' and 'Hospital Sunday' funds. Complaints from medical sources that hospital charity was being abused by working-class people who could afford to pay for outpatient medical care were not new.... Medical practitioners attending patients at the voluntary hospitals received no payment" (p. 193).

8.787
Lysons, C.K., "Some Aspects of the Historical Development and Present Organisation of Voluntary Welfare Societies for Adult Deaf Persons in England, 1840-1963," M.A. thesis, Univ. of Liverpool, 1965.

8.788
Barrows, Beverley M., **A COUNTRY AND ITS HEALTH: A HISTORY OF THE DEVELOPMENT OF THE WEST RIDING HEALTH SERVICES 1889-1974.** West Riding, 1974. Administrative bodies, primarily on the local government level, have been responsible for the development of public health services in England. Consequently, provision for preventive medicine and environmental control has been discontinuous. Barrows' introduction surveys this situation historically, and provides a necessary understanding of the role of government structures in the gradual growth of health care. This author does not consider voluntary effort, but her omission shows that any researcher of charitable effort should understand the complexities of governmental provision.

8.789
Woodward, John, **TO DO THE SICK NO HARM: A STUDY OF THE BRITISH VOLUNTARY HOSPITAL SYSTEM TO 1875.** 1974. Surveys the establishment and operation of hospitals as philanthropic institutions and centers of health care for "the poor" above the class of "pauper." Woodward analyzes hospital services in terms of the results obtained, especially with regard to the effects that these services had on mortality. Discusses the qualification, roles and work of matrons and nurses.

8.790
Lewis, Jane, **THE POLITICS OF MOTHERHOOD: CHILD AND MATERNAL WELFARE IN ENGLAND, 1900-1939.** 1980. "During the early twentieth century the *bete noir* of those who sought to improve maternal and child welfare was the mother who claimed to know all about childbearing and childrearing because she had 'borne 12 and buried 8.' The cover of MOTHER AND CHILD, a magazine serving the maternal and child welfare societies... showed a Madonna-like mother watching over a healthy, contented baby-in-arms with a well-cared-for older child standing in the protective shadow of its mother. The campaign to 'glorify, dignify and purify' motherhood and to transform this image into reality began in earnest

soon after the Boer War" (p. 13). Lewis also shows that the scope of the services offered for women's health were in fact very limited, and failed to meet the needs and demands of women's groups campaigning for improvement in maternal and infant welfare services. She gives some attention to voluntary efforts.

8.791
Armour, Philip K., **THE CYCLES OF SOCIAL REFORM: MENTAL HEALTH POLICY MAKING IN THE U.S., ENGLAND AND SWEDEN.** 1981.

8.792
HISTORY WORKSHOP JOURNAL: Summers, A., *"Pride and Prejudice: Ladies and Nurses in the Crimean War,"* no. 16 (1983) 33-55.

8.793
Green, David G., **WORKING-CLASS PATIENTS AND THE MEDICAL ESTABLISHMENT. SELF-HELP IN BRITAIN FROM THE MID-NINETEENTH CENTURY TO 1948.** New York, 1985. "The friendly societies were so successful that their arrangements for social insurance and primary medical care formed the model for the early welfare state" (p. 2). The focus of this book is working-class self-organized medical care. It is related to both the development of professional medical organization and governmental involvement, particularly with the National Insurance Act of 1911. Includes discussion of the medical treatment of women under voluntary organization and state provision.

* * *

8. SLUM CLEARANCE AND NEW HOUSING

8.794
Metropolitan Association for Improving the Dwellings of the Industrious Classes, **CHARTER OF INCORPORATION, ETC.** 1845; **HEALTHY HOMES. REPORT OF A PUBLIC MEETING TO CONSIDER THE BEST METHOD OF EXTENDING THE OPERATIONS OF THE METROPOLITAN ASSOCIATION, ETC.** [1854].

8.795
Roberts, Henry, **THE DWELLINGS OF THE LABOURING CLASSES.** 1850; **HOME REFORM: OR, WHAT THE WORKING CLASSES MAY DO TO IMPROVE THEIR DWELLINGS.** 1852; **HOME REFORM; OR, ADVICE TO THE LABOURING CLASSES ON THE IMPROVEMENT OF THEIR DWELLINGS AND KEEPING THEM IN GOOD CONDITION.** [1855]; **THE IMPROVEMENT OF THE DWELLINGS OF THE LABOURING CLASSES THROUGH THE OPERATION OF GOVERNMENT MEASURES, BY THOSE OF PUBLIC BODIES AND BENEVOLENT ASSOCIATIONS AS WELL AS INDIVIDUAL EFFORTS.** 1859.

8.796
Gore, Montagu, **ON THE DWELLINGS OF THE POOR, AND THE MEANS OF IMPROVING THEM.** 1851.

8.797
Society for Improving the Condition of the Labouring Classes, **PLANS AND DESCRIPTIONS OF THE MODEL DWELLINGS IN LONDON ERECTED BY THE SOCIETY.** 1851; **PROSPECTUS OF THE SOCIETY... TOGETHER WITH PLANS AND DESCRIPTIONS OF THEIR MODEL DWELLINGS IN LONDON.** 1857.

8.798
HOUSEHOLD WORDS: Morley, H., *"Death's Doors,"* 9 (1854) 398-402. Discusses the dwellings of the London poor; Morley, H., *"Frost-Bitten Homes,"* 11 (1855) 193-196. Examines living conditions of the poor in Bethnal Green; Morley, H., *"Wild Court Tamed,"* 12 (1855) 85-87; Morley, H., *"Day-Workers at Home,"* 13 (1856) 77-78. Discusses lodging homes for working girls; Morley, H., *"Many Needles in One Housewife,"* 15 (1856) 234-236. Discusses lodging homes for working girls.

8.799
Grant, James, **PICTURES OF LIFE: THE DWELLINGS OF THE POOR.** 1855.

8.800
Allen, C. Bruce, **RUDIMENTARY TREATISE ON COTTAGE BUILDING OR HINTS FOR IMPROVING THE DWELLING OF THE LABOURING CLASSES.** 3rd ed., 1857. Asserts that higher quality homes with gardens would discourage drunkenness, decrease pauperism, and help instill moral virtues in the working-class.

8.801
Gatliff, Charles, **ON IMPROVED DWELLINGS AND THEIR BENEFICIAL EFFECT ON HEALTH, MORALS, ETC.** 1857.

8.802
Bayly, Ada Ellen (Mrs. Mary), **RAGGED HOMES AND HOW TO MEND THEM.** 1859; **MENDED HOMES, AND WHAT REPAIRED THEM.** 1861.

8.803
FRIEND OF THE PEOPLE: B., W., *"Homes for Young Women,"* 1 (1860) 258.

8.804
Hole, James, **THE HOMES OF THE WORKING CLASSES WITH SUGGESTIONS FOR THEIR IMPROVEMENT.** 1866. Discusses reasons why dwellings of the poor and working classes were unsanitary and endangered health. Cites ignorance, rapid growth of urban areas, and the separation of the classes due to the migration of the upwardly mobile away from poor neighborhoods as among the chief causes. Includes illustrated plans of improved dwellings.

8.805
FORTNIGHTLY REVIEW: Hill, O., *"Cottage Property in London,"* 6 (1866) 681-687. Concerns a good landlady's duties towards her tenants and the friendship which grows from intimate knowledge; Phillips, E.M., *"A Dock Lodging House,"* 57 (1892) 668-677. The proprietress' idyllic description is intended to dispel the notion that all men's lodging houses are "detestable dens." Mentions the concern prevalent that dock workers and casual laborers might marry early in order to escape living in such places.

8.806

TRANSACTIONS OF THE NATIONAL ASSOCIATION FOR THE PROMOTION OF SOCIAL SCIENCE: Hill, O., *"An Account of a Few Houses Let to the London Poor,"* (1866) 625.

8.807

MACMILLAN'S MAGAZINE: Hill, O., *"Teaching the Poor the Virtues of a Good Home,"* 24 (1871) 456-459; Hill, O., *"The Homes of the London Poor,"* 30 (1874) 131-138; Hill, J.M., *"Homes for the Homeless,"* 32 (1875) 133-140; Hill, O., *"Space for the People,"* 32 (1875) 328-332; Hill, O., *"Our Common Land,"* 33 (1876) 536-539; McCullagh, W.T., *"What Is To Be Done With The Slums?"* 39 (1879) 533-545; Phillips, J.R., *"London Landowners, London Improvements, and the Housing of the Poor,"* 49 (1883) 1-9. "When our working classes are properly housed, a great change will come over the community, and as long as they live as they have now to do there lurks a real danger which may involve society in an overwhelming overthrow" (p. 8).

8.808

Charity Organisation Society, **DWELLINGS OF THE POOR. REPORT OF THE DWELLINGS COMMITTEE OF THE CHARITY ORGANISATION SOCIETY... NOVEMBER 3, 1873.** 1873; **DWELLINGS OF THE POOR. REPORT OF THE DWELLINGS COMMITTEE OF THE CHARITY ORGANISATION SOCIETY... AUGUST 2, 1881, ETC.** 1881.

8.809

CORNHILL MAGAZINE: Lathbury, D.C., *"Homes of the Poor in Towns,"* 30 (1874) 74-83; Jones, H., *"Homes of the Town Poor,"* 42 (1880) 452-463.

8.810

Hill, Octavia, **HOMES OF THE LONDON POOR.** 1875; 1883; *rpt. in:* **HOMES OF THE LONDON POOR AND THE BITTER CRY OF OUTCAST LONDON. AN INQUIRY INTO THE CONDITION OF THE ABJECT POOR.** 1970. Collection of articles from periodicals dated 1866-1875. "The people's homes are bad, partly because they are badly built and arranged; they are tenfold worse because the tenants' habits and lives are what they are. Transplant them tomorrow to healthy and commodious homes, and they would pollute and destroy them" (p. 10). Granddaughter of the renowned public health worker, Dr. Southwood Smith, Hill directed the work of poor children in a short-lived Co-Operative Guild during her teens. She, her mother, and sisters began inviting the neighboring women of poor families into their home one evening a week for sewing and sociability. John Ruskin, from whom she took painting lessons, bought three working-class houses in Paradise Place, Marylebone, for Hill to manage. Hill is considered the first professional caseworker and in Marylebone she worked out and applied the principles of housing management as part of social work. Her co-workers were women whom she trained in voluntary service and rent collectors who were also "friendly visitors." Their responsibility was to get to know their families by providing decent housing, giving advice in personal affairs, and encouraging thrift amongst their tenants; ...**ESSAYS, BY OCTAVIA HILL...** Boston, [1880]. See especially: "District Visiting"; **EXTRACTS FROM OCTAVIA HILL'S "LETTERS TO FELLOW WORKERS," 1864 TO 1911.** compiled by Elinor Southwood Ouvrey. 1933. ——*see also:* Maurice, C.E., ed., **LIFE OF OCTAVIA HILL AS TOLD IN HER LETTERS.** 1913; Tabor, Margaret Emma, **PIONEER WOMEN.** 1927. Includes a section on Octavia Hill; Maurice, Emily S., ed., **OCTAVIA HILL: EARLY**

IDEALS. 1928. Composed mainly of excerpts from correspondence with Ruskin; Bell, Enid Moberly, OCTAVIA HILL: A BIOGRAPHY. 1942; 1965; Hill, William Thompson, OCTAVIA HILL: PIONEER OF THE NATIONAL TRUST AND HOUSING REFORMER. 1956; JOURNAL OF BRITISH STUDIES: Wohl, A.S., *"Octavia Hill and the Homes of the London Poor,"* 10 (1971) 105-131. Sympathetic and humane, Miss Hill believed "in the ability of the upper classes to reach the poor and help them to raise themselves," and thus overcome class distinctions. She underestimated "the real crises which had to be met—widespread poverty, widespread overcrowding and the inconsistency of wages and rents" (p. 131). Hill opposed rent subsidies; McGaffey, B.A.K., "Three Founders of the British Conservation Movement, 1865-1895: Sir Robert Hunter, Octavia Hill, and Hardwicke Drummond Rawnsley," Ph.D. diss., Texas Christian Univ., 1978; Boyd, Nancy, "Octavia Hill" in THREE VICTORIAN WOMEN WHO CHANGED THEIR WORLD. by Nancy Boyd. New York, 1982.

8.811
Soldiers' Daughters' Home, Hampstead, ANNUAL REPORT. 1875; 1877-1886; MEMORANDUM. 1881.

8.812
JOURNAL OF THE ROYAL STATISTICAL SOCIETY: Gatliff, C., *"On Improved Dwellings and Their Beneficial Effects on Health and Morals, with Suggestions for Their Extension,"* 38 (1875) 33-35. Includes a map which shows the localities of the buildings and the agencies responsible for providing them.

8.813
NINETEENTH CENTURY: Stanley, M., *"West-End Improvements,"* 9 (1881) 849-855. Discusses the positive and negative ramifications of the Artisans' Dwelling Act; Cross, R.A., *"Homes of the Poor in London,"* 12 (1882) 231-241; Hill, O., *"Common Sense and the Dwellings of the Poor: I. Improvement Now Practicable,"* 14 (1883) 925-933. Against public assistance for dwellings for the poor. Describes an alternative which would help the poor help themselves. Article also includes plans for housing the poor with compatible spaces; Arnold-Forster, H.O., *"The Dwellings of the Poor: III. The Existing Law,"* 14 (1883) 940-951. Contends that there is no need for more legislation. Suggests strong voluntary committees to enforce existing laws; Cooper, A.A., *"The Dwellings of the Poor, the Mischief of State Aid,"* 14 (1883) 934-939; Howell, G., *"The Dwellings of the Poor,"* 13 (1883) 992-1007; Glazier, W., *"The Mischief of State Aid,"* 14 (1883) n.p. Details voluntary efforts to reform poor and working-class housing and argues against state intervention on the basis that it may alleviate poor physical conditions while destroying the "moral energies" of the laboring classes; Cross, R.A., *"Homes of the Poor,"* 15 (1884) 150-166; Hill, O., *"Colour, Space and Music for the Poor,"* 15 (1884) 741-752; Cross, R.A., *"Housing of the Poor,"* 17 (1885) 926-947; Hill, O., *"On the Dwellings of the Poor,"* 30 (1891) 161-170; Marleborough, C., *"Hostels for Women,"* 69 (1911) 858-866. Describes several inexpensive municipal lodging houses for working women and recommends the construction of such hostels to facilitate the reform of casual wards and rescue homes which are neither respectable nor sanitary.

8.814
Forwood, Arthur B., THE DWELLINGS OF THE INDUSTRIAL CLASSES IN THE DIOCESE OF LIVERPOOL, AND HOW TO IMPROVE THEM. Liverpool, 1883.

8.815
Williams, Robert, **LONDON ROOKERIES AND COLLIERS' SLUMS.** 1883. An architect reports on the poor design of urban apartments and advocates stricter municipal codes; **MORE LIGHT AND AIR FOR LONDONERS.** 1894.

8.816
QUARTERLY REVIEW: Dildin, L.T., *"Dwellings of the Poor,"* 157 (1884) 144-168.

8.817
ENGLISHWOMAN'S REVIEW: *"A Working Women's Dwelling,"* 20 (1889) 337-342. Discusses "what may be done to add a little comfort and happiness to the lives of the great body of struggling, respectable women who earn daily wages" (p. 337).

8.818
NATIONAL REVIEW: Newton, W., *"The Housing of the Poor,"* 12 (1889) 830-841.

8.819
Lazarus, Henry, **LANDLORDISM.** 1892. Contends that landlords are partially responsible for the housing conditions of the poor.

8.820
Fabian Society, **HOUSES FOR THE PEOPLE: A SUMMARY OF THE POWERS OF LOCAL AUTHORITIES UNDER THE HOUSING OF THE WORKING CLASSES ACTS, 1890 TO 1909, AND THE USE WHICH HAS BEEN AND CAN BE MADE OF THEM.** 1897; 5th ed., 1910. "In the poorest districts of our large towns and cities the artisan in search of a house must make his choice between grim and gloomy model dwellings, erected by thrifty philanthropists of the five per cent school, and dilapidated insanitary tenements which yield fat revenues to the rack-renting proprietor and constant work for the doctor and undertaker" (p. 2).

8.821
Twining, Louisa, **THE LOSSES AND GAINS OF FIFTY YEARS.** 1897.

8.822
Women's Cooperative Guild, **THE HOUSING OF THE PEOPLE.** nos. 1-3, 5. Manchester, 1898.

8.823
HOUSES FOR THE WORKING CLASSES: HOW TO PROVIDE THEM IN TOWN AND COUNTRY. [1900].

8.824
How, George, **NO ROOM TO LIVE: THE PLAINT OF OVERCROWDED LONDON.** 1900.

8.825
CONTEMPORARY REVIEW: Zimmern, A., *"Ladies' Dwellings,"* 77 (1900) 96-104. Discusses housing for educated working women and the different criteria for housing for men and women; Osborn, C., *"Rowton Houses for Women,"* 99 (1911) 707-717. Argues against lodging-houses, claiming that they are "in [their] very nature anti-social" (p. 711).

8.826

ECONOMIC JOURNAL: Bosanquet, H., *"People and Homes,"* 10 (1900) 47-59.

8.827

Crolch, W. Walter, THE COTTAGE HOMES OF ENGLAND: THE CASE AGAINST THE HOUSING SYSTEM IN RURAL DISTRICTS. 2nd ed., 1901.

8.828

Lawrence, F.W., "The Housing Problem" in THE HEART OF THE EMPIRE. ed. by C.F. Masterman, 1901; rpt., New York, 1973.

8.829

Sutter, Julie, BRITAIN'S NEXT CAMPAIGN. 3rd ed., 1904. Delineates slum conditions, especially homelessness, evaluating philanthropic attempts to alleviate these problems. Concludes that "Individually, we are powerless... [This] book insists on the necessity of our individual efforts being municipalized" (p. 4). "Thanks to the British land system, there is not a more homeless race than the masses of our prosperous country" (p. 14).

8.830

Meakin, James Budgett, MODEL FACTORIES AND VILLAGES: IDEAL CONDITIONS OF LABOUR AND HOUSING. 1905. Compares industrial communities in England, Europe and America.

8.831

Kaufmann, Mauritz, THE HOUSING OF THE WORKING CLASSES AND OF THE POOR. 1907; rpt., Yorkshire, 1975. An effort to raise the consciousness of the wealthier classes to help improve living conditions of the poor.

8.832

Johnston, J., "Motherhood, Housing and Children" in WASTAGE OF CHILD LIFE AS EXEMPLIFIED BY CONDITIONS IN LANCASHIRE. by J. Johnston. 1909. Correlates the insanitary housing conditions in poor and working-class districts with childhood disease and infant mortality.

8.833

Higgs, Mary Kingsland, HOW TO DEAL WITH THE UNEMPLOYED. 1904; (and Hayward, Edward), WHERE SHALL SHE LIVE? THE HOMELESSNESS OF THE WOMAN WORKER. 1910. Publication of the National Association for Women's Lodging-Houses. Chapters include "The Home of the Woman Worker," "The Common Lodging-House for Women" and "The Urgency of the Need for Reform." Also see Appendix for a "List of Safe Lodging-Homes"; COMFORTABLE QUARTERS. 1912; HOW TO START A WOMEN'S LODGING HOME. 1912; GLIMPSES INTO THE ABYSS. 1916.

8.834

Alston, Francis C.W., PROVISION OF LODGING HOMES FOR RESPECTABLE WOMEN IN LONDON. 1911.

8.835

Dale, Mrs. Hylton, NECESSITY FOR PROVISION OF MUNICIPAL LODGING HOUSES FOR WOMEN. 1911.

8.836
National Association for Women's Lodging-Homes, **REPORT OF THE PROCEED-INGS OF THE NATIONAL CONFERENCE ON LODGING-HOUSE ACCOMMODATION FOR WOMEN... 17TH MAY, 1911, ETC.** 1911. Discusses prevention of female destitution.

8.837
Bramwell-Booth, Florence E., "The Housing of Homeless Women" in **MOTHERS OF THE EMPIRE AND OTHER ADDRESSES.** compiled by the Salvation Army. 1914. Author may be cataloged as Booth, Florence E. Bramwell.

8.838
Adderley, James Granville, **IN SLUMS AND SOCIETY.** 1916.

8.839
Nevinson, Margaret, **LIFE'S FITFUL FEVER: A VOLUME OF MEMORIES BY RENT COLLECTORS.** 1926.

8.840
Quigley, Hugh and Goldie, Ismay, **HOUSING AND SLUM CLEARANCE IN LONDON.** [1934].

8.841
Turner, F.L., "The Movement to Provide Improved Working-Class Housing in England, 1840-1860," Ph.D. diss., North Carolina Univ., 1960.

8.842
Dyos, H.J., "The Making of a Suburban Slum" in **VICTORIAN SUBURB: A STUDY OF THE GROWTH OF CAMBERWELL.** by H.J. Dyos. Edinburgh, 1961.

8.843
Hole, W.V., "The Housing of the Working Classes in Britain, 1850-1914: A Study of the Development of Standards and Methods of Provision," Ph.D. diss., London Univ., 1965.

8.844
DICKENSIAN: Fielding, K.J., *"Dickens's Work with Miss Coutts: I., 'Nova Scotia Gardens and What Grew There', II., 'Casby and the Westminster Landlords',"* 61 (1965) 112-119; 155-160. Examines the housing developments made by Angela Burdett-Coutts and Charles Dickens in East London.

8.845
Wohl, Anthony S., "The Housing of the Artisans and Labourers in Nineteenth Century London," Ph.D. diss., Brown Univ., 1966; "The Housing of the Working Classes in London; 1815-1914" in **THE HISTORY OF WORKING CLASS HOUSING: A SYMPOSIUM.** ed. by Stanley D. Chapman. Newton Abbot, 1971. The enormous rise in population during the period between the reigns of George III and George V caused various social and economic difficulties, the worst of which was providing the working classes with adequate housing; "Unfit for Human Habitation" in **THE VICTORIAN CITY: IMAGES AND REALITIES.** ed. by H.J. Dyos and Michael Wolff. vol. 2, 1973. Concentrates on the difficulties of overcrowding and the role of medical officers in its exposure; **THE ETERNAL SLUM: HOUSING AND SOCIAL POLICY IN VICTORIAN LONDON.** 1978.

8.846
VICTORIAN STUDIES: Tarn, J.N., *"The Peabody Donation Fund: The Role of a Housing Society in the Nineteenth Century,"* 10 (1966) 7-38; Dyos, H.J., *"The Slums of Victorian London,"* 11 (1967) 5-40; Dyos, H.J., *"The Speculative Builders and Developers of Victorian London,"* Supplement 11 (1968) 641-690.

8.847
Pike, E. Royston, "Housing the Workers" in **HUMAN DOCUMENTS OF THE AGE OF THE FORSYTES.** by E. Royston Pike. 1969. Compilation of Parliamentary papers dealing with the issues of clean, safe, and affordable housing for the working classes. Also discusses tenements, labourers' cottages, defects in structures, sanitation problems, etc.

8.848
Steffel, R.V., "Housing for the Working Classes in the East End of London, 1890-1907," Ph.D. diss., Ohio State Univ., 1969. Examines the governmental handling of the urban housing crisis as well as the public opinion generated by this issue during the period.

8.849
Wilson, L.F., "The State and the Housing of the English Working Classes, with Special Reference to Nottingham, 1851-1909," Ph.D. diss., Univ. of California, Berkeley, 1970.

8.850
Chapman, Stanley D., ed., **THE HISTORY OF WORKING-CLASS HOUSING: A SYMPOSIUM.** Newton Abbot, 1971. Chapters include: "The Housing of the Working Classes in London, 1815-1914," "Working-Class Housing in Glasgow, 1851-1914," "The Back-to-Back House in Leeds, 1787-1937," "Working-Class Housing in Nottingham During the Industrial Revolution," "Liverpool Working-Class Housing, 1801-51," "The Contribution of Building Clubs and Freehold Land Society to Working-Class Housing in Birmingham," "The Architecture of the Domestic System in South-East Lancashire and the Adjoining Pennines," and "Housing in an Industrial Colony: Ebbw Vale, 1778-1914."

8.851
Ferguson, Neal A., "Working-Class Housing in Bristol and Nottingham, 1868-1919," Ph.D. diss., Univ. of Oregon, 1971.

8.852
Stedman-Jones, Gareth, "Housing and the Casual Poor" in **OUTCAST LONDON.** by Gareth Stedman Jones. 1971. "Attempts to improve working-class housing and to abate the danger of 'rookery' areas took four main forms in the period from the 1840's to the 1870's: street clearance, model dwellings, sanitary regulation, and the schemes initiated by Octavia Hill" (p. 179). Author may be cataloged as Jones, Gareth Stedman.

8.853
Kunze, Neil L., "English Working Class Housing: A Problem of Social Control [in the 1880's]," Ph.D. diss., Univ. of California, Los Angeles, 1971.

8.854
Tarn, John N., **WORKING CLASS HOUSING IN NINETEENTH CENTURY BRITAIN.** 1971; **FIVE PERCENT PHILANTHROPY: AN ACCOUNT OF HOUSING IN URBAN AREAS BETWEEN 1840 AND 1914;** Cambridge, 1973. "Expound[s] the complex philosophy behind the developing housing movement and [the homes] which were constructed specifically to house the poor" (p. xiii). Illustrated with photographs and drawings; *reviewed in:* JOURNAL OF URBAN HISTORY: Gardner, D., 7 (1981) 403-38.

8.855
BULLETIN OF THE SOCIETY FOR THE STUDY OF LABOUR HISTORY: Sutcliffe, A., *"Working-Class Housing in Nineteenth Century Britain: A Review of Recent Research,"* 7 (1972) 40-51.

8.856
Roberts, Robert, **THE CLASSIC SLUM.** 1973.

8.857
Sutcliffe, Anthony, ed., **MULTI-STOREY LIVING: THE BRITISH WORKING-CLASS EXPERIENCE.** 1974. Valuable compilation of essays that explore issues surrounding housing for the poor and working class. Includes illustrations, tables and appendices. Notes a basic unity in the format of planned working-class housing which included a trend away from communal facilities towards more private dwellings.

8.858
Blyth, A.W., "Tenement Dwellings" in **TRANSACTIONS OF THE SOCIETY OF MEDICAL OFFICERS OF HEALTH, 1882-1883.** 1978. Describes the "savage life" of the poor and working classes.

8.859
Burnett, John, **A SOCIAL HISTORY OF HOUSING 1815-1890.** 1978. It wasn't until after the second World War that "the housing experience of many people showed little major change... from 5.11 persons per dwelling in 1861 to 2.97 in 1966" (p. 304). Demonstrates how middle-class housing reflected Victorian values of privacy, respectability, social standing, comfort, and the material display of affluence. Also discusses rural housing.

8.860
Merrett, Stephen, **STATE HOUSING IN BRITAIN.** 1979; *reviewed in:* HISTORICAL JOURNAL: Pennybacker, S.D., *"Unfit for Heroes? The Housing Question and the State in Britain, 1890 to the Present,"* 26 (1983) 499-508. "As recently as 1967, Merrett discovers, government statements referred to the efficacy of the 'Octavia Hill' system" (p. 506).

8.861
Melling, Joseph, ed., **HOUSING, SOCIAL POLICY AND THE STATE.** 1980; *reviewed in:* HISTORICAL JOURNAL: Pennybacker, S.D., *"Unfit for Heroes? The Housing Question and the State in Britain, 1890 to the Present,"* 26 (1983) 499-508. "As late as 1911, sixty per cent of Glasgow's working class were living in accommodation of only one or two rooms" (p. 502).

8.862

White, Jerry, **ROTHSCHILD BUILDINGS: LIFE IN AN EAST END TENEMENT BLOCK 1887-1920.** Boston, 1980. "The philanthropy which provided Rothschild Buildings was far from unconditional. With it went a detailed programme of class control which stipulated the tenant's duties and obligations to his landlord.... In housing terms, the rule book passed blame for the housing problem to the people affected by it, making slum life appear a conscious choice which must be eliminated by restrictions and threats" (p. 54).

8.863

King, S., "The Formation and Development of Slums: East London in the Second Half of the Nineteenth Century," Ph.D. diss., London School of Economics, 1981.

8.864

Daunton, M.J., "Public Place and Private Space: The Victorian City and the Working-Class Household" in **THE PURSUIT OF URBAN HISTORY.** ed. by Derek Fraser and Anthony Sutcliffe. 1983. Study aims to "move beyond a mere description of the physical structure of cities" and to view development "from below through the eyes of the slum dweller or the cottage tenant" (p. 213).

* * *

9. *SETTLEMENTS*

8.865

Knapp, John M., ed., **THE UNIVERSITIES AND THE SOCIAL PROBLEM: AN ACCOUNT OF THE UNIVERSITY SETTLEMENTS IN EAST LONDON.** 1895. See especially: Maud Corbett, "Mayfield House (Cheltenham Ladies' College Settlement)" and Mary Talbot, "St. Margaret's House, Bethnal Green (Ladies' Branch of the Oxford House)." University settlements were established for the same purposes as industrial settlements: to overcome isolation and loneliness, to promote cooperation, and to provide a safe habitation for women. Middle-class philanthropists took up residence in poor neighborhoods to manage these houses.

8.866

ECONOMIC REVIEW: Talbot, M., *"Women's Settlements,"* 5 (1895) 489-500. "Several women's settlements have, within the last few years, been established in London. The first was the Women's University Settlement in Southwark... also the Canning Town Settlement in connection with Mansfield House, the Wesleyan Settlement in Bermondsey, the Friends' Settlement in Tottenham, the Roman Catholic Settlement lately opened in Bow, the Cheltenham Ladies' College Settlement at Mayfield House, St. Margaret's House... the Rochester Diocesan Settlement at Blackheath, and the North London Settlement at York House" (p. 493). St. Margaret's House, established by the Christian Social Union in Bethnal Green, occupied its tenants in parish work, and in hospital and workhouse visiting.

8.867

GOOD WORDS AND SUNDAY MAGAZINE: Mace, Mrs., *"Women's Settlements in*

Bethnal Green," 36 (1895) 613-614. Concerns women who do volunteer social service work in girls's clubs, first aid, and home nurseries.

8.868

Bliss, William D.P., et al., eds., **THE ENCYCLOPEDIA OF SOCIAL REFORM.** 1897. See especially: "College Women's Settlements." "By the establishment of a home in the midst of the working people, not with any spirit of patronage or curiosity, but with a desire for a life of simplicity with a wish to know as friends those who are bearing a large part of the real work of the world, would the women interested in settlements express their ideals" (p. 1417).

8.869

Woods, Robert Archey, **ENGLISH SOCIAL MOVEMENTS.** 3rd ed., New York, 1897. See especially: "University Settlements."

8.870

NINETEENTH CENTURY: Barnett, S.A., *"The Ways of 'Settlements' and of 'Missions,'"* 42 (1897) 975-984. Explains that the objectives of a mission are to convert its audience whereas the objectives of a settlement are to disseminate mutual knowledge; Free, R., *"Settlements or Unsettlements?,"* 63 (1908) 365-380. "It is little short of impertinence for such a society as a Settlement to establish itself in the midst of a parish, even with the consent of the incumbent, a society the very purpose of whose being is confessedly to supplement the deficiencies of the parish.... Sooner or later trouble will supervene" (p. 368); Creighton, L., *"Women's Settlements,"* 63 (1908) 607-613. "Settlements may either be institutions which aim at doing a great deal of work within their own building, having their own clubs and classes, being themselves a centre for philanthropic, social, and religious work; or they may be merely houses in which a number of workers live together so as to be within convenient reach of the district in which they hope to work, as well as to have the advantage of association and intercourse with those who share their interests and duties" (p. 608); Marlborough, C., *"Hostels for Women,"* 69 (1911) 858-866. Recognizes a gap in philanthropic services to working girls. "The fact that a woman cannot obtain decent accommodation in any of our large towns except through the charity of a religious institution or by entering a rescue home is an intolerable injustice to the worker" (p. 860).

8.871

Reason, Will, ed., **UNIVERSITY AND SOCIAL SETTLEMENTS.** 1898. Contains a Directory of Settlements. See especially: "Women's Settlements in England" by Margaret A. Sewell and E.G. Powell. "The 'idea' common to all Settlements is that persons of various callings and standards should, in some measure, share a common life, that rich and poor, educated and uneducated, cultured and uncultured, should meet, and know each other, and help each other" (p. 94). Describes women's settlements, their history, and specific functions.

8.872

Portal, Ethel M., "The Work of the Ladies' Settlement [St. Margaret's House, Bethnal Green]" in **GOOD CITIZENSHIP.** ed. by J.E. Hand. 1899.

8.873

Fortescue, Miss, "Settlement Work in Connection with the Catholic Social Union" in **WOMEN IN SOCIAL LIFE. THE TRANSACTIONS OF THE SOCIAL SECTION OF THE INTERNATIONAL CONGRESS OF WOMEN. LONDON, JULY 1899.** ed.

by Ishbel Aberdeen. 1900. "Settlements for women are a necessary outcome of the philanthropic movement" (p. 118). Gives advice on starting settlement work and examples of those benefitting from the settlements.

8.874
Simmons, [Mary], "Discussion [of] Social Settlements" in **WOMEN IN SOCIAL LIFE. THE TRANSACTIONS OF THE SOCIAL SECTION OF THE INTERNATIONAL CONGRESS OF WOMEN. LONDON, JULY, 1899.** ed. by Ishbel Aberdeen. 1900.

8.875
CHARITY ORGANISATION REVIEW: Urwick, E.J., *"Settlement Ideals,"* n.v. (Dec. 1903) 328-329; Matheson, M., *"Birmingham Women's Settlement,"* n.v. (Jan. 1915) 24-30.

8.876
Wilson, Philip Whitwell, "The Settlement Ideal" in **THE RELIGIOUS LIFE OF LONDON.** ed. by Richard Mudie-Smith. 1904. "A lady settler, who sought refuge from her blinding successes at the University of Cambridge, once remarked that, after staying and working [in a Settlement] among South Londoners, a visit to Bond Street gave her a peculiar feeling. She expressed it by saying that the people there struck her as being quite mad [in the superficiality of their dress and behavior, in the calm of their landscape].... They resembled the Willow pattern on a tea-cup (p. 298). By contrast, the settlers observe how South Londoners are engaged in meeting practical imperatives of daily life. From their reports it's possible to say that "for the first time in the recent history of London the poor are respected and understood" (p. 298).

8.877
Hodson, Alice Lucy, **LETTERS FROM A SETTLEMENT.** 1909.

8.878
Addams, Jane, "The Subjective Necessity for Social Settlements" in **TWENTY TEARS OF HULL HOUSE.** New York, 1910; 1938; subsequent eds. "It is easy to see why the settlement movement originated in England, where the years of education are more constrained and definite than they are here, where class distinctions are more rigid" (p. 95). Addams writes that "the word 'settlement,' which we have borrowed from London, is apt to grate a little on American ears" in its implication of a movement of one class into another's territory in the name of philanthropy, and she wrestled with this problem and its relation to the democratic ideal. See pp. 44-45 for a description of her visit to London and her enthusiasm at seeing the work that had been done there in municipal housing for the poor, schools and public baths; "The Objective Value of a Social Settlement" in **PHILANTHROPY AND SOCIAL PROGRESS.** No editor listed. New York, 1893.

8.879
Picht, Werner, **TOYNBEE HALL AND THE ENGLISH SETTLEMENT MOVEMENT.** 1914. Includes an annotated list of settlements.

8.880
Women's University Settlement, **ANNUAL REPORTS, 1887-1923.** 1923.

8.881
Pimlott, A.R., **TOYNBEE HALL: FIFTY YEARS OF SOCIAL PROGRESS (1884-**

1934). 1935.

8.882
Brodie, D.M., **WOMEN'S UNIVERSITY SETTLEMENT, 1887-1937.** 1937. ——*see also:* Oldfield, Sybil, **SPINSTERS OF THIS PARISH: THE LIFE AND TIMES OF F.M. MAYOR AND MARY SHEEPSHANKS.** 1984. "The 'Settlements' were emphatically not soup-kitchens or coal-and-blanket depots or any other such charitable headquarters for middle-class, religious 'slummers.' They were centres where young university-educated people went first to learn of life in poverty and then to share whatever knowledge and abilities they had with the poorest. Instead of hand-outs, they were offering themselves" (p. 48).

8.883
King, Constance M. and King, Harold, (Warden of the Liverpool University Settlement), **"THE TWO NATIONS": THE LIFE AND WORK OF LIVERPOOL UNIVERSITY SETTLEMENT AND ITS ASSOCIATED INSTITUTIONS 1906-1937.** Liverpool, 1938.

8.884
Grant, Clara Ellen, **FROM 'ME' TO 'WE': FORTY YEARS ON BOW COMMON.** 1939.

8.885
Stocks, Mary, **FIFTY YEARS IN EVERY STREET. THE STORY OF THE MANCHESTER UNIVERSITY SETTLEMENT.** Manchester, 1945; 2nd ed. with an additional chapter by Brian Rodgers, 1956. Established 1885 by Owens College in Ancoats, a slum which had a death rate of 28.32 per thousand as compared with Manchester's 21.6 (p. 9). Among the first "settlers" were Dr. Annie Anderson and C. Helen Stoehrs. "Miss Octavia Hill's highly individualized system of house-property management... contained within itself a germ of municipal socialism which was no part of her vision of a happier world.... [She demonstrated] that slumdwellers are made by slums rather than slums by slumdwellers" (p. 1).

8.886
SOCIAL SERVICE REVIEW: Abel, E.K., *"Middle-Class Culture for the Urban Poor: The Educational Thought of Samuel Barnett,"* 52 (1978) 596-620.

8.887
Vicinus, Martha, "Settlement Houses: A Community Ideal for the Poor" in **INDEPENDENT WOMEN: WORK AND COMMUNITY FOR SINGLE WOMEN 1850-1920.** by Martha Vicinus. Chicago, 1985. "The roots of the settlements for women were both revolutionary and evolutionary, domestic and public. During the years from the late nineteenth century until after World War I, the work of middle-class women settlers——helping poor women and girls——changed from social outreach to social welfare. But women always remained ideologically and practically distinct from their male counterparts, bringing to the slums both different services and different goals" (p. 214).

*   *   *

10. PROTECTION OF AND ASSISTANCE TO CHILDREN

8.888

Foundling Hospital, A COPY OF THE ROYAL CHARTER ESTABLISHING AN HOSPITAL FOR THE MAINTENANCE AND EDUCATION OF EXPOSED AND DESERTED YOUNG CHILDREN. 1739. Founded in 1739, in 1760 the Foundling Hospital amended its rules to accept the illegitimate children of poor mothers. The Committee had to be satisfied of the previous good character of the mother. Handel and Hogarth were among its most liberal benefactors and the President was the Duke of Cambridge; THE REPORT OF THE GENERAL COMMITTEE FOR DIRECTING... AND TRANSACTING THE BUSINESS... OF THE CORPORATION OF THE GOVERNORS AND GUARDIANS OF THE HOSPITAL FOR THE MAINTENANCE... OF EXPOSED AND DESERTED YOUNG CHILDREN. 1740; REGULATION FOR MANAGING THE HOSPITAL FOR THE MAINTENANCE AND EDUCATION OF EXPOSED AND DESERTED YOUNG CHILDREN, ETC. 1757; THE GENUINE SENTIMENTS OF AN ENGLISH COUNTRY GENTLEMAN, UPON THE PRESENT PLAN OF THE FOUNDLING HOSPITAL IN RELATION TO THE DANGER OF BRINGING CHILDREN TO LONDON, OR ESTABLISHING MORE RECEIVING HOSPITALS IN THE COUNTRY, ETC. 1759; THE RISE AND PROGRESS OF THE FOUNDLING HOSPITAL CONSIDERED: AND THE REASONS FOR PUTTING A STOP TO THE GENERAL RECEPTION OF ALL CHILDREN. 1761; A LIST OF THE GOVERNORS AND GUARDIANS, OF THE HOSPITAL FOR THE MAINTENANCE AND EDUCATION OF EXPOSED AND DESTITUTE YOUNG CHILDREN. 1767; AN ACCOUNT OF THE HOSPITAL FOR THE MAINTENANCE AND EDUCATION OF EXPOSED AND DESERTED YOUNG CHILDREN. [1796]; 2nd ed., 1799; 3rd ed., 1807; 1826. ——*see also:* [Holliday, J.], AN APPEAL TO THE GOVERNORS OF THE FOUNDLING HOSPITAL ON THE PROBABLE CONSEQUENCES OF COVERING THE HOSPITAL LANDS WITH BUILDINGS. IN THIS APPEAL THE ORIGINAL INSTITUTION OF CHARITY AND THE PRESENT STATE OF ITS REVENUES ARE INVESTIGATED. 1787; LONDON: Saunders, J., *"The Foundling Hospital,"* 3 (1841) 337-352. Survey history of the evolution of policies and practices, told in a dramatic, literary style. Statistics and reported opinions included; Brownlow, John, MEMORANDA: OR, CHRON-ICLES OF THE FOUNDLING HOSPITAL, INCLUDING MEMOIRS OF CAPTAIN CORAM, ETC. 1847; Brownlow, John, THE HISTORY AND DESIGN OF THE FOUNDLING HOSPITAL, WITH A MEMOIR OF THE FOUNDER. 1858; 1881. Defends the institution; Nichols, R.H. and Wray, F.A., THE HISTORY OF THE FOUNDLING HOSPITAL. 1935; McClure, Ruth K., CORAM'S CHILDREN: THE LONDON FOUNDLING HOSPITAL IN THE EIGHTEENTH CENTURY. 1981. Discusses the hospital as the world's first incorporated charity. Handles issues such as debts, disease, morals and manners, the role of women, illegitimacy, poverty, etc.

8.889

Female Orphan Asylum For Poor, Friendless and Deserted Girls, AN ACCOUNT OF THE INSTITUTION, AND PROCEEDINGS OF THE GUARDIANS OF THE ASYLUM OR HOUSE OF REFUGE; SITUATED ON THE SURRY SIDE OF WESTMINSTER BRIDGE: FOR THE RECEPTION OF ORPHAN GIRLS RESIDING WITHIN THE BILLS OF MORTALITY, WHOSE SETTLEMENT

CANNOT BE FOUND. 1763; 1809. The asylum was founded in 1758 by Sir John Fielding.

8.890
Society For the Relief of the Widows and Orphans of Medical Men, **PROPOSALS FROM THE SOCIETY FOR THE RELIEF OF THE WIDOWS AND ORPHANS OF MEDICAL MEN IN THE CITY OF LONDON AND ITS VICINITY. INSTITUTED... 1788.** 1788; **SOCIETY FOR RELIEF OF WIDOWS AND ORPHANS OF MEDICAL MEN, IN LONDON AND ITS VICINITY.** 1818; **A SHORT ACCOUNT... FROM ITS FOUNDATION IN OCTOBER 1788 TO DECEMBER 1856.** 1859.

8.891
INFANT ASYLUM FOR THE PRESERVING OF THE LIVES, OF CHILDREN OF HIRED WET-NURSES, AND OTHERS. 1799.

8.892
Asylum for Orphan Girls, **CONSTITUTION AND LAWS AND REGULATIONS OF THE ASYLUM, ETC.** 1801.

8.893
Gascoigne, H.B., **THE OLD VIEWS OF SOCIETY REVIVED: WITH REMARKS ON THE PRESENT STATE AND PROSPECTS OF ORPHAN AND PAUPER CHILDREN.** 1820.

8.894
THE ROYAL METROPOLITAN INFIRMARY, FOR SICK CHILDREN, IN MEMORY OF PRINCESS CHARLOTTE. 1823.

8.895
Society For the Suppression of Juvenile Vagrancy, **SOCIETY FOR THE SUPPRESSION OF JUVENILE VAGRANCY. NO. 1 REPORT OF THE HACKNEY-WICK SCHOOL SUB-COMMITTEE. (SUGGESTIONS TO THE MASTER OF THE... SCHOOL).** 1833.

8.896
Brenton, Edward Pelham, **OBSERVATIONS ON THE TRAINING AND EDUCATION OF CHILDREN IN GREAT BRITAIN.** 1834. Brenton and his associate Amelia Murray founded the Children's Friend Society.

8.897
Children's Friend Society, **FOURTH ANNUAL REPORT FOR THE YEAR 1834, ETC.** 1834. Argues against stigmatizing children in its institutions; **LIST OF SUBSCRIBERS TO THE CHILDREN'S FRIEND SOCIETY, FOR THE PREVENTION OF JUVENILE VAGRANCY.** 1838.

8.898
ROYAL UNIVERSAL INFIRMARY FOR CHILDREN. 1835.

8.899
Infant Orphan Asylum, Dalston, **REPORTS.** 1835-1836; 1838.

8.900

THE ASSOCIATED CATHOLIC CHARITIES FOR EDUCATING, CLOTHING, AND APPRENTICING THE CHILDREN OF POOR CATHOLICS, AND PROVIDING FOR DESTITUTE ORPHANS. 1836.

8.901

Hill, Frederic, **NATIONAL EDUCATION: THE PRESENT STATE AND PROSPECTS.** 2 vols. 1836. Discusses institutions for both vagrant and delinquent children such as the Refuge for the Destitute at Hoxton, the Metropolitan Modern School of Industry at Woolrich, and the Institution for the Reform of Female Children of Vicious Habits; **AN AUTOBIOGRAPHY OF FIFTY YEARS IN TIMES OF REFORM.** ed. by Constance Hill. 1893.

8.902

Mueller, Georg Friedrich, **OPENING OF THE ORPHAN HOUSE FOR DESTITUTE FEMALE CHILDREN, ESTABLISHED AT BRISTOL, IN CONNECTION WITH THE SCRIPTURAL KNOWLEDGE SOCIETY FOR HOME AND ABROAD...** Bristol, 1836; **BRIEF NARRATIVE OF THE FACTS RELATING TO THE NEW ORPHAN HOUSE OF ASHLEY DOWN, BRISTOL, AND THE OTHER OBJECTS OF THE SCRIPTURE KNOWLEDGE INSTITUTION, ETC.** 1857. ——*see also:* **GEORG MUELLER AND THE ORPHAN HOMES AT ASHLEY DOWN.** 1878.

8.903

School of Industry for the Instruction of the Female Children of the Industrious Poor, **[REPORT FOR 1837].** 1837; **[REPORT FOR 1839].** 1839.

8.904

St. Patrick's Charity, **ST. PATRICK'S CHARITY, FOR THE GRATUITOUS EDUCATION AND CLOTHING OF THE CHILDREN OF POOR CATHOLICS, AND ASYLUM FOR FEMALE ORPHANS.** 1838.

8.905

London Society for the Protection of Young Females and Prevention of Juvenile Prostitution, **FOURTH REPORT.** 1839. Blames street-walkers and brothel-keepers for corrupting youth. Seeks to suppress these houses and to punish those persons.

8.906

NEW MONTHLY MAGAZINE: Gore, C., *"The Orphan House of Brussels: A Confession,"* 68 (1843) 534-541.

8.907

Rotch, Benjamin, **SUGGESTIONS FOR THE PREVENTION OF JUVENILE DEPRAVITY.** 1846.

8.908

Metropolitan Working Classes Association for Improving the Public Health, **THE REARING AND TRAINING OF CHILDREN.** 1847.

8.909

Ragged School Union (afterwards Ragged School Union and Shaftesbury Society), **THE THIRD (-95TH, 120TH, 122ND, ETC.) ANNUAL REPORT, ETC.** 1847-.

8.910
Sailors' Orphan Girls' Episcopal School and Asylum, **ANNUAL REPORT [FOR 1847]...** 1848.

8.911
RAGGED SCHOOL UNION MAGAZINE: 1849 to 1873; vols. 1-25; *continued as:* **RAGGED SCHOOL UNION QUARTERLY RECORD:** Jan. 1876 to Oct. 1887; vols. 1-12; *continued as:* **IN HIS NAME. THE RECORD OF THE RAGGED SCHOOL AND MISSION UNION:** Jan. 1888 to Dec. 1907; vols. 1-20. Publication of the Ragged School Union.

8.912
THE ESTABLISHMENT OF DAY NURSERIES IN MANCHESTER AND SALFORD. Manchester, 1850.

8.913
HOUSEHOLD WORDS: Dickens, C., *"A Walk in the Workhouse,"* 1 (1850) 204-207; Wells, W.H., *"A Day in a Pauper Palace,"* 1 (1850) 361-364. Discusses an institution for pauper children at Swinton; Jerrold, W.B., *"Protected Cradles,"* 2 (1850) 108-112. Discusses day nurseries for the infants of working mothers; Jerrold, W.B., *"Anybody's Child,"* 8 (1854) 551-552. On slum children; *"Nobody's Philanthropist,"* 19 (1859) 605-608.

8.914
REPORT OF THE LIVERPOOL FEMALE ORPHAN ASYLUM. Liverpool, 1851.

8.915
Kingsley, Charles, **THE MASSACRE OF THE INNOCENTS.** 1858. Pamphlet encouraging the Ladies Sanitary Association to confront the problem of infant mortality "to help the increase of the English race as much as possible" (p. 10).

8.916
A FEW WORDS IN BEHALF OF ORPHANS IN UNION HOUSES. 1859.

8.917
Archer, Hannah, **A SCHEME FOR BEFRIENDING ORPHAN PAUPER GIRLS.** 1861; **TO THE RESCUE: REMARKS ON THE EDUCATION OF POOR AND ORPHAN CHILDREN.** [1870].

8.918
Cobbe, Frances Power, **FRIENDLESS GIRLS AND HOW TO HELP THEM...** 1861. Describes the work of the Preventive Mission at Bristol.

8.919
TRANSACTIONS OF THE NATIONAL ASSOCIATION FOR THE PROMOTION OF SOCIAL SCIENCE: Carpenter, M., *"What Shall We Do With Our Pauper Children?"* (1861) 687.

8.920
Reformatory and Refuge Union, **ANNUAL REPORT.** 1863. The Union worked with a far wider range of children than were sent to the reformatories. It became a clearing house for information and published a classified list of institutions with accommodations and ages of admission, to inform workers where to send different

types of children. It also held conferences for governesses and matrons; **FIFTY YEARS' RECORD OF CHILD-SAVING AND REFORMATORY WORK, 1856-1906.** 1906.

8.921
French, W.S., **A PAPER ON EXCESSIVE INFANT MORTALITY.** Liverpool, 1864. High incidence is related to working mothers and unsanitary conditions. Stresses the need for charitable female volunteers, sanitary improvements, and new legislation regulating housing.

8.922
Alexandra Orphanage for Infants, **ALEXANDRA ORPHANAGE FOR INFANTS, ALBERT ROAD, ST. JOHN'S VILLE.** 1866.

8.923
Confraternity For Girls and Young Women, **THE MANUAL OF THE CONFRATERNITY OF ALL SAINTS FOR GIRLS AND YOUNG WOMEN.** 1866.

8.924
Curgenven, J. Brendon, **THE WASTE OF INFANT LIFE.** 1867; **ON BABY-FARMING AND THE REGISTRATION OF NURSES.** 1869; **INFANT LIFE PROTECTION SOCIETY PROSPECTUS.** [1870]; 1871; **REPLY OF THE INFANT LIFE PROTECTION SOCIETY TO A MEMORIAL OF MEMBERS OF THE NATIONAL SOCIETY FOR WOMEN'S SUFFRAGE OBJECTING TO THE PROPOSED MEASURE.** 1870; **A BILL FOR THE BETTER PROTECTION OF INFANT LIFE.** 1871.

8.925
Hill, Florence Davenport, **CHILDREN OF THE STATE: THE TRAINING OF JUVENILE PAUPERS.** 1868; 2nd ed., 1889; 1968.

8.926
ALL THE YEAR ROUND: *"Canker in the Bud,"* 1 (1868) 540-544. Describes the Children's Home and Laundry at Leytonstone, which housed "poor little girls who have been led into habits of impurity; often in entire ignorance of sin; sometimes through curiosity or self-will. They are too young and too childish to be received into Penitentiaries; too deeply tainted with evil to be admitted into ordinary industrial schools and orphanages" (p. 540).

8.927
Grant, C.W., **A PRACTICAL GUIDE TO THE BOARDING OUT SYSTEM FOR PAUPER CHILDREN.** [1870].

8.928
WESTMINSTER REVIEW: *"Pauper Girls,"* 93 (1870) 461-476; Offen, C.R.W., *"The Pseudo and the Real Cottage Homes For Pauper Children. A Reply,"* 147 (May 1897) 570-581. Argues in response to another article that the critique of cottage homes and barrack schools is unfair: "It has been demonstrated that at such barrack schools as Swinton and Kirkdale, where the most enlightened and humanitarian methods have been adopted in the education and development of the child-life, that exceedingly satisfactory results have occurred" (p. 570); Sewi, *"Save the Children: A Plea,"* 160 (1903) 559-562.

8.929
Smith, George, **THE CRY OF THE CHILDREN FROM THE BRICKYARDS OF ENGLAND: A STATEMENT AND APPEAL WITH REMEDY.** 3rd ed., 1871; **GYPSY LIFE: BEING AN ACCOUNT OF OUR GYPSIES AND THEIR CHILDREN, WITH SUGGESTIONS FOR THEIR IMPROVEMENT.** 1880; **GYPSY CHILDREN.** 1893.

8.930
MACMILLAN'S MAGAZINE: Oldfield, L., *"The Children of the Poor,"* 27 (1873) 335-344; Norris, Mrs., *"A Note on a Good Work (Holidays in the Country For City Children),"* 49 (1884) 309-311.

8.931
LITTLE SERVANTS: HOW TO HELP THEM. Bristol, 1874.

8.932
ENGLISHWOMAN'S REVIEW: *"The Vigilance Association,"* 5 (1874) 48-52. Details of a case involving treatment of an illegitimate child and its support; *"Friendless Girls in Marylebone,"* 5 (1874) 234-235; T., M., *"Homes For Working Girls,"* 5 (1874) 251-252. Discusses the assistance of young servant girls who, after the age of 16, are no longer under the supervision of the workhouse authorities; *"Young Women Servants Temporary Home,"* 6 (1875) 89-90; Boucherett, J., *"Protection of Girls Brought Up as Paupers,"* 6 (1875) 104-106. Discusses the task of finding situations for pauper girls brought up in large workhouses or District Schools. The article contains a large quote from Mrs. Nassau Senior; as a result of her remarks an association of ladies had been formed to aid such girls in an unofficial manner; *"Homes For Working Girls,"* 9 (1878) 324-327; *"A Visit to the Albion Hill Home,"* 9 (1878) 481-486. "Hard work is the order of the day, but it is hard work cheered by intervals of study and recreation, and by affectionate sympathy and personal solicitude. The young women lead a cheerful, natural, homely life" (p. 481); *"The Act for Prevention of Cruelty to Children,"* 20 (1889) 439-444. Defines the Act in detail.

8.933
Society for the Relief of the Necessitous Widows and Children of Protestant Ministers, **THE HUNDRED AND FORTY-SECOND (HUNDRED AND FORTY-NINTH, HUNDRED AND FIFTY-FIRST) REPORT OF THE SOCIETY...** 1875-1884.

8.934
National Committee for Boarding Out Pauper Children, **PAUPER CHILDREN IN METROPOLITAN SCHOOLS.** [1876].

8.935
Waugh, Benjamin, **THE GAOL CRADLE, WHO ROCKS IT?** 3rd ed., 1876; **SOME CONDITIONS OF CHILD LIFE IN ENGLAND.** 1889; **THE RESULTS OF CHILD-LIFE INSURANCE.** 1891; **A NEW PUBLIC POLICY FOR CHILDREN.** 1894. — *see also:* Waugh, Rosa, **THE LIFE OF BENJAMIN WAUGH.** 1915.

8.936
Letchworth, William Pryor, **REPORT ON DEPENDENT AND DELINQUENT CHILDREN.** 1877.

8.937
Preusser, Anette, **FOURTH REPORT ON BOARDING OUT PAUPER CHILDREN.**
1877.

8.938
Hopkins, Jane Ellice, **LADIES ASSOCIATIONS FOR THE CARE OF
FRIENDLESS GIRLS. BEING AN ACCOUNT OF WORK IN BRIGHTON.** 1878;
ON PENITENTIARY WORK. 1880. Hopkins attempts to deal with the problem of
children raised in immoral surroundings in three ways: encouraging more workers to
help children raised in brothels; establishing societies to protect young girls from
prostitution; and denouncing male attitudes towards prostitution; **PREVENTIVE
WORK: OR, THE CARE OF OUR GIRLS.** 1881; **THE LEGAL PROTECTION OF
THE YOUNG.** [1882]; **DRAWN UNTO DEATH: A PLEA FOR THE CHILDREN
COMING UNDER THE INDUSTRIAL SCHOOLS AMENDMENT ACT, 1880.** 1884;
**"GOD'S LITTLE GIRL"... FACTS CONCERNING A... "WAIF" ADMITTED INTO
"DR. BARNARDO'S VILLAGE HOME,"** ETC. [1885].

8.939
Pike, Godfrey Holden, **THE VILLAGE HOME FOR GIRLS AT ILFORD ESSEX.**
1878.

8.940
Hart, Mary H., **THE CHILDREN OF THE STREETS.** 1880.

8.941
Wines, Enoch Cobb, **THE STATE OF PRISONS AND OF CHILD-SAVING
INSTITUTIONS IN THE CIVILIZED WORLD.** 1880; rpt., 1968. See especially:
"Child-Saving Work in England" for a brief history of institutions designed to aid
delinquent, pauper, and deviant children.

8.942
GIRL'S OWN PAPER: *"How to Make Poor Children's Clothing,"* 1 (1880) 125-126;
"Sunday School Treats," 1 (1880) 365-366; Butson, Mrs. S., *"The Standing Evil: a
Plea for Shop Girls,"* 1 (1880) 612; Hope, D., *"Girls' Own Societies,"* 1 (1880) 239;
Reany, Mrs. G.S., *"The Working Girls of London,"* 1 (1880) 574-575; Barnett, Mrs.
S.A., *"What Girls Can do to Hush 'The Bitter Cry',"* 5 (1884) 691-692. Paper read at
a meeting of the Metropolitan Society of Voluntary Workers; Corne, Marquess of,
"Miss Rye's Girls' Homes," 5 (1884) 488-490. Describes the home, the response
given to Lord Shaftesbury when he visited and a journey taken by the children;
King, A., *"Parish Work,"* 5 (1884) 712-713; Brewer, E., *"The Flower Girls of
London,"* 13 (1891) 78-79; 166-168; 200-202; 283-285; Willson, T.B., *"What Girls are
Doing for South London: The United Girls' Schools Mission,"* 21 (1900) 418-420.

8.943
Barnardo, Thomas John, **TAKEN OUT OF THE GUTTER.** 1881; **A CITY WAIF.**
1883; **A YEAR'S WORK IN "DR. BARNARDO'S HOMES."** 1884; **"THESE FORTY
YEARS." BEING THE 40TH ANNUAL REPORT OF DR. BARNARDO'S HOMES.**
[1906]. ——*see also:* Bready, J. Wesley, **DOCTOR BARNARDO.** 1930; Williams,
A.E., **BARNARDO OF STEPNEY: THE FATHER OF NOBODY'S CHILDREN.**
1943; 2nd ed., 1953. Barnardo established homes for the rescue of children. In the
course of his life his homes provided care for over sixty thousand boys and girls;
Wagner, Gillian, "Doctor Barnardo and the Charity Organisation Society: a
Reassessment of the Arbitration Case of 1877," Ph.D. diss., London Univ., 1977;

Wagner, Gillian, "The Custody of Children" in **BARNARDO.** by Gillian Wagner. 1979. On the influence and work of Barnardo. "All through the 1880s public awareness of the injustices suffered by children... was becoming more widespread" (p. 214). A member of Barnardo's committee wrote in 1885 that "if expression were given to public opinion, more severe provisions would be found... against indecent assaults against young girls, and more effectual powers of dealing with parents who neglected or ill used their children would be granted to courts" (p. 214).

8.944
Rowe, Richard, **PICKED UP IN THE STREETS.** 1881.

8.945
NINETEENTH CENTURY: Rossiter, E., *"Child Life for Children,"* 10 (1881) 567-572; Trench, M., *"Girl-Children of the State,"* 13 (1883) 76-87; Brabazon, R., *"Public Playgrounds for Children,"* 34 (1893) 267-271. Discusses the work of the Metropolitan Public Gardens Association and the Kyrle Society to establish public open spaces, gardens and playgrounds; Leake, D.M., *"A Girls' Lodging House,"* 44 (1898) 1015-1023; Russell, A., *"The St. Pancras School for Mothers,"* 63 (1908) 763-770. Argues for state intervention to educate women in child-rearing practices and pre-natal care. Uses the St. Pancras School for Mothers as an example of what can be done; Elliott, C.A., *"State Funding of School Children in London,"* 65 (1909) 862-874; Lane-Claypon, J.E., *"Waste of Infant Life,"* 65 (1909) 48-64; Scharlieb, M., *"The Nation's Children and Our Duty Towards Them,"* 81 (1917) 1277-1289. Eugenicist article traces the causes of children's diseases to lack of proper sanitation in the home due to poverty and contests the view that faults working-class women for their slovenliness. Advocates state-funded ante-natal care and simplification and unification of health services to the needy.

8.946
Shaen, William, **THE PROTECTION OF YOUNG GIRLS. OBSERVATIONS ON THE REPORT OF THE SELECT COMMITTEE OF THE HOUSE OF LORDS ON THE LAWS RELATING TO THE PROTECTION OF YOUNGER GIRLS IN ENGLAND.** 1882.

8.947
Humble, Richard of Leeds, **BOARDING OUT OF ORPHAN AND DESERTED PAUPER CHILDREN VERSUS WORKHOUSE SCHOOLS.** Leeds, 1883.

8.948
Barlee, Ellen, **PANTOMIME WAIFS: OR, A PLEA FOR OUR CITY CHILDREN.** 1884.

8.949
Sharp, Amy, **THE LEGAL PROTECTION OF YOUNG GIRLS.** 1884.

8.950
CHILD'S GUARDIAN: 1884 to present. Publication of the Society for the Prevention of the Cruelty to Children.

8.951
GOOD WORDS AND SUNDAY MAGAZINE: Collier, J.F., *"The Prevention of Cruelty to Children,"* 25 (1884) 537-540.

8.952
THE HISTORY OF THE WORKHOUSE, OR POOR'S HOSPITAL FROM 1739-1818: ITS BOYS' HOSPITAL FROM 1818-1852, GIRLS' HOSPITAL FROM 1828-1852 AND ITS BOYS' AND GIRLS' HOSPITALS FROM 1852-1885. Aberdeen, 1885.

8.953
Colam, Robert Frederick, **PREVENTION OF CRUELTY TO CHILDREN: A MANUAL.** 1885.

8.954
THE FORTY-FIRST REPORT OF THE NATIONAL REFUGES FOR HOMELESS AND DESTITUTE CHILDREN. 1886.

8.955
Mager, Alfred W., **CHILDREN'S RIGHTS: A SOCIAL AND PHILANTHROPIC QUESTION.** Bolton, 1886.

8.956
Mitchell, William, **RESCUE THE CHILDREN.** 1886.

8.957
CHARITY ORGANISATION REVIEW: P., T., *"Creches,"* 2 (1886) 103-105. "Creches have a twofold use.... They supply the mother's care when she herself is compelled to go from home to earn her living, and the restriction to such cases will seem a sound one to all who recognise the value of family life; and they may well be made the means, as in Sweden, of instruction to growing girls, who will one day be mothers, in the tendance of infants" (p. 105).

8.958
Hall, Wilhelmina, **BOARDING-OUT AS A METHOD OF PAUPER EDUCATION AND A CHECK ON HEREDITARY PAUPERISM.** 1887.

8.959
Clotten, Francis Egon, **THE NECESSITY OF SANITARY REFORM IN INFANT REARING: WHY AND HOW IT SHOULD BE EFFECTED.** Liverpool, 1888.

8.960
CONTEMPORARY REVIEW: Waugh, B., *"Street Children,"* 53 (1888) 825-835; Waugh, B., *"Baby Farming,"* 57 (1890) 700-714; Waugh, B., *"Child-Life Insurance,"* 58 (1890) 40-63.

8.961
Rossiter, [W.], ed., **ELIZABETH ROSSITER, FOUNDER OF COUNTRY LIFE FOR POOR TOWN CHILDREN.** Huntington, 1890.

8.962
WRONGS RIGHTED: BEING A BRIEF RECORD OF THE WORK OF THE MANCHESTER AND SALFORD SOCIETY FOR THE PREVENTION OF CRUELTY TO CHILDREN. 1892.

8.963
Exeter Hall, **CHILDREN'S MISSIONARY MEETING.** 1892.

8.964
Riis, Jacob A., **THE CHILDREN OF THE POOR**. 1892.

8.965
Smith, Nora, "How Shall We Govern Our Children?" in **CHILDREN'S RIGHTS**. ed. by Kate Douglas Wingate. Cambridge, 1892.

8.966
TRANSACTIONS OF THE 7TH INTERNATIONAL CONGRESS OF HYGIENE AND DEMOGRAPHY: *"Neglected Children in Our Towns and Cities,"* 4 (1892) 131-137.

8.967
CHILDREN'S LEAGUE OF PITY PAPER: 1893 to 1911.

8.968
Legitimation League, **THE RIGHTS OF NATURAL CHILDREN. VERBATIM REPORT OF THE INAUGURAL PROCEEDINGS OF THE LEGITIMATION LEAGUE.** [1893].   ——*see also:* Dawson, Oswald, **THE BAR SINISTER AND LICIT LOVE: THE FIRST BIENNIAL PROCEEDINGS OF THE LEGITIMATION LEAGUE WITH FOUR PORTRAITS.** 1895. "The object of the Legitimation League... is to place acknowledged illegitimate children upon the same footing as children born in wedlock, thus giving legal recognition to the obligations of unmarried parents" (p. 167).

8.969
Molesworth, Mrs., "For the Little Ones——'Food, Fun, and Fresh Air'" in **WOMAN'S MISSION**. ed. by Angela Georgina Burdett-Coutts. 1893.

8.970
Sellers, Miss E., "Women's Work for the Welfare of Girls" in **WOMAN'S MISSION**. ed. by Angela Georgina Burdett-Coutts. 1893. Emphasizes the importance of preventing young women from "falling" rather than trying to save them after they have fallen. Lauds the YWCA, Girls' Friendly Society, Travellers' Aid Society and others for their preventive work in philanthropy.

8.971
Stretton, Hesba, "Women's Work for Children" in **WOMAN'S MISSION**. ed. by Angela Georgina Burdett-Coutts. 1893.

8.972
JOURNAL OF THE ROYAL STATISTICAL SOCIETY: Warner, F., *"Results of an Inquiry as to the Physical and Mental Condition of Fifty Thousand Children Seen in One Hundred and Six Schools,"* 56 (1893) 71-95. Report of an investigation promoted by the C.O.S. and the Medical Association. The inquiry concerns nutrition, nervousness, and alertness in an effort to relate factors that produce health or illness and handicaps; Jones, H.R., *"The Perils and Protection of Infant Life,"* 57 (1894) 1-98; Warner, F., *"Mental and Physical Conditions Among Fifty Thousand Children, Seen 1892-1894, and the Methods of Studying Recorded Observations with Special Reference to the Determination of the Causes of Mental Dullness and Other Defects,"* 59 (1896) 125-162; Drake, Mrs., *"A Study of Infant Life in Westminster,"* 71 (1908) 678-685. Examines infant mortality and its causes,

among which are poverty and working mothers who must neglect their children; includes an exploration of the controversy between breast feeding and hand feeding. The visitor can improve the lot of the infant by encouraging the mother to benefit the child.

8.973
NEW REVIEW: Harkness, M.E., *"The Children of the 'Unemployed,'"* 8 (1893) 228-236; Jeune, M., *"Holidays for Poor Children,"* 2 (1890) 455-465. On the success of a program to send parish children to live with country families for a week or two, where they are well-fed and allowed to thrive on the beauties of nature.

8.974
Lewis, Gerald C. and Barrows, Harold Murdoch, **PREVENTION OF CRUELTY TO CHILDREN ACT, 1894.** 1894.

8.975
Tuckwell, Gertrude M., **THE STATE AND ITS CHILDREN.** 1894. Addresses the public sentiment that child reform interferes with the privacy of the classes to which it is aimed.

8.976
Bosanquet, Helen (Dendy), "The Children of Working London" in **ASPECTS OF THE SOCIAL PROBLEM.** ed. by Bernard Bosanquet. 1895; "The Children" in **THE STRENGTH OF THE PEOPLE: A STUDY IN SOCIAL ECONOMICS.** by Helen Bosanquet. 2nd ed., 1903. Contends that the family is the main institution in which the child is protected, and it should therefore be strengthened.

8.977
McCallum, M., "The Protection of Children" in **ASPECTS OF THE SOCIAL PROBLEM.** ed. by Bernard Bosanquet. 1895.

8.978
Hallowes, J.L., **THE RIGHTS OF CHILDREN IN SPIRIT, MIND AND BODY.** 1896.

8.979
National Society for the Prevention of Cruelty to Children, **THE POWER FOR THE CHILDREN. BEING THE REPORT FOR 1895-1896.** 1896; **THE WAYS OF CHILD TORTURERS ILLUSTRATED.** 1909. ——*see also:* **SATURDAY REVIEW:** *"The Society for the Prevention of Cruelty to Children,"* 55 (1883) 596-597; Webster, Richard E., **SPEECH OF THE RIGHT HONORABLE THE LORD CHIEF JUSTICE OF ENGLAND ON THE NATIONAL SOCIETY FOR THE PREVENTION OF CRUELTY TO CHILDREN WORKING UNDER A ROYAL CHARTER.** 1910; Leis, Gordon L., "A Sociological Study of Voluntary Organization with Special Reference to the National Society for the Prevention of Cruelty to Children," M.A. thesis, London School of Economics, 1959.

8.980
Chance, William, **CHILDREN UNDER THE POOR LAW.** 1897.

8.981
Hilton, J. Deane, **MARIE HILTON: HER LIFE AND WORK, 1821-1896.** 1897. Hilton was the founder of the creche system which provided childcare for working

mothers.

8.982
State Children's Aid Association, [LEAFLETS]. [1897, etc.].

8.983
REPORT OF THE COMMITTEE ON VAGRANT CHILDREN. 1899.

8.984
Freeman, Flora Lucy, **RELIGIOUS AND SOCIAL WORK AMONGST GIRLS.**
1901.

8.985
Gilman, Charlotte Perkins, **CONCERNING CHILDREN.** Boston, 1901. Advocates
child care for the improvement of the race. See chapter entitled "Mothers: Natural,
Unnatural."

8.986
Greenwood, Florence J., **IS THE HIGH INFANTILE DEATH-RATE DUE TO
THE OCCUPATION OF MARRIED WOMEN?** 1901.

8.987
Bray, Reginald A., "The Children of the Town" in **THE HEART OF THE EMPIRE.**
ed. by C.F.G. Masterman. 1902; rpt., New York, 1973; **THE TOWN CHILD.** 1907.

8.988
Folks, Homer, **THE CARE OF DESTITUTE, NEGLECTED, AND DELINQUENT
CHILDREN.** New York, 1902.

8.989
Trevelyan, William Pitt, **SOME RESULTS OF BOARDING OUT POOR LAW
CHILDREN.** 1903.

8.990
Jevons, W. Stanley, "Married Women in Factories" in **METHODS OF SOCIAL
REFORM AND OTHER PAPERS.** 1904; *rpt. from:* **CONTEMPORARY REVIEW:**
n.v. (1882) n.p. Correlates infant mortality rates to the fact that working mothers
had to leave children for up to ten hours at a time "to the care of other, usually
careless hands" (p. 151). Provides statistics and examines the Infant Life Protection
Act.

8.991
McCleary, G.F., **THE INFANTS' MILK DEPOT: ITS HISTORY AND FUNCTION.**
1904; **INFANTILE MORTALITY AND INFANTS' MILK DEPOTS; MUNICIPAL
MILK DEPOTS AND MILK STERILISATION.** 1905.

8.992
Fabian Society, **AFTER BREAD, EDUCATION: A PLAN FOR THE STATE
FEEDING OF SCHOOL CHILDREN.** 1905.

8.993
Infants' Health Society, **THE PRESENT CONDITIONS OF INFANT LIFE AND
THEIR EFFECT ON THE NATION.** 1905.

8.994
Sherard, Robert Harborough, **THE CHILD-SLAVES OF BRITAIN.** 1905. Series of articles originally printed in LONDON MAGAZINE. "I followed the half-timer into the mills of Lancashire and Scotland, the devil's holes of Bradford, and the starvation-sheds of Bromsgrove and of Cradley Heath. I talked with many hundred little merchants, male and female, of our cities' streets. I did not neglect to visit police-courts, workhouses and one county gaol. These are, all three, institutions which are part of the set scenes of the squalid little life-dramas which it was mine to study" (p. xi).

8.995
EMPIRE REVIEW: Rogers, C.F., *"The Free Feeding of School Children. Theory and Practice,"* 9 (1905) 526-533. Objects to "wholesale and indiscriminate feeding" and insists on parental responsibility. Claims that actual cases of underfed children are few and implies that they are often the children of parents who waste money on drink.

8.996
Gorst, Sir John, **THE CHILDREN OF THE NATION: HOW THEIR HEALTH AND VIGOUR SHOULD BE PROMOTED BY THE STATE.** 1906.

8.997
Maddison, Arthur J.S., compiler, **THE LAW RELATING TO CHILD-SAVING AND REFORMATORY EFFORTS. BEING EXTRACTS FROM ACTS OF PARLIAMENT AND OTHER INFORMATION.** 1906. Valuable collection of documents.

8.998
National League for Physical Education and Improvement, **FIRST [-TWENTY-THIRD] ANNUAL REPORT, 1906-1928.** [1906-1928]; **INTERIM REPORT, 1906.** [1906]; **MISCELLANEOUS PAMPHLETS, LEAFLETS AND POSTERS.** [1909-38]; **MILK SUPPLY: INSTRUCTIONS FOR ENSURING THE SUPPLY OF CLEAN MILK... PREPARED BY THE JOINT COMMITTEE ON MILK OF THE NATIONAL HEALTH SOCIETY AND THE NATIONAL LEAGUE FOR PHYSICAL EDUCATION AND IMPROVEMENT.** [1910]; **REPORT OF THE PROCEEDINGS OF THE FIFTH ANNUAL GENERAL MEETING OF THE NATIONAL LEAGUE... AND OF THE FIRST CONFERENCE OF HEALTH-PROMOTING INSTITUTIONS, ETC.** 1911.

8.999
Spargo, John, **THE BITTER CRY OF THE CHILDREN.** 1906; 1913. See especially: Appendix A., "How Foreign Municipalities Feed Their School Children." The book is concerned with the poverty of children in New York City and makes comparisons with London.

8.1000
HEALTH OF THE NATION: 1906+. Edited by L.E. Creasy. Journal of the National League for Physical Education and Improvement.

8.1001
Heath, Harry L., **THE INFANT, THE PARENT, AND THE STATE: A SOCIAL STUDY AND REVIEW...** 1907.

8.1002
Kanthack, Emelia, **THE PRESERVATION OF INFANT LIFE.** 1907.

8.1003
Malvery, Olive Christian (MacKirdy), **BABY TOILERS.** 1907.

8.1004
National Society of Day Nurseries, **HINTS ON HOW TO START A CRECHE.** 1907. Formerly the National Society of Children's Nurseries.

8.1005
Webb, Sidney, **THE DECLINING BIRTHRATE.** 1907. Recommends as incentives to child-bearing "a munipal supply of milk to all infants, and a free meal on demand to all mothers actually nursing their babies... food for school children and scholarships to foster middle-class parents" (pp. 16-17).

8.1006
Barnett, Henrietta, ed., **DESTITUTE, NEGLECTED, AND DELINQUENT CHILDREN.** 1908.

8.1007
MacDonald, Arthur, **STATISTICS OF CHILD SUICIDE.** [1908].

8.1008
CHILD-STUDY; THE JOURNAL OF THE CHILD-STUDY SOCIETY: 1908 to 1920; 13 vols.

8.1009
ECONOMIC REVIEW: Craske, M., *"Girl Life in a Slum,"* 18 (1908) 184-189; Iselin, H., *"The Story of A Children's Care Committee,"* 22 (1912) 42-64. Presents arguments for and against the Education (Provision of Meals) Act, 1906.

8.1010
Johnston, J., **WASTAGE OF CHILD LIFE AS EXEMPLIFIED BY CONDITIONS IN LANCASHIRE.** 1909.

8.1011
Parr, Robert J., **THE BABY FARMER: AN EXPOSITION AND AN APPEAL...** 2nd ed., 1909. In 1897 a law was passed regulating the commercial care of children with local authorities merely enforcing the registration of children placed to nurses. Parr, the director of the Society for the Prevention of Cruelty to Children, made an inquiry about changing and improving this law; **THE CARE AND CONTROL OF THE FEEBLE MINDED.** 1909; **PREVENTION OF CRUELTY TO CHILDREN ACT 1904.** 1909; [WILFUL] **WORK: THE NATION'S RESPONSIBILITY FOR ITS CHILDREN.** 1910; **MAIMED OR WHOLE? A STATEMENT RELATING TO OPERATIONS ON CHILDREN.** 1912.

8.1012
ESSAYS ON DUTY AND DISCIPLINE: A SERIES OF PAPERS ON THE TRAINING OF CHILDREN IN RELATION TO SOCIAL AND NATIONAL WELFARE. 3 vols., 1910.

8.1013
Harben, Henry D., **THE ENDOWMENT OF MOTHERHOOD**. 1910. Advocates assistance to pregnant women to reduce infant mortality and "raise the economic status of women by a method which would emphasize and appreciate at full value their work as mothers of the race" (p. 37).

8.1014
National Society of Children's Nurseries, **YEARBOOK FOR 1910 [ETC]**. [1911, etc].

8.1015
Samuelson, James, **THE CHILDREN OF OUR SLUMS**. Liverpool, 1911.

8.1016
[Payne, W.], **THE CRUELTY MAN: ACTUAL EXPERIENCES OF AN INSPECTOR OF THE N.S.P.C.C. GRAPHICALLY TOLD BY HIMSELF**. 1912.

8.1017
Percival, Tom, **POOR LAW CHILDREN**. 1912.

8.1018
Phillips, Marion, **THE SCHOOL DOCTOR AND THE HOME: RESULTS OF AN INQUIRY INTO MEDICAL INSPECTION AND TREATMENT OF SCHOOL CHILDREN**. [1912]. Published by the Women's Labour League.

8.1019
Women's Labour League, **THE NEEDS OF LITTLE CHILDREN: REPORT OF A CONFERENCE ON THE CARE OF BABIES AND YOUNG CHILDREN. PAPERS BY MISS MARGARET MCMILLAN, MRS. PEMBER-REEVES, DR. ETHEL BENTHAM, MRS. DESPARD**. 1912.

8.1020
Birt, Lilian M., **THE CHILDREN'S HOME-FINDER: THE STORY OF ANNIE MACPHERSON AND LOUISA BIRT**. 1913. Discusses "revival homes" founded for needy boys by McPherson and Birt.

8.1021
Bondfield, Margaret, **THE NATIONAL CARE OF MATERNITY**. 1914; 1915.

8.1022
National Conference on Infant Mortality, **REPORT ON THE PROCEEDINGS OF THE NATIONAL CONFERENCE ON INFANT MORTALITY, HELD AT ST. GEORGE'S HALL, LIVERPOOL, ON JULY 2 AND 3, 1914...** 1914.

8.1023
Women's Cooperative Guild, **MATERNITY: LETTERS FROM WORKING WOMEN**. 1915; rpt., ed. by Margaret Llewelyn Davies. 1978.

8.1024
Marlborough, Consuelo Spencer Churchill (Duchess of), **SAVING THE CHILDREN: THE LADY PRIESTLEY MEMORIAL LECTURE FOR 1916**. 1916.

8.1025
Kerr, James, **THE CARE OF THE SCHOOL CHILD. A COURSE OF LECTURES**

DELIVERED... MAY TO JULY 1916. [1916].

8.1026
Simeral, Isabel, "Anglican Promotion of Education For the Children of the Poor in England——Its Antecedents, Its Setting and Its Interpretation" in "Reform Movements in Behalf of Children in England of the Early Nineteenth Century, and the Agents of Those Reforms," Ph.D. diss., Columbia Univ., 1916. Examines the origins of Charity Schools and includes a discussion on Sarah Trimmer's work in educating poor children.

8.1027
Hall, William Clark, **THE STATE AND THE CHILD**. 1917.

8.1028
Kirk, John, **THIS WAY AND THAT: A BACKWARD LOOK AND A FORWARD LOOK AT THE PROBLEMS AND PROGRESS OF CHILD WELFARE AMONG THE VERY POOR**. 1917.

8.1029
Martin, Anna, **THE MOTHER AND SOCIAL REFORM**. 1917. Traces poverty and depravity in the lower classes to the subordination of women and the laws that perpetuate it. Discusses at length ill-treatment of wives and the need to remedy their plight. Sees child health as consequent upon such reform. Published by the National Union of Women's Suffrage Societies.

8.1030
EQUAL PAY AND THE FAMILY; A PROPOSAL FOR THE NATIONAL ENDOW- MENT OF MOTHERHOOD. 1918. Includes report of the Family Endowment Committee; *also published as:* **THE ENDOWMENT OF MOTHERHOOD**.

8.1031
Edmondson, W., **MAKING ROUGH PLACES PLAIN: FIFTY YEARS' WORK OF THE MANCHESTER AND SALFORD BOYS' AND GIRLS' REFUGES AND HOMES 1870-1920**. Manchester, 1921.

8.1032
Agnew, T.A., **WORK IN EARLY DAYS FOR THE PREVENTION OF CRUELTY TO CHILDREN**. 1925.

8.1033
Meath, Mary, **DIARIES OF THE COUNTESS OF MEATH, EDITED BY HER HUSBAND**. 2 vols. 1928. Meath did philanthropic and social work for distressed women and children.

8.1034
Greville, Frances Evelyn (Countess of Warwick), **LIFE'S EBB AND FLOW**. New York, 1929. Autobiography. See especially: "Succoring the Little Children and Teaching the Big Ones." Concerns her work with crippled children. Argues in favor of state intervention.

8.1035
Rawlinson, Francis William, **THE ROYAL MERCHANT SEAMEN'S ORPHANAGE: AN HISTORICAL OUTLINE**. Kelihen, 1929.

8.1036
Cowper, C.L.H., "An Historical Study of The Provision Made for the Social Welfare of Children and Young People in England Since 1800," M.A. thesis, London Univ., 1930.

8.1037
Jeffs, Ernest H., **MOTHERLESS: THE STORY OF ROBERT THOMSON SMITH AND THE FIRST HOME FOR MOTHERLESS CHILDREN.** foreword by Lady Bertha Dawkins. Marshall, 1930.

8.1038
Buxton, D.F. and Fuller, E., **THE WHITE FLAME: THE HISTORY OF THE SAVE THE CHILDREN FUND.** 1931.

8.1039
Caulfield, Ernest, **THE INFANT WELFARE MOVEMENT IN THE EIGHTEENTH CENTURY.** New York, 1931.

8.1040
Mansbridge, Albert, **MARGARET MCMILLAN, PROPHET AND PIONEER, HER LIFE AND WORK (1858-1931).** 1932. McMillan worked for the health of schoolchildren of working-class families and the improvement of school sanitary conditions, inaugurating school baths.

8.1041
McCleary, George F., **THE EARLY HISTORY OF THE INFANT WELFARE MOVEMENT.** 1933. Traces the progress of children's health legislation. A "measure of far-reaching effect... was the development of health visiting at Huddersfield, which was exceptional in at least two respects: the two principal health visitors were qualified medical women, and the work was done under a local act of Parliament that required the notification to the Medical Officer of health of all births occurring in the borough" (pp. 111-112); **THE MATERNITY AND CHILD WELFARE MOVEMENT.** 1935; **THE DEVELOPMENT OF BRITISH MATERNITY AND CHILD WELFARE SERVICES.** 1945.

8.1042
Uttley, Alison, **THE COUNTRY CHILD.** 1933; Harmondsworth, 1977.

8.1043
Cuthbert, V.I., **WHERE DREAMS COME TRUE: A RECORD OF 95 YEARS OF NATIONAL REFUGES FOR HOMELESS AND DESTITUTE CHILDREN.** 1937.

8.1044
THE CHILDREN'S AID SOCIETY: ITS WORK AND ITS AIMS. 1938.

8.1045
Wrong, R.M., "Some Voluntary Organizations for the Welfare of Children" in **VOLUNTARY SOCIAL SERVICES: THEIR PLACE IN THE MODERN STATE.** ed. by Anne Francis Claudine Bourdillon. 1945.

8.1046
Fuller, Edward, **THE RIGHT OF THE CHILD: ,A CHAPTER IN SOCIAL**

HISTORY. Boston, 1951. Discusses Eglantyne Jebb, founder of the Save the Children Fund, an organization which aimed its endeavor at the welfare and development of the "rescued" child in order to create productive citizens.

8.1047
Hopkinson, Diana, FAMILY INHERITANCE: A LIFE OF EVA HUBBACK. 1954. Hubback worked for the reform of education and the welfare of children.

8.1048
Housden, Leslie George, THE PREVENTION OF CRUELTY TO CHILDREN. 1955. Multi-dimensional perspective of the history of the movement based upon the records and writings of early participants.

8.1049
Chambers, Mary, THEY FOUGHT FOR CHILDREN: SHORT BIOGRAPHIES OF SOME PIONEERS OF CHILD WELFARE. 1956.

8.1050
Ross, A.M., "Care and Education of Pauper Children in England and Wales, 1834-96," Ph.D. diss., Univ. of London, 1956.

8.1051
Rooff, Madeline, "The Maternity and Child Welfare Movement" in VOLUNTARY SOCIETIES AND SOCIAL POLICY. by Madeline Rooff. 1957.

8.1052
Heywood, Jean S., CHILDREN IN CARE: THE DEVELOPMENT OF THE SERVICE FOR THE DEPRIVED CHILD. 1959. Chapters on philanthropic care of children, state care through the Poor Law, the growth of state obligation, and the importance of the family. Includes details on the work of Mary Carpenter and backgrounds of the vagrant and delinquent children in whose service she spent her life. Appendix lists primary sources.

8.1053
Allen, Anne and Morton, Arthur, THIS IS YOUR CHILD: THE STORY OF THE NATIONAL SOCIETY FOR THE PREVENTION OF CRUELTY TO CHILDREN. 1961. Details the founding of the N.S.P.C.C. by Benjamin Waugh in the 1880s and covers the society's development through the next 100 years.

8.1054
Baker, C.F., "The Care and Education of Children in Union Workhouses of Somerset, 1834-70," M.A. thesis, London Univ., 1961.

8.1055
Middleton, Nigel Gordon, "The Child in Public Care 1900 to 1939: A Historical Study," M.A. thesis, London Univ., 1962; WHEN FAMILY FAILED: THE TREATMENT OF CHILDREN IN THE CARE OF THE COMMUNITY DURING THE FIRST HALF OF THE TWENTIETH CENTURY. 1971. See especially: "Children's Institutions 1896-1914" and "Some Results of the System," which discusses poor girls.

8.1056
Edwards, George, THE VICTORIA HOSPITAL FOR CHILDREN, TITE STREET

CHELSEA: A SHORT COMMEMORATIVE HISTORY 1866-1964. 1964.

8.1057
Paisley, M.E., "The Historical Development from the Mid-Nineteenth Century of Services for Physically Handicapped Children...," M.A. thesis, London Univ., 1964.

8.1058
Wilson, Francesca M., **REBEL DAUGHTER OF A COUNTRY HOUSE: THE LIFE OF EGLANTYNE JEBB, FOUNDER OF THE SAVE THE CHILDREN FUND.** 1967. She believed her "mission was to save first of all the children of our enemies and later the children of the world, not only from death through starvation, but from growing up crippled morally as well as physically because of hunger and neglect in childhood" (p. 9).

8.1059
PAST AND PRESENT: Henriques, U., *"Bastardy and the New Poor Law,"* no. 37 (1967) 103-29; Plumb, J.H., *"The New World of Children in Eighteenth Century England,"* no. 67 (1975) 64-95.

8.1060
Schupf, Harriet Warm, "The Perishing and Dangerous Classes: Efforts to Deal with the Neglected, Vagrant and Delinquent Juvenile in England, 1840-1875," Ph.D. diss., Columbia Univ., 1971. Asserts that it was voluntary philanthropy, not the state, that launched the movement to treat the problems of disadvantaged children. Discusses organizations and institutions and the work of Mary Carpenter.

8.1061
Pinchbeck, Ivy and Hewitt, Margaret, **CHILDREN IN ENGLISH SOCIETY: FROM THE EIGHTEENTH CENTURY TO THE CHILDREN ACT 1948.** 2 vols. 1973. Discusses the status of children in general and the condition of those in disadvantaged classes. Surveys philanthropic and reform activities initiated to improve the child's position.

8.1062
Grist, Donald, **"A VICTORIAN CHARITY": THE INFANT ORPHAN ASYLUM AT WANSTEAD.** 1974. The orphanage was established in 1841 and operated until 1971. Only children whose parents were "of good social position" were accepted.

8.1063
Stanford, Jean and Patterson, A. Temple, **THE CONDITION OF THE CHILDREN OF THE POOR IN MID-VICTORIAN PORTSMOUTH.** Portsmouth, 1974.

8.1064
MANCHESTER REVIEW: Hughes, R.E., *"The Boys' and Girls' Welfare Society, 1870-1894,"* 13 (1974) 1-14. Contains notes regarding the society's records.

8.1065
Manton, Jo, **MARY CARPENTER AND THE CHILDREN OF THE STREETS.** 1976. Examination of Carpenter's reform work with ragged and poor children set in a biographical context; *reviewed in:* **MEDICAL HISTORY:** 21 (1977) 476.

8.1066
Behlmer, George, "The Child Protection Movement in England," Ph.D. diss.,

Stanford Univ., 1977. Chapters include "Deadly Motherhood: Infanticide in Mid-Victorian England," "The Stirrings of Reform," and "Organizing in Defense of the Young"; **CHILD ABUSE AND MORAL REFORM IN ENGLAND, 1870-1918.** Menlo Park, 1982. Analyzes the actions of various voluntary organizations in gaining protective legislation for children and in reshaping public opinion on the heretofore private matter of parental power and behavior in the home. Sheds light on pressure group techniques and politics and helps to clarify Victorian attitudes toward poverty, the family, social class, and state interference. "As it grew, the NSPCC became increasingly reliant on two elements for its financial health. First was the loyalty of its local militia, the lady collectors... [especially] the system... of leaving the renewal of subscriptions to a special branch committee of lady collectors.... These women [made] house-to-house calls.... saturated both rich and poor neighborhoods with an assortment of leaflets. By mid-1897, nearly 6,000 upper-middle-class women were engaged in this promotional campaign across England, Wales and Ireland" (pp. 193-194).

8.1067
BRITISH JOURNAL OF EDUCATIONAL STUDIES: Musgrave, P.W., *"Morality and the Medical Department: 1907-1974,"* 25 (1977) 136-154. Explores the contention that school health service initially began because of the high rejection rate of recruits in the Boer War.

8.1068
JOURNAL OF SOCIAL HISTORY: Dyhouse, C., *"Working-Class Mothers and Infant Mortality in England, 1895-1914,"* 12 (1978) 248-267. Argues that the growing interest of social reformers in infant care was often expressed in a patronizing and condescending manner towards working-class mothers and that the ideology that women's place was in the home blinded investigators to evidence showing that children of working mothers actually fared better than those of the same social class whose mothers stayed at home; *rpt. in:* **BIOLOGY, MEDICINE AND SOCIETY 1840-1940.** ed. by Charles Webster. 1981.

8.1069
Heineman, Helen, **MRS. TROLLOPE: THE TRIUMPHANT FEMININE IN THE NINETEENTH CENTURY.** Athens, 1979. "Boldly she described factory conditions and the processes of child labor among the machines, using her story to familiarize middle-class readers with the settings, procedures, and terminology of industrialization. She brought her sheltered and comfortable public inside Sir Matthew's extensive factory, behind walls customarily locked and silent, to that place from which the delights of childhood have been banished for ever" (p. 175).

8.1070
EIGHTEENTH CENTURY STUDIES: Taylor, J.S., *"Philanthropy and Empire: Jonas Hanway and the Infant Poor of London,"* 12 (1979) 285-305. Hanway, governor of the Foundling Hospital, also had extensive interests in mercantile trade. His philanthropy was geared toward securing the national interest, hence his concern for "prostitutes who might become mothers, foundlings who might become productive subjects, domestic servants who might become parents" (p. 287).

8.1071
Lewis, Jane, **THE POLITICS OF MOTHERHOOD, CHILD AND MATERNAL WELFARE IN ENGLAND 1900-1939.** 1980. Discusses the work and accomplishments of women's pressure groups such as the Women's Cooperative Guild in

securing state assistance for maternity and health care for dependent wives and children. "The campaign to 'glorify, dignify and purify' motherhood... began... soon after the Boer War... child and maternal welfare services were developed earlier than most other health services. They were not connected with the Poor Law and were thus free from the stigma.... Infant welfare services were strictly educational; health visitors and infant welfare clinics were not permitted to offer medical treatment and confined themselves to instructing mothers in infant hygiene" (pp. 13-14).

8.1072
Prochaska, F.K., "Little Vessels" in **WOMEN AND PHILANTHROPY IN 19TH CENTURY ENGLAND.** by F.K. Prochaska. 1980. "Where women worked children were likely to follow. Christian parents from all walks of life were anxious to give their children a religious training and wives and mothers, whose educational role within the family was rarely challenged, took up this responsibility with enthusiasm" (p. 73).

8.1073
TEACHERS COLLEGE RECORD: Reese, W.J., *"After Bread, Education: Nutrition and Urban School Children, 1890-1920,"* 81 (1980) 496-525. Examines the conflict between those who advocated free lunch programs and those who felt they would create greater dependency upon the state.

8.1074
Bowder, Bill, **CHILDREN FIRST: A PHOTO-HISTORY OF ENGLAND'S CHILDREN IN NEED WRITTEN AND COMPILED BY BILL BOWDER FOR CHURCH OF ENGLAND CHILDREN'S SOCIETY, 1881-1981.** 1981.

8.1075
Cruickshank, Marjorie, **CHILDREN AND INDUSTRY: CHILD HEALTH AND WELFARE IN NORTH-WEST TEXTILE TOWNS DURING THE NINETEENTH CENTURY.** Manchester, 1981. Extensive research into valuable sources; *reviewed in:* **HISTORY WORKSHOP JOURNAL:** Davin, A., no. 14 (1982) 156-157.

*   *   *

11. FEMALE YOUTH ORGANIZATIONS

8.1076
Caulfield, S.F.A., **DIRECTORY OF GIRLS' SOCIETIES.** 1886.

8.1077
Hopkins, Jane Ellice, Paton, C., et al., **GIRLS' CLUBS, AND RECREATIVE EVENING HOMES: HOW TO WORK THEM.** 1887.

8.1078
Fraser, Donald, **MARY JANE KINNAIRD.** 1890. Kinnaird did work with girls'

clubs.

8.1079
Stanley, Maude, **CLUBS FOR WORKING GIRLS**. 1890; rev. ed., 1904. Emphasizes that over-population is the result of early marriages and the cause of poverty. By belonging to a girl's club, the working girl will occupy herself with other interests rather than needing "the idle companionship of lads" which leads to early marriage. See the appendix for "Clubs Belonging to the Girls' Club Union"; "Clubs for Working Girls" in **WOMAN'S MISSION: A SERIES OF CONGRESS PAPERS ON THE PHILANTHROPIC WORK OF WOMEN BY EMINENT WRITERS**.. compiled by Angela Georgina Burdett-Coutts. 1893; *also published in:* **NINETEENTH CENTURY**: 25 (1889) 73-83. Discusses how to start these organizations. "Slowly and gradually the girls have learned that order conduces more to the general well-being and comfort than disorder, and that culture and refinement are to a certain extent within their reach" (p. 83).

8.1080
Sellers, E., "Women's Work for the Welfare of Girls" in **WOMAN'S MISSION: A SERIES OF CONGRESS PAPERS ON THE PHILANTHROPIC WORK OF WOMEN BY EMINENT WRITERS**. compiled by Angela Burdett-Coutts. 1893. Discusses the trials borne by visitors: "It must not be forgotten that she has no legal right to interfere with the movements of these young women, and that many of them keenly resent anything that savours of dictation. Her only chance of influencing them, therefore, lies in convincing them that she regards them as friends" (p. 37).

8.1081
ENGLISHWOMAN'S REVIEW: *"Working Girls' Clubs in Bristol,"* 28 (1897) 68-70. "Bristol was one of the earliest towns to begin this work, which for nearly forty years has been carried on here with quiet perseverance" (p. 68).

8.1082
Pethick, Emmeline, "Working Girls' Clubs" in **UNIVERSITY AND SOCIAL SETTLEMENTS**. ed. by Will Reason. 1898.

8.1083
NINETEENTH CENTURY: Hobart-Hampden, A., *"The Working Girl of To-Day,"* 43 (1898) 724-730. Concerned with working girls and their activities after work. Author attributes the success of clubs to personal influence rather than financial motivation.

8.1084
Freeman, Flora Lucy, **RELIGIOUS AND SOCIAL WORK AMONGST GIRLS**. 1901.

8.1085
Cadbury, Edward, Matheson, M. Cecile, and Shann, George, "Girls' Clubs, Classes, etc." in **WOMEN'S WORK AND WAGES: A PHASE OF LIFE IN AN INDUSTRIAL CITY**. by Edward Cadbury, M. Cecile Matheson and George Shann. Chicago, 1907. Discusses clubs aimed at the factory girl whose purpose is to refine "its members by offering opportunities for wholesome recreation and development" (p. 272).

8.1086
Federation of Working Girls' Clubs (Factory Helpers' Union), **IN PERILS IN THE CITY.** 1909; **29TH YEAR [ETC.]. ANNUAL REPORT.** 1914, etc.

8.1087
National Association of Mixed Clubs and Girls' Clubs, **MISCELLANEOUS PUBLICATIONS.** 1909-1952; **GIRLS' CLUB DIRECTORY.** 3rd ed., 1913.

8.1088
GIRLS' CLUB JOURNAL: FOR WORKERS AND THOSE INTERESTED IN THE GIRLS' CLUB MOVEMENT: 1909. Edited by Grace A. Tong; published by the organization of the Federation of Working Girls' Clubs.

8.1089
Cecilia, Madame, **GIRLS' CLUBS AND MOTHERS' MEETINGS.** 1911. A handbook for establishing such organizations with the view to "refine, Christianise and catholicise" working girls. "We must provide something even more attractive than the questionable or impure enticements which they find so enticing" (p. 4). Club administrators should "avoid arousing that spirit of independence which characterises the working girl and often leads her to do what is wrong simply in order to assert her right to go where she pleases and do what she likes" (p. 20).

8.1090
Moor, Lucy M., **GIRLS OF YESTERDAY AND TODAY: THE ROMANCE OF THE YWCA.** [1910]. An important pioneer in the YWCA's activity was Mary Jane Kinnaird, who started by assisting young nurses travelling to serve with Florence Nightingale in the Crimean War. She then expanded her mission to include all girls coming to London from the provinces.

8.1091
GIRLS' CLUB NEWS: 1912 to 1924; nos. 1-129.

8.1092
Girl Guides Association, **A.B.C. TO THE GIRL GUIDE HANDBOOK.** [1914]. — *see also:* Baden-Powell, Agnes Smyth and Baden-Powell, Robert, **THE HANDBOOK FOR GIRL GUIDES OR HOW GIRLS CAN HELP BUILD THE EMPIRE...** 1912. "Its aim is to get girls to learn how to be women——self-helpful, happy, prosperous, and capable of keeping good homes and of bringing up good children.... Training has been found attractive to all classes, but more especially to those by whom it is so vitally needed——the girls of the factories and of the alleys of our great cities, who, after they leave school, get no kind of restraining influence, and who, nevertheless, may be the mothers, and should be the character trainers of the future men of our nation" (p. 1); Baden-Powell, Olave, **TRAINING GIRLS AS GUIDES: HINTS TO COMMISSIONERS AND ALL WHO ARE INTERESTED IN THE WELFARE OF GIRLS.** 1917; Kerr, Rose, **THE STORY OF THE GIRL GUIDES.** 1932. The purpose of the organization was to instruct slum-girls on moral and practical matters to prevent the decaying of morals in Britain. Contains photos and many accounts by members concerning their participation in the Guides. "The jobs which fell to the lot of the Guides were many and varied. They were used as interpreters and guides to foreign visitors, and had several lost children to take care of" (p. 97); Wade, Eileen, K.,**THE WORLD CHIEF GUIDE, OLAVE, LADY BADEN-POWELL.** 1957; Wade, Eileen K., **OLAVE BADEN-POWELL: THE AUTHORISED BIOGRAPHY OF THE WORLD CHIEF GUIDE.**

1971; Baden-Powell, Olave, **WINDOW ON MY HEART: THE AUTOBIOGRAPHY OF OLAVE, LADY BADEN-POWELL, AS TOLD TO MARY DREWERY.** 1973.

8.1093
Beard, P.F., "Voluntary Youth Organizations" in **VOLUNTARY SOCIAL SERVICES: THEIR PLACE IN THE MODERN STATE.** ed. by Anne Francis Claudine Bourdillon. 1945. See p. 150 for statistics on youth groups.

8.1094
Lochhead, Marion, **A LAMP WAS LIT: GIRLS' GUILDRY THROUGH FIFTY YEARS.** Edinburgh, 1949. Founded by Dr. William F. Somerville and modeled after the Boy's Brigade, the Guildry's main purpose was to de-emphasize class lines and biases. It was religious in orientation and offered classes in physical exercise and practical lessons in first aid.

8.1095
Percival, Alicia C., **YOUTH WILL BE LED: THE STORY OF THE VOLUNTARY YOUTH ORGANIZATIONS.** 1951. Includes a chronological table. Part two covers the nineteenth century. See especially: "The Village Girls' Club: The G.F.S." The Girls' Friendly Society "helped to give continuity to the home-loving and home-making tendencies of girls" (p. 42).

8.1096
Duguid, Julian, **THE BLUE TRIANGLE.** 1955. Discusses the work of the Y.W.C.A. "It is strange, and rather moving, to look back upon these women: to see what they were and what they did.... They had a good firm middle-class spread, with the aristocratic spear-tip so necessary for getting things done... It is reputed that Lady Kinnaird's daughter, the Hon. Emily Kinnaird, begged from many of her friends before breakfast, arriving at their houses and refusing to allow them to eat until she had milked them of a cheque" (p. 17).

8.1097
Leicester, James H. and Farndale, W.A. James, **TRENDS IN THE SERVICES FOR YOUTH.** 1967.

8.1098
EDUCATIONAL RESEARCH: Dearnaley, E.J. and Fletcher, M.H., *"Cubs and Brownies: Social Class, Intelligence and Interests,"* 2 (1968) 149-151.

8.1099
PAST AND PRESENT: Harrison, B., *"For Church, Queen and Family: The Girls' Friendly Society, 1874-1920,"* no. 61 (1973) 107-38.

8.1100
Springhall, John, **YOUTH, EMPIRE AND SOCIETY: THE BRITISH YOUTH MOVEMENTS, 1883-1940.** 1977. Refers to girls' organizations in Appendix 1, "Girls in Uniform." Contends that youth organizations were designed to reinforce social conformity. "Basically derivative products of the early twentieth century, youth movements for girls are, at least in origin, imitations of the organizations intended solely for boys" (p. 130).

* * *

12. TEMPERANCE WORK

8.1101
A COMPLETE CATALOGUE OF TEMPERANCE LITERATURE: THE BOOKS, TRACTS AND OTHER REQUISITES HERE BROUGHT TOGETHER, COMPRISE NEARLY ALL THE KNOWN PUBLICATIONS ON THE TEMPERANCE QUESTION IN GREAT BRITAIN. [18??].

8.1102
London Temperance Society (afterwards British and Foreign Temperance Society), REPORT, ETC. 1832-1835; THE THIRD REPORT OF THE NEW BRITISH AND FOREIGN TEMPERANCE SOCIETY. 1840.

8.1103
TEMPERANCE PENNY MAGAZINE: 1836 to 1848; vols. 1-14.

8.1104
ENGLISH CHARTIST CIRCULAR, AND TEMPERANCE RECORD FOR ENGLAND AND WALES: 1841 to 1843; vols. 1-3; rpt., New York, 1968. Valuable material on women and the movement.

8.1105
NATIONAL TEMPERANCE SOCIETY... SECOND REPORT. 1844.

8.1106
NATIONAL TEMPERANCE CHRONICLE: *incorporating the* TEMPERANCE GAZETTE: July 1843 to Dec. 1850; July 1851 to Dec. 1856; vols. 1-4. Published by the Committee of the National Temperance League.

8.1107
Balfour, Clara Lucas, WOMAN AND THE TEMPERANCE REFORMATION: AN EXPOSTULATION. 1849; MORNING DEWDROPS; OR THE JUVENILE ABSTAINER. 1862; OUR "OLD OCTOBER":BEING A TRUE SKETCH OF A TEMPERANCE MEETING IN THE EARLIEST DAYS OF THE TEMPERANCE REFORMATION. 1868.

8.1108
United Kingdom Alliance, UNITED KINGDOM ALLIANCE, ETC. (REPORT OF PROVISIONAL COMMITTEE). Manchester, 1853; THE POLITICS OF TEMPERANCE: THE UNITED KINGDOM ALLIANCE MONTHLY PAPERS. 8 parts, 1859. Suggests a Bill to prevent trafficking of liquor. ——*see also:* Hayler, Mark H.C., THE VISION OF A CENTURY, 1853-1953. 1953. History of the United Kingdom Alliance.

8.1109
AN EARNEST APPEAL TO CHRISTIAN MOTHERS ON BEHALF OF THE TEMPERANCE MOVEMENT. 1856.

8.1110
Band of Hope Union, **TEMPERANCE HYMNS AND MELODIES**. 1856; **THE BAND OF HOPE MANUAL**. [1894]. Discusses the formation and management of Bands of Hope; **EASY STEPS TO TEMPERANCE KNOWLEDGE: BEING A PRIMARY CATECHISM FOR CHURCH BANDS OF HOPE, BASED UPON THE AUTHORISED SYLLABUSSES OF THE SOCIETY**. [1898]. — *see also:* Garrett, Charles, **STOP THE GAP! A PLEA FOR BANDS OF HOPE...** 3rd ed., Manchester, 1863; South, Frederic, ed., **THE JUBILEE OF THE BAND OF HOPE MOVEMENT**. 1897; Harrison, Brian, "Pubs" in **THE VICTORIAN CITY: IMAGES AND REALITIES**. ed. by H.J. Dyos and Michael Wolff. vol. 1, 1973. Examines the impact of the Band of Hope Movement; **VICTORIAN STUDIES: THE VICTORIAN CHILD: A SPECIAL ISSUE:** Shiman, L.L., *"The Band of Hope Movement: Respectable Recreation for Working-Class Children,"* 8 (1973) 49-74. Examines the function of the Band of Hope, a temperance movement that tried to reform the moral behavior of working-class children; Pope, Norris, "Missions and Missionaries" in **DICKENS AND CHARITY**. by Norris Pope. 1978. See especially: pp. 136-139 on Band of Hope movement.

8.1111
BAND OF HOPE INSTRUCTOR AND UNION RECORD: 1856 to 1857; vol. 1; *continued as:* **BAND OF HOPE RECORD:** 1858 to 1861; vols. 2-5; 1861 to 1864; vols. 1-4.

8.1112
Marsh, Catherine, **ENGLISH HEARTS AND ENGLISH HANDS**. Nisbet, 1857. Discusses work with the navvies and temperance. —*see also:* O'Rorke, L.E., **THE LIFE AND FRIENDSHIPS OF CATHERINE MARSH**. 1917.

8.1113
Holyoake, George Jacob, **SOCIAL MEANS OF PROMOTING TEMPERANCE**. 1859.

8.1114
National Temperance League, **ANNUAL REPORT AND REGISTER OF... MEMBERS... DECEMBER 31, 1858, ETC.** 1859; **WOMEN'S WORK IN THE TEMPERANCE REFORMATION: BEING PAPERS PREPARED FOR A LADIES CONFERENCE HELD IN LONDON, MAY 26, 1868 WITH AN INTRODUCTION BY MRS. S.C. HALL**. 1868; **WOMAN'S WORK IN THE TEMPERANCE REFORMATION: BEING PAPERS [BY C.L. BALFOUR AND OTHERS], ETC.** 1868; **THE LADIES NATIONAL TEMPERANCE CONVENTION OF 1876. WITH AN INTRODUCTION BY MRS. W.H. SMITH**. 1876; **THE NATIONAL TEMPERANCE LEAGUE ANNUAL FOR 1880**. ed. by R. Rae. 1881; **THE NATIONAL TEMPERANCE CONGRESS LIVERPOOL... 1884**. [1885]; **NATIONAL TEMPERANCE CONGRESS OF BIRMINGHAM... 1889**. [1890]; **REPORT FROM APRIL 21, 1890, TILL APRIL 20, 1891**. 1891; **THE NATIONAL TEMPERANCE CONGRESS CHESTER... 1895**. [1896].

8.1115
Wightman, Julia Bainbrigge (Mrs. Charles), **'HASTE TO THE RESCUE' OR, WORK WHILE IT IS DAY**. 1859; 1862; **ANNALS OF THE RESCUED**. 1861; **THOUGHTS ON HASTE TO THE RESCUE**. 1861. Wightman established a total abstinence society at Shrewsbury which became the pattern for temperance societies working in conjunction with charitable organizations all over England. —*see also:*

How, F.D., **NOBLE WOMEN OF OUR TIME**. 1901. Includes information on Wightman; Fletcher, James M., **MRS. WIGHTMAN OF SHREWSBURY: THE STORY OF A PIONEER IN TEMPERANCE WORK**. 1906.

8.1116
TEMPERANCE MESSENGER AND DOMESTIC JOURNAL: 1859; vol. 1; *continued as:* **DOMESTIC MESSENGER AND TEMPERANCE JOURNAL**: 1860 to 1867; vols. 2-9. Edited by J. DeFraine.

8.1117
TEMPERANCE SPECTATOR: 1859 to 1866; vols. 1-8.

8.1118
WOMAN AND TEMPERANCE. THOUGHTS ON WOMAN'S DUTY IN REGARD TO THE TEMPERANCE CAUSE. Lancaster, 1862.

8.1119
Temperance Congress of 1862, **CONGRESS PAPERS**. 1862.

8.1120
WOMAN'S WORK IN THE TEMPERANCE REFORMATION. 1868. With an introduction by Mrs. S.C.H.

8.1121
National Union for the Suppression of Intemperance, **ANNUAL REPORTS**. Manchester, 1871-1905.

8.1122
Ritchie, James Ewing, **BESSBOOK AND ITS LINEN MILLS: A SHORT NARRATIVE OF A MODEL TEMPERANCE TOWN**. 1872.

8.1123
Arthur, Timothy Shay, **WOMAN TO THE RESCUE: A STORY OF THE NEW CRUSADE**. Cincinnati, [1874]. Novel that dramatizes the evils of intemperance and the women who waged the campaign against it.

8.1124
British Women's Temperance Association, **ANNUAL REPORTS**. 1876-1877. ——*see also:* Heath, Henry J.B., **MARGARET BRIGHT LUCAS: THE LIFE STORY OF A BRITISH WOMAN: BEING A MEMOIR**. 1890. Margaret Bright Lucas (1818-1890) became President of the British Women's Temperance Association in 1878. She worked for women's suffrage and for the repeal of the Contagious Diseases Act; Stewart, Louisa and Fowler, Jessie A., eds., **MEMOIR OF MARGARET BRIGHT LUCAS, PRESIDENT OF THE BRITISH WOMEN'S TEMPERANCE ASSOCIATION**. 1890; Stewart, Eliza (Daniel), **THE CRUSADER IN GREAT BRITAIN, OR THE HISTORY OF THE ORIGIN AND ORGANIZATION OF THE BRITISH WOMEN'S TEMPERANCE ASSOCIATION**. Springfield, 1893. Personal reminiscences. Includes letters sent to the author.

8.1125
National Temperance League, **THE LADIES' NATIONAL TEMPERANCE CONVENTION OF 1876**. introduction by Mrs. W.H. Smith. 1876.

8.1126
Cotton, Elizabeth (Reid), (Lady Hope), **LINES ON A DARK GROUND.** 1879.
Cotton opened a coffee house in Dorking. Due to the publication of this work,
about 3,000 coffee houses opened up all over the country.

8.1127
ENGLISHWOMAN'S REVIEW: *"Women and Temperance,"* 10 (1879) 181-182.
"Nobody can deny that women are... interested in the temperance question. This is
especially true of the working classes, who form the main army of the public house
customers" (p. 181).

8.1128
Sharman, Henry Risborough, **A CLOUD OF WITNESSES AGAINST GROCERS'
LICENSES: THE FRUITFUL SOURCE OF FEMALE INTEMPERANCE.** [188?].

8.1129
YOUNG STANDARD BEARER: 1880 to 1910; vols. 1-30. Publication of the Church
of England Temperance Society.

8.1130
BRITISH WOMEN'S TEMPERANCE JOURNAL: 1886 to 1892; *continued as:*
WINGS: 1892 to 1925. The official journal during 1903 of the National British
Women's Total Abstinence Union; *superseded by:* **WHITE RIBBON:** 1926+.

8.1131
A COMPLETE CATALOGUE OF TEMPERANCE LITERATURE. 1887.

8.1132
Church of England Temperance Society, **JUVENILE UNION: OUTLINE
ADDRESSES AND READINGS.** 3 vols. 1887-1889. Appeal to young members;
FAMILY PLEDGE CARD: ABSTAINING DECLARATION. 1890; **HARD FACTS
LEAFLET.** Westminster, 1890; **THE ILLUSTRATED TEMPERANCE
MONTHLY/AND HAND AND HEART: THE MONTHLY MAGAZINE OF THE
CHURCH OF ENGLAND TEMPERANCE SOCIETY.** 1890; **ALCOHOL AND
CHILDHOOD: A REPORT OF TWO CONFERENCES PROMOTED BY THE...
SOCIETY, ETC.** 1891; **JUVENILE UNION RECITERS.** 1891; **CHILDREN'S
LEAFLETS.** 8 vols. 1894; **HISTORY AND WORK OF THE CHURCH OF
ENGLAND TEMPERANCE SOCIETY: A LECTURE, ETC.** [1894]; **POPULAR
TRACTS FOR THE PEOPLE.** 1894; **CHURCH OF ENGLAND TEMPERANCE
SOCIETY LEAFLETS.** Westminster, 1894; **CATALOGUE OF TEMPERANCE
BOOKS, PUBLICATIONS, ETC., PUBLISHED BY THE CHURCH OF ENGLAND
TEMPERANCE SOCIETY.** Westminster, 1895; **THE JUVENILE MANUAL.
CONTAINING SUGGESTIONS FOR THE FORMATION OF JUNIOR AND
SENIOR BRANCHES, ETC.** Westminster, 1895; **MISSIONARY EFFORTS OF THE
CHURCH OF ENGLAND TEMPERANCE SOCIETY: A LECTURE, ETC.** [1895];
TEMPERANCE STORIES WITH SONG. 1895 to 1897; **YOUNG CRUSADER'S
UNION MANUAL.** 1895; **LEAFLETS.** [1920]. "The Women's Union is a Department
of the C.E.T.S. organised with a view to special Temperance work among women....
Membership of the Women's Union shall be in accordance with the General
Constitution of the Society, and shall be open to all women who shall have signed
one or both of the Society's declarations.... Membership of the Union should remind
each mistress of a household that she has abundant opportunities in the management
of her domestic affairs to be a worker for Temperance" (n.p.; Leaflet no. 79). —

see also: Hird, J. Dennis, **THE GUIDE TO THE CHURCH OF ENGLAND TEMPERANCE SOCIETY WORK IN THE LONDON DIOCESE.** 1889.

8.1133
National Temperance Publication Depot, **[ANONYMOUS TRACTS].** [1888, 1892]; **CATALOGUE OF TEMPERANCE LITERATURE, ETC.** [1887].

8.1134
WOMEN'S PENNY PAPER: 1888 to 1893; *superseded by:* **WOMEN'S HERALD:** 1893 to 1894; *superseded by:* **JOURNAL:** 1894 to 1899.

8.1135
Burns, Dawson, **TEMPERANCE HISTORY.** 1889; **TEMPERANCE HISTORY, VOLUME 2, 1862-90.** 1891; **TEMPERANCE IN THE VICTORIAN AGE: SIXTY YEARS OF TEMPERANCE, TOIL AND TRIUMPH, FROM 1887 TO THE GREAT DIAMOND JUBILEE OF QUEEN VICTORIA'S REIGN.** 1898.

8.1136
THE CYCLOPEDIA OF TEMPERANCE AND PROHIBITION: A REFERENCE BOOK OF FACTS, STATISTICS, AND GENERAL INFORMATION ON ALL PHASES OF THE DRINK QUESTION, THE TEMPERANCE MOVEMENT AND THE PROHIBITION AGITATION. 1891.

8.1137
Winskill, Peter Turner, **THE TEMPERANCE MOVEMENT AND ITS WORKERS.** 1892.

8.1138
Somerset, Isabella Caroline (Lady Henry Somerset), **OUR POSITION AND OUR POLICY. A REPLY TO CHARGES MADE AGAINST A MINORITY OF THE EXECUTIVE COMMITTEE OF THE BRITISH WOMEN'S TEMPERANCE ASSOCIATION.** 1893.   ——*see also:* Fitzpatrick, Kathleen, **LADY HENRY SOMERSET.** 1923. Somerset founded the World's Women's Christian Temperance Union.

8.1139
World's Woman's Christian Temperance Union, **MINUTES OF THE THIRD BIENNIAL CONVENTION OF THE WORLD'S WOMAN'S CHRISTIAN TEMPERANCE UNION.** 1893. Lady Henry Somerset established this group which set up a political department to integrate the causes of temperance and female suffrage.

8.1140
National British Women's Total Abstinence Union, **FIRST ANNUAL REPORT OF THE WOMEN'S TOTAL ABSTINENCE UNION FOR THE YEAR 1893-4.** [1894].

8.1141
WOMEN'S SIGNAL: LADY SOMERSET'S NEW PAPER: 1894 to 1895.

8.1142
CHURCH FRIENDLY: 1895 to 1929; functioned as a monthly publication from Nov. 1895 to July 1914; went into quarterly form from Nov. 1915 to Feb. 1929. Publication of the Church of England Temperance Benefit Society.

8.1143
Roundtree, Joseph and Sherwell, Arthur, **THE TEMPERANCE PROBLEM AND SOCIAL REFORM.** 1899.

8.1144
Chant, Mrs. Ormiston, "Temperance" in **WOMEN IN SOCIAL LIFE. THE TRANSACTIONS OF THE SOCIAL SECTION OF THE INTERNATIONAL CONGRESS OF WOMEN. LONDON, JULY 1899.** ed. by Ishbel Aberdeen. 1900. Claims that it is men, not women, who are responsible for the evils of intemperance as well as "the fatal cowardice of... legislators" (p. 159); It is, however, woman's moral and social responsibility to work for temperance reform.

8.1145
THE CHILDREN AND THE DRINK. 1901.

8.1146
Buxton, Noel and Hoare, Walter, "Temperance Reform" in **THE HEART OF THE EMPIRE.** ed. by C.F.G. Masterman. 1901; rpt., New York, 1973.

8.1147
TEMPERANCE RECORD: 1903 to 1907. Edited by J.T. Rae; *superseded by:* **NATIONAL TEMPERANCE QUARTERLY AND MEDICAL REVIEW:** 1908 to 1942. Publication of the National Temperance League.

8.1148
WESTMINSTER REVIEW: Dowman, J., *"Science and Sentiment in Temperance Reform,"* 160 (1903) 522-530. "The woman who has occasion to bemoan the burden of a drunken husband might be convinced, were she amenable to reason, that her own tongue and temper were the breeders of subsequent woe and tribulation" (p. 527); Joel, J.E., *"Husbands and Wives Under the New Licensing Act of 1902,"* 160 (1903) 68-76. Delineates this piece of legislation which allows the married "to secure protection, the wife from the husband and the husband from the wife when one or the other has given way to the vice of drunkenness" (p. 68).

8.1149
True Temperance Association, **REPORT OF THE INAUGURAL MEETING, ETC.** [1909-]; **WOMEN'S TRUE TEMPERANCE COMMITTEE STUDY CIRCLE PAPERS.** 1927.

8.1150
Weston, Agnes Elizabeth, **MY LIFE AMONG THE BLUEJACKETS.** 1909. ——*see also:* Wintz, Sophia G., **OUR BLUE JACKETS: MISS WESTON'S LIFE AND WORK AMONG OUR SAILORS.** 1890; Tomkinson, E.M., "Agnes Weston, The Sailor's Friend" in **THE WORLD'S WORKERS: SARAH ROBINSON, AGNES WESTON, MRS. MEREDITH.** by E.M. Tomkinson. 1894. Weston established temperance societies on board navy ships.

8.1151
International Congress of Women, **REPORT OF THE 1909 CONGRESS.** 1910. Session on temperance work is included.

8.1152
Robinson, Sarah, **THE SOLDIER'S FRIEND: A PIONEER'S RECORD.** 1913. —
see also: Tomkinson, E.M., "Sarah Robinson, the Soldier's Friend" in **THE
WORLD'S WORKERS: SARAH ROBINSON, AGNES WESTON, MRS.
MEREDITH.** by E.M. Tomkinson. 1894. Robinson visited soldiers in their barracks,
extolling the virtues of abstinence. She established the Soldier's Institute and the
Sailor's Welcome, as well as a Temperance Society called "The Helping Hand."

8.1153
BLACKWOOD'S MAGAZINE: *"A Woman—To Women,"* 206 (1919) 653-666.
Discusses the Temperance (Scotland) Act, 1913 and its advantages and effects; also
examines American Prohibition.

8.1154
Malcolm, Christie, **THE NATIONAL BRITISH WOMEN'S TEMPERANCE
ASSOCIATION: ITS ORIGIN AND PROGRESS.** 1926.

8.1155
Tillyard, Aelfrida Catharine, **AGNES E. SLACK; TWO HUNDRED THOUSAND
MILES' TRAVEL FOR TEMPERANCE IN FOUR CONTINENTS.** Cambridge,
1926.

8.1156
Roberts, Charles, **THE RADICAL COUNTESS: THE HISTORY OF THE LIFE OF
ROSALIND, COUNTESS OF CARLISLE.** Carlisle, 1962. In 1887 helped to form
the Women's Liberal Rederation, and was elected president of the National British
Women's Temperance Association in 1903. Also worked for suffrage.

8.1157
Fryer, Peter, "The Teetotalitarians" in **MRS. GRUNDY: STUDIES IN ENGLISH
PRUDERY.** by Peter Fryer. New York, 1963.

8.1158
HISTORY TODAY: Harrison, B., *"Drunkards and Reformers: Early Victorian
Temperance Tracts,"* 13 (1963) 178-185. Quotes Shaftesbury as stating that "nearly
all our most interesting and effective stories [moral tales on alcoholism] were
written by women" (p. 184).

8.1159
Longmate, Norman, **THE WATERDRINKERS: A HISTORY OF TEMPERANCE.**
1968. "[Some] reformers specialized in providing practical alternatives to the public
house. The most famous worker in this field was Elizabeth Cotton.... Demand from
her customers compelled Cotton to start a Total Abstinence Society but she had no
sympathy with 'young ladies,' who 'pledge book in hand... persecute the unfortunate
tired guests of the coffee room' until the latter signed for peace and then retired to
the public house. She was clearly motivated by a real respect for the working class"
(pp. 206-208).

8.1160
Harrison, Brian and Trinder, Barrie, **DRINK AND SOBRIETY IN AN EARLY
VICTORIAN COUNTRY TOWN: BANBURY 1830-1860.** 1969. "By the 1850s one
could assess the respectability of a Banbury woman by observing her attitude to
public houses" (p. 9).

8.1161
Shiman, Lilian Lewis, "Crusade Against Drink in Victorian England," Ph.D. diss., Univ. of Wisconsin, 1970. Traces the temperance movement from 1829, and analyzes the very complicated organizational and ideological elements. Illustrates the difficulties of tracing women's roles in the various aspects of the movement; "'Changes are Dangerous': Women and Temperance in Victorian England" in RELIGION IN THE LIVES OF ENGLISH WOMEN, 1760-1930. ed. by Gail Malmgreen. 1986. Points out that the early temperance movement required moderation rather than total abstinence, and that many temperance reformers saw their work as a means for conversion to religion rather than as an end in itself. The movement "as a whole was male-dominated" and a "conservative reform effort which saw nothing wrong in the existing society that the elimination of drink could not solve" (p. 210).

8.1162
INTERNATIONAL REVIEW OF SOCIAL HISTORY: Harrison, B., *"The British Prohibitionist 1853-1872: A Biographical Analysis,"* 15 (1970) 375-467. "To a limited extent the nineteenth century temperance movement was in itself a feminist movement——defending the interests of women and children against the selfishness of men. Prohibitionism is a noteworthy example of that alliance between feminism and middle-class puritanism which Bernard Shaw so detested" (p. 402). Yet women's role in the prohibition movement was subordinate until they formed their own temperance organizations: "Women were wanted primarily for routine work behind the scenes——for raising funds, organising bazaars, distributing propaganda" (p. 403).

8.1163
Harrison, Brian, DRINK AND THE VICTORIANS: THE TEMPERANCE QUESTION IN ENGLAND, 1815-1872. 1971. Presents analogies between the temperance movement and the feminist movement; "State Intervention and Moral Reform" in PRESSURE FROM WITHOUT IN EARLY VICTORIAN ENGLAND. ed. by Patricia Hollis. 1974.

8.1164
National Temperance Hospital, ALIVE AND LIVELY 100 YEARS AFTER. A CENTENNIAL REPORT ON THE NATIONAL TEMPERANCE HOSPITAL, 1873-1973. 1973.

8.1165
Paulson, Ross Evans, WOMEN'S SUFFRAGE AND PROHIBITION: A COMPARATIVE STUDY OF EQUALITY AND SOCIAL CONTROL. Glenview, 1973. See especially: "Women and English Values 1800-1840," "The Background of Prohibition in England and America 1826-1856," and "Prohibition and Politics in Norway, Sweden, and England." "The 'woman question' of the nineteenth and early twentieth centuries was an aspect of the debate on the meaning of equality, and that the temperance and prohibition movements involved questions concerning the nature of democracy and the means of social control within society" (preface).

8.1166
HISTORICAL STUDIES: Hyslop, A., *"Temperance, Christianity and Feminism: The Woman's Christian Temperance Union of Victoria, 1887-97,"* 17 (1976) 27-49. Examines the work done by temperance reformers for women's suffrage.

8.1167
Dingle, Anthony Edward, **THE CAMPAIGN FOR PROHIBITION IN VICTORIAN ENGLAND.** 1980.

8.1168
Williams, Gwylmor Prys and Brake, George Thompson, **DRINKING IN GREAT BRITAIN 1900 TO 1979.** 1980. See especially: "The Emergence of an Alcohol Problem in Britain," "Temperance Takes Over," and "Children and Drink." Parliament's passage of laws in 1889 and 1894, which made cruelty to children an offense, called public attention to child abuse, the effects on children of parental intoxication, and the sale of liquor to children.

8.1169
Epstein, Barbara Leslie, **THE POLITICS OF DOMESTICITY: WOMEN, EVANGELISM, AND TEMPERANCE IN NINETEENTH CENTURY AMERICA.** Middletown, 1981. Useful as a theoretical approach to studying similar activity in great Britain. Argues that, in developing a proto-feminist politic, the WTCU opposed what they saw as uniquely male cultural institutions.

8.1170
HISTORICAL MAGAZINE OF THE PROTESTANT EPISCOPAL CHURCH: Shiman, L.L., *"The Blue Ribbon Army: Gospel Temperance in England,"* 50 (1981) 391-408. Introduced in England in the 1870's, the movement differed from other temperance movements in that there was "no rescuing of drunkards, no distribution of anti-drink literature, no political activities in support of anti-drink principles, no involvement in public demonstrations" (p. 403).

8.1171
ALCOHOL IN HISTORY: A MULTIDISCIPLINARY NEWSLETTER: Gutzke, D. and Fahey, D.M., *"Drink and Temperance in Britain,"* 9 (1984) 3-5.

* * *

13. ANIMAL PROTECTION AND THE ANTI-VIVISECTION MOVEMENT

8.1172
Royal Society for the Prevention of Cruelty to Animals, **OBJECTS AND ADDRESS OF THE SOCIETY, ETC.** 1829; **DOMESTIC ANIMALS AND THEIR TREATMENT.** 1855; 1857; **VIVISECTION.** 1876; **BAND OF MERCY ALMANAC.** 1881; 1883-1885; 1887-1901; 1904-1906. ——*see also:* Moss, Arthur W., **VALIANT CRUSADE: THE HISTORY OF THE ROYAL SOCIETY FOR THE PREVENTION OF CRUELTY TO ANIMALS.** 1961. "The Ladies' Committee, as a separate body, was apparently discontinued, but many years afterwards was revived under the presidency of the Baroness Burdett-Coutts, and did magnificent work in the field of humane education. Even as late as 1886, however, ladies were not permitted to serve on the General Committee that controlled the Society's work.... The result was that the committee of gentlemen had to go cap in hand to their ladies to re-start

working for them and they also had to face the handicap that, in the meantime, a purely women's animal welfare organization had been begun, and to it funds were flowing in vast quantities!" (p. 24); ENGLISH HISTORICAL REVIEW: Harrison, B., "Animals and the State in Nineteenth-Century England," 88 (1973) 786-820. History of the RSPCA and the establishment of legislation concerning cruelty to animals; rpt. in: PEACEABLE KINGDOM: STABILITY AND CHANGE IN MODERN BRITAIN. by Brian Harrison. 1982.

8.1173
Gompertz, L., FRAGMENTS IN DEFENCE OF ANIMALS. 1852.

8.1174
ANIMAL WORLD: AN ADVOCATE OF HUMANITY: 1869 to 1870.

8.1175
BAND OF MERCY ADVOCATE: 1869 to 1934. A journal which advocated the humane treatment of animals.

8.1176
Cobbe, Frances Power, THE NINE CIRCLES; OR, THE TORTURE OF THE INNOCENT. BEING RECORDS OF VIVISECTION, ENGLISH AND FOREIGN. 2nd rev. ed., 1873; THE MORAL ASPECTS OF VIVISECTION. 1875; THE FALLACY OF RESTRICTIONS APPLIED TO VIVISECTION. 1886. Written for the London Victoria Street Society for the Protection of Animals from Vivisection, united with the International Association for the Total Suppression of Vivisection; ILLUSTRATIONS ON VIVISECTION; OR, EXPERIMENTS ON LIVING ANIMALS. Philadelphia, 1889; THE MODERN RACK: PAPERS ON VIVISECTION. 1893; THE LIFE OF FRANCES POWER COBBE BY HERSELF. 3rd ed., 1894; LORD LISTER AND PAINLESS VIVISECTION... Bristol, 1898.

8.1177
Society for the Protection of Animals Liable to Vivisection, STATEMENT OF THE SOCIETY... ON THE REPORT OF THE ROYAL COMMISSION ON VIVISECTION. 1876.

8.1178
MACMILLAN'S MAGAZINE: Greenwood, G., "Vivisection," 40 (1879) 523-530. Discriminates between types of animal experimentation and whether they are justified or unjustified, according to their usefulness to mankind.

8.1179
ZOOPHILIST AND ANIMAL'S DEFENDER: 1881 to 1915; vols. 1-35. Publication of the Victoria Street and International Society for the Protection of Animals from Vivisection.

8.1180
NINETEENTH CENTURY: Kingsford, A., "Uselessness of Vivisection," 11 (1882) 171.

8.1181
Victoria Street and International Society for the Protection of Animals from Vivisection (National Anti-Vivisection Society), THE VIVISECTION CONTROVERSY; A SELECTION OF SPEECHES AND ARTICLES... FROM THE

PUBLICATIONS OF THE VICTORIA STREET AND INTERNATIONAL SOCIETY. 20 parts, 1883; 22 parts, 1890; THE COMING ELECTION: WORKING MEN AND LICENSED VIVISECTION—THEIR PART AND LOT IN IT. [1892]; [PAMPHLETS AND LEAFLETS]. [1895-]; TWENTIETH (-THIRTY-SEVENTH, ETC.) ANNUAL REPORT... 1895 (1912, ETC.). 1895+.

8.1182
Kingsford, Anna (Bonus), "Unscientific Science. Moral Aspects of Vivisection" in SPIRITUAL THERAPEUTICS. ed. by William J.L. Colville. 1888.

8.1183
Independent Anti-Vivisection League, VIVISECTION. [1890].

8.1184
Mackenzie, Mrs. Muir, "Woman's Work for Animals" in WOMAN'S MISSION. ed. by Angela Burdett-Coutts. 1893.

8.1185
ABOLITIONIST: THE JOURNAL OF THE BRITISH UNION FOR THE ABOLITION OF VIVISECTION: April 1899 to Nov./Dec. 1948; vols. 1-49.

8.1186
London Anti-Vivisection Society, THE DYNAMITARDS OF SCIENCE. BY G. BERNARD SHAW. [1900].

8.1187
LAW QUARTERLY REVIEW: De Montmorency, J.E.G., *"State Protection of Animals at Home and Abroad,"* 18 (1902) 31-48.

8.1188
WESTMINSTER REVIEW: Gordon, G.P., *"The Progress of Legal Protection to Animals,"* 166 (1906) 218-223. Reviews legislation on animal cruelty.

8.1189
Kidd, Beatrice Ethel, THE POLITICS OF ABOLITION: BEING THE REPORT OF A SPEECH DELIVERED... AT THE INTERNATIONAL CONGRESS OF THE WORLD ANTI-VIVISECTION LEAGUE... BRITISH LEAGUE... BRITISH UNION FOR THE ABOLITION OF VIVISECTION. 1909.

8.1190
World League Against Vivisection, FOURTH TRIENNIAL INTERNATIONAL CONGRESS OF THE WORLD LEAGUE... LONDON, FROM JULY 19TH TO 24TH, 1909. 1910.

8.1191
British Union for the Abolition of Vivisection, FOURTEENTH [ETC.] ANNUAL REPORT... FOR THE YEAR ENDING MAY 1912 [ETC.]. 1912+.

8.1192
Fairholme, Edward G. and Wellesley, Pain, A CENTURY OF WORK FOR ANIMALS. 1924.

8.1193
French, Richard D., "Medical Science and Victorian Society: the Anti-Vivisection Movement," Ph.D. diss., Univ. of Oxford, 1972; **ANTIVIVISECTION AND MEDICAL SCIENCE IN VICTORIAN SOCIETY.** 1975.

8.1194
Pearsall, Ronald, "Cruelty to Animals" in **NIGHT'S BLACK ANGELS: THE MANY FACES OF VICTORIAN CRUELTY.** by Ronald Pearsall. New York, 1975. Details the work of the R.S.P.C.A. and the anti-vivisection movement. "The anti-vivisection movement sheltered temperance advocates, women's rights, devotees of spiritualism and animal magnetism, and theosophists. One of the latter group was Anna Kingsland, who put a curse on two of the leading French vivisectionists; much to her pleasure, they died shortly afterwards" (p. 224).

8.1195
Turner, James C., "Kindness to Animals: The Animal Protection Movement in England and America During the Nineteenth Century," Ph.D. diss., Harvard Univ., 1975; **RECKONING THE BEAST. ANIMALS, PAIN AND HUMANITY IN THE VICTORIAN MIND.** 1980.

8.1196
Harrison, Brian, "Animals and the State in Nineteenth-Century England" in **PEACEABLE KINGDOM.** by Brian Harrison. 1982. "Nor do we always acknowledge the centrality of animals in nineteenth-century commerce, recreation, and transport. That subject is also important for pressure-group history, for the RSPCA was among the most successful continuous influences on nineteenth-century opinion" (p. 83).

8.1197
Lansbury, Coral, **THE OLD BROWN DOG: WOMEN, WORKERS, AND VIVISECTION IN EDWARDIAN ENGLAND.** 1985. The title refers to a 1907 battle between suffragettes, antivivisectionists, and trade unionists against a group of London University medical students over an experiment on a dog. Author addresses the question of why the antivivisection movement attracted the support of feminists and labor unionists, arguing that the issue reflected their own plight as subjects of medical abuses. In the chapter "A Woman is Being Beaten," a parallel is drawn between Victorian pornographic bondage imagery and the devices used to strap animals to the operating table; *excerpt rpt. in:* **VICTORIAN STUDIES:** *"Gynaecology, Pornography, and the Antivivisection Movement,"* 28 (1985) 413-438.

* * *

14. THE PEACE MOVEMENT

8.1198
Wright, Frances D'Arusmont, **VIEWS OF SOCIETY AND MANNERS IN AMERICA.** 1821; rpt., ed. by Paul R. Baker. Cambridge, Mass., 1963; **BIOGRAPHY, NOTES, AND POLITICAL LETTERS OF FRANCES WRIGHT D'ARUSMONT.** New York, 1844. ——*see also:* **TENNESSEE HISTORICAL MAGAZINE:** Parks, E.W., *"Dreamer's Vision: Frances Wright at Nashoba (1825-30),"* 2 (Jan. 1932) 74-86; Emerson, O.B., *"Frances Wright: Her Nashoba Experiment,"* 6 (1947) 291-314; Gilbert, Amos, **MEMOIRS OF FRANCES WRIGHT: THE PIONEER WOMAN IN THE CAUSE OF HUMAN RIGHTS.** Cincinnati, 1855; Perkins, Alice Jane Gray and Wolfson, Theresa, **FRANCES WRIGHT, FREE ENQUIRER: THE STUDY OF A TEMPERAMENT.** New York, 1939; **INDIANA MAGAZINE OF HISTORY:** Elliott, H., *"Frances Wright's Experiment with Negro Emancipation,"* 35 (1939) 141-157; **CONTEMPORARY REVIEW:** Lane, M., *"Frances Wright (1795-1852): The Great Experiment,"* 218 (1971) 7-11; Lane, Margaret, **FRANCES WRIGHT AND THE GREAT EXPERIMENT.** Manchester, 1972.

8.1199
HERALD OF PEACE AND INTERNATIONAL ARBITRATION: [1821 to 1908]. Published by the International Peace Society.

8.1200
NEW HARMONY GAZETTE: Wright, F.D'A., *"A Plan for the Gradual Abolition of Slavery in the United States, Without Danger of Loss to the Citizens of the South,"* 1 (Oct. 1825) 4-5; Wright, F.D'A., *"Explanatory Notes Respecting the Nature and Objects of One Institution of Nashoba and of the Principles Upon Which it is Founded,"* 3 (Jan. and Feb. 1828) n.p.

8.1201
[Heyrick, Elizabeth], **APOLOGY FOR LADIES' ANTI-SLAVERY ASSOCIATIONS, BY THE AUTHOR OF "IMMEDIATE NOT GRADUAL ABOLITION, ETC."** 1828.

8.1202
Female Society for Birmingham, West Bromwich, Wednesburg, Walsall and the Respective Neighborhoods, for the Relief of British Negro Slaves, **WHAT DOES YOUR SUGAR COST? A COTTAGE CONVERSATION ON THE SUBJECT OF BRITISH NEGRO SLAVERY.** Birmingham, 1829; **FIFTH REPORT.** Birmingham, 1830.

8.1203
Trollope, Frances, **DOMESTIC MANNERS OF THE AMERICANS.** 2 vols. 1832. Trollope notes the laws designed to keep slaves in ignorance; how they are discussed in their own presence as if they did not possess human feelings and comprehension; the deliberate breeding of slaves in the upper South for sale in the markets of the deep South; and the impact of the institution of slavery upon the morals of the whites.

8.1204
Stephen, George, **ANTI-SLAVERY RECOLLECTIONS**. 1854.

8.1205
Stowe, Harriet Beecher, **SUNNY MEMORIES OF FOREIGN LANDS**. 1854. Includes her contacts with British women abolitionists.

8.1206
Ladies' London Emancipation Society, **FIRST ANNUAL REPORT**. 1864. Quotes from tracts warning against English working-class sympathies with the South. "There are various considerations connected with the institution of slavery which make it, far more than is the case in ordinary politics, a question especially and deeply interesting for women, and demanding the fullest exercise of their influence and activity" (p. 4); **SECOND ANNUAL REPORT**. 1865. The Society took up contributions for aid to freedmen, and recorded contributions and exhortations to the membership (pp. 10-11). Blacks "may not only be helped, but educated and habituated to self-help" (p. 24).

8.1207
Ladies' Negro's Friend Society for Birmingham, **THIRTY-NINTH ANNUAL REPORT**. 1864. Members should provide assistance to American blacks. Cites their ability and willingness to work "under the stimulus of the same motives that influence other races to labour" (p. 7).

8.1208
Edinburgh Ladies' Emancipation Society, **ANNUAL REPORT**. 1867. Details reports from the London Society.

8.1209
Martineau, Harriet, **SOCIETY IN AMERICA**. 3 vols. 1837; **RETROSPECT OF WESTERN TRAVEL**. 1838; **THE MARTYR AGE OF THE UNITED STATES OF AMERICA**. 1840; **AUTOBIOGRAPHY. WITH MEMORIAL BY M.W. CHAPMAN**. 3 vols. 1877. ——*see also:* Webb, Robert Kiefer, **HARRIET MARTINEAU. A RADICAL VICTORIAN**. New York, 1960. Discusses her antislavery activities, writings and American friends.

8.1210
Tayler, Maria, **WOMEN AND WAR! A REPLY TO THE QUESTIONS: HOW DOES WAR AFFECT WOMEN? AND HOW CAN WOMEN PREVENT WAR?** 1877.

8.1211
ENGLISHWOMAN'S REVIEW: *"The Peacemakers,"* 9 (1878) 207-211. "On the present occasion when so many true-hearted Englishmen have been expressing their determination to oppose war by every means in their power, Englishwomen have stood side by side with them to second their efforts.... Little doubt can be felt by any one that the Peace Party in the country would have received a larger augmentation of force if women had equally with men possessed the authority by citizens to elect their governor" (p. 211). Names women petitioners opposing government war policy. Signers include 10,076 women in Birmingham alone, among them well-known feminists; *"Women's Peace and Arbitration Auxiliary of the London Peace Society,"* 11 (1880) 271-276; *"Peace and Arbitration,"* 11 (1880) 275-276. Urges greater organization among women to introduce the 'principle of Arbitration.' Offers an outline on "How to Organize a Local Peace Association in

Your Own Neighborhood" (p. 276).

8.1212
Stoddart, Anna M., **ELIZABETH PEASE NICHOL.** 1899.

8.1213
Hallowes, Frances S., **WOMEN AND WAR; AN APPEAL TO THE WOMEN OF ALL NATIONS.** 1914.

8.1214
SOCIALIST REVIEW: Lawrence, E.P., *"The Women's Crusade For Peace. A New Chapter in the History of Internationalism,"* 12 (1915) 642-651. "In women's latent consciousness [lies]... a collective responsibility for the welfare of the human family" (pp. 642-643).

8.1215
Hirst, Margaret E., **THE QUAKERISM IN PEACE AND WAR.** 1923.

8.1216
Klingberg, Frank J., **THE ANTI-SLAVERY MOVEMENT IN ENGLAND.** New Haven, 1926.

8.1217
Mathieson, W.L., **BRITISH SLAVERY AND ITS ABOLITION 1823-1838.** 1926.

8.1218
Phelps, Christina, **THE ANGLO-AMERICAN PEACE MOVEMENT IN THE MID-NINETEENTH CENTURY.** New York, 1930.

8.1219
NEW ENGLAND QUARTERLY: Bloore, S., *"Miss Martineau Speaks Out,"* 9 (1936) 403-416. Reaction to Martineau's first speech on abolition.

8.1220
Howse, Ernest M., **PAINTS IN POLITICS: THE "CLAPHAM SECT" AND THE GROWTH OF FREEDOM.** Toronto, 1952.

8.1221
Tolles, Frederick, **SLAVERY AND THE WOMAN QUESTION: LUCRETIA MOTT'S DIARY.** 1952.

8.1222
Lee, Amica, **LAURELS AND ROSEMARY: THE LIFE OF WILLIAM AND MARY HOWITT.** Oxford, 1955.

8.1223
Thistlethwaite, Frank, **THE ANGLO-AMERICAN CONNECTION IN THE EARLY NINETEENTH CENTURY.** Philadelphia, 1959.

8.1224
THE ESTLIN PAPERS, 1840-1884. 1961. Microfilm collection of original papers illustrating connections between British and American antislavery reformers, including Mary Anne Estlin.

8.1225
Bolt, Christine, **THE ANTI-SLAVERY MOVEMENT AND RECONSTRUCTION: A STUDY IN ANGLO-AMERICAN COOPERATION 1833-1877**. 1969. Includes quotations from correspondence between American and English women abolitionists. Indicates the nature of their thought, activity and relationships, for example, Harriet Beecher Stowe and Maria Weston Chapman of the U.S. and Mary Estlin in England. "After as before 1863, women of sufficient leisure and philanthropic bent were entreated to form serving circles and make clothes for the Negroes" (p. 118); (and Drescher, Seymour, eds.), **ANTI-SLAVERY, RELIGION, AND REFORM**. 1980.

8.1226
Fladeland, Betty, **MEN AND BROTHERS, ANGLO-AMERICAN ANTISLAVERY COOPERATION**. Urbana, 1972; "Harriet Martineau" in **ABOLITIONISTS AND WORKING-CLASS PROBLEMS IN THE AGE OF INDUSTRIALIZATION**. by Betty Fladeland. 1984. "For many years Harriet sent articles to the NATIONAL ANTI-SLAVERY STANDARD in the United States.... Up until her death, she wrote over 1600 leading pieces for the LONDON DAILY NEWS including her arguments for the Northern side" (p. 92).

8.1227
Temperley, Howard, **BRITISH ANTISLAVERY 1833-1870**. 1972. Excellent for background of the antislavery crusades. Includes a discussion of the rejection of women's participation in the World Antislavery Convention held in London in 1840. See pp. 87-90; "British and American Abolitionists Compared" in **THE ANTISLAVERY VANGUARD: NEW ESSAYS ON THE ABOLITIONISTS**. ed. by Martin Duberman. Princeton, 1965. "[The] stern attitude toward the American abolitionists is the more puzzling when compared to the very different treatment afforded their British counterparts" (p. 344).

8.1228
Hurwitz, Edith F., **POLITICS AND THE PUBLIC CONSCIENCE: SLAVE EMANCIPATION AND THE ABOLITIONIST MOVEMENT IN BRITAIN**. 1973. "Like Dissenters, women could find in the slave society the perfect image of tyranny and despotism greater, powerful and more enormous for them.... The pages of the ANTI-SLAVERY REPORTERS were filled with authentic descriptions of feminine travails and exploitation.... Women's organizations reached national proportions. This was reflected in the petition of females of Great Britain that was presented to both houses of parliament in 1833. It had over 350,000 signatures on it.... George Stephen... [admitted] that 'none of our anti-slavery meetings were well attended until after it was agreed to admit ladies to be present' (p. 90).... Much of the back-up work in terms of fundraising, distribution of literature, and securing petitions was done by women" (p. 91).

8.1229
Taylor, Clare, **BRITISH AND AMERICAN ABOLITIONISTS: AN EPISODE IN TRANSATLANTIC UNDERSTANDING**. Edinburgh, 1974. "The Garrisonian [antislavery] connection... is characterized by the leading role which women played in it. The link of the anti-slavery campaign to the movement for women's rights both in Britain and America... was very largely through the channels of the Garrison organization.... [But] the letters between the British and American women... show that their first loyalty was to the anti-slavery cause (p. 4)....

Important as Mary Estlin was, the most influential woman in British anti-slavery circles was undoubtedly Elizabeth Pease Nichol" (p. 11).

8.1230
Sager, Eric W., "Pacifism and the Victorians: A Social History of the English Peace Movement, 1816-1878," Ph.D. diss., Univ. of British Columbia, 1975.

8.1231
Lorimer, Douglas A., **COLOUR, CLASS AND THE VICTORIANS: ENGLISH ATTITUDES TO THE NEGRO IN THE MID-NINETEENTH CENTURY.** Leicester, 1978. "Those mid-Victorians who interested themselves in the welfare of blacks through missionary and anti-slavery charities were drawn from a broad spectrum of English society.... but in the main, supporters... came from the middle classes associated either with the Evangelical wing of the Established Church or with the various Nonconformist denominations.... Two groups played a particularly active part.... middle-class women, who had the leisure and were attracted by the social prestige of anti-slavery and missionary works; and members of the Society of Friends, who had the money and the zeal to spend their time and wealth in acts of charity" (p. 114).

8.1232
HISTORICAL JOURNAL: Tyrrel, A., *"Making the Millenium: The Mid-Nineteenth Century Peace Movement,"* 21 (1978) 75-95.

8.1233
Ceadel, Martin, **PACIFISM IN BRITAIN 1914-1945: THE DEFINING OF A FAITH.** Oxford, 1980. See chapter 3, "Before the Great War." Outlines "the pacifist tradition as it affected Britain before 1914."

8.1234
Harrison, Brian, "A Genealogy of Reform in Modern Britain" in **ANTI-SLAVERY, RELIGION AND REFORM.** ed. by Christine Bolt and Seymour Drescher. Folkestone, 1980.

8.1235
VICTORIAN STUDIES: Sager, E.W., *"The Social Origins of Victorian Pacifism,"* 23 (1980) 211-236. "Women were always prominent among Peace Society supporters. Of the 203 most generous subscribers to the Peace Society in 1873 and 1874, fourteen percent were women. Women were admitted to the peace congresses as visitors rather than delegates, but no less than thirty percent of all delegates and visitors at the Paris Peace Congress were women. Pacifist women were not feminists: they did not provoke the kind of debate which occurred in the abolitionists movement... but attended congresses in a subordinate role and formed their own female societies" (p. 220).

8.1236
Oldfield, Sybil, "Mary Sheepshanks and the First World War: 1914-1918" in **SPINSTERS OF THIS PARISH: THE LIFE AND TIME OF F.M. MAYOR AND MARY SHEEPSHANKS.** by Sybil Oldfield. 1984. Discusses the work of suffragists for the cause of international peace. See footnote 1 for a list of women activists, including Maude Royden, Helena Swanwick, Margaret Ashton, Alice Clark, Eva Gore-Booth, Sylvia Pankhurst, Hannah Mitchell, Ada Nield Chew, Selina Cooper, Margaret Llewelyn Davies, and Vernon Lee.

* * *

15. THE ANTI-SLAVERY MOVEMENT IN BRITAIN

8.1237
More, Hannah, **CHEAP REPOSITORY TRACTS.** 1795-1798. Includes anti-slavery propaganda: BABAY, THE TRUE STORY OF A GOOD NEGRO WOMAN. (1795); THE SORROWS OF YAMBA, OR THE NEGRO WOMAN'S LAMENTATIONS. (1795); TRUE STORIES OF TWO GOOD NEGROES. (1798); and THE BLACK PRINCE. (1798); **STORIES FOR THE MIDDLE RANKS OF SOCIETY, AND TALES FOR THE COMMON PEOPLE.** 2 vols. 1818. ——*see also:* Roberts, William, ed., **MEMOIRS OF THE LIFE AND CORRESPONDENCE OF MRS. HANNAH MORE.** 4 vols. 1834; Jones, M.G., **HANNAH MORE.** 1968. See especially: "The Saints" for material on More's anti-slavery efforts.

8.1238
Female Anti-Slavery Society, London, **A VINDICATION OF FEMALE ANTI-SLAVERY ASSOCIATIONS.** [18??].

8.1239
Heyrick, Elizabeth (Coltman), **IMMEDIATE, NOT GRADUAL ABOLITION: OR, AN INQUIRY INTO THE SHORTEST, SAFEST, AND MOST EFFECTUAL MEANS OF GETTING RID OF WEST INDIAN SLAVERY, WITH AN APPENDIX CONTAINING CLARKSON'S COMPARISON BETWEEN THE STATE OF THE BRITISH PEASANTRY AND THAT OF SLAVES IN THE COLONIES.** 1824. — *see also:* Corfield, Kenneth, "Elizabeth Heyrick: Radical Quaker" in RELIGION IN THE LIVES OF ENGLISH WOMEN, 1760-1930. ed. by Gail Malmgreen. 1986. Heyrick and her female followers demanded immediate emancipation and the evidence suggests that their radical views had little impact on "the male abolitionist leaders [who] adhered to their gradualist policy" (p. 44). The movement attracted women who were brazen enough to "step out of their usual sphere" (p. 50). Yet Heyrick did not translate her zeal to the feminist cause as did other female abolitionists.

8.1240
Scrope, G.P., **PLEA FOR THE ABOLITION OF SLAVERY IN ENGLAND, AS PRODUCED BY AN ILLEGAL ABUSE OF THE POOR LAW, COMMON IN THE SOUTHERN COUNTIES.** 1829.

8.1241
Newcastle Ladies' Anti-Slavery Association, **A CONCISE VIEW OF COLONIAL SLAVERY.** 1830.

8.1242
Ivimey, Joseph, **THE UTTER EXTINCTION OF SLAVERY AS AN OBJECT OF SCRIPTURE PROPHECY; A LECTURE... DELIVERED AT THE ANNUAL MEETING OF THE CHELMSFORD LADIES' ANTI-SLAVERY ASSOCIATION.**

1832.

8.1243

Martineau, Harriet, **TALE OF DEMERARA: ILLUSTRATIONS OF POLITICAL ECONOMY.** 1832. Reform novel whose protagonist concludes that free labor is more humane and economically efficient than slavery; "Views of Slavery and Emancipation" in **SOCIETY IN AMERICA.** by Harriet Martineau. New York, 1837.

8.1244

Glasgow Female Anti-Slavery Society, **AN APPEAL TO THE LADIES OF GREAT BRITAIN IN BEHALF OF THE AMERICAN SLAVE.** 1841.

8.1245

Bristol and Clifton Ladies' Anti-Slavery Society, **SPECIAL REPORT OF THE BRISTOL AND CLIFTON LADIES' ANTI-SLAVERY SOCIETY FROM JANUARY 1851 TO JUNE 1852.** 1852; **STATEMENTS RESPECTING THE AMERICAN ABOLITIONISTS, BY THEIR OPPONENTS AND THEIR FRIENDS: INDICATING THE PRESENT STRUGGLE BETWEEN SLAVERY AND FREEDOM IN THE UNITED STATES OF AMERICA.** Dublin, 1852.

8.1246

TIMES: Sutherland, Duchess of, *"The Affectionate and Christian Address of Many Thousands of the Women of England to Their Sisters, the Women of the United States of America,"* (Nov. 29, 1852) 8. Complete text of a memorial composed by the Duchess of Sutherland, et al., calling for the abolition of slavery. It became known as "The Stafford House Address." ──*see also:* **SPECTATOR:** *"The Lady Abolitionists,"* 25 (1852) 1164; *rpt. in:* **NEW YORK TIMES:** (Jan. 1853) 3. Criticizes the Duchess of Sutherland and her friends for their denouncement of slavery; **SOUTHERN LITERARY MESSENGER:** Tyler, J.G., *"To the Duchess of Sutherland and the Ladies of England,"* 19 (1853) n.p.; **VIRGINIA MAGAZINE OF HISTORY AND BIOGRAPHY:** Pugh, E.L., *"Women and Slavery: Julia Gardiner Tyler and the Duchess of Sutherland,"* 88 (1980) 186-202. "To the defensive South, Julia Gardiner Tyler was the perfect respondent to British abolitionists.... The major portion of Mrs. Tyler's reply [to the Duchess of Sutherland], which so incensed English newspapers, had remarkably little to do either with slavery as an institution or with proslavery arguments.... But one of the themes of her essay was a pointed reminder to English aristocrats that Americans resented foreign intrusion into their domestic affairs. She also repeated a theme... [that] the white worker of England was more to be pitied than the black slave of the South" (p. 193).

8.1247

DE BOW'S REVIEW: McCord, L.S., *"British Philanthropy and American Slavery,"* 14 (1853) 278.

8.1248

Kemble, Frances Ann (Butler), **JOURNAL OF A RESIDENCE ON A GEORGIAN PLANTATION IN 1838-1839.** 1863; New York, 1961; 1969. The journal was published in the interest of preventing the British from entering the American Civil War in support of the South. It records the observations of a former British actress who married an American and was shocked by conditions on his southern plantation. She recorded "the day-to-day operations of the estate as a business enterprise, the lives of several 'classes' of Negro slaves and their white masters, and the plantation's landscape of swamps and woods, canals and rivers, stately houses and decrepit hovels" (bookjacket). Written 25 years previously, the journal was rejected by British publishers. ——*see also:* JOURNAL OF NEGRO HISTORY: Scott, J.A., *"On the Authenticity of Fanny Kemble's Journal of a Residence on a Georgian Plantation in 1838-39,"* 46 (1961) 233-242; Driver, Leota Stulz, FANNY KEMBLE. Westport, 1969.

8.1249
Ladies' London Emancipation Society, FIRST ANNUAL REPORT. 1864. "There are numerous considerations connected with the institution of slavery, which make it... a question especially and deeply interesting for women, and demanding of the fullest excess of their influence and activity" (p. 4).

8.1250
Klingberg, Frank J., THE ANTI-SLAVERY MOVEMENT IN ENGLAND: A STUDY IN ENGLISH HUMANITARIANISM. New Haven, 1926. Discusses the Clapham Sect, in which women were involved.

8.1251
Abel, Annie H. and Klingberg, Frank J., eds., CORRESPONDENCE OF LEWIS TAPPAN AND OTHERS WITH THE BRITISH AND FOREIGN ANTI-SLAVERY SOCIETY. Washington, 1927. Includes information on the media battle waged between the Duchess of Sutherland, an English abolitionist, and Julia Gardiner Tyler, a Southern apologist.

8.1252
AMERICAN HISTORICAL REVIEW: Klingberg, F.J., *"Harriet Beecher Stowe and Social Reform in England,"* 43 (1937-1938) 542-552.

8.1253
JOURNAL OF NEGRO HISTORY: Merrill, L.J., *"The English Campaign for Abolition of the Slave Trade,"* 30 (1945) 382-399.

8.1254
VICTORIAN STUDIES: Spring, D., *"The Clapham Sect: Some Social and Political Aspects,"* 5 (1961) 35-58.

8.1255
Billington, Louis, "Some Connections Between British and American Reform Movements 1830-1860, With Special Reference to the Anti-Slavery Movement," M.A. thesis, Univ. of Bristol, 1966.

8.1256
Bolt, Christine, THE ANTI-SLAVERY MOVEMENT AND RECONSTRUCTION: A STUDY IN ANGLO-AMERICAN COOPERATION, 1833-77. 1969. Includes a discussion of women's work in the movement; (and Drescher, Seymour, eds.), ANTI-SLAVERY, RELIGION AND REFORM. 1980. Series of articles examine women's participation in the abolition and other reform movements.

8.1257
Fladeland, Betty, MEN AND BROTHERS: ANGLO-AMERICAN ANTISLAVERY COOPERATION. Urbana, 1972. Women abolitionists who were rejected by the world antislavery convention in London, 1840, "enjoyed a great deal more publicity... than if they had been quietly seated. Relegated to the gallery, they were

openly 'on display' and were joined from time to time by such British celebrities as Lady Byron and the novelist Amelia Opie" (p. 267).

8.1258
Temperley, Howard, **BRITISH ANTI-SLAVERY 1833-1870.** 1972. While the men in anti-slavery organizations "heartily supported the participation of women in anti-slavery work, and [were] active in sponsoring female auxiliaries [they] did not believe that women... should interfere" (p. 88); "Anti-Slavery" in **PRESSURE FROM WITHOUT IN EARLY VICTORIAN ENGLAND.** ed. by Patricia Hollis. 1974. Examines the predominant role played by Quakers in the abolition movement.

8.1259
Wright, Frances D'Arusmont, **LIFE, LETTERS AND LECTURES. 1834/1844.** New York, 1972. Author may be cataloged as D'Arusmont, Frances Wright.

8.1260
Hurwitz, Edith F., "Anti-Slavery and British Society" in **POLITICS AND THE PUBLIC CONSCIENCE: SLAVE EMANCIPATION AND THE ABOLITIONIST MOVEMENT IN BRITAIN.** 1973. "Women's intense involvement in the Anti-slavery crusade was rooted in the attack on their self image which came from the power structure of the slave society.... Anti-slavery tracts written in the 1820's often addressed themselves directly to women for theirs was a special interest in getting slavery abolished" (pp. 89-90).

8.1261
Taylor, Clare, ed., **BRITISH AND AMERICAN ABOLITIONISTS: AN EPISODE IN TRANSATLANTIC UNDERSTANDING.** Edinburgh, 1974.

8.1262
Chambers-Schiller, Lee V., "The CAB: A Transatlantic Community, Aspects of Nineteenth-Century Reform," Ph.D. diss., Univ. of Michigan, 1977. The Anglo-American community was formed by radical Garrisonians committed to expand the membership of the antislavery movement to include women. CAB ("There were not enough of us to fill a good sized cab") was also dedicated to women's rights and a single moral standard for both male and female behavior. Chambers-Schiller's study is from a multi-dimensional perspective.

8.1263
ANNALS OF THE NEW YORK ACADEMY OF SCIENCES: Walvin, J., *"The Impact of Slavery on British Radical Politics: 1787-1838,"* 292 (1977) 343-355. "The most notable new groups to side with Emancipation were female. In the 1790s, on the other hand, with the exception of Mary Wollstonecraft's contribution, women played no part in the radical societies. But in the 1820s and 1830s female emancipationists provided certain women with their first organized and coherent political role in modern British society. A female Anti-Slavery Society, founded in 1825 in Sheffield with a membership of 80, within a year had distributed 1400 pamphlets, printed 2,000 copies of tracts, and published a collection of antislavery poetry" (p. 351).

8.1264
Wyatt-Brown, Bertram, "Conscience and Career: Young Abolitionists and Missionaries" in **ANTI-SLAVERY, RELIGION AND REFORM.** ed. by Christine Bolt and Seymour Drescher. 1980. "Antislavery women were bound to be unusually

imaginative and alive to moral and political questions.... Yet the road for women was a difficult one. Even in evangelical households, too aggressive an approach to scholarly competition was considered unladylike" (p. 191).

* * *

16. ASSISTED EMIGRATION: CONTEMPORARY AND HISTORICAL PERSPECTIVES

8.1265
Holditch, Robert, **THE EMIGRANT'S GUIDE TO THE UNITED STATES OF AMERICA: CONTAINING THE BEST ADVICE AND DIRECTIONS RESPECTING THE VOYAGE, PRESERVATION OF HEALTH, CHOICE OF SETTLEMENT, ETC. 1818. OBSERVATIONS ON EMIGRATION TO BRITISH AMERICA, AND THE UNITED STATES... FOR THE USE OF PERSONS ABOUT TO EMIGRATE.** [1818].

8.1266
Curtis, C.G., **AN ACCOUNT OF THE COLONY OF THE CAPE OF GOOD HOPE, WITH A VIEW TO THE INFORMATION OF EMIGRANTS; AND AN APPENDIX, CONTAINING THE OFFERS OF GOVERNMENT TO PERSONS DISPOSED TO SETTLE THERE. 1819.**

8.1267
Savage, William, **OBSERVATIONS ON EMIGRATION TO THE UNITED STATES.** 1819. Opposes emigration to the United States, especially to Kentucky. Based on material from the 1790s.

8.1268
Watson, William, **THE EMIGRANT'S GUIDE TO THE CANADAS. 1822.**

8.1269
Faux, William, **MEMORABLE DAYS IN AMERICA: BEING A JOURNAL OF A TOUR TO THE UNITED STATES, PRINCIPALLY UNDERTAKEN TO ASCERTAIN, BY POSITIVE EVIDENCE, THE CONDITION AND PROBABLE PROSPECTS OF BRITISH EMIGRANTS; INCLUDING ACCOUNTS OF MR. BIRBECK'S SETTLEMENT IN THE ILLINOIS: AND INTENDED TO SHOW MEN AND THINGS AS THEY ARE IN AMERICA. 1823.**

8.1270
Cobbett, William, **THE EMIGRANT'S GUIDE; IN TEN LETTERS, ADDRESSED TO THE TAX-PAYERS OF ENGLAND; CONTAINING INFORMATION OF EVERY KIND, NECESSARY TO PERSONS WHO ARE ABOUT TO EMIGRATE; INCLUDING SEVERAL AUTHENTIC AND MOST INTERESTING LETTERS FROM ENGLISH EMIGRANTS, NOW IN AMERICA, TO THEIR RELATIONS IN ENGLAND. 1824.**

8.1271
Boulton, Henry J., **A SHORT SKETCH OF THE PROVINCE OF UPPER CANADA FOR THE INFORMATION OF THE LABOURING POOR THROUGHOUT ENGLAND.** 1826.

8.1272
Traill, Catherine Parr, **THE YOUNG EMIGRANTS; OR PICTURES OF CANADA.** 1826; rpt., Yorkshire and New York, 1969. Children's story of a young woman's experience as an emigrant; **THE BACKWOODS OF CANADA, BEING LETTERS FROM THE WIFE OF AN EMIGRANT OFFICER.** 1846; **THE FEMALE EMIGRANT'S GUIDE, HINTS ON CANADIAN HOUSEKEEPING.** Toronto, 1854; **THE CANADIAN SETTLER'S GUIDE.** Toronto, 1855; 1969. "My female friends must bear in mind that it is one of the settler's great objects to make as little outlay of money as possible. Everything that is done... by the hands of the family, is so much saved or... earned towards the paying for the land, of building houses and barns" (p. 2).

8.1273
HINTS ON EMIGRATION, AS THE MEANS OF EFFECTING THE REPEAL OF THE POOR LAWS. 1828.

8.1274
Buchanan, Alexander Carlisle, **EMIGRATION PRACTICALLY CONSIDERED; WITH DETAILED DIRECTIONS TO EMIGRANTS PROCEEDING TO BRITISH NORTH AMERICA, PARTICULARLY TO THE CANADAS; IN A LETTER TO THE RIGHT HON. F. WILMOT NORTON M.P.** 1828.

8.1275
Head, Francis Bond, **A FEW PRACTICAL ARGUMENTS AGAINST THE THEORY OF EMIGRATION.** 1828; **THE EMIGRANT. BY SIR FRANCIS B. HEAD, BART...** 2nd ed., 1846.

8.1276
NEW MONTHLY MAGAZINE: *"English Residents Abroad, Part II,"* 23 (1828) 559-565. "Another inducement for many a prudent and anxious mother of a family to travel, and even to reside abroad, is the view of marrying her daughters; and this end is not seldom answered" (p. 563).

8.1277
QUARTERLY REVIEW: Southey, R., *"Emigration Report,"* 37 (1828) 539-578. Asserts that emigration will cure the surplus population problem in England and relieve poverty; Palgrave, R.H.I., *"Census of England and Wales, 1871,"* 139 (1875) 525-550. "[The Report] remarks... that in order to induce a corresponding emigration among women to the emigration among men... [female] education should be directed so as to suit the circumstances of country and colonial life" (p. 542); *"Climate and Colonization,"* 190 (1899) 268-270. Supposes women and children to be particularly susceptible to the high heat and humidity of colonial environments in Africa, India, and Canada.

8.1278
Collins, S.H., **THE EMIGRANT'S GUIDE TO AND DESCRIPTIONS OF THE UNITED STATES OF AMERICA... BY S.H. COLLINS.** 1830; rpt., New York, 1971.

8.1279
HINTS TO EMIGRANTS RESPECTING NORTH AMERICA, BY AN EMIGRANT.
Quebec, 1831.

8.1280
THOUGHTS ON EMIGRATION AS THE MEANS OF SURMOUNTING OUR PRESENT DIFFICULTIES. 1831.

8.1281
Colton, Calvin, **MANUAL FOR EMIGRANTS TO AMERICA.** 1831. Encourages artisans and businessmen and their families to emigrate, but not professionals.

8.1282
WESTMINSTER REVIEW: Rainsford, E., *"24 Letters From Labourers in America to Their Friends in England,"* 15 (1831) 138-142. One emigrant, Mary Watson, writes, "I can enjoy a silk and white frock... without a parish grumbling about it. If you are not dressed well here, you are not respected" (p. 141).

8.1283
THE EMIGRANT'S GUIDE; CONTAINING PRACTICAL AND AUTHENTIC INFORMATION, ETC. Westport, 1832.

8.1284
Dunlop, William, **STATISTICAL SKETCHES OF UPPER CANADA, FOR THE USE OF EMIGRANTS: BY A BACKWOODSMAN.** 1832.

8.1285
Ferrall, Simon Ansley, **A RAMBLE OF SIX THOUSAND MILES THROUGH THE UNITED STATES OF AMERICA.** 1832.

8.1286
HINTS AND OBSERVATIONS ON THE DISADVANTAGES OF EMIGRATION TO BRITISH AMERICA, BY AN EMIGRANT. 1833.

8.1287
CONTINUATION OF LETTERS FROM SUSSEX EMIGRANTS IN UPPER CANADA FOR 1833. 1834.

8.1288
Carmichael, Henry, **HINTS RELATING TO EMIGRANTS AND EMIGRATION.** 1834.

8.1289
Doyle, Martin, **HINTS ON EMIGRATION TO UPPER CANADA.** 1834.

8.1290
Marshall, John, **A REPLY TO THE MISREPRESENTATIONS WHICH HAVE BEEN PUT FORTH RESPECTING FEMALE EMIGRATION TO AUSTRALIA.** 1834.

8.1291
Rosier, Ellik, **THE EMIGRANT'S FRIEND... THIRD EDITION, IMPROVED AND**

ENLARGED. 1834.

8.1292

CHAMBERS'S EDINBURGH JOURNAL: *"The Working Classes on the Subject of Emigration,"* 3 (1834) 151-152. Provides information on emigration to Kentucky and adjacent areas. "Men with families find no difficulty in getting them employed... girls, as helps, get, if fifteen years old, one to two dollars per week; they can make well out in sewing, and washing is well paid for" (p. 152).

8.1293

QUARTERLY REVIEW: Barrow, J., *"Emigration—Letters From Canada,"* 54 (1835) 413-429. One woman wrote to her parents: "I never knew the want of victuals or drink since I entered my aunt's house" (pp. 426-427).

8.1294

Peck, John Mason, A NEW GUIDE FOR EMIGRANTS TO THE WEST, CONTAINING SKETCHES OF OHIO, INDIANA, ILLINOIS, MISSOURI, MICHIGAN, WITH THE TERRITORIES OF WISCONSIN AND ARKANSAS, AND THE ADJACENT PARTS. BY J.M. PECK... Boston, 1836.

8.1295

LETTERS FROM SUSSEX EMIGRANTS GONE OUT FROM THE SOUTH SIDE OF THE HILLS TO UPPER CANADA. 1837.

8.1296

TEGG'S HANDBOOK FOR EMIGRANTS. 1839. A "do-it-yourself" handbook aimed at a middle-class audience.

8.1297

Wakefield, Edward Gibbon, A LETTER FROM SIDNEY. 1839. Advocates emigration to extend British markets, relieve population pressure in the U.K. and provide a new field for capital investment. The book emerged from an extensive study of colonial affairs; A VIEW OF THE ART OF COLONIZATION, IN LETTERS BETWEEN A STATESMAN AND A COLONIST. introduction by James Collier. 1849. Correpondence between two public officials, who sign as "The Statesman" and "The Colonist." A section concerning women colonists discusses women's religious nature and their extreme importance to colonization. Asserts that if men like a settlement, women still may find it wanting, but if women find a settlement satisfactory, then that place is truly civilized. *—see also:* BLACKWOOD'S EDINBURGH MAGAZINE: *"Colonisation—Mr. Wakefield's Theory,"* 65 (1849) 509-528; Mills, Richard Charles, THE COLONIZATION OF AUSTRALIA 1839-1842. THE WAKEFIELD EXPERIMENT IN EMPIRE BUILDING. 1915. Credits the advent of responsible government in Australia to the 1829 movement for colonial reform led by Edward Gibbon Wakefield.

8.1298

MONTHLY CHRONICLE: *"Colonies and Emigration: South Australia,"* 4 (1839) 193-208. Encourages adoption of systematic emigration to wastelands, mentioning several programs of assistance. Provides data broken down by age and sex, on the number of emigrants to South Australia in 1838.

8.1299

Colonial Land and Emigration Commission, FIRST SEVEN GENERAL REPORTS

OF THE COLONIAL LAND AND EMIGRATION COMMISSIONERS. 1840-1847. The duties of the commission included reporting on laws and questions relating to colonial areas, collecting statistics, administering the Passenger Acts, dispatching immigrants to the colonies and slave labor to the West Indies, and providing information regarding settlement prospects in the British Colonies; **EIGHTH GENERAL REPORT, ETC...** 1847. Contains information on the destination of male and female emigrants and reports on the districts of Natal and the Cape of Good Hope; **NINTH GENERAL REPORT, ETC...** 1848; **TENTH GENERAL REPORT, ETC...** 1849. Reports on the selection of female emigrants. Single women "of bad character" and women abandoned by their husbands received passages. Discusses religious instruction available in Southern Australia and the different denominations in Cape Town; **FOURTEENTH ANNUAL REPORT, ETC...** 1854. Examines proportion of male to female emigrants, medical examinations performed prior to embarkation, and the number of men and women sent to Victoria in 1852 and 1853; **FIFTEENTH GENERAL REPORT, ETC...** 1855. Reports on the character of emigrants. Shows an unfavorable regard for single women; **SIXTEENTH GENERAL REPORT, ETC...** 1856. Delineates the principal causes for declining emigration and the reasons for the Commissioners' selection of Irish women; **SEVENTEENTH ANNUAL REPORT.** 1857. Reports on Irish emigration, the distribution of men and women, complaints of Irish emigrants, criteria adopted for obtaining more eligible classes to the destitute, and the causes for the decrease in emigration; **EIGHTEENTH GENERAL REPORT, ETC.** 1858. Discusses matrons and schoolmasters in government ships, the demand for female domestic servants in South Australia, and regulations for immigrants from Cape Town; **NINETEENTH GENERAL REPORT, ETC...** 1859. ——*see also:* Hitchins, Fred H., **THE COLONIAL LAND AND EMIGRATION COMMISSION, 1840-1878.** Philadelphia, 1931. Provides background information concerning state-assisted emigration, of which women especially benefited.

8.1300
COLONISATION CIRCULAR: [1840 to 1858]; nos. 1-18. Issued by Her Majesty's Emigration Commission; *"Regulations on the Selection of Labourers,"* no. 6 (1846) 16-19. Lists criteria for the selection of male and female emigrants.

8.1301
Chisholm, Caroline, **FEMALE IMMIGRATION CONSIDERED IN A BRIEF ACCOUNT OF THE SYDNEY IMMIGRANT'S HOME.** Sydney, 1842. Caroline Chisholm (1808-1877) opened an office in Sydney in 1841 to aid emigrants. In 1846 she founded the Female Immigrant's Home and the Female Colonization Society; **COMFORT FOR THE POOR! MEAT THREE TIMES A DAY! VOLUNTARY INFORMATION FROM THE PEOPLE OF NEW SOUTH WALES.** 1847; **EMIGRATION AND TRANSPORTATION RELATIVELY CONSIDERED IN A LETTER DEDICATED TO EARL GREY.** 1847. Introduces a plan to segregate men and women during the voyage; **FAMILY COLONIZATION LOAN SOCIETY, OR, A SYSTEM OF EMIGRATION TO THE COLONIES OF NEW SOUTH WALES, PORT PHILLIP, AND SOUTH AUSTRALIA.** 1850. Chisholm founded this agency to assist the wives and children of ex-convicts in joining their husbands. **THE A.B.C. OF COLONIZATION IN A SERIES OF LETTERS BY MRS. CHISHOLM. NO. I. ADDRESSED TO THE FAMILY COLONIZATION LOAN SOCIETY.** 1850; 1859. Delineates the evils in the existing mode of emigrant transportation; **STORY OF THE LIFE OF MRS. CAROLINE CHISHOLM, THE EMIGRANT'S FRIEND, AND HER ADVENTURES IN AUSTRALIA.** 1852. Autobiography; **THE EMIGRANT'S GUIDE TO AUSTRALIA.** 1860. Specifies who should emigrate and

gives advice about emigration societies, choice of ship, preparation, stores, and outfits. ——*see also:* HOUSEHOLD NARRATIVE: *"Progress of Emigration and Colonisation,"* 1 (1850) 116. *"Progress of Emigration and Colonisation,"* 1 (1850) 140; *"Progress of Emigration and Colonisation,"* 1 (1850) 164-165; *"Progress of Emigration and Colonisation,"* 2 (1851) 210-211. On Caroline Chisholm and the Family Colonization Loan Society; *"Progress of Emigration and Colonisation,"* 3 (1853) 142-143; *"Progress of Emigration and Colonisation,"* 3 (1853) 235. Report of Chisholm's farewell address prior to her departure for Australia; HOUSEHOLD WORDS: Wills, W.H., *"Safety for Female Emigrants,"* 3 (1851) 228. Describes Chisholm's scheme to protect single women by having them migrate with families; MacKenzie, Eneas, MEMOIRS OF MRS. CAROLINE CHISHOLM, AND SKETCHES OF HER PHILANTHROPIC LABOURS IN INDIA, AUSTRALIA AND ENGLAND. 1852. Includes a history of the Female Emigrant's Home; PUNCH: *"A Carol on Caroline Chisholm,"* 25 (1853) 71; RAMBLER: *"Mrs. Chisholm and Emigration,"* 11 (1853) 148-166; Smiles, Samuel, "Mrs. Chisholm" in BRIEF BIOGRAPHIES. by Samuel Smiles. Boston, 1861. Although her mission was to place emigrants as servants, she remarks that "one of the most serious impediments I met with in transacting business in the country, was the application made for wives. Men came to me and said 'Do make it known in Sidney what miserable men we are; do send wives to us'" (p. 514); Harris, R., WHAT HAS MRS. CHISHOLM DONE FOR THE COLONIZATION OF NEW SOUTH WALES? Sydney, 1862; Anstruther, George Eliot, CAROLINE CHISHOLM, THE EMIGRANT'S FRIEND. 1916. Briefly outlines Chisholm's life; Felton, M.P.A., "A Study of Emigration from Great Britain 1802-1860," Ph.D. diss., Univ. of London, 1931. Describes Chisholm's emigration reform efforts; Kiddle, Margaret, CAROLINE CHISHOLM. Melbourne, 1950. Based on material from the United Kingdom and Australia; Hoban, Mary, FIFTY-ONE PIECES OF WEDDING CAKE. Kilmore, 1973. Biography; ATLANTIS: A WOMEN'S STUDIES JOURNAL: Roberts, B., *"Daughters of the Empire and Mothers of the Race: Caroline Chisholm and Female Emigration in the British Empire,"* 1 (1976) 106-127. Contends that Chisholm and her associates were consciously engaged in "empire building," hoping their assistance would enable emigrants to establish model Victorian families in the colonies.

8.1302
EMIGRATION. WHO SHOULD GO; WHERE TO GO; HOW TO GET THERE; AND WHAT TO TAKE. 1843. Aimed at working-class families. Advises against emigration to the United States.

8.1303
Butler, Samuel, THE EMIGRANT'S HAND-BOOK OF FACTS CONCERNING CANADA, NEW ZEALAND, AUSTRALIA, CAPE OF GOOD HOPE, ETC. 1843.

8.1304
Abbott, Joseph, THE EMIGRANT TO NORTH AMERICA. 1844. Based on the experiences of an emigrant family who settled in Canada and later, the western United States. The author, a former missionary of the Society for the Propagation of the Gospel, offers advice to emigrants.

8.1305
Beavan, F., SKETCHES AND TALES. 1845. Woman emigrant describes life in New Brunswick in the 1820s.

8.1306
Mills, Arthur, SYSTEMATIC COLONIZATION. 1847. Sees emigration as the means to reduce the number of public pensioners among women.

8.1307
QUEEN; THE LADY'S NEWSPAPER: 1847 to 1906; vols. 1-119. Contains numerous articles on the emigration of middle-class women; "*Emigration of Educated Women,*" 82 (1886) n.p.; "*The Work of the Women's Emigration Society,*" 44 (1890) 613; "*Women's Emigration Association,*" 60 (1906) 272; "*Training for English Girls as Colonists,*" 91 (1891) n.p.

8.1308
Burton, John Hill, THE EMIGRANT'S MANUAL. AUSTRALIA-AMERICA AND THE UNITED STATES OF AMERICA—NEW ZEALAND, CAPE OF GOOD HOPE, PORT NATAL, ETC. EMIGRATION IN ITS PRACTICAL APPLICATION TO INDIVIDUALS AND COMMUNITIES. 1848; THE EMIGRANT'S MANUAL; AUSTRALIA, NEW ZEALAND, AMERICA AND SOUTH AMERICA. Edinburgh, 1851. Comprehensive guide for the working-class emigrant family.

8.1309
Byrne, J.C., TWELVE YEARS' WANDERINGS IN THE BRITISH COLONIES FROM 1835 TO 1847. 1848. See especially: "Van Dieman's Land; or; Tasmania," for a description of male and female convict life, and "Emigration and Colonization," for remarks on contemporary emigration policies.

8.1310
Maury, Sarah Mytton, AN ENGLISHWOMAN IN AMERICA... AN APPENDIX CONTAINS THE HISTORY OF THE EMIGRANT SURGEON'S BILL. 1848.

8.1311
[Sidney, Samuel and Sidney, John], SIDNEY'S AUSTRALIAN HANDBOOK. HOW TO SETTLE AND SUCCEED IN AUSTRALIA, COMPRISING EVERY INFORMATION FOR INTENDING EMIGRANTS... 1848; SIDNEY'S EMIGRANT JOURNAL: INFORMATION, ADVICE, AND AMUSEMENT FOR EMIGRANTS AND COLONIZERS. 1849.

8.1312
NINETEENTH CENTURY: Holyoake, G.J., "*Emigrant Education,*" 44 (1848) 427-436. Questions whether emigrants of the British Empire can receive adequate education when the Empire is having trouble supporting its labor force. "Where is the manliness of man when women are *compelled* to seek employment? Yet if men do not know how to obtain wages enabling them to keep wives and daughters at home, women must enter the labour market. That women should have to work in factories, *whether able to or not*, is a misfortune to society, present and future. The children of badly paid men are ill-fed and therefore ignorant—for ill-fed children cannot be taught" (p. 435); Morgan, G.O., "*On Well-Meant Nonsense About Emigration,*" 21 (1877) 596-610. "There are persons who think that to draft men and women from the thickly to the thinly inhabited portions of the globe is as easy as to avert water from a higher to lower level" (p. 600); Brabazon, R., "*State-Directed Emigration: It's Necessary,*" 19 (1884) 764-787. "Think of the different future which is in store for the girl who returns from the pauper school to the East End of London, and for her who has been fortunate enough to find her way under the guidance of Miss Rye, or of some other benevolent lady, to a happy country

household in the colonies of England. This is no idle dream. It has been realised over and over again, and might be the destiny of thousands of our destitute boys and girls if only the country could once be made thoroughly to understand that it is not only a wiser, but a more economical policy to give these children a chance of becoming contented and independent citizens in a new country than to coop them up in workhouses or district schools in the old" (p. 771); Campbell, J.D.S., "*A Suggestion for Immigrants,*" 25 (1889) 608-614; Campbell, J.D.S., "*Planting Out State Children in South Africa,*" 47 (1900) 609-611; Hutchinson, M.H., "*Female Emigration to South Africa,*" 51 (1902) 71-87. "The greatest impediment to progress in South Africa from the mother's... point of view is the impossibility of obtaining efficient domestic servants" (p. 71).

8.1313
RAMBLER: Jerningham, F.W., "*Emigration; Now Possible for the Poor,*" 3 (1848) 30-33.

8.1314
SIDNEY'S EMIGRANT JOURNAL: 1848.

8.1315
Cooper, Anthony Ashley, THE SPEECH OF THE RT. HON. LORD ASHLEY, M.P., ON SUBMITTING HIS MOTION, THAT MEANS MAY BE ANNUALLY PROVIDED FOR THE VOLUNTARY EMIGRATION OF A CERTAIN NUMBER OF YOUNG PERSONS OF BOTH SEXES WHO HAVE BEEN EDUCATED IN THE RAGGED SCHOOLS. IN THE HOUSE OF COMMONS, TUESDAY, JULY 24, 1849. 1849.

8.1316
Herbert, Sidney, THE NEEDLEWOMEN AND SLOPWORKERS. 1849. Presents an occupation-specific emigration plan to remedy the problems caused by a surplus of female labor. ——see also: ECONOMIST: "*Mr. Sidney Herbert's Emigration Scheme,*" 7 (1849) 1445-1447. A critic says that sending women to the colonies will only lure more young women to seek their fortunes in London; Sidney, Samuel, FEMALE EMIGRATION——AS IT IS——AS IT MAY BE: A LETTER TO THE RT. HON. SIDNEY HERBERT, M.P.. 1850; Stanmore, Arthur Hamilton-Gordon, SIDNEY HERBERT, LORD HERBERT OF LEA; A MEMOIR. 1906.

8.1317
Harris, Alexander, THE EMIGRANT FAMILY; OR, THE STORY OF AN AUSTRALIAN SETTLER. 3 vols. 1849.

8.1318
Hodgson, Arthur, EMIGRATION TO THE AUSTRALIAN SETTLEMENTS; BEING THE SUBSTANCE OF LECTURES DELIVERED IN 1849. SECOND EDITION. 1849.

8.1319
Kingston, William Henry Giles, A LECTURE ON COLONIZATION. 1849.

8.1320
Prentice, Archibald, A TOUR OF THE UNITED STATES. Manchester, 1849. Advice for emigrating professionals.

8.1321
Ross, Alexander, **ADVENTURES OF THE FIRST SETTLERS ON THE OREGON OR COLUMBIA RIVER: BEING A NARRATIVE OF THE EXPEDITION FITTED OUT BY JOHN JACOB ASTOR, TO ESTABLISH THE "PACIFIC FUR COMPANY"; WITH AN ACCOUNT OF SOME OF THE INDIAN TRIBES ON THE COAST OF THE PACIFIC. BY ALEXANDER ROSS. ONE OF THE ADVENTURERS...** 1849; **THE RED RIVER SETTLEMENT: ITS RISE, PROGRESS, AND PRESENT STATE. WITH SOME ACCOUNT OF THE NATIVE RACES AND ITS GENERAL HISTORY, TO THE PRESENT DAY. BY ALEXANDER ROSS...** 1856.

8.1322
Society for the Promotion of Colonization, **REPORT OF THE GENERAL COMMITTEE. FEBRUARY 1849.** [1849]. The Society would not sponsor single women emigrants under eighteen unless they were with their families or under the immediate care of nearby married relatives. Membership was determined by contributions and members were entitled to receive the society's publications and recommend candidates for emigration at reduced fares. The Society also operated a school fund which financed religious and scholastic instruction on each ship.

8.1323
ECONOMIST: *"The Needlewomen and Emigration,"* 9 (1849) 1447. Contends that exporting 11,000 surplus needlewomen to the colonies would ruin those who serve them, i.e., bakers, grocers, drapers, etc.

8.1324
PLANS OF COMMITTEES FORMED IN TORONTO TO COOPERATE WITH A SOCIETY IN ENGLAND FOR PROMOTING FEMALE EMIGRATION, OF WHICH THE RIGHT HONOURABLE SIDNEY HERBERT IS PRESIDENT. Toronto, 1850.

8.1325
Druitt, Robert, "Medical Hints for Immigrants" in **EMIGRANT TRACTS.** 1850.

8.1326
Kingston, William Henry Giles, **HOW TO EMIGRATE; OR, THE BRITISH COLONISTS, A TALE FOR ALL CLASSES. WITH AN APPENDIX, FORMING A COMPLETE MANUAL FOR INTENDING COLONISTS, AND FOR THOSE WHO MAY WISH TO ASSIST THEM.** 1850.

8.1327
Low, Sampson, Jr., **THE CHARITIES OF LONDON, COMPREHENDING THE BENEVOLENT, EDUCATIONAL AND RELIGIOUS INSTITUTIONS, THEIR ORIGIN AND DESIGN, PROGRESS AND PRESENT POSITION.** 1850; 1852; 1862. Includes information on organizations which assisted female emigrants.

8.1328
Sidney, Samuel, **"THE SETTLERS' NEW HOME"——GUIDE TO EMIGRANTS.** 1850; **THE THREE COLONIES OF AUSTRALIA: NEW SOUTH WALES, VICTORIA, SOUTH AUSTRALIA: THEIR PASTURES, COPPER-MINES, AND GOLDFIELDS... WITH NUMEROUS ENGRAVINGS.** 1852.

8.1329
Society for Promoting Christian Knowledge, EMIGRANT TRACTS. 1850-1852.
Collection of pamphlets containing information and advice for emigrants; THE
EMIGRANT'S CALL. 1872; THE EMIGRANT'S VOYAGE. 1872.

8.1330
HOUSEHOLD NARRATIVE OF CURRENT EVENTS: 1850 to 1856; vols. 1-5;
supplement to: HOUSEHOLD WORDS: *"Progress of Emigration and Colonisation,"*
1 (1850) 18-19. Discusses family colonization, Female Emigration Fund, and aid for
distressed needlewomen to emigrate; *"Progress of Emigration and Colonisation,"* 1
(1850) 260. Describes the arrival in Australia of the first parties of female
emigrants sponsored by Sidney Herbert's organization, the Female Emigration Fund;
"Progress of Emigration and Colonization," 2 (1851) 18-19. Discusses the Female
Emigration Association in Van Dieman's Land, a penal colony in Australia. The
Association's objective was to cooperate with Sidney Herbert's society in England;
"Progress of Emigration and Colonization," 2 (1851) 93. Describes the Family
Colonization Loan Society; *"Progress of Emigration and Colonization,"* 3 (1852) 210.
Contains Caroline Chisholm's advice to young, unmarried female emigrants: "A
female should never remain on deck one minute after the married females retire.
Your character cannot be preserved if you did" (p. 210). Discourse on British Ladies
Female Emigration Society.

8.1331
HOUSEHOLD WORDS: Chisholm, C., *"A Bundle of Emigrant Letters,"* 1 (1850) 19-
24; Chisholm, C., *"Pictures of Life in Australia,"* 1 (1850) 307-310. Discusses church
attendance, dinner in the bush, the need for good wives, and cottages; Wills, W.H.
and Gwynne, F., *"Two Letters From Australia,"* 1 (1850) 475-480; Sidney, S.,
"Family Colonization Loan Society," 1 (1850) 514-515. The purpose of the
organization was to establish "a self-supporting system of emigration for assisting
industrious people and for promoting the spread of sound moral principles" (p. 514);
Cole, A.W., *"Cape Sketches: Cape of Good Hope,"* 2 (1850-1851) 118-120. Describes
colonial women's unsuccessful attempts to employ native women as servants;
Harrold, C.B. and Harrold's sister, *"A Woman's Experience in California,"* 2 (1850-
1851) 450-451. Letters from a young woman who first emigrated to New Zealand
with her brother and entered domestic service with a family there. She later
married and followed the family (with her husband and brother) to California.
Encourages her sister to join her; Wills, W.H., *"Safety for Female Emigrants,"* 3
(1851) 228; Harrold, C.B. and Harrold's sister, *"A 'Ranch' in California,"* 3 (1851)
471-472. Continued from *"A Woman's Experience in California."* Paints a glowing
picture of economic opportunity in the American west. "If a woman has a mind to
work in this country, she can earn as much, or more than, a man" (p. 471); *"A
Rainy Day on the Euphrates,"* 4 (1851-1852) 409-415; Horne, R.H., *"Look Before
You Leap,"* 4 (1851-1852) 497-499; Sidney, S., *"Better Ties Than Red Tape Ties,"* 4
(1851-1852) 529-534. Discusses the Family Colonization Loan Societies; *"From a
Settler's Wife,"* 4 (1851-1852) 585-588. Discusses the Auckland settlement; George,
F., *"An Emigrant's Glance Homeward,"* 5 (1852) 80. Poem and extracts of letters to
England; Wills, W.H., *"Official Emigration,"* 5 (1852) 155-156. Discusses
government assistance; Sidney, S., *"What to Take to Australia,"* 5 (1852) 364-366;
Sidney, S., *"Climate of Australia,"* 5 (1852) 391-392; Morely, H. and Capper, J.,
"Off to the Diggings," 5 (1852) 405-410. Describes an emigrant ship; Sala, G.A.,
"Cheerily, Cheerily," 6 (1852-1853) 25-31. Describes emigrant ships departing from
Liverpool; Sidney, S., *"Lost and Found in the Gold Fields,"* 7 (1853) 84-88. Notices
in Australian newspapers; Capper, J. and Wills, W.H., *"First Stage to Australia,"* 8

(1853-1854) 42-45; Procter, A.A., *"Home-Sickness,"* 9 (1854) 104-105. A poem; *"The New Colonists of Norfolk Island,"* 16 (1857) 476-477; Marryat, Miss, *"Friends in Australia,"* 19 (1859) 584-588.

8.1332
JOURNAL OF THE ROYAL STATISTICAL SOCIETY: *"Return of the Number of Emigrants Embarked, with the Number of Births and Deaths During the Voyage and in Quarantine; the Total Number Landed in the Colony;... with the Number of Souls From Each Country,"* 13 (1850) 275. Provides statistics on men, women and children from Ireland, England, Scotland, Germany, and the Lower Ports; *"Emigration and Immigration in 1892,"* 56 (1893) 312-315.

8.1333
THE EMIGRANT'S FRIEND. SCRIPTURAL INSTRUCTION FOR A LONG VOYAGE. Montrose, 1851.

8.1334
Brown, James Bryce, **VIEWS OF CANADA AND THE COLONISTS. WITH INFORMATION FOR INTENDING EMIGRANTS...** 1851.

8.1335
Chambers, William and Chambers, Robert, "The Emigrant's Manual, British America and the United States" in **CHAMBERS' INSTRUCTIVE AND ENTERTAINING LIBRARY.** 1851. Circulated especially among farm servants and artisans.

8.1336
Fund for Promoting Female Emigration, **FIRST REPORT, MARCH 1851.** 1851. Founded by Sidney Herbert to balance the unequal sex ratio in the colonies and to give destitute working women a means of effective self-support.

8.1337
THE EMIGRANT'S FRIEND; A SELECTION OF [18] TRACTS; BEING A COMPANION FOR THE VOYAGE, ETC. 1852.

8.1338
Meredith, Louisa Anne (Twamley), **MY HOME IN TASMANIA, DURING A RESIDENCE OF NINE YEARS.** 2 vols. 1852; **NOTES AND SKETCHES OF NEW SOUTH WALES, DURING A RESIDENCE IN THAT COLONY, 1839-42.** rpt., Harmondsworth, 1973. Details the voyage and makes numerous observations of colonial society contrasting with that of England. "Bad servants" were the main topic of conversation among Australian sheep farmers' wives.

8.1339
Moodie, Susanna, **ROUGHING IT IN THE BUSH.** 1852. Moodie emigrated to Canada with her husband where, due to bad luck and poor judgement, they went into debt. She subsequently wrote this book to discourage others from following her family's example; **LIFE IN THE CLEARINGS VERSUS LIFE IN THE BUSH.** 1853. The Moodies' experiences in Belleville, a Canadian town, after six years in the wilderness.

8.1340
MacKenzie, Eneas, **MACKENZIE'S AUSTRALIAN EMIGRANT'S GUIDE.** 1852;

THE EMIGRANT'S GUIDE TO AUSTRALIA. 1855.

8.1341
Perley, Moses H., **A HANDBOOK OF INFORMATION FOR EMIGRANTS TO NEW BRUNSWICK.** 1854; rpt., 1857.

8.1342
AINSWORTH'S MAGAZINE: Reeves, A.R., *"Physiology of an Australian Emigrant Ship,"* 25 (1854) 306-317.

8.1343
Foster, Vere Henry Lewis, **WORK AND WAGES; OR, THE PENNY EMIGRANT'S GUIDE TO THE UNITED STATES AND CANADA, FOR FEMALE SERVANTS, LABORERS, MECHANICS, FARMERS, ETC.** 1855.

8.1344
THE EMIGRANT'S DAUGHTER. A TALE THAT IS TOLD. DESCRIPTIVE OF VICTORIA DURING THE STIRRING TIMES THAT FOLLOWED THE DISCOVERY OF GOLD. Tasmania, 1856.

8.1345
Murray, D.A.B., **INFORMATION FOR THE USE OF EMIGRANTS.** 1857.

8.1346
Jukes, Harriet Maria, **THE EARNEST CHRISTIAN. MEMOIR, LETTERS, AND JOURNALS OF HARRIET MARIA, WIFE OF THE LATE REV. MARK R. JUKES.** ed. by Mrs. H.A. Gilbert. 1858. Discusses her experiences as a settler in Canada and later, Ohio.

8.1347
ENGLISH WOMAN'S JOURNAL: Craig, I., *"Emigration as a Preventive Agency,"* 2 (1859) 289-297. Examines emigration as a means to reduce female crime rates and to rehabilitate women criminals; *"British Ladies' Female Emigration Society,"* 5 (1860) 32-36. Details the work of the society and its results; *"Emigrant Ship Matrons,"* 5 (1860) 24-36. Discusses discipline on emigrant ships, harassment of matrons, and the British Ladies Emigration Society; *"On Assisted Emigration,"* 5 (1860) 235-240; 326-335. Suggests assistance for educated ladies to the colonies, especially to New Zealand. Includes letters from female emigrants describing their experiences; Parkes, B.R., *"A Year's Experience in Woman's Work,"* 6 (1860) 112-121. Includes a discussion of bureaucratic reform of female emigration agencies; *"Emigration for Educated Women,"* 7 (1861) 1-19. Advocates government support for educated women to emigrate in order to ease the overcrowded condition of the female work force; W., B., *"Stray Letters on Emigration,"* 9 (1862) 109-117; N., L., *"Our Emigrant,"* 9 (1862) 181-186; *"Letters from Australia and New Zealand,"* 9 (1862) 407-411; Rye, M., *"Female Middle-Class Emigration,"* 10 (1862) 20-30; Rye, M., *"Middle-Class Female Emigration Impartially Considered: The Emigration of Educated Women Examined from a Colonial Point of View. By a Lady Who Has Resided Eleven Years in One of the Australian Colonies,"* 10 (1862) 73-85; Parkes, B.R., *"The Departure of Miss Rye for the Colonies,"* 10 (1862) 261-264; *"The Last News of the Emigrants,"* 11 (1863) 180; Rye, M., *"Another Mail from Miss Rye,"* 11 (1863) 260; Lewin, J., *"Female Middle Class Emigration,"* 12 (1864) 313-317; *"Prospectus of Female Emigrants to South Australia,"* 21 (1873) 271-272.

8.1348
TAIT'S EDINBURGH MAGAZINE: *"Emigration and the Sexes,"* 25 (1859) 509; *"The Three Kingdoms and Their Colonies,"* 25 (1859) 623-634. Contains population, birth and death statistics. "A surplus of 348,364 females in England presents the unnatural consequences of our immigration system" (p. 629). Recommends state support to families to emigrate.

8.1349
TRANSACTIONS OF THE NATIONAL ASSOCIATION FOR THE PROMOTION OF SOCIAL SCIENCE: Stephen, J., *"Colonization as a Branch of Social Economy,"* (1859) n.p.; Rye, M., *"Report on Female Emigration,"* (1862) 811; Hill, F., *"The Emigration of Educated Women Examined from a Colonial Point of View,"* (1862) 812; Lewin, J., *"Female Middle-Class Emigration,"* (1864) 612-616; Layton, E., *"On the Superintendence of Female Emigrants,"* (1864) 616-618. Established in 1849, the British Ladies' Female Emigrant Society provided matrons for the superintendence and training of single women on emigrant ships and supplied homes in London for returning voyagers. Society members also visited emigrants at ports, distributed bibles, tracts, and employment guides, and organized corresponding committees in the colonies.

8.1350
MY EXPERIENCES IN AUSTRALIA. BEING RECOLLECTIONS OF A VISIT TO THE AUSTRALIAN COLONIES 1856-57. BY A LADY. 1860. Written for middle-class emigrants.

8.1351
Brown, James, NEW BRUNSWICK AS A HOME FOR EMIGRANTS: WITH THE BEST MEANS OF PROMOTING IMMIGRATION. 1860; PLAIN AND PRACTICAL LETTERS TO WORKING PEOPLE CONCERNING AUSTRALIA, NEW ZEALAND AND CALIFORNIA, AND SHOWING THE BEST COUNTRY TO WHICH TO EMIGRATE. 1889.

8.1352
Female Middle Class Emigration Society, REPORTS. 1861; 1862-1872; 1880-1882; 1883-1885; LETTER BOOK NUMBER ONE. 1862-1876; LETTER BOOK NUMBER TWO. 1877-1882. The society was founded by Maria S. Rye and Jane Lewin to aid educated women to emigrate and work as nursery governesses.

8.1353
Rye, Maria S., EMIGRATION OF EDUCATED WOMEN... A PAPER READ AT THE SOCIAL SCIENCE CONGRESS IN DUBLIN 1861. 1861. A call for qualified women to emigrate: Rye co-founded with Jane Lewin the Female Middle Class Emigration Society in 1862, to aid educated women who would perform duties as nursery governesses. The Society loaned money for passage, bought necessary cabin fittings, and sent full information about each emigrant to overseas correspondents.

8.1354
HOME AND FOREIGN REVIEW: Moule, H., *"Emigration in the Nineteenth Century,"* 6 (1863) 472-496. Calls emigration a secondary source of national wealth, the primary source being increased home population and production. Advocates government provision of emigration information. Applauds the increasing numbers of female emigrants because they are approaching parity with the number of male emigrants.

8.1355
VICTORIA MAGAZINE: Rye, M., *"Report from Miss Rye From Kaipoi,"* 1 (1863) 571; Taylor, M., *"Redundant Women,"* n.v. (1870) n.p. Proposes emigration as a means to relieve the surplus female population.

8.1356
Rawlings, Thomas, EMIGRATION, WITH SPECIAL REFERENCE TO MINNE-SOTA, U.S., AND BRITISH COLUMBIA. [1864].

8.1357
JOURNAL OF SOCIAL SCIENCE: Rye, M., *"On Female Emigration,"* n.v. (1865-1866) 445-450. Describes colonial climate and conditions as much less severe than that in England. Contends that emigrants fail because of their own deficiencies.

8.1358
GENERAL HINTS TO EMIGRANTS: CONTAINING NOTICES OF THE VARIOUS FIELDS FOR EMIGRATION, WITH PRACTICAL HINTS ON PREPARATION FOR EMIGRATING. 1866.

8.1359
THE CAPE COLONY IN 1868. A HANDYBOOK FOR INTENDING SETTLERS. 1868.

8.1360
THE REAL EXPERIENCES OF AN EMIGRANT. 1868; *also published as:* EXPERIENCES OF AN EMIGRANT.

8.1361
Barker, William T., EMIGRATION PAPERS FOR THE WORKING CLASSES. EMIGRATION TO IOWA. ed. by Ellen Barlee. 1869.

8.1362
Bate, John, EMIGRATION. FREE, ASSISTED, AND FULL-PAYING PASSAGES. [1869]. Tract.

8.1363
Boucherett, Jessie, "How to Provide for Superfluous Women" in WOMAN'S WORK AND WOMAN'S CULTURE. ed. by Josephine Butler. 1869. Response to W.R. Greg's article "Why are Women Redundant?" Whereas Greg recommends the compulsory emigration of women to redress the numerical balance between the sexes, Boucherett responds by advocating the compulsory emigration of men. She claims that male emigration would drive working wages up, thus allowing married women to remain at home while alleviating the economic distress of single women who must compete with men for work.

8.1364
Herring, Armine Styleman, EMIGRATION FOR POOR FOLKES. 1869; LETTERS FROM ABROAD WITH ADVICE TO EMIGRANTS. 1871.

8.1365
MacLeod, Malcolm, PRACTICAL GUIDE FOR EMIGRANTS TO THE UNITED STATES AND CANADA. Manchester, 1870.

8.1366
FRASER'S MAGAZINE: Froude, J.A., *"The Colonies Once More,"* 82 (1870) 269-287. Supports emigration for relief of overpopulation.

8.1367
Conroy, James, **THE EMIGRANT'S WIFE OR ONE IN TEN THOUSAND.** 1871.

8.1368
EMIGRATION! THE EMIGRANTS GUIDE TO THE BRITISH COLONIES AND AMERICA, ETC. 1871.

8.1369
ENGLISHWOMAN'S REVIEW: Hill, F., *"Prospects of Female Emigrants to South Australia,"* 5 (1873) 271-272. "I much fear from what I have heard that women above the hard-working servant class are practically as 'redundant' here as at home. I am amazed by the number of unmarried women of the middle class, many of whom had a hard struggle to maintain themselves" (p. 271); *"Emigration,"* 5 (1874) 96-102. Discusses the importance of emigrant women and children developing skills for employment abroad; *"Emigration of Pauper Children,"* 6 (1875) 132-133; *"Women's Emigration Society,"* 9 (1878) 52-61. "There are an immense number of women in England of all classes who are not at present qualified for remunerative employment in the Colonies, but who are willing so to qualify themselves, and who could so qualify themselves, under proper instruction at very small expenditure of time and money.... There is real need of an organization... which shall seek out, among our redundant female population, those who are able and willing to undertake work in the Colonies; shall aid them, where necessary, in completing their qualifications for such work; shall make all arrangements for their passage out to the colony; and shall there hand them over to some trustworthy and responsible agents, who will find them work as soon as possible, give them a home until that work is found, and act as their friends at any subsequent time, should circumstances require it" (p. 60); Leslie, J., *"Notes on Employments of Women in South Australia,"* 10 (1879) 212-217; *"The Women's Emigration Society,"* 11 (1880) 492-495. "The Colonial Governments have endeavoured to meet this demand, so far as domestic labour goes, by making liberal arrangements for the emigration of women servants, but they have not done anything to help women in their ranks of life" (p. 493); *"Our Surplus Girls,"* 11 (1880) 248-250. "The great disproportion between the sexes continues to increase, injuring both the colonies and the older Country. The excess of the male population over women——in New South Wales, 66,000; in Victoria 84,000, cannot fail to induce many evils; while in England the difficulty of marrying, and the overcrowding of women into every employment, lower the position, morally and socially, of the female sex.... Would these girls not be much happier with their brothers in a new Colony, certain to marry if they wished, and if not, working for good pay where work is not a degradation?" (p. 248).

8.1370
LEISURE HOUR: *"Progress of New Zealand [Immigration and Emigration],"* no. 1194 (1874) 734-735. Presents statistics for male and female emigrants and immigrants of 1872.

8.1371
[King, Harriet Barbara], **LETTERS FROM MUSKOKA BY AN EMIGRANT LADY.**

1878. —*see also:* Dunae, Patrick, **GENTLEMAN EMIGRANTS**. 1981. Quotes King: "It is one thing to sit in a pretty drawing room, to play, to sing, to study, to embroider, and to enjoy social and intellectual converse with a select circle of kind friends, and it is quite another to slave and toil in a log-house, no better than a kitchen, from morning till night, at cleaning, washing, baking, preparing meals for hungry men (not always of one's own family) and drying incessant changes of wet clothes" (p. 28).

8.1372

Clayden, Arthur, **THE ENGLAND OF THE PACIFIC, OR NEW ZEALAND AS AN ENGLISH MIDDLE CLASS EMIGRATION FIELD, A LECTURE**. 1879.

8.1373

Browne, E.L. (Mrs. Walter Browne), **EMIGRATION FOR WOMEN**. [c. 1880-1884]; **EMIGRATION FOR MEMBERS OF THE GIRLS FRIENDLY SOCIETY**. 1883.

8.1374

WORK AND LEISURE: Blanchard, E.L., *"The Emigration of Women."* 5 (1880) 129-134.

8.1375

MACMILLAN'S MAGAZINE: Ross, A., *"Emigration for Women,"* 45 (1882) 312-317. Lists writers, organizations, periodicals and societies who have emigration information about women.

8.1376

Boyd, J.F., **STATE-DIRECTED EMIGRATION**. Manchester, 1883.

8.1377

Brabazon, Reginald, **THE PREVENTION OF THE DEGRADATION OF WOMEN AND CHILDREN**. 1883. Discusses emigration as a preventive measure; **STATE-DIRECTED COLONIZATION: ITS NECESSITY**. 1886.

8.1378

Ffolkes, E.G.E., **LETTERS FROM A YOUNG EMIGRANT IN MANITOBA**. ed. by C.H. Everard. 1883.

8.1379

Potter, George, **IMPERIAL EMIGRATION**. 1883. Supports state-assisted emigration for the poor and working classes.

8.1380

Duncan, Sinclair Thomas, **JOURNAL OF A VOYAGE TO AUSTRALIA BY THE CAPE OF GOOD HOPE, SIX MONTHS IN MELBOURNE, AND RETURN TO ENGLAND BY CAPE HORN, INCLUDING SCENES AND SAYINGS ON SEA AND LAND**. Edinburgh, 1884. Daily experiences on board ship, with personal anecdotes of various passengers. "We found our lady passengers to be, ever ready... to enliven and elevate us, the sterner sex, with their appearance and demeanour, as also with their desire to assist in any times of sickness, and their presence on such occasions was a great source of comfort" (p. 125).

8.1381

Joyce, Ellen, **LETTERS ON EMIGRATION**. 1884; **EMIGRANT'S REST FOR**

WOMEN AND CHILDREN... [1887]; THIRTY YEARS WORK WITH THE GIRLS' FRIENDLY SOCIETY. 1912.

8.1382
Hetherington, Frederick Wallace, **HETHERINGTON'S USEFUL HANDBOOK FOR INTENDING EMIGRANTS. LIFE AT SEA AND THE IMMIGRANT'S PROSPECTS IN AUSTRALIA AND NEW ZEALAND.** 1884.

8.1383
Potter, George, **THE CANADIAN EMIGRANT; BEING A COMPLETE GUIDE TO THE VARIOUS PROVINCES OF CANADA.** 1884.

8.1384
British Women's Emigration Association (afterwards United Englishwomen's Emigration Association), **FINANCE COMMITTEE RECORDS.** 1885-1886. Founded in 1884; **ANNUAL REPORTS.** 3 vols. 1888-1918; **SOUTH AFRICAN COMMITTEE CORRESPONDENCE.** 1889-1900; **MINUTE BOOK.** 1896-1901; **HOSTEL MINUTE BOOK.** 1900-1912; **SUB-COMMITTEE FOR DIFFUSING INFORMATION.** 1903-1905; **PAMPHLETS.** 1905. ——*see also:* Ross, Adelaide, **EMIGRATION FOR WOMEN. BY A MEMBER OF THE UNITED ENGLISHWOMAN'S EMIGRATION ASSOCIATION.** 1886.

8.1385
Paton, Walter B., **STATE-AIDED EMIGRATION.** 1885.

8.1386
Cooke, Bella, **RIFTED CLOUDS OR THE LIFE STORY OF BELLA COOKE.** New York, 1886. An English Methodist, Cooke emigrated to America in 1847. She describes the voyage and her adjustment to the new life.

8.1387
East End Emigration Fund (afterwards British Dominions Emigration Society), **REPORT FOR 1884-1886.** 1886.

8.1388
Paton, Walter B., **THE HANDY GUIDE TO EMIGRATION TO THE BRITISH COLONIES.** 1886. Urges women to emigrate and lists organizations which will aid them; **HANDBOOK OF BRITISH COLONIES.** 1888; 1905.

8.1389
NATIONAL REVIEW: Boyd, J.F., *"The Depression of Trade and State Directed Colonization,"* 7 (1886) 40-53; Brabazon, R., *"State Directed Colonization,"* 9 (1887) 525-537; Narley, R., *"Compulsory Emigration of English Paupers to Western Australia,"* 11 (1888) 142-144; Paterson, A., *"Canadian Immigrants,"* 25 (1895) 399-409.

8.1390
Daly, Harriet W., **DIGGING, SQUATTING AND PIONEERING LIFE IN THE NORTHERN TERRITORY OF SOUTHERN AUSTRALIA.** 1887.

8.1391
Self-Help Emigration Society, **THE OLD COUNTRY AND THE NEW. AN ACCOUNT OF THE WORK OF THE SOCIETY.** 1887.

8.1392
EMIGRANT; THE OFFICIAL ORGAN OF THE CHURCH EMIGRATION
SOCIETY: 1887 to 1889; vols. 1-8.

8.1393
WESTMINSTER REVIEW: *"State-Directed Colonization,"* 127 (1887) 71-82. The
state "assisted family migration or emigration... [to create] settlements of selected
families, not competing for wages... but farming their own lands under the joint
direction of the Imperial and Colonial Governments" (pp. 1-2); MacFie, M.,
"Cultured Colonization," 142 (1894) 673-680. Discusses opportunities for educated
English ladies and gentlemen to place their cultural stamp on the colonies.

8.1394
FORTNIGHTLY REVIEW: Collier, R., *"State Colonisation,"* 44 (1888) 387-398.
Agrees with Canadian women settlers that the male settler should bring his wife and
family to the colony in order to marry off their daughters as soon as possible;
Harkness, M.E., *"Week on a Labour Settlement in Australia,"* 62 (1894) 206-213.
Discusses poor planning and government of the Pitt settlement in Australia,
intended as an opportunity for unemployed men and women to return to the land.

8.1395
JOURNAL OF THE ROYAL SOCIETY OF ARTS: Rankin, J.H., *"Duty of the State
Towards Emigration,"* 36 (1888) 722-733. Advocates state-assisted emigration "so
that persons may be emigrated when they are fit and proper cases for emigration,
and when they will make good emigrants" (p. 731).

8.1396
WOMAN'S WORLD: Joyce, E., *"Emigration,"* 1 (1888) 173-176.

8.1397
Mayo-Smith, Richmond, EMIGRATION AND IMMIGRATION; A STUDY IN
SOCIAL SCIENCE, BY RICHMOND MAYO-SMITH. 1890. Author may be
cataloged as Smith, Richmond Mayo.

8.1398
Church of England, Church Emigration Society, ...THE SOCIETY AND ITS
EMIGRANTS. 1891; QUARTERLY NOTES. 1902; THE ANNUAL REPORT... FOR
THE WORK OF THE YEAR 1907, ETC. [1908].

8.1399
CONTEMPORARY REVIEW: White, A., *"The Colonization Report,"* 59 (1891) 609-
619. Discusses several women involved in the endowment of colonization. Comments
on the confusion and ambiguity of terms rampant in the Report, implying a lack of
systematization in the state's implementing of colonization; Berry, J., Denison, E.L.,
Ossington, Lady, and Phillmore, A., *"Labour Colonies in South Australia,"* 67 (1895)
665-670. Discusses village settlements in Australia for unemployed men, women,
and children.

8.1400
NEW REVIEW: Parker, G., *"Women in the Colonies,"* 11 (1894) 409-417. Concludes
that women who emigrate have a chance to move upward in society. Describes the
healthful and self-sufficient life that emigrants enjoy.

8.1401
BLACKWOOD'S EDINBURGH MAGAZINE: O'Neill, M., *"A Lady's Life on a Ranche,"* 163 (1898) 1-16. Nesta Skrine, wife of a rancher, comments: "In England, on a narrow income, there is no such thing as freedom. You cannot go where you please.... But with the same income in a country like this, you can live on equal terms with your neighbors" (pp. 15-16).

8.1402
Robinson, Miss, "Emigration to South Africa" in **WOMEN IN SOCIAL LIFE. THE TRANSACTIONS OF THE SOCIAL SECTION OF THE INTERNATIONAL CONGRESS OF WOMEN, LONDON, 1899.** ed. by Ishbel Aberdeen. 1900. Presents an emigration scheme for girls to enter domestic service in the colonies and advocates carrying out the plan on a small-scale, personal level of organization.

8.1403
South African Colonization Society, **MINUTES OF COMMITTEE MEETINGS.** 1902-1919.

8.1404
IMPERIAL COLONIST: ORGAN OF THE BRITISH WOMEN'S EMIGRATION SOCIETY AND SOUTH AFRICAN EXPANSION COMMITTEE JOURNAL: 1902 to 1927; vols. 1-25. Edited by Louisa Mary Knightley, Baroness of Fawsley. Published by the Society for the Overseas Settlement of British Women; Ross, E., *"Some Views of the Emigration of Women to South Africa,"* 1 (1902) 79-82; Chitty, [J.R.], *"Imperial Patriotism,"* 3 (1904) 15-16. Contends that female emigration is a patriotic enterprise; Orpen, L., *"Governesses in South Africa,"* 3 (1904) 50-53; Perkins, S.R., *"Openings for Women in South Africa,"* 4 (1905) 87-88; Hopkinson, J., *"On Colonisation of Women in South Africa,"* 5 (1906) 37-43; Joyce, E., *"On Openings for Educated Women in Canada,"* 5 (1906) 100-104; Chitty, J.R., *"The Young Old Maid as Emigrant,"* 5 (1906) 116-118; Clark, G.B., *"Women's Chances in the West,"* 7 (1909) 39-41; *"Are Educated Women Wanted in Canada?"* 8 (1910) 22-24; *"A Visit to the Colonial Training College for Ladies at Stoke Prior,"* 10 (1912) 102-105; Dutton, P., *"Rhodesia for Women,"* 11 (1913) 131-132; *"Overseas Training School for Women,"* 11 (1913) 225-226.

8.1405
Vernon, Miss, **LEATON COLONIAL TRAINING HOME.** Winchester, 2nd ed., 1905.

8.1406
EMPIRE REVIEW: Cooke, C.K., *"The Emigration of State Children,"* 9 (1905) 208-228. The emigration system should be "more in accordance with the rules of public business, which does not impose upon private charity, and which will ensure for the [Poor Law] child some practice-training for a life's work in a new country" (p. 228); *"A State-Aided and State-Directed Scheme of Emigration and Colonization,"* 10 (1905) 1; *"State-Aided Emigration: A National Programme Wanted,"* 11 (1906) 97.

8.1407
Salvation Army, **THE SURPLUS.** 1909. Describes the emigration work of the Salvation Army.

8.1408
EMIGRANTS' INFORMATION OFFICE HANDBOOK. 1910. See especially: "Circular on the Emigration of Women."

8.1409
Colonial Intelligence League, ANNUAL REPORTS. 1911-1915; RECORDS OF COMMITTEES AND COUNCIL MINUTES. 1911-1919.

8.1410
Simcoe, Mrs. John Graves, DIARY OF MRS. JOHN GRAVES SIMCOE. ed. by John Ross Robertson. 1911. Emigrant's diary.

8.1411
Samuelson, James, "Emigration of Poor Children and Youths" in THE CHILDREN OF OUR SLUMS: THEIR SUFFERING, PROTECTION, RESCUE, TRAINING AND AFTER-LIFE. by James Samuelson. Liverpool, 1911. Mentions several of the benevolent associations engaged in seeing that children emigrants from some English slums to Canada are well-settled. Relates a positive report from an emigration reformer named Miss Quarries, which outlines the conditions for children in Canada and the eventual success of many of them in adult colonial life. For example: "After going on to speak of 'our young men taking business courses at college,' and of 'thirty-four marriages during the year,' Miss Quarrier ends her narrative thus: 'Surely few, if any, better investment for a ten pound note can be found than that of placing a Scottish orphan boy or girl in such conditions as those referred to above'" (p. 95).

8.1412
Johnson, Stanley C., A HISTORY OF EMIGRATION FROM THE UNITED KINGDOM TO NORTH AMERICA, 1763-1912. 1913; rpt., 1966. "Women immigrants are of two classes: the escorted and the unescorted" (p. xiii). Examines the work of Emigration Societies and Commissions designed to assist women and discusses opportunities and transportation for middle-class women.

8.1413
Morris, Elizabeth Keith, AN ENGLISHWOMAN IN THE CANADIAN WEST. Bristol, 1913. Contains advice for women emigrants.

8.1414
Thomas, Mary, DIARY AND LETTERS OF M. THOMAS, BEING A RECORD OF THE EARLY DAYS OF SOUTH AUSTRALIA. ed. by E.K. Thomas. 2nd ed., Adelaide, 1915.

8.1415
Marchant, James, "Migration" in BIRTH RATE AND EMPIRE. by James Marchant. 1917. Maintains that a lack of state-sponsored emigration is the reason both for a female surplus in England and a dearth of women in the colonies. Argues that there is "a moral need" for women to migrate to the colonies and links womens' emigration with empire-building.

8.1416
Society for the Overseas Settlement of British Women, ANNUAL REPORTS. 1919, etc. ——see also: Plant, Geoffrey Frederick, S.O.S.B.W.: A SURVEY OF VOLUNTARY EFFORT IN WOMEN'S EMPIRE EMIGRATION. 1950; Plant,

Geoffrey Frederick, **OVERSEAS SETTLEMENT. MIGRATION FROM THE UNITED KINGDOM TO THE DOMINIONS.** 1951.

8.1417
Belcher, Ernest Albert Crossley and Williamson, James A., **MIGRATION WITHIN THE EMPIRE.** Glasgow, 1924. Examines the migration of boys and girls to Canada and includes a summary of Maria Rye's plan of child emigration.

8.1418
Morehouse, F.M.I., "Migration from the United Kingdom to North America, 1840-1850," Ph.D. diss., Univ. of Manchester, 1926.

8.1419
Cowan, Helen I., **BRITISH EMIGRATION TO BRITISH NORTH AMERICA, 1783-1837.** Toronto, 1928.

8.1420
Archer, S.A., compiler, **A HEROINE OF THE NORTH: MEMORIES OF CHARLOTTE SELINA BOMPAS (1830-1917), WIFE OF THE FIRST BISHOP OF SELKIRK (YUKON).** Toronto, 1929. Details experiences at Fort Simpson on the MacKenzie River.

8.1421
Carrothers, William Alexander, **EMIGRATION FROM THE BRITISH ISLES. WITH SPECIAL REFERENCE TO THE DEVELOPMENT OF THE OVERSEAS DOMINIONS.** 1929.

8.1422
Walpole, Kathleen Annette, "Emigration to British North America Under the Early Passenger Acts, 1803-1842," M.A. thesis, London University, 1929; **THE HUMANITARIAN MOVEMENT OF THE NINETEENTH CENTURY TO REMEDY ABUSES ON EMIGRANT VESSELS TO AMERICA.** 1931. Discusses the Passenger Acts, which were intended to protect immigrants, especially women, from abuses during their voyage.

8.1423
Page, Monica Glory, "A Study of Emigration from Great Britain 1802-1860," Ph.D. diss., London School of Economics and Political Science, 1931. Contains information about female emigration societies. Concludes that charitable emigration societies, of which women were significant beneficiaries, were a failure. "They failed to realize... that men and women who had worked and lived always in towns would be useless and unhappy as servants on lonely farms; that life in a mill or a factory is no satisfactory training for hard work in the open air" (p. 217).

8.1424
Lowe, Clara M.S., "Emigration of Families: Emigration of the Young" in **GOD'S RECORD OF ANNIE MACPHERSON'S WORK.** by Clara M.S. Lowe. 1932.

8.1425
Harris, M., "British Migration to Western Australia, 1829-1850," Ph.D. diss., London School of Economics and Political Science, 1934.

8.1426
Woodruff, Douglas, "Expansion and Emigration" in **EARLY VICTORIAN ENGLAND, 1830-1865**. ed. by George Malcolm Young. 2 vols. 1934. Background discussion of colonial policy and transportation in emigration to Canada, Australia, New Zealand, Africa, the West Indies, India, and Ceylon.

8.1427
Madgwick, Robert Bowden, "The Quality of Emigration into Eastern Australia Before 1851," Ph.D. diss., Univ. of Oxford, 1935; **IMMIGRATION INTO EASTERN AUSTRALIA, 1788-1851**. 1937.

8.1428
RECORD OF THE PIONEER WOMEN OF VICTORIA 1835-60. Osbolstone, 1937.

8.1429
Guillet, Edward Clarence, **THE GREAT MIGRATION, THE ATLANTIC CROSSING BY SAILING SHIP SINCE 1870**. 1937. Describes experiences of emigrants from England, Scotland, Ireland travelling on board ship to America.

8.1430
Pickard, O.G., "Midland Emigration," M.A. thesis, Univ. of Birmingham, 1940.

8.1431
Simpson, Helen MacDonald, **THE WOMEN OF NEW ZEALAND**. Wellington, 1940. Intends to give the women their due for the establishment of the colony. Describes the voyage and living conditions of the early settlers.

8.1432
Woodhouse, Airini Elizabeth (Rhodes), **TALES OF PIONEER WOMEN**. 1940. Stories of female British emigrants to Australia during the nineteenth century compiled from notes and testimonies of the women themselves.

8.1433
Huxley, Elspeth Josceline, **ATLANTIC ORDEAL: THE STORY OF MARY CORNISH**. 1941; (and Curtis, Arnold, eds.), **PIONEERS' SCRAPBOOK: REMINISCENCES OF KENYA 1890-1968**. 1980. Foreword by Princess Alice, Duchess of Goucester. Compiled by the East Africa Women's League.

8.1434
Hockly, Harold Edward, **THE STORY OF THE BRITISH SETTLERS OF 1820 IN SOUTH AFRICA**. Capetown, 1948; 1966.

8.1435
Godley, Charlotte, **LETTERS FROM EARLY NEW ZEALAND 1850-1853**. Christchurch, 1951. Traveled to New Zealand in 1849 with her husband, a member of the Canterbury Association which sponsored a colonial settlement there. Text begins with her granddaughter's memoir, which emphasizes Godley's civilizing influence on the colony, "an influence all the more marked for being so largely unconscious." Family had servants and Godley did little, if any, household labor.

8.1436
Plant, George Frederick, **OVERSEAS SETTLEMENT: MIGRATION FROM THE U.K. TO THE DOMINIONS**. 1951. Discusses Wilmot Horton's schemes for

colonization in Canada which advocated state-controlled, state-funded emigration for paupers and intended women to be the chief beneficiaries. Discourses on female emigrants and the training of women to be colonists.

8.1437
Wainright, Miss M.D., "Agencies For the Promotion or Facilitation of Emigration from England to the United States of America, 1815-1861," M.A. thesis, London Univ., 1951.

8.1438
Carrier, Norman H. and Jeffrey, James R., **EXTERNAL MIGRATION: A STUDY OF THE AVAILABLE STATISTICS, 1815-1950.** 1953. See especially: "A Century of Emigration, 1815-1914."

8.1439
Brinley, Thomas, **MIGRATION AND ECONOMIC GROWTH. A STUDY OF GREAT BRITAIN AND THE ATLANTIC ECONOMY.** Cambridge, 1954. See especially: "The Classical View of Emigration," "The Outflow of the United Kingdom," "Demographic Determinants of British and American Building Cycles," and "The Atlantic Economy." Important background work.

8.1440
McCleary, G.F., **PEOPLING THE BRITISH COMMONWEALTH.** 1955. See especially: "British Emigration Before the First World War." Also contains brief general histories of Australia, Canada, New Zealand and South Africa.

8.1441
Shepperson, Wilbur Stanley, **BRITISH EMIGRATION TO NORTH AMERICA: PROJECTS AND OPINIONS IN THE EARLY VICTORIAN PERIOD.** Oxford, 1957. Discusses the general economic causes and popular attitudes which led to the formulation of state-aided emigration policies and the establishment of emigration societies. Also notes how women benefited from such policies and societies.

8.1442
POPULATION STUDIES: Brown, L.B., *"Applicants for Assisted Migration from the United Kingdom to New Zealand,"* 11 (1957) 89-91. "The majority of the applications are from single [men and women] under the age of 30" (p. 91); Erickson, C., *"Emigration from the British Isles to the U.S.A. in 1831,"* 35 (1981) 175-197. "One could conclude that emigration did not help where help was most needed, in the adaptation to urbanization and industrial methods... the contract [of internal migration] with overseas movement appears striking. Women predominated instead of men; young people moved internally with not so wide a spread of age groups as in the overseas movement; single people rather than families were the internal migrants" (pp. 196-197).

8.1443
ALBERTA HISTORICAL REVIEW: May, E.G., *"A British Bride-to-Be Comes to Calgary,"* n.v. (1958) 19-22; Bailey, M.C., *"Reminiscences of a Pioneer,"* 15 (1967) 17-25. Describes settler life in Red Deer, Alberta, 1904-1911.

8.1444
Drummond, Alison, ed., **MARRIED AND GONE TO NEW ZEALAND. BEING EXTRACTS FROM THE WRITINGS OF WOMEN PIONEERS.** Hamilton, 1960.

Profiles of eight emigrant women whose journals, letters, and biographies provide a detailed picture of emigrant life. Well-documented and includes numerous anecdotes, for example, meetings between transplanted English and native New Zealanders. "A story is told of Hannah King, who was boiling rice on her outside-fire, attended by an interested chief. When her back was turned he thrust his hand into the pot to catch the dancing grains. He had never seen boiling water before" (p. 13).

8.1445
Bray, Kenneth, "Government-Sponsored Immigration into South Australia 1872-1886," M.A. thesis, Univ. of Adelaide, 1961. "Of especial interest in South Australia was the high proportion of females in Shetland and Orkney, where so many men were lost fishing" (p. 136).

8.1446
MacDonagh, Oliver, A PATTERN OF GOVERNMENT GROWTH, 1800-1860; THE PASSENGER ACTS AND THEIR ENFORCEMENT. 1961. Identifies seven essential problems associated with voluntary emigration: inequality between parties bargaining on a basic contract; the supplying of many persons outside the settled community; contagious diseases and malnutrition; unsanitary living conditions; sexual promiscuity and sexual offenses arising from co-habitation; physical dangers as a result of poor equipment and careless management; and technical issues derived from new inventions which were successively implemented due to advances in the natural sciences.

8.1447
Wrong, Dennis H., "Migration" in POPULATION AND SOCIETY. by Dennis H. Wrong. New York, 1962. A comprehensive introduction to migration as part of demographics study. Clear and useful, especially for orientation to migration in historical terms.

8.1448
Monk, Una, NEW HORIZONS: A HUNDRED YEARS OF WOMEN'S IMMIGRATION. 1963. Written for the Women's Migration and Overseas Appointments Society. Includes information on agencies designed to assist female emigrants. Also discusses various occupations these women sought.

8.1449
Musgrove, Frank, "The Movement Out (II): The Superfluous Female" in THE MIGRATORY ELITE. by Frank Musgrove. 1963. "Young women of superior education and occupation are probably seeking overseas careers... for substantially the same reason as educated young men: at school they have formed a self-image which includes a period of foreign experience if not actual settlement; and they have been subjected through their education to the forces of 'dislodgement'" (pp. 42-43).

8.1450
ECONOMICA: Ghosh, G.N., "Malthus on Emigration and Colonization," 30 (1963) 45-62.

8.1451
HISTORICAL STUDIES: Robson, L.L., *"The Origins of Women Convicts Sent to Australia, 1781-1852,"* 9 (1963) 43-53; Hammerton, A.J., *"'Without Natural*

Protectors': Female Immigration to Australia, 1832-1836," 16 (1965) 539-566. Analyzes attitudes which inspired state-sponsored emigration of large numbers of single women from England to the colonies, a practice which continued long after both the "surplus woman" argument and state-assisted emigration had ceased to exist; Shultz, R.J., *"Immigration to Eastern Australia 1788-1851,"* 14 (1970) 273-282.

8.1452
Langton, Anne, **A GENTLEWOMAN IN UPPER CANADA, THE JOURNALS OF ANNE LANGTON.** ed. by H.H. Langton. rpt., 1964. ——*see also:* Dunae, Patrick A., **GENTLEMEN EMIGRANTS.** 1981. Langton was unmarried and kept house for her brother John Langton in Canada. An 1840 entry states: "I am afraid women deteriorate in this country more than the other sex" (p. 28).

8.1453
Robson, Lloyd L., **THE CONVICT SETTLERS TO AUSTRALIA.** Melbourne, 1965. Contains accounts of female convicts.

8.1454
ONTARIO HISTORY: Brock, D.J., *"The Account of Two Families who Settled Near Simcoe, 1834-1838,"* 58 (1966) 43-68.

8.1455
McCorkell, Harry Allen, ed., **THE DIARIES OF SARAH MIDGLEY AND RICHARD SKILBECK: A STORY OF AUSTRALIAN SETTLERS, 1857-64.** Melbourne, 1967.

8.1456
Hammerton, Anthony James, "A Study of Middle-Class Female Emigration From Great Britain, 1830-1913," Ph.D. diss., Univ. of British Columbia, 1969. Investigation of emigration as a means for destitute, unmarried gentlewomen to seek and find employment. Based on the documents of women's emigration societies and emigrants' personal communications; "Feminism and Female Emigration, 1861-1886" in **A WIDENING SPHERE: CHANGING ROLES OF VICTORIAN WOMEN.** ed. by Martha Vicinus. Bloomington, 1977; 1980. "Between 1862 and 1914 voluntary societies helped more than twenty thousand women of various classes to emigrate to the British colonies.... The Female Middle Class Emigration society [which] operated from 1862 to 1886... was a feminist organization; its activities touched feminist principles at some sensitive points and brought to the surface some deeply held feminist opinions on class, employment, and marriage" (p. 53); **EMIGRANT GENTLEWOMEN: GENTEEL POVERTY AND FEMALE EMIGRATION, 1830-1914.** 1979. Chapters include "The Problem of the Distressed Gentlewoman," "Pioneer Emigrants, 1832-1836," "Mary Taylor in New Zealand: A Case Study," "Emigration and Respectability, 1849-1853," "Feminism and Female Emigration, 1861-1886," and "Emigration Propaganda and the Distressed Gentlewoman, 1880-1914."

8.1457
Washburn, Enga, **COURAGE AND CAMP OVENS: FIVE GENERATIONS AT GOLDEN BAY.** Sydney and Melbourne, 1970. See appendices for information about emigrant families and their experiences upon arrival in New Zealand.

8.1458
Burton, Clive M., **SETTLERS TO THE CAPE OF GOOD HOPE.**

ORGANIZATION OF THE NOTTINGHAMSHIRE PARTY 1819-1920. Port Elizabeth, 1971. Account of the ruined families who emigrated from Nottinghamshire. Many were rural hosiery makers.

8.1459

Coleman, Terry, **GOING TO AMERICA.** New York, 1972. See especially: "Who Should Go and Why," "Hard-Driven Ships and Brutal Crews," "The Voyage" and "Washed Away; Drowned Altogether."

8.1460

Erickson, Charlotte, **INVISIBLE IMMIGRANTS: THE ADAPTATION OF ENGLISH AND SCOTTISH IMMIGRANTS IN 19TH CENTURY AMERICA.** Coral Gables, Florida, 1972. Consists of collected letters of male and female emigrants. "'[Nov.] 17th, a head wind with a heavy sea, sometimes water on deck. A man struck his wife. So we called our comitty to try him and sentance him and his sentance was that there should be 6 whomen chosen and give him 6 slaps with a handsaw on his backside. So the[y] began and laid him on a barrel. But Mary Fairbrother being the 4th and being inraged, gave him 7 slaps wich made his friends fly in. So it was agreed to let him go'" (p. 149); **EMIGRATION FROM EUROPE, 1815-1914: SELECT DOCUMENTS.** 1976. See especially: "Liverpool As An Emigration Port; 1850," "A Bad Crossing on the Steamship 'Washington'" and "Problems of Regulating Emigrant Vessels" for description of the experiences of emigrant families on board ship.

8.1461

Johnston, Hugh J.M., **BRITISH EMIGRATION POLICY "SHOVELING OUT PAUPERS."** Oxford, 1972. Examines government-supported emigration schemes designed to adjust population growth and increase agricultural production. Asserts that the vast tracts of under-developed colonial land prompted the creation of pauper settlements; *reviewed in:* **HISTORICAL STUDIES:** Buckner, P.A., 16 (1979) 132-134.

8.1462

Steven, John, ed., **MARY TAYLOR: FRIEND OF CHARLOTTE BRONTE. LETTERS FROM NEW ZEALAND AND ELSEWHERE.** 1972. Taylor was a British emigrant to New Zealand where she opened a shop. She emphasized the importance of financial self-sufficiency for women.

8.1463

EMIGRATION IN THE VICTORIAN AGE—DEBATES ON THE ISSUE FROM 19TH CENTURY CRITICAL JOURNALS. introduction by Oliver MacDonagh. 1973. A selection of essays from periodicals.

8.1464

Capper, John, **THE EMIGRANT'S GUIDE TO AUSTRALIA IN THE EIGHTEEN FIFTIES.** Melbourne, 1973. "Should the emigrant be married, so much the better provided the wife be frugal and industrious; such a helper will not only be no expense, but she will often earn nearly as much as the husband" (p. 7). Also speaks of the usefulness of children for the extra household labor they provided.

8.1465

Morris, John, "The Assisted Emigrants to New Zealand, 1871-1879: A Statistical Study," M.A. thesis, Univ. of Auckland, 1973.

8.1466
Summers, Anne, **DAMNED WHORES AND GOD'S POLICE: THE COLONIZATION OF WOMEN IN AUSTRALIA.** 1975. Multi-disciplinary overview. Chapters 8, 9, and 10 deal expressly with the emigration of women to Australia and concentrate on the social difficulties engendered by the huge disproportion of men to women in the colonies. "Female immigrants were subjected to the same kind of treatment as the women convicts [i.e. abuse and enforced whoredom]. Whenever news spread that a shipload of female immigrants was due to arrive hordes of men would assemble at the docks, waiting to claim their share of the imported goods" (p. 277).

8.1467
McLeod, Ellen, **DEAR LOUISA: HISTORY OF A PIONEER FAMILY IN NATAL, 1850-1888. ELLEN MCLEOD'S LETTERS TO HER SISTER IN ENGLAND FROM THE BYRNE VALLEY.** ed. by R.E. Gordon. Durban, 1976.

8.1468
Taylor, P.A.M., "Emigration" in **POPULATION AND EMIGRATION.** by David Victor Glass and P.A.M. Taylor. Dublin, 1976. The commissioners in the Canadian province of Victoria "became obsessed by the problem of the balance of the sexes.... [They] concluded that England could not produce female emigrants in the numbers required, and recommended the resumption of Irish pauper emigration" (p. 79).

8.1469
Kingston, Beverly, **THE WORLD MOVES SLOWLY. A DOCUMENTARY HISTORY OF AUSTRALIAN WOMEN.** 1977. Two chapters examine the issues of criminal transportation and emigration and include discussion of Caroline Chisholm.

8.1470
HECATE: Buckley, S., *"British Female Emigration and Imperial Development: Experiments in Canada, 1885-1931,"* 3 (1977) 26-40. Account of committees in Canada who took care of new emigrants until they found jobs. Highlights the imperialist motives of emigration societies.

8.1471
CANADIAN WOMEN'S STUDIES: *"Pioneer Woman's Advice to Immigrant Women,"* 1 (1978-1979) 29-30. Response to a questionnaire about conditions for immigrants.

8.1472
Malchow, Howard L., **POPULATION PRESSURES: EMIGRATION AND GOVERNMENT IN LATE NINETEENTH-CENTURY BRITAIN.** 1979. An account of the efforts of Maria Rye and Jane Lewin to raise money for emigration assistance to females while also helping them find employment in England as clerks and journalists. Rye eventually "came to despair of opening further employment for women in England and was inclined more and more towards the establishment of some scheme, by which educated women... [could] with safety be introduced into the colonies where social barriers to working women were less onerous and entailed less loss of caste" (p. 59); Discusses such organizations of the National Emigration League and the National Association for Promoting State-Directed Emigration and Colonization; *reviewed in:* **VICTORIAN STUDIES:** Brundage, A., 24 (1981) 364-366.

8.1473
Roberts, Barbara, "A 'Work of Empire': Canadian Reformers and British Female Emigration" in A NOT UNREASONABLE CLAIM: WOMEN AND SOCIAL REFORM IN CANADA, 1880'S TO 1920'S. ed. by Linda Kealey. Toronto, 1979. Argues that reformers intended to build an enduring empire by inculcating middle-class domestic values in their working-class emigrant clients.

8.1474
Colebrook, Vera, ELLEN. Dublin, 1980. Describes the repressed and unhappy life of late Victorian emigrant Ellen Ellis, her emigration to Australia and publication of a novel depicting marriage as legalized slavery.

8.1475
King, Hazel, ELIZABETH MACARTHUR AND HER WORLD. Sydney, 1980; rpt., 1981. "This is the study of a pioneer woman whose colonial experiences began with the arrival of the Second Fleet in Sydney in 1790, and ended with her death in 1850, on the eve of the gold discoveries. Because the hub of her life was her love for her husband and children, this is in part a study of her family, although it has not been possible... to deal with them as fully as they deserve" (p. 1).

8.1476
Parr, Joy, LABOURING CHILDREN: BRITISH IMMIGRANT APPRENTICES TO CANADA, 1869-1924. 1980. Discusses the efforts of evangelical social workers who sent 80,000 children to Canada as laborers and servants.

8.1477
HISTORICAL JOURNAL: Dunkley, P., *"Emigration and the State, 1803-1842: The 19th Century Revolution in Government Reconsidered,"* 23 (1980) 353-380. "If the history of emigrant protection tells us anything, it is that individual initiative and imagination remained fundamental to administrative evolution in the early nineteenth century" (p. 379).

8.1478
REPORTS AND TRANSACTIONS, DEVONSHIRE ASSOCIATION: Brayshay, M., *"Government Assisted Emigration from Plymouth in the Nineteenth Century,"* 112 (1980) 185-211.

8.1479
Arnold, Rollo, THE FARTHEST PROMISED LAND—ENGLISH VILLAGERS, NEW ZEALAND EMIGRANTS OF THE 1870'S. Wellington, 1981. Study of state-assisted emigrants chosen from among English farm laborers.

8.1480
Dunae, Patrick A., GENTLEMAN EMIGRANTS FROM THE BRITISH PUBLIC SCHOOLS TO THE CANADIAN FRONTIER. Vancouver, 1981. See especially pp. 13-29 for the experiences of female settlers in Canada.

8.1481
Light, Beth and Prentice, Alison, eds., PIONEER AND GENTLEWOMEN OF BRITISH NORTH AMERICA, 1713-1867. Toronto, 1981. Oral and written statements from nineteenth-century immigrants themselves. Each personal account is classified according to activities and economic class and gives insight into the

variety of emigrant life. Some examples are "Two Views of Dancing," "An Irish Servant," "On Civil Disobedience," "John Wishes It," "Learning to be Gentlewomen," and "Runaway Wives."

8.1482
ALBION: Blakeley, B.L., *"Women and Imperialism: the Colonial Office and Female Emigration to South Africa 1901-1910,"* 13 (1981) 131-149. Discusses South Africa as a case-in-point demonstrating how imperialist goals necessitated the emigration of women to colonies. Shows how private emigration societies, though funded by the state, ultimately failed. Nevertheless, between "1902-1914, 5,740 women and children were sent to South Africa, a remarkable attempt to strengthen the empire" (p. 148).

8.1483
HISTOIRE SOCIALE/SOCIAL HISTORY: Baehre, R., *"Pauper Emigration to Upper Canada in the 1830s,"* 14 (1981) 339-367. "Of this entire group, 52.1 percent were male, 28.2 percent were female and 19.6 were under fourteen and of either sex. Assuming for the moment that all the females were married, then at least 6.634 men were single" (p. 347).

8.1484
Jackel, Susan, ed., **A FLANNEL SHIRT AND LIBERTY: BRITISH EMIGRANT GENTLEWOMEN IN THE CANADIAN WEST 1880-1914.** Vancouver, 1982. Discusses reasons why people saw a need for female emigration to Canada.

8.1485
Clarke, Patricia, **THE GOVERNESSES: LETTERS FROM THE COLONIES 1862-1882.** 1985. These letters from middle-class women who financed their own voyages abroad reveal the "shocks, disappointments and joys of life in strange and often isolated places" (p. xi).

IX. CRIME AND DEVIANCE

INTRODUCTION*

Any study of the criminality and social deviance of Victorian women must include the journalistic and sociologically minded writings of Henry Mayhew and his collaborators. Beginning publication of his social investigations with articles in THE MORNING CHRONICLE in the 1840s, Mayhew reprinted these and more in several volumes in the 1860s:

9.1int
Mayhew, Henry, **LONDON LABOUR AND THE LONDON POOR**. 4 vols. 1861-1862; rpt., New York, 1968. The fourth volume is subtitled, "Those That Will Not Work, Comprising, Prostitutes, Thieves, Swindlers, and Beggars." It includes an introductory chapter by William Tuckniss, "The Agencies At Present In Operation Within the Metropolis, For the Suppression of Vice and Crime." Mayhew's reports of his investigatory explorations among the "non-workers" include vivid descriptions of women involved in criminal activity and anti-conventional behavior. Lucid prose, graphic illustrations, maps and statistical tables bring the Victorian female underworld to life.

9.2int
Mayhew, Henry and Binny, John, **THE CRIMINAL PRISONS OF LONDON AND SCENES OF PRISON LIFE**. 1862; rpt., 1968. Brings the reader into the prison houses and into the wards where women of all ages were undergoing incarceration and punishments. Graphic illustrations and Mayhew's typically Victorian discourse provide the reader with insights into these women's experiences, and also into Mayhew's own moralistic perspective and beliefs.

Other journalistic social investigators and philanthropic social explorers committed their observations to writing. Thereby, they provided the reading public, philanthropic organizations and governmental agencies with information, interpretations and suggestions for remedial activity on behalf of those they viewed as fallen women. Were relief and control to fail, their suggestions for suitable punishment were not far behind. Books, pamphlets, periodical essays, speeches and testimony before parliamentary committees are the forms in which these contemporary renderings are encased. They comprise important though thoroughly biased sources for the modern researcher in pursuit of female Victorian criminality and deviance. (For references to social investigation of the poor and criminal population, see in this volume, Chap. 8, "Philanthropy, Social Service and Social Welfare," section 2.)

Supplementing sources that represent personal investigations and governmental inquiries are criminal statistics. Valuable discussions of the extent to which these contemporary demographics and calculations of the criminal scene are accurate or problematical include:

9.3int

HARVARD LIBRARY BULLETIN: Peirce, D., "Crime and Society in London: 1700-1900: A Bibliographical Survey," 20 (1972) 430-435. Peirce notes that the London Central Criminal Court Sessional Papers (1835-1913) take up nearly 500 volumes and are a source that is "virtually untapped by historians" (p. 432).

9.4int

Gatrell, V.A.C. and Hadden, T.B., "Criminal Statistics and Their Interpretation" in **NINETEENTH-CENTURY SOCIETY: ESSAYS IN THE USE OF QUANTITATIVE METHODS FOR THE STUDY OF SOCIAL DATA.** ed. by E.A. Wrigley. Cambridge, 1972.

> In any series of criminal statistics the number of offences officially recorded inevitably falls short of the number of offences actually committed. The real incidence of criminal activity, the so-called 'dark figure,' must always remain a matter for informed judgment rather than precise quantification.... Some crimes are more easily detected than others. Serious crimes are more frequently reported than minor ones.... In many cases there will be real difficulty in defining what constitutes a separate crime. But if the actual incidence of crime must in varying degrees remain obscure.... other, more direct, measures of criminal activity... are resorted to.... The officially recorded figures are in fact used by modern criminologists on the unproved, though generally uncontested, assumption that they do bear a fairly constant relationship to the real incidence of the offence in question (pp. 350-351).

9.5int

Gatrell, V.A.C., Lenman, Bruce and Parker, Geoffrey, eds., **CRIME AND THE LAW: THE SOCIAL HISTORY OF CRIME IN WESTERN EUROPE SINCE 1500.** 1980. "It is no wonder that many historians today follow the 'new' criminologists into wholesale scepticism about the legitimacy of using recorded crime rates as indices of 'real' patterns of criminal behavior in society. The tendency nowadays is to see even large aggregations of data as reflecting mainly what ruling groups thought was happening. Court records may be used to build up a picture of how crimes were dealt with, of which social groups were most vulnerable to the attentions of the law, and of the changing preoccupations of the courts. But beyond that, agreement among scholars ceases" (p. 5).

The question of criminal statistics is of special importance in studying rates of female crime. It is generally accepted that women's criminal activity has been underreported from the beginning of official statistics. Historians of crime in England who have included questions of female criminality have speculated that one of the reasons for the great discrepancy in reported crime rates between women and men is that women's criminal deviance may be significantly hidden in the "dark figure" described by Gatrell and Hadden (above). The question of underreported female crime has been undertaken by J.M. Beattie in his pioneering work

9.6int
JOURNAL OF SOCIAL HISTORY: "The Criminality of Women in Eighteenth
Century England," 8 (1975) 80-116; *rpt. in:* **WOMEN AND THE LAW: A SOCIAL
HISTORICAL PERSPECTIVE.** Vol. I, "Women and the Criminal Law," ed. by D.
Kelly Weisberg. 1982.

It is... possible that the underreporting of two... offences, shoplifting and
picking pockets, might have had relatively more effect on the apparent rate
of women's crime than on men's.... Clearly women engaged prominently in
both.... Women frequently worked in pairs, for example, one distracting the
attention of the shopkeeper while the other lifted something; others
contrived special pockets in their clothes... and employed a great variety of
ruses.... Shoplifting by women was certainly very much more common than
the mere number of cases suggests. Women were also prominent among
pickpockets.... both capital offences... and the relative ease with which a
practised thief could make a hit and get away undetected together help
explain the small numbers prosecuted. In addition, many of the women
charged with 'stealing from the person' were prostitutes accused of robbing
their clients. This clearly must have added to the reluctance of many victims
to bring a prosecution.... Far fewer women than men were indicted for the
most serious offences... [accounting] for almost 27 percent of all male
property crime and only 13 percent of female.... Given these broad
tendencies it may be that women's crime was relatively less well reported
than men's (pp. 212-214).

Beattie analyzes female crime in terms of the specifics that are yielded by court
records for Sussex, Surrey and London. He discusses them in the context of these
local societies. He considers rural/urban contrasts of environment, life styles,
relationships and expectations. His interpretations are manifestly informed by
contemporary ideas of women's social and economic position and he does not omit
comparisons within men's. It is a classic work in social history. See also:

9.7int
Beattie, J.M., **CRIME AND THE COURTS IN ENGLAND, 1660-1800.** Princeton,
1986. Beattie includes analysis of the patterns of offenses charged against eighteenth-
century English women and the place of women in the crime/justice milieu under
the following headings: I. Offenses and Offenders Before the Courts: prosecution;
violent offenses; property offenses and offenders; patterns of prosecution and the
character of property crime. II. The Administration of Justice: coming to trial; the
criminal trial; verdicts and pardons; punishment 1660-1750: Transportation;
Punishment, 1750-1800: emergence of imprisonment. His handling of the evidence
is informed by recent theoretical and critical writings.

Another historical work that is focused geographically within a homogeneous
community and compares male and female patterns in criminal and social deviance
is

9.8int
Philips, David, **CRIME AND AUTHORITY IN VICTORIAN ENGLAND: THE
BLACK COUNTRY 1835-1860.** 1977. Coal mining districts had a reputation for
bad moral conditions and a crime rate above the national average; they also had a
particularly high proportion of female offenses. Philips quotes the **MORNING
CHRONICLE:** "Labour and the Poor," 3 (Jan. 1850), linking this to the fact that
"the women work at rude and unsexing labor at the pit mouth, partly assuming the

habiliments and altogether adopting the coarseness of the men" (p. 34 in Philips)....
In 1850-60, men were committed to trial in a ratio of 3 to 1 over women. Ninety
percent of the female committals were for larceny——receiving stolen goods, fraud
and currency offences——acts which required no physical strength for their
commission.... [But] why there is this marked difference in male and female rates at
all is one of the unsolved mysteries of criminology, and very little has been written
which seriously approaches this topic (p. 148).... [also there is] no clear link with
economic conditions for the female committals. This point must be left
inconclusive. And one must not forget that women also figured in some quantity in
offences other than larceny.... The female rate was as high as 1:3 to the male crime
rate... and female criminals, though fewer in number than male, were regarded as
morally worse and more hardened criminals than the men" (p. 150). Philips deals
with additional specific offenses, comparisons and tentative interpretations
throughout the book.

How regional differences, socioeconomic conditions, changes in thought and social
structure as well as administration affected gender-differentiated crime rates in
Wales, London, and Manchester over the Victorian age are among the major the
concerns of

9.9int
Jones, David, **CRIME, PROTEST, COMMUNITY AND POLICE IN NINETEENTH-
CENTURY BRITAIN.** 1982.

> Contemporaries and historians have paid special attention to three groups of
> offenders: females, juveniles and middle-class prisoners.... In the towns [of
> the eighteenth century] women were responsible for a quarter of the
> offences. In the next century between one-fifth and one-third of all
> prisoners in England and Wales were females, the proportion being even
> higher in places like Liverpool and Merthyr Tydfil during the 1840s and
> 1850s.... The peak of female crime in Britain was reached in the years 1857-
> 65, and of those committed to gaol at this time 25.6 per cent (males 30.5)
> were aged under 20 years. Female criminality is, as modern criminologists
> indicate, a difficult subject; women at this time had fewer opportunities to
> commit offences and those that did often received preferential treatment at
> every stage of the legal process. The character of their crime is a good
> index of the kind of pressures to which women, especially single, deserted
> and widowed persons, were subjected in the years before the welfare state
> (p. 7).... There is a wealth of material awaiting the historian of female
> crime, especially in the Liverpool Record Office (p. 211, fn17).

Undertaking a unique approach to the broad question of crime in early nineteenth
century society, George Rude has undertaken "to tackle the old but little explored
question of 'who robbed whom?'" (p. 2) by designing a study that gives equal
weight to both criminal and victim. The three distinctive areas that Rude selected
for close study are Sussex, Gloucester and Middlesex (virtually synonymous with
London) during the period 1800 to 1850. He enumerates the rich archival resources
for records of the courts, prisons and police (pp. 4-5)——notably the Old Bailey
Sessions Papers, "the richest source for case-studies of criminals and victims in the
country" (p. 4):

9.10int
Rude, George, **CRIMINAL AND VICTIM: CRIME AND SOCIETY IN EARLY**

NINETEENTH-CENTURY ENGLAND. Oxford, 1985. Like Beattie, Philips and Jones, Rude's major goal is to penetrate the patterns of crime in particular geographical areas over a specific time period as a methodological approach that will contribute ultimately to the history of criminality in modern Britain. In the course of his study he pointedly contributes to the history of the criminality of English women. An example of how he approaches and considers the available legal and statistical evidence concerns the situation in Sussex:

> There were about 2,000 prisoners tried at quarter sessions in Sussex in our five-year sample between 1805 and 1850... and about half that number at assizes in our ten-year sample between 1810 and 1850. Of those tried at quarter sessions 88.9 per cent were male and 11.1 per cent were female, while at the assizes the latter percentage fell to under 5. Moreover about 70 per cent of all prisoners committed for trial were found guilty by the courts and, therefore, became 'criminal' by definition. So if we are willing to accept that 'criminal' is one who has been convicted by law, we must further conclude that the proportion of the male 'criminals' to female was something in the order of 12 to 1. But was there such a thing as a distinctly female type of crime or criminal?... The more immediate question... is to which social group or class did the prisoner belong?... What proportion were laborers? How many were skilled?... How do the answers... vary between counties? (p. 41).

Rude does not entirely confine himself to convicted criminals. He also considers women and men whose behavior was anti-social and immoral. He illustrates, for example, in his "cases" the proximity of prostitution to criminal activity. Like Beattie, however, he proves that women are represented in crimes of larceny more than in any other category.

On the question of punishment, there are two outstanding studies on the sentence of Transportation to Australia that not only expose the configuration of indictment-to-conviction, but also trace the female convicts from place of sentencing to their destinations. More than the historical considerations of the convicted women discussed above, they focus closely on the actual experiences of those undergoing punishment:

9.11int
Beddoe, Deidre, **WELSH CONVICT WOMEN: A STUDY OF WOMEN TRANS-PORTED FROM WALES TO AUSTRALIA, 1787-1852.** 1979.

> Many contemporary writers denounced the female transportees *en masse* and regarded them as a sub-species, an untouchable caste of near monsters.... [A witness before] the 1837 Commission of Inquiry into Transportation... says, 'They are as bad as is possible for human beings to be'.... When asked if they were dissolute women, he replied, 'Shockingly so; they are drunken... the most disgusting objects that ever graced the female form... far worse than men'.... [But] we should not unquestioningly accept these criticisms and we must recognize the prejudices behind them.... The second fact, which needs to be stated... concerns the reason why women were transported [besides that] they had committed crimes.... There is ample evidence to confirm that the main reason women were transported was for the sexual gratification of both free and convict males (p. 16).

9.12int
Hughes, Robert, **THE FATAL SHORE: THE EPIC OF AUSTRALIA'S FOUND-
ING.** 1986. This is perhaps the most complete description of convict conditions in
the penal colonies of Australia in the early nineteenth century. A woman convict
could have been sentenced to Transportation for having stolen a small article of
clothing from her employer. Life-style, let alone the punishments, was severe. Some
aspects of servitude were veritable slavery:

> And there was punishment by humiliation, whose most hated form was
> shaving the woman's head. This could produce rebellions, as the
> superintendent of the Hobart Factory found in 1827: 'She screamed most
> violently.... She then entered my Sitting Room screaming, swearing, and
> jumping about the Room as if bereft of her senses'.... Naturally this was
> seen as the action of a crazed termagant, not the protest of a woman whose
> physical rights were brutally transgressed.... the pervasive belief in their
> whorishness and worthlessness must have struck deep into the souls of these
> women (pp. 257-258).

When the sentence of Transportation was abolished for both sexes in the mid-
nineteenth century government administrators and social reformers turned new and
more concentrated attention upon the criminal justice system generally and prisons
specifically. Many of the philanthropically-inspired, individualistic reform ideas
and practices of the earlier nineteenth century gave way to conceptions of the
prison houses as impersonal recycling institutions. Whereas the former focused
attention on the prisoner's individual soul, the latter considered the prison
population in the aggregate and in accordance with conceptions of "a criminal class"
or type. Tracing the dynamics of this and other developments over the last century
is the admirable text:

9.13int
Dobash, Russell P., Dobash, R. Emerson, and Gutteridge, Sue, **THE IMPRISON-
MENT OF WOMEN.** 1986. This is the most comprehensive, able work available that
traces from pre-industrial times the ideas, circumstances and practices that led from
local control to systematic incarceration of female offenders who were sentenced to
be punished for breaking the law. The work and recommendations of reformers
such as Elizabeth Fry and Mary Carpenter are studied alongside of the official
decisions and applications of administrators of prisons and penitentiaries. Prisons
under examination are compared and contrasted for their physical structures and
functions as well as for their regimes that provided such punishments as deliberate
humiliation, perpetual surveillance, "irksome toil" and isolation.

> The imprisonment of women in Britain and the United States today reflects
> the end product of a process that has its roots in early nineteenth-century
> British prisons.... A Prison was meant to be a world that would lead to
> physical discipline and moral transformation. From the very beginning,
> women in prison were treated differently from men, considered more
> morally depraved and corrupt and in need of special, closer forms of control
> and confinement.... [The regimes] were shaped by an early emphasis on
> work and religion.... With the development of each new regime something of
> the old has usually remained, resulting in a composite of over a hundred
> years of experimentation blended into routines that shape the daily life of
> the prisoner and the prison. Images of the nature of criminal women and
> theories about the causes of their crimes... often informed the development
> of unique responses to them. The fear, disgust and outrage revealed in these

ideas help to explain the kinds of regimes that were developed to deal with criminal women (p. 1).

Dobash, Dobash and Gutteridge discuss these ideas and their practical application in the prison environment. "Until recently, contemporary research on women in prison was dominated by bio-psychological perspectives about women and girls" (p. 6). In the chapter, "Experts and the Female Criminal" the authors consider the ideas about the nature of criminal women that dominated during the third quarter of the nineteenth century and into the twentieth, focusing on those about environment, physiognomy, physiology and psychiatry. Theories of the philanthropist, Elizabeth Fry; the reformer, Mary Carpenter; the investigator, Henry Mayhew; and the moralist, Frederick W. Robinson (pseud., A Prison Matron) are set into context with the new "scientific" approaches of the medical profession. The leading nineteenth-century theorist in the latter category, Caesare Lombroso, viewed women criminals as pathological anomalies who failed to develop the "natural instincts" of their sex. Dobash, Dobash and Gutteridge show that the formulation and application of parallel and competing theories posed serious consequences to women inmates of penological institutions of the era. They suggest that this impact remains a factor in women's imprisonment, which is a theme also of

9.14int
Box, Steven, "Powerlessness and Crime——The Case of Female Crime" in **POWER, CRIME AND MYSTIFICATION.** 1983. Box is interested even more in comparing crimes and the rate of criminality of women as compared with men. His chapter surveys sociological, criminological and feminist theory and criticism:

> Of course, these various theories of criminal deviance do not explain why females differ from males in their exposure to or possession of just those factors which are more criminogenic.... A supporter of feminism might regard women's social existence in our culture as bad enough without their collective attempts to achieve liberty and equality being viewed pejoratively as criminogenic (p. 188).

Pervading all discussion of the "nature" of female criminality is the fascination of historians and criminologists with the perpetually vast differentials in the rates of indictments and imprisonments of men and women. Especially feminist criminologists have been harsh in their criticism of the attempts that have been made since the last century to account for them philosophically and scientifically. For example:

9.15int
Leonard, E.B., **WOMEN, CRIME AND SOCIETY.** New York, 1982. "Theoretical criminology was constructed by men, about men. It is simply not up to the analytical task of explaining female patterns of crime. Although some theories work better than others, they all illustrate what social scientists are slowly recognizing within criminology and outside the field: that our theories are not the general explanations of human behavior they claim to be, but rather particular understandings of male behavior" (pp. 1-2).

9.16int
Windschuttle, Elizabeth, "Women, Crime and Punishment" in **WOMEN AND CRIME.** ed. by Satyanshu K. Mukherjee and Jocelynne A. Scutt. 1981. "Theories of crime and punishment, both in the past and today, have reflected the ideas and social conflicts of the period and the society they have served. Theories currently

dominating the criminology of women [still] are based on biological and psychological accounts of causality. Women [have been and] are assumed to be subject to unique drives and urges.... Theories of causality... have been incorporated into legal definitions of female crime and lead to uncritical acceptance of official crime statistics" (p. 31).

9.17int

Klein, Dorie, "The Etiology of Female Crime: A Review of the Literature" in WOMEN, CRIME AND JUSTICE. ed. by Susan K. Datesman and Frank R. Scarpitti. Oxford and New York, 1980; *rpt. from:* ISSUES IN CRIMINOLOGY: 8 (Fall 1973) 3-30; *also rpt. in:* Adler, Freda and Simon, Rita James, THE CRIMINOLOGY OF DEVIANT WOMEN. Boston, 1979. Klein examines the theoretical writings of Caesare Lombroso and William Ferrero (1895); W.I. Thomas (1907 and 1923); Sigmund Freud (1933); Kingsley Davis (1961); Otto Pollak (1950); Gisela Konopka 1966); Clyde Vedder and Dora Somerville (1970); as well as John Cowie, Valerie Cowie and Eliot Slater (1968). "The emphasis is on the continuity between these works, because it is clear that, despite recognizable differences in analytical approaches and specific theories, the authors represent a tradition to a great extent. It is important to understand, therefore, the shared assumptions made by the writers that are used in laying the groundwork for their theories" (p. 71 in Datesman and Scarpitti).

9.18int

Smart, Carol, "Criminological Theory: Its Ideology and Implications Concerning Women" in WOMEN AND THE LAW: A SOCIAL HISTORICAL PERSPECTIVE. Vol. 1: "Women and the Criminal Law." ed. by D. Kelly Weisberg. 1982. "There has been virtually no development of our knowledge in [the theoretical] area with the result that ostensibly scientific works predicated upon unexplicated ideologies have been allowed to stand uncriticized.... As a consequence... the ideology and methodological limitation inherent in some of the classical works on female criminality still inform contemporary studies" (pp. 284-285). Smart covers ground similar to that of Klein, applying her own knowledge and insights.

Besides their criticism of theories that have been or need to be discredited and replaced, feminist criminologists urge research that may explain the persistent and profound male-female differentials recorded in criminal statistics since the last century. One alternative assumption to the possibility that the records are wrong is that, if they are right, causation of low female crime may lie in consistent social conditioning of women away from "serious," violent crime. An example might be the indoctrination of "the Victorian feminine ideal." Another possibility is that women's criminal behavior has tended to be contemplated in a mirror that distorts its reflection in terms of contemporary belief, expectations and prejudices. It has been shown that regimes in prisons were designed to train inmates in conformity with ideal types; and that resistance or deviation from expectations of femininity were met with either punishment or treatment for mental illness. Do official records also bear the biases of the authorities responsible for keeping them? With these and related questions in currency, recent feminist writing reflects a distinct trend to revise interpretations of female criminality. Some relevant statements by feminist criminologists include:

9.19int

Dobash, Russell P., Dobash, R. Emerson, and Gutteridge, Sue, THE IMPRISON-MENT OF WOMEN. Oxford, 1986.

The Victorian ideal exalted the cult of domesticity and characterized normal, proper or good women as mothers, dependent wives, sexually passive and morally perfect. By contrast, criminal women were by definition flawed, frequenters of the public world, unchaste, sexually deviant, morally aberrant, unmotherly and the like. At best, they were simply not proper women. At worst, they were monsters, perhaps not even human. This ideal of the private, perfect woman served as the backdrop for evaluating all women and helps to explain the ferocity of those who set about the task of constructing a view of women who found their way into prison (p. 98).

9.20int
Edwards, Susan S.M., **WOMEN ON TRIAL: A STUDY OF THE FEMALE SUSPECT, DEFENDANT, AND OFFENDER IN THE CRIMINAL LAW AND CRIMINAL JUSTICE SYSTEM.** Manchester, 1984. Edwards' unifying theme is an examination of whether women

as suspects, defendants or offenders are dealt with in part in accordance with the degree to which their criminal behavior deviates from what is expected of them in their appropriate gender role. Thus the expression 'women on trial' denotes a lived experience which is double-edged, encompassing not only a consideration of the female defendant's [passage] through the criminal justice system, but also the way in which... [her] culpability... [is] influenced by the degree to which [she]... is a good wife, mother, homemaker, honest, decent and moral, and above all, feminine (p. 1).

9.21int
Carlen, Pat, ed., **CRIMINAL WOMEN: AUTOBIOGRAPHICAL ACCOUNTS.** Cambridge, 1985. "Recent research into sentencing patterns has... suggested that [prison] sentences translate... beliefs concerning the relationships between non-fulfillment of gender role-expectations and female lawbreaking into a sentencing logic which discriminates against women who are not, at the time of their court appearances, able to demonstrate that they are committed to conventional gender roles" (p. 4).

9.22int
Weisberg, D. Kelly, ed., **WOMEN AND THE LAW: A SOCIAL HISTORICAL PERSPECTIVE.** Vol. 1: "Women and the Criminal Law." Cambridge, Mass., 1982.

The essays dramatically illustrate the relation between societal expectations about proper sex-role behavior and the development of the social institutions which embody and reinforce socially defined behavioral norms. Delinquency, deviance, crime and insanity may thus be viewed as departures from social norms or societal expectations about proper sex-role identification. Punishment, treatment and rehabilitation become the societal response to this form of deviance (p. 5).

9.23int
CRIMINOLOGY: Philips, D.M. and De Fleur, L.B., "Gender Ascription and the Stereotyping of Deviants," 20 (1982) 431-448. "The benefits accruing to a female defendant by virtue of her sex may be decreased or lost if her deviant behavior contradicts other sex stereotypic expectations" (p. 436). There are "masculine crimes" and feminine. How does this influence judgment and sentences in courts? "Offenders characterized as 'feminine' will be judged by the general public as mentally ill and nonculpable. Offenders categorized as 'masculine' will be judged as

rational. Feminine offenders will receive less punitive sentencing" (pp. 436-437).

9.24int

Widom, Cathy Spatz, "Perspectives of Female Criminality: A Critical Examination of the Literature" in **WOMEN AND CRIME: PAPERS PRESENTED TO THE CROPWOOD ROUND-TABLE CONFERENCE, DECEMBER 1980.** ed. by Allison Morris with the assistance of Loraine Gelsthorpe. 1981.

> Casual explanations of women's crimes have focused on gender-role expectations (and deviations from such expectations); hypotheses have ranged from physical abnormalities... to various forms of psychological and social pathology. Whereas males have been characterized as 'acting-out' against others, females have traditionally been thought to direct these feelings inwardly against themselves. For women to do otherwise was inappropriate and against societal standards for proper sex-role behavior.... Such assumptions have not only colored our *understanding* of the female offender, but have also influenced the rehabilitative and treatment facilities available (p. 33).

It would seem that these critical, revisionist writers on criminology urge new research strategies and criteria for study and for framing new explanations for female criminality in the past and present. They suggest abandonment of the prejudicial stereotypes of deviant women that have been misguided from the start. Fresh examinations of records should deal fairly with women criminals and bring them into the mainstream of the discipline with new theses for exploration and testing. For example, there is value in the hypothesis that previously held beliefs about female criminality functioned as mechanisms to control and limit their behavior in gender-defined patterns. Representative examples of critical, revisionist writings are:

9.25int

Hutter, Bridget and Williams, Gillian, "Controlling Women: The Normal and the Deviant" in **CONTROLLING WOMEN** ed. by Bridget Hutter and Gillian Williams. 1981.

> Neglect of the study of female criminality and deviance mirrors a general sociological and academic disregard of women as an important or even fit topic of research.... Several writers have pointed out that the reason for the small proportion of women involved in crime may simply be that much illegal behavior of women is masked or invisible.... [or it] occurs in private rather than in public space and thus remains undetected.... Part of women's invisibility in the deviance literature stems from the common assumptions about normal women which prevent a series of questions from being posed and explored (pp. 13-14).

9.26int

Smart, Carol, **WOMEN, CRIME AND CRIMINOLOGY.** 1977.

> Criminology as a subject discipline is... in no way unique in its consistently male-oriented bias, but as a policy-oriented social science it may be seen to have special implications for women which extend beyond the narrow confines of academia to the actual treatment of women in the courts and in penal institutions (p. 1).... Traditionally it has been argued that there has been little research or interest in the area of female criminality because

statistically the numbers of female offenders have been so small and insignificant.... Consequently it has been maintained that there is not enough subject material to justify research. But statistical quantity alone is not sufficient to explain why female offenders are not yet treated as a social problem (p. 2).... Our knowledge of the character and causes of female criminality is at the same stage of development that characterized our knowledge of male criminality some thirty or more years ago.... An important consequence of this lack of development has been the total neglect of any critical analysis of the common-sense perceptions of female criminality informing classical... and contemporary studies (p. 3).

9.27int
CRIME AND DELINQUENCY: Price, R., "The Forgotten Female Offender," 23 (1977) 101-108. "Officially, statistics have supported the assumption that women have been seven to twenty times less involved in criminal behavior than men. But if we correct for overlooking, excusing, forgiving, reluctance to report, unwillingness to hold, and general leniency all along the line from original complaint to imprisonment, the figures may well be more comparable to those for men" (p. 104).

9.28int
Hartman, Mary S., "Introduction" in **VICTORIAN MURDERESSES: A TRUE HISTORY OF THIRTEEN RESPECTABLE FRENCH AND ENGLISH WOMEN ACCUSED OF UNSPEAKABLE CRIMES.** 1977.

> Unsurprisingly, fewer women than men were accused of murder in both England and France, although the percentage of women charged with murder was (and remains) higher than for many other sorts of crime. For example, in England from 1855 to 1874 the annual totals of women tried for murder, which ranged from twelve to forty-two, twice exceeded those for men and normally were at least half as high, whereas women were only a fifth to a quarter of those tried in assize courts for all felonies.... Admittedly women's representation in statistics of those tried for murder (and in crime statistics generally) is probably artificially low for several reasons. The records of coroners' inquests reveal that only a fraction of the known cases of infanticide led to an indictment for what is largely a woman's crime, and infanticides which were never detected are also believed to have been numerous. Moreover, the demonstrated greater popularity of poison among women and the fact that several women were multiple poisoners... supports the view that many deaths by poison which went undetected were women's crimes (pp. 6-7).

9.29int
Millman, Marcia, "She Did It All for Love: A Feminist View of the Sociology of Deviance" in **ANOTHER VOICE: FEMINIST PERSPECTIVES ON SOCIAL LIFE AND SOCIAL SCIENCE.** ed. by Marcia Millman and Rosabeth Moss Kanter. New York, 1975. "Since there haven't been many sociologists who take note of women as deviants, women have largely been ignored in the literature or else abandoned to a few deviant categories (mental illness, prostitution and shoplifting)" (p. 258). ——*see also:* "Images of Deviant Women" in **THE WOMAN QUESTION** ed. by M. Evans. 1982.

9.30int
SOCIAL PROBLEMS: Anderson, E.A., "The 'Chivalrous' Treatment of the Female Offender in the Arms of the Criminal Justice System," 23 (1976) 350-357. "Criminologists... have described the woman offender as receiving more 'lenient'

and/or 'chivalrous' handling in the justice system than her male counterpart. Yet [there is] little if any evidence to support them.... Why has [this claim] been so frequently espoused" (p. 351)? Women are said to have been instigators of crimes while men committed them as the result of female manipulation and seduction. "The thesis that the female criminal is motivated [to act on her own] by economic and/or social reasons is seldom posed, much less explored" (p. 352).

9.31int
Heidensohn, Frances, **WOMEN AND CRIME.** 1985. Heidensohn reaffirms and expands upon statements in her article, **BRITISH JOURNAL OF SOCIOLOGY:** "The Deviance of Women: A Critique and an Enquiry," 19 (1968) 160-175. Two key themes are restated: "the remarkable, indeed perverse exclusion of females from consideration in criminological literature and the distortion of the experiences of women offenders to fit certain inappropriate stereotypes. Notable among these was the tendency to over-sexualize female crime, so that prostitution, for instance, was seen only as sexual deviance and not as the rational choice for some women who need the financial support for themselves and their children. The only remedy for the neglect and distortion of female deviance is a crash programme of research which telescopes decades of comparable studies of males" (p. 161).

It would seem that Heidensohn's suggestion of a "crash program" in criminology research has already begun with the feminist critical writings themselves. It seems also that they have, and will continue to have, a creative influence on the study of the criminality of women that has recently penetrated social history and other scholarly disciplines. No doubt, it will take even further interdisciplinary cooperation in order to reconstruct theoretical, methodological and interpretive bases for building new knowledge in such a neglected field.

*NOTE: For additional references on relevant questions see section 7 in Chapter 4, "Law and the Amendment of the Law," and sections 2 and 3 in Chapter 8, "Philanthropy, Social Service and Social Reform."

* * *

1. A SURVEY OF BACKGROUND WRITINGS FOR FEMALE CRIME AND PUNISHMENT

9.1
Hanway, Jonas, **THE DEFECTS OF THE POLICE, THE CAUSE OF IMMORALITY, AND THE CONTINUAL ROBBERIES COMMITTED, PARTI-CULARLY IN AND ABOUT THE METROPOLIS: WITH VARIOUS PROPOSALS FOR PREVENTING HANGING AND TRANSPORTATION: LIKEWISE FOR THE ESTABLISHMENT OF SEVERAL PLANS OF POLICE ON A PERMANENT BASIS WITH RESPECT TO COMMON BEGGARS; THE REGULATION OF PAUPERS; THE PEACEFUL SECURITY OF SUBJECTS; AND THE MORAL AND POLITICAL CONDUCT OF THE PEOPLE: OBSERVATIONS ON THE REV. MR. HETHERINGTON'S CHARITY: AND THE MOST PROBABLE MEANS OF RELIEVING THE BLIND. IN TWENTY-NINE LETTERS TO A MEMBER OF**

PARLIAMENT. 1775. Complains of general lawlessness and the proliferation of organized crime in London.

9.2
Colquhoun, Patrick, **A TREATISE ON THE POLICE OF THE METROPOLIS CONTAINING A DETAIL OF THE VARIOUS CRIMES AND ARE, AT PRESENT, INJURED AND ENDANGERED: AND SUGGESTING REMEDIES FOR THEIR PREVENTION.** 1796; 7th ed., 1806; rpt., Montclair, 1969. Suggests expansion of the scope of law to encompass crimes against religion and virtue. Recommends modifications in criminal penalties, after-care of prisoners, and invigilation of public houses, and condemns the corruptive influence of certain types, such as ballad singers.

9.3
Philanthropic Society, **AN ACCOUNT OF THE NATURE AND VIEWS OF THE PHILANTHROPIC SOCIETY, INSTITUTED IN... 1788 FOR THE PREVENTION OF CRIMES, ETC. [WITH THE ANNUAL REPORT FOR 1788].** 1799; 1803; 1804; [ANOTHER EDITION. WITH THE REPORT FOR 1813 AND LISTS OF MEMBERS AND SUBSCRIBERS]. 1814.

9.4
Cobbett, William, et al., **COBBETT'S COMPLETE COLLECTION OF STATE TRIALS AND PROCEEDINGS FOR HIGH TREASON AND OTHER CRIMES AND MISDEMEANORS FROM THE EARLIEST PERIOD TO THE PRESENT TIME.** 33 vols. 1809-1826.

9.5
AN ACCOUNT OF THE ORIGIN AND OBJECT OF THE SOCIETY FOR THE DIFFUSION OF KNOWLEDGE UPON THE PUNISHMENT OF DEATH, AND THE IMPROVEMENT OF PRISON DISCIPLINE. [1812].

9.6
STRONG ADMONITIONS TO THE SEVERAL CITIZENS OF LONDON AND WESTMINSTER; WHEREIN ARE SUGGESTED MEANS OF SECURITY AGAINST FIRE, THIEVES, MURDERERS, AND PROSTITUTES, ETC. BY A REFLECTING STRANGER. 1812.

9.7
THE LONDON GUIDE AND STRANGER'S SAFEGUARD AGAINST THE CHEATS, SWINDLERS AND PICKPOCKETS THAT ABOUND WITHIN THE BILLS OF MORTALITY. 1818.

9.8
Russell, W.O., **A TREATISE ON CRIME AND MISDEMEANORS.** 2 vols. 1819; 4th ed., 1865.

9.9
Forsyth, J.S., **A SYNOPSIS OF MODERN MEDICAL JURISPRUDENCE, ANATOMICALLY, PHYSIOLOGICALLY, AND FORENSICALLY, ILLUS-TRATED; FOR THE FACULTY OF MEDICINE, MAGISTRATES, LAWYERS, CORONERS, AND JURYMEN.** 1829. See chapters 33-35, covering infanticide, abortion, concealed birth, rape, and illegitimacy.

9.10
Wade, John, **A TREATISE ON THE POLICE AND CRIME OF THE**

METROPOLIS. 1829; HISTORY OF THE MIDDLE AND WORKING CLASSES, WITH A POPULAR EXPOSITION OF THE ECONOMICAL AND POLITICAL PRINCIPLES... CRIMES, SCHOOLS, EDUCATION, OCCUPATION... 1835.

9.11

Wakefield, Edward Gibbon, FACTS RELATING TO THE PUNISHMENT OF DEATH IN THE METROPOLIS. 1832.

9.12

NEW MONTHLY MAGAZINE: Williams, D.E., *"The Machinery of Crime in England,"* 40 (1834) 487-496.

9.13

FRASER'S MAGAZINE: *"Principles of Police, and Their Application to the Metropolis,"* 16 (1837) 169-178.

9.14

Miles, W.A., POVERTY, MENDICITY AND CRIME; OR THE FACTS, EXAMINATIONS ETC., UPON WHICH THE REPORTED WAS FOUNDED, PRESENTED TO THE HOUSE OF LORDS BY W.A. MILES, ESQ. TO WHICH IS ADDED A DICTIONARY OF FLASH OR CANT LANGUAGE, KNOWN TO EVERY THIEF AND BEGGAR. BY A SOCIOLOGICAL INVESTIGATOR. ed. by H. Brandon. 1839. Condemns the harsh imprisonment of juveniles and women, blaming the poor state of prisons on the increasing prevalence of crime. Contains excerpts of testimony describing poor conditions of prisons by Elizabeth Fry and past inmates. Gives detailed descriptions of frequenters of flash houses and "low lodging houses."

9.15

JOURNAL OF THE ROYAL STATISTICAL SOCIETY: Rawson, R.W., *"An Inquiry into the Statistics of Crime in England and Wales"* 2 (1839) 316-344. Uses judicial statistics for 1835-1839 as a basis for examining the influence of age and sex upon the full volume of crime and on specific types of crimes; Fletcher, J., *"Moral and Educational Statistics of England and Wales"* 11 (1848) 344-366; 12 (1849) 151-335. Changing patterns of social institutions are important factors affecting public morality. Claims that expanding employment opportunities for women are a "moral evil" because they lead to early marriages, illegitimacy, disorder, and general laxity in morals; Clay, J., *"On the Relation Between Crime, Popular Instruction, Attendance on Religious Worship, and Beer-houses,"* 20 (1857) 22-32. "The amount of crime in a county mainly depends on the number of low drinking houses which are suffered to infest it... our present system of popular education is of little or no efficacy in saving the industrial classes from the moral dangers created by those drinking-houses"; Grey, W.A., *"On the Executions for Murder that Have Taken Place in England and Wales During the Last Seventy Years,"* 38 (1875) 463-486. See p. 480 for a table enumerating the number of men and women committed to trial for murder from 1836 to 1874, and p. 485 for a table indicating the relationship of the victims to both male and female murderers; Ogle, W., *"Suicides in England and Wales in Relation to Sex, Season and Occupation,"* 49 (1886) 101-126; 127-135. Statistics indicate that female suicides outnumbered that of males in the 15-20 and the 45-55 age groups. These rates are explained by the "sudden shock given to the female system" at menopause and at puberty, periods also associated with "female lunacy." Women are also said to employ more varied means of self-destruction; *"Discussion on Dr. Ogle's Paper,"* 49 (1886) 127-135.

9.16
Winslow, Forbes, **THE ANATOMY OF SUICIDE**. [1840]. The act of suicide was equated with rebellion against God and the State.

9.17
Bentley, Joseph, **STATE OF EDUCATION, CRIME, ETC.** 1842.

9.18
BLACKWOOD'S EDINBURGH MAGAZINE: Alison, A., *"The Causes of the Increase in Crime,"* 55 (1844) 533-545; 56 (1844) 1-14. Attributes the rising crime rate to accelerated migrations from country to town, and the consequent urban density. Suggests alienation as a factor among London dwellers.

9.19
Symons, Jelinger C., **TACTICS FOR THE TIMES, AS REGARDS THE CONDITION AND TREATMENT OF THE DANGEROUS CLASSES**. 1849. With useful tables showing the number of offenses committed by females in every 10,000 of the population, the proportion of female to male crime in separate industrial areas, and the influence of various employments on female criminal statistics.

9.20
Beames, Thomas, **THE ROOKERIES OF LONDON, PAST, PRESENT AND PROSPECTIVE**. 1850.

9.21
Mayhew, Henry, **LONDON LABOUR AND THE LONDON POOR: THOSE THAT WILL NOT WORK, COMPRISING PROSTITUTES, THIEVES, SWINDLERS AND BEGGARS**. vol. 4, 1851; 1861; 1862; rpt., New York, 1968. Without entirely disassociating the professions, this indispensable source provides descriptions of prostitution, robbery, smuggling, begging, pimping, sharping, and thievery of every variety and provides maps and tables of government statistics on crime, paying attention to women as "partners" as well as criminals. See especially: "Agencies for the Suppression of Vice and Crime" by William Tuckniss.

9.22
Vanderkiste, R.W., **NOTES AND NARRATIVES OF SIX YEARS MISSION PRINCIPALLY AMONG THE DENS OF LONDON**. 1852. Eyewitness accounts of deviant behavior in groups of young criminals, with strong moralistic overtones.

9.23
A Governor, "Gaol Revelations" in **MELIORA. OR, BETTER TIMES TO COME**. ed. by Charles John Chetwynd Talbot, Viscount Ingestre. 1853; rpt., 1971. "The greatest evil and cause of crime is vagrancy [produced by] 1. Poverty and destitution from want of employment. 2. Love of a wandering life, idleness and dissipation. 3. Early habits of loose morality caused by want of proper parental care and instruction. 4. The encouragement given to crime by parents' bad instruction and bad example. 5. The loss of one or both parents" (p. 216).

9.24
Hill, Frederic, **CRIME: ITS AMOUNT, CAUSES AND REMEDIES**. 1853.

9.25
AINSWORTH'S MAGAZINE: Lascelles, M.A., *"The Seven Ages of Poverty and Crime in the Nineteenth Century,"* 24 (1853) 537-545; 25 (1854) 107-118.

9.26
Cave, S., **PREVENTION AND REFORMATION: THE DUTY OF THE STATE OR INDIVIDUALS?** 1856.

9.27
Kingsmill, Joseph, **ON THE PRESENT ASPECT OF SERIOUS CRIME IN ENGLAND AND THE MEANS USED FOR ITS PUNISHMENT AND REPRESSION BY GOVERNMENT; WITH REMARKS ON THE REFORMATORY SCHOOL MOVEMENT.** 1856.

9.28
Neate, Charles, **CONSIDERATIONS ON THE PUNISHMENT OF DEATH.** 1857.

9.29
Society for Promoting the Amendment of the Law, **REPORT FROM THE CRIMINAL LAW COMMITTEE UPON A PAPER BY MR. F. HILL, "ON THE MEANS OF FREEING THE COUNTRY FROM DANGEROUS CRIMINALS," READ... 1857, ETC.** [1857].

9.30
HOUSEHOLD WORDS: Smith, A.R., *"Rogue's Walk,"* 16 (1857) 262-264. On the section of Piccadilly and Haymarket frequented by the underworld.

9.31
MELIORA: *"The Vices of the Streets,"* 1 (1858) 70-79.

9.32
TRANSACTIONS OF THE NATIONAL ASSOCIATION FOR THE PROMOTION OF SOCIAL SCIENCE: Hubback, J., *"Prevention of Crime,"* n.v. (1858) 344-349; Ford, C.R., *"Efforts on Behalf of Criminal Women,"* n.v. (1868) 373-375. Contradicts common opinion that "when once a woman [gives] herself up to a course of crime it [is] hopeless to attempt reformation" (p. 374). Discharged prisoners' homes, "female agents to visit women in their haunts of vice" and other structures turn women away from a criminal lifestyle.

9.33
Pinks, William J., **THE HISTORY OF CLERKENWELL.** ed. by J. Wood., 1865; 2nd ed., 1881. Includes a description of a flash house called the Red Lion Tavern which was a haven for female criminals.

9.34
Taylor, Alfred S., **THE PRINCIPLES AND PRACTICE OF MEDICAL JURIS-PRUDENCE.** 1865. This medical guide covers several varieties of crimes related to women: poisoning, drowning, infanticide and violent wounds.

9.35
Greenwood, James, **THE SEVEN CURSES OF LONDON.** 1869. The seven evils are: neglected children, professional thieves, professional beggars, fallen women, drunkenness, gamblers, and waste of charity. Contains interesting views of women as the objects of crime: "Generally [the door-to-door beggar] is successful. Women—young mothers and old mothers alike——find it hard to resist the artless allusion to the wife, 'weak and ill from her confinement,' and the amazingly well-acted sudden outburst of emotion that the actor is so anxious to conceal under cover of blowing his nose" (p. 251).

9.36
Ritchie, J. Ewing, **THE NIGHT SIDE OF LONDON**. 1869. "Crime must be the natural result of a pictorial literature filthy, sensational, obscene. The annual statistical return furnished from Guildhall to the Home Secretary.... showed that... there had been 6571 prisoners, of whom 5723 were males and 848 females. Of these... 5 females were known thieves; 10 were prostitutes... 4 females were suspicious characters; 2 males and 1 female were habitual drunkards; 154 males and 9 females had previous good characters, and 53 males and 4 females had characters which were unknown" (pp. 30-31).

9.37
JOURNAL OF MENTAL SCIENCE: Thompson, J.B., *"The Hereditary Nature of Crime,"* 15 (1869) 487-498. Claims that crime and insanity are closely allied and presents statistics that show women are just as prone to crime as men.

9.38
SAINT PAUL'S MAGAZINE: Greg, W.R., *"The Disposal and Control of Our Criminal Classes,"* 3 (1869) 599-613.

9.39
Carpenter, Mary, "The Duty of Society to the Criminal Classes" in **AN ADDRESS DELIVERED TO THE CHURCH OF MESSIAH, MONTREAL, SUNDAY, JULY 6, 1873.** [1873].

9.40
Cooper, William M., "Anecdotes of Domestic Birch at Home" and "Extracts from the Diary of a Lady of Quality" in **FLAGELLATION AND THE FLAGELLANTS: A HISTORY OF THE ROD IN ALL AGES AND COUNTRIES.** 1873. Stories of birching of children, servants and apprentices in the home, and beating of wives. Relates an 1856 newspaper article wherein a man refused to abide an injunction to stop beating his wife, saying, "'Am I to obey the laws of God or the laws of man?'" The reverend of his congregation had held that "it was perfectly scriptural for a man to beat his wife" (pp. 396-397).

9.41
MACMILLAN'S MAGAZINE: Ponsonby, C.F.A.C., *"Crime, Criminals and Punishment,"* 29 (1873) 145-154; Moggridge, M.W., *"Reformed Public Houses,"* 38 (1878) 467-474.

9.42
QUARTERLY REVIEW: Gregory, R., *"Criminal Statistics,"* 137 (1874) 526-542; Gregory, R., *"Crime in England,"* 185 (1897) 408-432. Surveys the decrease in crime rates in England due to compulsory education, a decline in pauperism, and a greater number of boys and girls committed to reformatories, day truant schools, and day industrial schools. Statistics reflect the statements that "'In the case of boys and girls under the age of 14, there is practically no difference in social functions. Children under this age are brought up in the same way; they are subjected to almost the same supervision; their social life is the same in all its essential features, and yet boys under fourteen are five times more likely to become offenders than girls of the same age'" (p. 423-424).

9.43
WOMEN'S SUFFRAGE JOURNAL: Becker, L.E., *"Who Are the 'Dregs'?"* 5 (1874) 2-3.

9.44
Hoyle, William, **CRIME IN ENGLAND AND WALES IN THE NINETEENTH CENTURY.** 1876. Includes analysis that breaks down general crime rate by decades, considering such variables as the price of wheat, the state of trade, and substitution of hand labour by machinery. Emphasizes that "by far the greatest proportion of crime of the country results from the intemperance" caused by the proliferation of liquor shops (p. 115).

9.45
Pike, Luke Owen, **A HISTORY OF CRIME IN ENGLAND ILLUSTRATING THE CHANGES OF THE LAWS IN THE PROGRESS OF CIVILIZATION.** vol. 2, 1879. See especially: "And by Comparison of the Crimes of Women With the Crimes of Men." "It follows that, so far as crime is determined by external circumstances, every step made by woman towards her independence is a step towards that precipice at the bottom of which lies a prison" (p. 527).

9.46
Wolstenholme-Elmy, Elizabeth C., **THE CRIMINAL CODE IN ITS RELATION TO WOMEN.** Manchester, 1880. A paper read before the Dialectical Society. Argues that changes in those provisions of the criminal code which affect women are "of the highest importance, inasmuch as it puts an end, for the purposes of criminal prosecutions, to the legal fiction of a wife's absolute subordination to her husband, and recognizes a married woman as a free and responsible moral agent" (p. 5). Author may also be cataloged as Elmy, Elizabeth C. Wolstenholme.

9.47
NATIONAL REVIEW: Hoare, H.E., *"Homes of the Criminal Classes,"* 1 (1883) 224-239; 824-840. A personal account of the author's experiences living among criminals; Gregory, R., *"Is Crime Increasing or Diminishing with the Spread of Education?"* 6 (1886) 772-783; Barnett, H.O., *"The Social Problem of East London Crime,"* 12 (1888) 433-443.

9.48
NINETEENTH CENTURY: Stephen, J.F., *"Variations in the Punishment of Crime,"* 17 (1885) 755-776. In general, proposes granting wide discretion to judges rather than using a pre-determined set of sentences, since circumstances and public sentiment vary widely. As regards rape, for example, "the degree to which a woman resists, her character and conduct, all affect the question of punishment.... I do not remember more than one case in which the punishment was imprisonment and hard labor. If the circumstances justify such a sentence, they are generally such as would justify, if the law permitted it (which I wish it did), an acquittal for rape and a conviction for indecent assault" (p. 774); Bramwell, G.W.W., *"Insanity and Crime,"* 18 (1885) 893-894; Tuke, J.B., *"Lunatics as Patients, not Prisoners,"* 25 (1889) 595-607; Skelton, R.A., *"Statistics of Suicide,"* 48 (1900) 465-482.

9.49
Pelham, Camden, **THE CHRONICLES OF CRIME, OR THE NEW NEWGATE CALENDAR.** 2 vols. 1886.

9.50
Dugdale, Richard Louis, **THE JUKES; A STUDY IN CRIME, PAUPERISM, DISEASE AND HEREDITY.** 1888. The Jukes, a family of criminals, are a case study for the thesis that criminality is inherited.

9.51
Baker, Thomas Banwick Lloyd, 'WAR WITH CRIME': BEING A SELECTION OF
REPRINTED PAPERS ON CRIME, REFORMATORIES, ETC... ed. by Herbert
Philips and Edmund Verney. 1889.

9.52
Ellis, Havelock, THE CRIMINAL. 1891; 1901; rpt., 1977. Gives "a critical summary
of the results of the science now commonly called criminal anthropology" (p. xxix).
"It is worth while to enumerate briefly the probable causes of the sexual variation
in criminality. There are perhaps five special causes acting on women: 1) physical
weakness, 2) sexual selection, 3) domestic seclusion, 4) prostitution, 5) maternity"
(p. 263).

9.53
Morrison, William Douglas, CRIME AND ITS CAUSES. 1891. "It has also to be
born to mind that women are very frequently the instigators of crime and escape
punishment because they are not actually engaged in its commission.... Household
extravagance, extravagance in dress, the mad ambition of many English women to
live in what they call 'better style' than their neighbours sends not a few men to
penal servitude" (p. 154). Crime decreases when financial stability allows women to
devote their lives to their children, "after having themselves been educated mainly
with a view to that great end" (p. 157).

9.54
NEW REVIEW: Hawkins, H., *"Crime and Punishment,"* 8 (1893) 617-620; Hopwood,
H., *"Crime and Punishment,"* 8 (1893) 620-626; Poland, H.B., *"Crime and
Punishment,"* 8 (1893) 626-630; Jay, A.O., *"The East-End and Crime,"* 11 (1894) 401-
408. Crime in the East-End is cyclical and inherited. A way must be devised to
break the cycle since education, philanthropy, religion and law have all failed to do
so; Ferrero, W., *"Suicide Among Women,"* 11 (1894) 637-646. Women who are
destitute do not usually kill themselves. Rather, women kill themselves "when the
tortures of hopeless love become too strong to be longer endured" (p. 640). Asserts
that female love enjoys pain and finds its greatest pleasure in abnegation.

9.55
Lombroso, Cesare and Ferraro, William, THE FEMALE OFFENDER. 1895; New
York, 1897; 1920. A study in "criminal biology" which finds physiological
peculiarities such as "cranial capacity," weight, height, and color and quantity of
hair characteristic of particular types of female criminals and their crimes; *reviewed
in:* PSYCHOLOGICAL REVIEW: Boas, F., 4 (1897) 212. ——*see also:* Mann,
Coramae Richey, "Biological/Constitutional Theories of Female Deviance" in
FEMALE CRIME AND DELINQUENCY. by Coramae Richey Mann. University,
Alabama, 1984.

9.56
MacDonald, Arthur, ABNORMAL WOMAN, A SOCIOLOGIC AND SCIENTIFIC
STUDY OF YOUNG WOMEN, INCLUDING LETTERS OF AMERICAN AND
EUROPEAN GIRLS IN ANSWER TO PERSONAL ADVERTISEMENTS, WITH A
BIBLIOGRAPHY. Washington, D.C., 1895.

9.57
Bliss, William D.P., ed., "With the Cooperation of Many Specialists" in THE
ENCYCLOPEDIA OF SOCIAL REFORM. ed. by William D.P. Bliss. 1897.

9.58
INTERNATIONAL JOURNAL OF ETHICS: Kellor, F.A., *"Sex in Crime,"* 9 (1898) 74-85. Proposes that judicial leniency towards women produces the discrepancy in the amounts of male and female criminality.

9.59
Burnhill, J., **THE MORALS OF SUICIDE**. 2 vols. 1900. Irreligious Board Schools have exacerbated the heathenism of the urban poor and contributed to their rebelliousness against God and their suicidal tendencies.

9.60
Carpenter, Edward, **PRISONS, POLICE AND PUNISHMENT. AN INQUIRY INTO THE CAUSES AND TREATMENT OF CRIMES AND CRIMINALS**. 1905. Drink and property, Carpenter believes, account for nine-tenths of crime in his day. He condemns the harsh punishment of infanticidal mothers and those whose crimes are caused by temporary insanity.

9.61
DICKENSIAN: Dickens, C., *"Ignorance and Crime,"* 3 (1907) 286-288; *rpt. from:* **EXAMINER:** n.v. (April 22, 1848) n.p. Comments on published statistics on persons taken into custody by London's Metropolitan Police. "One extraordinary feature of the tables is the immense number of persons who have no trade or occupation... 17,100 out of 20,500 women. Of these... 9,000 can neither read nor write, 11,000 can only read or read and write imperfectly and only 14 can read and write well!" (p. 288).

9.62
Adam, Hargrave Lee, **THE STORY OF CRIME FROM THE CRADLE TO THE GRAVE**. 1908; **WOMEN AND CRIME**. 1912. "Wrongdoing in the female was an outcome of the malevolent male influence" (p. 4); criminal women are slavishly devoted to brutal men yet female influence causes male crime. Asserts that sexual attraction is the basis for all inclinations towards crime and as women drift away from their responsibilities in maternity, they become more involved in crime; **POLICE WORK FROM WITHIN—WITH SOME REFLECTIONS UPON WOMEN, THE LAW AND LAWYERS**. 1913. Relates the participation of women in crime to late nineteenth- and early twentieth-century feminist protests against Victorian feminine ideals and roles. Contends that feminists are "social hermaphrodites" who have a negative influence on men. "It is a well-established fact with the police and criminologists generally that female criminals are infinitely worse than the worst of male criminals" (p. 37).

9.63
Devon, James, **THE CRIMINAL AND THE COMMUNITY**. 1912. Extensive theoretical discussion of crime as a social question. Many references to women's participation in such crimes as bigamy and theft, and women as "decoys" in collaboration with men.

9.64
Ives, George, **A HISTORY OF PENAL METHODS: CRIMINALS, WITCHES, LUNATICS**. 1914; rpt., Montclair, 1970. General history of crimes and criminals with revealing examples of contemporary thought on women as targets of violence and as offenders of all types.

9.65
Read, Alfred Baker, **SOCIAL CHAOS AND THE WAY OUT**. 1914. Traces the

cause of crime to overpopulation and the poverty it engenders.

9.66

HOWARD JOURNAL OF PENOLOGY AND CRIME PREVENTION: 1921; vol. 1.

9.67

Thomas, William I., **THE UNADJUSTED GIRL. WITH CASES AND STANDPOINT FOR BEHAVIOR ANALYSIS.** ed. by Benjamin Nelson. introduction by Michael Parenti. 1923; 1967. Draws on such social observers as the Webbs and Havelock Ellis. Valuable for its rich accounts by women who became prostitutes and deviants, exploring how they were introduced to sex, their attitudes toward sex and prostitution, and the influence of rigid control by their Victorian parents.

9.68

Philips, Margaret and Tomkins, W.S., "The Woman Criminal" in **ENGLISH WOMEN IN LIFE AND LETTERS.** by Margaret Philips and W.S. Tomkins. 1926. Discusses some of the methods of punishment meted out to women during the eighteenth century and includes a brief account of reforms realized by Elizabeth Fry.

9.69

London School of Economics and Political Science, **THE NEW SURVEY OF LONDON LIFE AND LABOUR.** 9 vols. 1930-1935.

9.70

Wilson, Margaret, **THE CRIME OF PUNISHMENT.** New York, 1931. Criticizes traditional methods of civil punishment for men and women. Advises women to take action, be critical, and evaluate their relation to crime and the law in comparison to men.

9.71

Dangerfield, George, **THE STRANGE DEATH OF LIBERAL ENGLAND 1910-1914.** New York, 1935. See especially: "The Women's Rebellion" and "The Pankhursts Provide a Clew." Author describes the Militant Suffragette Movement in which suffragists engaged in criminal acts in agitating for women's rights. "The record of suffragette arson for the first seven months of 1914 was an impressive one——no less than 107 buildings were set on fire" (p. 368). Suffragists were a target for abuse as well. In a demonstration on Parliament, later known as Black Friday, police responded brutally: "Women were struck with fists and knees, knocked down.... They were pummelled and they were pinched, their thumbs were forced back, their arms twisted, their breasts gripped, their faces rubbed against the pailings... indeed, one woman is said to have died, a year later, as the result of having been indecently assaulted in a side street" (pp. 159-160).

9.72

Henderson, William, ed., **VICTORIAN STREET BALLADS.** 1937. See "Introduction" and "Crime and Horror," which includes such songs as "Execution of Alice Holt," "Ladies Don't Go Thieving," "Female Transport," "Shocking Rape and Murder," and "Penal Servitude for Mrs. Maybrick." Interesting illustrations.

9.73

JOURNALISM QUARTERLY: Peterson, T., *"British Crime Pamphleteers: Forgotten Journalists"* 22 (1945) 305-316. Gives history of crime pamphleteering, most popular from the mid-1700's to the mid-1800's. The pamphlets describe crimes with fearless attention to detail, catering to the public fancy for gore and sentiment.

9.74
Partridge, Eric, **A DICTIONARY OF THE UNDERWORLD**. 1949; 1961. Subtitled: "Being the Vocabularies of Crooks Criminals Racketeers Beggars and Tramps Convicts The Commercial Underworld The Drug Traffic The White Slave Traffic Spivs." Excellent source for uncovering general women's history as well as women's association with crime in the 19th century. Examples: The definition of "abbess" is "a bawd, a female brothel-keeper," an "abishag" is "an illegitimate child of a mother who has been seduced by a married man," and an "arch dell" is "the female head of a gang of criminals and/or vagabonds." See pp. 248-250 for accounts of criminals associated with flash houses.

9.75
Pollak, Otto, **THE CRIMINALITY OF WOMEN**. Philadelphia, 1950. The amount of female crime has been greatly underestimated by traditional opinion, one reason being that crime is considered part of the male sphere. Women's criminality "reflects their biological nature in a given cultural setting"; *reviewed in:* **PSYCHOANALYTIC QUARTERLY**: Mohr, G., 21 (1952) 262-264. Reviewer sums Pollak's view: "Woman's predilection toward concealment, social attitudes toward women, and the nature of the crimes committed, all tend toward concealing crime committed by women" (p. 263). Stresses biological analysis: "Predilection toward concealment is postulated as an expression of woman's physiologically determined capacity for concealment of her true feelings in the sphere of sexual relations.... Women can feign sexual responsiveness; men cannot" (p. 263).

9.76
Fry, S. Margery, "Tides of Opinion" in **ARMS OF THE LAW**. by S. Margery Fry. 1951. Surveys eighteenth- and early nineteenth-century social critics whose philosophies were instrumental in nineteenth-century penal reform movements.

9.77
Abrahamsen, David, **WHO ARE THE GUILTY? A STUDY OF EDUCATION AND CRIME**. 1954.

9.78
Gowers, Ernest, "The Punishment" in **A LIFE FOR A LIFE: THE PROBLEM OF CAPITAL PUNISHMENT**. 1956. Gowers, Chairman of the Royal Commission on Capital Punishment, presents the arguments for and against the death penalty. Contains brief allusion to the execution of women within a history of the procedure and technique of hanging in the 19th century.

9.79
Radzinowicz, Leon, **A HISTORY OF ENGLISH CRIMINAL LAW AND ITS ADMINISTRATION FROM 1750: THE CLASH BETWEEN PRIVATE INITIATIVE AND PUBLIC INTEREST IN THE ENFORCEMENT OF THE LAW**. vol. 2, 1956; 1974. Generally presents crime in Victorian England as "evil licensed by a corrupt system" (p. 292). See pp. 297-306 for information on flash houses, and their "elaborate underground organisation," as "Centres of Criminal Activity" and the role of "Police as Protective Customers." "These houses generally harbored 'flash women,' defined as a "prostitute under the protection of a bully" (p. 301). Concerning these gaming houses, titled ladies in the 18th century indulged in gaming as in the case of Lady Mirdington and Lady Cassilis "who contended that the privilege of peerage made them immune from any prosecution, or proceeding, for keeping a gaming house" (p. 286, footnote 64).

9.80
Morris, Terrence, "Some Ecological Studies of the 19th Century" in **THE CRIMINAL AREA: A STUDY IN SOCIAL ECOLOGY.** by Terrence Morris. 1957. Criminological studies in the 19th century were based largely on the work of "zealous social reformers and administrators, anxious about the moral welfare of the community" (n.p.).

9.81
Havard, J.D.J., **THE DETECTION OF SECRET HOMICIDE: A STUDY OF THE MEDICO-LEGAL SYSTEM OF INVESTIGATION OF SUDDEN AND UNEXPLAINED DEATHS.** 1960. Describes the origins of forensics.

9.82
Hollingsworth, Keith, **THE NEWGATE NOVEL 1830-1847: BULWER, AINSWORTH, DICKENS AND THACKERAY.** Detroit, 1963. Between 1830 and 1847 a series of novels was published in which the protagonists were criminals. Contemptuous critics called them Newgate fiction. Inquires into the significance of these novels as a group and critically examines their individual character against the background of a turbulent period in English political and social development.

9.83
Macnab, K.K., "Aspects of the History of Crime in England and Wales Between 1805-1960," Ph.D. diss., Univ. of Sussex, 1965.

9.84
Tobias, John Jacob, **CRIME AND INDUSTRIAL SOCIETY IN THE 19TH CENTURY.** 1967; *also titled:* **URBAN CRIME IN VICTORIAN ENGLAND.** New York, 1972; This excellent reference surveys contemporary views of W.D. Morrison, DuCane, Mayhew, etc. on crime believed committed by a separate criminal class. See especially: "Juveniles and Women." Extensive bibliography.

9.85
Peirce, David, "Crime and Society in Mid-Victorian London," Ph.D. diss., Harvard Univ., 1969.

9.86
Chesney, Kellow, **THE VICTORIAN UNDERWORLD.** 1970; *also titled:* **THE ANTI-SOCIETY: AN ACCOUNT OF THE VICTORIAN UNDERWORLD.** New York, 1970. Includes roles of women in describing criminal and deviant activities in slums, dens of thieves, "baby farms," crowded areas of towns, the highways, and places of entertainment and recreation.

9.87
Box, Steven, **DEVIANCE, REALITY AND SOCIETY.** Canterbury, 1971; 1981. Shows how 19th-century traditional assumptions about delinquency influence modern sociological analysis. "Not only were the strain and cultural theories based on the belief that delinquency was a lower-class phenomenon, but they were also intended to explain why delinquency was a male preserve. Faithful to a long and 'dishonourable' tradition in criminology, these theories rendered invisible, trivialized or ignored female delinquency" (p. 143); **POWER, CRIME AND MYSTIFICATION.** 1983.

9.88
De Vries, Leonard, **'ORRIBLE MURDER: AN ANTHOLOGY OF VICTORIAN CRIME AND PASSION COMPILED FROM "THE POLICE ILLUSTRATED**

NEWS." New York, 1971.

9.89
Schur, Edwin M., **LABELING DEVIANT BEHAVIOR: ITS SOCIOLOGICAL IMPLICATIONS.** New York, 1971. The labeling approach to deviance is strongly grounded in traditional cultural and psychological formulations appropriate to specific times and places. It is an important reminder to researchers that definitions of "deviance" therefore depend upon relevant contexts.

9.90
Gatrell, V.A.C. and Hadden, T.B., "Criminal Statistics and Their Interpretation" in **NINETEENTH-CENTURY SOCIETY: ESSAYS IN THE USE OF QUANTITATIVE METHODS AND STUDY OF SOCIAL DATA.** by E.A. Wrigley. Cambridge, 1972.

9.91
HARVARD LIBRARY BULLETIN: Peirce, D., *"Crime and Society in London 1799-1900: A Bibliographical Survey,"* 20 (1972) 430-435. A guide to doing research on crime in London.

9.92
Cooper, David D., **THE LESSON OF THE SCAFFOLD: THE PUBLIC EXECUTION CONTROVERSY IN VICTORIAN ENGLAND.** Athens, Ohio, 1974. Examines public opinion over punishments and criminal law reform movements.

9.93
VICTORIAN STUDIES: O'Kell, R., *"'The Victorian Counterculture': An Interdisciplinary Conference,"* 17 (1973-1974) 431-435. Historians of nineteenth-century England categorized many patterns of behavior as "deviant" which were actually prominent among the Victorians; Senelick, L., *"Ladykillers and Lady Killers: Recent Popular Victoriana,"* 21 (1978) 493-500. Reviews six monographs, some of which deal with criminal acts.

9.94
Rosen, Andrew, **RISE UP WOMEN! THE MILITANT CAMPAIGN OF THE WOMEN'S SOCIAL AND POLITICAL UNION, 1903-1914.** 1974. Traces the "shocking" militant tactics employed by the WSPU, often violent and illegal, to secure women's suffrage and legislation.

9.95
FEMINIST STUDIES: Hartman, M.S., *"Crime and the Respectable Woman: Toward a Pattern of Middle-Class Female Criminality in Nineteenth-Century France and England,"* 2 (1974) 38-56. Crimes of middle-class women in general resulted from domestic situations and reflect the changing position of women. Criminal activity centered in three traumatic periods of life: immediately prior to marriage, just after marriage, and in later, restless periods in married life. These periods are marked by the severe adjustments that the customs and conventions of courtship and marriage demanded; Monheimer, J., *"Murderous Mothers: The Problem of Parenting in the Victorian Novel,"* 5 (1979) 530-546. "The rash of terrible mothers in the novel is an expression of outrage against such a fierce economy. These women reveal terrible failings in their world... [that] drains the self of all possibilities of self-interest, sexuality, activity outside the home" (p. 545).

9.96
JOURNAL OF SOCIAL HISTORY: Lane, R., *"Crime and Industrial Revolution: British and American Views,"* 7 (1974) 287-303. While British historians view the

Industrial Revolution as one reason for the increase in disruptive social behavior, American historians have not made this connection. Offers some reasons for this difference and suggests that the British experience might be a model for an understanding of the American past; Beattie, J.,*"The Criminality of Women in Eighteenth Century England,"* 8 (1975) 80-116; Storch, R.D., *"The Policeman as Domestic Missionary: Urban Discipline and Popular Culture in Northern England, 1850-1880,"* 9 (1976) 480-509; Graff, H.J., *"Pauperism, Misery and Vice: Illiteracy and Criminality in the Nineteenth Century,"* 11 (1977) 245-268; O'Brien, P., *"Crime and Punishment as an Historical Problem,"* 11 (1978) 508-520. Surveys the development of social-historical thoughts on the criminal in society by Foucault, Marx, and others. "The different aims of institutional rehabilitation according to sex were grounded in the dominant social values.... We need not talk here about institutions mirroring each other; we must talk here about mediations by which values come to be dominant on different institutional levels and how these values interact and reinforce one another" (p. 517).

9.97
Adler, Freda, SISTERS IN CRIME: THE RISE OF THE NEW FEMALE CRIMINAL. New York, 1975. "Part of the difficulty in understanding changes in female crime stems from the blind spots which have obstructed society's vision of women in general. Throughout centuries of male domination, even men of good will have persistently tried to unravel the mystery of women as if women were a species apart, as if women did not share the male need for status and security" (p. 9).

9.98
Bailey, Victor, "The Dangerous Classes in Late Victorian England: Some Reflections on the Social Foundations of Disturbance and Order with Special Reference to London in the 1880s," Ph.D. diss., Warwick Univ., 1975.

9.99
Hay, Douglas, Linebaugh, Peter, Rule, John, Thompson, E.P. and Winslow, Cal, ALBION'S FATAL TREE: CRIME AND SOCIETY IN EIGHTEENTH CENTURY ENGLAND. New York, 1975. Includes women offenders in this examination of "criminality itself, the offenses, the offenders and the popular myths of offenders... as part hero, part dreadful moral exemplars" (p. 13); *reviewed in:* PAST AND PRESENT: Langbein, J.H., *"Albion's Fatal Flaws,"* no. 98 (1983) 96-120; ——*see also:* Thompson, E.P., WHIGS AND HUNTERS. New York, 1975.

9.100
Klein, Dorie, "The Etiology of Female Crime: A Review of the Literature" in THE FEMALE OFFENDER. ed. by Laura Crites. Lexington, 1976. Survey of historical literature from the turn-of-the-century writings of Lombroso to the present.

9.101
Smart, Carol, WOMEN, CRIME AND CRIMINOLOGY: A FEMINIST CRITIQUE. 1976. Argues that there has been a "total neglect of any critical analysis of the common-sense perceptions of female criminality informing classical... and contemporary... studies. Hence many unexplicated, culturally specific assumptions about the 'true nature' of women.... It is not surprising therefore that many myths, from the theological belief in the fundamental evil and weakness of Woman to the paternalistic belief in Woman's frailty and gentleness, still prevail in accounts of female criminality" (p. 3).

9.102
Zeher, H., CRIME AND THE DEVELOPMENT OF MODERN SOCIETY. 1976.

Constructs a new methodology with which to examine crime and its meaning in society. Implicates the modernization process in rising crime rates: "Modernity implies a decline in respect for conventions, a reduction in social controls, a lessening of appreciation for the rights and property of others" (p. 11).

9.103
BRITISH JOURNAL OF LAW AND SOCIETY: Young, F., *"A Sociological Analysis of the Early History of Probation,"* 3 (1976) 44-58.

9.104
Bayley, David H., "Introduction" in **POLICE AND SOCIETY**. ed. by David H. Bayley. Beverly Hills, 1977. Addresses the relationship between social status and police behavior.

9.105
Donajgrodzki, Tony, **SOCIAL CONTROL IN NINETEENTH CENTURY BRITAIN**. 1977.

9.106
Foucault, Michel, **DISCIPLINE AND PUNISH: THE BIRTH OF THE PRISON**. trans. by Alan Sheridan. New York, 1977; *reviewed in:* **NEW SOCIETY:** Laslett, P., *"Under Observation,"* 42 (1977) 474-475.

9.107
Miller, Wilbur R., "Never on Sunday: Moralistic Reformers and the Police in London and New York City, 1830-1870" in **POLICE AND SOCIETY**. ed. by David H. Bayley. Beverly Hills, 1977. The movement against Sabbath-breaking "aroused serious political conflict during the mid-nineteenth century.... The London and New York police forces' response... provides a case study of the influence of reforming pressure groups upon the police, of alternative methods of dealing with 'victimless crimes' and of the broader problems of police legitimization in two heterogeneous societies" (p. 128). ——*see also:* Miller, Wilbur R., **COPS AND BOBBIES: POLICE AUTHORITY IN NEW YORK AND LONDON**. Chicago, 1977.

9.108
Philips, David, **CRIME AND AUTHORITY IN VICTORIAN ENGLAND: THE BLACK COUNTRY 1835-1860**. 1977. "Nineteenth-century commentators on crime drew attention to [the] differing sex ratio in crime, mostly because they were disturbed that the female rate was as high as 1:3 to the male crime rate; this was seen as a product of 'the collection of large masses of population in crowded cities' and of female industrial labour, since the female crime rate was higher in cities and industrial areas than [that of] the men" (p. 150). Women's involvement in crime within a given cultural period is correlated with their social role and the strength and skills they employ; *reviewed in:* **LABOUR HISTORY:** Merritt, A., *"Methodological and Theoretical Implication of the Study of Law and Crime,"* 37 (1979) 108-119; *also reviewed in:* **NEW SOCIETY:** Ditton, J., 42 (1977) 480-481.

9.109
Taylor, I., Walton, P. and Young, J., **THE NEW CRIMINOLOGY: FOR A SOCIAL THEORY OF DEVIANCE**. 1977. Analyzes the impact that biological, medical and atavistic criminal theories had on society from the late nineteenth to the early twentieth century.

9.110
BRITISH JOURNAL OF SOCIOLOGY: Smart, C., *"Criminological Theory; Its*

Ideology and Implication Concerning Women," 28 (1977) 89-100. Critiques basic background material on female criminology studies such as Lombroso, explicating the ideological underpinnings of their logic, assumptions which still largely determine how female criminals are considered; Hagan, J., Simpson, J.H. and Gillis, A.R., *"The Sexual Stratification of Social Control: A Gender-Based Perspective on Crime and Delinquency,"* 30 (1979) 25-38.

9.111

INTERNATIONAL JOURNAL OF CRIMINOLOGY AND PENOLOGY: Adler, F., *"Interaction Between Women's Emancipation and Female Criminality—A Cross-Cultural Perspective,"* 5 (1977) 101-112. Study shows that as women integrate socially and economically, there is an associated rise in female crime.

9.112

JOURNAL OF INTERDISCIPLINARY HISTORY: Graff, H.J., *"Crime and Punishment in the Nineteenth Century: A New Look at the Criminal,"* 7 (1977) 477-491. Prescribes methodological options for historical criminology based on class divisions rather than on systems and institutional analysis.

9.113

Cornish, W.R., Hart, Jenifer, Manchester, A.H., and Stevenson, J., CRIME AND LAW IN NINETEENTH CENTURY BRITAIN. Dublin, 1978. Discusses criminal law, punishment, transportation of criminals, juvenile offenders, legal administration, civil disorder, and police.

9.114

Whitmore, Richard, VICTORIAN AND EDWARDIAN CRIME AND PUNISHMENT FROM OLD PHOTOGRAPHS. 1978. A photographic essay. See pp. 60-74 for women and children.

9.115

NEW SOCIETY: Weightman, G., *"Before 999,"* 43 (1978) 57. Deals with the establishment of the metropolitan police force in nineteenth-century England, describing evolution of the force, as well as fire departments and ambulance service; Ignatieff, M., *"Police and People: The Birth of Mr. Peel's 'Blue Locusts,'"* 30 (1979) 443-445. The metropolitan police force was instituted amid much popular opposition.

9.116

VICTORIAN PERIODICALS NEWSLETTER: Rutenberg, D., *"From Praise of Hanging to the Femme Fatale: Capital Punishment in Nineties Periodicals,"* 11 (1978) 95-104.

9.117

McGowen, Randall E., "Rethinking Crime: Changing Attitudes Toward Law Breakers in Eighteenth and Nineteenth Century England," Ph.D. diss., Univ. of Illinois, 1979.

9.118

LABOUR HISTORY: Merritt, A., *"Methodological and Theoretical Implications of the Study of Law and Crime,"* 37 (1979) 108-119. Includes discussion of problems in gauging female crime.

9.119

SIGNS: Cloward, R.A. and Piven, F.F., *"Hidden Protest: The Channeling of Female*

Innovation and Resistance," 4 (1979) 651-669. The authors hypothesize that deviant behavior is purposeful and that women deviate differently from men. Our preoccupation with mental health may have contributed to a rise in female deviance in the twentieth century.

9.120
Jones, Ann, **WOMEN WHO KILL**. New York, 1980. "A woman can't kill a man, no matter what he has done to her, and get away with it" (p. 331). Discusses social and intellectual traditions behind treating women accused of crime. Shows that they were judged from a different set of criteria than that established for men. Details crime and punishment of women from the seventeenth century, including the penalty of death by burning for English women who murdered husbands, the last burned in 1779. Also includes a chapter on infanticide.

9.121
HISTORY TODAY: Brewer, J., *"An Ungovernable People? Law and Disorder in Stuart and Hanoverian England,"* 30 (1980) 18-27. "When a parish constable... tried to serve a warrant on a laborer's wife, she siezed the document, tore it into several pieces... spit it out on the ground and immediately struck him" (p. 22); Storch, R.D., *"Crime and Justice in 19th Century England,"* 30 (1980) 32-37. Includes discussion of prison conditions, police efforts, legislative progress, demographics, and trends. Considering broad influences: "Victorian society created a new, massive problem that challenged the police mission of ensuring order and decorum in public spaces: the spectacle of open and casual street prostitution in the West End" (p. 35).

9.122
PAST AND PRESENT: Anderson, O., *"Did Suicide Increase with Industrialization in Victorian England?"* no. 86 (1980) 149-173. "Already in the 1860s industrialization had given each stage of the life cycle a new meaning for male industrial workers, but that for women, even in places where many of them were factory operatives, the traditional dominance of biological factors had only been modified slightly, and then more by the advent of big cities than by industrialization" (p. 172). Suicide was far more common among men than women except in youth and old age.

9.123
SOCIETY FOR THE STUDY OF LABOUR HISTORY BULLETIN: Bailey, V., *"Crime, Criminal Justice and Authority in England: A Bibliographic Essay,"* 40 (1980) 36-46. Advocates a comparative approach to the assessment of past patterns of criminality with scrupulous attention paid to historical detail and context. Historians should cleave to the precept that the definition and development of crime are functions of distinct economic and cultural formations. Identifies a polemic useful to female criminological methodology that questions whether criminal indictment indicates an act of crime or whether it is a record of a particular legal system during a point in time.

9.124
Hirsch, Miriam, "When She is Bad, She is Horrid: Women and Crime" in **WOMEN AND VIOLENCE.** by Miriam Hirsch. 1981. Observes how social conceptions of "normal" behavior for women shape conceptions of deviance and its causes. Discusses Caesare Lombroso, a nineteenth-century criminologist whose study of physical attributes and criminality "explained" why prostitutes were particularly disposed to crime. He also believed that "women were naturally more impervious to pain than men and therefore less compassionate" (p. 140).

9.125
Scutt, Jocelynne A., "Sexism in Criminal Law" in **WOMEN AND CRIME**. ed. by Satyanshu K. Mulkherjee and Jocelynne A. Scutt. Sydney, 1981. In regard to felonies and misdemeanors, "'the husband and wife are one person in law, that is, the very being or legal existence of the wife is suspended during marriage....' Under this doctrine it was considered at law that where a wife committed a crime in the presence of her husband, she was presumed to have committed it under coercion..., entitled to an acquittal... with no requirement... of threats, pressure, or instruction from the husband" (p. 2). Married women had therefore the legal rights of children. The law encouraged husbands to be in control of wives. Ultimately without this protection she was "subjected to a more severe penalty" (p. 3).

9.126
Smith, Roger, "Medico-Legal Views of Women" in **TRIAL BY MEDICINE: INSANITY AND RESPONSIBILITY IN VICTORIAN TRIALS**. by Roger Smith. Edinburgh, 1981. Arguments of inherent moral and physical weakness abound as justification for certain kinds of female madness. In fact, women's "nature" by and large overruled giving her any responsibility in crime.

9.127
ECONOMIC HISTORY REVIEW: Thompson, F.M.L., *"Social Control in Victorian Britain,"* 34 (1981) 180-208.

9.128
Jones, David, **CRIME, PROTEST, COMMUNITY AND POLICE IN NINETEENTH CENTURY BRITAIN**. 1982. Female criminals often received preferential treatment by legal authorities. "The character of their crime is a good index of the kind of pressures to which women, especially single, deserted and widowed persons, were subjected in the years before the Welfare State... the great majority of female offences were theft (notably from the person, from shops and employers), drunkenness and disorderly conduct" (p. 7).

9.129
Pearson, Geoffrey, **HOOLIGAN: A HISTORY OF RESPECTABLE FEARS**. 1983. "We have encountered girl garotters in the 1860s, as well as 'Hooligan Girls' in the 1890s throwing their weight about the streets indistinguishable from their hooligan brothers" (p. 225).

9.130
Beattie, J.M., **CRIME AND THE COURTS IN ENGLAND 1660-1800**. Princeton, 1986. See especially: "Women Offenders." "Simple larceny charges made up three-quarters of the charges against women.... Some of the differences [in male versus female accusations] arose no doubt from the greater reluctance of victims to charge women than men (p. 238).... Some of the differences in the prosecution of women in urban and rural parts of the country are the comparative ease of access to [the quarter sessions] court.... by the middle of the eighteenth century the quarter sessions were likely to deal harshly with simple larceny... and there was by then no certainty that a woman prosecuted before the sessions for a relatively trivial crime would be treated lightly" (p. 241). ——*see also:* **PAST AND PRESENT:** *"The Pattern of Crime in England, 1660-1800,"* no. 62 (1974) 47-95; "The Criminality of Women in Eighteenth Century England" in **WOMEN AND THE LAW: A SOCIAL HISTORICAL PERSPECTIVE**. ed. by D. Kelly Weisberg. 1982.

9.131a
Carlen, Pat, and Worrall, Anne, eds., **GENDER, CRIME AND JUSTICE**. Oxford,

1987.

* * *

2. VIOLENCE AGAINST WOMEN AND CHILDREN

9.131
Farr, Samuel, **ELEMENTS OF MEDICAL JURISPRUDENCE**. 1788. Expounds one of the basic tenets of medical jurisprudence: that conception does not occur unless the woman responds pleasurably in the sexual act, therefore intercourse which produces a child cannot be considered forcible rape.

9.132
THE FEMALE HERO, OR BOLD STAFFORDSHIRE GIRL. CONTAINING AN AUTHENTIC ACCOUNT OF A SERVANT GIRL, WHO... WAS OVERTAKEN BY A ROBBER... AFTER ACCOMPANYING HER INTO A NARROW LANE HE MADE HER STOP... AND ATTEMPTED TO ROB HER, WHEN SHE RESOLUTELY KNOCKED HIM DOWN WITH HIS OWN STICK, AND BEAT HIS BRAINS OUT. ALSO AN ACCOUNT OF THE APPREHENDING HIS ASSOCIATES, ETC. [1815].

9.133
FEMALE'S FRIEND: 1846; vols. 1-4. Published by the Associate Institution for Improving and Enforcing the Laws for the Protection of Women.

9.134
ELIZA COOK'S JOURNAL: *"Treatment of Women,"* 5 (1851) 225-227. Comments on wife-beating and abuse of female agricultural workers. "In the horrible case of Tomlinson vs. Tomlinson, the miscreant corrupted a daughter of his wife by a former husband, and the ecclesiastical judge rewarded the monster by presenting him with half of his wife's property, which she had derived from her previous husband" (p. 226).

9.135
NORTH BRITISH REVIEW: Kaye, J.W., *"Outrages Against Women,"* 25 (1856) 233-256. An emotional examination of domestic violence toward women as regards both the upper and the lower classes. Wife-beating and seduction are crimes for which there is no atonement.

9.136
Taylor, Alfred S., **THE PRINCIPLES AND PRACTICE OF MEDICAL JURISPRUDENCE.** 1865. Extensive and factual chapter on rape. Advises medical men called to examine a case of rape to be precise about empirical details like time and information provided by the "prosecutrix." Statistics show that "70 percent of all rapes are perpetrated on girls below the age of twelve years" (p. 990). Also discusses what evidence legally constitutes rape, and at what age these considerations change. Differs with the previously held notion that conception depends on the volition of the female.

9.137
LAW JOURNAL: *"Savage Assaults Upon Wives,"* 9 (1874) 500-501.

9.138
ENGLISHWOMAN'S REVIEW: *"Inefficacy of Corporal Punishment,"* 6 (1875) 58-61. Reports the Vigilance Association's position on punishing, wife-beating and other "extreme cruelties." The Association comes out against reviving "the punishment of the lash" in favor of a different set of suggestions for legal consideration.

9.139
JOURNAL OF THE ROYAL STATISTICAL SOCIETY: Grey, W.A., *"On the Executions For Murder That Have Taken Place in England and Wales During the Last 70 Years,"* 38 (1875) 480-486. See p. 455, table VII, which shows "the large proportion in which women brought into close relationship and contact with men become victims of their murderous assaults" (p. 478).

9.140
WOMEN'S SUFFRAGE JOURNAL: Becker, L.E., *"The Epidemic of Brutality,"* 6 (1875) 2-3.

9.141
Hoyle, William, **CRIME IN ENGLAND AND WALES IN THE NINETEENTH CENTURY, AN HISTORICAL AND CRITICAL RETROSPECTIVE.** 1876. Examines crime decade by decade from 1805 to 1874. See chapter on "Crime of the Country" which points out that in 1853, aggravated assault on women and children was made a non-indictable crime.

9.142
Cobbe, Frances Power, **WIFE TORTURE IN ENGLAND.** 1878; *rpt. from:* **CONTEMPORARY REVIEW:** 32 (1878) 55-87.

9.143
SPECTATOR: *"The Protection of Children,"* (July 1884) 910; *"One Unavoidable Cause of Cruelty,"* (May 1893) 637-638.

9.144
Colam, Robert Frederick, **PREVENTION OF CRUELTY TO CHILDREN: A MANUAL.** 1885. Published by the Society for the Prevention of Cruelty to Children.

9.145
Fox, Richard Kyle, **THE HISTORY OF THE WHITECHAPEL MURDERS: A FULL AND AUTHENTIC NARRATIVE.** New York, 1888.

9.146
BRITISH MEDICAL JOURNAL: *"The East End Murders: Detailed Lessons,"* 2 (1888) 768-769. Calls for more urgent police action.

9.147
DAILY TELEGRAPH: See articles from 1888 to 1892 for coverage of the Ripper murders.

9.148
LONDON CITY MISSION MAGAZINE: *"The East End Atrocities,"* 52 (1888) 258-

260.

9.149
STAR: Shaw, G.B., *"Blood Money For White Chapel,"* 1 (1888) n.p. Socialist perspective.

9.150
Hayne, W.J., **JACK THE RIPPER: OR THE CRIMES OF LONDON.** 1889.

9.151
Waugh, Benjamin, **SOME CONDITIONS OF CHILD-LIFE IN ENGLAND.** 1889.

9.152
Geary, William Nevill, "Crimes" in **THE LAW OF MARRIAGE AND FAMILY RELATIONS.** by William Nevill Geary. 1892. Includes rape, assault, and forcible marriage.

9.153
MEDICO-LEGAL JOURNAL: Dailey, A., *"The Conflict Between Parental Authority and the Society for the Prevention of Cruelty to Children,"* 10 (1892) 376-385.

9.154
Holmes, Thomas, "Husbands and Wives" in **PICTURES AND PROBLEMS FROM LONDON POLICE COURTS.** 1900. Extensive descriptions of battered wives seeking protection from the magistrates. "A good number of Englishmen seem to think that they have as perfect a right to thrash or kick their wives as the American had to 'lick his nigger'" (p. 73).

9.155
FORTNIGHTLY REVIEW: Cooper, E.H., *"The Punishment of Children,"* 73 (1903) 1060-1067. Denies that children respond at all to reasonableness in their disciplining and regrets the shift in opinion against corporal punishment. Sympathizes with some convicted child abusers: "Two or three of the hysterically denounced 'tortures' which I read of... struck me as highly original and harmless punishments, which would be worth remembering and recommending if their use had not been rendered practically impossible by popular hysteria" (p. 1064).

9.156
Hall, G. Stanley, **ADOLESCENCE. ITS PSYCHOLOGY AND ITS RELATION TO PHYSIOLOGY, ANTHROPOLOGY, SEX CRIME, RELIGION AND EDUCATION.** 2 vols. New York, 1904.

9.157
CONTEMPORARY REVIEW: Loane, M.E., *"Husband and Wife Among the Poor,"* 87 (1905) 222-230. On husband and wife beating, and relations between spouses and their children among the poor.

9.158
QUARTERLY REVIEW: *"The Cry of the Children,"* 408 (1906) 29-53. On child-labor, improvement of juvenile facilities, child abuse in the home, "baby-farming" and infant life insurance.

9.159
THE WAY OF CHILD TORTURERS. 1909. Illustrated.

9.160

[Payne, W.], **THE CRUELTY MAN: ACTUAL EXPERIENCES OF AN INSPECTOR OF THE N.S.P.C.C. GRAPHICALLY TOLD BY HIMSELF.** 1912.

9.161

Moll, Albert, "The Child as an Object of Sexual Practices" in **THE SEXUAL LIFE OF THE CHILD.** trans. by Eden Paul. New York, 1913. General discussion of paedophiles and their various forms of abuse, by a German doctor.

9.162

Chapman, Cecil, "The Position and Treatment of Women" in **THE POOR MAN'S COURT OF JUSTICE: TWENTY-FIVE YEARS AS A METROPOLITAN MAGISTRATE.** by Cecil Chapman. 1925. Deals with the "persistent cruelty" of many domestic relations which came before this Magistrate's court. Chapman was an advocate of sexual equality.

9.163

Fry, S. Margery, "Capital Punishment" in **ARMS OF THE LAW.** by S. Margery Fry. 1951. See especially: pp. 189-191 for comparison of criminal motives for women and men in 1905 and an analysis of the victims of male murderers, 1900-1948. Of "all the murders considered (61 per cent of those committed by men) the victims were women, wives, sweethearts or others; of these woman-murders, over 64 per cent were due to drink... [and quarrels] accounted for less than one-tenth of the total" (p. 190).

9.164

Cullen, Tom, **WHEN LONDON WALKED IN TERROR.** Boston, 1965. "The important thing is that Jack the Ripper has never died as far as the average Londoner is concerned. Mothers frighten their children with his name. Headline writers keep it alive.... The Ripper is remembered for the wrong reasons" (pp. 277-278).

9.165

Altick, Richard D., **VICTORIAN STUDIES IN SCARLET.** New York, 1970. "The greatest single class of murders was domestic.... In a sampling which includes approximately 480 cases that resulted in the execution of a murderer, 1837-1901, no fewer than 127 included the killing of a wife" (p. 286).

9.166

McCormick, Donald, **THE IDENTITY OF JACK THE RIPPER.** 1970.

9.167

Gelles, Richard, **THE VIOLENT HOME.** 1972.

9.168

Harrison, Michael, **CLARENCE: WAS HE JACK THE RIPPER?** 1973.

9.169

Kelly, Alexander Garfield, **JACK THE RIPPER; A BIBLIOGRAPHY AND REVIEW OF THE LITERATURE.** 1973.

9.170

de Mause, Lloyd, **THE HISTORY OF CHILDHOOD.** 1974. The eighteenth century saw the biggest decrease in child-beating. "As beatings began to decrease, substitutes had to be found. For instance, shutting children up in the dark became quite popular in the eighteenth and nineteenth centuries" (p. 43).

9.171
Symons, Julian, "The Criminal Classes" in **RULE BRITANNIA: THE VICTORIAN WORLD**. ed. by George Perry and Nicholas Mason. 1974. See pp. 218-219 on Jack the Ripper. Includes brief account of his violent crimes and photographs of victims.

9.172
Brownmiller, Susan, **AGAINST OUR WILL: MEN, WOMEN, AND RAPE**. New York, 1975. States that, both then and now, "Jack the Ripper's grip on the masculine imagination is so out of proportion to the case of an unknown man who stalked, mutilated and murdered five prostitutes in London's East End in the autumn of 1888 that we wonder what his attraction holds" (p. 325); *reviewed in:* SIGNS: Shorter, E., *"On Writing the History of Rape,"* 3 (1977) 471-482. Shorter considers rape to be a result of "pent-up sexual frustration on the part of the lunatic male fringe" (p. 471). He also denies the crime's political nature at any point before the French Revolution. Never outrightly vindicating rape, Shorter does, in a sense, remove responsibility, explaining the act in terms of "sheer, accumulated misere sexuelle" (p. 475). ——*see also:* SIGNS: Hartmann, H.I. and Ross, E., *"Review of 'On Writing the History of Rape,'"* 3 (1978) 931-935. Calls Shorter down for several of his presuppositions, including the "pent-up sexual frustration" theory.

9.173
Jones, Elwyn, ed., **RIPPER FILE**. 1975. Written as "a dossier——compiled as if it were by two policemen." Extensive bibliography exclusively dealing with Jack the Ripper.

9.174
Pearsall, Ronald, **NIGHT'S BLACK ANGELS: THE FORMS AND FACES OF VICTORIAN CRUELTY**. New York, 1975. The institution of marriage provided legal protection for men accused of cruelty. In one case of wife-beating in 1861, a husband "had taken his wife by the throat and thrown her to the floor, but she did not get her hoped-for divorce for one violent act under excitement did not constitute cruelty" (p. 18). See index under "children" for discussion of various forms of child abuse, including flogging, incestuous rape, child labor, and white slavery/prostitution.

9.175
Rumbelow, Donald, **THE COMPLETE JACK THE RIPPER**. New York, 1975.

9.176
Whittington-Egan, Richard, **A CASEBOOK OF JACK THE RIPPER**. 1975. Author may also be cataloged as Egan, Richard Whittington.

9.177
Knight, Stephen, **JACK THE RIPPER: THE FINAL SOLUTION**. 1976.

9.178
PRACTITIONER: Gayford, J.J., *"Battered Wives One Hundred Years Ago,"* 219 (1977) 122-128. Examines marital violence of the nineteenth century within the context of the "coming of women's rights." "Nineteenth-century cartoons usually depict domestic violence among the poorer classes... alcohol is usually in evidence in some shape or form.... There is evidence that women of the upper social classes were also treated with violence" (p. 123).

9.179
Gibson, Ian, **THE ENGLISH VICE: BEATING, SEX AND SHAME IN VICTORIAN ENGLAND AND AFTER**. 1978.

9.180
May, Margaret, "Violence in the Family: An Historical Perspective" in **VIOLENCE IN THE FAMILY**. ed. by John Powell Martin. New York, 1978. Discusses wife and child battering, implications for different classes, and the problems of source accuracy and documentation. Examines legal rights accorded women and social patterns that keep the institution of domestic violence intact.

9.181
Spiering, Frank, **PRINCE JACK: THE TRUE STORY OF JACK THE RIPPER**. New York, 1978. Advances the theory that Jack the Ripper was Albert Victor, grandson of Queen Victoria. Uses primary sources.

9.182
JOURNAL OF SOCIAL HISTORY: Tomes, N., *"A 'Torrent of Abuse': Crimes of Violence Between Working-Class Men and Women in London, 1840-1875,"* 2 (1978) 328-345. "In mid-nineteenth century London, working-class women were offered relief from male violence by a paternalistic system of values and institutions, in exchange for their right to fight. In the process they gained a new image of male-female relationships, one in which men were 'natural protectors' and women were in need of protection" (p. 342).

9.183
Dobash, Rebecca Emerson and Dobash, Russell, **VIOLENCE AGAINST WIVES: A CASE AGAINST THE PATRIARCHY**. New York, 1979; "The Violent Event" in **THE CHANGING EXPERIENCE OF WOMEN**. ed. by Elizabeth Whitelegg, et al. Oxford, 1982. "Kicking and standing on women was practiced with hobnail boots in Yorkshire during the late nineteenth century and was called 'purring'" (p. 205).

9.184
NEW SOCIETY: Edwards, S., *"Sex Crimes in the 19th Century,"* 49 (1979) 562-563. "Attitudes to rape and indecent assault in 19th century England depended on who was doing what to whom and when.... The differences in sentences often varied according to the social class of the convicted offender.... Women [of the working class] were thought to get what they deserved, since it was assumed that rape and sexual illicitness was a common feature of working class life" (p. 562).

9.185
Davis, Jennifer, "The London Garotting Panic of 1862: A Moral Panic and the Creation of a Criminal Class in Mid-Victorian England" in **CRIME AND THE LAW: THE SOCIAL HISTORY OF CRIME IN WESTERN EUROPE SINCE 1500**. ed. by V.A.D. Gatrell, Bruce Lenman, and Geoffrey Parker. 1980. In the Garotting Panic of 1862, (caused by increasing incidences of highway assault and robbery), not only was the "crime wave" created by the media before it happened, but the media presented it in such a way as to curtail women's freedom outside her home, claiming that this would leave them particularly vulnerable to moral and physical assault.

9.186
Weber, Donna-Lee, "Fair Game: Rape and Sexual Aggression on Women in Some Early Eighteenth-Century Prose Fiction," Ph.D. diss., Univ. of Toronto, 1980.

9.187
Morrell, Caroline, 'BLACK FRIDAY' AND VIOLENCE AGAINST WOMEN IN THE SUFFRAGE MOVEMENT. 1981.

9.188
HISTORICAL JOURNAL: Sharpe, J.A., *"Domestic Homicide in Early Modern England,"* 24 (1981) 29-48. Examines the period between 1560 and 1709. Useful for comparative research.

9.189
WOMEN'S STUDIES INTERNATIONAL QUARTERLY: Rodmell, S., *"Men, Women and Sexuality: A Feminist Critique of the Sociology of Deviance"* 4 (1981) 145-155. Contributes to conceptualizing approaches and frameworks for studying male sexual crimes against women from female and feminist perspectives. "Many scholars of deviance fail to situate their analyses within a broader framework of socio-sexual power structures in male-dominated societies" (p. 146). One way the "failure to specify the difference between non-criminal deviance and non-deviant criminality" has affected perception of heterosexual crimes against women is the "process of transferring the deviant label of the offender from the offender to the victim" (p. 149).

9.190
Behlmer, George K., **CHILD ABUSE AND MORAL REFORM IN ENGLAND, 1870-1908.** Stanford, 1982. Excellent account of changing attitudes toward parental abuse of children and state intervention in the private sphere. Details the reforms of the Society for the Prevention of Cruelty to Children and others, with a chronological history of child-welfare legislation (see appendix A).

9.191
FEMINIST STUDIES: Ross, E., *"Fierce Questions and Taunts: Married Life in Working-Class London, 1870-1914,"* 8 (1982) 575-602. This was "a culture where husband-wife violence was incredibly frequent, where pubs were regularly invaded by angry wives, where husbands cheated on their wives, wives stole from husbands, and music halls nightly unfolded new chapters in the domestic struggle over power" (p. 577); Walkowitz, J.R., *"Jack the Ripper and the Myth of Male Violence,"* 8 (1982) 543-574. "Over the past hundred years, the Ripper murders have achieved the status of a modern myth of male violence against women... whose 'moral' message is clear: the city is a dangerous place for women, when they transgress the narrow boundaries of home and hearth and dare to enter public space" (p. 544). — *see also:* FEMINIST REVIEW: Hollway, W., *"I Just Wanted to Kill a Woman, Why? The Ripper and Male Sexuality,"* 9 (1981) 33-40.

9.192
INTERNATIONAL JOURNAL OF WOMEN'S STUDIES: Bauer, C. and Ritt, L., *"'A Husband is a Beating Animal': Frances Power Cobbe Confronts the Wife-Abuse Problem in Victorian England,"* 6 (1983) 99-118. "Although Cobbe observed that wife-beating was exacerbated by drink, prostitution and appalling living conditions, she clearly recognized that the fundamental cause of wife-abuse could only be seen in the context of conventional attitudes toward the female sex." Cobbe's efforts were instrumental in the enactment of the Matrimonial Causes Act of 1858 (p. 99); Bauer, C. and Ritt, L., *"Wife-Abuse, Late-Victorian English Feminists, and the Legacy of Frances Power Cobbe,"* 6 (1983) 195-207. Feminists "denounced the lenient sentences continually handed out to wife-beaters; the difficulty in obtaining separation orders from brutal husbands (and the near impossibility of securing divorces); and the courts almost invariably awarding custody of the children to the

husbands" (p. 195).

9.193
SIGNS: Pleck, E., *"Feminist Responses to Crimes Against Women,"* Special Issue, 8 (1983) 451-470.

9.194
DARK LANTERN: Krone, K.A., *"In Search of Jack the Ripper,"* 2 (1985) 13-31. Reviews the social milieu, existing evidence and some theories that have been advanced.

9.195
Ayers, Pat and Lambertz, Jan, "Marriage Relations, Money and Domestic Violence in Working-Class Liverpool, 1919-1939" in **LABOUR AND LOVE: WOMEN'S EXPERIENCE OF HOME AND FAMILY, 1850-1940.** ed. by Jane Lewis. Oxford, 1986.

* * *

3. FEMALE CRIMINALS AND DEVIANTS

9.196
AN ACCOUNT OF MARY DAVIS WHO WAS EXECUTED AND AFTERWARDS HUNG IN CHAINS FOR THE MURDER OF HER SIX HUSBANDS BY POURING MELTED LEAD INTO THEIR EARS, WHICH WAS WONDERFULLY DISCOVERED BY HER SEVENTH HUSBAND. [1800].

9.197
Johnson, Mary, **THE LIFE, TRIAL AND EXECUTION... OF MISS. M. JOHNSON, WHO WAS EXECUTED AT... LONDON... FOR BEING CONCERNED IN THE MURDER AND ROBBERY OF HER OWN MISTRESS.** 1822.

9.198
A MURDERESS. A FULL AND PARTICULAR ACCOUNT OF THE TRIAL AND SENTENCE OF CATHARINE DAVIDSON, WHO IS TO BE EXECUTED AT ABERDEEN, ON THE 8TH OF OCTOBER NEXT... FOR THE MURDER OF HER OWN HUSBAND, JAMES HUMPHREY, BY ADMINISTERING VITRIOL TO HIM, WHILE ASLEEP! 1830.

9.199
Huish, Robert, **THE PROGRESS OF CRIME OR THE AUTHENTIC MEMOIRS OF MARIA MANNING (MURDERESS).** 1849.

9.200
HOUSEHOLD WORDS: *"Innocence and Crime: An Anecdote,"* 1 (1850) 431-432. Relates a friend's experience of being pickpocketed trying to help a little girl who was crying that she'd been beaten by her mother. It appears that the punishment was for failure in a pocket picking lesson.

9.201
TRANSACTIONS OF THE NATIONAL ASSOCIATION FOR THE PROMOTION OF SOCIAL SCIENCE: INAUGURAL ADDRESSES AND SELECT PAPERS, 1857. 1858. See especially: William Acton, "Prostitution," pp. 605-608. "No delusion should be encouraged as to the possible extirpation of the evil; as long as man was strong and woman weak, as long as a woman's honour might be bartered as her last resource against starvation or crime, she would be liable to fall" (p. 606).

9.202
TEMPLE BAR: Browne, C.T., *"Criminal Lunatics,"* 1 (1860) 135-143.

9.203
Stapleton, Joseph W., **THE GREAT CRIME OF 1860: BEING A SUMMARY OF THE FACTS RELATING TO THE MURDER COMMITTED AT ROAD.** 1861. Examines a domestic murder case where several women were implicated.

9.204
JOURNAL OF MENTAL SCIENCE: Boyd, R., *"Vital Statistics, and Observations on the First Thousand Female Patients Admitted to the Somerset Country Lunatic Asylum, The Results Compared with an Equal Number of Male Patients, Together with an Analysis of the Causes of Death in Both Sexes,"* 10 (1864) 491-513; Baker, J., *"Female Criminal Lunatics,"* 48 (1902) 13-28.

9.205
Archer, Thomas, **THE PAUPER, THE THIEF AND THE CONVICT: SKETCHES OF SOME OF THEIR HOMES, HAUNTS AND HABITS.** 1865.

9.206
EDINBURGH REVIEW: Martineau, H., *"Life in the Criminal Class,"* 122 (1865) 337-371.

9.207
CORNHILL MAGAZINE: *"Criminal Women,"* 14 (1866) 152-160. "Criminal women, as a class, are found to be more uncivilized than the savage, more degraded than the slave, less true to all natural and womanly instincts than the untutored squaw of a North American Indian tribe.... As a class they are guilty of lying, theft, unchastity, drunkenness, slovenliness" (p. 153).

9.208
GOOD WORDS AND SUNDAY MAGAZINE: Crofton, W., *"Female Criminals and Their Children's Fate,"* 14 (1873) 170-174.

9.209
Meredith, Susanna, **A BOOK ABOUT CRIMINALS.** 1881.

9.210
THE MARRIAGE LAWS CONSIDERED WITH THE VIEW OF DIMINISHING PROSTITUTION AND INFANTICIDE. Birmingham, 1883.

9.211
Beale, Edward, ed., **THE TRIAL OF ADELAIDE BARTLETT FOR MURDER: HELD AT THE CENTRAL CRIMINAL COURT... APRIL... 1886.** 1886.

9.212
Ribton-Turner, Charles James, **A HISTORY OF VAGRANTS AND VAGRANCY,**

AND BEGGARS AND BEGGING. 1887. Valuable source with many examples of female beggars and legislation regarding the removal of the poor: In 1800 in Gloucestershire, six women committed the crime of "hedge pulling," or damaging wood on another's property for means of a fire or walking stick. Each was "stripped to the waist and flogged till the blood ran down their backs" (p. 205). Author may also be cataloged as Turner, Charles James Ribton.

9.213
ALL THE YEAR ROUND: *"Female Gamblers,"* 1 (1889) 81-84.

9.214
MACMILLAN'S MAGAZINE: Yonge, E.S., *"The Insanity of the Criminal,"* 79 (1898) 50-55.

9.215
WESTMINSTER REVIEW: Foard, I., *"The Criminal: Is He Produced by Environment or Atavism?"* 150 (1898) 90-103. "Criminal women often give far more trouble than men. They are very revengeful, easily take offence, and noisily resent a fancied insult or slight. Some are sullen and taciturn. Prognathism is a marked characteristic amongst them, together with that Mongolian type of face that has been so much observed by the Italian school of criminologists as distinctly belonging to the criminal. These women are not very amenable to softening influences; they seem to have no sense of right or wrong, and by a kind of illogical reasoning difficult to understand, look upon themselves as the injured parties!" (pp. 92-93).

9.216
Griffiths, Arthur George Frederick, CRIMINALS I HAVE KNOWN... WITH ILLUSTRATIONS, ETC. 1895; MYSTERIES OF POLICE AND CRIME: A GENERAL SURVEY OF WRONGDOING AND ITS PURSUIT. 2 vols. 1899. See especially: vol. 1, "Some Female Criminals" and vol. 2, "Female Poisoners"; THE HISTORY AND ROMANCE OF CRIME FROM THE EARLIEST TIMES TO THE PRESENT DAY. 12 vols. [19??].

9.217
Vincent, Arthur, ed., TWELVE BAD WOMEN; ILLUSTRATIONS AND REVIEWS OF FEMININE TURPITUDE SET FORTH BY IMPARTIAL HANDS. 1897; 1911. Three of these twelve Englishwomen could be termed Victorian, strictly speaking. Their crimes range from pickpocketing to polygamy to sadism to simply being taken advantage of. A few noblewomen are included, as well as some lower-class women of literary significance.

9.218
Waters, W.G., "Mary Anne Clarke (1776-1852)" in LIVES OF TWELVE BAD WOMEN. ed. by Arthur Vincent. 1897. A biographical account of Mrs. Clarke's criminal life as a courtesan and extortionist.

9.219
Ashton, John, HISTORY OF GAMBLING IN ENGLAND. 1898. See pp. 60 and 76-83 for gambling women.

9.220
FORTNIGHTLY REVIEW: Orme, E., *"Our Female Criminals,"* 69 (1898) 790-796.

9.221

Deane, Augusta, **BETTING AND GAMBLING AMONG WORKING WOMEN AND GIRLS.** 1908.

9.222

Weidensall, Jean, **THE MENTALITY OF THE CRIMINAL WOMAN: A COMPARATIVE STUDY OF THE CRIMINAL WOMAN, THE WORKING GIRL, AND THE EFFICIENT WORKING WOMAN IN A SERIES OF MENTAL AND PHYSICAL TESTS.** New York, 1916. Utilizes the tests developed by Helen B. Thompson Woolley. The institutionalized criminal women tested demonstrated "decidedly less ability" than the average 15-year-old working girl.

9.223

Burke, William, **BURKE AND HARE.** 1921. Part of a series entitled: **NOTABLE BRITISH TRIALS.** William Burke, William Hare, Mrs. Hare and Helen McDougal were associated in the murder of more than 16 persons. Deals especially with the trial of William Burke and Helen McDougal who were indicted for the murder of three of the victims in 1828.

9.224

Scott, Stanley, "Some Curious Stories of Women Criminals" in **THE HUMAN SIDE OF CROOK AND CONVICT LIFE.** by Stanley Scott. 1924. "On the whole, the type of the woman criminal is more uniform, and of a lower standard, than that of the male convict. Her first offence is nearly always connected with some sexual transgression, her latter ones with drink or drugs" (p. 219). Also comments on the undercover prostitution prevalent in London "massage-manicure establishments."

9.225

O'Donnell, Elliott, ed., **THE TRIAL OF KATE WEBSTER.** 1925. Part of a series entitled: **NOTABLE BRITISH TRIALS.** Sensationalized story of Kate Webster, hanged for the murder of her mistress. Dwells on her sinister attractiveness: "I believe the magnet that drew men to her was her extraordinary virility and primitiveness, the wildness and savagery of her native surrounding manifesting through her and appealing to them" (p. 13). Contains the transcript of her trial in 1879.

9.226

Parry, Edward Abbott, **VAGABONDS ALL.** New York, 1926. Tells the lively tales of two female imposters——Mary Anne Clarke, The Courtesan and Mary Bateman, The Fortune-Teller. Mary Bateman, "the Yorkshire Witch," "could rob her dupes thoroughly and deliberately without losing their friendship, support and gratitude. It is for this reason, I should imagine, that women, who are more dependant than men upon human sympathy, are attracted to this class of crime in which pleasant friendship of imposter and dupe is an essential condition" (p. 215).

9.227

Ferrier, J. Kenneth, **CROOKS AND CRIME: DESCRIBING THE METHODS OF CRIMINALS FROM THE AREA SNEAK TO THE PROFESSIONAL CARD SHARPER FORGER OR MURDERER AND THE VARIOUS WAYS IN WHICH THEY ARE CIRCUMVENTED AND CAPTURED.** 1928. In virtually every category of crime, women practitioners are mentioned, but there are also chapters on "feminine" crimes such as "Women Swindlers," "Matrimonial Frauds," "Fortune-Telling," and "White Slave Traffic." "The general public, which is often thrilled by the reading of the perpetration of audaciously planned jewel thefts, does not quite realize to what extent women figure in these crimes. Frequently it has been found that the woman jewel thief is more skillful than the man" (p. 78).

9.228
Roughead, William, **MALICE DOMESTIC**. Edinburgh, 1928. Contains sensational-ized descriptions of women poisoners.

9.229
Lambert, Richard S., "The Reprieve of Charlotte Winsor" and "Mrs. Cotton's Profession" in **WHEN JUSTICE FALTERED: A STUDY OF NINE PECULIAR MURDER TRIALS**. by Richard S. Lambert. 1935.

9.230
Hunt, Peter, **THE MADELEINE SMITH AFFAIR**. Liverpool, 1950. Re-examines the circumstances and trial surrounding the acquittal of Madeleine Smith of the murder of her lover Pierre Emile L'Angelier. While revealing the damning evidence of her correspondence, censored in court because of its "pornographic" nature, author interprets the evidence with marked animosity: "All he wanted was a 'lady' for his wife; she was out for her un-Victorian desires" (p. viii).

9.231
Bridges, Yseult, **THE TRAGEDY AT ROAD-HILL HOUSE**. New York, 1955. Re-opens the case of Constance Kent who refused to defend herself from the charge of murdering her stepbrother in 1860. The case had never been submitted to a jury's consideration because of her confession.

9.232
Morland, Nigel, **THAT NICE MISS SMITH**. 1957. Comments on Smith's murder trial: "The verdict meant the jury had compromised with itself. Not Proven does not settle complete innocence or complete guilt, being exactly what it says. That the party at the receiving end is neither washed white nor left black is obvious, but left with a permanently smeared character.... What mattered was whether the prisoner who so escaped could take it——Madeleine could, and did" (p. 179).

9.233
Harrison, Michael, "Courtship By Forgery" and "Trials of a Titled Journalist" in **PAINFUL DETAILS: TWELVE VICTORIAN SCANDALS**. 1962. "No court today has been more lenient than that which permitted Mary Smith, the letter-writer of Austry, to go scot-free, when strict justice should have ordered her to be transported for forgery" (p. 24).

9.234
Christie, Trevor L., **ETCHED IN ARSENIC: A NEW STUDY OF THE MAYBRICK CASE**. Harrap, 1969. Florence Maybrick, an American, was charged with poisoning her British husband, a lifelong addict to arsenic and other drugs.

9.235
Altick, Richard D., **VICTORIAN STUDIES IN SCARLET**. New York, 1970. Examines the cases of several men and women murderers. A major theme is the heightened sensationalism of murder in Victorian times by "balladmongers," the press, and, paradoxically, upper-class women. "We are told that in 1877, when the jury returned in the sordid case of the Stauntons, the benches 'were filled even at this dread hour with the bevy of smartly dressed, over jewelled women who had drunk champagne in the luncheon internal and skimmed the pages of PUNCH when the interest flagged'" (p. 42).

9.236
Sparrow, Gerald, **WOMEN WHO MURDER**. 1970. "Women being different from men in their mentality, thought-processes, intuition, emotional reactions and in their whole approach to life and death, when they murder, do the deed in a way that a man often would not contemplate. Their crime does not bear the mark of Cain, it is stamped with that characteristic subtlety and horror that has distinguished the rare evil women of all times" (p. 7); **VINTAGE VICTORIAN MURDER**. Bristol, 1971. Discusses the Victorian perception of murder. See especially: "Liverpool Society" for an account of the trial of Florence Maybrick who allegedly poisoned her husband. He points to the dubious evidence contributing to her conviction, the unlawful circumstances of her release, and the attraction of murder cases by the upperclass.

9.237
Wilson, Patrick, **MURDERESS: A STUDY OF WOMEN EXECUTED IN BRITAIN SINCE 1843**. 1971. The first year in which the Home Office statistics indicated the sex of those executed was 1843. More than 60 cases were reported over 68 years.

9.238
VICTORIAN STUDIES: Hartman, M.S., *"Murder for Respectability: The Case of Madeleine Smith,"* 16 (1973) 381-400. Examines the case and popular sentiment concerning a socially prominent woman who was tried for the murder of her lover and then released after a scandalous trial. Offers an understanding of a much larger group of women.

9.239
Symons, Julian, "The Criminal Classes" in **RULE BRITANNIA: THE VICTORIAN WORLD**. ed. by George Perry and Nicholas Mason. 1974. See p. 212 for photographs of three female criminals.

9.240
HISTORY WORKSHOP JOURNAL: Knight, T. and McGrath, P., *"History on Stage: Grimsby,"* no. 1 (1976) 121-126. Discusses the play, DEATH BY BATTLE'S VERMIN KILLER, based on the true story of a servant girl who was convicted in 1871 of stealing a postage stamp, spent one day in prison, and then committed suicide.

9.241
Hartman, Mary S., **VICTORIAN MURDERESSES**. New York, 1977. Gives an account of thirteen French and English women who committed murder during the period 1840-1890 including Madeleine Smith and Florence Maybrick, showing how these cases reflect the confines that middle-class women experienced in the home. On the phenomenon of women filling the courtrooms to sympathize with the accused: "Without acknowledging their real alarm over what these women's behavior meant, the men's remarks often display that they understood precisely what was happening, namely, that the 'female element' was showing a supportive identification with women accused of adultery and murder" (p. 357); *reviewed in:* **SOCIAL HISTORY:** Heppenstal, R., *"Lady Killers,"* n.v. (1977) 1326; *also reviewed in:* **JOURNAL OF PSYCHOHISTORY:** Robertson, P., 5 (1977-1978) 143-144.

9.242
Winn, Dilys, compiler, **MURDERESS INK: THE BETTER HALF OF THE MYSTERY**. New York, 1979. Gives accounts of notorious female criminals.

9.243
Borowitz, Albert, **THE WOMAN WHO MURDERED BLACK SATIN: THE BERMONDSEY HORROR.** Columbus, Ohio, 1980. Gives a spirited history of the investigation and public fanfare of the murder of Patrick O'Connor in Bermondsey, 1849, for which Maria Manning and her husband were convicted and executed. Includes material on murder, capital punishment, and crime journalism in Victorian England; *reviewed in:* **DICKENS QUARTERLY:** Cahill, P., 1 (1984) 112-114. Borowitz' book contrasts factual information with Manning's publicized image in the fictional account by Huish, AUTHENTIC MEMOIRES OF MARIA MANNING.

9.244
Harrison, Brian, "The Act of Militancy: Violence and the Suffragettes, 1904-1914" in **PEACEABLE KINGDOM: STABILITY AND CHANGE IN MODERN BRITAIN.** by Brian Harrison. Oxford, 1982.

9.245
CONTEMPORARY CRISES: Miller, E., *"International Trends in the Study of Female Criminality,"* 7 (1983) 59-70.

9.246
DARK LANTERN: Krone, K.A., *"One Woman's Poisons: The Preferred Poisons of the Victorian Era,"* 1 (1984) 19-27. "The black market poisons were 'marketed' under many names, including 'spouse removers,' 'inheritance powders,' and 'aqua toffana'" (p. 20). Tells of such murderesses as Mary Ann Cotton of Durham who had "the distinction of holding the title of Britain's greatest mass murderer. Until she was executed in March of 1873, no one was safe from her fatal ministrations. In her 41 years of life, her victims included 2 husbands, 1 lover, 9 children, 5 stepsons, and even her own mother!" (p. 23).

* * *

4. UNWED MOTHERS AND ILLEGITIMATE CHILDREN

9.247
Blackstone, William, "Of Parent and Child" in **COMMENTARIES ON THE LAWS OF ENGLAND.** ed. by Edward Christian. vol. 1, 1800. Distinguishes between legitimate children and bastards. "The rights [of a bastard] are very few, being only such as he can acquire, for he can inherit nothing, being looked upon as the son of nobody" (p. 458).

9.248
Nicolas, Nicholas Harris, **A TREATISE ON THE LAW OF ADULTERINE BASTARDY.** 1836.

9.249
Head, Edmund Walker, **REPORT ON THE LAW OF BASTARDY; WITH A SUPPLEMENTARY REPORT ON A CHEAP CIVIL REMEDY FOR SEDUCTION.** 1840.

9.250
LONDON: Saunders, J., *"The Foundling Hospital,"* 3 (1841) 337-352. When the orphan institution was full with 20 infants, "probably five times as many mothers with their infants [were] rejected... gazing upon the notice with all the heartburning and rage of the unsuccessful" (p. 342).

9.251
JOURNAL OF THE ROYAL STATISTICAL SOCIETY: Acton, W., *"Observations on Illegitimacy in London Parishes at St. Marylebone, St. Pancras and St. Georges, Southwark, During the Year 1857,"* 22 (1857) 491-502; *"Illegitimacy in England and Wales, 1879,"* 44 (1881) 394-398. "As regards the effect of town life, as opposed to country life, it will be noticed that London and the immediately adjoining counties have the lowest rates of illegitimacy" (p. 396).

9.252
Wright, Henry Clarke, THE UNWELCOME CHILD; OR, THE CRIME OF AN UNDESIGNED AND UNDESIRED MATERNITY. Boston, 1858.

9.253
Mayhew, Henry, "Appendix" in LONDON LABOUR AND THE LONDON POOR. by Henry Mayhew. vol. 4, 1862. See pp. 468-469 for charts and tables, and p. 489 for map.

9.254
Chaflin, Lady Cook Tennessee, ILLEGITIMACY. [188?]; 1910. Illegitimacy occurs more in rural areas than urban, and among the well educated rather than not. In manufacturing districts "a woman with several young illegitimate children is more sought after by some than one who has never borne, no matter how estimable her character" (p. 5). One explanation is the profitability of child labour and the value of a woman's proven fertility. Also, "the chances of life in the first year alone are at least four times greater for a legitimate than for an illegitimate child" (p. 7). Proposes reforms to remove the temptations to infanticide.

9.255
Cramond, William, ILLEGITIMACY IN BANFFSHIRE. Banff, 1888.

9.256
Hill, Florence Davenport, CHILDREN OF THE STATE. 2nd ed., 1889. Gives statistics on the number of homeless and illegitimate children in England and describes state institutions caring for them. Advocates the boarding-out system over large pauper boarding schools, citing better care and lower cost.

9.257
WESTMINSTER REVIEW: Hannigan, D.F., *"The Legitimacy of Children,"* 133 (1890) 619-624. Criticizes the laws of England as they relate to illegitimate children. Derides as hypocritical the accepted doctrine of British "respectability" whereby promiscuity is denounced yet tolerated at the same time. "The very persons who exhibit this shameful disregard of the growth and propagation of vice are the most strenuous upholders of the distinction between legitimacy and illegitimacy. Their contention is 'We must not encourage immorality. Therefore we must attach a stigma to every child not born in wedlock'.... How is immorality checked by calling an innocent child a bastard" (pp. 621-622); *"A Crime and Its Causes,"* 151 (1899) 131-139. The crime referred to is the practice of abortion, and its cause the stigma and unsupportive legislation regarding illegitimacy. "The cruelty inflicted upon the mother, the injustice which suffers the father to escape practically scot free, these

are paralleled by the criminal carelessness of the state, as to the future of the children who spring from irregular unions" (p. 138).

9.258
Leffingwell, Albert, ILLEGITIMACY AND THE INFLUENCE OF THE SEASONS UPON CONDUCT. 1892.

9.259
Legitimation League, THE RIGHTS OF NATURAL CHILDREN: VERBATIM REPORT OF THE INAUGURAL PROCEEDINGS OF THE LEGITIMATION LEAGUE. 1893. The League's founders did not believe in civil or religious marriage, and their goal was to "create a machinery for acknowledging offspring born out of wedlock, and to secure for them equal rights with legitimate children"; THE BAR SINISTER AND LICIT LOVE. THE FIRST BIENNIAL PROCEEDINGS OF THE LEGITIMATION LEAGUE. ed. by Oswald Dawson. 1895.

9.260
ADULT; THE JOURNAL OF SEX: 1897 to 1899; vols. 1-3. Published by the Legitimation League.

9.261
JOURNAL OF THE SOCIETY OF COMPARATIVE LEGISLATION: Fitzpatrick, D., *"Legitimation by Subsequent Marriage,"* 6 (1904) 22-45.

9.262
Heath, Harry Llewellyn, THE INFANT, THE PARENT AND THE STATE. 1907. Reports that illegitimate infants suffer a mortality rate four times as high as that of legitimate infants, and attributes this to feeble-mindedness of the parents, inferior physical condition of the mother, and lack of legal protection.

9.263
Great Britain Bastardy Orders Committee, REPORT FROM THE SELECT COMMITTEE TOGETHER WITH THE PROCEEDINGS OF THE COMMITTEE. 1909.

9.264
Chesser, Elizabeth Sloan, "The Unmarried Mother" in WOMEN, MARRIAGE AND MOTHERHOOD. by Elizabeth Sloan Chesser. 1913. "Our moral code and the law alike deal lightly with the unmarried father, whilst we make of unwedded maternity an almost insurmountable disgrace" (p. 58). Favors legitimation by subsequent marriage.

9.265
ENGLISH REVIEW: Gallichan, C.G., *"The Unmarried Mother,"* 18 (1914) 78-90. Condemns the laws which perpetuate hardships for unwed mothers, such as those pertaining to alimony and paternity. The State should take an interest in aiding illegitimate children, as is done in France. "The life of every child must be safeguarded, not on ethical grounds, but for the sake of the health and efficiency of the race" (p. 89). Decries the wastage of human life represented by the startlingly high mortality rates of illegitimate children.

9.266
CONTEMPORARY REVIEW: Barnes, A., *"The Unmarried Mother and Her Child,"* 112 (1917) 556-559. "In all we try to do let us hold firmly to the faith that every mentally normal mother, whether married or single, should be enabled to keep her

baby with her for the first year of its life at least" (p. 558).

9.267
Darwin, L., **DIVORCE AND ILLEGITIMACY.** 1918; *rpt. from:* EUGENICS REVIEW: 8 (1918) 296-306.

9.268
ENGLISH WOMAN: Fisher, H.A.L., *"Illegitimacy,"* 46 (1920) 81-90.

9.269
LAW QUARTERLY REVIEW: White, J.D., *"Legitimation by Subsequent Marriage,"* 36 (1920) 255-267.

9.270
Williams, Arthur Edmund, **BARNARDO OF STEPNEY: THE FATHER OF NOBODY'S CHILDREN.** 1953. The subject was founder of homes for destitute children. "Barnardo had never made illegitimacy a bar to admission to his homes, but this special type of case [young, unmarried woman and unwanted child] was in a category by itself, and bristling with difficulties. If he freely admitted such children, he might well be charged with putting a premium on immorality" (p. 124). The Auxiliary Boarding Out branch (1889) of his work made the father of the child contribute to the cost of its maintenance, placed the mother in domestic service, and boarded the child outside his other institutions.

9.271
BRITISH JOURNAL OF SOCIOLOGY: Pinchbeck, I., *"Social Attitudes to the Problem of Illegitimacy,"* 5 (1954) 309-333. Urges new legislation in England to replace the existing Bastardy Act of 1872. "Throughout history, the law dealing with children born out of wedlock has reflected to a considerable degree the changing mores concerning illegitimacy... as monogamy won favour owing to the desire to hand on property to the heirs of the blood, the bastard's position in the family deteriorated and changed rapidly for the worse under the influence of the Church, which gave exclusive sanction to that form of marriage, with the consequence that all progeny so begotten were deemed unlawful" (p. 312).

9.272
PAST AND PRESENT: Henriques, U.R.Q., *"Bastardy and the New Poor Law,"* no. 37 (1967) 103-129. "Perhaps the old bastardy laws, with all their abuses, to some extent weighted the scales in favour of the woman in search of a husband, and ensured that wooing customs did not disrupt local society" (p. 129). New laws that penalized women as a way to mend public morality largely failed.

9.273
Dewar, Diana, **ORPHANS OF THE LIVING: A STUDY OF BASTARDY.** 1968.

9.274
Middleton, Nigel, "The Treatment of Unmarried Mothers, 1900-1946" in **WHEN FAMILY FAILED: THE TREATMENT OF CHLDREN IN THE CARE OF THE COMMUNITY DURING THE FIRST HALF OF THE TWENTIETH CENTURY.** by Nigel Middleton. 1971.

9.275
JOURNAL OF INTERDISCIPLINARY HISTORY: Shorter, E., *"Illegitimacy, Sexual Revolution and Social Change in Modern England,"* 2 (1971) 261-269; Tilly, L.A., Scott, J.W. and Cohen, M., *"Women's Work and European Fertility Patterns,"* 6

(1976) 447-476; Fairchilds, C., *"Female Sexual Attitudes and the Rise of Illegitimacy: A Case Study,"* 8 (1978) 627-667. Study relates to France, but the generalization can be tested for England. Considers the thesis that "traditional sexual attitudes persisted in changing economic circumstances" and therefore were not the cause of the puzzling rise in illegitimacy (p. 629); Meteyard, B., *"Illegitimacy and Marriage in Eighteenth Century England,"* 10 (1979) 479-489. A steep rise in illegitimate children can be attributed to the effects of Lord Hardwicke's Act on Clandestine Marriages, 1753, which prevented the clergy from registering children from long term common unions as legitimate yet did nothing to restrain the sexual assaults on lower class women by their employers or other socially superior men.

9.276
POPULATION STUDIES: Laslett, P. and Oosterveen, K., *"Long-Term Trends in Bastardy in England and Wales: A Study of the Illegitimacy Figures in the Parish Registers and in the Reports of the Registrar General, 1561-1960,"* 27 (1973) 255-286. "It must never be forgotten that bastardy may have meant various things to an Englishman in Tudor times, to a Hanoverian, or a Victorian, or a citizen of the Lloyd George era. The causes of illegitimacy must have varied as well as its extent" (p. 256); Crafts, N.R., *"Illegitimacy in England and Wales in 1911,"* 36 (1982) 327-331. Discusses the role of economic variables as well as locality and late marriage as factors in illegitimate fertility.

9.277
Stone, Lawrence, **THE FAMILY, SEX AND MARRIAGE IN ENGLAND, 1500-1800.** New York, 1977. Discusses illegitimacy in the eighteenth century.

9.278
FEMINIST STUDIES: Gillis, J.R., *"Servants, Sexual Relations, and the Risks of Illegitimacy in London, 1801-1900,"* 5 (1979) 142-173. Explores the reasons for the many illegitimate children born to a higher class of London servants in the nineteenth century.

9.279
Laslett, Peter, Oosterveen, Karla and Smith, Richard M., eds., **BASTARDY AND ITS COMPARATIVE HISTORY: STUDIES IN THE HISTORY OF ILLEGIT-IMACY AND MENTAL NON-CONFORMISM IN BRITAIN, FRANCE, GERMANY, SWEDEN, NORTH AMERICA, JAMAICA AND JAPAN.** Cambridge, Mass., 1980. Part one deals exclusively with Britain in eight separately authored papers. The book as a whole proposes that "sexual behaviour has never anywhere been confined to procreative behaviour, procreative behaviour confined to marriage, and marriage confined to the official celebrations established by society" (n.p.).

9.280
Steinberg, Janice Burke, "The Development of a Social Policy Towards Illegitimacy in England 1870-1918," Ph.D. diss., Univ. of Cincinnati, 1980. "The policy the English followed... failed to provide adequate services for unmarried mothers and their children, and its ineffectiveness stemmed primarily from the inability of policy makers to separate their assistance programs from their moral disapproval of the recipients" (p. 1).

* * *

5. INFANTICIDE

9.281
THE TRIAL, INCLUDING AN ACCOUNT OF THE EXECUTION OF MARIA DAVIS AND CHARLOTTE BOBETT FOR THE WILFUL MURDER OF RICHARD DAVIS, AN INFANT FIFTEEN MONTHS OLD. Bristol, 1802.

9.282
Hunter, William, ON THE UNCERTAINTY OF THE SIGNS OF MURDER IN THE CASE OF BASTARD CHILDREN. 1812.

9.283
Arnold, Anne, MURDER!!! THE TRIAL AT LARGE OF ANNE ARNOLD FOR THE WILFUL MURDER OF HER INFANT CHILD, ETC. Bury at St. Edmond's, 1813.

9.284
Mahon, Paul Augustin Olivier, AN ESSAY ON THE SIGNS OF MURDER IN NEWBORN CHILDREN. Lancaster, 1813.

9.285
Beck, John B., AN INAUGURAL DISSERTATION ON INFANTICIDE. New York, 1817.

9.286
Hutchinson, William, A DISSERTATION ON INFANTICIDE IN ITS RELATIONS TO PHYSIOLOGY AND JURISPRUDENCE. 1820. A manual for the detection of feticide and infanticide.

9.287
Paris, John Ayrton and Fonblanque, J.S.M., "Physiological Illustrations.— Infanticide" in MEDICAL JURISPRUDENCE. by John Aryton Paris and J.S.M. Fonblanque. 1823. Discusses "the various means by which death of the newly born infant is usually accomplished; such as by wounding, suffocating, strangling, poisoning, etc." (p. 129). Pleads for the courts' sympathies for the "modest female" under "temporary insanity." Tells of a respectable married woman's acquittal of charges via an insanity plea, yet warns that "had this woman been of doubtful character, though innocent, she might have been executed, for want of medical evidence to prove the nature and frequency of puerperal insanity" (p. 130).

9.288
Simpson, James, A PROBATIONARY ESSAY ON INFANTICIDE. Edinburgh, 1825.

9.289
Scott, John, THE FATAL CONSEQUENCES OF LICENTIOUSNESS; A SERMON, OCCASIONED BY THE TRIAL OF A YOUNG WOMAN FOR THE ALLEGED MURDER OF HER ILLEGITIMATE CHILD. 1828.

9.290
Cumin, William, ed., THE PROOF OF INFANTICIDE CONSIDERED INCLUDING DR. HUNTER'S TRACT ON CHILD MURDER. 1836.

9.291
Easton, J.A., **CONTRIBUTIONS TO LEGAL MEDICINE; BEING OBSERVA-TIONS ON THE MEDICAL JURISPRUDENCE OF INFANTICIDE.** Edinburgh, 1852.

9.292
Clay, John, **BURIAL CLUBS AND INFANTICIDE IN ENGLAND: A LETTER TO W. BROWN, ESQ., M.P.** Preston, 1854. Clay was Chaplain to the Preston House of Correction.

9.293
DUBLIN REVIEW: *"On Some of the Circumstances Influencing the Practice of Exposure and Child Murder in Different Ages,"* 45 (1858) 55.

9.294
INFANTICIDE AND ITS CAUSE: AN APPEAL FOR THE UNREPRESENTED. 1859.

9.295
Moore, W.R., **REPORT ON FEMALE INFANTICIDE.** 1859.

9.296
INFANTICIDE MEMORANDA. 1861. Newspaper cuttings.

9.297
INFANTICIDE AND ITS CAUSE. BY A NORTH-COUNTRY WOMAN. 1862.

9.298
Greaves, George, **OBSERVATIONS ON SOME OF THE CAUSES OF INFANTICIDE.** Manchester, 1862-63; **OBSERVATIONS ON THE LAWS RELATING TO CHILD MURDER AND CRIMINAL ABORTION, WITH SUGGESTIONS FOR THEIR AMENDMENT.** Manchester, 1864. Advocates more stringent laws covering infanticide.

9.299
Ryan, William B., **INFANTICIDE: ITS LAW, PREVALENCE, PREVENTION AND HISTORY.** 1862.

9.300
TRANSACTIONS OF THE MANCHESTER STATISTICAL SOCIETY: Greaves, G., *"Observations on Some Causes of Infanticide,"* 11 (1862-1863) n.p.

9.301
J., B., **THOUGHTS AND SUGGESTIONS HAVING REFERENCE TO INFANTICIDE.** 1864.

9.302
Dymond, Alfred H., **THE LAW ON TRIAL: OR PERSONAL RECOLLECTIONS OF THE DEATH PENALTY AND ITS OPPONENTS.** 1865. See pp. 96-108, 125-147.

9.303
JOURNAL OF SOCIAL SCIENCE: Baines, M.A., *"A Few Thoughts Concerning Infanticide,"* 1 (1865-1866) 535-540. Infanticide has increased due to an apathetic

police force and public. "Hitherto the misguided erring woman has been compelled to bear the whole of the burden and obloquy while the partner of her sin has enjoyed all but complete immunity, not only from its legal penalty, but from his own share of the censure which society has so unmercifully pronounced upon her" (p. 537).

9.304
NATION: *"England: Infanticide Amongst the Poor,"* 1 (1865) 270.

9.305
GUIDE: *"Infanticide,"* 1 (1866-1867) 332.

9.306
Curgenven, John Brendon, **THE WASTE OF INFANT LIFE.** 1867.

9.307
BRITISH MEDICAL JOURNAL: *"Baby-Farming,"* 2 (1867) 570. Condemns the practice of hiring wet-nurses, claiming it contributes to high infant mortality. Recommends regulation of wet nurses and laws against profiteering on the life or death of a child.

9.308
BRITISH AND FOREIGN MEDICO-CHIRURGICAL REVIEW: Ballard, E., *"Baby Killing,"* 45 (1870) 346-370.

9.309
FRASER'S MAGAZINE: Froude, J.A., *"The Colonies Once More,"* 82 (1870) 269-287. Discusses infanticide as an adjunct to the problem of overpopulation and stresses the importance of aid for emigration.

9.310
LANCET: *"Infanticide,"* 2 (1873) 426; *"Remedies for Baby-Farming Evils,"* 2 (1911) 925. Reports on a paper entitled "Protection of Illegitimate Children Nursed for Hire." Suggests that protective legislation not be limited to illegitimate children.

9.311
Gardener, Augustus K., "Infanticide, Historically and Morally Considered" in **THE CONJUGAL RELATIONSHIPS AS REGARDS PERSONAL HEALTH AND HEREDITARY WELL BEING.** by Augustus K. Gardener. New York, 1874; 1892; rpt., 1974. "We can forgive the poor, deluded girl——seduced, betrayed, abandoned—who, in her wild frenzy, destroys the mute evidence of her guilt. We have only sympathy and sorrow for her. But for the married shirk, we have nothing but contempt" (p. 112).

9.312
THE MARRIAGE LAWS CONSIDERED WITH THE VIEW OF DIMINISHING PROSTITUTION AND INFANTICIDE. Birmingham, 1883.

9.313
Taylor, Alfred S., **THE PRINCIPLES AND PRACTICE OF MEDICAL JURIS-PRUDENCE.** 3rd ed., 1883. A legal guide for doctors that includes a scientific chapter on infanticide——its medical and legal definition, its proof even without bodily signs of evidence on the victim, and its status under the law.

9.314

SANITARY RECORD: Curgenven, J.B., *"Infanticide, Baby-Farming, and the Infant Life Protection Act,"* (1888-1889) 409-410; 461-463.

9.315

Parr, Robert John, **THE BABY FARMER; AN EXPOSITION AND AN APPEAL.** 1904. Published by the National Society for the Prevention of Cruelty to Children.

9.316

Read, Alfred Baker, **SOCIAL CHAOS AND THE WAY OUT.** 1914. Overpopulation is the greatest evil of society, causing poverty which in turn causes crime. "Infanticide your only remedy——When you can realise that your only salvation lies in having the overwhelming numbers of the riff-raff thinned down, you will see that there is only one way of doing this——by giving them lawful permission to reduce their own numbers." States that "it is a woman's affair (not a politician's, or a parson's, or the public's), whether she shall keep her uncounted children alive in misery, or not.... What is it now that stands between women and free love, between men and free love? Children; nothing else" (p. 355).

9.317

MODERN LAW REVIEW: Davies, D.S., *"Child-Killing in English Law,"* 1 (Dec. 1937 and March 1938) 269-287.

9.318

Williams, G., **THE SANCTITY OF LIFE AND THE CRIMINAL LAW.** 1958. History of abortion legislation in England.

9.319

Dickens, B.M., **ABORTION AND THE LAW.** Bristol, 1966. Details the history of statutory provisions pertaining to abortion in 1803, 1828, 1837 and 1861, on pp. 23-38.

9.320

Radbill, Samuel X., "A History of Child Abuse and Infanticide" in **THE BATTERED CHILD.** ed. by Ray Helfer and Henry Kempe. Chicago, 1968.

9.321

Walker, Nigel, "Infanticide" in **CRIME AND INSANITY IN ENGLAND: THE HISTORICAL PERSPECTIVE.** by Nigel Walker. vol. 1, Edinburgh, 1968. "Not all infanticides are committed in disordered states of mind.... Both Aschaffenbury [1903] and Grunhut [1948] recognized that in many cases this is the inexperienced girl's substitute for contraception or abortion" (p. 124). It was debated among justices of the Capital Punishment Commission that infanticide was a result of "temporary madness" and one "was even bold enough to hint that less harm was done by such homicides than in other cases: you cannot estimate the loss to the child itself, you know nothing about it at all. With regard to the public it causes no alarm, because it is a crime which can be committed only by mothers upon their newly born children" (p. 128). There were repeated attempts by judges aimed at amending this part of the capital punishment laws.

9.322

HARVARD LIBRARY BULLETIN: Peirce, D., *"Crime and Society in London 1799-1900: A Bibliographical Survey,"* 20 (1972) 430-435. Eighty-three criminals out of 117 sampled were women, most of whom had been convicted for the murder of infants or children. Pierce calls the volumes he searched a "source virtually untapped by historians" (p. 432).

9.323
Aykroyd, Peter, **EVIL LONDON: THE DARK SIDE OF A GREAT CITY.** 1973. Diverse references to crimes by women, such as the "celebrated babyfarmer" convicted in 1896. "She was Mrs. Dyer who strangled 46 of the babies she was paid to adopt and threw them into the Thames. Babyfarming thrived at this time because there were strong pressures, social and economic, on Victorian unmarried mothers to get rid of their children" (p. 107).

9.324
HISTORY OF CHILDHOOD INFANTICIDE QUARTERLY: Langer, W.L., *"Infanticide: A Historical Survey,"* 3 (1974) 353-365. Discusses infanticide as the accepted procedure of population control for economic and health-related reasons within a community.

9.325
NEW YORK REVIEW OF BOOKS: Stone, L., *"The Massacre of the Innocents,"* (November 14, 1974) 25-31.

9.326
Malcolmson, R.W., "Infanticide in the Eighteenth Century" in **CRIME IN ENGLAND 1550-1800.** ed. by J.S. Cockburn. 1977. Lists common characteristics of infanticide: babies were most often killed by women, usually their own mother; those accused were unmarried or widowed and were rarely of the genteel or middle-class family but from laboring, mechanic or farming backgrounds; of suspected and convicted women the majority were servant maids; recorded infanticides occurred immediately after birth; and sex of the baby was irrelevant. "In considering the tragic circumstances of infanticide, one is impressed, not only with the brute fact of the snuffing out of a young life, but also with the large burden of private responsibility which was borne by these unwed mothers in situations of almost total isolation" (p. 207).

9.327
Piers, Maria W., **INFANTICIDE.** New York, 1978. Gives a cross-cultural historical account of the motivations and techniques of infanticide: "As far as the past is concerned, that the value of a human life depended primarily on its muscular potential is also borne out by the preponderance of female victims of infanticide. Men were worth more than women.... All in all, then, it is the female condition that is at the root of considerations like the one that woman is the worthless sex and often not worthy of living" (p. 43).

9.328
MEDICAL HISTORY: Damme, C., *"Infanticide: The Worth of an Infant Under Law,"* 22 (1978) 1-24. Traces the evolution of attitudes toward infanticide in ecclesiastical, secular and common law in England. Illustrates "the lower status in which the infant was held by society," shown by a history of legislation "which prescribe lesser penalties than those for homicide as well as establish a very liberal insanity defence" (p. 24).

9.329
POPULATION STUDIES: Sauer, R., *"Infanticide and Abortion in Nineteenth-Century Britain,"* 32 (1978) 81-93. Examines the role and extent of infanticide, who practiced it, trends in its use, and the public opinion it generated.

9.330
HUMAN ECOLOGY: Hansen, E.D.G.R., *"'Overlaying' in 19th-Century England: Infant Mortality or Infanticide?"* 7 (1979) 333-352. "The attribution of infant deaths among the poor to more or less willful 'overlaying' may have been an expression of social distance by middle and upper-income people from working-class people" (p. 347).

9.331
JOURNAL OF THE HISTORY OF MEDICINE AND ALLIED SCIENCES: Behlmer, G.K., *"Deadly Motherhood: Infanticide and Medical Opinion in Mid-Victorian England,"* 34 (1979) 403-427. Investigates the reasons why, between 1860 and 1865, infanticide suddenly emerged as an issue of national concern. The "most obvious explanation was that child-murder had reached such epidemic proportions by the 1860s as to demand [public] attention." But the issue also provided sensational press and reinforced elitist sentiments. The rise in coroners' inquests during the period may also be a factor, as well as the general difficulty in determining the viability of an infant at birth.

9.332
SOCIETY FOR THE SOCIAL HISTORY OF MEDICINE BULLETIN: Clarke, K., *"Infanticide, Illegitimacy and the Medical Profession in Nineteenth Century England,"* 26 (1980) 11-14. Examines "the discussions of infanticide which appeared in the medical press and are reported in parliamentary papers, in order to throw light on attitudes to the newborn infant in nineteenth century England.... Most cases reaching the courts involved the death of an illegitimate child, often the child of a domestic servant" (p. 11).

9.333
Hoffer, Peter and Hull, N.E.H., **MURDERING MOTHERS: INFANTICIDE IN ENGLAND AND NEW ENGLAND, 1558-1803.** 1981. Good general background. Focuses on the emergence of modern laws on infanticide and treatment of suspects in the criminal justice systems.

9.334
Behlmer, George K., **CHILD ABUSE AND MORAL REFORM IN ENGLAND, 1870-1908.** Stanford, 1982. See especially: "Doctors and Baby-Farmers," covering the sordid history of "professional adoption" houses that were often centers of infanticide.

9.335
Parssinen, Terry M., *"'Mother's Friend': Opium as an Escape"* in **SECRET PASSIONS, SECRET REMEDIES: NARCOTIC DRUGS IN BRITISH SOCIETY 1820-1930.** by Terry M. Parssinen. Philadelphia, 1983. Opium, in the form of laudanum and Godfrey's Cordial, was a common means of infanticide, whether deliberate or not. It was said that working-class mothers fed their children opiates to quiet them and suppress their appetite. "An observer noted 'the heavy, deathlike sleep, accompanied by convulsive twitchings, the scorched, swollen eyelids, the bluish pallor of countenance and growing heaviness of expression' that characterized opium-fed infants" (p. 44).

9.336
McLaren, Angus, **REPRODUCTIVE RITUALS: THE PERCEPTION OF FERTILITY IN ENGLAND FROM THE SIXTEENTH CENTURY TO THE NINETEENTH CENTURY.** 1984. Abortion became a statutory crime in 1803. The statute held that any attempt, by poison or instrument, to effect miscarriage in the

first four months of gestation was a criminal act. Discusses the history of infanticide laws and the role of doctors in abortion legislation on pp. 113-144.

9.337
Rose, Lionel, THE MASSACRE OF THE INNOCENTS: INFANTICIDE IN BRITAIN 1800-1939. 1986. Includes discussion of "Baby Farmers"; Infant Life Protection Society; and burial insurance as factors to consider in researching infanticide.

*   *   *

6. ALCOHOLISM AND DRUG ABUSE

9.337
De Quincey, Thomas, **CONFESSIONS OF AN ENGLISH OPIUM EATER.** 1822; rpt., 1971. Glorifies the "pleasures of opium"; this was the first writing to alert the public to opium use by industrial workers and as a stimulant.

9.338
MEDICAL TIMES AND GAZETTE: *"Increased Consumption of Opium in England,"* (April 25, 1857) 426.

9.339
CHEMIST AND DRUGGIST: *"An Opium Den in Whitechapel,"* 9 (1868) 275. "Seated on a mattress in a room lighted by a dim lamp is an old woman with dishevelled white hair, thin face, and dull-looking eyes, blowing a cloud of smoke and coughing every now and then like a person in the last stage of consumption. She casts a stupefied gaze upon us, then throws herself back and continues to puff away at her pipe of opium" (p. 275); W., A.C., *"Opium Smoking in Bluegate Fields,"* 11 (1870) 259-261. Describes a visit to a den in Victoria-street run by a Chinese named Osee. "Leaving Osee and his friends, we stepped again into the court, and were hailed from the opposite side by a woman who asked if we should like to see her smoke opium. We accepted the invitation, and found her alone. She was evidently poorer, and doing less business than her thriving neighbour, but she seemed much more intelligent. I think she said that she was the only female opium smoker in London, and certainly Osee said that none of his customers were women" (p. 260); *"Homoeopathic Cure for the Opium Habit,"* 20 (1878) 319. Reports an American doctor's homoeopathic treatment (Ipecac) which he says has cured 38 out of 40 patients treated; *"A Lady on the Effects of Opium,"* 20 (1878) 337-338. A not altogether convincing attempt to demonstrate to readers that the "pleasures of opium" (as Thomas De Quincey put it) are outweighed by the side effects. The lady quoted is a consul's daughter who mistook a cigarette offered her for tobacco. "Presently, I felt a strange languor creeping over me, my head whirled, my ears began to tingle, my eye-sight dimmed, and my eyelids heavily closing, I soon found myself in the fool's paradise of opium-eaters. All sorts of sweet dreams took possession of my imagination, crossed by the most ludicrous thoughts and desires. I imagined that trains were running down my arms; next my travelling-boots... took to my deluded vision the proportions of a grotto, towards which I made a desperate rush, and soon fell exhausted with the efforts I made to enter it. My hostess took the form of a rat, from whose presence I vainly tried to escape... the twinkle of the

myriad bright stars raised my mind to higher thoughts, and sensations of an indescribably delicious character took possession of me.... On awakening next morning I felt uncomfortable; in fact, I was ill" (p. 338); *"Green Tea as an Opium Antidote,"* 20 (1878) 267. A Quebec doctor successfully administered a green tea enema to a woman on the point of death from swallowing 28 drachms of a liquid opiate preparation.

9.340
LONDON SOCIETY: AN ILLUSTRATED MAGAZINE OF LIGHT AND AMUSING LITERATURE FOR THE HOURS OF RELAXATION: *"East London Opium Smokers,"* 14 (1868) 68-72. Author visits a den in Bluegate Fields whose customers are chiefly sailors arriving in London ports. Describes the Chinese proprietor and his English wife, and details the methods and implements of preparation for smoking. Says Mrs. Chi Ki, "It don't often make me ill; it makes me silly. I am ill sometimes, though. I was ill a-bed when the Prince of Wales and the other gentlemen came up here to see the smokers.... I was sorry that the place was in such a muddle; but the Prince didn't seem to mind" (p. 72).

9.341
LANCET: *"Female Drunkenness,"* 2 (1880) 706. "Scarcely a day passes but the bench have a number of feminine inebriates to pass judgement on, and the number of confirmed cases that often came under their consideration is truly lamentable" (p. 706); *"Drinking Among Englishwomen"* 1 (1890) 187; *"Inebriety in Women,"* 2 (1900) 1292. Discusses the more visible drinking by Englishwomen of all classes. In 1880 James Wakely suggested that if the women's rights advocates wanted to turn their attention to a real issue they should concern themselves with female alcoholics.

9.342
Campbell, Hugh, **THE DRINK-HUNGER IN WOMEN, ITS CAUSES, CONSE-QUENCES AND CURATIVE TREATMENT.** 1890. Alcoholism in women may be traced in origin to problems of the digestive system.

9.343
PUBLIC HEALTH: *"Opium-Eating in Lincolnshire,"* 5 (1893) 190.

9.344
Horsley, J.W., **PRISON AND PRISONERS.** 1898. Contains descriptions of female criminals and the nature of crimes related to alcoholism.

9.345
Holmes, Thomas, **PICTURES AND PROBLEMS FROM LONDON POLICE COURTS.** 1900. Includes extensive criminal records on female inebriates and addresses the inadequecy of incarceration for deliquency and inebriation of the mentally ill. "We have heard so much of women's rights that there is a danger of the rights of men being over-looked, so on their behalf I contend that the sober husband of a drunken wife should have the power of summoning her before the magistrate" (p. 105). Cites the case of the murder of a drunken wife by her husband, and deems his six-month prison charge unjust.

9.346
ILLUSTRATED TEMPERANCE MONTHLY: Melynock, Mrs., *"Alcoholism Amongst Women,"* 12 (1902) 217.

9.347
BRITISH JOURNAL OF INEBRIETY: Zanetti, F., *"Inebriety in Women and Its*

Influence on Child-Life," 1 (1903) n.p.

9.348
ECONOMIC REVIEW: *"Alcoholism,"* 16 (1906) 305-314. "Another factor which in recent years without doubt has been responsible for the increased drinking habits of women is the granting of grocers' licences to sell intoxication drinks; this has led to an enormous amount of drinking amongst this sex" (p. 307).

9.349
Scharlieb, Mary Ann Dacomb, "Alcoholism in Relation to Women and Children" in THE DRINK PROBLEM IN ITS MEDICO-SOCIOLOGICAL ASPECTS. BY FOURTEEN MEDICAL AUTHORITIES. ed. by Theophilus Nicholas Kelynack. 1907; 1916. "During the present generation women have through the franchise and by increased legal control of their own affairs——become more independent of men, and these changes have rendered them less amenable to 'communal vigilance.' Women are also now not ashamed to be seen in public-houses as they used to be... the unexpected result [of emancipation]... is more drinking" (p. 232).

9.350
WESTMINSTER REVIEW: Houghton, B., *"Elimination by Alcohol,"* 169 (1908) 299-308. Illuminates the startlingly high incidence of alcohol abuse.

9.351
Johnson, J., "Motherhood-Heredity-Alcohol" in WASTAGE OF CHILD LIFE AS EXEMPLIFIED BY CONDITIONS IN LANCASHIRE. 1909. Discusses alcohol abuse by women and its effects on their children during and after pregnancy.

9.352
Barrington, Amy and Pearson, Karl, EUGENICS LABORATORY MEMOIRS: A PRELIMINARY STUDY OF EXTREME ALCOHOLISM IN ADULTS. vol. 14, 1910. Contends that, on the basis of statistics, "Roman Catholic inebriates are less frequently prostitutes than the Protestants" (p. 22).

9.353
Devon, James, "The Inebriate Home" in THE CRIMINAL AND THE COMMUNITY. 1912. Informs on the successes and failures of the Gergenti Inebriate Home. "The habits of housekeeping acquired by the inmates of a home may tend to make them good servants, but they are certainly not the kind likely to make them more fit than they were to undertake the management of a house of their own; for they do not manage, they are managed" (p. 283).

9.354
Heron, David, EUGENICS LABORATORY MEMOIRS: A SECOND STUDY OF EXTREME ALCOHOLISM IN ADULTS WITH SPECIAL REFERENCE TO THE HOME OFFICE INEBRIATE REFORMATORY DATA. vol. 17, 1912. Contains tables comparing convictions of male and female inebriates; discusses inebriate reformatories for women.

9.355
Booth, Mrs. Bramwell, "The Management of the Inebriate Woman" and "A Plea For the Woman Inebriate" in MOTHERS AND THE EMPIRE AND OTHER ADDRESSES. St. Albans, 1914. Published by the Salvation Army.

9.356
NINETEENTH CENTURY: Martin, A., *"Working-Women and Drink,"* 78 (1915)

1378-1395. "It may safely be asserted that the evil of inebriety among women is less widespread than the diatribes of platform and press have led the general public to believe" (n.p.); *"Working-Women and Drink II,"* 78 (1916) 85-104. "Even when there has been no abnormal strain, many elderly women after their children have grown up and left home tend to give way to drink. They are nearly always more or less ailing, have never had any interests or pursuits apart from their families, and they suffer from loneliness and depression" (p. 87). Includes accounts of several female inebriates.

9.357
Gordon, Mary, "The Inebriate Vagabond" in **PENAL DISCIPLINE.** by Mary Gordon. 1922.

9.358
Cunnington, Cecil Willett, **FEMININE ATTITUDES IN THE NINETEENTH CENTURY.** 1935. See pp. 206-209 for alcoholism and women.

9.359
Walker, Nigel, "Automatism and Drunkenness" in **CRIME AND INSANITY IN ENGLAND: THE HISTORICAL PERSPECTIVE.** by Nigel Walker. vol. 1, Edinburgh, 1968. The criminal responsibility of the drunken person is compared with that of the automatist or sleepwalker, because in neither case does the person have complete volition. Both defenses were frowned upon in English courts, from the nineteenth century through the 1960's.

9.360
BULLETIN OF THE INSTITUTE OF THE HISTORY OF MEDICINE: Lomax, E., *"The Uses and Abuses of Opiates in Nineteenth-Century England,"* 47 (1973) 167-176. "Officially, opium and its preparations were responsible for more premature deaths than any other chemical agent." Opiates accounted for 186 of the 543 deaths by poison recorded in 1837-38.

9.361
Cotterell, Gareth, "A Night in an Opium Den" in **LONDON SCENE FROM THE STRAND.** 1974. ed. by Gareth Cotterell.

9.362
Watney, John, **MOTHER'S RUIN: THE STORY OF GIN.** 1976.

9.363
BRITISH JOURNAL OF ADDICTION: Berridge, V., *"Our Own Opium: Cultivation of the Opium Poppy in Britain, 1740-1823,"* 72 (1977) 90-94. The reports of several doctors who compared the efficacy of British opium to the Turkish variety "indicate a contemporary medical acceptance of dependence which had survived any furor created by the publication of De Quincey's 'Confessions [of an English Opium Eater]'" (p. 93); Berridge, V., *"Fenland Opium Eating in the Nineteenth Century,"* 72 (1977) 275-284. Opium was sold in large quanitities and took the place of drink in Fenland towns and villages. Article analyzes the demographics of its use in the area in the context of prevailing attitudes and debates about drug use in the nineteenth century; Berridge, V., *"Opium Eating and the Working Class in the Nineteenth Century: The Public and Official Reaction,"* 73 (1978) 107-112. Debates were catalyzed by concern over opium's debilitating effects on the industrial work force, Indian involvement in the Chinese opium trade, and the struggle for professionalization by pharmacists. Sensationalist journalism helped to obscure rational consideration of the problem; Berridge, V., *"Working-Class Opium Eating*

in the Nineteenth Century: Establishing the Facts," 73 (1978) 363-374. Most working-class addiction began with use of the drug for medical reasons, not for luxury, and "women seem to have been major consumers" (p. 371); Berridge, V., *"Drugs and Social Policy: The Establishment of Drug Control in Britain 1900-1930,"* 79 (1984) 17-30; Bynum, W.F., *"Alcoholism and Degeneration in 19th Century European Medicine and Psychiatry,"* 79 (1984) 59-70. Reports the controversy that followed a study in which it was reported that drunkenness was a heritable tendency; Gutzke, D.W., *"'The Cry of the Children': The Edwardian Medical Campaign Against Maternal Drinking,"* 79 (1984) 71-84. To Edwardians... beset with unpropitious falls in the birth rate and alarmed at the proportion of recruits rejected as physically unfit during the Boer War, mother drunkenness... assumed importance in what they regarded as unacceptable infant deaths and 'race deterioration'" (p. 71). Good bibliography.

9.364

BULLETIN FOR THE SOCIAL HISTORY OF MEDICINE: Berridge, V., *"Victorian Opium Eating: Responses to Opiate Use in 19th Century Society,"* 22 (1978) 11-16.

9.365

PHARMACY IN HISTORY: Berridge, V., *"Opium Over the Counter in Nineteenth Century England,"* 20 (1978) 91-100. "The surprise shown by doctors when working people were revealed to be dependent on the drug when their supplies were curtailed suggests that addiction often may have been masked because most managed their opium consumption without much disruption, and because few among the laboring population would, in any case, have seen a doctor" (p. 94).

9.366

JOURNAL OF THE HISTORY OF MEDICINE AND ALLIED SCIENCES: Berridge, V., *"Opium in the Fens in Nineteenth-Century England,"* 34 (1979) 293-313. There was a high incidence of malaria in the low-lying marshland of the Fens, and ague was extremely common. "The use of opiates was most obvious among the labouring population and their children. Without ready access even to free medical treatment, opiates formed a cheap and accessible form of self-medication, culturally sanctioned and accepted" (p. 301).

9.367

Berridge, Virginia and Edwards, Griffith, **OPIUM AND THE PEOPLE: OPIATE USE IN 19TH CENTURY ENGLAND.** 1981. Comprehensive with good bibliography. See especially: Part Two, "Opium Use in the First Half of the Nineteenth Century" and Part Four, "Class Tensions." "Morphine was undoubtedly popular in the treatment of specifically female complaints——for period pains, in pregnancy and during labour——and also for those ailments such as neuralgia, sleeplessness and 'nerves' in general, which were considered to have a hysterical origin and so to be particularly common among female patients. There were well-known female addicts like G.B. Shaw's actress friend Janet Achurch" (pp. 148-149).

9.368

Parssinen, Terry M., **SECRET PASSIONS, SECRET REMEDIES: NARCOTIC DRUGS IN BRITISH SOCIETY 1820-1930.** Philadelphia, 1983. Reports of opium use were relatively rare, considering the "fastidiousness with which the medical and pharmaceutical press reported such exotic indulgences as chloroform-inhaling in London, eau-de-cologne tippling in Liverpool, and ether-drinking in Glasgow." In Nottingham, "a local chemist estimated, in 1801, that women [opium] users outnumbered men by three to one" (pp. 46-47). Opium users were considered much more civil and benign than alcoholics.

9.369
ALCOHOL IN HISTORY: A MULTIDISCIPLINARY NEWSLETTER: Gutzke, D.
and Fahey, D.M., *"Drink and Temperance in Britain,"* 9 (1984) 3-5.

* * *

7. PRISONS, PRISONERS AND PENAL REFORM

9.370
Howard, John, **STATE OF PRISONS IN ENGLAND AND WALES WITH
PRELIMINARY OBSERVATIONS AND AN ACCOUNT OF SOME FOREIGN
PRISONS.** 1784; **JOHN HOWARD AND THE PRISON WORLD OF EUROPE.**
1850. —*see also:* Aiken, John, **A VIEW OF THE LIFE, TRAVELS AND
PHILANTHROPIC WORK OF THE LATE JOHN HOWARD.** Boston, 1794;
Howard, D.L., **JOHN HOWARD: PRISON REFORMER.** 1958.

9.371
Bentham, Jeremy, **MANAGEMENT OF THE POOR: OR A PLAN, CONTAINING
THE PRINCIPLE AND CONSTRUCTION OF AN ESTABLISHMENT, IN WHICH
PERSONS OF ANY DESCRIPTION ARE TO BE KEPT UNDER INSPECTION,
AND IN PARTICULAR PENITENTIARY HOUSES, PRISONS,... MADHOUSES,...
ETC.** Dublin, 1796.

9.372
Neild, James, **STATE OF THE PRISONS IN ENGLAND, SCOTLAND AND
WALES.** 1812. Contains lists and brief description of prisons in England. Valuable
statistics on woman criminals incarcerated in 1805-1806.

9.373
Buxton, Thomas Fowell, **AN INQUIRY INTO WHETHER CRIME AND MISERY
ARE PRODUCED OR PREVENTED, BY OUR PRESENT SYSTEM OF PRISON
DISCIPLINE... AND THE PROCEEDINGS OF THE LADIES' COMMITTEE OF
NEWGATE IN 1813.** 1813; 2nd ed., 1818. Advocates reform, maintaining the prison
system promotes crime. Reports that lack of separation between male and female
prisoners encourages promiscuity, prisoners are severely underfed, and they are
often allowed no labor or schooling. —*see also:* Binney, T., **LIFE OF SIR
THOMAS FOWELL BUXTON.** 1853. Elizabeth Fry wrote to Buxton, who solicited
the Prime Minister's permission for Fry to visit prisons.

9.374
Bennett, Henry Grey, "A Letter to the Common Council and Livery of the City of
London, on the Abuses Existing at Newgate..." in **THE PAMPHLETEER.** ed. by
A.J. Valpy. 29 vols. 2nd ed., 1818.

9.375
EDINBURGH REVIEW: Jeffrey, F., *"Prison Discipline,"* 30 (1818) 463-486; Smith,
S., *"Council for Prisoners,"* 45 (1826) 74-95; Greg, W.R., *"The Management and
Disposal of our Criminal Population,"* 100 (1854) 563-632; Martineau, H., *"The
Convict System in England and Ireland,"* 117 (1863) 241-268; Martineau, H., *"Life*

in the Criminal Class," 122 (1865) 337-371.

9.376
Fry, Elizabeth, **OBSERVATIONS ON THE VISITING, SUPERINTENDING AND GOVERNMENT OF FEMALE PRISONERS.** 1819; 1827; **ON VISITING PRISONS.** 1827; **SKETCH OF THE ORIGIN AND RESULTS OF LADIES' PRISON ASSOCIATIONS: WITH HINTS FOR THE FORMATION OF LOCAL ASSOCIATIONS.** 1827; **HINTS ON THE ADVANTAGES AND DUTIES OF LADIES' COMMITTEES WHO VISIT PRISONS.** 1840. ——*see also:* Gurney, Joseph John, **NOTES ON A VISIT MADE TO SOME OF THE PRISONS IN SCOTLAND AND THE NORTH OF ENGLAND, IN COMPANY WITH ELIZABETH FRY.** 1819; **FRIEND:** *"Elizabeth Fry,"* 3 (1845) 263-264; **AINSWORTH'S MAGAZINE:** *"Mrs. Fry in Newgate; or Female Delinquency,"* 9 (1846) 123-131; Fry, Katherine and Cresswell, Rachel E., eds., **MEMOIR OF THE LIFE OF ELIZABETH FRY.** 2 vols. 1847; rpt. Montclair, 1974; Timpson, Thomas, **MEMOIRS OF MRS. ELIZABETH FRY: INCLUDING A HISTORY OF HER LABOURS IN PROMOTING THE REFORMATION OF FEMALE PRISONERS, AND THE IMPROVEMENT OF BRITISH SEAMEN.** New York, 1847; Clay, Walker Lowe, **THE PRISON CHAPLAIN: A MEMOIR OF THE REV. JOHN CLAY, B.D.** 1861; 1969. In section on women reformers, there is a decided reverence for the self-sacrificing Sarah Martin over Elizabeth Fry, who is, ironically, almost satirically described as a "spiritual dictatress" whose "thorough goodness" and "peculiar gift for exhortation" led her to ministry in the prisons. "She unconsciously assumed a position of plenary authority among her select followers and a tone of placid dogmatism with the general public. Her nursery and housekeeping were scarcely so congenial as her public pursuits" (p. 82); **ALL THE YEAR ROUND:** *"Chronicles of London Streets,"* 7 (1872) 490-491. On Mrs. Fry and the Newgate prisoners; Pitman, Emma Raymond, "Elizabeth Fry" in **EMINENT WOMEN SERIES.** ed. by John H. Ingram. 1883; Griffiths, Arthur, **THE CHRONICLES OF NEWGATE.** New York, 1884. See pp. 375-384; Pitman, Emma Raymond, **LIFE OF ELIZABETH FRY.** Boston, 1884; 1901; Ashby, Irene, **ELIZABETH FRY.** 1892; Render, William, **THROUGH PRISON BARS. THE LIVES AND LABOURS OF JOHN HOWARD AND ELIZABETH FRY...** 1894; Lewis, Georgina King (Stouton), **ELIZABETH FRY.** 1903; 3rd ed., 1909; Homes, Marion, **ELIZABETH FRY: A CAMEO LIFE SKETCH.** 1913; Richards, Laura Elizabeth, **ELIZABETH FRY: THE ANGEL OF THE PRISONS.** New York, 1916; Wakeford, Constance, **THE PRISONERS' FRIENDS: JOHN HOWARD, ELIZABETH FRY AND SARAH MARTIN.** 1917; Johnson, R. Brimley, ed., **ELIZABETH FRY'S JOURNEYS ON THE CONTINENT.** 1931; Whitney, Janet, **ELIZABETH FRY: QUAKER HEROINE.** 1937; Hinde, R.S.E., "Elizabeth Fry and Her Contemporaries" in **THE BRITISH PENAL SYSTEM 1773-1950.** by R.S.E. Hinde. 1951; Bardens, Dennis, **THE TRUE BOOK ABOUT ELIZABETH FRY.** 1961; Kent, John, **ELIZABETH FRY.** 1962; Rose, June, "The National Crusade" in **ELIZABETH FRY 1780-1845.** by June Rose. 1980. Fry wished to establish a local Ladies' Association in every area, as well as set and enact high standards for female prisoners to live by; Rose, June, **ELIZABETH FRY: A BIOGRAPHY.** New York, 1981; *reviewed in:* ALBION: Knox, T.R., 13 (1981) 404-405.

9.377
Committee of the Society for the Improvement of Prison Discipline, and for the Reformation of Juvenile Offenders, **RULES FOR THE GOVERNMENT OF GAOLS, HOUSES OF CORRECTION, AND PENITENTIARIES, TO WHICH ARE ADDED, PLANS OF PRISONS ON IMPROVED PRINCIPLES, AND A DESCRIPTION, WITH PLATES OF A CORN MILL AND WATER MILL ADAPTED TO THE EMPLOYMENT OF PRISONERS.** 1821. Outlines the

regulations regarding the architecture of prisons and management of male and female prisoners. The plans appear designed to protect rather than to actively discipline. For example: "No officer of the prison, or any other person shall enter the cell of any female prisoner, under solitary confinement, but in the presence of the matron; or her female assistant, in the event of the matron being necessarily absent" (p. 32); SIXTH REPORT. 1824.

9.378
Reid, Thomas, TWO VOYAGES TO NEW SOUTH WALES AND VAN DIEMAN'S LAND, WITH A DESCRIPTION OF THE PRESENT CONDITION OF THAT INTERESTING COLONY:... CONVICTS OF BOTH SEXES... 1822.

9.379
QUARTERLY REVIEW: Taylor, G., *"Prisons and Penitentiaries,"* 30 (1824) 404-440. Reports eleven deaths due to scurvy among prisoners at Millbank in 1822: "To inexperienced persons like ourselves there appears to be an insufficiency on the face of it; the only portion of animal food in the whole was a single ox-head boiled in soup for 100 males, and the same for 120 females per diem; but prison diet is so purely a question of experience that no one can impute the slightest blame to those who adopted it as sufficient under such recommendations and authority" (p. 433); Armstrong, J., *"Female Penitentiaries,"* 83 (1848) 359-376.

9.380
British Ladies' Society for Promoting the Reformation of Female Prisoners, FOURTH ANNUAL REPORT OF THE COMMITTEE. 1825; SKETCH OF THE ORIGIN AND RESULTS OF LADIES' PRISON ASSOCIATIONS. 1827; 1840; A CONCISE VIEW OF THE ORIGIN AND PROGRESS OF THE BRITISH LADIES' SOCIETY FOR PROMOTING THE REFORMATION OF FEMALE PRISONERS. 1839; 1840. ——*see also:* TRANSACTIONS OF THE NATIONAL ASSOCIATION FOR THE PROMOTION OF SOCIAL SCIENCE: Frazer, C., *"The Origins and Progress of 'The British Ladies' Society for Promoting the Reformation of Female Prisoners,' Established by Mrs. Fry in 1821,"* 6 (1862) 495-501.

9.381
FRASER'S MAGAZINE: *"The Schoolmaster's Experience in Newgate,"* 6 (1832) 460-498. Discusses the various crimes committed by those incarcerated in Newgate and establishes guidelines for the incarceration and rehabilitation of various criminals; Carpenter, M., *"On the Treatment of Female Convicts,"* 67 (1863) 31-46. "The first and obvious intention of a prison is punishment of crime. Suffering must always follow sin.... The gaol must not be made a more desirable place than the workhouse" (p. 34); Skene, F., *"Prison Visiting,"* 22 (1880) 762-774. Prison visiting organizations are the best "restorative agenc[ies]" that can be utilized in prison reform and rehabilitation of female prisoners.

9.382
Maconochie, Alexander, THOUGHTS ON CONVICT MANAGEMENT, AND OTHER SUBJECTS CONNECTED WITH THE AUSTRALIAN PENAL COLONIES. Hobart Town, 1838. See p. 128 for information on the management of female prisoners.

9.383
MONTHLY CHRONICLE: De Morgan, E., *"Reform of Prison,"* 3 (1839) 173-184; Innes, M., *"Transportation,"* 6 (1840) 159-162. On punishment by transportation.

9.384
Tristan, Flora, "Prisons" in **FLORA TRISTAN'S LONDON JOURNAL: A SURVEY OF LONDON LIFE IN THE 1830S.** orig. French ed., 1840; rpt., trans. by Dennis Palmer and Gisell Penceti. 1980. Contains detailed descriptions of women's incarceration and the differentiation between male and female prisoners in Newgate and Coldbath prisons. Describes several encounters with female prisoners such as a three-year-old girl: "The poor little thing was at Coldbath with her mother, who usually worked in the garden and took the child with her, but the mother had made the double mistake of breaking silence and of asking one of her companions for what reason she was in prison. Such questions are punishable by fifteen days in solitary confinement and the poor child was serving the sentence along with her mother" (p. 127).

9.385
LONDON: Platt, J.C., *"Prisoners and Penitentiaries,"* 5 (1841) 321-336. Includes valuable crime statistics: "In the year 1839, taken into custody... 22,467 females and 43,498 males. Numbers taken up for drunkenness were 13,952 males and 7317 females" (p. 321). Also describes women at Newgate.

9.386
Martin, Sarah, **PRISON JOURNALS.** 1844. Martin was a poor working woman who established schools and vocational training for women prisoners. Includes a brief sketch of her life and parliamentary reports on prisons. ——*see also:* Religious Tract Society, **A BRIEF SKETCH OF THE LIFE OF THE LATE SARAH MARTIN OF GREAT YARMOUTH, WITH EXTRACTS FROM HER WRITINGS AND PRISON JOURNALS.** Yarmouth, 1845; **SELECTIONS FROM THE POETICAL REMAINS OF... MISS. S. MARTIN, ETC. (INTRODUCTORY NOTICE OF THE AUTHORESS).** Yarmouth, 1845; von Eckart, F., **SARAH MARTIN... EINE LEBENSGESCHICHTE.** 1849; Balfour, Clara Lucas, **A SKETCH OF SARAH MARTIN.** 1854; Mogridge, George, **SARAH MARTIN, THE PRISON VISITOR OF GREAT YARMOUTH. WITH EXTRACTS FROM HER WRITINGS AND PRISON JOURNALS.** [1854]; Smiles, Samuel, "Sarah Martin" in **BRIEF BIOGRAPHIES.** Boston, 1861; 1869; 1874; 1876; 1877; 1881. The author was a well-known English popular philanthropist; Mogridge, George, **SARAH MARTIN: THE PRISON VISITOR OF GREAT YARMOUTH. A STORY OF A USEFUL LIFE.** 1872; Buckle, John, **SARAH MARTIN: THE PRISONER'S FRIEND.** 1910; Wakeford, Constance, **THE PRISONER'S FRIENDS: JOHN HOWARD, ELIZABETH FRY AND SARAH MARTIN.** 1917.

9.387
BLACKWOOD'S EDINBURGH MAGAZINE: Alison, A., *"Imprisonment and Transportation: The Increase of Crime,"* 55 (1844) 533-545; *"Causes of the Increase in Crime,"* 56 (1844) 1-14; *"Colonisation——Mr. Wakefield's Theory,"* 65 (1849) 509-528; Alison, A., *"The Transportation Question [Punishment of Convicts],"* 66 (1849) 519-538.

9.388
Adshead, Joseph, **PRISONS AND PRISONERS... WITH ILLUSTRATIONS.** 1845; **OUR PRESENT GAOL SYSTEM DEEPLY DEPRAVING TO THE PRISONER AND A POSITIVE EVIL TO THE COMMUNITY.** Manchester, 1847.

9.389
LONDON TIMES: *"Prison for Female Vagrants,"* n.v. (Nov. 24, 1848) 5. "In the present case the persons to be dealt with are for the most part idle, profligate, reckless women and girls, vagrants, tramps and paupers, many of whom actually

break windows, riot in workhouses and maliciously destroy property that they may get into gaol and share the comforts which our prisons afford" (p. 5).

9.390
Dixon, Hepworth, THE LONDON PRISONS: WITH AN ACCOUNT OF THE MORE DISTINGUISHED PERSONS WHO HAVE BEEN CONFINED IN THEM. 1850. Surveys and criticizes conditions of incarceration at the Tower, the Queen's Prison, the Hulks, Millbank, Pentonville, Parkhurst, Newgate, the House of Detention, Coldbath-Fields, etc.

9.391
Wrench, Matilda, ed., VISITS TO FEMALE PRISONERS AT HOME AND ABROAD. EDITED AT THE REQUEST OF THE COMMITTEE OF THE BRITISH LADIES' SOCIETY FOR PROMOTING THE REFORMATION OF FEMALE PRISONERS, ETC. 1852. Discusses London prisons, country associations, patronage, refuges, convict ships and penal colonies as well as associations in continental Europe and America.

9.392
Kingsmill, Joseph, CHAPTERS ON PRISONS AND PRISONERS, AND THE PREVENTION OF CRIME. 3rd ed., 1854.

9.393
Chesterton, George Laval, REVELATIONS OF PRISON LIFE WITH AN ENQUIRY INTO PRISON DISCIPLINE AND SECRETARY PUNISHMENTS. 2 vols. 1856. Chesterton governed Middlesex House of Correction which included female prisoners. Proponent of education and rehabilitation for prisoners.

9.394
Seebohm, B., MEMOIRS OF THE LIFE OF STEPHEN GRELLET. 1860. Grellet was an American Quaker who visited many London prisons, among them the women's ward at Newgate. His description is quoted.

9.395
Clay, Walter Lowe, THE PRISON CHAPLAIN: A MEMOIR OF THE REV. JOHN CLAY, B.D. LATE CHAPLAIN OF THE PRESTON GAOL, WITH SELECTIONS FROM HIS REPORTS AND CORRESPONDENCE, AND A SKETCH OF PRISON DISCIPLINE IN ENGLAND. 1861; rpt., Montclair, 1969. "The Fuhan refuge has not been without many good results, but they are far from commensurate with the expense. The women are grossly overfed; there is a lack of moral power in the discipline, there is too much routine and restraint" (p. 403). Recommends entrusting the refuge to the care of ladies, namely Caroline Neave, a longtime associate of Elizabeth Fry.

9.396
CORNHILL MAGAZINE: Hunt, T., "The English Convict System," 3 (1861) 708-733. Discusses Millbank, Brixton, and Fulham. At Millbank, "For the first two months after reception, the women are employed in coir picking; the next five months in bag-making, or other rough work; then in coarse needlework. From the first class are selected the cooks, cleaners, and laundry-women" (p. 726); Hunt, T., "The Convict Out in the World," 4 (1861) 229-250. See p. 250 for graphs illustrating the number, percentage, and nature of the crimes per annum of female convicts returned to convict prisons, either by revocation of license, or under fresh sentence, to penal servitude or transportation from 1853 to 1861; Holland, H.W. and Greenwood, F., "Revelations of Prison Life," 7 (1863) 638-648; "A Visit to a Convict

Lunatic Asylum," 10 (1864) 448-460.

9.397
Robinson, Frederick William (pseud. "A Prison Matron"), **FEMALE LIFE IN PRISON.** 2 vols. 1862; *excerpt rpt. in:* McConville, Sean, **A HISTORY OF ENGLISH PRISON ADMINISTRATION 1750-1877.** vol. 1, 1981. Female convicts are described as "desperately wicked—deceitful, crafty, malicious, lewd, and void of common feeling.... In the penal classes of the male prisons there is not one man to match the worst inmates of our female prisons" (p. 414); **MEMOIRS OF JANE CAMERON, FEMALE CONVICT.** 1864. A "chronicle of a woman's fall and rescue." Warns of the "grave mistake which has lately been asserted, that prisoners do not care for prison. Its confinement has no terrors, but its monotony has, and the comfort of a prison is as nothing in the balance with the horror of a life measured by the square and rule. To the dissolute and dissatisfied it is a living death; the old prison-birds never get used to prison life in their hearts, however lightly they may affect to regard" (p. 226); *reviewed in:* **VICTORIA MAGAZINE:** 2 (1863-64) 285; **PRISON CHARACTERS DRAWN FROM LIFE, WITH SUGGESTIONS FOR PRISON GOVERNMENT.** 2 vols. 1866.

9.398
Mayhew, Henry and Binny, John, **THE CRIMINAL PRISONS OF LONDON AND SCENES OF PRISON LIFE.** 1862; rpt., 1968. "In 1818 only 23 out of 518 prisons in the United Kingdom were separated and divided as the law dictated; in 59 of the number there was no division whatever—not even separation of males and females" (p. 97). See especially: "The Female Convict Prison at Brixton," "The House of Detention, Clerkenwell," "The Female House of Correction, Holloway," "Horsemonger Lane Jail," "The Female Convict Prison at Millbank," "Newgate Jail," "The Female Prison at Tothill Fields, and Female Prisons Generally," "The Interior of the Female Prison," "The Female Prison, Wandsworth," and "Of the Interior of the Female Prison at Westminster." —*see also:* Morris, Terrence, "Some Ecological Studies of the 19th Century" in **THE CRIMINAL AREA: A STUDY IN SOCIAL ECOLOGY.** by Terrence Morris. 1957. "[Mayhew's] primary view was that crime was not the result of moral laxity alone, any more than of some supernatural forces of determinism, but very largely of contemporary social conditions, a view re-echoed in the writings of other reformers of that time, like Mary Carpenter and Walter Buchanan" (p. 63).

9.399
CHRISTIAN REMEMBRANCER: A Prison Matron, *"Female Life in Prison,"* 44 (1862) 365-387. Describes female convicts as a "miserable class" and calls attention to the plight of both prisoners and prison matrons who are overworked and underpaid.

9.400
ENGLISH WOMAN'S JOURNAL: Parkes, B.R., *"Female Life in Prison,"* 10 (1862) 1-8; Carpenter, M., *"On the Treatment of Female Convicts,"* 8 (1863) 251-259. Advises the enlistment of female reformers in efforts to rescue female convicts from their criminal life.

9.401
Crofton, Walter, **CONVICT SYSTEMS AND TRANSPORTATION; A LECTURE.** 1863.

9.402
NORTH BRITISH REVIEW: Greg, W.R., *"Convicts and Transportation,"* 38 (1863)

1-35.

9.403

VICTORIA MAGAZINE: *"Woman Convicts,"* 2 (1863-1864) 518. Discusses discharge of female prisoners and their children, and problems in placement of female ex-convicts. Women's status as a convict implies a long series of offenses since they are seldom sentenced to punishment on first or second offenses; *"Female Convicts— Discharged Without Protection—Consignment to Ruin,"* 2 (1863-1864) 518-532. Advocates equal treatment of English and Irish women discharged from prison. The latter were discharged to refuge homes where they learned discipline and a trade before being integrated into the general public; Carpenter, M., *"Our Convicts,"* 5 (1865) 1-13; *"Carlisle Memorial Refuge for Female Convicts,"* 5 (1865) 89-90.

9.404

Carpenter, Mary, **OUR CONVICTS.** 2 vols. 1864. Contains extensive quotes from newspapers and women convicts telling their own stories. See especially: vol. 2, "Female Convicts." Prisons "are not reforming women and decreasing the crime of the country, but the reverse" (p. 239); *reviewed in:* **MONTH:** *"Miss Carpenter on Our Convicts,"* 1 (1864) 649.

9.405

MELIORA: Hill, R., *"The Petting and Fretting of Female Convicts,"* 6 (1864) 45-59. A lengthy review of a book of the same name, written by "A Prison Matron." Details the life of England's women prisoners. Strict enforcement of unbecoming haircuts and dress, as well as insufficient activity, are seen to drive the prisoners to extremes of manic behavior and "obscure communications." Hill suggests humane alternatives, and outlines the nature of women convicts.

9.406

TRANSACTIONS OF THE NATIONAL ASSOCIATION FOR THE PROMOTION OF SOCIAL SCIENCE: Carpenter, M., *"On the Treatment of Female Convicts,"* n.v. (1864) 415-422; Nugent, J., *"Incorrigible Women: What Are We To Do With Them?"* n.v. (1876) 375-377; Ford, C.R., *"Efforts On Behalf of Criminal Women,"* n.v. (1968) 373-375. Successful efforts include discharged prisoners homes and "female agents to visit women in their haunts of vice."

9.407

REPORT OF MISSION TO WOMEN DISCHARGED FROM PRISON. 1868.

9.408

DUBLIN REVIEW: Lockhart, E., *"Female Life in Prison,"* 62 (1868) 117-150.

9.409

Woods, Caroline H., **WOMAN IN PRISON.** New York, 1869. Reports management negligence due to discrimination by a male deputy. Extensive details of prison life.

9.410

Cooper, William M., **FLAGELLATION AND THE FLAGELLANTS: A HISTORY OF THE ROD IN ALL COUNTRIES FROM THE EARLIEST PERIOD TO THE PRESENT TIME.** 1870. See especially: "Whipping of Theives and Garrotters" and "Whipping in Bridewell and Other Prisons." The law for public whipping of women was abolished in 1817 and private whipping was abolished three years later.

9.411

Antrobus, Edmund Edward, **THE PRISON AND THE SCHOOL. AN APPEAL**

FOR THE GIRLS. 1871.

9.412
DuCane, Edmund Frederick, **AN ACCOUNT OF THE MANNER IN WHICH SENTENCES OF SERVITUDE ARE CARRIED OUT IN ENGLAND.** 1872. From a report on assistance to discharged women convicts: "We were particularly fortunate, and not only have many women obtained respectable situations... but have evinced their thankfulness by writing most grateful letters and... bringing in more than one instance contributions from their scanty wages to 'help some other poor thing'" (p. 27); **THE PUNISHMENT AND PREVENTION OF CRIME.** 1885. General empirical information on contemporary crime and penal systems. The chapter on transportation is a good background in the history of, reasons for, and opinions on exporting prisoners to the colonies. Mentions women convicts frequently throughout; **PRISONS.** Philadelphia, 1891.

9.413
International Penal and Prison Congress, First, London, **PRISONS AND REFORMATORIES AT HOME AND ABROAD, BEING THE TRANSACTIONS OF THE INTERNATIONAL PENITENTIARY CONFERENCE HELD IN LONDON, JULY 3-13, 1872.** 1872.

9.414
Church Penitentiary Association, **PENITENTIARY WORK OF THE CHURCH OF ENGLAND. PAPER PREPARED FOR DISCUSSION AT THE ANNIVERSARY MEETING.** 1873.

9.415
GOOD WORDS AND SUNDAY MAGAZINE: Crofton, W., *"Female Criminals and Their Children's Fate,"* 14 (1873) 170-174.

9.416
Griffiths, Arthur, **MEMORIALS OF MILLBANK AND CHAPTERS IN PRISON HISTORY.** 2 vols. 1875. See especially: "The Women." "It is a well established fact in prison logistics that the women are far worse than the men" (p. 255); **CHRONICLES OF NEWGATE.** New York, 1884. Impropriety in the separation of male and female prisoners as well as the governor's "habit of drawing frequently upon the female prisoners to act as domestic servants in his own private dwelling" are examples of injustices done to female prisoners at Newgate (p. 411); **A PRISON PRINCESS. A ROMANCE OF MILLBANK PENITENTIARY.** 1893; **SECRETS OF THE BRITISH PRISON HOUSE.** 2 vols. 1894. Chap. 1 discusses female prisoners and Part 4 discusses types of prisoners. "Although women can thus be proved to lapse less frequently into crime than men, it must not be overlooked that though not always criminal themselves, they are often the cause of criminality in others of the opposite sex.... They may not always exactly know how the money is gained that is to be spent in gratifying their caprices, although they may shrewdly guess its origin.... Crime in fact is largely committed for them if not by them" (p. 6).

9.417
CONTEMPORARY REVIEW: Synnot, H.L., *"Institutions and Their Inmates,"* 26 (1875) 487-504; Amos, S.M., *"Prison Treatment of Women,"* 73 (1898) 803-813.

9.418
Saint George's and Saint James's Dispensary, **SIXTIETH (-SIXTY-FIFTH) ANNUAL REPORT...** 1877-1882.

9.419

NINETEENTH CENTURY: Wills, A., *"Should Prisoners be Examined?"* 3 (1878) 169-182; DuCane, E.F., *"The Prison Committee Report,"* 38 (1895) 278-294; West, A., *"English Prisons,"* 39 (1896) 150-157; DuCane, E.F., *"The Prisons Bill and Progress in Criminal Treatment,"* 43 (1898) 809-821. Explains the changes to be effected by a bill introduced in Parliament relating to prisons; Harris, V., *"The Female Prisoner,"* 61 (1907) 780-797; Bedford, A., *"Fifteen Years Work in a Female Convict Prison,"* 68 (1910) 615-630. Discusses the work of the Association of Lady Visitors to Prisons; Wallis, H.M., *"The Case of Gwendoline Casson Misdemeanant,"* 69 (1911) 704-713. Casson was a sixteen-year old girl incarcerated at Whitestone Gaol where no juvenile class existed.

9.420

Hopkins, Jane Ellice, **NOTES ON PENITENTIARY WORK.** 1879.

9.421

Wines, Enoch Cobb, **THE STATE OF PRISONS AND OF CHILD-SAVING INSTITUTIONS IN THE CIVILIZED WORLD.** Cambridge, Mass., 1880. The third book of this series discusses the prison systems of Great Britain and its dependencies.

9.422

Meredith, Susanna, **A BOOK ABOUT CRIMINALS.** 1881; **SAVED REHAB! AN AUTOBIOGRAPHY.** 1881. Meredith worked to help women in prison as well as those newly discharged. ——*see also:* Lloyd, Mary Anne, **SUSANNA MEREDITH: A RECORD OF A VIGOROUS LIFE.** 1903. Includes extracts of her writings on various women's prisons and punishments.

9.423

ALL THE YEAR ROUND: *"Convict Angelina Simpson. A Prison Matron's Story,"* 29 (1882) 330-336; 348-353. An attractive lady-prisoner who, in her kindness and strength of character, saves a prison matron from losing her job.

9.424

Sweeting, Richard Deane Roker, **ESSAY ON THE EXPERIENCES AND OPINIONS OF JOHN HOWARD ON THE PRESERVATION OF THE HEALTH OF INMATES OF SCHOOLS, PRISONS, WORKHOUSES, HOSPITALS...** 1884.

9.425

Skene, Felicia Mary Frances (pseud. Scougal, Francis), **SCENES FROM A SILENT WORLD, OR PRISONS AND THEIR INMATES.** 1889. A personal and direct account of prison life by a novelist who was a prison visitor.

9.426

Merrick, George Purnell, **WORK AMONG THE FALLEN, AS SEEN IN THE PRISON CELL. A PAPER READ BEFORE THE RUDI-DECANAL CHAPTER OF ST. MARGARET'S AND ST. JOHN'S, WESTMINSTER, IN THE JERUSALEM CHAMBER, ON THURSDAY, JULY 17, 1890.** [1891]. Discusses several "female" crimes and reasons why women turn criminal, including seduction and betrayal by men and abandonment. "I am convinced that there are many poor men and women who do not in the least understand what is implied in the term 'immorality.' Out of courtesy to you, they may assent to what you say, but they do not comprehend your meaning when you talk of virtue or purity; you are simply talking over their heads" (p. 48).

9.427
Balgarnie, Florence, **A PLEA FOR THE APPOINTMENT OF POLICE MATRONS AT POLICE STATIONS.** 1894.

9.428
HINTS TO LADIES APPOINTED, AS PRISON VISITORS. 1896.

9.429
Lytton, Constance Georgina Bulwer, **PRISONS AND PRISONERS.** 1898; 1914. Discusses personal experiences of those jailed for suffrage activities.

9.430
FORTNIGHTLY REVIEW: Orme, E., *"Our Female Convicts,"* 69 (1898) 790-796; Johnston, M.F., *"Life of a Woman Convict,"* 69 (1901) 559-567.

9.431
Klare, Hugh J., **ANATOMY OF A PRISON.** Hutchinson, 1900.

9.432
WESTMINSTER REVIEW: Pike, G.H., *"Why Prisoners' Wives are Helped,"* 166 (1906) 100-105. Argues that philanthropic aid to prisoners' wives contributes to the lessening of crime.

9.433
Adam, Hargrave Lee, "Life at Aylesbury Convict Prison" in **THE STORY OF CRIME: FROM THE CRADLE TO THE GRAVE.** by Hargrave Lee Adam. 1908. Contains glorified but elaborate descriptions of prisoners, their routines and characteristics.

9.434
Quinton, R.F., **CRIME AND CRIMINALS 1876-1910.** 1910. Author performed prison medical work and eventually became Govenor at Holloway Prison. Defends English prisons, citing progress in such areas as the decrease in convicts and improvements in conduct. In general, women were less idle than men in prison, and "confirmed female criminals [were] specially dangerous as corrupters of novices" (p. 239). Mentions Millbank prison in 1880 where there was "pandemonium" due to its govenor's opinion that "all women were mad" (p. 42).

9.435
Russell, C.E.B., **YOUNG GAOL BIRDS.** 1910.

9.436
Blagg, Helen and Wilson, Charlotte, **WOMEN AND PRISONS.** 1912; rpt., 1913. "Crime among women, while confined to a much smaller class than among men, proceeds from an ineradicably unmoral nature.... Prison treatment is better suited to men than to women.... Owing to the state of public opinion imprisonment affects the future social and economic life of women more adversely than that of men" (p. 13). Offers relative statistics for men and women concerning average daily population of prisons, periods of detention in local prisons, ages of prisoners, etc.

9.437
Chesser, Elizabeth Sloan, "Women Prisoners" in **WOMAN, MARRIAGE AND MOTHERHOOD.** by Elizabeth Sloan Chesser. 1913. "Our women prisoners are the founders of criminal stocks, because our methods... often fail to reform" (p. 183). Complains of lack of funds to rehabilitate discharged prisoners and calls for better

medical care for inmates, as well as fresh air, exercise, baths, and activities to occupy idle minds and hands.

9.438
Ives, George, **A HISTORY OF PENAL METHODS: CRIMINALS, WITCHES, LUNATICS.** 1914; Montclair, 1970. Contains various references to female crimes and convicts: "Both men and women (the latter up to 1817) were flagellated in public, being either tied up to a post, or fastened behind a cart and so thrashed along the road" (p. 54).

9.439
PSYCHOLOGICAL REVIEW: Weidensall, J., *"Psychological Tests as Applied to the Criminal Women,"* 21 (1914) 370.

9.440
Osborn, Thomas Mott, **SOCIETY AND PRISONS (INCLUDES THE OLD PRISON SYSTEMS).** New Haven, 1916.

9.441
Battersea, Constance, "Prison Work" in **REMINISCENCES.** by Constance Battersea. 1922. Recounts her experiences as visitor to Aylesbury prison.

9.442
Gordon, Mary, **PENAL DISCIPLINE.** New York, 1922. Contains much commentary on the characteristics of women prisoners. On tattooed prisoners "the marks are a difficulty in the way of getting respectable situations for the women, and many of the women themselves bitterly regret being so marked" (p. 142). Contains illustrations.

9.443
Webb, Sidney and Webb, Beatrice, **ENGLISH PRISONS UNDER LOCAL GOVERNMENT.** introduction by George Bernard Shaw. 1922. This general source covers male and female incarceration from the 16th through the 19th centuries with interesting theoretical discussion of criminality by Bernard Shaw. "I cannot add too emphatically that the people who imagine that criminals can be reformed by setting chaplains to preach at them, by giving them pious books and tracts to read, by separating them from their companions in crime and locking them up in solitude to reflect on their sins and repent, are far worse enemies both to the criminal and to society than those who face the fact that these are merely additional cruelties" (p. xxxviii).

9.444
Ruggles-Brise, Evelyn, **PRISON REFORM AT HOME AND ABROAD: A SHORT HISTORY OF THE INTERNATIONAL MOVEMENT SINCE THE LONDON CONGRESS, 1872.** 1924. Author may be cataloged as Brise, Evelyn Ruggles.

9.445
Fairs, G.H., "Criminal Transportation: Its Theory and Practice, with Special Reference to Australia," M.A. thesis, Bristol Univ., 1931.

9.446
Ayscough, H.H., "An Account of the Progress of Penal Reform in England from 1810 to 1930, Together with Some Conclusions," Ph.D. diss., Univ. of London, 1932.

9.447
Rhodes, Albert John, **DARTMOOR PRISON, 1806-1932.** 1933.

9.448
Hooper, W. Eden, **THE HISTORY OF NEWGATE AND THE OLD BAILEY.** 1935.

9.449
Carter, M., **A LIVING SOUL IN HOLLOWAY.** 1938. Glorifies prison life; author worked as a lady volunteer at Holloway Prison for 15 years. See especially: "Y.P.'s" (young prisoners), "Convicts," "Recidivists" and "Thieves of the Well Dressed Classes." —*see also:* **HOWARD JOURNAL:** Faulkner, D., *"The Redevelopment of Holloway Prison,"* 13 (1971) 122-132.

9.450
Koenig, M.L., "English Parliamentary Legislation on Prison Reform, 1850-1908," Ph.D. diss., Univ of Iowa, 1938.

9.451
Blackton, C.S., "The Australian Colonial Movement Against Penal Transportation from Great Britain, 1837-67," Ph.D. diss., Univ. of California, Los Angeles, 1939.

9.452
Lonsdale, Kathleen, **SOME ACCOUNT OF LIFE IN HOLLOWAY PRISON FOR WOMEN.** 1943. Published by the Prison Medical Reform Council.

9.453
Fry, S. Margery, "Tides of Opinion" in **ARMS OF THE LAW.** by S. Margery Fry. 1951. Briefly surveys the social philosophies of John Howard, Casare Bonesana, Jeremy Bentham, Samuel Romilly, and Elizabeth Fry; also explores their ramifications for 19th and 20th century penal reform. "It is very much the fashion at present to run down the effect of their efforts. It is pointed out, with justice, that in many respects the old, filthy, promiscuous, venal goals, with all their brutality, were less inhuman than the repressive, silent, cold-storage institutions of the nineteenth century" (p. 54). —*see also:* Jones, Enid H., **MARGERY FRY: THE ESSENTIAL AMATEUR.** 1966.

9.454
Dendrickson, George and Thomas, Frederick, **THE TRUTH ABOUT DARTMOOR.** 1952.

9.455
Howard League for Penal Reform, **ENGLISH PENAL METHODS.** 1954.

9.456
Jones, Howard, **CRIME AND THE PENAL SYSTEM.** 1956.

9.457
Radzinowicz, Leon, **A HISTORY OF ENGLISH CRIMINAL LAW AND ITS ADMINISTRATION FROM 1750: THE CLASH BETWEEN PRIVATE INITIATIVE AND PUBLIC INTEREST IN THE ENFORCEMENT OF THE LAW.** vol. 2, 1956. See especially: "Trading in Police Services." Surveys the evolution of crime enforcement in England. "The fees which constables and police officers were officially permitted to charge to private persons for any of the multifarious services which it was part of their duty to perform, seldom, if ever, bore any relation to the charges which were in fact made." Tells the story of Mary Ann Cramer who was

charged 20 shillings for her release.

9.458

Young, Agnes Freda and Ashton, E.T., "The Penal Services" in **BRITISH SOCIAL WORK IN THE NINETEENTH CENTURY**. by Agnes Freda Young and E.T. Ashton. 1956. On Elizabeth Fry, Mary Carpenter, Sarah Martin, Discharged Prisoners' Aid Societies, Reformatory and Industrial Schools and Probation.

9.459

Elkin, Winfred Adeline, **THE ENGLISH PENAL SYSTEM**. 1957. Survey of the prison system with a brief historical account.

9.460

Playfair, Giles and Sington, Derrick, **THE OFFENDERS; SOCIETY AND THE ATROCIOUS CRIME**. 1957.

9.461

Size, Mary, **PRISONS I HAVE KNOWN**. 1957. Autobiographical account of forty-seven years' work in prison service. Contains details on prison procedure, meals, and dress at Manchester, Aylesbury, Leeds, and Borstal training. In 1906 "there was at that time little if any scope within the prison system for reform or rehabilitation. Separate confinement and the rule of silence prevailed. The humiliating, shapeless clothing, with its sprinkling of broad arrows, and a diet that left a good deal to be desired, did not make for reform. Retribution and deterence were the order of the day; it was difficult to find any humanizing elements. The self-respect of the prisoner, where it existed, was crushed and any moral instinct she possessed was starved. She had no opportunity to render a kindness to a fellow being, and if she were found trying to do this she was punished; if she were found receiving a kindness she was punished too" (p. 32).

9.462

Crooke, Robert, **THE CONVICT**. Hobart, Tasmania, 1958. Transportation to Tasmania (Van Dieman's Land), stretched from 1828 to 1840. "The female servants too in most families were convicts, women of abandoned character, the sweepings of the streets of London, Liverpool, Dublin and Cork, and it will be matter of surprise to none, that licentiousness and depravity were rife in a community so constituted" (p. 3).

9.463

Grew, Benjamin Dixon, **PRISON GOVERNOR**. 1958. Autobiography of a prison administrator.

9.464

Bateson, Charles, **THE CONVICT SHIPS, 1787-1868**. Glasgow, 1959. Covers transportation of female convicts.

9.465

Howard, D.L., **THE ENGLISH PRISONS: THEIR PAST AND THEIR FUTURE**. 1960. "It was in the women's wards at the New Newgate that conditions were at their worst.... The women slept on the stone floors, without bedding; many were drunk, and all were nearly starving" (pp. 34-36).

9.466

Rose, Gordon, **THE STRUGGLE FOR PENAL REFORM: THE HOWARD LEAGUE AND ITS PREDECESSORS**. 1961. Among the solutions for overcrowding in mid-nineteenth century prisons was the establishment by the state of "intermediate" or "open" prisons where supervision was very light. "For women, refuges set up by voluntary effort were used instead" (p. 5).

9.467
TASMANIAN HISTORICAL RESEARCH ASSOCIATION: Payne, H.S., *"A Statistical Study of Female Convicts in Tasmania 1843-1853,"* 9 (1961) 56-64. From the sample group of women, information is given on who they were socially, what crimes they were transported for, how they were deported, what they found in Van Dieman's Land in terms of servitude and opportunity, and their various capacities to assimilate the new conditions.

9.468
Blumenthal, Walter H., BRIDES FROM BRIDEWELL: FEMALE FELONS SENT TO COLONIAL AMERICA. 1962.

9.469
Smith, Ann D., WOMEN IN PRISON: A STUDY OF PRISON METHODS. 1962. Gives a sense of the indecision accompanying most of the legislation on women in English prisons, the ineffectiveness of standard treatment for female convicts, and special allowances made for them: "A nursery was provided for the children of women transferred to Brixton from other prisons. After some years the Secretary of State put a stop to this practice, but if a child was actually born in Brixton, it appears to have remained with its mother until the end of her sentence which might be six years or over" (n.p.).

9.470
Field, Xenia, UNDER LOCK AND KEY: A STUDY OF WOMEN IN PRISON. Parrish, 1963. Organization of the book offers insights into Victorian studies and women's criminality. Divided into general catagories: "Borstals," "Medicine," "The Mind and Venereal Diseases," and "Entertainment."

9.471
HISTORICAL STUDIES OF AUSTRALIA AND NEW ZEALAND: Robson, L.L., *"The Origin of the Women Convicts Sent to Australia, 1787-1852,"* no. 11 (1963) 43-63. Transcribes comments, brief histories, and reputations of transported women, and gives some demographics. "Tales of the misbehaviour, impertinence and brazenness of women convicts abound... 'four or five hundred of the most abandoned women of the empire' threw everything over the walls of the prison yard on one occasion" (p. 43).

9.472
Carpenter, Edward, PRISONS, POLICE, AND PUNISHMENT: AN INQUIRY INTO THE CAUSES AND TREATMENT OF CRIME AND CRIMINALS. 1965. Recommends abandoning the solitary system, converting prisons into industrial reformatories, cultivation of farm lands in connection with all reformatories, substitution of short sentences with first warnings or fines, the establishment of a widespread probationary system like the Borstal system, the transfer of corporeal punishment from the courts to the heads of reformatories, the complete abolition of capital punishment and the establishment of a court of appeal (pp. 78-79).

9.473
Hattersley, Alan Frederick, THE CONVICT CRISIS: THE GROWTH OF UNITY: RESISTANCE TO TRANSPORTATION IN SOUTH AFRICA AND AUSTRALIA, 1848-1853. Pietermaritzburg, 1965.

9.474

Melville, Henry, **THE HISTORY OF VAN DIEMAN'S LAND FROM 1824 TO 1835.** 1965. See pp. 140-141 for detailed information of the emigration of families and married and single women to a convict colony.

9.475

Robson, Lloyd L., **THE CONVICT SETTLERS TO AUSTRALIA.** Melbourne, 1965. Contains accounts of female convicts.

9.476

Shaw, A.G.L., **CONVICTS AND THE COLONIES.** 1966. See appendix for statistics. Examines the reasons why convict transportation to the colonies was instituted and then abandoned: "In fact, transportation and assignment was the most effective reformatory punishment that was widely adopted before 1850; but at that time few accepted the principle that aim of punishment and prison discipline should be reformation rather than infliction of suffering, and most agreed with Sir James F. Stephan that the 'criminal law system is mainly a system of licensed revenge'" (p. 359). Contains references to misconduct of female convicts in the colonies.

9.477

Babington, Anthony, **THE POWER TO SILENCE. A HISTORY OF PUNISHMENT IN GREAT BRITAIN.** 1968. Brief references to women in the general context of the history of the English Penal System. Concerning corporeal punishment, between 1820 and 1830 "women were excluded from the penalty [of whipping] and vagrants became less likely to receive it; on the other hand, the range of offences for which it could be ordered was considerably extended" (p. 18). Also during this decade "women prisoners were ordered to be kept in different buildings from men and were to be supervised by a female staff" (p. 98); **A HOUSE IN BOW STREET. CRIME AND THE MAGISTRACY LONDON 1740-1881.** 1969. This general study of crime enforcement and the Bow Street Police Office, 1740-1887, rarely differentiates male and female criminality but points out that "shoplifting in those days was almost wholly a female offence" (p. 225).

9.478

Playfair, Giles, "Women and Children" in **THE PUNITIVE OBSESSION: AN UNVARNISHED HISTORY OF THE ENGLISH PRISON SYSTEM.** by Giles Playfair. 1971. "But one may see in retrospect that the preferential treatment of women under the prison system... is above all owed to their own peculiar emotional resistance to a male-made and male-administered punishment. 'It is a well established fact in prison logistics,' Major Arthur Griffiths wrote in his history of Millbank (1875) 'that the women are far worse than the men'... while female crime is a very minor problem by comparison with male crime, imprisonment is harder for them to bear philosophically——to bear, that is, without losing whatever mental balance or emotional stability they may once have possessed" (p. 147).

9.479

Camp, John, "Women Only" and "Famous Names and Recidivists" in **HOLLOWAY PRISON: THE PLACE AND THE PEOPLE.** by John Camp. Newton Abbot, 1974. In 1902 Holloway became an all female prison, housing drunks, prostitutes, baby farmers, petty thieves, and suffragettes. It emphasized reform over punishment and, in 1907, received the first inspector of womens' prisons, Dr. Mary Gordon, who ultimately achieved many improvements in the conditions and laws concerning women prisoners.

9.480
O'Keeffe, Mamie, **A BRIEF ACCOUNT OF THE MORETON BAY PENAL SETTLEMENT 1824-1839.** Queensland, Oxley Memorial Library, 1974. "135 women are known to have been sentenced to Moreton Bay between 1829 and 1837." Their occupations included laundry and farm work; "those who had young children had their children with them" (p. 6).

9.481
Heidensohn, Frances, "The Imprisonment of Females" in **THE USE OF IMPRISONMENT: ESSAYS IN THE CHANGING STATE OF ENGLISH PENAL POLICY.** ed. by Sean McConville. 1975. "For most of its history the prison system of England and Wales has not significantly differentiated beween its male and female inmates; in more recent times, however, this approach has changed somewhat" (n.p.).

9.482
HARVARD LIBRARY BULLETIN: Singleton, R.R., *"Defoe, Moll Flanders and the Ordinary of Newgate,"* 24 (1976) 407-413.

9.483
Dixon, William H., **THE LONDON PRISONS.** 1977.

9.484
Sheehan, W.J., "Finding Solace in Eighteenth-Century Newgate" in **CRIME IN ENGLAND: 1550-1800.** by V.S. Cockburn. 1977. Describes the various diversions and consolations made available to Newgate prisoners in the 18th century. These included drinking, having the family live with the prisoner in prison, gaming, religion (only insofar as worshippers could mock the services), reading, writing, whoring and sex in general. "Illicit sex offered a pleasurable gate and enhanced the gaol's notorious reputation... [nevertheless] overcrowding and the physical shortcomings of the prison made effective separation impossible so that the sexes intermingled freely.... Indeed, in 1702 a group from the society for Promoting Christian Knowledge visited the gaol several times and was scandalized to see the female prisoners openly soliciting in hope of becoming pregnant so that they could 'plead their belly' and be pardoned by the justices at sessions" (p. 243).

9.485
CARMARTENSHIRE ANTIQUARY: Beddoe, D., *"Carmartenshire Women and Criminal Transportation to Australia, 1787-1852,"* 13 (1977) 65-71. Crimes by women were committed in every case against property, and not against people. Examines the contention that female criminals are "as bad as it is possible for human beings to be." ——*see also:* Beddoe, Deidre, **WELSH CONVICT WOMEN: A STUDY OF WOMEN TRANSPORTED FROM WALES TO AUSTRALIA, 1787-1852.** Wales, 1979.

9.486
Ignatieff, Michael, **A JUST MEASURE OF PAIN: THE PENITENTIARY IN THE INDUSTRIAL REVOLUTION, 1750-1850.** New York, 1978. Alludes to the influence and abuse of the penal system on women: "The new prisons [in Gloucester]... played a role in the enforcement of family discipline. Imprisonments for desertion of family and for bastardy increased markedly after the new prisons were opened" (p. 109). Also, the son of Thomas Aris, "a corrupt, violent, and indolent administrater" (p. 127) of Coldbath Fields Prison, was formally charged with having sexual relations with female prisoners "but took the curious position that Aris senior could not be held responsible for his son's conduct in the

institution" (p. 141). Also, tells of public outrage over the Mary Rich case in July, 1800. She was a fourteen-year-old workingman's daughter that alleged she had been raped by a lawyer. "Astonishing as it may seem, it was common in cases where accusers were indigent to commit them to prison as material witnesses, while setting the defendants free on bail" (p. 133). After over a month in Coldbath Fields prison she showed signs of starvation and fainted on the witness stand; an investigation found that material witnesses such as Mary Rich were fed bread and water and held in solitary confinement while awaiting trial; *reviewed in:* SOCIAL HISTORY: King, W., 14 (1981) 544-546.

9.487

Henriques, Ursula R.Q., **BEFORE THE WELFARE STATE**. 1979. Describes how some of the main branches of social administration developed amidst the stresses and strains of the Industrial Revolution and beyond. Includes an examination of the Poor Law, Factory Acts and prisons.

9.488

QUAKER HISTORY: THE BULLETIN OF FRIENDS' HISTORICAL SOCIETY: Cooper, R.A., *"The English Quakers and Prison Reform, 1809-1823,"* 68 (1979) 3-19. "Through superior organization the Quakers had secured the legislation they wanted [Prison Act of 1823]" (p. 19).

9.489

Bailey, Victor, ed., **POLICING AND PUNISHMENT IN NINETEENTH CENTURY BRITAIN**. 1981.

9.490

Freedman, Estelle B., **THEIR SISTERS' KEEPERS. WOMEN'S PRISON REFORM IN AMERICA 1830-1930**. Ann Arbor, 1981. Cites such British influences as Elizabeth Fry and Mary Carpenter.

9.491

McConville, Sean, **A HISTORY OF ENGLISH PRISON ADMINISTRATION: 1750-1877**. vol. 1, 1981. See pp. 413-428 for brief but detailed section on basic facts of women's imprisonment, such as more favorable treatment than men in the remission of their sentences, and distinct disciplinary arrangements: "Odd little foibles were allowed which certainly would have met with severe punishment had they been attempted on the male side.... One reads of mouse-training and sparrow-taming, of attempts to mix punishments and threats with persuasion, of the humoring of the obdurate offender and of her affection between staff and inmates" (p. 428); (as editor), **THE USE OF IMPRISONMENT: ESSAYS IN THE CHANGING STATE OF ENGLISH PENAL POLICY**. 1975. For example, see "The Imprisonment of Females" by Frances Heidensohn.

9.492

ABOLITIONIST: Sim, J., *"Women in Prison: A Historical Analysis,"* 8 (1981) 14-18.

9.493

JOURNAL OF THE HISTORY OF IDEAS: Cooper, R.A., *"Jeremy Bentham, Elizabeth Fry, and English Prison Reform,"* 42 (1981) 675-690. "Bentham's pleasure-pain principle and Mrs. Fry's fervent evangelicalism brought them both to positions supporting classification of prisoners and productive labor in prisons, as well as to a shared concern for the maintenance of healthful prison conditions. Their supposed followers, on the other hand, shared a confidence in solitary confinement and hard labor. Perhaps the best explanation... is that both Bentham and Mrs. Fry belonged to a generation of reformers concerned primarily with salvation (sociological and religious) of the prisoner, while Benthamites and Quakers active in the 1830's were primarily concerned with deterring crime" (p. 675).

9.494
Evans, Robin, **THE FABRICATION OF VIRTUE: ENGLISH PRISON ARCHI-TECTURE 1750-1840.** Cambridge, 1982. Ideologies of punishment and reformation of prisoners are reflected in architectural design. Unique study.

9.495
Melossi, Dario and Pavarini, Massimo, **THE PRISON AND THE FACTORY: ORIGINS OF THE PENITENTIARY SYSTEM.** trans. by Glynis Cousin. 1981. A study of the development of capitalistic modes of production and its influence on the prison system. See pp. 33-47 on nineteenth-century developments in England.

9.496
Priestley, Philip, **VICTORIAN PRISON LIVES: ENGLISH PRISON BIOGRAPHY 1830-1914.** 1985. See pp. 69-73 for descriptions of women prisoners, and pp. 209-210 for examples of punishment. "There was, also, a special mode of restraint reserved to women, called 'hobbling,' which consisted 'in binding the wrists and ankles of the prisoner then strapping them together behind her back'" (p. 210).

9.497a
Harding, Christopher, Hines, Bill, Ireland, Richard and Rawlings, Philip, **IMPRISONMENT IN ENGLAND AND WALES: A CONCISE HISTORY.** 1985.

*   *   *

8. JUVENILE OFFENDERS, DELINQUENTS AND REFORMATORIES

9.497
Philanthropic Society, **AN ADDRESS TO THE PUBLIC, FROM THE PHILANTHROPIC SOCIETY FOR THE PROMOTION OF INDUSTRY AND REFORM OF THE CRIMINAL POOR.** 1792; **AN ACCOUNT OF THE NATURE AND PRESENT STATE OF THE PHILANTHROPIC SOCIETY INSTITUTED IN THE YEAR 1788 AND INCORPORATED IN 1806 FOR THE PREVENTION OF CRIMES, BY THE ADMISSION OF THE OFFSPRING OF CONVICTS, AND THE REFORMATION OF CRIMINAL POOR CHILDREN.** 1818.

9.498
REPORT OF THE COMMITTEE FOR INVESTIGATING THE CAUSES OF THE ALARMING INCREASE OF JUVENILE DELINQUENCY IN THE METROPOLIS. 1816. Primary causes of juvenile delinquency cited are improper conduct of parents, lack of education and suitable employment, violation of the Sabbath, and gambling in public streets. Secondary influences include severity of the criminal code, inefficiency of the police and existing prison discipline.

9.499
PHILANTHROPIST: *"Report on Juvenile Delinquency,"* 4 (1816) 202-208.

9.500
Society for the Improvement of Prison Discipline, and for the Reformation of Juvenile Offenders, **REPORT OF THE COMMITTEE OF THE SOCIETY FOR THE IMPROVEMENT OF PRISON DISCIPLINE AND FOR THE REFORMATION OF JUVENILE OFFENDERS.** 1818; 6TH ANNUAL REPORT... 1824. ——*see also*: Highmore, Anthony, "Society For the Improvement of Prison Discipline, and For the Reformation of Juvenile Offenders" in **PHILANTHROPIA METROPOLITANA; A VIEW OF THE CHARITABLE INSTITUTIONS ESTABLISHED IN AND NEAR LONDON, CHIEFLY DURING THE LAST TWELVE YEARS.** by Anthony Highmore. 1822.

9.501
Eardley-Wilmot, John, **A SECOND LETTER TO THE MAGISTRATES OF WARWICKSHIRE ON THE INCREASE OF CRIMINALITY IN GENERAL, BUT MORE PARTICULARLY OF JUVENILE DELINQUENCY WITH A FEW OBSERVATIONS ON THE CAUSES AND REMEDIES OF THE INCREASING EVIL.** 1820.

9.502
Reformatory and Refuge Union, **ADDENDA.** 1820; **A SHORT ACCOUNT OF THE REFUGE... 1831; THE ANNUAL REPORT OF THE REFUGE... 1832.** 1833; **ARNOS COURT GIRLS' REFORMATORY BRISTOL. ROMAN CATHOLIC INSTITUTION.** 1854; **THE METROPOLITAN REFORMATORIES AND REFUGES.** 1856; 4th ed., 1859; **FIRST ANNUAL REPORT.** 1856-1857; **A HANDBOOK OF INDUSTRIAL WORK IN VARIOUS REFORMATORIES, REFUGES AND INDUSTRIAL SCHOOLS IN GREAT BRITAIN AND IRELAND.** 2nd ed., 1857; **THE PROVINCIAL REFORMATORIES, REFUGES, INDUSTRIAL SCHOOLS.** 2nd ed., 1857; **SECOND ANNUAL REPORT OF THE REFORMATORY AND REFUGE UNION.** 1858. See especially: "Allesley Reformatory Farm for Girls, Coventry, 1856," "Birmingham Girls' Reformatory 1854," "Good Shepherd Reformatory 1857——Hammersmith-Roman Catholic Institution," "Liverpool Girls' Reformatory 1857," "Toxteth Park Girls' Reformatory School Liverpool, 1854," and "West Riding Female Refuge and Reformatory School 1848"; **THE METROPOLITAN REFORMATORIES, REFUGES AND INDUSTRIAL SCHOOLS. AUTHENTIC ACCOUNTS OF 54 INSTITUTIONS.** 1859; **THIRD ANNUAL REPORT.** 1859; **A GUIDE TO THE RE-FEMALE MISSION IN CONNECTION WITH THE REFORMATORY AND REFUGE UNION. REPORT OF THE SUB-COMMITTEE.** 1859; **A CLASSIFIED LIST OF REFORMATORIES, REFUGES, INDUSTRIAL SCHOOLS...** 1859; 2nd ed., 1861; Female Mission, in Connexion with the Reformatory and Refuge Union, **REPORT OF THE SUBCOMMITTEE.** 1859; **FOURTH ANNUAL REPORT.** 1860; **A GUIDE TO THE REFORMATORY INSTITUTIONS OF LONDON AND ITS VICINITY.** 1862; **CLASSIFIED LIST OF CHILD SAVING INSTITUTIONS.** 1900; **THE LAW RELATING TO CHILD SAVING AND REFORMATORY EFFORTS.** 1900; Reformatory and Refuge Union Provident and Benevolent Fund, **TWENTY-FOURTH [ETC.] ANNUAL REPORT...** 1900, ETC. [1900, etc.]; **FIFTY YEARS' RECORD OF CHILD-SAVING AND REFORMATORY WORK 1856-1906.** 1906; "The Children's Dangerous Performance Act, 1879" in **FIFTY YEARS RECORD OF REFORMATORY AND REFUGE UNION.** 1906; **RULES AND ANNUITY TABLES, ETC.** [1910]; **THE CLASSIFIED LIST OF CHILD-SAVING INSTITUTIONS.** 20th ed., 1912-1935; **CONFERENCE OF PREVENTATIVE AND RESCUE WORKERS... RECORD OF PROCEEDINGS.** 1923; Reformatory and Refuge Union Provident Benevolent Fund, **RULES OF THE...** [1927]. ——*see also*: **TRANSACTIONS OF THE NATIONAL ASSOCIATION FOR THE PROMOTION OF SOCIAL SCIENCE:** Hanbury, R., *"The Reformatory and Refuge Union,"* n.v. (1857) 398-402. The

Union, established in 1856, had placed "fifty-two fallen and un-fallen women and girls" in institutions and established a "Girls' Laundry" to protect and train young women for future employment; *"On the Disposal of Girls from Reformatory Schools,"* n.v. (1858) 413-419.

9.503
Hill, Frederic, **NATIONAL EDUCATION; ITS PRESENT STATE AND PROSPECTS.** vol. 1, 1836. Extensive survey of schools of industry, day schools, factory schools, schools for paupers, and infant schools as means to combat juvenile delinquency.

9.504
Brenton, Edward, **THE BIBLE AND THE SPADE; OR CAPTAIN BRENTON'S ACCOUNT OF THE RISE AND PROGRESS OF THE CHILDREN'S FRIEND SOCIETY: SHOWING ITS TENDENCY TO CRIME AND POVERTY, AND EVENTUALLY TO DISPENSE WITH CAPITAL PUNISHMENT AND IMPRISONMENT.** 1837. Brenton was the driving force behind the Children's Friend Society, a private philanthropic organization intended to aid and reform juvenile delinquents of both sexes. Founded in the 1830's, the society defended the participation of private reform agencies working parallel with government efforts. Brenton believed that government prisons and workhouses provided corrupt environments for children. The society worked with young criminals of both sexes, emphasizing domestic training for girls and agricultural work for boys. It aimed to replace physical punishment with "psychological pressure." After incarceration, the children were sent abroad to British colonies for work assignments. Bad publicity about the treatment of these child emigrants led to its eventual end in the 1840's. — *see also*: Brenton, Jaheel, **MEMOIRS OF CAPTAIN EDWARD PELHAM BRENTON... AND EXERTIONS IN THE CAUSE OF HUMANITY, AS CONNECTED WITH THE CHILDREN'S FRIEND SOCIETY...** 1842.

9.505
Hawes, [Benjamin], **OBSERVATIONS ON THE TREATMENT OF JUVENILE OFFENDERS.** 1837.

9.506
Mirehouse, John, **CRIME AND ITS CAUSES: WITH OBSERVATIONS ON SIR E. WILMOT'S BILL, AUTHORISING THE SUMMARY CONVICTION OF JUVENILE OFFENDERS IN CERTAIN CASES OF LARCENY AND MISDEMEANOUR.** 1840.

9.507
Neale, William Beaver, **JUVENILE DELINQUENCY IN MANCHESTER; ITS CAUSES AND HISTORY; ITS CONSEQUENCES, ETC.** Manchester, 1840; *excerpt printed in:* Tobias, John Jacob, **URBAN CRIME IN VICTORIAN ENGLAND.** New York, 1972. "It is well known that young children are often employed by more experienced thieves, to bring them information as to where and how property is situated; and they are also employed by house-breakers, to enter through windows and small apertures, and at the proper time to open the doors for the admission of their older accomplices" (p. 124). See Appendix B for an account of a girls' asylum.

9.508
MONTHLY CHRONICLE: *"Proposed Remedy for Juvenile Delinquency,"* 6 (1840) 122-131.

9.509

Buchanan, Walter, **REMARKS ON THE CAUSES AND STATE OF JUVENILE CRIME IN THE METROPOLIS WITH HINTS FOR PREVENTING ITS INCREASE.** 1846.

9.510

The Philanthropic, **ANNUAL REPORT. REFORMATION OF JUVENILE OFFENDERS.** 1846; **REFORMATION OF JUVENILE OFFENDERS. REPORT FOR 1848.** 1848. Youthful crime should be dealt with early, yet with compassion.

9.511

Turner, Sydney and Paynter, Thomas, **REPORT ON THE SYSTEM AND ARRANGEMENTS OF 'LA COLONIE AGRICOLE' AT METTRAY, PRESENTED TO THE COMMITTEE OF THE PHILANTHROPIC SOCIETY, ST. GEORGE'S FIELDS, 19TH AUGUST, 1846.** 1846. The French reformatory emphasized rehabilitation through teaching agricultural skills rather than physical punishment. This system was considered worthy of emulation by English penal reformers and social commentators who idealized the rural setting for its remedial quality.

9.512

Barclay, Hugh, **JUVENILE DELINQUENCY: ITS CAUSES AND CURE. BY A COUNTY MAGISTRATE.** Edinburgh, 1848.

9.513

Dufton, John, **THE PRISON AND THE SCHOOL: A LETTER TO LORD JOHN RUSSELL, M.P.** 1848.

9.514

Turner, Sydney, **THE PHILANTHROPIC REPORT FOR 1848.** 1848.

9.515

NORTH BRITISH REVIEW: Ivory, W., *"Juvenile Criminals,"* 10 (1848) 1-38. For girls, see p. 7.

9.516

REFUGE FOR THE DESTITUTE REPORT. 1849; 1850. During the years 1846, 1847, and 1848, the government gave grants of 1,000 pounds in support of this institution.

9.517

Beggs, T., **AN INQUIRY INTO THE EXTENT AND CAUSES OF JUVENILE DEPRAVITY.** 1849. Complains that, in general, juvenile delinquency in the professional class was less reprimanded by the police than crime committed by the working classes; **JUVENILE DELINQUENCY AND REFORMATORY INSTITU-TIONS. A LECTURE, ETC.** 1857.

9.518

ENGLISH JOURNAL OF EDUCATION: *"The Colony of Mettray and the Reformation of the Juvenile Criminal,"* 3 (1849) 375-378; 415-420; 459-462.

9.519

HOGG'S WEEKLY INSTRUCTOR: *"Juvenile Depravity—Its Causes and Cure. I— The Importance of the Subject,"* 21 (1849) 148-149; *"Juvenile Depravity. II—Its More Prominent and Prevailing Forms,"* 21 (1849) 185-187; *"Juvenile Depravity III— Its Extent,"* 21 (1849) 340-342. Gives demographical statistics on age and number of juvenile offenders.

9.520
RAGGED SCHOOL UNION MAGAZINE: 1849 to 1875. Informs philanthropists and donors to ragged schools of what the organizations are doing to prevent future criminality.

9.521
Vanderkiste, R.W., **NOTES AND NARRATIVES OF A SIX YEARS' MISSION, PRINCIPALLY AMONG THE DENS OF LONDON.** 1849. See p. 295 for female crime and p. 297 for juveniles.

9.522
Worsley, Henry, **JUVENILE DEPRAVITY.** 1849. Juvenile delinquency continues due to the "strong tendencies in the system of manufacturing to moral evil," "drunkenness," and lack of education. "As long as we have myriads of drunken dissolute parents, we must expect still to have myriads of sons and daughters, who will be in a manner forced to earn a wretched livelihood by thieving and by prostitution" (p. 193).

9.523
CHAMBERS'S EDINBURGH JOURNAL: *"Juvenile Crime and Destitution,"* 12 (1849) 281-285; *"The Red Hill Reformatory Arm,"* 12 (1849) 347-350.

9.524
REPORT OF THE PROCEEDINGS OF A CONFERENCE ON THE SUBJECT OF PREVENTIVE AND REFORMATORY SCHOOLS HELD AT BIRMINGHAM ON THE 9TH AND 10TH OF DECEMBER, 1851. 1851. Claims present systems of juvenile reformation have failed completely and advocates adoption of some new means to stem the tide of "juvenile depravity." Includes information about the role of Amelia Murray, an original member of the Children's Friend Society who worked toward passage of the Infant Felon's Act.

9.525
Carpenter, Mary, **REFORMATORY SCHOOLS FOR THE CHILDREN OF THE PERISHING AND DANGEROUS CLASSES AND FOR JUVENILE OFFENDERS.** 1851; rpt., New York, 1969. Examines the virtues of schools for the poor and juvenile offenders. "Their present mode of life is so lucrative and so pleasant, that they will not exchange it for another presenting far greater advantages" (p. 72); *reviewed in:* HISTORY OF EDUCATION QUARTERLY: Harrison, J.F.C., *"Review Essay II: Education in Victorian England,"* 10 (1970) 488-489; **JUVENILE DELINQUENTS, THEIR CONDITIONS AND TREATMENT.** 1853. On the unequal treatment of offenders from working-class and upper-class backgrounds: Carpenter concludes that along with considerable prejudice between classes, there was reluctance to prosecute children from respectable backgrounds, due to the well-known contaminating effects of incarceration; **REFORMATORY PRISON DISCIPLINE AS DEVELOPED BY THE RT. HON. SIR WALTER CROFTON IN THE IRISH CONVICT PRISONS.** 1872; rpt., 1967; **AN ADDRESS ON PRISON DISCIPLINE AND JUVENILE REFORMATORIES.** Calcutta, 1876. ——*see also*: Carpenter, J. Estlin, **THE LIFE AND WORK OF MARY CARPENTER.** 1879; Browne, Phyllis (pseud. for Hamer, Sarah Sharp), **MRS. SOMERVILLE AND MARY CARPENTER.** 1887. See p. 61 for Carpenter; Tabor, Margaret Emma, **PIONEER WOMEN.** 1927. See the second series for Mary Carpenter.

9.526
Conference on the Subject of Preventive and Reformatory Schools, Birmingham, **REPORT OF THE PROCEEDING... HELP... ON THE 9TH AND 10TH OF DECEMBER, 1851.** 1851.

9.527
Neal, Stephen, **SPECIAL REPORT ON THE STATE OF JUVENILE EDUCATION AND DELINQUENCY IN THE BOROUGH OF SALFORD.** 1851.

9.528
Tuckness, William, "Agencies For the Suppression of Vice and Crime" in **LONDON LABOUR AND THE LONDON POOR.** by Henry Mayhew. vol. 4, 1851; 1861; New York, 1968.

9.529
HOUSEHOLD NARRATIVE: *"Social, Sanitary and Municipal Progress,"* 2 (1851) 272-274. On the National Public School Association and preventive and reformatory schools.

9.530
HOUSEHOLD WORDS: *"A Free (and Easy) School,"* 4 (1851) 169-173; Hannay, J., *"Lambs to be Fed (Mary Carpenter, Reformatory Schools),"* 3 (1851) 544-549; *"In and Out of Jail,"* 7 (1853) 241-245; Dickens, C., *"Home for Homeless Women,"* 7 (1853) 169-175; *"A Mighty Scene in London,"* 13 (1856) 25-27.

9.531
LAW REVIEW AND QUARTERLY JOURNAL OF BRITISH AND FOREIGN JURISPRUDENCE: *"Juvenile Offenders: Preventative and Reformatory Schools,"* 15 (1851-52) 344-357; *"Mettray: A Lecture Read Before the Leeds Philosophical and Literary Society by Robert Hall,"* 20 (1854) 389-392. Review of a guide/lecture to the juvenile reformatory colony in France, held up as a possible model for the English to follow. This was a popular consideration among the social reformers at a peak time in forming legislation that would set juvenile criminals apart from adults.

9.532
Antrobus, Edmund E., **THE PRISON AND THE SCHOOL. THE CHIEF ASCERTAINED CAUSES OF CRIME CONSIDERED, WITH SUGGESTIONS FOR THE CARE, RELIEF, AND REFORMATION OF THE NEGLECTED, DESTITUTE AND CRIMINAL CHILDREN OF THE METROPOLIS.** 2nd ed., 1853.

9.533
Fulford, Captain, "On Prison Discipline" in **MELIORA: OR BETTER TIMES TO COME.** ed. by Charles John Chetwynd Talbot, Viscount Ingestre. 1853; rpt., 1971. "Children are sent here so small and so babyish that it really has been difficult to carry out the rules in their cases, and they have been sent into female prisons to spend their term in the nursery with the women who have infants" (p. 143).

9.534
Hill, Micaiah and Cornwalles, C.F., **TWO PRIZE ESSAYS ON JUVENILE DELINQUENCY.** 1853. Concludes that between 1836 and 1845, juvenile delinquency fell 13 per cent while adult crime increased. Observes the inadequacy of statistical returns that count committals, not offenders.

9.535
Leigh, John, "Juvenile Offenders and Destitute Pauper Children" in **MELIORA: OR**

BETTER TIMES TO COME. ed. by Charles John Chetwynd Talbot, Viscount Ingestre. 1853; rpt., 1971. "Nothing short of the direct interference of the legislature can adequately restrain the increase of juvenile delinquency" (p. 81).

9.536
AINSWORTH'S MAGAZINE: Desmond, W., *"The Institution at Mettray [French Vocational School for Youthful Criminals],"* 23 (1853) 69-72.

9.537
ENGLISH WOMAN'S JOURNAL: *"Women's Work in the Reformatory Movement,"* 1 (1853) 289-295. A call to Christian women; *"Manchester and Salford Reformatory For Juvenile Criminals,"* 3 (1859) 406-411.

9.538
PROSPECTIVE REVIEW: Wickstead, C., *"Society in Danger from Children,"* 9 (1853) 165-182. Relates Mary Carpenter's views on juvenile delinquency.

9.539
WESTMINSTER REVIEW: Cornwallis, C.F., *"Young Criminals,"* 60 (1853) 137-164; *"What to Do With Our Juvenile Paupers,"* 150 (1898) 282-288.

9.540
TREATMENT OF CRIMINAL CHILDREN. REPORT OF THE SOCIETY FOR THE AMENDMENT OF THE LAW. 1854.

9.541
Murray, Patrick John, **REFORMATORY SCHOOLS IN FRANCE AND ENGLAND.** 1854.

9.542
Parkes, William, **THE DESTITUTE AND CRIMINAL JUVENILES OF MANCHESTER.** Manchester, 1854.

9.543
LAW MAGAZINE: *"The Birmingham Conference on the Reformation of Young Criminals,"* 51 (1854) 51-59.

9.544
Administrative Reform Association, **ADDRESS OF THE COMMITTEE TO THE PEOPLE OF ENGLAND. MAY 19, 1855.** 1855.

9.545
Baker, T.B.L., **REPORT OF THE CHILDRENS FRIEND REFORMATORY.** Gloucester, 1855.

9.546
Hill, Matthew Davenport, **PRACTICAL SUGGESTIONS TO THE FOUNDERS OF REFORMATORY SCHOOLS.** 1855.

9.547
Turner, Sydney, **REFORMATORY SCHOOLS. A LETTER TO C.B. ADDERLY, ESQ., M.P.... ON THE REFORMATION OF YOUNG OFFENDERS, ETC.** 1855.

9.548
EDINBURGH REVIEW: Greg, W.R., *"The Correction of Juvenile Offenders,"* 101

(1855) 383-394. Presents a portrait of juvenile delinquents as a class and attacks the economic problem of their public maintenance as well as the maintenance of adult criminals. Argues on economic and moral grounds against the punitive system and for reformatories for juvenile delinquents; Greg, W.R., *"Reformatories Are Not Places of Punishment,"* 101 (1855) 394-415.

9.549
PHILANTHROPIST AND PRISON REFORMATORY GAZETTE AND SOCIAL SCIENCE GAZETTE: 1855 to 1861.

9.550
QUARTERLY REVIEW: Northcote, S., *"Reformatory Schools,"* 98 (1855) 32-65.

9.551
Kingsmill, Joseph, **ON THE PRESENT ASPECT OF SERIOUS CRIME IN ENGLAND WITH REMARKS ON THE REFORMATORY SCHOOL MOVEMENTS.** 1856.

9.552
Macgregor, John, **THE LAW OF REFORMATORIES.** 1856.

9.553
McClelland, James, **ON REFORMATORIES FOR THE DESTITUTE AND FALLEN.** Glasgow, 1856.

9.554
CHURCH OF ENGLAND MONTHLY REVIEW: *"Reformatory Institutions,"* 1 (1856) 4-12.

9.555
Adshead, Joseph, **ON JUVENILE CRIMINALS, REFORMATORIES, AND THE MEANS OF RENDERING THE PERISHING AND DANGEROUS CLASSES SERVICEABLE TO THE STATE...** Manchester, 1857.

9.556
Beggs, Thomas, **JUVENILE DELINQUENCY AND REFORMATORY INSTITU-TIONS. A LECTURE, ETC.** 1857.

9.557
JOURNAL OF THE ROYAL STATISTICAL SOCIETY: Carpenter, M., *"On the Importance of Statistics to the Reformatory Movement, with Returns from Female Reformatories, and Remarks on Them,"* 20 (1857) 33-40. "Orphanage is not the cause of crime among these children, little more than one-tenth of them having lost both parents. Nearly one-half, however, have lost one parent, and a large proportion of these have a step-father or mother. In delinquency of the child [it] is directly traceable to the bad character of the parents, or, if the surviving parent is respectable, to the unkind treatment of a stepmother" (p. 37); Barrett, R.M., *"The Treatment of Juvenile Offenders: Together with Statistics of Their Numbers,"* 63 (1900) 183-261. "Boy criminals are five to six times as numerous as girls.... Of those under 21 the proportion is 87 boys to 13 girls; of those committed to reformatories there are 88 percent boys to 12 percent girls" (p. 189); *"Discussion on Miss Barrett's Paper,"* 63 (1900) 261-271. Includes a response from Miss Barrett.

9.558
TRANSACTIONS OF THE NATIONAL ASSOCIATION FOR THE PROMOTION

OF SOCIAL SCIENCE: Carpenter, M., *"Reformatories for Convicted Girls,"* n.v. (1857) 338-346. "Girls are far the most hardened and difficult to manage" (p. 339) due to the incarceration which is invoked when more lenient means of correction prove ineffective. Advocates preparing girls for domestic service and gives guidelines for training schools; Hanbury, R., *"Facts and Statistics Respecting the London Reformatories, Refuges, Industrial Schools and Penitentiaries,"* n.v. (1861) 480-483; Carpenter, M., *"On the Supplementary Measures Needed for Reformatories for the Diminution of Juvenile Crime,"* n.v. (1861) 489-497; Carpenter, M., *"On the Essential Principles of the Reformatory Movement,"* n.v. (1862) 443; *"The Reformatory Movement,"* n.v. (1864) 471-472; Carpenter, M., *"On the Consolidation of the Reformatory and Industrial Schools' Act,"* n.v. (1866) 217; Gainsford, R.J., *"Reformatory Schools and Especially the North of England Catholic Girls Reformatory School at Howard Hill, Near Sheffield,"* n.v. (1866) 261.

9.559
Day, Samuel Phillips, **JUVENILE CRIME; ITS CAUSES, CHARACTER, AND CURE.** 1858. Assumes the largest group of female criminals is juvenile prostitutes who commit robbery. Links promiscuity and working class status to crime: "Robberies of a daring character are being almost daily committed through the instrumentality of prostitutes, and it seems all but certain, that the plunder of dwelling-houses is chiefly effected by the connivance of servants or domestics; women, whose conduct would in any other country but England have placed them on the list of 'the suspected'" (p. 319).

9.560
Discharged Prisoners Aid Society, **THE SECOND ANNUAL REPORT OF THE REFORMATORY AND REFUGE UNION.** 1858; 12th report, 1869. See especially: "Devon and Exeter Refuge, 1836," "Durham Refuge for Discharged Prisoners, 1849: Males and Females," and "Discharged Prisoners, 1857"; **DISCHARGED PRISONERS' AID SOCIETIES. [A CORRESPONDENCE WITH THE HOME SECRETARY, SIR WILLIAM HARCOURT, 1882, ON THE MODIFICATION OF THE RULES ISSUES IN MARCH, 1880]. THE GOVERNMENT INSPECTOR'S 25TH REPORT ON THE REFORMATORY AND INDUSTRIAL SCHOOLS OF GREAT BRITAIN.** 1882.

9.561
PHILANTHROPIST AND SOCIAL SCIENCE GAZETTE: *"Reformatory Movement: The Birmingham Reformatory Institution,"* 3 (1858) 101-102. Work is the antidote to juvenile crime.

9.562
ENGLISH WOMAN'S JOURNAL: *"Manchester and Salford Reformatory for Juvenile Criminals,"* 3 (1859) 406-411.

9.563
HAMPSTEAD REFORMATORY SCHOOL FOR GIRLS. 1860. Accommodates fifty girls, ages 7-16, convicted under the "Youthful Offenders Act"; a donation of L5/5 was required.

9.564
JOURNAL OF THE STATISTICAL SOCIETY OF LONDON: *"Abstracts and Inferences Founded Upon the Official Criminal Returns of England and Wales For the Years 1854-1859, With Special Reference to the Results of Reformatories,"* 23 (1860) 427-439. See p. 439 for statistics relating to girls committed to prisons.

9.565
REFORMATORY AND REFUGE JOURNAL: 1861 to 1899; vols. 1-13; *continued as:* **SEEKING AND SAVING:** 1900 to ?; vols. 1-14. Published by the Reformatory and Refuge Union.

9.566
Mayhew, Henry and Binny, John, **THE CRIMINAL PRISONS IN LONDON AND SCENES OF PRISON LIFE.** 1862; rpt., 1968. "The great mass of crime in this country is committed by those who have been bred and born to the business... living as systematically by robbery or cheating as others do by commerce or the exercise of intellectual or manual labour" (p. 383). See pp. 578-579 on the Juvenile Wing of Holloway Prison.

9.567
Hill, Florence Davenport, **CHILDREN OF THE STATE: THE TRAINING OF JUVENILE PAUPERS.** 1868; 1889. On female juvenile paupers from workhouse schools: "80 percent of the girls they send to service are failures" (p. 16).

9.568
Mission to Women Discharged from Prison, **REPORT OF MISSION...** 1868.

9.569
Fish, Ismael, **THE IMPRISONMENT OF CHILDREN PRIOR TO BEING SENT TO A REFORMATORY.** 1869.

9.570
MONTH: A MAGAZINE AND REVIEW: Todd, W.G., *"English Reformatories and Industrial Schools,"* 13 (1870) 319-339.

9.571
Howard Association, **IMPRISONMENT OF CHILDREN.** 1871; **JUVENILE OFFENDERS. A REPORT BASED ON AN INQUIRY INSTITUTED BY THE COMMON, IMPRISONMENT OF CHILDREN.** 1871; **JUVENILE OFFENDERS. A REPORT BASED ON AN INQUIRY INSTITUTED BY THE COMMITTEE OF THE HOWARD ASSOCIATION.** 1898; **CHILDREN'S COURTS AND THE PROBATION SYSTEM.** 1904.

9.572
ALL THE YEAR ROUND: *"How We Make Thieves,"* 7 (1872) 279-283.

9.573
Waugh, Benjamin, **THE GAOL CRADLE: WHO ROCKS IT?** 1876. Author founded the National Society for the Prevention of Cruelty to Children. Calls for the abolishment of juvenile imprisonment.

9.574
Harris, Elisha, **THE EDUCATIONAL AND CORRECTIONAL TREATMENT OF JUVENILE DELINQUENTS AND OF DEPRAVED, NEGLECTED, ABANDONED AND OTHER CHILDREN IN DANGER OF FALLING INTO A CRIMINAL CAREER.** New York, 1877.

9.575
VICTORIA MAGAZINE: *"Reformatory Prisons for Women,"* 31 (1878) 331.

9.576
Hopkins, Jane Ellice, **NOTES ON PENITENTIARY WORK**. 1879. Discusses the understanding and treatment of delinquent girls as well as the organization and management of institutions; **DRAWN UNTO DEATH**. 1884.

9.577
Rowe, Richard, **PICKED UP IN THE STREETS; OR, STRUGGLES FOR LIFE AMONGST THE LONDON POOR**. 1880. See p. 19 for material on juveniles.

9.578
Smith, George, **GIPSY LIFE: BEING AN ACCOUNT OF OUR GIPSIES AND THEIR CHILDREN WITH SUGGESTIONS FOR THEIR IMPROVEMENT**. 1880. "It is a black, burning shame and disgrace to see herds of healthy-looking girls and great strapping youths growing up in ignorance and idleness.... Their highest ambition is to learn slang, roll in the ditch, spread small pox and fevers" (p. 285).

9.579
Wines, Enoch Cobb, **THE STATE OF PRISONS AND OF CHILD-SAVING INSTITUTIONS IN THE CIVILIZED WORLD**. 1880.

9.580
GOOD WORDS AND SUNDAY MAGAZINE: Crofton, W., *"On the Treatment of Our Juvenile Offenders,"* 22 (1881) 458-463. Calls for greater parental responsibility for child offenders and argues that children under twelve should not be sent to reformatories.

9.581
NINETEENTH CENTURY: Surr, E., *"The Child Criminal,"* 9 (1881) 649-663. Recommends the workhouse, where delinquents may be "trained to good behaviour under moral and religious influences" (p. 653), as well as segregation of criminals from other schoolchildren; White, R., *"On the Prison Treatment of Juvenile Offenders,"* 42 (1897) 326-335.

9.582
Mem. (pseud.), **FARM LIFE FOR REFORMATORY GIRLS: BEING AN ACCOUNT OF A VISIT TO "BROOKSIDE" PRIVATE REFORMATORY**. Melbourne, 1890.

9.583
Hill, Frederic, **AN AUTOBIOGRAPHY OF FIFTY YEARS IN TIMES OF REFORM**. 1894.

9.584
Bosanquet, Helen (Dendy), "The Children of Working London" in **ASPECTS OF THE SOCIAL PROBLEM**. ed. by Bernard Bosanquet. 1895.

9.585
Morrison, Arthur, **CHILD OF THE JAGO**. 1896. Fictional treatment of upbringing in "Jago," the famous criminal slum of late-Victorian London.

9.586
Morrison, William Douglas, **JUVENILE OFFENDERS**. 1896; New York, 1897. Author was Chaplain of Wandsworth Prison from 1883 to 1898. ——*see also*: Mannheim, Hermann, "Previous Investigations" in **YOUNG OFFENDERS: AN ENQUIRY INTO JUVENILE DELINQUENCY**. by A.M. Carr-Sanders, Herman

Mannheim, and E.C. Rhodes. 1897; Cambridge, 1942. Outlines seven aspects of Morrison's analysis: local distribution of juvenile delinquency, relationship with pauperism, physical condition, mental condition, parental condition, economic condition, and recidivism.

9.587
Chance, William, **CHILDREN UNDER THE POOR LAW**. 1897.

9.588
JUVENILE OFFENDERS. A REPORT BASED ON AN INQUIRY INSTITUTED BY THE HOWARD ASSOCIATION, 1898. 1898.

9.589
Wilde, Oscar, **CHILDREN IN PRISONS AND OTHER CRUELTIES OF PRISON LIFE**. 1898.

9.590
LAW MAGAZINE AND REVIEW: Atkinson, C.M., *"The Punishment of Juvenile Offenders,"* 23 (1898) 289-299.

9.591
Legge, T.C., "The Treatment of Children in Reformatories" in **WOMEN IN SOCIAL LIFE. THE TRANSACTIONS OF THE SOCIAL SECTION OF THE INTERNATIONAL CONGRESS OF WOMEN. LONDON, JULY, 1899**. ed. by Ishbel Maria Gordon (Countess of Aberdeen). 1900. Children "sent to reformatories are generally 12 years of age, and on the high road to a criminal career; that 71 percent of these are arrested in their downward course is a result to be profoundly thankful" (p. 28). Delineates methods utilized in successful reformation.

9.592
CONTEMPORARY REVIEW: Holmes, T., *"Youthful Offenders and Parental Responsibility,"* 77 (1900) 845-854.

9.593
National Association of Certified Reformatory and Industrial Schools, **REPORT OF THE NATIONAL... 1900, ETC**. [1901, etc.].

9.594
Holmes, H.T., **REFORM AND REFORMATORIES AND INDUSTRIAL SCHOOLS**. 1902. Warns against overcrowding at such institutions and recommends their transference from "private hands to public bodies" (p. 14). Bibliography included.

9.595
Taylor, William J., **THE STORY OF THE HOMES**. 1907.

9.596
Alden, Margaret (Pearse), "Juvenile Offenders and Children's Courts" in **CHILD LIFE AND LABOUR**. by Margaret Alden. 1908; 1909; 1913. Discusses reformatory schools, the Industrial School system, separate detention for children, children's courts, and probation officers. "Science has taught us that in the great majority of cases, the juvenile offender is a boy or a girl of poor physique and low mental development, underfed or wrongly fed from earliest years, condemned by the will of parents or relatives to be a child beggar or street seller years before school age is over" (p. 144).

9.597
Jones, Llewellyn Archer Atherley and Bellot, Hugh Hale Leigh, LAW OF CHILDREN AND YOUNG PERSONS IN RELATION TO PENAL OFFENCES, INCLUDING THE CHILDREN ACT, 1908. 1909.

9.598
Samuelson, James, THE CHILDREN OF OUR SLUMS. 1911.

9.599
Barnett, Mary G., YOUNG DELINQUENTS: A STUDY OF REFORMATORY AND INDUSTRIAL SCHOOLS... New York, 1913.

9.600
Gorst, John, "Girls' Reformatory and Industrial Schools" in YOUNG DELINQUENTS, A STUDY OF REFORMATORY AND INDUSTRIAL SCHOOLS. by Mary G. Barnett. New York, 1913.

9.601
PSYCHOLOGICAL REVIEW: Rowland, E., *"Report of Experiments at the State Reformatory for Women at Bedford, New York,"* 20 (1913) 245-249. Attempt to discover in advance whether the women would benefit, and be sufficiently "normal" to be released, from the reformatory.

9.602
Simeral, Isabel, "The Newgate Prison Schools and Their Development" in "Reform Movements in Behalf of Children in England and Wales of the Early Nineteenth Century and the Agents of Those Reforms," by Isabel Simeral. Ph.D. diss., Columbia Univ., 1916.

9.603
Russell, Charles, THE PROBLEM OF JUVENILE CRIME. Oxford, 1917.

9.604
Burt, Cyril, THE YOUNG DELINQUENT. 1919; 1931; 4th ed., 1948. A classic examination of the causes of juvenile delinquency.

9.605
CHILD-STUDY: Burt, C., *"Facial Expression as an Index of Mentality,"* 12 (1919) n.p.

9.606
ENGLISHWOMAN: Mills, E., *"Juvenile Delinquency,"* 43 (1919) 15-20.

9.607
Barman, S., "The Girl Offender" and "Borstal for Girls, Aylesbury" in THE ENGLISH BORSTAL SYSTEM: A STUDY OF THE TREATMENT OF YOUNG OFFENDERS. 1934. Study is divided into environmental, mental, psychological, and physical factors. Links a woman's sexual appetite to crime. Since a large percentage come from slum areas, "members of the family sleep together in the home room, with the consequence that the young ones are influenced in acquiring evil sexual habits... [thus a girl] lacks naturally the power of self-control, for she was never brought up to exercise it" (pp. 112-110).

9.608
Hinde, R.S.E., "Treatment of Juveniles" and "Further Developments in the Treat-

ment of Juveniles" in **THE BRITISH PENAL SYSTEM 1773-1950.** by R.S.E. Hinde. 1951. Both chapters chronicle the growth of legislation which led to the removal of delinquent children from prisons to reformatories and schools. "Section 11 of the [Parkhurst] Act [1838] further provided for a royal pardon on condition that the offender put himself under the care of a charitable organization. Thus males would go to the Redhill Reformatory and females to the Refuges at Dalston or Chelsea" (p. 97).

9.609
SOCIAL SERVICE REVIEW: Marks, R., *"Treatment of Delinquent Women: A Nineteenth-Century Experiment Reported in the Letters of Charles Dickens,"* 27 (1953) 408-418. Dickens and Angela Burdett-Coutts established the Urania Cottage, a home for fallen women. Article describes Dickens' businesslike advice on how to set up the home which, despite high ambitions, failed in practice.

9.610
Size, Mary, **PRISONS I HAVE KNOWN.** 1957. See especially: Chap. 3 for a description of the newly implemented Borstal System provided by the Prevention of Crimes Act, 1908. "Outside school hours the girls were employed on housework, cookery, laundry work, garden and farm work and poultry keeping" as well as needlework and dressmaking (p. 43). "French knots came to be known as 'Borstal Knots' and were lavishly used for decoration" (p. 44).

9.611
Collins, Philip, "The Home for Homeless Women" in **DICKENS AND CRIME.** by Philip Collins. 1962.

9.612
BRITISH JOURNAL OF CRIMINOLOGY: Knell, B.E.F., *"Capital Punishment: Its Administration in Relation to Juvenile Offenders in the Nineteenth Century and its Possible Administration in the Eighteenth,"* 5 (1965) 198-207. Shows number and age of juvenile offenders sentenced to death between the years 1801 and 1836 with their respective offences, one of which was Mary Crawley, age 10, for shoplifting. A child under 14 that was sentenced to death most often remained in the school, and was "treated like all other prisoners of their own age" (p. 199). Study contradicts many modern social historians' conclusions as to the preponderance of children executed in the 18th and 19th century.

9.613
Boss, Peter, "The Historical Background—From Retribution to Reform" in **SOCIAL POLICY AND THE YOUNG DELINQUENT.** by Peter Boss. 1967. In the nineteenth century, "relaxation of trial procedures, different treatment of delinquents after finding of guilt in the court and a generally less rigid attitude toward juveniles' misbehavior brought about through better understanding of the social problems which give rise to it, produced a new climate of opinion... resulting in the juvenile court system of the 20th century" (p. 32).

9.614
Tobias, John Jacob, "Juveniles and Women" in **CRIME AND INDUSTRIAL SOCIETY IN THE 19TH CENTURY.** by John Jacob Tobias. 1967. Excellent discussion of juvenile offenders—their behavior in court, in jail, to police and to each other. Also describes their living situations, including sexual pairing at early ages, their diversions, and stories about criminal heroes.

9.615
Lamb, Felicia and Prickthorn, Patricia, **LOCKED-UP DAUGHTERS**. 1968.

9.616
Platt, Anthony M., **THE CHILD SAVERS: THE INVENTION OF DELINQUENCY**. Chicago, 1969. Traces the concept of juvenile delinquency from nineteenth-century origins. The focus is American, but there is discussion and comparison with England and the work of Mary Carpenter.

9.617
ANNALS: Platt, A.M., *"The Rise of the Child Saving Movement: A Study in Social Police and Correctional Reform,"* 381 (1969) 21-38.

9.618
Sanders, Wiley B., ed., **JUVENILE OFFENDERS FOR A THOUSAND YEARS. SELECTED READINGS FROM ANGLO-SAXON TIMES TO 1900**. Chapel Hill, 1970.

9.619
ISSUES IN CRIMINOLOGY: Platt, A.M., *"Saving and Controlling Delinquent Youths: A Critique,"* 5 (1970) 1-24.

9.620
Middleton, Nigel, **WHEN FAMILY FAILED: THE TREATMENT OF CHILDREN IN THE COMMUNITY IN THE FIRST HALF OF THE TWENTIETH CENTURY**. 1971.

9.621
Playfair, Giles, "Women and Children" in **THE PUNITIVE OBSESSION**. by Giles Playfair. 1971.

9.622
Kanner, S. Barbara, "Victorian Institutional Patronage: Angela Burdett-Coutts, Charles Dickens and Urania Cottage, Reformatory for Women, 1846-1858," Ph.D. diss., Univ. of California, Los Angeles, 1972. A case study in the development of institutions for social reform in mid-Victorian England. Urania Cottage, the institution investigated, was a reformatory-rehabilitation home for young delinquent women.

9.623
Schupf, Harriet Warm, "The Perishing and Dangerous Classes: Efforts to Deal with the Neglected, Vagrant and Delinquent Juvenile in England, 1840-1875," Ph.D. diss., Columbia Univ., 1971. "By 1870 more than 20,000 juveniles had been admitted to the reformatories, about a third of whom were girls... too often children were sent without any record of prior conviction" (pp. 309-310). Discusses the training of girls for domestic service and some of the institutions established for young female criminals who, "while less numerous than the male[s], presented a more serious problem in one respect, for [they were] generally considered to be the more hardened of the two" (p. 357).

9.624
HISTORY OF EDUCATION QUARTERLY: Houston, S.E., *"The Victorian Origins of Juvenile Delinquency,"* 12 (1972) 254-280.

9.625

VICTORIAN STUDIES: May, M., *"Innocence and Experience: The Evolution of the Concept of Juvenile Delinquency in the Mid-Nineteenth Century,"* 17 (1973-1974) 7-29. Special Issue: "The Victorian Child." Traces the evolution of the treatment of juvenile delinquents: "A reformatory system which clearly distinguished a child's offence from an adult's crime replaced a penal system which made little specialised provision for children. This departure culminated in Herbert Samual's Children Act of 1908" (p. 8); Dunae, P., *"Penny Dreadfuls: Late Nineteenth Century Boys' Literature and Crime,"* 22 (1979) 133-150.

9.626

Gillis, John R., **YOUTH AND HISTORY.** 1974. See especially: "Conformity and Delinquency: The Era of Adolescence, 1900-1950." Traces the trend toward protectionism of minors, beginning with the establishment of reformatory and industrial schools in the 1850s. "The imposition of adolescence provoked strong resistance from a sizeable part of the population, particularly the laboring poor, with the result that for most of the period 1900-1950 the lines between conformity and delinquency were drawn along what were essentially class divisions" (p. 134).

9.627

Horn, Pamela, "Crime and Punishment" in **THE VICTORIAN COUNTRY CHILD.** by Pamela Horn. Kineton, 1974. Petty larceny was the charge most often levied against juveniles, probably because they were stealing badly needed food.

9.628

Stack, John Andrew, "Social Policy and Juvenile Delinquency in England and Wales, 1815-1875," Ph.D. diss., Univ. of Iowa, 1974. Examines how reformers reacted to the inadequacies of juvenile prisons, how the treatment of delinquency relates to the current debate of the nineteenth century "Revolution in Government" and how the new reformatory system operated.

9.629

PAST AND PRESENT: Gillis, J.R., *"The Evolution of Juvenile Delinquency in England 1890-1914,"* no. 67 (1975) 96-126. Explains how the institutionalization of adolescence affected perceptions of delinquency. Types of juvenile behavior previously dealt with informally became subject to prosecution.

9.630

Smith, C.J., "Changes in Provision for Juvenile Offenders in Mid-Nineteenth Century England with Particular Reference to Merseyside," M.A. thesis, Univ. of Liverpool, 1977.

9.631

HISTORIAN: Stack, J.A., *"The Juvenile Delinquent and England's Revolution in Government, 1825-1875,"* 42 (1979) 42-57. Surveys the anomalous progress of England's treatment of juvenile offenders which, instead of becoming a nationalized institution, was increasingly handled in the second half of the century by private concerns.

9.632

HISTORY OF EDUCATION JOURNAL: Stack, J.A., *"The Provision of Reformatory Schools, the Landed Class and the Myth of Superiority of Rural Life in Mid-Victorian England,"* 8 (1979) 33-43. Most reformatories for girls were in the city because it was thought that rural life was less suited to rehabilitating criminal girls. "By the early 1850s... a few magistrates and judges, some prison officials and assorted reformers had become disenchanted with the prevailing punishment alternatives for convicted juvenile offenders.... Consequently these critics lobbied vigorously for the establishment of 'reformatory schools' to which convicted juvenile offenders might be sent for longer periods, and in which they might be subjected to a form of discipline more appropriate to their youthful condition" (p. 45).

9.633
Humphries, Stephan, "Reformatories: Resistance To Repression" in **HOOLIGANS OR REBELS? AN ORAL HISTORY OF WORKING CLASS CHILDHOOD AND YOUTH 1889-1939.** by Stephan Humphries. Oxford, 1981. Contains "recollections of the rigid classification of inmates, the formalized and regimented daily routine and the harsh discipline and the brutal punishments inflicted upon working-class children" (p. 209). "For whether a working-class child was an orphan, vagrant, a truant, a rebel at home or school or a thief, the assumption was that he or she was the offspring of a degenerate and deprived class, requiring intensive disciplinary treatment in a reformatory" (p. 211).

9.634
ORAL HISTORY: Humphries, S., *"Steal to Survive: The Social Crime of Working-Class Children, 1890-1940,"* 9 (1981) 24-34.

9.635
O'Brien, Patricia, "Youth in Prison" in **THE PROMISE OF PUNISHMENT: PRISONS IN NINETEENTH-CENTURY FRANCE.** by Patricia O'Brien. Princeton, 1982. Though French laws differed greatly from the English, both were characterized by fears about juvenile crime and a reliance on male-dominated means of discipline.

9.636
JOURNAL OF EDUCATIONAL AND ADMINISTRATIVE HISTORY: Stack, J.A., *"Interests and Ideas in Nineteenth Century Social Policy: The Mid-Victorian Reformatory School,"* 14 (1982) 36-45.

X. SEXUAL ISSUES

INTRODUCTION*

That the subject of sexuality is a valid and useful category for scholarly analysis is borne out by the expanding number of books and papers appearing over the last dozen years. These writings represent virtually all the academic disciplines within the humanities and social sciences. The major justification that authors give for establishing the new sub-field of sexual studies is that studying sexual matters yields new understandings about societies past and present. Questions about sexuality and sexual issues are analyzed with relevance to social organization and control, as well as to ideas and ideologies, private and public behaviors, gender and class relationships, and to cultural developments. For the historical study of Victorian and Edwardian England, however, modern scholarly work on sex and society is a comparatively recent development.

As long ago as 1967 Brian Harrison attempted to open up the field in his review of Steven Marcus' literary study of Victorian pornography. His critique included suggestions to historians of alternative areas of inquiry and historiographical questions. But almost ten years later, Vern Bullough found it still appropriate to exhort: "In my opinion the investigation of sexual behavior offers many... opportunities to make major breakthroughs.... For those willing to do some pioneering, the study of the history of sex offers only virgin fields" (p. 15). See:

10.1int
VICTORIAN STUDIES: Harrison, B., _"Underneath the Victorians,"_ 10 (1967) 239-262.

10.2int
Marcus, Steven, **THE OTHER VICTORIANS: A STUDY OF SEXUALITY AND PORNOGRAPHY IN MID-NINETEENTH-CENTURY ENGLAND.** New York, 1964.

10.3int
Bullough, Vern, "Sex in History: A Virgin Field" in **SEX, SOCIETY, AND HISTORY.** New York, 1976.

Another decade later, in a wide-ranging commentary on twenty-five books unevenly representing historical sexual studies, Lawrence Stone could still critique the neglect of the history of sexuality: "There is something very illogical about the way we scrutinize... our individual sexual history on the psychoanalyst's couch, but inquire so little about our collective sexual history as heirs——and prisoners——of an ancient sexual culture" (p. 26) in

10.4int
NEW REPUBLIC: Stone, L., *"Sex in the West: The Strange History of Human Sexuality,"* n.v. (July 8, 1985) 25-37. Stone explores the very great extent to which human sexuality has been discussed and exploited over the span of Western history.

> Human beings... have managed to erect around the simple physiological arrangements for perpetuating the species some of the most bizarre, complex and glittering edifices of moral, religious, and medical prescriptions and taboos in the whole history of mankind.... Men and women have always invented elaborate refinements upon the simple 90-second act of penetration and ejaculation that fertilizes the egg (p. 25).... [They have] proceeded to enmesh sexual reproduction with a massive array of moral and aesthetic injunctions, ascetic codes of conduct and theological laws and prescriptions of the most extraordinary complexity, variety, and severity. For long periods of time, the full moral, administrative and judicial powers of church and state have been directed toward controlling the libido and directing it into strictly delimited channels.... [Yet] sexuality in the nineteenth century is still much of a mystery. It combined what seems like the all-time pinnacle of hypocritical prudery and sexual asceticism, evidenced by a fairly widespread concept of women as sexless, domesticated childbearing machines.... On the other hand, it is known that large numbers of the urban proletariat were living in casual concubinage, that a vast army of prostitutes and highly specialized brothels serviced all classes of men, and that some of the most elaborate and obscene pornography... [was] produced.... The reasons for the most salient aspect of the nineteenth century, the evident attempts at sexual repression, are even more obscure than the facts of actual behavior (p. 35).

It is of course analyses of the *reasons* behind Victorian sexuality that concern modern social historians who are otherwise skeptical of the old tales and myths of Victorian prudery and hypocrisy.

In a review of a reprint series of nineteenth-century books on sex, marital advice and morality published in 1974, Peter Gay compares old popular cliches about sexless wives and sexually insensitive husbands with the contradictory content in the sex manuals under his inspection.

10.5int
AMERICAN SCHOLAR: Gay, P., *"Victorian Sexuality: Old Texts and New Insights,"* 49 (1980) 372-378. The series of reprints is

10.6int
Rosenberg, Charles E. and Smith-Rosenberg, Carroll, eds., **SEX AND SOCIETY.** New York, 1974.

Besides surveying the reprinted books, Gay takes the opportunity to critique some of the vintage 1970s sex-in-history scholarship on the Victorian age that appeared around the time the series was published:

> If we have long believed that the Victorians were arrant hypocrites engaged in a conspiracy of silence about the human body, these books will assist us in seeing that this pharisaic view of our nineteenth-century forbears is all nonsense, or at best a superficial reading of pathology. Paradoxically, our

recent candor in sexual matters has only served to lend this self-satisfied cluster of cliches the prestige of what parades as serious, responsible scholarship.... Historians of varying degrees of competence have indulged in higher gossip amounting, in long, luxuriant passages, to a kind of soft pornography.... I have no intention of questioning the facts or the quotations that this modern crop of candor has gathered... I have drawn instruction from all these [recent] titles. But I question the representativeness of their anecdotes and the sobriety of their analyses.... However portentous their tone, however earnest their footnotes, they have perpetrated myths.... To be sure, this consensus has not remained unbroken (pp. 372-373).... Much more needs to be done by scholars at once liberated from what I have called the Victorian myth and immune to the desire to revise for revision's sake.... This much, though is plain now... the Victorians... had a far more positive view of sexuality than has been supposed. They were often ambivalent; there were areas of ignorance and repression that helped to produce... 'neurasthenia'.... [However] I think we can conclude with some confidence: it is a mistake to think that nineteenth-century bourgeois did not know what they did not discuss, did not practice what they did not confess, or did not enjoy what they did not publish (p. 377).

Like Gay, other serious revisionists have sought contexts and frameworks not only to transcend the old myths and bare facts but also to better comprehend how Victorian sexuality operated in the systems of private and public spheres. Considerable inspiration for posing new questions has come from the philosophically-oriented writings on sexuality of

10.7int
Foucault, Michel, **THE HISTORY OF SEXUALITY, VOLUME I: AN INTRO-DUCTION.** trans. by Robert Hurley. New York, 1978; 1980.

Foucault is not so interested in the factual bases of Victorian sexual life and thought as he is in the discourses that transpired about sex and the categories of experience about which discussions took place. He acknowledges the appropriateness of positing a hypothesis of sexual repression in Western society beginning in the seventeenth century, but he is more interested in asking: "Do the workings of power... really belong primarily to the category of repression? Are prohibition, censorship, and denial truly the forms through which power is exercised" (p. 10). More than sexual repression in the Victorian age, Foucault prefers to inquire: "Why has sexuality been so widely discussed, and what has been said about it? What were the effects of power generated by what was said? What are the links between these discourses, these effects of power, and the pleasures that were invested by them? What knowledge is formed as a result of this linkage? The object, in short, is to define the regime of power-knowledge-pleasure that sustains the discourse on human sexuality in our part of the world. The central issue... is to account for the fact that it is spoken about, to discover who does the speaking, the positions and viewpoints from which they speak, the institutions which prompt people to speak about it and which store and distribute the things that are said" (p. 11).

The history of sexuality, then, is a history of discourses about sexuality. And sex is far from simply a means of reproduction or a source of pleasure. From the perspective of discourse in the context of social relations, sexuality is central to self and society.

The most recent writings of revisionist historians do take their questions about sexuality well beyond the mainsprings of biology and into social-cultural contexts. One valuable discussion that appears to be informed by Foucault is

10.8int
RADICAL HISTORY REVIEW: Padgug, R.A., *"Sexual Matters: On Conceptualizing Sexuality in History,"* 20 (1979) 3-24:

> Biology as a set of potentialities and insuperable necessities provides the material of social interpretations and extensions; it does not *cause* human behavior, but conditions and limits it.... Human biology and culture are both necessary for the creation of human society. It is as important to avoid a rigid separation of "Nature" and "Culture" as it is to avoid reducing one to the other or simply uniting them as an undifferentiated reality (p. 9).... The content of sexuality is ultimately provided by human social relations, human productive activities, and human consciousness. The *history* of sexuality is therefore the history of a subject whose meaning and contents are in a continual process of change. It is the history of social relations (p. 11).

The introduction to the following important anthology pertains explicitly to female sexuality and features the bio-social theme:

10.9int
Stimpson, Catherine R. and Person, Ethel Spector, eds., **WOMEN: SEX AND SEXUALITY.** Chicago, 1980:

> We distrust any theory of female sexuality that burnishes it as the mirror image of the male, that universalizes it, or that reifies it. We suggest instead that sexuality is a biological process that both follows certain development patterns and that responds to the mediation of culture. Biology may set the outer boundaries of sexual possibility, but cultures work effectively within them. Paradoxically, a common consequence of cultural toil has been to reduce the female to her sexuality, her active being to her flesh. No mere reflex arc, human sexuality, like the process of birth with which it is so entwined, is embedded with meaning. To understand female sexuality then, is to explore the power of social constructions of reality and symbolic transformations of what seem to be matters of natural fact. Moreover, as feminists rightly warn us, sexuality cannot be assigned only to the domains of psychology and of our private lives. Public production and reproduction, social structures and sexuality are linked as irrevocably as the brain and our five senses (pp. 1-2).

This brings us to the sphere of overt behavior. Probing the question of interaction of ideology, norms, and other social constructs with behavior is:

10.10int
Smith-Rosenberg, Carroll, "Hearing Women's Words" in **DISORDERLY CONDUCT: VISIONS OF GENDER IN VICTORIAN AMERICA.** New York, 1985.

> One critical factor... [is] the impact of the larger social structure.... Categories, ideology, behavior are all equally social constructs, reactions to, reflections of underlying structures and power relations. Conceptual systems,

colloquial usages, formal ideologies, informal sexual norms all grow out of and reflect specific structural arrangements.... The shape [that] both sexual and nonsexual ideas assume... affects our sexual options, feelings, acts. Ideas thus function as a conduit (usually unself-consciously) linking fundamental material and social forces to sexual behavior. But economic, demographic, and institutional forces act directly as well as indirectly upon sexual behavior.... Once formed, sexual norms and sexual behavior each takes on a life of its own, reacting back upon the social and material forces that initially brought it into being. To examine sexual values and categories solely for the information they can reveal concerning sexual behavior narrows our field of vision just at the moment when it should be most broadly focused. Studied in relation to the world that created them, sexual values and categories will tell us as much about the social construction of power as they do about actual sexual behavior (pp. 37-38).

Applying theories about the social construction of sexuality, sexual preference and behavior, Jeffrey Weeks explores the organization and regulation of sexuality in Britain from the beginning of the nineteenth century until today.

10.11int
Weeks, Jeffrey, **SEX, POLITICS AND SOCIETY: THE REGULATION OF SEXUALITY SINCE 1800.** 1981. Weeks studies sexual phenomena as areas of social concern along with reform efforts and social policies that were established to deal with the issues. He devotes some discussion to the place of sexuality in consciousness, and also traces scientific investigation of human sexual nature and deviation. Considerable attention is paid to beliefs about and prescriptions for Victorian women within the family and in wider society. Lesbianism and homosexuality in Victorian culture are especially well considered. Weeks' text is by way of a clearing of the ground for later work, and points towards the importance of studying "the central symbolic and moral significance assigned to sexuality in our culture" (p. 16).

This crucial status for sexuality was translated into both symbolic and functional roles within Victorian society. Women undertook key parts in so many of the categories, representations and discourses associated with sexuality that, in colloquial parlance, they were "The Sex." Primarily they represented the body, and as Snitow, Stansell and Thompson show, "its mixed pleasures and pains for everyone" (p. 10):

10.12int
Snitow, Ann, Stansell, Christine, and Thompson, Sharon, **POWERS OF DESIRE: THE POLITICS OF SEXUALITY.** New York, 1983.

To the Victorians, the body came to represent an increasing number of motifs, concepts, and occupations. The female body figured importantly in the process of feminization of ideology that included the dichotomous images of "the Victorian feminine ideal" and "the fallen woman." Other relevant representations that adorned or augmented the body image followed: dress, manners, taste, speech, posture, life-style and so forth. Nuances indicated class as well as gender and not infrequently indicated power status. These images took on meanings and values that became further associated with, for example, praise or blame, pleasure or pain, respectable or outcast. "The Sex" was a highly charged and multidimensional metaphor.

Periodical literature popularized the infinite variety of femininity by the 1840s:

10.13int
QUARTERLY REVIEW: Kinglake, A.W., *"The Rights of Women,"* 75 (1844-1845) 94-125. "This subject of 'Woman' is so splendid, so terrifying, so enchanting, so vast" (n.p.). For this kind of perspective see:

10.14int
Palmegiano, E.M., "Introduction" in WOMEN AND BRITISH PERIODICALS 1832-1867: A BIBLIOGRAPHY. New York, 1976. —*see also:* VICTORIANS INSTITUTE JOURNAL: *"The Propaganda of Sexuality: Victorian Periodicals and Women,"* no. 6 (1977) 21-30.

There is also the element of anxiety. Contemporary writings—popular, social science, and pornographic—testify to its being enmeshed with female sexuality. There were attempted solutions for this through prudery, silence, denial, restriction, and abuse. But these appear only to have exaggerated eroticism. On this theme see for example:

10.15int
Kern, Stephen, ANATOMY AND DESTINY: A CULTURAL HISTORY OF THE HUMAN BODY. New York, 1975. See especially: "The Onset of Victorian Sexual Morality" and "Pure Women and Superb Men."

Anatomical and physiological studies of the late eighteenth century greatly impacted medical ideas on sex differences. These are important to an understanding of transformations in ideas on the relative position of the sexes. For example, Thomas Laqueur shows how the abandonment of the belief in the early biological link that had been made between female erotic excitation and conception also broke "the link of pleasure to infusion of life to matter." Thus, ideas on differences between the sexes were now based in scientific facts. Ultimately, these came to be applied to concomitant social thought, rooted in ideas about sexuality.

10.16int
REPRESENTATIONS: Laqueur, T., *"Orgasm, Generation, and the Politics of Reproductive Biology,"* Special Issue (Spring 1986) 1-35. The new model of sex differences that were based upon biological distinctions reinforced the theory of lesser biological position of women. However, says Laqueur, the new knowledge did not have as much consequence in the sphere of science as it did in "representing and... constituting social realities." Here Laqueur reminds us that in the dominant world-view and political theory of eighteenth-century England the image of the body was treated as an image of society: "the body politic."

> The new biology, with its search for fundamental differences between the sexes and its tortured questioning of the very existence of women's sexual pleasure, emerged at precisely the time when the foundations of the old social order were irremediably shaken, when the basis for a new order of sex and gender became a critical issue of political theory and practice (p. 4).... The political, economic and cultural transformations of the eighteenth century created the context in which the articulation of radical differences between the sexes became culturally imperative.... New claims and counterclaims regarding the public and private roles of women were thus contested through questions about the nature of their bodies as distinguished

from those of men. In these new discursive wars feminists as well as antifeminists sacrificed the idea of women as inherently passionate; sexual pleasure as a sign in the flesh of reproductive capacity fell victim to political exigencies (p. 35).

The nineteenth and early twentieth centuries witnessed debates on women's capability for sexual passion. A wide range of motives underscored a diversity of discourses in medical, scientific and social settings and in print. The vast majority of public participants were men of the medical profession and the social sciences, including sexologists. Much of the writing was prescriptive for what was conventionally considered to be appropriate sexual attitudes and behavior. In recent years this ground has been covered and debated by feminist historians and literary scholars. The most frequent point of departure for discussing dominant Victorian thinking on female sexual response and behavior are the writings of William Acton, surgeon and urologist, a popular writer on medical subjects.

10.17int
Acton, William, **THE FUNCTIONS AND DISORDERS OF THE REPRODUCTIVE ORGANS**. 1857; many subsequent eds. to 1894. This book is primarily about men and male sexuality. Only a few passages are exclusively on women; **PROSTITUTION, CONSIDERED IN ITS MORAL, SOCIAL, AND SANITARY ASPECTS, IN LONDON AND OTHER LARGE CITIES AND GARRISON TOWNS, WITH PROPOSALS FOR THE CONTROL AND PREVENTION OF ITS ATTENDANT EVILS.** 1870.

Acton's portrayal of female sexuality epitomizes the well-known stereotype of the passionless Victorian middle-class woman. It is possibly for that reason that his name has appeared as the cardinal source on the subject more frequently than any other Victorian author. His conclusions about basic female sexual nature and behavior have been largely discredited, although we have yet to discover to what extent some Victorian women followed his modeling. The most recent debates about Acton have stood on the question of how well he reflected the opinion of his time. By now a wide majority of scholars consider him to have been more prescriptive than descriptive for women of his society. There is undoubtedly considerable value in reviewing the literature of the debate on Acton. In reading the arguments for and against his representativeness, we are exposed to the opinions of both his contemporaries and modern scholars. This allows us to ponder how such a controversial authority could have held sway for so long as spokesman for the sexual nature of the women of his time.

Literary scholar Steven Marcus figured early in the Acton debates. In THE OTHER VICTORIANS (see above) he compares Acton's imagination and prose with the style and setting of Victorian pornography. Marcus does not believe in Acton's observations of female sexlessness, but he quotes and comments on passages to illustrate Acton's own Victorian vision. On FUNCTIONS AND DISORDERS OF THE REPRODUCTIVE ORGANS Marcus writes:

> We need not pause to discuss the degree of truth or falsehood in these assertions. What is of more immediate concern is that these assertions indicate a system of beliefs. These beliefs are in the first place associated with class.... [They] express yet again the notion that sex is a curse and a torture, and that the only hope of salvation for man lies in marriage to a woman who has no sexual desires and who will therefore make no sexual demands upon her husband. At this point we can observe how sexual

responsibility is being projected onto the role of woman; she is being required to save man from himself; and conversely if she is by some accident endowed with a strongly responsive nature, she will become the agent of her husband's ruin. In either event, she is being regarded as essentially a function of masculine needs, whatever direction in which those needs may run (p. 32).

Marcus has been criticized for having relied on Acton's stance as typically Victorian. In a leading article, Barry Smith not only rejects the possibility that Acton's views were "standard," but he destroys Acton's credibility as a medical authority on sexuality.

10.18int
UNIVERSITY OF NEWCASTLE HISTORICAL JOURNAL: Smith, F.B., *"Sexuality in Britain, 1800-1900,"* 2 (1972-1976) 19-32; *rev. rpt. in:* **A WIDENING SPHERE: CHANGING ROLES OF VICTORIAN WOMEN** ed. by Martha Vicinus. Bloomington, 1977.

Going even further than Smith in refuting Acton's status as a medical authority and comparing his views with those of other physicians, especially James Paget, is the valuable paper,

10.19int
VICTORIAN STUDIES: Peterson, M.J., *"Mr. Acton's Enemy: Medicine, Sex and Society in Victorian England,"* 29 (1986) 569-590.

Perhaps the most severe critic of Acton's beliefs and on his status as a leading authority is historian Carl N. Degler. It is Degler who has made the strongest case to deny Acton's credibility about Victorian sexual relations in marriage. The major writings in which Degler attacks Acton are:

10.20int
AMERICAN HISTORICAL REVIEW: Degler, C.N., *"What Ought to Be and What Was: Women's Sexuality in the Nineteenth Century,"* 79 (1974) 1467-1490.

10.21int
Degler, Carl N., **AT ODDS: WOMEN AND THE FAMILY FROM THE REVOLUTION TO THE PRESENT.** New York, 1980.

Degler offers citations from a veritable library of marriage manuals and advice books on sexual questions and birth control as explicit evidence that Acton's views ran counter to a strong stream, if not the main stream of opinion.

Using statements and bibliography similar to Degler's, and supplementing these with evidence from diaries and letters that detail the sexual involvements of a number of passionate nineteenth-century women, Peter Gay joins the corps of historians against Acton:

10.22int
Gay, Peter, **THE BOURGEOIS EXPERIENCE, VICTORIA TO FREUD: VOLUME I. EDUCATION OF THE SENSES.** New York, 1984.

But cautioning that revisionist historians such as Degler and Gay may be too extreme in correcting the record as written by Acton is the provocative article:

10.23int
JOURNAL OF SOCIAL HISTORY: Stearns, C.Z. and Stearns, P.N., *"Victorian Sexuality: Can the Historians Do It Better?"* 18 (1985) 625-634. Stearns and Stearns suggest that Degler and Gay go too far in the opposite direction when they counter Acton's thesis with another that posits a Victorian population of generally passionate, orgasmic women. Aside from criticism of their evidence, the Stearns show that interpretive problems remain. They point also to sources as yet untapped by systematic analysis. They ask about Victorian patterns of cautioning children on sexual dangers and taboos, prevailing middle-class values on keeping daughters "innocent," and schools and other institutions that repressed attitudes and behavior in order to discourage female sexual stimulation. They remind us of the repetition of myths about masturbation and menstruation that seem calculated to cause anxiety, as did the possibilities of too frequent pregnancy. In addition, they recall, there was the traditional association of sex with sin.

The Stearns' questions have not been formally addressed by the revisionists. However, in AT ODDS, Carl Degler makes the point that the later nineteenth-century manuals indicate a trend toward sexual repression. This was the era of purity crusades which defined and attacked areas of sexual immorality. The organized reform campaigns that instigated public discourses on child prostitution and white slavery inculcated sexual anxiety along with the resolutions for abolition of vice. Published feminine protests against the double standard in sex relations, and warnings of rampant venereal disease that husbands might bring to the marriage bed undoubtedly encouraged sexual repression and fear among both sexes. A buildup of articulated sexual issues centering around sexual morality and disease posited danger to sexually active women, whether they were respectable wives and daughters or fallen prostitutes. A provocative article that discusses the various sex-oriented campaigns, varieties of feminine response and consequences of social purity's narrow focus on the dangers posed by sexual life to women's health and control of their bodies is:

10.24int
FEMINIST STUDIES: Gordon, L. and DuBois, E., *"Seeking Ecstasy on the Battlefield: Danger and Pleasure in Nineteenth Century Feminist Sexual Thought,"* 13 (1983) 42-54.

> The weight of the nineteenth century concern was with protection from danger. This approach, usually known as social purity, reflected an experienced reality and was overwhelmingly protectionist in its emphasis.... Social purity thought emphasized the importance of consensual sex for women, and insisted that even married women should not be coerced into any sexual activities they did not choose freely.... The negative consequences of social purity's single-minded focus on sexual danger come into focus when we look at their vigorous campaign against prostitution. Over time the repressive tendencies of this campaign overwhelmed its liberatory ones and threw a pall over feminism's whole approach to sexuality (p. 46).

At least some women who felt threatened by public sexual issues sought to reduce their vulnerability by joining organized groups in which they could express their concerns and possibly plan remedies. An unusual opportunity for membership in a small group came with the inception of the The Men and Women's Club. It was established by Karl Pearson in the 1880s to discuss relationships between the sexes. Discussion topics included marriage and marital sex. One valuable article that explores the women's experiences as members is:

10.25int
Bland, Lucy, "Marriage Laid Bare: Middle-Class Women and Marital Sex, c. 1880-1914" in **LABOUR AND LOVE: WOMEN'S EXPERIENCE OF HOME AND FAMILY 1850-1940.** ed. by Jane Lewis. 1986.

> The Men and Women's Club [was] committed to the free and unreserved discussion of all matters connected with the mutual position and relation of men and women (p. 126).... As for marital sex, nearly all the women and a couple of the men felt there was much need for change. One male member proposed that 'forcing the wife' (presumably he meant rape) should be treated as cruelty.... Mrs. Walters... was the only one to suggest explicitly that marriage reform, first and foremost required the reform of *man*—particularly his sexual behavior. Men 'must change and become altruistic,' treating marriage as 'only sexual for race ends'.... Emma Brooke.... claimed that women's economic independence would force men to learn self-restraint and 'to stop being a beast of prey.' As we shall see, their views prefigured the opinions of many feminists writing ten to twenty years later (pp. 126-127).

A second important article on the Club and its significance is:

10.26int
HISTORY WORKSHOP JOURNAL: Walkowitz, J.R., *"Science, Feminism and Romance: The Men and Women's Club 1885-1889."* Issue 21 (Spring 1986) 37-59.

> They took a more rigid and unspeculative position than the men, because more was personally at stake; their own identity was organized around the figure of the prostitute; they could not consider sexual relations abstractly or disinterestedly, for it was precisely the region where women are possibly bodies only to men that cast a dark shadow across their own relations to the other sex. In these discussions, men self-confidently assumed the position of innovators and explorers, while women were forced into a defence of traditional values and customs. There were episodes, however, where a role reversal between male innovator and female traditionalist occurred——where a woman adopted a more avant-garde position on sex than Pearson and placed him on the defensive (p. 51).

But women did not take only defensive positions. For example, a number chose to abandon heterosexual relationships in favor of lesbian ones. Scholars have only just begun serious inquiry into this aspect of Victorian/Edwardian women's sexual lives. Discussing the seriousness of the omission of historical analysis is:

10.27int
RADICAL HISTORY REVIEW: Cook, B., *"The Historical Denial of Lesbianism,"* 20 (Spring 1977) 60-65.

> Even if they did renounce all physical contact we can still argue that they were lesbians: they chose each other, and they loved each other. Women who love women, who choose women to nurture and support and to form a living environment in which to work creatively and independently are lesbians. Genital 'proofs' to confirm lesbianism are never required to confirm the heterosexuality of men and women who live together for 20 or

50 years. Such proofs are not demanded even when discussing ephemeral love relations between adult men and women (p. 64).

Gordon and DuBois discuss women's option of intense emotional and physical relationships with each other in "Seeking Ecstasy on the Battlefield" (above, p. 42). Jeffrey Weeks also devotes sections of his text to lesbian relationships (See "The Construction of Homosexuality" in SEX, POLITICS AND SOCIETY, above). A more lengthy and sustained analysis is in

10.28int
SIGNS: Vicinus, M., *"Distance and Desire: English Boarding-School Friendships,"* 9 (1984) 600-622.

> Recovering lost lesbians of the past and establishing bases for self-definition have been to this point the chief concerns of lesbian historiography. The vexed question of when and why single-sex genital contact became labeled deviant has absorbed much energy. Scholars have concentrated, for example, on such issues as whether the famous sexologists of the late nineteenth and early twentieth centuries were detrimental or helpful to women's single-sex friendships (p. 600).... In this essay I examine one aspect of the most widely known of women's friendships, the adolescent crush.... I am concerned with its social origins, its various phases, and its impact on both the younger woman and the older recipient of her love.... Neither the ingredients that make up an intense friendship nor its impact on the participants may have changed over time, but I believe that beginning in the late nineteenth century we find a different conjunction of public demands and private needs; these will be explored here (p. 601).

See also:

10.29int
FEMINIST STUDIES: Vicinus, M., *"'One Life to Stand Behind Me': Emotional Conflicts in First-Generation College Women in England,"* 8 (Fall 1982) 603-628.

10.30int
FEMINIST STUDIES: Vicinus, M., *"Sexuality and Power: A Review of Current Work in the History of Sexuality,"* 8 (Spring 1982) 147-151.

For a relatively small number of highly articulate middle-class women, political activism became concomitant with the social issues that involved sexual questions. Besides permeating the preoccupations of the anti-Contagious Diseases Acts movement, and later the social purity movements and the neo-Malthusian movement, issues involving sexuality pervaded debates about advancing women's political status. Suffrage politics could not escape facing pointed questions on sex differences, concepts of masculinity and femininity, sex equality and inequality, sex-roles in nature and society and so forth. The champions of the movement to grant women a greater share in public life and political power, as well as their their opponents, invariably resorted to arguments based upon sexual components in masculine-feminine dichotomies.

Activists who worked for changes in women's status and roles comprised a diversified political population that has been discussed under the umbrella term, "feminist." Although the varieties and degrees of Victorian/Edwardian feminisms and feminist ideologies have been traditionally analyzed in socio-political terms, the scholarly trend has been altered to expose the sexual components of feminist and anti-feminist discourses and activities. Jeffrey Weeks gives a clear and judicious introduction to this subject in SEX, POLITICS AND SOCIETY, including the observation of the more radical feminist sector:

> The very existence of agitation for women's rights did raise vital questions about female sexuality, and in confronting these the feminists can be aligned with more obviously radical strands of thought. Questions of women's role in the family could not be divorced from sexual questions. One participant remembered her very frequent discussions with older suffragettes of the more sordid problems of sex.... And a memory comes of a pallid individual who raised her head from her pillow to whisper that her wedding night had been a dreadful revelation to her (p. 162).... Feminists were conspicuously silent over neo-Malthusianism. But to see the question purely in terms of support for artificial birth control is to misconstrue the actual complexity of the beliefs and feelings that come into play.... But where the division amongst feminists could take place was over the nature of the controls that should be exercised.... The goal in all cases was the same: for women to gain a degree of control of their own bodies.... The fundamental task for feminists was therefore to protect womanhood from male lusts. Although outwardly on the extreme fringe of feminist propaganda, Christabel Pankhurst's pamphlet, THE GREAT SCOURGE, published in 1913... is a useful index of many feminist views on sexuality. The arguments of this tract were clear enough. Male sexual lust was the real reason why men prevented women getting the vote.... Ruling-class men wanted to protect prostitution and the sexual abuse of women. Prostitution wasted the energy of men and sacrificed women on the altar of the double standard.... [There was the] "doctrine that woman is sex and beyond that nothing".... The only way out of this male nightmare was for women to get the vote, and enforce chastity and the female standard.... Similar themes to this, despite the overheated and emotional tone, can be traced to... the 1870s and 1880s (pp. 163-164).

Since the public arena, including parliament, hosted oral and written debates on social reform and moral crusade movements, published sources are rich in evidence that questions of sexuality often predominated in dialogues relevant to both specific causes, and to those that spilled over into general feminist and anti-feminist argumentation. The written record includes radical feminist critiques of social science theorists (including sexologists), politicians and popular social commentators. Isolating these writings for discussion in a book on the sexual emphasis in suffrage politics is:

10.31int

Kent, Susan Kingsley, **SEX AND SUFFRAGE IN BRITAIN 1866-1914**. Princeton, 1987. Kent deliberately magnifies any coherence that existed among a body of feminist writers, and she intentionally attributes greater power to the part they played in the overall history of Victorian/Edwardian politics. As she compiles, stacks up and abstracts their statements, Kent projects the kinds of images required for her chapter title, "Sex War":

> Feminists asserted that in truth men despised and were contemptuous of women. The Elmys described patriarchal institutions as "woman-reviling

systems." THE FREEWOMAN charge that the majority of men hated women. Try as they might to conceal their feelings, hatred of women dominated male emotions and had led to antagonism and ultimately to war between the sexes. "However much they love the individual of their fancy," observed Maud Braby, "a kind of veiled distrust seems to obtain between the sexes collectively, but more especially on the part of men." Men had always found fault with women, she believed, but the revolt of women against the "old man-made conditions" had intensified their contempt and antagonism. Where formerly, men's diatribes against women had contained a certain good humor and were along the lines of genial chaff, they had taken on a "bitterness, a distinct animus," with the rise of the women's movement, Braby noted. Writing in FRASER'S MAGAZINE in 1880, "M.O.W.O. [described how women's] demands for equality were met with an insolent laugh, a storm of ridiculous epithets... hinting... threats of violence from men, threats that often succeeded in frightening women away".... The ideology of separate spheres, contended feminists, exaggerated the differences between men and women and confined women to an exclusively sexual role.... Gasquoine Hartley [wrote], "Extreme outward sex attraction has come to veil but thinly a deep inward sex-antipathy, until it seems almost impossible that women and men can really understand one another.... Olive Schreiner articulated what was perhaps a typical feminist opinion in writing to Havelock Ellis in 1884, "in that you are a man I am afraid of you and shrink from you." (pp. 167-168).

Kent also quotes from and discusses sections from private correspondence among feminists. For example, a letter from Elizabeth Wolstenholme Elmy to Harriet McIlquham reads in part: "It is the fear of men that women will cease to be any longer their sexual slaves either in or out of marriage that is at the root of the whole opposition to their just claim.... No doubt their fear is justified, for that is precisely what we mean" (p. 14).

The isolation and telescoping of this stream of writing sometimes taken out of context no doubt distorts the history of feminism and the suffrage movement. But as it provokes (perhaps irritates) more traditionalist social historians, it contributes the important insight that some vital areas of women's history have either been missed, underplayed or insufficiently investigated as to their proper weight in the ultimate analysis of the record. In this case, it is the factor of sexuality.

*NOTE: For additional references on sexuality set in a specific context see Chapter 2, section 4, "Marriage Manuals"; Chapter 2, section 5, "Birth Control as a Family Issue"; Chapter 3, section 7, "Gynecological Surgery and Moral Ideas"; and Chapter 11, "Science, Social Science and Their Social Applications."

* * *

1. PROSTITUTION AND SOCIETY

1a. Prostitution, "Fallen Women" and the "Great Social Evil"

10.1
THE WOMEN OF LONDON: DISCLOSING THE TRIALS AND TEMPTATIONS OF A WOMAN'S LIFE IN LONDON WITH OCCASIONAL GLIMPSES OF A FAST CAREER. n.d.

10.2
Fielding, John, **AN ACCOUNT OF THE ORIGINS AND EFFECTS OF A POLICE... TO WHICH IS ADDED A PLAN FOR PRESERVING THOSE DESERTED GIRLS IN THIS TOWN WHO BECOME PROSTITUTES FROM NECESSITY.** 1757.

10.3
HARRIS'S LIST OF COVENT GARDEN LADIES... FOR... 1788. 1788; rpt., New York, 1984. An alleged catalog of London prostitutes; provides names, addresses, descriptions, and prices.

10.4
MODERN PROPENSITIES; OR, AN ESSAY ON THE ART OF STRANGLING. 1793. Appeared shortly after the trial of London prostitute Susannah Hill, who was tried and acquitted for strangling Francis Kotzwara. For erotic stimulus, he requested that she strangle him to death.

10.5
Colquhoun, Patrick, **POLICE AND METROPOLIS.** 1797. Calls prostitutes "brazen lower-class hussies" whom the police should keep out of sight.

10.6
HINTS TO THE PUBLIC AND THE LEGISLATURE ON THE PREVALENCE OF VICE AND ON THE DANGEROUS EFFECTS OF SEDUCTION. 1811.

10.7
Hale, William, **CONSIDERATIONS ON THE CAUSES AND PREVALENCE OF FEMALE PROSTITUTION AND ON THE MOST PRACTICABLE AND EFFICIENT MEANS OF ABATING AND PREVENTING THAT AND ALL OTHER CRIMES AGAINST THE VIRTUE AND SAFETY OF THE COMMUNITY.** 1812. "How easy it is to arrest the progress of abandoned harlots... taken the next morning before a magistrate, who would gladly commit them to the house of correction for a month, there to endure solitary confinement, where... the mind would recoil upon itself, and force them to those reflections, which might tend to harrow up the pangs of a guilty conscience" (p. 58).

10.8
STRONG ADMONITIONS TO THE SEVERAL CITIZENS OF LONDON AND WESTMINSTER, WHEREIN ARE SUGGESTED MEANS OF SECURITY AGAINST FIRE, THIEVES, MURDERERS, AND PROSTITUTES ETC. BY A REFLECTING STRANGER. 1812. Mentions fees levied by a local watchman to prostitutes for safe, unchecked walks down his beat, amounting to a substantial income for the watchman.

10.9
London Society for the Protection of Young Females, and the Prevention of Juvenile Prostitution, **FOURTH REPORT PRESENTED AND ADOPTED AT THE ANNUAL MEETING... 7TH MAY 1839.** 1839.

10.10
Ryan, Michael, **PROSTITUTION IN LONDON, WITH A COMPARATIVE VIEW OF THAT OF PARIS AND NEW YORK, AS ILLUSTRATIVE OF THE CAPITALS AND LARGE TOWNS OF ALL COUNTRIES; AND PROVING MORAL DEPRIVATION TO BE THE MOST FERTILE SOURCE OF CRIME, AND OF PERSONAL AND SOCIAL MISERY; WITH AN ACCOUNT OF THE NATURE AND TREATMENT OF THE VARIOUS DISEASES, CAUSED BY THE ABUSES OF THE REPRODUCTIVE FUNCTION.** 1839. Ryan was a senior physician at the Metropolitan Free Hospital. "About the year 1793, a magistrate of police concluded, after tedious investigations, that there were 50,000 prostitutes in this metropolis. At that period the population was one million, and it is now doubled, the number of abandoned women might perhaps be supposed to have doubled" (p. 89).

10.11
Tait, William, **MAGDALENISM: AN INQUIRY INTO THE EXTENT, CAUSES AND CONSEQUENCES OF PROSTITUTION IN EDINBURGH.** Edinburgh, 1840. Claims that for every 8 adult males in Edinburgh, there is one prostitute, compared to London, where the ratio is 60 to one.

10.12
Edgar, John, **FEMALE VIRTUE, ITS ENEMIES AND FRIENDS. A DISCOURSE ON THE STATISTICS, EVILS, AND CURE OF PROSTITUTION, DELIVERED ON BEHALF OF THE LONDON SOCIETY FOR THE PROTECTION OF YOUNG FEMALES.** 1841.

10.13
Tristan, Flora, "Prostitutes" in **FLORA TRISTAN'S LONDON JOURNAL: A SURVEY OF LONDON LIFE IN THE 1830'S.** Paris, 1842; trans. ed., 1982. "Put the blame therefore on the social order and let women be exonerated. As long as she is under the yoke of men or of prejudice, as long as there is no professional education for her, as long as she is deprived of her civil rights, there can be no moral law for woman" (p. 73).

10.14
Wardlaw, Ralph, **LECTURES ON FEMALE PROSTITUTION: ITS NATURE, EXTENT, EFFECTS, GUILT, CAUSES AND REMEDY.** Glasgow, 1842. According to one Victorian observer, "with regards to the average duration of life among female victims of prostitution... not above one in eleven survives twenty-five years of age" (p. 36).

10.15
Bevan, William, **PROSTITUTION IN THE BOROUGH OF LIVERPOOL.** Liverpool, 1843.

10.16
Logan, William, **AN EXPOSURE FROM PERSONAL OBSERVATION OF FEMALE PROSTITUTION IN LONDON, LEEDS, AND ROCHDALE, AND ESPECIALLY IN THE CITY OF GLASGOW; WITH REMARKS ON THE CAUSE, EXTENT, RESULTS, AND REMEDY OF THE EVIL.** Glasgow, 1843; **THE GREAT SOCIAL EVIL: ITS CAUSES, EXTENT, RESULTS AND REMEDIES.** 1871. Social

investigation-style tract about prostitution in London.

10.17
Associate Institution for Improving and Enforcing the Laws for the Protection of Women, **REMEDIES FOR THE WRONGS OF WOMEN**. 1844. Advocates preventing organized prostitution and seeks to raise the age of consent for girls.

10.18
Talbot, James Beard, **THE MISERIES OF PROSTITUTION**. 1844. Talbot was secretary of the London Society for the Protection of Young Females. This book, written to publicize the agency's work, calls for virtuous women to help eliminate prostitution and reform prostitutes.

10.19
Reed, John, **THREE LECTURES ON PROSTITUTION ADDRESSED TO GEORGE COOKMAN, ESQ. BOROUGH MAGISTRATE**. 1846.

10.20
LANCET: Acton, W., *"Observations on Venereal Disease in the United Kingdom,"* 3 (1846) 369-372. "It is supposed that females do not perish directly from syphilis, but linger on under other complaints, and die in large numbers in our asylums and workhouses.... I have visited most of these houses, and conversed with medical officers, who are not cognizant of these supposed cases.... Dr. Pidduck, Physician to the London Female Mission, who has opportunities of seeing large numbers of this class of females for several years, writes to me that he had not observed the young females who come under his care subject to any complaint other than those to which female servants in private families are liable" (p. 372); *"Prostitution—The Need for Its Reform,"* n.v. (1857) n.p.; *"Sin in the Streets,"* 1 (1858) 95-96. "Public morality is now outraged. But by such blind coercive measures as the wholesale arrest of prostitutes, driving them at once from their haunts, public safety will be in danger" (p. 96).

10.21
Beggs, Thomas, "Prostitution" in **THREE LECTURES ON THE MORAL ELEVATION OF THE PEOPLE**. by Thomas Beggs. 1849. See "Prostitution: Its Extent and Causes." Illustrates the popular middle-class conception of the genesis of prostitution: "The poor girl who yields to a misplaced passion, no matter how her ruin has been effected... is irremediably fallen. She has passed the threshold over which there is no return, and she is cast forth to beg, sin, or starve.... The dashing colonel, or handsome and accomplished roue does not lose caste, nor forfeit position, although he has committed a crime for which he ought to be spurned from the path of every honest man. He has only become more interesting by the event" (p. 99).

10.22
Beames, Thomas, **THE ROOKERIES OF LONDON: PAST, PRESENT AND PROSPECTIVE**. 1850. Observations on the haunts of young prostitutes and their male friends. Descriptions of lifestyles and conditions of behavior.

10.23
Acton, William, **PROSTITUTION IN RELATION TO PUBLIC HEALTH**. 1851. "A very superficial consideration of the laws which regulate the animal economy in a state of health and disease... are sufficient, I think, in warranting the pathologist of the present day to infer, that many of the various affections, both organic and functional, now recognised as following sexual intercourse, and which I have here

included under the collective term 'venereal diseases,' must have livelihood in the streets" (p. 5); **PROSTITUTION, CONSIDERED IN ITS MORAL, SOCIAL AND SANITARY ASPECTS IN LONDON AND OTHER LARGE CITIES, WITH PROPOSALS FOR THE MITIGATION AND PREVENTION OF ITS ATTENDANT EVILS.** 1857; 1870; 1970. Presents statistics on prostitution in London and incidence of venereal disease. "Such women, ministers of evil passions, not only gratify desire, but also arouse it. Compelled by necessity to seek for customers, they throng out streets and public places, and suggest evil thoughts and desires which might otherwise remain undeveloped" (p. 119); *reviewed in:* **JOURNAL OF MENTAL SCIENCE:** 4 (1858) 276-296. ——*see also:* Marcus, Steven, "Mr. Acton of Queen Anne Street, or, the Wisdom of Our Ancestors" in **THE OTHER VICTORIANS. A STUDY OF SEXUALITY AND PORNOGRAPHY IN MID-NINETEENTH-CENTURY ENGLAND.** by Steven Marcus. New York, 1964; 1965; 1966. "One of Acton's chief purposes in [PROSTITUTION, CONSIDERED...] is to humanize the prostitute, to educate or persuade his respectable audience to regard her not as some alien and monstrous creature but as a fellow human being. To this end, he explodes the popular myth of the harlot's progress" (p. 5).

10.24
Gaskell, Elizabeth Cleghorn, **RUTH.** 1853. A novel dramatizing the issues connected to the fallen woman. Heroine is an unwed mother. Serialized in HOUSEHOLD WORDS, to the astonishment of many proper Victorians; *reviewed in:* **NORTH BRITISH REVIEW:** Forbes, J.M., 19 (1853) 151-174. "Ruth the seduced girl is made a noble Christian by the very consequences of her sin. Satan sent the sin— God sends the child. The new sense of responsibility which his birth brings forth... [is] the means of her sanctification" (p. 155). ——*see also:* Haldane, E.S., **MRS. GASKELL AND HER FRIENDS.** 1930; Rubenius, Ana, "The 'Fallen Women'" in **THE WOMAN QUESTION IN MRS. GASKELL'S LIFE AND WORKS.** by Ana Rubenius. Cambridge, 1950; Hopkins, A.B., **ELIZABETH GASKELL: HER LIFE AND WORK.** 1952; Easson, Angus, "Ruth: 'An Unfit Subject for Fiction'" in **ELIZABETH GASKELL.** by Angus Easson. 1979.

10.25
Greg, William Rathbone, **THE GREAT SIN OF GREAT CITIES.** 1853.

10.26
AINSWORTH'S MAGAZINE: *"The Dens of London,"* 24 (1853) 172-180.

10.27
Craik, Dinah Maria (Mulock), "Lost Women" in **A WOMAN'S THOUGHTS ABOUT WOMAN.** by Dinah Maria Mulock Craik. 1857; 1858. Recommends the redemption of unchaste women back into states upon repentance: "I think it cannot be doubted that even this loss does not indicate total corruption or entail permanent degradation; that after it, and in spite of it, many estimable and womanly qualities may be found existing" (p. 262).

10.28
Richelot, Gustave Antoine, **THE GREATEST OF OUR SOCIAL EVILS: PROSTITUTION, AS IT NOW EXISTS IN LONDON, LIVERPOOL, MAN-CHESTER, GLASGOW, EDINBURGH AND DUBLIN; AN ENQUIRY INTO THE CAUSE AND MEANS OF REFORMATION, BASED ON STATISTICAL DOCUMENTS. BY A PHYSICIAN.** trans. by Robert Knox. 1857.

10.29
TAIT'S EDINBURGH MAGAZINE: *"The Greatest Social Evil,"* 24 (1857) 747-752.

10.30
TRANSACTIONS OF THE NATIONAL ASSOCIATION FOR THE PROMOTION OF SOCIAL SCIENCE: Acton, W., *"Prostitution,"* 1 (1857) 605-608.

10.31
Smith, W.A., **THE SOCIAL EVIL; ALSO THE POWER AND CONDUCT OF THE POLICE.** 1858.

10.32
Whitehorne, James Charles, **THE SOCIAL EVIL PRACTICALLY CONSIDERED.** 1858.

10.33
BRITISH AND FOREIGN MEDICO-CHIRURGICAL REVIEW: *"Prostitution: Its Causes and Remedies,"* 21 (1858) 388-415.

10.34
MELIORA: *"Timid Legislation,"* 1 (1858-1859) 70-79. "In this Christian land of England, many-thousands of women are leading lives of open notorious profligacy; many of the streets of our great cities are thronged at night with shameless creatures, who, not content with parading their dishonour before the world, do not scruple to annoy and disgust even unwilling men with their solicitations" (pp. 70-71); *"Prostitution,"* 3 (1860-1861) 145-157.

10.35
PHILANTHROPIST AND SOCIAL SCIENCE GAZETTE: *"The Social Evil,"* n.v. (1858) n.p.

10.36
THE SIN OF GREAT CITIES; OR, THE GREAT SOCIAL EVIL, A NATIONAL SIN. 1859.

10.37
Miller, James, **PROSTITUTION CONSIDERED IN RELATION TO ITS CAUSE AND CURE.** Edinburgh, 1859.

10.38
Noel, Babtist W.R., **THE FALLEN AND THEIR ASSOCIATES.** 1860; 1870.

10.39
SATURDAY REVIEW: *"The Literature of the Social Evil,"* 10 (1860) 417-418. "As soon as [female] unchastity is looked upon as merely a misfortune, rather than a social wrong——we are not now speaking of the religious side of the matter——it is practically encouraged" (p. 418).

10.40
Hemying, Bracebridge and Mayhew, Henry, **THE PROSTITUTE CLASS GENERALLY.** 1861; "Prostitution in London" in **LONDON LABOUR AND THE LONDON POOR.** ed. by Henry Mayhew. 1862; rpt., 1967. "A woman who has fallen like a star from heaven, may flash like a meteor in a lower sphere, but only with a transitory splendour. In time her orbit contracts, and the improvidence that has been her leading characteristic through life now trebles and quadruples the misery she experiences" (p. 214).

10.41
Drysdale, Charles Robert, **PROSTITUTION MEDICALLY CONSIDERED WITH SOME OF ITS SOCIAL ASPECTS.** 1866. Claims that sex-appetite is the prime mover to prostitution in both sexes. Connects prostitution with infanticide and implies that prostitutes are neither womanly nor human: "Hysteria, a disease admitted by all medical authorities to be very common among the... female sex, appears to be unknown among prostitutes" (p. 15).

10.42
West London Association for the Suppression of Public Immorality, **PROPOSAL FOR AN ACT TO AMEND THE CLAUSE OF THE METROPOLITAN POLICE ACT, WHICH PROHIBITS THE LOITERING AND SOLICITATION OF PROSTITUTES IN THE PUBLIC THOROUGHFARES. [BY H. DOLBY AND T. SMITH].** 1866.

10.43
Butler, Josephine, **REBECCA JARETT.** [1855]. Jarett was a reformed prostitute who enlisted in the Salvation Army to help eliminate prostitution; **THE EDUCATION AND EMPLOYMENT OF WOMEN.** 1868. Relates poor economic status and lack of education to the prevalence of prostitution; **ON THE MORAL RECLAIMABILITY OF PROSTITUTES.** 1870. Butler reveals that there were many virtuous fallen women and prostitutes. She opposed the rescue work done by individual men and accused men of being responsible for the women who "fell." Butler believed that women alone could perform adequate reforming work since they could gain the trust of their condemned sisters.

10.44
Greenwood, James, **THE SEVEN CURSES OF LONDON.** 1869; rpt., 1982. "She is but one of a thousand walking the streets of London, the most cruelly used and oppressed of all the great family to which they own relationship.... They are infinitely worse off than the female slaves.... these slaves of the London pavement may boast of neither soul nor body, nor the gaudy skirts and laces and ribbons with which they are festooned. They belong utterly and entirely to the devil in human shape who owns the den that the wretched harlot learns to call her 'home'" (p. 287).

10.45
Lecky, William Augustus, **THE HISTORY OF EUROPEAN MORALS. FROM AUGUSTUS TO CHARLEMAGNE.** 1869. Discusses the status of the prostitute and her effect on the monogamous family.

10.46
WESTMINISTER REVIEW: Greg, W.R., *"Prostitution,"* 53 (1850) 238-268. Pleads for sympathy and compassion for prostitutes condemned as "outcast, Pariahs, lepers," quoting extensively from Mayhew. Argues that desire is not what brings their fall, since women only develop desire after sexual initiation. Recognizes the rampant gin usage that betrays their misery, and puts much of the blame on men. "For one woman who thus, of deliberate choice, sells herself to a lover, ten sell themselves to a husband," the only difference between the transactions being "the price that is paid down" (p. 243); *"Prostitution in Relation to the National Health,"* 36 (1869) 179-234; *"Prostitution; Its Sanitary Superintendance by the State,"* 36 (1869) 556-569; *"Prostitution; Government Experiments in Controlling It,"* 37 (1870) 119-179. "The policy of indifference and laissez-faire [regarding prostitution] has in the United Kingdom had a long, full, and fair trial.... Among the causes... Christian purism, and the generally strong English feeling in favour of personal liberty" (p. 121); *"Prostitution; How to Deal With It,"* 93 (1870) 477-535. States that measures

taken to diminish venereal disease have largely failed. Sees extensive government intervention as insufficient and ineffective, as well as unjust; *"Prostitution—The Christian Harem,"* 122 (1884) 105-115.

10.47
Kirwan, Daniel Joseph, **PALACE AND HOVEL; OR PHASES OF LONDON LIFE.** 1870; 1963.

10.48
CONTEMPORARY REVIEW: *"Regulation, Cure and Prevention of Prostitution,"* 14 (1870) 220-235; Cowen, J., *"Music Halls and Morals,"* 110 (1916) 611-620. Discusses the availability of music halls as a "prostitution market" (p. 619).

10.49
Duffey, Eliza B., "Prostitution: Its History, and Effects, Causes and Remedies" in **THE RELATION OF THE SEXES.** New York, 1876; rpt., 1974. References to and examples from England are included.

10.50
MEDICAL ENQUIRER: Nevins, J.B., *"Enquiry Into the Condition of Prostitution,"* 2 (1876-1877) 17-28.

10.51
Griffiths, George Frederick, **A WAYWARD WOMAN.** 3 vols. 1879. A novel.

10.52
Hadden, Robert Henry, compiler, **AN EAST END CHRONICLE: ST. GEORGE'S-IN-THE-EAST PARISH AND PARISH CHURCH.** introduction by Harry Jones. 1880.

10.53
Stead, W.T., **THE MAIDEN TRIBUTE OF MODERN BABYLON.** 1881; *serialized in:* **PALL MALL GAZETTE:** 6, 7, 8, 10 (1885) n.p. Determined to raise the age of legal consent from 13 to 16 for girls, Stead actually purchased a virgin to prove the accessibility of child prostitutes and published this embellished account. He was sentenced to two months in prison for fraudulent custody, but the necessary legislation passed Parliament soon afterwards; *rpt. in:* **HUMAN DOCUMENTS OF THE AGE OF THE FORSYTES.** ed. by E. Royston Pike. 1969. Describes "a house, kept apparently by a highly respectable midwife, where children were taken by procurers to be certified as virgins before violation, and where, after violation, they were taken to be 'patched up,' and where, if necessary, abortion could be procured" (p. 290); **W.T. STEAD IN THE CENTRAL CRIMINAL COURT.** 1885; **MR. STEAD BEFORE HIS COUNTRYMEN.** 1886; **MY FIRST IMPRISONMENT.** 1886. *—see also:* MacGlashan, W., **ENGLAND ON HER DEFENCE! REPLY TO THE MAIDEN TRIBUTE.** Newcastle, 1885; Stead, Estelle W., **MY FATHER: PERSONAL AND SPIRITUAL REMINISCENCES.** 1913; Harper, E.K., **STEAD, THE MAN OF PERSONAL REMINISCENCES.** 1914; Whyte, Frederick, **THE LIFE OF W.T. STEAD.** 2 vols. 1925. See especially: "The Maiden Tribute of Modern Babylon"; **VICTORIAN PERIODICALS NEWSLETTER:** Robson, A., *"The Significance of the 'Maiden Tribute of Modern Babylon,'"* 11 (1978) 51-57; Gorham, D., *"The 'Maiden Tribute of Modern Babylon' Re-examined: Child Prostitution and the Idea of Childhood in Late-Victorian England,"* 21 (1978) 353-379. Contends that reformers like W.T. Stead failed to recognize the social and economic factors that lead to child prostitution.

10.54
C., H.J., BABYLON; OR THE "PALL MALL GAZETTE" AND SALVATION
ARMY ON THE CORRUPTION, CRUELTIES AND CRIME OF LONDON. 1885.

10.55
Lowndes, F.W., PROSTITUTION IN LIVERPOOL. 1886.

10.56
Newman, F.W., REMEDIES FOR THE GREAT SOCIAL EVIL, WITH SPECIAL
REFERENCE TO RECENT LAWS. 1889.

10.57
Merrick, G.P., WORK AMONG THE FALLEN: AS SEEN IN THE PRISON CELL.
A PAPER READ BEFORE THE RURI-DECANAL CHAPTER OF ST.
MARGARET'S AND ST. JOHN'S, WESTMINISTER, IN THE JERUSALEM
CHAMBER, ON THURSDAY, JULY 17, 1890. introduction by F.W. Farrar. 1890.
"Many women have told me that when they married, they with great delight
renounced all intention of leading an immoral life, honestly purposing to be good
and faithful wives to their husbands. Finding, however, that their husbands had no
such respectable thoughts concerning them, and were hoping to make a 'market' out
of them, they left them, and went back to the life from which they had expected
they were set free" (p. 43).

10.58
Moore, George, ESTHER WATERS. A NOVEL. 1894. Story of a "fallen" woman—
an unwed mother——who seeks a good and penitent way of life.

10.59
NEW REVIEW: Mary, A. (signed T. Sparrow), *"In a Woman's Doss-House,"* 11
(1894) 174-185. Describes a house of prostitution.

10.60
Sanger, William, HISTORY OF PROSTITUTION: ITS EXTENT, CAUSES AND
EFFECTS THROUGHOUT THE WORLD. New York, 1897; 1910; 1937. See
especially: "Great Britain——Syphilitic Diseases." Details the business practices of
brothels and their keepers.

10.61
Despard, Lena, THE CONFESSIONS OF A FAST WOMAN. 1898.

10.62
Drysdale, George, THE ELEMENTS OF SOCIAL SCIENCE: OR PHYSICAL,
SEXUAL AND NATURAL RELIGION. AN EXPOSITION OF THE TRUE CAUSE
AND ONLY CURE OF THE THREE PRIMARY SOCIAL EVILS: POVERTY,
PROSTITUTION AND CELIBACY. 35th ed., 1905. "If the heart of the prostitutes
remains in general icy cold towards the common crowd of those with whom they
consort, it is always warm towards some favourite lover, who is really dear to them,
and on whom they lavish all their fondness. These, their real lovers, are not only
admitted in general to their favours free of expense, but may receive presents from
their mistresses" (p. 252).

10.63
Campbell, Reginald John, WOMEN'S SUFFRAGE AND THE SOCIAL EVIL:
SPEECH DELIVERED ON DECEMBER 17, 1907... UNDER THE AUSPICES OF
THE MEN'S LEAGUE FOR WOMEN'S SUFFRAGE. 1907. Argues that women

should be given political power in order to release them from their dependence upon men. "Man is woman's capitalist... women sell themselves to men because men have control of the sources of wealth... politics and industry" (pp. 2-3).

10.64

Bloch, Iwan, "Prostitution" in **SEXUAL LIFE IN ENGLAND**. by Iwan Bloch. trans. by William H. Forstern. 1908. "Ryan estimates the number of brothels in London in the year 1840 as 1,500! And this must have been only half the real number, as many of these houses concealed their true character under other designations, such as 'Institution for the Care of Children,' in the rooms of which, every night, [were] an incredible number of young women... the brothels were perfectly erected in the neighborhood of the churches, and did a good business there, 'so that often the preacher from the chancel could see the happenings in a neighborhood brothel'" (p. 127).

10.65

Nevill, Ralph, **PICCADILLY TO PALL MALL**. 1908. "With regards to the cruel hounding of poor women from the houses which they occupy, blame can hardly be laid upon the police, who in most cases are forced to take action by the urgent representations of Puritans, some sincere, others merely creatures seeking notoriety by slimy dabblings with filth" (p. 151).

10.66

Rappaport, Philip, **LOOKING FORWARD: A TREATISE ON THE STATUS OF WOMAN AND THE ORIGIN AND GROWTH OF THE FAMILY AND THE STATE**. Chicago, 1908. Traces the source of prostitution to the extreme differentiations of wealth in capitalist society and the "extreme precariousness of existence for millions of people, especially women, and... [the] steady decrease of the number of marriages by reason of positive or relative inability to support a family" (p. 143).

10.67

Wales, Hubert, **THE YOKE**. 1908. A didactic novel protraying man-woman relationships and urging men to avoid prostitutes because they are the source of diseases that ruin the lives of men as well as their families. The key figure is an older woman who becomes mentor-mistress to the young anti-hero.

10.68

Ellis, Havelock, "Prostitutes" in **THE CRIMINAL**. by Havelock Ellis. New York, 1910. "Prostitutes may fairly be compared to the great class of vagabonds among men who live on the borderlands of criminality, and who also present a larger proportion of abnormalities than even criminals" (p. 269).

10.69

Addams, Jane, **A NEW CONSCIENCE AND AN ANCIENT EVIL**. New York, 1912. American, but applicable to the English context. Blames the isolation and alienation characteristic of city life for a girl's beginning in prostitution: "when desire for companionship in itself constitutes a grave danger" (p. 89).

10.70

Chesser, Elizabeth Sloan, "Motherhood and the Social Evil" in **WOMEN, MARRIAGE AND MOTHERHOOD**. by Elizabeth Sloan Chesser. 1913.

10.71

Pankhurst, Christabel, **PLAIN FACTS ABOUT A GREAT EVIL**. New York, 1913.

"The disenfranchisement of women is an insult to motherhood.... Prostitution is to be condemned on the same grounds... because [it] makes slaves and outcasts of the women used for purposes of vice, and degrades their high sex function... poison[ing] men's idea of the sex-relationship" (p. 114); **THE GREAT SCOURGE AND HOW TO END IT**. 1913. Pamphlet.

10.72
Royden, Agnes Maude, et al., **DOWNWARD PATHS: AN INQUIRY INTO THE CAUSES WHICH CONTRIBUTE TO THE MAKING OF THE PROSTITUTE**. 1913; 1916. Personal investigations of prostitution in a social context. Cites the following causes in the making of a prostitute: bad homes and the desecration of childhood, the perils of adolescence, deliberate choice, gain, homelessness, feeblemindedness, and seduction and desertion; *reviewed in:* **SOCIALIST REVIEW**: 3 (1917) 190-192. Establishes itself as "a book which recognises that prostitution cannot be dealt with as an isolated phenomenon, but that for its cure, or that for the cure of its worst evils, there is essential a resanation of our entire sexual life... a book by women with a detailed knowledge of the physiology and psychology as well as the economics of sex" (p. 192).

10.73
Wilson, Helen, **ON SOME CAUSES OF PROSTITUTION WITH SPECIAL REFERENCE TO ECONOMIC CONDITIONS. A PAPER READ AT THE 11TH CONGRESS OF THE INTERNATIONAL ABOLITIONISTS FEDERATION HELD IN PARIS, JUNE 9-12, 1913**. 1913.

10.74
Flexner, Abraham, **PROSTITUTION IN EUROPE**. New York, 1914.

10.75
Hartley, Catharine Gasquoine, "Prostitution" in **THE TRUTH ABOUT WOMAN**. by Catharine Gasquoine Hartley. 1913. "It is a mistake of sentiment to believe they have any real dislike to this traffic.... This was first made clear to me in a conversation with a member of the higher demi-monde, a woman of education and considerable character. 'After all,' she said, 'it is really a very small thing to do, and gives one very little trouble, and men are almost always generous.' This remarkable statement seems to me representative of the attitude of most prostitutes. They are much better paid, if at all successful, than they ever could be as workers" (pp. 365-366).

10.76
Ives, George, **A HISTORY OF PENAL METHODS: CRIMINALS, WITCHES, LUNATICS**. 1914; Montclair, New Jersey, 1970. Mentions the state-sponsored emigration of English prostitutes to outposts in West Africa, "who were made 'honest women' through marriage... however, the African fever destroyed these unfortunates" (p. 124).

10.77
Martindale, Louisa, **UNDER THE SURFACE**. Brighton, [1920]. "Prostitution is only possible in a class economically dependent upon another. Among free women, who have full liberty, who are able to earn a living wage, and who are therefore independent of all other means of support, it could not exist for a moment. At the present time, women are in large majority ill-fitted by their education, or by their circumstances to earn a living, hence we find that close connection between poverty and prostitution" (p. 69).

10.78
La Croix, Paul, **HISTORY OF PROSTITUTION**. 3 vols. Chicago, 1926. Discusses prostitution from ancient antiquity to the present Christian era.

10.79
Hall, Gladys Mary, **PROSTITUTION IN THE WORLD: A SURVEY AND A CHALLENGE**. introduction by Charles E. Raven. 1933; New York, 1936. Considers promiscuity unpaid prostitution. Regarding England, discusses the white slave traffic, laws relating to prostitution and how the practice is carried on in rural areas.

10.80
Gotto, Sybil Katherine (Neville-Rolfe), **POVERTY AND PROSTITUTION. COMPRISING ECONOMIC CONDITIONS IN RELATION TO PROSTITUTION.** 1934; **UNEMPLOYMENT AND PROSTITUTION OF YOUNG GIRLS**. 1934.

10.81
Scott, George Ryley, **A HISTORY OF PROSTITUTION FROM ANTIQUITY TO THE PRESENT**. [1936]; 1954; New York, 1976. "Marriage and prostitution are inextricably interlinked. Every bond which makes the monogamous marriage system more secure coincidentally extends promiscuity in the form of prostitution, free love or adultery. It is the realisation of all this that has led the clergy and the moralists either to lament the necessity for prostitution or to wink at its indulgence" (p. 40).

10.82
Unsworth, Madge, **MAIDEN TRIBUTE, A STUDY IN VOLUNTARY SOCIAL SERVICE**. 1949. See especially: "The Essential Link" for an account of the rehabilitation of a prostitute and her subsequent work for the Salvation Army.

10.83
Turner, Ernest S., "A Flourish of Strumpets" in **ROADS TO RUIN: THE SHOCKING HISTORY OF SOCIAL REFORM**. by Ernest S. Turner. 1950. "It was only the more successful prostitutes——those who could behave in public and produce a five-shillings entrance fee——who had access to such luxurious marts and promenades of the Empire Theatre. Their bedraggled sisters swarmed in the streets of theatreland or were tolerated in some of the Popular Restaurants of Lower Regent Street, when at closing time... were carefully shepherded into the street.... They looked for all the world like a rather disreputable girls' school going home from church" (p. 210).

10.84
Anderson, Mosa, **H.J. WILSON: FIGHTER FOR FREEDOM, 1833-1914**. 1953. Presents the social context of prostitution in this biography of a leader in the campaign for the repeal of the Contagious Diseases Acts.

10.85
Pearl, Cyril, **THE GIRL WITH THE SWANSDOWN SEAT**. 1955. A somewhat glamorized portrayal of poor women, who were either inclined or desperate to work as prostitutes, and who left "a vicious squalid poverty" in hopes to pursue "the vicious brilliant opulence" of the upper-class whore or "pretty horsebreaker."

10.86
Radzinowicz, Leon, **A HISTORY OF ENGLISH CRIMINAL LAW AND ITS ADMINISTRATION FROM 1750**. vol. 2, 1956; 1974. Gives extensive statistics on

regional prostitute populations. "In 1817 a return from three parishes totalling about fifty-nine thousand inhabitants, disclosed the existence of three hundred and sixty disorderly houses employing about 2,000 prostitutes" (p. 287).

10.87
Partridge, Burgo, "The Victorians" in **A HISTORY OF ORGIES**. by Burgo Partridge. 1958; 1959. "The prostitute was the scapegoat of the nineteenth century, and the Victorians used her to carry their lusts for them, just as the Medieval Church had loaded all the sins of the world on the heads of the witches" (p. 191). Describes Kate Hamilton's famous brothel that was immortalized in the epic poem "The Siliad."

10.88
Taylor, Gordon Rattray, **THE ANGEL MAKERS: A STUDY IN THE PSYCHOLOGICAL ORIGINS OF HISTORICAL CHANGE 1750-1850**. 1958. "The fact that 'good' women were the severest condemners of prostitutes is easily explicable, of course, by the fact that they resented (at the unconscious level) having unrestricted right to the sexual and social freedom which they were denied: this of course is a common mechanism——if I can't have it, you must not either. And no doubt they feared the rivalry of the 'bad' woman who had so much to offer which they had not" (p. 263).

10.89
Bateson, Charles, **THE CONVICT SHIPS 1787-1868**. Glasgow, 1959. "On the passage to Port Jackson the *Lady Juliana* was nothing more than a floating brothel," recalls Nicol, "every man on board took a wife from among the convicts, they nothing loath" (p. 106).

10.90
Association for Moral and Social Hygiene, **PROSTITUTION**. 1960.

10.91
Epton, Nina Consuelo, **LOVE AND THE ENGLISH**. 1960. "Several English courtesans made a name abroad. Cora Pearl captivated the emperor's cousin, in Paris, and a Monsieur Duval committed suicide unnecessarily on her doorstep when she had left him for a count" (p. 308).

10.92
Kirnan, Daniel J., "The Legion of the Lost" in **PALACE AND HOVEL**. by Daniel J. Kirnan. 1963. "A high officer of the London police informed me that there were in that city about seven thousand lost women who are always well dressed, well gloved, and well shod, who live comfortably, and many of them elegantly. These women, of course, are all Free Lances, and prey upon the fashionable young men of London and strangers who visit the Great Babylon" (p. 183).

10.93
Cullen, Tom A., **WHEN LONDON WALKED IN TERROR**. Cambridge, 1965. In the voice of prostitutes: "We, your murdered sisters, are what the dreadful homes where we live have made us. Behind your fine squares and handsome streets you continue to leave our wild beast lairs unchanged and uncleansed. The slums kill us, body and soul, with filth and shame and spread fever and death among your gentry also" (p. 282).

10.94
Henriques, Fernando, **THE IMMORAL TRADITION: PROSTITUTION AND**

SOCIETY. 1965; 1966; 1968. "The connection between whoredom and politics is not a flight of the imagination. 'During the election for members of parliament, it is not unusual to see these ladies refuse to barter their charms for large sums of money, and reserve their charms for the purchase of votes, in favour of certain patriots, whom they esteem.' Could loyalty to the party system go further?" (p. 142).

10.95
Robson, L.L., "The Female Convicts" in THE CONVICT SETTLERS OF AUSTRALIA. by L.L. Robson. 1965. Details the histories of female sexual offenders on convict ships bound for Australia.

10.96
Laver, James, "Poverty and Prostitution" in AGE OF OPTIMISM. by James Laver. 1966. "It is probable that at no other time in English history, before or since, has prostitution been so rampant as in the mid-Victorian era. It was taken for granted that man, unlike woman, had sexual impulses which he could, perhaps with difficulty, control but could never entirely extinguish" (p. 90).

10.97
Tobias, J.J., CRIME AND INDUSTRIAL SOCIETY IN THE NINETEENTH CENTURY. 1967. See pp. 93-96 on prostitutes; "Juveniles and Women" in URBAN CRIME IN VICTORIAN ENGLAND. by J.J. Tobias. New York, 1972. Details activities of brothels where both customers and prostitutes were under sixteen. Some of this information is taken from an investigation by the Select Committee on Juvenile Offenders of 1816-1818. Representatives of the Magdalen Hospital and the London Female Penitentiary considered the usual age for prostitution to be 14 and 15, and the lowest 11 or 12.

10.98
Hugill, Stan, SAILORTOWN. 1967. "Many of the dives had only a single waitress-harlot or barmaid-harlots or hostess-harlots.... Harlots would call from the doorways an endless chant of 'Jiggy-jiggy, Johnny-garmarouche!'" (p. 143).

10.99
Babington, Anthony, "Prostitutes" in THE POWER TO SILENCE. A HISTORY OF PUNISHMENT IN GREAT BRITAIN. by Anthony Babington. 1968. "One of the most serious aspects of prostitution was the comparative ease with which a very young girl could drift into the trade. Even during the nineteenth century there were no social services and few accredited societies to provide for the guidance and protection of youth" (p. 148).

10.100
Burn, W.L., THE AGE OF EQUIPOISE: A STUDY OF THE MID-VICTORIAN GENERATION. 1968. "The interest taken in prostitution was very considerable. Prostitutes or ex-prostitutes or 'fallen women' on their way to reformation made controversial (if not always credible) appearances in books and pictures——for instance in Mrs. Gaskell's RUTH (1853), in Holman Hunt's THE AWAKENED CONSCIENCE (1853) and in Trollope's THE VICAR OF BULLHAMPTON (1870)" (p. 292).

10.101
Scott, George Ryley, LADIES OF VICE: A HISTORY OF PROSTITUTION FROM ANTIQUITY TO THE PRESENT DAY. 1968.

10.102
Pearsall, Ronald, **THE WORM IN THE BUD: THE WORLD OF VICTORIAN SEXUALITY**. 1969; rpt., Harmondsworth, 1974. See Chap. 6 in part II for a discussion of various aspects of prostitution, including the Stead case and the Whitechapel murders. Valuable discussion of child prostitution.

10.103
Seymour-Smith, Martin, **FALLEN WOMEN: A SCEPTICAL INQUIRY INTO THE TREATMENT OF PROSTITUTES, THEIR CLIENTS AND THEIR PIMPS, IN LITERATURE**. 1969. Discusses prostitution in conjunction with MY SECRET LIFE. "Walter's account of his sexual life with whores... is certainly a testament to the tyranny of genital organization in himself.... His hundreds of prostitutes [are] symbolic of the dissatisfaction felt by most of the clients of brothels and street prostitutes: the urge to polymorphous perversity——the urge to indulge in non-genital affectionate physical play is——frustrated by the notion of genital duty" (p. 148).

10.104
Ware, Helen, "Prostitution and the State: The Recruitment, Regulation and Role of Prostitution in the Nineteenth and Twentieth Century," Ph.D. diss., Univ. of London, 1969.

10.105
Blyth, Henry, **SKITTLES. THE LAST VICTORIAN COURTESAN. THE LIFE AND TIMES OF CATHERINE WALTERS**. 1970. Biography of a poor Liverpool girl who migrated to London where she "became the mistress of several wealthy and influential men. She was therefore a whore, but this does not imply that she was ready to sell herself to anyone who had enough money to pay for her services" (p. xi). The first chapter delineates employment opportunities for females of the poor and working classes.

10.106
Chesney, Kellow, **THE VICTORIAN UNDERWORLD**. 1970. "In the cheapest of dockside prostitution, the woman simply retired with her customer down the nearest dark alley, where their perfunctory business was done against a wall" (p. 321).

10.107
Rover, Constance, **LOVE, MORALS AND FEMINISTS**. 1970. Details the dispute among authorities, including Havelock Ellis, over the economic motive of prostitution. "The argument runs that with better wages and fuller employment for women, the price a prostitute could obtain would rise, therefore the calling would be more attractive" (p. 68).

10.108
Crow, Duncan, **THE VICTORIAN WOMAN**. New York, 1971. "According to Bracebridge Hemyng, the kept mistresses, of whom Laura Bell and Skittles were the stars, were usually uneducated women, although, as he admitted, 'they undeniably have ability'.... They were recruited from a class where education was not much in vogue" (p. 219).

10.109
Pearson, Michael, **THE FIVE POUND VIRGINS**. New York, 1972. Examines issues of rights and sexuality centered on the prostitute; **THE AGE OF CONSENT: VICTORIAN PROSTITUTION AND ITS ENEMIES**. Newton Abbot, 1972. Examines the work of reformers such as William Stead, Josephine Butler, Catherine,

William, and Bramwell Booth, and others. Considers Stead's expose in detail. "To the new feminists, the concept of the prostitute, as a state-supported institution, was intolerable. By implication, it approved and even encouraged sexual licence by men. The issue sparked the western world's first feminine revolt of any stature.... [It was] the first militant reaction against male dominance. It was more basic, and commanded more support, than the suffragette campaign, still only in its very early stages, because it involved the ordinary women's menfolk" (p. 19).

10.110
Sigsworth, E.M. and Wyke, T.J., "A Study of Victorian Prostitution and Venereal Disease" in SUFFER AND BE STILL: WOMEN IN THE VICTORIAN AGE. ed. by Martha Vicinus. 1972. Valuable discussion and analysis.

10.111
Thompson, E.P. and Yeo, Eileen, THE UNKNOWN MAYHEW. New York, 1972. Discusses the contributions of Henry Mayhew as a social investigator of the Victorian times. Mayhew recorded the following statement from a young female slop worker: "I am a daughter of a minister of the gospel. My father was an Independent preacher, and I pledge my word... that it was the low price paid for my labour that drove me to prostitution" (p. 150).

10.112
PROSTITUTION IN THE VICTORIAN AGE: DEBATES ON THE ISSUE FROM 19TH CENTURY CRITICAL JOURNALS. introduction by Keith Nield. 1973. Compilation of articles previously published during the nineteenth century. Important introduction outlining the course of the debates. "Great efforts are made to protect the soldiers from infection by the women; but the idea of protecting the women from infection by the soldiers though a much more practicable idea is scarcely entertained at all" (pp. 505-506).

10.113
Gagnon, John H. and Simon, William, "The Prostitution of Females" in SEXUAL CONDUCT: THE SOCIAL SOURCES OF HUMAN SEXUALITY. Chicago, 1973. "The combined reforming and condemning impulse of the Victorian middle classes stylized the image of the prostitute, giving her motives and a life history and, indeed, inventing an entire social apparatus through which she could be experienced directly or in fantasy and put to social use" (p. 220).

10.114
Trudgill, Eric, "Prostitution and Paterfamilias" in THE VICTORIAN CITY: IMAGES AND REALITIES. ed. by H.J. Dyos and Michael Wolff. vol. 2, 1973. "The prostitute... was a natural corollary of the Victorian's idealistic view of feminine purity. Many Victorians, without Freud's perception, were shrewd enough to see this connection clearly. Some even argued that prostitution was not only inevitable because of society's economic structure, it was also in fact desirable because of society's marriage system. Without this channel for middle-class men's illicit sexual indulgence the purity of the home, the peace and chastity of British maids and matrons would be undoubtedly less secure" (p. 702); "The Fortunes of the Magdalen" in MADONNAS AND MAGDALENS: THE ORIGINS AND DEVELOPMENT OF VICTORIAN SEXUAL ATTITUDES. by Eric Trudgill. New York, 1976.

10.115
Longmate, Norman, "Fallen Women" in THE WORKHOUSE. by Norman Longmate. 1974. Maintains that the workhouses, lying-in wards, and dayrooms often converted "poor, sinful girls" into "depraved, degraded women." "It was the lying-in ward, the

nursery and the able-bodied women's dayroom, which threw a basically decent and perhaps tearfully repentant girl into the company of hardened older women, so that, as one speaker told a conference in 1857, they 'laugh at her simplicity and too often shame her out of her repentance'" (n.p.).

10.116

Walkowitz, Judith R., "'We Are Not the Beasts of the Field': Prostitution and the Campaign Against the Contagious Diseases Acts, 1869-1886," Ph.D. diss., Univ. of Rochester, 1974. Argues that Victorians regarded the prostitute's offence as economic as well as sexual: "By giving up her chastity, she had wrongfully disposed of property not her own... in fact, she was the property of her husband and male guardian" (p. 4); "The Making of An Outcast Group: Prostitutes and Working Women in Nineteenth-Century Plymouth and Southampton" in A WIDENING SPHERE. CHANGING ROLES OF VICTORIAN WOMEN. ed. by Martha Vicinus. 1977; PROSTITUTION AND VICTORIAN SOCIETY: WOMEN, CLASS AND THE STATE. Cambridge, 1980. Discusses the common prostitute, contagious disease advocates, the repeal campaign, class and gender conflict in the repeal movement, and two case studies: Plymouth and Southampton under the Contagious Diseases Acts. Reformers acknowledged that men from their own class comprised most of the demand for prostitutes; *reviewed in:* AMERICAN HISTORICAL REVIEW: Kanner, B., 86 (1981) 840-841. "The nineteenth-century controversies over sex, disease, vice, and regulation yielded no positive assertions of female sexuality.... Walkowitz exposes the void that still exists in the historical explanation of changes in ideas and policies on sexual and social relations of the sexes that have transpired since late Victorian times" (p. 841); *also reviewed in:* VICTORIAN STUDIES: Banks, J.A., 24 (1981) 513-515. "The choice of prostitution as their solution for poverty... was made by these women—in contrast to so many of their gender and class peers—because their broken family background may have released them "from the stranglehold of standard female socialization. Without an emotional attachment to a mother and/or father, it may have been easier for a young woman to act against conventional norms" (pp. 16-17, 20); *also reviewed in:* M/F: Wood, N., *"Prostitution and Feminism in Nineteenth-Century Britain,"* 7 (1982) 61-77. Analyzes Walkowitz' study especially with regard to the extent of "feminist discourse" among members of the L.N.A. Wood also follows the connections between the Contagious Diseases Acts repeal campaign and social purity advocation. Contends that Walkowitz's book does not adequately resolve the "policing" question.

10.117

Summers, Anne, DAMNED WHORES AND GOD'S POLICE: THE COLONIZA-TION OF WOMEN IN AUSTRALIA. 1975. Feminist viewpoint asserting that prostitutes were treated as commodities, to be shipped to Australia in order to satisfy male colonists' urges, make homes and thus stabilize the social situation.

10.118

CONFERENCE GROUP FOR SOCIAL AND ADMINISTRATIVE HISTORY, TRANSACTIONS: Bullough, V.L., *"Women: Birth Control. Prostitution. and the Pox,"* 6 (1976) 20-31. Identifies the increase in prostitution as a sexual outlet for males who wanted no more children as a reason for the declining fertility rate during the nineteenth century.

10.119

Bullough, Vern, Deacon, Margaret, Elcano, Barrett, and Bullough, Bonnie, eds., A BIBLIOGRAPHY OF PROSTITUTION. 1977; PROSTITUTION: AN ILLUS-TRATED SOCIAL HISTORY. New York, 1978. "Women had little control over their own affairs, and in a man's world the only thing women had to advance themselves was their sex" (p. 117).

10.120
Harrison, Fraser, "Prostitution" in **THE DARK ANGEL: ASPECTS OF VICTORIAN SEXUALITY**. 1977. by Fraser Harrison. "Despite the sacredness of her task, the prostitute received no thanks; on the contrary, she was cruelly vilified and despised. Although her job was to relieve men of their uncontrollable urges, it was deemed essential that she was herself stripped of all sexuality" (p. 245).

10.121
Rosen, Ruth and Davidson, Sue, eds., **THE MAIMIE PAPERS**. Old Westbury, 1977. Rare, authentic memoir of a prostitute. Letters written by Maimie Pinzer, a former prostitute who was both cured of syphilis and of her addiction to morphine. They were written to Fanny Quincy Howe, a prominent Bostonian. These are among the few fully authenticated memoirs of prostitutes in existence.

10.122
Saville, John, "Robert Owen on the Family and the Marriage System of the Old Immoral World" in **REBELS AND THEIR CAUSES**. ed. by Maurice Comforth. 1978. "Prostitution flowed directly from the institution of the single-family marriage, for where there was not 'unbiased affection' only evils could follow" (p. 116).

10.123
ART BULLETIN: Nochlin, L., *"Lost and Found: Once More the Fallen Woman."* 60 (1978) 139-153. The image of the fallen woman "exerted a peculiar fascination on the imagination of nineteenth-century artists... an interest that reaches its peak in England in the middle years of the nineteenth century, and that perhaps received its characteristic formulation in the circle of Pre-Raphaelites and their friends" (p. 139). The theme obsessed such artists as Dante Gabriel Rossetti.

10.124
Evans, Hilary, **HARLOTS, WHORES AND HOOKERS**. New York, 1979. "Virgins were at a premium throughout the period; brothels housing children aged fourteen or less were a standard feature of the London underworld" (p. 127).

10.125
Finnegan, Frances, **POVERTY AND PROSTITUTION. A STUDY OF VICTORIAN PROSTITUTES IN YORK**. New York, 1979. Includes: "Houses and Haunts," "The Prostitutes and Brothel-Keepers," "The Clients," "Drink, Destitution and Disease," and "Rescue and Reform." Examines previously ignored facets of the history of prostitution: that prostitutes did not always engage in sexual affairs for money; that many middle-class marriages were sexually satisfying for both partners; and that prostitutes catered to all classes. Numerous case histories; *reviewed in:* ECONOMIC HISTORY REVIEW: Armstrong, W.A., 33 (1979-1980) 425-426; *also reviewed in:* HISTORY: Floud, R., 65 (1979-1980) 323-324; *also reviewed in:* NEW SOCIETY: Thane, P., 49 (1979) 416.

10.126
Rickert, Marilou, "The Fallen Woman in the Victorian Novel," Ph.D. diss., Univ. of Colorado, Boulder, 1979. Traces the literary theme of the working-class virgin woman who is successfully seduced by a middle-class man and then is labelled "fallen" since her chastity is lost.

10.127
VICTORIAN STUDIES: Engel, A.J., *"'Immoral Intentions': The University of Oxford and the Problem of Prostitution, 1827-1914,"* 23 (1979) 79-107.

10.128
Nash, Stanley D., "Social Attitudes Towards Prostitution in London from 1752 to 1829," Ph.D. diss., New York Univ., 1980. "Eighteenth and early-nineteenth century opinion held that prostitutes were mostly orphaned girls, deserted girls, girls left with one parent, or country girls who were corrupted upon arrival in London" (p. 456).

10.129
Summer, M., "Prostitution and Images of Women: A Critique of the Victorian Censure of Prostitution," M.A. thesis, Univ. of Wales, Aberystwyth, 1980.

10.130
SIGNS: Walkowitz, J.R., *"The Politics of Prostitution,"* 6 (1980) 123-136. "Prostitution also served as a paradigm for the female condition; it established the archetypal relationship between men and women, repeated in a more subtle manner within genteel society. Feminists realized that the popular sentimentalization of 'female influence' and motherhood only thinly masked an older contempt and distrust for women as 'The Sex,' as sexual objects to be sold by men. The treatment of prostitutes under the [Contagious Diseases] Acts epitomized this underlying misogyny" (p. 125); *rpt. in:* **WOMEN: SEX AND SEXUALITY.** ed. by Catharine R. Stimpson and Ethel Spector Person. 1980; *reviewed in:* **JOURNAL OF SOCIAL HISTORY:** Lewis, J.S., 15 (1982) 534-536. "Walkowitz may be the first to persuade us——as she does——that legal control of prostitution isolated prostitutes from the working class as a whole.... In the public mind, this isolation served to segregate prostitution as a moral issue, divorced from the social-economic concerns of the working class as a whole" (p. 535).

10.131
Mitchell, Sally, **THE FALLEN ANGEL: CHASTITY, CLASS AND WOMEN'S READING 1835-1880.** Bowling Green, 1981; *reviewed in:* **VICTORIAN PERIODICALS REVIEW:** Robson, A., 14 (1981) 162-164. "The image of the fallen angel in 1880 seemed not very different from that of 1835; there was always sympathy for the repentant sinner from Urania to Josephine Butler's spare room, and this sympathy showed in the fiction" (p. 164).

10.132
Symanski, Richard, **THE IMMORAL LANDSCAPE: FEMALE PROSTITUTION IN WESTERN SOCIETIES.** Toronto, 1981; *reviewed in:* **AMERICAN JOURNAL OF SOCIOLOGY:** Goldman, M.S., 90 (1984) 235-237. Symanski draws on classic studies of prostitution in England, France and Germany. "Explores 19th- and 20th-century women's prostitution in Europe and the United States in terms of its visibility and relationship to social space. According to Symanski, 'Much of the social problem of [female] prostitution and its solution are eminently geographic'" (p. 235).

10.133
Weeks, Jeffrey, "'That Damned Morality': Sex in Victorian Ideology" in **SEX, POLITICS, AND SOCIETY.** by Jeffrey Weeks. 1981. "The lifestyle of the bourgeois lady was purchased at the expense of a large class of servants, often prone to sexual depredations, and an equally vulnerable group of prostitutes" (p. 30).

10.134
STUDIES IN EIGHTEENTH-CENTURY CULTURE: Kern, J.B., *"The Fallen Woman, From the Perspective of Five Early Eighteenth-Century Women Novelists,"* 10 (1981) 457-468.

10.135
Auerbach, Nina, "The Rise of the Fallen Woman" in **WOMAN AND THE DEMON: THE LIFE OF A VICTORIAN MYTH.** by Nina Auerbach. 1982; Contrasts Victorian perceptions of the "fallen woman" with previous incarnations of the stereotype. For example, whereas Milton makes the earth shudder in pain when Eve sins, "in Victorian revisions, it is the woman done who is wounded, sighs, laments, and is lost; indifferent Nature simply reclaims her" (p. 34).

10.136
Rosen, Ruth, **THE LOST SISTERHOOD: PROSTITUTION IN AMERICA, 1900-1918.** 1982. See especially: "Prostitution: Symbol of an Age" and "The Lost Sisterhood: The Causes of Prostitution." Good background for comparison to English studies of prostitution.

10.137
HISTORY WORKSHOP JOURNAL: Walkowitz, J., *"Male Vice and Female Virtue: Feminism and the Politics of Prostitution in Nineteenth-Century Britain,"* no. 13 (1982) 79-83; *rpt. in:* **POWERS OF DESIRE: THE POLITICS OF SEXUALITY.** ed. by Ann Snitow, Christine Stansell and Sharon Thompson. New York, 1983. "In their defense of prostitutes and their concern to protect women from male sexual aggression, feminists were limited by their own class bias and by their continued adherence to a separate-sphere ideology that stressed women's purity, moral supremacy and domestic virtues" (p. 434).

10.138
MacPike, Loralee, "The Fallen Woman's Sexuality: Childbirth and Censure" in **SEXUALITY AND VICTORIAN LITERATURE.** ed. by Don Richard Cox. Knoxville, 1984. "It is with the fallen woman that we see most clearly how judgement of female sexuality operates through the metaphor of childbirth. Anna Karenina's adultery is punished by a difficult birth of a girl child whom Anna does not love, while Kitty's legitimate sexuality is rewarded by the joyful birth of a son whom she cherishes" (p. 57).

10.139
Watt, George, **THE FALLEN WOMAN IN THE NINETEENTH-CENTURY ENGLISH NOVEL.** 1984. "From the twentieth-century perspective there is a difference, and a distinct one, between a prostitute and a girl who makes one mistake. An element of Victorian society did not allow for such a distinction" (p. 2).

10.140
Bristow, Edward J., **PROSTITUTION AND PREJUDICE: THE JEWISH FIGHT AGAINST WHITE SLAVERY 1890-1939.** Oxford, 1982; *reviewed in:* **HISTORY:** Copley, A.R.H., 69 (1984) 80-81. Bristow traces "the link between a Jewish campaign against Jewish white slavery and the anti-semitic slur of the Jewish white slavery of Christian women, [and] between Jewish prostitution and anti-semitic prejudice" (p. 80).

10.141
Kishtainy, Khalid, **THE PROSTITUTE IN PROGRESSIVE LITERATURE.** 1982; *reviewed in:* **VICTORIAN STUDIES:** Mitchell, S., 27 (1983-1984) 395-397. The

"introductory chapter indicates the theoretical underpinning of his book: to socialists, the prostitute represents the evil brought about by capitalists. Dramatists and novelists critical of society are therefore drawn to the prostitute as subject" (p. 395). Such writers are "progressive" in that they view prostitution as a social problem.

10.142
JOURNAL OF SOCIAL HISTORY: Nash, S.D., *"Prostitution and Charity: The Magdalen Hospital, A Case Study,"* 17 (1984) 617-628. "Repentance, they were told, meant 'sorrow for sin,' and if they were 'really sorry and amend,' they would be peaceful and contented" (p. 620).

1b. "Rescue Work": Missions, Penitentiaries and Magdalen Homes

10.143
Lock Hospital Asylum and Chapel, **LOCK HOSPITAL ASYLUM AND CHAPEL.** 1746. The Lock Hospitals treated prostitutes who had venereal disease. No one received a second time after having been cured; **AN ACCOUNT OF THE PROCEEDINGS OF THE GOVERNORS OF THE LOCK-HOSPITAL NEAR HYDE-PARK CORNER. SEPTEMBER 29, 1749 FROM THE FIRST INSTITUTION JULY 4, 1746.** 1749; **A SERMON PREACHED AT THE PARISH-CHURCH OF ST. GEORGE, HANOVER-SQUARE, FOR THE BENEFIT OF THE LOCK-HOSPITAL ON TUESDAY, FEBRUARY 25, 1777.** 1777; **AN ACCOUNT OF THE PROCEEDINGS OF THE GOVERNORS OF THE LOCK-HOSPITAL, NEAR HYDE-PARK-CORNER BY ORDER OF THE ANNUAL GENERAL COURT, HELD THURSDAY, APRIL 18, 1776.** 1777; **AN ACCOUNT OF THE INSTITUTIONS OF THE LOCK ASYLUM FOR THE RECEPTION OF THE PENITENT FEMALE PATIENTS, WHEN DISCHARGED CURED FROM LOCK HOSPITAL, ETC.** 1796; 1805; **AN ACCOUNT OF THE NATURE AND INTENTION OF THE LOCK HOSPITAL, NEAR HYDE-PARK-CORNER; THE PROCEEDINGS OF THE GOVERNORS, AND THE IMPROVEMENTS LATELY ADOPTED: WITH AN ABSTRACT OF ITS INCOME AND EXPENDITURE, THE STATE OF FINANCES TO LADY-DAY 1802, AND A LIST OF THE GOVERNORS AND SUBSCRIBERS BY ORDER OF THE ANNUAL GENERAL COURT APRIL 23, 1802.** 1802; **A SHORT HISTORY OF THE LONDON LOCK HOSPITAL AND RESCUE HOME, 1746-1906.** 1906. —*see also:* Highmore, Anthony, **PIETAS LONDINENSIS: THE HISTORY, DESIGN AND PRESENT STATE OF THE VARIOUS PUBLIC CHARITIES IN AND NEAR LONDON.** 2 vols. 1810. Writes about the prejudice the Lock hospital suffered and says the spouses emphasized how "many innocent women of irreproachable character themselves have received infection from the profligacy of their husbands" (p. 143); **MEDICAL HISTORY:** Wyke, T.J., *"Manchester and Salford Lock Hospital 1818-1917,"* 19 (1975) 73-90.

10.144
Massie, Joseph, **A PLAN FOR THE ESTABLISHMENT OF CHARITY HOUSES FOR EXPOSED OR DESERTED WOMEN AND GIRLS, AND FOR PENITENT PROSTITUTES.** 1758.

10.145
Magdalen Hospital, **RULES, ORDERS AND REGULATIONS OF THE MAGDALEN HOSPITAL... WITH A LIST OF THE GOVERNORS.** 1759; 1787; **PLAN FOR THE MAGDALEN HOUSE FOR THE RECEPTION OF PENITENT PROSTITUTES.** 1759; 1769; 1787; **THE HISTORIES OF SOME OF THE PENITENTS IN THE MAGDALEN HOUSE, AS SUPPOSED TO BE RELATED BY THEMSELVES.** 1760; **THE RULES AND REGULATIONS OF THE MAGDALEN CHARITY... WITH INSTRUCTIONS TO THE WOMEN WHO ARE ADMITTED AND PRAYERS FOR THEIR USE.** 4th ed., 1769; **GENERAL STATE OF THE MAGDALEN HOSPITAL IN ST. GEORGE'S FIELDS, FOR THE RECEPTION OF PENITENT PROSTITUTES, INSTITUTED IN 1758.** 1777; **BYE-LAWS AND REGULATIONS OF THE MAGDALEN HOSPITAL.** 1791; 1802; 1816; 1821; 1832. Inmates were given religious instruction and put into laundry work; **A LIST OF THE GOVERNORS OF THE MAGDALEN HOSPITAL.** 1798; 1803; 1805; 1821; **SOCIETY FOR THE ESTABLISHMENT OF A MAGDALEN ASYLUM IN LIVERPOOL. INTRO. REPORT OF THE SOCIETY... PARTICULARS OF A PLAN SUCCESSFULLY ADOPTED IN THE LONDON FEMALE PENITENTIARY.** Liverpool, 1809; **REGULATIONS.** 1816; **A SHORT ACCOUNT OF THE MAGDALEN HOSPITAL.** 1822; 1823; 1831; **A LIST OF THE GOVERNORS... CORRECTED TO JUNE 24, 1824.** 1824; **A LIST OF THE GOVERNORS AND SUBSCRIBERS TO THE MAGDALEN HOSPITAL.** 1833; **SPECIAL APPEAL: THE CENTENARY OF THE MAGDALEN HOSPITAL, BLACKFRIARS ROAD.** 1858; **THE ORIGIN OF THE LONDON MAGDALEN HOSPITAL.** 1890. ——*see also:* Hanway, Jonas, **THOUGHTS ON THE PLAN FOR A MAGDALEN HOUSE FOR REPENTANT PROSTITUTES, WITH THE SEVERAL REASONS FOR SUCH AN ESTABLISHMENT, ETC.** 1758; Dodd, William, **AN ACCOUNT OF THE RISE, PROGRESS, AND PRESENT STATE OF THE MAGDALEN CHARITY TO WHICH ARE ADDED, THE REV. MR. DODD'S SERMON, VICE-PRESIDENTS, AND GOVERNORS, ETC.** 1761; 1776; rpt., New York, 1981; Butler, John, **A SERMON PREACHED IN THE CHAPEL OF THE MAGDALEN-HOSPITAL ON OCCASION OF THE ANNIVERSARY MEETING OF THE PRESIDENT, VICE-PRESIDENTS, AND GOVERNORS OF THAT CHARITY; ON THURSDAY, MAY 11, 1786 BY JOHN BUTLER, LORD BISHOP OF OXFORD.** 1786; Manning, Henry Edward, **PENITENTS AND SAINTS. A SERMON PREACHED ON BEHALF OF THE MAGDALEN HOSPITAL.** 1844; Compston, Herbert Fuller Bright, **THE MAGDALEN HOSPITAL, THE STORY OF A GREAT CHARITY.** 1917; 1923; Pearce, Samuel Birt Perry, **AN IDEAL IN THE WORKING: THE STORY OF THE MAGDALEN HOSPITAL 1758-1958.** 1958. "There was an occasion when an inmate, over-mastered by the return of an old fierce appetite, told the head-matron of her wish to leave the home. The matron took her to the bundle room where the discarded clothes were kept, pointed to those she had worn on her arrival and said, 'You must change into these, you know.' There they were, all the poor tawdry things——the old hat, the shabby ulster and the leaky worn-out boots which had seen such hard service as their wearer tramped the streets in search of the wages-of-sin. This saved her. The contrast was too great and she made no more request to go" (p. 49).

10.146
AN ADDRESS TO THE UNFORTUNATE FEMALE, SHOWING HOW SHE MAY BE DELIVERED FROM TROUBLE, AND BECOME TRULY HAPPY. [1802].

10.147
London Female Penitentiary, **AN ADDRESS TO THE BENEVOLENT PUBLIC IN BEHALF OF THE LONDON FEMALE PENITENTIARY.** 1807; **FIRST, SECOND, FOURTH, TWENTY-NINTH, THIRTY-FOURTH, THIRTY-FIFTH ANNUAL**

REPORT OF THE COMMITTEE OF THE LONDON FEMALE PENITENTIARY TO THE GENERAL MEETING... 1808-1842; REPORT OF THE COMMITTEE OF THE LONDON FEMALE PENITENTIARY TO THE GENERAL MEETING, MAY 14, 1808. 1808; BY-LAWS AND REGULATIONS OF THE LONDON FEMALE PENITENTIARY. 1809; THE FOURTH REPORT OF THE LONDON FEMALE PENITENTIARY. 1811. —see also: Juvenis, CURSORY REMARKS ON A RECENT PUBLICATION... UPON THE DANGEROUS TENDENCY OF THE LONDON FEMALE PENITENTIARY, ETC. 1809; Hale, William, A REPLY TO THE PAMPHLETS LATELY PUBLISHED IN DEFENSE OF THE LONDON FEMALE PENITENTIARY. [1809]; Hale, William, AN ADDRESS TO THE PUBLIC UPON THE DANGEROUS TENDENCY OF THE LONDON FEMALE PENITENTIARY; WITH HINTS RELATIVE TO THE BEST MEANS OF LESSENING THE SUM OF PROSTITUTION. 1809; Hodson, G., STRICTURES ON MR. HALE'S REPLY TO THE PAMPHLETS IN DEFENCE OF LONDON FEMALE PENITENTIARY TO WHICH IS ADDED A LETTER TO THE AUTHOR ON THE INADEQUACY OF THE POOR LAWS, UNFORTUNATE FEMALES DESTITUTE OF WORK—IN ANSWER TO MR. HALE'S REPLY BY MR. BLAIR SURGEON OF THE LOCK HOSPITAL, ETC. 1809; THE THIRTY-FIFTH ANNUAL REPORT OF THE COMMITTEE OF THE LONDON FEMALE PENITENTIARY. 1842. "The object proposed, therefore, is to withdraw from society a fallen and injured member, who by her guilt has become an outcast from its reputable portion, but is desirous to reform, to train her to habits of diligence, order and industry; to teach her the truths and duties of Christianity" (p. 29).

10.148
Fund of Mercy, FUND OF MERCY: OR AN INSTITUTION FOR THE RELIEF AND EMPLOYMENT OF DESTITUTE AND FORLORN FEMALES, ETC. 1813.

10.149
Guardian Society, REPORT OF THE PROVISIONAL COMMITTEE OF THE GUARDIAN SOCIETY, FOR THE PRESERVATION OF PUBLIC MORALS BY PROVIDING TEMPORARY ASYLUMS FOR PROSTITUTES, REPROVED BY THE OPERATION OF THE LAWS FROM THE PUBLIC STREETS AND AFFORDING TO SUCH OF THEM AS ARE DESTITUTE EMPLOYMENT AND RELIEF ETC. 1816; 1817; SECOND (EIGHTH, NINTH, TENTH, TWELFTH) REPORT OF THE COMMITTEE OF THE GUARDIAN SOCIETY. 1817; 1827; 1828; 1832; 1838; AN ADDRESS TO THE GUARDIAN SOCIETY. 1817. Suggests that the Guardian Society should concentrate on combatting the seduction of young girls. Considers professional prostitutes beyond reclamation; REPORT OF THE COMMITTEE OF THE GUARDIAN SOCIETY FOR THE PRESERVATION OF PUBLIC MORALS, PROVIDING TEMPORARY ASYLUMS FOR PROSTITUTES, REMOVED BY THE OPERATION OF THE LAWS FROM THE PUBLIC STREETS AND AFFORDING TO SUCH OF THEM AS ARE DESTITUTE EMPLOYMENT AND RELIEF. SUBMITTED TO A GENERAL MEETING HELD AT THE EGYPTIAN HALL, MANSION HOUSE ON THURSDAY, 30 OCTOBER. 1817. 1817; EIGHTEENTH REPORT OF THE COMMITTEE OF THE GUARDIAN SOCIETY. 1848.

10.150
Metropolitan Female Asylum, THE REPORT OF THE PROVISIONAL COMMITTEE... WITH AN ADDRESS FROM THE PERMANENT COMMITTEE, EXPLANATORY OF THE OBJECTS OF THE INSTITUTION. 1830.

10.151
Westminster Asylum, TWELFTH REPORT OF THE WESTMINSTER ASYLUM.

1834. Lists subscribers and donations.

10.152
Maritime Penitent Female Refuge, **THE REFUGE, CONDUCTED BY THE COMMITTEE IN THE YEAR 1835.** 1835; **TENTH ANNUAL REPORT OF THE MARITIME FEMALE PENITENT REFUGE, FOR POOR, DEGRADED FEMALES.** 1839.

10.153
London Society for the Protection of Young Females and Prevention of Juvenile Prostitution, **FOURTH REPORT.** 1839. ——*see also:* **MAGDALEN'S FRIEND AND HOMES INTELLIGENCER:** *"The London Society for the Protection of Young Females,"* 1 (1860) 215-223. "It has saved from ruin more than 800 young females under fifteen years of age, many of whom are married, while others are in domestic service, or are governesses in private families and public schools" (p. 216); Edgar, John, **FEMALE VIRTUE: ITS ENEMIES AND FRIENDS.** 1891.

10.154
TOWN: A JOURNAL OF ORIGINAL ESSAYS, CHARACTERISTIC OF THE MANNERS, SOCIAL, DOMESTIC, AND SUPERFICIAL, OF LONDON AND LONDONERS: *"Society for the Protection of Young Females and the Prevention of Prostitution,"* 3 (1839-1840) 1220.

10.155
Cambridge Female Refuge, **THE SECOND (...FIFTH, EIGHTH) ANNUAL REPORT OF THE CAMBRIDGE REFUGE, INSTITUTED IN CAMBRIDGE, OCT. 1838 WITH THE RULE AND REGULATIONS AND A LIST OF SUBSCRIBERS.** Cambridge, 1840-1846.

10.156
Manning, Henry Edward, **PENITENTS AND SAINTS: A SERMON, PREACHED IN BEHALF OF THE MAGDALEN HOSPITAL AT ST. GEORGE-IN-THE-FIELDS, MAY 8, 1844.** 1844. "In one hour, daughter, sister, wife, hath become that thing from which the fondest shrink; the very name of which they dare not utter.... A fallen woman the world counts it righteous to forsake and scorn. Even her own kindred turn their back, and shut the door of home upon her" (p. 18).

10.157
FEMALES' ADVOCATE: Jan. 1844 to Dec. 1844; nos. 73-74. Published under the superintendence of the Committee of the London Female Mission.

10.158
Associate Institution for Improving and Enforcing the Laws for the Protection of Women, **THE FIRST REPORT, PRESENTED TO THE GENERAL MEETING HELD AT THE HANOVER SQUARE ROOMS, ON TUESDAY, 21ST JULY, 1846, THE RT. HON. LORD ROBERT GROSVENOR, M.P.** 1846. Founded to obtain stringent laws against acts of indecency such as dancing, inebriety, and obscenity. Operating on voluntary contributions, the agency also helped to find houses of refuge for rape victims. Their efforts were met with opposition both within and outside of Parliament. Called for their endeavors to be accomplished by moral rather than legal means; "[The Committee] deem it sufficient at present to state, that their object is not, and never has been, the suppression of voluntary prostitution, but the suppression of trading in seduction and prostitution by third parties" (p. 18); **REMEDIES FOR THE WRONGS OF WOMEN.** 4th ed., 1884. Calls for better enforcement of laws protecting women from sexual crime. Seeks to raise the age of

consent and greater punishment for proven "seducers"——i.e., rapists. Advocates making trade in prostitution a penal offence.

10.159
FEMALE FRIEND: 1846; vols. 1-4. Published by the Associate Institution for Improving and Enforcing the Laws for the Protection of Women.

10.160
QUARTERLY REVIEW: Armstrong, J., "Female Penitentiaries," 133 (1848) 359-377. "It costs a woman, covered with her own shame, no slight effort to present herself at the door of a penitentiary. Is there not something awful in the thought of turning away even one applicant——of stifling the feeling of repentance when an actual step has been taken towards an altered life" (p. 363).

10.161
CHRISTIAN REMEMBRANCER: [Armstrong, J.], "The Church and Her Female Penitents," 17 (1849) 1-17.

10.162
Carter, Thomas Thelluson, IS IT WELL TO INSTITUTE SISTERHOODS IN THE CHURCH OF ENGLAND FOR THE CARE OF FEMALE PENITENTS? Oxford, 1851; THE FIRST FIVE YEARS OF THE HOUSE OF MERCY, CLEWER. 1855. Describes the procedures of the House of Mercy in rescuing prostitutes. The intent of such procedures was to keep them from corrupting the sisters and isolate them from the outside agents which caused their "fall"; MERCY FOR THE FALLEN. TWO SERMONS IN AID OF THE HOUSE OF MERCY. 1856; THE FIRST TEN YEARS OF THE HOUSE OF MERCY. 1861; HARRIET MONSELL, A MEMOIR. 1884.

10.163
Vincent, Thomas V., SOME ACCOUNT OF ST. MARY'S HOME FOR PENITENTS AT WANTAGE, BERKSHIRE. Oxford, 1852. Housed a "miserable class of women who had fallen by the sin of impurity." See especially the Armstrong article.

10.164
Female Temporary Home, LONDON BY MOONLIGHT; OR, MISSIONARY LABOURS FOR THE FEMALE TEMPORARY HOME. 1853; 1854. Compilation of five pamphlets describing their work.

10.165
HOUSEHOLD WORDS: Dickens, C., "Home For Homeless Women," 7 (1853) 169-175. Describes Miss Burdett-Coutts' Urania Cottage.

10.166
Society for the Rescue of Women and Children, EIGHTH ANNUAL REPORT. 1861. Lists the occupations of destitute women in order of prominence: domestic servants living at home, needlewomen, dressmakers, milliners and shopwomen, etc. The Society sheltered fallen and destitute young women and encouraged good character and preparation for service; THE GREATEST MORAL HYPOCRISY OF THE DAY. 1873; "Twenty-Fifth Annual Report of the London Society For the Rescue of Women and Children, 1877" in RESCUE SOCIETY REPORTS. 1877-1892. See especially: "Representative Cases"; A MORE EXCELLENT WAY; ON VOLUNTARY HOSPITALS VS. STATE HOSPITALS AND THE REGULATION OF VICE. 1878.

10.167

Church Penitentiary Association, ACCOUNT OF THE HOUSE OF REFUGE FOR FALLEN WOMEN. 1854; A FEW WORDS TO SERVANTS ABOUT THE CHURCH PENITENTIARY ASSOCIATION. 1854; PENITENTIARY WORK OF THE CHURCH OF ENGLAND. PAPER PREPARED FOR DISCUSSION AT THE ANNIVERSARY MEETING. WITH A PREFACE BY H.P. LIDDON, ETC. 1873.

10.168

London Female Dormitory, A LETTER TO LT. JOHN BY A MARRIED INCUMBENT: A COMMENT ON THE MISSIONARY ENTERPRISES CARRIED ON IN CONNEXION WITH THE OPERATIONS OF THE FEMALE TEMPORARY HOME AND THE LONDON FEMALE DORMITORY. 1854; THE FIFTH ANNUAL REPORT OF THE LONDON DORMITORY, CARRIED ON IN CONNECTION WITH THE LONDON BY MOONLIGHT MISSION. 1856.

10.169

Open-Air Mission, 1ST (4TH, 10TH, 26TH, 80TH...) REPORT OF THE OPEN-AIR MISSION. 1854; 1857; 1863; 1878; 1879; 1933; subsequent eds.

10.170

McClelland, James, ON REFORMATION FOR THE DESTITUTE AND FALLEN. Glasgow, 1856.

10.171

Reformatory and Refuge Union, FIRST ANNUAL REPORT. 1856-1857; A HANDBOOK OF INDUSTRIAL WORK IN VARIOUS REFORMATORIES, REFUGES AND INDUSTRIAL SCHOOLS IN GREAT BRITAIN AND IRELAND. 1857; A GUIDE TO THE RE-FEMALE MISSION IN CONNECTION WITH THE REFORMATORY AND REFUGE UNION: REPORT OF THE SUB-COMMITTEE. 1859; FEMALE MISSION IN CONNEXION WITH THE REFORMATORY AND REFUGE UNION. REPORT OF THE SUBCOMMITTEE. 1859-1868. Reports on the work of two female missionaries who were employed to enter the streets at night, "speak kindly" to prostitutes, and attempt to convince them to end "their lives of sin"; FIFTY YEARS RECORD. 1906. THE CLASSIFIED LIST OF CHILD-SAVING INSTITUTIONS CERTIFIED BY GOVERNMENT OR CONNECTED WITH THE REFORMATORY AND REFUGE UNION... TO WHICH ARE ADDED COMPLETE LISTS OF DISCHARGED PRISONERS' AID SOCIETIES, MAGDALEN INSTITUTIONS, AND INEBRIATE RETREATS. 1912. The Union was established as a center of information and encouragement for reformatories, refuges, industrial schools and other similar institutions. Collected and dispersed information to these organizations. The number of associated societies rose from about 450 in the 1870's to more than 11,000 by 1900. It is estimated that about 600 of these cared for young women. ——*see also:* TRANSACTIONS OF THE NATIONAL ASSOCIATION FOR THE PROMOTION OF SOCIAL SCIENCE: Hanbury, R., *"The Reformatory and Refuge Union,"* n.v. (1857) 398-402; Hatch, H.J., *"The Reformatory and Refuge Union,"* n.v. (1858) 333-334.

10.172

THE HOUSE OF MERCY AT DITCHINGHAM. 1859.

10.173

Blackmore, John, THE LONDON BY MOONLIGHT MISSION: BEING AN ACCOUNT OF MIDNIGHT CRUISES ON THE STREETS OF LONDON DURING THE LAST THIRTEEN YEARS. 1860; *reviewed in:* MAGDALEN'S FRIEND AND FEMALE HOME INTELLIGENCER: 1 (1860) 221.

10.174
Female Mission to the Fallen, REPORTS. 1860-1867. ——see also: Charles, A.O., THE FEMALE MISSION TO THE FALLEN. 1860.

10.175
Sheppard, Emma, AN OUT-STRETCHED HAND TO THE FALLEN. [1860].

10.176
MAGDALEN'S FRIEND AND FEMALE HOME INTELLIGENCER: 1860 to 1864; vols. 1-5. The editor, a clergyman, believed that rescue work was properly a "woman's mission," and opposed indisciminate reintegration of fallen women into the community; "New Penitentiary at Birmingham," 1 (1860) 217; "The Saturday Review and the Magdalen's Friend," 1 (1860) 265; "Prevention and Cure," 3 (1862) 33; "Missionary Sketches," 3 (1862) 79-90. "Many poor girls who are on the streets know what it is to feel real love all the while towards some individual they know, and many of them resign their own sinful earnings to maintain such persons, if out of employment, whilst many of them still devotedly love the very persons who first brought them to this ruin" (p. 82).

10.177
Midnight Meeting Movement, STATEMENT OF THE ORIGIN, PROCEEDINGS AND RESULTS OF THE MIDNIGHT MEETINGS FOR THE RECOVERY OF FALLEN WOMEN. 5th ed., [1860]. Authored by Theophilus Ahijah Smith, secretary of the Midnight Mission; THE FIRST ANNUAL REPORT OF THE MIDNIGHT MEETING FOR THE RECOVERY OF FALLEN WOMEN: CONTAINING A SKETCH OF THE MOVEMENT AND ITS PROGRESS DURING THE PAST YEAR: WITH MANY INTERESTING CASES AND RESULTS, BOTH IN LONDON AND THE PROVINCES. ALSO, A LIST OF CONTRIBUTIONS AND THE BALANCE SHEET. 1861; 1891.

10.178
Wightman, Julia, ANNALS OF THE RESCUED. 1861.

10.179
REFORMATORY AND REFUGE JOURNAL: 1861 to 1899; vols. 1-13; continued as: SEEKING AND SAVING: 1900+; vol. 14+.

10.180
Homes of Hope, EIGHTH ANNUAL REPORT OF THE HOMES OF HOPE, 1868. 1869.

10.181
Hopkins, Jane Ellice, HOME THOUGHTS FOR MOTHERS AND MOTHERS' MEETINGS... 2nd ed., 1869; WORK AMONG THE LOST [A SHORT ACCOUNT OF THE WORK OF MRS. FANNY VICARS AND THE ALBION HILL HOME FOR FEMALE PENITENTS, BRIGHTON]. 1870; LADIES' ASSOCIATION FOR THE CARE OF FRIENDLESS GIRLS. 1878. ——see also: Barrett, Rosa, ELLICE HOPKINS: A MEMOIR. introduction by H. Scott Holland. 1907. Ellice Hopkins was active in the rescue movement of prostitutes; however, her approach was not evangelical. She also worked in creating a Soldier's Institute at Portsmouth to teach purity and provide an atmosphere free from alcoholic consumption and prostitution. She then founded the Ladies Association for the Care of Friendless Girls.

10.182
Rescue Society, **ANNUAL REPORTS.** 1869-1877. Dedicated to the reform of prostitutes and vagrant women. Employed male as well as female volunteer and paid workers.

10.183
TRANSACTIONS OF THE NATIONAL ASSOCIATION FOR THE PROMOTION OF SOCIAL SCIENCE: Acton, W., *"Medical Moonlight Mission in the Streets of Birmingham, With a View to Estimate and Improve the Moral Condition of the Inland Towns,"* (1872) 381-382.

10.184
Robinson, Sarah, "Journal" in **THE VISITATION OF DENS: AN APPEAL TO THE WOMEN OF ENGLAND.** by Ellice Hopkins. 1874.

10.185
ENGLISHWOMAN'S REVIEW: *"Women's Protective and Provident League,"* 6 (1875) 84-85; *"Protection of Young Girls Brought Up as Paupers,"* 6 (1875) 104-106. "At present, in a few of the schools, the matron or one of the female under officers, is sent to see the mistress applying for a servant, and to ascertain whether the place is a fit one. This system is attended by very satisfactory results. The situations which I found these girls were, it appeared to me, more suitable than those chosen by relieving officers, and the girls themselves were as a rule doing better" (p. 105).

10.186
Thomas, Edward W., **TWENTY-FIVE YEARS' LABOUR AMONG THE FRIENDLESS AND FALLEN.** 1879; 2nd ed., 1886. When Commander John Blackmore was seeking a shelter for a young woman desirous of forsaking a "sinful life," he received help from Maria Thomas (1823-1868) who took her into her home. In 1850, when Blackmore opened his first home, he appointed Maria Thomas matron. In 1857, she and her husband, E.W. Thomas, founded the Reformatory Institution. ——*see also:* Taylor, William J., **THE STORY OF THE HOMES, BEING A RECORD OF THEIR ORIGIN, DEVELOPMENT AND WORK FOR 50 YEARS.** 1907. Usually cataloged under London Female Preventive and Reformatory Institution.

10.187
Guardian Society for the Preservation of Public Morals, **REPORT OF THE COMMITTEE FOR PROVIDING TEMPORARY ASYLUM... FOR FEMALES WHO HAVE DEVIATED FROM THE PATHS OF VIRTUE.** 1880. The Society was established in 1815.

10.188
Blackwell, Elizabeth, **RESCUE WORK IN RELATION TO PROSTITUTION AND DISEASE. READ BEFORE THE ASSOCIATION FOR THE ADVANCEMENT OF WOMEN, AT ITS ANNUAL CONGRESS, HELD AT BUFFALO, NEW YORK, OCT. 1881.** New York, 1882. "An important field of work is here presented to those who devote themselves to the rescue of unfortunate women and men. A special and wisely organized mission to influence those unhappy ones, and strengthen their lost self-command, might be of great utility" (p. 6); *rpt. in:* **ESSAYS IN MEDICAL SOCIOLOGY.** by Elizabeth Blackwell. 1902.

10.189
Prynne, G.R., **THIRTY-FIVE YEARS OF MISSION WORK IN A GARRISON AND SEAPORT TOWN.** Plymouth, 1883.

10.190
Sharp, Amy, THE LEGAL PROTECTION OF YOUNG GIRLS. 1884.

10.191
Brinkman, Arthur, NOTES ON RESCUE WORK. 1885. A manual for philanthropists.

10.192
Church Mission to the Fallen, SIXTH (SEVENTH) ANNUAL REPORT. 1886; 1887.

10.193
Weigall, Mrs. Arthur, SEEKING AND SAVING: BEING RESCUE WORK OF THE MANCHESTER MISSION. 1889.

10.194
NEW REVIEW: Cavendish, L.C.F., "What is to Be Done With the Morally Deficient?" 2 (1890) 212-220. Qualifies certain fallen women as "morally imbecile" because they lack "the power of self-control when free from external restraint" (p. 214). Claims that certain proposals such as euthanasia and compulsory confinement are not as satisfactory as voluntary religious institutions.

10.195
Bristol and Clifton Ladies' Association for the Care of Girls, WOMEN WORKERS. PAPERS READ AT A CONFERENCE CONVENED BY THE... ASSOCIATION... November, 1892. Bristol, 1893.

10.196
Steer, Mary H., "Rescue Work by Women Among Women" in WOMEN'S MISSION: A SERIES OF CONGRESS PAPERS ON THE PHILANTHROPIC WORK OF WOMEN BY EMINENT WRITERS. ed. by Angela Burdett-Coutts. 1893. "A missionary told me just lately that she has succeeded in speaking to some of these girls who are living in what are called 'the doubles,' i.e. those lodging-houses intended for the use of couples, the keepers of which make no inquiries and it is needless to say that the marriage bond rarely links the men to women who frequent them" (p. 152); OPALS FROM SAND, A STORY OF EARLY DAYS AT THE BRIDGE OF HOPE. [1912].

10.197
Maddison, Arthur John Stewart, HINTS ON RESCUE WORK: A HANDBOOK FOR MISSIONARIES, SUPERINTENDENTS OF HOMES, CLERGY AND OTHERS. 1898.

10.198
Railton, George, WOMEN'S SOCIAL WORK: TALKS WITH RESCUERS. 1898. Salvation Army.

10.199
TALKS WITH RESCUERS: BEING A GENERAL REVIEW OF THE WORK DURING 1898 INCLUDING A SPECIAL REPORT OF THE CARDIFF BRANCH. 1898.

10.200
Booth, Mrs. Bramwell, "Principles of Rescue Work" in WOMEN IN SOCIAL LIFE, THE TRANSACTIONS OF THE SOCIAL SECTION OF THE INTERNATIONAL

CONGRESS OF WOMEN. LONDON, JULY 1899. ed. by Ishbel Aberdeen. 1900. "Exactly as with other forms of sin, and in common with them, the path of recovery will lie in the direction of self-renunciation, of self-abasement, of self-reliance. The weak and wobbling nature must be attacked where it is weakest and most uncertain. The untamed and brutal spirit must be approached exactly at the seat of rebellion, rather than in its expressions of unruly conduct. The half-crazy and suspicious creature must be won by the restoration of confidence" (pp. 52-53).

10.201
Salvation Army, **BETSY BOBBET... BEING THE ANNUAL REPORT OF THE WOMEN'S SOCIETY AND RESCUE WORK OF THE SALVATION ARMY.** 1905. —*see also:* Search, Pamela, **HAPPY WARRIORS. THE STORY OF THE SOCIAL WORK OF THE SALVATION ARMY.** 1956. Describes Catherine Booth's involvement with the Army. Contains information about Army's work for unwed and abandoned mothers and prostitutes in foreign countries.

10.202
Higson, Jessie E., **THE STORY OF THE BEGINNING: AN ACCOUNT OF PIONEER WORK FOR MORAL WELFARE.** 1955. Recounts her life of reform work in England. "In one of these slum streets I opened a club for girls over twelve, and through the kindness of friends in Yorkshire village two houses were bought. 'Sledmore House' became the centre of new life and interest for the roughest and poorest girls of the neighborhood. It contained the only bath in the parish! Best of all, it was a home for many who knew the world only as a place of drunkeness and quarreling" (p. 2).

10.203
Young, A.F. and Ashton, E.T., "Moral Welfare" in **BRITISH SOCIAL WORK IN THE NINETEENTH CENTURY.** by A.F. Young and E.T. Ashton. 1956. Brief overview of moral reform work and its pioneers. "Having mapped out a field of social work these pioneers set out to strengthen their work by their training schemes, especially for women workers.... Thus rescue workers became specialists in their sphere" (p. 221).

10.204
Heasman, Kathleen, "The Reform of the Prostitute" in **EVANGELICALS IN ACTION: AN APPRAISAL OF THEIR SOCIAL WORK IN THE VICTORIAN ERA.** by Kathleen Heasman. 1962. "The Evangelical homes had certain characteristics in common. The majority of them cultivated a homely atmosphere where the girls were allowed, as far as possible, to develop their own personalities, and some of them, like the Church Army homes, were organised as family groups under the care of a housemother, each girl having her own cubicle and her possessions around her" (p. 155).

10.205
Collins, Philip, **DICKENS AND CRIME.** 1965. Dickens co-founded Urania Cottage, a home for homeless women and prostitutes. "He could... be firm and even ruthless, and he insisted that the girls should acknowledge to themselves the error of their past ways; but thereafter, there were to be no reproaches about the past. The girls were forbidden to discuss it, and even the superintendents were generally kept in ignorance of their charges' histories" (p. 104).

10.206
Deacon, Richard, **THE PRIVATE LIFE OF MR. GLADSTONE.** 1965. William Ewart Gladstone, who believed in applying the principles of Christianity to politics,

was one of Britain's most illustrious Prime Ministers. He became very involved in the rescue movement. "Not only did Gladstone visit the brothels of London in his quest for prostitutes whom he might persuade to quit their profession, but he literally prowled the streets looking for them. Most of his contemporaries who indulged in this kind of work confined their activities to sitting on committees, but Gladstone maintained——with admirable logic——that merely talking about the subject was a negative approach, that the only way to reform these women was to seek them out directly" (p. 13). Many of his contemporaries gossiped about his "true" intentions for entering the brothel district; others thought him to be indiscreet.

10.207
Laver, James, **MANNERS AND MORALS IN THE AGE OF OPTIMISM, 1848-1914.** New York, 1966. "One of the most extraordinary developments at this period was the founding in 1860 of the Midnight Movement. This took the novel form of having a number of cards printed with the words 'Madam, will you favour a few friends with your company at the above address. Refreshment is provided.' The address was the St. James Restaurant, Piccadilly.... A contemporary print show us the astonishing spectacle of a room full of women in all the finery of bonnets and crinolines listening with the utmost decorum to a sermon by the Reverend Baptist Noel in which he urged them with considerable eloquence to give up their way of life" (p. 106).

10.208
Kanner, S. Barbara, "Victorian Institutional Patronage: Angela Burdett-Coutts, Charles Dickens and Urania Cottage, Reformatory for Women, 1846-1858," Ph.D. diss., University of California, Los Angeles, 1972. Discusses the founding of Urania Cottage by Burdett-Coutts and Dickens. "The policies established by Miss Coutts and Dickens were significantly influenced by and involved with current reform movements which, at least in some respects, related to the question of women's roles and social position in English society. For example, the expansion of inquiry into educational opportunity, the innovations in penology, the increasing rationalization of charity organization, the revision of emigration policy, and the modification of social policy and legislation relative to women's status were programs which were recognized by patrons of Urania Cottage as bearing a direct relationship to their rehabilitation scheme" (p. 3).

10.209
Bristow, Edward J., "Repression and Rescue of Prostitutes, 1750-1860" in **VICE AND VIGILANCE: PURITY MOVEMENT IN BRITAIN SINCE 1700.** by Edward J. Bristow. Bristol, 1977. "The voluntary confinement of prostitutes in rescue homes grew out of the ever-widening circle of Georgian humanitarianism. Through the next century the impressive expansion of this 'peculiar form of philanthropy,' as it was called by one of its many enemies, was largely a manifestation of the Christian workers' struggle with sexual sin. While the double standard drove some men to prostitutes, fear and trembling about lust moved others, and women as well, to patrol the streets and even enter brothels to rescue harlots from Satan's grasp" (pp. 62-63).

10.210
Prochaska, F.K., "In Streets and 'Dens of Vice'" in **WOMEN AND PHILANTHROPY IN 19TH CENTURY ENGLAND.** by F.K. Prochaska. Oxford, 1980.

*1c. The Contagious Diseases Acts and Other Legislation Regulating
Women's Sexual Behavior*

10.211
Davis, James Edward, **PRIZE ESSAY ON THE LAWS FOR THE PROTECTION
OF WOMEN.** 1854. Argues that until recently a woman not only had to have
surrendered herself to a man to have been seduced, but the man also had to make
her erotically aroused. Discusses child prostitution.

10.212
BRITISH CONTROVERSIALIST: *"Can the Government Interfere Beneficially in the
Suppression of the Social Evil?"* 1 (1859) 180.

10.213
Nightingale, Florence, **NOTE ON THE SUPPOSED PROTECTION AFFORDED
AGAINST VENEREAL DISEASE, BY RECOGNIZING PROSTITUTION AND
PUTTING IT UNDER POLICE REGULATION.** [1863].

10.214
MELIORA: *"The Contagious Diseases Acts,"* 12 (1864) 336-354. Opposes the
proposed extension of the Act. "A very rapid glance at this new law reveals its
exceedingly one-sided character, as relates to the two sexes. All its artillery is
pointed at the woman. The man, though equally dangerous to public health, is let
off scot free" (p. 345).

10.215
Association for Promoting the Extension of the Contagious Diseases Act, 1866 to
the Civil Population of the United Kingdom, **REPORT ON THE EXTENT OF
VENEREAL DISEASE; ON THE OPERATION OF THE CONTAGIOUS
DISEASES ACT, AND THE MEANS ON CHECKING CONTAGION.** 1868;
**REPORT OF THE SUB-COMMITTEE OF THE ASSOCIATION... WITH A LIST
OF ITS MEMBERS.** 1869; **MOTION FOR REPEAL OF THE CONTAGIOUS
DISEASES ACTS. SPEECH OF DR. L. PLAYFAIR, ETC.** 1870; **THIRD
(FOURTH, SIXTH-EIGHTH) REPORT OF THE OPERATION OF THE
CONTAGIOUS DISEASES ACTS, ETC.** 1870-1878; **THE EFFECTS OF THE
CONTAGIOUS DISEASES ACTS IN DIMINISHING DISEASE... BEING AN
EXAMINATION OF A PAPER READ BEFORE THE STATISTICAL SOCIETY OF
LONDON BY THE RIGHT HON. J. STANSFIELD... REPRINTED FROM THE
BRITISH MEDICAL JOURNAL.** 1876; **COPY OF THE REPORT FROM THE
SELECT COMMITTEE OF THE HOUSE OF COMMONS ON CONTAGIOUS
DISEASES ACTS, AUG., 1882.** 1882.

10.216
Dolby, Henry and Smith, T., **PROPOSAL FOR AN ACT TO AMEND THE
CLAUSE OF THE METROPOLITAN POLICE ACT WHICH PROHIBITS THE...
SOLICITATION OF PROSTITUTES, ETC.** [1866].

10.217
LONDON MEDICAL PRESS AND CIRCULAR: *"The Contagious Diseases Act of
1866,"* 2 (1866) 275-276; T.C.S., *"A Plea for the Control of Prostitution,"* 8 (1869) 50-
54; *"The Contagious Diseases Act,"* 8 (1869) 127-128; Worth, T., *"Remarks on the
Contagious Diseases Act,"* 8 (1869) 512-513.

10.218
Select Committee on the Contagious Diseases Acts, REPORT FROM THE SELECT
COMMITTEE... (1866); WITH THE PROCEEDINGS OF THE COMMITTEE.
[1869]; REPORT[S] FROM THE SELECT COMMITTEE... TOGETHER WITH
THE PROCEEDINGS OF THE COMMITTEE, MINUTES OF EVIDENCE, AND
APPENDIX. 1879-1882; INDEX TO THE REPORT FROM THE SELECT
COMMITTEE... ORDERED BY THE HOUSE OF COMMONS TO BE PRINTED 7
AUG., 1882. [1882]; COPY OF THE REPORT FROM THE SELECT
COMMITTEE... AUG., 1882, WITH MEMORIALS FROM THE BOROUGHS OF
PORTSMOUTH AND DAVENPORT. 1882.

10.219
Society for the Rescue of Women and Children, "THE REMEDY WORSE THAN
THE DISEASE": A PROTEST AGAINST LEGISLATIVE MEASURES FOR THE
REGULATION (AND TENDING TO THE ENCOURAGEMENT) OF
PROSTITUTION, AS EXEMPLIFIED IN THE PROVISIONS AND WORKING OF
THE CONTAGIOUS DISEASES ACT, 1866. [1867]; EXTRACT FROM THE 20TH
ANNUAL REPORT, 1872. 1873. Mostly contains CD Acts papers.

10.220
BRITISH MEDICAL JOURNAL: Hill, M.B., "Illustrations of the Workings of the
Contagious Diseases Acts," 1 (1867) 583-585.

10.221
AN APPEAL TO THE PEOPLE OF ENGLAND ON THE RECOGNITION AND
SUPERINTENDENT OF PROSTITUTION BY GOVERNMENTS. Nottingham,
1869.

10.222
Kingsford, Douglas, A CRITICAL SUMMARY OF THE EVIDENCE BEFORE THE
ROYAL COMMISSION UPON THE CONTAGIOUS DISEASES ACTS, 1866-1869.
1869.

10.223
Ladies' National Association for the Repeal of the Contagious Diseases Acts,
MANIFESTO. 1869; rpt. in: DAILY NEWS: (Dec. 11, 1869) n.p.; ANNUAL
REPORTS. 1870-1915; NATIONAL ASSOCIATION FOR THE REPEAL OF THE
CONTAGIOUS DISEASE ACTS: A GRAVE SUBJECT. 1870; rpt. from: THE
SEVENTEENTH ANNUAL REPORT OF THE RESCUE SOCIETY, ETC. 1870;
FOUR LETTERS BY "AN ENGLISHWOMAN..." Bristol, n.d.

10.224
Newman, Francis William, THE CURE OF THE GREAT SOCIAL EVIL WITH
SPECIAL REFERENCE TO RECENT LAWS DELUSIVELY CALLED
CONTAGIOUS DISEASES ACTS. 1869; THE THEORY AND RESULTS OF THE
CONTAGIOUS DISEASES ACTS OF 1864, 1866 AND 1869. [1870].

10.225
Royal Commission on Contagious Diseases Acts, A CRITICAL SUMMARY OF THE
EVIDENCE BEFORE AND ROYAL COMMISSION UPON THE CONTAGIOUS
DISEASES ACTS 1866-1869. 8 vols. [1869]. See chaps. 4-6; REPORT OF THE
ROYAL... ACTS. 2 vols. 1871; ROYAL COMMISSION UPON THE ADMIN-
ISTRATION AND OPERATION OF THE CONTAGIOUS DISEASES ACTS. 1871.

10.226
TRANSACTIONS OF THE NATIONAL ASSOCIATION FOR THE PROMOTION OF SOCIAL SCIENCE: Hill, B., *"Should the Principle of the Contagious Diseases Act be Applied to the Civil Population,"* (1869) 428-438.

10.227
WESTMINSTER REVIEW: Chapman, J., *"Prostitution in Relation to the National Health,"* 92 (1869) 179-234; Chapman, J., *"Prostitution; its Sanitary Superintendence by the State: an Extract from the Eleventh Report of the Medical Officer of the Privy Council,"* 92 (1869) 556-569; Chapman, J., *"Prostitution; How to Deal With It: the Contagious Diseases Acts, 1866 and 1869,"* 93 (1870) 477-535; Chapman, J., *"Prostitution: Governmental Experiments in Controlling It,"* 93 (1870) 119-179; Ethelmer, E., *"Contagious Diseases Acts: A Warning,"* 147 (1897) 477-483; 152 (1899) 249-260; 397-443; 448-509; 608-627. Calls the Acts "a pretext of the most hollow kind for the continuous subjugation of a slave class of women to the untempered sensuality of vicious men" (pp. 482-483); Elmy, B.W., *"Contagious Diseases Acts,"* 152 (1899) 249-260; *"The Contagious Diseases Acts (Women) Part I,"* 152 (1899) 397-443; *"Do the Contagious Diseases Acts Succeed?"* Part II, 152 (1899) 488-509; Part III, 152 (1899) 608-627; *"Contagious Diseases Acts. Do They Succeed?"* 153 (1900) 135-158.

10.228
Acton, William, **THE CONTAGIOUS DISEASES ACT. SHOULD THE CONTAGIOUS DISEASES ACT BE APPLIED TO THE CIVIL POPULATION?... A PAPER, ETC.** 1870.

10.229
Amos, Sheldon, **THE POLICY OF THE CONTAGIOUS DISEASES ACTS OF 1866 AND 1869, TESTED BY THE PRINCIPLES OF ETHICAL AND POLITICAL SCIENCE.** 1870; **THE PRESENT STATE OF THE CONTAGIOUS DISEASES ACTS CONTROVERSY.** 1870; **A COMPARATIVE SURVEY OF THE LAWS IN FORCE FOR THE PROHIBITION, REGULATION AND LICENSING OF VICE IN ENGLAND AND OTHER COUNTRIES.** 1877. A detailed presentation on the laws regulating vice, licensed houses, certified rescue hospitals, and the functions of the state and parliamentary system in regulation.

10.230
Ash, Edward, **CONTAGIOUS DISEASES ACTS CONSIDERED IN RELATION TO RELIGION AND MORALS.** 1870.

10.231
Bright, Jacob, **THE CONTAGIOUS DISEASES ACTS: SPEECH... DELIVERED IN THE HOUSE OF COMMONS... JULY 20, 1870, ETC.** Manchester, 1870.

10.232
Butler, Josephine Elizabeth (Grey), **AN APPEAL TO MY COUNTRYMEN.** 1870; Butler's main contribution to social reform was her crusade against the Contagious Diseases Acts which made women subject to arrest, forced medical examination and, if they resisted, imprisonment at hard labor. The Acts were finally repealed in 1886. **AN APPEAL TO THE PEOPLE OF ENGLAND ON THE RECOGNITION AND SUPERINTENDANCE OF PROSTITUTION BY GOVERNMENT.** 1870; **THE CONSTITUTION VIOLATED.** 1871; **SURSUM CORDA; ANNUAL ADDRESS TO THE LADIES' NATIONAL ASSOCIATION.** Liverpool, 1871; **A LETTER ON THE SUBJECT OF MR. BRUCE'S BILL ADDRESSED TO THE REPEALERS OF THE CONTAGIOUS DISEASES ACTS.** Liverpool, 1872; **NEW ERA: CONTAINING A**

RETROSPECT OF THE HISTORY OF THE REGULATION SYSTEM IN BERLIN... Liverpool, 1872; SOME THOUGHTS ON THE PRESENT ASPECT OF THE CRUSADE AGAINST THE STATE REGULATION OF VICE. Liverpool, 1874; SPEECH DELIVERED... AT THE FOURTH ANNUAL MEETING OF THE "VIGILANCE ASSOCIATION FOR THE DEFENCE OF PERSONAL RIGHTS" HELD AT BRISTOL, OCTOBER 15TH, 1874. [1874]; A LETTER TO THE MEMBERS OF THE LADIES' NATIONAL ASSOCIATION. Liverpool, 1875; THE HOUR BEFORE THE DAWN: AN APPEAL TO MEN. 1876; GOVERNMENT BY POLICE. 1879; 2nd ed., 1880; 1888; THE PRINCIPLES OF THE ABOLITION-ISTS, AN ADDRESS DELIVERED AT EXETER HALL FEBRUARY 20, 1885. 1885; A GRAVE QUESTION (THE SYSTEM OF OFFICIALLY ORGANIZED PROSTITUTION) THAT NEEDS ANSWERING BY THE CHURCHES OF GREAT BRITAIN [1886]; SIMPLE WORDS FOR SIMPLE FOLK ABOUT THE REPEAL OF THE CONTAGIOUS DISEASES ACTS. Bristol, 1886; REVIVAL OF THE ABOLITIONIST CAUSE. Winchester, 1887; RECOLLECTIONS OF GEORGE BUTLER: PERSONAL REMINISCENCES OF A GREAT CRUSADE. 1892; 1896; 1898; 1910; 1911. Butler details her actions to repeal the Contagious Diseases Acts. "I saw this great social iniquity (based on shameful inequality of judgement concerning sexual sin in man and woman) devastating the world, contentedly acquiesced in, no great revolt proclaimed against it" (p. 8); JOSEPHINE E. BUTLER: AN AUTOBIOGRAPHICAL MEMOIR. Bristol, 1909; 1911; ed. by George W. Johnson and Lucy A. Johnson. 3rd rev. ed., Bristol, 1928. A selection from Butler's other work: RECOLLECTIONS OF GEORGE BUTLER, PERSONAL REMINISCENCES OF A GREAT CRUSADE, and some of her principal publications. Argued that prostitutes and their exploiters could be reclaimed; THE VOICE OF ONE CRYING IN THE WILDERNESS. BEING HER FIRST APPEAL MADE IN 1874-75 TO CONTINENTAL NATIONS AGAINST THE SYSTEM OF REGULATED VICE. trans. by Osmond Airy. Bristol, 1913. ——see also: Stead, W.T., JOSEPHINE BUTLER: A LIFE SKETCH. 1887; Marchant, James K.B.E., A RECORD OF A GREAT MORAL CRUSADE IN CHATHAM... WITH A SPECIAL INTRODUCTORY LETTER FROM MRS. J. BUTLER. 1904; Stuart, James, "Mrs. Josephine Butler's Work" in REMINISCENCES. by James Stuart. 1911; Holmes, Marion, JOSEPHINE BUTLER. A CAMEO LIFE SKETCH. 8th ed., 1913; Hay-Cooper, L., JOSEPHINE BUTLER AND HER WORK FOR SOCIAL PURITY. 1922. "Wherever Mrs. Butler went, leadership was required of her. She was a leader in the movement for women's rights; she was instantly acknowledged leader of the crusade against regulation" (p. 133); Turner, E.M., THE JOSEPHINE BUTLER CENTENARY 1828-1928: AN APPRECIATION. 1927. "The Contagious Diseases Acts were a distinct violation of English Law. They deprived women of legal safeguards, and every guarantee of personal security hitherto established by law; they punished an offence which had not been defined as an offence... they entailed on women the liability to arrest, forced surgical examination, and (if this were resisted) imprisonment with hard labour" (p. 4); Association for Moral and Social Purity, NOTES FOR SPEAKERS ON THE WORK AND PRINCIPLES OF JOSEPHINE BUTLER. SPECIALLY PREPARED IN CONNECTION WITH THE JOSEPHINE BUTLER CENTENARY 1828-1928 1928; Crawford, Virginia M., JOSEPHINE BUTLER. [1928]; Turner, E.M., JOSEPHINE BUTLER. 1935; Butler, A.S.G., PORTRAIT OF JOSEPHINE BUTLER. 1954. "She practically identified herself with fallen women in her scorn of the hypocrisy among men of her period. She even said she would enjoy speaking to two or three hundred harlots on the subject of profligate men much more than addressing an assembly of respectable people on fallen women" (p. 84); Bell, Enid H.C.M., JOSEPHINE BUTLER: FLAME OF FIRE. 1962; Stocks, Mary, JOSEPHINE BUTLER AND THE MORAL STANDARDS OF TODAY. 1967; Boyd, Nancy, "Josephine Butler" in THREE VICTORIAN WOMEN WHO CHANGED THEIR WORLD. by Nancy Boyd. Oxford,

1982; Forster, Margaret, "Sexual Morality: Josephine Butler 1828-1906" in SIGNIFICANT SISTERS: THE GRASSROOTS OF ACTIVE FEMINISM 1839-1939. by Margaret Forster. 1984.

10.233
Garrett-Anderson, Elizabeth, AN ENQUIRY INTO THE CHARACTER OF THE CONTAGIOUS DISEASES ACTS OF 1866-69. 1870. Author may also be cataloged as Anderson, Elizabeth Garrett.

10.234
Hume, Catherine Mary (Rothery), A LETTER ADDRESSED TO THE RIGHT HON. W.E. GLADSTONE... TOUCHING THE CONTAGIOUS DISEASES' ACTS OF 1866 AND 1869, ETC. 1870.

10.235
Martineau, Harriet, THE CONTAGIOUS DISEASES ACTS, AS APPLIED TO GARRISON TOWNS AND NAVAL STATIONS: BEING A SERIES OF LEADING ARTICLES FROM THE DAILY NEWS OF 1863. Liverpool, 1870. Critiques the army's management of its soldiers in encouraging the base instincts and neglecting their moral character.

10.236
National Anti-Contagious Diseases Acts Association (changed to National Association for the Repeal of the Contagious Diseases Acts), NATIONAL ASSOCIATION FOR THE REPEAL OF THE CONTAGIOUS DISEASES ACTS. A GRAVE SUBJECT. [1870]. A CRITICAL SUMMARY OF THE EVIDENCE BEFORE THE ROYAL COMMISSION UPON THE CONTAGIOUS DISEASES ACTS, 1866-1869. [1872].

10.237
Taylor, Charles Bell, THE CONTAGIOUS DISEASES ACTS (WOMEN): FROM A SANITARY POINT OF VIEW, SHOWING HOW AND WHY SUCH DESPOTIC MEASURES NOT ONLY FAIL TO REPRESS VENEREAL DISEASE BUT TEND TO INCREASE ITS MOST SERIOUS MANIFESTATIONS. 1870; OBSERVATIONS ON THE CONTAGIOUS DISEASES ACT, (WOMEN, NOT ANIMALS)... BEING A REPLY TO MR. W.P. SWAIN'S PAPER ON THE WORKING OF THE ACT AT DEVONPORT. Nottingham, [1871]; THE STATISTICAL RESULTS OF THE CONTAGIOUS DISEASES ACTS... SHOWING THEIR TOTAL FAILURE IN A SANITARY POINT OF VIEW. Nottingham, 1872; A SPEECH DELIVERED AT EXETER IN REFERENCE TO THE PROPOSED EXTENSION OF THE CONTAGIOUS DISEASES ACTS TO THAT CITY. 1880; NOTTINGHAM PARLIAMENTARY DEBATING SOCIETY... SPEECH... ON THE SECOND READING AT THE BILL FOR THE REPEAL OF THE CONTAGIOUS DISEASES ACT, 1866-1869. 1883.

10.238
Wilkinson, James John Garth, THE FORCIBLE INTROSPECTION OF WOMEN FOR THE ARMY AND NAVY BY THE OLIGARCHY, CONSIDERED PHYSICALLY. 1870.

10.239
Worth, Thomas, A SECOND LETTER TO THE RIGHT HON. W. EWART GLADSTONE, FIRST LORD OF THE TREASURY, OPPOSING THE ATTEMPT UNDER THE TITLE OF A "CONTAGIOUS DISEASES BILL," TO INTRODUCE INTO THIS COUNTRY THE CONTINENTAL SYSTEM, OF LICENSED

PROSTITUTION, WITH ITS ATTENDANT EVILS. Nottingham, 1870.

10.240
CONTEMPORARY REVIEW: Butler, J., *"The Lovers of the Lost,"* 13 (1870) 16-40; *"Regulation, Cure and Prevention of Prostitution,"* 14 (1870) 220-235; Fawcett, M.G., *"Speech or Silence,"* 48 (1885) 326-331.

10.241
FORTNIGHTLY REVIEW: Morley, J., *"A Short Letter to Some Ladies,"* 13 (1870) 372-376; Venturi, E.A., *"A Short Answer to Mr. Morley's Short Letter,"* 13 (1870) 633-638. "Nothing could be easier than for the government to employ the same detectives in plain clothes, who now watch over and entrap the women, to watch over and entrap the male frequenters of brothels (who are well known to them), and to classify them at once. God forbid that I should advocate such a system; but those who consider it just and wise to apply it to the weak, should be the first to recommend its extension to the strong" (p. 636).

10.242
JOURNAL OF THE ROYAL STATISTICAL SOCIETY: Hill, B., *"Statistical Results of the Contagious Diseases Acts,"* 33 (1870) 463-485. "Now, every known prostitute is examined, but before 1868 the want of sufficient hospital accommodation rendered it useless to examine ali the women, for the wards could be kept full by only taking such as were suspected, or avowed themselves to be diseased. Consequently at the present time a very much larger number of women free from disease are examined than formerly, and partly from this, the ratio of diseased to the number of examinations has lessened" (p. 475); Stansfeld, J., *"On the Validity of the Annual Government Statistics of the Operation of the Contagious Diseases Acts,"* 39 (1876) 540-561; Lawson, R., *"The Operation of the Contagious Diseases Acts Among the Troops in the United Kingdom, and Men of the Royal Navy on the Home Station, From their Introduction in 1864 to their Ultimate Repeal in 1884,"* 54 (1891) 31-62; *"Discussion on Inspector-General Lawson's Paper,"* 54 (1891) 62-69.

10.243
Collingwood, Charles Edward Stuart, SOME OF THE RELIGIOUS AND MORAL ASPECTS OF THE CONTAGIOUS DISEASES ACTS. 1871.

10.244
Mill, John Stuart, THE EVIDENCE OF JOHN STUART MILL TAKEN BEFORE THE ROYAL COMMISSION OF 1870, ON THE ADMINISTRATION AND OPERATION OF THE CONTAGIOUS DISEASES ACTS OF 1866 AND 1869. 1871.

10.245
North Eastern Counties Association, ANNUAL REPORTS. 1871-1886.

10.246
Wilson, Robert, PROSTITUTION SUPPRESSIBLE AND RESISTANCE TO THE CONTAGIOUS DISEASES (WOMEN'S) ACTS A DUTY. 1871.

10.247
Thomas, Edward W. (of the London Female Preventive and Reformatory Association), AN EXPOSURE OF THE FALSE STATISTICS OF THE CONTAGIOUS DISEASES ACT (WOMEN) CONTAINED IN PARLIAMENTARY NO. 149, ON THE RETURN OF THE ASSISTANT COMMISSIONER OF METROPOLITAN POLICE. BY THE MANAGERS OF METROPOLITAN FEMALE

REFORMATORIES [E.W. THOMAS, W. HORNIBROOK, AND OTHERS]. 1873.

10.248
THE CONTAGIOUS DISEASES ACTS. OBSERVATIONS SUGGESTED BY THE QUERIES: 1. ARE THE CONTAGIOUS DISEASES ACTS NECESSARY IN ENGLAND? 2. DO THEY SUCCEED? 3. WOULD NO LESS OBJECTIONABLE MEASURES SUFFICE?... BY A PHYSICIAN. PT. 1. 1874, etc.

10.249
THE DISEASES OF WOMEN... BY A PHYSICIAN. 1878.

10.250
Midland Counties Electoral Union, ANNUAL REPORTS. 1874-1883; OCCASIONAL PAPERS. 1879-1886.

10.251
Nevins, John Birkbeck, STATEMENT OF THE GROUNDS UPON WHICH THE CONTAGIOUS DISEASES ACTS ARE OPPOSED, ETC. 1874; THE HEALTH OF THE NAVY: AN ANALYSIS OF THE OFFICIAL REPORT FOR 1876, AND OF THE SPECIAL RETURN RELATING TO FIVE PORTS UNDER AND FIVE PORTS NOT UNDER THE CONTAGIOUS DISEASES ACTS, ETC. 1878; EXAMINATION OF THE WAR OFFICE AND ADMIRALTY RETURN AS TO THE AMOUNT OF VENEREAL DISEASE IN THE ARMY AND NAVY, SINCE THE SUSPENSION OF THE COMPULSORY EXAMINATIONS OF WOMEN, ETC. 1884.

10.252
British Continental and General Federation for the Abolition of Government Regulation of Prostitution, FIRST, [SECOND] ANNUAL REPORTS. 1875-1876; 1876-1877; 1877-1914; THE NEW ABOLITIONISTS. 1876.

10.253
NATIONAL LEAGUE JOURNAL: 1875 to 1884; *continued as:* SENTINEL: 1884+. Published by the Working Men's National League for the Repeal of the Contagious Diseases Acts.

10.254
Association for Extending the Contagious Diseases Act, THE EFFECTS OF THE CONTAGIOUS DISEASES ACTS IN DIMINISHING DISEASE IN THE ARMY AND NAVY AND AMONG THE CIVIL POPULATION. 1876.

10.255
Lowndes, Frederick Walter, PROSTITUTION AND SYPHILIS IN LIVERPOOL, AND THE WORKING OF THE CONTAGIOUS DISEASES ACTS, AT ALDERSHOT, CHATHAM, PLYMOUTH, AND DEVONPORT. 1876; THE EXTENSION OF THE CONTAGIOUS DISEASES ACTS TO LIVERPOOL AND OTHER SEAPORTS, PRACTICALLY CONSIDERED. Liverpool, 1886.

10.256
Stuart, James, THE NEW ABOLITIONISTS. A NARRATIVE OF A YEAR'S WORK. BEING AN ACCOUNT OF THE MISSION UNDERTAKEN TO THE CONTINENT OF EUROPE, AND OF THE EVENTS SUBSEQUENT THEREUPON. 1876.

10.257
Ladies' National Association for the Abolition of Government Regulation of Vice, **ANNUAL REPORT.** Manchester, 1879-1880; **REPORT, 10TH, FOR 1882.** Bristol, 1883; **SEVENTEENTH REPORT.** Bristol, 1887; **WOMEN AND THE REGULATION SYSTEM.** 1906. Pamphlet by Emily Ford; **GIRLS OVER SIXTEEN IN MORAL DANGER OR RE-EDUCATION.** 1912. Pamphlet by Emily Ford; **THE CONTAGIOUS DISEASES ACTS AND THE NECESSARIAN PHILOSOPHY.** n.d.

10.258
Stansfeld, James, **ON THE FAILURE OF THE CONTAGIOUS DISEASES ACTS AS PROVED BY THE OFFICIAL EVIDENCE.** 1881; **REPEAL OF THE CONTAGIOUS DISEASES ACTS.** 1884. —*see also:* Hammond, J.L. and Hammond, Barbara, **JAMES STANSFELD: A VICTORIAN CHAMPION OF SEX EQUALITY.** 1932. Stansfeld fought for the repeal of the Contagious Diseases Acts. "Far wider and deeper issues than the immediate and local operation of these Acts are at stake. If we probe to their roots the ideas and motives out of which they have sprung, we shall find... the necessity of prostitution; the desirableness of frankly, 'without hypocrisy,' accepting that necessity; of treating prostitution as a recognised social institution, and of making state provision to render it physically as innocuous as possible by compulsory state medical supervision and inspection of a pariah class of women set apart for the 'necessities' of men" (p. 191).

10.259
H., S., **STATE LEGALIZATION OF VICE.** 1882.

10.260
Barcroft, W., **THE CONTAGIOUS DISEASES ACTS.** 1883.

10.261
Bentinck, G.C., **THE GOVERNMENT AND THE CONTAGIOUS DISEASES ACTS.** 1883.

10.262
Blackwell, Elizabeth, **WRONG AND RIGHT METHODS OF DEALING WITH SOCIAL EVIL, AS SHOWN BY ENGLISH PARLIAMENTARY EVIDENCE.** New York, 1883.

10.263
An Ex-Constable of the Davenport Division, **THE SOCIAL EVIL, WITH SUGGESTIONS FOR ITS SUPPRESSION, AND REVELATIONS OF THE WORKING OF THE CONTAGIOUS DISEASES ACTS.** Bristol, [1883].

10.264
City of London Committee for Obtaining the Repeal of the Contagious Diseases Acts, **SEVEN REASONS FOR THE REPEAL OF THE (SO-CALLED) CONTAGIOUS DISEASES ACTS, 1866-1869.** 1883.

10.265
Booth, Charles, **THE INIQUITY OF STATE REGULATED VICE.** 1884.

10.266
Scott, Benjamin, **STATE REGULATED VICE AS IT EXISTED IN LONDON.** 1886; **A STATE INIQUITY. ITS RISE, EXTENSION AND OVERTHROW.** 1890; 1968. Provides a detailed account of the establishment and repeal of the Contagious Diseases Acts.

10.267
London Moral Reform Union, HISTORY OF THE CONTAGIOUS DISEASES ACTS. 1892.

10.268
NEW REVIEW: Hart, E., *"Women, Clergymen and Doctors,"* 7 (1892) 708-718; Wilberforce, B., *"'Women, Clergymen and Doctors': a Reply,"* 8 (1893) 85-95.

10.269
Friends Association for Abolishing State Regulation of Vice, THE CROWNING CRIME OF CHRISTENDOM. 1893; SOME FACTS WITH REGARD TO STATE REGULATION OF VICE. 1898; ANNUAL REPORTS. n.d.

10.270
Bebel, August, A REVOLTING INJUSTICE. WHAT DEPUTY BEBEL SAYS ON THE STATE REGULATION OF VICE. 1896.

10.271
STORM BELL: Butler, J., *"To the Friends of Freedom Throughout Our Land,"* n.v. (1898) 1-5. "During the first years of this law, a certificate on paper was given to every woman who had passed through this cruel ordeal, on this paper was the name of the woman, and of the doctor who certified her to be fit for bad men to consort with, and the date of the last examination" (p. 3).

10.272
Gregory, Maurice, THE CROWNING CRIME OF CHRISTENDOM WITH A SHORT HISTORY OF THE EFFORTS OF THE SOCIETY OF FRIENDS FOR ITS ABOLITION. 1896; A SHORT SUMMARY OF THE PARLIAMENTARY HISTORY OF STATE-REGULATED VICE IN THE UNITED KINGDOM. 1900.

10.273
Morrow, Prince A., SOCIAL DISEASES AND MARRIAGE: SOCIAL PROPHYL-AXIS. New York, 1904. "Venereal disease, declares a distinguished authority, is... a fatal gift that the courtesan repays her virtuous sister for the scorn and contempt which are heaped upon her, and by a strange irony of fate the husband is made the bearer of this venom and administers it to his family" (p. 343).

10.274
Wilson, Henry J., COPY OF A ROUGH RECORD OF EVENTS AND INCIDENTS CONNECTED WITH THE REPEAL OF THE CONTAGIOUS DISEASES ACTS, 1874-1869 IN THE UNITED KINGDOM, AND OF THE MOVEMENT AGAINST STATE REGULATION OF VICE IN INDIA AND THE COLONIES 1858-1906. Sheffield, 1907.

10.275
VOTES FOR WOMEN: Webbe, A.J., *"War and the Social Evil,"* n.v. (1914) 29-30. "Why, in fine, should women's stand for the woman's movement be against Regulation? Because more than perhaps anything else, state regulation of vice helps to keep alive the subjection of women; because it helps keep alive an unequal moral standard" (p. 29).

10.276
SHIELD: A REVIEW OF MORAL AND SOCIAL HYGIENE: January 1916; March 1916 to December 1931. First issued by the International Federation for the

Abolition of State Regulation of Vice, and later by the Association for Moral and Social Hygiene.

10.277
Gordon, Mary, **PENAL DISCIPLINE AS APPLIED TO WOMEN**. New York, 1922. See especially: "The Young Prostitute" and "The Making of the Common Prostitute." "How does a woman become a 'common prostitute'? She becomes one by the simple process of the policeman moving her on, probably telling her she is one, warning her he will arrest her, and finally arresting her, swearing in court that she is one, and that she had loitered with the intention of soliciting, or that he has seen her soliciting" (p. 97).

10.278
Reiss, Erna, **RIGHTS AND DUTIES OF ENGLISH WOMEN: A STUDY IN LAW AND PUBLIC OPINION**. 1934. See Chap. 6 for a discussion of the Metropolitan Police Act of 1839 which attempted to remove prostitutes from "fashionable" streets.

10.279
James, Thomas Egbert, **PROSTITUTION AND THE LAW**. Altrincham, 1951. Calls prostitution an emotional disturbance and examines the profession from a legal perspective. See especially: "The Law Relating to Prostitution and Other Kindred Offences" for a delineation of the statutes implemented to curtail prostitution from 1824 to 1898. "Most of the offences in England and Wales with which the law relating to prostitution and kindred offences is concerned are not indictable. Procuration and offences under the Vagrancy Act of 1898, may or may not be tried summarily. This fact narrows the scope of the legal aspect of the problem to a considerable extent" (p. 28).

10.280
MARXISM TODAY: Ramelson, M., *"The Fight Against the Contagious Diseases Acts,"* 8 (1964) 78-84. Chronicles the repeal of the Acts and the career of Josephine Butler.

10.281
Deacon, Richard, **THE PRIVATE LIFE OF MR. GLADSTONE**. 1965. On the effects of the Contagious Diseases Acts on prostitutes: "The fact that the law now allowed plain-clothes policemen to examine and then 'register' girls on the streets without adequate safeguards for the women themselves to be protected against gross abuse or discrimination, forced some Victorians to realise that the time was ripe for a change in the position of women in a society ruled by men for man's enjoyment" (p. 97).

10.282
Ramelson, Marion, **THE PETTICOAT REBELLION**. 1967. Traces the development of female activism for women's emancipation which includes the following chapters on the Contagious Diseases Acts: "The Dialogue" and "People and Parliament."

10.283
JOURNAL OF THE SOCIETY FOR ARMY HISTORICAL RESEARCH: Bianco, R.L., *"The Attempted Control of Venereal Disease in the Army of Mid-Victorian England,"* 45 (1967) 234-241. Under the Act for the Better Prevention of Contagious Diseases, "any suspected prostitute within a five mile radius of certain military garrisons could be detained for medical examination" (p. 240).

10.284

HISTORICAL STUDIES: Smith, F.B., *"Ethics and Disease in the Later Nineteenth Century: the Contagious Diseases Acts,"* 15 (1971) 118-135. "Examinations were done at one a minute. At Aldershot the women were housed in a single-storied building, which meant that blinds had to be drawn all day to prevent the women from attracting the soldiers passing by, with the result that the women lived in semi-darkness for weeks on end" (p. 126).

10.285

Sigsworth, E.M. and Wyke, T.J., "A Study of Victorian Prostitution and Venereal Disease" in **SUFFER AND BE STILL: WOMEN IN THE VICTORIAN AGE.** ed. by Martha Vicinus. 1972.

10.286

BULLETIN OF THE SOCIETY FOR THE STUDY OF LABOUR HISTORY: L'Esperance, J., *"The Work of the Ladies' National Association for the Repeal of the Contagious Diseases Acts,"* 26 (1973) 13-16. "The L.N.A. sought political solutions for the problem of prostitution and the oppression of women; instead of personal intervention in social problems they engaged in the usual activities of Victorian pressure groups" (p. 15); L'Esperance, J., *"Middle-Class Women, Working-Class Men and Working-Class Women: A Case Study of the Campaign to Repeal the Contagious Diseases Acts,"* 26 (1973) 9-14.

10.287

Walkowitz, Judith R., "'We Are Not Beasts of the Field': Prostitution and the Campaign Against the Contagious Diseases Acts, 1869-1886," Ph.D. diss., Univ. of Rochester, 1974. Chapter three provides a chronology of the Contagious Diseases Acts and the repeal movement; "The Repeal Campaign" in **PROSTITUTION AND VICTORIAN SOCIETY: WOMEN, CLASS, AND THE STATE.** by Judith R. Walkowitz. 1982. After the repeal of the Contagious Diseases Acts, "repealers and regulationists collaborated in the new purity campaigns that offered moralistic goals in a noncontroversial and nonpolitical framework. In the transition to social purity, moral concerns had been disconnected from larger feminist issues, and the feminist context of the repeal movement had been subverted" (p. 245).

10.288

McHugh, Paul, "The Campaign to Repeal the Contagious Diseases Acts: Some Organizational Aspects," Ph.D. diss., Oxford Univ., 1976; **PROSTITUTION AND VICTORIAN SOCIAL REFORM.** 1980; *reviewed in:* **TIMES LITERARY SUPPLEMENT:** Shannon, R.T., *"Better Free Than Healthy,"* 25 (1980) 852; *also reviewed in:* **ECONOMIC HISTORY REVIEW:** Davidoff, L., 34 (1981) 327-238; *also reviewed in:* **VICTORIAN STUDIES:** Banks, J.A., 24 (1981) 513-515.

10.289

Buckley, Suzann, "The Failure to Resolve the Problem of Venereal Disease Among the Troops in Britain During World War One" in **WAR AND SOCIETY.** ed. by Brian Bond and Ian Roy. 1977.

10.290

Skelley, Alan Ramsay, **THE VICTORIAN ARMY AT HOME: THE RECRUIT-MENT AND TERMS AND CONDITIONS OF THE BRITISH REGULAR, 1859.** 1977. Contains information on government regulation of prostitution around army encampments.

10.291
Storch, Robert D., "Police Control of Street Prostitution in Victorian London: A Study in the Contexts of Police Action" in **POLICE AND SOCIETY**. ed. by David H. Bayley. Beverly Hills, 1977. Details methods of police control of prostitution and enforcement of the CD Acts.

10.292
Trustram, Myna, **WOMEN OF THE REGIMENT: MARRIAGE AND THE VICTORIAN ARMY.** by Myna Trustram. 1984. See especially: "Prostitution and Venereal Disease." "The origins of the Acts lay very much in the military concern for venereal disease amongst soldiers and sailors; they were conceived as exceptional legislation for a specific military problem" (p. 121). The Acts were soon extended to the civilian population. Trustram cites Walkowitz' argument that the Acts led to professionalization of prostitutes.

10.293
ALBION: Hamilton, M., *"Opposition to the Contagious Diseases Act, 1864-1886,"* 10 (1978) 14-27. "Those opposed also argued that the Acts were unjust in that they were directed against women only. In her testimony before the Royal Commission, Josephine Butler said, 'Let your laws be put in force, but let them be for male as well as female'" (p. 17).

10.294
MEDICAL HISTORY: Post, J.B., *"A Foreign Office Survey of Venereal Disease and Prostitution Control, 1869-70,"* 22 (1978) 327-334.

10.295
Ballhatchet, Kenneth, **RACE, SEX AND CLASS UNDER THE RAJ: IMPERIAL ATTITUDES AND POLICIES AND THEIR CRITICS, 1793-1905.** 1980. Details the enforcement of the Contagious Disease Acts in army camps in India. "It was generally recognized that religious attitudes were less rigid in India than in England, though social structures were more rigid: prostitutes were not denounced as sinners, but society permitted no alternative occupation" (p. 20).

1d. White Slavery

10.296
Cobden, John C., "Mental and Moral Condition of the White Slaves in Great Britain" in **THE WHITE SLAVES OF ENGLAND.** by John C. Cobden. 1853. Discusses concubinage among costermongers and patteners. Attributes the practice to poverty, lack of education, and bad working conditions. "Mr. Mayhew estimates that only one-tenth of the couples living together and carrying on the costermonging trade are married. There is no honour attached to the marriage state and no shame to concubinage" (p. 424).

10.297
Napheys, George H., "White Slaves" in **THE PHYSICAL LIFE OF WOMAN.** by George H. Napheys. 1872. "The reason this fearful trade exists and flourishes in the midst and under the very noses of good, proper living people is, primarily, becuase of the existence of despicable creatures known as 'pimps' and 'bludges'" (p. 24).

10.298
Borel, Thomas, THE WHITE SLAVERY OF EUROPE... WITH SUPPLEMENT RELATING TO THE FOREIGN TRAFFIC IN ENGLISH, SCOTCH AND IRISH GIRLS. 1880.

10.299
Dyer, Alfred Stace, THE EUROPEAN SLAVE TRADE IN ENGLISH GIRLS: A NARRATIVE OF FACTS. 1880; SIX YEARS' LABOUR AND SORROW: BEING THE FOURTH REPORT OF THE LONDON COMMITTEE FOR SUPPRESSING THE TRAFFIC IN BRITISH GIRLS FOR PURPOSES OF CONTINENTAL PROSTITUTION. 1885. Discussion of the Criminal Law Amendment Bill of 1883 which raised the age of consent to 16 years and allowed police to search brothels for underage girls. Also allowed police to close brothels and attempted to limit solicitation through stricter regulation; SLAVE TRADE IN EUROPEAN GIRLS IN INDIA. Bombay, 1893.

10.300
Committee for the Suppression of Traffic in English Girls, REPORT. 1881.

10.301
CONTEMPORARY REVIEW: Hopkins, J.E., *"The Apocalypse of Evil,"* 48 (1885) 332-342; Bunting, M.H.L., *"The White Slave Traffic Crusade,"* 103 (1913) 49-52. "We see that to put down this traffic there must be international agreement and understanding. These foreign agents advertise in *our* newspapers, make use of *our* ships, have their offices in *our* great cities, entice, defraud, and force into slavery not only girls of other countries, but *our* English girls" (p. 4).

10.302
Bloch, Iwan, "Pandering, Bullies, and Traffic in Young Girls (Defloration Mania)" in SEXUAL LIFE IN ENGLAND. by Iwan Bloch. 1908. "London was for a long time the central market for the traffic in young girls, which was carried on there on a huge scale and under the most shameful conditions" (p. 153).

10.303
Bell, Ernest Albert, FIGHTING THE TRAFFIC IN YOUNG GIRLS; OR, WAR ON THE WHITE SLAVE TRADE. 1910. Describes techniques which men used to lure country girls and trap them in houses of prostitution, including courtship and false marriage. Refers to them as "demons in human form."

10.304
International Bureau for the Suppression of the White Slave Traffic, PROSPECTUS. 1910.

10.305
Jewish Association for the Protection of Girls and Women, OFFICIAL REPORT OF THE JEWISH INTERNATIONAL CONFERENCE ON THE SUPPRESSION OF TRAFFIC IN GIRLS AND WOMEN. 1910.

10.306
Knight, G. Kerschener, THE WHITE SLAVES OF ENGLAND. Denham, 1910.

10.307
THE WHITE SLAVE TRAFFIC. ARTICLES AND LETTERS REPRINTED FROM "THE SPECTATOR." 1912.

10.308
THE WHITE SLAVE TRAFFIC. 1912. ——*see also:* IN THE GRIP OF THE WHITE SLAVE TRADER. BY THE AUTHOR OF "THE WHITE SLAVE TRAFFIC." 1911.

10.309
Addams, Jane, A NEW CONSCIENCE AND AN ANCIENT EVIL. New York, 1912. American, but applicable to the English case.

10.310
Malvery, Olive Christian (MacKirdy) and Willis, W.N., THE WHITE SLAVE MARKET. 1912. See especially: "Slaves," "Haunts of the White Slave Traffic," "Madame V.'s Story: the Devil's Ambassador," "Pleas," "Martyrs," and "Remedies."

10.311
Metropolitan Police Force, WHITE SLAVE TRAFFIC. 1913.

10.312
National Vigilance Association, THE FIFTH INTERNATIONAL CONGRESS FOR THE SUPPRESSION OF THE WHITE SLAVE TRAFFIC. HELD IN LONDON FROM MONDAY, JUNE 30TH, TO FRIDAY, JULY 4TH, 1913, AT CAXTON HALL, VICTORIA STREET, WESTMINSTER. 1913. Includes transcript of the congress meeting. A former white slave describes her passage across the ocean for exploitation: "The manner in which the sailors, stewards, firemen, and others mingled with the women passengers was thoroughly revolting. Their language and the topics of conversation were vile. Their comments about the women, and made in their presence, were coarse. What was far worse and of continual occurrence was their handling of the women and girls. Some of the crew were always on deck, and took all manner of liberties with the women, in broad daylight as well as after dark. Not one young woman in the steerage escaped attack" (p. 74). ——*see also:* Coote, William Alexander, A VISION AND ITS FULFILLMENT. BEING THE HISTORY OF THE ORIGIN AND WORK OF THE NATIONAL VIGILANCE ASSOCIATION FOR THE SUPPRESSION OF THE WHITE SLAVE TRAFFIC. [1910]. Relates what was supposed to be a typical case of a young woman who "had answered an advertisement for a situation as companion or governess to a family abroad.... The facts were nearly always the same——the girl had been met on her arrival by an apparently very kind lady, who for the first day would study her comfort, and under that genial influence the girl had written home the satisfactory letter above referred to. After that she would be taken away from the hotel and neighborhood, cut off from communications with the outside world, and gradually led into the way of shame and sorrow, never to be heard again by those near and dear to her" (p. 20); (as editor), A ROMANCE OF PHILANTHROPY. BEING A RECORD OF SOME OF THE PRINCIPAL INCIDENTS CONNECTED WITH THE EXCEPTIONALLY SUCCESSFUL THIRTY YEARS' WORK OF THE NATIONAL VIGILANCE ASSOCIATION. 1916. Case studies. The Association, dedicated to the eradication of white slavery, was determined "to enlist in the army of those who would wage war against the men and women who, for the greed of gain, seek victims to satisfy the insatiable lust of men, of whom it might truly be said that their appetite grows with the eating" (p. 17).

10.313
Willis, William Nicholas, THE WHITE SLAVES OF LONDON, BY W.N. WILLIS... INCORPORATING APPEALS TO THE NATION BY HIS GRACE THE ARCHBISHOP OF CANTERBURY, THE LORD BISHOP OF BIRMINGHAM

AND MRS. BRAMWELL BOOTH. Boston, 1913. Gruesome stories which emphasize the dangers of the trade to the girls and to society, particularly in the spread of venereal disease. "On examination at the station the girl [white slave] was found to be in a very serious state of health, for she was suffering from an advanced state of a dreadful disease. When she regained consciousness, she was ordered to the Women's Lock Hospital, where, after much suffering, she went the way of thousands of her unfortunate class. The nurse told me her death was dreadful, her hands, neck, and body being covered with gangrene" (p. 145); **WHITE SLAVES IN A PICCADILLY FLAT.** [1915]. Purportedly written by a journalist to satisfy the curiousity of the public clamouring to know more about procuress "Queenie Gerald" and her "den of vice." She was charged with "living on the immoral earnings of young girls." Mostly in the form of "interviews."

10.314
British Social Biology Council, Joint Standing Committee of the British Society Hygiene Council and the Conference of British Missionary Societies, **TRAFFIC IN WOMEN. OFFICIAL AND NON-OFFICIAL CO-OPERATIVE ACTION IN COMBATTING THE TRAFFIC IN THE EAST. REPORT OF A CONFERENCE OF BRITISH AND INTERNATIONAL REPS.** 1934.

10.315
Scott, John William Robertson, **THE STORY OF THE PALL MALL GAZETTE.** Oxford, 1950. The GAZETTE featured editor W.T. Stead's famous expose of white slave traffic.

10.316
Turner, Ernest S., "A Flourish of Strumpets" in **ROADS TO RUIN: THE SHOCKING HISTORY OF SOCIAL REFORM.** 1950. "In 1885 W.T. Stead had run his famous exposure of the white slave traffic... and the oft-postponed Criminal Law Amendment Act had been rushed through a shocked Parliament. Until the Act was passed, the age at which a girl might consent to her seduction was 13" (pp. 207-208).

10.317
Young, A.F. and Ashton, E.T., "Moral Welfare" in **BRITISH SOCIAL WORK IN THE NINETEENTH CENTURY.** by A.F. Young and E.T. Ashton. 1956. Contains material on white slavery. "In the year 1884 there had appeared at the door of the refuge a girl of about seventeen, wearing a red silk dress. She had come up from the country to London, she said, and there had met a very nice lady, who had introduced her to a friend. They had gone with the lady, and the girl found herself virtually imprisoned. Attempts were made to seduce her, but finally she escaped to the Salvation Army" (p. 209).

10.318
British Vigilance Association and the National Committee for the Suppression of Traffic in Persons, **68TH ANNUAL REPORT. SINCE THE FOUNDATION OF THE NATIONAL VIGILANCE ASSOCIATION IN 1885.** [1955]; **72ND ANNUAL REPORT.** 1959.

10.319
Terrot, Charles, **THE MAIDEN TRIBUTE: A STUDY OF THE WHITE SLAVE TRAFFIC.** 1959. "A high percentage of them were 'broken in'——a term used in the trade to denote summary raping, followed by a period of mental conditioning which had something in common with modern brainwashing techniques. A girl would be put amongst confirmed old prostitutes whose task it was to give her compulsory sex

education and also to fill her mind with lewd horrible stories" (p. 41).

10.320
Deacon, Richard, **THE PRIVATE LIFE OF MR. GLADSTONE**. 1965. Gladstone rescued a young child from a London brothel run by Mrs. Jeffries. Girls aged three to seven were often chloroformed and raped by old men at Jeffries' brothel. Gladstone sought the enactment of age of consent legislation, and his life was subsequently threatened.

10.321
O'Callaghan, Sean, **THE WHITE SLAVE TRAFFIC**. 1965. "Prostitution and white slavery flourished in the latter half of the nineteenth century as it did at no other period of England's history.... Mrs. Josephine Butler could make a formal declaration before a board of magistrates in 1880 that, 'English, Scots, Welsh and Irish girls were being bought daily for exportation to Brussels and Paris, and there detained in the horrible slavery, and that large numbers of young girls under the age of twenty-one, many as young as twelve, had been bought or induced to go abroad and then placed in brothels; that the placeurs had received from eighteen pounds to thirty-two pounds for each girl after buying them for as little as five pounds each, and that these girls and children had no power to escape'" (p. 20).

10.322
Petrie, Glen, **A SINGULAR INIQUITY: THE CAMPAIGNS OF JOSEPHINE BUTLER**. New York, 1971. Discusses the climate of Victorian sexuality which Butler exposed. "The real profits were to be found in the exploitation of 'fresh girls' up from the country. West-End club-men would pay anything up to twenty-five guineas for a teenage virgin, and up to a hundred for the privilege of raping or tormenting a young child.... In such establishments, girls who attempted to defend themselves were strait-jacketed, strapped to their beds or simply held down by servants of the house. When fastidious clients wished to take their pleasure undisturbed by screams, the children——mostly between the ages of ten and sixteen but not infrequently much younger——were chloroformed, or drugged with 'drowsers' (a medicated snuff), or most freqently of all, were gagged with the leather thong which was employed in the armed services for those undergoing field punishment by flogging. Young girls frequently died from the combined effects of shock, mental and physical, and suffocation from the gag and the pressure of their assailant's body lying on top of them" (p. 249).

10.323
UNIVERSITY OF MICHIGAN PAPERS IN WOMEN'S STUDIES: Strauss, S., *"Raising the Victorian Woman's Consciousness: White Slavery and the Women's Movement,"* 2 (1978) 13-30. Discusses the impact on the women's movement of the crusade against white slavery: "Traumatic is not too strong a word to describe the reactions of women, shielded from such realities, to the evidence of the sexual abuse of children and the forcing of women into prostitution. It achieved a solidarity among women that the earlier attempt to expose the exploitation of what were thought to be willing prostitutes failed to do" (p. 24).

10.324
VICTORIAN STUDIES: Gorham, D., *"The 'Maiden Tribute of Modern Babylon' Re-examined: Child Prostitution and the Idea of Childhood in Late-Victorian England,"* 21 (1978) 353-379. "In much of the reform rhetoric, the young prostitutes are portrayed as sexually innocent, passive victims of individual men. This imagery of individual sin, with its corresponding possibility of individual redemption, may have been comforting to these late-Victorian middle-class reformers because it did

not threaten the images of womanhood, childhood, and family life that formed an essential part of their world view" (p. 355). Suggests that the real cause of white slavery was an exploitative economic structure whose impoverished victims had little choice.

10.325
Marchant, James, **THE MASTER PROBLEM.** 1979. Provides an overview of the white slave traffic and its regulation. "The white slave traffic is... the more or less organized relationship of the sexes outside the bonds of matrimony, a relationship which has everywhere and in all times existed, and is seemingly inevitable in numerous instances in all classes throughout the world" (n.p.).

10.326
WOMEN'S STUDIES INTERNATIONAL FORUM: Kaplan, M., *"Prostitution, Morality Crusades and Feminism: German-Jewish Feminists and the Campaign Against White Slavery,"* 5 (1982) 619-627. "This 'traffic in flesh' was condoned by large portions of society and most governments. Victorians despised prostitutes, but they used them. They and their governments dismissed the cause of prostitution—destitution——in a vast 'conspiracy of silence'" (p. 619).

* * *

2. EROTIC LITERATURE, PORNOGRAPHY, VIOLENT PORNOGRAPHY, OBSCENITY LAWS AND CENSORSHIP

10.327
THE FORCED VIRGIN; OR, UNNATURAL MOTHER. A TRUE SECRET HISTORY. 1730.

10.328
Shenstone, William, **THE SCHOOLMISTRESS.** Oxford, 1742; 1924. A poem romanticizing flagellation, a popular source of erotic stimulation and interest for many Victorians.

10.329
Richardson, Samuel, **CLARISSA; OR THE HISTORY OF A YOUNG LADY. 1747-1748.** 1747. Establishes England as the home of the Gothic horror school. Moral story of heroine's progression downhill from seduction to prison to death. At one point she dreams that her lover stabs her in a churchyard and buries her amid half-decayed bodies. Presages later Romantic period in two respects: interest in psychology of the protagonist; established a pattern of rather sadistic treatment of female characters, which continued in both pornographic and pulp literature.

10.330
VARIOUS RECOLLECTIONS OF DOMESTIC SCENES AND LITTLE LOVE AFFAIRS; WHICH OCCURRED IN MY FAMILY. COMPILED AND WRITTEN FOR MY DEARLY BELOVED HUSBAND AT MARTINIQUE. BY MADAME MARIE DE T... 1748; 1844; 1863; *also printed as:* **DOMESTIC DISCIPLINE; OR, EVERY ONE TO HIS TASTE.** n.d.

10.331
Cleland, John, **FANNY HILL, OR MEMOIRS OF A WOMAN OF PLEASURE.**
[1748-1749]; New York, 1963. Famous English pornographic novel that describes
the experiences of a "high class" prostitute who later "repents," marries, and raises a
family.

10.332
**SATAN'S HARVEST HOME OR THE PRESENT STATE OF WHORECRAFT,
ADULTERY, FORNICATION, PROCURING, PIMPING, SODOMY, AND THE
GAME AT FLATTS, (ILLUSTRATED BY AN AUTHENTIC AND ENTER-
TAINING STORY) AND OTHER SATANIC WORKS, DAILY PROPAGATED IN
THIS GOOD PROTESTANT KINGDOM... TO WHICH IS ADDED, THE PETIT
MAITRE, A POEM, BY A LADY OF DISTINCTION.** 1749. "Most women, indeed,
let them be ever so fully resolved to comply, make as great a show of Resistance as
they can conveniently counterfeit; and this the sex would palm upon the World for
a kind of innate modesty. Not to mention the actual Pleasure a woman receives in
struggling, it is a Justification of her, in the eye of the man, and a kind of Salvo to
her Honour and Conscience, that she never did fully comply, but was in a manner
forc'd into it. This is the plain Reason, why most women refuse to surrender upon
Treaty, and why they delight so much in being storm'd" (p. 8).

10.333
**THE PLEASURES OF LOVE. CONTAINING A VARIETY OF ENTERTAINING
PARTICULARS AND CURIOSITIES, IN THE CABINET OF VENUS.** 1755.

10.334
THE AMOUROUS FRIARS: OR, THE INTRIGUES OF A CONVENT. 1759.

10.335
**DID YOU EVER SEE SUCH DAMNED STUFF? OR, SO-MUCH-THE-BETTER.
A STORY WITHOUT HEAD OR TAIL, WIT OR HUMOUR.** 1760.

10.336
**THE BATTLE OF VENUS. A DESCRIPTIVE DISSERTATION OF THE
VARIOUS MODES OF ENJOYMENT: COMPRISING PHILOSOPHICAL
DISCUSSION OF THE MOST INTERESTING AND AFFECTING QUESTIONS.
DEMONSTRATIVE THAT THE LOOSEST THOUGHTS AND SENSATIONS MAY
BE CONVEYED WITHOUT AN EXPRESSION VERGING ON IMMODESTY.** 1760;
also printed as: **THE BATTLE OF VENUS. A DESCRIPTIVE DISSERTATION
ON THE VARIOUS MODES OF ENJOYMENT OF THE FEMALE SEX, AS
PRACTISED IN DIFFERENT COUNTRIES, WITH SOME CURIOUS
INFORMATION ON THE RESOURCES OF LUST, LECHERY, AND LICEN-
TIOUSNESS, TO REVIVE THE DROOPING FACULTIES AND STRENGTHEN
THE VOLUPTUOUS AND EXHAUSTED. FROM THE FRENCH.** [1850-60].
Comments on the best positions for intercourse; claims that sex with a virgin is "the
acme of sexual delight" and also that women enjoy intercourse more than men since
they are subject to the pain of pregnancy and delivery.

10.337
Borewell, Pego (pseud. for John Pego), **AN ESSAY ON WOMEN.** 1761; 1763; *rpt.
as:* **AN ESSAY ON WOMEN AND OTHER PIECES... TO WHICH ARE ADDED
EPIGRAMS AND MISCELLANEOUS POEMS NOW FIRST COLLECTED.** 1871.
Privately printed. A parody of Pope's ESSAY ON MAN. Assumes sexual equality
between men and women. "Prick, cunt and bollocks in convulsions hurl'd/ And now
a hymen burst, and now a world" (p. 19).

10.338
THE HISTORY OF THE YOUNG HUMAN HEART OR, THE ADVENTURES OF A YOUNG GENTLEMAN. 1769; *rpt. as:* MEMOIRS OF A MAN OF PLEASURE; OR, THE AMOURS, INTRIGUES, AND ADVENTURES, OF SIR CHARLES MANLY... 1827.

10.339
THE AMOURS, ADVENTURES, AND INTRIGUES OF TOM JOHNSON. WRITTEN BY HIMSELF. 1770; rev. rpt., 1870.

10.340
THE AUTHENTIC MEMOIRS OF THE COUNTESS DE BARRE THE FRENCH KING'S MISTRESS, CAREFULLY COLLATED FROM A MANUSCRIPT IN THE POSSESSION OF THE DUCHESS OF VILLEROY, BY SIR FRANCIS N_____. 2nd ed., 1771; 1772; 1775; 1777; *rpt. as:* THE LOVER'S FESTIVAL, OR MELTING MOMENTS. Compilation of 24 letters which detail the adventures of Emily Palmer. Supposedly written by a man in Paris to a friend in England.

10.341
Melmoth, Courteney, THE PUPIL OF PLEASURE: OR, THE NEW SYSTEM ILLUSTRATED... 1776.

10.342
EXHIBITION OF FEMALE FLAGELLANTS IN THE MODEST AND INCONTINENT WORLD. PROVING FROM INDUBITABLE FACTS THAT A NUMBER OF LADIES TAKE A SECRET PLEASURE IN WHIPPING THEIR OWN AND CHILDREN COMMITTED TO THEIR CARE; AND THAT THEIR PASSION FOR EXERCISING AND FEELING THE PLEASURE OF A BIRCH-ROD, FROM OBJECTS OF THEIR CHOICE, OF BOTH SEXES, IS TO THE FULL AS PREDOMINANT AS THAT OF MANKIND. NOW FIRST PUBLISHED, FROM AUTHENTIC ANECDOTES, FRENCH AND ENGLISH, FOUND IN A LADY'S CABINET. 1777; [18??]; PART THE SECOND OF THE EXHIBITION OF FEMALE FLAGELLANTS... 1785.

10.343
Buckle, Henry Thomas, LIBRARY ILLUSTRATIVE OF SOCIAL PROGRESS. EXHIBITION OF FEMALE FLAGELLANTS. 1777.

10.344
NOCTURNAL REVELS OR, THE HISTORY OF KING'S PLACE, AND OTHER MODERN NUNNERIES. CONTAINING THEIR MYSTERIES, DEVOTIONS, AND SACRIFICES. COMPRISING ALSO, THE ANCIENT AND PRESENT STATE OF PROMISCUOUS GALLANTRY: WITH THE PORTRAITS OF THE MOST CELEBRATED DEMIREPS AND COURTEZANS OF THE PERIOD: AS WELL AS SKETCHES OF THEIR PROFESSIONAL AND OCCASIONAL ADMIRERS. BY A MONK OF THE ORDER OF ST. FRANCIS. 2 vols. 1779.

10.345
A CABINET OF AMOROUS CURIOSITIES. IN THREE TALES. HIGHLY CALCULATED TO PLEASE THE VOTARIES OF VENUS. 1786. Includes "The Village Bull," "Memoirs of a Feather-Bed" and "Adventures of a Droll One."

10.346
DIALOGUE BETWEEN A WOMAN AND A VIRGIN. 1786.

10.347
Birch, R. (pseud.), **VENUS SCHOOLMISTRESS; OR, BIRCHEN SPORTS**. 1788; rpt., 1898. Flagellation manual. Divides male devotees into three groups: masochists, sadists, and voyeurs.

10.348
de Sade, Marquis A.F., **JUSTINE, OU LES MALHEURS DE LA VERTU**. 2 vols. Paris, 1791; *also printed as:* **THE COMPLETE JUSTINE, PHILOSOPHY IN THE BEDROOM AND OTHER WRITINGS**. trans. by Richard Seaver and Austryn Wainhouse. New York, 1965; **ALINE ET VALCOUR OU LE ROMAN PHILOSOPHIQUE**. Paris, 1792; Brussels, 1883; **LA PHILOSOPHIE DANS LE BOUDOIR**. 2 vols. Paris, 1795; **JULIETTE OU LES PROSPERITES DU VICE**. 1796; 1797; trans. by Austryn Wainhouse. New York, 1968; **LA NOUVELLE JUSTINE**. Paris, 1797; **ZOLOE ET SES DEUX ACOLYTES, OU QUELQUES DECADES DE LA VIE DE TROIS JOLIES FEMMES**. Paris, 1800; 1912; **LES CRIMES DE L'AMOUR**. Paris, 1881; 1927; trans. by Lowell Blair. New York, 1964; **LES 120 JOURNEES DE SODAME OU L'ECOLE DU LIBERTINAGE**. [Paris], 1904; ed. by Maurice Heine. Paris, 1930; trans. by Pieralessandro Cascavini. Paris, 1954; **SELECTED LETTERS**. trans. by W.J. Strachman. 1965; **OEUVRES COMPLETES**. 16 vols. Paris, 1966-1967; **MARQUIS DE SADE: THE MAN AND HIS AGE**. trans. by James Bruce. Newark, 1931; New York, 1958. —*see also:* de Beauvoir, Simone, **THE MARQUIS DE SADE**. 1953. Analyzes the role of women in de Sade's writings. His pornographic imagination reveals a sensibility not dissimilar from some Victorian pornography. "We may also wonder whether Sade did not hate women because he saw in them his double rather than his complement and because there was nothing he could get from them.... Sade felt himself to be feminine, and he resented the fact that women were not the males he really desired" (pp. 36-37); Gorer, Geoffrey, **THE LIFE AND IDEAS OF THE MARQUIS DE SADE**. 1953. "La Nouvelle Justine is above everything an attempt to explain why the revolution failed.... His conclusion is that by far the greater number of people desire to hurt and oppress their fellows.... To illustrate this point he allows his characters to do whatever their imaginations suggest.... They mostly tend to torture, cruelty and murder.... The people who imagine that de Sade intended Justine or Juliette to be incitements to cruelty show extraordinarily little insight" (pp. 189-90); Chanover, E. Pierre, **THE MARQUIS DE SADE: A BIBLIOGRAPHY**. New Jersey, 1973; Hayman, Ronald, **DE SADE: A CRITICAL BIOGRAPHY**. New York, 1978. Investigates the origin of Sade's taste for flagellation and argues that "le vice anglaise" actually originated in England; **MOTHER JONES**: Dworkin, A., *"The Prophet of Perversion: A New Reading of the Marquis de Sade,"* 5 (1980) 24-60. Recounts Sade's real-life abuses of women and his various imprisonments. It was the class of old, aristocratic libertines that presided over Sade's sexual hell and everyone socially inferior to them became fodder for their fantasies. "Wives, daughters and mothers are particularly singled out for humiliation, ridicule and contempt. Servants of both sexes and female prostitutes are the main population of the abused, dismembered, executed" (p. 58).

10.349
THE BAGNIO MISCELLANY CONTAINING THREE INTERESTING DIA-LOGUES BETWEEN A JEW AND A FEMALE CHRISTIAN. THE ADVENTURES OF MISS LAIS LOVECOCK, AT MISS TWIG'S BOARDING SCHOOL. THE FORCE OF INSTINCT, A DROLL STORY, DEVELOPING AN ODD CONTRIVANCE TO FACILITATE THE GROWTH OF THE 'LANUGO' ON THE 'LABIA' OF A YOUNG LADY. EROTIC ANECDOTES; MARIA ANTOINETTE, QUEEN OF FRANCE—THE WIDOW AND THE PARSON'S BULL, OR THE

BENEFIT OF FLAGELLATION. 1792. Illustrated.

10.350
THE CHERUB: OR, GUARDIAN OF FEMALE INNOCENCE. EXPOSING THE ARTS OF BOARDING SCHOOLS, HIRED FORTUNE TELLERS, CORRUPT MILLINERS, APPARENT LADIES OF FASHION. 1792.

10.351
ELEMENTS OF TUITION, AND MODES OF PUNISHMENT. IN LETTERS, FROM MADEMOISELLE DUBOULEAU, A CELEBRATED PARISIAN TUTORESS, TO MISS SMART-BUM, GOVERNESS OF A YOUNG LADIES' BOARDING SCHOOL AT-. WITH SOME SECRETS DEVELOPED OF MOCK TUTORS, WHO HAVE TAKEN A DELIGHT IN ADMINISTERING BIRCH DISCIPLINE TO THEIR FEMALE PUPILS. 1794.

10.352
VOLUPTUOUS CONFESSIONS OF A FRENCH LADY OF FASHION. [18??]. — *see also:* Gay, Peter, THE BOURGEOIS EXPERIENCE FROM VICTORIA TO FREUD: THE EDUCATION OF THE SENSES. 1984. "Pornographic climaxes are moments of uncontrollable impulsiveness. Protagonists will not even take the time to undress to slake their sexual thirst; and they will brave the risk of discovery, not just to enhance the erotic thrill of their coupling, but simply because they cannot brook delay" (p. 374).

10.353
Euston, Arabella, LOVER'S LOOKING GLASS. [1800]. Account of a Devonshire milkmaid's affair.

10.354
SCENES IN THE SERAGLIO BY THE AUTHOR OF THE LUSTY TURK. [1820-1830]; [1855-1860]. Story of an abducted virgin, Adelaide, who is sold by the corsair Tiek to a Turkish Sultan.

10.355
THE LIFE OF MISS LOUISA SELBY. BEING THE SECOND PART OF THE ADVENTURES, INTRIGUES, AND AMOURS OF A LADY'S MAID. WRITTEN BY HERSELF. NEVER BEFORE PUBLISHED. EMBELLISHED WITH EIGHT ENGRAVINGS. 1822; *also titled:* THE ADVENTURES, INTRIGUES, AND AMOURS OF A LADY'S MAID! 1822. Seduced by her father, sold by her mother, Louisa travels to France, Italy and England, "employed" by various families to satisfy their sexual needs.

10.356
THE CRIMES OF THE CLERGY, OR THE PILLARS OF PRIEST-CRAFT SHAKEN... 1823.

10.357
HOW TO MAKE LOVE OR, THE ART OF MAKING LOVE IN MORE WAYS THAN ONE, EXEMPLIFIED IN A SERIES OF LETTERS BETWEEN TWO COUSINS. 1823; *printed with a sequel as:* HOW TO RAISE LOVE; OR THE ART OF MAKING LOVE, IN MORE WAYS THAN ONE; BEING THE VOLUPTUOUS HISTORY AND SECRET CORRESPONDENCE OF TWO YOUNG LADIES, (COUSINS), HANDSOME AND ACCOMPLISHED. MINUTELY DETAILING THEIR FIRST SEXUAL EMOTIONS; THEIR FEELINGS AT ITS INTRODUCTION; AND THEIR DELICIOUS ENJOYMENT OF THE

ENCHANTING REVELRIES OF LOVE. 1848; 1865.

10.358
Coates, Henry, THE BRITISH DON JUAN; BEING A NARRATIVE OF THE SINGULAR AMOURS, ENTERTAINING ADVENTURES, REMARKABLE TRAVELS ETC. OF THE HON. EDWARD W. MONTAGUE, SON OF THE CELEBRATED LADY MARY WORTLEY MONTAGUE. 1823.

10.359
THE MODERN RAKE OR, THE LIFE AND ADVENTURES OF SIR EDWARD WALFORD: CONTAINING A CURIOUS AND VOLUPTUOUS HISTORY OF HIS LUSCIOUS INTRIGUES, WITH NUMEROUS WOMEN OF FASHION, HIS LAUGHABLE FAUX PAS, FEATS OF GALLANTRY, DEBAUCHERY, DISSIPATION AND CONCUBISM! HIS NUMEROUS RAPES, SEDUCTIONS AND AMATORY SCRAPES. MEMOIRS OF THE BEAUTIFUL COURTEZANS WITH WHOM HE LIVED; WITH SOME TICKLISH SONGS, ANECDOTES, POETRY, ETC. 1824.

10.360
THE VOLUPTUARIAN CABINET: BEING A FAITHFUL REPRINT OF SUCH FACETIOUS FACTS AS HAVE BECOME SCARCE... 1824.

10.361
THE ACCOMPLISHED WHORE. TRANSLATED FROM THE PUTTANA ERRANTE OF PIETRO ARETINO BY MARY WILSON, SPINSTER. 1827.

10.362
THE FESTIVAL OF THE PASSIONS. OR, VOLUPTUOUS MISCELLANY. BY AN AMATEUR. 1828. Three separate stories.

10.363
THE LUSTFUL TURK. PART THE FIRST. A HISTORY FOUNDED ON FACTS, CONTAINING AN INTERESTING NARRATIVE OF THE CRUEL FATE OF TWO YOUNG ENGLISH LADIES, NAMED SYLVIA CAREY, AND EMILY BARLOW. FULLY EXPLAINING HOW EMILY BARLOW AND HER SERVANT, ELIZA GIBBS, ON THEIR PASSAGE TO INDIA, WERE TAKEN PRISONER BY AN ALGERINE PIRATE, AND MADE A PRESENT TO THE DEY OF ALGIERS; WHO, ON THE VERY NIGHT OF THEIR ARRIVAL DEBAUCHED EMILY— CONTAINING ALSO, EVERY PARTICULAR OF THE ARTFUL PLANS LAID BY THE DEY, TO GET POSSESSION OF THE PERSON OF SYLVIA CAREY— HOW HE EFFECTED HIS PURPOSE—WITH THE PARTICULARS OF HER BECOMING A VICTIM TO HIS LIBIDINOUS DESIRES. WHICH RECITAL IS ALSO INTERSPERSED WITH THE HISTORIES OF SEVERAL OTHER LADIES CONFINED IN DEY'S HAREM. ONE OF WHICH GIVES AN ACCOUNT OF THE HORRID PRACTICES THEN CARRYING ON IN SEVERAL FRENCH AND ITALIAN CONVENTS BY A SOCIETY OF MONKS, ESTABLISHED AT ALGIERS, UNDER PRETENCE OF REDEEMING CHRISTIAN SLAVES; BUT WHO, IN REALITY, CARRIED ON AN INFAMOUS TRAFFIC IN YOUNG GIRLS.——ALSO AN ACCOUNT OF THE SUFFERINGS OF ELIZA GIBBS, FROM THE FLOGGING PROPENSITIES OF THE DEY ON TUNIS... THE WHOLE COMPILED FROM ORIGINAL LETTERS... 1828; 1860; *rpt. as:* THE LUSTFUL TURK; OR SCENES IN THE HAREM OF AN EASTERN POTENTATE, FAITHFULLY AND VIVIDLY DEPICTED IN A SERIES OF LETTERS FROM A YOUNG AND BEAUTIFUL ENGLISH LADY TO HER COUSIN IN ENGLAND——THE FULL PARTICULARS OF HER RAVISHMENT,

OF HER COMPLETE ABANDONMENT TO ALL THE SALACIOUS TASTES OF THE TURKS, DESCRIBED WITH THAT ZEST AND SIMPLICITY, WHICH ALWAYS GIVES GUARANTEE FOR ITS AUTHENTICITY. 1864. —*see also:* Marcus, Steven, "The World of Fiction" in THE OTHER VICTORIANS. A STUDY OF SEXUALITY AND PORNOGRAPHY IN MID-NINETEENTH-CENTURY ENGLAND. by Steven Marcus. New York, 1964; 1965; 1966. The sexual fantasies in the novel "have largely to do with the sexuality of domination, and with that conception of male sexuality in which the aggressive and sadistic components almost exclusively prevail" (p. 211). In each story a prideful virgin, through beating, flogging, and rape, is molded into the responsive instrument of male desire.

10.364
MEMOIRS OF ROSA BELLEFILLE OR, A DELICIOUS BANQUET OF AMOUROUS DELIGHTS! DEDICATED TO THE GODDESS OF VOLUPTUOUS PLEASURE AND HER SOUL-ENAMOURED VOTARIES. 1828; 1865. Narrated by Rosa, a nymphomaniac.

10.365
THE VIRGIN'S OATH; OR THE FATE OF SONTAG. AN HISTORICAL DRAMA, IN TWO ACTS. [1828-30].

10.366
THE BED-FELLOWS: OR YOUNG MISSES MANUEL [SIC] IN SIX CONFI-DENTIAL DIALOGUES BETWEEN TWO BUDDING BEAUTIES, WHO HAVE JUST FLEDGED THEIR TEENS. ADAPTED TO THE CAPACITY OF EVERY LOVING VIRGIN WHO HAS WIT ENOUGH IN HER LITTLE FINGER TO KNOW THE VALUE OF THE REST. [1830]; rpt., 1860.

10.367
THE SCHOOL-FELLOWS OR, YOUNG LADIES GUIDE TO LOVE. IN A SERIES OF LETTERS. INCLUDING SOME CURIOUS ANECDOTES OF FLAGELLATION. TO WHICH IS ADDED, THE SINGULAR AND DIVERTING HISTORY OF THE LIFE AND DEATH OF A GODEMICHE, ENRICHED WITH FINE ENGRAVINGS. [1830]. Stories of birching and masturbation recounted in nine letters between two young women.

10.368
THE WOMAN OF PLEASURE'S POCKET COMPANION WITH ENGRAVINGS. rpt., Paris, 1830.

10.369
LeDuck, Madame, THE SEDUCING CARDINAL, OR, ISABELLA PETO. A TALE FOUNDED ON FACTS. 1830.

10.370
Spanker, Colonel, EXPERIMENTAL LITERATURE... ON THE EXCITING AND VOLUPTUOUS PLEASURES TO BE DERIVED FROM CRUSHING AND HUMILIATING THE SPIRIT OF A BEAUTIFUL AND MODEST YOUNG LADY; AS DELIVERED BY HIM IN THE ASSEMBLY ROOM OF THE SOCIETY OF ARISTOCRATIC FLAGELLANTS. 1836. Privately printed.

10.371
AWFUL DISCLOSURES BY MARIA MONK, OF THE HOTEL DIEU NUNNERY OF MONTREAL: WITH AN APPENDIX... rev. by J.J. Slocum. 2nd ed., 1837.

10.372
EVELINE; OR, THE AMOURS AND ADVENTURES OF A LADY OF FASHION, WRITTEN BY HERSELF. [1840]. Depicts the sexual episodes of a young woman who sleeps with men of an inferior class. When she finally marries a British baronet, he "allows" her to have relations with other men.

10.373
EXQUISITE: 1842 to 1844; vols. 1-3. Pornographic periodical.

10.374
Forberg, F.K., **MANUAL OF CLASSICAL EROTOLOGY.** Manchester, 1844.

10.375
Rowlandson, Thomas, **PRETTY LITTLE GAMES FOR YOUNG LADIES AND GENTLEMEN. WITH PICTURES OF GOOD OLD ENGLISH SPORTS AND PASTIMES.** 1845. Collection of ten erotic etchings with verse. —*see also:* Fryer, Peter, ed., **FORBIDDEN BOOKS OF THE VICTORIANS. HENRY SPENCER ASHBEE'S BIBLIOGRAPHIES OF EROTICA...** by Henry Spencer Ashbee. 1970. See pp. 152-172 for a descriptive list of Rowlandson's erotic or obscene etchings and drawings; Von Meier, Kurt, compiler, **THE FORBIDDEN EROTICA OF THOMAS ROWLANDSON 1756-1827.** 1970. An Academy painter, Rowlandson created these erotic paintings and etchings. Text accompanying the reproduction is by Von Meier.

10.376
THE LIFE, INTRIGUES, AND ADVENTURES OF AN AMOUROUS QUAKER; DEVELOPING THE MOST CURIOUS SCENES OF INTRIGUES, SEDUCTIONS AND AMOURS EVER OFFERED TO THE PUBLIC. [1848].

10.377
LA ROSE D'AMOUR OR, THE ADVENTURES OF A GENTLEMAN IN SEARCH OF PLEASURE. 2 vols. Philadelphia, 1849; 1852; rpt., 1864; *also rpt. in:* **PEARL:** n.d. Mainly a narrative of a young, wealthy Frenchman who abducts virgins and rapes them in his chateau.

10.378
Couture, Thomas, **A YOUNG BATHER.** 1849. Sensual photographs of children.

10.379
ABISHAG; A LUSCIOUS TALE OF A SUCCESSFUL PHYSIOLOGICAL SEARCH AFTER REJUVENESCENCE, FULLY DISCLOSING THE SECRET OF THE ONLY NATURAL AND TRUE ELIXIR CAPABLE OF EFFECTING SUCH A DESIRABLE NECESSITY. BY DAVID II. Jerusalem, 1851.

10.380
CREMORNE: 1851. Victorian pornographic magazine.

10.381
THE AMOURS OF SANGFROID AND EULALIA: BEING THE INTRIGUES AND AMOURS OF A JESUIT AND A NUN; DEVELOPING THE PROGRESS OF SEDUCTION OF A HIGHLY EDUCATED YOUNG LADY, WHO BECAME, BY THE FOULEST SOPHISTRY AND TREACHERY, THE VICTIM OF DEBAUCHERY AND LIBERTINISM. New York, 1854.

10.382
Thompson, George, THE BRIDAL CHAMBER, AND ITS MYSTERIES: OR, LIFE
AT OUR FASHIONABLE HOTELS... New York, 1856.

10.383
[Bertram, James G.], THE MERRY ORDER OF SAINT BRIDGET. PERSONAL
RECOLLECTIONS OF THE USE OF THE ROD BY MARGARET ANSOM. York,
1857.

10.384
AN ACCOUNT OF A YOUNG WOMAN'S EXPERIMENTS IN DEBAUCHERY.
[186?]. Illustrated.

10.385
THE ADVENTURES OF SIR HENRY LOVEALL, IN A TOUR THROUGH
ENGLAND, IRELAND, SCOTLAND AND WALES. 2 vols. 1860.

10.386
THE CONFESSIONS OF A VOLUPTUOUS YOUNG LADY OF HIGH RANK.
DISCLOSING HER SECRET LONGINGS AND PRIVATE AMOURS BEFORE
MARRIAGE. FORMING A CURIOUS PICTURE OF FASHIONABLE LIFE AND
REFINED SENSUALITY [TO WHICH IS ADDED] TEN YEARS OF THE LIFE OF
A COURTEZAN; OR, THE MEMOIRS OF MADEMOISELLE CELESTINA.
DETAILING HER FIRST LESSONS IN LUST, HER SEDUCTION, AND
VOLUPTUOUS LIFE, THE PIQUANT PENCHANTS OF HER VARIOUS
LOVERS, ETC, ETC, ETC, FORMING A PICTURE OF SENSUALITY SELDOM
OFFERED TO THE PUBLIC. [1860].

10.387
INTRIGUES IN A BOARDING SCHOOL; OR, THE ADVENTURES OF DR.
PHOOKALL, WITH HIS SERVANT GIRL... [1860].

10.388
THE FESTIVAL OF LOVE; OR, REVELS AT THE FOUNT OF VENUS,
DISCLOSED IN A SERIES OF LUSCIOUS DIALOGUES AND AMATORY
LETTERS BETWEEN FLORA AND THE VOLUPTUOUS ALDABELLA. BY THE
PRINCESS PICCOLOMINI... 1860.

10.389
THE PHILOSOPHICAL THERESA OR MEMOIRS OF A GAY GIRL. [c. 1860].
[trans. by J.C. Reddie]. English edition of a French work.

10.390
Reade, W. Winwood, LIBERTY HALL OXON. [1860]; *reviewed in:* SATURDAY
REVIEW: 9 (1860) 84. Calls the book "the filthiest... that has been issued by a
respectable English publisher" (p. 84).

10.391
BOUDOIR: A MAGAZINE OF SCANDAL, FACETIAE, ETC.: 1860; nos. 1-6.
Reprinted by Grove Press, New York, 1971.

10.392
MYSTERIES OF FLAGELLATION OR, A HISTORY OF THE SECRET
CEREMONIES OF THE SOCIETY OF FLAGELLANTS. THE SAINTLY
PRACTICE OF THE BIRCH! ST. FRANCIS WHIPPED BY THE DEVIL! HOW

TO SUBDUE THE PASSIONS, THE ART OF FLOGGING! WITH MANY CURIOUS ANECDOTES OF THE PREVALENCE OF THIS PECULIAR PASTIME IN ALL NATIONS AND EPOCHS WHETHER SAVAGE OR CIVILIZED. 1863. Provides a history of flagellation and describes some of the well known London houses of flagellation.

10.393
AMOURS OF A MODEST MAN BY A BACHELOR. 1864. Describes the adventures between a man, a pretty widow, and Mary, the maid, in a New York boarding house.

10.394
THE LADIES' TELL TALE OR, DECAMERON OF PLEASURE. A RECOLLECTION OF AMOUROUS TALES, AS RELATED BY A PARTY OF YOUNG FRIENDS TO ONE ANOTHER. 1865. Stories of virgin boys and girls and their initiations to sex. While the girls are seduced by older men, the boys are seduced by older women.

10.395
Sellon, Edward (pseud. for William Potter), **THE NEW EPICUREAN.** 1865; **THE ROMANCE OF LUST.** 1873. Includes details of incestuous relationships; **THE NEW EPICUREAN; OR, THE DELIGHTS OF SEX, FACETIOUSLY AND PHILOSOPHICALLY CONSIDERED, IN GRAPHIC LETTER ADDRESSED TO YOUNG LADIES OF QUALITY.** 1865. Although the title page is dated 1740, it is generally acknowledged that Sellon authored this book; **PHOEBE KISSAGEN; OR, THE REMARKABLE ADVENTURES, SCHEMES, WILES AND DEVILRIES OF UNE MAQUERELLE; BEING A SEQUEL TO THE NEW EPICUREAN.** 1866; **THE UPS AND DOWNS OF LIFE. A FRAGMENT.** 1867. Story of an English captain stationed in India, where he has sex with both European and native women.

10.396
LASCIVIOUS GEMS SET TO SUIT EVERY FANCY, BY SEVERAL HANDS. 1866. Accounts of nymphomania, prostitution, rape, "open" marriage, flagellation, oral sex, necrophilia, and intercourse.

10.397
THE NEW LADIES' TICKLER; OR THE ADVENTURES OF LADY LOVESPORT AND THE AUDACIOUS HARRY. 1866.

10.398
NUNNERY TALES OR CRUISING UNDER FALSE COLOURS: A TALE OF LOVE AND LUST. 3 vols. 1866; 1867; 1868. Adventures of a young man disguised as a woman who enters a convent and sleeps with his aunt, the mother superior. He is later aided by her in sleeping with every nun there.

10.399
THE YOUTHFUL ADVENTURER DEPICTING THE CAREER OF A YOUNG MAN AMONG THE FAIR SEX—WITH MANY VARIOUS CHOICE ANECDOTES OF THE WAYS OF INDULGING THE LUSTFUL PASSIONS, BOTH IN MAN AND WOMAN, FORMING A GUIDE TO YOUNG AND OLD IN THEIR PURSUIT OF PLEASURE. 1866.

10.400
Reade, Charles, **GRIFFITH GAUNT.** 1866; "The Prurient Prude" in **REAPIANA.** by Charles Reade. 1883. ——*see also:* St. John-Stevas, Norman, **OBSCENITY AND**

THE LAW. 1956. THE ROUND TABLE "had called the book indecent and immoral and opined that 'the modesty and purity of women could not survive its perusal'" (p. 56).

10.401
Campbell, James, **THE ADVENTURES OF A SCHOOL-BOY OR THE FREAKS OF YOUTHFUL PASSION.** 1866. Depicts the "seduction" of two young girls by two Eton students; **THE AMATORY EXPERIENCES OF A SURGEON.** Moscow, 1881. —*see also:* Marcus, Steven, "The World of Fiction" in **THE OTHER VICTORIANS. A STUDY OF SEXUALITY AND PORNOGRAPHY IN MID-NINETEENTH CENTURY ENGLAND.** by Steven Marcus. New York, 1964; 1965; 1966. Argues that the fantasies concerning seminal fluid that abound in this work were a reaction against the idea that emission was a waste of a finite resource. "This is demonstrated most clearly in that image which I take to be the final, or most inclusive, form of this particular notion: a man and woman, reversed upon each other, sucking away, 'spending' and swallowing each other's juices.... Intake and outake are beautifully balanced; production is plentiful, but nothing is lost, wasted or spent, since the product is consumed only to produce more of the raw material by which the system is sustained. The primitive dream of capitalism is fulfilled in the primitive dream of the body" (pp. 243-244).

10.402
THE VICTIM OF LUST OR SCENES IN THE LIFE OF ROSA FIELDING. DEPICTING THE CRIMES AND FOLLIES OF HIGH LIFE AND THE DISSIPATION AND DEBAUCHERIES OF THE DAY. 1867. Story of a farmer's daughter who is seduced by a gentleman. ——*see also:* Marcus, Steven, "The World of Fiction" in **THE OTHER VICTORIANS. A STUDY OF SEXUALITY AND PORNOGRAPHY IN MID-NINETEENTH-CENTURY ENGLAND.** by Steven Marcus. New York, 1964; 1965; 1966. The novel expresses the fantasy of female ejaculation, a theme that recurs in more modern pornography. "Its universality and persistence indicate how unflagging is the need among men to deny the existence of two sexes" (p. 233).

10.403
INTRIGUES AND CONFESSIONS OF A BALLET GIRL: DISCLOSING STARTLING AND VOLUPTUOUS SCENES BEFORE AND BEHIND THE CURTAIN... AND A FULL DISCLOSURE OF THE SECRET AND AMATORY DOINGS IN THE DRESSING ROOM... BY ONE WHO HAS HAD HER SHARE. [1868-1870].

10.404
Cooper, William M. (pseud. for James Glass Bertram), **FLAGELLATION AND FLAGELLANTS. A HISTORY OF THE ROD IN ALL COUNTRIES FROM THE EARLIEST PERIOD TO THE PRESENT TIME.** 1870; 1873.

10.405
THE QUINTESSENCE OF BIRCH DISCIPLINE. A SEQUENCE TO THE ROMANCE OF CHASTISEMENT. 1870. Privately printed. Although one of the main characters is named Miss Martinet, H.S. Ashbee claims that the author is not the same author of romance, etc.

10.406
PRIVATE RECREATIONS, OR THE UPS AND DOWNS OF LIFE. BY ONE WHO HAS BEEN BEHIND THE SCENES, AND TAKEN PART IN THE PERFORMANCE. Belfast, 1870.

10.407
Society for Promoting Useful Knowledge, CYTHERA'S HYMNAL; OR, FLASKES
FROM THE FORESKIN. A COLLECTION OF SONGS, POEMS, NURSERY
RHYMES, QUIDDITIES, ETC., ETC. NEVER BEFORE PUBLISHED. Oxford,
1870.

10.408
Stock, St. George H., THE ROMANCE OF CHASTISEMENT OR REVELATIONS
OF THE SCHOOL AND BEDROOM. BY AN EXPERT. 1870. Portrays women as
taking enjoyment in both chastising and being chastised. Describes the sexual
undertakings of a Miss Martinet, headmistress of a girl's boarding school, and her
pleasure in flogging her pupils.

10.409
THE ROMANCE OF LUST OR, EARLY EXPERIENCES. 1873. Describes the
carnal activities of a young man noted for his endurance. Scenes of flagellation and
incest are frequent.

10.410
LETTERS FROM A FRIEND IN PARIS. 1874. Detailed descriptions of sodomy and
incest.

10.411
Chiniquy, Pere, THE PRIEST, THE WOMAN AND THE CONFESSIONAL. 1874.

10.412
CURIOSITIES OF FLAGELLATION. A SERIES OF INCIDENTS AND FACTS
COLLECTED BY AN AMATEUR FLAGELLANT. 5 vols. 1875.

10.413
THE NAMELESS CRIME, A DIALOGUE ON STAYS, UNDUE CURIOSITY, THE
DOLL'S WEDDING, THE WAY TO PEEL, THE VAIL AND THE STIFF DREAM.
1875.

10.414
Besant, Annie, IS THE BIBLE INDICTABLE? 1877. Essay questions what
constitutes obscenity and argues that even classical art and the Bible may be ruled
obscene. Concludes that the court's prerogative in establishing criteria for obscenity
is merely another form of censorship. Besant published the essay after being
arrested for distributing "obscene" literature—pamphlets on contraceptive
techniques.

10.415
Fraxi, Pisanus (pseud. for Henry Spencer Ashbee), INDEX LIBRORUM
PROHIBITORUM. 1877; CENTURIA LIBRORUM ABSCONDITORUM. 1879;
CATENA LIBRORUM TACENDORUM. 1885; all three vols. *rpt. in:* FORBIDDEN
BOOKS OF THE VICTORIANS: HENRY SPENCER ASHBEE'S BIBLIO-
GRAPHIES OF EROTICA. ed. by Peter Fryer. 1970. "Improper books, however
useful to the student, or dear to the collector, are not 'virginibus puerisque'; they
should, I consider be used with caution even by the mature; they should be looked
upon as poisons, and treated as such; should be (so to say) distinctly and treated as
such; should be (so to say) distinctly labelled, and only confided to those who
understand their potency, and are capable of rightly using them" (p. 19). Lists many
books anonymously published and some undated and privately printed. Brief

descriptions accompany each entry; MY SECRET LIFE. 11 vols. Amsterdam, [1888-1894]; rpt., New York, 1966; *also titled:* WALTER. THE ENGLISH CASANOVA. A PRESENTATION OF HIS UNIQUE MEMOIRS 'MY SECRET LIFE.' ed. by William Eberhard Kronhausen and Phyllis Kronhausen. New York, 1967. Editors note, with satisfaction, that Walter's 1,200 women are not pallid, weak, and sexless but are "rather lusty, sexy, responsive females, ready to meet Walter's approaches at least half way-and not always for financial gain either" (p. 42). *——see also:* Marcus, Steven, "Pisanus Fraxi, Pornographer Royal" in THE OTHER VICTORIANS: A STUDY OF SEXUALITY AND PORNOGRAPHY IN MID-NINETEENTH-CENTURY ENGLAND. New York, 1964; 1965; 1966. Concludes that for Ashbee what began as an investigation of a literary genre became a "propaganda of reality." He began to project male sexual fantasies onto the behavior of women; "The Secret Life——I" and "The Secret Life——II" in THE OTHER VICTORIANS, ETC. Concerning MY SECRET LIFE: "In its very emphasis on sex, in its obsessive and exclusive concern with it, this work was in its own time subversive. It was subversive of that characteristic Victorian arrangement in which the existence of a whole universe of sexuality and sexual activity was tacitly acknowledged and actively participated in, while at the same time one's consciousness of all this was, as far as possible, kept apart from one's larger, more general, and public consciousness of both self and society" (p. 163); Fryer, Peter, "Editor's Introduction" in FORBIDDEN BOOKS OF THE VICTORIANS. HENRY SPENCER ASHBEE'S BIBLIOGRAPHIES OF EROTICA... ed. by Peter Fryer. 1970. "It has been shown that interest in pornography is not correlated with deviant sexual activity; it may, or may not be, a substitute for it... there is not a shred of evidence to support the hypothesis that he was the compulsive chaser after women and memorialist of his encounters who as 'Walter,' wrote... MY SECRET LIFE" (p. 2); Kronhausen, Phyllis and Kronhausen, Eberhard, MORE WALTER. BEING A FURTHER EXAMINATION OF 'MY SECRET LIFE.' 1970. Examines the controversy among moralists on the popularity of MY SECRET LIFE. "Walter's almost totally uncritical account of all kinds of unorthodox sexual behavior will upset members of both the old and the new moral guard" (pp. 6-7).

10.416
Bennett, Dr. M., ANTHONY COMSTOCK. HIS CAREER OF CRUELTY AND CRIME. [1878]. Argues that Comstock, a moralist who insisted on clearing literature of its sexual references, was himself obsessed with sex.

10.417
Coote, Rose Belinda, THE CONVENT SCHOOL, OR EARLY EXPERIENCES OF A YOUNG FLAGELLANT. 1879. Privately printed.

10.418
PEARL: A JOURNAL OF FACETIAE AND VOLUPTUOUS READING: July 1879 to December 1880; nos. 1-18. Published by the Society of Vice; rpt., introduction by Jack Kirschman. 3 vols. North Hollywood, 1967; rpt. in one volume, New York, 1968. *——see also:* SWIVIA OR THE BRIEFLESS BARRISTER. THE EXTRA SPECIAL NUMBER OF THE PEARL, CONTAINING A VARIETY OF COMPLETE TALES... [Paris], 1879. Account of four young men who celebrate Christmas Eve by having an orgy with two girls. THE HAUNTED HOUSE OR THE REVELATION OF THERESA TERENCE. 'AN O'ER TRUE TALE...' BEING THE CHRISTMAS NUMBER OF THE PEARL. Privately printed, 1880. Detailed story of gang rape and flagellation; THE EROTIC CASKET BOOK FOR 1882. CONTAINING VARIOUS FACETIAE OMITTED IN THE PEARL CHRISTMAS ANNUAL FOR WANT OF SPACE. Privately printed, [1882].

10.419
INDECENT WHIPPING. [1880]. Letters and a story on the subject of flogging girls.

10.420
LOVE'S TELL TALE, THE SAILOR'S YARN. A DELICIOUS ADVENTURE IN THE BAY OF NAPLES. Moscow, 1880.

10.421
THE POWER OF MESMERISM. A HIGHLY EROTIC NARRATIVE OF VOLUPTUOUS FACTS AND FANCIES. Moscow, 1880. Detailed account of incest perpetrated by a young man using mesmerism.

10.422
THE STORY OF A DILDOE. A TALE IN FIVE TABLEAUX. 1880. Privately printed.

10.423
THE BIRCHEN BOUQUET; OR CURIOUS AND ORIGINAL ANECDOTES OF LADIES FOND OF ADMINISTERING THE BIRCH DISCIPLINE, AND PUBLISHED FOR THE AMUSEMENT AS WELL AS THE BENEFIT OF THOSE LADIES WHO HAVE UNDER THEIR TUITION SULKY, STUPID, WANTON, LYING OR IDLE YOUNG LADIES OR GENTLEMEN. 1881.

10.424
THE LOVES OF VENUS OR THE YOUNG WIFE'S CONFESSION, A TRUE TALE FROM REAL LIFE. Dublin, 1881. Written as a letter between an incestuous brother and sister pair, describes the brother's wife's defloration.

10.425
THE SINS OF THE CITIES OF THE PLAIN; OR THE RECOLLECTIONS OF A MARY-ANN. WITH SHORT ESSAYS ON SODOMY AND TRIBADISM. 1881.

10.426
Hardcastle, Mrs., LIFE OF LORD CHANCELLOR CAMPBELL, LORD HIGH CHANCELLOR OF GREAT BRITAIN, CONSISTING OF A SELECTION FROM HIS AUTOBIOGRAPHY, DIARIES, AND LETTERS. 2 vols. 1881. Campbell was the principal framer of the Obscene Publications Act.

10.427
KATE HANDCOCK OR, A YOUNG GIRL'S INTRODUCTION TO FAST LIFE. 1882. Privately printed. Account of a young girl who begins her sexual encounters at age twelve with her female servant. Her curiosity leads her to watching her maid having intercourse with the groom who later rapes her, to her "delight." After leaving home under the threat of disgrace, Kate winds up in a London brothel.

10.428
Etonensis, THE MYSTERIES OF VERBENA HOUSE OR, MISS BELLASIS BIRCHED FOR THIEVING. 1882. Flagellation at a girls' seminary.

10.429
RADIANA; OR EXCITABLE TALES; BEING THE EXPERIENCES OF AN EROTIC PHILOSOPHER. New York, 1884. Compilation of stories which delineate sexual activities of all natures—flagellation, incest, lesbian sex, orgiastic encounters, defloration, and intercourse.

10.430

Clowes, W.C. (Speculator Morum), **BIBLIOTHECA ARCANA SEU CATOLOGUS LIBRORUM PENETRALIUM, BEING BRIEF NOTICES OF BOOKS THAT HAVE BEEN SECRETLY PRINTED, PROHIBITED BY LAW, SEIZED, ANATHEMA-TISED, BURNT OR BOWDLERISED.** 1884-1885.

10.431

THE INUTILITY OF VIRTUE. A TALE OF LUST AND LICENTIOUSNESS, EXEMPLIFIED IN THE HISTORY OF A YOUNG AND BEAUTIFUL LADY MODEST AND VIRTUOUS, WHO, BY A SERIES OF UNFORTUNATE CIRCUMSTANCES, IS FIRST RAVISHED BY A ROBBER, THEN BECOMES SUCCESSIVELY THE VICTIM OF LUST AND SENSUALITY; TILL OVERPOWERED BY DEBAUCHERY, HER PASSIONS BECOME PREDOMINANT, HER MIND REMAINING PURE, WHILE HER BODY IS CONTAMINATED. THE WHOLE RICHLY AND BEAUTIFULLY NARRATED, SHOWING THE TRIUMPHS OF VICE AND THE DEGRADATION OF VIRTUE. 1830; 1885.

10.432

SHEAVES FROM AN OLD ESCRITOIRE. 1887; 1896. Details the incestuous relationship of a sister and brother.

10.433

Swinburne, Algernon Charles, **CONTRIBUTIONS TO THE WHIPPINGHAM PAPERS.** 1888; **LESBIA BRANDON.** [18??]. Masochistic novel; **FLOSSIE, A VENUS OF FIFTEEN, BY ONE WHO KNEW THIS CHARMING GODDESS AND WORSHIPPED AT HER SHRINE. PRINTED AT CARNOPOLIS FOR THE DELECTATION OF THE AMOROUS AND THE INSTRUCTION OF THE AMATEURS.** n.d. ——*see also:* Lang, Cecily, **THE SWINBURNE LECTURES.** 6 vols. 1958-1962. Contains material which reveals Swinburne's masochistic tendencies; Wilson, Edward, ed., **THE NOVELS OF A.C. SWINBURNE.** 1963.

10.434

ASTRID CANE. 1891; rpt., New York, 1983. Instructed by Julia Tingle, Astrid Cane is seduced by both men and women, often against her will. After her "apprenticeship," she becomes the seducer of both innocent girls and curious young men.

10.435

[Avery, Edward], **CONFESSIONS OF MADAME VESTRIS; IN A SERIES OF FAMILIAR LETTERS TO HANDSOME JACK, GIVING A GLOWING PICTURE OF: HER EARLY SEDUCTIONS; HER INTRIGUES WITH CAPTAIN ANSTRUTHER; HER CURIOUS ADVENTURES ON THE WEDDINGS NIGHT, PARISIAN FROLICS. INCLUDING CURIOUS AND ORIGINAL ANECDOTES OF MANY EMINENT PERSONS, HER EARLY YOUTH AND TIMES, ETC.** 1891.

10.436

THE BAGLIO MISCELLANY, CONTAINING THE ADVENTURE OF MISS LAIS LOVECOCK, WRITTEN BY HERSELF; AND WHAT HAPPENED TO HER AT MISS TWIG'S ACADEMY, AND AFTERWARDS. DIALOGUE BETWEEN A JEW AND A CHRISTIAN, A WHIMSICAL ENTERTAINMENT LATELY PERFORMED IN DUKE'S PLACE. THE FORCE OF INSTINCT: A TRUE STORY, WHEREIN IS DETAILED THE CURIOUS EXPERIMENT RESORTED TO BY A YOUNG LADY IN ORDER TO MAKE THE HAIR GROW ON THE BOTTOM OF HER BELLY, WITH OTHER DROLL MATTERS AND QUAINT CONCEITS. 1892; rpt., Atlanta,

Georgia, 1967.

10.437
Farrar, J.A., **BOOKS CONDEMNED TO BE BURNT**. 1892.

10.438
**GYNECOCRACY: A NARRATIVE OF THE ADVENTURES AND PSYCHOLO-
GICA EXPERIENCES OF JULIAN ROBINSON (AFTERWARDS VISCOUNT
LADYWOOD) UNDER PETTICOAT RULE, WRITTEN BY HERSELF.** 1893. On
female sadism.

10.439
CONTEMPORARY REVIEW: Noble, J.A., *"Fiction of Sexuality,"* 67 (1895) 490-
498. Contests the view that the new "fiction of sexual sensualism which has lately
made itself such a nuisance to ordinarily decent and wholesome readers" is a
reflection of actual goings-on in society. Rather, he claims these books are written
to arouse the prurient interest of the public and to make money.

10.440
LADY GAY SPANKER'S TALES OF FUN AND FLAGELLATION. 1896.

10.441
**PRIVATE LETTERS FROM PHYLLIS TO MARIE, OR (SIC) THE ART OF
CHILD-LOVE, OR THE ADVENTURES AND EXPERIENCES OF A LITTLE
GIRL. SHOWING HOW PRETTY LITTLE MAIDENS INDULGE THOSE SECRET
PASSIONS, ALONE AND WITH OTHERS, WHICH BUT TOO OFTEN LEAD TO
THEIR SEDUCTION AT AN EARLY AGE.** 1898.

10.442
Crowley, Aleister, **WHITE STAINS, THE LITERARY REMAINS OF GEORGE
ARCHIBALD BISHOP, A NEUROPATH OF THE SECOND EMPIRE.** 1898; rpt.,
ed. by John Symonds, 1973; **THE SCENTED GARDEN OF ABDULLAH THE
SATIRIST OF SHIRAZ.** 1910.

10.443
**HOW TO RISE LOVE; OR, MODERN STUDIES IN THE SCIENCE OF
STROKING: THE HORN BOOK: A GIRL'S GUIDE TO THE KNOWLEDGE OF
GOOD AND EVIL.** [Paris], 1899; 1901; *also published as:* **THE HORN BOOK.**

10.444
Grassal, George, **MEMOIRS OF DOLLY MORTON.** 1899. Tale of flagellation.

10.445
[Holmes, James, et al.], **MEMOIRS OF PRIVATE FLAGELLATION.** [1899].

10.446
An Old Bibliophile, **FORBIDDEN BOOKS.** Paris, 1902.

10.447
**LETTERS FROM LAURA AND EVELINE GIVING AN ACCOUNT OF THEIR
MOCK MARRIAGE, WEDDING-TRIP, ETC...** 1903.

10.448
**THE LUSTFUL MEMOIRS OF A YOUNG AND PASSIONED (SIC) GIRL,
WRITTEN BY HERSELF.** 1904.

10.449
Beardsley, Aubrey, LAST LETTERS OF AUBREY BEARDSLEY. with introductory note by John Gray. 1904; UNDER THE HILL, AND OTHER ESSAYS IN PROSE AND VERSE... WITH ILLUSTRATIONS. with introductory note by John Lane. 1904; THE STORY OF VENUS AND TANNHAUSER... A ROMANTIC NOVEL, ETC. privately printed. 1907; 1927; ed. with introduction by Robert Oresko. 1974; THE UNCOLLECTED WORK OF AUBREY BEARDSLEY. introduction by C. Lewis Hind. 1925; THE BEST OF BEARDSLEY. collected and edited by R.A. Walker. 1948; AUBREY BEARDSLEY'S EROTIC UNIVERSE. introduction and illustrations selected by Derek Stanford. 1967; DRAWINGS. New York, 1967; THE BEST OF AUBREY BEARDSLEY. compiled by Kenneth Clark. New York, 1978. —*see also:* Beckson, Karl, ed., AESTHETES AND DECADENTS OF THE 1890S; AN ANTHOLOGY. New York, 1966. Includes 16 illustrations by Beardsley; Reade, Brian, AUBREY BEARDSLEY. introduction by John Rothenstein. 1966; New York, 1967. Quotes Roger Fry's assessment of Beardsley as "the Fra Angelico of Satanism." "[Beardsley's] black-and-white conceptions of erotic, mischevious-looking females in exaggerated versions of the clothes of the 'nineties merged for a time with the aspirations of the New Woman of the period into a mythical entity called The Beardsley Woman" (p. 8); Brophy, Brigid, BLACK AND WHITE: A PORTRAIT OF AUBREY BEARDSLEY. New York, 1970. "Beardsley's subject matter, by his own choice, encompasses virtually the whole sexual spectrum, from delicate bestiality (Venus, in his novel, masturbates her pet unicorn, Adolphe, every morning before breakfast) to flagellation" (pp. 28, 32); Benkovitz, Miriam J., AUBREY BEARDSLEY. AN ACCOUNT OF HIS LIFE. 1981.

10.450
FORBIDDEN FRUIT. 1905; rpt. in the United States, 1968.

10.451
MARGOT, THE BIRCHING BEAUTY. HER WHIPPING ADVENTURES AS CONFIDED TO REBECCA BIRCH, HER FRIEND, LATE TEACHER AT MRS. BUSBY'S YOUNG LADIES' BOARDING SCHOOL. 1905.

10.452
THE MEMOIRS OF A VOLUPTUARY. 1905. Erotic novel.

10.453
Wales, Hubert (pseud. for William Pigott), THE YOKE. New York, 1907; 1908. Fictional account that explores the theme of danger of venereal disease from casual sex. Daring for the time, it examines the exploits of a younger man with an older lover.

10.454
MAUDIE: REVELATIONS OF LIFE IN LONDON. 1909.

10.455
Sackville, Charles (pseud.), MR. HOWARD GOES YACHTING AND SUBJECTS TO HIS VOLUPTUOUS CAPRICES WITH YOUNG LADIES CAPTURED AND IMPRISONED ON BOARD. 1908; WHIPPING AS A FINE ART, BEING AN ACCOUNT OF EXQUISITE AND REFINED CHASTISEMENT INFLICTED BY MR. HOWARD ON GROWN-UP SCHOOLGIRLS. 1909.

10.456
Fowell, F. and Palmer, F., CENSORSHIP IN ENGLAND. 1913. "The human body is

no longer a God-like thing made in the image of its creator, but a thing of shame and indecency, to be mutually concealed and suppressed. It was not in a comic opera, but in Great Britain, in the year of our Lord 1909, that a harmless poster representation of a baby's back was solemnly adjudicated on a town council and ordered to be concealed" (p. 237).

10.457
NEW STATESMAN: *"Pornography,"* 2 (1913) 140-142. Decries censorship.

10.458
Calverton, Victor Francis, **SEX EXPRESSION IN LITERATURE**. New York, 1926.

10.459
Committee on Evil Literature, **REPORT**. Dublin, 1926.

10.460
Ernst, Morris L. and Seagle, William, **TO THE PURE... A STUDY OF OBSCENITY AND THE CENSOR**. 1929.

10.461
Gallichan, Walter M., "Pornography and Prudery" and "The Banning of Books" in **THE POISON OF PRUDERY**. by Walter M. Gallichan. 1929. Although Gallichan views pornographic literature as "an intellectual and moral poison which spreads, like cancer and suicide... [and] one of the chief incitements to sexual vice" (p. 126), he opposes censorship on the grounds that it encourages its popularity.

10.462
Cruse, Amy, **THE ENGLISHMAN AND HIS BOOKS IN THE EARLY NINETEENTH CENTURY**. 1930; **THE VICTORIANS AND THEIR BOOKS**. 1935; **AFTER THE VICTORIANS**. 1938. Discusses popular literature between 1887 and 1914.

10.463
Ellis, Havelock, "The Revaluation of Obscenity" in **MORE ESSAYS OF LOVE AND VIRTUE**. by Havelock Ellis. 1931. "The test of 'obscenity' can, obviously, only be subjective. Nothing is in itself obscene apart from the human observer" (p. 23).

10.464
Armitage, Gilbert, **BANNED IN ENGLAND**. 1932. History of laws regulating obscene literature in Victorian England.

10.465
Ernst, Morris L., "Sex and Censorship" in **SEX IN THE ARTS. A SYMPOSIUM**. ed. by John Francis McDermott and Kendall B. Taft. 1932.

10.466
Hallis, F., **THE LAW AND OBSCENITY**. 1932.

10.467
Jackson, Holbrook, **THE FEAR OF BOOKS**. New York, 1932.

10.468
Ladd, H.A., **THE VICTORIAN MORALITY OF ART**. New York, 1932.

10.469
Lawrence, D.H., **PORNOGRAPHY AND SO ON**. 1936. "We take it, I assume, that pornography is something base, something unpleasant. In short we don't like it. And why don't we like it? Because it arouses sexual feelings?" (p. 19); **SEX, LITERATURE AND CENSORSHIP**. ed. by H.T. Moore. 1955. "This is the secret of really vulgar and of pornographical people: the sex flow and the excrement flow is the same thing to them. It happens when the psyche deteriorates, and the profound controlling instincts collapse. Then sex is dirt and dirt is sex, and sexual excitement becomes a playing with dirt, and any sign of sex in a woman becomes a show of her dirt... this is the source of all pornography" (p. 70).

10.470
Reade, Rolfe S. (A. Rose), **REGISTRUM LIBRORUM EROTICORUM**. 1936.

10.471
Atkinson, Edward Tindal, **OBSCENE LITERATURE IN LAW AND PRACTICE**. 1937. "While books and photographs of a grossly pornographic character, produced mainly in Paris, but also in other towns on the continent, present no sort of difficulty, a large number of publications have to be judged in the light of a tolerance in public opinion represented by a swing of the pendulum" (p. 10).

10.472
Craig, Alec, **THE BANNED BOOKS OF ENGLAND**. 1937. Provides a history of the voluntary societies established to promote enforcement of obscenity laws, such as the Society for the Suppression of Vice, the Society for the Encouragement of Pure Literature, and the national Vigilance Association; "Censorship of Sexual Literature" in **THE ENCYCLOPEDIA OF SEXUAL BEHAVIOUR**. ed. by A. Ellis and A. Abarbanel. 2 vols. New York, 1961; **SUPPRESSED BOOKS. A HISTORY OF THE CONCEPTION OF LITERARY OBSCENITY**. New York, 1963. "The subject of this book is the conception of literary obscenity as found in law and practice and its cultural and social effects. My primary concern is the restraint which the conception exercises on serious literature and consequently on intellectual freedom and artistic creation" (p. 9). Much discussion of England because of its peculiar legal structure.

10.473
McCabe, J., **THE HISTORY OF FLAGELLATION**. Girard, 1946.

10.474
Legman, Gershon, **LOVE AND DEATH: A STUDY IN CENSORSHIP**. New York, 1949; 1963. See especially: "Avatars of the Bitch" and "Open Season on Women" for brief accounts of pornographic works that deal with women either as dominators or victims; **THE HORN BOOK: STUDIES IN EROTIC FOLKLORE AND BIBLIOGRAPHY**. New York, 1964. "Erotic literature exists because it serves an important need. The need is twofold: the education of the inexperienced young, and the excitation of the impotent and old... these two main groups... are the principal searchers after and the main buyers of erotic literature" (p. 71).

10.475
Pope-Hennessy, James, **MONCKTON MILNES: THE FLIGHT OF YOUTH, 1851-1885**. 1951. Milnes, a Member of Parliament, was famous for his erotic book collection.

10.476
Haight, Anne Lyon, **BANNED BOOKS**. New York, 1955.

10.477
St. John-Stevas, Norman, **OBSCENITY AND THE LAW.** 1956. By examining literature considered obscene by Victorian standards, reveals attitudes about sexuality and the rising phenomenon of nineteenth-century prudery. "Undergraduates at Oxford and Cambridge were keen buyers of pornography, especially in the form of snuff boxes, in which there was a flourishing trade. These also found their way into boarding schools for young ladies" (p. 37). Valuable book. See the appendices for English obscenity laws, comparisons with other countries, censorship sponsored by the Church, and a selected list of banned books.

10.478
Ginzburg, Ralph, **AN UNHURRIED VIEW OF EROTICA.** New York, 1958; 1959.

10.479
Brusendorff, Ove and Henningsen, Poul, **THE COMPLETE HISTORY OF EROTICISM.** Copenhagen and Secaucus, N.J., 1961. See especially: "From the Time of the Marquis de Sade" and "Victoriana." Many illustrations. Although England produced few erotic novels compared to France and Germany, it published a surfeit of erotic journals, such as THE COVENT GARDEN, THE RAMBLER'S MAGAZINE, THE BON TON, THE RANGER'S MAGAZINE, THE EXQUISITE, and THE PEARL, that printed obscene poetry and short stories.

10.480
Loth, David, "The Pornography of the Victorians" in **THE EROTIC LITERATURE: A HISTORICAL SURVEY OF PORNOGRAPHY AS DELIGHTFUL AS IT IS INDISCREET.** by David Loth. New York, 1961. "So, just as the female sex now could be divided unquestionably into the two classes of good or bad, chaste or unchaste, books were classified as moral and uplifting or obscene and degrading" (p. 120).

10.481
Chandos, John, ed., **TO DEPRAVE AND CORRUPT: ORIGINAL STUDIES IN THE NATURE AND DEFINITION OF "OBSCENITY."** 1962.

10.482
Wedeck, Harry E., **DICTIONARY OF EROTIC LITERATURE.** New York, 1962. "The term erotic is here taken... to include all normal and perverted sexual and amatory phenomena depicted in the field of literature" (Introduction). Lists authors and titles, with brief descriptive passages, arranged alphabetically.

10.483
Hyde, H. Montgomery, **A HISTORY OF PORNOGRAPHY.** 1964; New York, 1966. "The seal was set on Victorian propriety by the passing of the Obscene Publications Act... in 1857. This unfortunate piece of legislation did not create any new offence. What it did was to give magistrates throughout the country statutory power to order the destruction of 'any obscene publication held for sale or distribution on information laid before a court of summary jurisdiction.' Thus it turned the magistrate into a censor of literary morals" (p. 12). Discusses many books, especially those cited in Ashbee's bibliographies, their content, and reasons for their censorship.

10.484
Klaf, Franklin and Hurwood, Bernhardt, **A PSYCHIATRIST LOOKS AT EROTICA.** New York, 1964. Discusses unintentional pornography produced by

public lawsuits of English husbands against their wives' lovers. The press was allowed to print all the details of the cases for public titillation. The practice was discontinued by the Matrimonial Causes Act of 1857.

10.485
Marcus, Steven, **THE OTHER VICTORIANS: A STUDY OF SEXUALITY AND PORNOGRAPHY IN MID-NINETEENTH-CENTURY ENGLAND**. New York, 1964; 1965; 1966. Examines "the sexual culture——more precisely, perhaps, the sexual subculture of Victorian England" (p. xiv) as reflected in Ashbee's bibliographies, MY SECRET LIFE, flagellation literature, and other popular pornographic literature.

10.486
Fryer, Peter, **PRIVATE CASE. PUBLIC SCANDAL**. 1966. Describes erotic literature and pornography concealed in the private cases of the British museum. Very valuable book; **THE MAN OF PLEASURE'S COMPANION. A NINETEENTH CENTURY ANTHOLOGY OF AMOROUS ENTERTAINMENT**. 1968. "If female emancipation has been only partial, the male attitudes which sustain female servitude and are nourished by it, and which are so abundantly reflected in these pages, are still a prominent feature of sexual and family relationships" (p. 40). Collection of extracts from primary sources; (as editor), **FORBIDDEN BOOKS OF THE VICTORIANS: HENRY SPENCER ASHBEE'S BIBLIOGRAPHIES OF EROTICA**. 1970. Synopsizes the plots of many Victorian publications, including THE HAUNTED HOUSE, THE PHOENIX OF SODOM, PRETTY LITTLE GAMES, MYSTERIES OF VERBENA HOUSE, and many others.

10.487
Fryer, Peter and De Vries, Leonard, compilers, **VENUS UNMASKED OF AN INQUIRY INTO THE NATURE AND ORIGIN OF THE PASSION OF LOVE, INTERSPERSED WITH CURIOUS AND ENTERTAINING ACCOUNTS OF SEVERAL MODERN AMOURS: A COLLECTION OF EIGHTEENTH-CENTURY BAWDRY**. New York, 1967. Asserts that literary prudery and its consequences "seem to be associated with the ascendancy of a middle class bent on self-improvement. The female members of this increasingly literate class demanded reading matter free from disturbing sexual realism" (p. 7).

10.488
A MAN WITH A MAID. rpt., New York, 1968. An "underground" novel of the Victorian period recounts the tale of Jack, who rapes the virgin Alice. After this episode, she is "won over" to her sexuality and aids him in the seduction of several other women, including her maid. Two features of the book——the seduced female minion, and sexual coupling between women and between classes——illustrate the Victorian fears that illicit sexual passion converted chaste women into monsters as well as threatened social stability.

10.489
Boyer, Paul S., **PURITY IN PRINT**. New York, 1968. "The average editor publisher knew a 'bad book' when he saw one, but he didn't waste much time brooding over precisely what made it bad or what the nature of its baneful impact might be" (p. 20).

10.490
Kronhausen, Phyllis and Kronhausen, Eberhard, **EROTIC FANTASIES: A STUDY OF THE SEXUAL IMAGINATION**. New York, 1969. Selections from pornography of the seventeenth to the twentieth centuries, some of which is English.

10.491

Pearsall, Ronald, "Pornography" in **THE WORM IN THE BUD: THE WORLD OF VICTORIAN SEXUALITY.** by Ronald Pearsall. 1969. Documents various cases of censorship or attempted banning; the popular pornographic works and magazines; sexual humor; and public reaction to pornographic literature and attempts to censor it.

10.492

Pecham, Morse, **ART AND PORNOGRAPHY.** New York, 1969.

10.493

Rolph, Cecil Hewitt (pseud.), "The Nineteenth Century 'Readership' Explosion" in **BOOKS IN THE DOCKS.** by Cecil Hewitt Rolph. 1969. "Pornography poured from the printing presses——long erotic novels of absolutely no survival value, whose heroes staggered from one bed to another; weekly and monthly magazines which pandered to all those appetites that the 'Vice Societies' were working vainly to eliminate. There was a huge flagellation literature (to which Swinburne enthusiastically contributed).... The 'readership explosion' had taken the class out of pornography and merely rearranged its prices to suit all purses" (p. 51). Examines the obscenity laws as they related to literature, and the political implications inherent in various censorship cases. Reveals many nuances concerning Victorian sexual attitudes.

10.494

Sontag, Susan, "The Pornographic Imagination" in **STYLES OF RADICAL WILL.** by Susan Sontag. New York, 1969. "The imagination pursuing its outrageous pleasures in THE STORY OF O and THE IMAGE remains firmly anchored to certain notions of the formal consummation of intense feeling, of procedures for exhausting an experience, that connect as much with literature and recent literary history as with the ahistorical domain of eros. And why not? Experiences aren't pornographic; only images and representations——structures of the imagination——are" (p. 49).

10.495

Thomas, Donald, **A LONG TIME BURNING: THE HISTORY OF LITERARY CENSORSHIP IN ENGLAND.** 1969. Identifies three main areas of banned literature: political treason or libel, blasphemy, and pornography. "There was not a great deal of sadistic or flagellant literature in England until the humanitarianism of the nineteenth century abolished the judicial flogging of women and curtailed it in the case of men. As women achieved emancipation in life, they became enslaved in literature" (p. 314).

10.496

VICTORIAN STUDIES: Thomas, D., *"MY SECRET LIFE: The Trial of Leeds,"* 12 (1969) 448-451. The book was the first pre-twentieth century work to be brought to trial under the Obscene Publications Act of 1959, where its value as an historical document was debated; Banks, J.A., Best G., Irwin, M., and Thomas, D., *"'MY SECRET LIFE': Theme and Variations. A Symposium on the Obscenity Case,"* 13 (1969) 204-215. Geoffrey Best comments that Walter's historical value is not as a "sex-obsessed egoist" but as the "sharp observer of contemporaries in postures and situations open as well as secret" (p. 211).

10.497

Atkins, John, **SEX IN LITERATURE.** 3 vols. 1970-1978.

10.498
Goldfarb, Russell M., **SEXUAL REPRESSION AND VICTORIAN LITERATURE**. Lewisburg, 1970.

10.499
Barber, D.F., **PORNOGRAPHY AND SOCIETY**. 1972. "The trouble is, apparently, that a great many people do not find sexual arousal and orgasm entertaining and seek to frustrate those who do. As a result, pornography has become the scapegoat for a general sexual neurosis and has consequently suffered as a genre" (pp. 102-103).

10.500
Altick, Richard D., "Literature and Circulating Library Morality" in **VICTORIAN PEOPLE AND IDEAS**. by Richard D. Altick. 1973. Claims that Evangelical prudery not only banned much valuable literature but also prevented contemporary authors from addressing social and sexual topics directly and honestly.

10.501
Drakeford, John W. and Hamm, Jack, **PORNOGRAPHY: THE SEXUAL MIRAGE**. New York, 1973.

10.502
Hess, Thomas B. and Nochlin, Linda, **WOMAN AS SEX OBJECT: STUDIES IN EROTIC ART, 1730-1970**. New York, 1973. Explains the lack of female contributions to erotic art and literature by arguing that "women were never even permitted to dream about such things, much less bring them to life on canvas" (p. 10).

10.503
Miles, Henry, **FORBIDDEN FRUIT: A STUDY OF THE INCEST THEME IN EROTIC LITERATURE**. 1973. "There is little doubt that the fictional treatment of incest in the 19th century served as a form of protest literature, whether conscious or not, opposing the cosy artificial world of the Victorian family presented by the penny novels and general fiction of the circulating libraries" (p. 9).

10.504
Ovenden, Graham, **NYMPHETS AND FAIRIES: THREE VICTORIAN CHILDREN'S ILLUSTRATORS**. 1976. Illustrated booklet with highly suggestive photographs of children.

10.505
Gibson, Ian, **THE ENGLISH VICE: BEATING, SEX AND SHAME IN VICTORIAN ENGLAND AND AFTER**. 1978. Psychoanalytic view. Asserts that the flagellation fantasies were rooted in the early childhood experience of being whipped in public school, the point of the practice being to overcome impotence.

10.506
Carter, Angela, **THE SADEIAN WOMAN. AN EXERCISE IN CULTURAL HISTORY**. 1979. "Female castration is an imaginary fact that pervades the whole of men's attitudes towards women and our attitude towards ourselves, that transforms women from human beings into wounded creatures who were born to bleed" (p. 23).

10.507
Dworkin, Andrea, **PORNOGRAPHY: MEN POSSESSING WOMEN**. New York,

1979. Analyzes contemporary and Victorian definitions of pornography. "The fact that pornography is widely believed to be 'sexual representations' or 'depictions of sex' emphasizes only that the valuation of women as low whores is widespread and that the sexuality of women is perceived as low and whorish in and of itself" (p. 201); *reviewed in:* FEMINIST REVIEW: no. 11 (1982) 101-104. ——*see also:* FEMINIST REVIEW: Wilson, E., *"Interview with Andrea Dworkin,"* no. 11 (1982) 23-30. Argues that pornography is a representation of real life for women: "The reality is that men commit acts of forced sex against women systematically. That is precisely what the women's movement has been based upon" (p. 26).

10.508
Robertson, Geoffrey, **OBSCENITY: AN ACCOUNT OF CENSORSHIP LAWS AND THEIR ENFORCEMENT IN ENGLAND AND WALES.** 1979. Discusses the prosecutions of the Society for the Suppression of Vice, which "was convinced that Britain stood in peril of continental pollution" (p. 27).

10.509
Thompson, Roger, **UNFIT FOR MODEST EARS. A STUDY OF PORNOGRAPHIC, OBSCENE AND BAWDY WORKS WRITTEN OR PUBLISHED IN ENGLAND IN THE SECOND HALF OF THE SEVENTEENTH CENTURY.** 1979. Despite the focus on the late seventeenth century, provides an interesting contrast comparison to Victorian pornography. Maintains that seventeenth-century erotica displayed a degree of sexual realism not found in the Victorian literature.

10.510
Byerly, Greg, **PORNOGRAPHY: THE CONFLICT OVER SEXUALLY EXPLICIT MATERIALS IN THE UNITED STATES. AN ANNOTATED BIBLIOGRAPHY.** 1980. See index for material on Great Britain.

10.511
Faust, Beatrice, **WOMEN, SEX AND PORNOGRAPHY. A CONTROVERSIAL AND UNIQUE STUDY.** New York, 1980. Discusses current issues of female sexuality including the following: "Why is There No Pornography for Women?," "Pornography —What is It?," and female physiologic sexual response. Draws comparisons with the Victorian period.

10.512
MOTHER JONES: English, D., *"The Politics of Porn: Can Feminists Walk the Line?"* 5 (1980) 20-23. Compares the modern feminist attack on pornography with nineteenth-century feminists' war against alcohol; both were errant in their object of attack. Sees a need for distinction between porn and erotica, and a focus on the underlying attitudes toward women that are responsible for violent fantasies.

10.513
Charney, Maurice, "Two Sexual Lives, Entrepreneurial and Compulsive: Fanny Hill and My Secret Life" in **SEXUAL FICTION.** by Maurice Charney. 1981. "Unlike the public and ritualized sex in Sade and his followers, these books insist that sex must be secret in order to be tantalizing, but Walter is obsessed and tormented by his secret life in a way that is unknown to Fanny Hill and her complaisant nymphs" (p. 77).

10.514
Griffin, Susan, **PORNOGRAPHY AND SILENCE: CULTURE'S REVENGE AGAINST NATURE.** New York, 1981. "Pornography is an expression of a fear of bodily knowledge, and a desire to silence eros... the bodies of women in

pornography, mastered, bound, silenced, beaten, and even murdered, are symbols for natural feeling and the power of nature... 'the woman' in pornography, like the 'Jew' in anti-Semitism and 'the black' in racism, is simply a lost part of the soul, that region of being the pornographic or the racist mind would forget and deny" (pp. 1-2); *reviewed in:* FEMINIST REVIEW: no. 11 (1982) 97-100.

10.515
Bold, Alan, "Introduction" in THE SEXUAL DIMENSION IN LITERATURE. ed. by Alan Bold. 1982. Describes the prudish affectation of bibliographers of erotic literature, such as Henry Spencer Ashbee, Patrick Kearney, Gershon Legman and the British Museum Library authorities, who he claims pretend that the interest is purely academic. The present study is "a collective discussion of erotic literature by writers who understand its appeal" (p. 10).

10.516
Kearney, Patrick J., A HISTORY OF EROTIC LITERATURE. 1982.

10.517
Webb, Peter, "Victorian Erotica" in THE SEXUAL DIMENSION IN LITERATURE. ed. by Alan Bold. 1982. Comments on the wide range of sexual activity in erotic literature, from incest to male and female homosexuality to rape and flagellation. Finds the more frequent recurrence of the latter two to be symptomatic of a "totally male-dominated" culture.

10.518
THE AUTOBIOGRAPHY OF A FLEA. rpt., New York, 1983. Originally published in the late nineteenth century, this novel relates the story of Bella, her deflowering, and the subsequent discovery by a local priest who "punishes" her for her carnal explorations by engaging with her himself.

10.519
PAST AND PRESENT: McCalman, I., *"Unrespectable Radicalism, Infidels and Pornography in Early 19th Century London,"* no. 104 (1984) 74-110. Discusses certain members of the radical political underground of the early nineteenth century, (including George Cannon, William Dugdale, John Duncombe, Robert Wedderburn, and John Ascham), who involved themselves in libertinism, running brothels, printing eccentric pornography, and pirating legitimate poetry. "If anyone deserved the title of sexual radicals during this period it was the Carlilean Zetetics and Owenite feminists who hated pornography but challenged sexual orthodoxy in the name of greater freedom and dignity for men and women alike" (p. 109).

10.520
M.S.: Blakely, M.K., *"Is One Woman's Sexuality Another Woman's Pornography?"* 13 (1985) 37-123. Modern feminist analysis of how pornography is regulated by law and the various frameworks of support for anti-pornography laws. Provides valuable insights for study of Victorian pornography and censorship. Argues that the current regulatory framework rests on "some kind of intellectual axis between sexual repression on the one hand and sexual freedom on the other," a conception that obscures the harm pornography does to women. "Essentially, the laws 'make the harm to women invisible'" (p. 40).

10.521
VICTORIAN STUDIES: Lansbury, C., *"Gynaecology, Pornography, and the Antivivisection Movement,"* 28 (1985) 413-439. "There is an uneasy similarity between the devices made to hold women for sexual pleasure and those tables and

chairs, replete with stirrups and leather straps, which made women ready for the surgeon's knife. When Dr. Elizabeth Blackwell saw a woman exposed in this fashion, she was horrified, and her sense of outrage was deepened by its unconscious reference to the darkest male fantasies" (p. 421); Roberts, M.J.D., *"Morals, Art and the Law: The Passing of the Obscene Publications Act, 1857,"* 28 (1985) 609-629. This legislation gave "police the right to enter and search premises on the authority of any magistrate who could be convinced of the likelihood that obscene publications were being kept for sale or exhibition there. Police were to seize any such materials found and 'to burn or otherwise destroy them'" (p. 610).

* * *

3. LESBIANISM AND ROMANTIC OR EROTIC FEMALE FRIENDSHIPS

10.522
[Fielding, Henry], **THE FEMALE HUSBAND: OR, THE SURPRISING HISTORY OF MRS. MARY, ALIAS MR. GEORGE HAMILTON, WHO WAS CONVICTED OF HAVING MARRIED A YOUNG WOMAN OF WELLS, ETC.** 1746. Biography of Mrs. Mary, born on the Isle of Man in August 1721, who masqueraded as George Hamilton. She had her first lesbian relationship with Anne Johnson, a young woman who seduced her. Johnson went through a Methodist conversion, eventually married a man and moved to Ireland. Mary followed Anne to Ireland to win back her affections. Still disguised as George, she married several wealthy women in succession. Upon their discovery of her sex in the nuptial bed, Mary would flee to a new town and continue her exploits. She was finally arrested, publicly flogged and imprisoned.

10.523
THE ADDITIONAL PETITION OF MISS MARY-ANN WOODS AND MISS JANE PIRIE. Edinburgh, 1811. Mistresses of a girls' boarding school, Woods and Pirie were accused of "improper and criminal conduct" by a student who claimed to overhear them making love. ——*see also:* Faderman, Lillian, **SCOTCH VERDICT.** 1984. Detailed history of the Woods and Pirie relationship.

10.524
Kitchener, Henry Thomas, "Clitoridian Defilement" in **LETTERS ON MARRIAGE, ON CAUSES OF MATRIMONIAL INFIDELITY, AND ON THE RECIPROCAL RELATIONS OF THE SEXES.** by Henry Thomas Kitchener. 1812. Describes lesbianism as defilement and self-pollution. Refers to lesbians as "clitoridians." Speculates that some women become homosexual because their clitoris is enlarged.

10.525
Chesterton, George Laval, **REVELATIONS OF PRISON LIFE; WITH AN ENQUIRY INTO PRISON DISCIPLINE AND SECONDARY PUNISHMENTS.** 2 vols. 1856. Observes that sexual liasons between female prisoners was a common feature of life at this institution.

10.526
LE CHASSEPOT. [1865 or 1866]. The writer George Sand is portrayed as "an utter slave to lesbian passion"; the actress Leonie Leblanc is depicted as a procuress of

young girls; other accounts of well-known men and women are included in this pamphlet whose author claims authenticity for all documents.

10.527
Alger, William Rounseville, **THE FRIENDSHIPS OF WOMEN**. Boston, 1868. "A little after the middle of the eighteenth century, Lady Eleanor Butler and Miss Sarah Ponsonby, two young women of wealth and high station, formed an extreme mutual attachment, and were possessed with each other. Taking measures accordingly, they departed to an obscure retreat in the country. Their relatives frowned on this eccentricity, traced them out in their hiding place, and, despite their protestations, separated them, and brought them back. But they soon effected a second elopement, which proved a successful and permanent one" (p. 294).

10.528
Griffiths, Arthur, **THE CHRONICLES OF NEWGATE**. New York, 1884. In this general history of Newgate prison homosexual marriage is made reference to within the context of bigamy: "Ann Marrow, who had been guilty of the strange offence of disguising herself as a man, and as such marrying three different women, was sentenced to three months' imprisonment, and exposure on the pillory, at Charing Cross. So great was the resentment of the populace, principally those of the female sex, that they pelted her till they put out both her eyes.... This was not an uncommon offence. One Mary Hamilton was married fourteen times to members of her own sex" (p. 152fn).

10.529
Symonds, John Addington, **A PROBLEM IN MODERN ETHICS. BEING AN ENQUIRY INTO THE PHENOMENON OF SEXUAL INVERSION.** [1890]. Argues that congenital homosexuality is one avenue of population control.

10.530
BLACKWOOD'S MAGAZINE: Pilkington, W.T., *"Modern Mannish Maids,"* 147 (1890) 252-264. Contends that too much attention to athletics fosters homosexuality in women.

10.531
Ireland, Mrs. Alexander, ed., **SELECTIONS FROM THE LETTERS OF GERALDINE ENDSOR JEWSBURY TO JANE WELSH CARLYLE.** 1892. The two women were romantically involved. ——*see also:* **TIMES LITERARY SUPPLE-MENT:** Woolf, V., *"Geraldine and Jane,"* (Feb. 28, 1929) 1-2.

10.532
Arnold, Edith, **PLATONICS: A STUDY.** 1894. Novel that deals with romantic love between two women, interspersed with temporary heterosexual episodes.

10.533
MacDonald, Arthur, **ABNORMAL WOMAN: A SOCIOLOGICAL AND SCIENTIFIC STUDY OF YOUNG WOMEN, INCLUDING LETTERS OF AMERICAN AND EUROPEAN GIRLS IN ANSWER TO PERSONAL ADVERTISE-MENTS. WITH A BIBLIOGRAPHY.** 1895.

10.534
AMERICAN JOURNAL OF INSANITY: Hamilton, A.M., *"The Civil Responsibility of Sexual Perverts,"* 52 (1896) 503-509.

10.535
Carpenter, Edward, **AN UNKNOWN PEOPLE**. 1897. "Presently, a journey of the married pair led to another meeting with the female friend——who had now been wedded (but also unhappily) for three years. Both ladies trembled with joy and excitement as they fell into each other's arms, and were thenceforth inseparable. The man found that this friendship relation was a singular one, and hastened the departure. When the opportunity occurred, he convinced himself from the correspondence between his wife and her 'friend' that their letters were exactly like those of two lovers. It appears that the loves of such women are often very intense, and life-long" (p. 20); **THE INTERMEDIATE SEX**. 1908; 1930. Speculates on the creative power of homosexuality. "[The lesbian's love] is of a heroic type and inspiring to great deeds; and when held duly in leash may sometimes become an invaluable force in the teaching and training of girlhood, or in creation of a school of thought or action among women" (p. 36); **LOVE'S COMING OF AGE. A SERIES OF PAPERS ON THE RELATION OF THE SEXES**. 1911. See especially: "The Intermediate Sex" in which he uses the term to describe those whose romantic sentiments flow toward others of the same sex. Instead of narrowly categorizing, Carpenter points out the "immense diversity of human temperament and character in matters relating to sex and love" (p. 122). ——*see also:* **HISTORY WORKSHOP JOURNAL**: Rowbotham, S., *"In Search of Carpenter,"* no. 3 (1977) 121-133. "When Ellis eventually married another member of the Fellowship, Edith Lees, they lived apart and did not have sexual intercourse because Edith Lees was attracted to women" (p. 125); Tsuzuki, Chushichi, **EDWARD CARPENTER, 1844-1929. PROPHET OF HUMAN FELLOWSHIP**. 1980. Carpenter, a gay socialist, was an advocate of working class, women's, and lesbian and gay rights. "He was... encouraged to write, not merely in defence of homosexuality, but also in praise of its unique virtues. He somehow believed that 'there is an organic connection between the homosexual temperament and unusual psychic or divinatory powers'" (p. 146).

10.536
Ellis, Havelock, "Sexual Inversion in Women" in **STUDIES IN THE PSYCHOLOGY OF SEX: SEXUAL INVERSION**. by Havelock Ellis. 1897; Philadelphia, 1901; rev. ed., 1926. Ellis was a foremost sex researcher whose wife was lesbian. Here, he asserts that inversion (homosexuality) in women is found most frequently in places where there are all-women groups, such as in schools, convents, and prisons. While Ellis believed that insanity is not a cause or result of lesbianism, he does claim that incidents of violent crimes and suicide are greater among homosexual women than their heterosexual counterparts. Contending that many great women in history had homosexual or bisexual tendencies, Ellis justifies this information by adding that the women concerned exhibited many masculine traits. Believed homosexuality to be a congenital condition, aggravated, he implied, by sexual frustration; **MY LIFE**. Boston, 1939. "It might be true that I was heterosexual and she [Edith Ellis] was not, and that therefore there was no demand on me to go outside marriage for love. But it was also true that the very qualities in her nature which made her largely homosexual were qualities which, fortifying as they might be to our comradeship, were inimical to the purely feminine qualities of sweetness and repose which a man seeks in a woman, and therefore opposed in our case to a strict conjugal fidelity" (p. 310). ——*see also:* Rowbotham, Sheila and Weeks, Jeffrey, **SOCIALISM AND THE NEW LIFE. THE PERSONAL AND SEXUAL POLITICS OF EDWARD CARPENTER AND HAVELOCK ELLIS**. 1977; Brome, Vincent, "His Wife's Lesbian Experience" in **HAVELOCK ELLIS: PHILOSOPHER OF SEX: A BIOGRAPHY**. by Vincent Brome. 1979; Grosskurth, Phyllis, **HAVELOCK ELLIS: A BIOGRAPHY**. New York, 1980. Notes that it is questionable whether Ellis was aware of Edith's lesbianism when they married.

10.537
NEW YORK MEDICAL JOURNAL: Howard, W.L., *"Effeminate Men and Masculine Women,"* 71 (1900) 686.

10.538
Howard, William Lee, THE PERVERTS. 1901. Fictional anti-lesbian work.

10.539
Rosenbaum, Julius, THE PLAGUE OF LUST. vols. 1 and 2, Paris, 1901. "For as women that are called Tribades, because they practise the love of either sex, are eager to have intercourse with women more than with men, and pursue these with a jealousy almost as violent as a man's, and when they have been deserted by their love or for the time being superseded, seek to do to other women what they are known to suffer, and winning from their double sex a pleasure in giving pleasure" (p. 165).

10.540
Leland, Charles Godfrey, THE ALTERNATE SEX OR THE FEMALE INTELLECT IN MAN, AND THE MASCULINE IN WOMAN. New York, 1904. Argues in favor of a more tolerant attitude toward homosexuality in men and women. "The Greeks recognised that such a being could exist even in harmony with Nature, and so beautified and idealized it as Sappho. But, in fact, the Sappho soul, though latent or hidden, exists unsuspected in innumerable women, and it would reveal itself in poetry and art as in her, if those who have it would, instead of following worn-out models, as all women do, develop their own Imaginations" (p. 58).

10.541
Ellis, Edith, THE LOVER'S CALENDAR, COMPILED AND EDITED BY MRS. HAVELOCK ELLIS. 1912. Edith Ellis was married to Havelock Ellis but was sexually attracted to other women and refused intercourse with her husband. "In this anthology I have tried to represent the whole course of Love in its birth, its slow growth, its inevitable sorrow and its joyous fruition" (preface); ESSAYS BY MRS. HAVELOCK ELLIS. WITH A PREFACE BY GEORGE IVES. REMINISCENCES BY F.W. STELLA BROWNE AND A NOTE BY HAVELOCK ELLIS. DECORATIONS BY M. DUVALET. New Jersey, 1924. ——*see also:* Goldberg, Isaac, HAVELOCK ELLIS: A BIOGRAPHICAL AND CRITICAL SURVEY. WITH A SUPPLEMENTARY CHAPTER ON MRS. EDITH ELLIS. ILLUSTRATED AND DOCUMENTED. New York, 1926.

10.542
AMERICAN JOURNAL OF UROLOGY: McMurtie, D., *"Some Observations on the Psychology of Sexual Inversion in Women,"* 9 (1913) 38-45; McMurtie, D., *"Principles of Homosexuality and Sexual Inversion in the Female,"* 9 (1913) 144-153. Describes his perception of the development of a lesbian relationship as a progression from infatuation to cohabitation highlighted by an intense mutual passion——similar to the relationship between heterosexual couples.

10.543
Ives, George, A HISTORY OF PENAL METHODS: CRIMINALS, WITCHES, LUNATICS. Montclair, New Jersey, 1914; rpt., 1970. "The sexual inverts may be compared to the left-handed. They are indeed always a minority in every population, but an eternal minority which neither laws nor even religious systems have ever altogether swept away" (p. 292).

10.544
Dane, Clemence, **REGIMENT OF WOMEN**. New York, 1917; 1922. Novel focusing on intense love relationships among women.

10.545
Bartley, Nalbro, **A WOMAN'S WOMAN**. 1919. An amusing satire of gender stereotypes from a lesbian-feminist perspective, showing a playful contempt of heterosexual couplings.

10.546
PSYCHOANALYTIC REVIEW: Hinkle, B., *"On the Arbitrary Use of the Terms Masculine and Feminine,"* 7 (1919) 15-30; Riggall, R.M., *"Homosexuality and Alcoholism,"* 10 (1923) 157-169; Case, I. and Sherman, M., *"The Factor of Personal Attachment in Homosexuality,"* 13 (1925) 32-37; Freud, S., *"Concerning the Sexuality of Woman,"* 1 (1932) 191-209. "It is clear that the bisexuality which, we have claimed, is inherent in mankind appears much more distinctly in women than in men" (p. 194).

10.547
INTERNATIONAL JOURNAL OF PSYCHOANALYSIS: Freud, S., *"Certain Neurotic Mechanisms in Jealousy, Paranoia, and Homosexuality,"* 4 (1923) 1-10.

10.548
JOURNAL OF SEXOLOGY AND PSYCHOANALYSIS: Browne, F.W.S., *"Studies in Feminine Inversion,"* 1 (1923) 51-58.

10.549
Freud, Sigmund, "The Psychogenesis of a Case of Homosexuality in a Woman" in **COLLECTED PAPERS**. by Sigmund Freud. vol. 2. orig. ed., 1924; trans. by Joan Riviere. New York, 1959. Freud concludes that his patient had developed a repudiation of her mother in childhood that is normally seen in boys and in her love of women was searching for a mother-substitute. She had "adopted the characteristic masculine type of love"——humility in her pursuit of her beloved, and a desire to be lover, not loved. And "she in fact was a feminist; she felt it to be unjust that girls should not enjoy the same freedom as boys, and rebelled against the lot of woman in general" (p. 228).

10.550
Lucas, Netley, **LADIES OF THE UNDERWORLD: THE BEAUTIFUL, THE DAMNED AND THOSE WHO GET AWAY WITH IT**. Cleveland, 1927. See especially: "Women Who Have Posed as Men." "To assume male attire and pose as a man on a single occasion is, possibly, not a very difficult matter, but to live, work and mingle with companions of both sexes, without incurring suspicion, is a different task, yet many women have achieved it and carried through the imposture with so great a measure of success that their real sex was discovered only on their death beds. Of course, a great number of these are homosexual.... Most of them do not partake in crime and are generally of a much higher order of intelligence" (pp. 191-192).

10.551
JOURNAL OF PSYCHOANALYSIS: Jones, E., *"The Early Development of Female Sexuality,"* 8 (1927) 59-472. Analysis links lesbianism with sadism.

10.552
Vyver, Bertha, **MEMOIRS OF MARIE CORELLI, BY BERTHA VYVER, WITH**

AN EPILOGUE BY J. CUMING WALTERS. 1930. Vyver and Corelli had an extremely close friendship with homosexual overtones.

10.553

Gordon, Mary Louisa, **CHASE OF THE WILD GOOSE; THE STORY OF LADY ELEANOR BUTLER AND MISS SARAH PONSONBY, KNOWN AS THE LADIES OF LLANGOLEN.** 1936. Novelesque account of the Ponsonby-Butler relationship. Suggests that women found much comfort, sympathy and love in friendly relationships which was lacking in the familial context. "Five years ago, when they were all at Woodstock, she and Lady Betty had remarked on the politeness of Miss Butler and Sarah towards one another. 'Exaggerated, don't you think?' Lady Betty had said. 'Oh! Affected, my dear, and no more likely to last than the usual endearments between lovers. To see much of it would make one tired'" (p. 160).

10.554

Hirschfeld, Magnus, "Homosexuality" in **THE ENCYCLOPEDIA SEXUALIS: A COMPREHENSIVE ENCYCLOPAEDIA—DICTIONARY OF THE SEXUAL SCIENCES.** ed. by Victor Robinson. New York, 1936.

10.555

Bigland, Eileen, **MARIE CORELLI, THE WOMAN AND THE LEGEND; A BIOGRAPHY.** 1953. Includes a narrative of the longstanding relationship between Bertha Vyver and Corelli, characterized as a non-sexual, "romantic, emotional friendship." Also shows that Corelli and Vyver were so close in part because they received little sympathy or unselfish aid from Corelli's father and half-brother.

10.556

Scott, William Stuart, **MARIE CORELLI: THE STORY OF A FRIENDSHIP.** 1955. On Bertha Vyver's extraordinary devotion to Marie Corelli.

10.557

Foster, Jeanette, **SEX VARIANT WOMEN IN LITERATURE.** Baltimore, 1956; 1975. "Feminine variance has persisted in human experience since the beginning of literary records... the odds [against this] have been two very different sorts— religious taboo and masculine distaste" (p. 353). Examines fictional accounts of romantic female friendship and lesbianism.

10.558

LADDER; A LESBIAN REVIEW: Oct. 1956 to Sept. 1972; vols. 1-16. Contains some historical articles.

10.559

McKenzie, K.A., **EDITH SIMCOX AND GEORGE ELIOT.** New York, 1961. Simcox was enamored of Eliot.

10.560

Braun, Walter, **LESBIAN LOVE OLD AND NEW.** trans. by Rudolf Schlesinger. Los Angeles, 1966. "In the nineteenth century generally, however, female homosexuality almost disappeared from the scene. Middle-class women were not yet emancipated. Women of the working-class were glad if they had enough to eat for their families and it was only during the industrial revolution that intimate companionships arose" (p. 38).

10.561

Pearsall, Ronald, "Lesbianism" in **THE WORM IN THE BUD. THE WORLD OF**

VICTORIAN SEXUALITY. by Ronald Pearsall. 1969. "Lesbianism is not, nor has been, a crime in Britain, but this is not because of a permissive or forward-looking policy on the parts of mysterious legislators of the past.... No one could think of a way to explain to Queen Victoria what homosexual acts between women were" (p. 474).

10.562
Karlen, Arno, **SEXUALITY AND HOMOSEXUALITY.** 1971. "A nightmare vision of sex appeared more and more frequently in Western literature through the nineteenth century, darker and more frightful even as the anti-Victorian reaction gained momentum.... In paintings, lesbians were usually seen as written pornography had always tended to show them——sensual and uninhibited, like the unfettered pagans of libidinous imagination, who would indulge any and all desires. They were female Casanovas and roues who went from pleasure to pleasure, excess to excess" (pp. 200-201).

10.563
Katz, Jonathan, ed., **HOMOSEXUALITY: LESBIANS AND GAY MEN IN SOCIETY, HISTORY AND LITERATURE.** New York, 1971.

10.564
Nicolson, Nigel, **PORTRAIT OF A MARRIAGE.** New York, 1973. Account of the marriage of Nicolson's parents, Vita Sackville-West and Harold Nicolson. Both had strong homosexual tendencies, although Sackville-West's lesbianism seemed to have developed after her marriage.

10.565
Lauristen, John and Thorstad, David, **THE EARLY HOMOSEXUAL RIGHTS MOVEMENT (1864-1935).** New York, 1974. "Lesbians and lesbian feminism played a small role in the early movement. One obvious reason for this is the fact that the main focus of the early movement, opposition to anti-gay laws, was not one that could be immediately or directly related to homosexual women, since those laws applied only to men" (p. 18).

10.566
Rosen, David H., **LESBIANISM: A STUDY OF FEMALE HOMOSEXUALITY.** Springfield, 1974. "Our culture encourages heterosexuality, and marriage is prized above all. Homosexuality symbolically threatens this cultural value as it used to threaten the continuation of our species, although this should be no problem with our present hope of curtailing overpopulation" (p. 68).

10.567
SIGNS: Smith-Rosenberg, C., *"The Female World of Love and Ritual: Relations Between Women in 19th Century America,"* 1 (1975) 1-29. Provides a useful analytical viewpoint for England. Argues that historians, "influenced by Freud's true libidinal theory, have discussed these relationships almost exclusively within the context of individual psychosexual developments, or, to be more explicit, psychopathology" (p. 2). Suggests an alternative approach that would view female friendships within a social and cultural context; Claus, R.F., *"Confronting Homosexuality: A Letter from Frances Wilder,"* 2 (1977) 928-935. Quotes Wilder in a letter to Edward Carpenter: "I have come to the conclusion that [the lesbian] relationship can never be as degrading as the normal sex relationship can be and usually is... it will be true whenever and so long as women are in economic slavery to men" (p. 932); Fassler, B., *"Theories of Homosexuality as Sources of Bloomsbury's Androgyny,"* 5 (1979) 237-251; Rich, A., *"Compulsory Heterosexuality*

and Lesbian Existence," 5 (1980) 631-660. Examines "how and why women's choice of women as passionate comrades, life partners, co-workers, lovers, tribe, has been crushed, invalidated, forced into hiding and disguise," reflected in "the virtual or total neglect of lesbian existence in a wide range of writings, including feminist scholarship" (p. 632); Vicinus, M., *"Distance and Desire: English Boarding-School Friendships,"* 9 (1984) 600-622. "Many women... appear to have found a more complete love as an adolescent than they ever were to find with a man, possibly because they found that the male ego continually demanded that a woman be Echo to its needs and desires, whereas a woman permitted the full range of self-expression, enabling the youthful lover to be both Narcissus and Echo, creator and respondent" (p. 609).

10.568
Bullough, Vern L., Legg, Dorr W., Elcano, Barrett W., and Kepner, James, AN ANNOTATED BIBLIOGRAPHY OF HOMOSEXUALITY. 2 vols. 1976. "Bibliographies and indices ignored the topic or if perchance it was included listed it under the rubric of sexual perversion or some similiar pejorative terminology" (p. vii).

10.569
Vivien, Renee, A WOMAN APPEARED TO ME. trans. from the French by Jeanette Foster. introduction by Gayle Rubin. Reno, 1976. Account of her relationship with Natalie Barney. Renee Vivien was born Pauline Tarn in London in 1877. In 1899, she had her first sexual relationship with Barney. "From the beginning of the affair, Renee was both exhilarated and terrorized by its carnality and its power. Natalie was the incarnation of her dreams, a lover who could inspire incinerating passion. But Renee was conflicted about such a passion. She had a curious kind of chastity, both emotional and physical" (p. xxi); AT THE SWEET HOUR OF HAND IN HAND. Weatherby Lake, 1979. Translation of Vivien's poetry. From "Sappho Lives Again": "We women live with an infinite candor,/With the amazement of an astonished child/For whom a whole new world has opened up.../Sappho lives again now that we love as only women can" (p. 2). ——*see also:* Klaich, Dolores, "The Belle Epoque" in WOMAN AND WOMAN: ATTITUDES TOWARD LESBIANISM. by Dolores Klaich. New York, 1974. Highlights the artistic careers of lesbian women in the latter nineteenth century with particular attention to Vivien. "Her early poems are languorously sensual and full of wide-eyed, earnest rebellion... none has written so openly, so erotically and so prolifically of lesbian love" (p. 163).

10.570
HISTORY WORKSHOP JOURNAL: Weeks, J., *"'Sins and Diseases': Some Notes on Homosexuality in the Nineteenth Century,"* no. 1 (1976) 211-219. "Although it has been socially condemned at various times... attitudes towards homosexuality are inextricably linked to wider questions of the function and importance of the family, the evolution of sex roles, and attitudes to sexual behaviour generally" (p. 211). Observes that part of the reason why homosexuality seems so inexplicable is that it has been traditionally examined in isolation from other issues.

10.571
Cockshut, A.O.J., "The Lesbian Theme" in MAN AND WOMAN: LOVE AND THE NOVEL FROM 1740-1940. by A.O.J. Cockshut. 1977. "The lesbian, in the years before 1930... was often the mother of a family, appearing to the world much like other wives and mothers. It is even possible that, in some cases, husbands... were unaware" (p. 187).

10.572
Weeks, Jeffrey, **COMING OUT: HOMOSEXUAL POLITICS IN BRITAIN FROM THE NINETEENTH CENTURY TO THE PRESENT.** 1977. See especially: Part 3 on Lesbianism. Discusses Edith Lees Ellis and Violet Paget. "Male homosexuality and lesbianism have different social implications. For men, homosexuality is seen as a rejection of maleness, with all its socially approved connotations. For women, it can be an assertion of femaleness, of separateness from men, and of identity" (p. 101); *reviewed in:* **VICTORIAN STUDIES:** Meyers, J., 22 (1979) 211-213. "Lesbians escaped punishment under the English law, but this was the exception. Women were burned, hanged and drowned in France, Italy, and Switzerland.... But the lesbian was the invisible woman of Victorian times" (p. 212).

10.573
JOURNAL OF SOCIAL HISTORY: Trumbach, R., *"London's Sodomites: Homosexual Behavior and Western Culture in the Eighteenth Century,"* 11 (1977) 1-33. "Female homosexuality was certainly abstractly condemned, but, like adultery in men, it was not much noticed. It was not even illegal in England. Sir Edward Coke took for granted that a woman's action came under the sodomy statute primarily 'if she commits buggery with a beast'" (p. 13).

10.574
Masters, Brian, **NOW BARABBAS WAS A ROTTER: THE EXTRAORDINARY LIFE OF MARIE CORELLI.** 1978. "Such matters [lesbianism] were seldom discussed at the end of the last century, and to women like Marie Corelli and Bertha Vyver they were barely imaginable. No doubt they embraced, they held hands, they proclaimed unashamedly their love for each other" (p. 277).

10.575
JOURNAL OF HOMOSEXUALITY: Faderman, L., *"The Morbidification of Love Between Women by Nineteenth Century Sexologists,"* 4 (1978) 73-89. "Medical science and psychology for the past 100 years have morbidified intense love relationships between women by inventing a syndrome of ills that supposedly accompany such affection, and by denying the validity or seriousness of the affection where such ills are clearly not present. The result has been that (until the lesbian-feminist movement) 20th century women were largely forced to deny their love for other women unless they were willing to acknowledge their concomitant morbidity" (p. 73).

10.576
JOURNAL OF POPULAR CULTURE: Faderman, L., *"Lesbian Magazine Fiction in the Early Twentieth Century,"* 11 (1978) 800-817.

10.577
Bullough, Vern L., **HOMOSEXUALITY: A HISTORY.** New York, 1979. Includes a chapter on lesbianism; *reviewed in:* **JOURNAL OF THE HISTORY OF MEDICINE:** Crompton, L., 36 (1981) 372.

10.578
Wolf, Deborah Goleman, **THE LESBIAN COMMUNITY.** 1979. See especially: "Socio-Historical Background." "Not until... the introduction of the Napoleonic Code in 1810, which was influenced by the social and political reforms sweeping through Europe in the eighteenth century, were laws against homosexual behavior... dropped from the books. Similar reforms were adopted in all Western countries except England, Germany, and America" (p. 28).

10.579

FRONTIERS: Simmons, C., *"Companionate Marriage and the Lesbian Threat,"* 4 (1979) 54-60. "Defensive sexual advisors [during Victorian times] turned to attack. 'Some married women thought to dislike coitus only because of a superior modesty, in reality are deceiving themselves and others. Their frigidity is on a homosexual basis, all their interests being feminine.' Another man described the 'nightmare' of marriage to a lesbian: After intercourse 'they feel cold, and do not experience the normal glow; they talk as though nothing important had happened'.... In normal heterosexual intercourse 'something important' did happen——when a woman expressed or feigned love and desire for a man in spite of the socially determined inequality among them, she symbolized some acceptance of her position, whether from having achieved an individually satisfactory relationship or from the need to please him. Overt sexual coldness destroyed the illusion of harmony" (p. 58).

10.580

RADICAL HISTORY REVIEW: Weeks, J., *"Movements of Affirmation, Sexual Meanings and Homosexual Identities,"* 20 (1979) 164-177. "The historical evidence points to the latter part of the nineteenth century as the crucial period in the conceptualisation of homosexuality as the distinguishing characteristic of a particular type of person, the 'invert,' or 'homosexual,' and the corresponding development of a new awareness of self amongst 'homosexuals.' The word 'homosexuality' itself was not invented until 1869, and did not enter English usage until the 1880's and 90's, and then largely as a result of the work of Havelock Ellis" (p. 164).

10.581

Todd, Janet, **WOMEN'S FRIENDSHIPS IN LITERATURE.** New York, 1980. "Diderot's THE NUN is the first novel in English or French to treat lesbianism seriously, explicitly, and decently.... The women in the book are pitiful because they have been wrongfully imprisoned either with or without their consent. They are more pitiful, the novel seems to assert, because in many cases they have embraced their imprisonment and accepted that an exclusive female society can satisfy all their needs. In this acceptance they have gone against nature and their fate must be madness, sickness and death" (n.p.).

10.582

Faderman, Lillian, "The Nineteenth Century. A. The Loving Friends" and "The Nineteenth Century. B. The Reaction" in **SURPASSING THE LOVE OF MEN. ROMANTIC FRIENDSHIP AND LOVE BETWEEN WOMEN FROM THE RENAISSANCE TO THE PRESENT.** by Lillian Faderman. New York, 1981. Analyzes lesbian activities in the socio-economic context for women of the period. Also evaluates both fictional and non-fictional "scientific" works of the period dealing with female homosexuality and romantic friendship; *reviewed in:* **HISTORY WORKSHOP JOURNAL:** Ruehl, S., no. 14 (1982) 157-160. Objects to "the conflation of lesbianism and feminism within Faderman's view, and the place her lesbian-feminism assigns——or rather denies——to lesbian sexual desire. That women actually do experience spontaneous, explicit desires for sexual contact with other women is a fact which Faderman's brand of lesbian-feminism finds hard to accommodate" (p. 159).

10.583

Holledge, Julie, **INNOCENT FLOWERS: WOMEN IN THE EDWARDIAN THEATRE.** 1981. "Chris [St. John] chose Edy [Ellen Terry's daughter] as the object of her love and when Ellen went to America at the end of the year, the two women set up house together at Smith Square. Some years later Chris wrote a thinly

disguised account of her relationship with Edy in a novel called HUNGERHEART"
(p. 117).

10.584
Mavor, Elizabeth, **THE LADIES OF LLANGOLLEN**. 1981. "It was the conception
of the relationship, one more nearly akin to the modern idea of marriage, that
Eleanor Butler and Sarah Ponsonby were to make their own" (p. 92).

10.585
FEMINIST STUDIES: Vicinus, M., *"'One Life to Stand Beside Me': Emotional
Conflicts in First-Generation College Women in England,"* 8 (1982) 603-628. "Middle-
class observers... remained deeply suspicious of a woman who gave up marriage,
and never fully validated public service as an alternative to motherhood. Women's
homoerotic friendships became especially suspect because they symbolized the single
woman's sexual autonomy and economic freedom" (p. 605); Wilson, E., *"Forbidden
Love,"* 10 (1984) 213-227. "The possibility of being a femme damnee, a
Baudelairean lesbian, disappeared when the women's movement came along, and I
[Elizabeth Wilson] was left caught between the two——for me——impossibilities. On
one side was the 'lesbian continuum' and woman bonding, on the other the
fetishistic specificity of hankey codes, leather, and colored handkerchiefs.
Romanticism was no magical third way. I do believe, though, that it is far more
pervasive than we realize, an attitude to life so deeply woven into our culture that
it permeates even radical ideologies——even sadomasochist outlawry and woman
bonding are ultimately romanticizations" (p. 223).

10.586
Cox, Don Richard, "Passion Between Women in the Victorian Novel" in
SEXUALITY AND VICTORIAN LITERATURE. by Don Richard Cox. Knoxville,
1984.

10.587
Fitzgerald, Penelope, **CHARLOTTE NEW AND HER FRIENDS**. 1984. Poet
Charlotte New (1869-1928) spoke openly about her lesbian attractions to Lucy
Harrison, Ella D'Arcy and May Sinclair, although these relationships were never
consummated. New was often attracted to unavailable lesbians, heterosexual women,
or asexual women.

10.588
Baker, Michael, **OUR THREE SELVES: THE LIFE OF RADCLYFFE HALL**. 1985.
Radclyffe Hall, author of THE WELL OF LONELINESS (1928), believed that she
was actually a man trapped in a woman's body and subscribed to a good deal of
Havelock Ellis' psycho-sexual theory. She was the "husband" in her long relationship
with Una Troubridge. Title refers to Hall, Troubridge, and Mabel (Lady) Veronica
Batten, Hall's first lover who had died unexpectedly during their relationship.
Batten became a spiritual inspiration in the lives of both women.

10.589
Jeffreys, Sheila, "Women's Friendships and Lesbianism" in **THE SPINSTER AND
HER ENEMIES: FEMINISM AND SEXUALITY 1880-1930**. 1985.

10.590
Parker, William, **HOMOSEXUALITY BIBLIOGRAPHY: SECOND SUPPLEMENT,
1976-1982**. 1985. Includes books, newspaper articles, court cases, religious journals,
legal journals, popular magazines, and gay publications.

* * *

4. MORAL REFORM AND "SOCIAL PURITY" AS SOCIAL ISSUES AND SOCIAL MOVEMENTS

10.591

Society for the Reformation of Manners, AN ACCOUNT OF THE SOCIETIES FOR REFORMATION OF MANNERS IN ENGLAND AND IRELAND WITH A PERSUASIVE TO PERSONS OF ALL RANKS TO BE ZEALOUS AND DILIGENT IN PROMOTING THE EXECUTION OF THE LAWS AGAINST PROPHANENESS AND DEBAUCHERY FOR THE EFFECTING A NATIONAL REFORMATION. 1700; AN ACCOUNT OF THE PROGRESS OF THE REFORMATION OF MANNERS IN ENGLAND, SCOTLAND AND IRELAND AND OTHER PARTS OF EUROPE AND AMERICA, ETC. 1704; 1705; THE FOURTEENTH ACCOUNT OF THE PROGRESS MADE IN SUPPRESSING PROPHANENESS AND DEBAUCHERY BY THE SOCIETIES FOR REFORMATION OF MANNERS, IN THE CITIES OF LONDON AND WESTMINSTER, AND PLACES ADJACENT. 1709; THE TWO AND TWENTIETH ACCOUNT OF THE PROGRESS MADE IN THE CITIES OF LONDON AND WESTMINSTER, AND PLACES ADJACENT, BY THE SOCIETIES FOR PROMOTING A REFORMATION OF MANNERS; BY FURTHERING THE EXECUTION OF THE LAWS AGAINST PROPHANENESS AND IMMORALITY, AND BY OTHER CHRISTIAN METHODS. 1717; FOUR AND TWENTIETH (SIXTH AND, SEVENTH AND, THIRTIETH, ONE AND THIRTIETH, THREE AND, SIX AND, EIGHT AND, FORTIETH, FORTY-FIRST, FORTY-THIRD, FORTY-FOURTH) ACCOUNT. 1719; many subsequent eds.

10.592

Moral Society, PLAN OF THE MORAL SOCIETY, WITH SOME ACCOUNT OF THEIR UNDERTAKING;... TO WHICH IS ADDED THE MORAL CATECHISM. 1729.

10.593

Proclamation Society, A NARRATIVE OF PROCEEDINGS, TENDING TOWARD A NATIONAL REFORMATION PREVIOUS TO AND CONSEQUENT UPON, HIS MAJESTY'S ROYAL PROCLAMATION FOR THE SUPPRESSION OF VICE AND IMMORALITY IN A LETTER TO A FRIEND... 1787; STATEMENT AND PROPOSITIONS FROM THE SOCIETY FOR GIVING EFFECT TO HIS MAJESTY'S PROCLAMATION AGAINST VICE AND IMMORALITY... 1790; SEVENTH REPORT OF THE COMMITTEE OF THE SOCIETY FOR CARRYING INTO EFFECT HIS MAJESTY'S PROCLAMATION AGAINST VICE AND IMMORALITY, AND TOGETHER WITH A BRIEF STATEMENT OF THE ORIGIN AND NATURE OF SOCIETY, AND A LIST OF THE MEMBERS. 1795; REPORT OF THE COMMITTEE OF THE SOCIETY FOR CARRYING INTO EFFECT HIS MAJESTY'S PROCLAMATION AGAINST VICE AND IMMORALITY, FOR THE YEAR 1799. 1800.

10.594

Society for the Suppression of Vice, PROPOSAL FOR ESTABLISHING A

SOCIETY FOR THE SUPPRESSION OF VICE, AND THE ENCOURAGEMENT OF RELIGION AND VIRTUE, THROUGHOUT THE UNITED KINGDOM, ETC. [1801]; ADDRESS TO THE PUBLIC FROM THE SOCIETY FOR THE SUPPRESSION OF VICE. 1803; PART THE SECOND OF AN ADDRESS TO THE PUBLIC FROM THE SOCIETY FOR THE SUPPRESSION OF VICE. 1803; AN ABSTRACT OF THE LAWS AGAINST VICE AND IMMORALITY. [1810]; OCCASIONAL REPORTS OF THE SOCIETY FOR THE SUPPRESSION OF VICE, NOS. VI, VII, IX. 1812; 1816; 1822; OBJECTS. 1825. Objects included prevention of profanation of Sabbath, suppression of blasphemous and obscene publications and eradication of brothels and fortune tellers; REPORT OF THE SOCIETY FOR THE SUPPRESSION OF VICE. 1825. ——*see also:* Thomas, Donald, "Guardians of Public Morality: The Society for the Suppression of Vice" in A LONG TIME BURNING: THE HISTORY OF LITERARY CENSORSHIP IN ENGLAND. by Donald Thomas. 1969; HISTORICAL JOURNAL: Roberts, M.J.D., *"Communications: The Society for the Suppression of Vice and its Early Critics, 1802-1892,"* 26 (1983) 159-176. "The particular forms of vice which the founders of the society selected for suppression they eventually listed as follows: profanation of the Lord's Day and profane swearing; publication of blasphemous, licentious and obscene books and prints; selling by false weights and measures; keeping of disorderly public houses; brothels and gaming houses" (p. 159).

10.595
OBSOLETE IDEAS IN SIX LETTERS ADDRESSED TO MARIA, BY A FRIEND. 1805. Recommends to "Maria" that, whereas she should not prudishly isolate herself from men, she should definitely keep the "libertine man" or "libertine woman" at arm's length. "The moment the breath of impurity assails you, you must, like the sensitive plant, shut up in yourself" (p. 86).

10.596
Beggs, Thomas, THREE LECTURES ON THE MORAL ELEVATION OF THE PEOPLE. 1849.

10.597
Sewell, Elizabeth, "Purity" in PRINCIPLES OF EDUCATION DRAWN FROM NATURE AND REVELATION AND APPLIED TO FEMALE EDUCATION IN THE UPPER CLASSES. by Elizabeth Sewell. 2 vols. 1865. "We feel that God has mercifully left a remnant of the innocence of Paradise in the natural purity of a young girl's mind.... And, acting upon this theory we leave——or at least we think we leave——young girls to themselves; taking, perhaps, one precaution, that the books they read should be... unobjectionable.... And what is the result? Most highly satisfactory" (p. 67).

10.598
Drysdale, George R., THE ELEMENTS OF SOCIAL SCIENCE: OR, PHYSICAL, SEXUAL, AND NATURAL RELIGION. BY A GRADUATE OF MEDICINE. 7th ed., 1867. Decries the double standard which tolerates male sexual indulgences but punishes those of women. States that such a standard "confuses all ideas of morality" (p. 410).

10.599
Hopkins, Jane Ellice, WORK AMONG THE LOST [A SHORT ACCOUNT OF THE WORK OF MRS. FANNY VICARS AND THE ALBION HILL HOME FOR FEMALE PENITENTS, BRIGHTON]. 1870; AN ENGLISH WOMAN'S WORK AMONG WORKINGMEN. 1875. introduction by Elihu Burritt. Account of Hopkins' work for moral purity among working men as well as women; A PLEA FOR THE

WIDER ACTION OF THE CHURCH OF ENGLAND IN THE PREVENTION OF THE DEGRADATION OF WOMEN, AS SUBMITTED TO A COMMITTEE OF CONVOCATION. 1879; GRAVE MORAL QUESTIONS ADDRESSED TO THE MEN AND WOMEN OF ENGLAND. 1882; THE PURITY MOVEMENT: CANNOT WE USE EXISTING ORGANIZATIONS? 1885; THE PRESENT MORAL CRISIS: AN APPEAL TO WOMEN. [1886]. —*see also:* Barrett, Rosa, ELLICE HOPKINS. 1907.

10.600
National Association for the Promotion of Social Purity, CONSTITUTION OF THE NATIONAL ASSOCIATION FOR THE PROMOTION OF SOCIAL PURITY. [1870]; ANNUAL REPORT. 1875; LAWS OF THE SOCIETY. 1875.

10.601
Butler, Josephine, ADDRESS DELIVERED IN CRAIGIE HALL, EDINBURGH, 24 FEBRUARY 1871. Manchester, 1871; SOCIAL PURITY (AN ADDRESS GIVEN AT CAMBRIDGE, IN MAY 1879). 1879; 1881; 1882.

10.602
National Vigilance Association [for the Defence of Personal Rights and for the Amendment of the Law in Points wherein it is Injurious to Women], ANNUAL REPORTS. 1871-1885. REPORT TO THE ANNUAL MEETING BY THE COMMITTEE FOR AMENDING THE LAW IN POINTS WHEREIN IT IS INJURIOUS TO WOMEN, LIVERPOOL, NOVEMBER 14, 1871. Manchester, 1871; SHORT MANUAL ON THE ENGLISH LAW ON THE SUBJECT (OF THE REPRESSION OF IMMORALITY): WITH... PRACTICAL SUGGESTIONS, AND AN APPENDIX OF STATUTES. 1883; TWELFTH ANNUAL REPORT. 1883; ANNUAL REPORT OF THE EXECUTIVE COMMITTEE. 1888, etc.; EXECUTIVE COMMITTEE MINUTES. 5 July 1887 and 29 April 1890; PUBLIC MORALS. [1903]; A FRIENDLY WARNING. 1904. —*see also:* Butler, Josephine, SPEECH DELIVERED... AT THE FOURTH ANNUAL MEETING OF THE VIGILANCE ASSOCIATION FOR THE DEFENCE OF PERSONAL RIGHTS, HELD AT BRISTOL, OCTOBER 15TH, 1874. 1874; THE PROTECTION OF YOUNG GIRLS. OBSERVATIONS ON THE REPORT OF THE SELECT COMMITTEE OF THE HOUSE OF LORDS, ON THE LAW RELATING TO THE PROTECTION OF YOUNG GIRLS IN ENGLAND... 1882; Coote, William and Baker, Miss A., eds., A ROMANCE OF PHILANTHROPY: BEING A RECORD OF THE PRINCIPAL INCIDENTS CONNECTED WITH THE EXCEPTIONALLY SUCCESSFUL THIRTY YEARS' WORK OF THE NATIONAL VIGILANCE ASSOCIATION. 1916. Discusses medical and preventive homes established by the preventive committee, the repatriation of undesirable foreign women, and the Association's national purity crusade. "Fifty years ago only a very small band of brave men and women spoke out in the cause of social purity. They were held to be troublesome enthusiasts, cranks, disturbers of public decency, because they removed the veil that covered those sores that were poisoning our social life" (p. xiii); Bewes, Wyndham A., A MANUAL OF VIGILANCE LAW. 3rd ed., 1913.

10.603
Brown, James Baldwin, OUR MORALS AND MANNERS. 1872.

10.604
Social Purity Alliance, ANNUAL REPORTS 1873-1890; LAWS AND OPERATIONS AND ADDRESS. Leeds, 1880; SINS OF THE FLESH. A SERMON BY J.M. WILSON. 1880; SPEECH OF MRS. ORMISTON CHANT AT THE ANNUAL MEETING OF THE S.P.A., JUNE, 13, 1883. 1883.

10.605
Platt, Smith H., **QUEENLY WOMANHOOD. A PRIVATE TREATISE; FOR FEMALES ONLY, ON THE SEXUAL INSTINCT, AS RELATED TO MORAL AND CHRISTIAN LIFE**. 1875; 2nd ed., 1877.

10.606
Blackwell, Elizabeth, **COUNSEL TO PARENTS ON THE MORAL EDUCATION OF THEIR CHILDREN**. New York, 1878; 2nd ed., 1879; 1883; 8th ed., 1913. Emphasizes that a pure and moral heart will save society from degradation and debauchery. "All the young women of the middle and upper classes of society, no matter how pure and innocent their natures, are brought, by these customs of society, into direct competition with prostitutes! The modest grace of pure young womanhood... will not compare for a moment with the force of attraction which sensual indulgence and the excitement of debauch exert upon the youth who is habituated to such intoxications" (p. 73).

10.607
SENTINEL: 1879 to 1900. Journal of the Association for the Improvement of Public Morals; Hill, S., *"Fallen Men,"* n.v. (1880) n.p.

10.608
JOURNAL OF THE VIGILANCE ASSOCIATION FOR THE DEFENCE OF PERSONAL RIGHTS: 1881 to 1886; nos. 1-62; *continued as:* **PERSONAL RIGHTS JOURNAL:** 1886 to 1903; nos. 63-240. During the 1880's and the 1890's, this journal, published by the Personal Rights Association, condemned the National Vigilance Association for persecuting "the poorest, most helpless of womankind."

10.609
Moral Reform Union, **THE FIRST ANNUAL REPORT**. 1882; **SPEECH DELIVERED BY W.T. STEAD AT THE CENTRAL CRIMINAL COURT... NOV. 4, 1885**. 1885; **A COLLECTION OF PAMPHLETS ISSUED BY THE MORAL REFORM UNION**. 1888; **HISTORY OF THE CONTAGIOUS DISEASES ACTS**. 1892.

10.610
Central Vigilance Committee for the Repression of Immorality, **SHORT MANUAL ON THE ENGLISH LAW ON THE SUBJECT [OF THE REPRESSION OF IMMORALITY]; WITH... PRACTICAL SUGGESTIONS, AND AN APPENDIX OF STATUTES**. 1883; **REPORT OF THE FIRST ANNUAL MEETING, ETC.** 1884.

10.611
Dyer, Alfred S., **FACTS FOR MEN ON MORAL PURITY AND HEALTH**. 1884.

10.612
Scott, B., **IS LONDON MORE IMMORAL THAN PARIS OR BRUSSELS?** 1884.

10.613
CONTEMPORARY REVIEW: *"The Speech of Silence,"* 48 (1885) 326-331. "A hideously perverted state of morals has been exposed, running through, so far as one sex is concerned, the whole of society, from the highest to the lowest; whilst, so far as the other sex is concerned, it condemns the poorest, most ignorant and most helpless to a life of unspeakable degradation, and drags down certain others, through appeals to their cupidity, to much lower depth of infamy and shame, that of living in luxury on the trade of decoying and selling children and their fellow-

women" (p. 327); Hopkins, J.E., *"The Apocalypse of Evil,"* 48 (1885) 332-342. Argues in favor of chastity for men and women alike: "This, yea, this equal obligation of the law of purity on men and women alike is the great natural law of the kingdom... and the day is at hand when women will insist on its recognition" (p. 342); Noble, J.A., *"The Fiction of Sexuality,"* 67 (1895) 493-494.

10.614
White Cross League, **THE PRACTICAL WORKING OF THE WHITE CROSS MOVEMENT.** 1886; **TWENTY-EIGHTH TO FIFTY FIFTH ANNUAL REPORTS, 1894-1938.** 1910-1911; 1937-1938. (Lacks the 29th, 31st and 33rd reports); **"MANNERS MAKETH" THE MAN: DEDICATED TO THE GENTLEMEN OF ENGLAND.** edited for the League by Lieutenant-Colonel H. Everitt. 1906. ——*see also:* **THE WHITE CROSS ARMY. A STATEMENT OF THE BISHOP OF DURHAM'S MOVEMENT.** 1883; **THE WHITE CROSS SERIES ETC.** 1883; **CONTEMPORARY REVIEW:** Dunelm, J.B., *"The White Cross,"* 48 (1885) 262-268. The members of the White Cross Army "do not profess to be pure.... They place an ideal definitely before themselves, which they endeavour to realize in themselves, and which they commend to others. The chief points of this ideal are two. It upholds the principle that purity is an obligation on men not less than on women, and it maintains a chivalrous respect for the honour of woman as woman" (p. 266).

10.615
Beale, Lionel Smith, **OUR MORALITY AND THE MORAL QUESTION: CHIEFLY FROM THE MEDICAL SIDE.** 1887. "Bad bringing up in the home, bad example, and bad management at school have at least as much to do with a bad moral result as regards victim as well as aggressor, as the inherent badness of disposition" (p. 69).

10.616
THE VIGILANCE RECORD. 1888.

10.617
Vox Clamantis (pseud.), **PUBLIC MORALITY: OUR STREETS.** 1890.

10.618
Church of England Purity Society, **PROPOSALS CONCERNING THE MORAL CONDITIONS OF GARRISON AND SEAPORT TOWNS.** 1893. Argues that more power should be given to police against brothel keepers and prostitutes.

10.619
Claflin, Tennesse (Lady Cook), **ESSAYS ON SOCIAL TOPICS.** [1898]. Argues that mothers should prepare their daughters for the shock of sexual relations after marriage. See especially: "Ideal Woman," "Prudery," "Woman's Purity"; **THE NEED OF REVISING MORALS AND LAWS: A LECTURE.** 1910. "When we mothers see that over a million girls die every four years, as one of the effects of unbridled lust, so that our young men may 'sow their wild oats,' and that old roues may run the gamut with many mistresses and not only debauch themselves but teach their sons to follow in their tracks——then, I say, it is time that we rebelled. It is not necessary for a man to 'sow his wild oats.' Every man can be as continent and pure as any woman" (p. 12).

10.620
International Congress of Women, **REPORT.** 1899; **AN EQUAL MORAL STANDARD FOR MEN AND WOMEN; A REPORT OF THE PAPERS READ AT A SPECIAL MEETING FOR WOMEN HELD IN CONNECTION WITH THE**

SOCIAL SECTION AT THE INTERNATIONAL CONGRESS OF WOMEN, CHURCH HOUSE, JUNE 30, 1899. 1900. "In demanding an equal moral standard for men and women, we do not mean the right to the disposal of the body, a right to be immoral; that would be to lower the moral level. It is only when an equal standard means an improvement in the morality of all, and when the good members of society are protected from the bad, that mankind will make any progress" (p. 10); "Social Necessity for an Equal Moral Standard for Men and Women" in WOMEN IN SOCIAL LIFE: THE TRANSACTIONS OF THE SOCIAL SECTION OF THE INTERNATIONAL CONGRESS OF WOMEN. LONDON, JULY 1899. 1900. "Morality, justice and liberty demanded a single moral standard and equal responsibility for both sexes. Mothers should cease to inculcate unjust ideas in the minds of their daughters——ideas which were largely accountable for the actual state of affairs and tended to make women a hindrance rather than a help to advancement towards the desired goal" (p. 130).

10.621
Scott, James Foster, THE SEXUAL INSTINCT: ITS USES AND DANGERS AS AFFECTING HEREDITY AND MORALS. New York, 1899.

10.622
Wilson, James M., "The Progress of Morality in the Relations of Men and Women" in GOOD CITIZENSHIP. ed. by J.E. Hand. 1899. Contends that only Christianity can prevent the corruption of sexual relations and the moral degradation of the nation which follows.

10.623
London Council for the Promotion of Public Morality (Public Morality Council), ANNUAL REPORT. 1901.

10.624
Wintz, Sophia Gertrude, OUR BLUE JACKETS: MISS WESTON'S LIFE AMONG OUR SAILORS. 1903. By providing meeting places, food, recreation, etc., Miss Weston sought to prevent drunkenness, licentious sexual activity, gambling and fighting among the navy men.

10.625
National Social Purity Crusade, THE NATIONAL PURITY CRUSADE... WITH AN INTRODUCTION BY MISS E. HOPKINS. [1904]; THE NATIONAL PURITY CRUSADE, ITS ORIGIN AND RESULTS. A BRIEF RECORD. rpt. from: CHRISTIAN: n.d.; THE CLEANSING OF A CITY. 1908; THE NATION'S MORALS. 1910.

10.626
Westermarck, Edvard Alexander, THE ORIGIN AND DEVELOPMENT OF MORAL IDEAS. 2 vols. 1906-1908. Argues that "with regard to sexual relations bewteen unmarried men and women Christianity has done little more than establish a standard which, though accepted perhaps in theory, is hardly recognized by the feelings of the lage majority of people——or at least of men——in Christian communities, and has introduced the vice of hypocrisy, which apparently was little known in sexual matters by pagan antiquity" (II, p. 434).

10.627
WESTMINISTER REVIEW: Boyle, H.R., *"Sexual Morality,"* 166 (1906) 334-340. "A woman may be anatomically pure, for lack of opportunity, from excess of caution, or for many other reasons, and yet her mind may be a hotbed of impurity" (p. 339).

10.628
Moral Instruction League, **MORAL INSTRUCTION, WHAT IT IS NOT AND WHAT IT IS.** 1908; **MORAL INSTRUCTION IN ELEMENTARY SCHOOLS IN ENGLAND AND WALES.** 1908; **A GRADUATED SYLLABUS OF MORAL AND CIVIC INSTRUCTION FOR SECONDARY SCHOOLS.** 1908; **A SCHEME FOR THE CORRELATION OF CERTAIN SUBJECTS OF INSTRUCTION IN SUBORDINATION TO THE AIM OF CHARACTER-TRAINING.** 1912.

10.629
Douglas, Mary Tew, **PURITY AND DANGER: AN ANALYSIS OF POLLUTION AND TABOO.** 1910; New York, 1966.

10.630
Moral Education League, (afterwards Civic and Moral Education League), **NOBLE PATH. A VOLUME OF MORAL INSTRUCTION DESIGNED FOR THE USE OF CHILDREN, PARENTS AND TEACHERS, AND MAINLY BASED ON EASTERN TRADITION, POETRY AND HISTORY.** 1911.

10.631
MORAL EDUCATION LEAGUE QUARTERLY: 1911 to 1914. Published by the Moral Education League.

10.632
Gallichan, Catherine Gasquoine Hartley, (Mrs. Walter Gallichan), **WOMEN AND MORALITY BY A MOTHER, MEN AND MORALS BY A FATHER: THE SEXES AGAIN.** by Catherine Gasquoine Hartley. Chicago, 1913.

10.633
More, P. McCarthy, **TRUE CONFLICT BETWEEN LOVE AND MORALITY.** 1913.

10.634
Pankhurst, Christabel, **THE GREAT SCOURGE AND HOW TO END IT.** 1913. Collection of articles advocating "chastity for men" to prevent spreading venereal disease. Presents a strident argument that women are the victims of a double standard of morality and are made extremely vulnerable to venereal disease by their husbands' relations with prostitutes. "If a woman can earn an adequate living by the work of her hand or brain, then it will be much the harder to compel her to earn her living by selling her sex.... So long as men have the monopoly of political power, it will be impossible to restrain their impulse to keep women in economic dependence and so sexually subservient" (p. 45). —*see also:* Morrow, Prince A., **SOCIAL DISEASES AND MARRIAGE: SOCIAL PROPHYLAXIS.** New York, 1904. Pankhurst used this as a basis for her work THE GREAT SCOURGE.

10.635
Creighton, Louise, **THE SOCIAL DISEASE AND HOW TO FIGHT IT: A REJOINDER.** 1914. "If women are condemned to degradation because of unchastity of men, the same sin condemns men to degradation. Women must struggle not only for the purity of women but for the purity of men, and in this struggle they have not got to fight against men but win more men to fight with them" (pp. 34-35).

10.636
Michels, Robert, **SEXUAL ETHICS: A STUDY OF BORDERLAND QUESTIONS.** 1914. Discusses sexual education, nature and the limits of modesty, intermediate

stages of sexual morality in woman, the prostitute as the "old maid" of the proletariat, dualism of woman in primary sexual love, value and limits of chastity, and outward manifestations of the subjection of woman in marriage.

10.637
ATLANTIC MONTHLY: Repplier, A., *"The Repeal of Reticence,"* 113 (1914) 301-309. "All the studies of seduction... conspire to lift the burden of blame from the woman's shoulders, to free her from any sense of human responsibility. It is assumed that she plays no part in her own undoing, that she is as passive as the animal bought for vivisection, as mute and helpless in the tormentor's hands. The tissue of false sentiment woven about her has resulted in an extraordinary confusion of outlook, a perilous nullification of honesty and honor" (p. 307).

10.638
Association for Moral and Social Hygiene, **PAMPHLETS.** 1916-1938; **SECOND [ETC.] REPORT.** 1917+.

10.639
Begbie, Harold, "The Purity Crusade" in **THE LIFE OF GENERAL WILLIAM BOOTH, THE FOUNDER OF THE SALVATION ARMY.** by Harold Begbie. vol. 2, New York, 1920. Details the Salvation Army's work in the reclamation of prostitutes and the eradication of prostitution.

10.640
Brittain, Vera, "Morals in the Post-Victorian Era 1900-1930" in **HALCYON OR THE FUTURE OF MONOGAMY.** by Vera Brittain. 1929. Claims that World War I had the positive effect of bringing the reality of sex to the light of day. "Released from sheltered dependence by war work, and from the trivial cowardice of shame by the constant threat of disaster, young women, as we learn from the conversations of the heroines in the fiction of the period did not shrink from admitting both to themselves and to their lovers the mutual character of sex-desire" (p. 12). Speaks of the subsequent attempts to perpetuate "the Victorian illusion"; "Women and Sex Morals" in **LADY INTO WOMAN.** by Vera Brittain. 1953.

10.641
Gallichan, Walter M., **THE POISON OF PRUDERY: AN HISTORICAL SURVEY.** 1929. "While ignorant, prudish women were discussing whether one should speak of 'legs' in polite company, and boys and girls were being reared in 'the sheltered home,' without any effort to guide them rightly in sex conduct and hygiene, syphilis raged throughout the United Kingdom, prostitution was being practised in its grossest and most callous forms, and schools were often breeding places of vice. Such was Victorian pseudomorality" (p. 49).

10.642
Markun, Leo, **MRS. GRUNDY: A HISTORY OF FOUR CENTURIES OF MORALS INTENDED TO ILLUMINATE PRESENT PROBLEMS IN GREAT BRITAIN AND THE UNITED STATES.** 1930. "In the 1880's and 1890's the precise moralists of England thought that immorality was being imported from France. Tennyson in his old age took up the cry about the degenerate times. In 'Locksley Hall Sixty Years After,' which was published in 1886, he exclaims: 'Authors——atheist, essayist, novelist, realist, rhymster play your part, Paint the mortal shame of nature with the living hues of Art'" (p. 314).

10.643
May, Geoffrey, **SOCIAL CONTROL OF SEX EXPRESSION.** 1930. May's thesis is

that legal control of extramarital sex throughout Western civilization has persisted not because of moral reasons or for the protection of individuals, but because illegitimacy weakens society. He presents as evidence statistics that show a higher infant mortality among illegitimate children and a lower birth rate among prostitutes than among married women.

10.644
Wagner, Donald O., **THE CHURCH OF ENGLAND AND SOCIAL REFORM SINCE 1854.** 1930. Discussion of the activities of Anglican sisterhoods to curb illicit sexual activity in the slums.

10.645
Calverton, Victor F., **THE BANKRUPTCY OF MARRIAGE.** [1931]. Discusses the dissolution of moral and sexual repression required of women during the Victorian age. Women's increased social and political freedom resulted in "a new feminine psychology and a new morality" (p. 8).

10.646
Unsworth, Madge, **MAIDEN TRIBUTE: A STUDY IN VOLUNTARY SOCIAL SERVICE.** 1949; 1950. Account of the Salvation Army, Whitechapel Refuge, Josephine Butler, Mrs. Bramwell Booth, poor children, and fallen women.

10.647
BRITISH JOURNAL OF VENEREAL DISEASES: Fessler, A., *"Advertisements on the Treatment of Venereal Disease and the Social History of Venereal Disease,"* 25 (1949) 84-87. "The conviction that venereal disease had to be treated as taboo, an attitude typical of the Victorian period, was prevalent" (p. 86).

10.648
Higson, Jessie E., **THE STORY OF A BEGINNING: AN ACCOUNT OF PIONEER WORK FOR MORAL WELFARE.** 1955.

10.649
Young, Agnes Freda and Ashton, Elwyn Thomas, "Moral Welfare" in **BRITISH SOCIAL WORK IN THE NINETEENTH CENTURY.** 1956.

10.650
Fryer, Peter, **MRS. GRUNDY: STUDIES IN ENGLISH PRUDERY.** New York, 1964. "Prudery is fear and hatred of pleasure, primarily of sexual pleasure; and Mrs. Grundy is a prude who carries this fear and hatred to the stage of more or less organized interference with other people's pleasures. The private prude and the prude-at-large are both obsessed by an awareness of the vast amount of unregulated pleasure that is being enjoyed in the world; this they call sin" (p. 18). Discusses the various manifestations of prudery in Victorian England, lewd language, teetotalitarians, and nudity.

10.651
Hall, Mary Penelope and Howes, Ismene, **THE CHURCH IN SPECIAL WORK, A STUDY OF MORAL WELFARE WORK.** 1965. "By specific reforms and practical measures of help, they sought to make it less easy for girls to 'go wrong,' to hinder those inviting them to do so, and to substitute compassion towards them for the current hostility and condemnation" (p. 23).

10.652
Playfair, Giles, "Scandal 1885: The Battle for Purity" in **SIX STUDIES IN**

HYPOCRISY. by Giles Playfair. 1969. Discussion of Parliament's passage of the bill to raise the age of consent to sexual intercourse to sixteen.

10.653
Pivar, David J., **PURITY CRUSADE, SEXUAL MORALITY AND SOCIAL CONTROL 1868-1900.** Westport, 1973; 1978. American, but useful for studying the English case. "Since urbanization destroyed the close kinship ties of a pre-industrial era, and the urban culture lacked the restraints of the small town, reformers developed agencies for single women to serve as a substitute for family environments. For years, the Young Women's Christian Associations had been 'homes away from home.' A major social function of the YWCA and similar agencies was the preservation of individual purity" (p. 105).

10.654
Harrison, Brian, "State Intervention and Moral Reform" in **PRESSURE FROM WITHOUT IN EARLY VICTORIAN ENGLAND.** ed. by Patricia Hollis. New York, 1974. "The nineteenth century debate on State intervention cannot be fully understood unless the historian, like the Victorians themselves, discusses both moral and social reform together; for attitudes generated in the moral sphere carried over into the social" (p. 289). The support for moral reform cut across party allegiance and religious denomination. The Evangelicals and the Benthamites cooperated in the movement. "Josephine Butler, like other moral reformers, began with an extremely elevated concept of law. She saw her movement as 'a great school of principle,' and insisted that the State should concern itself with morality; to deny this was 'the cardinal heresy of the Liberal Party'" (p. 312).

10.655
McGregor, O.R., "The Double Standard" in **RULE BRITANNIA: THE VICTORIAN WORLD.** ed. by George Perry and Nicholas Mason. 1974. "Given the late age of marriage of middle-class men, the expectation that they would have some wild oats to sow and the rule of chastity for their sisters, it is easy to understand why Lecky, in common with other Victorian moralists, described prostitutes as eternal priestesses of humanity, blasted for the sins of the people, preserving the purity of upper-class womanhood" (p. 178).

10.656
UNIVERSITY OF NEWCASTLE HISTORICAL JOURNAL: Smith, F.B., *"Sexuality in Britain 1800-1900,"* 2 (1974) 19-32. The Victorians supported "the notion that only a purified leadership can survive challenges from religious infidelity of the lower orders. This grand fear directly linked sexual pollution with the threat of social chaos and the fall of the Empire" (p. 29).

10.657
TRANSCRIPT OF THE CONFERENCE GROUP FOR SOCIAL AND ADMINI-STRATIVE HISTORY: Burstyn, J., *"The Two Faces of Moral Reform in Women's Education in Victorian England,"* 6 (1976) 4-19.

10.658
Pearsall, Ronald, **PUBLIC PURITY, PRIVATE SHAME.** 1976. "Many Victorians behaved in an ostensibly moral manner through fear, fear of social obloquy, fear of offending those to whom they owed their livelihood, and fear of God. God was all-knowing and all-seeing, could see a shop-assistant purloining change from the till and a respectable middle-class man playing, as it was called, High Life in London. As more and more people ceased to believe in God and vengeance on high, an inhibition was removed. The stern exhortations to be pure were no more regarded

than cracker mottoes" (p. 135).

10.659
LITERATURE AND HISTORY: Curtis, T.C. and Speck, A., *"The Societies for the Reformation of Manners: A Case Study in the Theory and Practice of Moral Reform,"* no. 3 (1976) 45-64.

10.660
Bristow, Edward J., **VICE AND VIGILANCE: PURITY MOVEMENTS IN BRITAIN SINCE 1700.** Dublin, 1977. "Up to 1914 and even through the interwar years, the social purity movement made its influence felt. It proceeded along a number of more or less distinct fronts: for the diffusion of information about chastity and the rescue and protection of females, against prostitution and commercialised vice as well as sex expression in literature, art, entertainment and advertising" (p. 121). "Finally the message for all men was the wickedness of the double standard. As Josephine [Butler] stated, 'Vain Sophistry! Sirs, you cannot hold us in mire so long as you drag our sisters in the mire. As you are unjust and cruel to them, you will become unjust and cruel to us... we... turn away in disgust from the thought of a family life whose purity is preserved at the price of her degradation'" (p. 83).

10.661
Watson, J.S., "The Role of the Purity Movement in the Development of Sex Education for Young People, 1850-1914," M.Phil. diss., London School of Economics, 1979.

10.662
FEMINIST STUDIES: Ryan, M., *"The Power of Women's Networks: Female Moral Reform in Utica, New York,"* 5 (1979) 66-85. This study of an American reform movement is useful as a background for investigation of the motivations and outcome of similar efforts in England. "Female Moral Reform... presents two apparently contradictory uses of woman's power: to attack the double standard, on the one hand, and to celebrate a domestic feminine stereotype, on the other" (p. 67).

10.663
Degler, Carl, "Organizing to Control Sexuality" in **AT ODDS: WOMEN AND THE FAMILY IN AMERICA FROM THE REVOLUTION TO THE PRESENT.** Oxford, 1980. "Women's activity in behalf of social purity was... quite in conformity with the doctrine of separate spheres, as other causes, like woman suffrage, would never be" (p. 281).

10.664
Firth, Violet, (Fortune, Dion), **THE PROBLEM OF PURITY.** rpt., New York, 1980. See especially: "Our Attitudes Towards Sex," "The Sex Life of the Child," "Control of the Sex Force."

10.665
Isaacs, Tina Beth, "Moral Crime, Moral Reform and the State in Early Eighteenth Century England," Ph.D. diss., Univ. of Rochester, 1980.

10.666
Snitow, Ann, Stansell, Christine, and Thompson, Sharon, eds., **POWERS OF DESIRE: THE POLITICS OF SEXUALITY.** New York, 1983. From the introduction: "Social purity, however, quickly reached beyond the feminist intentions of many of its first adherents and became an attack on sexually active

working-class youth, poor women, homosexuals, and female boardinghouse keepers
—those whose erotic activity outside of marriage placed them at odds with Victorian
norms. If social purity afforded feminists the possibility of exercising some control
over sexual politics, the terms of discourse the feminists established ultimately
allowed men, not women, to dominate the movement. An abstract image of woman
as sexual victim, originated by feminists, became a weapon with which the male
ruling class on both sides of the Atlantic strengthened its hegemony over women,
sexual outlaws, and the poor by establishing a state apparatus of protectionist sexual
policies" (p. 22).

* * *

5. MODERN COMMENT AND SCHOLARSHIP ON SEXUALITY IN THE VICTORIAN AND EDWARDIAN ERAS

10.667
Craig, Alec, **SEX AND REVOLUTION**. 1934. "The Victorians knew romance,
comradeship and inspiration in love, and knew that these things can exist apart
from child-bearing... The subjection of women was implicit in this system. Girls
were educated for housewifery only. Those who missed success in the marriage
market were condemned to social obloquy and often to economic distress. The
system was supported and strengthened by the following expedients. (1)
Prostitution, though officially frowned upon, was recognized as a necessary safety-
valve. It diverted surplus virility into channels where it was not a menace to the
'virtue' of 'respectable' women. (2) A general ignorance of contraceptive technique
was carefully preserved, although prostitutes and their medical advisors must have
been well acquainted with these matters. (3) The vigorous persecution of 'anti-
social' (i.e. anti-propagatory) sexual activities... (a) Abortion. (b) Male
homosexuality. (c) 'Illicit relationships'... (4) a very effective taboo on all sexual
information and discussion was maintained... (5) Erotic desire was artificially
inflamed... by various means. For example: (a) The accentuation of secondary sexual
characteristics (tight lacing, bustles, fantastic whiskers, male corsets and padding
jackets). (b) The exaggeration of sex-distinction behaviour (fainting, military
swagger). (c) Strict concealment of the body, especially as between the two sexes"
(pp. 12-14).

10.668
Hodann, Max, **HISTORY OF MODERN MORALS**. trans. by Stella Browne. 1937.
"Sexual knowledge has still to wage constant battle with the vestiges of
Victorianism; and these are often the more powerful for being implicit and
subconscious. We must overcome this peculiar legacy of the nineteenth century, to
which even the most enlightened amongst us are co-heirs" (p. 31).

10.669
Leach, William, **TRUE LOVE AND PERFECT UNION: THE FEMINIST REFORM
OF SEX AND SOCIETY**. 1944; 1980. See especially: "The Rationalization of Sexual
Desire." This chapter discusses the contributions of George Napheys and Edward
Carpenter. Napheys denied that sexual passion in women was degrading. "Carpenter
maintained that both sexes needed sexual release, and that female desire was
particularly strong during the 'period of menstruation' and 'by no means wanting at
other times'" (pp. 94-95).

10.670
Beales, H.L. and Glover, Edward, "Victorian Ideas of Sex" in **IDEAS AND BELIEFS OF THE VICTORIANS**. ed. by Harman Grisewood. 1949. Reveals that taboos had their class character. Claims that "to get to know Victorian beliefs on this subject it is necessary to examine behavior rather than books" (p. 351).

10.671
Comfort, Alex, **SEXUAL BEHAVIOUR IN SOCIETY**. 1950; *rev. and rpt. as:* **SEX IN SOCIETY**. 1963. A sociological investigation, mainly modern. Argues that throughout history, medical literature of sex "was helping most shamelessly to work the oracle for convention... medical men only echoed the anti-sexual tone of the 'overt culture'——meaning the moral posture of society" (p. 15); **THE ANXIETY MAKERS: SOME CURIOUS PREOCCUPATIONS OF THE MEDICAL PROFESSION**. 1967. Contends that the medical profession has helped society to incorporate prohibition and fostering of sexual anxiety into the culture as a main driving power behind ethical and religious life. Sees the doctor as the guardian of the status quo, especially evident in his "non-acceptance of women as people and as professional equals... his claims to paternal status vis a vis his patients, and in his whole conscious and unconscious orientation towards advice-giving and social responsibility" (p. 9).

10.672
Neville-Rolfe, Sybil, **SEX IN SOCIAL LIFE**. New York, 1950. Foreword by Cyril Norwood. See especially: "The Misuse of Sex," "Sex Education in the Home," "Why Marriages Fail," and "The Psychology and Biology of Sex." "The wife may be the companion of her husband and the guardian of the legitimate family, but as a 'virtuous woman' is expected to take no interest or pleasure in sex relations. As a 'good woman' she is expected to face these as an unpleasant 'duty.' We have only to read our Victorian novels with understanding to see that this attitude still persisted in England until the end of the last century" (p. 454).

10.673
Anderson, Mosa, **H.J. WILSON, FIGHTER FOR FREEDOM 1833-1914**. 1953. "It was not easy in Victorian days for a woman to come out into the open on any public question whatsoever. The effort was vastly greater when the issue concerned the forbidden subject of sex. No 'respectable female' was expected to know anything of the dark underworld where immortality and vice were enthroned" (pp. 19-20).

10.674
de Beauvoir, Simone, **THE SECOND SEX**. trans. and ed. by H.M. Parshley. New York, 1953; 1974. Philosophical treatise on woman as "The Other." Discusses the origins of the imagery of sexuality and devotes a chapter to the Victorian woman.

10.675
Taylor, Gordon Rattray, **SEX IN HISTORY**. New York, 1953; 1954; 1964; 1970. Psychological explanation for changing sexual attitudes in Western civilization. The Victorians regarded themselves as more civilized than people of the previous century, and needed to reconcile their moral superiority with the undignified sexual act. See especially: "Sex Denied." "Women, ex definitione sexless, hardly existed below the waist; or, if they did, they were not bifurcated. When advertisements of underclothing first began to appear in Victorian papers, the bifurcated garments were always shown folded, so that the bifurcation would not be remarked. Any complaints between the neck and the knees was referred to as 'liver,' and when it

was necessary for a doctor to examine a female patient, he was sometimes handed a doll upon which the location of the affected part might be pointed out" (p. 214); **THE ANGEL-MAKERS**. 1958. "Women, especially, were expected to model themselves on angels, and in the seventeenth century Jeremy Taylor had said that virgins were like angels and must therefore spend much of their time in 'angelic employments.' And Dr. Gregory warned his daughters that women would not 'regain their ascendancy' over the male sex 'by the fullest display of their personal charms' because this actually reduced the angel to a very ordinary girl.... Angels are mothers who have no sexual interests" (p. xiv).

10.676
Hewitt, Margaret, "Cotton-Mill Morality" in **WIVES AND MOTHERS IN VICTORIAN INDUSTRY**. by Margaret Hewitt. 1958. A Lancashire observer at the end of the nineteenth century remarked that although "there is a good deal of sexual intercourse between young persons," it is not considered promiscuous as it is between couples engaged to be married (p. 55).

10.677
Bailey, Derrick Sherwin, "Towards a Theology of Sex" in **SEXUAL RELATIONS IN CHRISTIAN THOUGHT**. by Derrick Sherwin Bailey. New York, 1959. Discusses woman's position in Judeo-Christian thought and the influence of Christianity on Victorian morality.

10.678
Devlin, Patrick, **THE ENFORCEMENT OF MORALS**. 1959. "The greater part of the law relating to sexual offences [in the Victorian era] is the creation of statute and it is difficult to ascertain any logical relationship between it and the moral ideas which most of it upholds. Adultery, fornication, and prostitution are not, as the report points out, criminal offences: homosexuality between males is a criminal offence, but between females it is not" (p. 1).

10.679
Lewinsohn, Richard, **A HISTORY OF SEXUAL CUSTOMS**. trans. by Alexander Mayce. New York, 1959. "The first modern water-closets, baths and showers came from England and Scotland, but bidets——a French invention dating from the age of Pompadour——were unknown in Great Britain. Regular washing of the genitals might induce impure thoughts in a girl and lead to masturbation, if nothing worse. That alone was enough to ban it from any Victorian home" (p. 294).

10.680
JOURNAL OF THE HISTORY OF IDEAS: Thomas, K., *"The Double Standard,"* 20 (1959) 195-216. "It seems that the English insistence on female chastity cannot be explained by reference to the fact of child birth and elaborations thereon, but that the solution is more likely to be found in the desire of men for absolute property in women" (p. 216).

10.681
Epton, Nina, **LOVE AND THE ENGLISH**. New York, 1960. See especially: "Courtships," "Passion and Aspidistras," "The Image of Cupid," and "Expensive Ladies." Includes accounts of female childhood love and sexuality.

10.682
Ellis, Albert and Abarbanel, Albert, eds., **THE ENCYCLOPEDIA OF SEXUAL BEHAVIOR**. vols. 1 and 2, New York, 1961. Entries include the spectrum of sexual expression: abortion, autoeroticism, censorship of sexual literature, sex in Great

Britain, homosexuality, and pornography.

10.683

Brewer, Leslie, **THE GOOD NEWS: SOME SIDELIGHTS ON THE STRANGE STORY OF SEX EDUCATION**. 1962. See especially: "Does Mother Know?" In an anecdotal style, author describes the Victorian woman's affectation of sexual ignorance and the recognition of prostitution by reforming ladies, or "prudes on the prowl," as they were sometimes called.

10.684

Harrison, M., **PAINFUL DETAILS: TWELVE VICTORIAN SCANDALS**. 1962. Discusses famous court cases which detail Victorian marital and extramarital sexual habits in twelve cases.

10.685

Masters, R.E.L., **FORBIDDEN SEXUAL BEHAVIOUR AND MORALITY**. New York, 1962. Broad, general survey including homosexuality, aphrodisiacs, adult-child sex, miscegenation and bestiality. Mentions the occultist Aleister Crowley, whose "Love is the Law" cult is said to have engaged in "acts of bestiality with a sacred goat. These acts of 'Sex Magick' were supposed to 'generate magical currents,' and to be useful in divining the future, attracting wealth, smiting one's enemies, etc." (pp. 51-52).

10.686

Burne, Glenn S., **REMY DE GOURMANT: HIS IDEAS AND INFLUENCE IN ENGLAND AND AMERICA**. Carbondale, 1963. Presents the life and ideas of editor/writer Gourmant. "The theme of mysticism versus carnality, in one form or another, runs through all of Gourmant's plays and fiction. Woman appears as 'the artful creature that humiliates man by securing him with carnal chains'" (p. 17).

10.687

INTERNATIONAL REVIEW OF SOCIAL HISTORY: Cominos, P.T., *"Late-Victorian Sexual Respectability and the Social System,"* 8 (1963) 18-48; 216-250. Three part article. "A comprehensive system of interlocking institutions of Respectable celibacy and Respectable marriage on the one hand, and of celibacy and prostitution and marriage and prostitution on the other hand, were regulated by two systems of morality; firstly, the single standard of purity or continence and secondly the double standard of impurity or incontinence. Perceptive late Victorians understood prostitution to be an integral part of the whole matrimonial system" (p. 230).

10.688

WILLIAM AND MARY QUARTERLY: Beall, O.T., *"Aristotle's Masterpiece in America: A Landmark in the Folklore of Medicine,"* 20 (1963) 206-222. Discusses Aristotle's writings on sexuality which were the first reprinted manuals on sex for Victorian England.

10.689

Banks, Olive and Banks, Joseph Ambrose, **FEMINISM AND FAMILY PLANNING IN VICTORIAN ENGLAND**. Liverpool, 1964. Nineteenth-century feminists fought against the double standard of morality. Even they argued that woman "was victim of man's sex desires" (p. 111).

10.690

Hays, Hoffman Reynolds, **THE DANGEROUS SEX: THE MYTH OF THE**

FEMININE EVIL. New York, 1964. See especially: "The Bell-Shaped Woman" in which the author draws on Victorian literature and popular journals to elucidate the repression of sexuality. "The woman who was all eros was degraded to the role of hired instrument of pleasure and the male's extreme hostility toward her was expressed by physical brutality, exploitation and indifference to her sufferings. Thus the split concept, virgin and prostitute, was born" (p. 232).

10.691
Young, Wayland H., **EROS DENIED. SEX IN WESTERN HISTORY.** New York, 1964. Discusses Victorian sexual attitudes. "We imagine that women feel and fuck like men, we imagine that the ancients fucked more than we do, and that foreigners and animals still do. That which we deny and distrust in ourselves, we have to place somewhere. We know well enough that there is fucking, lots of it going on, but it can't be us who are doing it" (p. 329).

10.692
Hurwood, Bernhardt, **THE GOLDEN AGE OF EROTICA.** Los Angeles, 1965. "No more perfect example of Victorian extremism can be found than the unbelievable breast piercing craze that swept London in the 1890's. This barbaric practice achieved fantastic popularity among seemingly sane, civilized Englishwomen, who submitted to the excruciating pain of having their nipples pierced in order to insert decorative gold and jeweled rings... a fashionable London modiste wrote a letter to a popular magazine, which said in part 'So I had my nipples pierced, and when the wounds healed, I had rings inserted.... With regard to wearing these rings, I can only say that they are not in the least uncomfortable or painful. On the contrary, the slight rubbing and slipping of the rings causes in me an extremely titillating feeling' And so gentle reader——as the writers of old used to say——now you know the truth. Anyone who believes that our forbearers were dull, dry and sexless, has not yet found the closet wherein they locked the family skeletons" (p. 306).

10.693
Ludovici, L.J., **THE FINAL INEQUALITY: A CRITICAL ASSESSMENT OF WOMEN'S SEXUAL ROLE IN SOCIETY.** 1965. "Experience had shown that the public relationships of men and women, which had no sexual implications, were not only safe and beneficial but actually raised the tone of public morality" (p. 185).

10.694
Coveny, Peter, "The End of the Victorian Child" in **THE IMAGE OF CHILDHOOD.** by Peter Coveny. 1967. "Did a sexually-fearful society create a myth of childhood as a period in life when the Devil, in the guise of Sex, could not assail the purity of man?... Freud and his associates... revolutionized the whole attitude of Western society to its children" (p. 302).

10.695
VICTORIAN STUDIES: Harrison, B., *"Underneath the Victorians,"* 10 (1967) 239-262; Gross, C., *"Mary Cowden, 'The Girlhood of Shakespeare's Heroines,' and the Sex Education of Victorian Women,"* 16 (1972) 37-58. "By taking slight hints from the plays, by ignoring what it did not suit her purpose to recognize, and by spinning from her own imagination intricate webs of character and incident, Mrs. [Mary Cowden] Clarke was able to borrow some seeming sanction from Shakespeare for the morality she wished to instill in her feminine audience" (p. 44).

10.696
Barker-Benfield, G.J. Ben, "The Horrors of the Half Known Life: Aspects of the Exploitation of Women by Men," Ph.D. diss., Univ. of California, Los Angeles,

1968; **THE HORRORS OF THE HALF-KNOWN LIFE: MALE ATTITUDES TOWARD WOMEN AND SEXUALITY IN NINETEENTH-CENTURY AMERICA.** New York, 1976. Examines medical and cultural history to determine the factors contributing to the American male's exploitative attitude toward women and nature in general; "The Spermatic Economy: A Nineteenth-Century View of Sexuality" in **THE AMERICAN FAMILY IN SOCIAL HISTORICAL PERSPECTIVE.** ed. by Michael Gordon. New York, 1973; *rpt. from:* **FEMINIST STUDIES:** 1 (1972) 45-74. Observes that an increasingly economic view of sexuality pervaded medical doctrine, to the extent that loss of semen represented a concomitant loss of vitality; conjugal sex had to be kept at a minimum in order to "keep the male's sperm souped up to a particular level of richness" for procreation of healthy offspring. Focuses on American society but useful for the English case. Author may be cataloged as Benfield, G.J. Ben Barker.

10.697
Wright, Helena, **SEX AND SOCIETY.** 1968. "By the mid-nineteenth century the Victorian attitude towards women had crystallized into a rigid form. Not only were women regarded as a lower kind of being than men, but they were held incapable of sexual feeling" (p. 28).

10.698
Pearsall, Ronald, **THE WORM IN THE BUD: THE WORLD OF VICTORIAN SEXUALITY.** 1969; rpt., Harmondsworth, 1974. General overview of the various aspects of Victorian sexuality. See especially: "Prostitution," "Perversion," "The Psychology of Victorian Sex," "Pornography," and "Against the Norm"; "Sexual Cruelty" in **NIGHT'S BLACK ANGELS: THE MANY FACES OF VICTORIAN CRUELTY.** by Ronald Pearsall. New York, 1975. "Women were persuaded into taking a resigned pessimistic view of themselves, and in 1868 the phrase 'redundant women' became fashionable. Women who had not succeeded in getting married often looked on themselves as failures. The word spinster carried bleak connotations, and for a woman not to want to get married was considered unnatural, a slap in the face of all that was holy" (p. 41); **PUBLIC PURITY, PRIVATE SHAME: VICTORIAN SEXUAL HYPOCRISY EXPOSED.** 1976.

10.699
Playfair, Giles, **SIX STUDIES IN HYPOCRISY.** 1969. Discusses several Victorian sexual scandals. See especially: "An Actor's Adultery," "Indecent Assault by a Colonel" and "A Doctor's Trust; A Woman's Honor."

10.700
Greer, Germaine, **THE FEMALE EUNUCH.** 1970. "The 'normal' sex roles that we learn to play from infancy are no more natural than the antics of a transvestite. In order to approximate those shapes and attitudes which are considered normal and desirable, both sexes deform themselves, justifying the process by referring to the primary, genetic differences between the sexes" (p. 29); **SEX AND DESTINY: THE POLITICS OF HUMAN FERTILITY.** 1984.

10.701
Crow, Duncan, **THE VICTORIAN WOMAN.** New York, 1971. "Ideally women would produce children by parthenogenesis; failing that, male impregnation should take place in a dark bedroom into which the husband would creep to create his offspring in silence while the wife endured the connection in a sort of coma" (p. 25).

10.702
Delavenay, Emile, **D.H. LAWRENCE AND EDWARD CARPENTER: A STUDY IN EDWARDIAN TRANSITION.** 1971. "Carpenter advocates sexual intercourse 'in the open air, in touch with the great and abounding life of Nature' rather than 'in closed and stuffy rooms, the symbols of mental darkness and morbidity, and the breeding ground of the pettier elements of human nature'" (p. 96).

10.703
Cecil, Robert, "The State of Morals and the Rights of Women" in **LIFE IN EDWARDIAN ENGLAND.** 1972. "Hell-fire still illuminated sermons in chapel, if not in church, and for Anglo-Saxon Protestantism sexual morality remained the touchstone for all morality. Woman was the source of temptation, as Adam had found" (p. 157).

10.704
Cohen, Morton N., **LEWIS CARROLL, PHOTOGRAPHER OF CHILDREN; FOUR NUDE STUDIES.** New York, 1972; **THE LETTERS OF LEWIS CARROLL.** ed. by Morton N. Cohen with the assistance of Roger Lancelyn Green. 2 vols. 1979. Many of these letters were written to young girls with whom he formed intimate attachments. However, the question still remains whether Carroll had any sexual encounters with them; **LEWIS CARROLL AND THE KITCHINS. CONTAINING TWENTY-FIVE LETTERS NOT PREVIOUSLY PUBLISHED AND NINETEEN OF HIS PHOTOGRAPHS.** ed. with an introduction and notes by Morton N. Cohen. 1980. Carroll's letters reveal his relationship with the Kitchins family and their daughters whom he photographed. Regarding the allegations that he may have been sexually involved with some of the young girls he photographed, Carroll appears to subtly confront people's mistrust of his intentions in a letter to Mrs. Kitchins. He questions why she repeatedly sends two boys, possibly her sons, who barge through his studio while he is in the middle of photographing her daughter. "To go back a little further in History——to your sending these mysterious boys: what have I done, that I should be supposed desirous of photographing boys! Or perhaps you thought that two boys were a sufficient substitute for one girl? Never!" (p. 38).

10.705
Cominos, Peter, "Innocent Femina Sensualis in Unconscious Conflict" in **SUFFER AND BE STILL: WOMEN IN THE VICTORIAN AGE.** ed. by Martha Vicinus. 1972. Describes the "battle between sensual desire and duty" that unconsciously dominated the lives of respectable Victorian women. Their role as harbinger of "Paradisiacal innocence" conflicted with erotic desire; adherence to the model effectively eliminated moral choice "and, hence, autonomy.

10.706
Neale, R.S., **CLASS AND IDEOLOGY IN THE NINETEENTH CENTURY.** 1972. See especially: "Middle Class Morality and the Systematic Colonizers." Critiques Steven Marcus' and Peter Cominos' approach to questions of sexuality. "I propose to try to relax some of the premises underlying their arguments in order to portray the middle strata of society as less ideologically homogeneous and, therefore, more flexible and capable of generating change from within than Marcus permits, and able to choose from more alternatives than Cominos is willing to allow" (p. 121).

10.707
Oakley, Ann, **SEX, GENDER AND SOCIETY.** 1972. "In Victorian times, a large group of Western females were denied their sexuality altogether, but the twentieth century has seen the emergence (or re-emergence, after the inhibitions of the eighteenth and nineteenth centuries) of the female's right to sexuality, which has

come to be defined at least partly in terms of her own sexual needs" (p. 99).

10.708
Ovenden, Graham and Melville, Robert, eds., **VICTORIAN CHILDREN**. New York, 1972. Editors ignore the very evident sexual perversion reflected in these often pornographic photographs, focusing on their artistic merit. Valuable composite that provides a rare view of Victorian sexual deviance and how it applied to children.

10.709
Plumb, J.H., "The Victorians Unbuttoned" in **IN THE LIGHT OF HISTORY**. by J.H. Plumb. New York, 1972. "In some ways the girl's life was more rigorous, certainly more sheltered than a boy's, and her innocence was protected so meticulously that many middle-class brides had no idea of the consequences of marriage. A boy could not be ignorant, but girls could be and were; and on their honeymoons they were shocked into frigidity" (p. 240).

10.710
Roberts, Helene E., "Marriage, Redundancy or Sin: The Painter's View of Women in the First Twenty-Five Years of Victoria's Reign" in **SUFFER AND BE STILL: WOMEN IN THE VICTORIAN AGE**. ed. by Martha Vicinus. 1972. Discusses how paintings illuminate conceptions of woman's mission, "redundant" women (the unfortunates who didn't marry and often lived in economic distress), and "fallen" women.

10.711
Vicinus, Martha, ed., **SUFFER AND BE STILL: WOMEN IN THE VICTORIAN AGE**. 1972; **A WIDENING SPHERE: CHANGING ROLES OF VICTORIAN WOMEN**. 1977. Includes important essays by Judith Walkowitz, Carol Christ, Sheila Ryan Johansson and F. Barry Smith; *reviewed in:* **VICTORIAN STUDIES**: Welter, B., 22 (1979) 213-215. "As Martha Vicinus admits in her introduction, 'the area which has most fascinated our generation looking back at the Victorians is sexuality.' What is not admitted, although the essays on the subject offer mute testimony to its truth, is that this area is precisely the most difficult both to document and to evaluate. The kind of doublethink needed to make explicit what the Victorians refused to say, or to interpret what they did say in the light of what really they meant, leads at best to murky prose and frequently to murky documentation as well" (p. 214).

10.712
JOURNAL OF SOCIAL POLITICS: McGregor, O.R., *"Equality, Sexual Values and Permissive Legislation: the English Experience,"* 1 (1972) 44-59. An examination of "the social and legal evolution of some forms of so-called permissiveness" and how changing values are connected with the equal rights movement. In economic terms, "a rule of chastity had been easily imposed on women whose excess of numbers in the marriageable age groups forced them to compete for a limited number of husbands" (p. 46).

10.713
JOURNAL OF THE HISTORY OF MEDICINE: Bullough, V., *"Sex in History: A Virgin Field,"* 8 (1972) 101-116.

10.714
Black, Eugene C., **VICTORIAN CULTURE AND SOCIETY**. 1973. Discusses the sexual beliefs of the Victorians. See especially: "Sexual Roles: Victorian Progress?" This chapter includes essays by Michael Ryan and S. Herbert. "Man reaches the

climax very much sooner, the orgasm in woman being attained more slowly. Her sex feeling is altogether more diffuse, more extensive, while in man it is intensive, focused, as it were, in a single point. For this reason, the sex impulse in woman is in need of stimulation" (p. 394).

10.715
Walker, Benjamin, **SEX AND THE SUPERNATURAL: SEXUALITY IN RELIGION AND MAGIC.** 1973. "Altogether, in matters of sex expression a woman was not to be allowed full freedom. Her role was that of a passive vessel for the pleasure of the male, since she was created to give and not take. 'A lady,' stated one of the Victorian dicta, 'does not shake'" (p. 34).

10.716
AMERICAN QUARTERLY: Rosenberg, C.E., *"Sexuality, Class and Role in Nineteenth-Century America,"* 25 (1973) 131-153. Historians have argued that "sexual impulse was systematically repressed and deformed" during the Victorian period. (p. 132). Discusses formal proscriptions for sex and gender roles and "the ways in which these roles may have related to the actual expression of sexuality" (p. 133).

10.717
JOURNAL OF MARRIAGE AND FAMILY: Strong, B., *"Toward a History of the Experiential Family: Sex and Incest in the Nineteenth-Century Family,"* 35 (1973) 457-466. "The sexual anxieties which men experienced in the nineteenth century may be traced to their incestuous fears which arose from their family relations. The hypothesis suggests that the reason men tended to divide women in good and bad according to whether they were passionate was related to their inability to unite sexual desire with love" (p. 466).

10.718
Burlage, Dorothy D., "Judaeo-Christian Influences on Female Sexuality" in **SEXIST RELIGION AND WOMEN IN THE CHURCH. NO MORE SILENCE!** ed. by Alice L. Hageman. New York, 1974.

10.719
Haller, John S. and Haller, Robin M., **THE PHYSICIAN AND SEXUALITY IN VICTORIAN AMERICA.** 1974. Discusses the regulation of female sexuality by Victorian physicians. Emphasizes that many women accepted strict sexual morality in order to retain autonomy within the family. "The Victorian woman cultivated beauty in the same manner that she attended to her private thoughts. With her sexuality circumscribed by society's harsh moral incantations, she turned for relief toward narcissism" (p. 141); *reviewed in:* **JOURNAL OF THE HISTORY OF MEDICINE:** Bullough, V., 29 (1974) 429-431. "By denying their sexuality, by resorting to marital continence and abstinence, [women] insisted that they were no longer to be regarded simply as sex objects. If this thesis is accepted, the prudery of the Victorian woman then becomes a mask to hide her effort to achieve freedom of person" (p. 430).

10.720
MacGregor, O.R., "The Double Standard" in **RULE BRITTANIA: THE VICTORIAN WORLD.** ed. by George Perry and Nicholas Mason. 1974. "The Victorian conspiracy of silence about sex was an aspiration not an achievement. It is partly the invention of those who have looked at life in the period through the double meanings of some novels" (p. 180). Illustrated with Victorian pin-ups and advertisements that use women's sexuality to sell products.

10.721

Murstein, Bernard, LOVE, SEX AND MARRIAGE THROUGH THE AGES. New York, 1974.

10.722

Walter, Ronald G., PRIMERS FOR PRUDERY: SEXUAL ADVICE TO VICTORIAN AMERICA. New Jersey, 1974. "Complexities of female sexual response and a fashionable image of woman clearly reinforced each other. Woman's apparently cooler passions signified an inherent chastity and, therefore, an inherent moral refinement superior to man's" (p. 66).

10.723

HISTORY OF CHILDHOOD QUARTERLY: Hartman, M., *"Child Abuse and Self-Abuse: Two Victorian Cases,"* 2 (1974) 221-248. Analyzes legal cases concerning two upper-middle class families in England, revealing attitudes toward moral standards and addressing issues of female sexuality, masturbation, and child abuse.

10.724

UNIVERSITY OF NEWCASTLE HISTORICAL JOURNAL: Smith, F.B., *"Sexuality in Britain 1800-1900,"* 2 (1974) 19-32. Smith points out that recent historians have relied too heavily on sources that serve to perpetuate the Victorian stereotype. "The emphasis upon [William] Acton and Walter [pseudonymous author of MY SECRET LIFE] has displaced the knowledge that a great many Victorian families and liaisons in widely different classes, temporal and local situations were richly happy... and this happiness must have had at least some basis in the parents' mutual sexual satisfaction" (p. 22); *rpt. revised and expanded in:* A WIDENING SPHERE: CHANGING ROLES OF VICTORIAN WOMEN. ed. by Martha Vicinus. 1980.

10.725

Branca, Patricia, SILENT SISTERHOOD: MIDDLE-CLASS WOMEN IN THE VICTORIAN HOME. 1975. Questions the myth that women in the nineteenth century had a distaste for sex.

10.726

Brander, Michael, THE VICTORIAN GENTLEMAN. 1975. See especially: "Birth and Childhood" and "Morality and Sex." "That a gentleman could and did have his mistress, or visit prostitutes, was fully accepted by everyone with the provision that it was 'done discreetly.' As ever the Victorians preferred not to face the facts of life, but took refuge in turning a blind eye, or employing a euphemism. In this instance the term 'pretty horse breakers' was the common one used for the hordes of kept women who daily rode in Rotten Row in the afternoon" (n.p.).

10.727

Johnson, Wendell Stacy, SEX AND MARRIAGE IN VICTORIAN POETRY. 1975. Suggests that the contrast between "moderns" and "Victorians" was their view of the source of spiritual love and its impact on sex: Victorians felt such love came from the soul or God and transformed the physical relationship to a spiritual one; moderns like Swinburne insisted "on the earthy, the physical, the lowly basis of spiritual love" (p. 257); LIVING IN SIN: THE VICTORIAN SEXUAL REVOLUTION. Chicago, 1979. "The nineteenth century was the first since ancient times that generally regarded sex as a terrifying power, one that could virtually be a religion or replace religion. This obsession with the sexual urge that lay beneath the Victorian surface... had a quality and an intensity that were new to the Western world" (p. 4).

10.728
Kern, Stephen, ANATOMY AND DESTINY: A CULTURAL HISTORY OF THE
HUMAN BODY. New York, 1975. See especially: "The Onset of Victorian Sexual
Morality" and "The Body Electric." Describes the literary genre of Whitman, Zola
and Nietzsche and its reclaiming of corporeality and sensuality in the latter half of
the nineteenth century. "Fear of the body, they agreed, led to various wrong turns
in the history of morality, and their works were intended to assist the return to a
more rewarding sexual ethic" (p. 93). Also discusses the impact of "bourgeois-
ification" on sexuality, whereby the human body was transformed "from an
instrument of pleasure to an instrument of production" (p. 6).

10.729
Rinehart, Nana Merte, "Anthony Trollope's Treatment of Women, Marriage, and
Sexual Morality Seen in the Context of Contemporary Debate," Ph.D. diss., Univ. of
Maryland, 1975.

10.730
Seymour-Smith, Martin, SEX AND SOCIETY. 1975. Observes that the Victorian
idealization of good women as asexual and bad women as insatiable was rooted in a
male desire to conserve semen. "'Gaping quims cessation fear,' as a piece of
clandestine Victorian verse put it" (p. 23).

10.731
Bullough, Vern L., "Nineteenth Century Attitudes Toward Sex" in SEXUAL
VARIANCE IN SOCIETY AND HISTORY. by Vern L. Bullough. 1976. Discusses
the developing importance of the private sphere, isolation of women, motherhood,
the medical idea that sex dissipates energy and debilitates the nervous system, the
fascination with flagellation, and homosexuality; *reviewed in:* JOURNAL OF
PSYCHOHISTORY: Malkin, E.E., 5 (1977-78) 144-147; SEX, SOCIETY AND
HISTORY. 1976; (and Bullough, Bonnie), SIN, SICKNESS AND SANITY: A
HISTORY OF SEXUAL ATTITUDES. 1977; *reviewed in:* JOURNAL OF THE
HISTORY OF MEDICINE: Benedek, T.G., 35 (1980) 120-121; THE FRONTIERS
OF SEX RESEARCH. New York, 1979;

10.732
Robinson, Paul, THE MODERNIZATION OF SEX. New York, 1976. Observes that
Havelock Ellis believed women embodied a passive sexuality. "Men were propulsive,
women receptive. In sexual relations the woman was the 'instrument' from which
the man 'evoked' music" (p. 19).

10.733
Trudgill, Eric, MADONNAS AND MAGDALENS: THE ORIGINS AND
DEVELOPMENT OF VICTORIAN SEXUAL ATTITUDES. New York, 1976. "If
[the Victorian bride] has been told of sex at all, she might have been told that only
the lascivious woman experienced genuine physical pleasure" (p. 62).

10.734
BULLETIN OF THE SOCIETY FOR THE SOCIAL HISTORY OF MEDICINE:
Rugen, H.M., *"Women on the Borderland of Pathology: Dominant Conceptions of
Female Sexuality 1900-1920,"* 18 (1976) 11-12; Banks, J.A., *"The Attitude of the
Medical Profession to Sexuality in the Nineteenth Century,"* 22 (1978) 9-10.
Attitudes were governed by pressures both within and without the profession.
Discusses doctors' attitudes about the innocence of women and children and their
reticence in providing information on birth control. Doctors' "attitude to hysteria
and hysterical 'counterfeits' were coloured by the degree to which they regarded

women to be very similar or very different from men in their sexuality, and their sensuality... and this division between them was derived from their interpretation of the Christian conception of innocence as applicable to women and children but not to men" (p. 9); Edwards, S., *"Femina Sexualis: Medico-Legal Control in Victoriana,"* 28 (1981) 17-20. Any deviation from passive female behavior was considered abnormal. Treatment ranged from resocialisation to clitoridectomy.

10.735
EIGHTEENTH CENTURY STUDIES: LeGates, M., *"The Cult of Womanhood in Eighteenth-Century Thought,"* 10 (1976) 21-39. "The dichotomy is not between the chaste bourgeoisie and the licentious lady, but between the virtuous woman of the upper classes (whether by merit or birth) and the loose woman of the lower orders (whether by choice or circumstance)" (p. 37).

10.736
SOCIETAS: A REVIEW OF SOCIAL HISTORY: Walters, R.G., (Societas), *"Sexual Matters as Historical Problems: A Framework of Analysis,"* 6 (1976) 157-175. "Sex roles, sexuality, values, norms, and behavior are not the only conceivable analytic categories available to us: they merely are useful ones. They can become... logic-tight little boxes... but these little boxes serve the purpose for a time; in any event, historians (like naughty children) delight in overturning them" (p. 172).

10.737
Blackman, Janet, "Popular Theories of Generation: The Evolution of Aristotle's Works, the Study of an Anachronism" in **HEALTH CARE AND POPULAR MEDICINE IN 19TH CENTURY ENGLAND.** ed. by John Woodward and David Richards. 1977. Examines Aristotle's works as an indicator of attitudes towards sexuality and childbirth. The publication (variously edited) remained a popular manual for centuries.

10.738
Christ, Carol, "Victorian Masculinity and the Angel in the House" in **A WIDENING SPHERE: CHANGING ROLES OF VICTORIAN WOMEN.** ed. by Martha Vicinus. 1977; 1980. Concerned with Victorian men's conception of woman's passivity and asexuality as a reflection of their wish to sublimate their own distasteful aggressive tendencies.

10.739
Cockshut, A.O.J., **MAN AND WOMAN: A STUDY OF LOVE AND THE NOVEL 1740-1940.** 1977; 1978. "Every writer on the relation of the sexes who is worth serious discussion at all knows he is not dealing with an isolated part of life.... As with religious questions, the response, whatever it is, is that of the whole personality, not just of the... mind, or the... heart, or the... body" (p. 209). Divides Victorian writers into topical rather than chronological catagories, e.g., The Pessimists, The Optimists, etc. Discusses the double sexual standard and devotes a chapter to the Lesbian theme in English literature.

10.740
Harrison, Fraser, **THE DARK ANGEL: ASPECTS OF VICTORIAN SEXUALITY.** 1977. The book is divided into three parts: Middle-Class Sexuality, Working-Class Sexuality, and Prostitution. "Marriage was not common among working people who on the whole obtained their wives and husbands simply by taking up residence with them" (n.p.).

10.741

Phayer, Michael J., "The Secularization of Sex" in **SEXUAL LIBERATION AND RELIGION IN NINETEENTH CENTURY EUROPE.** by Michael Phayer. 1977. "The rustic never gave the morality of sexual behavior a second thought. Once he took it to mind that God was unconcerned about sexuality because He did not punish bastardy, his attitude towards sex became secular... thus around 1800 the literate bourgeoisie required guidelines for sexual conduct and emerged with... secular considerations to gain compliance: 'your hair will fall out'" (pp. 26-27); *reviewed in:* **SOCIAL HISTORY:** Kaplow, J., 3 (1978) 399-402. Phayer singles out the rural proletariat as the social group which "first benefitted from the relaxation of community control.... Not only that they were alone, for the bourgeoisie was also 'easing their sexual inhibitions and dallying with sex for pleasure.' But the bourgeoisie needed order in its relationships (for reasons of property?), and their moralists quickly supplied it" (p. 400).

10.742

Rowbotham, Sheila, **A NEW WORLD FOR WOMEN: STELLA BROWNE— SOCIALIST FEMINIST.** 1977. Browne, a Canadian-born activist, asserted women's right to sexual pleasure and birth control. She was one of the founding members of the Abortion Law Reform Association. Her radicalism stems from her support of Havelock Ellis' writings on the psychology of sex.

10.743

HISTORY WORKSHOP JOURNAL: Rowbotham, S., *"In Search of Carpenter,"* no. 3 (1977) 121-133. "Carpenter believed that the liberation of women required both real economic freedom and a change of women's consciousness.... It also necessitated 'her complete freedom as to the disposal of her sex'" (p. 127).

10.744

VICTORIANS INSTITUTE JOURNAL: Palmegiano, E.M., *"The Propaganda of Sexuality: Victorian Periodicals and Women,"* no. 6 (1977) 21-30. "Like other Christian societies before them, the English of the nineteenth century believed that all females were descendants of Eve, that all inherited the ability to destroy man and his world by exploiting his sexual needs. What this notion inferred about female intelligence or male physiology was never pursued. Instead, determined to insulate the danger, Victorians tried to convince woman that she had neither body nor wit.... In magazine after magazine that women might read, the joys of marriage and maternity were constantly extolled but nothing was even hinted about female sexuality" (p. 21).

10.745

Foucault, Michel, **THE HISTORY OF SEXUALITY.** New York, 1978. Vol. 1 of two volumes. Argues that the first stereotype to be "sexualized" was the "idle" woman. "She inhabited the outer edge of the 'world,' in which she always had to appear as a value, and of the family, where she was assigned a new destiny charged with conjugal and paternal obligations" (p. 121). Considers sexuality "the effect of prohibition and the return of the repressed, but also as a consistent consciously implanted by power into the body of society" (p. 1); *reviewed in:* **SIGNS:** Shaffer, E., 5 (1980) 812-820; **THE USE OF PLEASURE.** New York, 1985. Volume two of THE HISTORY OF SEXUALITY.

10.746

Hayman, Ronald, **DE SADE: A CRITICAL BIOGRAPHY.** New York, 1978. Biography of de Sade and the development of his sadistic sexuality. Details many of his sexual encounters and his love of flagellation——a sexual taste shared by the

Victorians.

10.747
Honore, Anthony, **SEX LAW IN ENGLAND**. 1978. "According to Victorian standards, a wife was simply expected to 'submit to her husband's embraces' and was not thought to have any rights in matters of sex except perhaps the right to have children if she wished" (p. 22).

10.748
Jacobus, Mary, "Tess: The Making of a Pure Woman" in **TEARING THE VEIL; ESSAYS ON FEMININITY**. ed. by Susan Lipshitz. 1978.

10.749
Martin, John Rutledge, "Sexuality and Science: Victorian and Post-Victorian Scientific Ideas on Sexuality," Ph.D. diss., Duke Univ., 1978. Surveys "analysis of scientific thought on sexuality in Britain from 1840 to 1920.... The major conclusion is that Victorian scientific writers... evaluated sexuality in terms of 'nature' and 'natural law' while post-Victorian writers... evaluated sexuality in terms of 'normality'.... The standard of nature may be characterized as static, mechanistic, and Newtonian, while standards of normality was [sic] dynamic, developmental and Darwinian" (pp. iii-iv).

10.750
Smith-Rosenberg, Carroll, "Sex as Symbol in Victorian Purity: An Ethnohistorical Analysis of Jacksonian America" in **TURNING POINTS. HISTORICAL AND SOCIOLOGICAL ESSAYS ON THE FAMILY**. ed. by John Demos and Sarane Spence Boocock. 1978. American, but a useful comparison to the English case. Suggests that female sexuality was seen as a powerful force which could be channeled in such a way as to benefit both the woman and society. "A woman devoted her sexuality exclusively to reproduction and thus to the service of the transgenerational family.... Moral reformers conceived of the body as a closed energy system. Health was a product of an orderly balance maintained within the body itself and between the body and its social and physical environment" (p. 244).

10.751
BULLETIN OF THE JOHN RYLANDS UNIVERSITY LIBRARY OF MANCHESTER: Chaloner, W.H., *"How Immoral Were the Victorians? A Bibliographical Reconsideration,"* 60 (1978) 362-375. Argues that Victorians were more obsessed with death than with sex. Concludes that any interest in Victorian sexuality is a purely modern one.

10.752
JOURNAL OF INTERDISCIPLINARY HISTORY: Fairchilds, C., *"Female Sexual Attitudes and the Rise of Illegitimacy: A Case Study,"* 8 (1978) 627-667. Claims that the rise in illegitimacy reported in France in the last half of the 18th century was due neither to urbanization nor to increasing sexual adventurism. Rather, it was caused by depressed economic conditions which in turn had several effects: young couples couldn't afford to marry, girls were more susceptible to promises of marriage, and rape and prostitution were on the rise.

10.753
SOCIAL SCIENCE QUARTERLY: Fee, E., *"Psychology, Sexuality and Social Control in Victorian England,"* 58 (1978) 632-646. "The familiar pattern of sexual repression characterized the bourgeoisie——at least as an ideal of conduct, if not as an exact description of reality——while less constrained forms of sexual expression

characterized the new working class" (p. 632).

10.754
Cott, Nancy F., "Passionlessness: An Interpretation of Victorian Sexual Ideology, 1790-1851" in **HERITAGE OF HER OWN.** ed. by Nancy F. Cott and Elizabeth H. Pleck. New York, 1979. Sources used are women's private and public writings in New England and prescriptive works, mostly religious. "The serviceability of passionlessness to women in gaining social and familial power should be acknowledged as a primary reason that the ideology was quickly and widely accepted" (p. 175).

10.755
Doherty, Dennis, **DIMENSIONS OF HUMAN SEXUALITY.** New York, 1979. "Of course, the hypocrisy of the Victorian age is also well documented. It was important in that age to defend the strict norms of sexual morality, even if one did not follow them oneself, since without the seriousness of the work ethic society could not pursue its aim" (p. 89)

10.756
Sullerton, Evelyne, **WOMEN ON LOVE: EIGHT CENTURIES OF FEMININE WRITING.** trans. from the French by Helen R. Lane. Garden City, 1979. See especially: "Nineteenth Century; The Liberation of Feeling." Argues that "libertines rediscover religion and invent spiritual discipline through passion, the salvation of the soul through profane love. But this is accomplished by sacrificing the body: Women use modesty for their own ends—and are sick from it. Marriage triumphs, but it is the century of mistresses who are saints of love" (p. viii).

10.757
CRIMINAL LAW REVIEW: Bailey, V. and Blackburn, S., *"The Punishment of Incest Act 1908: A Case Study in Law Creation,"* n.v. (1979) 708-718. "The overcrowded homes of the poor similarly provided the back-cloth to William Booth's provocative statement in 1890: 'Incest is so familiar as hardly to call for remark'" (p. 710).

10.758
FEMINIST STUDIES: Davidoff, L., *"Class and Gender in Victorian England. The Diaries of Arthur J. Munby and Hannah Cullwick,"* 5 (1979) 87-141. Discusses the dual nature of woman as symbolized by the madonna/whore dichotomy, and how this idea manifested in class relations. "What makes the analysis of the interaction of class and gender so difficult, however, is that the same forces which produced a world view dividing the society between masculine and feminine, working class and middle (upper) class, urban and rural, also separated physicality, e.g., bodily functions in general and sexuality in particular, from the public gaze. This is an example of the privatization we have come to associate with the development of industrial capitalism and was part of a changing view of men's and women's positions in the cosmos and their relation to Nature" (p. 88); Walkowitz, J.R., *"Jack the Ripper and the Myth of Male Violence,"* 3 (1982) 543-574. "One cannot emphasize too much the role of the popular press, itself a creature of the 1880's, in establishing Jack the Ripper as a media hero, in amplifying the terror of male violence, and in elaborating and interpreting the meaning of the Ripper murders to a 'mass' audience.... Embedded in this convention was a titillating 'sexual script,' based on the association of sex and violence, male dominance and female passivity, and the crossing of class boundaries in the male pursuit of female objects of desire" (p. 546); Vicinus, M., *"Sexuality and Power: A Review of Current Work in the History of Sexuality,"* 8 (1982) 133-156.

10.759
JOURNAL OF SOCIAL HISTORY: L'Esperance, J.L., *"Woman's Mission to Woman: Explorations in the Operation of the Double Standard and Female Solidarity in Nineteenth Century England,"* 12 (1979) 316-338. "The study of how women themselves tried to overcome the separation of their sex into pure and impure by involving themselves in charitable work with the fallen, dramatically illustrates the development of the female solidarity within the Women's Movement" (p. 316); Special Issue: "Social History with Love," 15 (1982) 337-425; Holtzman, E.M., *"The Pursuit of Married Love: Women's Attitudes Toward Sexuality and Marriage in Great Britain, 1918-1939,"* 16 (1982) 39-53. Discusses Marie Stopes' ideas about the legitimacy of female sexual pleasure. "Stopes was, in effect, providing women with a sexual role within marriage. Moreover, her descriptions of the heights of ecstasy a woman could reach during sex gave women a goal to strive for within the confines of their domestic life" (p. 42); Stearns, C.Z. and Stearns, P.N., *"Victorian Sexuality: Can Historians Do It Better?"* 18 (1985) 625-634. Calls for a new interpretation that integrates traditional conceptions with the more recent revisions postulating the "sexy middle-class Victorian." Raises questions about how modern sexual standards influence historical study of sexuality.

10.760
RADICAL HISTORY REVIEW: Interrante, J. and Lasser, C., *"Victims of the Very Songs They Sing: A Critique of Recent Work on Patriarchal Culture and the Social Construction of Gender,"* 20 (1979) 25-40. Concerns "how forms of sexual domination emerge from, and in turn shape the relations of production, consumption, and reproduction in which they are embedded" (p. 26); Sahli, N., *"Sexuality in 19th and 20th Century America: The Sources and Their Problems,"* 20 (1979) 89-96.

10.761
Ballhatchet, Kenneth, **RACE, SEX AND CLASS UNDER THE RAJ: IMPERIAL ATTITUDES AND POLICIES AND THEIR CRITICS, 1793-1905.** 1980. Study of the role of racial, sexual and class attitudes in the state regulation of sex relations between Englishmen and Indian women. "Curzon [Viceroy from 1899-1905] and his colleagues assumed that the social hierarchy should correspond to the political hierarchy and that sexual behaviour should be subordinated to the need of both" (p. 8).

10.762
Degler, Carl, "Women's Sexuality in 19th Century America" in **AT ODDS: WOMEN AND THE FAMILY IN AMERICA FROM THE REVOLUTION TO THE PRESENT.** by Carl Degler. New York and Oxford, 1980. Although nineteenth-century marriage manuals recognized female sexuality, the recognition became "disguised as an admonition to woman and a warning to men." Notes that historians have mistakenly looked to such contemporaries as William Acton for a representation of popular opinion.

10.763
Janeway, Elizabeth, "Who is Sylvia? On the Loss of Sexual Paradigms" in **WOMEN: SEX AND SEXUALITY.** ed. by Catharine R. Stimpson and Ethel Spector Person. 1980. Uses Thomas Kuhn's fourfold definition of paradigm as a model for explaining the sexual paradigm of Eve the temptress and Mary the virgin and mother. The paradigm is seen as the historical outcome of inheritance patterns in a patriarchal society. With the development of a cash economy, however, it has steadily lost its usefulness and consequently, its currency. New paradigms created by women must "reach the deep layers of repressed and denied mind and feeling"

and "widen the range of personal connection... beyond the strictly and narrowly sexual" (p. 19).

10.764
Jordanova, Ludmilla, "Natural Facts: A Historical Perspective on Science and Sexuality" in **NATURE, CULTURE AND GENDER.** ed. by Carol MacCormack and Marilyn Strathern. Cambridge, 1980.

10.765
Leach, William, **TRUE LOVE AND PERFECT UNION: THE FEMINIST REFORM OF SEX AND SOCIETY.** New York, 1980. Surveys traditional ideas including sexual ownership, sentimental love, sexual stereotypes, romantic love, and "the vindication of love." "The sentimentalization of women as mothers made sexual expression between the sexes difficult and at times impossible. The transformation of the home into a haven infused with feminine virtues of frailty and passivity cut to the core of male narcissistic vulnerability: it generated fears of impotence that could be met only by escape from the home or by assertion of power within it in often sadistic ways" (p. 101).

10.766
Stimpson, Catharine R. and Person, Ethel Spector, eds., **WOMEN: SEX AND SEXUALITY.** 1980. A collection of essays, including "Who is Sylvia? On the Loss of Sexual Paradigms" by Elizabeth Janeway and "Social and Behavioral Constructions of Female Sexuality" by Patricia Y. Miller and Martha R. Fowlkes.

10.767
Tannahill, Reay, "The Nineteenth Century" in **SEX IN HISTORY.** by Reay Tannahill. New York, 1980; *reviewed in:* **NEW SOCIETY:** Carter, A., *"Between the Sheets,"* 52 (1980) 239-240; *also reviewed in:* **TIMES LITERARY SUPPLEMENT:** Grosskurth, P., n.v. (1980) 634. "Tannahill is inclined to the view that incest, not cannibalism, was the world's first taboo——a complete contradiction of Havelock Ellis" (p. 634).

10.768
AMERICAN SCHOLAR: Gay, P., *"Victorian Sexuality: Old Texts and New Insights,"* 49 (1980) 372-378. Examines reprints made available by the Arno Press of books on health, medicine, and marriage. "The Victorians were repressed and repressive.... In the age of the queen who was not amused, respectable husbands used their wives to make children and prostitutes to have pleasure" (p. 372).

10.769
INTERNATIONAL JOURNAL OF WOMEN'S STUDIES: Griffin, G.B., *"'Your Girls that You All Love are Mine': Dracula and the Victorian Sexual Imagination,"* 3 (1980) 454-465. Analysis of Bram Stokes' DRACULA (1897). Argues that "the threat of Dracula is not the predatory male sexuality of the Count, who is nearly absent from the novel, but the much more vivid sexuality of his female surrogates" (p. 454). "The worst horror [the author] can imagine is not Dracula at all but the released, transforming sexuality of the Good Woman" (p. 464).

10.770
LABOUR HISTORY: McCalman, I., *"Females, Feminism and Free Love in an Early Nineteenth Century Radical Movement,"* 38 (1980) 1-25. "One of the most sadistic characteristics of the established sexual code was the fact that the greater the idealisation of female chastity, the more men enjoyed seducing women and persecuting them for succumbing" (p. 18).

10.771
Edwards, Susan, **FEMALE SEXUALITY AND THE LAW**. Oxford, 1981. The legal questions dealt with pertain mostly to the mid-twentieth century. "The period from 1850 to 1900, in particular, was characterized by a rapidly growing gynaecologiza-tion of female sexuality and behaviour, whilst from 1900 onwards psychoanalysis redefined the structural basis of female sexual expression by relocating it in the structure of the unconscious mind" (p. 100).

10.772
Gathorne-Hardy, Jonathan, **LOVE, SEX, MARRIAGE AND DIVORCE**. 1981. Discusses the role of adultery as a romantic love vehicle for the middle classes.

10.773
Girouard, Mark, **THE RETURN OF CAMELOT: CHIVALRY AND THE ENGLISH GENTLEMAN**. New Haven, 1981. See especially: "Modern Courtly Love." Contains several extracts from the manuscript diary of Wilfred Scawen Blunt, anti-imperialist Home Ruler, country gentleman, poet, and womanizer. He compared himself to Lancelot when "he saw himself as being torn between the life of love and the life of the spirit." He wrote about his affair with Minny Pollen: "How happy I could be serving God with Minny and sinning sin with her, for which we should both sit in sackcloth" (p. 205).

10.774
Mitchell, Sally, **THE FALLEN ANGEL**. Bowling Green, 1981. "Marriage required a woman to give up her name, her identity, her right to her own body, her property, her legal existence and her ability to act independently. With the end of innocence, it became scarcely possible unless she were overwhelmed by a mystic, metaphysical love. The romantic ethic supplied a pseudo-solution: the individual bond between one man and one woman, made possible because he loved her as a person in her own right, allowed them to establish a union that would forget the inequities of the matrimonial contract" (p. 175).

10.775
Weeks, Jeffrey, **SEX, POLITICS AND SOCIETY: THE REGULATION OF SEXUALITY SINCE 1800**. 1981. See especially: "Sexuality and the Historian," "'That Damned Morality': Sex in Victorian Ideology," and "The Public and the Private: Moral Regulation in the Victorian Period"; **SEXUALITY AND ITS DISCONTENTS: MEANINGS, MYTHS AND MODERN SEXUALITIES**. 1985.

10.776
JOURNAL OF THE HISTORY OF MEDICINE AND ALLIED SCIENCES: Colp, R., *"Charles Darwin, Dr. Edward Lane and the 'Singular Trial' of Robinson v. Robinson and Lane."* 36 (1981) 205-213. Identifies attitudes towards women, madness and sexuality. In 1858, Mr. Robinson sued his wife for divorce on the grounds that she committed adultery with Dr. Lane. Her diary was submitted as evidence. Leading doctors of the day described it a "shocking sexual delusion" caused by gynecological problems.

10.777
Barickman, Richard, MacDonald, Susan, and Stark, Myra, **CORRUPT RELATIONS: DICKENS, THACKERAY, TROLLOPE, COLLINS, AND THE VICTORIAN SEXUAL SYSTEM**. New York, 1982. "The Victorian novel in general shifts attention from courtship as a relation between individuals to courtship as a ritual conditioned by family life. Courtship continues to provide the main plot structures

of most Victorian novels, but it often seems a framework for other, broader social concerns.... As part of the shift from an erotic to a domestic center, the courted woman tends to be valued for her ability to sustain family life, to maintain or restore moral, emotional, and spiritual integrity for the household, rather than for any distinct erotic qualities" (pp. 8-9).

10.778

Bland, Lucy, "'Guardians of the Race', or 'Vampires Upon the Nation's Health'?: Female Sexuality and its Regulation in Early Twentieth-Century Britain" in THE CHANGING EXPERIENCE OF WOMEN. ed. by Elizabeth Whitelegg, et al. Oxford, 1982. Examines the roles of sex education, racial purity campaigns and the venereal disease panic in maintaining a dual stereotype of females: the ideal mother and the "amateur prostitute"; "Purity, Motherhood, Pleasure or Threat? Definitions of Female Sexuality 1900-1970s" in SEX AND LOVE: NEW THOUGHTS ON OLD CONTRADICTIONS. ed. by Sue Cartledge and Joanna Ryan. 1984. Changing conceptions of women's sexuality throughout the century. Bland discusses the various definitions of "natural" and "desirable." She shows that women have been fairly inarticulate in expressing their needs. She examines feminist debates on sexual topics; "Cleansing the Portals of Life: The Venereal Disease Campaign in the Early Twentieth Century" in CRISES IN THE BRITISH STATE, 1880-1930. ed. by Mary Langan and Bill Schwartz. 1985. "In the early years of the twentieth century feminists campaigned against venereal disease, transferring the blame away from the prostitute and onto her male client" (p. 194); "Marriage Laid Bare: Middle-Class Women and Marital Sex c. 1800-1914" in LABOUR AND LOVE: WOMEN'S EXPERIENCE OF HOME AND FAMILY 1850-1940. ed. by Jane Lewis. 1986. "If taboos around sex were so extensive in 'polite' society, and if most middle-class women (and many working-class ones too) were in reality entering marriage with so little sexual knowledge, what made it possible for them suddenly to question and challenge the sexual practices of married men within their marriage as well as outside them?" (p. 125).

10.779

Bouce, Paul Gabriel, ed., SEXUALITY IN EIGHTEENTH-CENTURY BRITAIN. Totowa, 1982. Includes chapters on sexual mores and attitudes, nymphomania, pornography, the veil of chastity, and scatology. "Enlightenment values strongly opposed the blind and merely animal indulgence of sexual cravings. For sexuality to be enjoyable, it had to be refined, decent, polite. The Enlightenment legitimated sexuality at the cost of making it decorous" (p. 18).

10.780

Brake, Mike, ed., HUMAN SEXUAL RELATIONS: TOWARDS A REDEFINITION OF SEXUAL POLITICS. 1982.

10.781

Kunzle, David, FASHION AND FETISHISM. New Jersey, 1982. "The charge that females used the corset for forbidden autoerotic purposes has been largely unspoken since the late 18th century.... But the Schnepfenthal Institute prize essays of 1788 by Soemmerring etc. give a specific account.... 'But I must leave it to doctors and moralists for further consideration, whether girls from a young age do not find something pleasurable in leaning with the front (lower) point of the corset and the busk inserted therein, against the corner of a chair, a table etc., resting or even rubbing there, and whether they do not provoke thereby innocently and unperceived sensations.... Adults of course oppose such bad habits as soon as they notice them, but are not children left alone to themselves?'" (pp. 170-171).

10.782
Pratt, J.D., "Sexuality and Social Control," Ph.D. diss., Univ. of Sheffield, 1982.

10.783
Robertson, Priscilla, **AN EXPERIENCE OF WOMEN: PATTERN AND CHANGE IN 19TH CENTURY EUROPE**. Philadelphia, 1982. See especially: "Extramarital Affairs," "If Ignorance is Bliss," and "To Have and to Hold."

10.784
Shorter, Edward, **A HISTORY OF WOMEN'S BODIES**. New York, 1982. "Evidence on the subject of female sexuality, among middle-class and aristocratic women, starts to accumulate during the eighteenth and early nineteenth centuries, precisely at the time when modern attitudes toward family life, which value emotional expressiveness among women, begin to appear among these classes.... the overwhelming body of evidence suggests that, for married women in the past, sex was a burden to be dutifully, resentfully borne throughout life rather than a sense of joy" (p. 13). Also examines medical problems associated with the female body, childbirth, abortion, and physical differences between men and women; *reviewed in:* **LOS ANGELES TIMES:** Kendall, E., *"Were Women Victims of Their Bodies?"* (Dec. 21, 1982) n.p.

10.785
CRITICAL INQUIRY: Yeazel, R.B., *"Podsnappery, Sexuality, and the English Novel,"* 9 (1982) 339-359. "To make the young girl's innocence the measure of everything that may be said is implicitly to convert all knowledge into sexual knowledge, to translate every possible speech into the very language which no Young Person may hear. In the Podsnap drawing room [of Dickens' OUR MUTUAL FRIEND], as so often in the English novel, all history waits on the young girl's awakening; but in the Podsnap drawing room there is to be no awakening, no story at all" (p. 340).

10.786
RADICAL AMERICA: Dubois, E., *"Beyond the Victorian Syndrome: Feminist Interpretations of the History of Sexuality,"* 16 (1982) 149-153. "Women found that the new ideology of passionlessness could be made to serve them in many ways: it replaced a despised definition of womanhood with an esteemed one; it allowed women a respected role in social life; it linked women together in their common distaste for (male) sexuality; and last but not least, it gave women the right to reject unwanted sexual intercourse" (p. 151).

10.787
REVIEWS IN AMERICAN HISTORY: Freedman, E.B., *"Sexuality in Nineteenth-Century America: Behavior, Ideology, and Politics,"* 10 (1982) 196-215.

10.788
WOMEN'S STUDIES INTERNATIONAL FORUM: Jeffreys, S., *"'Free From All Uninvited Touch of Man': Women's Campaigns Around Sexuality, 1880-1914,"* 5 (1982) 629-645. "Feminists within social purity fought the assumption that prostitution which they saw as a sacrifice of women for men, was necessary because of the particular biological nature of male sexuality, and stated that the male sexual urge was a social and not a biological phenomenon. They were particularly outraged at the way in which the exercise of male sexuality created a division of women into 'pure' and the 'fallen' and prevented the unity of the 'sisterhood of women'" (p. 632); Jackson, M., *"Sexual Liberation or Social Control?,"* 6 (1983) 1-19. Examines the relationship between women's liberation and sexual liberation from 1914-1939.

Focuses on the ideas of Havelock Ellis.

10.789
Gillis, John R., "Servants, Sexual Relations and the Risks of Illegitimacy in London, 1801-1900" in **SEX AND CLASS IN WOMEN'S HISTORY**. ed. by Judith L. Newton, Mary P. Ryan, and Judith R. Walkowitz. 1983. Servants were particularly vulnerable to illegitimacy, owing to class dynamics, rather than to the supposed sexual promiscuity attributed to them; *rpt. from:* **FEMINIST STUDIES:** 5 (1979) 142-173.

10.790
Nelson, James B., **BETWEEN TWO GARDENS**. New York, 1983. "The historical roots of sexual alienation are not hard to find. They emerged as two intertwining dualisms. Spiritualistic dualism (spirit over body, mind over matter) emerged.... The good life and, indeed, salvation itself required escape from flesh into spirit. Sexist or patriarchal dualism (man over woman) is the twin of spiritualism... the two dualisms became inextricably intertwined as men assumed to themselves superiority in spirit and reason while identifying women with body, earthiness, irrationality, and instability" (p. 7).

10.791
Newton, Judith L., Ryan, Mary P. and Walkowitz, Judith R., eds., **SEX AND CLASS IN WOMEN'S HISTORY**. 1983.

10.792
Rose, Phyllis, **PARALLEL LIVES: FIVE VICTORIAN MARRIAGES**. New York, 1983. Rose provides a detailed account, including intimate sexual relations, of the marriages of Jane Welsh and Thomas Carlyle, Effie Gray and John Ruskin, Harriet Taylor and John Stuart Mill, Catherine Hogarth and Charles Dickens, and George Eliot and George Henry Lewes. "I prefer to see the sexless marriages I discuss as examples of flexibility rather than abnormality.... Many cultural circumstances worked against the likelihood of sexual satisfaction within Victorian marriages" (p. 12). John Ruskin and Effie Gray never consummated their marriage, possibly because Ruskin was horrified by the mature female body, contrasting with the pre-pubescent, mythic female nudes he admired as an art critic; *reviewed in:* **TIME MAGAZINE:** *"Sex, Scandal and Sanctions,"* (Oct. 24, 1983) 94-95. "Three of the unions were devoid of passion, one degenerated into widely publicized scandal, and the sole happy one was the most shocking of all. George Eliot dared to live with a man without the sanction of either religion or the state" (p. 94).

10.793
Ross, Ellen and Rapp, Rayna, "Sex and Society: A Research Note from Social History and Anthropology" in **POWERS OF DESIRE: THE POLITICS OF SEXUALITY**. ed. by Ann Snitow, Christine Stansell and Sharon Thompson. New York, 1983.

10.794
Peiss, Kathy, "'Charity Girls' and City Pleasures: Historical Notes on Working-Class Sexuality, 1880-1920" in **POWERS OF DESIRE: THE POLITICS OF SEXUALITY**. ed. by Ann Snitow, Christine Stansell and Sharon Thompson. New York, 1983. Peiss "describes an urban subculture of young women who orchestrated their premarital social lives in the street, dance hall, theater, and at work, places that did not exist for their rural or immigrant mothers, or that would have been out of bounds for them" (p. 74). American study that provides useful insights for the English case.

10.795
Sokolow, Jayme A., **EROS AND MODERNIZATION: SYLVESTER GRAHAM, HEALTH REFORM, AND THE ORIGINS OF VICTORIAN SEXUALITY IN AMERICA.** 1983.

10.796
FEMINIST REVIEW: Gordon, L. and DuBois, E., *"Seeking Ecstasy on the Battlefield: Danger and Pleasure in Nineteenth Century Feminist Sexual Thought,"* no. 13 (1983) 42-54.

10.797
DuBois, Ellen Carol and Gordon, Linda, "Seeking Ecstasy on the Battlefield: Danger and Pleasure in Nineteenth-Century Feminist Sexual Thought" in **PLEASURE AND DANGER: EXPLORING FEMALE SEXUALITY.** ed. by Carole S. Vance. 1984.

10.798
Cox, Don Richard, ed., **SEXUALITY AND VICTORIAN LITERATURE.** Knoxville, 1984. Many important articles, including: "Lewis Carroll and Victorian Morality" by Morton Cohen, "The Fallen Woman's Sexuality: Childbirth and Censure" by Loralee MacPike, "Passion Between Women in the Victorian Novel" by Sara Putzell-Korab, and "The Worlds of Victorian Sexuality: Work in Progress" by John Maynard.

10.799
Gay, Peter, **THE BOURGEOIS EXPERIENCE, VICTORIA TO FREUD: THE EDUCATION OF THE SENSES.** 1984. Substantial amount of material from England. "That treasured, almost miraculous encounter, happy marital sexual intercourse suffused with tenderness, was the business of lovers alone. Its very mystery, often taken as a symptom of the shame with which prudish bourgeois approached the marriage bed, was something of a tribute to their high regard for loving, erotic pleasures.... The bourgeois experience was far richer than its expression, rich as that was; and it included a substantial measure of sensuality for both sexes and of candor——in sheltered surroundings" (p. 458); *reviewed in:* **HISTORY TODAY:** Weeks, J., 34 (1984) 54; **LISTENER:** Ryan, A., 111 (1984) 23-24; **THE TENDER PASSION.** 1986.

10.800
Harris, Kevin, **SEXUAL IDEOLOGY AND RELIGION: THE REPRESENTATION OF WOMEN IN THE BIBLE.** 1984. The sexual ideology and double standard of the Victorian era finds its root in the writings of the Bible. "Men are advised, and at times even commanded to take virgins for wives; and women are advised, commanded and expected to retain their virginity until their wedding night.... On the other hand women can be enticed and/or raped and thus lose their virginity through little or no fault of their own. In this latter case the offending male, if caught, must marry the woman he has deflowered" (p. 57).

10.801
Hartcup, Adeline, **LOVE AND MARRIAGE IN THE GREAT COUNTRY HOUSES.** 1984.

10.802
MacPike, Loralee, "The Fallen Woman's Sexuality: Childbirth and Censure" in **SEXUALITY AND VICTORIAN LITERATURE.** ed. by Don Richard Cox. Knoxville, 1984. "It is with the fallen woman that we see most clearly how judgement of female sexuality operates through the metaphor of childbirth. Anna Karenina's adultery is punished by a difficult birth of a girl child whom Anna does

not love, while Kitty's legitimate sexuality is rewarded by the joyful birth of a son whom she cherishes" (p. 57).

10.803
Maynard, John, CHARLOTTE BRONTE AND SEXUALITY. 1984. Bronte created a discourse that anticipated much of twentieth-century thought on sexuality. "Her work is centrally focused on the nature of sexual experience, especially the major stage of transition or awakening to adult sexuality.... Bronte realizes, in her artistic vision, most of the major assumptions of the sexual revolution of Havelock Ellis, Freud, and their successors" (p. viii).

10.804
Aries, Philippe and Bejin, Andre, eds., WESTERN SEXUALITY: PRACTICE AND PRECEPT IN PAST AND PRESENT TIMES. Oxford, 1985. A broad survey of relevant questions including the changing attitudes towards sexual practices between men and women, the origins of homosexuality and lesbianism, and attitudes towards femininity and masculinity.

10.805
Brophy, Janet and Smart, Carol, WOMEN IN LAW: EXPLORATIONS IN LAW, FAMILY AND SEXUALITY. 1985.

10.806
Mort, Frank, "Purity, Feminism and the State: Sexuality and Moral Politics, 1880-1914" in CRISES IN THE BRITISH STATE, 1880-1930. ed. by Mary Langan and Bill Schwartz. 1985. On representations of female sexuality and about the role of the state.

10.807
NEW REPUBLIC: Stone, L., *"Sex in the West: The Strange History of Human Sexuality,"* n.v. (July 8, 1985) 25-37. Surveys scholarship that covers Western sexuality from the Roman Empire to present. Posits several explanations of nineteenth-century sexual repression: a "moral panic" arising from the threat to the upper classes posed by the French Revolution, evangelistic asceticism, and the theory of "spermatic economy" as a "sexual ethic peculiarly appropriate to the acquisitive and retentive bourgeoisie of the Victorian era" (p. 35).

10.808
Jeffreys, Sheila, ed., THE SEXUALITY DEBATES. 1987. A collection of documents consisting of major articles of the nineteenth and early twentieth centuries that represent feminist campaigns against government regulation of prostitution, the prevalence of domestic violence, medical pronouncments on sexuality, and policies reflecting the double standard of sexual expectations and prescriptions. The final sections are on "The Impact of Sex Reform" and "Mothers, Spinsters and Lesbians."

XI. SCIENCES, SOCIAL SCIENCES AND THEIR SOCIAL APPLICATION

INTRODUCTION

11.1
Loewenberg, Bert James, DARWINISM; REACTION OR REFORM? New York, 1957.

> Once man was swept into the evolutionary orbit, the logic of science became applicable to all forms of human activity.... Hence the logic of science and the dynamics of evolution applied to the mind, to morals, and to society. This was the Darwinian revolution... not in science alone; it was a revolution in man's conception of himself and his works.... The Darwinian synthesis permeated every sector of thought (p. 1).

11.2
Darwin, Charles, ON THE ORIGIN OF THE SPECIES. 1859; THE DESCENT OF MAN, AND SELECTION IN RELATION TO SEX. 2 vols. 1871.

That the publication of Darwin's theories was a catalyst in launching new developments in biology and psychology and in charting new paths for anthropology and sociology has been supported by scholarly defenders since the nineteenth century.

11.3
Irvine, William, APES, ANGELS AND VICTORIANS: THE STORY OF DARWIN, HUXLEY AND EVOLUTION. 1955.

11.4
Houghton, Walter E., "Darwinism, Chauvinism, Racism" in THE VICTORIAN FRAME OF MIND. by Walter E. Houghton. New Haven, 1959.

11.5
Vorzimmer, Peter J., CHARLES DARWIN: THE YEARS OF CONTROVERSY. Philadelphia, 1970.

11.6
Hull, David L., DARWIN AND HIS CRITICS: THE RECEPTION OF DARWIN'S THEORY OF EVOLUTION IN THE SCIENTIFIC COMMUNITY. Cambridge, 1973.

On the question of psychology:

11.7
Flugel, J.C., **A HUNDRED YEARS OF PSYCHOLOGY**. 1933; 1970:

> In so far as Darwinism was accepted, psychology was itself compelled henceforward to adopt the evolutionary point of view (p. 95).... The individual mind could no longer be considered in the artificial isolation of the philosopher's study... the developmental aspect of consciousness of behavior... could no longer be lost sight of. From now onwards, psychology was related not only to philosophy... and to physiology... but to the general study of life (p. 99).

Regarding biology:

11.8
Singer, Charles, **A HISTORY OF BIOLOGY TO ABOUT THE YEAR 1900**. 1959.

> The whole of modern biology has been called a commentary on ORIGIN OF THE SPECIES... the generations to which the ORIGIN was delivered followed Darwin blindly. The last decade of the nineteenth century showed some reaction. This lasted until the discovery of Mendel's work [in genetics] ushered in a new era (p. 311).

On anthropology and the rise of evolutionary anthropological theory:

11.9
Harris, Marvin, **THE RISE OF ANTHROPOLOGICAL THEORY**. New York, 1968:

> Competition, progress, perfection, expansion, struggle, conquest——these were themes, dynamic and optimistic, which awaited a joining with the biological interpretation of history. The fusion of all these diverse elements into one grand scientific theory was the achievement of Herbert Spencer and Charles Darwin (p. 105).... it is almost impossible to read [Darwin's] DESCENT OF MAN without being struck by its almost total advocacy of the struggle for survival as the means of understanding sociocultural evolution (p. 120).

The labels Darwinism and Social Darwinism have prevailed since the nineteenth century among social scientists and in public opinion as the identifying terminology for theories that link the biological determinations represented in Darwin's writings with the theoretical constructs that were employed in attempts to define sociocultural evolution. See:

11.10
Ellegard, Alvar, **DARWIN AND THE GENERAL READER; THE RECEPTION OF DARWIN'S THEORY OF EVOLUTION IN THE BRITISH PERIODICAL PRESS, 1859-1872**. Goteborg, 1958.

11.11
SOCIAL SCIENCE REVIEW: Pantin, C.F.A., *"Darwin's Theory and the Causes of Its Acceptance,"* October 1950, March 1951 and June 1951, pp. 75-83, 197-205, 313-321.

On the aims of Social Darwinists:

11.12
JOURNAL OF THE HISTORY OF IDEAS: Rogers, J.A., *"Darwinism and Social Darwinism,"* 33 (1972) 265-280. Rogers concludes that "Social Darwinism... wanted to view society through Darwin's vision of the animal world... (and to have) Darwin's belief in biological progress linked to Spencer's belief in social progress" (p. 265).

The practical task of interpreting the translation of Darwinian thought into social theory has been and remains a complex undertaking. This question is explored in:

11.13
Himmelfarb, Gertrude, **DARWIN AND THE DARWINIAN REVOLUTION.** New York, 1959; 1962. "[ORIGIN] did not revolutionize... beliefs so much as give public recognition to a revolution that had already occurred. It was belief made manifest, revolution legitimized" (p. 452, 1962 ed.).

11.14
PHILOSOPHY OF SCIENCE: Bock, K.E., *"Darwin and Social Theory,"* 22 (1955) 123-134. Bock asserts the "need of discriminating between perspectives that are blatantly Darwin ['biologism'] and others that have subtler and more elusive roots" (p. 132).

This theme is closely detailed in the important book:

11.15
Burrow, J.W., **EVOLUTION AND SOCIETY: A STUDY IN VICTORIAN SOCIAL THEORY.** 1966.

and in:

11.16
Mandelbaum, Maurice, **HISTORY, MAN AND REASON: A STUDY IN NINETEENTH CENTURY THOUGHT.** Baltimore, 1971.

11.17
VICTORIAN STUDIES: 3 (Sept. 1959) entire; Halliday, R.J., *"Social Darwinism: A Definition,"* 14 (1971) 388-405.

11.18
Jones, Greta, **SOCIAL DARWINISM AND ENGLISH THOUGHT: THE INTERACTION BETWEEN BIOLOGICAL AND SOCIAL THEORY.** Brighton, 1980.

Notwithstanding the permeation of Darwinism in late nineteenth-century thought, conflict and controversy reigned among the anthropologists and sociologists as their theories and prescriptions irregularly accommodated or clashed with traditional views about mankind and social processes. Gertrude Himmelfarb has observed (see above entry):

> In the spectrum of opinion that went under the name of Social Darwinism almost every variety of belief was included.... Some complained because it exalted men to the level of supermen and gods; others because it degraded them to the state of animals. Political theorists read it as an assertion of the need for inequality... alternatively as an egalitarian tract (p. 431).

A uniting principle, however, concerned the mutual aspiration to develop the social sciences into structured disciplines:

11.19
AMERICAN HISTORICAL REVIEW: Soffer, R.N., *"The Revolution in English Social Thought, 1880-1914,"* 75 (1970) 1938-1964:

> From the 1880s until 1914 there was in England a genuine vital revolution in the contents of methodology and purposes of thought. An inductive behavioral science bent on effecting practical sociology overthrew deductive social theory that assumed inherent laws of human nature and society (p. 1938).

But in:

11.20
JOURNAL OF BRITISH STUDIES: Soffer, R.N., *"New Elitism: Social Psychology in Pre-War England,"* 8 (1969) 111-140:

> The social psychologists, like other social evolutionists, could not give up the idea of progress though it contradicted their analysis of human nature in society (p. 126).

The theme and idea of "progress" permeates the writings of the mid and late nineteenth-century anthropological and sociological writings with important ramifications for questions about women. For example, when "the evolution" of matriarchal structures of early societies to the patriarchal forms of recent times was traced, the trend was invariably attributed to "advance in civilization." This and similar questions are the concern of Elizabeth Fee who discusses social anthropological theory and its application in social thought:

11.21
FEMINIST STUDIES: Fee, E., *"The Sexual Politics of Victorian Social Anthropology,"* 2 (1973) 23-40; *rpt. in:* **CLIO'S CONSCIOUSNESS RAISED.** ed. by Mary Hartman and Lois Banner. New York, 1974:

> Social anthropology demonstrated that the idealized family in the Victorian middle class was dictated by no law of nature, that monogamous marriage was only one of various human sexual possibilities, and that women were not necessarily born only to domestic and decorative functions (p. 24).

But in reviewing the writings of Maine, Bachofen, McLennan, Lubbock, and Herbert Spencer, she concludes that the assertions of these early social scientists nevertheless assured that:

> Patriarchalism was now inextricably linked with the progress of civilization; Victorian culture and its attendant social relations represented the capstone of all evolution. Male superiority, then, was sanctified not by nature but by civilization (p. 38).

By the 1880s argumentation on questions of women's intellectual and physical nature as well as their domestic, social, and political roles (past and present) began to rely perhaps as much on social science investigations and findings as on the traditional outlook, religion, myth, irrational prejudice and socioeconomic status.

The extent to which the new sciences preserved myths and beliefs is still not precisely estimated. The following sections on the new sciences and social sciences relate almost exclusively to more theoretical developments in the various categories of study that are tied to questions about roles, status and responsibility of Victorian and Edwardian women. The interests, attitudes and techniques of the nineteenth and early twentieth-century social scientists were generally so similar as to be overlapping, but, recognizably, anthropology, sociology and evolutionary biology are represented. There is little resemblance between mid-twentieth-century social science disciplines and nineteenth-century counterparts.

* * *

1. ANTHROPOLOGY, SOCIOLOGY, EVOLUTIONARY BIOLOGY AND PSYCHOLOGY: VIEWS OF WOMEN'S MIND AND NATURE

Note: "Psychology" here denotes the "transitional psychology" described by Reba Soffer (see section 2 in this chapter), that grew out of an application of the new biology to the study of the mind. Modern clinical psychology is a more recent development and is therefore not considered in the present study.

11.22
Spencer, Herbert, **SOCIAL STATICS; OR, THE CONDITIONS ESSENTIAL TO HUMAN HAPPINESS SPECIFIED, AND THE FIRST OF THEM DEVELOPED.** 1851; 1868; New York, 1886; 1910; New York, 1903. Endorses the idea that a society based upon individual freedom requires individual liberty of women. However, by the second edition, Spencer changed his view in accordance with theories of social and biological evolution; **EDUCATION: INTELLECTUAL, MORAL AND PHYSICAL.** 1861. Discusses women's physiology in relation to college studies and exercise. Overeducation is disastrous; **PRINCIPLES OF BIOLOGY.** New York, 1864; **THE STUDY OF SOCIOLOGY.** New York, 1873; **PRINCIPLES OF SOCIOLOGY.** 3 vols. 1876; 1904. See especially: vol. 1, part 3, "Domestic Institutions"; **ESSAYS: SCIENTIFIC, POLITICAL, SPECULATIVE.** New York, 1899; **AN APPENDIX TO THE PRINCIPLES OF SOCIOLOGY.** New York, 1905; **ON SOCIAL EVOLUTION.** ed. by J.D.Y. Peel. 1972. ——*see also:* Carneiro, Robert, **THE EVOLUTION OF SOCIETY: SELECTIONS FROM HERBERT SPENCER'S PRINCIPLES OF SOCIOLOGY.** Chicago, 1967.

11.23
FRASER'S MAGAZINE: Buckle, H.T., *"Influence of Women on the Progress of Knowledge,"* 57 (1858) 395-407; Greg, W.R., *"On the Failure of 'Natural Selection' in the Case of Man,"* 78 (1868) 353-362. Relates the tenets of Darwinism and considers the issues of marriage and offspring as they affect "the race"; Cusack, M.F., *"Woman's Place in the Economy of Creation,"* 91 (1874) 200-207.

11.24
Darwin, Charles, **THE ORIGIN OF THE SPECIES BY MEANS OF NATURAL SELECTION IN THE PRESERVATION OF FAVORED RACES IN THE STRUGGLE FOR LIFE.** 1859; **THE DESCENT OF MAN AND SELECTION IN RELATION TO SEX.** 1871; Princeton, 1981. "The chief distinction in the intellectual powers of the two sexes is shown by man attaining to a higher eminence, in whatever he takes up, than woman can attain——whether requiring

deep thought, reason, or imagination, or merely the use of the senses and hands.... in order that woman should reach the same standard as man, she ought, when nearly adult, to be trained to energy and perseverence, and to have her reason and imagination exercised to the highest point; and then she would probably transmit these qualities chiefly to her adult daughters.... [men] generally have to undergo, during manhood, a severe struggle in order to maintain themselves and their families, and this will tend to keep up or even increase their mental powers, and as a consequence, the present inequality between the sexes" (pp. 327-329, 1981 ed.).
—*see also:* SOCIAL SCIENCE REVIEW: Pantin, C.F.A., *"Darwin's Theory and the Causes of its Acceptance,"* in 3 parts. n.v. (Oct. 1950) 75-83; n.v. (March 1951) 197-205; n.v. (June 1951) 313-321. Describes Darwin's background and career, and the intellectual climate of the time. "It was often said that towards the end of that time [the years previous to publication of ORIGIN OF THE SPECIES], evolution was in the air" (part I, 79); Irvine, William, APES, ANGELS AND VICTORIANS: THE STORY OF DARWIN, HUXLEY AND EVOLUTION. New York, 1955.

11.25
Reeve, Isaac, THE INTELLECT OF WOMAN NOT NATURALLY INFERIOR TO THAT OF MAN. 1859.

11.26
Allan, James MacGrigor, THE INTELLECTUAL SEVERANCE OF MEN AND WOMEN. 1860. Marriage is unfavorable to the intellectual process.

11.27
WESTMINSTER REVIEW: Spencer, H., *"The Social Organism,"* 17 (1860) 90-121; Harvey, H.E., *"Science and the Rights of Women,"* 148 (1897) 205-207; Bulley, A., *"The Political Evolution of Women,"* 134 (1890) 1-8; Johnson, E., *"Capacity in Men and Women,"* 153 (1900) 567-576. Uses cross-cultural and mythical accounts of women exercising their capacities to argue that "talent and capacity are non-sexual"; Swinburne, J., *"Feminine Mind Worship,"* 158 (1902) 187-198. The feminine mind is dependent upon memory and being reproductive whereas the masculine mind is dependent on reason and being creative.

11.28
Bachofen, Johann Jakob, DAS MUTTERECHT. Stuttgart, 1861. Title translates as "Mother-Right." The classic study of matriarchy as the original societal form, and prototype for many subsequent speculations. Uses poetic and historical sources to defend his thesis of a primitive "gynocracy" eventually superseded by patriarchy; MYTH, RELIGION AND MOTHER RIGHT: SELECTED WRITINGS OF JOHANN JAKOB BACHOFEN. trans. by R. Manheim. 1967. "Bachofen's theory of a matriarchal society out of which modern patriarchal societies evolved was accepted pretty generally among sociologists until about the beginning of the twentieth century" (xviii).

11.29
Maine, Henry James Sumner, ANCIENT LAW: ITS CONNECTION WITH THE EARLY HISTORY OF SOCIETY AND ITS RELATION TO MODERN IDEAS. 1861. Claims that the patriarchal system was the original, universal system; directly opposes Bachofen's DAS MUTTERECHT, published the same year.

11.30
Lubbock, John William, (Baron Avebury), PRE-HISTORIC TIMES. 1865; ORIGIN OF CIVILIZATION AND THE PRIMITIVE CONDITION OF MAN. 1870. Theory of wife capture.

11.31
McLennan, J.F., **PRIMITIVE MARRIAGE: AN INQUIRY INTO THE ORIGIN OF THE FORM OF CAPTURE IN MARRIAGE CUSTOMS.** Edinburgh, 1865; **THE PATRIARCHAL THEORY BASED ON THE PAPERS OF THE LATE JOHN FERGUSON MCLENNAN.** ed. by Donald McLennan. 1885. Theory of patriarchal society based upon a primordial patriarchal family structure. The theory supposedly explains the genesis of nations and the state. Includes an extended study of patriarchy, totemism, agnation, and exogamy in ancient civilizations.

11.32
Tylor, Edward B., **RESEARCHES INTO THE EARLY HISTORY OF MANKIND.** 1865. Explicitly separated his own theory of progression as it applied to the elements in culture from the modern naturalist's doctrine of progressive development; **PRIMITIVE CULTURE.** 1871.

11.33
ANTHROPOLOGICAL REVIEW: Ecker, A., *"On a Characteristic Peculiarity in the Form of the Female Skull, and its Significance for Comparative Anthropology,"* 6 (1868) 350-356; Allan, J.M., *"On the Real Differences in the Minds of Men and Women,"* 7 (1869) 195-221. Argues that there are "radical, natural, permanent distinctions in the mental and moral conformation, corresponding with those in the physical organisation of the sexes" (p. 196).

11.34
ENGLISHWOMAN'S REVIEW: Becker, L.E., *"Is There Any Specific Distinction Between Male and Female Intellect?"* 8 (1868) n.p.; C., T.G., *"Is There Sex in Mind?"* 6 (1875) 444-449. "The admission of the female element" would improve the legislative and judicial process by complementing the male tendency to "hasty generalization" with the female aptitude for particulars.

11.35
LANCET: *"Miss Becker on the Mental Characteristics of the Sexes,"* 2 (1868) 320-321. This review of Becker's paper synopsizes the disparaging pseudo-scientific view of women's capacities and its patronizing and condescending rhetoric; Roberts, C., *"Nature's Plan in the Determination of the Sexes and the Hereditary Transmission of Physical and Mental Qualities, and the Acquisition of New Ones,"* 2 (1880) 926-928; Browne, J.C., *"An Oration on Sex in Education,"* 1 (1892) 1011-1018. Indictment of high schools for girls and the "dangers to health that lurk in their aims and methods... all arising out of their forgetfulness of sexual differentiation, and out of the futile attempt to educate boys and girls on exactly the same lines" (p. 1013).

11.36
Mill, John Stuart, **THE SUBJECTION OF WOMEN.** Philadelphia, 1869. Represents the early foundation of feminist thought. In it, Mill argues that the innate differences between the sexes are impossible to determine apart from external circumstances, refutes the claim that anatomical differences reflect mental ones, and advocates expansion of education to develop the intellectual attributes that have been suppressed. ——*see also:* Seymour-Smith, Martin, "The Old Feminism" in **SEX AND SOCIETY.** by Martin Seymour-Smith. 1975. This work is "the clearest statement, and still the classic one, of the nineteenth-century feminist position." Mill argued that "'brute force and unthinking sentiment', not reason, are the foundations of male supremacy" (p. 71).

11.37
JOURNAL OF THE ANTHROPOLOGICAL SOCIETY OF LONDON: Harris, G., *"On The Distinctions, Mental and Moral, Occasioned by the Differences of Sex,"* 7 (1869) 189-195; 215-219; Pike, L.O., *"On the Claims of Women to Political Power,"* 7 (1869) 47-61. Anthropological view of "the proper position of the two sexes in matters of government" (n.p.). Questions how far the female intellect can be trained to imitate the male.

11.38
Amos, Sheldon, **DIFFERENCE OF SEX AS A TOPIC OF JURISPRUDENCE AND LEGISLATION.** 1870. Sex differences are "far too deep and subtle to admit of the application of coarse methods of legal description and enforcing. Every law or political institution that has fixed and perpetuated any differences between the men and women... has retarded civilization" (p. 9).

11.39
Harte, Richard, **THE LAWS AND CUSTOMS RELATING TO MARRIAGE... BEING A PAPER READ BEFORE THE DIALECTICAL SOCIETY.** 1870.

11.40
Morgan, Lewis Henry, **SYSTEMS OF CONSANGUINITY AND AFFINITY OF THE HUMAN FAMILY.** 1871; **ANCIENT SOCIETY.** 1877. ——*see also:* Engels, Friedrich, **THE ORIGIN OF THE FAMILY, PRIVATE PROPERTY AND THE STATE. IN LIGHT OF THE RESEARCHES OF LEWIS H. MORGAN.** orig. ed., Zurich, 1884; 1891; New York, 1942; 1972. Morgan's "rediscovery of the primitive matriarchal gens as the earlier stage of the patriarchal gens of civilized peoples has the same importance for anthropology as Darwin's theory of evolution has for biology and Marx's theory of surplus value for political economy" (preface to 4th ed.).

11.41
Greg, William R., "Non-Survival of the Fittest" in **ENIGMAS OF LIFE.** by William R. Greg. 1872.

11.42
Clarke, Edward H., **SEX IN EDUCATION: OR, A FAIR CHANCE FOR GIRLS.** Boston, 1873; **SEX IN MIND AND EDUCATION.** Boston, 1874. Higher education for women is detrimental to their reproductive capacity and can lead to "neuralgia, uterine disease, hysteria, and other derangements of the nervous system" (pp. 17-18). Clarke's arguments were later taken up by Henry Maudsley in England. ——*see also:* Greene, William B., **CRITICAL COMMENTS UPON CERTAIN PASSAGES IN THE INTRODUCTORY PORTION OF DR. EDWARD H. CLARKE'S BOOK ON "SEX IN EDUCATION."** Boston, 1874; Howe, J.W., ed., **SEX AND EDUCATION: A REPLY TO DR. E.H. CLARKE'S "SEX IN EDUCATION."** Boston, 1874.

11.43
Smith, Jerome Van Crowninshield, **THE WAYS OF WOMEN IN THEIR PHYSICAL, MORAL, AND INTELLECTUAL RELATIONS.** 1873.

11.44
CONTEMPORARY REVIEW: Carpenter, W.B., *"On the Hereditary Transmission of Acquired Psychical Habits,"* 21 (1873) 295-314; 779-795; 867-885. Insists that acquired characteristics are inherited; Spencer, H., *"The Inadequacy of 'Natural Selection,'"* 63 (1893) 153-166; 439-456; 743-760; Weismann, A., *"The All-*

Sufficiency of Natural Selection: A Reply to Herbert Spencer," 64 (1893) 309-338; 596-610; "A Rejoinder to Professor Weismann," 64 (1893) 893-912; Spencer, H., "Weismannism Once More," 66 (1894) 592-608; Weismann, A., "Heredity Once More," 68 (1895) 420-456; Reid, G.A., "The Alleged Transmission of Acquired Characters," 94 (1908) 399-412; Hartog, M., "The Transmission of Acquired Characters: A Rejoinder," 94 (1908) 635-640.

11.45
ANTHROPOLOGIA: Wallington, E., "The Physical and Intellectual Capacities of Woman Equal to Those of Man," 1 (1874) 552-565. "Where men and women, either in physical or intellectual labor, are placed under equal conditions, there you will have equality of power" (p. 555).

11.46
BLACKWOOD'S MAGAZINE: Cowell, H., "Sex in Mind and Education, a Commentary," 115 (1874) 736-749.

11.47
FORTNIGHTLY REVIEW: Maudsley, H., "Sex in Mind and Education," 21 (1874) 446-483. Expanding on Dr. Clarke's position on higher education for women in America, Maudsley warns that any attempt to rebel against the natural duty of women to produce offspring by engaging in the physical and mental strain of education would result in grave injury; Anderson, E.G., "Sex in Mind and Education, A Reply," 21 (1874) 582-594. Disagrees with Maudsley and argues that it is impossible to compare American and British systems since they are very different.

11.48
POPULAR SCIENCE MONTHLY: Spencer, H., "Psychology of the Sexes," 4 (1874) 30-38. Human evolution necessitated development of brutal males that were coped with by females that were compliant, intuitive, and had reverence for power. There is a "somewhat earlier arrest of individual evolution in women than in men, necessitated by the reservation of vital power to meet the cost of reproduction," hence, a "perceptible falling short in... the latest products of evolution——the power of abstract reasoning and that most abstract of the emotions, the sentiment of justice" (p. 33); Van De Warker, E., "The Genesis of Woman," 27 (1874) 269-276; White, F.E., "Woman's Place in Nature," 28 (1875) 292-300; "Biology and 'Woman's Rights,'" 14 (1879) 201-213. Contends that the women's rights movement is a process of "unnatural selection" which will create a race of monstrosities; Brooks, W.K., "The Condition of Women from a Zoological Point of View," 15 (1879) 145-155. There is a "fundamental and constantly increasing difference between the sexes" (p. 145); Delauney, G., "Equality and Inequality in Sex," 20 (1881) 184-192. "The supremacy of the female is... the first term of the evolution which sexuality undergoes, while the supremacy of the male is the last term" (p. 184); Hardaker, M.A., "Science and the Woman Question," 35 (1882) 577-584; Morais, N., "The Women Question," 21 (1882) 70-78; Gardener, H.H., "Sex and Brain Weight," 31 (1887) 266-269; Romanes, G.J., "Mental Differences in Men and Women," 31 (1887) 372-382; Patrick, G.T.W., "The Psychology of Woman," 47 (1895) 209-225. Woman's arrested development is manifested in her childlike mental traits and primitive dress. "Every woman is... a composite picture of the race, never much worse nor much better than all. Man is... Nature's experiment.... From her retarded development the educational and political reformer might learn that woman's cause may suffer irretrievable damage if she is plunged too suddenly into duties demanding the same strain and nervous expenditure that is safely borne by man" (p. 224); Ellis, H., "Variation in Man and Woman," n.v. (1903) n.p.; Glaser, O.C., "The

Constitutional Conservatism of Women," 64 (1911) 299-302. ——*see also:* Newman, Louise Michelle, ed., **MEN'S IDEAS/WOMEN'S REALITIES: POPULAR SCIENCE, 1870-1915.** New York, 1984.

11.49
Blackwell, Antoinette Brown, **THE SEXES THROUGHOUT NATURE.** New York, 1875; abridged version appears in **THE FEMINIST PAPERS.** ed. by Alice S. Rossi. New York, 1973. Points out the tenuousness of a theory of natural selection in which by mathematical progression males outstrip females. "Mr. Spencer scientifically *subtracts* from the female, and Mr. Darwin as scientifically *adds* to the male.... Where, then, is male superiority to end?.... There must be functional checks... to maintain a due balance" (pp. 358-359).

11.50
JOURNAL OF THE ROYAL ANTHROPOLOGICAL INSTITUTE: Distant, W.L., *"The Mental Differences Between the Sexes,"* 4 (1875) 78-87; Treagear, E., *"Sexual Inferiority,"* 25 (1896) 87-89; Tylor, E.B., *"On a Method of Investigating the Development of Institutions, Applied to Laws of Marriage and Descent,"* 28 (1899) 245-269.

11.51
Dugdale, Richard Louis, **"THE JUKES": A STUDY IN CRIME, PAUPERISM, DISEASE AND HEREDITY...** 1877; 4th ed., 1888. The Jukes family was used as a case study to show that criminality is hereditary.

11.52
Geddes, Patrick and Thomson, J. Arthur, **THE EVOLUTION OF SEX.** New York, 1880; 1889. Describes the existing state of knowledge about sex differentiation, leading to conclusions (mainly Geddes') on how the social position of women coincided with a preordained evolutionary design. Defends inheritance of acquired characteristics against Weismann's theory of germ-plasm, just being formed. ——*see also:* Thomson, J. Arthur, **THE POSITION OF WOMEN: BIOLOGICALLY CONSIDERED.** 1911.

11.53
Huxley, Thomas Henry, "Emancipation in Black and White" in **LAY SERMONS AND ESSAYS.** by Thomas Henry Huxley. 1880; New York, 1881. Following a discussion of reasons why negroes are inferior to whites, Huxley applies his argument to women, saying that their emancipation will only result in partial social equality since women's physical and mental strength can never match that of men.

11.54
JOURNAL OF SCIENCE: Fernseed, F., *"Sexual Distinctions and Resemblances,"* 3 ser. 33 (1881) 741-744.

11.55
KNOWLEDGE... A MONTHLY RECORD OF SCIENCE: Allan, J.M., *"Influence of Sex on Mind: Cranial Contour,"* 1 (1881-1882) 78-79; 230-231. "There is not in woman sufficient development of the abstract principles of justice, morality, truth, causality, inventive, and executive power to hold society together for one week" (pp. 230-231); Allan, J.M., *"Influence of Sex on Daily Experience,"* 1 (1881-1882) 321-322; Delauney, J.M., *"Women, Are They Inferior to Men?"* 1 (1881-1882) 456; Gay, S.E., *"Are Women Inferior to Men?"* 1 (1881-1882) 456-457. Response to Delauney. "Man is the tree, woman the flower, and when fully understood, they are too closely united to admit the question of the latter's 'inferiority'" (p. 456); Foster,

T., *"Volubility of Women,"* 8 (1885) 17.

11.56
Clouston, Thomas Smith, **FEMALE EDUCATION FROM A MEDICAL POINT OF VIEW.** Edinburgh, 1882; **CLINICAL LECTURES ON MENTAL DISEASES.** 1883; 1904. Claims adverse effects of higher education on the "tender organism"; **THE PSYCHOLOGICAL DANGERS TO WOMEN IN MODERN SOCIAL SCIENCE EXPERIMENTS.** 1911. "Equality of the sexes should be limited to opportunity, legal status and social position, and should not be attempted as to certain faculties and instincts" (n.p.).

11.57
INTERNATIONAL REVIEW: *"The Intellectuality of Women,"* 13 (1882) 123-136. Expresses a need for opportunities for mental culture.

11.58
Galton, Francis, **INQUIRIES INTO HUMAN FACULTY AND ITS DEVELOP-MENT.** 1883. Includes observations regarding marriage and women's faculties.

11.59
Ward, Lester, L., **DYNAMIC SOCIOLOGY.** New York, 1883. An early sociologist whose theories reflect social Darwinistic ideas.

11.60
JOURNAL OF MENTAL SCIENCE: Clouston, T.S., *"Female Education from a Medical Point of View,"* 29 (1883) 100-105.

11.61
Engels, Friedrich, **THE ORIGIN OF THE FAMILY, PRIVATE PROPERTY AND THE STATE. IN THE LIGHT OF THE RESEARCHES OF LEWIS H. MORGAN.** orig. ed., Zurich, 1884; many subsequent eds.; New York, 1942; 1972. Engels summarizes and clarifies Morgan's ANCIENT SOCIETY, a treatise on social evolution based on studies of American Indians. Marx and Engels found Morgan's anthropological data to corroborate their own historical-materialist theories of societal evolution. In his preface to the fourth edition, Engels reviews the development of studies of the history of the family from Bachofen and McLennan to Morgan.

11.62
Sidgwick, Mrs. Henry, **THE UNIVERSITY EDUCATION OF WOMEN.** 1884; **HEALTH STATISTICS OF WOMEN OF CAMBRIDGE AND OXFORD AND OF THEIR SISTERS.** Cambridge, 1890. Purpose of the study was to investigate the alleged ill effects of education on women.

11.63
Thorburn, John, **FEMALE EDUCATION FROM A PHYSIOLOGICAL POINT OF VIEW.** Manchester, 1884. Series of six lectures.

11.64
Ploss, Hermann Heinrich, Bartels, Max and Bartels, Paul, **WOMAN: AN HISTORICAL, GYNAECOLOGICAL AND ANTHROPOLOGICAL COMPENDIUM.** 3 vols. 1885; 1887; 1927 (in German); ed. and trans. by Eric Dingwall, 1935. Dingwall claims that this work was utilized in England from the first edition. Extremely valuable with important photographic illustrations and lengthy bibliography; *vol. 1 rpt. as:* **FEMINA LIBIDO SEXUALIS.** New York, 1965; *also*

titled: WOMAN IN THE SEXUAL RELATION: AN ANTHROPOLOGICAL AND HISTORICAL SURVEY. rev. and enlarged by F.F. Reitzenstein. New York, 1964.

11.65
Woodward, Emma Hosken, "Women and Evolution" in MEN, WOMEN AND PROGRESS. by Emma H. Woodward. 1885.

11.66
Maudsley, Henry, PHYSIOLOGY AND PATHOLOGY OF THE MIND. 1886.

11.67
QUARTERLY REVIEW: Maine, H.J.S., *"The Patriarchal Theory,"* 162 (1886) 181-209; Colquhoun, E., *"Modern Feminism and Sex-Antagonism,"* 219 (1913) 143-166. "The keynote of the new relations" is the word "individualism" (n.p.).

11.68
NINETEENTH CENTURY: Romanes, G.J., *"Mental Differences Between Men and Women,"* 21 (1887) 654-672. Quotes passages from Darwin's THE DESCENT OF MAN in which Darwin claims that by natural selection, the male has surpassed the female both physically and mentally; Symcox, E., *"The Capacity of Women,"* 21 (1887) 391-402. Response to Romanes. Asserts that cultural rather than biological influences are the decisive factors; Tylor, E.B., *"The Matriarchal Family System,"* 40 (1896) 81-96; Sutherland, A., *"Woman's Brain,"* 47 (1900) 802-810. Surveys theories relating brain weight to intelligence. Concludes that 90 percent of women are at least equally as intelligent as men, and about 40 percent are of superior intelligence.

11.69
Carpenter, W.B., "Darwinism in England" in NATURE AND MAN. by W.B. Carpenter. 1888.

11.70
Grove, Agnes Geraldine (Fox-Pitt-Rivers), "The Re-Subjection of Women" in THE HUMAN WOMAN. by Agnes Grove. 1888; 1908. A suffragist's attack on ideas from "the new sciences" that nourished the anti-suffrage campaign. Grove especially attacks the principle that physical-force superiority should be applied in sociopolitical arrangements.

11.71
Nisbet, John Ferguson, MARRIAGE AND HEREDITY: A VIEW OF PSYCHOLOGICAL EVOLUTION. 1889. Unlike other acquired characteristics, mental states may be transmissible; Weismann's genetic theory set limitations upon the variability of the species.

11.72
Weismann, August, ESSAYS UPON HEREDITY AND KINDRED BIOLOGICAL PROBLEMS. Oxford, 1889; THE GERM-PLASM: A THEORY OF HEREDITY. 1893. Weismann's work challenged the concept of inheritance of acquired characteristics suggested by Darwin and held by biologists of the period. After Weismann's publication, discussion and controversy developed at a rapid pace; THE EFFECT OF EXTERNAL INFLUENCES UPON DEVELOPMENT. 1894; THE EVOLUTION THEORY. 1904. ——*see also:* NATURE: Mosely, H.N., *"Dr. August Weismann on the Importance of Sexual Reproduction for the Theory of Selection,"* 34 (1886) 629-632; Mosely, H.N., *"The Continuity of the Germ Plasm Considered as the Basis of a Theory of Heredity,"* 33 (1895) 154-157. In 1875 Weismann expressed the

conviction that "the physiological value of the sperm cell and egg cell are identical" (p. 157); Romanes, George J., **AN EXAMINATION OF WEISMANNISM.** 1893; **MONIST:** Morgan, C.L., *"Dr. Weismann on Heredity and Progress,"* 4 (1893-1894) 20-30. Asserts that there is no definite proof that transmission of acquired characteristics is not inherited; see above **CONTEMPORARY REVIEW** entries for the debate between Weismann and Spencer.

11.73
MONIST: Cope, E.D., *"On the Maternal Relations of Sex in Human Society,"* 1 (1890-1891) 38-47. Women's needs from the environment are the same as men's but women have two disabilities: physical and mental incompetence; Ferrero, G., *"The Problem of Woman, From the Bio-Sociological Point of View,"* 4 (1893-1894) 261-274. Contends that it is "natural law that the woman should neither labor nor struggle for her existence" (p. 262); Ward, L., *"The Exemption of Women from Labor,"* 4 (1893-1894) 385-395. Responds to Ferrero.

11.74
Campbell, Harry, **DIFFERENCES IN THE NERVOUS ORGANIZATION OF MAN AND WOMAN: PHYSIOLOGICAL AND PATHOLOGICAL.** 1891. An evolutionary viewpoint.

11.75
Westermarck, Edward, **THE HISTORY OF HUMAN MARRIAGE.** 3 vols. 5th ed., 1891. Defends the theory of patriarchy as the original society; **THE ORIGIN AND DEVELOPMENT OF MORAL IDEAS.** 1908; *reviewed in:* **SOCIOLOGICAL REVIEW:** Hobhouse, L.T., *"Ethical Evolution,"* 2 (1909) 402-405. "The primary object of the study of ethical evolution is not to discover what is ethically sound or unsound. A system of moral philosophy cannot be logically based on historical facts of moral development" (p. 402).

11.76
Mitchell, Charles Pitfield, **THE ENLARGEMENT OF THE SPHERE OF WOMEN: AN ESSAY IN SOCIAL BIOLOGY.** [1892].

11.77
AMERICAN JOURNAL OF OBSTETRICS: Morris, R.T., *"Is Evolution Trying to Do Away With the Clitoris?"* 26 (1892) 847-858. Application of Darwinistic principles to medicine.

11.78
Gamble, Eliza Burt, **THE EVOLUTION OF WOMEN: AN INQUIRY INTO THE DOGMA OF HER INFERIORITY TO MAN.** 1894; *revised ed. rpt. as:* **THE SEXES IN SCIENCE AND HISTORY.** Westport, 1975. Critiques Bachofen, Lubbock, McLennan, Morgan (all of whom she calls "naturalists") and Darwin's **THE DESCENT OF MAN; WOMAN, EVOLUTION, INFERIORITY.** 1894.

11.79
Bebel, August, **WOMAN IN THE PAST, PRESENT, AND FUTURE.** San Francisco, 1897.

11.80
EDUCATIONAL REVIEW: Browne, J.C., *"Sex in Education,"* 4 (1892) 164-178.

11.81
NEW REVIEW: Buchner, L., *"The Brain of Women,"* 9 (1893) 166-176.

11.82
Ellis, Havelock, **MAN AND WOMAN: A STUDY OF HUMAN SECONDARY SEXUAL CHARACTERS.** 1894; Boston, 1929; "It cannot be said that... we have reached any very definite results. A few careful experiments, which need confirmation and extension; a certain number of observations on irregular masses of data, accumulated in the practical experiences of life, which have their value, although they are open to various misinterpretations,——that is about all that experimental psychology has yet to show us in regard to the intellectual differences of men and women" (n.p.); *reviewed in:* **PSYCHOLOGICAL REVIEW:** Brinton, D.G., 1 (1894) 532-534. According to Ellis, "women have the 'infantile diathesis.' They share their special characteristics with children. 'We have found over and over again that, when women differ from men, it is the latter who have diverged, leaving women nearer to the child-type.' This sounds ominous for the fair sex. Immature in their essential differences, children all their lives, how can they claim equality with men? But with a *tour de force,...* Mr. Ellis saves his science and his chivalry at once. The child, the infant, in fact, alone possesses in their fulness 'the chief distinctive characters of humanity.' 'The highest human types, as represented in men of genius, present a striking approximation to the child-type'.... Hence, the true tendency of the progressive evolution of the race is to become childlike——to become feminine" (pp. 533-534). ——*see also:* Klein, Viola, "The Biological Approach: Havelock Ellis," in **THE FEMININE CHARACTER: HISTORY OF AN IDEOLOGY.** by Viola Klein. 1946.

11.83
Kidd, Benjamin, **SOCIAL EVOLUTION.** 2nd ed., 1894. Kidd was co-founder of the British Sociological Society. ——*see also:* Crook, David Paul, **BENJAMIN KIDD: PORTRAIT OF A SOCIAL DARWINIST.** Cambridge, 1984. Kidd conceived of the concept of woman as "the psychic centre of the world" whose increasing social participation would lead to the world's being saved within a single generation. A civil service clerk, his SOCIAL EVOLUTION became a landmark in the history of social Darwinism and a world-wide bestseller.

11.84
Lee, Alice Elizabeth, **CONTRIBUTION TO THE MATHEMATICAL THEORY OF EVOLUTION BY KARL PEARSON.** 1894; 1900; **DATA FOR THE PROBLEM OF EVOLUTION IN MAN. A FIRST STUDY OF THE CORRELATION OF THE HUMAN SKULL.** 1901. Lee was a student of Pearson.

11.85
von Hartmann, Carl Robert Edward, **THE SEXES COMPARED AND OTHER ESSAYS...** ed. and trans. by A. Kenner. 1895.

11.86
PSYCHOLOGICAL REVIEW: Calkins, M., *"Wellesley College Psychological Studies,"* 2 (1895) 360-363. Calkins' study failed to repeat Jastrow's findings that women's thinking was less abstract and therefore showed less evolution than men's; Nevers, C.C., *"Dr. Jastrow on Community of Ideas of Men and Women,"* 2 (1895) 363-367; Jastrow, J., *"Community of Ideas of Men and Women,"* 3 (1896) 68-71. Letter; Calkins, M.W., *"Community of Ideas of Men and Women,"* 3 (1896) 426-430. Followed by a letter from Joseph Jastrow, pp. 430-431; Tanner, A., *"The Community of Ideas of Men and Women,"* 3 (1896) 548-550; Angell, J.R., *"The Influence of Darwin on Psychology,"* 16 (1909) 152-169.

11.87
SATURDAY REVIEW OF POLITICS, LITERATURE, SCIENCE AND ART: Dies Dominae, *"The Maternal Instinct,"* 79 (1895) 752-753.

11.88
Hansson, Laura (Mohr), MODERN WOMEN. 1896; THE PSYCHOLOGY OF WOMAN. 1899; STUDIES IN THE PSYCHOLOGY OF WOMAN. New York, 1899. Philosophical rather than scientific writing.

11.89
Pearson, Karl, THE CHANCES OF DEATH AND OTHER STUDIES IN EVOLUTION. 2 vols. 1897. Pearson's anatomical statistics finally put to rest the controversy over the supposed relation between brain size and intelligence. Guards against drawing conclusions with regard to "social evolution" without first using precise definitions and careful statistical investigation. "The word evolution has been so terribly abused, first by biologists, then by pseudo-scientists, and lastly by the public, that it has become a cant term to cover any muddle-headed reasoning" (p. 103). Criticizes Havelock Ellis for perpetuating "some of the worst of the pseudo-scientific superstitions, notably that of the greater variability of the male human being" (p. 256).

11.90
AMERICAN JOURNAL OF SOCIOLOGY: Thomas, W.I., *"On a Difference in the Metabolism of the Sexes,"* 3 (1897) 60-66. Builds on the anabolic/katabolic model of Thomson and Geddes to explain sex differences.

11.91
Schenk, Samuel Leopold, THE DETERMINATION OF SEX. Chicago, 1898. Assumes biological inferiority of women and asserts that less developed ova produce females; *reviewed in:* JOURNAL OF THE ROYAL ANTHROPOLOGICAL INSTITUTE: Garson, J.G., 28 (1899) 182-183.

11.92
Walker, A., WOMAN PHYSIOLOGICALLY CONSIDERED AS TO MIND, MORALS, MARRIAGE, MATRIMONY, SLAVERY, INFIDELITY AND DIVORCE. Birmingham, 1898.

11.93
Swiney, Frances, THE AWAKENING OF WOMEN, OR WOMAN'S PART IN EVOLUTION. 1899. Despite her debilitating "pathological habit of periodic occurrence," woman remains far superior to man both physically and psychologically. In her "essentially female attributes," most notably her "intuitive religious perception" and "capacity for faith," rests the moral evolution of mankind. This book relies upon religious mysticism perhaps more than scientific theory. The word "evolution" here is broadly interpreted; THE COSMIC PROCESSION; OR, THE FEMININE PRINCIPLE IN EVOLUTION. ESSAYS OF ILLUMINATION. 1906; WOMAN AND NATURAL LAW. 2nd ed., 1912. Revised from OCCASIONAL PAPERS, 1906.

11.94
LIVERPOOL MEDICAL-CHIRURGICAL JOURNAL: Oliver, J., *"Women, Physically and Ethically Considered,"* 9 (1899) 219-226.

11.95
ALIENIST AND NEUROLOGIST: Mobius, J.P., *"The Physiological Mental*

Weakness of Woman," 22 (1901) 624-642. Extensive treatise on women's inferior mind and nature. "Supposing the feminine faculties were developed equally with the masculine, the maternal organs would wither and we would have an ugly and useless mongrel" (p. 634).

11.96
GUNTON'S MAGAZINE: Sedgwick, M.K., *"Some Scientific Aspects of the Woman Suffrage Question,"* 20 (1901) 333-334. Anti-suffrage attempt to relate social science arguments to the question of enfranchisement.

11.97
Bateson, William, **MENDEL'S PRINCIPLE OF HEREDITY.** 1902; **THE METHODS AND SCOPE OF GENETICS.** Cambridge, 1908; **BIOLOGICAL FACT AND THE STRUCTURE OF SOCIETY.** Oxford, 1912. Discusses the phenomena related to the biological aspects of society. Darwinian eugenics influence.

11.98
PROCEEDINGS OF THE ROYAL SOCIETY OF LONDON: Pearson, K., *"On the Correlation of Intellectual Ability with the Size and Shape of the Head,"* 69 (1902) 333-342; *rpt. in:* **BIOMETRIKA:** 5 (1906) 105-146.

11.99
Shaw, George Bernard, **MAN AND SUPERMAN.** 1903. "The bubble of Heredity has been pricked: the certainty that acquirements are negligible as elements in practical heredity has demolished the hopes of the educationists as well as the terrors of the degeneracy mongers; and we know now that there is no hereditary 'governing class' any more than a hereditary hooliganism" (p. xxiv).

11.100
Thompson, Helen Bradford (Woolley), **PSYCHOLOGICAL NORMS IN MEN AND WOMEN.** Chicago, 1903; *also published as:* **MENTAL TRAITS OF SEX; AN EXPERIMENTAL INVESTIGATION OF THE NORMAL MIND IN MEN AND WOMEN.** The first sophisticated statistical analysis of mental aptitude. Thompson found females slightly superior in memory and males slightly superior in ingenuity, findings which she attributes to social factors. —*see also:* Klein, Viola, "First Investigations in Experimental Psychology: Helen B. Thompson" in **THE FEMININE CHARACTER: HISTORY OF AN IDEOLOGY.** by Viola Klein. 1946; Thompson may also be cataloged as Woolley, Helen Bradford.

11.101
Leland, Charles Godfrey, **THE ALTERNATE SEX, OR THE FEMALE INTELLECT IN MAN, AND THE MASCULINE IN WOMEN.** 1904. Maintains that all humans are equal before God in Christ's original teaching. Emphasizes the uniqueness of each individual. "To assume the absolute equality, likeness or identity of the female mind or 'intelligence' with that of the male, is not only contrary to experience, but it also renders impossible the clear intelligence and development of what are really woman's faculties or capacities. And these, as I hope to show, are far greater than any writer as yet known to me has ever dreamed of" (p. 6). Mentions mystical teachings such as Theosophy and the Occult and the hidden capacities these teachings allude to.

11.102
PSYCHOLOGICAL BULLETIN: Thompson, H., *"A Review of the Recent Literature on the Psychology of Sex,"* 7 (1910) 335-342. Questions the validity of studies purporting to show a biological basis for women's inferiority.

11.103

SOCIOLOGICAL PAPERS: Westermarck, E., *"On the Position of Woman in Early Civilization,"* 1 (1905) 145-160.

11.104

Hobhouse, Leonard Trelawney, MORALS IN EVOLUTION: A STUDY IN COMPARATIVE ETHICS. 2 vols. New York, 1906. See especially: Part I, Chap. 4, "Marriage and the Position of Women." Important sociologist of the period.

11.105

Weininger, Otto, SEX AND CHARACTER. 1906; rpt., New York, 1975. Attempts "not to collect the greatest possible number of distinguishing characters... but to refer to a single principle the whole contrast between man and woman" and to transcend Positivism and Biology to establish "an enduring position for non-biological, non-physiological psychology" (n.p.). —*see also:* Klein, Viola, "A Philosophical Approach: Otto Weininger" in THE FEMININE CHARACTER: HISTORY OF AN IDEOLOGY. by Viola Klein. 1946. "Respect for Life as the world's greatest miracle, love and admiration for the dynamic forces of existence, for growth and evolution, which were such characteristic features of Havelock Ellis' personality, are conspicuously absent in Otto Weininger.... Amidst the crumbling ruins of a hitherto apparently stable culture he holds up his shield of eternal ideas and permanent, unchangeable values." He paints a "portrait, seen through a magnifying glass, of bourgeois woman in his contemporary society" (pp. 53-54).

11.106

Densmore, Emmet, SEX EQUALITY: A SOLUTION TO THE WOMAN PROBLEM. 1907. Relies heavily on Darwin's DESCENT OF MAN, emphasizing the importance of environment in shaping sexual differences.

11.107

Thomas, William I., SEX AND SOCIETY: STUDIES IN THE SOCIAL PSYCHOLOGY OF SEX. 1907. Thomas was an important early British sociologist. "In the animal world the female is noted for her indirection. On account of the necessity of protecting her young, she is cautious and cunning, and in contrast with the open and pugnacious methods of the more untrammeled male, she relies on sober colors, concealment, evasion, and deception of the senses. This quality of cunning is, of course, not immoral in its origin, being merely a protective instinct developed along with maternal feeling. In woman, also, this tendency to prevail by passive means rather than by assault is natural; and especially under a system of male control, where self-realization is secured either through the manipulation of man or not at all, a resort to trickery, indirection, and hypocrisy is not to be wondered at (pp. 232-233).... Difference in natural ability is, in the main, a characteristic of the individual, not of race or of sex" (p. 257); THE UNADJUSTED GIRL. WITH CASES AND STANDPOINT FOR BEHAVIOR ANALYSIS. ed. by Benjamin Nelson. introduction by Michael Parenti. 1923; 1967. Fascinating case histories documenting how and why girls become prostitutes and deviants. —*see also:* Klein, Viola, "A Sociological Approach: W.I. Thomas" in THE FEMININE CHARACTER. by Viola Klein. 1946.

11.108

AMERICAN MAGAZINE: Thomas, W.I., *"The Mind of Woman,"* 67 (1908) n.p. Refutes the argument that brain weight is a measure of intelligence.

11.109
McDougall, William, AN INTRODUCTION TO SOCIAL PSYCHOLOGY. 1908; PSYCHOLOGY: THE STUDY OF BEHAVIOUR. 1912. One of the first prominent British psychologists with a scientific background, McDougall insisted on the importance of physiology for the study of psychology.

11.110
Staars, David, THE ENGLISH WOMAN. STUDIES IN HER PSYCHIC EVOLUTION. trans. from the French by Jane M.E. Brownlow. 1909. Capitalizes on the recent fervor over theories of biological evolution as a rhetorical device in validating a "Social Psychology," or study of the "psychic evolution" of the English woman. Surveys the history of England in a social context, comparing English women of the Renaissance with those of the last half of the nineteenth century "who gave the impulse to the woman movement (p. 80).... The desire for property, independence, education, knowledge, intercourse with others... it would be very interesting to trace these feelings and ideas historically in the English woman, and this would enable us to understand a little better how the important actions of female life in their turn influence her conception of love" (pp. 79-80).

11.111
Lawrence, Robert Means, PRIMITIVE PSYCHO-THERAPY AND QUACKERY. 1910.

11.112
Marshall, Francis Hugh Adam, THE PHYSIOLOGY OF REPRODUCTION. 1910. Discusses controversies among biologists on sex characteristics.

11.113
BRITISH MEDICAL JOURNAL: Edinburgh Correspondent, *"The Position of Women: Actual and Ideal; A Report of the Lectures by T.S. Clouston,"* 2 (1910) 1885-1886.

11.114
Schreiner, Olive, WOMAN AND LABOR. New York, 1911. Chapter 5, "Sex Differences," discusses the psychology of sex differences as determined by environment. "Where psychic sex differences appear to exist, subject to rigid analysis they are found to be artificial creations" (n.p.).

11.115
Thomson, J. Arthur, THE POSITION OF WOMAN: BIOLOGICALLY CONSIDERED. 1911.

11.116
Christie, Jane Johnstone, THE ADVANCE OF WOMEN FROM THE EARLIEST TIMES TO THE PRESENT. 1912. Asserts that woman has always been the backbone of civilization. "There is no field of human activity in which man has been the pioneer except in the devising and inventing of weapons of destruction.... In every regard she is his biological superior" (pp. 281-282).

11.117
McMahon, Theresa Schmid, "The Status of Women and Primitive Industry" and "The Effects of Industrial Changes Upon Marriages" in WOMEN AND ECONOMIC EVOLUTION OR THE EFFECTS OF INDUSTRIAL CHANGES UPON THE STATUS OF WOMEN. by Theresa Schmid McMahon. Madison, 1912. Anthropological perspective.

11.118
Finot, Jean, **PROBLEMS OF THE SEXES**. 1913. "According to Herbert Spencer, woman is only a man paralysed and arrested in his evolution while according to Darwin, man is only a woman who has finished the cycle of her evolution" (p. 130).

11.119
Hartley, Catherine Gasquoine (Gallichan), **THE TRUTH ABOUT WOMAN**. 1913. See especially: "Sexual Differences in Mind and the Artistic Impulse in Women"; **MOTHERHOOD AND THE RELATIONSHIPS OF THE SEXES**. 1914; **THE AGE OF MOTHER-POWER**. 1914; **THE POSITION OF WOMAN IN PRIMITIVE SOCIETY; A STUDY OF THE MATRIARCHY**. 1914.

11.120
Heape, Walter, **SEX ANTAGONISM**. 1913. Woman is in violation of biological laws when she is ignorant of man's sexual requirements and tries to suppress his sexual instincts——she is at her best when she is breeding.

11.121
Housman, Laurence, **THE 'PHYSICAL FORCE' FALLACY**. 1913. State and society have placed undue emphasis on the value of physical force, whereas claims based on other factors can be more reasonably applied to questions of enfranchisement and contributions to the economy. Addresses "the argument which the physical force theorists seek to draw from these very unstable premises——namely, that as women 'cannot fight,' therefore they must not vote" (p. 5).

11.122
Parsons, Elsie W. Clews, **THE OLD-FASHIONED WOMAN: PRIMITIVE FANCIES ABOUT THE SEX**. 1913. Social science commentary.

11.123
NEW STATESMAN: Harrison, J., *"Scientiae Sacra Fames,"* Special Supplement (1913) 6-8. Addressing the argument against women's education based on inferior biology: "This release from self which comes through knowledge, this imaginative altruism, do not women need it? In a sense, more than men.... If indeed she be more 'resonant,' she is, *ipso facto*, more religious... a religious woman without knowledge is like a lunatic armed with an explosive" (p. 7).

11.124
SCIENCE PROGRESS: Pembrey, M.S., *"Woman's Place in Nature,"* 8 (1913) 133-140. "The old-fashioned view of women's place in nature is the one supported by biological knowledge. Woman's sphere was the home and family, for there she found ample opportunities for the exercise of her special gifts of patience, kindness and love of offspring" (p. 134).

11.125
Scharlieb, Mary Ann Dacomb, **THE SEVEN AGES OF WOMAN: A CONSIDERATION OF THE SUCCESSIVE PHASES OF WOMAN'S LIFE**. 1915; **REMINISCENCES**. 1924. Scharlieb was a physician and activist in the Eugenics movement.

11.126
George, Walter Lionel, **THE INTELLIGENCE OF WOMAN**. Boston, 1916; London, 1917.

11.127
SCIENTIFIC MONTHLY: Lowie, R.H. and Hollingwort, L.S., *"Science and Feminism,"* (Sept. 1916) n.p. Concludes that "no rational grounds have been established that should lead to artificial limitation of woman's activity on the ground of inferior efficiency" (p. 284).

11.128
PSYCHOANALYTIC REVIEW: Hinkle, B.M., *"On the Arbitrary Use of the Terms 'Masculine' and 'Feminine,'"* 1 (1920) 15-30. "My wish is to point out the bondage in which both men and women are held by thinking of themselves in the collective terms of masculine and feminine, and to suggest that the error has occurred through the mistake of confusing type distinctions with those of sex" (p. 20). These "types" correspond with C.G. Jung's categories of extrovert and introvert.

11.129
Briffault, Robert, THE MOTHERS: THE MATRIARCHAL THEORY OF SOCIAL ORIGINS. 3 vols. New York, 1927; rpt. 1959; 1963. Thoroughly critiques Maine's ANCIENT LAW.

11.130
Calverton, Victor Frances and Schmalhausen, S.D., eds., SEX IN CIVILIZATION. introduction by Havelock Ellis. New York, 1929. Excellent compendium of articles dedicated to "women who have led in the struggle for sex emancipation and a better civilization." See especially: "The Role of Sex in Behavior" and "Sex and Psycho-Sociology."

11.131
Jastrow, Joseph, "The Implications of Sex" in SEX IN CIVILIZATION. ed. by Victor F. Calverton and S.D. Schmalhausen. New York, 1929. "A masculine body implies a masculine mind, and a feminine body carries even more significant implications, though we take our chances in tracing their issues by confusing what and how much is set by nature, what and how much shaped by nurture; which is often man's interpretation of nature's intentions" (p. 130).

11.132
Flugel, J.C., A HUNDRED YEARS OF PSYCHOLOGY. New York, 1933. See especially: Part 3, "1860-1900."

11.133
Gallichan, Walter M., THE EVOLUTION, THEORY, PHYSIOLOGY, PSYCHOLOGY, AND IDEAL PRACTICE OF HUMAN LOVE. New York, 1939. Discourse traversing a variety of topics relating to sex, love, and marriage. Relies on ethnographic accounts as well as on contemporary "scientific" notions.

11.134
BRITISH JOURNAL OF PSYCHOLOGY: Edgell, B., *"The British Psychological Society,"* 37 (1947) 113-132. Founded in 1901. At that time, psychology was emerging from a field within philosophy into a discipline in its own right, using scientific methodologies.

11.135
BULLETIN OF THE BRITISH PSYCHOLOGICAL SOCIETY: Hearnshaw, L.S., *"Sixty Years of Psychology,"* no. 46 (1962) 2-10.

11.136
Hearnshaw, Leslie Spencer, **A SHORT HISTORY OF BRITISH PSYCHOLOGY, 1840-1940.** 1964. See especially: "The Rise of Comparative Psychology," with discussion of Darwin, Romanes and Hobhouse, and "Galton and the Beginning of Psychometrics."

11.137
Abrams, Philip, **THE ORIGINS OF BRITISH SOCIOLOGY, 1834-1914.** Chicago, 1968.

* * *

2. *MODERN COMMENT AND FEMINIST CRITIQUES OF NINETEENTH AND EARLY TWENTIETH-CENTURY SOCIAL SCIENCE RELATED TO WOMEN*

11.138
Mead, Margaret, **SEX AND TEMPERAMENT IN THREE PRIMITIVE SOCIETIES.** 1935. "Two of these tribes have no idea that men and women are different in temperament... any idea that temperamental traits of the order of dominance, bravery, aggressiveness, objectivity, malleability, are inalienably associated with one sex (as opposed to the other) is entirely lacking" (p. xiii); **MALE AND FEMALE.** New York, 1949. Data is drawn mainly from seven peoples of the Pacific Islands. "I try... to bring a greater awareness of the way in which the differences and the similarities in the bodies of human beings are the basis on which all our learning about our sex, and our relationship to the other sex, are built" (p. 4). ——*see also:* Klein, Viola, "The Anthropological Approach: Margaret Mead" in **THE FEMININE CHARACTER: HISTORY OF AN IDEOLOGY.** by Viola Klein. 1946; Chicago, 1972.

11.139
Klein, Viola, "Psychometric Tests: L.M. Terman and C.C. Miles" in **THE FEMININE CHARACTER: HISTORY OF AN IDEOLOGY.** by Viola Klein. 1946; "Introduction" in **THE FEMININE CHARACTER: HISTORY OF AN IDEOLOGY.** by Viola Klein. 1946; Chicago, 1972. "Scientific knowledge, especially in the social sciences, does not exist in splendid isolation, but is an organic part of a coherent cultural system" (p. 2).

11.140
Herschberger, Ruth, **ADAM'S RIB.** New York, 1948. See "Society Writes Biology" for a feminist view of biological conception, pointing up the absurdity of the male-oriented paradigm in biology.

11.141
De Beauvoir, Simone, **THE SECOND SEX.** orig. French ed., 1949; trans. and ed. by H.M. Parshley. New York, 1952. Phenomenological approach to the question of sex equality. See especially, "The Data of Biology." "Biology is not enough to give an answer to the question that is before us: why is woman the *Other*?" (p. 37).

11.142
BULLETIN OF THE HISTORY OF MEDICINE: Bullough, V. and Voght, M., *"Women, Menstruation, and Nineteenth-Century Medicine,"* 25 (1951) 132-148. Shows

how physicians' ideas about the menstrual cycle were influenced by prevailing views of women, and how they were utilized by such men as Maudsley and Clarke in excluding women from education; Fee, E., *"Nineteenth-Century Craniology: The Study of the Female Skull,"* 53 (1979) 415-433. Comprehensive historical account of anthropology's attempts to legitimize women's inferiority.

11.143
Montagu, Ashley, THE NATURAL SUPERIORITY OF WOMEN. New York, 1952. Re-evaluates traditional "scientific" claims of women's inferiority as an early contribution towards the modern Women's Movement.

11.144
AMERICAN PHILOSOPHICAL SOCIETY PROCEEDINGS: Murphree, I.L., *"The Evolutionary Anthropologists: the Progress of Mankind. The Concepts of Progress and Culture in the Thought of John Lubbock, Edward B. Tylor and Lewis H. Morgan,"* 105 (1961) 265-272.

11.145
Hays, H.R., THE DANGEROUS SEX: THE MYTH OF FEMININE EVIL. New York, 1964. Historical, cross-cultural account of ways in which men have institutionalized fear of women.

11.146
Evans-Pritchard, E.E., "The Position of Women in Primitive Societies and in Our Own" in THE POSITION OF WOMEN IN PRIMITIVE SOCIETIES AND OTHER ESSAYS IN SOCIAL ANTHROPOLOGY. by E.E. Evans-Pritchard. 1965. "In all [societies], regardless of the form of social structure, men are always in the ascendancy, and this is perhaps the more evident the higher the civilization.... The facts seem... to suggest that there are deep biological and psychological factors, as well as sociological factors, involved, and that the relation between the sexes can only be modified by social changes, and not radically altered by them" (pp. 54-55).

11.147
Forde, Daryll, "Anthropology——The Victorian Synthesis and Modern Relativism" in IDEAS AND BELIEFS OF THE VICTORIANS. by Daryll Forde. New York, 1966.

11.148
PAST AND PRESENT: Young, R.M., *"Malthus and the Evolutionists: The Common Context of Biological and Social Theory,"* no. 43 (1969) 109-145.

11.149
ANNALS OF THE NEW YORK ACADEMY OF SCIENCE: Reeves, N., *"Anatomy and Destiny,"* 175 (1970) 793-809. "The tyranny of biology as normative absolute remains an unexamined assumption about the status of women across the centuries... woman was femina genitalis... pre-programmed, and static... the condition of woman is her relation to the nest" (p. 793).

11.150
Burstyn, Joan N., "Brain and Intellect: Science Applied to a Social Issue 1860-1875" in HISTOIRE DES SCIENCES DE L'HOMME. Paris, 1971; rpt. in ACTES: 9 (1971) 13-16. The demand for higher education for women was argued against on the grounds that differences in skull measurement between men and women proved that "women... in the course of evolution, had not kept pace with man's development.... It was suggested that this had occurred through sexual selection, since women had always been chosen for beauty rather than for brains" (p. 15).

11.151
Chinas, Beverly, "Women as Ethnographic Subjects" in **WOMEN IN CROSS-CULTURAL PERSPECTIVE: A PRELIMINARY SOURCEBOOK.** ed. by Sue Ellen Jacobs. Limited printing by Univ. of Illinois, Department of Urban and Regional Planning, Nov. 1971.

11.152
JOURNAL OF MARRIAGE AND THE FAMILY: Schwendinger, J. and Schwendinger, H., *"Sociology's Founding Fathers: Sexists to a Man,"* 33 (1971) 783-799. Summarizes the theories of Lester Ward and W.I. Thomas. Both sociologists "envisioned prehistoric women as born superior or equal to man. Eventually, however, women were made biologically inferior by adapting to circumstances created by their passive nature or man's greater passion" (p. 783).

11.153
Safilios-Rothschild, Constantina, **TOWARD A SOCIOLOGY OF WOMEN.** Toronto and Lexington, 1972. Concerned with "building a sociology of women, or a sociology of sex roles... [as a] new, important sociological field... [which] may lead to a reformulation of existing sociological theories and the development of new ones" (p. v). See especially: "Sex Roles and Social Change."

11.154
JOURNAL OF SOCIAL ISSUES: Carlson, R., *"Understanding Women: Implications for Personality Theory and Research,"* Special issue entitled "New Perspectives on Women," 28 no. 2 (1972) 17-32. Aimed at fostering new research paradigms.

11.155
Campbell, Bernard, ed., **SEXUAL SELECTION AND THE DESCENT OF MAN, 1871-1971.** 1973. Examines Darwin's work in the context of modern research.

11.156
Conway, Jill, "Stereotypes of Femininity in a Theory of Sexual Evolution" in **SUFFER AND BE STILL: WOMEN IN THE VICTORIAN AGE.** ed. by Martha Vicinus. Bloomington, 1973. "The guiding rule of the early social sciences... required sociologists to develop their discipline on the basis of a biology in which the significance of sex differences was far from clear (p. 140).... in the English interpretation of Weismann's germ-plasm theory we have the perfect case study of the way in which sexual stereotypes could be adapted to new scientific formulations. The inheritance of acquired characteristics [had] permitted Spencer to explain the existing stereotypes of female character,... [but] once environmental factors were removed (by Weismann) as major sources of variation, evolutionary theorists were compelled to look for other explanations of the supposed psychic differences between the sexes and other ways to explain... the inferiority of women" (p. 142).

11.157
Diner, Helen, **MOTHERS AND AMAZONS: THE FIRST FEMININE HISTORY OF CULTURE.** New York, 1973. Inspired by Johann Jakob Bachofen's DAS MUTTER-ECHT, this is intended as the "first feminine history of culture" (p. xviii).

11.158
JOURNAL OF AMERICAN HISTORY: Smith-Rosenberg, C. and Rosenberg, C., *"The Female Animal: Medical and Biological Views of Woman and Her Role in Nineteenth-Century America,"* 60 (1973) 332-356. Examines the medical and

psychological attack made on women as they began to demand educational opportunities and the right to use birth control. A quote by the president of the American Gynecological Society in 1900 illustrates the authoritative view: "'Many a young life is battered and forever crippled in the breakers of puberty; if it crosses these unharmed and is not dashed to pieces on the rock of childbirth, it may still ground on the ever-recurring shallows of menstruation, and lastly, upon the final bar of the menopause ere protection is found in the unruffled waters of the harbor beyond the reach of sexual storms'" (pp. 336-337).

11.159
PROCEEDINGS OF THE AMERICAN PHILOSOPHICAL SOCIETY: Burstyn, J.N., *"Education and Sex: The Medical Case Against the Higher Education for Women in England, 1870-1900,"* 117 (1973) 79-89. As evidence on the relationship of brain size to mental capacity was becoming inconclusive, opponents to higher education for women turned to medical theories purporting to show the adverse effects of mental strain on the female reproductive system.

11.160
Bamberger, Joan, "The Myth of Matriarchy: Why Men Rule in Primitive Society" in **WOMEN, CULTURE, AND SOCIETY.** ed. by Michelle Zimbalist Rosaldo and Louise Lamphere. Stanford, 1974. Objects to modern glorification of myths of original matriarchy, on the grounds that they "constantly reiterate that women did not know how to handle power when they had it" (p. 280) as indicated by the domination of the patriarchal form.

11.161
Ortner, Sherry B., "Is Female to Male as Nature is to Culture?" in **WOMEN, CULTURE, AND SOCIETY.** ed. by Michelle Zimbalist Rosaldo and Louise Lamphere. Stanford, 1974. "What could there be... that would lead every culture to place a lower value upon women? Specifically, my thesis is that woman is being identified with——or... a symbol of——something that every culture defines as being of a lower order of existence than itself... and that is 'nature'" (pp. 71-72).

11.162
Rosaldo, Michelle Zimbalist, "Woman, Culture, and Society: A Theoretical Overview" in **WOMAN, CULTURE, AND SOCIETY.** ed. by Michelle Zimbalist Rosaldo and Louise Lamphere. Stanford, 1974. Relates the cross-cultural asymmetrical valuation of men's and women's work with a universal, structural opposition between public and domestic spheres.

11.163
Rosaldo, Michelle Zimbalist and Lamphere, Louise, eds., **WOMAN, CULTURE, AND SOCIETY.** Stanford, 1974. "The authors... all believe that anthropology has suffered from a failure to develop theoretical perspectives that take account of women as social actors (p. 2).... Most previous descriptions of social processes have treated women as being theoretically uninteresting. Women who exercise power are seen as deviants, manipulators, or, at best, exceptions" (p. 9).

11.164
AMERICAN QUARTERLY: Trecker, J.L., *"Sex, Science and Education,"* 26 (1974) 352-366. The attempts to bar women from education or learning were based on "scientific" arguments that women's achievements in education "were dangerous for the woman's health, for the survival of the race, for the continued progress of the species" (p. 355).

11.165

Kern, Stephen, "Sexual Alienation and Sexual Selection" in ANATOMY AND DESTINY: A CULTURAL HISTORY OF THE HUMAN BODY. by Stephen Kern. New York, 1975. "Darwin's theory made four revolutionary changes in the going conception of human nature at that time. The theory of the animal origins of man contradicted the idea of a special creation of man; the explanation of animal rudiments demolished the idea of man's having been fashioned in God's image; the theory of sexual selection introduced in DESCENT OF MAN overturned the romantic conception of human love and emphasized the animal nature of human relations; and his philosophical materialism brought the human mind into nature and viewed it as dependent upon the body" (p. 62).

11.166

Reed, Evelyn, WOMEN'S EVOLUTION FROM MATRIARCHAL CLAN TO PATRIARCHAL FAMILY. New York, 1975. Claims that "the maternal clan system was the original form of social organization" (p. xiii).

11.167

Reiter, Rayna R., ed., TOWARD AN ANTHROPOLOGY OF WOMEN. 1975. A collection of essays. "Most anthropologists read rather directly from biology to culture, asserting that women's role in reproduction is responsible for the earliest forms of the division of labor, and that male supremacy flows from this division" (pp. 11-12). See especially: "Perspectives on the Evolution of Sex Differences" by Lila Leibowitz, "Woman the Gatherer: Male Bias in Anthropology" by Sally Slocum, "Matriarchy: A Vision of Power" by Paula Webster, and "The Traffic in Women: Notes on the 'Political Economy' of Sex" by Gayle Rubin.

11.168

Seymour-Smith, Martin, SEX AND SOCIETY. 1975. Excellent resource. See especially: "The Differences Between Men and Women," discussing Mead, Bachofen, Briffault and Westermarck.

11.169

FEMINIST STUDIES: Rosenberg, R., "In Search of Woman's Nature, 1850-1920," 3 (1975) 141-154. Valuable survey of scientific interest in women's nature. "For a generation Darwinism proved to be all things to all people, principally because neither feminists nor antifeminists were yet willing to challenge the ancient belief in female uniqueness" (p. 142); Spelman, E., "Woman As Body: Ancient and Contemporary Views," 8 (1982) 103-131. Demonstrates that misogynous attitudes pervading Western philosophy go hand-in-hand with the traditional idea that flesh is to be loathed and the mind extolled.

11.170

Bleier, Ruth H., "Brain, Body and Behavior" in BEYOND INTELLECTUAL SEXISM. ed. by Joan L. Roberts. New York, 1976; "Social and Political Bias in Science: An Examination of Animal Studies and Their Generalizations to Human Behavior and Evolution" in GENES AND GENDER II: PITFALLS IN RESEARCH ON SEX AND GENDER. ed. by Ruth Hubbard and Marian Lowe. New York, 1979. Examines the assumptions implicit in studies of sex hormones and behavior, male aggression and dominance, and animal behavior as a model for human behavior.

11.171

Fee, Elizabeth, "Science and the Woman Problem: Historical Perspectives" in SEX DIFFERENCES: SOCIAL AND BIOLOGICAL PERSPECTIVES. ed. by Michael S. Teitelbaum. New York, 1976. "Physical anthropologists also hewed to the evolutionary line. Seeking to measure comparative intelligence, they [developed] a 'science' that came to be known as craniology.... Male brains developed considerably with civilization, while women's brains had grown only slowly" (p. 194); "Science and the 'Woman Question', 1860-1920: A Study of English Scientific Periodicals," Ph.D. diss., Princeton Univ., 1978. "There was, in the 1860's and 1870's, a general conviction that natural physiological and psychological sex differences dictated a restricted social role for women." However, "popular science journals consistently promoted feminist positions, due in part to their relatively high proportion of women writers and subscribers" (p. iii); "Women's Nature and Scientific Objectivity" in WOMAN'S NATURE: RATIONALIZATIONS OF INEQUALITY. ed. by Marian Lowe and Ruth Hubbard. Oxford and New York, 1983.

11.172
Rich, Adrienne, OF WOMAN BORN: MOTHERHOOD AS EXPERIENCE AND INSTITUTION. New York, 1976. Offers rich and thoughtful insights on the myth of matriarchy with references to Bachofen, Briffault, Diner, and de Beauvoir, among others. See especially: "The Kingdom of the Fathers" and "The Primacy of the Mother."

11.173
HISTORY OF EDUCATION JOURNAL: Dyhouse, C., *"Social Darwinistic Ideas and the Development of Women's Education in England, 1880-1920,"* 5 (1976) 41-58. "There were... those who felt that education... was rendering women physiologically unfit for motherhood... [and] there were a large number of writers who believed that educational arguments... were calculated to disincline women from the prospect of motherhood as a worthwhile or sufficient goal in life" (p. 44).

11.174
UNIVERSITY OF MICHIGAN PAPERS IN WOMEN'S STUDIES: Bleier, R.H., *"Myths of the Biological Inferiority of Women: An Exploration of the Sociology of Biology Research,"* 2 (1976) 39-63. Discusses conceptual and methodological flaws in a variety of studies. "The overriding determinant of human behavior is the social milieu operating from the day of birth upon a broad range of biological potentialities" (p. 55).

11.175
HECATE: Trenfield, K., *"On the Role of Biology in Feminist Ideology,"* 3 (1977) 41-56. Summarizes the history of biological determinism into the present "nature-nurture" debate, along with feminist counter-arguments.

11.176
JOURNAL OF THE HISTORY OF IDEAS: Alaya, F., *"Victorian Science and the Genius of Women,"* 38 (1977) 261-280. "Nineteenth-century science... gave such vigorous and persuasive reinforcement to the traditional dogmatic view of the sexual character that it not only strengthened the opposition to feminism but disengaged the ideals of feminists themselves from their philosophic roots" (p. 262).

11.177
Duffin, Lorna, "Prisoners of Progress: Women and Evolution" in THE NINETEENTH CENTURY WOMAN: HER CULTURAL AND PHYSICAL WORLD. ed. by Sara Delamont and Lorna Duffin. 1978. "Evolutionary arguments were used as a rationale for confining women to the domestic sphere, justified by the past and in order to safeguard the future" (p. 58).

11.178
Fisher, Elizabeth, **WOMAN'S CREATION: SEXUAL EVOLUTION AND THE SHAPING OF SOCIETY.** New York, 1978. A re-examination of anthropology from the female perspective.

11.179
Soffer, Reba N., **ETHICS AND SOCIETY IN ENGLAND: THE REVOLUTION IN THE SOCIAL SCIENCES 1870-1914.** 1978. "In the transitional period from 1855 to 1890, four independent departures from traditional psychology competed for acceptance in the United States, Europe, and England." These include phrenology and psychophysics, both relying on anatomical and neurological studies, and the comparative method, introduced by Darwin (pp. 116-117).

11.180
ISIS: Daston, L.J., *"British Responses to Psycho-Physiology, 1860-1900,"* 69 (1978) 192-208. "This essay deals with the various attempts made by British psychologists, philosophers, and scientists during this period to reconcile an ethically meaningful doctrine of volition with the so-called new, or physiological, psychology" (p. 193).

11.181
JOURNAL OF THE HISTORY OF BIOLOGY: Mosedale, S.S., *"Science Corrupted: Victorian Biologists Consider 'The Woman Question,'"* 11 (1978) 1-55. See especially the section on Jean Finot, a moralist who spoke against "biology-based" theories of female inferiority and was ahead of his time in doing so.

11.182
SIGNS: Aldrich, M.L., *"Women in Science,"* 4 (1978) 126-135. Reviews the Victorian period; Shields, S.A., *"The Variability Hypothesis: The History of a Biological Model of Sex Differences in Intelligence,"* 7 (1982) 769-797. "The belief that 'biology is destiny' was not invented by Freudian theorists.... Beliefs about specific behavioral sex differences presumed to emerge from biological sex differences show great stability over time" (p. 769); Rose, H., *"Hand, Brain, and Heart: A Feminist Epistemology for the Natural Sciences,"* 9 (1983) 73-90. Marxist orientation.

11.183
SOCIAL SCIENCE QUARTERLY: Fee, E., *"Psychology, Sexuality, and Social Control in Victorian England,"* 58 (1978) 632-646. "The psychologists took the idea of ideal bourgeois character and redefined it as not simply *virtuous*, but as mentally healthy and as morally 'sane,'" (p. 633).

11.184
VICTORIAN STUDIES: Rainger, R., *"Race, Politics and Science: The Anthropological Society of London in the 1860s,"* 22 (1978) 51-70. "While most scientific organizations... concentrated on the examination of scientific problems and largely avoided discussions of religious and political issues, the Anthropological Society consciously mixed science and politics" (p. 51).

11.185
WOMEN'S STUDIES INTERNATIONAL QUARTERLY: Dyhouse, C., *"Towards a 'Feminine' Curriculum for English Schoolgirls: The Demands of Ideology 1870-1963,"* 1 (1978) 291-311. Includes a summary of social science and medical views on the dangers of education to girls' health; McCormack, T., *"Good Theory or Just Theory? Toward a Feminist Philosophy of Social Science,"* Special issue: Women in Futures Research, 4 no. 1 (1981) 1-12. "A just theory... excludes any principle of

explanation which accounts for the biological or social necessity of social inequality" (p. 5).

11.186
Eichler, Magrit, **THE DOUBLE STANDARD: A FEMINIST CRITIQUE OF FEMINIST SOCIAL SCIENCE.** New York, 1979. Claims that the social sciences are androcentrically biased and proposes a non-sexist "feminist science"; *reviewed in:* SOCIOLOGICAL REVIEW: Deem, R., 28 (1980) 666-667.

11.187
Griffiths, Dorothy and Saraga, Esther, "Sex Differences and Cognitive Abilities: A Sterile Field of Enquiry?" in **SEX-ROLE STEREOTYPING.** ed. by Oonagh Hartnett, Gill Boden, and Mary Fuller. 1979. Takes issue with both biological and environmental determinism; sex-role stereotypes must be analyzed by examining women's role in the capitalist system.

11.188
Hubbard, Ruth, "Have Only Men Evolved?" in **WOMEN LOOKING AT BIOLOGY LOOKING AT WOMEN.** by Ruth Hubbard, Mary Sue Henifin, and Barbara Fried. Cambridge, 1979; 1982. Discusses evolutionary biology studies. Shows that Victorian ideas of sex roles permeate current research in sociobiology.

11.189
Hubbard, Ruth and Marian Lowe, eds., **GENES AND GENDER II: PITFALLS IN RESEARCH ON SEX AND GENDER.** New York, 1979. "Scientists of the nineteenth century were not hypocrites who were willing to distort their science to prove a political point. They were almost entirely university-trained, privileged sons of the upper and middle classes who accepted the social order... as founded on natural law that science could be called on to explicate" (p. 12). Contains chapters by Lila Leibowitz, Ruth Bleier, Freda Salzman, and Susan Leigh Star; **WOMAN'S NATURE: RATIONALIZATIONS OF INEQUALITY.** Oxford and New York, 1983. Claims that modern sociobiology is being conducted on the same male-oriented assumptions as nineteenth-century biological determinism. See especially: "Social Effects of Some Contemporary Myths About Women" by Ruth Hubbard, "Women's Nature and Scientific Objectivity" by Elizabeth Fee, "The Dialectic of Biology and Culture" by Marian Lowe, and "Origins of the Sexual Division of Labor" by Lila Leibowitz.

11.190
Leibowitz, Lila, "'Universals' and Male Dominance Among Primates: A Critical Examination" in **GENES AND GENDER II: PITFALLS IN RESEARCH ON SEX AND GENDER.** ed. by Ruth Hubbard and Marian Lowe. New York, 1979; "Origins of the Sexual Division of Labor" in **WOMEN'S NATURE: RATIONALIZATIONS OF INEQUALITY.** ed. by Marian Lowe and Ruth Hubbard. Oxford and New York, 1983. Critique of traditional anthropology.

11.191
Dyhouse, Carol, **GIRLS GROWING UP IN LATE VICTORIAN AND EDWARDIAN ENGLAND.** 1981. See "Feminism and 'Femininity,'" p. 151-161, for a historical perspective on scientific views of women and its use as a justification against women's struggle for higher education.

11.192
Easley, Brian, "Biology, Medicine and 'Viriculture' in Nineteenth-Century Britain" in **SCIENCE AND SEXUAL OPPRESSION: PATRIARCHY'S CONFRONTATION**

WITH WOMAN AND NATURE. by Brian Easley. 1981. See especially: "Clitoridectomy and Ovariotomy in Britain and America," pp. 133-136 and "The Scientists' 'Proof' of Female 'Inferiority,'" pp. 138-149.

11.193
Hirsch, Miriam, "'When She is Bad, She is Horrid': Women and Crime" in WOMEN AND VIOLENCE. by Miriam Hirsch. 1981. Discusses how views of women's biological nature permeated nineteenth-century studies of female crime and deviance.

11.194
McMillan, Carol, WOMEN, REASON, AND NATURE: SOME PHILOSOPHICAL PROBLEMS WITH FEMINISM. Oxford, 1982. Criticizes feminists for embracing the same assumptions as sexists, namely, the duality of logic/intuition. "The very notion of an 'androgynous culture'——the fusion of the 'masculine' and the 'feminine'——is dependent on the idea of a division of knowledge between the sexes which does not... exist" (p. 39).

11.195
Rosenberg, Rosalind, BEYOND SEPARATE SPHERES: INTELLECTUAL ORIGINS OF MODERN FEMINISM. New Haven, 1982. Contains a biography of Helen B. Thompson detailing her original contributions to psychology.

11.196
Sayers, Janet, BIOLOGICAL POLITICS: FEMINIST AND ANTI-FEMINIST PERSPECTIVES. 1982. "Feminists are divided as to how biology shapes women's social status... some feminists argue that the influence of biology on women's status... is mediated by the way their biology is interpreted and construed within a given society... others, by contrast, argue that biology does affect women directly, [endowing them] with an essential and particular 'feminine' character from which they have become alienated as a result of living in a male-dominated world" (p. 3).

11.197
Coward, Rosalind, PATRIARCHAL PRECEDENTS: SEXUALITY AND SOCIAL RELATIONS. 1983. Chapters on "mother-right," theories of sex in the social sciences, and "the woman question and the early marxist left."

11.198
Jaggar, Alison M., FEMINIST POLITICS AND HUMAN NATURE. 1983. Explores the conceptions of human nature implicit in classical political theories and their influence on feminist politics. "Earlier feminists accepted... prevailing conceptions of human nature that took the male as paradigm... both liberal and Marxist feminists insisted on a sharp distinction between the biological attribute of sex and the cultural attribute of gender, and they argued that biological differences were, by and large, irrelevant to political theory... contemporary feminists have seen the need to reconsider the political and philosophical significance of biology. In some parts of the women's movement this has led to a resurrection of biological determinism" (pp. 21-22). See especially: "Political Philosophy and Human Nature" and "Feminist Theories of Human Nature."

11.199
Lewin, Miriam, "'Rather Worse Than Folly?' Psychology Measures Femininity and Masculinity, 1: From Terman and Miles to the Guilfords" in IN THE SHADOW OF THE PAST: PSYCHOLOGY PORTRAYS THE SEXES: A SOCIAL AND INTELLECTUAL HISTORY. ed. by Miriam Lewin. New York, 1984. Summarizes

the psychological testing whose questionable methodologies were made to fit underlying assumptions about innate sex differences; "The Victorians, the Psychologists, and Psychic Birth Control" in **IN THE SHADOW OF THE PAST: PSYCHOLOGY PORTRAYS THE SEXES: A SOCIAL AND INTELLECTUAL HISTORY.** ed. by Miriam Lewin. New York, 1984. "The ideology of Psychic Birth Control [sexual repression] and Victorian sex roles, explained and defended in the vocabulary of Darwinian evolution and of [Herbert Spencer's] Conservation of Force, were the building blocks for nineteenth century psychology" (p. 39).

11.200
Lewontin, R.C., Rose, Steven, and Kamin, Leon J., **NOT IN OUR GENES: BIOLOGY, IDEOLOGY, AND HUMAN NATURE.** New York, 1984; *reviewed in:* WOMEN'S REVIEW OF BOOKS: Hubbard, R., *"Putting Genes in Their Place,"* 2 no. 4 (1985) 7-8. "This is a book about inequality and about the role science, in the persons of biologists, psychologists and anthropologists, has played in maintaining it" (p. 7).

11.201
Newman, Louise Michele, ed., **MEN'S IDEAS/WOMEN'S REALITIES: POPULAR SCIENCE, 1870-1915.** New York, 1984. Collection of articles from POPULAR SCIENCE MONTHLY. Includes sections on "The 'Woman Question'" and "The Problem of Biological Determinism (1870-1890)."

11.202
SOCIAL PROBLEMS: Stacey, J. and Thorne, B., *"The Missing Feminist Revolution in Sociology,"* 32 (April 1985) 4.

* * *

3. EUGENICS AND NEO-MALTHUSIANISM

Neo-Malthusianism and Eugenics spurred two social-theoretical movements that were closely allied with science, social science and medicine. Both were concerned with "the population question"——a phrase which actually raised multiple issues about how to influence or control the quantity, quality and demographic distribution of the English people by socioeconomic status and biological inheritance. The neo-Malthusians promoted family limitation and the techniques to accomplish it on the theory that poverty among the lower classes and economic strain among the higher were caused by the burden of large families. Their views on "checking" family size were based upon those of

11.203
Malthus, Thomas R., **AN ESSAY ON THE PRINCIPLE OF POPULATION AS IT AFFECTS THE FUTURE IMPROVEMENT OF SOCIETY.** 1798.

as well as those of the early "birth controllers" who spread family limitation information during the earlier years of the nineteenth century:

11.204
Fryer, Peter, **THE BIRTH CONTROLLERS.** 1965.

Experiencing a virtual population explosion along with industrialization and urbanization, England was transformed over the nineteenth century from a largely rural and uncrowded country of about nine million inhabitants to a populous, modern, industrial society of nearly thirty-seven million. The birthrate reached a record peak of about thirty-six births per one thousand persons by 1876. Cities became overcrowded, social problems accompanied periodic economic distress, philanthropy and local social service agencies could not meet the challenges that questions of poverty, illness, illiteracy and and alienation presented. The neo-Malthusians, following perspectives associated with Utilitarianism and Secularism, sought solutions through self-conscious family planning. Since Malthus himself had been opposed to "artificial" as compared with natural "checks" to family size, the organized movement of the later nineteenth and earlier twentieth century that promoted contraception identified themselves as neo-Malthusians. Under the leadership of Charles Bradlaugh, they organized the Malthusian League in 1877. This was the first organization in the world to unite formally to promote popular acceptance as well as state cooperation in spreading knowledge of "the law of population." The League campaigned for the abolition of legal penalties for public discussion of contraception. It published the monthly periodical, THE MALTHUSIAN and distributed many thousands of tracts and pamphlets explaining the relationship between poverty and large families and how the use of devices and preventive measures could keep them small. Bradlaugh, with Annie Besant, re-published and publicized in 1876 an early American manual,

11.205
Knowlton, Charles, **THE FRUITS OF PHILOSOPHY: THE PRIVATE COMPANION OF YOUNG MARRIED PEOPLE.** 1834; 1876.

This was the fullest account of contraceptive methods yet available. Bradlaugh and Besant were brought to trial when a bookseller added questionable material, and this widely publicized the thought and work of the neo-Malthusians. For an indispensable, comprehensive, chronological account of the League in the context of the movement, see:

11.206
Ledbetter, Rosanna, **A HISTORY OF THE MALTHUSIAN LEAGUE, 1877-1927.** Columbus, Ohio, 1976.

A thoughtful discussion of its background and valuable evaluation of its development, challenges and decline is

11.207
POPULATION STUDIES: Micklewright, F.H., *"The Rise and Decline of English Neo-Malthusianism,"* 15 (July 1961) 32-51.

The campaign for reducing family size became involved with religious, moral, educational and political questions as well as with the complicated networks of other movements. Examining its possible relationship to feminism, for example, and determining that neo-Malthusianism and the organized women's movement were not directly related, is

11.208
Banks, J.A. and Banks, Olive, **FEMINISM AND FAMILY PLANNING IN VICTORIAN ENGLAND.** Liverpool, 1964; many subsequent eds.

In the 1890s there occurred a dramatic reversal of population trends. The birthrate plunged rapidly. By 1901 fertility was reported down by more than twenty-four percent. By 1914, it was down thirty-three percent. Without directly crediting the organized neo-Malthusians, investigators attributed the cause to widespread family planning. "The population question" took on new dimensions and opinions, especially when it was determined that the middle and upper classes were reducing their numbers while the proportionate birthrate among the poor, uneducated and ethnic sectors of society was comparatively high. Responding energetically to these new demographic trends, the eugenicists in the science/social science community contemplating the population question were highly articulate on the prospect of the geometric proliferation of those biologically lesser-endowed or comparatively "unfit." Excellent discussions of the views of prominent eugenicists Francis Galton, Karl Pearson, Caleb Saleeby, Havelock Ellis, and others are found in:

11.209
Soloway, Richard Allen, **BIRTH CONTROL AND THE POPULATION QUESTION IN ENGLAND, 1877-1930.** Chapel Hill, 1982.

11.210
Kevles, Daniel J., **IN THE NAME OF EUGENICS: GENETICS AND THE USES OF HUMAN HEREDITY.** New York, 1985.

Soloway describes the viewpoints of Ellis and Saleeby:

> Ellis was an optimistic eugenist in an era of racial pessimism. A majority of his contemporaries who explained the declining birthrate in biological, evolutionary terms feared that before the blessings of individuation reached the less cerebral lower classes their numbers would overwhelm their more complex, highly differentiated countrymen and reverse the progressive course of race development. Well aware that concerns about the birthrate were entwined with broader worries about the possibility of race degeneration in an age of real and imagined challenges to Britain's economic, political and imperial position in the world.... Saleeby promoted a national eugenics program to encourage the marriage and procreation of the more individuated 'fit' people in society who were readily identified by their professional, intellectual, economic or social achievements (p. 18).

On the question of control of "race improvement" for English society, Kevles shows that eugenicists were split along the lines of voluntarism and state interference in the matter of reproducing more children from the fit, and less from the unfit.

> Many eugenicists expected their program... to rest on voluntarism—— thus the stress on education, moral injunction, and the need for contraception.... Voluntarism was also deemed essential because... little was yet known about the laws of heredity in human beings.... Yet a number of British and American eugenicists came to the view... that perhaps with regard to certain critical problems—— notably the proliferation of degenerates——the situation [warranted] state intervention of a coercive nature in human reproduction (p. 91).

Some eugenicists were to go to extremes in proposing legalized sterilization and other severe governmental controls without success. Others considered perhaps less drastic measures of state intervention, not only on "the population question," but also on the merits of providing social welfare services to improve life, health and education of the lower classes——despite their being allegedly fixed in inferiority by heredity. Some eugenicists were at least able to reconcile standing relief and improvement programs for the poor with the eugenic pronouncements about the "congenitally unfit":

11.211

Elderton, Ethel, **REPORT ON THE ENGLISH BIRTH-RATE.** 1914. In the conclusion to her study of fertility patterns in nine counties, avowed eugenicist Elderton states, "No one who has even a feeble belief in the power of heredity can regard [differential fertility] as anything but an unmixed evil" (p. 219).... [However,] no community can allow its children to suffer more than can possibly be avoided from the carelessness of their parents, but by thus interfering with natural processes the community probably lays up racial trouble for the future.... We must continue to help the helpless, [but] can nothing be done to increase the fertility of the racially fit?" (p. 232).

11.212

Marchant, James, **BIRTH-RATE AND EMPIRE.** 1917. Marchant agreed that the "problem is to find some remedy for the persistently diminishing birthrate of our growing Empire and the serious decrease of men of ability born to the better-educated classes" (p. ix). However, he endorsed the policy of State welfare assistance to the existing poor, especially mothers and children.

A widespread belief among eugenicists was that nature (heredity) was stronger than nurture (environment), as both Francis Galton and Karl Pearson attempted to demonstrate:

11.213

JOURNAL OF THE ROYAL ANTHROPOLOGICAL INSTITUTE OF GREAT BRITAIN AND IRELAND: Pearson, K., *"On the Inheritance of the Mental and Moral Characteristics in Man and Its Comparison with the Inheritance of the Physical Characters,"* 33 (1903) 179-237. "We have placed our money on Environment when Heredity wins in a canter.... No training or education can *create* [intelligence].... You must breed it" (p. 182).

Neo-Malthusians extended their interests to eugenics at least by the time the Eugenics Society was founded in 1907. The Society was divided in its approach to the question of "race-betterment." There was the Positive (or neo-Darwinian) School that promoted increased reproduction among the fit and promising sectors of the population, and was not concerned with demographic numbers as a whole. The other side represented Negative Eugenics: the deliberate restriction of propagation by those with undesirable biological or psychological traits, or who were suffering from hereditary peculiarities or diseases. The neo-Malthusians tended toward the Negative school.

11.214

MALTHUSIAN: Drysdale, C.R., *"Twenty-Third Annual Meeting,"* 24 no. 3 (1900) 22. "Nothing could teach the poor so quickly and so clearly as a statute law imposing some slight penalty for the producing of an over-numerous offspring" (p. 43). Actually, Drysdale proposed to penalize all overproducing families regardless of class when population was perceived to be on the rise, and before the eugenics issue was paramount; Drysdale, C.V., *"The 'Eugenics Review' and the Malthusian League,"* 33 no. 12 (1909) 90. "We neo-Malthusians are Negative eugenists to the core.... [However, we prefer] voluntary abstention from procreation on the part of the unfit to sterilization or other compulsion, except where there is absolutely no possibility of self-control being exercised" (p. 90). Drysdale goes on to explain that the Positive program seemed to be intended to produce "Supermen"——a ruling elite.

Neo-Malthusians, he said, feel it is better to decrease births among the unfit than to promote an increase among the fit.

The question of breeding inevitably involves the contemporary view of the role of women in eugenic thought and activity. Widely expressed was the concern that "emancipated" women who had taken advantage of opportunities for higher education and careers were electing not to marry and bear children, thus altering the biological makeup and reproductive potential of females of their class as they spurned domestic roles. For a useful historical discussion of this question:

11.215
Soloway, Richard Allen, "The Woman Question" in **BIRTH CONTROL AND THE POPULATION QUESTION IN ENGLAND 1877-1930.** by Richard Allen Soloway. Chapel Hill, 1982; "Feminism, Fertility, and Eugenics in Victorian and Edwardian England" in **POLITICAL SYMBOLISM IN MODERN EUROPE.** ed. by Seymour Drescher, et al. New Brunswick, N.J., 1982.

A widely noted contemporary work on reduced fertility among the educated classes of women was written by a physicist and his colleague-wife, parents of six:

11.216
Whetham, William C.D. and Whetham, Catherine, **THE FAMILY AND THE NATION: A STUDY IN NATURAL INHERITANCE AND SOCIAL RESPONSIBI-LITY.** 1909. The authors view the diminished reproduction among the "abler classes" as an imminent danger to the country and high treason to the human race, and urge that the trend be reversed. On women: "Woe to the nation whose best women refuse their natural and most glorious burden!" (pp. 198-199). The Whethams were considered the most anti-feminist sector of the Eugenics Education Society.

Kevles discusses the question of women related to eugenics throughout his book. He shows the high participation of women in the eugenics movement, including the fact that fully half the membership of the British Eugenics Society consisted of women, and so did about a quarter of its officers (p. 64). He refers to Karl Pearson's Men and Women's Club for exploring relations between the sexes, and shows a probable connection between the social purity movement and developments in the eugenics campaign. "Honoring motherhood, the movement aimed to make motherhood voluntary, an achievement that it claimed would not only benefit women but would promote the eugenic interest of the race (p. 65).... Within... mainline eugenics, it was a morally injunctive commonplace that middle- and upper-class women should remain at home, hearth, and cradle——that was their duty——to marry and bear children" (p. 88). Advanced education need not be a bar. Some eugenicists could reconcile personal feminist goals with domestic duties, and argued that more "emancipated" single women should try to find greater fulfillment in marriage.

Eugenicists as well as eugenic-minded social service agencies virtually created an institution of Motherhood largely to implement the goals of race improvement. Here, working-class and poor mothers were also targeted. A valuable and provocative analytic discussion of the late-Victorian and Edwardian writing and activity that focused on "training" for and ideology of motherhood for English society and the expanding empire is

11.217
HISTORY WORKSHOP JOURNAL: Davin, A., *"Imperialism and Motherhood,"* no.

5 (1978) 9-65.

Women must be taught how to 'exercise her great natural function of choosing fathers of the future' and to understand 'the age at which she should marry, and the compatibility between discharge of her incomparable functions of motherhood and the lesser functions which some women now assume.' Motherhood though a destined and natural function nevertheless needed to be taught; there were skills to be learnt so that the eugenically conceived baby would also be reared to its best advantage. The responsible mother would study expert opinion and put herself and her family under the supervision of a doctor... whose instructions she would then execute (p. 21).... 'Endowment of motherhood' was a demand for financial recognition by the state that mothers' work rearing children contributed to the good of society.... As proposed in the 1900s by [Sidney] Webb and the Fabians it was effectively an economic version of the eugenists' 'elevation of motherhood' (p. 23).

Thus social movements and personal pressures relative to both family limitation and family expansion along the lines of eugenic ideology involved English women crucially over the nineteenth and into the twentieth century. The guide to sources that follows should assist in exploring the relevant questions and in opening new areas for research. They supplement the fine bibliographies that are included in the writings described above.

11.218
NATIONAL REFORMER: 1860 to 1893; vols. 1-62; issues from 1881-1887 edited by Charles Bradlaugh assisted by Annie Besant. Became an important forum for the avid debate on family limitation. Volume 29 of 1877 contains many articles on incidents before and after the Bradlaugh-Besant trial, including the start of the Malthusian league; volume 32 of 1878 and 33 of 1879 have information on the League's early activities; *"Account of the Trial of Henry Loader,"* 59 (1892) n.p.; *"The Neo-Malthusian Prosecution at Newcastle,"* 59 (1892) n.p.

11.219
Galton, Francis, **HEREDITARY GENIUS: AN INQUIRY INTO ITS LAWS AND CONSEQUENCES.** 1865; rpt. 1952. Galton was the first to treat "hereditary genius" in a statistical manner and to introduce the "law of deviation from an average" into discussion of heredity. Apologizes for not including women in his cases; **RECORD OF FAMILY FACULTIES.** 1884. Attempts to trace ancestry so as to forecast the mental and bodily faculties of offspring and to further the science of heredity; **NATURAL INHERITANCE.** 1889. On marriage selection; **EUGENICS: ITS DEFINITION, SCOPE AND AIMS.** 1905; **ESSAYS IN EUGENICS.** 1905-1906; **FOUNDATIONS OF EUGENICS.** 1907. Urges improvement of the quality of man in society, society being a "complex organism, with a consciousness of its own" (n.p.). ——*see also:* **JOURNAL OF THE HISTORY OF BIOLOGY:** Cowan, R.S., *"Francis Galton's Contribution to Genetics,"* 5 (1972) 389-412; **HISTORY TODAY:** Corning, C.H., *"Francis Galton and Eugenics,"* 23 (1973) 724-732. Biographical essay focusing on Galton's studies of racial qualities. Galton was Charles Darwin's younger cousin.

11.220
FRASER'S MAGAZINE: Jenkins, J.E., *"Two Solutions,"* 83 (1871) 451-456. "The true problem is not how to stop the increase of a noble race but how to distribute its active forces over our vast estate" (p. 455); Newman, F.W., *"Malthusianism, True and False,"* 83 (1871) 584-598. Condemns contraception as a "harlot's habit."

11.221
Greg, William R., "Malthus Notwithstanding" and "Non-Survival of the Fittest" in ENIGMAS OF LIFE. by William R. Greg. New York, 1872; rpt., New York, 1972.

11.222
CONTEMPORARY REVIEW: Darwin, G., *"On Beneficial Restrictions to Liberty in Marriage,"* 22 (1873) 412-426. "Civilization has so diminished the force of Natural Selection, that we cannot... afford to neglect some process of artificial selection" (p. 426). Advocates state interference to restrict marriages in order to improve the race; Galton, F., *"A Theory of Heredity,"* 27 (1875) 80-95; Hutchinson, W., *"Evolutionary Ethics of Marriage and Divorce,"* 88 (1905) 397-410. "Husband and wife unite not to enjoy themselves, but to rear and train healthy, happy, worthy offspring" (p. 407); Sprigge, S.S., *"Mating and Medicine,"* 96 (1909) 578-587. Argues against the eugenists' proposal for medical examinations for prospective partners; Shelton, S., *"Eugenics,"* 101 (1912) 84-95. Considers the "state endowment of motherhood"; Ellis, H., *"Eugenics and Genius,"* 106 (1913) 519-527. Genius is not threatened by the elimination of "corrupt stocks."

11.223
Besant, Annie, THE LAW OF POPULATION: ITS CONSEQUENCES AND ITS BEARING UPON HUMAN CONDUCT AND MORALS. [1877-1879]; *rpt. in:* FERTILITY CONTROLLED! THE BRITISH ARGUMENT FOR FAMILY LIMITATION: SEX, MARRIAGE AND SOCIETY. ed. by Charles Smith-Rosenberg and Carroll Smith-Rosenberg. New York, 1974. Sets out Malthus' theory that population always outgrows its capacity for subsistence. Besant suggests a variety of contraceptive techniques as checks to fertility and argues that merely delaying marriage, as proposed by Malthus, will only increase prostitution, besides being unacceptable to the majority of young people; THE SOCIAL ASPECTS OF MALTHUSIANISM. 1880; 1881. Discusses the roles of women other than that of mother and homemaker; AUTOBIOGRAPHICAL SKETCHES. 1885; AN AUTOBIOGRAPHY. 1893; THEOSOPHY AND THE LAW OF POPULATION. 1904; (with Bradlaugh, Charles), DEFENDENTS IN THE HIGH COURT OF JUSTICE. 1877. Account of their trial (Queen v. Bradlaugh and Besant), including affadavits presented to the Court. —*see also:* QUEEN V. CHARLES BRADLAUGH AND ANNIE BESANT. [1877]. A transcript of the trial; Besterman, Theodore, A BIOGRAPHY OF ANNIE BESANT. 1924; Bradlaugh, Charles, THE TRUE STORY OF MY PARLIAMENTARY STRUGGLE. 1882; Shaw, George Bernard, DR. ANNIE BESANT: FIFTY YEARS IN PUBLIC WORK. 1924; West, Geoffrey, THE LIFE OF ANNIE BESANT. 1929; Williams, Gertrude M., THE PASSIONATE PILGRIM: A LIFE OF ANNIE BESANT. 1932; Besterman, Theodore, MRS. ANNIE BESANT: A MODERN PROPHET. 1934; POPULATION STUDIES: Banks, J.A. and Banks, O., *"The Bradlaugh-Besant Trial and the English Newspapers,"* 8 (1954) 22-34. "The decline in the English fertility was brought about by factors other than the Bradlaugh-Besant trial and the furors it aroused; yet without it, the spread of family limitation might well have been delayed" (p. 33); Nethercot, A.H., THE FIRST FIVE LIVES OF ANNIE BESANT. 1961; Prakasa, Sri, ANNIE BESANT AS A WOMAN AND AS LEADER. 3rd ed., Bombay, 1962; Nethercot, A.H., THE LAST FOUR LIVES OF ANNIE BESANT. 1963; A SELECTION OF THE SOCIAL AND POLITICAL PAMPHLETS OF ANNIE BESANT. ed. by John Saville. New York, 1970; INDIAN REVIEW: Sivasankar, W.S., *"Dr. Annie Besant: A Profile,"* 68 (1972) 23-27; Manvell, Roger, THE TRIAL OF ANNIE BESANT AND CHARLES BRADLAUGH. 1976; Chadrasekhar, Sripati, "A DIRTY FILTHY BOOK": THE WRITINGS OF CHARLES KNOWLTON AND ANNIE BESANT ON REPRODUCTIVE PHYSIOLOGY AND BIRTH CONTROL

AND AN ACCOUNT OF THE BRADLAUGH-BESANT TRIAL. Berkeley, 1981.

11.224
Watts, Charlie, A REFUTATION OF MR. BRADLAUGH'S INACCURACIES AND MISREPRESENTATIONS... 1877.

11.225
MALTHUSIAN: 1879 to 1921; vols. 1-45; *continued as:* NEW GENERATION: 1922-1949; *continued as:* MALTHUSIAN LEAGUE: October 1949+; Kautsky, K., *"The Law of Population and its Influence on the Well-Being of Society,"* 8 (1886) 14 ff; Vickery, A.D., *"Certain Points in Which the Population Difficulty Affects the Life and Happiness of Women,"* 8 (1886) 52-54; *"The Bitter Cry of the Mother,"* 8 (1886) 76; *"A Debate Between Ladies on the Malthusian Question,"* 9 (1887) 57-59; *"Eleventh Annual Meeting of the Malthusian League: Speeches by Mrs. Annie Besant, Dr. Alice Vickery, Mrs. Snowden, Miss Thorton Smith, Mr. Hember and Others,"* 10 (1888) 50-52; Fisher, M.C., *"Ought Women to be Punished for Having too Many Children?"* 10 (1888) 68-69; 75-76; An Indignant Woman, *"A Woman's Protest Against the Limitation of Families,"* 10 (1888) 78; A Well-Wisher to the Cause, *"Reply,"* 10 (1888) 92; A Health Reformer, *"The Horrors of Overbearing,"* 13 (1891) 54; Vickery, A.D., *"A Women's Population Committee,"* 13 (1891) 59-60; Weale, K., *"A Lady's Views,"* 18 (1894) 37-38; Drysdale, C.R., *"Darwinian Objections to Neo-Malthusian Doctrines,"* 18 (1894) 73-74; *"Social Purity Ideals,"* 18 (1894) 81-82; Vickery, A.D., *"A Women's Malthusian League,"* 28 (1904) 67-69; *"Extracts Reprinted form the January 1917 Issue,"* (1917).

11.226
Malthusian League, PAMPHLETS, LEAFLETS, TRACTS. 1885-1915; OPINIONS OF EMINENT MEN ON THE CAUSE OF POVERTY AND ITS CURE. various dates; J.S. MILL ON SMALL FAMILIES. 1877; THE MALTHUSIAN HANDBOOK. 1893; A PROGRAMME OF WOMEN'S EMANCIPATION. 1905; UNEMPLOYMENT: ITS CAUSE AND REMEDY. 1908; HYGIENIC METHODS OF FAMILY LIMITATION. 1913; INTERNATIONAL NEO-MALTHUSIAN BUREAU OF CORRESPONDENCE AND DEFENCE. 1915; MALTHUSIAN LEAGUE: A RECRUITING LEAFLET. 1915; FORTIETH ANNUAL REPORT. 1918; FORTY-SECOND ANNUAL REPORT. 1920; PRACTICAL METHODS OF FAMILY LIMITATION. 1920; BIRTH CONTROL: WHAT IT AIMS AT. 1922; PUBLIC MEETING AT KENSINGTON TOWN HALL. [1922]; JUBILEE YEAR. 1927; THE MALTHUSIAN LEAGUE. 1877-1927. 1927. ——*see also:* Drysdale, Bessie I., THE MALTHUSIAN LEAGUE FOR RATIONAL BIRTH CONTROL FOUNDED IN 1877. n.d.

11.227
Routh, Charles Henry Felix, THE MORAL AND PHYSICAL EVILS LIKELY TO FOLLOW IF PRACTICES INTENDED TO ACT AS CHECKS TO POPULATION BE NOT STRONGLY DISCOURAGED AND CONDEMNED. 1878; *rpt. from:* MEDICAL PRESS AND CIRCULAR: n.v. (October 1878) n.p.

11.228
Truelove, Edward, IN THE HIGH COURT OF JUSTICE... QUEEN VS. EDWARD TRUELOVE FOR PUBLISHING OWEN'S "MORAL PHYSIOLOGY." 1878. Bound with a pamphlet titled INDIVIDUAL, FAMILY AND NATIONAL POVERTY.

11.229
Drysdale, Charles Robert, LARGE FAMILIES AND OVER-POPULATION. 1879; (as editor), MEDICAL OPINIONS ON THE POPULATION QUESTION. 1879; rpt.,

1901; THE POPULATION QUESTION AT THE MEDICAL SOCIETY OF LONDON; OR THE MORTALITY OF THE RICH AND POOR. 1879; THE PRINCIPLE OF POPULATION. [1885]; THE CAUSE OF POVERTY. 1891; THE POPULATION QUESTION ACCORDING TO T.R. MALTHUS AND J.S. MILL. 1892; CLERICAL OPINIONS ON THE POPULATION QUESTION. 1902; THE SMALL FAMILY SYSTEM, IS IT INJURIOUS OR IMMORAL? rev. ed., 1917. "Of course one may preach very late marriages, as advocated by Malthus. But this means the delaying of marriage in the case of women of the poorest classes till the age of 35 or over. Even then families of six or more children would still be common.... On the contrary, early marriage... is the one and only possibility of reducing or eliminating the evils of prostitution" (p. 135); OVERPOPULATION CONSIDERED AS A PROMINENT CAUSE OF MISERY AND EARLY DEATH. n.d.

11.230
LIBERAL: Jewel, H., "Population Restriction and the Progress of the Race," 1 (1879) 154-158; King, W.G., "Population and Progress," 1 (1879) 398-407.

11.231
Aveling, Edward B., DARWINISM AND SMALL FAMILIES. 1882. "I hope to show that the principle of Natural Selection, a part of Darwinism, is all in favor of small families" (p. 2) for the working classes, because "as the low forms of organic beings last, so do the low forms of man persist" (p. 3).

11.232
Oxoniensis (pseud.), EARLY MARRIAGE AND LATE PARENTAGE: THE ONLY SOLUTION OF THE SOCIAL PROBLEM. 1883; 1889; 1906; rpt. in: FERTILITY CONTROLLED! THE BRITISH ARGUMENT FOR FAMILY LIMITATION. SEX, MARRIAGE AND SOCIETY. ed. by Charles Smith-Rosenberg and Carroll Smith-Rosenberg. New York, 1974.

11.233
MACMILLAN'S MAGAZINE: Cunningham, W., "On the Statement of the Malthusian Principle," 49 (1883) 81-86. Critiques those who condemn over-population as the "chief cause of social degradation," arguing that if numbers were kept in check, social evils would still exist.

11.234
Clapperton, Jane Hume, SCIENTIFIC MELIORISM AND THE EVOLUTION OF HAPPINESS. 1885. See especially: "Heredity, or Natural Selection Counteracted and a Policy for Race Regeneration"; A VISION OF THE FUTURE BASED ON THE APPLICATION OF ETHICAL PRINCIPLES. 1904.

11.235
OUR CORNER: Besant, A., "The Law of Population in Relation to Socialism," 7 (1886) 324-331.

11.236
BRITISH MEDICAL JOURNAL: Albutt, M.A., "The Royal College of Physicians and Modern Malthusianism," 1 (1887) 754; "Malthusian Principles and Practice," 1 (1887) 1176-1177. On Dr. Albutt's case; Elderton, E.M., "Report of Galton Lectures on 'National Eugenics'... The Topic was: Fertility as Related to the 'Social Value' of the Parents," 1 (1913) 536; Heron, D., "Report of Galton Lectures on 'National Eugenics' Delivered by Heron," 1 (1913) 591; "Report of Comments from Prof. John Edgar, on the Disproportionate Slowing of the Birth-Rate, in Which the Wealthier

and More Educated Classes had Begun to Decline in Births, While the Lower Classes Had Not," 1 (1913) 974-975; *"The Declining Birth Rate,"* 1 (1913) 1179-1180. "Do the environmental advantages which thus accrue to the diminished numbers of offspring outweigh the disadvantages of a slackening of the intensity of natural selection operating upon a larger number of children, some of whom must be 'weeded out?'" (p. 1179); Dunlop, Dr., *"Correspondence on Birth Control,"* 1 (1913) 1404; Standring, C., *"The Declining Birth Rate: Correspondence in Support of Birth-Control,"* 2 (1913) 56.

11.237
FORTNIGHTLY REVIEW: Galton, F., *"Good and Bad Temper in English Families,"* 48 (1887) 21-30; Wallace, A.R., *"Human Selection,"* 54 (1890) 325-337. Anti-legislative eugenics; Pearson, K., *"Woman and Labour,"* 61 (1894) 561-577. Calls for national insurance for motherhood; Sully, J., *"The New Study of Children,"* 64 (1895) 723-737. Women as investigators in this field must get rid of their attachment and attraction to babies; Crackenthorpe, M., *"The Friends and Foes of Eugenics,"* 92 (1912) 740-748. Debaters of socialism vs. eugenicism should ignore biology in favor of improving the environment; Alec-Tweedie, E., *"Eugenics,"* 97 (1912) 854-865. "It is to the women of the country we must look in this great eugenics movement" (p. 857).

11.238
Blackwell, Elizabeth, A MEDICAL ADDRESS ON THE BENEVOLENCE OF MALTHUS CONTRASTED WITH THE CORRUPTIONS OF NEO-MALTHUSIAN-ISM. 1888; (with Newman, Francis W.), THE CORRUPTION CALLED NEO-MALTHUSIANISM. 1889.

11.239
Wright, Henry C., MARRIAGE AND PARENTAGE: OR, THE REPRODUCTIVE ELEMENT IN MAN AS A MEANS TO HIS ELEVATION AND HAPPINESS. 1888.

11.240
WESTMINSTER REVIEW: Drysdale, C.R., *"The Malthusian Theory of Population,"* 131 (May 1889) 561-573; Ogilvie, A.J., *"The Malthusian Doctrine,"* 136 (1891) 289-297; Foard, I., *"The Power of Heredity,"* 151 (1899) 538-553; Tayler, J.L., *"The Social Application of Eugenics,"* 170 (1908) 416-424. Describes two distinct fields for the study of eugenics: the genetic-physiological and the socio-environmental. Popular assistance is needed to improve the environment and spread the "teachings" and "truth" of eugenics; Hill-Climo, W., *"A Healthy Race: A Woman's Vocation,"* 173 (1910) 11-19; Laski, H.J., *"The Scope of Eugenics,"* 174 (1910) 25-34; Herbert, S., *"The Discovery of the Fittest: A Eugenic Problem,"* 175 (1911) 39-45; MacGregor, M.E., *"A Plea for the Reduction of the Birth Rate,"* 177 (1912) 348-352; Herbert, S., *"Eugenics in Relation to Social Reform,"* 180 (1913) 377-386.

11.241
Gaskell, George Arthur, SOCIAL CONTROL OF BIRTH RATE AND ENDOWMENT OF MOTHERS. 1890. "A state-supported motherhood is essential to the emancipation of women from dependence on individual men.... Evolutionists are agreed in tracing the subjection of women to her reproductive disabilities; it follows that her subjection can only be put an end to by those reproductive disabilities being constituted by the State" (p. 11).

11.242
Holmes, James Robins, TRUE MORALITY; OR, THE THEORY AND PRACTICE OF NEO-MALTHUSIANISM. 1891. Includes rules for the married and unmarried;

AN ILLUSTRATED PRICE LIST OF NEO-MALTHUSIAN APPLIANCES AND HYGIENIC REQUISITES. 1914. In this edition, all the passages objected to by the Prosecuting Council are omitted and thus blanks occur; SUPPLEMENTARY PRICE LIST OF NEO-MALTHUSIAN APPLIANCES. 1922; A DESCRIPTIVE PRICE LIST... BOOKS... 1931; A SHORT LIST OF THE MORE IMPORTANT ARTICLES WHICH ARE USED IN THE PRACTICE OF NEOMALTHUSIANISM. 1936.

11.243
Woodhull, Victoria, THE RAPID MULTIPLICATION OF THE UNFIT. 1891. Criticizes healthy classes for postponing marriage and family on the basis of need to propagate a stronger race. Argues that the pauper classes are unfit not because they are unthrifty or intemperate, but because of their "organically defective" inherited traits.

11.244
Strahan, Samuel A.K., MARRIAGE AND DISEASE: A STUDY OF HEREDITY AND THE MORE IMPORTANT FAMILY DEGENERATIONS. New York, 1892. "Imbeciles, confirmed epileptics and drunkards, those who have been insane more than once, and habitual criminals... should [all] be at once denied the right of procreation" (p. 9).

11.245
NINETEENTH CENTURY: Dunn, H.P., *"Is Our Race Degenerating?"* 36 (1894) 301-314; Elsdale, H., *"Why Are Our Brains Deteriorating?"* 46 (1899) 262-272; Crackenthorpe, M., *"Eugenics as a Social Force,"* 63 (1908) 962-972. Concerning alcoholics: "The Eugenist... rather than eliminate the drink would eliminate *them*" (p. 968); *"The Extinction of the Upper Classes,"* 66 (1909) 97-108; Crackenthorpe, M., *"Marriage, Divorce and Eugenics,"* 68 (1910) 686-702. Justifies eugenics theory based on historical examples and seeks appropriate social policy and legislation; Whetham, W.C.D., *"Eminence and Heredity,"* 69 (1911) 818-832; Lindsay, J.A., *"The Case For and Against Eugenics,"* 72 (1912) 546-557. Defends eugenics; Martin, A., *"The Mother and Social Reform II,"* 73 (1913) 1235-1255; Rigby, J.A., *"The Diminishing Birth-Rate: Is It a National Danger?,"* 75 (1914) 434-445.

11.246
Bonner, Hypatia Bradlaugh and Robertson, John M., CHARLES BRADLAUGH: A RECORD OF HIS LIFE AND WORK. 2 vols. 1896; 5th. ed., 1902.

11.247
Bliss, William D.P., "Malthusianism" in THE ENCYCLOPEDIA OF SOCIAL REFORM. by William D.P. Bliss. 1897.

11.248
Pearson, Karl, "Variation in Man and Woman" in CHANCES OF DEATH. by Karl Pearson. 1897; NATIONAL LIFE FROM THE STANDPOINT OF SCIENCE. 2nd. ed., 1905. "The greatness of a nation depends on the dominant fertility of its fitter stocks" (p. viii); (and Elderton, Ethel M.), EUGENICS LABORATORY MEMOIRS XIII. A SECOND STUDY OF THE INFLUENCE OF PARENTAL ALCOHOLISM ON THE PHYSIQUE AND ABILITY OF THE OFFSPRING. BEING A REPLY TO CERTAIN MEDICAL CRITICS OF THE FIRST MEMOIR AND AN EXAMINATION OF THE REBUTTING EVIDENCE CITED BY THEM. 1910; THE SCOPE AND IMPORTANCE TO THE STATE OF THE SCIENCE OF NATIONAL EUGENICS. 3rd ed., 1911. Optimistic on the future of eugenics, Pearson believes "that every university twenty years hence will offer its students training in the

science that makes for race-efficiency and in the knowledge which alone can make a reality of statecraft" (p. 44); DARWINISM, MEDICAL PROGRESS AND EUGENICS. 1912; EUGENICS AND PUBLIC HEALTH. 1912; THE GROUND-WORK OF EUGENICS. 1912.

11.249
Smith, Henry, A PLEA FOR THE UNBORN. 1897. See especially: "An Argument that Children Should be Born with a Sound Mind in a Sound Body."

11.250
Ussher, Richard, NEO-MALTHUSIANISM: AN ENQUIRY INTO THAT SYSTEM WITH REGARD TO ITS ECONOMY AND MORALITY. 1897. A critical viewpoint that suggests alternatives. "All classes seem to be smitten by the Neo-Malthusian craze, now rapidly spreading, fondly imagining that it will remove all human woes and totally eradicate poverty and wretchedness... [but] those who think at all must see that to voluntarily cause the population of a civilized country to decline... need to be shown how utterly mistaken they are" (pp. 10-11).

11.251
Standring, George and Reynolds, William, THE MALTHUSIAN HANDBOOK, DESIGNED TO INDUCE MARRIED PEOPLE TO LIMIT THEIR FAMILIES WITHIN THEIR MEANS. 4th ed., 1898. Replaced Annie Besant's LAW OF POPULATION.

11.252
Drysdale, Bessie I., WANTED—BEAUTIFUL BABIES. 1900; SHOULD WORKING MEN AND WOMEN BE URGED TO HAVE LARGE FAMILIES AT THE PRESENT TIME? 1914; TO WORKING MEN AND WOMEN! 1915.

11.253
Vickery, Alice Drysdale, A WOMAN'S MALTHUSIAN LEAGUE. 1900.

11.254
NATURE: Galton, F., *"The Possible Improvement of the Human Breed Under the Existing Conditions of Law and Sentiment,"* 64 (1901) 659-665. "An enthusiasm to improve the race would probably express itself by granting diplomas to a silent class of young men and women by encouraging their inter-marriages, by hastening the time of marriage of women of that high class and by provision for rearing healthy children" (p. 663); *rpt. from:* SMITHSONIAN INSTITUTION ANNUAL REPORT. 1901; Washington, 1902.

11.255
Rentoul, Robert R., PROPOSED STERILIZATION OF CERTAIN MENTAL AND PHYSICAL DEGENERATES. 1903. Includes "sexual degeneracy" dypsomania; RACE CULTURE: OR, RACE SUICIDE? A PLEA FOR THE UNBORN. 1906. Deterioration and degeneracy of the population are directly related to poor choices in marriage, work patterns, intemperance, use of abortion, drugs, venereal disease, etc.

11.256
Drysdale, George R., THE STATE REMEDY FOR POVERTY: BY A DOCTOR OF MEDICINE (BIRTH CONTROL). 1904.

11.257
Finch, A. Elley, MALTHUSIANA: ILLUSTRATIONS OF THE INFLUENCE OF

NATURE'S LAW. 1904. Chapters include "The Population Question" and "If Malthus Were Living Now, Would He Be A Neo-Malthusian?"

11.258
SOCIOLOGICAL PAPERS: Galton, F., *"Eugenics: Its Definition, Scope and Aims,"* 1 (1905) 45-89. The aim of eugenics is to influence the "useful" classes "to contribute more than their proportion to the next generation" (p. 47) in order to raise the quality of the nation; *"Restriction in Marriage,"* 2 (1906) 1-47. Argues against those that believe "human nature would never brook interference with the freedom of marriages" by citing different kinds of marriages in different countries that are influenced by custom and religion; Galton, F., *"Studies in National Eugenics,"* 2 (1906) 14-25. Gives an outline of the required investigation of national eugenics; McDougall, W., *"A Practicable Eugenic Suggestion,"* 3 (1907) 53-104. Suggests a system of financial reward to certain desirable classes (e.g., civil servants) to have larger families.

11.259
Greville, Frances E., A NATION'S YOUTH: PHYSICAL DETERIORATION, ITS CAUSES AND SOME REMEDIES. 1906.

11.260
Swift, Morrison Isaac, MARRIAGE AND RACE DEATH. New York, 1906.

11.261
POPULAR SCIENCE MONTHLY: Webb, S., *"Physical Degeneration or Race Suicide,"* 69 (1906) 512-529. Essay on how to avoid race deterioration.

11.262
Webb, Sidney, THE DECLINE OF THE BIRTH RATE 1907; 1910. Fabian Tract no. 131. "In Great Britain at this moment, when half or perhaps two-thirds of all the married people are regulating their families, children are being freely born to the Irish Roman Catholics, and the Polish, Russian and German Jews, on the one hand, and the thriftless and irresponsible——largely the casual laborers and the other denizens of our great cities——on the other.... This can hardly result in anything but national deterioration" (pp. 16-17); EUGENICS AND THE POOR LAW. 1909.

11.263
Whatham, Arthur Edward, NEO-MALTHUSIANISM: A DEFENCE. 10th ed., 1907.

11.264
Eder, Montagne David, THE ENDOWMENT OF MOTHERHOOD. 1908. To improve the health and "quality of the race."

11.265
Haycraft, John B., DARWINISM AND RACE PROGRESS. 1908.

11.266
Ravenhill, Alice, EUGENIC EDUCATION FOR WOMEN AND GIRLS. 1908.

11.267
Saleeby, C.W., THE CREED OF EUGENICS. BIOLOGY AND HISTORY. 1908; PARENTHOOD AND RACE CULTURE. 1909; METHODS OF RACE-REGENERATION. 1911; WOMAN AND WOMANHOOD: A SEARCH FOR PRINCIPLES. 1912; THE PROGRESS OF EUGENICS. 1914.

11.268
Johnston, J., "National Degeneration" in **WASTAGE OF CHILD LIFE AS EXEMPLIFIED BY CONDITIONS IN LANCASHIRE**. by J. Johnston. 1909. Examines statistics concerning height, mortality and dental quality of children indicating that the national standard is declining.

11.269
Whetham, William C.D. and Whetham, Catherine, **EUGENICS AND UNEMPLOYMENT**. 1910. A lecture to future factory and landowners to encourage the "healthier stocks" of workers to produce large families. This will create a more efficient workforce; **HEREDITY AND SOCIETY**. 1912. Contends that environmental improvement will not help the lot of the race; improvement can only come from "selective breeding"; **AN INTRODUCTION TO EUGENICS**. 1912.

11.270
EUGENICS REVIEW: Slaughter, J.W., *"Selection in Marriage,"* 1 (1909-1910) 150-162; Scharlieb, M., *"Adolescent Girlhood Under Modern Conditions. With Special Reference to Motherhood,"* 1 (1909-1910) 174-183; Ravenhill, A., *"Eugenic Ideals for Motherhood,"* 1 (1909-1910) 265-274. If women are not eugenists, they betray their trust amongst one another; Hughes, E.M., *"Sex Teaching in Girls' Schools,"* 2 (1910-1911) 144-146; Murray, L., *"Woman's Progress in Relation to Eugenics,"* 2 (1910-1911) 282-298. It is women's responsibility to develop the faculties of their children. Speculates on the state endorsement of maternity to insure adequate nourishment during pregnancy, "the performance of her great race function"; Ewart, R.J., *"The Aristocracy of Infancy and the Conditions of its Birth,"* 3 (1911-1912) 143-175; Kingham, R.D., *"Ellen Key's LOVE AND MARRIAGE from the Viewpoint of Eugenics,"* 3 (1911-1912) 178-179; Tredgold, A.F., *"Marriage Regulation and National Family Records,"* 4 (1912-1913) 74-90; Thomson, M.R., *"Women and Eugenics: A Review of Olive Schreiner's WOMAN AND LABOUR,"* 4 (1912-1913) 307-312; Darwin, L., *"Notes on the Report of the Royal Commission on Divorce and Matrimonial Causes,"* 4 (1912-1913) 363-372; Carr-Saunders, A.M., *"A Criticism of Eugenics,"* 5 (1913-1914) 316-342; Cobb, J.A., *"The Problem of the Sex Ratio,"* 6 (1914-1915) 157-163; Clay, A., *"Eugenics and the Poor,"* 7 (1915) 107-122.

11.271
SOCIOLOGICAL REVIEW: Chatterton-Hill, G., *"Race Progress and Race Degeneracy,"* 2 (1909) 140-151; 250-259. Claims unhealthy parents may produce healthy children if they procreate at an early age, and regrets that early marriages are discouraged by social and economic conditions; Saleeby, C.W., *"The Obstacles of Eugenics,"* 2 (1909) 228-240. Expresses the need for mothers of the "higher type"— educated women who show no interest in giving up liberty for marriage and motherhood. Advocates education for parenthood; *"The Methods of Eugenics,"* 3 (1910) 277-286. Discusses three categories: positive, negative and preventive; Marvin, E.M.D., *"Reply,"* 2 (1909) 400-401. "It is obviously impossible that society shall be so regulated as to give women the most favourable conditions for child-bearing until women themselves can speak freely on the subject and take their share in the counsels of the nation" (p. 401); Atkinson, M., *"The Feminist Movement and Eugenics,"* 3 (1910) 51-56. Argues that eugenics and the principles of the feminist movement are compatible; Hobhouse, L.T., *"The Value and Limitation of Eugenics,"* 4 (1911) 281-302; Hobson, J.A., *"Olive Schreiner: WOMAN AND LABOUR,"* 4 (1911) 149; Hutchins, B.L., *"The Position of Women, Active and Ideal,"* 4 (1911) 360; Tayler, J.M., *"Heredity and the Social Outlook,"* 4 (1911) 131-140.

11.272
Elderton, Ethel M. (with the assistance of Karl Pearson), **EUGENICS**

LABORATORY MEMOIRS. X. A FIRST STUDY OF THE INFLUENCE OF PARENTAL ALCOHOLISM ON THE PHYSIQUE AND ABILITY OF THE OFFSPRING. 1910. "Alcoholism in the parent may, like insanity, be the somatic mark of a defective germ plasm in the stock" (p. 1); (and Barrington, Amy, Jones, H. Gertrude, Lamotte, Edith M.M. De G., Laski, H.J., and Pearson, Karl), EUGENICS LABORATORY MEMOIRS XVIII. ON THE CORRELATION OF FERTILITY WITH SOCIAL VALUE. A COOPERATIVE STUDY. 1913. "It has been shown that if fertility be correlated with any anti-social hereditary character, then a population will fairly rapidly degenerate. It has further been demonstrated that the more intellectual and energetic, the more prudent and well-to-do classes in this country have a lower fertility" (p. 1).

11.273
Harben, Henry D., THE ENDOWMENT OF MOTHERHOOD. 1910. Advocates pensions and insurance to compensate for the expenses of maternity.

11.274
Hawkes, Mrs. R.J.J., WHAT IS EUGENICS? 1910. Chapters include "National Degeneracy and its Cause" and "A Pressing Problem: Some Suggested Remedies."

11.275
Heron, David, EUGENICS LABORATORY MEMOIRS. VIII. THE INFLUENCE OF DEFECTIVE PHYSIQUE AND UNFAVOURABLE HOME ENVIRONMENT ON THE INTELLIGENCE OF SCHOOL CHILDREN, BEING A STATISTICAL EXAMINATION OF THE LONDON COUNTY COUNCIL PIONEER SCHOOL SURVEY. 1910. Considers observations made at 12 boys' schools and 13 girls' schools. Includes tables of compared mental capacities of the children investigated.

11.276
MacGregor, Margaret, THE WHITE SLAVES OF MORALITY. 1910. On family limitation.

11.277
Pinsent, E.F., SOCIAL RESPONSIBILITY AND HEREDITY. 1910.

11.278
ENGLISHWOMAN: Arnold, E., *"Training for Motherhood,"* 5 (1910) 294; Newmarch, E., *"Woman and the Race,"* 10 (1912) 33-39; Humphries, M., *"Racial Responsibility,"* 18 (1913) 97-104.

11.279
Barr, James, THE AIM AND SCOPE OF EUGENICS. Edinburgh, 1911. Chapters include "Desirable Traits" and "Purification of the British Race."

11.280
Beale, Octavius C., ed., RACIAL DECAY: A COMPILATION OF EVIDENCE FROM WORLD SOURCES. 1911.

11.281
Drysdale, Charles Vickery, FREEWOMEN AND THE BIRTHRATE. 1911. "It is continuously cast up against advanced women by Imperialists and Eugenicists that education and freedom unfit them for their divine function of motherhood... but before women apologize... it would be well for them to consider a little more fully what have been the results of this positive maternity in the past, not only for themselves but for the community and the Empire" (p. 203); NEO-

MALTHUSIANISM AND EUGENICS. 1912; CAN EVERYONE BE FED? 1913; THE SMALL FAMILY SYSTEM: IS IT INJURIOUS OR IMMORAL? WITH THIRTEEN DIAGRAMS OF POPULATION MOVEMENTS, ETC., AT HOME AND ABROAD, AND PREFATORY NOTE BY DR. BINNIE DUNLOP. 1913; New York, 1917; THE EMPIRE AND THE BIRTH RATE. 1914. A paper read before the Royal Colonial Institute on March 24, 1914. Reprint by permission from the JOURNAL OF THE ROYAL COLONIAL INSTITUTE; THE MALTHUSIAN DOCTRINE AND ITS MODERN ASPECTS. 1917. Justifies the Malthusian doctrine; SMALL OR LARGE FAMILIES? New York, 1917; "Birth-Control and the Wage Earners" in POPULATION AND BIRTH CONTROL ed. by Maurice Eden Paul and Cedar Paul. New York, 1917; THE NEO-MALTHUSIAN IDEAL AND HOW IT CAN BE REALIZED. 1921.

11.282
Ellis, Havelock, THE PROBLEM OF RACE-REGENERATION. New York, 1911; THE TASK OF SOCIAL HYGIENE. 1912. Maintains that the practice of family limitation would "diminish death, disease and misery, making possible the finer ends of living, and at the same time indirectly or even directly improving the quality of the race" (p. 172).

11.283
Field, James A., THE PROGRESS OF EUGENICS. Cambridge, 1911; "The Early Propagandist Movement in English Population Theory" in ESSAYS ON POPULATION AND OTHER PAPERS. ed. by Helen F. Hohman. Chicago, 1931; 1967; *rpt. from:* BULLETIN OF THE AMERICAN ECONOMICS ASSOCIATION: no. 2 (1911) 207-236.

11.284
Hobhouse, Leonard Trelawney, "Value and Limit of Eugenics" in SOCIAL EVOLUTION AND POLITICAL THEORY. by Leonard Trelawney Hobhouse. 1911.

11.285
Newsholme, Arthur, THE DECLINING BIRTH RATE: ITS NATIONAL AND INTERNATIONAL SIGNIFICANCE. 1911. Notes the high birth rate "among the poorest classes," and states that "this implies the survival of a disproportionate number who are relatively ill-fed, ill-nourished and brought up under conditions rendering them less fitted to become serviceable citizens" (p. 50).

11.286
Scharlieb, Mary Ann Dacomb, WOMANHOOD AND RACE-REGENERATION. introduction by James Marchant. New York, 1911. Among the issues dealt with are "the commercial employment of married women, resulting, to a serious extent, in the neglect and disruption of family life" (p. 2). Chapters on "The Training of Women," "Woman's Influence on the Race," and "Women as Citizens."

11.287
Taylor, John W., "The Diminishing Birth-Rate: Its Causes, Its Tendency and Possible Remedy" in RACIAL DECAY: A COMPILATION OF EVIDENCE FROM WORLD SOURCES. ed. by Octavius C. Beale. 1911.

11.288
LANCET: *"The International Eugenics Congress,"* 2 (1911) 1345; *"Darwinism, Medical Progress and Eugenics,"* 2 (1912) 1525; *"Neo-Malthusianism and Eugenics,"* 2 (1912) 960. "The Neo-Malthusian doctrine is detrimental to the interest of the community" (n.p.); Adami, J.G., *"A Study in Eugenics: 'Unto the Third and Fourth*

Generation,'" 2 (1912) 1199-1204. Discusses heredity and the germ plasm, and gives statistical examples; Darwin, L., *"The Need for Eugenic Reform,"* 2 (1913) 1324-1325. Advocates the sterilization and/or segregation of undesirable citizens.

11.289
NEW TRACTS FOR THE TIMES. Series, 1911-1913

11.290
Darwin, Leonard, FIRST STEPS TOWARDS EUGENIC REFORM. 1912; EUGENICS AND NATIONAL ECONOMY: AN APPEAL. 1913; REPORT OF AN ADDRESS ON PRACTICAL EUGENICS. 1914.

11.291
Edgar, J., EUGENICS AND PATRIOTISM. 1912.

11.292
Horsely, J.W., HOW CRIMINALS ARE MADE AND PREVENTED. 1912.

11.293
International Eugenics Society; Eugenics Education Society, PROBLEMS IN EUGENICS: PAPERS COMMUNICATED TO THE FIRST INTERNATIONAL CONGRESS AT THE UNIVERSITY OF LONDON. 1912.

11.294
Isaacson, Edward, THE MALTHUSIAN LIMIT: A THEORY OF A POSSIBLE STATIC CONDITION FOR THE HUMAN RACE. 1912.

11.295
Schuster, Edgar, EUGENICS. A SCIENCE AND AN IDEAL. [1912-1913].

11.296
FORTNIGHTLY REVIEW: Alec-Tweedie, E., *"Eugenics,"* 91 (1912) 854-865. Supports the eugenics movement and also discusses the role of environment in shaping human behavior. Looks to educated women for their participation. "Women of fine build and brain make fine men" (p. 857).

11.297
QUARTERLY REVIEW: Tredgold, A.F., *"The Study of Eugenics,"* 217 (1912) 43-67. Despite environmental improvements, "the people of England are showing undoubted indications of a failure to adapt themselves to the requirements of progress... the number of the dependent and parasitic class is increasing" (p. 57).

11.298
Chesser, Elizabeth Sloan, "Motherhood and Eugenics" in WOMEN, MARRIAGE AND MOTHERHOOD. by Elizabeth Sloan Chesser. 1913.

11.299
Gorst, John E., EDUCATION AND RACE REGENERATION. 1913. Emphasizes practical education of girls for motherhood. See especially: "Special Education for Girls."

11.300
Hecht, Charles E., ed., REARING AN IMPERIAL RACE: CONTAINING A FULL REPORT OF THE SECOND GUILDHALL SCHOOL CONFERENCE. 1913. Discusses diet, cookery, hygiene, etc.

11.301

NEW STATESMAN: Balfour, B., *"Motherhood and the State,"* 2 (1913) Special Supplement; Lens, *"The Birth-Rate Commission,"* 2 (1913) 170-171; *"Special Supplement on Motherhood and the State,"* 3 (1914) 1-12.

11.302

Billington-Grieg, Theresa, COMMONSENSE ON THE POPULATION QUESTION. 1914. Published by the Malthusian League. Author may also be cataloged as Grieg, Theresa Billington.

11.303

Key, Ellen Karolina Sofia, THE RENAISSANCE OF MOTHERHOOD. 1914.

11.304

NATIONAL REVIEW: Selborne, M., *"Imperialism and Motherhood,"* 43 (1914) 985-988.

11.305

International Neo-Malthusian Bureau of Correspondence and Defence, REPORTS AND ACCOUNTS FOR 1916. 1916.

11.306

Marchant, James, CRADLES OR COFFINS? 1916. Chapters include "Is the Large Family Dreaded?" and "The Great Discovery: Dangerous Methods of Limitation"; BIRTH RATE AND EMPIRE. 1917. Chapters include "The New Motherhood," "Penalties on Parenthood," "Heredity and Environment," and "Birth Control and the Racial Instinct." High infant mortality is largely due to inadequate conditions which could be remedied by state intervention. However, "who... can doubt that motherhood, and not industry or politics, will in the end control womanhood; that the primal duties of the home and not the double task of factory and maternity will prevail; that the child will take its place in our midst again; that sex will remain enthroned, and gifts of frankincense and myrrh be offered at her shrine? Of this ultimate revival of love and family there can be little doubt" (p. 182).

11.307

National Birth-Rate Commission, THE DECLINING BIRTH-RATE: ITS CAUSES AND EFFECTS. 1916. James Marchant was secretary to the Commission.

11.308

Paul, Maurice Eden and Paul, Cedar, eds., POPULATION AND BIRTH CONTROL: A SYMPOSIUM. New York, 1917. Pro-birth control and pro-abortion. Critiques Malthus' theory as propounded in his ESSAY ON POPULATION. "There is no general excess of population over food supply... [but] an excess of people in relation to the privately owned capital which is able to secure profitable investment" (p. 263). Includes "Dysgenic Tendencies of Birth Control and of the Feminist Movement" by S.H. Halford and "Women and Birth Control" by Stella F.W. Browne.

11.309

Browne, Stella F.W., "Women and Birth Control" in POPULATION AND BIRTH CONTROL: A SYMPOSIUM. ed. by Maurice Eden Paul and Cedar Paul. New York, 1917. "The birth control movement... is the expression of a more intelligent and discriminating maternal love" (p. 253). ——see also: Rowbotham, Sheila, A NEW WORLD FOR WOMEN. STELLA BROWNE: SOCIALIST FEMINIST. 1977. Browne was an advocate for birth control and abortion during the Neo-Malthusian era. She was active in the Malthusian League and worked with associates Eden Paul and Havelock Ellis in the Eugenics Education Society.

11.310
ECONOMIC HISTORY: Blackmore, J.S. and Mellonie, F.C., *"Family Endowment and the Birth-Rate in the Early Nineteenth Century,"* 1 (1927) 205-213. Argues that a family allowance would decrease the birth rate; Blackmore, J.S. and Mellonie, F.C., *"Family Endowment and Birth-Rate in the Nineteenth Century. A Second Analysis,"* 1 (1928) 412-418; Himes, N., *"John Stuart Mill's Attitude Toward Neo-Malthusianism,"* 1 (1929) 457-484; Himes, N., *"Bentham and the Genesis of Neo-Malthusianism,"* 3 (1937) 267-276.

11.311
NEW GENERATION: Drysdale, C.V., *"After 50 Years,"* 6 (1927) 138-140.

11.312
NEW ENGLAND MEDICAL JOURNAL: Himes, N., *"Charles Knowlton's Revolutionary Influence on the English Birth Rate,"* 199 (1928) 461-465.

11.313
QUARTERLY JOURNAL OF ECONOMICS: Himes, N., *"The Influence of John Stuart Mill and of Robert Owen in the History of English Neo-Malthusianism,"* 42 (1928) 627-640.

11.314
JOURNAL OF POLITICAL ECONOMY: Himes, N., *"McCulloch's Relation to the Neo-Malthusian Propaganda of the Time: An Episode in the History of English Neo-Malthusianism,"* 37 (1929) 73-86.

11.315
How-Martyn, Edith and Breed, Ruth, **THE BIRTH CONTROL MOVEMENT IN ENGLAND.** 1930. Contains sections on "The Malthusian League," "Popular Propaganda," "The Eugenics Society," and "Recent Parliamentary Propaganda."

11.316
MEDICAL JOURNAL AND RECORD: Himes, N., *"Notes on the Origin of the Terms Contraception, Birth Control, Neo-Malthusianism, Etc.,"* 135 (1932) 495-496.

11.317
Himes, Norman, **MEDICAL HISTORY OF CONTRACEPTION.** Baltimore, 1936; 1963; 1970.

11.318
ECONOMIC JOURNAL: Himes, N., *"Jeremy Bentham and the Genesis of English Neo-Malthusianism,"* Historical Supplement (January 1936).

11.319
Glass, D.V., **CHANGES IN FERTILITY IN ENGLAND AND WALES, 1851-1931.** 1938; "Population and Population Movements in England and Wales" in **POPULATION POLICIES AND MOVEMENTS IN EUROPE.** by D.V. Glass. Oxford, 1940. Includes a survey of early practices and propaganda in England. Discusses Malthus and his opponents, Place, Carlile, Owen, and Knowlton; (with Banks, Joseph Ambrose), "A List of Books, Pamphlets and Articles on the Population Question Published in Britain in the Period 1793 on to 1880" in **INTRODUCTION TO MALTHUS.** ed. by D.V. Glass. Watts, 1953.

11.320
Innes, John W., **CLASS FERTILITY TRENDS IN ENGLAND AND WALES, 1876-1934.** Princeton, 1938.

11.321
Smith, Kenneth, **THE MALTHUSIAN CONTROVERSY.** 1951. See especially: "Birth Control."

11.322
Banks, Joseph Ambrose, **PROSPERITY AND PARENTHOOD.** 1954.

11.323
POPULATION STUDIES: Banks, J.A. and Banks, O., *"The Bradlaugh-Besant Trial and the English Newspapers,"* 8 (1954) 22-34; D'Arcy, F., *"The Malthusian League and the Resistance to Birth Control Propaganda in Late Victorian Britain,"* 31 (1977) 429-448.

11.324
Boner, Harold A., **HUNGRY GENERATIONS: THE NINETEENTH-CENTURY CASE AGAINST MALTHUSIANISM.** New York, 1955.

11.325
Eversley, David Edward Charles, **SOCIAL THEORIES OF FERTILITY AND THE MALTHUSIAN DEBATE.** 1959. See especially: "The Status of Women," pp. 154-162.

11.326
Semmel, Bernard, **IMPERIALISM AND SOCIAL REFORM: ENGLISH SOCIAL IMPERIAL THOUGHT, 1895-1914.** 1960. See especially: "Social Darwinism: Benjamin Kidd and Karl Pearson." Both Kidd and Pearson "asserted that England's first concern——if she meant to maintain her world position——was with the welfare of her own people at the expense, if need be, of other inferior peoples" (p. 31). Francis Galton believed that with "the application of eugenic methods, it would be possible to assure... England... of a population healthy and strong and intelligent, rather than sickly, weak and incompetent" (p. 45).

11.327
POLITICAL QUARTERLY: Jeger, L.M., *"The Politics of Family Planning,"* 33 (1962) 48-58. A study of the birth control movement in England.

11.328
Arnstein, Walter L., **THE BRADLAUGH CASE: A STUDY IN LATE VICTORIAN OPINION AND POLITICS.** 1965; rpt., 1967. Annie Besant, Edward Aveling and Charles Bradlaugh "became the 'trinity' for older free-thinkers, some of whom considered the pace of their advance within the movement too rapid" (p. 15).

11.329
Hutchinson, Edward P., **THE POPULATION DEBATE: THE DEVELOPMENT OF CONFLICTING THEORIES UP TO 1900.** 1967.

11.330
PAST AND PRESENT: Young, R.M., *"Malthus and the Evolutionists: The Common Context of Biological and Social Theory,"* no. 43 (1969) 109-145.

11.331
Farrall, Lyndsey A., "The Origins and Growth of the English Eugenics Movement, 1865-1925," Ph.D. diss., Indiana Univ., 1970.

11.332
Wood, Clive and Suitters, Beryl, THE FIGHT FOR ACCEPTANCE: A HISTORY OF CONTRACEPTION. Aylesbury, 1970. Helpful survey; *reviewed in:* JOURNAL OF SOCIAL HISTORY: Smith, D.S., 8 (1974) 124-126.

11.333
Pearsall, Ronald, "Eugenics and Birth Control" in EDWARDIAN LIFE AND LEISURE. by Ronald Pearsall. 1973. "The readers of MYRA'S JOURNAL in 1905 would soon acquire a second-hand knowledge which would place them on an equal footing with an experienced prostitute" (p. 152). States that tracts on induced abortion were explicit on making use of pills of lead plaster, a liquor in which copper coins had been boiled, quinine crystals, and various salts.

11.334
Royle, Edward, "Bradlaugh and National Unity" in VICTORIAN INFIDELS: THE ORIGIN OF THE BRITISH SECULARIST MOVEMENT. by Edward Royle. Manchester, 1974.

11.335
Kern, Stephen, "Physiology and the Victorian Family" in ANATOMY AND DESTINY. by Stephen Kern. Indianapolis, 1975.

11.336
Searle, Geoffrey R., EUGENICS AND POLITICS IN BRITAIN, 1900-1914. Leyden, 1976. See especially: pp. 119-139 for useful bibliographical information; "Eugenics and Class" in BIOLOGY, MEDICINE AND SOCIETY, 1840-1940. ed. by Charles Webster. 1981. "The eugenist impulse was accordingly important in the movements for birth-control, sterilization, euthanasia, and the control of deviant groups ranging from the blind to the mentally handicapped (p. 8).... Eugenists encountered vigorous medical and lay opposition in their campaigns for negative eugenics measures" (p. 9).

11.337
ALBION: Soloway, R.A., *"Neo-Malthusians, Eugenists and the Declining Birth Rate in England, 1900-1918,"* 10 (1979) 264-268. Explores agreements and conflicts between Neo-Malthusians and eugenists prior to the first World War.

11.338
ENGLISH HISTORICAL REVIEW: Quinault, R.E., *"The Fourth Party and the Conservative Opposition to Bradlaugh 1880-1888,"* 91 (1976) 315-340.

11.339
Leathard, Audrey Mary, "The Development of Family Planning Services in Britain," Ph.D. diss, London Univ., 1978.

11.340
Soffer, Reba N., ETHICS AND SOCIETY IN ENGLAND: THE REVOLUTION IN THE SOCIAL SCIENCES, 1870-1914. Berkeley, 1978. "Galton's faith in the determining force of heredity meant that natural random selection had to be directed to socially desirable ends through a scheme by which only nationally desirable physical and mental qualities would be reproduced in future generations

(p. 91).... It was even argued by eugenicists that social problems in the working classes could only be alleviated by selective breeding since those problems were due to inferior biological stock (p. 92).... Galton's cultural perspective was hopelessly parochial, and his methods of measurement were simplistic" (p. 144).

11.341
Eyler, John M., "Farr on the Population Question: Farr's Eugenic Ideas" in VICTORIAN SOCIAL MEDICINE. by John M. Eyler. 1979.

11.342
ANNALS OF SCIENCE: Farrall, L.A., *"The History of Eugenics: A Bibliographical Review,"* 36 (1979) 111-123; Love, R., *"Alice in Eugenics-Land: Feminism and Eugenics in the Scientific Careers of Alice Lee and Ethel Elderton,"* 36 (1979) 145-158. Lee was one of the first women to have a successful academic career at London University.

11.343
EDUCATIONAL FORUM: Seldon, S., *"Eugenics and Curriculum: 1860-1929,"* 43 (1979) 67-82.

11.344
HISTORICAL JOURNAL: Freeden, M., *"Eugenics and Progressive Thought: A Study in Ideological Affinity,"* 22 (1979) 645-671.

11.345
Jones, Greta, "Theories of Heredity: The Eugenics Movement" in SOCIAL DARWINISM AND ENGLISH THOUGHT. by Greta Jones. Sussex, 1980. Links early twentieth-century social reform to eugenics movement.

11.346
BULLETIN OF THE HISTORY OF MEDICINE: Mazumdar, P.M.H., *"The Eugenists and the Residuum: The Problem of the Urban Poor,"* 54 (1980) 204-215. In connection with the concerns of the urban poor, British eugenists are distinguished "from those in other countries, such as the United States and Germany, where eugenics was concerned primarily with the politics of race rather than class" (p. 205).

11.347
SOCIETY FOR THE SOCIAL HISTORY OF MEDICINE BULLETIN: Buchanan, I., *"Infant Mortality and Social Policy: The Eugenists and the Social Ameliorators, 1900-1914,"* 27 (1980) 5-8. Those who offered alternative views on the eugenic position of infant mortality were usually medical officers.

11.348
Weeks, Jeffrey, "The Population Question in the Early Twentieth Century" in SEX, POLITICS AND SOCIETY: THE REGULATION OF SEXUALITY SINCE 1800. by Jeffrey Weeks. 1981. Examines the early twentieth-century emphasis on the functions of motherhood and the enthusiasm for direct intervention in family planning which was associated with the eugenics movement.

11.349
JOURNAL OF CONTEMPORARY HISTORY: Soloway, R.A., *"Counting the Degenerates: The Statistics of Race Deterioration in Edwardian England,"* 17 (1982) 137-164. "Concentrates upon three areas of concern to those Edwardians pursuing the evidence and causation of decline: the effects of urbanization and rural

depopulation on the health and vigour of the working classes; the problems of military recruitment; and the explanations and implications of the falling birth-rate" (p. 138).

* * *

4. SEXOLOGY: VICTORIAN/EDWARDIAN STUDIES IN SEX

11.350

Starkweather, George Briggs, **SONS OR DAUGHTERS? CHOOSE! AN ELUCIDATION OF THE PROBLEM OF SEX, SHOWING ITS NATURE AND ORIGIN, AND HOW IT MAY BE ABSOLUTELY CONTROLLED IN DIFFERENT SPECIES. ALSO, THE IMPORTANT BEARING OF THIS DISCOVERY ON THE MOST VITAL ISSUES OF THE DAY—"THE WOMAN QUESTION", DARWINISM, POPULATION, POLYGAMY.** Hartford, 1877; **THE LAW OF SEX; BEING AN EXPOSITION OF THE NATURAL LAW BY WHICH THE SEX OF OFFSPRING IS CONTROLLED IN MAN AND THE LOWER ANIMALS.** 1883.

11.351

Blackwell, Elizabeth, **THE HUMAN ELEMENT IN SEX: BEING A MEDICAL ENQUIRY INTO THE RELATION OF SEXUAL PHYSIOLOGY TO CHRISTIAN MORALITY.** 1884; 2nd ed., 1885; 1894.

11.352

Ellis, Havelock, **WOMEN AND MARRIAGE: OR, EVOLUTION IN SEX.** 1888. Illustrated; **STUDIES IN THE PSYCHOLOGY OF SEX.** 7 vols. New York, 1897-1928; Philadelphia, 1898-1902; 1911; 1926-1928. Ellis describes sexuality as a healthy, rather than sinful, function. See especially: vol. 3, "The Analysis of Sexual Impulse, Love and Pain, The Sexual Impulse in Women" and vol. 6, "Sex in Relation to Society"; **A NOTE ON THE BEDBOROUGH TRIAL.** 1898. Bedborough was a bookseller who was jailed for selling Ellis' STUDIES IN THE PSYCHOLOGY OF SEX, deemed obscene at the time; **THE EVOLUTION OF MODESTY: THE PHENOMENON OF SEXUAL PERIODICITY, AUTO-EROTICISM.** 1899. "There is, however, an allied and corresponding desire which is very often clearly or latently present in the woman: a longing for pleasure that is stolen or forbidden.... We may trace its recognition at a very early stage of history in the story of Eve and the forbidden fruit that has so often been the symbol of the masculine organs of sex" (p. 45); **ANALYSIS OF THE SEXUAL IMPULSE.** Philadelphia, 1908. Discusses erotic symbolism, scatological imagery, bestiality, exhibitionism, foot fetishism, the relationship of maternal and sexual emotion, and the constituents of semen; "The Problem of Sexual Hygiene" in **THE TASK OF SOCIAL HYGIENE.** by Havelock Ellis. Boston and New York, 1912; **THE EROTIC RIGHTS OF WOMEN, AND THE OBJECTS OF MARRIAGE.** 1918. Two essays; **THE PLAY-FUNCTION OF SEX.** 1924; **MORE ESSAYS OF LOVE AND VIRTUE.** 1931; "Women's Sexual Nature" in **WOMAN'S COMING OF AGE: A SYMPOSIUM.** ed. by Samuel D. Schmalhausen and Victor Frances Calverton. New York, 1931. "The woman is free to know what she latently feels and what she desires, but she is not yet usually free to manifest these feelings and desires. The result is that we have today a far larger body of women who definitely know what they want but definitely know also that to make that clear would cause misunderstanding" (n.p.); **MY LIFE.** 1939; 1967. — *see also:* Goldberg, Isaac, **HAVELOCK ELLIS: A BIOGRAPHICAL AND**

CRITICAL STUDY. 1926; Klein, Viola, "The Biological Approach: Havelock Ellis" in THE FEMININE CHARACTER. by Viola Klein. 1946; 2nd ed., Chicago, 1972; Collis, John Stewart, HAVELOCK ELLIS, ARTIST OF LIFE: A STUDY OF HIS LIFE AND WORK. New York, 1959; ENCOUNTER: Brome, V., *"Sigmund Freud and Havelock Ellis: The Dialogue and the Debate,"* 12 (1959) 46-53. "Freud and Ellis broke the conspiracy of silence about sex which choked investigation in the late nineteenth century" (p. 48); Calder-Marshall, A., *"Havelock Ellis and Company: Lewd, Scandalous and Obscene,"* 37 (1971) 8-23; Robinson, Paul, "Havelock Ellis" in THE MODERNIZATION OF SEX. by Paul Robinson. New York, 1976. Monograph which explores Ellis' ideas, assumptions and biases; Rowbotham, Sheila and Weeks, Jeffrey, SOCIALISM AND THE NEW LIFE: THE PERSONAL AND SEXUAL POLITICS OF EDWARD CARPENTER AND HAVELOCK ELLIS. 1977. "It was Ellis' boast that he was one of the first to produce a major study of sex psychology which dealt with the 'normal' manifestations of sex as opposed, for example, to the work of the Austrian Richard Krafft-Ebing, whose massive PSYCHOPATHIA SEXUALIS details sex in all its varieties, as a 'nauseous disease'" (p. 149). The first part of STUDIES IN THE PSYCHOLOGY OF SEX to be published (in 1897) was "Sexual Inversion," a study of homosexuality; Brome, Vincent, HAVELOCK ELLIS: PHILOSOPHER OF SEX. A BIOGRAPHY. 1979; *reviewed in:* NEW SOCIETY: Rowbotham, S., *"A Man of Study,"* 48 (1979) 100; LISTENER: Johnson, J., *"Havelock Ellis: The Sage of Sex,"* 101 (1979) 19-20; Grosskurth, Phyllis, HAVELOCK ELLIS: A BIOGRAPHY. New York, 1980. "Havelock Ellis was a revolutionary, one of the seminal figures responsible for the creation of a modern sensibility.... As a late Victorian, he rebelled against the general conspiracy of silence surrounding sex. As a youth of sixteen, miserable and guilty with strange, incomprehensible forces stirring within him, he made an unusual resolve: he determined to make his life's work the exposure, the explanation, and the understanding of sex in all its manifestations" (introduction); HISTORY TODAY: Grosskurth, P., *"Reviewing the Reviews,"* 31 (1981) 52-53. After bookseller George Bedborough was arrested for selling three copies of STUDIES IN THE PSYCHOLOGY OF SEX, Ellis had no choice but to publish his work in the United States with a medical publisher. "While ostensibly confined to a readership of doctors and lawyers, the STUDIES had an enormous underground circulation, and there were few young people whose groping knowledge of sex was not in some way associated with the name Havelock Ellis" (p. 52).

11.353
Pearson, Karl, "The Woman Question" in THE ETHIC OF FREE THOUGHT. by Karl Pearson. 1888. Pearson conducted the first rigorously scientific studies of differences in sex characteristics between men and women and was at the forefront of the eugenics movement. "Not until we have ample statistics of the medico-social results of the various regular and morbid forms of sex-relationship, will it be possible to lay the foundations of a real science of sexualogy.... It is the complete disregard of sexualogical difficulties which renders so superficial and unconvincing much of the talk which proceeds from the 'Women's Rights' platform" (p. 371).

11.354
Thomson, J. Arthur and Geddes, Patrick, THE EVOLUTION OF SEX. 1889; PROBLEMS OF SEX. 1911; New York, 1912. Important reference. "Two principles must be kept in mind. (1) A sexually vicious habit of mind and body is something far more evil and destructive than is any single or even occasional lapse through extreme temptation. (2) Irregularities in sexual behaviour or conduct have to be judged not merely by their effect on the individual, but by their influence on the race" (p. 29). Describes "the dismal treatises on the pathology of sex, full of records of the abnormalities of behaviour which ensue when satisfaction can no longer be

found in normal ways," such as the old woman who, instead of declining in sexual desire, becomes "the sensualist witch among the three traditional types of her perversion" (p. 47).

11.355
BRITISH MEDICAL JOURNAL: Barnes, R., *"The Correlation of the Sexual Functions and Mental Disorders of Women,"* 2 (1890) 901; 1013; Jones, H.M., *"A Discussion of the Correlation Between Sexual Function, Insanity and Crime,"* 2 (1900) 789-792.

11.356
Campbell, Harry, DIFFERENCES IN THE NERVOUS ORGANIZATION OF MAN AND WOMAN. 1891. "One fact which strikes one forcibly in the preceding observations is the tendency for the sexual instinct in the woman to change from time to time: not only may it be temporarily altered, with menstruation, pregnancy and lactation, but it may, I have now to add, disappear for months, or even years, to reappear again suddenly.... The most important conclusion, however, which our inquiry establishes is that the sexual instinct is very much less intense in woman than in man" (pp. 209-210).

11.357
von Krafft-Ebing, Richard, PSYCHOPATHIA SEXUALIS. orig. ed., 1892; trans. by Harry E. Wedeck from Latin, 1965. Editor observes that Krafft-Ebing lapsed into Latin "whenever he thought things might get too lively——whenever he had to describe the specific means used by his patients for their sexual gratification" (p. 7). Considers the book to be "the most comprehensive collection of case histories of sexual deviation available" (p. 8). ——*see also:* ~Sulloway, Frank J., ~FREUD, BIOLOGIST OF THE MIND: BEYOND THE PSYCHOANALYTIC LEGEND. New York, 1979. Excellent discussion of the development in Europe of the scientific study of sex.

11.358
Carpenter, Edward, SEX-LOVE AND ITS PLACE IN A FREE SOCIETY. Manchester, 1894; LOVE'S COMING OF AGE: A SERIES OF PAPERS ON THE RELATIONS OF THE SEXES. Manchester, 1896; London, 1902. Believed increased sexual freedom would engender better marital relations. "There are signs... of a new order in the relations of the sexes; and the following papers are, among other things, an attempt to indicate the inner laws which, rather than the outer, may guide Love when——some day——he shall have come to his full estate" (dedication); THE INTERMEDIATE SEX: A STUDY OF SOME TRANSITIONAL TYPES OF MEN AND WOMEN. 1908; subsequent eds. to 1930. Carpenter was the first English author to argue the social benefits of homosexuality; THE DRAMA OF LOVE AND DEATH... 1912. ——*see also:* Hynes, Samuel, "Science, Seers and Sex" in THE EDWARDIAN TURN OF MIND. by Samuel Hynes. Princeton, 1968. "His books draw on current work in biology and physics and on the researches of European psychologists like Krafft-Ebing, but they are not scientific books... he was a seer, and his methods were the methods of sermon and prophecy" (p. 150); Rowbotham, Sheila and Weeks, Jeffrey, SOCIALISM AND THE NEW LIFE: THE PERSONAL AND SEXUAL POLITICS OF EDWARD CARPENTER AND HAVELOCK ELLIS. 1977. "[Carpenter's] acceptance of the range and variety of human sexual feeling, his willingness to accept the irrational and contradictory came from his own sexual predicament [his homosexuality], and from the studies of early sex psychologists like [Havelock] Ellis. He was in contact with sexual radicals in Germany who were discussing all aspects of human sexuality, seeking a science of sexual relations.... Edward Carpenter's writing was thus important in popularising the development of

German sex psychology and in carrying the radical utopian insistence on the significance of sexual pleasure and control over the body to British socialists" (p. 110).

11.359
Ethelmer, Ellis, THE HUMAN FLOWER: BEING A BRIEF AND PLAIN STATEMENT OF THE PHYSIOLOGY OF BIRTH AND THE RELATIONS OF THE SEXES. Congleton, 1894.

11.360
Gallichan, Walter M., (pseud. Geoffrey Mortimer), CHAPTERS ON HUMAN LOVE. 1898; 1900. Advocates free love and liberal divorce laws. Discusses modesty, monogamy and polygamy, selection of mates, celibacy, "romantic love and chivalry," frigidity, perversions, and spiritual love. Argues that "attempts to divorce the carnal from the spiritual element in love have frequently ended in celibacy" and cites the Shakers and Roman Catholic ascetics as examples. "But in more than one of these sects of celibates and spiritual lovers, the flesh has repeatedly triumphed and asserted itself" (p. 259). Gives credence to the belief of phrenologists that "amativeness" is located in the cerebellum. "Persons of the passionate temperament are seldom stout.... In the amative there is usually a fair development of the neck and lower jaw, and a fullness of the lips" (p. 172). Some disorders related to sexual excess are "various ailments of the female generative system, neurasthenia... [and] sometimes insanity" (n.p.); THE GREAT UNMARRIED. [1916]. Social Darwinist work. Asserts that "there is some weight of proof that modern industrial life tends to stimulate the evolution of a neuter type" (p. 19). Claims that "nature has marked the cold man or the woman as undesirable for the reproduction of the species. As working units of the community, natural celibates may be exceedingly valuable" (p. 16). Yet, "the majority of women, through ignorance, inexperience, and conventional suppression of inquiry into vital questions, are fatally apt to deceive themselves concerning fundamental desires" (p. 18); THE POISON OF PRUDERY. AN HISTORICAL SURVEY. 1929. Condemns prudery on the grounds that it breeds ignorance and therefore vice and obscenity. Encourages sex education and reverence for the human body, male and female. Traces prudish attitudes from tribal communities to the nineteenth century. Cites cases of hysteria and madness in young boys and girls punished, or threatened with punishment, for innocent sexual curiosity.

11.361
Scott, James Foster, HEREDITY AND MORALS AFFECTED BY THE USE AND ABUSE OF THE SEXUAL INSTINCT. [c. 1898]; 1899; 2nd ed., 1908; THE SEXUAL INSTINCT: ITS USES AND DANGERS AS AFFECTING HEREDITY AND MORALS. ESSENTIALS TO THE WELFARE OF THE INDIVIDUAL AND THE FUTURE OF THE RACE. 1908. Discusses several subject areas on Victorian sexuality including: the sexual instinct, sexual immorality, prostitution, abortion, onanism, and marital and extra-marital intercourse. "Sexual passion in its full force exercises far more influence over the life of a woman, for not only is her corporeal condition dominated by her physical sex, but her husband represents the only means of gratification for her sexual longings——meaning by this far more than the mere voluptuous embrace" (p. 140).

11.362
PSYCHOLOGICAL REVIEW: Ellis, H., *"The Evolution of Modesty,"* 6 (1899) 134-135.

11.363
Godfrey, John Allen, THE SCIENCE OF SEX: AN ESSAY TOWARDS THE PRACTICAL SOLUTION OF THE SEX PROBLEM. 1901. Part I——the evolution, physiology and psychology of sex; Part II——marriage, celibacy, masturbation, prostitution, sexual inversion, population limitation, and "the sexual ideal."

11.364
AMERICAN JOURNAL OF PSYCHOLOGY: Bell, *"A Preliminary Study of the Emotion of Love Between the Sexes,"* 13 (1902) 325-354. "The love emotion, while fed by sights and sounds, and even by odors, reaches its climax in touch; and, if so, it must be more completely identified with this sensibility than with any other" (p. 333).

11.365
WESTMINSTER REVIEW: Mortimer, G. (pseud. for Walter Gallichan), *"The Work of Havelock Ellis,"* 158 (1902) 540-544. "Respect is due to those sincere and direct teachers who endeavour to drag a noble passion from the slough of ignorance and iniquity into which we have allowed it to sink. Until we understand the relation of the sexes we understand little indeed of humanity" (p. 542).

11.366
Hall, G.S., ADOLESCENCE: ITS PSYCHOLOGY AND PHYSIOLOGY, ETC. 2 vols. New York, 1904. See especially: "Adolescent Love." "The first crude impulse of coyness often impels her to open scorn of what is secretly fascinating.... She might upon occasion slap him and afterward fancy or wish it had been a kiss" (p. 105). The author's questionnaire found that "seven percent of the girls specify broad shoulders; ten percent regular and six percent white teeth; long lashes charm five percent of the young men; long, clean fingernails are often specified; arched eyebrows among girls find a special susceptibility in four percent of the youth, while cowlicks charm three percent" (p. 113).

11.367
Walling, William H., ed., SEXOLOGY: FAMILY MEDICAL EDITION. 1904. Addressed to married persons.

11.368
Freud, Sigmund, THREE CONTRIBUTIONS TO SEXUAL THEORY. orig. ed. 1905; trans. by A.A. Brill. New York, 1910; 1938; *also published as:* THREE ESSAYS ON THE THEORY OF SEXUALITY. ed. and trans. by James Strachey. 1949; 1962. The three essays are: "The Sexual Aberrations," "Infantile Sexuality," and "The Transformations of Puberty." Includes an appendix list of writings by Freud dealing predominantly with sexuality; "The Psychology of Women" in NEW INTRODUCTORY LECTURES ON PSYCHOANALYSIS. trans. by W.J.H. Sprott. New York, 1933; FREUD: ON WAR, SEX AND NEUROSIS. New York, 1947. Contains "'Civilized' Sexual Morality and Modern Nervousness"; THE STANDARD EDITION OF THE COMPLETE PSYCHOLOGICAL WORKS OF SIGMUND FREUD. ed. and trans. by James Strachey. 24 vols. 1953-1974; COLLECTED PAPERS. 5 vols. New York, 1959. In vol. 1, see especially: "Sexuality in the Aetiology of the Neuroses." In vol. 2, see especially: "The Sexual Enlightenment of Children," "Character and Anal Erotism," "Hysterical Fantasies and Their Relation to Bisexuality," "On the Sexual Theories of Children," "'Civilized' Sexuality and Modern Nervousness," "On the Transformation of Instincts with Special Reference to Anal Erotism," "'A Child is Being Beaten': A Contribution to the Study of the Origin of Sexual Perversions," "The Psychogenesis of a Case of Homosexuality in a Woman," "Certain Neurotic Mechanisms in Jealousy, Paranoia and Homosexuality,"

"The Infantile Genital Organization of the Libido: A Supplement to the Theory of Sexuality," "The Economic Problem in Masochism," "The Passing of the Oedipus Complex." In vol. 3, see especially: "Fragment of an Analysis of a Case of Hysteria." In vol. 4, see especially: "Contributions to the Psychology of Love: The Most Prevalent Form of Degradation of Erotic Life," "Contributions to the Psychology of Love: The Taboo of Virginity." In vol. 5, see especially: "The Libido Theory," "Fetishism," "Libidinal Types," and "Female Sexuality"; CHARACTER AND CULTURE. ed. by Philip Rieff. New York, 1963; SEXUALITY AND THE PSYCHOLOGY OF LOVE. ed. by Philip Rieff. New York, 1963; "On the Universal Tendency to Debasement in the Sphere of Love" in ON SEXUALITY. by Sigmund Freud. 1977.

11.369
Forel, August, THE SEXUAL QUESTION: A SCIENTIFIC, PSYCHOLOGICAL, HYGIENIC AND SOCIOLOGICAL STUDY FOR THE CULTURAL CLASSES. 1906; 1922; Brooklyn, 1936. Includes "The sexual appetite in man and woman— Flirtation," "Sexual pathology" including masturbation and homosexuality, and "Psychic irradiations of love in woman: old maids, passiveness and desire, abandon and exaltation, desire for domination, petticoat government, desire of maternity and maternal love,... jealousy, coquetry, prudery, and modesty"; SEXUAL ETHICS. 1908. Every sexual union should be a sacrament.

11.370
Weininger, Otto, SEX AND CHARACTER. 1906. The sexual impulses in men and women differ not in degree but in quality. "These forces may be termed the 'liberating' and the 'uniting' impulses. The first appears in the form of the discomfort caused by the accumulation of ripe sexual cells; the second is the desire of the ripe individual for sexual completion. Both impulses are possessed by the male; in the female only the latter are present" (p. 88). ——*see also:* Klein, Viola, "A Philosophical Approach: Otto Weininger" in THE FEMININE CHARACTER: HISTORY OF AN IDEOLOGY. by Viola Klein. 1946; 1971.

11.371
Thomas, William I., SEX AND SOCIETY: STUDIES IN THE SOCIAL PSYCHOLOGY OF SEX. 1907. Sociological/anthropological study. "When woman lost the temporary prestige which she had acquired in the maternal system through her greater tendency to associated life, and particularly when her person came more absolutely into the control of man through the system of marriage by purchase, she also accepted and reflected naively the moral standards which were developed for the most part through male activities" (p. 171). ——*see also:* Klein, Viola, "A Sociological Approach: W.I. Thomas" in THE FEMININE CHARACTER: HISTORY OF AN IDEOLOGY. by Viola Klein. 1946; 1971.

11.372
Bloch, Iwan, THE SEXUAL LIFE OF OUR TIME IN ITS RELATION TO MODERN CIVILIZATION. trans. by Maurice Eden Paul. 1908; 1920. See especially: "Physical Differential Sexual Characteristics and the Woman's Question," "Appendix: Sexual Sensibility in Women," "The Social Forms of Sexual Relationship-Marriage," and "Misogyny." Bloch introduced the term "Sexualwissenschaft"——the science of sex. "The sexual impulse exhibits in woman greater variability, a greater extent of variation, than in man——alike when we examine separate feminine individuals, and when we compare the different phases in the life of the same woman. This greater extension of feminine sexual sphere is illustrated... by the case reported by Mongolia, of a woman who was able to induce sexual excitement by the masturbation of fourteen different areas of her body" (p. 85); STRANGE SEXUAL

PRACTISES. New York, 1933; ETHNOLOGICAL AND CULTURAL STUDIES OF THE SEX LIFE IN ENGLAND AS REVEALED IN ITS EROTIC AND OBSCENE LITERATURE AND ART. trans. and ed. by Richard Deniston. New York, 1934; A HISTORY OF ENGLISH SEXUAL MORES. 1936; SEX LIFE IN ENGLAND. trans. by William Farst. 1934; 1938. Includes: "Indecent Fashions," "Sexual Quacks," "Homosexuality," "Sadism and Masochism," "Curious Sexual Instruments," "Flagellation," "Erotic Dancing and Pastimes," "Obscene Art," and "Pornographic Literature."

11.373

Pratt, Sarah J., REGULATION OF SEX: A HANDBOOK FOR MARRIED WOMEN. EVERY WOMAN TO PREDETERMINE AND REGULATE THE SEX OF HER CHILDREN. Manchester, 1908.

11.374

McDougall, William, INTRODUCTION TO SOCIAL PSYCHOLOGY. 1908; PSYCHOLOGY: THE STUDY OF BEHAVIOR. 1912; CHARACTER AND THE CONDUCT OF LIFE. n.d.   —*see also:* Roback, A.A., "Sex in Dynamic Psychology" in SEX IN CIVILIZATION. ed. by Victor Frances Calverton and S.D. Schmalhausen. New York, 1929. "McDougall has presented a naturalistically frank analysis of the sex instinct, perhaps to the discomfiture of [his] American publishers" (p. 150).

11.375

Schroeder, Theodore Albert, LEGAL OBSCENITY AND SEXUAL PSYCHOLOGY. New York, 1908; rpt., 1934.

11.376

Kisch, Enoch Heinrich, THE SEXUAL LIFE OF WOMAN IN ITS PHYSIOLOGICAL, PATHOLOGICAL AND HYGIENIC ASPECTS. trans. by Maurice Eden Paul. 1910. Illustrated. Comprehensive medical text by a German physician. Under the section entitled "Competence for Marriage of Women Suffering From Disease" the author considers the consequences of marriage on "women suffering from neurasthenic states (p. 250).... The favorable influence which marriage is often observed to exercise upon the course of nervous disorders is explicable with reference to psychical considerations of a very different nature. Sexual abuses, masturbation, and the use of preventive measures, give rise in women far less often than in men to neurasthenic and hysterical conditions" (p. 257-258).

11.377

Blount, Elizabeth Anne Mould, THE ORIGIN AND NATURE OF SEX. 1911. Published by the Health and Vim Co.

11.378

Foerster, Friedrich W., MARRIAGE AND THE SEX PROBLEM. trans. by Meyrick Booth. 1911. Discusses the ethics of sex including the value of the monogamous ideal, the social significance of monogamy, love and marriage, sex and health, and religion and sex.

11.379

Moll, Albert, THE SEXUAL LIFE OF THE CHILD. trans. by Maurice Eden Paul. 1912. Discusses sexual development, pathology, morality, and sex education. Argues that the onset of puberty occurs much earlier than at the appearance of first menstruation or first ejaculation.

11.380
AMERICAN JOURNAL OF INSANITY: McDougall, W., *"The Sources and Direction of Psychophysical Energy,"* 69 (1913) n.p. Makes use of the concept of sublimation of drives.

11.381
Doncaster, L., THE DETERMINATION OF SEX. Cambridge, 1914. On how parents may exercise choice of gender of their child at conception.

11.382
Michels, Robert W.E., SEXUAL ETHICS: A STUDY OF BORDERLAND QUESTIONS. 1914. Part of the Contemporary Science Series edited by Havelock Ellis. "In former times England was a country in which sexual problems—although, as everywhere, they were then exiled from the domain of science—had a free right of entry into the field of letters. During the nineteenth century, however... England became fiercely hostile to all literary study or discussion of questions of sex. Whilst elsewhere, and above all in France, Germany, Russia, and Scandinavia, there sprang into existence a new literature, in part fictional, and in part scientific, dealing, under infinite shades of tendency and with an almost maternal care, with the supreme problems of the human sexual life, England appeared to veil its countenance before such problems" (p. v). Contains sections on: "Hunger and Love," "Nature and Limits of Modesty," "Dualism of Woman in Primary Sexual Love," and "Outward Manifestations of the Subjection of Women in Marriage."

11.383
PROCEEDINGS OF THE ROYAL SOCIETY OF MEDICINE: McDougall, W., *"The Definition of the Sexual Instinct,"* 7 (1914) n.p.

11.384
Browne, Frances Worsley Stella, SEXUAL VARIETY AND VARIABILITY AMONG WOMEN AND THEIR BEARING UPON SOCIAL RECONSTRUCTION. 1915. Publication no. 3 of the British Society for the Study of Sex Psychology, founded in 1914.

11.385
Starr, L., THE ADOLESCENT PERIOD: ITS FEATURES AND MANAGEMENT. 1915.

11.386
Herbert, Solomon, AN INTRODUCTION TO THE PHYSIOLOGY AND PSYCHOLOGY OF SEX. 1917; FUNDAMENTALS IN SEX ETHICS; AN INQUIRY INTO MODERN TENDENCIES. 1920.

11.387
Housman, Lawrence, THE RELATION OF FELLOW-FEELING TO SEX. 1917. Publication no. 4 of the British Society for the Study of Sex Psychology.

11.388
Meisel-Hess, Grete, THE SEXUAL CRISIS: A CRITIQUE OF OUR SEX LIFE. trans. by Maurice Eden Paul and Cedar Paul. introduction by William J. Robinson. 1917; 1933. Covers a broad spectrum of sexual issues: free love, illegitimate erotic intimacy, man's ideal woman, sexual hygiene, the metamorphosis of sexual impulse into obscenity, the necessity of prostitution, love-witchery, reform of prostitutes, sexual crisis and the race, "the wellborn," and capitalism as the root of sexual

misery. Sexual misery is the most important problem confronting humankind, more important than economic problems.

11.389
JOURNAL OF MEDICAL SCIENCE: Ellis, H., *"Psychoanalysis in Relation to Sex,"* 63 (1917) 537-552.

11.390
PSYCHOANALYTIC QUARTERLY: Freud, S., *"Concerning the Sexuality of Women,"* 1 (1932) 191-209.

11.391
British Society for the Study of Sex Psychology, **POLICY AND PRINCIPLES: GENERAL AIMS.** 1920. Discussion of sex is considered as being on "equal footing."

11.392
Fielding, W.J., **SANITY IN SEX.** 1920; "The Art of Love" in **SEX IN CIVILIZATION.** ed. by Victor Frances Calverton and S.D. Schmalhausen. Garden City, 1929. "As sexual feeling in women is usually heightened during menstruation, the question not infrequently arises whether intercourse may be engaged in at this time. Sexual congress should be avoided during these periods. In the first place, it is unaesthetic and unhygienic; and in the second place it is apt to lead to congestion and disturbances of the uterus and other parts of the woman's genital system" (p. 644).

11.393
Summers, Montague, **THE MARQUIS DE SADE: A STUDY IN ALGOLAGNIA.** 1920. Publication no. 6 of the British Society for the Study of Sex Psychology. Algolagnia, or pleasure in inflicting and suffering pain, is derived from the Latin *algo* (pain) and *lagneia* (lust).

11.394
Knight, Melvin Moses, Peters, Iva Lowther and Blanchard, Phyllis, **TABOO AND GENETICS; A STUDY OF THE BIOLOGICAL, SOCIOLOGICAL AND PSYCHO-LOGICAL FOUNDATION OF THE FAMILY.** 1921. "The institutionalized forms of social control into which the old sex taboos have developed impose upon all members of the group a uniform type of sexual relationship. These socially enforced standards which govern the sex life are based upon the assumption that men and women conform closely to the masculine and feminine ideals of tradition. The emphasis is much more strongly placed on feminine conformity, however" (pp. 220-221).

11.395
Paul, Maurice Eden, **THE SEXUAL LIFE OF THE CHILD.** 1921. Publication no. 12 of the British Society for the Study of Sex Psychology.

11.396
Westermarck, Edvard Alexander, **THE ORIGIN OF SEXUAL MODESTY.** 1921. Publication no. 8 of the British Society for the Study of Sex Psychology; **THREE ESSAYS ON SEX AND MARRIAGE.** 1934. With bibliography.

11.397
Stekel, Wilhelm, **TWELVE ESSAYS ON SEX AND PSYCHOANALYSIS.** trans. and ed. by S.A. Tennenbaum. New York, 1922; **SADISM AND MASOCHISM.** New York, 1953. Supports the theories of Krafft-Ebing on sado-masochism. Cites case

histories.

11.398
THE SOCIAL PROBLEM OF SEXUAL INVERSION. 1923. Abridged translation of a 1903 German treatise published by the British Society for the Study of Sex Psychology.

11.399
Goldschmidt, R., **THE MECHANISM AND PHYSIOLOGY OF SEX DETERMINA-TION.** 1923.

11.400
Picton, Harold Williams, **THE MORBID, THE ABNORMAL AND THE PERSONAL.** 1923. Publication no. 12 of the British Society for the Study of Sex Psychology.

11.401
Bousfield, Paul, **SEX AND CIVILIZATION.** 1925. See especially: "Physiological Inefficiency in Woman and Its Remedy" and "Bi-Sexuality and Normal Sex Evolution." "Psychological research has shown that psychically we are even more bi-sexual than we are physically. An important instance is that when a woman is normally developed the pleasure obtained by her in any sexual encounter is centered chiefly in the nerves of the clitoris, i.e. in her so-called 'male' organ" (p. 88).

11.402
BRITISH JOURNAL OF MEDICAL PSYCHOLOGY: Hadfield, J.A., *"The Conception of Sexuality (I),"* 5 (1925) 161-174; Glover, J., *"The Conception of Sexuality (II),"* 5 (1925) 175-188; Shand, A.F., *"The Conception of Sexuality (III),"* 5 (1925) 189-195; Glover, J., *"The Conception of Sexuality (IV),"* 5 (1925) 196-207; Hadfield, J.A., *"The Conception of Sexuality (V),"* 5 (1925) 208-211. A discussion among Freudian analysts about the origins and development of human sexuality.

11.403
Calverton, Victor Frances and Schmalhausen, S.D., eds., **SEX IN CIVILIZATION.** introduction by Havelock Ellis. New York, 1929. Dedicated to "women struggling for sex emancipation and a better civilization." Valuable compendium of essays, of which the following are particularly important: "Should All Taboos Be Abolished?" by William McDougall. "It has long been recognized that the production of great art seems somehow related to the sex instinct.... If, then, we were all as sensitive to beauty and ugliness as Shelley and Byron and Dante, and if all women were as beautiful as Beatrice, we should need no sex taboos. But unfortunately the majority of us fall far short" (pp. 91-92); "Sex in Religion" by Robert Briffault. "The sentimental development of sexual love acquires... a greatly increased importance with reference to religion as this passes from the stage of primitive magic to the more philosophic and emotional phases of its development" (p. 50); "Sex in Dynamic Psychology" by A.A. Roback. "Dynamic psychology harbors sex radicals——and Freud is not the extremist among them——as well as Puritans, who like McDougall applaud the rigidity of the law against homosexuals" (p. 149); "The Art of Love" by William J. Fielding; and "Sex and Normal Human Nature" by Ira S. Wile.

11.404
Hirschfeld, Magnus, **THE SEXUAL HISTORY OF THE WORLD WAR.** New York, 1934. A study based on documents from World War I. Useful in shedding light on the transition from Victorian/Edwardian sexual mores. "The dammed-up instincts,

which had frequently broken through the moral repressions that were no longer regarded as sacred, rushed out in a veritable moral chaos which reached its peak... in the first post-war years (p. 21).... The female types which the war brought forth, must be judged from the erotic realm, even though they seem to draw life from the economic and social status only (p. 20).... It was quite clear that a considerable portion of the female nurses were impelled to nursing by quite other than patriotic and humanitarian motives" (p. 53).

11.405
Charles, Edward (pseud. for Edward Charles Hempstead), **AN INTRODUCTION TO THE STUDY OF THE PSYCHOLOGY AND PHYSIOLOGY AND BIO-CHEMISTRY OF THE SEXUAL IMPULSE AMONG ADULTS IN MENTAL AND BODILY HEALTH.** [1935].

11.406
Ploss, Hermann Heinrich, Bartels, Max and Bartels, Paul, **WOMAN: AN HISTORICAL GYNAECOLOGICAL AND ANTHROPOLOGICAL COMPENDIUM.** ed. by Eric Dingwall. vol. 1, 1935. Extremely rich and diverse cross-cultural material with an abundance of illustrations. Includes sections on development of sexuality, conceptions of feminine beauty, artificial culture of beauty, the sexual organs in folklore, castration of women, relationships between the sexes, and the anthropology of menstruation.

11.407
Bonaparte, Marie, **FEMALE SEXUALITY.** New York, 1953. Discusses female sexuality and sexual function from a Freudian perspective. "As Freud has so well shown in his paper FEMALE SEXUALITY (1931), women, it appears, may be divided into three main types, each of which responds, in its own way, to the traumatic shock that every little girl experiences on first realizing the differences between the sexes" (p. 1).

11.408
Keating, Walter S., **SEX STUDIES FROM FREUD TO KINSEY.** New York, 1954. See especially: "The Sex Impulse: An Examination of the Work of Sigmund Freud" and "Psychology of Sex: The Contribution of Havelock Ellis."

11.409
Brecher, Edward M., **THE SEX RESEARCHERS.** Boston, 1969. Includes chapters on Havelock Ellis and Sigmund Freud.

11.410
Nichols, Thomas Low, **ESOTERIC ANTHROPOLOGY (THE MYSTERIES OF MAN): A COMPREHENSIVE AND CONFIDENTIAL TREATISE ON THE STRUCTURE, FUNCTIONS, PASSIONAL ATTRACTIONS AND PERVERSIONS, TRUE AND FALSE PHYSICAL AND SOCIAL CONDITIONS, AND THE MOST INTIMATE RELATIONS OF MEN AND WOMEN.** 15th ed., n.d.; rpt., New York, 1972.

11.411
HISTORY OF CHILDHOOD QUARTERLY: Kern, S., *"Freud and the Discovery of Child Sexuality,"* 1 (1973) 117-141. Surveys the climate of thought regarding child sex development which preceded and influenced Freud in his formulation. "The sum of evidence that counters Freud's claim that he was the first to recognize the regular existence of sexuality in children is substantial. By 1905, statements affirming the existence of normal sexual feelings in children were made by

Maudsley, Perez, Sollier, Barnes, Dallemagne, Ribot, Dessoir, Bell, Ellis, and Terman" (p. 120).

11.412
Murstein, Bernard I., "Havelock Ellis and Sigmund Freud: Philosophers of Sex" in **LOVE, SEX AND MARRIAGE THROUGH THE AGES.** by Bernard I. Murstein. New York, 1974. Shows that "their very different life styles and personalities led them to favor certain views at the expense of other options... [and] that their findings stemmed, in part, from unresolved personal conflicts (in the case of Ellis) or the blinders which Viennese culture placed on otherwise acute observational powers (in the case of Freud)" (p. 282).

11.413
Kern, Stephen, **ANATOMY AND DESTINY: A CULTURAL HISTORY OF THE HUMAN BODY.** New York, 1975. See especially: "The Scientific Study of Sex" and "Sexual Pathology of Homosexuality." "The reintroduction of the sense of smell in human sexual life offered by Iwan Bloch and Havelock Ellis, and by implication Freud, were the direct historical consequence of Krafft-Ebing's exploration of this subject.... The idea that anal stimulation might be sexual was given elaboration in Krafft-Ebing's most disapproving account of it. Twenty years later, Freud only had to revise Krafft-Ebing's evaluation of this process to derive a large section of his own theory of the sexual significance of the anal region" (pp. 141-142); Also: "The Discovery of the Meaning of the Body" on the development of the idea of human corporeality; Also: "Pure Women and Superb Men." "There is some evidence... that beginning in the 1870's ideas started to change. One historian has concluded that 'although most doctors had denied or remained silent about the female orgasm, after 1870 it began to get objective consideration by a number of physicians.'" Clitoridectomy, first used in 1822 in Berlin, was popularised by a London surgeon as a treatment for excessive masturbation. Quoted from an 1881 medical encyclopedia: "'This operation had attracted much attention during the past few years, but although it has produced some favorable results when employed by conscientious surgeons, today it is not generally used. There is just too much evidence to show that the clitoris does not play either an exclusive or a preponderant role in orgasms'" (p. 102).

11.414
Seymour-Smith, Martin, **SEX AND SOCIETY.** 1975. See especially: "The Victorians and Sex" with a discussion of Krafft-Ebing, Hirschfeld, Carpenter and Ellis. Well written with interesting anecdotes.

11.415
Robinson, Paul A., "Havelock Ellis" and "Epilogue/Sexual Modernism and Romanticism" in **THE MODERNIZATION OF SEX: HAVELOCK ELLIS, ALFRED KINSEY, WILLIAM MASTERS, AND VIRGINIA JOHNSON.** by Paul A. Robinson. New York, 1976. "Against the Victorians, the modernists held that sexual experience was neither a threat to moral character nor a drain on vital energies... where the Victorians had all but denied woman a sexual existence, the modernists argued her sexual parity with the male, even at the risk of transforming her into an exclusively sexual being.... The central figure in the emergence of this modern sexual ethos was not Freud,... but rather Henry Havelock Ellis," whose STUDIES IN THE PSYCHOLOGY OF SEX "established the basic moral categories for nearly all subsequent sexual theorizing (p. 3).... Havelock Ellis is the most unambiguously Romantic of the great modernists... a proper affair, in his opinion, was a matter of the heart, not merely of the flesh" (p. 194).

11.416
HISTORY WORKSHOP JOURNAL: Rowbotham, S., *"In Search of Carpenter,"* no.
3 (1977) 121-133. Quotes Carpenter: "Too long have women acted the part of mere
appendages to the male, suppressing their own individuality and fostering their self-
conceit" (p. 127).

11.417
Martin, John Rutledge, "Sexuality and Science: Victorian and Post-Victorian
Scientific Ideas on Sexuality," Ph.D. diss., Duke Univ., 1978. See especially:
"Havelock Ellis and the Post-Victorian Synthesis: Normality is Destiny."

11.418
JOURNAL OF HOMOSEXUALITY: Faderman, L., *"The Morbidification of Love
Between Women by Nineteenth Century Sexologists,"* 4 (1978) 73-89.

11.419
Brewer, Joan Scherer and Wright, Rod W., compilers, **SEX RESEARCH: BIBLIO-
GRAPHIES FROM THE INSTITUTE FOR SEX RESEARCH.** Phoenix, 1979.
Collection of over 34,000 entries. Emphasizes modern works.

11.420
Fineman, Joel, "Psychoanalysis, Bisexuality, and the Difference Before the Sexes" in
PSYCHOSEXUAL IMPERATIVES: THEIR ROLE IN IDENTITY FORMATION.
ed. by Marie Coleman Nelson and Jean Ikenberry. New York, 1979. "When it was
discovered in the middle of the nineteenth century that the urogenital systems of
the two sexes derive from a common embryonic origin, the elegant hypothesis of
human bisexuality seemed once and for all to have been established as biological
fact (p. 109)... These speculations... define the quasi-scientific ambience within
which Freud began to work out his own understanding of human sexuality and
gender" (p. 111).

11.421
FEMINIST STUDIES: Benjamin, J., *"The Bonds of Love: Rational Violence and
Erotic Domination,"* 6 (1980) 144-174. Uses THE STORY OF O to demonstrate ways
in which sadomasochism and erotic domination derive from male identity
formation, which relies on differentiation from and repudiation of the mother.
Argues that differentiation of the self can be understood alternatively as mutual
recognition, and discusses the political and social ramifications of such a paradigm.

11.422
NEW YORK: Comfort, A., *"Oh! Pioneers! A Review of HAVELOCK ELLIS by
Phyllis Grosskurth and FREUD, THE MAN AND THE CAUSE by Ronald W. Clark,"*
n.v. (1980) 55-56. "Both saw sexuality veiled in nonsensical fig leaves at great cost
in human suffering. If pulling off fig leaves is a human compulsion going back to
the curiosities of toddlerhood, no matter the project was worthwhile in itself, and
we are in their debt for our diminished anxieties" (p. 56).

11.423
SEX RESEARCH: EARLY LITERATURE FROM STATISTICS TO EROTICA.
Woodbridge, 1981; 1983.

11.424
Brake, Mike, ed., **HUMAN SEXUAL RELATIONS.** 1982. Discusses early sexology.

11.425
Farley, John, **GAMETES AND SPORES: IDEAS ABOUT SEXUAL REPRODUCTION, 1750-1914.** 1982. Includes prevailing concepts of male and female roles in the reproductive process.

11.426
Jackson, Margaret, "Sexology and the Social Construction of Male Sexuality (Havelock Ellis)" in **THE SEXUALITY PAPERS: MALE SEXUALITY AND THE SOCIAL CONTROL OF WOMEN.** 1984. ed. by Lal Coveney, Margaret Jackson, Sheila Jeffreys, Leslie Kay, Pat Maloney. Reviews some recent socialist and radical feminist appraisals and critiques of Ellis' work. Then goes on to survey and critique some of Ellis' most important ideas on homosexuality, fluctuation of feminine sexuality according to the menstrual cycle, the legitimation of male sexuality, sado-masochism and abstinence. Also see subsequent chapter in the book, "Sexology and the Universalization of Male Sexuality (From Ellis to Kinsey, and Masters and Johnson)," also by Margaret Jackson.

11.427
Bejin, Andre, "The Decline of the Psycho-Analyst and the Rise of the Sexologist" in **WESTERN SEXUALITY: PRACTICE AND PRECEPT IN PAST AND PRESENT TIMES.** ed. by Philippe Aries and Andre Bejin. trans. by Anthony Forster. Oxford, 1985. Differentiates between the sexology represented by Krafft-Ebing in the late 1800s which was concerned with sexual aberrations, and the newer sexology beginning in the 1920s, that emphasized therapeutics. "It is precisely because they have managed to confront the psycho-analysts over the question of therapeutic success that the sexologists are on their way to winning a probably decisive advantage" (p. 184).

11.428
Weeks, Jeffrey, "'Nature Had Nothing to Do With It': The Role of Sexology" in **SEXUALITY AND ITS DISCONTENTS: MEANINGS, MYTHS AND MODERN SEXUALITIES.** 1985. Though sexology constructed limiting definitions of individuals, "it also put into language a host of definitions and meanings which could be played with, challenged, negated, and used. Against its intentions usually, countering its expectations often, sexology did contribute to the self-definition of those subjected to its power of definition" (p. 95).

* * *

5. EARLY TWENTIETH-CENTURY PSYCHOANALYSIS: ORIGINAL WORKS AND HISTORIES

First and foremost, Freud was the discoverer of the first instrument for the scientific examination of the human mind. Creative writers of genius had had fragmentary insight into mental processes, but no systematic method of investigation existed before Freud.... The forgotten trauma in... hysteria provided the earliest problem and perhaps the most fundamental of all, for it showed conclusively that there were active parts of the mind not immediately open to inspection either by an onlooker or by the subject himself. These parts of the mind were described by Freud... as the unconscious (pp. xii-xiii).

Thus James Strachey introduces the starting point from which Sigmund Freud was to develop psychoanalysis as an instrument for research into the power of the unconscious in mental life:

11.429
Strachey, James, "Sigmund Freud: A Sketch of his Life and Ideas," introduction to **ON THE HISTORY OF THE PSYCHO-ANALYTIC MOVEMENT** by Sigmund Freud. rev. and ed. by James Strachey. trans. by Joan Riviere. 1962; New York, 1967.

Freud only gradually developed his methods, interpretations and theories of psychoanalysis. In the 1880s he completed his medical studies, conducted research and published work on biology, specialized in neurology, followed this interest into work with Jean-Martin Charcot at the Salpetriere (hospital for nervous diseases) in Paris, turned his attention to studying the nervous disorder, hysteria, and practiced hypnosis in its treatment. Work with neurologist Joseph Breuer on cathartic hypnosis, including its application to the famous case of "Anna O.," revealed the suffering from hidden unacceptable ideas. Breuer and Freud formulated the idea that hysterical patients suffer from the repressed memory of upsetting——perhaps traumatic——events that could not be acknowledged at the time they occurred. They concluded that the forgotten events as well as the manifest symptoms associated with hysteria had to be given free expression. Together they published an early landmark in the history of psychoanalysis:

11.430
Breuer, Joseph and Freud, Sigmund, **STUDIES ON HYSTERIA.** trans. by A.A. Brill from the 1895 German edition. New York, 1912; also trans. by James Strachey in collaboration with Anna Freud. New York, 1957; *also printed in:* **STANDARD EDITION OF THE COMPLETE WORKS OF SIGMUND FREUD.** ed. and trans. by James Strachey. New York, 1966.

Freud continued these studies alone, soon investigating, discovering, and analyzing the meaning of the phenomenon of "transference":——the patient's emotional involvement with the doctor. With the understanding of transference, "psychoanalysis as a therapeutic approach became established." See:

11.431
Alexander, Franz G. and Selesnick, Sheldon T., "Freud's Scientific Evolution" in **THE HISTORY OF PSYCHIATRY: AN EVALUATION OF PSYCHIATRIC THOUGHT AND PRACTICE FROM PREHISTORIC TIMES TO THE PRESENT.** New York, 1966.

Hysteria and other nervous disorders had been treated by both neurologists and medical psychologists/psychiatrists as a largely somatic problem and therefore considered in the context of physiological ailments by the majority of medical men. Freud broke with medical psychology, and set psychoanalytic research into the category of psychology rather than medicine. See:

11.432
Freud, Sigmund, "The Question of Lay Analysis" in **STANDARD EDITION OF THE COMPLETE PSYCHOLOGICAL WORKS OF SIGMUND FREUD**. ed. and trans. by James Strachey. New York, 1966. Written 1926. Freud had held these opinions since the turn of the century.

> In his medical school a doctor receives a training which is more or less the opposite of what he would need as a preparation for psychoanalysis.... His interest is not aroused in the mental side of vital phenomena... [It] is supposed to deal with the disturbances of mental functions.... It looks for the somatic determinants of mental disorders and treats them like other causes of illness (pp. 230-231).

See also:

11.433
Freud, Sigmund, "Postscript to Discussion on Lay Analysis" in **THE HISTORY OF THE PSYCHOANALYTIC MOVEMENT AND OTHER PAPERS**. ed. by Philip Rieff. New York, 1963. Written 1927.

11.434
Freud, Sigmund, "Psycho-Analysis and Psychiatry" in **INTRODUCTORY LEC-TURES ON PSYCHOANALYSIS**. ed. and trans. by James Strachey. New York, 1966. Written 1916-1917. Freud explains:

> Psychiatry does not employ the technical methods of psycho-analysis; it omits to make any inferences from the *content* of a delusion, and, in pointing to heredity, it gives us a very general and remote aetiology instead of indicating first the more special and proximate causes.... Psycho-analysis is related to psychiatry approximately as histology is to anatomy: the one studies the external forms of the organs, the other studies their construction out of tissues and cells.... It is to be expected that in the not too distant future it will be realized that a scientifically based psychiatry is not possible without a sound knowledge of the deeper-lying unconscious process of mental life (pp. 254-255).

Freud was very knowledgeable about contemporary thought: the concepts, methodologies and findings of researchers in the human and social sciences. There is little doubt of their influence on psychoanalysis, particularly the impact of Darwin and evolutionary biology. There were the developing fields of association psychology; anthropology; sexology; and sociology. Not to be overlooked is Freud's interest in literature and history. Freud knew ancient theory as he had been "steeped in the study of antiquity." See:

11.435
Fine, Reuben, **A HISTORY OF PSYCHOANALYSIS**. New York, 1979. This book is extremely useful for the context of relevant past and contemporary thought. Fine traces the development of psychoanalysis from its inception to the present.

Antecedents of Freud's views should be kept in mind in everything that follows. Much has been made of Freud's biological bias, but it has been overlooked that his biology and neurology were not original at all; it was his psychology that was revolutionary.... In terms of the future course of psychoanalysis, the most significant paper of... [the 1890s] was "The Defense of Neuropsychoses" (1894).... [introducing] the idea, ever since fundamental, that all neurosis involves a [psychological] defense against unbearable ideas. In one sense much of the history of psychoanalysis can be viewed as an elaboration and clarification of this formula (pp. 24-25).

11.436

Sulloway, Frank, J. **FREUD, BIOLOGIST OF THE MIND: BEYOND THE PSYCHOANALYTIC LEGEND.** New York, 1979. Makes an important contribution toward comprehending Freud's work in the context of other researches in the human sciences—particularly the nascent "science of sex," sexology. Sulloway evaluates the influence of the work of Havelock Ellis, Richard von Krafft-Ebbing, Magnus Hirschfield, P.J. Mobius, Albert Moll and others on Freud's work and his upon theirs. Sulloway contends that Freud remains one of the most misunderstood thinkers in the history of Western thought, and he offers an "intellectual biography" that elucidates Freud's scientific career. He includes a detailed section on contemporary reception as well as opposition to Freud's work on the continent and in England. He explains the differences between continental and English reaction to Freud's ideas, asserting that Ernest Jones describes only the "peculiar" English reaction. See:

11.437

Jones, Ernest, **FREE ASSOCIATIONS: MEMORIES OF A PSYCHO-ANALYST.** New York, 1959. Jones, a young London neurologist, read Freud's work in German in 1898 and "came away with the deep impression of there being a man in Vienna who actually listened with attention to every word his patients said to him.... Here for the first time was a man who took a scientific interest in them.... a man who was seriously interested in investigating the mind" (pp. 159-160). Jones became Freud's first English adherent and psychoanalyst in England. In his autobiography Jones records the inhospitable attitudes that were expressed about Freud by medical specialists in neurology, and medical psychology/psychiatry.

The whole attack was on... a vulgar and non-intellectual level: no scientific arguments were to be found. Since the libido theory played a central part in the psychoanalytical doctrine, the whole range of sexual bawdiness was opened up... What a loathsome atmosphere it all was! I was simply staggered to discover to what depths men of scientific standing could descend when their unconscious minds were stirred by new teachings (p. 225).

Freud began to publish his findings on sexual factors just subsequent to his work on hysteria and the unconscious. For the chronological details see also:

11.438

Jones, Ernest, **THE LIFE AND WORK OF SIGMUND FREUD.** 3 vols. New York, 1953-1957.

Freud constantly revised his methods of investigation, interpretation, theory and treatment. Fine and Sulloway explain how, from about 1886 to 1900, Freud worked on documenting unconscious phenomena from cases of hysteria. He also made an intensive investigation and documentation of dreams that brought him to his theory of dream interpretation. This work was related also to his intensive "self-analysis" (1897) from which he reconstructed the libidinal emotions of his childhood—including incestuous feelings about his mother, aggressive attitudes toward his father, rivalry with his brothers——that formed the basis of his theory of the Oedipus complex which he then identified within the nucleus of all neurotic problems.

Frank Sulloway describes the reaction to Freud's revelation of infantile sexuality and the Oedipus complex in his chapter, "Evolutionary Biology Resolves Freud's Three Psychoanalytic Problems, (1905-1939)" in FREUD, BIOLOGIST OF THE MIND (cited above):

> Readers... were both shocked and fascinated by what he had to say... that sexuality is the one and only *specific* cause of neurosis. 'None of the theses of psycho-analysis,' Freud frankly confessed in 1923, 'has met with such tenacious scepticism or such embittered resistance as this assertion of the preponderating aetiological significance of sexual life in the neuroses' (pp. 375-376).

Freud had manifested his findings in his early publications:

11.439
Freud, Sigmund, "Sexuality in the Aetiology of the Neurosis" in **COLLECTED PAPERS.** vol. 1, trans. by Joan Riviere. New York, 1959. Written 1898. Links sexual experiences, frustrations and practices considered perverse (masturbation, types of coitus, etc.) with neurasthenia and other psychoneurosis.

11.440
Freud, Sigmund, "My Views on the Part Played by Sexuality in the Aetiology of the Neurosis" in **COLLECTED PAPERS.** vol. 1, trans. by Joan Riviere. New York, 1959. Written in 1905. Opened the subject of bisexuality.

11.441
Freud, Sigmund, **THREE ESSAYS ON THE THEORY OF SEXUALITY.** ed. and trans. by James Strachey. 1962. New York, 1965. Written 1905. Here Freud broadens the concept of sexuality, extending it to include all physical pleasure as well as affection, love, and the tender emotions. The term "psychosexual" comes into use.

These newer concepts of sexuality led to a revised framework of neurosis which Freud included in his libido theory. By 1915 he largely abandoned the direct sexual theory of neurosis in favor of the concept of an individual's "instinctual drives," and the supposition that "the ego"——another new concept——was libidinally charged. Of course Freud's investigations and conclusions went against the current of dominant Victorian codes and culture, especially placing sexual matters at the center of both neurotic and normal psychology, and by insisting that sexual life should be a subject for consideration by medical as well as psychological specialists. By the turn of the century, however, at least *avant garde* intellectuals were attuned to Freud's work. See:

11.442
Glover, Edward, "Psychoanalysis in England" in **PSYCHOANALYTIC PIONEERS.** ed. by Franz Alexander, Samuel Eisenstein, and Martin Grotjahn. New York, 1966. The influence of cultural groups had been far greater than professional groups in circulating knowledge of psychoanalysis. "By the early twenties, few Cambridge

undergraduates having any pretensions to advanced thought failed to profess an interest in Freudian psychology" (p. 535).

Intellectual, social and moral implications of Freudian psychoanalysis are the special concern of:

11.443
Rieff, Philip, **FREUD: THE MIND OF THE MORALIST.** New York, 1959. In his chapter, "Sexuality and Domination," Rieff raises the question of Freud's concepts of sexual difference and his unequal considerations of male and female neurotic patients:

> By insisting that the emotions generated in an analysis are part of the analytic *situation* and arise without regard to the individual personalities of either patient or physician, Freud seems to say that it does not matter who is involved: certain characteristic erotic responses will occur. Yet it made a great difference to Freud, as therapist, who was being analyzed——whether male or female. Not so much in his case histories as in his theoretical remarks, Freud shows condescension toward his female patients. The mental evolution which he traces through childhood is invariably predicated of the boy-child; he usually adds that the same mechanism (with the appropriate reversal of parental objects) applies to the little girl——in simpler and less assertive form (pp. 173-174).

Rieff details Freud's "special attitude toward women" showing how misogynistic elements permeated his psychoanalytical explanations. That is, the masculine/feminine dichotomy helped him to exemplify the sexual meaning he ascribed even to objects. (see especially pp. 176-183). Rieff says,

> His misogyny, like that of his predecessors, is more than prejudice; it has a vital intellectual function in his system. In the nineteenth century strong links, the forging of which have not yet been closely studied, existed between irrationalist philosophy and misogyny. Freud's views echo those of Schopenhauer... and Nietzsche.... Neo-Freudians (led by eminent women analysts like Karen Horney) would like to omit that part of Freud's work as mere culture-prejudice.... But actually the pejorative image of woman serves as a measure of the general critical component in Western philosophies" (p. 182).

Freud's tenets about feminine inferiority include the idea that men have higher claims to culture building while women represent family and sexual life; that women are congenitally passive; and that women express the primal and static while men exude dynamism. One of the most controversial is women's "castration complex"——also described as her "penis envy." Perhaps the most clear of Freud's statements on the masculine/feminine dichotomy is his paper that summarizes his findings to 1931:

11.444
Freud, Sigmund, "Femininity" in **NEW INTRODUCTORY LECTURES ON PSYCHOANALYSIS.** ed. and trans. by James Strachey. New York, 1965-1966. Written 1931.

> Unless we can find something that is specific for girls and is not present or not in the same way present in boys, we shall not have explained the

termination of the attachment of girls to their mother. I believe we have found this specific factor, and indeed where we expected to find it.... for it lies in the castration complex. After all, the anatomical distinction [between the sexes] must express itself in psychical consequences (p. 110).... One cannot very well doubt the importance of envy for the penis.... The discovery that she is castrated is a turning point in a girl's growth.... The little girl has hitherto lived in a masculine way, has been able to get pleasure by the excitation of her clitoris and has brought this activity into relation with her sexual wishes directed towards her mother, which are often active ones; now, owing to the influence of her penis-envy, she loses her enjoyment in her phallic sexuality (pp. 111-112).... We are now struck by a difference between the two sexes... in regard to the relation of the Oedipus complex to the castration complex.... The formation of the super-ego must suffer... and feminists are not pleased when we point out to them the effects of this factor upon the average feminine character (p. 114).

Since Freud considered women to be intellectually inferior to men, what is to be made of Freud's close, respectful and professional relationships with the women analysts whom he trained and with whom he worked for so many years? First, he identified them as above average. Second, he made it clear that they nurtured his continuing queries into questions of female passivity and intellectuality. Freud promoted the work of these women and admitted that he incorporated their contributions into his thinking. In "Femininity" (above) he writes:

Since the subject is woman, I will venture on this occasion to mention by name a few of the women who have made valuable contributions to this investigation. Dr. Ruth Mack Brunswick [1928] was the first to describe a case of neurosis which went back to a fixation in the pre-Oedipus stage and had never reached the Oedipus situation at all.... Dr. Jeanne Lampl-de Groot [1927] has established the incredible phallic activity of girls towards their mother by some assured observations, and Dr. Helene Deutsch [1932] has shown that the erotic actions of homosexual women reproduce the relations between mother and baby (p. 115).

These women analysts are known to have consistently followed their mentor's teachings. Perhaps their writings should be evaluated in terms of their intellectual dependence upon him and their consistent physical proximity within his circle. See:

11.445
Roazen, Paul, "The Women" in **FREUD AND HIS FOLLOWERS**. New York, 1975. The discussion includes: Ruth Mack Brunswick: "The Rabbi May" and "Dependency and Addiction"; Anna Freud: "Child Analysis" and "Ladies in Waiting" and "Ego Psychology"; Helene Deutsch: "The Theory of Femininity"; Melanie Klein, "The English School." Roazen also discusses other women analysts in Freud's menage—for example, Princess Marie Bonaparte.

Freud encouraged the transference Marie had set up toward him. She fit into the category of those beautiful and narcissistic women for whom Freud seems to have had a special fascination.... In the inner circle around Freud, Princess Marie was one of the prime figures. She and Ruth Brunswick were the closest to Freud.... Over summers, these women——Marie Bonaparte, Ruth Brunswick, Dorothy Burlingham, Eva Rosenfeld——formed a colony around Freud (p. 451).

Freud ramified his theory of female inferiority by employing in "Femininity" (p.

114) the term "*average* feminine character" (my italics). He seems also to have wavered about having come to the last word on this subject. For example, in 1908 he made allowances for the cultural, rather than psychobiological, suppression of mental growth:

11.446
Freud, Sigmund, "'Civilized' Sexuality and Modern Nervousness" in **COLLECTED PAPERS**. ed. by Ernest Jones. trans. by Joan Riviere. vol. 2, New York, 1959. Written in 1908.

> A particular application of the general statement that the course of the sexual life is typical for the way in which other functions are exercised is easily demonstrable in the entire female sex. Their training excludes them from occupying themselves intellectually with sexual problems, in regard to which naturally they have the greatest thirst for knowledge, and terrifies them with the pronouncement that such curiosity is unwomanly and a sign of immoral tendencies. And thus they are thoroughly intimidated from all mental effort, and knowledge in general is depreciated in their eyes. The prohibition of thought extends beyond the sexual sphere.... I do not support Mobius in the view he has put forward, which has met with so much opposition, that the biological contrast between intellectual work and sexual activity explains the 'physiological mental weakness' of women. On the contrary, I think that the undoubted fact of the intellectual inferiority of so many women can be traced to that inhibition of thought necessitated by sexual suppression (p. 94).

In 1931, he was still wavering somewhat when he ended "Femininity":

> That is all I have to say to you about femininity. It is certainly incomplete and fragmentary and does not always sound friendly. But... I have only been describing women in so far as their nature is determined by their sexual function.... But we do not overlook the fact that an individual woman may be a human being in other respects as well. If you want to know more about femininity, enquire from your own experiences of life, or turn to the poets, or wait until science can give you deeper and more coherent information (p. 119).

The question of women's nature and status *vis-a-vis* men's has persisted into the twentieth century as a matter of scientific and social debate. To some extent Freud's contribution has worked toward proving gender equality in terms of libidinous drives, thereby influencing relaxation of most nineteenth-century myths in matters of sexual/emotional makeup and behavior. Nevertheless, Freud's early construct of innate feminine psychological difficulties and consequent inferiority— however tentatively they were sometimes expressed——appears to have merged with other Victorian social science theories in a way that has retarded acceptance of an alternative theory of full gender equality in both intellectual and social spheres.

The histories, theoretical works and critical writings listed below should help to illuminate the development of Freudian psychology during the Victorian/Edwardian period. They should also assist in re-evaluating the teachings of psychoanalysis relative to the male/female dichotomy from a female-centered perspective.

11.447
Freud, Sigmund, **SELECTED PAPERS ON HYSTERIA AND OTHER**

PSYCHONEUROSES. trans. by A.A. Brill. 1909; *reviewed in:* **LANCET:** 1 (1913) 1105; **THREE CONTRIBUTIONS TO SEXUAL THEORY**. orig. ed., 1905; trans. by A.A. Brill. 1910; New York, 1938; *also published as:* **THREE ESSAYS ON THE THEORY OF SEXUALITY**. ed. and trans. by James Strachey. 1949; 1962. The three essays are: "The Sexual Aberrations," "Infantile Sexuality," and "The Transformations of Puberty." Also includes an appendix list of writings by Freud dealing predominantly with sexuality; **ON CREATIVITY AND THE UNCONSCIOUS**. trans. by Joan Riviere. 1912; New York, 1958; **PSYCHOPATHOLOGY OF EVERYDAY LIFE**. 1914; **NEW INTRODUCTORY LECTURES ON PSYCHOANALYSIS**. trans. by W.J.H. Sprott. New York, 1933. See especially: "The Psychology of Women"; **AN AUTOBIOGRAPHICAL STUDY**. orig. German ed., 1934; New York and London, 1935; **FREUD: ON WAR, SEX AND NEUROSIS**. New York, 1947. Selection of essays, with glossary; **THE STANDARD EDITION OF THE COMPLETE PSYCHOLOGICAL WORKS OF SIGMUND FREUD**. 24 vols. trans. and ed. by James Strachey. 1953-1974. Vol. 7 contains the famous case of Dora, "Fragment of an Analysis of a Case of Hysteria"; **THE ORIGINS OF PSYCHOANALYSIS. LETTERS TO WILHELM FLIESS; DRAFTS AND NOTES, 1887-1902**. ed. by Marie Bonaparte, Anna Freud and Ernst Kris. introduction by Steven Marcus. New York, 1954; **THE INTERPRETATION OF DREAMS**. ed. and trans. by James Strachey. 1956. "All the material making up the content of a dream is in some way derived from experience" (p. 11); **COLLECTED PAPERS**. 5 vols. 1st American ed., New York, 1959. Vols. 1 and 2 trans. by Joan Riviere, vol. 3 trans. by Alix Strachey and James Strachey, vol. 4 trans. by Joan Riviere, vol. 5 trans. by James Strachey. In vol. 1, see especially: "Sexuality in the Aetiology of the Neuroses" (1898) and "My Views on the Part Played by Sexuality in the Aetiology of the Neuroses" (1905). The first is a defense of the psycho-analytical study of sex, with emphasis on clinical practice. "Neither is it true that patients themselves raise insuperable objections to an investigation of their sexual life. After some slight hesitation, grown-up persons usually adjust themselves to the situation by saying: 'I am at the doctor's; I can say anything to him.' Numerous women who find it difficult enough to go through life with the task of concealing their sexual feelings are relieved to find that to the physician their recovery is the paramount issue, and are grateful to him for allowing them for once to behave quite naturally in regard to sexual matters" (p. 223). In vol. 2, see especially: "The Sexual Enlightenment of Children" (1907). A letter to an editor in which Freud wholeheartedly advocates providing sexual information to children, at the proper time and in a proper manner; "Character and Anal Erotism" (1908); "Hysterical Phantasies and their Relation to Bisexuality" (1908); "On the Sexual Theories of Children" (1908). Via evidence from adult neurotics' testimony as well as his observation of children, Freud makes this basic statement: "It is my conviction that no child——none, at least, who is mentally sound, still less none who is mentally gifted——can avoid being occupied with sexual problems in the years *before* puberty" (p. 60); "'Civilized' Sexual Morality and Modern Nervousness" (1908); "On the Transformation of Instincts with Special Reference to Anal Erotism" (1916); "'A Child is Being Beaten' A Contribution to the Study of the Origin of Sexual Perversions" (1919); "The Psychogenesis of a Case of Homosexuality in a Woman" (1920). Freud explains the case-study's lesbianism as a frustrated Oedipal desire for her mother and for the role of mother, resulting in repudiation of "her wish for a child, the love of a man, and womanhood altogether" (p. 215); "Certain Neurotic Mechanisms in Jealousy, Paranoia and Homosexuality" (1922); "The Infantile Genital Organization of the Libido. A Supplement to the Theory of Sexuality" (1923); "The Economic Problem in Masochism" (1924). A revision of the pleasure principle theory based on the anomaly of masochism. Freud discusses the three basic kinds of masochism: erotogenic, feminine, and moral; "The Passing of the Oedipus Complex" (1924). In vol. 3, see especially: "Fragment of an Analysis of a Case of Hysteria"

(1905). Dora's famous case of hysteria, including accounts of her two dreams; "Analysis of a Phobia in a Five Year-old Boy" (1909). The case of Little Hans. In vol. 4, see especially: "Contributions to the Psychology of Love: The Most Prevalent Form of Degradation in Erotic Life" (1912); "Contributions to the Psychology of Love: The Taboo of Virginity" (1918). Freud discusses the emphasis on a bride's virginity as a characteristic of the "sexual life of primitive races," then moves on to a general discussion of frigidity. In vol. 5, see especially: "The Libido Theory" (1922). The second half of an article on psychoanalysis. Deals particularly with the sexual instincts as opposed to the ego instincts; "Some Psychological Consequences of the Anatomical Distinction Between the Sexes" (1925). Further refining of theories of childhood sexuality; "Fetishism" (1927). "Probably no male human being is spared the terrifying shock of threatened castration at the sight of the female genitals. We cannot explain why it is that some of them become homosexual in consequence of this experience, others ward it off by creating a fetish, and the great majority overcome it" (p. 201); "Libidinal Types" (1931); "Female Sexuality" (1931). The pre-Oedipal stage in women is shown to be more important than previously supposed. The famous dependence upon the father in women is viewed as "merely" a replacement for this attachment to the mother, which Freud decides is longer-lasting than he had anticipated; **LETTERS OF SIGMUND FREUD, 1873-1939.** ed. by Ernst L. Freud. trans. by Tania Stern and James Stern. 1961; **ON THE HISTORY OF THE PSYCHOANALYTIC MOVEMENT.** trans. by Joan Riviere. revised and ed. by James Strachey. New York, 1962; 1966; 1967. Includes a sketch of Freud's life and ideas and a chronological table; **THE HISTORY OF THE PSYCHOANALYTIC MOVEMENT AND OTHER PAPERS.** ed. by Philip Rieff. New York, 1963; 4th ed., 1972. Freud's personal account relating public response to the sexual theories he proposed. "This is a work of determined self-interest, to exclude, on his own terms, those among his disciples who had already departed on terms he could no longer permit to be theirs... the HISTORY is a masterpiece of polemic" (p. 9); **CHARACTER AND CULTURE: A COLLECTION OF PAPERS BY SIGMUND FREUD.** ed. by Philip Rieff. New York, 1963; 1972. See especially: "The Resistances to Psychoanalysis." "Society refuses to consent to the ventilation of the question because it has a bad conscience.... It has set up a high ideal of morality... and insists that all its members shall fulfill that ideal without troubling itself with the possibility that obedience may bear heavily upon the individual" (p. 259); **SEXUALITY AND THE PSYCHOLOGY OF LOVE.** ed. by Philip Rieff. New York, 1963; **DORA—AN ANALYSIS OF A CASE OF HYSTERIA.** ed. by Philip Rieff. New York, 1971; **A GENERAL INTRODUCTION TO PSYCHOANALYSIS.** trans. by Joan Riviere. New York, 1972; **THE FREUD-JUNG LETTERS.** ed. by W. McGuire. 1974; **ON SEXUALITY.** Harmondsworth, 1977. See especially: "On the Universal Tendency to Debasement in the Sphere of Love"; **THE COMPLETE LETTERS OF SIGMUND FREUD TO WILHELM FLIESS, 1887-1904.** ed. and trans. by Jeffrey Moussaieff Masson. 1985. With list of principal works cited, and subject index that includes Freud's references to symptoms of various neuroses in women.

11.448

Nunberg, Herman and Federn, Ernst, eds., **MINUTES OF VIENNA PSYCHO-ANALYTIC SOCIETY.** vol. 1, 1906-1908; vol. 2, 1908-1910; vol. 3, 1910-1911.

11.449

Hart, Bernard (and other contributors), **SUBCONSCIOUS PHENOMENA.** 1911; **THE PSYCHOLOGY OF INSANITY.** 1912. Objectifies "prudery" and other Victorian attitudes and interprets, in psychological terms, the phenomena behind them. Represents the beginning of modern psychological explanation; **THE MODERN TREATMENT OF MENTAL AND NERVOUS DISORDERS.** 1918;

PSYCHOPATHOLOGY, ITS DEVELOPMENT AND ITS PLACE IN MEDICINE.
Cambridge, 1927; 2nd ed., 1929.

11.450
BRAIN: Ormerod, J.A., *"Two Theories of Hysteria,"* 33 (1911) 269-287. Believes that psychoanalysis, if it means the freedom of suppressed sexual ideas, might hurt patients more than heal them; Hart, B., *"Freud's Conception of Hysteria,"* 33 (1911) 339-366. Summary of Freud's concepts and methodology.

11.451
Miller, H.C., **HYPNOTISM AND DISEASE. A PLEA FOR RATIONAL PSYCHO-THERAPY.** 1912.

11.452
BRITISH MEDICAL JOURNAL: Ash, E.L., *"Treatment of Neurasthenia,"* 1 (1913) 390; Glynn, T.R., *"The Bradshaw Lecture on Hysteria in Some of its Aspects,"* 2 (1913) 1193-1198; *"Report: A Paper by Dr. Yates on 'Some Recent Conceptions of Hysteria,'"* 1 (1913) 825-826.

11.453
PSYCHOANALYTIC REVIEW: November 1913; vol. 1; published by the National Psychological Association for Psychoanalysis; title varies: 1958-1962; absorbed **PSYCHOANALYSIS:** Spring/Summer 1958; Jung, C.G., *"The Theory of Psychoanalysis,"* 1 (1913) 1-40; 153-186; 415-430. Continued in a subsequent volume; Emerson, L.E., *"The Case of Miss A: A Preliminary Report of a Psychoanalytic Study and Treatment of a Case of Self-Mutilation,"* 1 (1913) 41-54; Jung, C.G., *"Letter From Dr. Jung,"* 1 (1913) 117-118. In this inauguration issue, Jung describes the current state of the science of psychology and what psychoanalysis has to offer to the discipline. He expects this journal to "fill the gap that the existing forms of psychology have rendered painfully evident. Each of these forms deals with a special domain, such as philosophical psychology, which is largely transcendental, experimental or physiological psychology, which has been accused, not without cause, of being physiology rather than psychology, and medical psychology, which through the psychoanalytic method of Freud has now come to encroach freely upon the domain of normal psychology. The complex psychic phenomena are left practically unexplained by the first two forms of psychology, whereas the psychoanalytic method of medical psychology has started a line of inquiry which would seem to have a general range of application" (p. 117).

11.454
Jones, Ernest, **PAPERS ON PSYCHOANALYSIS.** 1913; rev. and enlarged ed., New York, 1919; Boston, 1961. Jones was the major British proponent of the Freudian school and an intimate associate of Freud. See especially: "The Early Development of Female Sexuality" (1927) and "The Phallic Phase" (1932); **THE LIFE AND WORK OF SIGMUND FREUD.** 3 vols. New York, 1953-1957. In volume 1, chap. 9, "Personal Life," appears an extract from a letter of Freud to Martha Bernays concerning J.S. Mill: "He lacked in many matters the sense of the absurd; for example, in that of female emancipation and in the woman's question altogether.... His autobiography is so prudish or so ethereal that one could never gather from it that human beings consist of men and women and that this distinction is the most significant one that exists.... He finds the suppression of women an analogy to that of negroes. Any girl, even without a suffrage or legal competence, whose hand a man kisses and for whose love he is prepared to dare all, could have set him right... Nature has determined woman's destiny through beauty, charm, and sweetness. Law and custom have much to give women that has been withheld from them, but the

position of women will surely be what it is: in youth an adored darling and in mature years a loved wife" (pp. 166-167); **FREE ASSOCIATIONS: MEMORIES OF A PSYCHOANALYST.** New York, 1959. "Freud himself once said to me that the simplest way of learning psychoanalysis was to believe that all he wrote was true and then, after understanding it, one could criticize it in any way one wished" (p. 204).

11.455
Brill, A.A., **PSYCHANALYSIS [SIC]: ITS THEORIES AND PRACTICAL APPLICATION.** Philadelphia, 1914.

11.456
PRACTITIONER: Long, C.E., *"Psychoanalysis,"* 93 (1914) 84-97. Praises psychoanalysis as a valuable method for dealing with cases of hysteria and other obsessions.

11.457
PROCEEDINGS OF THE FIRST INTERNATIONAL CONFERENCE OF WOMEN PHYSICIANS: Long, C.E., *"Fantasy in the Child and the Authority Complex,"* 3 (1919) 128-149; Long, C.E., *"A Psychoanalytic Study of the Basis of Character,"* 4 (1919) 67-82.

11.458
Bjerre, Poul Carl, **THE HISTORY AND PRACTICE OF PSYCHANALYSIS [SIC].** 1920.

11.459
Long, Constance Ellen, **COLLECTED PAPERS ON THE PSYCHOLOGY OF PHANTASY.** 1920.

11.460
Stekel, Wilhelm, **TWELVE ESSAYS ON SEX AND PSYCHOANALYSIS.** trans. and ed. by S.A. Tannenbaum. New York, 1922.

11.461
Jung, Carl Gustav, **PSYCHOLOGICAL TYPES.** trans. by H.G. Baynes. New York, 1923; **CONTRIBUTIONS TO ANALYTICAL PSYCHOLOGY.** trans. by H.G. Baynes and Cary F. Baynes. 1928. See especially: "Women in Europe" pp. 164-188. "How is a man to write about woman, his exact opposite?... For woman stands just where man's shadow falls" (p. 164); **THE BASIC WRITINGS.** New York, 1938; **COLLECTED WORKS. VOL. 17. THE DEVELOPMENT OF THE PERSONALITY.** Princeton, 1954; **COLLECTED WORKS. VOL. 5. SYMBOLS OF TRANSFORMATION.** New York, 1956. Includes an account of mother symbolism.

11.462
INTERNATIONAL JOURNAL OF PSYCHOANALYSIS: Horney, K., *"On the Genesis of the Castration Complex in Women,"* 5 (1924) n.p.; Horney, K., *"The Flight from Womanhood,"* 7 (1926) 3; Jones, E., *"The Early Development of Female Sexuality,"* 8 (1927) n.p.; Klein, M., *"Early Stages of the Oedipus Conflict,"* 9 (1928) 167-180; Deutsch, H., *"Summary on Frigidity,"* 50 (1930) n.p.; Horney, K., *"The Dread of Women,"* 13 (1932) 348-360; Jones, E., *"Early Female Sexuality,"* 16 (1935) 263-273; Bonaparte, M., *"Passivity, Masochism and Femininity,"* 16 (1935) 325-333; Lampl-de Groot, J., *"Re-Evaluation of the Role of the Oedipus Complex,"* 33 (1952) 335-342.

11.463
Jastrow, Joseph, **THE HOUSE THAT FREUD BUILT**. New York, 1932; *also published as:* **FREUD: HIS DREAMS AND SEX THEORIES**. New York, 1948.

11.464
Klein, Melanie, **THE PSYCHOANALYSIS OF CHILDREN**. 1932; Klein's work influenced British analysts and her concept of "object relations"——the introjection and projection of objects into the ego——laid the foundation for W.R.D. Fairbairn's later work on "object-relations" theory; **CONTRIBUTIONS TO PSYCHO-ANALYSIS, 1921-1945**. 1948.

11.465
PSYCHOANALYTIC QUARTERLY: Freud, S., *"Concerning the Sexuality of Women,"* 1 (1932) 191-209; Lampl-de Groot, J., *"Problems of Femininity,"* 2 (1933) 489-518.

11.466
Freud, Anna, **THE EGO AND THE MECHANISMS OF DEFENCE**. 1937; "On the Theory of Analysis of Children" in **THE FIRST FREUDIANS**. ed. by Hendrik M. Ruitenbeek. New York, 1973. Analysis of children differs from that of adults; their superegos haven't come to the point of independence. In an account given of the treatment of a girl and boy, the girl's neurosis was based on the dread of loss of love while the boy's was based on dread of castration. Paper first appeared in 1914.

11.467
Hartmann, Heinz, **EGO PSYCHOLOGY AND THE PROBLEM OF ADAPTATION**. 1939. Differs with Freud as to the child's psychological configuration; the child is an "undifferentiated ego-id matrix" rather than "all id." For further discussion and comparison with object-relations theory, see: Chodorow, Nancy, **THE REPRODUCTION OF MOTHERING**. 1978. Chaps. 3 and 4, "Psychoanalysis and Sociological Inquiry" and "Early Psychological Development."

11.468
D[oolittle], H[ilda], **TRIBUTE TO FREUD**. orig. ed., 1944; New York, 1974. Informal account by one of Freud's patients describing her therapy.

11.469
Zilboorg, Gregory (with Henry, George W.), **A HISTORY OF MEDICAL PSYCHOLOGY**. New York, 1941; **SIGMUND FREUD: HIS EXPLORATION OF THE MIND OF MAN**. 1951. Uncritical view.

11.470
Deutsch, Helene, "Feminine Masochism" and "Feminine Passivity" in **THE PSYCHOLOGY OF WOMEN**. by Helene Deutsch. New York, 1944. Offers a full extrapolation of Freud's views on women: "Women's intellectuality is to a large extent paid for by the loss of valuable feminine qualities: it feeds on the sap of the affective life and results in impoverishment of this life either as a whole or in specific emotional qualities" (p. 290);   —*see also:* **PSYCHOANALYTIC QUARTERLY**: Wimpfheimer, M.J. and Schafer, R., *"Psychoanalytic Methodology in Helene Deutsch's THE PSYCHOLOGY OF WOMEN,"* 46 no. 2 (1977) 287-318. Deutsch offers a valuable descriptive account of women's psychology, but her adherence to Freud's orientation toward biology underestimates the role of society and learning.

11.471
Fenichel, Otto, **THE PSYCHOANALYTIC THEORY OF NEUROSIS.** New York, 1945.

11.472
Fliess, Robert, ed., **THE PSYCHOANALYTIC READER: AN ANTHOLOGY OF ESSENTIAL PAPERS WITH CRITICAL INTRODUCTIONS.** New York, 1948; 1969.

11.473
BULLETIN OF THE HISTORY OF MEDICINE: Riese, W., *"An Outline of a History of Ideas in Psychotherapy,"* 25 (1951) 442-456. "The nineteenth century offered two intellectual tools enabling Freud to conceive his analytic therapy, namely the doctrine of evolution and the experimental thought" (pp. 445-446); Veith, I., *"On Hysterical and Hypochondriacal Afflictions,"* 30 (1956) 233-240.

11.474
Munroe, Ruth L., **SCHOOLS OF PSYCHOANALYTIC THOUGHT.** New York, 1955. "'Psychoanalysis' began around 1890 as an offshoot of psychiatry——the branch of *medicine* concerned with mental illness. Many of its peculiarities as a scientific field are due to the fact that it was conceived and guided for forty years by a towering genius, Sigmund Freud" (p. v).

11.475
Grinstein, Alexander, **THE INDEX OF PSYCHOANALYTIC WRITINGS.** New York, 1956. Supplements from 1953.

11.476
Wittels, Fritz, **FREUD AND HIS TIME.** 1956. Quotes Freud: "The theory of Darwin in its beginning at that time attracted me mightily because it promises to advance tremendously a knowledge of the world" (p. 4).

11.477
Riese, Walther, "The History of the Term and Conception of Neurosis" in **SCIENCE AND PSYCHOANALYSIS.** by Walther Riese. 1958.

11.478
Rieff, Philip, **FREUD: THE MIND OF THE MORALIST.** New York, 1959. See especially: chap. 5, "Sexuality and Domination." "Freud faced the great problem created by the emancipation of women: 'intellectual training' may cause them 'to depreciate the feminine role for which [they are] intended.' The romantic in Freud saw a happy destiny for the sexually relaxed 'caretaker's daughter': she 'will find a lover; perhaps bear a child... perhaps become a popular actress, and end as an aristocrat.' Meanwhile, the poor little upper-class girl, too well brought up, is destined to become the more neurotic half of a wretched marriage. In thus charging that sexual and intellectual are incompatible in women, Freud exhibits again his belief that the two qualities are basically opposed. This opposition between sex and intellect remained an unquestioned part of Freud's doctrine of human nature" (p. 174).

11.479
INTERNATIONAL RECORD OF MEDICINE: Riese, W., *"The Impact of Nineteenth Century Thought on Psychiatry,"* 173 (1960) 7-19.

11.480
Brown, J.A.C., **FREUD AND THE POST-FREUDIANS.** 1961. See especially: "The British Schools."

11.481
Fine, Reuben, **FREUD: A CRITICAL RE-EVALUATION OF HIS THEORIES.** 1963; **A HISTORY OF PSYCHOANALYSIS.** New York. 1979. See especially: "Neurosis: Psychoanalysis and Psychiatry" for a history of the development of Freud's ideas.

11.482
Hunter, Richard and Macalpine, Ida, **THREE HUNDRED YEARS OF PSYCHIATRY, 1535-1860.** 1963.

11.483
Veith, Ilza, **HYSTERIA: THE HISTORY OF A DISEASE.** 1965. "It was specifically [Freud's] interest in and study of hysteria that formed the starting point of psychoanalysis and led to the formulation of those final new ideas on the illness which have as yet not been superseded" (p. 258). See especially: "Hysteria and the Evolution of Psychoanalysis."

11.484
Ruitenbeek, Hendrik M., ed., **PSYCHOANALYSIS AND FEMALE SEXUALITY.** New Haven, 1966; (as editor), **THE FIRST FREUDIANS.** New York, 1973. Includes: "The Origin and Structure of the Superego" by Ernest Jones; "Sexuality and its Role in the Neuroses" by A.A. Brill; "The Wish To Be a Man" by Hanns Sachs; "On the Theory of Analysis in Children" by Anna Freud; "Some Biophysical Aspects of Sado-Masochism" by Marie Bonaparte; "A Discussion of Certain Forms of Resistance" by Helene Deutsch; and "The Early Development of Conscience in the Child" by Melanie Klein.

11.485
Brome, Vincent, **FREUD AND HIS EARLY CIRCLE: THE STRUGGLES OF PSYCHOANALYSIS.** 1967. See appendix, "Havelock Ellis and Freud," detailing the influence each had on the other's work; **ERNEST JONES: FREUD'S ALTER EGO.** New York, 1983.

11.486
Horney, Karen, **FEMININE PSYCHOLOGY.** New York, 1967. ed. by Harold Kelman. Horney is an important figure among Freud's second generation who provided one of the first feminine-oriented perspectives in psychoanalytic theory. This publication is a collection of papers, the earliest of which was presented in 1923; introduction relates the different living and working milieus of Horney and Freud with their respective theoretical stances.

11.487
Stewart, Walter A., **PSYCHOANALYSIS: THE FIRST TEN YEARS 1888-1898.** 1967.

11.488
Roazen, Paul, **FREUD: POLITICAL AND SOCIAL THOUGHT.** New York, 1968.

11.489
Lampl-de Groot, Jeanne, "The Evolution of the Oedipus Complex in Women" (1927) in **THE PSYCHOANALYTIC READER: AN ANTHOLOGY OF ESSENTIAL**

PAPERS WITH CRITICAL INTRODUCTIONS. ed. by Robert Fliess. 1969. Lampl-de Groot was an early participant in the debate over female psychology.

11.490
Schur, Max, FREUD: LIVING AND DYING. New York, 1972. By a student of Freud who later became his physician.

11.491
SYNTHESIS: Baxter, P., *"The Evolution of Freud's Theory of Female Sexuality 1888-1933,"* 2 (1974) 18-40. Outlines Freud's theory.

11.492
Chertok, Leon and De Saussure, Raymond, THE THERAPEUTIC REVOLUTION FROM MESMER TO FREUD. trans. by R.H. Ahrenfeldt. New York, 1979. Contrasts the psychotherapy introduced by Freud with that of his predecessors.

11.493
Clark, Ronald W., FREUD: THE MAN AND THE CAUSE. A BIOGRAPHY. New York, 1980; *reviewed in:* NEW SOCIETY: Brome, V., *"Risen From the Dead?"* 53 (1980) 139-140. "The first full-scale account by a professional biographer" (p. 139).

* * *

6. *COMMENT AND FEMINIST CRITICISM OF FREUDIAN PSYCHOANALYSIS*

11.494
Horney, Karen, NEW WAYS IN PSYCHOANALYSIS. New York, 1939. Neo-Freudian critique of Freud's views on women; "The Flight from Womanhood: The Masculinity Complex in Women as Viewed by Men and Women" in FEMININE PSYCHOLOGY. ed. with introduction by Harold Kelman. New York, 1967. On cultural bias in Freud's psychology of women. Horney was a sharp critic of Freudian disciple Helene Deutsch, and emphasized the non-innate, environmental influences in the shaping of feminine sexuality; "The Flight From Womanhood: The Masculinity Complex in Women as Viewed by Men and by Women" in WOMEN AND ANALYSIS: DIALOGUES ON PSYCHOANALYTIC VIEWS OF FEMININITY. ed. by Jean Strouse. New York, 1974; *rpt. from:* INTERNATIONAL JOURNAL OF PSYCHOANALYSIS: 7 (1926) 324-339; "The Problem of Feminine Masochism" in PSYCHOANALYSIS AND WOMEN. ed. by Jean Baker Miller. 1973.
——*see also:* Rubin, Jack L., KAREN HORNEY: THE GENTLE REBEL OF PSYCHOANALYSIS. New York, 1978. "She was a bridge builder between the psychobiological man of Freud's psychology and the sociocultural man of today" (p. xiv); Westkott, Marcia, THE FEMINIST LEGACY OF KAREN HORNEY. New Haven, 1986.

11.495
AMERICAN JOURNAL OF SOCIOLOGY: Ellis, H., *"Freud's Influence on the Changed Attitude Toward Sex,"* 45 (1939) 309-317.

11.496
Klein, Viola, "The Psychoanalytical Approach: Sigmund Freud" in THE FEMININE CHARACTER: HISTORY OF AN IDEOLOGY. by Viola Klein. 1946. "Although Freud would not go so far as to ascribe to women an inferior intelligence, he prejudices judgments about their intellectual capacity by the rather axiomatic statement that, owing to their libidinal organization, women have only a limited urge for sublimation. Translated into ordinary language, this means that women are, by their organic nature, excluded from participation in cultural and creative activities" (p. 76).

11.497
PSYCHOANALYTIC QUARTERLY: *"The So-Called English School of Psychoanalysis,"* 16 (1947) 69-93; Fliegel, Z.O., *"Feminine Psychosexual Development in Freudian Theory: A Historical Reconstruction,"* 42 (1973) 385-408. History of the debate taken up by Freud, Horney, Lampl-de Groot, Deutsch, Jones, Klein, and Fenichel in the 1920s and early 1930s; Perman, J.M., *"The Search For the Mother: Narcissistic Regression as a Pathway of Mourning in Childhood,"* 48 (1979) 448-464. Recent clinical evidence sheds light on the disagreement over Freud's formulations in "Mourning and Melancholia"; Myers, W.A., *"A Transference Dream With Superego Implications,"* 49 (1980) 284-307; Lehmann, H., *"Reflections on Freud's Reaction to the Death of His Mother,"* 52 (1983) 237-249. Freud's reaction may have influenced his conception of the oedipal mother. It was presented in his paper on "Female Sexuality," written shortly after his mother's death; Compton, A., *"The Current Status of the Psychoanalytic Theory of Instinctual Drives. I: Drive Concept, Classification, and Development,"* 52 (1983) 364-401.

11.498
De Beauvoir, Simone, THE SECOND SEX. orig. French ed., 1949; trans. and ed. by H.M. Parshley. New York, 1952. See especially: Chap. 2, "The Psychoanalytic Point of View."

11.499
Fairbairn, W.R.D., AN OBJECT-RELATIONS THEORY OF THE PERSONALITY. New York, 1952. Fairbairn's work originated from the child psychology of Melanie Klein, who departs from Freud over the time that the infant's ego differentiates from the id.

11.500
Thompson, Clara, Mazer, Milton and Witenberg, Earl, eds., AN OUTLINE OF PSYCHOANALYSIS. rev. ed., New York, 1955. See especially: "The Theory of the Instincts," "The Development of the Sexual Function," and "Character and Anal Erotism," by Sigmund Freud; "The Feminine Character" by Viola Klein; "Some Effects of the Derogatory Attitude Towards Female Sexuality" by Clara Thompson; and "The Psychosomatic Implications of the Primary Unit: Mother-Child" by Therese Benedek.

11.501
PSYCHOANALYTIC REVIEW: Gordon, S., *"Incest as Revenge Against the Pre-Oedipal Mother,"* 42 (1955) 284-292. Recounts the case of Helen, who acts out her revenge to her mother by open promiscuity with men in a masochistic attempt to seduce her father. The author uses the case as evidence that Oedipal behavior may mask deeper feelings which, in this instance, are revenge against a rejecting mother

and defense against dependence on her; Love, S. and Feldman, Y., *"The Disguised Cry for Help: Narcissistic Mothers and Their Children,"* 48 (1961) 52-67. Presents cases in which mothers bring their children for treatment of symptoms that mirror their own neuroses. "These mothers suffered such narcissistic damage themselves that they could not tolerate the rivalrous and defiant feelings aroused in them by their child's being nurtured by the treatment process" (pp. 57-58); Grinstein, A., *"Profile of a 'Doll'—A Female Character Type,"* 50 (1963) 321-334. Contemptuous analysis of the character of certain Jewish women who "doll" themselves up as a narcissistic defense "to secure the love which they felt was withheld from them and given to their brothers in childhood" (p. 334); Lewin, K.K., *"Dora Revisited,"* 60 (1974) 519-532; Kestenberg, J.S., *"The Three Faces of Femininity,"* 67 (1980) 313-335. "The prominent task of parents to act as organizers of their children's phase-specific identity makes it incumbent upon them to respond harmoniously to the innate biological trends that manifest themselves in their children's developmental phases. The gentle face of a mother resonates that that of her three-year-old. The mother's competitive face is mirrored by her four-year-old girl and her wooing face serves as a model for the seductive expression of the five-year-old temptress" (pp. 320-321); 69 (1982). Entire issue is devoted to female sexuality; Fliegel, Z.O., *"Half A Century Later: Current Status of Freud's Controversial Views on Women,"* 69 (1982) 7-28. Discusses the continuing reexamination of Freud's theories in light of accumulating contrary empirical evidence; Lachmann, F.M., *"Narcissism and Female Gender Identity: A Reformulation,"* 69 (1982) 43-61; Menaker, E., *"Female Identity in Psychosocial Perspective,"* 69 (1982) 75-83; Abraham, R., *"Freud's Mother Conflict and the Formulation of the Oedipal Father,"* 69 (1982) 441-453. "Amalie Nathanson Freud may have been the most influential figure in her son's life.... On the one hand she seemed to the boy to be the source of all nurturance and love. On the other hand she appeared overwhelmingly powerful, sexual and possessive.... He was torn by his love and hatred of her" (p. 441).

11.502
Bakan, David, **SIGMUND FREUD AND THE JEWISH MYSTICAL TRADITION.** 1958. Explores the cultural tradition with which Freud identified as a Jew. See especially: "Sexuality." "We find a conception of sexuality which is startlingly close to Freud's in the Kabbalistic tradition, mixed with many supernatural considerations which tend to turn the modern enlightened mind away from it" (p. 271).

11.503
Fromm, Erich, **SIGMUND FREUD'S MISSION: AN ANALYSIS OF HIS PERSONALITY AND INFLUENCE.** 1959. On the critical function of Freud's views on women.

11.504
Friedan, Betty, **THE FEMININE MYSTIQUE.** New York, 1963. See especially: "The Sexual Solipsism of Sigmund Freud." "The degradation of women was taken for granted by Freud—and is the key to his theory of femininity" (p. 106).

11.505
Thompson, Clara M., **ON WOMEN.** foreword by Erich Fromm. New York, 1964; 1971; "Cultural Pressures in the Psychology of Women," "'Penis Envy' in Women" and "Some Effects of the Derogatory Attitude Toward Female Sexuality" in **PSYCHOANALYSIS AND WOMEN.** ed. by Jean Baker Miller. New York, 1973. Also contains the article by Frieda Fromm-Reichmann and Virginia Gunst, "On the Denial of Women's Sexual Pleasure: Discussion of Dr. Thompson's Paper";

Thompson's three articles *rpt. from:* **PSYCHIATRY:** 5 (1942) 331-339; 6 (1943) 123-125; 13 (1950) 349-354.

11.506
JOURNAL OF THE AMERICAN PSYCHOANALYTIC ASSOCIATION: Sherfey, M.J., *"The Evolution and Nature of Female Sexuality in Relation to Psychoanalytic Theory,"* 14 (1966) 28-128; Responses to previous article, 16 (1968) n.p.; Mack, J.E., *"Psychoanalysis and Historical Biography,"* 19 (1971) n.p.; Schafer, R., *"Problems in Freud's Psychology of Women,"* 22 (1974) 459-485. Many of the problems follow from Freud's own ambivalence; Stoller, R., *"Primary Femininity,"* 24 (1976) 59-78; Muslin, H. and Gill, M., *"Transference in the Dora Case,"* 26 (1978) 311-328; Rogow, A., *"A Further Footnote to Freud's 'Fragment of an Analysis of a Case of Hysteria,'"* 26 (1978) 330-356; Harrison, I.B., *"On Freud's View of the Infant-Mother Relationship and of the Oceanic Feeling—Some Subjective Influences,"* 27 (1979) 399-421; Silverman, M.A., *"Cognitive Development and Female Psychology,"* 29 (1981) 581-605. Freudian psychology must be revised to include the multiple developmental factors in the child; Maleson, F.G., *"The Multiple Meanings of Masochism in Psychoanalytic Discourse,"* 32 (1984) 325-356.

11.507
Edinger, Dora, **BERTHA PAPPENHEIM: FREUD'S ANNA O.** Highland Park, Illinois, 1968.

11.508
Klein, George S., "Freud's Two Theories of Sexuality" in **CLINICAL-COGNITIVE PSYCHOLOGY: MODELS AND INTEGRATIONS.** by George S. Klein. Englewood Cliffs, 1969. The "clinical theory," centering on the "distinctive properties of human sexual experience," is contrasted to the drive-discharge theory.

11.509
Chassequet-Smurgel, Janine, ed., **FEMALE SEXUALITY: NEW PSYCHO-ANALYTIC VIEWS.** Ann Arbor, 1970. "One could argue that Freud's discoveries in this domain are definitive, but that would be to exaggerate greatly Freud's own estimation of his work on female psychology. Indeed, Freud was always reticent about the 'dark continent' of femininity, and constantly stressed the incomplete nature of his discoveries.... [says Freud:] 'If you want to know more about femininity, enquire from your own experiences of life, or turn to the poets, or wait until science can give you deeper and more coherent information'" (p. 1). See especially: "A Masculine Mythology of Femininity" by Christian David. Editor may also be cataloged as Smurgel, Janine Chassequet.

11.510
Cioffi, F., "Freud and the Idea of a Pseudo-Science" in **EXPLANATION IN THE BEHAVIOURAL SCIENCES.** ed. by R. Borger and F. Cioffi. Cambridge, 1970. Denounces Freud's theories and methodologies as unscientific, relegating psychoanalysis to the realm of the "pseudo-sciences" such as numerology, pyramidology, and astrology; *reviewed in:* **PHILOSOPHY; JOURNAL OF THE ROYAL INSTITUTE OF PHILOSOPHY:** Jupp, V.L., 52 (1977) 441-453. Defends Freud.

11.511
Greer, Germaine, "The Psychological Sell" in **THE FEMALE EUNUCH.** by Germaine Greer. 1970. On Helene Deutsch's Freudian view of femininity and

female sexuality.

11.512
Millett, Kate, SEXUAL POLITICS. New York, 1970. See especially: "Freud and the Influence of Psychoanalytic Thought." Freud was "beyond question the strongest individual counterrevolutionary force in the ideology of sexual politics during the period [1930-1960]" (p. 178).

11.513
Freeman, Lucy, THE STORY OF ANNA O. introduction by Karl A. Menninjer. New York, 1972; (and Strean, Herbert S.), FREUD AND WOMEN. New York, 1981. In four parts: "The Women in Freud's Personal Life," "Women Colleagues and Friends," "The Women in Freud's Cases," and "Freud's Contributions to Understanding Women."

11.514
ARCHIVES OF GENERAL PSYCHIATRY: Hollender, M.H., *"Conversion Hysteria; A Post-Freudian Reinterpretation of Nineteenth Century Psycho-Social Data,"* 26 (1972) 311-314.

11.515
JOURNAL OF INTERDISCIPLINARY HISTORY: Weinstein, F. and Platt, G., *"History and Theory: The Question of Psychoanalysis,"* 2 (1972) 419-434. Historians could benefit from the utilization of psychoanalytic theory, since they "have to impute motives to historical actors [and] to explain the fundamental reasons for behavior" (n.p.).

11.516
Sherfey, Mary Jane, THE NATURE AND EVOLUTION OF FEMALE SEXUALITY. New York, 1972; *excerpts rpt. in:* PSYCHOANALYSIS AND WOMEN. ed. by Jean Baker Miller. 1973. Recent biological data on "the embryonic female primacy" and from Masters and Johnson's research "will, in fact, strengthen psychoanalytic theory and practice in the area of female sexuality. Without the erroneous biological premises, the basic sexual constitution and its many manifestations will be seen as highly moldable by hormonal influences, which in turn are so very susceptible to all those uniquely human emotional, intellectual, imaginative, and cultural forces upon which psychoanalysis has cast so much light" (p. 153).

11.517
SOCIAL RESEARCH: Smith-Rosenberg, C., *"The Hysterical Woman: Sex Roles and Role Conflict in Nineteenth-Century America,"* 39 (1972) 652-658.

11.518
Chodoff, Paul, "Feminine Psychology and Infantile Sexuality" in PSYCHO-ANALYSIS AND WOMEN. ed. by Jean Baker Miller. 1973. The validity of Freud's views of women's sexuality rests on the cogency of his concept of infantile sexuality, which provides the framework.

11.519
Miller, Jean Baker, PSYCHOANALYSIS AND WOMEN. 1973. A collection of essays including: "The Flight From Womanhood" and "The Problem of Feminine Masochism" by Karen Horney; "Sex" by Alfred Adler; "'Penis-Envy' in Women" and

"Cultural Pressures in the Psychology of Women" by Clara Thompson; "On the Denial of Women's Sexual Pleasure" by Frieda Fromm-Reichmann and Virginia Gunst; "Masculine and Feminine: Some Biological and Cultural Aspects" by Gregory Zilboorg; "Feminine Psychology and Infantile Sexuality" by Paul Chodoff; and "A Survey and Re-Evaluation of the Concept of Penis-Envy" by Ruth Moulton. From the introduction: "It is striking to realize that in the psychoanalytic writings on the *psychology* of women, the greatest amount of material is on their *sexuality*. This finding is a comment in itself" (p. xiii); *reviewed in:* NEW YORK REVIEW OF BOOKS: Lasch, C., *"Freud and Women,"* 21 (Oct. 3, 1974) 12-17.

11.520
Moulton, Ruth, "A Survey and Re-Evaluation of the Concept of Penis Envy" in PSYCHOANALYSIS AND WOMEN. ed. by Jean Baker Miller. 1973. The little girl's awareness of the penis doesn't necessarily lead to envy but envy may be reinforced by secondary factors such as sibling rivalry, dependency on the mother, a remote father, and dread of assuming the ineffectual role of woman.

11.521
Zilboorg, Gregory, "Masculine and Feminine: Some Biological and Cultural Aspects" in PSYCHOANALYSIS AND WOMEN. ed. by Jean Baker Miller. 1973. Traces the androcentric bias in Freud's writing and points out that throughout, "the organic inferiority of woman, as Freud put it, and the superiority of man, both implied and asserted in psychoanalytic theory, continued to be treated with postulative conviction" (p. 100). Asks why male hostility toward women was admitted in Freud's writing, but never adequately explained in his psychoanalytic theory; *rpt. from:* PSYCHIATRY: 7 (1944) 257-296.

11.522
INTERNATIONAL JOURNAL OF PSYCHOANALYSIS: Balint, E., *"Technical Problems Found in the Analysis of Women by a Woman Analyst: A Contribution to the Question 'What Does A Woman Want?'"* 54 (1973) 195-220. In answer to Freud's famous question, "I suggest that women want, both in their relationship with men and with women, to use that primitive structure in human relations, namely the capacity for mutual concern" (p. 200); Chiland, C., *"Clinical Practice, Theory, and Their Relationship in Regard to Female Sexuality,"* 61 (1980) 359-365. Argues that Freud's determination to explain psychology as biologically determined blinded him to his own clinical evidence. Freud was mistaken when he explained feminine identification as a masochistic identification to a castrated man——not all women have castration anxiety; Fayek, A., *"Narcissism and the Death Instinct,"* 62 (1981) 309-322. Both concepts that Freud outlined need to be viewed in relation to one another; analyzes four of Freud's dreams from this perspective; Kohon, G., *"Reflections on Dora: The Case of Hysteria,"* Part 1, 65 (1984) 73-84. The author conceives the hysteric as one who cannot choose between mother or father as the object of her desire, and so is incapable of defining herself as a woman or a man; Chassequet-Smurgel, J., *"The Femininity of the Analyst in Professional Practice,"* 65 (1984) 169-178. Part two of a series.

11.523
Irigaray, Luce, SPECULUM OF THE OTHER WOMAN. orig. ed., Paris, 1974; trans. by Gillian Gill. Ithaca, 1985. On the metaphysical prejudices of Freud that structure his theories on women. Irigaray seeks equality *and* difference in the sexes as a reconcilable assumption for feminist and more traditional analysts; CE SEXE QUI N'EN EST PAS UN. Paris, 1977. Continues critique of Freud using Freudian

analytical methodology. ——*see also:* **FEMINIST STUDIES:** Burke, C., *"Irigaray Through the Looking Glass,"* 7 (1981) 288-306; Gallop, Jane, "The Father's Seduction" in **THE DAUGHTER'S SEDUCTION: FEMINISM AND PSYCHO-ANALYSIS.** by Jane Gallop. Ithaca, 1982. "This encounter between Irigaray's feminist critique and Freud's final text on women [his essay "Femininity"] is an important training ground for a new kind of battle, a feminine seduction/disarming/unsettling of the positions of phallocratic, metaphysical ideology. Irigaray's tactic is a kind of reading: close reading, which separates the text into fragments of varying size, quotes it, and then comments with various questions and associations. She never sums up the meaning of Freud's text, or binds all her commentaries, questions, associations into a unified presentation, a coherent interpretation.... As a result, the reader does not so easily lose sight of the incoherency and inconsistency of the text. So 'the philosophical order of [Freud's] discourse is shaken up' and reduced to an unredeemed disorder. That could be seen as a victory for feminism" (p. 56). ——*see also:* Garner, Shirley N., Kahane, Claire and Sprengnether, Madelon, "Introduction" in **THE (M)OTHER TONGUE: ESSAYS IN FEMINIST PSYCHO-ANALYTIC INTERPRETATIONS.** ed. by Shirley N. Garner, et al. 1985. "Irigaray, feminist, psychoanalyst, writer, and rebel Lacanian (whose expulsion from Lacan's academy can itself figure the volatile and still seductive relation between Father and Daughter), asserts with Lacanian ingenuity that Western discourse follows a male morphology, analogous in its linearity, unity, and visible form to the phallus.... Irigaray writes to open language to a different analogy, a female morphologic figured by the female genitals.... Like [Helene] Cixous, Irigaray attempts to map a new geography of female relations along the lines of the child's sensual pleasure in the mother's body, a pleasure prohibited and repressed by the fathers of psychoanalytic theory" (p. 23).

11.524
Klaich, Dolores, "Freud and a Poet/Patient" in **WOMAN AND WOMAN: ATTITUDES TOWARD LESBIANISM.** by Dolores Klaich. New York, 1974.

11.525
Maccoby, Eleanor E. and Jacklin, Carol N., **THE PSYCHOLOGY OF SEX DIFFERENCES.** Stanford, 1974. Reviews psychological studies of sex differences and finds that there is frequently as much or more variation in traits and capacities within the sexes as between them.

11.526
Mitchell, Juliet, **PSYCHOANALYSIS AND FEMINISM.** New York, 1974. Part 1, an exposition of Freud's conception of the female personality, is generally considered to be a uniquely accurate and insightful reading of Freud. In part 2, Mitchell critiques feminist revisionists such as de Beauvoir, Friedan, Firestone and Millett. Part 3 takes up the question of patriarchy as an aspect of psychoanalysis, suggesting "in tentative and schematic ways, how we might use it to help us understand the operations of a patriarchal system that must by definition oppress women" (p. xvii); *reviewed in:* **FEMINIST STUDIES:** Ortner, S., *"Oedipal Father, Mother's Brother, and the Penis,"* 2 (1975) 167-182. Critiques Mitchell's explanation of the origin of patriarchal society. In her final analysis, "capitalism and its agent, the nuclear family, while not seen as the causes of patriarchy, are nonetheless suddenly elevated to a central position in the argument, through the device of claiming that they produce a particularly vicious form of the Oedipus complex and hence a particularly pernicious form of patriarchal oppression" (p. 176); *also reviewed in:* **WOMEN'S STUDIES:** Stanford, C.M., *"Is Freud Really the Enemy?"* 3 (1975) 105-

110. "Mitchell contends that Freud's theory itself has radical implications; in other words, that Freud's psychoanalysis is a perceptive analysis of patriarchal society, not a mere self-seeking recommendation for that society" (p. 106); *also reviewed in:* NEW YORK REVIEW OF BOOKS: Lasch, C., *"Freud and Women,"* 21 (Oct. 3, 1974) 12-17; "Psychoanalysis: Child Development and the Question of Femininity" in WOMEN: THE LONGEST REVOLUTION. by Juliet Mitchell. 1984.

11.527
Person, Ethel Spector, "Some New Observations on the Origins of Femininity" in WOMEN AND ANALYSIS: DIALOGUES ON PSYCHOANALYTIC VIEWS OF FEMININITY. ed. by Jean Strouse. New York, 1974. Focuses on Marie Bonaparte's formulation of the origin of feminine masochism; "Sexuality as the Mainstay of Identity: Psychoanalytic Perspectives" in WOMEN, SEX, AND SEXUALITY. ed. by Catharine R. Stimpson and Ethel Spector Person. Chicago, 1980. Challenges the assumptions that "sexuality is an innate force that achieves its ideal expression when free from cultural inhibitions and that female sexuality is inhibited (hyposexual) while male sexuality represents the norm. On the contrary, individuals do internalize their culture, which shapes both their experience of desire and expression of sexuality.... sexuality must be understood... in relationship to the maintenance of identity" (p. 36); *rpt. from:* SIGNS: 5 (1980) 605-630.

11.528
Strouse, Jean, ed., WOMEN AND ANALYSIS: DIALOGUES ON PSYCHO-ANALYTIC VIEWS OF FEMININITY. New York, 1974; rpt. with new preface by Jean Strouse, 1985. Valuable anthology with original writings juxtaposed with responses. Includes papers by Freud, Abraham, Deutsch, Horney, and Thompson; *reviewed in:* NEW YORK REVIEW OF BOOKS: Lasch, C., *"Freud and Women,"* 21 (Oct. 3, 1974) 12-17.

11.529
Williams, Juanita H., "Psychoanalysis and the Woman Question" and "Woman and Milieu: Innovative Views" in PSYCHOLOGY OF WOMEN: BEHAVIOR IN A BIOSOCIAL CONTEXT. by Juanita H. Williams. New York, 1974. Discusses Freud, Deutsch, Horney, Thompson and Adler.

11.530
AMERICAN JOURNAL OF ORTHOPSYCHIATRY: Levine, S., Karin, L., and Levine, E.L., *"Sexism and Psychiatry,"* 44 (1974) n.p. Presents sociological factors bearing on theories and practice of psychoanalysis. Expresses the need for empirical data to substantiate theoretical claims, and to "push for societal innovations and alternatives [to the]... sexual role stereotypes imposed by society" (p. 334).

11.531
Marcus, Steven, "Freud and Dora: Story, History, Case History" in REPRESENTA-TIONS: ESSAYS ON LITERATURE AND SOCIETY. by Steven Marcus. New York, 1975. Freud's case histories are creative narratives. Marcus shows how his imaginative style could undermine the scientific goal of treatment; *also appears in:* IN DORA'S CASE: FREUD—HYSTERIA—FEMINISM. ed. by Charles Bernheimer and Claire Kahane. New York, 1985.

11.532
Nagera, Humberto, FEMALE SEXUALITY AND THE OEDIPUS COMPLEX. New York, 1975. See especially: "An Historical Perspective."

11.533
Seymour-Smith, Martin, **SEX AND SOCIETY**. 1975. See especially: "Freud" and "Women: Freudian, Post-Freudian and Other Views." "Freud's theory, in its earliest and in its final form, is a metaphorical construct——a massive and revolutionary fiction derived from his clinical experience of himself and a number of Viennese middle-class neurotics living in the final, rotten-ripe period of a great empire" (p. 49).

11.534
Rich, Adrienne, **OF WOMAN BORN: MOTHERHOOD AS EXPERIENCE AND INSTITUTION**. New York, 1976. Well-documented and insightful writing. See especially: "Mother and Son, Woman and Man." "Through the resolution of the Oedipus complex, the boy makes his way into the male world, the world of patriarchal law and order. Civilization——meaning, of course, patriarchal civilization —requires the introduction of the father (whose presence has so far not been essential since nine months before birth) as a third figure in the interrelationships of mother and child. The Oedipus complex thus becomes, in Juliet Mitchell's phrase, 'the entry into human culture.' But it is distinctively the father who represents not just authority but culture itself" (p. 196).

11.535
COMPREHENSIVE PSYCHIATRY: Manalis, S.A., *"The Psychoanalytic Concept of Feminine Passivity: A Comparative Study of Psychoanalytic and Feminist Views,"* 17 (1976) n.p. A brief overview of the objections raised regarding Freud's concept of feminine passivity.

11.536
SIGNS: Vaughter, R.M., *"Review Essay: Psychology,"* 2 (1976) 120-146. Academic sources of the distinction between the sexes; Irigaray, L., *"When Our Lips Speak Together,"* 6 (1977) 69-79; Baker, S.W., *"Biological Influences on Human Sex and Gender,"* 6 (1980) 80-96.

11.537
Blum, Harold P., "Masochism, the Ego Ideal, and the Psychology of Women" in **FEMALE PSYCHOLOGY: CONTEMPORARY PSYCHOANALYTIC VIEWS.** ed. by Harold P. Blum. New York, 1977.

11.538
Dinnerstein, Dorothy, **THE MERMAID AND THE MINOTAUR: SEXUAL ARRANGEMENTS AND HUMAN MALAISE**. 1977. "Freud called women 'the enemy of civilization,' and in a sense this is true. But he radically oversimplified. She is the loyal opponent, the indispensable defanged and domesticated critic, of what he himself identified as the essential, and imminently lethal, sickness of civilization. Without her sabotage, civilization as it is could not go on" (p. 225).

11.539
Foreman, Ann, **FEMININITY AS ALIENATION: WOMEN AND THE FAMILY IN MARXISM AND PSYCHOANALYSIS**. 1977. See especially: "Freud: the Importance of Sexuality" and "Marxism and Psychoanalysis."

11.540
Jahoda, Marie, **FREUD AND THE DILEMMAS OF PSYCHOLOGY**. 1977.

11.541
IDEOLOGY AND CONSCIOUSNESS: Irigaray, L., *"Women's Exile,"* no. 1 (1977) 62-76. Claims that female psychology is not to be explained in terms of responses to male anatomy. Rather, femininity is mainly developed by female biology. Women's desire is specifically female——a female libido. Freud demonstrates one libido for both sexes.

11.542
JOURNAL OF THE AMERICAN ACADEMY OF PSYCHOANALYSIS: Slipp, S., *"Interpersonal Factors in Hysteria: Freud's Seduction Theory and the Case of Dora,"* 5 (1977) 359-376; Spiegel, R., *"Freud and the Women in His World,"* 5 (1977) 377-402; Roth, N., *"The Roots of Mary Wollstonecraft's Feminism,"* 7 (1979) 67-77; Gilman, S., *"Freud and the Prostitute: Male Stereotypes of Female Sexuality in Fin-de-Siecle Vienna,"* 9 (1981) n.p.; Shainess, N., *"Antigone, the Neglected Daughter of Oedipus: Freud's Gender Concepts in Theory,"* 10 (1982) 443-455. Had Freud considered Antigone, Oedipus' daughter, as the symbol for feminine personality development, his theories would have reflected a more generous view of women's potential. "Antigone is not the average woman. But she is what the average woman might become: a person of autonomy, high principle, not narcissistically self-involved, and not defensively suffering, but willing to take risks to live authentically" (p. 450).

11.543
NEW SOCIETY: Taylor, L., *"Freud,"* 42 (1977) 515-518. Discusses Freud's contribution to social science.

11.544
Chodorow, Nancy, **THE REPRODUCTION OF MOTHERING: PSYCHOANALYSIS AND THE SOCIOLOGY OF GENDER.** Berkeley, 1978. See especially: Chapters 5 and 6. Integrates object-relations theory with classic psychoanalytic theory to account for the ways in which the family produces women as mothers. Chodorow accepts "psychoanalysis as a theory of psychological development, one that tells us how social forms and practices affect the individual, but not as a theory of the genesis of civilization and the nature of culture" (p. 53).

11.545
Krohn, Alan, **HYSTERIA: THE ELUSIVE NEUROSIS.** New York, 1978. Psychological Issues Monograph 45/46. See especially: pp. 174-196.

11.546
M/F: Rose, J., *"'Dora'——Fragment of an Analysis,"* 2 (1978) 5-21.

11.547
Chamberlain, Edward M., **FREUD'S INCREDIBLE CONCEPTION OF THE CONTEMPORARY FEMALE.** 1979.

11.548
Firestone, Shulamith, **THE DIALECTIC OF SEX: THE CASE FOR FEMINIST REVOLUTION.** 1979. A foundation for radical feminism that establishes "the missing link between Marx and Freud."

.1.549
Seidenberg, Robert, "Psychoanalysis and the Feminist Movement" in **PSYCHO-SEXUAL IMPERATIVES: THEIR ROLE IN IDENTITY FORMATION.** ed. by Marie Coleman Nelson and Jean Ikenberry. 1979. Points out the irony that Freud himself discovered cases of hysteria in male slum dwellers and never asked what these men had in common with the brilliant but stifled daughters of wealthy Viennese merchants——namely oppression and powerlessness.

11.550
AMERICAN JOURNAL OF PSYCHOANALYSIS: Paley, M.G., *"A Feminist's Look at Freud's Feminine Psychology,"* 39 (1979) 179-182; Kestenbaum, C.J., *"Fathers and Daughters: The Father's Contribution to Feminine Identification in Girls as Depicted in Fairy Tales and Myths,"* 43 (1983) 119-127); Lerner, J.A., *"Horney's Theory and Mother/Child Impact on Early Childhood,"* 43 (1983) 149-155; Snodgrass, J., *"Patriarchy and Phantasy: A Conception of Psychoanalytic Sociology,"* 43 (1983) 261-275. Discussion of the nature/nurture debate as it manifests in psychoanalytic theory and in the social sciences. Psychoanalytic sociology takes into account environmental influences on mental processes; Lopez, A.G., *"Karen Horney's Feminine Psychology,"* 44 (1984) 280-289; Chessick, R.D., *"Was Freud Wrong About Feminine Psychology?"* 44 (1984) 355-367.

11.551
DIACRITICS: Gearhart, S., *"The Scene of Psychoanalysis: The Unanswered Question of Dora,"* 9 (Spring 1979) 114-126; Kofman, S., *"The Narcissistic Woman: Freud and Girard,"* 10 (Fall 1980) 36-45; Cixous, H., *"Portrait of Dora,"* 13 (Spring 1983) 2-32.

11.552
SOCIALIST REVIEW: Chodorow, N., *"Feminism and Difference: Gender, Relation, and Difference in Psychoanalytic Perspective,"* 9 (1979) 51-69. "Gender difference is not absolute, abstract, or irreducible; it does not involve an essence of gender.... Psychoanalysis... provides a particularly useful means to see the relational and situated construction of difference and gender difference" (p. 53).

11.553
WOMEN'S STUDIES INTERNATIONAL QUARTERLY: Sayers, J., *"Anatomy is Destiny: Variations on a Theme,"* 2 (1979) 19-32.

11.554
Auerbach, Nina, "Magic and Maidens: The Romance of the Victorian Freud" in **WRITING AND SEXUAL DIFFERENCE.** ed. by Elizabeth Abel. Chicago, 1980. Critique of Freud's views on women based upon the context of the "popular mythic configuration of the 1890s... a rich, covert collaboration between documents of romance and the romance of science" (p. 111).

11.555
Barrett, Michele, "Femininity, Masculinity, and Sexual Practice" in **WOMEN'S OPPRESSION TODAY: PROBLEMS IN MARXIST FEMINIST ANALYSIS.** by Michele Barrett. 1980. Discusses problems for Marxist feminism in Juliet Mitchell's "feminist appropriation of Freud."

11.556
Eisenstein, Hester and Jardine, Alice, eds., **THE FUTURE OF DIFFERENCE.**

Boston, 1980.

11.557
BRITISH JOURNAL OF MEDICAL PSYCHOLOGY: Greenberg, R.P. and Fisher, S., *"Freud's Penis-Baby Equation: Exploratory Tests of a Controversial Theory,"* 53 (1980) 333-342. Results of experiments with pregnant women and phallic imagery support Freud's theory of the wish for a baby as a substitute for the penis.

11.558
FEMINIST STUDIES: Ramas, M., *"Freud's Dora, Dora's Hysteria: The Negation of a Woman's Rebellion,"* 6 (1980) 472-510. "Ida Bauer's [Dora's] hysteria——her repudiation of sexuality——is not explained by Freud, but, rather, explained away.... At the deepest level of meaning, [her] hysteria was exactly what it appeared to be— a repudiation of the meaning of heterosexuality... an attempt to deny patriarchal sexuality, and a protest against postoedipal femininity" (pp. 477-478); Hunter, D., *"Hysteria, Psychoanalysis, and Feminism: The Case of Anna O,"* 9 (1983) 465-488. "Bertha Pappenheim [Anna O.] invented the 'talking cure' in an epoch that needed to tell itself its troubles. An important figure in the history of consciousness, she expressed in the language of the body what psychoanalysis says in words" (p. 476).

11.559
MEDICAL HISTORY: Carter, K.C., *"Germ Theory, Hysteria, and Freud's Early Work in Psychopathology,"* 24 (1980) 259-274.

11.560
BULLETIN OF THE MENNINGER CLINIC: Klein, M., *"Freud's Seduction Theory: Its Implications for Fantasy and Memory in Psychoanalytic Theory,"* 45 (1981) n.p.

11.561
FEMINIST REVIEW: Moi, T., *"Representations of Patriarchy: Sexuality and Epistemology in Freud's Dora,"* 9 (1981) 60-74.

11.562
ISSUES IN HEALTH CARE OF WOMEN: Litchfield, L., *"Feminine Masochism as a Component of Psychoanalytic Femininity,"* 3 no. 3 (1981) 129-137.

11.563
JOURNAL OF SOCIAL HISTORY: Decker, H.S., *"Freud and Dora: Constraints on Medical Progress,"* 14 (1981) 445-464. History of Freud's most famous case of hysteria in the context of the general treatment of hysterical women by physicians.

11.564
PSYCHIATRY: Nathan, S.G., *"Cross-Cultural Perspectives on Penis-Envy,"* 44 (1981) 39-44. An inverse relationship between women's social position and penis envy fantasies was found in a study of twenty cultures, supporting Clara Thompson's view that what women really envy is not the physical organ but men's status and power.

11.565
YALE FRENCH STUDIES: Schor, N., *"Female Paranoia: The Case for Psychoanalytic Feminist Criticism,"* no. 62 (1981) 204-219.

11.566
Buckley, Nellie Louise, "Women Psychoanalysts and the Theory of Feminine Development: A Study of Karen Horney, Helene Deutsch, and Marie Bonaparte," Ph.D. diss., University of California, Los Angeles, 1982.

11.567
Gallop, Jane, THE DAUGHTER'S SEDUCTION: FEMINISM AND PSYCHO-ANALYSIS. Ithaca, 1982. A sophisticated and incisive analysis of the relation between contemporary feminist theory and the psychoanalysis of Jacques Lacan, centering on the language of psychoanalysis. The chapter entitled "Keys to Dora" is a dialogue revolving around Helene Cixous' PORTRAIT DE DORA (Paris, 1976; untrans.). The hysteric is a metaphor for all women attempting to break free of their role in the "family" (patriarchy, the analyst); *reviewed in:* SIGNS: Abel, E., 10 (1984) 152-156. "Gallop identifies the denial of paternal desire as the source of the paternal authority (law) that defines patriarchy. Historically, this denial became explicit in the 1890s with Freud's shift from a theory of paternal seduction to a theory of infantile sexuality (the Oedipus complex); desire is thus relocated in the daughter, not the father, who is thereby protected from his own desire and granted the authority to proscribe hers. Seducing the father, eliciting his disavowed desire, violating the paternal sanctuary then become feminist acts" (p. 154).

11.568
Mitchell, Juliet and Rose, Jacqueline, eds., FEMININE SEXUALITY: JACQUES LACAN AND THE ECOLE FREUDIENNE. trans. by Jacqueline Rose with introductions by Juliet Mitchell and Jacqueline Rose. 1982; 1985. A collection of papers by Lacan and articles by other analysts written for his journal. "Psychoanalysis is now recognised as crucial in the discussion of femininity——how it comes into being and what it might mean. Jacques Lacan, who addressed this issue increasingly during the course of his work, has been at the centre of the controversies produced by that recognition" (p. 27).

11.569
Sayers, Janet, "Freud and Feminism" in BIOLOGICAL POLITICS: FEMINIST AND ANTI-FEMINIST PERSPECTIVES. by Janet Sayers. 1982. "If we look at Freud's actual account of the development of psychological sex differences we find that he did not subscribe to a biologically determinist account of female psychology. Instead he regarded the development of the characteristically female (and male) personality as the effect of the way the child construes her (or his) biology. He did not regard psychological sex differences as the mechanistic effect of biology" (p. 127); SEXUAL CONTRADICTIONS: PSYCHOLOGY, PSYCHOANALYSIS AND FEMINISM. 1986. See especially: Part Two, "Post-Freudian Psychoanalysis."

11.570
Van Herik, Judith, FREUD, FEMININITY, AND FAITH. 1982; *reviewed in:* SIGNS: Abel, E., 10 (1984) 152-156. Valuable methodological contribution to feminist scholarship, relating "the internal critical direction of Freud's psychology of religion by making the category of gender its principle of interpretation" (p. 197).

11.571
AMERICAN JOURNAL OF PSYCHIATRY: Chodoff, P., *"Hysteria and Women,"* 139 (1982) 545-551.

11.572
COMPARATIVE STUDIES IN SOCIETY AND HISTORY: Burnham, J.C., *"The Reception of Psychoanalysis in Western Cultures: An Afterword on Its Comparative History,"* 24 (1982) 603-610. "Freud's teachings... were caught up in preexisting and developing hopes and fears about what was happening to the structure of society. Concern about the nastiness—and attractiveness—of psychoanalytic discussions of sex was overwhelming, regardless of... locality" (p. 604).

11.573
JOURNAL OF MEDICAL PHILOSOPHY: Rawlinson, M.C., *"Psychiatric Discourse and the Feminine Voice,"* 7 no. 2 (1982) 153-177.

11.574
Bell, Susan Groag and Offen, Karen M., eds., **WOMEN, FAMILY, AND FREEDOM: THE DEBATE IN DOCUMENTS. VOLUME TWO, 1880-1950.** Stanford, 1983. See especially: "Psychoanalysis and Woman's Character." Contains selections from Sigmund Freud and Karen Horney on female sexuality. Horney countered Freud's theory of penis-envy with evidence of womb-envy on the part of men, and implicated "the purely masculine character of our civilization" in shaping women's feelings of inferiority. "These typical motives for flight into the male role—motives whose origin is the Oedipus complex—are reinforced and supported by the actual disadvantage under which women labor in social life" (p. 337).

11.575
Coward, Rosalind, **PATRIARCHAL PRECEDENTS: SEXUALITY AND SOCIAL RELATIONS.** 1983. See especially: "The Patriarchal Family in Freudian Theory" and "Psychoanalysis and Anthropology: the Interpretation of Social Practices."

11.576
AMERICAN PSYCHOLOGIST: Hare-Mustin, R.T., *"An Appraisal of the Relationship Between Women and Psychotherapy. 80 Years After the Case of Dora,"* 38 (1983) 593-601; Caplan, P.J., *"The Myth of Women's Masochism,"* 39 (1984) 130-139.

11.577
CANADIAN JOURNAL OF PSYCHIATRY: Nadelson, C.C., *"The Psychology of Women,"* 28 (1983) 210-228. Presents classical psychoanalytic theory and its critiques, considers whether there are sex differences in psychopathology, and discusses some implications of psychotherapy with women in the current socio-cultural context.

11.578
INTERNATIONAL JOURNAL OF WOMEN'S STUDIES: Sayers, J., *"Is the Personal Political? Psychoanalysis and Feminism Revisited,"* 6 (1983) 71-86. "While Freud's work raises... problems, it also has an important advantage over that of Mitchell and Chodorow in that it draws attention to the contradictions that exist within personal consciousness—contradictions that have been a major motive force of the current contradictions that exist within personal consciousness—contradictions that have been a major motive force of the current women's movement" (p. 71).

11.579
Donchin, Anne, "Concepts of Women in Psychoanalytic Theory: The Nature-Nurture Controversy Revisited" in **BEYOND DOMINATION: NEW PERSPECTIVES**

ON WOMEN AND PHILOSOPHY. ed. by Carol C. Gould. Totowa, 1984. Discusses the role of biological determinants in formulating a feminist psychoanalytic theory.

11.580
Drinka, George Frederick, THE BIRTH OF NEUROSIS: MYTH, MALADY AND THE VICTORIANS. 1984.

11.581
Komter, Aafke, "Feminism and Psychoanalysis" in A CREATIVE TENSION: EXPLORATIONS IN SOCIALIST FEMINISM. 1st English ed., 1984. This Dutch publication compares English and American feminist thinkers with those of the French Lacanian tradition. Discusses Irigaray, Cixous, and Kristeva; Mitchell and Foreman; Chodorow, Dinnerstein and Rich, among others.

11.582
Wickert, Gabrielle, "Freud's Heritage: Fathers and Daughters in German Literature (1750-1850)" in IN THE SHADOW OF THE PAST: PSYCHOLOGY PORTRAYS THE SEXES: A SOCIAL AND INTELLECTUAL HISTORY. ed. by Miriam Lewin. New York, 1984. Describes and illustrates the tradition of sexual roles from which Freud emerged.

11.583
INTERNATIONAL JOURNAL OF HEALTH SERVICES: Brown, P., *"Marxism, Social Psychology, and the Sociology of Mental Health,"* 14 (1984) 237-264. Includes discussion of "Freudo-Marxism."

11.584
Bernheimer, Charles and Kahane, Claire, eds., IN DORA'S CASE: FREUD—HYSTERIA—FEMINISM. New York, 1985. Dora was an hysteric adolescent whose father "gave" her to his friend, Herr K., in return for Frau K., with whom Dora's father was having an affair. Dora's case amplified the phenomenon of transference in psychoanalytic therapy. This anthology contains important essays by Felix Deutsch, Erik Erikson, Jacques Lacan, Steven Marcus, Jaqueline Rose and Jane Gallop.

11.585
Eysenck, Hans J., DECLINE AND FALL OF THE FREUDIAN EMPIRE. 1985.

11.586
Garner, Shirley Nelson, Kahane, Claire, and Sprengnether, Madelon, eds., THE (M)OTHER TONGUE: ESSAYS IN FEMINIST PSYCHOANALYTIC INTERPRE-TATION. 1985. Introduction offers a lucid account of recent feminist revision of the Oedipus complex by Anglo-Americans contrasted to that of the French followers of Lacan. Part 1, "Feminists on Freud," contains "The Father's Seduction" by Jane Gallop, "Enforcing Oedipus: Freud and Dora" by Madelon Sprengnether, "The Hand That Rocks the Cradle: Recent Gender Theories and Their Implications" by Coppelia Kahn, and "Hysteria, Psychoanalysis, and Feminism: The Case of Anna O." by Diane Hunter.

11.587
Gay, Peter, FREUD FOR HISTORIANS. Oxford, 1985; *reviewed in:* LOS ANGELES TIMES BOOK REVIEW: (Nov. 3, 1985) 11. "Yielding to the persuasions of Freud will necessarily force historians to change... drastically the way they do

history, force them to dispense with prized convictions and to revise favorite conclusions" (n.p.).

11.588
Kofman, Sarah, **THE ENIGMA OF WOMAN: WOMAN IN FREUD'S WRITINGS.** trans. from the French by Catherine Porter. 1985. "The thesis of bisexuality... serves as his defense against accusations of anti-feminism; and it, too, is double-edged. It allows Freud to repeat the most tenacious, the most traditional, the most metaphysical phallocratic discourse: if you women are as intelligent as men, it is because you are really more masculine than feminine.... And it is as though Freud were loudly proclaiming the universality of bisexuality in order better to disguise his silent disavowal of his own femininity, his paranoia" (pp. 14-15).

11.589
Schor, Naomi, "Theory's Body: Female Paranoia: The Case for Feminist Psychoanalytic Criticism" in **BREAKING THE CHAIN: WOMEN, THEORY, AND FRENCH REALIST FICTION.** New York, 1985. Comments on the gap existing between feminist psychoanalytic theory that is not based on literary criticism, and literary critique of psychoanalysis that is not primarily feminist. "Basing myself on a respectful but, literally, perverse reading of one of Freud's minor essays on femininity, I shall propose a psychoanalytic feminist hermeneutics which turns to account the specific contribution of women to contemporary theory, that is, their militant feminism" (p. 150).

11.590
Weeks, Jeffrey, "Sexuality and the Unconscious" in **SEXUALITY AND ITS DISCONTENTS: MEANINGS, MYTHS AND MODERN SEXUALITIES.** by Jeffrey Weeks. 1985.

11.591
ADVANCES IN PSYCHOSOMATIC MEDICINE: Lothstein, L.M., *"Female Sexuality and Feminine Development: Freud and His Legacy,"* 12 (1985) 57-70. Reviews Freud's hypotheses and subsequent reconceptualizations. "Freud believed that... it was more difficult for the girl to achieve her femininity than for a boy to achieve his masculinity. What we know today suggests just the opposite" (p. 58).

11.592
Ragland-Sullivan, Ellie, **JACQUES LACAN AND THE PHILOSOPHY OF PSYCHOANALYSIS.** Urbana, 1986. See especially: "'Beyond the Phallus'?: The Question of Gender Identity," describing Lacan's formation of the Oedipus complex.

XII. WOMEN'S RIGHTS, FEMINISM, POLITICS AND SUFFRAGE

INTRODUCTION

By the 1850s English women reformers were establishing organizations to champion causes that would improve their social position just as they and their forebears had organized for charitable improvement of the disadvantaged in the decades before. The legal disabilities of married women, the insufficiency of female educational institutions, the absence of employment opportunities for impecunious single women were among the issues that brought into association a group of women in London who may be called early Victorian feminists. If we define "feminist" as one who tries to change the position of women, or theories about women, in the direction of attaining greater personal freedom for women, equal rights, or the equality of the sexes, then the group that formed in Langham Place in 1855 deserves the designation. Barbara Leigh Smith (later Bodichon), author of the pamphlet titled "A Brief Summary, in Plain Language, of the Most Important Laws Concerning Women" (1854), called the initial meeting. Others attending included Bessie Rayner Parkes, Emily Davies, and Jessie Boucherett. Subsequently, Bodichon and Parkes founded THE ENGLISH WOMAN'S JOURNAL to attend to questions of employment, education and the legal status of women. Davies launched a movement to gain the admission of women to the Examinations of the University of London. Boucherett started (with others) the Society for Promoting the Employment of Women. A second committee was organized to petition for passage of a bill to permit married women to own property. This enterprise launched what has been called, largely for analytical convenience, "the women's movement."

For an introduction to the Langham Place organization and also to a related association, The Kensington Society, see especially:

12.1int
JOURNAL OF BRITISH STUDIES: Rosen, A., *"Emily Davies and the Women's Movement, 1862-1867,"* 19 (1979) 101-121.

Other modern introductory discussions of these and subsequent early organizations of the women's movement include:

12.2int
Morgan, David, **SUFFRAGISTS AND LIBERALS: THE POLITICS OF WOMAN SUFFRAGE IN ENGLAND.** 1975.

12.3int
Holcombe, Lee, "'The Germs of an Effective Movement': Feminism in the 1850s" in
**WIVES AND PROPERTY: REFORM OF THE MARRIED WOMEN'S PROPERTY
LAW IN NINETEENTH CENTURY ENGLAND.** by Lee Holcombe. Toronto, 1983.

12.4int
Rendall, Jane, "Politics, Philanthropy and the Public Sphere" in **THE ORIGINS OF
MODERN FEMINISM: WOMEN IN BRITAIN, FRANCE AND THE UNITED
STATES, 1780-1860.** 1985.

12.5int
The question of enfranchisement also began to have wide currency by the 1850s.
The female population had not participated in parliamentary elections by tradition,
and in 1832, with the legislation of the Great Reform Bill, women were explicitly
excluded. In 1851 Harriet Taylor Mill, wife of feminist philosopher John Stuart
Mill, published strong feminist arguments for women's suffrage. Her most famous
article appeared in **WESTMINSTER REVIEW:** 55 (1851) 289-301 and was later
published as a pamphlet in 1868.

> The modern... modes of education of women abjure an education of mere
> show and profess to aim at solid instruction, but mean by that expression,
> superficial information on solid subjects.... High mental powers in women
> will be but an exceptional accident until every career is open to them and
> until they as well as men are educated for themselves and for the world, not
> one sex for the other (n.p.).... What is wanted for women is equal rights,
> equal admission to all social privileges, not a position apart, a sort of
> sentimental priesthood (p. 301).

Examples of other early feminist publications that were reprinted by suffrage
organizations over the century are:

12.6int
"Justicia" (Mrs. Henry Davis Pochin), **THE RIGHT OF WOMEN TO EXERCISE
THE ELECTIVE FRANCHISE.** 1855. Grievances are stated under the headings,
"Evils of the Present System" and "Benefits of the Adopted Reforms."

12.7int
Bodichon, Barbara L.S., **REASONS FOR THE ENFRANCHISEMENT OF WOMEN.**
1866. Read at the October 1866 meeting of the National Society for the Promotion
of Social Science, an organization for social reform that admitted members of both
sexes.

Universally regarded as the classic argument for the enfranchisement of women, the
"feminist bible" is

12.8int
Mill, John Stuart, **THE SUBJECTION OF WOMEN.** 1869.

Commenting on the "enormous impression which THE SUBJECTION made on the
minds of educated women all over the world" is

12.9int

Evans, Richard J., **THE FEMINISTS: WOMEN'S EMANCIPATION MOVEMENTS IN EUROPE, AMERICA AND AUSTRALASIA 1840-1920.** 1979.

> Mill's book was influential because it summed up the feminist case in a way that linked it firmly to the political theory of liberal individualism and tied it to the assumptions about society and politics held by its audience. It is often claimed that the appeal of THE SUBJECTION is timeless, and that its impact derives from the lack of any markedly 'Victorian' character. Nothing could be further from the truth. Its power derived precisely from the fact that it was in many ways a summary of the prejudices and preconceptions of the age. Its rhetoric is redolent of the optimism and arrogance of mid-Victorian liberalism (p. 19).

Evans emphasizes the importance of considering the economic and political context in which Mill guided the organized suffragists, proposed legislation for women's suffrage, and failed to achieve their goal. Making a historical evaluation of the fluidity of socioeconomic conditions, administrative structures, political crises and party politics is undoubtedly as crucial to a thorough analysis of English feminist and suffrage history as is unraveling the threads of what transpired throughout the women's movement. Among the basic questions for that history is how and why so many feminist goals were at least partially fulfilled while equal voting rights were so intransigently denied. What was at the bottom of the women's rights/women's suffrage dichotomy?

On the way toward answering the second question, primarily from the intellectual/emotional perspective of the anti-suffragists ("Antis") is the very important study,

12.10int

Harrison, Brian, **SEPARATE SPHERES: THE OPPOSITION TO WOMEN'S SUFFRAGE IN BRITAIN.** 1978. See especially Chap. 4, "The Heart of the Matter." "The general case made out against woman suffrage between 1867 and 1918 must be reconstructed in all its contemporary plausibility. It would be as wrong to equate anti-suffragism with anti-feminism as to equate suffragism with feminism, though on both sides there was an overlap between the two" (p. 55). Harrison illustrates that a number of anti-suffragists supported reforms proposed by feminists in areas such as family law, education and personal rights. As for suffrage, however, he gives a lengthy summary of the grounds upon which the Antis campaigned against granting women the parliamentary vote. Not the least of the Antis' derogatory arguments pertain to women as a sex.

Some contemporary feminists also appear to have recognized the dichotomy of feminism/suffrage. For example,

12.11int

Blackburn, Helen, **WOMEN'S SUFFRAGE: A RECORD OF THE WOMEN'S SUFFRAGE MOVEMENT IN THE BRITISH ISLES WITH BIOGRAPHICAL SKETCHES OF MISS BECKER.** 1902. "Do some still say: women have gained so much without having votes [and so] they really ought to be content? Then it is because they have not yet learned how insecure is every gain which has been won by those who are unrepresented. To bid women rest content with anything short of direct representation, is to bid them plant their feet on shifting sand rather than on solid ground" (p. 227).

12.12int
Snowden, Ethel, **THE FEMINIST MOVEMENT**. 1912. Snowden argues that feminism developed when women saw that the course of industrialization was "responsible for robbing women of their work [that was] not directly concerned with the bearing of children." However, she denies the accusation that feminists seek "freedom from the cares and obligations following upon the carrying out of woman's special and particular work as woman" (p. 37). What women want, she says, is freedom "in the exercise of those gifts and in the use of those qualities of soul and mind which are apart from the consequences of the sex-act" (p. 15). Her illustrations begin with "the struggle for educational opportunity," and then she surveys the areas of social and public life in which feminists were struggling for rights. After describing gains made over the century, she then suggests the road yet to be traveled. Mainly it is toward the goal of parliamentary enfranchisement. She asks how it is possible for

> an unrepresented class to wring beneficial legislation from those not answerable to it.... Privileges and rights are not secure without the power which the vote carries to protect them... [and] most of all... [suffragists] look upon the vote as a symbol of deep spiritual things and the hallmark of their individuality (pp. 147-148).

As Harrison's study indicates, self-protection and individuality are exactly the traits in women that the Antis decried.

Running throughout feminist rhetoric of the early twentieth century is the theme that, aside from questions of rights and justice, full enfranchisement held strong symbolic meaning. A few examples illustrate the tone:

12.13int
Pethick-Lawrence, Emmeline, **THE FAITH THAT IS IN US**. [1908]. Women activists were agitating for "not the Vote only, but what the Vote means——the moral, mental, economic, the spiritual enfranchisement of that great temple of womanhood, which has been so ruined and defaced" (p. 4).

12.14int
Billington-Grieg, Teresa, **THE MILITANT SUFFRAGE MOVEMENT: EMANCIPATION IN A HURRY**. 1907.

> I am a feminist, a rebel, and a suffragist——a believer, therefore, in sex-equality and militant action. I desire to see women free and human; I seek her complete emancipation from all shackles of law and custom, from all chains of sentiment and superstition, from all outer imposed disabilities and cherished inner bondages which unite to shut off liberty from the human soul borne in her body. I believe that woman is in freedom the equal of man, and that any disabilities imposed by man upon woman or by woman upon man are evil (pp. 1-2).... I shall be a militant rebel to the end of my days (p. 3).... but... our revolt itself was of very much greater value than the vote we demanded (p. 29).

Modern scholars, synthesizing the cumulative opinions of suffragists from their sources, concur with contemporary writers that, by and large, suffragists attributed to enfranchisement a value beyond practical improvements of their status and economic opportunities. For example:

12.15int
CANADIAN JOURNAL OF HISTORY: Robson, A.P.W., *"The Founding of the National Society for Women's Suffrage 1866-1867,"* 8 (1973) 1-22. "Although there were many battlegrounds——education, employment, professional status, and moral reform——the central fight was for the suffrage" (p. 1).

12.16int
Richardson, Mary R., **LAUGH A DEFIANCE.** 1953. In this autobiography, Mary Richardson reflects that the suffragette campaign was "much more than votes for women. We were inaugurating a new era for women and demonstrating for the first time in history that women were capable of fighting their own battle for freedom's sake. We were breaking down old senseless barriers which had been the curse of our sex, exploding men's theories and ideas about us" (p. 103).

12.17int
Vicinus, Martha, **INDEPENDENT WOMEN: WORK AND COMMUNITY FOR SINGLE WOMEN 1850-1920.** Chicago, 1985. Vicinus, like the subjects of her study, takes objective measurements of women's improved social position without achieving the vote:

> The numbers of women who had gained independence and an adequate income were small. Women had made little progress against political and economic inequalities. They were generally discouraged from pursuing any career into the upper levels of management. Indeed they had no voice whatever in such male preserves as the law, banking, commerce, and industry, even though they were often directly affected by the policies emanating from such powerful institutions. An increasingly complex industrial society needed the work of trained women but had successfully kept them back from the centers of power. The lack of the vote symbolized women's secondary status (p. 247).

No doubt, the symbolic significance of the vote also lay behind radicalization and militancy that developed in the most active sectors of the suffrage campaign in the early twentieth century. As is well known, the most militant wing, the Suffragettes of the Women's Social and Political Union (WSPU), became virtual terrorists. The more moderate and largest organization, the National Union of Women's Suffrage Societies (WUWSS), became more self-consciously feminist, even seeking legitimate feminist roots by identifying an ideological, political and feminist inheritance by, for example, identifying their cause with Mary Wollstonecraft, the eighteenth-century author of the equal-rights manifesto, **A VINDICATION OF THE RIGHTS OF WOMAN.** 1792. Helen Blackburn heads the bibliography of her book on suffrage history with the citation of Wollstonecraft's work. Also employing the eighteenth-century feminist as a model is

12.18int
Fawcett, Millicent Garrett, "Introduction" to Wollstonecraft, Mary, **A VINDICATION OF THE RIGHTS OF WOMAN.** rpt. ed. 1891; "A Pioneer of the Movement, Mary Wollstonecraft" in **THE CASE FOR WOMEN'S SUFFRAGE.** ed. by Brougham Villiers (pseud. for Frederick John Shaw). 1907. Writing as president of the largest of all women's suffrage organizations, Fawcett presents a lengthy

discussion of Wollstonecraft's ideas, experiences and writing: "I have here endeavoured to consider the character of the initiative which she gave to the women's rights movement in England, and I find that she stamped upon it from the outset the word Duty, and has impressed it with a character that it has never since lost" (p. 189).

For thoughtful discussions of Wollstonecraft and early feminism in relation to the nineteenth-century suffrage movement, see

12.19int
Rover, Constance, **LOVE, MORALS AND THE FEMINISTS.** 1970.

12.20int
Kramnick, Miriam Brody, "Introduction: The Liberation of Mary Wollstonecraft—Life and Writings" in **A VINDICATION OF THE RIGHTS OF WOMAN.** 1975; 1978. Pelican Classic.

On the value of examining the history of the suffrage movement in terms of the ideas and doctrines that were inherited from the past and incorporated into the rhetoric of the various suffrage organizations, see

12.21int
Banks, Joseph A. and Banks, Olive, **FEMINISM AND FAMILY PLANNING IN VICTORIAN ENGLAND.** Liverpool, 1964. Several subsequent eds.

> At one level we may think of [feminism] as a set of doctrines which have been developed over the past 150 years on the place of women in society, and more especially, on the extent to which women should have equal rights, opportunities and responsibilities with those of men. These doctrines are associated with the names of people such as Mary Wollstonecraft, William Thompson and John Stuart Mill, to mention three of the most famous of the early feminists (p. 8).... Of even greater significance for our purpose is the organized movement which sought, not always successfully, to translate doctrine into reality (p. 9).... Between 1850 and 1870 there was a development of an organized movement to right women's wrongs (p. 40).

12.22int
Rowbotham, Sheila, **HIDDEN FROM HISTORY: REDISCOVERING WOMEN IN HISTORY FROM THE SEVENTEENTH CENTURY TO THE PRESENT.** 1976. Rowbotham evaluates "a strong minority tradition in radicalism which questioned the whole social and sexual position of women" (p. 40), especially the eighteenth-century radical feminist writing of William Thompson and Anna Wheeler.

12.23int
Schnorrenberg, Barbara B. with Hunter, Jean, "The Eighteenth-Century Englishwoman" in **THE WOMEN OF ENGLAND FROM ANGLO-SAXON TIMES TO THE PRESENT: INTERPRETIVE BIBLIOGRAPHICAL ESSAYS.** ed. by Barbara Kanner. Hamden, Conn. 1979. "The first woman openly to challenge the political status quo was Catherine Macaulay Graham. A radical republican who began publishing in 1763, Macaulay Graham showed little evidence of feminism until her **LETTERS ON EDUCATION, WITH OBSERVATIONS ON RELIGIOUS AND METAPHYSICAL SUBJECTS.** 1790. It was this book, which stated firmly that there were no differences, except physical ones, between the sexes, that

Wollstonecraft cited approvingly in her VINDICATION.... The VINDICATION initiated the final and most intense debate of the century on the nature and rights of women (p. 203).... Just as it took the whole century for the idea of female equality to be clearly stated, so it took another for it to be achieved. Feminism is more than politics. Modern feminism, like modern society, begins in the eighteenth century" (p. 205).

12.24int
Garner, Les, **STEPPING STONES TO WOMEN'S LIBERTY: FEMINIST IDEAS IN THE WOMEN'S SUFFRAGE MOVEMENT, 1900-1918.** 1984. Garner discusses some of the main ideas developed within the National Union of Women's Suffrage Societies (NUWSS), the Women's Freedom League (WFL), and the Women's Social and Political Union (WSPU). Garner pursues the question of how these organizations "identified the oppression of women" and the solutions they proposed (p. vii). She discusses also the ideas communicated by the radical feminist paper, **THE FREEWOMAN:** 1912-1913:

> 'Mirroring thought' is perhaps the best way to describe THE FREEWOMAN for it did not have a programme but acted as a forum for a radical and revolutionary discussion of women-politics. The discussions of women's sphere, marriage, sexuality and reproduction were all the more outstanding for their explicit criticism of contemporary moral codes and values.... The initial emphasis of FREEWOMAN was critical of suffragism, but from a radical and feminist perspective. Indeed, the paper argued that 'feminism is the whole issue, political enfranchisement a branch' (pp. 62-63).

12.25int
Rendall, Jane, **THE ORIGINS OF MODERN FEMINISM: WOMEN IN BRITAIN, FRANCE AND THE UNITED STATES, 1780-1860.** 1985.

> It is often assumed that concern about the rights of women springs from the eighteenth-century Enlightenment, from the assertion of individual natural rights in a period of revolutionary political thinking. When Mary Wollstonecraft wrote her VINDICATION OF THE RIGHTS OF WOMAN in 1792, she seemed to be applying the arguments of RIGHTS OF MAN to the situation of women.... Few writers of the Enlightenment took a deep interest in the relationship between the sexes, and yet the implications of their work were fundamental. The position of women in western Europe was analyzed in new terms: it was to be justified by reference to what was natural for their sex, rather than divinely ordained, and at the same time, set into a particular historical framework. These terms were to dictate the grounds of debate for feminists and their opponents in the nineteenth century (pp. 7-8).

The theme of eighteenth-century intellectual foundations informing nineteenth- and early twentieth-century English feminism is perhaps most elaborated in the work of

12.26int
Banks, Olive, **FACES OF FEMINISM: A STUDY OF FEMINISM AS A SOCIAL MOVEMENT.** New York, 1981; **THE BIOGRAPHICAL DICTIONARY OF BRITISH FEMINISTS 1800-1930.** New York, 1985; **BECOMING A FEMINIST: THE SOCIAL ORIGINS OF 'FIRST WAVE' FEMINISM.** Brighton, 1986.

In FACES OF FEMINISM Banks distinguishes three streams of eighteenth-century thought: evangelical Christianity, Enlightenment philosophy and Owenite socialism.

Under the influence of the first,

> women began to emerge from domesticity and take on a public role, as they became increasingly involved in issues of moral, and later social reform. Accompanied by ideas of the moral superiority of women, it finds its most modern expression in the 'pro-woman' sections of radical feminism. The second tradition is that of the Enlightenment philosophers. Among the principles they bequeathed to feminism is the appeal to human reason rather than tradition and its most influential feminist propagators have been Mary Wollstonecraft and John Stuart Mill.... Its whole tendency has been to emphasize the potential similarities between the sexes, rather than the differences.... It is from the Enlightenment thinkers, too, that the feminists draw their emphasis on self-realization, freedom and autonomy.... [Third is] Socialist feminism [which] has its roots, not in Marxism, but in the much earlier tradition of communitarian [Owenite] socialism.... [With its advocated] changes in family life went changes in the sexual relationships between men and women.... Deriving from separate origins representing different goals... those three traditions comprise the several faces of feminism with which this study is concerned (pp. 7-8).

In her introduction to THE BIOGRAPHICAL DICTIONARY, Banks emphasizes the dynamics of feminist ideology, changing and adapting over time to perpetually altering circumstances. She nevertheless continues to point out the touchstones between more modern versions of feminism and the intellectual foundations of the eighteenth century.

Banks designed BECOMING A FEMINIST as a companion volume to THE DICTIONARY. She analyzes the feminists treated in the dictionary after they are grouped into four cohorts arranged according to date of birth: 1) before 1828, representing the first generation of the women's movement; 2) between 1828 and 1848, covering most of the leaders of nineteenth-century feminist movements; 3) between 1849 and 1871, coming into the movement during the last decades of the century; and 4) between 1872 and 1891, representing the last generation of 'first-wave' feminism. Banks explains, "The main justification for the present study is its methodology which by examining the lives of individual feminists makes possible an exploration of the way in which personal experiences interact with ideological perspectives and indeed with the level of commitment to feminism itself" (p. 7). Ninety-eight women and eighteen men make up the sample. In her concluding chapter Banks draws together her data in provocative summaries that are worth close evaluation.

One limitation of Banks' otherwise valuable analysis is its pre-occupation with intellectual influences that conjures the world of feminism as the virtually exclusive preserve of educated middle-class thinkers and organizers. She seriously underplays the fact that the late eighteenth and early nineteenth centuries witnessed female working-class activism. Some recent studies drawing attention to female working-class politics of the early nineteenth century are

12.27int
Thomis, Malcolm I. and Grimmet, Jennifer, **WOMEN IN PROTEST, 1800-1850.** 1982. Following the Napoleonic wars women who had taken part in economic protests connected with industrialism began to be drawn into radical political movements in an organized way. For example, female reform societies were formed

in Blackburn, Stockport, Nottingham and Manchester "to assist the pale populations... to obtain their rights and liberties.... to use their utmost endeavors to instill into the minds of their children a deep and rooted hatred of their tyrannical rulers" (pp. 92-93).

On the organized working-class women's political and suffrage activities of the later nineteenth and early twentieth centuries, the scholarly study that has made the greatest impact is that of

12.28int

Liddington, Jill and Norris, Jill, **ONE HAND TIED BEHIND US: THE RISE OF THE WOMEN'S SUFFRAGE MOVEMENT.** 1978.

> The radical suffragists wanted the vote not just for a wealthy few but for women like themselves. They formulated a demand for 'womanhood suffrage' to include all women over the age of twenty-one.... And just as they rejected the limited aims of the existing suffrage societies, so, by the late 1890s, the radical suffragists realized that womanhood suffrage could never be won by the traditional methods of drawing-room meetings and discreet lobbying of individual MPs.... The only way was to build a mass movement of working women, firmly based in the Lancashire cotton unions (p. 26).

Other recent scholarship that has brought working-class women into the political and feminist spectrum, thus rejecting the notion of middle-class exclusivity in the development of feminism and women's emancipation movements include:

12.29int

Kanner, Barbara, "The Women of England in a Century of Social Change, 1800-1914: A Bibliography" in **SUFFER AND BE STILL: WOMEN IN THE VICTORIAN AGE.** ed. by Martha Vicinus. Bloomington, 1972. Draws attention to the activist roles of women Chartists, and suggests the potentiality of **THE ENGLISH CHARTIST CIRCULAR.** vols. 1-3, 1841-1843, rpt. New York, 1968 as a starting point in research.

12.30int

Martin, Caroline E., "Female Chartism: A Study in Politics," Masters thesis, Univ. of Wales, 1973.

12.31int

Thompson, Dorothy, "Women in Nineteenth-Century Radical Politics: A Lost Dimension" in **THE RIGHTS AND WRONGS OF WOMEN.** introduced and ed. by Juliet Mitchell and Ann Oakley. 1976; "The Women" in **THE CHARTISTS: POPULAR POLITICS IN THE INDUSTRIAL REVOLUTION.** New York, 1984. See especially: pp. 134-151.

12.32int

Liddington, Jill, "Women Cotton Workers and the Suffrage Campaign: the Radical Suffragists in Lancashire, 1893-1914" in **FIT WORK FOR WOMEN.** ed. by Sandra Burman. 1979.

12.33int

Malmgreen, Gail, **NEITHER BREAD NOR ROSES: UTOPIAN FEMINISM AND**

THE ENGLISH WORKING CLASS, 1800-1850. Brighton, 1978.

12.34int
Scott, Gillian, "The Politics of the Women's Cooperative Guild: Working Women and Feminism During the First World War," Masters thesis, Univ. of Sussex, 1980.

12.35int
Tank, Susan Patricia, "Social Change and Social Movements: Working-Class Women and Political Activity in Britain, 1880-1921," Ph.D. diss., London School of Economics, 1981.

12.36int
Chew, Ada Neild, THE LIFE AND WRITINGS OF A WORKING WOMEN. 1982. A collection composed by Chew's daughter, Doris, with an account of her mother as a working-class organizer for the suffrage movement.

12.37int
Walker, Linda E., "The Women's Movement in England in the Late Nineteenth and Early Twentieth Centuries," Ph.D. diss., Univ. of Manchester, 1984.

12.38int
HISTORY: Jones, D., *"Female Chartism,"* 68 (1983) 1-21. "Historians have underestimated the degree of female participation in the Chartist movement" (p. 9).

It is the imaginative historical scholarship of Barbara Taylor that links female working-class politics with middle-class intellectual currents as represented by the "democratic feminist" Mary Wollstonecraft, the Utopian socialist Robert Owen, and the radical feminist socialists ("of a Wollstonecraftian hue") William Thompson and Anna Wheeler. The almost seamless fabric of Taylor's exposition makes it difficult to offer extracts from her important work that are as valuable alone as they are in context.

12.39int
Taylor, Barbara, EVE AND THE NEW JERUSALEM: SOCIALIST FEMINISM OF THE NINETEENTH CENTURY. 1983. Taylor describes the mutuality of female experience that underscored cooperation and identification between early nineteenth-century middle-class and working-class feminists:

> When a woman had to labor for a living she could all too easily find herself inhabiting a region where class differences blurred in the face of a common female oppression. This may help to explain why women like Eliza Macauley and Emma Martin so strongly identified with the cause of working people——and why all Owenite feminists identified women's oppression as a trans-class phenomenon. The problems which united women from different backgrounds may have seemed more important than the social and cultural differences which divided them (p. 73).

By the end of the century, trans-class female co-operation was not so easily connected by such fluid lines as those that had been traversed by Owenite feminists. By Victorian/Edwardian times, at least in public life, much of female collaboration, or women-helping-women, appears to have followed more conventional hierarchical routes. Robin Jacoby identifies one pattern of middle-class/working-class female relationships in which the activism is for improvement of society in general and the status and conditions of women in particular. She designates this form of feminism as "social feminism"——ignoring whether or not suffragist or equal-rights goals were involved.

12.40int
Jacoby, Robin Miller, "Feminism and Class Consciousness in the British and American Women's Trade Union Leagues, 1890-1925" in **LIBERATING WOMEN'S HISTORY: THEORETICAL AND CRITICAL ESSAYS.** ed. by Berenice A. Carroll. Urbana, 1976. "Social feminists were women who expanded the scope of their role as moral guardians to include society at large as well as their individual families, and who then focused their reform energies on problems that particularly affected women they viewed as 'their less fortunate sisters.'" (p. 140).

Jacoby positions these middle-class feminists within the women's movement that "reflected both an attack on the restricted definition of what was considered to be women's sphere and an internalization of prevailing notions on the nature of women. The former led to the women's rights movement.... the latter was expressed through what has been termed social feminism" (p. 140). They entered public activity committed to improving the condition and position of working women in the home, the workplace and in labor organizations. They stimulated working women's interest in local government and suffragist politics, and they took leadership in trade union leagues.

Expanding on this definition of social feminism is

12.41int
Mappen, Ellen, **HELPING WOMEN AT WORK: THE WOMEN'S INDUSTRIAL COUNCIL, 1889-1914.** 1985. In the context of her short history of the Council, Mappen defines social feminists as "those women who were interested in social questions affecting women's lives and who wanted to obtain economic rights for women. For the most part, they also wanted the vote but they were not going to wait for it before they demanded certain rights and a place in public life. They did not necessarily espouse socialism, although many were involved with socialist groups such as the Fabian Society. They thus saw a connection between social reform and women's rights" (p. 27).

By the end of the nineteenth century many of these feminists were electors in local government. A number served on local boards. In the course of administrative reform, local councils had been charged with responsibility for social welfare measures. Women's votes were courted by political parties and their candidates. So were their volunteer political services. See:

12.42int
Snowden, Ethel, "Women in Public Service" in **THE FEMINIST MOVEMENT.** by Ethel Snowden. 1912. Valuable contemporary discussion.

12.43int
Rendel, Margherita, "The Contribution of the Women's Labour League to the Winning of the Franchise" in **WOMEN IN THE LABOUR MOVEMENT: THE BRITISH EXPERIENCE.** ed. by Lucy Middleton. 1977. "Local government was perhaps especially important in politicizing women, in making them aware of what could be done by their use of political organization and political power, whether it was to get a playground in Throckley, or to run a milk depot as in Woolwich. Much

of the work of local government directly and obviously affects women because local authorities provide services which women need as a result of the roles which society traditionally imposes upon them" (p. 79).

12.44int
Turnbull, Annie, "'So Extremely Like Parliament': The Work of Women Members of the London School Board, 1870-1904" in **THE SEXUAL DYNAMICS OF HISTORY: MEN'S POWER, WOMEN'S RESISTANCE.** compiled by The London Feminist History Group. 1983.

12.45int
Pennybacker, Susan, "The Labour Question and the London County Council, 1889-1919," Ph.D. diss., Cambridge Univ., 1985. See especially: Chap. I., Pt. 2, "The Political Culture of LCC Clerks."

12.46int
Rubinstein, David, "The Experience of Local Government" in **BEFORE THE SUFFRAGETTES: WOMEN'S EMANCIPATION IN THE 1890s.** 1986. Rubinstein discusses the election to local authorities of "not an inconsiderable number of working-class women, who took advantage of the easily satisfied conditions to stand for election to boards of guardians. Thirty-six members of the Women's Cooperative Guild served as guardians in 1898" (p. 170).

Another variety of middle-class/working class feminist relationship is introduced by

12.47int
Holton, Sandra Stanley, **FEMINISM AND DEMOCRACY: WOMEN'S SUFFRAGE AND REFORM POLITICS IN BRITAIN, 1900-1918.** 1986. In her chapter, "The ethos of the Women's Suffrage Movement," Holton shows that, parallel to feminist rhetoric that adhered to the Wollstonecraft tradition of arguing a rational case for individual liberty and equal-rights, there ran an "essentialist case for feminism"— perhaps traceable to evangelical as well as to socialist influences early in the century. This case argued that "women possessed a unique moral mission consequent on the very nature of of womanhood" (p. 11). Holton not only cites early socialists William Thompson and Anna Wheeler, but also mid-century feminists such as Frances Power Cobbe, Harriet Taylor Mill, Helen Taylor and Millicent Garrett Fawcett as infusing their suffragist rhetoric with the female "essentialist" position. For example, she quotes Millicent Fawcett's article in **NINETEENTH CENTURY:** 26 (1899) 96:

> We do not want women to be bad imitations of men; we neither deny nor minimize the differences between men and women. The claim of women to representation depends to a large extent on these differences. Women bring something to the service of the state different to that which can be brought by men (Holton, p. 12).

Holton further explains,

> The essentialist case for women's political emancipation was built upon an analysis of what it is to be female that conflated sex and gender.... Hence female enfranchisement could be argued to be essential to the creation of a more caring state through the furtherance of social reforms informed by feminine understanding and experience (p. 13).... In sum, British feminists

insisted on both the necessity of increasing state intervention in areas that had previously been part of women's domestic preserve and the concomitant need for women's participation in the work of the state. In asserting both, they challenged the notion that domestic and public matters could be kept apart as the separate concerns of women and men respectively (p. 15)....
Many socialists shared the bourgeois feminists' conviction of the fundamental need for women's presence in politics if extensive social reform were to be both rightly conceived and achieved. Middle-class or working-class, liberal or socialist, supporters of women's suffrage could unite in both a pragmatic sense of its expediency... and an ideological conviction of its rightness (p. 17).

Holton argues that this ethos allowed attempts to cross class divisions. It promoted analyses of women's social position as that of a "sex-class." Thus suffragists could "strengthen such claims of cross-social class identity among women and to make feminism pertinent to women from varying backgrounds.... Through the issues they chose to promote, notably those concerned with women's economic subordination and sexual exploitation, suffragists located the basis for a sense of sexual solidarity among women which could help militate against class tensions within the movement" (p. 27). The feminists within the National Union of Women Suffragist Societies who embraced this ethos——this "essentialist case" for a women's "sex-class," also represented "the pro-Labour alliance strand of opinion." Holton designates them as "democratic suffragists," building on an idea of Margaret Llewelyn Davies of the Women's Co-Operative Guild (p. 68). Their position was that women of all classes were to be enfranchised, and in "greater numbers than would have been the case in the simple equal-suffrage bills of the prewar years" (p. 150). Two years before World War I, democratic-suffragist strategy had played a large part in securing the firm commitment of the Labour Party to women's suffrage. Subsequent compromise politics resulted in the Representation of the People Act in 1918 which enfranchised all women on the local government register, or who were wives of men on the local government register and were over the age of thirty.

The full scope of the women's suffrage story has hardly been told and questions about the aftermath of the 1918 legislation has not yet been closely scrutinized for women's history. New studies are being undertaken, however, and innovative questions are being raised. There is, for example, the article

12.48int
Durham, Martin, "Suffrage and After: Feminism in the Early Twentieth Century" in **CRISES IN THE BRITISH STATE, 1880-1930.** 1985.

The suffrage movement before the war had been a force pitched against the dominant parties, generating a breadth of demands beyond that merely of enfranchisement. It expanded and reconstituted the very concept of 'citizenship' in order to address the problems of the cultural specificities of gender and sexuality. The success of 1918 was achieved at a cost of many of the specifically feminist aspects of these demands being drained away, with the residue squeezed into the programmes of the established parties.... The rights of citizenship which women had won were in the very process of being pared down to their most legalistic and abstract forms.... Once women received the vote they could be constituted in political discourse like any other legal subject, regardless of gender.... Before the war the movement for women's suffrage had embodied an active if volatile means of representation for women. But after 1918 the forms in which women were passively *represented* by the political parties... effectively contained (suppressed) much that was so crucial to the pre-war feminists (pp. 188-189).

This motif of loss-with-victory of course prompts a review of the general social-political context in which national and political imperatives were related to the female vote. Why the women's vote was granted just then is a question that historians are now re-opening. Durham's chapter goes a good way toward positing new explanations about the situation in 1918. But other recent studies allow us to consider the suggested dichotomy of loss/victory. Not the least is Sandra Holton's which questions why and how new networks of trans-class feminists turned their focus from franchise questions to, for example, "immerse themselves in movements for internationalism, for colonial freedom, for peace and against fascism" (p. 151).

Exemplifying recent studies of feminists and suffragists who shifted their emphasis from 1913-1914 and after to international cooperation and peace movements, there are:

12.49int

Tims, Margaret and Bussey, Gertrude, **PIONEERS FOR PEACE**. 1965. A history of the Women's International League for Peace and Freedom.

12.50int

Oldfield, Sybil, **SPINSTERS OF THIS PARISH: THE LIFE AND TIMES OF F.M. MAYOR AND MARY SHEEPSHANKS**. 1984. In 1913 Mary Sheepshanks became secretary of the International Women's Suffrage Alliance and editor of its monthly paper, JUS SUFFRAGII (Law of Suffrage). "The world-wide women's movement, right up to August 1914... had been positively internationalist. Whenever feminists had gathered, they had set themselves to work for international understanding as well as for the emancipation of women (p. 177).... At the end of July 1914... the leading British, German, French and American suffragists, then meeting in London... drew up a manifesto to all the governments.... It was drafted in Mary Sheepshanks' International Women's Suffrage Office" (pp. 177-178). This was an attempt to "stop the outbreak of the war." Ultimately, Sheepshanks and her colleagues were to form the Women's International League for Peace and Freedom (founded 1915).

12.51int

Wiltsher, Anne, **MOST DANGEROUS WOMEN: FEMINIST PEACE CAMPAIGNERS OF THE GREAT WAR**. 1985. Wiltsher shows that half the leading women of the British Suffrage movement opposed the First World War. They worked through international suffrage networks to campaign for a negotiated peace. By war's end there were active women's peace groups in eleven European countries as well as America.

12.52int

HISTORY WORKSHOP JOURNAL: Vellacott, J., *"Feminist Consciousness and the First World War,"* 23 (1987) 81-101. "The group that I want to look at is what became the dissident wing of the NUWSS in 1914-15 (p. 83).... Failing to get a mandate from the NU[WSS] Council, [Catherine] Marshall and [Kathleen] Courtney resigned from the executive council.... They turned at once to international peace work (p. 93).... Once the war was over, pacifist socialists, and especially the pacifist socialist feminists, were a small group in the larger body of Labour and of international socialism.... Their realistic assessment of the magnitude of social and political change needed did not prevent the feminist pacifists from rejoicing that the vote was won, but few there were who... any longer saw it as the earthshaking event they had expected" (p. 95).

The visions and revisions of feminist/suffragist history have expanded greatly in the 1980s, opening almost all aspects for new analytic work. Proposed perspectives that identify a range of feminisms require testing. Concomitant questions about the relationships among feminists of different hues within their own societies, and between the feminists of different organizations of the women's movement represent possible new approaches. That English women suffragists shared an identifiable political culture is a thesis awaiting careful treatment. The building of foundations for a "new feminism" that emerged post-war to attend to new conditions of women and new challenges of society still wants clarification. These and other wedges in the historical record are multiplying, leading ultimately to exciting ventures in research.

*   *   *

1. RIGHTS, EMANCIPATION AND THE FEMINIST CONTROVERSY

12.1

Astell, Mary, **A SERIOUS PROPOSAL TO THE LADIES FOR THE ADVANCEMENT OF THEIR TRUE AND GREATEST INTERESTS.** 1694. Addresses defects in education for women; **AN ESSAY IN DEFENSE OF THE FEMALE SEX.** 1697; *also published as:* **DEFENCE OF THE LADIES; REFLECTIONS ON MARRIAGE.** 1700. ——*see also:* **WESTMINSTER REVIEW:** McIlquham, H., *"Mary Astell: A Seventeenth Century Advocate for Women,"* 149 (1898) 440-449. Describes Astell's writings, calling her the "pioneer of the modern 'women's rights' movement" (p. 445); Janes, R., "Mary, Mary, Quite Contrary, Or Mary Astell and Mary Wollstonecraft Compared" in **STUDIES IN EIGHTEENTH-CENTURY CULTURE.** ed. by Ronald C. Rosbottom. vol. 5, 1976. "Separated by almost a hundred years, Mary Astell and Mary Wollstonecraft give us a common portrait of the position of women... and a common sense of the limitations imposed upon the women of the relevant classes (Middling and Quality)" (pp. 122-123); Perry, R., "The Veil of Chastity: Mary Astell's Feminism," vol. 9, 1979. This is an annual series; Kinnaird, Joan K., "Mary Astell: Inspired by Ideas (1668-1731)" in **FEMINIST THEORISTS. THREE CENTURIES OF WOMEN'S INTELLECTUAL TRADITIONS.** ed. by Dale Spender. 1983. Examines Astell's feminism which "was not born of liberal impulses but of conservative values. She preached not women's rights but women's duties——at a time when women were not thought worthy of duties and when they were accorded no role in the transmission of social values to the young" (p. 37); Hill, Bridget, ed., **THE FIRST ENGLISH FEMINIST: REFLECTIONS ON MARRIAGE AND OTHER WRITINGS BY MARY ASTELL.** 1986.

12.2

Defoe, Daniel, **AN ESSAY UPON PROJECTS.** 1698; 1969. "Ignorance and folly" is not more prevalent "among women than men" (pp. 302-303); **THE FAMILY**

INSTRUCTOR; OR, A SERIES OF MOST INTERESTING DIALOGUES, ON RELIGIOUS SUBJECTS. IN THREE PARTS... 19th ed., Newcastle-Upon-Tyne, 1715; many subsequent eds. "A man and his wife never quarrel, but there are faults on both sidides [sic]... if one is to blame for beginning it, the other's to blame for carrying it on" (pp. 420-421); RELIGIOUS COURTSHIP: BEING HISTORICAL DISCOURSES, ON THE NECESSITY OF MARRYING RELIGIOUS HUSBANDS AND WIVES ONLY. AS ALSO OF HUSBANDS AND WIVES BEING OF THE SAME OPINIONS IN RELIGION WITH ONE ANOTHER... 1722; THE FORTUNES AND MISFORTUNES OF THE FAMOUS MOLL FLANDERS, ETC... WRITTEN FROM HER OWN MEMORANDUMS. 1722; subsequent eds. Fictional account depicting the status of women; THE FORTUNATE MISTRESS: OR, A HISTORY OF THE LIFE AND VAST VARIETY OF FORTUNES OF MADEMOISELLE DE BALEAU, AFTERWARDS CALL'D THE COUNTESS OF WINTAELSHEIN, IN GERMANY, BEING THE PERSON KNOWN BY THE NAME OF THE LADY ROXANA, IN THE TIME OF KING CHARLES II. 1724; subsequent eds.; *also titled:* ROXANA. 1724. Fictional account of a woman deserted by her husband and the options open to her in eighteenth-century society for economic survival; CONJUGAL LEWDNESS: OR MATRIMONIAL WHOREDOM. 1727; *also titled:* A TREATISE CONCERNING THE USE AND ABUSE OF THE MARRIAGE BED, ETC. 1727. ——*see also:* Lee, William, DANIEL DEFOE: HIS LIFE, AND RECENTLY DISCOVERED WRITINGS. 1869; Backshielder, P., "Defoe's Women: Snares and Prey" in STUDIES IN EIGHTEENTH-CENTURY CULTURE. ed. by Ronald C. Rosbottom. vol. 5, 1976. Examines the characteristics of Defoe's female protagonists in the context of eighteenth-century social values; Rogers, Katherine, "The Feminism of Daniel Defoe" in WOMAN IN THE EIGHTEENTH CENTURY AND OTHER ESSAYS. ed. by Paul Fritz and Richard Morton. Toronto, 1976. Defoe advocated women's education as a means of emancipation. While he did not support "Female Government," he "went on to question [the] assumption which justified masculine government, pointing out that once women were properly educated, they would no longer be weak in judgement" (p. 3); Earle, Peter, DANIEL DEFOE. New York, 1977. See especially: "The Individual and His Wife"; Foot, Michael, "Daniel Defoe, Feminist" in DEBTS OF HONOUR. by Michael Foot. 1980. "MOLL FLANDERS... is a feminist tract, justifying the ways of woman to God and man" (n.p.).

12.3

Montagu, Mary Wortley (Lady), THE NONSENSE OF COMMON SENSE: 1737 to 1738; rpt., ed. by Robert Halsband. Evanston, 1947. An "anonymously-penned," short-lived journal, later verified through Montagu's letters to have been her work; THE COMPLETE LETTERS OF LADY MARY WORTLEY MONTAGU. ed. by Robert Halsband. 3 vols. Oxford, 1965; THE SELECTED LETTERS OF LADY MARY WORTLEY MONTAGU. ed. by Robert Halsband. 1970. See especially: "Girlhood and Courtship," "Domesticities and Politics," and "England Again." ——*see also:* FRASER'S MAGAZINE: Thomson, K., *"The Literary Circles of the Last Century: Mrs. Montagu and Her Friends,"* 36 (1847) 72-81; Doran, John, A LADY OF THE LAST CENTURY. 2nd ed., 1873; Blunt, Reginald, ed., MRS. MONTAGU, "QUEEN OF THE BLUES," HER LETTERS AND FRIENDSHIPS FROM 1762-1800. [1923]; Halsband, Robert, THE LIFE OF LADY MARY WORTLEY MONTAGU. Oxford, 1956; Benkovitz, Miriam J., "Some Observations on Woman's Concept of Self in the Eighteenth Century" in WOMAN IN THE EIGHTEENTH CENTURY AND OTHER ESSAYS. ed. by Paul Fritz and Richard Morton. Toronto, 1976. Focuses on Montagu and Fanny Burney and the attitudes manifested in their writings; Hanson, Marjorie, "Elizabeth Montagu: A Biographical Sketch and a Critical Edition of her Writings," Ph.D. diss., Univ. of Southern California, 1982.

12.4

WOMAN NOT INFERIOR TO MAN, OR A SHORT AND MODEST VINDICA-TION OF THE NATURAL RIGHTS OF A FAIR SEX TO A PERFECT EQUALITY OF POWER, DIGNITY, AND ESTEEM WITH THE MEN. BY SOPHIA: A PERSON OF QUALITY. 1739. —*see also:* **WESTMINSTER REVIEW:** McIlquham, H., *"Sophia: A Person of Quality. The Eighteenth Century Militant Champion of Women's Rights,"* 150 (1898) 533-547. Describes Sophia's radical pamphlet and the response it generated; includes excerpts.

12.5

FEMALE RIGHTS VINDICATED; OR THE EQUALITY OF THE SEXES MORALLY AND PHYSICALLY PROVED. BY A LADY. 1758.

12.6

Rousseau, Jean-Jacques, **EMILIUS AND SOPHIA: OR, A NEW SYSTEM OF EDUCATION.** trans. by William Kenrick. 4 vols. 1762. Introduces a concept later known as "the doctrine of female influence." —*see also:* **PUBLICATIONS OF THE MODERN LANGUAGE ASSOCIATION (PMLA):** Gutwirth, M., *"Madame de Stael, Rousseau and the Woman Question,"* 86 (1971) 100-109; **MIDWEST QUARTERLY:** Christenson, R., *"The Political Theory of Male Chauvinism: J.J. Rousseau's Paradigm,"* 13 (1972) 291-299; **AMERICAN HISTORICAL REVIEW:** Wexler, V.G., *"'Made for Man's Delight': Rousseau as Antifeminist,"* 31 (1976) 266-289. Delineates Rousseau's traditionalist views concerning women and the responses generated by these views (i.e., Wollstonecraft and Madame de Stael). Focuses on the female characters in Rousseau's fiction as illustrative of this radical thinker's misogyny; Okin, Susan Moller, "Part III. Rousseau" in **WOMEN IN WESTERN POLITICAL THOUGHT.** by Susan Moller Okin. Princeton, 1979. Chapters include "Rousseau and the Modern Patriarchal Tradition," "The Natural Woman and her Role," "Equality and Freedom—For Men," and "The Fate of Rousseau's Heroines." "In Rousseau's writings about women, we can clearly discern his consciousness that it was the women who aroused in him that sexuality which produced in him feelings of both fear and guilt" (p. 100).

12.7

Hays, Mary, **THE MEMOIRS OF EMMA COURTNEY.** 1769. Fictional account of an educated, career-oriented woman; (with Hays, Elizabeth), **LETTERS AND ESSAYS MORAL AND MISCELLANEOUS.** 1793. Supports Wollstonecraft's ideas and advocates women's insistence upon their rights; **APPEAL TO THE MEN OF GREAT BRITAIN IN BEHALF OF THE WOMEN.** 1798; rpt., New York, 1979. Calls for more equitable property and ownership laws; discusses the problems of marriage and argues for women's sexual freedom. See Gina Luria's introduction to the 1979 edition for biographical information on Hays; *reviewed in:* **GENTLE-MEN'S MAGAZINE:** 69 (1799) 310; **A VICTIM OF PREJUDICE.** 1799. Fictional account of an illegitimate daughter and her subsequent persecution; **FEMALE BIOGRAPHY.** 6 vols. 1803.

12.8

Foster, Frances, **THOUGHTS ON THE TIMES, BUT CHIEFLY ON THE PROFLIGACY OF OUR WOMEN, AND ITS CAUSES... IN TWO PARTS. SHEWING THE DANGER OF PUBLIC INCONTINENCE, THE ABSURDITY OF OUR FEMALE EDUCATION.** 1779. Example of the late eighteenth-century fear that English women, reacting to the unwholesome influence of the American revolution, were engaged in a destructive pursuit of their selfish interests.

12.9

Bentham, Jeremy, **AN INTRODUCTION TO THE PRINCIPLES OF MORALS AND LEGISLATION.** 1781; 1789; New York, 1965; **THE WORKS OF JEREMY BENTHAM.** 11 vols. New York, 1962. —*see also:* Stephen, Leslie, **THE ENGLISH UTILITARIANS.** 3 vols. 1900; subsequent eds.; New York, 1968; Letwin, Shirley Robin, **THE PURSUIT OF CERTAINTY: DAVID HUME, JEREMY BENTHAM, J.S. MILL AND BEATRICE WEBB.** 1965; Baumgart, David, **BENTHAM AND THE ETHICS OF TODAY.** New York, 1966; **JOURNAL OF THE HISTORY OF IDEAS:** Williford, M., *"Bentham on the Rights of Women,"* 36 (1975) 167-176. "Bentham's first defense of women came in his INTRODUCTION TO THE PRINCIPLES OF MORALS AND LEGISLATION where he attacks as an imbecility the practice of some nations that relegate women... to the status that men endure only when infants or insane" (p. 167). Bentham advocated women's suffrage but felt the time was not right to implement it.

12.10

Wollstonecraft, Mary, **THOUGHTS ON THE EDUCATION OF DAUGHTERS: WITH REFLECTIONS ON FEMALE CONDUCT, IN THE MORE IMPORTANT DUTIES OF LIFE.** 1787; 1788. Criticizes the popular methods of educating women in "accomplishments," etc. Disdainful of the lack of work for educated women; **MARY: A FICTION.** 1788. The author's first novel which examines the life of a contemporary woman who leaves an unhappy marriage, choosing instead to aid the sick and the poor; **ORIGINAL STORIES FROM REAL LIFE; WITH CONVERSATIONS CALCULATED TO REGULATE THE AFFECTIONS, AND FORM THE MIND TO TRUTH AND GOODNESS.** 1788; **A VINDICATION OF THE RIGHTS OF MAN.** 1790. A vivacious and angry response, then considered unwomanly in tone, to Edmund Burke's REFLECTIONS ON THE FRENCH REVOLUTION in which Wollstonecraft argues that civil and religious rights and freedoms are inherent in one's birthright; **A VINDICATION OF THE RIGHTS OF WOMAN: WITH STRICTURES ON POLITICAL AND MORAL SUBJECTS.** 1792; 1833; 1844; 1891; 1892; 1967; 1970; 1971; 1975. Radical treatise championing women's rights and responding to anti-female views, especially those manifested in the works of Jean-Jacques Rousseau; **AN HISTORICAL AND MORAL VIEW OF THE FRENCH REVOLUTION.** 1794. Expresses dismay over the course of the French Revolution but is optimistic that "a fairer government is rising" (p. 93), implying it is intended for women as well as for men; **LETTERS WRITTEN DURING A SHORT RESIDENCE IN SWEDEN, NORWAY AND DENMARK.** 1796; Lincoln, 1976. Poetic, critical travelogue styled as letters written to an absent lover; **MEMOIRS OF THE AUTHOR OF "A VINDICATION OF THE RIGHTS OF WOMAN."** ed. by William Godwin. 1798; **POSTHUMOUS WORKS OF THE AUTHOR OF A VINDICATION OF THE RIGHTS OF WOMAN.** ed. by William Godwin. 1798. Includes writings on infant and child training; **LETTERS TO IMLAY.** ed. by Paul C. Kegan. 1879. The letters to Wollstonecraft's lover reveal an emotional side of the author that she was unable to reconcile to her political ideals; **MEMOIRS OF MARY WOLLSTONECRAFT.** ed. by Clark W. Durant. 1927; **FOUR NEW LETTERS OF MARY WOLLSTONECRAFT AND HELEN M. WILLIAMS.** ed. by B.P. Kurtz and C.C. Autrey. Berkeley, 1937; **GODWIN AND MARY.** ed. by R.M. Wardle. 1967. A collection of letters; **MARIA; OR THE WRONGS OF WOMAN WITH AN INTRODUCTION BY MOIRA FERGUSON.** New York, 1975. This last and unfinished novel dramatizes the basic tenets of A VINDICATION OF THE RIGHTS OF WOMAN. This edition includes drafts that hint at what might have been the book's conclusion; **A WOLLSTONECRAFT ANTHOLOGY.** ed. by Janet Todd. Bloomington, 1977. Compilation of her works, with a biographical introduction by the editor; **COLLECTED LETTERS OF MARY WOLLSTONECRAFT.** ed. by R.M. Wardle. Ithaca, 1979. Includes biographical introduction, notes, and appendices. ——*see also:* **ECCENTRIC BIOGRAPHY; OR MEMOIRS OF REMARKABLE FEMALE CHARACTERS, ANCIENT AND MODERN**. Worcester, 1804. Praises Wollstonecraft and her work; Fessenden, Thomas G., **THE LADIES MONITOR, A POEM**. Bellows Falls, 1818. Wollstonecraft is mentioned in this anti-feminist work; Elwood, Anne Katherine, **MEMOIRS OF THE LITERARY LADIES OF ENGLAND FROM THE COMMENCEMENT OF THE LAST CENTURY**. 1843. Criticizes Wollstonecraft's radical political writings for their lack of femininity; **LEADER**: Eliot, G., *"Margaret Fuller and Mary Wollstonecraft,"* 6 (1855) 988-989. Wollstonecraft is praised and her work is compared to Fuller's; **DUBLIN UNIVERSITY MAGAZINE**: *"Mary Wollstonecraft Godwin,"* 73 (1869) 672-676. Biographical, anti-feminist sketch; Pennell, Elizabeth, **MARY WOLLSTONECRAFT GODWIN**. 1885; **ECLECTIC MAGAZINE OF FOREIGN LITERATURE, SCIENCE, AND ART**: *"Mary Wollstonecraft Godwin,"* 42 (1885) 100-107. Includes quotes from her letters and works; **WESTMINSTER REVIEW**: *"The Writings of Mary Wollstonecraft,"* 133 (1890) 10-23. Biographical sketch illustrated by Wollstonecraft's writings; Fawcett, Millicent Garrett, "Introduction" in **A VINDICATION OF THE RIGHTS OF WOMAN, ETC.** 1891. Fawcett discusses Wollstonecraft's prediction that women would use their greater rights and improved education in raising their children and attending to other domestic chores; Rauschen Busch-Clough, Emma, A **STUDY OF MARY WOLLSTONECRAFT AND THE RIGHTS OF WOMAN**. 1898; Staars, David, "The First Revolt——Mary Wollstonecraft" in **THE ENGLISH WOMAN. STUDIES IN HER PSYCHIC EVOLUTION**. by David Staars. trans. by J.M.E. Brownlow. 1909. Discusses Wollstonecraft's revolt at conventions proscribed for female behavior; **WESTMINSTER REVIEW**: Hamilton, C.J., *"The Romance of a Strong-Minded Woman,"* 174 (1910) 178-186. Examines Wollstonecraft's relationships with Fanny Blood and Gilbert Imlay; Jebb, Camilla, **MARY WOLLSTONECRAFT**. 1912; Brailsford, Henry Noel, **SHELLEY, GODWIN AND THEIR CIRCLE**. 1913. Commentary on Wollstonecraft; Bouten, Jacob, **MARY WOLLSTONECRAFT AND THE BEGINNINGS OF FEMALE EMANCIPATION IN FRANCE AND ENGLAND**. Amsterdam, 1922; Philadelphia, 1975. Compares the positions of early philosophers (i.e., Plato and Socrates) concerning women to Wollstonecraft's beliefs; Linford, Madeleine, **MARY WOLLSTONECRAFT**. 1924; James, Henry Rosher, **MARY WOLLSTONECRAFT, A SKETCH**. 1932; Woolf, Virginia, "Mary Wollstonecraft" in **THE SECOND COMMON READER**. by Virginia Woolf. 1932. Examines the conflicts between Wollstonecraft's feminist ideals and the dependent feelings towards her lover, Gilbert Imlay; Lawrence, Margaret, "Mary Wollstonecraft Who Walked an Emotional Tightrope" in **THE SCHOOL OF FEMININITY**. by Margaret Lawrence. New York, 1936; Preedy, George, **THIS SHINING WOMAN**. 1937; Wardle, R.M., **MARY WOLLSTONECRAFT: A CRITICAL BIOGRAPHY**. 1951; Taylor, George R.S., **MARY WOLLSTONECRAFT: A STUDY IN ECONOMICS AND ROMANCE**. New York, 1911; 1969; Hagelman, Charles W., "Introduction" in **A VINDICATION OF THE RIGHTS OF WOMAN, ETC.** 1967. Relates the ideological tenets of A VINDICATION OF THE RIGHTS OF MAN to the later RIGHTS OF WOMAN; George, Margaret, **ONE WOMAN'S "SITUATION"; A STUDY OF MARY WOLLSTONECRAFT**. Urbana, 1970; Nixon, Edna, **MARY WOLLSTONECRAFT: HER LIFE AND TIMES**. 1971; Flexner, Eleanor, **MARY WOLLSTONECRAFT**. New York, 1972; **BRITISH STUDIES MONITOR**: Todd, J., *"Mary Wollstonecraft: A Review of Research and Comment,"* 7 (1972) 3-23; Tomalin, Claire, **THE LIFE AND DEATH OF MARY WOLLSTONECRAFT**. 1974; **UNIVERSITY OF MICHIGAN PAPERS IN WOMEN'S STUDIES**: Sapiro, V., *"Feminist Studies and the Discipline: A Study of Mary Wollstonecraft,"* 1 (1974) 178-200. Political science feminist analysis of Wollstonecraft's work in its historical context; Detre, Jean, A **MOST EXTRAORDINARY PAIR: MARY WOLLSTONECRAFT AND WILLIAM GODWIN**. Garden City, 1975; Kramnick, Miriam Brody, "Introduction" in **A VINDICATION**

OF THE RIGHTS OF WOMAN, ETC. 1975. "Hannah More wrote that there was something so ridiculous in the very title [of Wollstonecraft's book] that she had no intention of reading [it].... The reaction in Paris, undergoing revolution, was quite different.... [Wollstonecraft] was welcomed into an international group of literary and political writers" (pp. 17-18); Sunstein, Emily W., A DIFFERENT FACE. THE LIFE OF MARY WOLLSTONECRAFT. 1975. Biographical account illuminated by quotes from Wollstonecraft's work and set in the social-historical context of the time; Tims, Margaret, MARY WOLLSTONECRAFT. A SOCIAL PIONEER. 1976; Todd, Janet, MARY WOLLSTONECRAFT: AN ANNOTATED BIBLIOGRAPHY. New York, 1976. "Includes works by Wollstonecraft, as well as most of the critical and biographical comment on her written in English between 1788 and 1975. Most book reviews are listed" (p. vii); *reviewed in:* STUDIES IN BURKE AND HIS TIME: Nussbaum, F.A., *"Eighteenth-Century Women,"* 19 (1978) 223-231; SIGNS: Todd, J., *"The Biographies of Mary Wollstonecraft,"* 1 (1976) 721-734; Walters, Margaret, "The Rights and Wrongs of Women: Mary Wollstonecraft, Harriet Martineau, Simone de Beauvoir" in THE RIGHTS AND WRONGS OF WOMEN. ed. by Juliet Mitchell and Ann Oakley. Harmondsworth, 1976; Janes, R., "Mary, Mary, Quite Contrary, Or Mary Astell and Mary Wollstonecraft Compared" in STUDIES IN EIGHTEENTH-CENTURY CULTURE. ed. by Ronald C. Rosbottom. vol. 5, 1976; Myers, M., "Politics from the Outside: Mary Wollstonecraft's First VINDICATION," 6 (1977) 113-132. Feminist analysis of Wollstonecraft's A VINDICATION OF THE RIGHTS OF MAN; Myers, Mitzi, "Mary Wollstonecraft's LETTERS WRITTEN DURING A SHORT RESIDENCE IN SWEDEN, NORWAY AND DENMARK: Toward Romantic Autobiography" n.v. (1979) n.p.; STUDIES IN BURKE AND HIS TIME: Guralnick, E.S., *"Radical Politics in Mary Wollstonecraft's A VINDICATION OF THE RIGHTS OF WOMAN,"* 18 (1977) 155-166. Examines the importance of the previous A VINDICATION OF THE RIGHTS OF MAN in relation to THE RIGHTS OF WOMAN; McGuinn, Nicholas, "George Eliot and Mary Wollstonecraft" in THE NINETEENTH CENTURY WOMAN. HER PHYSICAL AND CULTURAL WORLD. ed. by Sara Delamont and Lorna Duffin. 1978; JOURNAL OF THE HISTORY OF IDEAS: *"On the Reception of Mary Wollstonecraft's A VINDICATION OF THE RIGHTS OF WOMAN,"* 39 (1978) 294-302. Discusses contemporary reactions gleaned from reviews in periodicals of the period; Strauss, Claudia Marilyn, "A Pedagogy for Independence in an age of Constraints: The Educational Thought of Mary Wollstonecraft," Ph.D. diss., Columbia Univ., 1979; FEMINIST STUDIES: Wexler, A., *"Emma Goldman on Mary Wollstonecraft,"* 7 (1981) 113-133; Brody, Miriam, "Mary Wollstonecraft: Sexuality and Women's Rights (1759-1797)" in FEMINIST THEORISTS. THREE CENTURIES OF WOMEN'S INTELLECTUAL TRADITIONS. ed. by Dale Spender. 1983. Examines Wollstonecraft's ideals as set forth in her writings, in the context of eighteenth-century concepts of romance and female identity.

12.11

Macaulay, Catharine Graham, THE HISTORY OF ENGLAND. 8 vols. 1763-1783. Anti-royalist work considered bold for a woman at that time; LETTERS ON EDUCATION. 1790. ——*see also:* WILLIAM AND MARY QUARTERLY: Donnelly, L.M., *"The Celebrated Mrs. Macaulay,"* 6 (1949) 173-207; Beckwith, Mildred Chaffee, "Catharine Graham Macaulay: Eighteenth-Century English Rebel," Ph.D. diss., Ohio State Univ., 1953; JOURNAL OF BRITISH STUDIES: Donnelly, L.M. and Withey, L.E., *"Catharine Macaulay and the Uses of History: Ancient Rights, Perfectionism, and Propaganda,"* 16 (1976) 59-83; UNIVERSITY OF MICHIGAN PAPERS IN WOMEN'S STUDIES: Boos, F.S., *"Catharine Macaulay's LETTERS ON EDUCATION (1790): An Early Feminist Polemic,"* 2 (1976) 64-78. Discusses Macaulay's influence on Wollstonecraft; ALBION: Schnorrenberg, B., *"The Brood Hen of Faction: Mrs. Macaulay and Radical Politics, 1765-1775,"* 11 (1979) 33-45;

INTERNATIONAL JOURNAL OF WOMEN'S STUDIES: Boos, F.S. and Boos, W., *"Catharine Macaulay: Historian and Political Reformer,"* 3 (1980) 49-65. Analyzes Macaulay's writings and includes a biographical sketch.

12.12

Taylor, Thomas, A VINDICATION OF THE RIGHTS OF THOMAS TAYLOR. 1792; rpt., with introduction by Louise Shutz Boas. Gainesville, 1966. Parodies the radical ideas of Wollstonecraft and Thomas Paine; *also published as:* A VINDICATION OF THE RIGHTS OF BRUTES. [1792].

12.13

Polwhele, Richard, THE UNSEX'D FEMALES: A POEM. 1798; rpt., New York, 1974.

12.14

Wakefield, Priscilla, REFLECTIONS ON THE PRESENT CONDITIONS OF THE FEMALE SEX. 1798. Concludes that middle-class women have a duty to educate and improve lower-class working women for the good of society.

12.15

Radcliffe, Mary Ann, THE FEMALE ADVOCATE; OR AN ATTEMPT TO RECOVER THE RIGHTS OF WOMEN FROM USURPATION. 1799; Edinburgh, 1810; New York, 1974. "The subject of the following pages is... to delineate the situation of those poor helpless females whose sufferings... are too grievous to be borne" (p. 394); THE MEMOIRS OF MRS. M.A. RADCLIFFE IN FAMILIAR LETTERS TO HER FEMALE FRIEND. Edinburgh, 1810. Radcliffe is a good example of a manifest eighteenth-century advocate for women's rights. She is at the more radical end of the "feminist controversy" of the day. The reprint of her work is bound with Polwhele's THE UNSEX'D FEMALES: A POEM (above entry) in THE FEMINIST CONTROVERSY IN ENGLAND. New York, 1974. Valuable introduction by Gina Luria.

12.16

Randall, Anne-Frances, A LETTER TO THE WOMEN OF ENGLAND, ON THE INJUSTICE OF MENTAL SUBORDINATION: WITH ANECDOTES. 1799; *reviewed in:* GENTLEMEN'S MAGAZINE: 69 (1799) 311.

12.17

Southcott, Joanna, THE STRANGE EFFECTS OF FAITH. 1802. Southcott founded a religious sect which was popular among working-class men and women; LETTERS TO JANE TOWNLEY. 1804. —*see also:* Seymour, Alice, THE EXPRESS...: CONTAINING THE LIFE AND DIVINE WRITINGS OF THE LATE JOANNA SOUTHCOTT. 1909; Lane, Charles, LIFE AND BIBLIOGRAPHY OF JOANNA SOUTHCOTT. 1912; Robertson, Mary S., THE TRUE STORY OF JOANNA SOUTHCOTT. Ashford, 1923; Balleine, George Reginald, PAST FINDING OUT: THE TRAGIC STORY OF JOANNA SOUTHCOTT AND HER SUCCESSORS. 1956; Hopkins, J.K., "Joanna Southcott: A Study of Popular Religion and Radical Politics, 1789-1814," Ph.D. diss., Univ. of Texas, 1972; Oliver, William Hosking, "From the Southcottians to Socialism" in PROPHETS AND MILLENNIALISTS: THE USES OF BIBLICAL PROPHECY IN ENGLAND FROM 1790S TO THE 1840s. by William Hosking Oliver. Oxford, 1978. On the convergence of the ideas of Joanna Southcott, Robert Owen, and the Saint-Simonians; Taylor, Barbara, "The Woman-Power: Religious Heresy and Feminism in Early English Socialism" in TEARING THE VEIL; ESSAYS IN FEMININITY. ed. by Susan Lipshitz. 1978. Examines socialist, working-class, and women-oriented religious groups, such as the Southcottians and the Saint-Simonians, tracing their influence on Owenite feminism; *reviewed in:* RADICAL HISTORY REVIEW: Rowbotham, S., *"Women and Radical Politics in Britain 1820-1914,"* 19 (1978-1979) 149-159; Harrison, J.F.C., "The Woman Clothed in the Sun" in THE SECOND COMING: POPULAR MILLENARIANISM 1750-1850. by J.F.C. Harrison. 1979; Hopkins, James K., A WOMAN TO DELIVER HER PEOPLE: JOANNA SOUTH-COTT AND ENGLISH MILLENARIANISM IN AN ERA OF REVOLUTION. Austin, 1982. Discusses Southcott's socialism set in an idealized paternalistic system. Her audience consisted mainly of members of the artisan and servant classes.

12.18
Duff, William, LETTERS ON THE INTELLECTUAL AND MORAL CHARACTER OF WOMEN. Aberdeen, 1807. Anti-Wollstonecraft treatise on women's lives that studies the effects of feminism on society and its male members.

12.19
Owen, Robert, A NEW VIEW OF SOCIETY: OR, ESSAYS ON THE PRINCIPLE OF THE FORMATION OF THE HUMAN CHARACTER. 1813; THE BOOK OF THE NEW MORAL WORLD. 1836; 1844; 1849. Part 6 concerns women's roles, status, and education. "Women will be no longer made the slaves of, or dependent upon men... women may be trained to be equally useful and valuable as men" (pp. 35-37). ——*see also:* Morrison, Frances, THE INFLUENCE OF THE PRESENT MARRIAGE SYSTEM UPON THE CHARACTER OF INTERESTS OF FEMALES CONTRASTED WITH THAT OF ROBERT OWEN, ESQ. 1839; FRASER'S MAGAZINE: *"Women and the Social System,"* 21 (1840) 689-702. Criticizes Owenism; Kilham, John, "Robert Owen, Feminism and The Mechanics Institutions" in TENNYSON AND THE PRINCESS. REFLECTIONS OF AN AGE. 1958; 1967; Harrison, J.F.C., ROBERT OWEN AND THE OWENITES IN BRITAIN AND AMERICA, THE QUEST FOR THE NEW MORAL WORLD. 1969; Pollard, S. and Salt, J., ROBERT OWEN, PROPHET OF THE POOR. 1971; Garnett, Ronald G., CO-OPERATION AND THE OWENITE SOCIALIST COMMUNITIES IN BRITAIN, 1825-45. Manchester, 1972. "Owen viewed the family as a divisive influence because of its insularity and introspection. The family therefore reduced the effectiveness of his ambitions for the communal education of children. It also restrained improvement in the status of women.... [The enabling] of fuller personal development and participation of wives and mothers were salient factors to Owen's plan for communal living.... He aimed to loosen the child-parent bonds which... he regarded as the major obstacle to social conversion" (pp. 228-229); Saville, John, "Robert Owen on the Family and the Marriage System of the Old Immoral World" in REBELS AND THEIR CAUSES. ed. by Maurice Cornforth. 1978. Provides the most devastating analysis of the effects and consequences upon husbands, wives, and children of "the unnatural and artificial marriages of the world" during the nineteenth century (p. 114); Taylor, Barbara, "Feminism and Owenite Socialism," Ph.D. diss., Univ. of Sussex, 1980.

12.20
BLACKWOOD'S MAGAZINE: Neal, J., *"Men and Women,"* 16 (1824) 387-394. Argues that women have an inferior intellect to men but attributes it to an inadequate education, instead of an innate limitation; Wilson, J. (signed Jasper Sussex), *"Letter to Mrs. M. on the Equality of the Sexes,"* 20 (1826) 296-298; Eagles, J., *"The Wrongs of Women,"* 54 (1843) 597-607; Oliphant, M., *"The Condition of Women,"* 83 (1858) 139-154. "To hold fast still by the old assertion that womanhood is purer by native right than manhood, and than women are still next to the angels.... If they are, they ought to need rather less than more lecturing than falls to the share of the more obdurate rebel" (p. 154); Greenwood, F., *"Manners, Morals*

and Female Emancipation: Being a Familiar Letter from a Woman of Quality," 152 (1892) 463-470; Todd, M.G., *"Some Thoughts on the Woman Question,"* 156 (1894) 689-692; Stutfield, H.E.M., *"The Psychology of Feminism,"* 161 (1897) 104-117.

12.21
Thompson, William, **APPEAL OF ONE HALF OF THE HUMAN RACE, WOMEN, AGAINST THE PRETENSIONS OF THE OTHER HALF, MEN, TO RETAIN THEM IN POLITICAL AND THENCE IN CIVIL AND DOMESTIC, SLAVERY; IN REPLY TO A PARAGRAPH OF MR. MILL'S CELEBRATED "ARTICLE ON GOVERNMENT."** 1825; New York, 1970; rpt., 1983. Thompson acknowledges the participation of Anna Wheeler in producing this work. Examines the legal status of British women, writing that "equal political laws are requisite to secure to women equal civil and criminal laws, and through them equal enjoyments, with men" (p. xvi). ——*see also:* Pankhurst, Richard K.P., **WILLIAM THOMPSON (1775-1833), BRITAIN'S PIONEER SOCIALIST, FEMINIST, AND CO-OPERATOR.** 1954. Biography, illustrated by Thompson's writings and descriptions of his political milieu; **ATLANTIS:** McCrone, K.E., *"William Thompson and the APPEAL OF ONE HALF OF THE HUMAN RACE,"* 5 (1980) 34-51.

12.22
Jameson, Anna, **CHARACTERISTICS OF WOMEN, MORAL, POETICAL AND HISTORICAL.** 1832; 1833; Jameson was one of the early nineteenth-century feminists of the Langham Place circle; **MEMOIRS AND ESSAYS ON ART, LITERATURE AND SOCIAL MORALS.** 1846. Refutes the idea that man is "the natural guardian of women"; **SISTERS OF CHARITY.** 1855; 1859. ——*see also:* MacPherson, Geraldine, **MEMOIRS OF THE LIFE OF ANNA JAMESON.** 1878; Erskine, Beatrice C., ed., **ANNA JAMESON. LETTERS AND FRIENDSHIPS, 1812-1860.** 1915; Thomas, Clara, **LOVE AND WORK ENOUGH; THE LIFE OF ANNA JAMESON.** Toronto, 1967.

12.23
MONTHLY REPOSITORY: Fox, W.J., *"A Political and Social Anomaly,"* 6 (1832) 637-642; Adams, W.B., *"On the Condition of Women in England,"* 7 (1833) 217-231.

12.24
Martineau, Harriet, **ILLUSTRATIONS OF POLITICAL ECONOMY.** 9 vols. 1834. Didactic stories often illustrating women's roles; **SOCIETY IN AMERICA.** 3 vols. 1837. See especially: "Political Non-Existence of Women." Argues that American men circumscribe women's "sphere" more narrowly than "the broad and true conception... of a sphere appointed by God and bounded by the powers which He has bestowed" (p. 97); **WOMEN'S RIGHTS AND DUTIES CONSIDERED WITH RELATION TO THEIR INFLUENCE ON SOCIETY AND ON HER OWN CONDITION: BY A WOMAN [HARRIET MARTINEAU].** 1840. ——*see also:* **FRASER'S MAGAZINE:** *"Practical Reasoning versus Impracticable Theories,"* 19 (1839) 557-592. Criticizes Martineau's writings; Stanton, Elizabeth Cady, **[LETTERS]... TO THE WOMEN'S RIGHTS CONVENTION...** Syracuse, New York, 1852. A series of Women's Rights Tracts, no. 10. Includes resolutions passed by American feminists and a letter from Harriet Martineau read at this conference, praising the women's efforts and emphasizing the importance of female education; Law, Harriet, **AN HOUR WITH HARRIET MARTINEAU.** 1877; Staars, David, "Harriet Martineau" in **THE ENGLISH WOMAN. STUDIES IN HER PSYCHIC EVOLUTION.** by David Staars. trans. by J.M.E. Brownlow. 1909. Biographical essay delineating Martineau's work and the events in her life which predisposed her to reform work; Bosanquet, Theodora, **HARRIET MARTINEAU: AN ESSAY IN COMPREHENSION.** 1928; Rivenburg, Navrola E., **HARRIET MARTINEAU: AN**

EXAMPLE OF VICTORIAN CONFLICT. Philadelphia, 1932; Wheatley, Vera, THE LIFE AND WORK OF HARRIET MARTINEAU. 1957. Includes full bibliography of Martineau's writings; WOMEN'S STUDIES: Pichanick, V.R., *"An Abominable Submission: Harriet Martineau's Views on the Role and Place of Woman,"* 5 (1977) 13-32. In this biographical essay, Pichanick examines the motivations behind Martineau's writings; Pichanick, Valerie Kossew, HARRIET MARTINEAU: THE WOMAN AND HER WORK. Ann Arbor, 1978; 1980; Myers, Mitzi, "Unmothered Daughter and Radical Reformer: Reconstructing Some Interconnections in Harriet Martineau's Career" in EMBRACED AND EMBATTLED: THE HISTORY OF MOTHERS AND DAUGHTERS IN LITERATURE. ed. by C.N. Davidson and E.M. Boroner. New York, 1979; Myers, Mitzi, "Harriet Martineau's Autobiography: The Making of a Female Philosopher" in WOMEN'S AUTOBIOGRAPHY. ESSAYS IN CRITICISM. ed. by Estelle C. Jelinek. Bloomington, 1980; Weiner, Gaby, "Harriet Martineau: A Reassessment (1802-1876)" in FEMINIST THEORISTS. THREE CENTURIES OF WOMEN'S INTELLECTUAL TRADITIONS. ed. by Dale Spender. 1983. Looks at Martineau's career as a writer and advocate for women's educational reform.

12.25
CHRISTIAN'S PENNY MAGAZINE: *"The Rights of Woman Placed on Their Proper Basis,"* 6 (1837) 5-6.

12.26
METROPOLITAN MAGAZINE: *"An Outline of the Grievances of Women,"* 22 (1838) 16-27. Author identifies herself as a woman but beyond that little more is known. Article was released amid advance publicity and aroused furious debate. Finds "women's influence" no compensation for the "existing state of female bondage" and asserts that such influence has historically been exerted by "irreclaimably vicious" women rather than "the sensible, the modest, and the discreet." Recommends women's "passive resistance" as a means to agitate for equal civil rights.

12.27
WESTMINSTER REVIEW: Martineau, H., *"Criticism of Women,"* 32 (1838-1839) 454-475; Y., M.P., *"Woman and Her Social Position,"* 35 (1841) 13-27. Dissects the issues contained within the "woman question"——to what degree women should be subordinated to men and whether men have carried that subordination too far, whether the laws concerning women should be changed in their favor and whether restrictions on their individual lives should be reduced or abolished; Mill, H.T. and Mill J.S., *"Enfranchisement of Women,"* 55 (1851) 289-311. Disputes the assertion that women are inferior to men and argues that individuals of either sex should be allowed to develop their capacities to the full; Eliot, G., *"Three Novels [review of Frederika Bremer's novel HERTHA],"* 66 (1856) 571-578; Shore, L., *"The Emancipation of Women,"* 46 (1874) 137-174; *"The Relations of the Sexes,"* 111 (1879) 312-328. "Every man and woman, whether married or single, who upholds the doctrine that the pursuits of women should be made to conform to the views of men, must recognize the prostitute as fulfilling a righteous calling; for she is satisfying an imperious demand of men" (p. 328); *"Women's Rights as Preached by Women,"* 116 (1881) 469-478; Aveling, E. and Marx, E., *"Independent Section: The Woman Question from a Socialist Point of View,"* 69 (1886) 207-222. Concludes that female subordination to men is the inevitable result of a capitalist system. Charges that attempts to gain economic and political rights for women, i.e. the vote, treats the symptoms instead of the disease; *"The Emancipation of Women,"* 128 (1887) 165-173; *"Women Workers in the Liberal Cause,"* 128 (1887) 311-318. Liberal women's observations on Irish home rule reflect their opinions on women's rights: "Arguing from their own experience of home and life these women asked, What is Union? Is

it the narrow gold band worn since the wedding day: Is it the legal rite which pronounced 'husband and wife'? Is it not rather the linking of sympathies and aims, the independent yet correlated rule in each department of life and the full recognition of individual rights and common interests" (p. 316); *"Female Poaching on Male Preserves,"* 129 (1888) 290-297; Chapman, E.R., *"St. Paul and the Woman Movement,"* 131 (1889) 135-147; *"The Apple and the Ego of Women,"* 131 (1889) 374-382. Expresses a fear that women, given greater social and political freedom, will degrade male intellectual activity; *"Plea for Women by a Woman,"* 139 (1893) 282-285; Sykes, A.G.P., *"The Evolution of the Sex,"* 143 (1895) 396-400; Hewitt, E.C., *"The New Woman in Her Relation to the New Man,"* 147 (1897) 335-337; Harvey, H.E., *"Science and the Rights of Women,"* 148 (1897) 205-207; Ethelmer, E., *"Feminism,"* 149 (1898) 50-62. "Feminism, then, is a phase of larger civilisation; it is the recognition of the autonomy and human right of woman as equal with that of man. It is no lightly scoffed-at epicenism; not the affectation of a brusque masculinity on the part of women, or of a *dilettante* emasculateness on the part of man, but the acceptance and attainment by either sex of whatever is ennobling, be it mental or physical" (p. 60); Slater, E., *"Men's Women in Fiction,"* 149 (1898) 571-577; Lang, R.T., *"The Extra Woman,"* 150 (1898) 305-308. On the surplus of women, women's inequality in the workplace, the stigma attached to "fallen women," and the false ideal of monogamy; Arling, N., *"What is the Role of the 'New Woman'?"* 150 (1898) 576-587; Dennehy, A., *"The Woman of the Future,"* 152 (1899) 99-100. "The equality of the sexes may still be a moot question; but it cannot be denied that until of late the noblest and most gifted women were placed in a position of subjection to the vilest and most mindless of men" (p. 99); Wolstenholme-Elmy, E.C., (pseud. Ignota), *"Privileges vs. Justice to Women,"* 152 (1899) 128-141; Elmy, E.W. (pseud. Ethelmer, Ellis), *"The Individuality of Woman: From A Masculine Point of View,"* 158 (1902) 506-514. Points out the contradiction between woman's mission to elevate the race and man's attempts to hamper her intellectual development so that she can perform her function; McIlquham, H., *"Early Writers on the Woman Question,"* 158 (1902) 312-320; McIlquham, H., *"Some 18th Century Advocates of Justice for Women,"* 159 (1903) 167-179; *"Justice to Womanhood,"* 160 (1903) 77-83; Franklin, F.S., *"Women and Their Emancipation,"* 161 (1904) 407-419; Hill, W.K., *"The Essential Equality of Man and Woman,"* 160 (1903) 647-664. Argues that recognition of equality between the sexes will enhance the quality of marriage and strengthen the nation; Jones, G., *"Ruskin's Views on Women from a Woman's Point of View,"* 165 (1906) 685-688. "Ruskin is generally ready to acknowledge *pedestal* virtues in women. He finds in them an innate power for taking good and leaving evil.... This recognition of their discriminating capacity, is a consolation and encouragement, let us hope, for the suppression of individual development in other ways" (p. 686); Caird, M., *"The Lot of Women,"* 174 (1910) 52-59. Illustrates women's social and legal disadvantages, claiming that "the only real civil rights are those which are guaranteed by political rights" (p. 55); Cohen, P., *"Jews and Feminism,"* 180 (1913) 454-462.

12.28

Morgan, Lady Sydney (Owensen), **WOMAN AND HER MASTER.** 2 vols. 1840. — *see also:* **EIRE-IRELAND:** Atkinson, C., *"Sydney Owenson, Lady Morgan: Irish Patriot and First Professional Woman Writer,"* 15 (1980) 60-90. Delineates the career of this liberal female writer and describes the political and social climate in which she wrote.

12.29

Richardson, R.J., **THE RIGHTS OF WOMAN EXHIBITING HER NATURAL, CIVIL AND POLITICAL CLAIMS TO A SHARE IN THE LEGISLATIVE AND EXECUTIVE POWER OF THE STATE.** Edinburgh, 1840. A series of lectures. The author quotes the Bible, claiming that God ordained the natural equality of the sexes when Eve was created as Adam's helpmate.

12.30
WOMAN'S RIGHTS AND DUTIES CONSIDERED WITH RELATION TO THEIR INFLUENCE ON SOCIETY AND ON HER OWN CONDITION: BY A WOMAN. 2 vols. 1840. Acknowledges that women have some rights but claims that men, not women, define the limits of women's political and moral universe.

12.31
Bevan, Mrs., **DOMESTIC TYRANNY, OR WOMEN IN CHAINS; WITH AN ENQUIRY AS TO THE BEST MODES OF BREAKING HER BONDS ASUNDER... BY A PHILANTHROPIST.** 1841.

12.32
NEW MORAL WORLD: Barmby, J.G., *"The Man-Power, The Woman-Power, and the Woman-Man Power,"* 2 (1841) 268-269. "The question is... of woman-power and man-power, of gentleness and of force. These two powers will be equilibrated in community, in the bosoms of every individual, as in the conditions around then. Neither of the powers will be absolutely ascendant over the other, for although the woman-power will be higher than the man-power, inasmuch as love is higher than wisdom, still they will both work together in a system beautifully philosophical; constituting to themselves ordinated oneness, analogous to the oneness in which man and woman will form the social individual in communism" (p. 269).

12.33
EDINBURGH REVIEW: *"Rights and Condition of Women,"* 73 (1841) 189-209. Review essay on six books by contemporary female authors; Birrel, A., *"Women Under English Law,"* 184 (1896) 322-340.

12.34
Reid, Mrs. Hugo [Marion Kirkland], **A PLEA FOR WOMAN BEING A VINDICATION OF THE IMPORTANCE AND EXTENT OF HER NATURAL SPHERE OF ACTION.** 1843. Pleads for civil and legal equality for women. "We do not mean to assert that man and woman are strictly the same in their nature, or the character of their minds; but simply, that in the grand characteristics of their nature they are the same.... The weaker women are, the greater is their need for equal rights, that they may not fall under the tyranny of the stronger portion of their race"; *reviewed in:* **ATHENAEUM:** no. 854 (1844) 215-217.

12.35
Dryden, Anne Richelieu Lamb, **CAN WOMAN REGENERATE SOCIETY?** 1844. "Woman ought to prove herself, and examine whether or not she be indeed the mere being of impulse and instinct she is so frequently proclaimed to be" (p. 5).

12.36
QUARTERLY REVIEW: Barry, W., *"The Strike of a Sex [The 'New Woman'],"* 179 (1894) 289-318. Questions whether the improvement or degeneracy of a race depends upon the female; Colquhoun, E., *"Modern Feminism and Sex Antagonism,"* 219 (1913) 143-166. Review of nine contemporary books dealing with the women's emancipation movement and the feminist controversy.

12.37
Ossoli, Margaret Fuller, **WOMAN IN THE NINETEENTH CENTURY, AND OTHER KINDRED PAPERS RELATING TO THE SPHERE, CONDITION, AND**

DUTIES OF WOMAN. 1845; Boston, 1855; 1893; New York, 1971. A work that remains relevant to contemporary feminist issues.

12.38
Grey, Maria Georgina and Shirreff, Emily A.E., **THOUGHTS ON SELF CULTURE, ADDRESSED TO WOMEN.** 1850; 2nd ed., 1854. ——*see also:* Ellsworth, Edward W., **LIBERATORS OF THE FEMALE MIND: THE SHIRREFF SISTERS, EDUCATIONAL REFORM AND THE WOMEN'S MOVEMENT.** Westport, 1979.

12.39
ELIZA COOK'S JOURNAL: L., F., *"Wrongs of English Women,"* 3 (1850) 353-356. Describes women as slaves under a male-oriented "physical force supremacy," educated to amuse men as "an agreeable toy."

12.40
Ullathorne, William Bernard, **A PLEA FOR THE RIGHTS AND LIBERTIES OF RELIGIOUS WOMEN, WITH REFERENCES TO THE BILL PROPOSED BY MR. LACY.** 2nd ed., 1851.

12.41
HARPER'S NEW MONTHLY MAGAZINE: Bang, T.E., *"Woman's Emancipation. (Being a Letter Addressed to Mr. Punch, with a Drawing, by a Strong-Minded American Woman),"* 3 (1851) 424. Appeal to English women for sympathy with the American women's struggle for rights.

12.42
ROBERT OWEN'S JOURNAL: Owen, R., *"Rights of Women in the Old Immoral World,"* 2 (1851) 23-24; 45-47; 54-56; 61-64.

12.43
HOGG'S WEEKLY INSTRUCTOR: Blake, J., *"The Rights of Women,"* 10 (1853) 389-391.

12.44
LONDON JOURNAL: C., E., *"Women's Rights,"* 14 (1851-1852) 251-252.

12.45
NORTH BRITISH REVIEW: Patmore, C., *"The Social Position of Women,"* 14 (1851) 515-540; [Kaye, J.W.], *"The 'Non-Existence' of Women,"* 23 (1855) 536-562. "We make women what they are——we reduce them to dependence, and then taunt them with being incapable of independent action" (p. 558). Very good survey of the woman question relative to several popular books covering aspects of the subject; *"Outrages on Women,"* 25 (1856) 233-256; Kaye, J.W., *"Review of Eight Books on the Woman Question,"* 26 (1857) 157-182.

12.46
BRITISH CONTROVERSIALIST: O., T.F., et al., *"Is Woman Mentally Inferior to Man?"* 3 (1852) 218-227; 251-253; 296-299; 326-336; 366-372. Concludes that men have the superior intellect based on "empirical" evidence. Also argues that most intelligent women emerge from unusual and unfortunate circumstances (i.e. Caroline Norton) and abuse their mental powers by engaging in intrigue.

12.47
[N.A.], **BRITISH FEMALE OPPRESSION.** Manchester, 1853.

12.48
PUNCH'S ALMANAC FOR 1853: *"The Ladies of the Creation,"* bound with volume 24 (Dec. 1851). Pages not numbered. Collection of anti-feminist cartoons that satirize women's dress and behavior.

12.49
PUTNAM'S MONTHLY MAGAZINE: *"Woman and the Woman's Movement,"* 1 (1853) 279-289. "The very virtue of woman, her practical sense, which leaves her indifferent to past and future alike, and keeps her the busy blessing of the present hour, disqualifies her for all didactic dignity. Learning and wisdom do not become her" (p. 279).

12.50
Negginson, Thomas Wentworth, WOMAN AND HER WISHES: AN ESSAY. 1854.

12.51
HOUSEHOLD WORDS: Lynn, E., *"Rights and Wrongs of Women,"* 9 (1854) 158-161.

12.52
CHRISTIAN REMEMBRANCER: Armstrong, J., *"The Rights of Women,"* 30 (1855) 147.

12.53
Parkes, Bessie Rayner (Belloc), REMARKS ON THE EDUCATION OF GIRLS, WITH REFERENCES TO THE SOCIAL, LEGAL, AND INDUSTRIAL POSITION OF WOMEN IN THE PRESENT DAY. 2nd ed., 1856. —*see also:* VICTORIAN PERIODICALS REVIEW: Hunter, F., *"The Bessie Rayner Parkes Collection at Girton College, Cambridge,"* 16 (1983) 32-33. Discusses Parkes' role in establishing the ENGLISH WOMAN'S JOURNAL and her relationships with other early nineteenth-century feminists.

12.54
Milne, John Duguid, THE INDUSTRIAL AND SOCIAL POSITION OF WOMEN. 1857. Important work on women's employment with significance for the emancipation question.

12.55
Craik, Dinah Maria (Mulock), A WOMAN'S THOUGHTS ABOUT WOMEN. 1857; *reviewed in:* SATURDAY REVIEW: 5 (1858) 376-377. —*see also:* FEMINIST STUDIES: Showalter, E., *"Dinah Mulock Craik and the Tactics of Sentiment: A Case Study in Victorian Female Authorship,"* 2 (1975) 5-23.

12.56
Shirreff, Emily, INTELLECTUAL EDUCATION AND ITS INFLUENCE ON THE CHARACTER AND HAPPINESS OF WOMEN. 1858.

12.57
ENGLISH WOMAN'S JOURNAL: 1858 to 1864; *superseded by:* ALEXANDRA MAGAZINE: This journal was conducted by Bessie Rayner Parkes (later Belloc); may also be cataloged as ENGLISHWOMAN'S JOURNAL; *"The SATURDAY REVIEW and THE ENGLISH WOMAN'S JOURNAL: The Reviewer Reviewed,"* 1 (1858) 201-205; Hollings, J., *"On the Social Position of Woman in the Nineteenth Century,"* 1 (1858) 278-280; *"Social Science,"* 2 (1859) 122-124. Lauds the National

Association for the Promotion of Social Science for allowing women to participate in their sessions on social affairs.

12.58
SATURDAY REVIEW: *"Toasting the Ladies,"* 10 (1860) 418-419; *"Women's Friendships,"* 18 (1864) 176-177; *"What is Woman's Work?"* 25 (1868) 197-198; *"The Ladies at Guildhall,"* 13 (1862) 680-681; *"Women's Rights,"* 29 (1870) 662-664; *"Mere Man,"* 91 (1901) 733-734.

12.59
Brockett, Linus, WOMAN: HER RIGHTS, WRONGS, PRIVILEGES AND RESPONSIBILITIES. Hartford, 1859.

12.60
Le Plus Bas (pseud.), WOMAN'S RIGHTS AND WOMAN'S WRONGS, A DYING LEGACY. 1859.

12.61
W., B.A., THE WOMAN'S QUESTION AND THE MAN'S ANSWER. 1859.

12.62
Nightingale, Florence, CASSANDRA. privately printed, 1859; *also reprinted and heavily edited in:* Strachey, Ray, THE CAUSE. A SHORT HISTORY OF THE WOMEN'S MOVEMENT IN GREAT BRITAIN. 1928; 1969; rpt., with an introduction by Myrna Stark and epilogue by Cynthia MacDonald. 1979. —*see also:* Holmes, Marion, FLORENCE NIGHTINGALE: A CAMEO LIFE SKETCH. 1913; Allchin, A.M., "Florence Nightingale and the Status of Women" in THE SILENT REBELLION. by A.M. Allchin. 1958.

12.63
Boucherett, Jessie, HINTS ON SELF-HELP. 1863.

12.64
Cobbe, Frances Power, ESSAYS ON THE PURSUITS OF WOMEN. 1863; *rpt. from:* FRASER'S MAGAZINE and MACMILLAN'S MAGAZINE. Read at Guildhall before the Social Science Congress; CRIMINALS, IDIOTS, WOMEN AND MINORS: IS THE CLASSIFICATION SOUND? A DISCUSSION ON THE LAWS CONCERNING PROPERTY OF MARRIED WOMEN. Manchester, 1869; *also printed in:* FRASER'S MAGAZINE: 78 (1868) 777-794. "Much time and more temper have been lost in debating the sterile problem of the 'equality' of men and women, without either party seeming to perceive that the solution has no bearing on the practical matters at issue; since civil rights have never yet been reserved for 'physical, moral, and intellectual equals'... no class however humble, stupid, and even vicious, has been denied them since serfdom and slavery came to an end" (n.p.); "The Final Cause of Women" in WOMEN'S WORK AND WOMEN'S CULTURE. ed. by Josephine Butler. 1869. Describes two conceptions of the female character: "the final cause of the existence of Woman is the service she can do to man" and "the theory that Woman was created for an end proper to herself" (p. 6); THE DUTIES OF WOMEN. A COURSE OF LECTURES. 1881; LIFE OF FRANCES POWER COBBE, BY HERSELF. Boston and New York, 1894. Anticipates disruption to morality and society and corruption of women's nature as they "(very properly) pursue ends of their own" (p. 24).

12.65
VICTORIA MAGAZINE: 1863 to 1880. Conducted by Emily Faithfull; Andre, P.F.,

"*Civil and Political Status of Women,*" 5 (1865) n.p.; 6 (1865-1866) n.p.; 7 (1866) n.p.; 8 (1866-1867) n.p.; "*Social and Political Dependence of Women,*" 13 (1869) n.p.; Ayrton, J.C., "*Plea for Women,*" 14 (1869-1870) n.p.; Allan, J., "*The Woman Question: A Protest Against Women's Demands for the Privileges of Both Sexes,*" 15 (1870) n.p.; Roscoe, E., "*Opposition to the Movement on Behalf of Women,*" 16 (1870) n.p.; Wallington, "*Women as They are Supposed to Be,*" 15 (1870) n.p.; "*Woman Question,*" 18 (1871-1872) n.p.; Hoskins, J.T., "*Rights of Women,*" 18 (1871-1872) n.p.; Lewis, Mrs., "Position of Women Past and Present," 17 (1871) n.p.; "*Wrongs of Women,*" 17 (1871) n.p.; "*Natural Obstacles to the Culture of Women,*" 23 (1874) n.p.; "*Crusade Against Women,*" 36 (1880) 213.

12.66
CORNHILL MAGAZINE: King, R.A., "*A Tete a Tete Social Science Discussion,*" 10 (1864) 569-582. On the changing roles of women; Hall, E.B. and Scott, H.S., "*Character Note: The New Woman,*" 70 (1894) 365-368.

12.67
Spear, Mrs. C.H., **A BRIEF ESSAY ON THE POSITION OF WOMEN.** 1866. Contends that the problem in improving women's position is the lack of good education.

12.68
MACMILLAN'S MAGAZINE: T[aylor], H., "*Women and Criticism,*" 14 (1866) 335-340. Argues that it is impossible to anticipate results, catastrophic or otherwise, from the "experiments" in equal rights desired by women's rights advocates; Linton, E.L., "*The Modern Revolt [of Women],*" 23 (1870) 142-149. "The late remarkable outbreak of women against the restrictions under which they have hitherto lived— The Modern Revolt——has two meanings: the one is a noble protest against the frivolity and idleness into which they have suffered themselves to sink; the other a mad rebellion against the natural duties of the sex" (p. 142). Argues that women can take up any profession they choose, except for politics, the clergy, and the armed forces, professions for which they are constitutionally unfit; Myers, F.W.H., "*Local Lectures for Women,*" 19 (1869) 159-163. "Is it not disgraceful that men should be found to profane the names of wife and mother by speaking as if the fulfillment of the duties of those holy relationships were the exclusive privilege of fools" (p. 163); Holland, P., "*Two Girls of the Period (No. 1): The Upper Side, Our Offense, Our Defense, and Our Petition,*" 19 (1869) 323-331. Thoughtful reply to Linton's "A Girl of the Period." Describes the demoralization of young upper class women, who are told they have a lofty mission in society, but are confined to home and restricted to considering social engagements and marriage; "*The Ladies' Cry, Nothing to Do!*" 19 (1869) 451-454. Response to the SATURDAY REVIEW article entitled "*The Girl of the Period.*" "If she cannot be a pattern, let her at least be useful as a beacon. If it is too late for her to free herself from the deception of ignorance——if she must remain the wretched thrall of 'the accomplishments'——let her at least try to save her younger sisters and nieces from such a fate. Let her drop political and social agitation... and let her bend all her faculties to the task of winning a better education for her sex" (p. 454); Harberton, F., "*Individual Liberty for Women: A Remonstrance,*" 40 (1879) 282-288. Argues that unmarried women should enjoy greater social freedom because they are as rational and responsible as their male counterparts; Gwynn, S., "*Domesticity,*" 79 (1898) 56-61; "*The Characteristics of English Women,*" 51 (1889) 245-260; Sparay, W., "*Art and the Woman,*" 83 (1900) 29-34. Concludes that women are not creative because they are preoccupied with luxuries. Suggests that women suffer from their own peculiar varieties of materialism and spiritual impoverishment.

12.69

Christian Knowledge Society, A WOMAN'S VIEW OF WOMEN'S RIGHTS. 1867.

12.70

Mill, John Stuart, et al., SPEECHES OF MR. JACOB BRIGHT, M.P... MR. JOHN STUART MILL, M.P. AND MR. G. SHAW LEFEVRE, M.P., IN THE DEBATE ON THE SECOND READING OF THE BILL TO AMEND THE LAW WITH RESPECT TO THE PROPERTY OF MARRIED WOMEN. 1868. ——*see also:* CHRISTIAN OBSERVER AND ADVOCATE: *"Mill on the Condition of Women,"* 68 (1869) 629; Bain, Alexander, JOHN STUART MILL: A CRITICISM. 1882; West, Julius, JOHN STUART MILL. 1913. Sociological survey biography of Mill and his ideas and concepts of women's equality; von Hayek, Friedrick August, JOHN STUART MILL AND HARRIET TAYLOR: THEIR CORRESPONDENCE AND SUBSEQUENT MARRIAGE. 1951; Packe, Michael S., THE LIFE OF JOHN STUART MILL. 1954; Borchard, Ruth, JOHN STUART MILL. THE MAN. 1957. Biography; Pappe, H.O., JOHN STUART MILL AND THE HARRIET TAYLOR MYTH. Melbourne, 1960. Evaluates the extent to which Taylor influenced Mill in his political ideas and writings and the validity of his claim that she was an intellectual giant. Concludes that these claims are unsubstantiated and that there is "no valid evidence to show that Harriet turned Mill's mind towards new horizons or gave an unexpected significance to his thought" (p. 47); Magrid, Henry M., "John Stuart Mill" in HISTORY OF POLITICAL PHILOSOPHY. ed. by Leo Strauss and Joseph Cropsey. Chicago, 1963; Ellery, John B., JOHN STUART MILL. New York, 1964; Samson, Ronald V., "Power Corrupts" in THE PSYCHOLOGY OF POWER. by Ronald V. Samson. New York, 1966. See pp. 69-92 for an analysis of Mill's "mental crisis at the threshold of manhood," and an examination of THE SUBJECTION OF WOMEN and the criticisms it generated; QUEEN'S QUARTERLY: Robson, J.J., *"Harriet Taylor and John Stuart Mill: Artist and Scientist,"* 73 (1966) 167-186. Examines J.S. Mill's and Harriet Taylor's relationship prior to and after their marriage, in the context of their political beliefs regarding equality; Thomas, Donald, "Victoria: If All Mankind Minus One... J.S. Mill (1859)" in A LONG TIME BURNING: THE HISTORY OF LITERARY CENSORSHIP IN ENGLAND. by Donald Thomas. 1969; Rossi, Alice S., ed., "Sentiment and Intellect. The Story of John Stuart Mill and Harriet Taylor Mill" in ESSAYS ON SEX EQUALITY. by John Stuart Mill and Harriet Taylor Mill. Chicago, 1970. Confirms the independent intelligence of Harriet Taylor Mill; evaluates their partnership and feminism; VICTORIAN STUDIES: Millett, K., *"The Debate over Women: Ruskin and Mill,"* 14 (1970) 63-82; Sonstroem, D., *"Mill Versus Ruskin: A Defence of Ruskin's 'Of Queen's Gardens,'"* 20 (1977) 283-297; WESTERN SPEECH: Backes, J.G., *"J.S. Mill and his Preposterous Motion,"* 34 (1970) 90-99; Fletcher, Ronald, ed., JOHN STUART MILL: A LOGICAL CRITIQUE OF SOCIOLOGY. 1971. Collection of selected letters; Mineka, F. and Lindley, N., eds., THE LATER LETTERS OF JOHN STUART MILL. 1972; NEW ZEALAND JOURNAL OF HISTORY: Okin, S.M., *"John Stuart Mill's Feminism: THE SUBJECTION OF WOMEN and the Improvement of Mankind,"* 7 (1973) 105-127. This article pays tribute to Mill's influences in "the early struggle for women's rights" [and his impact on] "New Zealand feminists of the same period" (p. 105). Also examines ideological similarities and differences between Mill and his eventual wife, Harriet Taylor; SOUTHERN QUARTERLY: Tatalovich, A., *"John Stuart Mill THE SUBJECTION OF WOMEN: An Analysis,"* 12 (1973-74) 87-105. Sketches "the main lines of Mill's argument... his opinions on the female role as they are expressed within the larger framework of his political and ethical philosophy and his personal life" (p. 88); Himmelfarb, Gertrude, ON LIBERTY AND LIBERALISM: THE CASE OF JOHN STUART MILL. New York, 1974; CANADIAN HISTORICAL ASSOCIATION HISTORICAL PAPERS: Kornberg, J., *"Feminism and the Liberal Dialectic: John*

Stuart Mill on Women's Rights," n.v. (1974) 37-63. Outlines Mill's beliefs; discusses those who supported and disagreed with him; **QUADRANT:** Jackson, R.L.P., *"George Eliot, J.S. Mill and Women's Liberation,"* 19 (1975) 11-33. Comparative analysis; Thompson, Dennis, **JOHN STUART MILL AND REPRESENTATIVE GOVERNMENT.** Princeton, 1976. See pp. 158-173 for Mill's views on women's equality in general; Kamm, Josephine, **JOHN STUART MILL IN LOVE.** 1977. Examines Harriet Taylor's influence on Mill; **JOURNAL OF BRITISH STUDIES:** Zimmer, L.B., *"The Negative Argument in J.S. Mill's Utilitarianism,"* 17 (1977) 119-142; Himmelfarb, G., *"Reply to Louis B. Zimmer on Mill's 'Negative Argument,'"* 17 (1977) 138-140; **MILL NEWS LETTER:** Robson, J., *"Feminine and Masculine: Mill vs. Grote,"* 12 (1977) 18-23; Sobel, A., *"The Epistemology of the Natural and the Social in Mill's The Subjection of Women,"* 16 (1981) 3-9; **PHILOSOPHY: THE JOURNAL OF THE ROYAL INSTITUTE OF PHILOSOPHY:** Annas, J., *"Mill and the Subjection of Women,"* 52 (1977) 179-194. An analysis of the strengths and weaknesses in Mill's argument; **CANADIAN JOURNAL OF HISTORY:** Pugh, E.L., *"John Stuart Mill, Harriet Taylor, and Women's Rights in America, 1850-1873,"* 13 (1978) 423-442; **HISTORICAL STUDIES:** Caine, B., *"John Stuart Mill and the English Women's Movement,"* 18 (1978) 52-67. Outlines Mill's achievements and shortcomings; Okin, Susan Moller, "John Stuart Mill, Liberal Feminist" in **WOMEN IN WESTERN POLITICAL THOUGHT.** by Susan Moller Okin. Princeton, 1979. Examines Mill's ideas as manifested in his writings and compared to other political thinkers of his time; **CANADIAN JOURNAL OF POLITICAL SCIENCE:** Hughes, P., *"The Reality Versus the Ideal: J.S. Mill's Treatment of Women Workers and Private Property,"* 12 (1979) 523-542. Looks at the contradictions between Mill's writings and his actions; Feaver, G., *"Comment: Overcoming History? Ms. Hughes' Treatment of Mr. Mill,"* 12 (1979) 543-554. "A sharply critical verdict on Dr. Hughes' article" (p. 553); Gutmann, Amy, **LIBERAL EQUALITY.** Cambridge, 1980; **HISTORIAN:** Pugh, E.L., *"John Stuart Mill and the Women's Question in Parliament, 1865-1868,"* 42 (1980) 399-418. "This essay is broadened beyond a treatment of the 1867 amendment to include an examination and evaluation of his [Mill's] total program for women while he was a candidate for Parliament and during his brief term in office. His part in the married women's property bill of 1868 is considered and also his silence on the renewal of the Contagious Diseases Act of 1864" (p. 399); **POLITICAL THEORY:** Shanley, M.L., *"Marital Slavery and Friendship: John Stuart Mill's THE SUBJECTION OF WOMEN,"* 9 (1981) 229-247. Delineates Mill's views on marriage.

12.71
GIRL OF THE PERIOD MISCELLANY: March 1869; vol. 1; *continued as:* **GIRL OF THE PERIOD ALMANACK:** 1869 to 1870; vols. 1-2. An illustrated magazine written by women. Contains anti-feminist poems and articles on "society."

12.72
FORTNIGHTLY REVIEW: Morley, J., *"Critical Notice: The Social and Political Dependence of Women,"* 1 (1867) 764-765; Amberley, K., *"The Claims of Women,"* 9 (1871) 95-110; Grey, M.G., *"Men and Women, Part I,"* 32 (1879) 672-685; Allen, G., *"Plain Words on the Woman Question,"* 46 (1889) 448-458. Allen was a freethinker who condemned marriage for its constraints and hypocrisies, yet professed to believe that women could find fulfillment only in maternity. Contemporary feminists disputed his claim to be a spokesman for women's emancipation; Pennell, E.R., *"A Century of the Rights of Women,"* 48 (1890) 408; Harrison, F., *"The Emancipation of Women,"* 50 (1891) 437-452; Adam, J., *"Women's Place in Modern Life,"* 51 (1892) 522-529; Bury, J.B., *"The Insurrection of Women: A Criticism,"* 52 (1892) 651-666; Quilter, H., *"The Question of Courage and on Equality of Women,"* 57 (1895) 979-995; Smith, G., *"The Women of George Meredith,"* 59 (1896) 775-790;

Caird, M., "The Duel of the Sexes," 84 (1905) 109-122; Malet, L., "The Threatened Re-subjection of Women," 83 (1905) 806-819; Robins, E., "Shall Women Work?" 93 (1910) 899-911. Maintains that women should have free choice in decisions regarding work and marriage.

12.73
THE WOMAN OF THE FUTURE. 1869.

12.74
Butler, Josephine, MEMOIR OF JOHN GREY OF DILSTON. Edinburgh, 1869; (as editor), WOMAN'S WORK AND WOMAN'S CULTURE. 1869; ADDRESS DELIVERED AT CROYDEN, JULY 3, 1871. 1871; THE CONSTITUTION VIOLATED. Edinburgh, 1871; THE NEW ABOLITIONISTS. 1876; REBECCA JARRETT. 1885; PERSONAL REMINISCENCES OF A GREAT CRUSADE. 1896; Butler also published articles in: SHIELD (1870 to 1886), DAWN (quarterly; 1888 to 1896), and STORM BELL (monthly; 1898 to 1900). ——see also: Stead, William Thomas, JOSEPHINE BUTLER, A LIFE SKETCH. 1888; Johnson, George William and Johnson, Lucy A., JOSEPHINE BUTLER: AN AUTOBIOGRAPHICAL MEMOIR. Bristol, 1909; Holmes, Marion, JOSEPHINE BUTLER. A CAMEO LIFE SKETCH. 1913; Hay-Cooper, L., JOSEPHINE BUTLER. 1922; Fawcett, Millicent Garrett and Turner, Ethel Mary, JOSEPHINE BUTLER: HER WORKS AND PRINCIPLES. 1927; Butler, Arthur Stanley George, PORTRAIT OF JOSEPHINE BUTLER. 1954; Bell, Enid Moberly, JOSEPHINE BUTLER. FLAME OF FIRE. 1962; Petrie, Glen A., SINGULAR INIQUITY: THE CAMPAIGNS OF JOSEPHINE BUTLER. 1971; Harrison, Brian, "Josephine Butler" in EMINENTLY VICTORIAN: ASPECTS OF AN AGE. ed. by J.F.C. Harrison, Basil Taylor and Isobel Armstrong. 1974; Uglow, Jenny, "Josephine Butler: From Sympathy to Theory" in FEMINIST THEORISTS. THREE CENTURIES OF WOMEN'S INTELLECTUAL TRADITIONS. ed. by Dale Spender. 1983. "Butler argues for emancipation on two fronts, that the present inequitable treatment of women demands redress on straightforward egalitarian, civil-rights grounds, and that greater freedom will bring positive social benefits through releasing women's 'special qualities'" (p. 156).

12.75
Kinnear, John Boyd, "The Social Position of Women in the Present Age" in WOMAN'S WORK AND WOMAN'S CULTURE. ed. by Josephine Butler. 1869; THE RIGHTS OF WOMEN TO LABOUR. 1873.

12.76
Hoskins, James A., WOMEN'S RIGHTS. 1869.

12.77
Linton, Elizabeth Lynn, OURSELVES. A SERIES OF ESSAYS ON WOMEN. 1869. Anti-feminist observations on marriage roles, fashions and domestic responsibilities; THE GIRL OF THE PERIOD AND OTHER SOCIAL ESSAYS. 1883. ——see also: NINETEENTH CENTURY: Maxwell, H., "Walling the Cuckoo [Mrs. Linton] and Women's Rights," 32 (1892) 920-929; Layard, George Somes, THE LIFE OF ELIZA LYNN LINTON: HER LIFE, LETTERS, AND OPINIONS. 1901. Notes that THE GIRL OF THE PERIOD marked a turning point in Linton's career——her emphasis shifted from the rights to the limitations of women and she changed from an almost unknown writer to a household word. "I thought the lives of women should be as free as those of men... I have lived to see my mistake. Knowing in my own person all that women have to suffer when they fling themselves into the active fray, I would prevent with all my strength young girls from following my mistake" (p. 140). "Only to the new woman I am implacable" (p. 294); Anderson, Nancy F.,

"Eliza Lynn Linton and the Woman Question in Victorian England," Ph.D. diss., Tulane Univ., 1973; Belflower, James R., "The Life and Career of Elizabeth Lynn Linton and the Woman Question in Victorian England," Ph.D. diss., Tulane Univ., 1973; Vanthal, Herbert, **ELIZA LYNN LINTON: THE GIRL OF THE PERIOD, A BIOGRAPHY.** 1979; *reviewed in:* VICTORIAN STUDIES: Vicinus, M., 24 (1981) 369-370; VICTORIAN PERIODICALS REVIEW: Rinehart, N., *"The 'Girl of the Period' Controversy,"* 13 (1980) 3-9. Delineates Linton's career in journalism, her articles which criticized "the new woman," and the responses generated from readers. Although considered an "emancipated woman," Linton was an arch critic of many aspects of the women's movement.

12.78
Sewell, Sarah Ann, **WOMAN AND THE TIMES WE LIVE IN.** Manchester, 1869.

12.79
ALL THE YEAR ROUND: *"A Woman's Rights Convention,"* 2 (1869) 517-521.

12.80
ENGLAND'S DAUGHTERS: WHAT IS THEIR REAL WORK? 1870. Holds secular education responsible for the spreading "poison" of concern for woman's rights.

12.81
Kortright, Fanny Aikin, **THE TRUE RIGHTS OF WOMAN.** 2nd ed., [1870].

12.82
Morris, Francis O., **THE RIGHTS AND WRONGS OF WOMEN.** 1870.

12.83
Taylor, Mary, **THE FIRST DUTY OF WOMAN.** 1870; *a series of articles rpt. from:* VICTORIA MAGAZINE: 1865 to 1870.

12.84
CONTEMPORARY REVIEW: Cobbe, F.P., *"Wife Torture in England,"* 32 (1878) 55-87; Cobbe, F.P., *"The Little Health of Ladies,"* 31 (1878) 276-296; Leppington, B., *"Debrutalisation of Man,"* 67 (1895) 725-743; White, A., *"'La Politique ou la Politesse?': A Glance at Osborne Morgan's Review of Lady Jeune's 'London Society,'"* 239 (1981) 266-269.

12.85
ENGLISHWOMAN'S REVIEW: This periodical represents a nineteenth-century feminist perspective throughout; Crippen, T.G., *"The Testimony of Holy Scripture Concerning the Social Status of Woman,"* 3 (1870) 127-163; *"Are Duties and Rights the Same?"* 6 (1875) 301-306. Acknowledges that middle-class women may have all the rights they are conscious of wanting, but argues that such women have a duty to their poorer sisters who are protected neither by culture nor law from the viciousness of their menfolk; Drummond, A., *"The Rights of Women in 1798,"* 6 (1875) 248-252. Provides extracts from the book, AN APPEAL TO THE MEN OF GREAT BRITAIN ON BEHALF OF THE WOMEN and compares it with the writing of Mary Wollstonecraft. Urges women to press for political representation; Williams, C., *"Union Among Women,"* 6 (1875) 55-57; *"Three Decades of Progress,"* 9 (1878) 337-344; *"Women's Newspapers: A Sketch of the Periodical Literature Devoted to the Woman Question,"* 9 (1878) 433-440; *"Men's Views of Women's Duties,"* 10 (1879) 448-450; S., A., *"A Novelist on 'Women's Rights' to the editor of THE ENGLISHWOMAN'S REVIEW,"* 10 (1879) 115; *"Social Science,"* 10 (1879) 433-443; *"Bibliography on Women's Questions: Periodicals,"* 31 (1900) 217-220.

12.86
TINSLEY'S MAGAZINE: *"Modern Views About Women,"* 5 (1870) 660-664. "We think also that too much and too little has been expected of women. Men treat her as the negro does his fetish... but if she dares to assert any individuality... her worshipers turn on her and literally seem to question her right to exist" (p. 661).

12.87
H., A., ed., **WORDS OF WEIGHT ON THE WOMAN QUESTION. A BOOK OF QUOTATIONS.** 1871.

12.88
Bourke, John Walter, **THE EMANCIPATION OF WOMEN.** Dublin, 1871.

12.89
Brown, J. Baldwin, "Our Young Women" in **OUR MORALS AND MANNERS.** by J. Baldwin Brown. New York, 1871. Anti-feminist work that advocates allowing women what they want so they can fail and return to their proper place.

12.90
Cook, Tennessee Celeste (Claflin), **CONSTITUTIONAL EQUALITY A RIGHT OF WOMEN; OR, A CONSIDERATION OF THE VARIOUS RELATIONS WHICH SHE SUSTAINS AS A NECESSARY PART OF A BODY OF SOCIETY AND HUMANITY.** New York, 1871.

12.91
TEMPLE BAR: *"Women's Proper Place in Society,"* 33 (1871) 168-178.

12.92
MEN'S RIGHTS AND WOMEN'S POWERS. 1872.

12.93
THE WOMAN QUESTION. 1872. Twelve essays; *rpt. from:* **EXAMINER.**

12.94
Mylne, Margaret, **WOMAN, AND HER SOCIAL POSITION.** 1872.

12.95
Higginson, Thomas Wentworth, **OUGHT WOMEN TO LEARN THE ALPHABET?** Manchester, 1873; *rpt. from:* **ATLANTIC ESSAYS.**

12.96
Davis, Mrs., compiler, **A HISTORY OF THE WOMEN'S RIGHTS MOVEMENTS.** [1874]; *reviewed in:* **ENGLISHWOMAN'S REVIEW:** 5 (1874) 261-262.

12.97
WOMEN'S SUFFRAGE JOURNAL: *"The Women 'Parishioners' and 'Communicants,'"* 5 (1874) 83. Discusses a bill concerning public worship which would have the effect, according to the author, of ex-communicating women from the National Church, thereby withdrawing their right to participate in religion; *"Sir George Campbell, M.P. on Women's Rights,"* 6 (1875) 81.

12.98
WOMAN'S WORK: A WOMAN'S THOUGHTS ON WOMEN'S RIGHTS. 1875.

12.99
Lovett, William, **THE LIFE AND STRUGGLES OF WILLIAM LOVETT.** 2 vols. 1876.

12.100
BELGRAVIA: Linton, E.L., *"Women's Place in Nature and Society,"* 29 (1876) 362.

12.101
Oliphant, Margaret, **DAYS OF MY LIFE.** 1876; **THE AUTOBIOGRAPHY AND LETTERS OF MRS. M.O.W. OLIPHANT, ARRANGED AND EDITED BY MRS. HARRY COGHILL.** 3rd ed., 1899.

12.102
UNITARIAN REVIEW: L., M.P., *"Things at Home and Abroad. The Movements of Women,"* 8 (1877) 568-578.

12.103
NINETEENTH CENTURY: Orr, A., *"The Future of English Women,"* 3 (1878) 1010-1032; Fawcett, M.G., *"The Future of Englishwomen: A Reply [to A. Orr.],"* 4 (1878) 347-357; Simcox, E., *"The Capacity of Women,"* 22 (1887) 391-402; Gaskell, C.M., *"Women of Today, What is Expected of Them,"* 26 (1889) 776-784; Child-Villiers, M.E., *"Ourselves and Our Foremothers,"* 27 (1890) 56-64; Cowper, K., *"The Decline of Reserve Among Women,"* 27 (1890) 65-71. "Ladies who once would have thought that any work which necessitated their meeting the lower classes upon terms of intimacy and equality would be quite impossible, now acknowledge the immense advantage to be derived from doing so" (p. 69). "A crisis appears to have arisen" (p. 70); Linton, E.L., *"The Wild Women, No. 1. As Politicians,"* 30 (1891) 79-88. "This question of woman's political power is from the beginning to the end a question of sex——its moral and intellectual limitations, its emotional excesses, its personal disabilities, its social conditions" (p. 86); Linton, E.L., *"The Wild Women as Social Insurgents,"* 30 (1891) 596-605. "The Wild Woman as a social insurgent preaches the 'lesson of liberty' broadened into lawlessness and licence. Unconsciously, she exemplifies how beauty can degenerate into ugliness.... She repudiates the doctrine of individual conformity for the sake of the general good" (p. 596); Linton, E.L., *"Partisans of the Wild Women,"* 31 (1892) 455-464. Believes the "wild women," i.e., women who agitate for suffrage and increased political rights for themselves, to be fatally mistaken, yet declares her "moral respect in spite of strong intellectual deprecation" for wild women sincerely convinced of the merits of their case. Castigates women who capitalize on the suffrage issue for their own purposes and praises the less conspicuous efforts of professional women careerists who "keep the world of feminine activities pure and sweet" (p. 462); Caird, M., *"A Defense of the So-Called Wild Women,"* 31 (1892) 811-829. "The quarrel, in fact between Mrs. Lynn Linton and her opponents is... between decaying institutions and a new social faith.... There was a time when Mrs. Linton had sympathies with the struggle of a soul towards a new faith, but that is all over" (p. 828); Whibley, C., *"The Encroachment of Women,"* 41 (1897) 531-537; Sutherland, A., *"Women's Brain,"* 47 (1900) 802-810; Ponsonby, M.E., *"The Role of Women in Society,"* 49 (1901) 64-76; Harrison, E.B., *"The Victorian Women,"* 58 (1905) 951-957; Colquhoun, E., *"Quo Vadis, Femina?"* 73 (1913) 517-527; Pankhurst, R.K.P., *"Saint-Simonianism in England,"* 152 (1952) 449-512; Pankhurst, R.K.P., *"Saint Simonianism in England: II,"* 153 (1953) 47-58.

12.104
POPULAR SCIENCE MONTHLY: Bagehot, W., *"Biology and Women's Rights,"* 14 (1879) 210-213.

12.105
Clapperton, Jane Hume, **WHAT DO WOMEN WANT?** [188?]. "It is for educated women to re-organize domestic life and prepare on a wide scale for the ultimate triumph of socialism over individualism" (p. 7); **SOME EVOLUTIONAL ASPECTS OF THE WOMEN MOVEMENT.** 1899. "The International Congress of Women is a clear indication of the vitality of the movement and of its entering upon a new phase.... The woman movement is in perfect accord with the trend of the general evolution for while 'the old order changeth' all changes that mean progress inevitably involve enlargement of life and function" (p. 1).

12.106
Anthony, C., **SOCIAL AND POLITICAL DEPENDENCE OF WOMEN.** 1880.

12.107
FRASER'S MAGAZINE: Oliphant, M., *"The Grievances of Women,"* 101 (1880) 698–710. "The sentiment of men towards women is thoroughly ungenerous from beginning to end.... I have thought... that this was an old-fashioned notion.... But experience does not disprove it" (p. 710).

12.108
WOMEN'S RIGHTS AS PREACHED BY WOMEN, PAST AND PRESENT. BY A LOOKER ON. 1881.

12.109
Schreiner, Olive (pseud. Ralph Iron), **THE STORY OF AN AFRICAN FARM.** 1883; **DREAMS.** 1890. Short stories and allegories; **DREAM LIFE AND REAL LIFE.** 1893; 1912; **TROOPER PETER HALKETT OF MASHONOLAND.** 1897. Novella; **AN ENGLISH SOUTH AFRICAN'S VIEW OF THE SITUATION.** 1899; **THE WOMAN QUESTION.** New York, 1899; **WOMAN AND LABOUR.** Leipzig, 1911; New York, 1911; 1972; Toronto, 1978; **THOUGHTS ON SOUTH AFRICA.** 1923. Compilation of articles published during the years 1890-1892; Boston, 1924; **STORIES, DREAMS AND ALLEGORIES.** 1924; **MAN TO MAN.** 1926; **UNDINE.** 1929. —*see also:* Cronwright-Schreiner, S.C., ed., **THE LETTERS OF OLIVE SCHREINER, 1876-1920.** 1924; **THE LIFE OF OLIVE SCHREINER.** 1924; Hobman, D.L., **OLIVE SCHREINER, HER FRIENDS AND TIMES.** 1955; Greg, Lyndall, **MEMORIES OF OLIVE SCHREINER.** 1957; Meintjis, Johannes, **OLIVE SCHREINER: PORTRAIT OF A SOUTH AFRICAN WOMAN.** Johannesburg, 1965; Friedlander, Zelda, ed., **UNTIL THE HEART CHANGES: A GARLAND FOR OLIVE SCHREINER.** 1967; **FRONTIERS:** Berkman, J., *"The Nurturant Fantasies of Olive Schreiner,"* 3 (1977) 8-17. Links Olive Schreiner's "nurturant fantasies" as manifested in her writings, to "the social attitudes of the time" (p. 8); Berkman, Joyce Aurech, **OLIVE SCHREINER: FEMINISM ON THE FRONTIER.** Montreal, 1979; First, Ruth and Scott, Ann, **OLIVE SCHREINER.** 1980; **MICHIGAN OCCASIONAL PAPERS IN WOMEN'S STUDIES:** Winkler, B.S., *"Victorian Daughters: The Lives and Feminism of Charlotte Perkins Gilman and Olive Schreiner,"* no. 13 (Winter 1980) n.p.; **QUARTERLY BULLETIN OF THE SOUTH AFRICAN LIBRARY:** Cartwright, M.F., *"Portraits of Olive Schreiner: A Preliminary Guide,"* 35 (1981) 105-129. Delineates and lists portraits in the South African library and elsewhere; Stanley, Liz, "Olive Schreiner: New Women, Free Women, All Women (1855-1920)" in **FEMINIST THEORISTS: THREE CENTURIES OF WOMEN'S INTELLECTUAL TRADITION.** ed. by Dale Spender. 1983. Analyzes the majority of Schreiner's works for her feminist ideals and theories.

12.110
DUBLIN REVIEW: Cox, J.G., *"The Changed Position of Women,"* 92 (1883) 417-442.

12.111
NATIONAL REVIEW: Austin, A., *"Thoughts on Family Politics,"* 1 (1883) 810-823; Blackburn, H., *"Relation of Women to the State in Past Time,"* 8 (1886) 392-399; Linton, E.L., *"The Future Supremacy of Women,"* 8 (1886) 1-15; *"The Effects of Civilization on Women,"* 9 (1887) 26-38; Linton, E.L., *"The Threatened Abdication of Man,"* 13 (1889) 577-592; Jeune, M., *"Women of Today, Yesterday and Tomorrow,"* 2 (1889) 547-561; Wortley, V.S., *"Feminism in England and France,"* 51 (1905) 793-794.

12.112
OUR CORNER: Jan. 1883 to Dec. 1888; 12 vols. Edited by Annie Besant.

12.113
Stanton, Theodore, ed., **THE WOMAN QUESTION IN EUROPE.** New York, 1884; 1970.

12.114
Bebel, August, **WOMAN IN THE PAST, PRESENT, AND FUTURE.** trans. by Adams Walther. 1885. Argues that women must be given equality before the law, economic freedom and independence and "so far as possible" equality in mental development. Discusses women's role in the family with far greater specificity and realism than her role in public life. ——*see also:* MacMahon, William, **BEBEL'S LIBEL ON WOMEN.** 1912.

12.115
Besant, Annie, **WOMEN'S POSITION ACCORDING TO THE BIBLE.** 1885.

12.116
Woodward, Emma Hosken, ed., **MEN, WOMEN AND PROGRESS.** 1885.

12.117
SPECTATOR: *"Progress of Women,"* 58 (1885) 335-337; *"Advancing Influence of Women,"* 58 (1885) 1132-1133.

12.118
Aveling, Edward and Marx, Eleanor, **THE WOMAN QUESTION.** 1886; 1887; *rpt. in:* **MARXISM TODAY:** 16 (1972) 80-88. "The position of women... rests... on an economic basis... the woman question is one of the organisation of society as a whole" (p. 81). ——*see also:* Tsuzuki, Chushichi, **THE LIFE OF ELEANOR MARX 1855-1898: A SOCIALIST TRAGEDY.** 1967; Kapp, Yvonne, **ELEANOR MARX.** 2 vols. New York, 1972-1976; **MONTHLY REVIEW:** Rosebury, A., *"Eleanor, Daughter of Karl Marx: Personal Reminiscences,"* 24 (1973) 29-49. The author was a friend of Eleanor Marx.

12.119
Devey, Lousia, **LIFE OF ROSINA, LADY LYTTON.** 1887.

12.120
JOURNAL OF EDUCATION: *"The New Old Maid,"* 19 (1887) 77-80.

12.121
Gibson, John, **THE EMANCIPATION OF WOMEN**. Aberystwyth, 1888.

12.122
Hardy, Edward John, **THE FIVE TALENTS OF WOMAN: A BOOK FOR GIRLS AND WOMEN**. 1888.

12.123
Pearson, Karl, "The Woman's Question" in **THE ETHIC OF FREE THOUGHT: A SELECTION OF ESSAYS AND LECTURES**. by Karl Pearson. 1888.

12.124
Wolstenholme-Elmy, Elizabeth C., **THE EMANCIPATION OF WOMEN**. 1888. Author may be cataloged as Elmy, Elizabeth C. Wolstenholme.

12.125
Collet, Clara E., **THE ECONOMIC POSITION OF EDUCATED WORKING WOMEN**. 1890.

12.126
LUCIFER: Blavatsky, H.P., *"Diagnoses and Palliatives,"* 6 (1890) 353-364. Castigates Grant Allen's system of sexual ethics as illustrated in his novel THE WOMAN WHO DID. Responds that if Allen considers it an honor for a woman to be a mistress to Shelley or a mother of Newton "why should not the young ladies who resort to Regent Street... and who are soaked through and through with such 'honors,' why should not they we ask, receive public recognition and a vote of thanks from the nation?" (p. 364). Blavatsky was the founder of the Theosophical Society.

12.127
NEW REVIEW: *"Candour in English Fiction,"* 2 (1890) 6-21. Argues that the characterization of women in fiction must correspond with their increasing social emancipation by an honest portrayal of sexual relationships; Linton, E.L., *"Rights of Women Nearing the Rapids,"* 10 (1894) 302-310.

12.128
Fernald, James Champlin, **NEW WOMANHOOD**. Boston, 1891.

12.129
Harrison, Frederic, **THE EMANCIPATION OF WOMEN**. 1891.

12.130
Shaw, George Bernard, "The Womanly Woman" in **THE QUINTESSENCE OF IBSENISM**. 1891. Challenges the idea that women find ultimate fulfillment in attending only to the interests of husband and children, by arguing that no man ever found supreme satisfaction by adopting such a course; "Preface: The Revolt Against Marriage" in **GETTING MARRIED**. by George Bernard Shaw. 1909; **THE INTELLIGENT WOMAN'S GUIDE TO SOCIALISM, CAPITALISM, SOVIETISM, AND FASCISM**. 1928; rpt., 1972. ——*see also:* **SOCIALIST REVIEW:** Mansel, M.E., *"Bernard Shaw and Feminism,"* 9 (1912) 50-57. "Shaw's heroines are gigantically self-assertive, and not always agreeable. The ideal lady of his drama is jilted as often as she is married. To him, 'women are human beings just like men, only worse brought up, and therefore worse behaved.' They are not the womanly woman of man-made thought because that is a convention, and a convention denies them liberty and responsibility" (p. 56); Watson, Barbara Bellow, **A SHAVIAN**

GUIDE TO THE INTELLIGENT WOMAN. New York, 1972; Morgan, Margery M., THE SHAVIAN PLAYGROUND. AN EXPLORATION OF THE ART OF GEORGE BERNARD SHAW. 1972; Johnson, Josephine, FLORENCE FARR: BERNARD SHAW'S "NEW WOMAN." Totowa, 1975; 1976; CRITICAL INQUIRY: Holroyd, M., *"George Bernard Shaw: Women and the Body Politic,"* 61 (1979) 17-32; Holroyd, Michael, ed., THE GENIUS OF SHAW. New York, 1979. A symposium discussing Shaw's views on women and the politics of women; Peters, Margot, BERNARD SHAW AND THE ACTRESSES. Garden City, 1980. Discusses the influence actresses had on Shaw's work and the presence of the "new woman" in his plays.

12.131
Crepaz, Adele, THE EMANCIPATION OF WOMEN AND ITS POSSIBLE CONSEQUENCES. trans. from the German by Ellis Wright. Sonnenschein, 1893.

12.132
Ethelmer, Ellis (pseud. for Wolstenholme-Elmy, Elizabeth C.), WOMAN FREE. Congleton, 1893.

12.133
AN APPEAL AND A WARNING TO THE MEMBERS OF THE HOUSE OF COMMONS ON THE SUBJECT OF WOMEN'S RIGHTS. 1893.

12.134
Twining, Louisa, RECOLLECTIONS OF LIFE AND WORK; BEING THE AUTOBIOGRAPHY OF LOUISA TWINING. 1893; THE LOSSES AND GAINS OF FIFTY YEARS. 1897. ——*see also:* CANADIAN HISTORICAL ASSOCIATION HISTORICAL PAPERS: McCrone, K.E., *"Feminism and Philanthropy in Victorian England. The Case of Louisa Twining,"* n.v. (1976) 123-139. "Philanthropic work provided a back door through which some women entered public life. One such woman was Louisa Twining, the originator of the workhouse reform" (p. 125).

12.135
LAW TIMES: *"Women as Fellows of Scientific Societies,"* 95 (1893) 152.

12.136
MONIST: Ward, L., *"The Exemption of Women from Labor,"* 4 (1893-1894) 385-395. Ward examines from an anthropological perspective the "erroneous assumption that every adult female... is provided with a husband who is both able and willing to supply all her needs" (p. 390).

12.137
Carpenter, Edward, WOMAN, AND HER PLACE IN A FREE SOCIETY. Manchester, 1894; "Woman the Serf" and "Woman in Freedom" in LOVE'S COMING OF AGE. by Edward Carpenter. 1911. ——*see also:* Tsuzuki, Chushichi, EDWARD CARPENTER 1844-1929. PROPHET OF HUMAN FELLOWSHIP. Cambridge, 1980. Focuses on Carpenter as a socialist who advocated equal status for homosexuals and women.

12.138
Grundy, Sydney, THE NEW WOMAN. 1894.

12.139
Mason, Otis, WOMAN'S SHARE IN PRIMITIVE CULTURE. 1894.

12.140
Pellew, George, **WOMAN AND THE COMMONWEALTH**. Boston, 1894.

12.141
Allen, Grant, **THE WOMAN WHO DID**. 1895. Fictional account of a "new woman"; *reviewed in:* **CONTEMPORARY REVIEW:** Fawcett, M.G., 67 (1895) 625-631. "The central idea of Mr. Grant Allen's book is that marriage means slavery; but he only reiterates this again and again, without attempting to prove it.... He purports to write in the interests of women, but... his... book belongs... more to the unregenerate man than to women at all" (p. 631).

12.142
von Hartmann, Edward, **THE SEXES COMPARED AND OTHER ESSAYS**. trans. by A. Kenner. 1895.

12.143
SCOTTISH REVIEW: White, T.P., *"The Malcontent Women,"* 25 (1895) 270-290.

12.144
Stopes, Charlotte Carmichael, **THE WOMEN'S PROTEST. PAPER READ AT THE LONDON CONFERENCE. OCTOBER 15, 1896**. [1896]; **BRITISH FREEWOMEN: THEIR HISTORICAL PRIVILEGE**. 1909.

12.145
FORUM: Winston, E.W., *"Foibles of the New Woman,"* n.v. (1896) 196-202.

12.146
Caird, Mona, **THE MORALITY OF MARRIAGE AND OTHER ESSAYS ON THE STATUS AND DESTINY OF WOMEN**. 1897.

12.147
Dennehy, Annabella, **THE WOMAN OF THE FUTURE**. 1899.

12.148
Gilman, Charlotte Perkins, **WOMEN AND ECONOMICS**. 1899; 1906. ——*see also:* **MICHIGAN OCCASIONAL PAPERS IN WOMEN'S STUDIES:** Winkler, B.S., *"Victorian Daughters: The Lives and Feminism of Charlotte Perkins Gilman and Olive Schreiner,"* no. 13 (1980) n.p. "Both Schreiner and Gilman examined the reasons for and ramifications of women's exclusion from the public sphere, the psychological effects of women's economic dependence upon men, and the relationship between patriarchy and capitalism" (p. 1).

12.149
Swiney, Frances, **THE AWAKENING OF WOMEN, OR WOMEN'S PART IN EVOLUTION**. 1899; 1905. Claims that the sexes are equal in some respects, but that women are the more evolved beings; *reviewed in:* **WESTMINSTER REVIEW:** Ignota, 152 (1899) 69-72. This book should "be read with great profit by every earnest-minded man, desirous of comprehending the inner meaning of the 'woman movement'" (p. 1); *also reviewed in:* **ENGLISHWOMAN'S REVIEW:** 31 (1900) 130-132. Finds Swiney's belief in female superiority more typical of American than British thinking. "It inclines too much to the very questionable practice of regarding men and women as two distinct species, losing sight of the fact that they are both primarily human beings.... Mrs. Swiney is the first writer we have met with who has seriously maintained that woman is complete by herself and has no need of man, while he cannot get along without her" (p. 132).

12.150
International Council of Women, AN EQUAL MORAL STANDARD FOR MEN AND WOMEN. REPORT OF PAPERS READ AT A SPECIAL MEETING FOR WOMEN HELD IN CONNECTION WITH THE SOCIAL SCIENCE SECTION AT THE INTERNATIONAL CONGRESS OF WOMEN... 1899. 1900.

12.151
Vallance, Zona, "Women as Citizens" in ETHICAL DEMOCRACY: ESSAYS IN SOCIAL DYNAMICS. ed. by Stanton Coit. 1900.

12.152
NEW WORLD: Lee, G.S., *"The Sex-Conscious School in Fiction,"* 9 (1900) 77-84.

12.153
ARENA: Winchester, B., *"The New Woman,"* 1 (1902) 367-373.

12.154
Stead, William Thomas, THE DESPISED SEX. 1903.

12.155
Woolsey, Kate Trimble, REPUBLICS VS. WOMEN, CONTRASTING THE TREATMENT ACCORDED WOMEN IN ARISTOCRACIES WITH THAT METED OUT TO HER IN DEMOCRACIES. 1903.

12.156
Dixie, Florence, TOWARDS FREEDOM: AN APPEAL TO THOUGHTFUL MEN AND WOMEN. Watts, 1904.

12.157
Holyoake, George Jacob, "First Plan of the Women's Rights Agitation" in SIXTY YEARS OF AN AGITATOR'S LIFE. by George Jacob Holyoake. 1906. Details Holyoake's interest in political agitation in the 1840s and describes the reticence of English women at the start of the movement.

12.158
Densmore, Emmet, SEX EQUALITY. A SOLUTION OF THE WOMAN PROBLEM. 1907.

12.159
Murby, Millicent, THE COMMON SENSE OF THE WOMAN QUESTION. 1908.

12.160
JOURNAL OF THE ROYAL STATISTICAL SOCIETY: *"The Social Status of Women Occupiers,"* 71 (1908) 513-515.

12.161
NORTH AMERICAN REVIEW: Grand, S., (pseud. Frances Elizabeth McFall), *"The New Aspect of the Woman Question,"* 158 (1894) 270-276. Maintains that the mission of the New Woman is to enlighten men to the fact that women existed for their own purposes, not for men's purposes; Ouida, *"The New Woman,"* 158 (1894) 610-619. Opposes Grand's claims. Questions how the New Woman, man's moral and mental inferior, can teach anything of value; Aked, C.F., *"The Women's Movement In England,"* 188 (1908) 650-658. "Historically the Workman and the Woman have been alike the objects of exploitation. But the case of the woman has been worse"

(p. 650).

12.162
Aberconway, Laura Elizabeth (Pochin) McLaren, **THE WOMEN'S CHARTER OF RIGHTS AND LIBERTIES.** 1909; 1910; 1911.

12.163
Churchill, Consuelo Spencer (Duchess of Marlborough), (afterwards Balsan, Consuelo Vanderbilt), **THE POSITION OF WOMEN.** 1909; *rpt. from:* **NORTH AMERICAN REVIEW.**

12.164
Fletcher, Margaret, **FEMINISM.** Litchworth, 1909; **CHRISTIAN FEMINISM: A CHARTER OF RIGHTS AND DUTIES.** 1915.

12.165
Staars, David, "A Change in Public Opinion" and "Progressive Environments and First Steps" in **THE ENGLISH WOMAN. STUDIES IN HER PSYCHIC EVOLUTION.** by David Staars. trans. by J.M.E. Brownlow. 1909. First chapter discusses the contributions of Harriet Martineau, Mary Somerville, and Florence Nightingale to changing attitudes about female societal roles; second chapter examines the effects of legal reforms pioneered by women.

12.166
Thomas, J.M. Lloyd, **THE EMANCIPATION OF WOMEN.** 1909. Characterizes women's emancipation and emerging group consciousness as similar to religious conversion. Recounts women's accomplishments on behalf of the greater social welfare.

12.167
Tina, Beatrice, **WOMAN'S WORST ENEMY: WOMAN.** 1909.

12.168
Coit, Stanton, **WOMAN IN CHURCH AND STATE.** 1910.

12.169
Despard, Charlotte, **WOMEN IN THE NEW ERA.** 1910; **WOMAN IN THE NATION.** 1913.

12.170
Farr, Florence, **MODERN WOMAN, HER INTENTIONS.** 1910. Blames the subjection of women on the Jews, the Bible, and Mohammedanism. Discusses wages, marriage, and other contemporary issues concerning women.

12.171
Garnett, Richard and Garnett, Edward, **THE LIFE OF W.J. FOX, PUBLIC TEACHER AND SOCIAL REFORMER, 1786-1864.** 1910.

12.172
Hecker, Eugene Arthur, **A SHORT HISTORY OF WOMEN'S RIGHTS FROM THE DAYS OF AUGUSTUS TO THE PRESENT TIME WITH SPECIAL REFERENCE TO ENGLAND AND THE UNITED STATES.** 1910. See especially: "History of Women's Rights in England" in which Hecker discusses the sociopolitical ramifications of the legal differences between single and married women.

12.173
Housman, Lawrence, **ARTICLES OF FAITH IN THE FREEDOM OF WOMEN.** 1910.

12.174
James, Emily, **THE LADY: STUDIES OF CERTAIN SIGNIFICANT PHASES OF HER HISTORY.** 1910.

12.175
Wheeler, Ethel, **FAMOUS BLUE STOCKINGS.** 1910. Discusses the educated, middle-class salon ladies——largely authors——who tried to emulate the female French intelligentsia and nurtured movements for female emancipation, often unwittingly.

12.176
Sharp, Evelyn, **REBEL WOMEN.** 1910.

12.177
Halford, S.H., **A CRITICISM OF THE WOMAN MOVEMENT FROM THE PSYCHOLOGICAL STANDPOINT.** 1911.

12.178
Lumsden, Louisa Innes, "The Position of Women in History" in **THE POSITION OF WOMAN: ACTUAL AND IDEAL.** by Louisa Innes Lumsden. 1911. Preface by Sir Oliver Lodge. "There exist, biologists assure us, certain deep and fundamental distinctions between male and female.... Yet it seems certain that nothing can be predicated about the actions of man or woman save that the individual may and does override and set at naught all theories and generalizations" (p. 30).

12.179
Simms, Albert Ernest Nicholas, **ST. PAUL AND THE WOMAN MOVEMENT.** 1911.

12.180
Snowden, Ethel Annakin, **THE FEMINIST MOVEMENT.** 1911.

12.181
FREEWOMAN: A WEEKLY HUMANIST REVIEW: 1911 to 1912.

12.182
FRIEND: Grace, W., *"The Experience of Friends in Relation to the Position of Women,"* 51 (1911) 326; *"Friends and the Women's Movement,"* 54 (1914) 107; Taylor, G.R.S., *"'A Woman's Creed,'"* 54 (1914) 115-116; Wallis, H.M., *"A Gentle Protest,"* 54 (1914) 114-115; Cross, E.R., *"The Meeting for Sufferings and the Women's Movement,"* 54 (1914) 132-133; Bayes, A.H., et al., *"The Meeting for Sufferings and the Women's Movement,"* 54 (1914) 147-148; Thompson, J.S., et al., *"The Meeting for Sufferings and the Women's Movement,"* 54 (1914) 164-166; Sharp, A.J., et al., *"The Meeting for Sufferings and the Women's Movement,"* 54 (1914) 206-207; Jackson, H., *"The Meeting for Sufferings and the Women's Movement,"* 54 (1914) 258; Byles, H.B., *"The Women's Movement and the Meeting for Sufferings,"* 54 (1914) 276; Mennell, G.H., *"The Meeting for Sufferings and the Women's Movement,"* 54 (1914) 312-313; *"The Position of Women in the Society of Friends——Adopted by London Yearly Meeting, 1914,"* 54 (1914) 454.

12.183
Barnes, Earl, **WOMAN IN MODERN SOCIETY.** 1912.

12.184
Beveridge, William Henry, **JOHN AND IRENE; AN ANTHOLOGY OF THOUGHTS ON WOMAN**. 1912. Allegory in which a young man rallies his fiance to the "woman's cause" and then, dissatisfied with her resulting intellectual independence, breaks off the engagement. Portrays women as sophomoric. Implies that there is neither a "New Woman" nor a woman's movement, yet doubts whether men will get the comfortable domestic life which they want on their own terms.

12.185
Collegiate Church of St. Catherine, Tower, **THE RELIGIOUS ASPECTS OF THE WOMAN'S MOVEMENT. BEING A SERIES OF ADDRESSES DELIVERED AT MEETINGS HELD AT THE QUEEN'S HALL, LONDON, ON JUNE 19, 1912**. 2nd ed., 1913.

12.186
Ellis, Havelock, "The Changing Status of Women" in **THE SOCIAL TASK OF SOCIAL HYGIENE**. by Havelock Ellis. Boston and New York, 1912; *also printed in:* **WESTMINSTER REVIEW**: 128 (1887) 818-828. Examines women's societal roles in the eighteenth and nineteenth centuries; **MAN AND WOMAN**. 1914.

12.187
Keating, Joseph, **CHRISTIANITY AND "WOMEN'S RIGHTS."** 1912.

12.188
Key, Ellen Karolina Sofia, **THE WOMAN MOVEMENT**. trans. by Mamah Bouton Borthwick. 1912; 1913; **THE YOUNGER GENERATION**. 1914.

12.189
Paine, William, **SHOP SLAVERY AND EMANCIPATION**. introduction by H.G. Wells. 1912.

12.190
Schirmacher, Kathe, **THE MODERN WOMAN'S RIGHTS MOVEMENT; A HISTORICAL SURVEY**. trans. from the 2nd German ed., New York, 1912.

12.191
Sinclair, May, **FEMINISM**. 1912.

12.192
Blease, W. Lyon, **THE EMANCIPATION OF ENGLISH WOMEN**. 1913; New York, 1971; rpt., 1977. Historical survey supportive of the feminist movement.

12.193
Chesser, Elizabeth Sloan, "Motherhood and the Woman Movement" in **WOMAN, MARRIAGE AND MOTHERHOOD**. by Elizabeth Sloan Chesser. 1913. Examines the rights of mothers and their place in the feminist movement. Includes an appendix, "Laws of Parentage and Inheritance, Etc., in Different Countries." Chesser writes as a doctor and a mother.

12.194
Colquhoun, Ethel Maud (Cookson), **THE VOCATION FOR WOMEN**. 1913.

12.195
Dill, Floyd, **WOMEN AS WORLD BUILDERS: STUDIES IN MODERN FEMINISM**.

Chicago, 1913. Includes the Pankhursts, Charlotte Perkins Gilman, Olive Schreiner, and Beatrice Webb.

12.196
George, William Lionel, **WOMAN AND TOMORROW**. 1913.

12.197
Hartley, Catherine Gasquoigne (Gallichan), **THE TRUTH ABOUT WOMAN**. 1913.

12.198
Hutchins, B.L., **CONFLICTING IDEALS: TWO SIDES OF THE WOMAN'S QUESTIONS**. 1913; Includes analysis of ongoing debate over family roles, structure, and women's position; *reviewed in:* **WOMEN'S INDUSTRIAL NEWS:** Skinner, M.G., 18 (1914) 215-216.

12.199
Martin, Anna, **THE MOTHER AND SOCIAL REFORM**. 1913. "That the wife is in the disadvantageous position of being tied to only one possible employer [her husband] should have been the most powerful of reasons for [legal protection]. Inquiry, however, into the actual facts of the daily life of the humbler classes, as distinguished from legal fictions and conventional beliefs, reveals the truth that, as compared with the male worker, the wife suffers from two fundamental disabilities: firstly, the law does not enforce contract for her as against her employer-husband; secondly, it does not... protect her from his personal violence" (p. 8); *also printed in:* **NINETEENTH CENTURY:** 73 (1913) 1235-1255.

12.200
Mayreder, Rosa, **A SURVEY OF THE WOMAN PROBLEM**. trans. by H. Scheffauer. 1913.

12.201
Parsons, Elsie W. (Clews), **THE OLD FASHIONED WOMAN, PRIMITIVE FANCIES ABOUT SEX**. 1913. Elucidates "primitive" ethnological notions about women as "a distinct social class," and their historical subordination cross-culturally. This extensive bibliographic study lays the groundwork for a history of woman.

12.202
Robins, Elizabeth, **WAY STATIONS**. New York, 1913. Collection of speeches, lectures, and articles dealing with the women's movement in England.

12.203
Sapsworth, L., **THE EMANCIPATION AND THE EQUALITY OF WOMEN**. 1913.

12.204
Swanwick, Helena Maria, **THE FUTURE OF THE WOMEN'S MOVEMENT**. 1913. Discusses reasons for the rise of the movement, its economic aspect, and such issues as motherhood, male superiority, government and the vote; **I HAVE BEEN YOUNG**. 1935. Autobiography.

12.205
NEW FREEWOMAN; AN INDIVIDUALIST REVIEW: June to Dec. 1913; *continued as:* **EGOIST:** Jan. 1914 to Dec. 1919.

12.206
NEW STATESMAN: Webb, B., *"The Awakening of Women,"* 2 (1913) 3-26. "We shall

never understand the Awakening of Women until we realise that it is not mere feminism. It is one of three simultaneous world-movements towards a more equal partnership among human beings in human affairs" (n.p.); Balfour, B., *"Feminism: Pro and Con,"* 2 (1913) 408-409. Reviews three contemporary books; *"Motherhood and the State,"* Special Supplement 2 (1913) xii-xiii. Compares working-class and middle-class single mothers; Reeves, Mrs. P., *"Exclusions,"* Special Supplement 2 (1913) 23-24. Discusses the disparities between opportunities for men and women in professional capacities and blames this on the exclusion of women from the vote; Webb, B., *"Personal Rights and the Women's Movement: I. The Individual, Other Individuals and the Community,"* 3 (1914) 395-397; Webb, B., *"The Rights of the Women to Free Entry Into All Occupations,"* 3 (1914) 493-494; Webb, B., *"Equal Remuneration for Men and Women,"* 3 (1914) 525-527.

12.207
A., M., **THE ECONOMIC FOUNDATIONS OF THE WOMEN'S MOVEMENT.** 1914. Socialist-feminist analysis.

12.208
Fairfield, Zoe, **THE WOMAN'S MOVEMENT.** 1914; **SOME ASPECTS OF THE WOMAN'S MOVEMENT.** 1915.

12.209
Hale, Beatrice, **WHAT WOMEN WANT; AN INTERPRETATION OF THE FEMINIST MOVEMENT.** New York, 1914. "The movement is most advanced where democracy is best established, and most backward where autocracy is strongest" (p. 3).

12.210
MILITARISM VS. FEMINISM, AN INQUIRY AND A POLICY DEMON- STRATING THAT MILITARISM INVOLVES THE SUBJECTION OF WOMEN. 1915.

12.211
Martin, Edward Sandford, **THE UNREST OF WOMEN.** 1915.

12.212
National Mission of Repentance and Hope, **THE WOMAN'S MOVEMENT.** 1916.

12.213
Gollancz, Victor, "Introductory——A Restatement" and "Conclusion" in **THE MAKING OF WOMEN: OXFORD ESSAYS IN FEMINISM.** ed. by Victor Gollancz. 1917. Relates "the evils of [modern industrial] society" to the "subjection of women, which arises from the conscious or unconscious worship of physical strength as the supremely important element in human life" (p. 15).

12.214
Meikle, Wilma, **TOWARDS A SANE FEMINISM.** 1917.

12.215
Royden, A. Maude, "The Women's Movement of the Future" in **THE MAKING OF WOMEN: OXFORD ESSAYS IN FEMINISM.** ed. by Victor Gollancz. 1917. The movement was "transformed by the war.... A considerable number of people outside [it]... are now convinced that women are human beings, having a human value outside sex" (p. 132); **WOMEN AND THE SOVEREIGN STATE.** 1917.

12.216
Webb, Beatrice, **THE WAGES OF MEN AND WOMEN: SHOULD THEY BE EQUAL?** 1919.

12.217
Courtney, Janet Elizabeth, **FREETHINKERS OF THE NINETEENTH CENTURY.** 1920; **THE ADVENTUROUS THIRTIES: A CHAPTER IN THE WOMEN'S MOVE-MENT.** 1933; 1937; Freeport, 1967.

12.218
Flower, Constance (Baroness Battersea), **LADY BATTERSEA. REMINISCENCES.** 1922.

12.219
Strachey, Ray (pseud. for Rachel Costelloe), **MARCHING ON.** New York, 1923; **THE CAUSE: A SHORT HISTORY OF THE WOMEN'S MOVEMENT IN GREAT BRITAIN.** 1928; New York, 1969; rpt., 1978; 1983. History of the suffrage movement and the ideas behind it; *also published as:* **STRUGGLE: THE STORY OF WOMEN'S ADVANCE IN ENGLAND.** New York, 1930; (as editor), **OUR FREEDOM AND ITS RESULTS BY FIVE WOMEN.** 1936; 1938.

12.220
Johnson, George William, **THE EVOLUTION OF WOMEN: FROM SUBJECTION TO COMRADESHIP.** 1926.

12.221
Sharp, Evelyn, **HERTHA AYRTON 1854-1923: A MEMOIR.** 1926. Ayrton established herself as a scientist, the first woman to be elected to the Institute of Electrical Engineers in 1899. Supporter of women's suffrage and a member of Emmeline Pankhurst's organization of militant feminists, although she later became disillusioned with their tactics.

12.222
Challoner, Phyllis C. and Matthews, Vera Laughton, **TOWARDS CITIZENSHIP. A HANDBOOK OF WOMEN'S EMANCIPATION.** 1928.

12.223
Langdon-Davies, John, **A SHORT HISTORY OF WOMEN.** Cape, 1928.

12.224
Werth-Knudsen, K.A., **FEMINISM. A SOCIOLOGICAL STUDY OF THE WOMAN QUESTION FROM ANCIENT TIMES TO THE PRESENT DAY.** trans. by Arthur G. Chater. 1928. Views women as physiologically and intellectually inferior to men.

12.225
Greville, Frances Evelyn (Countess of Warwick), **LIFE'S EBB AND FLOW.** 1929. *—see also:* **SAN JOSE STUDIES:** Bell, S.G., *"Lady Warwick: Aristocrat, Socialist, Gardener,"* 8 (1982) 38-61.

12.226
Neff, Wanda Fraiken, **VICTORIAN WORKING WOMEN, 1832-1850.** New York, 1929; rpt., 1966. Relies on fiction and government documents to demonstrate a relationship between the social background of working women and the ideals of social change they strive to realize.

12.227
Wallas, Ada, **BEFORE THE BLUE STOCKINGS**. 1929. Good background for understanding the emergence of these female coteries.

12.228
SMITH COLLEGE STUDIES IN MODERN LANGUAGE: Horner, J.M., *"The English Women Novelists and Their Connection with the Feminist Movement, 1688-1797,"* 11 (1930) n.p. Recognizes their importance in commenting and communicating to readers on the social condition of women.

12.229
Beard, Mary Ritter, **ON UNDERSTANDING WOMEN**. 1931; **WOMAN AS FORCE IN HISTORY. A STUDY IN TRADITIONS AND REALITIES**. Examines "the tradition that women were members of a subject sex throughout history... [through] reference to historical realities——legal, religious, social, intellectual, military, political, and moral or philosophical" (preface).

12.230
Hargreaves, Reginald, **WOMEN AT ARMS. THEIR FAMOUS EXPLOITS THROUGHOUT THE AGES**. 1931. Explores the lives of various women who disguised themselves as men in order to work in professions closed to them.

12.231
Sadler, Michael, **BULWER AND HIS WIFE, A PANORAMA 1803-1836**. 1931.

12.232
Brittain, Vera, **TESTAMENT OF YOUTH. AN AUTOBIOGRAPHICAL STUDY OF THE YEARS 1900-1925**. 1933; *reviewed in:* **NEW SOCIETY:** Seaton, J., *"Reviews in Brief,"* 44 (1978) 675; **LADY INTO WOMAN: A HISTORY OF WOMEN FROM VICTORIA TO ELIZABETH II**. New York, 1953. Covers the British women's movement in which Brittain participated. Includes some photographs of her contemporaries.

12.233
Courtney, Janet E., **THE WOMEN OF MY TIME**. 1934. Sketches of various nineteenth-century women, including novelists, travelers, philanthropists, labor reformers, suffragettes, women in Parliament, and women scholars and educators.

12.234
Clephane, Irene, "Passing Panorama" in **OURSELVES**. by Irene Clephane. 1933; **TOWARD SEX FREEDOM**. 1935.

12.235
O'Malley, Ida Beatrice, **WOMEN IN SUBJECTION; A STUDY OF THE LIVES OF ENGLISHWOMEN BEFORE 1832**. 1933. "Subjection is, in the main, a spiritual matter" (p. 10).

12.236
Holtby, Winifred, **WOMEN AND A CHANGING CIVILIZATION**. 1934. A personal and emotional description of women's fight for social, legal, and economic rights.

12.237
Nesbitt, George L., **BENTHAMITE REVIEWING: THE FIRST TWELVE YEARS OF THE WESTMINSTER REVIEW**. 1934. Discusses the periodical's policy on women's issues.

12.238

Reiss, Erna, **RIGHTS AND DUTIES OF ENGLISHWOMEN: A STUDY IN LAW AND PUBLIC OPINION**. Manchester, 1934.

12.239

Rathbone, Eleanor, **THE HARVEST OF THE WOMEN'S MOVEMENT**. 1935. — *see also:* Stocks, Mary D., **ELEANOR RATHBONE: A BIOGRAPHY**. 1949; NEW SOCIETY: Lewis, J., *"Eleanor Rathbone,"* 27 (1983) 137-139. Rathbone was a feminist who advocated family wage allowances.

12.240

Lawrence, Margaret, **THE SCHOOL OF FEMININITY: A BOOK FOR AND ABOUT WOMEN AS THEY ARE INTERPRETED THROUGH FEMININE WRITERS OF YESTERDAY AND TODAY**. 1936.

12.241

Saywell, Ruby, "The Development of the Feminist Idea in England, 1789-1830," M.A. thesis, Univ. of London, 1936. English "women's rights" literature is related to the ideas of French radical philosophers. Details of women's inferior legal and social position are surveyed.

12.242

Russell, Bertrand and Russell, Patricia, eds., **THE AMBERLY PAPERS: LETTERS AND DIARIES OF BERTRAND RUSSELL'S PARENTS**. 2 vols. New York, 1937. Includes controversial questions about women's social and family roles.

12.243

Woods, Alice, **GEORGE MEREDITH AS CHAMPION OF WOMEN AND OF PROGRESSIVE EDUCATION**. Oxford, 1937.

12.244

Mineka, Francis E., **THE DISSIDENCE OF DISSENT: THE MONTHLY REPOSITORY 1806-38**. Chapel Hill, 1944. Details the contents of the MONTHLY REPOSITORY, an organ of the Unitarian movement, and the activities of its editors and contributors. The magazine "was a leader in breaking down religious dogmatism and in championing women's emancipation" (frontispiece).

12.245

MODERN LANGUAGE REVIEW: Humphreys, A.R., *"The 'Rights of Woman' in the Age of Reason,"* 41 (1946) 256-269. Part 1 covers John Dunton to Catharine Macaulay and part 2 discusses Mary Wollstonecraft. Humphreys traces sex equality and feminist progress from Socrates, who defended "rational equality——equality based on the primacy, in both sexes, of reason which demands similar education and rights" (p. 257).

12.246

Hamilton, Henry, "The Place of Women in Society" in **HISTORY OF THE HOMELAND**. by Henry Hamilton. 1947.

12.247

Ludovici, Anthony M., **ENEMIES OF WOMEN (THE ORIGINS IN OUTLINE OF ANGLO-SAXON FEMINISM)**. 1948. Anti-feminist work. The author differentiates between misogyny and anti-feminism, justifying the latter as "friendly to normal women"; **THE FINAL INEQUALITY: A CRITICAL ASSESSMENT OF WOMEN'S**

SEXUAL ROLE IN SOCIETY. 1965. Considers the emancipation of women from sexual slavery and passivity in a historical context.

12.248

Klein, Viola, **THE FEMININE CHARACTER: HISTORY OF AN IDEOLOGY.** New York, 1949; 1971. Fine bibliography; **CURRENT SOCIOLOGY:** *"Industrialization and the Changing Role of Women,"* 12 (1963-1964) 24-34.

12.249

United Nations, **POLITICAL RIGHTS OF WOMEN: 56 YEARS OF PROGRESS.** 1949; **THESE RIGHTS AND FREEDOMS.** 1950.

12.250

THE WOMAN QUESTION. SELECTIONS FROM THE WRITINGS OF KARL MARX, FREDERICK ENGELS, V.I. LENIN AND JOSEPH STALIN. New York, 1951; 1970. Compilation of excerpts.

12.251

Halevy, Elie, **A HISTORY OF THE ENGLISH PEOPLE IN THE NINETEENTH CENTURY.** 1952. See especially: "Domestic Anarchy: The Feminist Revolt" in vol. 6, part 3.

12.252

Dunbar, Janet, "Towards Emancipation" in **THE EARLY VICTORIAN WOMAN.** by Janet Dunbar. 1953.

12.253

Fussell, George Edwin and Fussell, Kathleen Rosemary, **THE ENGLISH COUNTRYWOMAN: THE INTERNAL ASPECT OF RURAL LIFE, 1500-1900.** 1953.

12.254

Kaplan, Justin, **WITH MALICE TOWARD WOMEN. A HANDBOOK OF WOMEN HATERS DRAWN FROM THE BEST MINDS OF ALL TIME.** 1953.

12.255

Gagen, Jean E., **THE NEW WOMAN: HER EMERGENCE IN ENGLISH DRAMA 1600-1730.** Twayne, 1954.

12.256

Pankhurst, Richard K.P., "Anna Wheeler and the Position of Women" in **WILLIAM THOMPSON: BRITAIN'S PIONEER SOCIALIST, FEMINIST AND CO-OPERATOR.** by Richard K.P. Pankhurst. 1954. Wheeler participated in the production of William Thompson's feminist manifesto, APPEAL OF ONE HALF THE HUMAN RACE, ETC; **THE SAINT-SIMONIANS, MILL AND CARLYLE: A PREFACE TO MODERN THOUGHT.** 1957. See especially: "The Emancipation of Women."

12.257

POLITICAL QUARTERLY: Pankhurst, R.K.P., *"Anna Wheeler: A Pioneer Socialist and Feminist,"* 25 (1954) 132-143. Biographical sketch set in the context of "early nineteenth century England [where] a married woman possessed no legal personality" (p. 132). Wheeler was close to Bentham and Owen.

12.258
Glyn, Anthony Geoffrey Leo Simon, **ELEANOR GLYN: A BIOGRAPHY**. Garden City, 1955.

12.259
BRITISH JOURNAL OF SOCIOLOGY: McGregor, O.R., *"The Social Position of Women in England, 1850-1914: A Bibliography,"* 6 (1955) 48-60. Readable as an essay as well as a bibliography.

12.260
Hobman, Daisy Lucie, **GO SPIN YOU JADE: STUDIES IN THE EMANCIPATION OF WOMEN**. 1957. Recounts the women's movement, illustrated by biographies of many important women involved in its history.

12.261
Stenton, Doris, M., **THE ENGLISH WOMAN IN HISTORY**. 1957. Focuses on exceptional contributions by women to social development.

12.262
Kilham, John, **TENNYSON AND THE PRINCESS. REFLECTIONS OF AN AGE**. 1958; 1967. Excellent bibliography in the notes. See especially: "Saint-Simonians and the New Feminism," "Feminism at Cambridge," "The Feminist Controversy in England Prior to THE PRINCESS——I" and "The Feminist Controversy in England Prior to THE PRINCESS——II."

12.263
Blount, Paul G., "Reputation of George Sand in Victorian England, 1832-1886," Ph.D. diss., Cornell Univ., 1961.

12.264
Melder, Keith, "The Beginnings of the Women's Movement, 1800-1840," Ph.D. diss., Yale Univ., 1963. Traces the movement, in part, to changes in social thought. Focuses mainly on the United States.

12.265
Titmuss, Richard, "The Position of Women" in **ESSAYS ON THE "WELFARE STATE."** ed. by Richard Titmuss. 1963; *rev. ed. rpt. as:* "The Position of Women: Some Vital Statistics" in **ESSAYS IN SOCIAL HISTORY**. ed. by M.W. Flinn and T.C. Smout. Oxford, 1974. "Draw[s] together some of the vital statistics of birth, marriage, and death for the light they shed on the changes that have taken place since the beginning of the century in the social position of women" (p. 277).

12.266
Banks, Joseph Ambrose and Banks, Olive, **FEMINISM AND FAMILY PLANNING IN VICTORIAN ENGLAND**. 1964. Examines the impact of the feminist movement on the decline in birth rate and concludes there is a negative connection between feminism and birth control.

12.267
Acworth, Evelyn, "Changes in Social and Economic Life" in **THE NEW MATRIARCHY**. by Evelyn Acworth. 1965. Discusses Hannah More and Mary Wollstonecraft as precursors to anti-feminist and feminist thinkers.

12.268
Harwick, Arthur, **THE DELUGE: BRITISH SOCIETY AND THE FIRST WORLD**

WAR. 1965. Evaluates women's activities during the shortage of manpower and how they rose to the occasion of filling "male occupations."

12.269
Kamm, Josephine, **RAPIERS AND BATTLEAXES: THE WOMEN'S MOVEMENT AND ITS AFTERMATH.** 1966. A useful survey.

12.270
Laver, James, **THE AGE OF OPTIMISM: MANNERS AND MORALS, 1848-1914.** 1966. See especially: "The Girl of The Period and The New Woman."

12.271
Cuddeford, Gladys, **WOMEN AND SOCIETY FROM VICTORIAN TIMES TO THE PRESENT DAY.** 1967.

12.272
Rover, Constance, **THE PUNCH BOOK OF WOMEN'S RIGHTS.** 1967. Collection of cartoons and excerpts relating to women from the journal PUNCH; **LOVE, MORALS AND THE FEMINISTS.** 1970. Examines the "interaction between feminism and morality" (p. 3), in terms of the relationship between such issues as prostitution, divorce and birth control.

12.273
Summerskill, Edith, **A WOMAN'S WORLD.** 1967.

12.274
CHAMBER'S ENCYCLOPEDIA: Douie, V., *"Women in the Social Order,"* 14 (1967) 619-623. Discusses women in government, diplomacy, and industry, as well as political and legal emancipation.

12.275
SOUTHERN REVIEW: Fernando, L., *"The Radical Ideology of the New Women,"* 2 (1967) 206-222. Traces the female emancipation movement in literature and politics, from 1865 to 1896, culminating in Hardy's JUDE THE OBSCURE.

12.276
Priestly, Harold, "The 'Woman Question'" in **VOICE OF PROTEST: A HISTORY OF CIVIL UNREST IN GREAT BRITAIN.** by Harold Priestly. 1968. Brief, informative account of the origins of English feminism from Hannah Wooley, Mary Astell, Mary Wortley Montagu, and Mary Wollstonecraft to Victorian-era reformers such as Florence Nightingale, Octavia Hill, Angela Burdett-Coutts, Josephine Butler, Louisa Twining, etc.

12.277
O'Neill, William L., **THE WOMAN MOVEMENT: FEMINISM IN THE UNITED STATES AND BRITAIN.** 1969. Includes documents by Victorian-era feminists. Main focus is on American women.

12.278
HISTORICAL JOURNAL: Anderson, O., *"Women Preachers in Mid-Victorian Britain. Some Reflections on Feminism, Popular Religion and Social Change,"* 12 (1969) 467-484. "Feminism explains less and popular religion more about the course of social change than has often been supposed" (p. 484).

12.279
Rossi, Alice S., ed., **JOHN STUART MILL AND HARRIET TAYLOR MILL: ESSAYS ON SEX EQUALITY.** Chicago, 1970.

12.280
White, Cynthia, **WOMEN'S MAGAZINES, 1693-1968.** 1970. Journals for women recognized as reflections of changes in women's roles and activities.

12.281
Leech, C.E., "The Feminist Movement in Manchester 1903-1914," M.A. thesis, Manchester, 1971.

12.282
McCrone, Kathleen Eleanor, "The Advancement of Women During the Age of Reform, 1832-1870," Ph.D. diss, New York Univ., 1971. Examines the feminist movement in terms of class representation.

12.283
CANADIAN HISTORICAL ASSOCIATION HISTORICAL PAPERS: *"The Assertion of Women's Rights in Mid-Victorian England,"* n.v. (1972) 39-53. "While its failure to cross the barriers of class is one of the women's movement's most important weaknesses, in its early stages feminism had to be primarily bourgeois. Although among the working classes the belief in the inferiority of women was as firmly established as in the higher ranks, the lot of the lower-class woman was so harsh and her educational level so low that the emancipation of her sex could mean little or nothing to her" (pp. 39-40).

12.284
Miller, John N., "Reform and Romanticism: Feminism and Anti-Feminism in the Nineteenth Century" in **A WORLD OF HER OWN. WRITERS AND THE FEMINIST CONTROVERSY.** by John Miller. Columbus, 1971. Analyzes the "woman question" as manifest in nineteenth and twentieth-century literature.

12.285
Millett, Kate, "The Debate Over Women: Ruskin vs. Mill" in **SUFFER AND BE STILL: WOMEN IN THE VICTORIAN AGE.** ed. by Martha Vicinus. Bloomington, 1971. "In Mill one encounters the realism of sexual politics, in Ruskin its romance and the benign aspect of its myth" (p. 121).

12.286
Vicinus, Martha, "Introduction" in **SUFFER AND BE STILL: WOMEN IN THE VICTORIAN AGE.** ed. by Martha Vicinus. Bloomington, 1971; "Introduction" in **A WIDENING SPHERE; CHANGING ROLES OF VICTORIAN WOMEN.** ed. by Martha Vicinus. Bloomington, 1977; 1980.

12.287
Showalter, Elaine, **WOMEN'S LIBERATION AND LITERATURE.** 1971; **A LITERATURE OF THEIR OWN. BRITISH WOMEN NOVELISTS FROM BRONTE TO LESSING.** Princeton, 1977. Examines women's roles, patterns and traditions these novelists transmitted in their literature.

12.288
VICTORIAN PERIODICALS NEWSLETTER: Palmegiano, E.M., *"Feminist Propaganda in the 1850s and 1860s,"* 2 (1971) 5-8; Fryckstedt, M.C., *"Charlotte Elisabeth Tonna and THE CHRISTIAN LADY'S MAGAZINE,"* 14 (1981) 43-51.

Tonna sought justice and improvement in status for women; Van Arsdel, R.T., *"Mrs. Florence Fenwick-Miller and THE WOMAN'S SIGNAL, 1895-1899,"* 15 (1982) 107-118; Nestor, P.A., *"A New Departure in Women's Publishing: THE ENGLISHWOMAN'S JOURNAL and THE VICTORIA MAGAZINE,"* 15 (1982) 93-104. Discusses the importance of these periodicals as a unifying force in the divided women's movement.

12.289
Adburgham, Alison, **WOMEN IN PRINT. WRITING WOMEN AND WOMEN'S MAGAZINES FROM THE RESTORATION TO THE ACCESSION OF VICTORIA.** 1972.

12.290
Cecil, Robert, "The State of Morals and the Rights of Women" in **LIFE IN EDWARDIAN ENGLAND.** by Robert Cecil. Newton Abbot, 1972.

12.291
Johnson, Diane, **THE TRUE HISTORY OF THE FIRST MRS. MEREDITH AND OTHER LESSER LIVES.** New York, 1972.

12.292
Wagner, Geoffrey Atheling, **FIVE FOR FREEDOM; A STUDY OF FEMINISM IN FICTION.** 1972.

12.293
VICTORIAN: Gross, G.C., *"Mary Cowden Clarke, the Girlhood of Shakespeare's Heroines and the Sex Education of Victorian Women,"* 16 (1972) 37-58. Clarke (1809-1898) was the first female editor of Shakespeare.

12.294
Goulianos, Joan, ed., **BY A WOMAN WRIT. LITERATURE FROM SIX CENTURIES BY AND ABOUT WOMEN.** Baltimore, 1973. Compilation of writings by women from the fourteenth to the twentieth century.

12.295
Holcombe, Lee, "The Women's Movement and Working Ladies" in **VICTORIAN LADIES AT WORK.** by Lee Holcombe. Hamden, 1973.

12.296
Rowbotham, Sheila, **WOMAN'S CONSCIOUSNESS, MAN'S WORLD.** Harmondsworth, 1973; 1974; **HIDDEN FROM HISTORY; REDISCOVERING WOMEN IN HISTORY FROM THE 17TH CENTURY TO THE PRESENT.** New York, 1974; *reviewed in:* **SOCIETY FOR THE STUDY OF LABOUR HISTORY BULLETIN:** Shankleman, J., 28 (1974) 83-86; **A NEW WORLD FOR WOMEN: STELLA BROWNE—SOCIALIST FEMINIST.** 1977.

12.297
JOURNAL OF POPULAR CULTURE: Gorsky, S.R., *"Old Maids and New Women: Alternatives to Marriage in Englishwomen's Novels, 1847-1915,"* 7 (1973) 68-85.

12.298
JOURNAL OF SOCIAL POLICY: Harris, A.K. and Silverman, B., *"Women in Advanced Capitalism,"* 4 (1973) 16-22. Discusses Marxism and modern feminist works; Dingwall, R.W.J., *"Collectivism, Regionalism and Feminism: Health Visiting and British Social Policy 1850-1975,"* 6 (1977) 291-315. Relates women's

emancipation to the development, growth, and decline of the public health movement as illustrated by health visitors.

12.299
VICTORIAN STUDIES: Cunningham, A.R., *"The New Woman Fiction of the 1890s,"* 17 (1973) 177-186. Discusses popular novels that broke the stereotypes created for women; Roe, J., *"Modernism and Sexism: Recent Writings on Victorian Women,"* 20 (1977) 179-192; Mitchell, S., *"Sentiment and Suffering: Women's Recreational Reading in the 1860s,"* 21 (1977) 29-45. Examines the sentimental novels of the period, designed to elicit emotional rather than intellectual responses from their female readers; Rubinstein, D., *"Cycling in the 1890s,"* 21 (1977) 47-71. Bicycles not only allowed girls some independence from chaperones but were responsible for the advent of "rational dress" for women, replacing their hitherto bulky and restrictive fashions.

12.300
Guettel, Charnie, **MARXISM AND FEMINISM**. Ontario, 1974. Marxist analysis of the liberal tradition as illustrated by Mill, Engels, and Bebel.

12.301
Luria, Gina, ed., **FEMINIST CONTROVERSY IN ENGLAND, 1788-1810.** New York, 1974. A series of reprints of fifty books by eighteenth-century authors on the subject of women. See BOOKS IN PRINT or NATIONAL UNION SERIES CATALOG.

12.302
LIBRARY: Fredeman, W.E., *"Emily Faithfull and the Victoria Press: An Experiment in Sociological Bibliography,"* 29 (1974) 139-164. With the establishment of the press, women were given the opportunity to learn the skills necessary to be compositors; Stone, J.S., *"More Light on Emily Faithfull and the Victoria Press,"* 33 (1978) 63-67. Corrects and amplifies some points in the previous article.

12.303
Thompson, Paul, "The Edwardian Crisis" in **THE EDWARDIANS**. by Paul Thompson. Bloomington, 1975.

12.304
Ruether, Rosemary, **NEW WOMEN, NEW EARTH: SEXIST IDEOLOGIES AND HUMAN LIBERATION**. New York, 1975.

12.305
Aubuchon, Andre, "Feminism and Women's Education in England," Ph.D. diss., Harvard Univ. 2 vols., 1976.

12.306
de Condorcet, Marquis, "On the Admission of Women to the Rights of Citizenship" in **CONDORCET, SELECTED WRITINGS**. ed. by Michael Baker Keith. Indianapolis, 1976. This revised translation by Dr. Alice Drysdale Vickery first appeared in 1912, during the women's suffrage movement. ——*see also:* Williams, D., "Condorcet, Feminism and the Egalitarian Principle" in **STUDIES IN EIGHTEENTH-CENTURY CULTURE**. ed. by Ronald C. Rosbottom. vol. 5, 1976. "Condorcet's attempts to create an issue of public conscience out of the melancholy position of women in his time constitute a clear landmark in the evolution of European political-sexual attitudes" (p. 151).

12.307
Jacoby, Robin, "Feminism and Class Consciousness in the British and American Women's Trade Union Leagues" in **LIBERATING WOMEN'S HISTORY: THEORETICAL AND CRITICAL ESSAYS.** ed. by Bernice A. Carroll. Urbana, 1976.

12.308
Ross, Ruth, "Tradition and the Role of Women in Great Britain" in **WOMEN IN THE WORLD: A COMPARATIVE STUDY.** ed. by Lynne B. Iglitzin and Ruth Ross. Santa Barbara and Oxford, 1976.

12.309
FEMINIST STUDIES: Bodek, E.G., *"Salonieres and Bluestockings: Educating Obsolescence and Germinating Feminism,"* 3 (1976) 185-199. Analytical treatment of women in England and France who began salons and advocated women's education; Taylor, B., *"'The Men are as Bad as Their Masters...': Socialism, Feminism and Sexual Antagonism in the London Tailoring Trade in the Early 1830s,"* 5 (1979) 7-40; Walkowitz, J.R., *"Jack the Ripper and the Myth of Male Violence,"* 8 (1982) 542-544; Vicinus, M., *"'One Life to Stand Behind Me': First Generation College Women in England,"* 8 (1982) 603-628. Delineates the personal and public conflicts in seeking sexual autonomy and economic freedom in a world that advocated domesticity and marriage; David, D., *"Ideologies of Patriarchy, Feminism and Fiction in 'The Odd Woman,'"* 10 (1984) 117-140.

12.310
JOURNAL OF GENERAL EDUCATION: Sargent, L.T., *"English and American Utopias: Similarities and Differences,"* 28 (1976) 16-22. Discusses women's rights in relation to nineteenth- and twentieth-century ideas about utopias, socialism, education, etc.

12.311
STUDIES IN LABOUR HISTORY: Burke, S., *"Letter from a Pioneer Feminist,"* no. 1 (1976) 19-23. Discusses Anna Wheeler and her participation in the cooperative and women's movements.

12.312
Evans, Richard J., **THE FEMINISTS: WOMEN'S EMANCIPATION MOVEMENTS IN EUROPE, AMERICA AND AUSTRALIA, 1840-1920.** 1977. Creates "a general framework of interpretation tracing the origins, developments and eventual collapse of women's emancipation movements in relation to the changing social formations and political structures... in the era of bourgeois liberalism" (preface).

12.313
Foreman, Ann, **FEMININITY AS ALIENATION. WOMEN AND THE FAMILY IN MARXISM AND PSYCHOANALYSIS.** 1977. Analysis of the separation of economics and sexuality in Marxist and socialist history.

12.314
Vann, Richard J., "Toward a New Lifestyle: Women in Preindustrial Capitalism" in **BECOMING VISIBLE: WOMEN IN EUROPEAN HISTORY.** ed. by Renate Bridenthal and Claudia Koonz. 1977.

12.315
FRONTIERS: Demetrakopoulos, S., *"Feminism, Sex Role Exchanges, and other Subliminal Fantasies in Bram Stoker's DRACULA,"* 2 (1977) 104-113. Analysis of

the Victorian-era novel as it reflects sexual repression; Chambers-Schiller, L., *"The Single Woman Reformer: Conflict between Family and Vocation 1830-1860,"* 3 (1978) 41-48.

12.316
HECATE: Caine, B., *"Women's 'Natural State': Marriage and the Nineteenth Century Feminists,"* 3 (1977) 84-102. Marriage is discussed as a propelling factor in the fight for emancipation.

12.317
Dyhouse, Carol, "The Role of Women: From Self-Sacrifice to Self-Awareness" in **THE VICTORIANS**. ed. by Lawrence Lerner. New York, 1978; "Feminism and the Family" and "Feminist Perspectives and Responses" in **GIRLS GROWING UP IN LATE VICTORIAN AND EDWARDIAN ENGLAND**. by Carol Dyhouse. 1981.

12.318
Kuhn, Annette and Wolpe, Ann Marie, eds., **FEMINISM AND MATERIALISM. WOMEN AND MODES OF PRODUCTION**. 1978. Theoretical context for considering women's roles and status.

12.319
Malmgreen, Gail, **NEITHER BREAD NOR ROSES: UTOPIAN FEMINISTS AND THE ENGLISH WORKING-CLASS, 1800-1850**. Brighton, 1978. Examines "the emergence of socialist-feminist ideas and attempts by the Utopians to find a constituency for these ideas among the organized working-class" (p. 3); *reviewed in:* **SOCIAL HISTORY**: Evans, R.J., *"Review Essay: Women's History: The Limits of Reclamation,"* 5 (1980) 273-281.

12.320
AMERICAN POLITICAL SCIENCE REVIEW: Butler, M., *"Early Liberal Roots of Feminism: John Locke and the Attack on Patriarchy,"* 72 (1978) 135-170. While [Locke] believed that women did suffer from some natural weaknesses, he had a classic liberal faith in the ability of the individual woman to overcome these natural obstacles... Locke was never explicit about women's roles in the formation of civil society" (p. 149).

12.321
CANADIAN MEDICAL ASSOCIATION JOURNAL: Garner, J., *"The Woman Question,"* 118 (1978) 685.

12.322
HISTORICAL STUDIES: Caine, B., *"John Stuart Mill and the English Women's Movement,"* 18 (1978) 52-67.

12.323
INTERNATIONAL JOURNAL OF WOMEN'S STUDIES: Heineman, H., *"Frances Trollope's Jessie Phillips: Sexual Politics and the New Poor Law,"* 1 (1978) 96-106. The novel, JESSIE PHILLIPS, A TALE OF THE PRESENT DAY (1843) depicted the sexual biases inherent in the New Poor Law of 1834; O'Connor, K. and McGlen, N.E., *"The Effects of Government Organization on Women's Rights: An Analysis of the Status of Women in Canada, Great Britain, and The United States,"* 1 (1978) 588-601; Weiner, N.F., *"Of Feminism and Birth Control Propaganda (1790-1840),"* 3 (1980) 411-430. Considers the activities and motivations of major birth control propagandists in England and America; Williamson, M.L., *"Who's Afraid of Mrs. Barbauld? The Blue Stockings and Feminism,"* 3 (1980) 89-102. "The Blue

Stockings were united by a desire to improve moral and intellectual life. The significance of the Blues for women's history is that although they were not, except for Elizabeth Carter, feminists, they led distinguished lives.... They also began the process of opening serious education and certain professions to women" (p. 89).

12.324
RADICAL HISTORY REVIEW: Lambertz, J., *"Feminist History in Britain,"* 19 (1978-1979) 137-142. Discusses the debate between feminists and historians over differing approaches to women's history.

12.325
SOUTH ATLANTIC QUARTERLY: Halperin, J., *"Trollope and Feminism,"* 527 (1978) 179-188. "Trollope's antipathy to the women's rights movement stems in large part from his conviction that women did and should wield great social power without resorting to the streets" (p. 187).

12.326
UNIVERSITY OF MICHIGAN PAPERS IN WOMEN'S STUDIES: Strauss, S., *"Raising the Victorian Woman's Consciousness: White Slavery and the Women's Movement,"* 2 (1978) 13-31. Delineates the activities of leading nineteenth-century feminists in the fight against prostitution and the Contagious Diseases Act.

12.327
Attrends, E., "Radicalism and Feminism in England in the Early 19th Century," M.A. thesis, Council for National Academic Awards, 1979.

12.328
Bauer, Carol and Ritt, Lawrence, eds., **FREE AND ENNOBLED. SOURCE READINGS IN THE DEVELOPMENT OF VICTORIAN FEMINISM.** Oxford, 1979. Compilation of excerpts by nineteenth-century writers with commentaries by the editors and extensive bibliography.

12.329
Chisolm, Anne, **NANCY CUNARD. A BIOGRAPHY.** 1979.

12.330
Cromwell, Victoria, **THE CHANGING ROLE OF WOMEN IN MODERN BRITAIN.** St. Louis, 1979. Examines the status of women from Wollstonecraft's time and the reforms made between 1850 and 1890 in the areas of divorce, education, employment, property, and suffrage.

12.331
Goldberg, Rita Bettina, "Female Sexuality and Eighteenth-Century Culture in England and France: Richardson and Diderot," Ph.D. diss., Princeton Univ., 1979.

12.332
Heineman, Helen, **MRS. TROLLOPE. THE TRIUMPHANT FEMININE IN THE NINETEENTH CENTURY.** Athens, 1979; **RESTLESS ANGELS: THE FRIEND-SHIPS OF SIX VICTORIAN WOMEN—FRANCES WRIGHT, CAMILLA WRIGHT, HARRIET GARNETT, FRANCES GARNETT, JULIA GARNETT PERTZ, FRANCES TROLLOPE.** Athens, Ohio, 1983. "The single thread that unifies their otherwise disparate destinies is their lifelong quest for self-definition, which centered around finding some serious occupation, either in place of or coexistent with their domestic tasks and assignments" (p. 2).

12.333
Hollis, Patricia, **WOMEN IN PUBLIC: THE WOMEN'S MOVEMENT 1850-1900. DOCUMENTS OF THE VICTORIAN WOMEN'S MOVEMENT.** 1979. Documents chosen to illustrate the wide range of women's public activity. Concludes that the English feminist movement began in the 1850s, motivated by three main concerns: "surplus women," the plight of governesses, and women's legal position. The demand for the vote followed in the 1860s; *reviewed in:* **SOCIETY FOR THE STUDY OF LABOUR HISTORY BULLETIN:** Hurt, G., no. 39 (1979) 90-94; *also reviewed in:* **SOCIAL HISTORY:** Evans, R.J., *"Review Essay: Women's History: The Limits of Reclamation,"* 5 (1980) 273-281.

12.334
Kanner, Barbara, ed., **THE WOMEN OF ENGLAND FROM ANGLO-SAXON TIMES TO THE PRESENT.** Hamden, 1979. See especially: "Women in the Mirror: Using Novels to Study Victorian Women" by Patricia Otto Klaus; "The Eighteenth-Century Englishwoman" by Barbara Schnorrenberg and Jean Hunter; "The Discovery of Women in Eighteenth-Century Political Life" by Karl von den Steinen; and "A Survey of Primary Sources and Archives for the History of Early Twentieth-Century English Women" by Jeffrey Weeks.

12.335
Lohman, Judith Sidnee, "Sex or Class? English Socialists and the Woman Question, 1884-1914," Ph.D. diss., Syracuse Univ., 1979. Examines the middle-class orientation of the feminist movement and its relationship to socialism.

12.336
Rogers, Katharine M., ed., **BEFORE THEIR TIME. SIX WOMEN WRITERS OF THE EIGHTEENTH CENTURY.** New York, 1979. Compilation of writings by Anne Finch, Mary Astell, Mary Wollstonecraft, Lady Mary Wortley Montagu, Charlotte Smith, and Frances Burney; **FEMINISM IN EIGHTEENTH-CENTURY ENGLAND.** 1982. "Most women made use of the new respect for feelings to articulate the emotions and sanction the values that were important to them as women" (p. 3).

12.337
Whittick, Arnold, **WOMAN INTO CITIZEN: THE WORLD MOVEMENT TOWARDS THE EMANCIPATION OF WOMEN IN THE 20TH CENTURY.** 1979.

12.338
ANNALS OF SCIENCE: Love, R., *"'Alice in Eugenics-Land': Feminism and Eugenics in the Scientific Careers of Alice Lee and Ethel Elderton,"* 36 (1979) 145-158. "Intellectual and economic factors involved in the choice of a career in eugenics are described together with some aspects of the relationship between eugenics and feminism" (p. 145).

12.339
DISSENT: Guttmann, A., *"Freud Versus Feminism,"* 26 (1979) 204-212.

12.340
JOURNAL OF BRITISH STUDIES: Rosen, A., *"Emily Davies and the Women's Movement 1862-1867,"* 19 (1979) 101-121.

12.341
Brink, Jeannie R., ed., **FEMALE SCHOLARS: A TRADITION OF LEARNED WOMEN BEFORE 1800.** Montreal, 1980. A compilation of critical biographical

essays, useful for cross-cultural comparison. See especially: "Bathsua Makin: Educator and Linguist (English, 1608?-1675?)" by J.R. Brink and "Elizabeth Elstob: The Saxon Nymph (English, 1683-1765)" by Mary Elizabeth Green.

12.342
Davis, Natalie Zemon, "Gender and Genre: Women as Historical Writers, 1400-1820" in **BEYOND THEIR SEX: LEARNED WOMEN OF THE EUROPEAN PAST.** ed. by Patricia H. Labalme. New York, 1980. Traces the careers of female historians from Christine de Pisan to Madame de Stael.

12.343
Doughan, David, **LOBBYING FOR LIBERATION: BRITISH FEMINISM 1918-1968.** 1980. Mimeographed pamphlet printed by the Fawcett Library, City of London Polytechnic; **FEMINIST PERIODICALS, 1855-1984: AN ANNOTATED CRITICAL BIBLIOGRAPHY OF BRITISH, IRISH, COMMONWEALTH AND INTERNATIONAL TITLES.** 1986.

12.344
Fletcher, Sheila, **FEMINISTS AND BUREAUCRATS! A STUDY IN THE DEVELOPMENT OF GIRL'S EDUCATION IN THE NINETEENTH CENTURY.** 1980.

12.345
Kaskebar, Veena P., "Power over Themselves: The Controversy about Female Education in England, 1660-1820," Ph.D. diss., Univ. of Cincinnati, 1980.

12.346
Rabkin, Peggy A., **FATHERS TO DAUGHTERS: THE LEGAL FOUNDATIONS OF FEMALE EMANCIPATION.** Westport, 1980.

12.347
Tax, Meredith, **THE RISING OF WOMEN: FEMINIST SOLIDARITY AND CLASS CONFLICT, 1880-1917.** New York, 1980. Contemporary feminists are viewed with historical allusions.

12.348
BRITISH JOURNAL FOR THE HISTORY OF SCIENCE: Allen, D.E., *"The Women Members of the Botanical Society of London: 1836-1856,"* 13 (1980) 240-254. Liberal policies allowed female participation at a time when women's public activities were generally restricted.

12.349
LABOUR HISTORY: McCalman, M., *"Females, Feminism and Free Love in an Early Nineteenth Century Radical Movement,"* no. 38 (May 1980) 1-25. Argues women were more active in popular radical movements than historians have conceded: for example, they contributed directly to Richard Carlile's "Zetetic" movement, a legal struggle to legitimize open discussion of unconventional ideas and practices such as free love and birth control. McCalman argues also that "significant advances were made by these early nineteenth century radicals in the area of sexual and feminist theory" (p. 3).

12.350
Banks, Joseph Ambrose, "The Emancipation of Women" in **VICTORIAN VALUES: SECULARISM AND THE SIZE OF FAMILIES.** by Joseph Ambrose Banks. 1981.

12.351
Banks, Olive, **FACES OF FEMINISM. 1981; THE BIOGRAPHICAL DICTIONARY OF BRITISH FEMINISTS. VOLUME ONE: 1800-1930. 1985; BECOMING A FEMINIST: THE SOCIAL ORIGINS OF 'FIRST WAVE' FEMINISM. 1986.** Examines early feminists in terms of family background, social ties, sexuality, religion and politics.

12.352
Eisenstein, Zillah, **THE RADICAL FUTURE OF LIBERAL FEMINISM.** 1981. See especially: Part II, chaps. 5 and 6 for the historical origins of a feminist critique of the male bias in liberal theory and an account of how Wollstonecraft and the Mills identified and appropriated the radical elements of liberal theory to construct a justification of women's civil and legal equality.

12.353
Hall, Catherine, "Gender Divisions and Class Formation in the Birmingham Middle Class, 1780-1850" in **PEOPLE'S HISTORY AND SOCIALIST THEORY.** ed. by Raphael Samuel. 1981.

12.354
Harrison, Brian, "Women's Health and the Women's Movement in Britain: 1840-1940" in **BIOLOGY, MEDICINE AND SOCIETY 1840-1940.** ed. by Charles Webster. 1981. Correlates improvements in women's health care, mortality rate and infant mortality to the emancipation of women. Describes the effects of Victorian attitudes on women's health care and doctors' responses to militant suffragettes.

12.355
Monaghan, David, **JANE AUSTEN IN A SOCIAL CONTEXT.** New York, 1981.

12.356
ARIEL: Gary, K., *"Amelia Opie, Lady Caroline Lamb and Maria Edgeworth: Official and Unofficial Ideology,"* 12 (1981) 3-24. Discusses the depiction of women's rights and duties in these authors' fictional works.

12.357
HISTORY OF EDUCATION JOURNAL: Purvis, J., *"Women's Life is Essentially Domestic, Public Life Being Confined to Men (Comte)': Separate Spheres and Inequality in the Education of Working Class Women, 1854-1900,"* 10 (1981) 227-243.

12.358
Boyd, Nancy, **THREE VICTORIAN WOMEN WHO CHANGED THEIR WORLD: JOSEPHINE BUTLER, OCTAVIA HILL, FLORENCE NIGHTINGALE.** New York, 1982.

12.359
Coote, Anna and Campbell, Beatrix, **SWEET FREEDOM: THE STRUGGLE FOR WOMEN'S LIBERATION.** 1982.

12.360
Hockstadt, Steve, "Appendix: Demography and Feminism" in **AN EXPERIENCE OF WOMEN: PATTERN AND CHANGE IN NINETEENTH CENTURY EUROPE.** by Priscilla Robertson. Philadelphia, 1982. Argues that upper-class liberties allowed for the formation of feminist thinking.

12.361
Murray, Janet, **STRONG MINDED WOMEN AND OTHER LOST VOICES FROM 19TH CENTURY ENGLAND.** New York, 1982. Collection of articles and excerpts by various Victorian writers concerned with the Woman Question, marriage, social service, motherhood, the poor, education, employment, and prostitution. A very good reader for an overview on women's position in society.

12.362
Myers, Mitzi, "Reform or Ruin: A Revolution in Female Manners" in **STUDIES IN EIGHTEENTH-CENTURY CULTURE.** ed. by Harry C. Payne. vol 2, 1982. Compares and contrasts the views of Mary Wollstonecraft and Hannah More on women's behavior.

12.363
Robertson, Priscilla, **AN EXPERIENCE OF WOMEN: PATTERN AND CHANGE IN NINETEENTH-CENTURY EUROPE.** Philadelphia, 1982.

12.364
Sarah, Elizabeth, ed., **REASSESSMENT OF 'FIRST WAVE' FEMINISM.** Oxford, 1982.

12.365
Smith, Hilda, **REASON'S DISCIPLES. SEVENTEENTH-CENTURY ENGLISH FEMINISTS.** 1982. Links early feminist views to later movements.

12.366
Spender, Dale, **WOMEN OF IDEAS——AND WHAT MEN HAVE DONE TO THEM. FROM APHRA BEHN TO ADRIENNE RICH.** 1982; *reviewed in:* **ATLANTIS:** Zaborszky, D., 9 (1983) 138-140.

12.367
Strauss, Sylvia, **"TRAITORS TO THE MASCULINE CAUSE": THE MEN'S CAMPAIGN FOR WOMEN'S RIGHTS.** Westport, 1982; *reviewed in:* **ATLANTIS:** McLaren, A., 9 (1984) 114-116. "Strauss provides a useful service in bringing together in one book the accounts of about fifty men who (by one criterion or another) could be considered to have been on the feminist side" (p. 115).

12.368
Thomis, Malcolm I. and Grimmett, Jennifer, **WOMEN IN PROTEST 1800-1850.** 1982. On working-class women and their participation in the food riots, and social and industrial protests.

12.369
ENGLISH LANGUAGE NOTES: Auerbach, N., *"Falling Alice, Fallen Women, and Victorian Dream Children,"* 20 (1982) 46-44. On ALICE IN WONDERLAND "as an amalgam of purity and subversive power, of propriety and holy exile. [Carroll's] Alice is a nursery avatar of a grand Pre-Raphaelite icon: the fallen woman, scandalous and blessed" (p. 47).

12.370
HISTORY WORKSHOP JOURNAL: Walkowitz, J.R., *"Male Vice and Feminist Virtue: Feminism and the Politics of Prostitution in Nineteenth Century Britain,"* no. 13 (1982) 79-93; Caine, B., *"Beatrice Webb and the Woman Question,"* no. 14 (1982) 23-43; Walkowitz, J., *"Science, Feminism and Romance: The Men's and Women's Club 1885-1889,"* no. 21 (1986) 37-59.

12.371

JOURNAL OF ECCLESIASTICAL HISTORY: Heeney, B., *"The Beginnings of Church Feminism: Women and the Councils of the Church of England 1897-1919,"* 33 (1982) 89-109. "Women became increasingly prominent in the day-to-day work and the worship of the church... two related developments emerged on the English scene: the feminist cause and the movement to provide the Church of England with the machinery for self-government" (p. 91).

12.372

QUAKER HISTORY: Malmgreen, G., *"Anne Knight and the Radical Subculture,"* 71 (1982) 100-113. In the standard suffrage histories, Knight is credited with authorship of the first pamphlet calling for women's suffrage, circa 1847. Malmgreen concludes that a radical subculture nurtured single women of independent means such as Knight, enabling them to argue the case for women's rights. Heterodox religion, in Knight's case Quakerism, was "both a component of, and a medium for the expression of, radical ideas" (p. 111).

12.373

WOMEN'S STUDIES INTERNATIONAL FORUM: Special Issue: "Reassessments of 'First Wave' Feminism," 5 (1982), ed. by Elizabeth Sarah; Caine, B., *"Feminism, Suffrage and the Nineteenth-Century English Women's Movement,"* 5 (1982) 537-550; Bacchi, C., *"'First Wave' Feminism in Canada: The Ideas of the English-Canadian Suffragists, 1877-1918,"* 5 (1982) 575-584; Register, C., *"Motherhood at Center: Ellen Key's Social Vision,"* 5 (1982) 599-610; Jeffreys, S., *"'Free From All Uninvited Touch of Man': Women's Campaigns Around Sexuality, 1880-1914,"* 5 (1982) 629-646; Lugones, M.C., and Spelman, E., *"Have We Got a Theory for You! Feminist Theory, Cultural Imperialism and the Demand for 'The Woman's Voice,'"* 6 (1983) 573-581; Zaborszky, D., *"Victorian Feminism and Gissing's THE ODD WOMEN: 'Why are Women Redundant?',"* 8 (1985) 489-496.

12.374

Bell, Susan Groag and Offen, Karen M., eds., **WOMEN, THE FAMILY, AND FREEDOM. THE DEBATE IN DOCUMENTS: VOLUME I. 1750-1880; VOLUME II. 1880-1950.** Stanford, 1983; *reviewed in:* **ALBION:** McBride, T., 16 (1984) 60-62. "Assesses the history of attitudes about women's rights, their place in the family, and their social roles. Focusing on the period in which women became ever more articulate about their rights, this collection highlights the ways in which women capitalized upon male claims to human rights to assert their own belief in equality" (p. 61).

12.375

Gaffin, Jean and Thomas, David, **CARING AND SHARING: THE CENTENARY HISTORY OF THE COOPERATIVE WOMEN'S GUILD.** 1983. Documentation of the activities of the Guild which was formed in 1883 in the cause against women's oppression. The Guild advocated provision of adequate child care and maternity benefits.

12.376

Greenburg, Reva Pollack, "Fabian Couples, Feminist Issues," Ph.D. diss., Univ. of California, San Diego, 1983.

12.377

Helsinger, Elizabeth K., Sheets, Robin Lauterbach, and Veeder, William, **THE WOMAN QUESTION: SOCIETY AND LITERATURE IN BRITAIN AND**

AMERICA, 1837-1883. 2 vols. 1983.

12.378
Mumford, Laura S., "Virile Mothers, Militant Sisters: British Feminist Theory and Novels, 1880-1920," Ph.D. diss., Univ. of Iowa, 1983. Examines the "first wave" feminist writers such as Olive Schreiner, Mona Caird, May Sinclair, Elizabeth Robins and anti-feminist Mrs. Humphrey Ward. Concludes that feminists idealized the mother-child bond and favored self-sacrifice to further political and artistic goals. Suggests the difficulty with which this group reconciled politics and art.

12.379
Spender, Lynne, **INTRUDERS ON THE RIGHTS OF MEN: WOMEN'S UNPUBLISHED HERITAGE.** 1983.

12.380
Taylor, Barbara, **EVE AND THE NEW JERUSALEM: SOCIALISM AND FEMINISM IN THE NINETEENTH CENTURY.** 1983; *reviewed in:* **ATLANTIS:** Kealey, L., 10 (1984) 133-136.

12.381
ANGLIA: *"The Emancipation of Women in Eighteenth-Century English Literature,"* 101 (1983) 78-98.

12.382
HISTORICAL JOURNAL: Harrison, B. and McMillan, J., *"Some Feminist Betrayals of Women's History,"* 26 (1983) 375-389.

12.383
HISTORY: Jones, D., *"Women and Chartism,"* 68 (1983) 1-21.

12.384
SIGNS: Pleck, E., *"Feminist Responses to Crimes Against Women,"* Special Issue 8 (1983) 451-470. Responses have been moralistic and punitive, and this has been a vehicle for the voicing of feminist claims and reform campaigns.

12.385
Atkins, Lynn R., "Expanding the Limits of Domesticity: Nineteenth-Century Non-Fiction by Women," Ph.D. diss., Wayne State University, 1984. Includes an extensive introduction followed by nine annotated essays by Dorothea Beale, Millicent Garrett Fawcett, Caroline Norton, Barbara Bodichon, Edith Simcox, Blanche Crackanthorpe, Sophia Jex-Blake, and Margaret Oliphant. Concludes that the feminist argument, presented in sexual terms and positioned in relation to the theme of domesticity, was conservative in thrust no matter how much writers argued in favor of adding professional dimensions to women's lives.

12.386
Forster, Margaret, **SIGNIFICANT SISTERS: THE GRASSROOTS OF ACTIVE FEMINISM, 1839-1939.** New York, 1985. Biographical essays on Caroline Norton, Elizabeth Blackwell, Emily Davies, Florence Nightingale, and Josephine Butler.

12.387
Rendall, Jane, **THE ORIGINS OF MODERN FEMINISM: WOMEN IN BRITAIN, FRANCE AND THE UNITED STATES, 1780-1860.** 1985.

12.388
VICTORIAN PERIODICALS REVIEW: Murray, J.H., *"Class vs. Gender Identification in the ENGLISHWOMAN'S REVIEW of the 1880's,"* 8 (1985) 138-142. Concludes that the REVIEW encouraged a belief in women's common virtues and their ability to correct male mistakes to the benefit of society. Nonetheless the periodical's appeal to working-class women was limited by the editorship's lack of experience in working women's lives and distrust of the lower classes.

12.389
Kuzmack, Linda Gordon, "The Emergence of the Jewish Women's Movement in England and the United States, 1881-1933: A Comparative Study," Ph.D. diss., George Washington Univ., 1986. "Nineteenth-century Jewish women began a campaign for a larger role in Jewish life that culminated in the demand for full equality and leadership roles in both communal and religious affairs. In both countries, Jewish women joined the general women's movement and translated the campaign for national civic and political rights into Jewish terms" (abstract).

12.390
Rubinstein, David, **BEFORE THE SUFFRAGETTES: WOMEN'S EMANCIPATION IN THE 1890'S.** New York, 1986.

* * *

2. POLITICS AND POLITICAL ORGANIZATIONS

12.391
Marcet, Jane, **CONVERSATIONS ON POLITICAL ECONOMY; IN WHICH THE ELEMENTS OF THAT SCIENCE ARE FAMILIARLY EXPLAINED.** 1816; 1827.

12.392
REPUBLICAN: *"Vindication of Female Political Interference,"* 1 (1819) n.p.

12.393
A CALL TO THE WOMEN OF ALL RANKS IN THE BRITISH EMPIRE, ON THE SUBJECT OF THE NATIONAL DEBT. 2nd ed., Aberdeen, 1833. Signed "A Sailor's Daughter."

12.394
NEW MORAL WORLD: *"Reports of Large Numbers of Female Teachers Attending Socialist Meetings in Leicester,"* 4 (1838) 330.

12.395
QUARTERLY REVIEW: Croker, J.W., *"Anti-Corn Law Agitation,"* 71 (1842) 261-265. Protests that the active participation of women in the opposition to the corn laws is unseemly.

12.396
Prentice, Archibald, **HISTORY OF THE ANTI-CORN LAW LEAGUE.** 1853; 1968. Work of women in the league is defended and probably understated.

12.397
Parker, Theodore, **THE PUBLIC FUNCTION OF WOMAN; A SERMON PREACHED AT THE MUSIC HALL, MARCH 27, 1853.** 1855.

12.398
MACMILLAN'S MAGAZINE: Cobbe, F.P., *"Social Science Congresses and Women's Part in Them,"* 3 (1861) 81-94; Seeley, J.R., *"Political Education of the Working Classes,"* 36 (1877) 143-145; Harberton, F.W., *"Individual Liberty for Women: A Remonstrance,"* 40 (1879) 282-288.

12.399
RAMBLER: Bastard, F.M., *"Women, Politics and Patriotism,"* 27 (1861) 349-362.

12.400
ENGLISH WOMAN'S JOURNAL: *"Women and Politics,"* 12 (1863) 1-6. Asserts that women don't have the quality of mind necessary for politics.

12.401
VICTORIA MAGAZINE: Andre, P.F., *"Civil and Political Status of Women,"* 5 (1865) n.p.; 6 (1865) n.p.; 7 (1866) n.p.; 8 (1866-67) n.p.

12.402
THE SOCIAL AND POLITICAL DEPENDENCE OF WOMEN. 1867.

12.403
Kingsley, Canon, **WOMEN AND POLITICS.** 1869; *also printed in:* **MACMILLAN'S MAGAZINE:** 20 (1869) 552-561.

12.404
JOURNAL OF THE ANTHROPOLOGICAL SOCIETY OF LONDON: Pike, L.O., *"On the Claims of Women to Political Power,"* 7 (1869) 47-61. Questions how far the female intellect can be trained to imitate the male.

12.405
SPECTATOR: *"Women and Politics,"* 64 (1870) 686-687; Twining, L., *"Women on County Councils,"* 62 (1889) 12.

12.406
ENGLISHWOMAN'S REVIEW: *"Election of School Boards,"* 2 (1871) 1-5; *"Election of School Boards,"* 5 (1871) 309; *"The Late School Board Elections,"* 5 (1874) 6-9; Williams, C., *"Shall a Women Householders' League be Formed?"* 5 (1874) 186-188; *"Women's Protective and Provident League,"* 6 (1875) 84-85; *"The Right of Women to Act on Deputations,"* 7 (1876) n.p.; *"Record of Events. Political Club for Women,"* 9 (1878) 569-570; *"Record of Events. Rights and Duties of Women in Local Government,"* 10 (1879) 83-85; *"Political Club for Women,"* 10 (1879) 180-181; *"Participation of Women in Local Franchises,"* 10 (1879) 206-212; Blackburn, H., *"Women on the London School Board,"* 10 (1879) 545-551; *"Women on School Boards,"* 10 (1879) 353-359; *"The Coming School Board Elections,"* 10 (1879) 443-448; *"Record of Events. School Board Elections,"* 10 (1879) 560-565; *"The Public Responsibilities of Women,"* 30 (1899) 1-9; Twining, L., *"The Official Work of Women,"* 30 (1899) 81-85. The rate of employment of women in official capacities has progressed such that at this date, over 1,000 are serving on 648 Boards in England; *"British Bibliography on Women's Questions,"* 30 (1899) 145-152.

12.407
Butler, Josephine, **SURSUM CORDA; ANNUAL ADDRESS TO THE LADIES'
NATIONAL ASSOCIATION.** Liverpool, 1871; **WOMEN AND POLITICS:
EXTRACT FROM A SPEECH BY MRS. JOSEPHINE BUTLER, AT A MEETING
OF THE PORTSMOUTH WOMEN'S LIBERAL ASSOCIATION, APRIL 11, 1888.**
1888.

12.408
Fawcett, Millicent Garrett and Fawcett, Henry, **ESSAYS AND LECTURES ON
SOCIAL AND POLITICAL SUBJECTS.** 1872.

12.409
Garrett, Rhoda, **THE ELECTORAL DISABILITIES OF WOMEN, A LECTURE
DELIVERED IN THE CORN EXCHANGE, CHELTENHAM, 3 APRIL 1872.**
Cheltenham, 1872.

12.410
Becker, Lydia E., **POLITICAL DISABILITIES OF WOMEN.** 1872; **THE RIGHTS
AND DUTIES OF WOMEN IN LOCAL GOVERNMENT.** Manchester, 1879.

12.411
WESTMINSTER REVIEW: *"The Political Disabilities of Women,"* 48 (1872) 60;
Hannigan, D.F. and Martyn, E., *"Women in Public Life,"* 132 (1889) 278-285;
Bulley, A.A., *"The Political Evolution of Women,"* 134 (1890) 1-8; Wolstenholme-
Elmy, E.C., *"The Part of Women in Local Administration,"* Part I, 150 (1898) 32-46;
Part II, 150 (1898) 248-260; Part III, 150 (1898) 377-389; Part IV, 151 (1899) 159-
171; Hawksley, J.M.A., *"Influence of the Woman's Club,"* 153 (1900) 455-457; Gill,
F.T., *"Woman Liberalism,"* 155 (1901) 130-132.

12.412
Fawcett, Henry, **SPEECHES ON SOME CURRENT POLITICAL QUESTIONS.**
1873. ——*see also:* Stephen, Leslie, **LIFE OF HENRY FAWCETT.** 1885.

12.413
Menzies, Sutherland and Stone, Elizabeth, **POLITICAL WOMEN.** 2 vols. 1873.

12.414
Robertson, Annie J., **WOMEN'S NEED OF REPRESENTATION.** Dublin, 1873.

12.415
WOMEN'S SUFFRAGE JOURNAL: Becker, L., *"The School Board Elections,"* 4
(1873) 166-167; Becker, L., *"The South Wales Strike,"* 4 (1873) 14-15; Becker, L.,
"The Sphere of Women in Politics," 6 (1875) 26-27; Becker, L., *"The Political
Functions of the Sovereign,"* 6 (1875) 92; Becker, L., *"Parliament Out of Session,"* 6
(1875) 129-130; Becker, L., *"Public Meetings,"* 6 (1875) 143; Becker, L., *"Curious
School Board Election,"* 6 (1875) 156.

12.416
Shore, Louisa, **THE CITIZENSHIP OF WOMEN SOCIALLY CONSIDERED.** 1874.

12.417
Wedgewood, Julia, **THE POLITICAL CLAIMS OF WOMEN.** 1876.

12.418
WOMAN'S GAZETTE: *"Ladies on School Boards,"* 2 (1877) 102-104; 153-155; 194-

196.

12.419
TIMES: *"Miss Taylor for Southwark,"* (August 31, 1878) 11.

12.420
Women's Local Government Society, **TO THE RIGHT HONORABLE SIR JOHN GORST, Q.C., M.P., VICE-PRESIDENT OF THE COMMITTEE OF COUNCIL. THE RESPECTFUL MEMORIAL OF THE... SOCIETY [ASKING HIM TO RECEIVE A DEPUTATION CONCERNING THE EDUCATION BILL].** 1879; 1896; **WOMEN AND THE MUNICIPAL CORPORATIONS ACT OF 1882.** 1882; **SHALL WOMEN BE ELIGIBLE TO SERVE ON COUNTY COUNCILS?** 1895; **WOMEN AS COUNTY COUNCILLORS.** 1896; **AN APPEAL TO WOMEN FROM THE WOMEN'S LOCAL GOVERNMENT SOCIETY...** 1913; **WOMEN OCCUPIERS AND THEIR VOTES.** 1913; **FIRST [ETC.] ANNUAL REPORT SINCE INCORPORATION.** 1916; **MISCELLANEOUS PAMPHLETS, LEAFLETS, ETC.** 1918.

12.421
Besant, Annie, **LIBERTY, EQUALITY, FRATERNITY.** [188?]; **ESSAYS, POLITICAL AND SOCIAL.** [1881]; **THE POLITICAL STATUS OF WOMEN.** 2nd ed., 1883; **THE LEGISLATION OF FEMALE SLAVERY IN ENGLAND.** 1885; **THE REDISTRIBUTION OF POLITICAL POWER.** 1885. On socialism; **THE EVOLUTION OF SOCIETY.** 1886; **MODERN SOCIALISM.** 1886; **WHY I AM A SOCIALIST.** 1886; **RADICALISM AND SOCIALISM.** 1887; **THE SOCIALIST MOVEMENT.** 1887; "Industry Under Socialism" in **FABIAN ESSAYS.** ed. by G.B. Shaw. 1889; 6th ed. with an introduction by Asa Briggs, 1962; **ESSAYS ON SOCIALISM.** 1893; **ANNIE BESANT: AN AUTOBIOGRAPHY.** 1893; **WOMEN AND POLITICS: THE WAY OUT OF PRESENT DIFFICULTIES.** 1914; **A SELECTION OF THE SOCIAL AND POLITICAL PAMPHLETS OF ANNIE BESANT.** compiled by John Saville. New York, 1970. —*see also:* Ball, William P., **MRS. BESANT'S SOCIALISM.** 1886; Besterman, Theodore, **A BIBLIOGRAPHY OF ANNIE BESANT.** 1924; **MRS. ANNIE BESANT: A MODERN PROPHET.** 1934; Nethercott, Arthur H., **THE FIRST FIVE LIVES OF ANNIE BESANT.** 1961; **INDIAN REVIEW:** Sivasankar, W.S., *"Dr. Annie Besant—A Profile,"* 68 (1972) 23-27. Biographical sketch illustrated by Besant's work in India and England; **DICTIONARY OF LABOUR BIOGRAPHY:** Rubinstein, D., *"Besant, Annie (1847-1933) Secularist, Socialist, Theosophist Indian Nationalist,"* 4 (1974) 21-31. Focuses on personal and political involvements. Includes good bibliography of Besant's biographies.

12.422
Primrose League, **RULES AND BY-LAWS. WITH A LIST OF MEMBERS.** [1883]. —*see also:* Hutton, Barbara, **THE PRIMROSE LEAGUE'S LADY'S LETTER AND REFERENCE BOOK WITH MOTTOES.** 1886; Robb, Janet, **THE PRIMROSE LEAGUE 1883-1906.** New York, 1942; rpt., 1968. Discusses the activities and political contributions of this women's organization, founded in 1883.

12.423
NINETEENTH CENTURY: Barnett, H.O., *"Practicable Socialism,"* 13 (1883) 554-560; Lonsdale, M., *"Platform Women,"* 15 (1884) 409-415; Galloway, M.A.A., *"Women and Politics,"* 19 (1886) 896-901; Huxley, J.H., *"Natural Rights and Political Rights,"* 27 (1890) 173-195; Linton, E.L., *"The Wild Women: As Politicians,"* 30 (1891) 79-88; Oakley, C.S., *"Of Women in Assemblies,"* 40 (1896) 559-566; Webb, B. and Webb, S., *"Arbitration in Labour Disputes,"* 40 (1896) 743-

758; McIlquham, H., *"Of Women in Assemblies: A Reply,"* 40 (1896) 777-781; Banks, E., *"Electioneering Women. An American Appreciation,"* 48 (1900) 791-800; Marriot, J.A.R., *"Reform of the House of Lords,"* 65 (1909) 34-47; Kingston, G., *"She Stoops to Canvass,"* 67 (1910) 324-334. Author canvasses because she has given up on getting the vote due to the acts of militant suffragists. Suggests that women may have had their own methods of canvassing. "In any case where the woman or man interviewed was more than humanly dirty, the man was almost more than fiercely Radical, and where I was taken into a moderately clean kitchen with 'a bit of gammon for supper' on the table, it was almost easy to predict the opposite trend of political opinion"; Dunraven, Lord, *"The Constitutional 'Sham Fight,'"* 67 (1910) 765-778.

12.424
JUSTICE: THE ORGAN OF THE SOCIAL DEMOCRATIC FEDERATION: 1884 to 1933; vols. 1-50; *also published as:* **JUSTICE: THE ORGAN OF SOCIAL DEMOCRACY:** 1884 to 1925; vols. 1-41.

12.425
PALL MALL GAZETTE: *"A Political Pioneer: An Interview with Miss Helen Taylor,"* (November 21, 1885) 2.

12.426
SATURDAY REVIEW: *"Playing at Politics,"* 59 (1885) 747-748. Comments on Helen Taylor; *"Rioting at the Late Elections,"* 60 (1885) 766. Account of violent disturbances at elections in some counties.

12.427
Reid, Anne, (Mrs. H.G. Reid), **WOMEN WORKERS IN THE LIBERAL CAUSE.** 1887. With prefatory note by Mrs. Gladstone. Calls for united action among women members of the Liberal Associations to defeat the Primrose League, a conservative women's group. Observes that women exert their most effective political influence at home; *rpt. in:* **WESTMINSTER REVIEW:** 128 (1887) 311-318.

12.428
NORTH AMERICAN REVIEW: Borthwick, A.B., *"English Women As A Political Force,"* 145 (1887) 81-85. Discusses the work of the Primrose League; Meath, R.B., *"British Women and Local Government,"* 157 (1893) 423-431. Urges female participation on county councils.

12.429
Webb, Sidney, **WHAT SOCIALISM MEANS; A CALL TO THE UNCONVERTED.** 4th ed., 1888; **THE BEST METHOD OF BRINGING CO-OPERATION WITHIN THE REACH OF THE POOREST OF THE POPULATION.** Manchester, 1891.

12.430
Women's Liberal Federation, **CIRCULARS, 1888-1900.** [1888-1900]; **ANNUAL REPORT OF THE EXECUTIVE COMMITTEE.** 1888-1910; **ANNUAL MEETING.** 1891-1900.

12.431
WOMEN'S GAZETTE AND WEEKLY NEWS: 1888 to ca. 1893. Edited by Miss Orme. Organ of the Women's Liberal Federation.

12.432
WOMEN'S PENNY PAPER: Oct. 1888 to 1890; vols. 1-4. Edited by H.B. Temple;

continued as: **WOMEN'S HERALD, A LIBERAL PAPER FOR WOMEN:** 1893 to 1894; vols. 4-8; Edited by Christina S. Bremner and afterwards by Lady Henry Somerset; *merged with:* **WOMAN'S SIGNAL:** 1894 to 1899; vols. 1-11. Edited by Lady Henry Somerset and Annie E. Holdsworth and in January, 1896 by Mrs. Fenwick Miller.

12.433
NATIONAL REVIEW: Payne, A.M., *"The Woman's Part in Politics,"* 14 (1889) 401-418.

12.434
Webb, Beatrice and Webb, Sidney, **PRINCIPLES OF THE LABOUR PARTY.** [189?]; **THE HISTORY OF TRADE UNIONISM.** 1894; 2nd ed., 1920; rpt., 1926; 1950; **INDUSTRIAL DEMOCRACY.** 1897; 2nd ed., 1902; 1920; **PROBLEMS OF MODERN INDUSTRY.** 1892; 2nd ed., 1902; 1920; **ENGLISH LOCAL GOVERNMENT: THE HISTORY OF LIQUOR LICENSING IN ENGLAND.** 1903; rpt., 1963; **THE PARISH AND THE COUNTY.** 1906; rpt., 1963; **THE MANOR AND THE BOROUGH.** 1908; rpt., 1963. ——*see also:* Warner, M., "The Webbs— A Study of the Influence of Intellectuals in Politics (largely between 1889-1918)," Ph.D. diss., Cambridge Univ., 1967; **DICTIONARY OF LABOUR BIOGRAPHY:** Cole, M., *"Webb, Beatrice (1858-1943) and Webb, Sidney James (1859-1947) (First Baron Passfield of Passfield Corner) Writers, Historians and Research Workers, Socialists and Labour Propagandists and Politicians,"* 2 (1974) 376-396. Includes bibliography.

12.435
Webb, Beatrice, **THE COOPERATIVE MOVEMENT IN GREAT BRITAIN.** 1891; 1931; (with Hutchins, B.L.), **SOCIALISM AND THE NATIONAL MINIMUM.** 1909; **MY APPRENTICESHIP.** 1926. Autobiography; **THE DISCOVERY OF THE CONSUMER.** 1928; **OUR PARTNERSHIP.** ed. by B. Drake and M.I. Cole. 1948; **BEATRICE WEBB'S DIARIES 1912-1924.** ed. by M.I. Cole. 1952; **BEATRICE WEBB'S DIARIES 1924-1932.** ed. and with an introduction by M.I. Cole. 1956. — *see also:* Letwin, Shirley Robin, "Beatrice Webb: Science and the Apotheosis of Politics" in **THE PURSUIT OF CERTAINTY: DAVID HUME, JEREMY BENTHAM, J.S. MILL AND BEATRICE WEBB.** by Shirley Robin Letwin. 1965; Hynes, Samuel, "The Fabians: Mrs. Webb and Mr. Wells" in **THE EDWARDIAN TURN OF MIND.** by Samuel Hynes. Princeton, 1968; 1969; **HISTORY WORKSHOP JOURNAL:** *"Beatrice Webb and the 'Woman Question,'"* no. 14 (1982) 23-43. Relates Webb's life to her social and political work.

12.436
IRIS: April 1892; several months only. The Organ of the Women's Progressive Society.

12.437
Shattuck, Harriette (Robinson), **THE WOMAN'S MANUAL OF PARLIAMENTARY LAW.** Boston, 1893. Informative book which offers instruction to women interested in organizing and agitating for political reform.

12.438
Independent Labour Party, **REPORT OF THE FIRST [-FIFTH] GENERAL CONFERENCE.** Glasgow, 1893-1897; **DIRECTORY AND BRANCH RETURNS FOR THE THREE MONTHS ENDING MAY 31ST, 1896.** 1896. ——*see also:* Joint Committee of the Independent Labour Party and the Fabian Society, **REPORT FOR THE TWO YEARS ENDED APRIL 30TH, 1913.** 1913.

12.439
LAW TIMES: *"Women in the Law Reform Congress,"* 95 (1893) 402.

12.440
Gammage, R.G., **HISTORY OF THE CHARTIST MOVEMENT 1837-1854**. 1894.
"At Birmingham the radical ladies formed themselves into a union" (p. 82).

12.441
Harper, Charles G., **REVOLTED WOMEN**. 1894.

12.442
Hill, Georgiana, "Women and Modern Politics" in **WOMEN IN ENGLISH LIFE**. by
Georgiana Hill. 1894. "Women of the middle classes have at present only an indirect
influence on politics. Singly they can do little or nothing, but by working in
numbers they are able to exert pressure, and to advance or retard social movements"
(p. 295). Also discusses the Primrose League; see also (in the same book): "The
Political Influence of Women," and "The Claim for Political Equality." Discusses
origins of the "claim," i.e., Wollstonecraft and Mill, Lydia Becker, and the suffrage
societies.

12.443
Sewell, May Wright, **THE WORLD'S CONGRESS OF REPRESENTATIVE
WOMEN**. Chicago and New York, 1894.

12.444
Blackburn, Helen, ed., **A HANDBOOK FOR WOMEN ENGAGED IN SOCIAL AND
POLITICAL WORK**. 2nd ed., Bristol, 1895. Offers practical advice concerning
public franchises, public appointments, education, employment, organizations, and
laws especially affecting women.

12.445
Pethick-Lawrence, Frederick William, **THE REFORMER'S YEAR BOOK**. 1895;
**THE BYE-ELECTION POLICY OF THE WOMEN'S SOCIAL AND POLITICAL
UNION**. [191?]. "The policy pursued by the WSPU has driven almost every
candidate to declare himself a 'sympathiser' with the cause [of suffrage], and it is
now almost unknown for any candidate to be unfavorable" (p. 4.). Includes
reproductions of figures from bye-elections in 1908 and accounts of women's
influence therein; **THE WOMAN'S BURDEN; HOW THE LABOUR PARTY
WOULD LIGHTEN IT**. [192?]. An appeal to women to enter into socialist politics;
FATE HAS BEEN KIND. 1943.   ——*see also:* Brittain, Vera, **PETHICK-
LAWRENCE. A PORTRAIT**. 1963. Delineates Pethick-Lawrence's career as a
writer, reformer, and political activist.

12.446
Twining, Louisa, **WOMEN AS OFFICIAL INSPECTORS**. 1895; *also printed in:*
NINETEENTH CENTURY: 35 (1894) 489-494.

12.447
FORTNIGHTLY REVIEW: Knodel, K., *"Sidelights on Socialism III. Woman and
Socialism,"* 57 (1895) 267-276. "The woman of the future must be independent of
her husband; she must do her own work in the world and receive her own wages,
or rather, in a collectivist state, her own share of rational enjoyment in return for
her services to the community" (p. 269).

12.448
QUARTERLY LEAFLET: 1895 to 1916; *superseded by:* **WOMEN'S LIBERAL MAGAZINE:** 1920; *superseded by:* **FEDERATION NEWS:** 1921 to 1924; *superseded by:* **LIBERAL WOMAN'S NEWS:** 1924-etc. Organ of the Women's Liberal Federation.

12.449
Mallet, Mrs. C., **SHALL WOMEN BE ELIGIBLE TO SERVE ON COUNTY COUNCILS?** 1896.

12.450
McIlquham, Harriet, **LOCAL GOVERNMENTS AND ITS LIMITATIONS FOR WOMEN.** 1896.

12.451
Stopes, Charlotte Carmichael, **THE WOMEN'S PROTEST. PAPER READ AT THE LONDON CONFERENCE OCT. 15, 1896.** [1896].

12.452
ECONOMIC JOURNAL: Webb, B. and Webb, S., *"The Method of Collective Bargaining,"* 6 (1896) 1-29; Butlin, F., *"International Congress of Women,"* 9 (1899) 450-455.

12.453
ECONOMIC REVIEW: Webb, B. and Webb, S., *"Are Trade Unions to Benefit Societies?"* 6 (1896) 441-455.

12.454
Bliss, William D.P., ed., **THE ENCYCLOPEDIA OF SOCIAL REFORM.** 1897.

12.455
BLACKWOOD'S MAGAZINE: Pilkington, W.T., *"Women in Politics,"* 161 (1897) 342-358.

12.456
LAW MAGAZINE AND REVIEW: *"The Legal Disqualification of Women for Election to School Boards,"* 23 (1897-1898) 99-106. "By the Common Law of England a woman is absolutely disqualified for being elected to or holding any office of a public nature" (p. 99).

12.457
Pratt, Edwin A., **CATHERINE GLADSTONE. LIFE, GOOD WORKS, AND POLITICAL EFFORTS.** 1898. On the work of William Gladstone's wife.

12.458
WOMEN AS COUNCILLORS. 1900.

12.459
Gordon, Ishbel Maria (Countess of Aberdeen), **WOMEN IN POLITICS.** 1900; (as editor), **INTERNATIONAL COUNCIL OF WOMEN, REPORTS.** 1900; 1910.

12.460
International Congress of Women, **REPORT OF THE TRANSACTIONS OF THE SECOND QUINQUENNIAL MEETING HELD IN LONDON, 1899, ETC.** 1900. — *see also:* **NINETEENTH CENTURY:** Gordon, I.M., *"The International Council of*

Women in Congresses," 46 (1899) 18-25; Low, F.H., *"A Woman's Criticism of the Women's Congress,"* 46 (1899) 192-202; Gaffney, F.H., *"A Woman's Criticism of the Women's Congress: A Reply,"* 46 (1899) 455-458.

12.461
PLATFORM: 1901 to 1904; nos. 1-168; Published by the Independent Labour Party; *continued as:* **TRACTS FOR THE TIMES:** 1903 [to 1906]; nos. 1-11.

12.462
King, Jessie Margaret, **WOMEN AND PUBLIC WORK: THEIR OPPORTUNITIES AND LEGAL STATUS IN ENGLAND, SCOTLAND AND IRELAND COMPARED.** 1902.

12.463
LADY'S REALM: Bennett, R., *"The Primrose League,"* 13 (1902) 3-12. Lauds the political efforts of the League, comprised mainly of women of the aristocracy.

12.464
Reddish, S., **WOMEN AND COUNTY AND BOROUGH COUNCILS. A CLAIM FOR ELIGIBILITY.** Manchester, 1903.

12.465
CHAMBERS'S EDINBURGH JOURNAL: Leach, H., *"The Great Ladies of Politics,"* 7 (1903-1904) 421-424.

12.466
Bebel, August, **WOMAN UNDER SOCIALISM.** trans. from the 33rd German ed. by Daniel De Leon. New York, 1903. "It is the common lot of woman and worker to be oppressed" (p. 1).

12.467
Ford, Isabella O., **WOMEN AND SOCIALISM.** 1904. Relates the women's movement to the socialist movement, briefly tracing the histories of both. Cites objections raised by the Labour Party to the women's movement.

12.468
Trevelyan, Caroline, **WOMEN IN LOCAL GOVERNMENT.** 1904; *also printed in:* **INDEPENDENT REVIEW:** n.v. (June 1904) n.p.

12.469
Williams, Constance, **HOW WOMEN CAN HELP IN POLITICAL WORK.** 1905.

12.470
Pethick-Lawrence, Emmeline, **THE NEW CRUSADE.** 1907. In this speech given at Exeter Hall, Pethick-Lawrence calls for women's support even though "women who work for women politically lose socially; women who work for men politically do not lose socially" (p. 4); **A CALL TO WOMEN.** [191?]; **DOES A MAN SUPPORT HIS WIFE?** New York, 1912. Discussion between Emmeline Pethick-Lawrence and Charlotte Perkins Gilman; **WHO SUPPORTS THE CHILDREN?** New York, 1912; **ENGLISH MILITANT METHODS.** New York, 1913; **MY PART IN A CHANGING WORLD.** 1938. Autobiography.

12.471
Snowden, Ethel (Annakin), **THE WOMAN SOCIALIST.** 1907; "Appendix" in **WOMAN: A FEW SHRIEKS! SETTING FORTH THE NECESSITY OF**

SHRIEKING TILL THE SHRIEKS BE HEARD. by "X." 1907.

12.472
NATION: Fordham, E.M., *"Women in Council,"* 1 (1907) 829-830; Massingham, H.W., *"The Task of the Prime Minister,"* 10 (1912) 687-689.

12.473
Montefiore, Dora, **THE POSITION OF WOMEN IN THE SOCIALIST MOVEMENT.** 1908. A critique, on an international comparative basis, with a focus on England. Relates female oppression to class oppression; **FROM A VICTORIAN TO A MODERN.** Autobiographical account.

12.474
SOCIALIST REVIEW: A MONTHLY REVIEW OF MODERN THOUGHT: March 1908 to Jan. 1926.

12.475
De Dino, Duchess, **MEMOIRS OF THE DUCHESS DE DINO, 1831-1835.** 1909; *reviewed in:* **QUARTERLY REVIEW:** *"Society and Politics in the Nineteenth Century,"* 212 (1910) 309-338.

12.476
McCabe, Joseph, **WOMEN IN POLITICAL EVOLUTION.** 1909.

12.477
Pole, Priscilla Wellesley (Countess of Westmoreland), **THE CORRESPONDENCE OF PRISCILLA, COUNTESS OF WESTMORELAND, 1813-1870.** 1909; *reviewed in:* **QUARTERLY REVIEW:** *"Society and Politics in the Nineteenth Century,"* 212 (1910) 309-338.

12.478
St. Helier, (Lady), **MEMORIES OF FIFTY YEARS.** 1909; *reviewed in:* **QUARTERLY REVIEW:** *"Society and Politics in the Nineteenth Century,"* 212 (1910) 309-338.

12.479
Staars, David, "The Introduction to Political Life" and "Claims and Conquests" in **THE ENGLISH WOMAN. STUDIES IN HER PSYCHIC EVOLUTION.** by David Staars. trans. by J.M.E. Brownlow. 1909. "A new element of social activity became evident in... [the Anti-Corn Law] agitation; women had been true helpers in the work. The starting point was a great tea in the Corn Exchange, Manchester in 1840, when many women were present. After this ladies were everywhere found canvassing and obtaining signatures to petitions" (p. 235). In "Claims and Conquests," Staars discusses the role of women's organizations, the mobilization of efforts to reform legislation concerning married women's property, and the move towards the fight for enfranchisement.

12.480
ENGLISHWOMAN: Feb. 1909 to Jan. 1921; vols. 1-49; Young, T.M., *"Women and Political Parties,"* 1 (1909) 321-327.

12.481
Goldman, Emma, **ANARCHISM AND OTHER ESSAYS.** New York, 1910.

12.482
QUARTERLY REVIEW: *"Society and Politics in the 19th Century,"* 212 (1910) 309-338. Discusses aristocratic women involved in various political circles and reviews three early Victorian memoirs recounting the participation of Priscilla, Countess of Westmoreland, the Duchess de Dino and Lady St. Helier in politics.

12.483
Brownlow, Jane M.E., **WOMEN'S WORK IN LOCAL GOVERNMENT, ENGLAND AND WALES.** 1911; **WOMEN IN LOCAL GOVERNMENTS IN ENGLAND AND WALES.** 1911.

12.484
Women's Cooperative Guild, **WORKING WOMEN AND DIVORCE. AN ACCOUNT OF EVIDENCE GIVEN ON BEHALF OF THE WOMEN'S COOPERATIVE GUILD BEFORE THE ROYAL COMMISSION ON DIVORCE.** 1911. ——*see also:* Gaffin, Jean and Thoms, David, **CARING AND SHARING: THE CENTENARY HISTORY OF THE COOPERATIVE WOMEN'S GUILD.** 1983.

12.485
Women's Labour League, **MY FAVORITE RECIPES. BY WOMEN MEMBERS OF THE LABOUR PARTY.** Woolwich, 1911.

12.486
Johnson, Olive M., **WOMEN AND THE SOCIALIST MOVEMENT.** New York, 1912. Investigates woman's "economic relation to society, her relation to the means of life, of production, and exchange" (p. 1).

12.487
Billington-Grieg, Teresa, **THE CONSUMER IN REVOLT.** 1912. Author may also be cataloged as Grieg, Teresa Billington.

12.488
MacDonald, J.R., **MARGARET ETHEL MACDONALD.** 1912. ——*see also:* Herbert, L., **MRS. RAMSAY MACDONALD.** 1924; Holmes, Marion I., **THE GIRLHOOD OF MRS. RAMSAY MACDONALD.** 1938; Baldwin, Arthur Windham, **THE MACDONALD SISTERS.** 1960; **VICTORIAN INSTITUTE JOURNAL:** Vines, A.G., *"Margaret MacDonald: A Socialist Pilgrimage,"* no. 6 (1977) 31-41.

12.489
TRANSACTIONS OF THE ROYAL HISTORICAL SOCIETY: Cunningham, W., *"The Family as a Political Unit,"* 3 (1912) 1-17. "The family has been and is the principle unit for political purposes" (p. 17).

12.490
Royden, Agnes Maude, **THE TRUE END OF GOVERNMENT: AN APPEAL TO THE MAN OF THE UNITED KINGDOM OF GREAT BRITAIN AND IRELAND.** 2nd ed., 1913.

12.491
Stobart, Mabel Annie Sinclair, **WAR AND WOMEN. FROM EXPERIENCE IN THE BALKANS AND ELSEWHERE.** 1913. Record of the achievements of the Women's Convoy Corps, whose members demonstrated their abilities without the aid of men.

12.492
LABOUR WOMAN: 1913-etc. Published by the Labour Party as a journal. From

1911 to 1913 published by the Women's Labour Party as a leaflet.

12.493
NEW STATESMAN: Anderson, A., *"Women in Public Administration,"* 2 (1913) Special Supplement; Hutchins, B.L., *"The Capitalist Versus the Home,"* 2 (1913) Special Supplement.

12.494
Fabian Society, **THE ECONOMIC FOUNDATIONS OF THE WOMEN'S MOVEMENT**. 1914.

12.495
Swanwick, Helena Maria, **WOMEN AND WAR**. 1915. Pacifist view; **WOMEN IN THE SOCIALIST STATE**. Manchester, 1921; **BUILDERS OF PEACE: BEING TEN YEARS' HISTORY OF THE UNION OF DEMOCRATIC CONTROL**. 1924. Suggests that women political activists dreamed of setting up a new world order. Some of the Cardinal Points of the Union bear a strong resemblance to Wilson's Fourteen Points, e.g., the third point which insists on abandonment of balance-of-power diplomacy and international agreements openly arrived at.

12.496
Key, Ellen Karolina, "Women and War" in **WAR, PEACE AND THE FUTURE... AND THE RELATION OF WOMEN TO WAR**. by Ellen Karolina Key. trans. by Hildgard Norberg. 1916.

12.497
Rosenblatt, Frank Ferdinand, **THE CHARTIST MOVEMENT IN ITS SOCIAL AND ECONOMIC ASPECTS**. New York, 1916.

12.498
Pease, Edward Reynolds, **HISTORY OF THE FABIAN SOCIETY**. 1916; 2nd ed., 1925; rpt., with an introduction by M.I. Cole, 1963.

12.499
Women's Local Government Society, **MISCELLANEOUS LEAFLETS AND PAMPHLETS 1894-1910**. 1916. The pamphlets include: "Shall Women Be Eligible to Serve on County Councils?" (1895) by Mrs. Charles Mallet; "Women As County Councillors" (1896); "An Appeal to Women from the Women's Local Government Society, LCC Election, 6 March 1913" (1913); and "Women Occupiers and Their Votes" (1913).

12.500
Phillips, Marion, ed., **WOMEN AND THE LABOUR PARTY**. 1918. Valuable anthology.

12.501
West, Julius, **A HISTORY OF THE CHARTIST MOVEMENT**. 1920.

12.502
Child-Villiers, Margaret Elizabeth, **LADY JERSEY. FIFTY-ONE YEARS OF VICTORIAN LIFE**. 1922. Author may be cataloged as Villiers, Margaret Elizabeth Child.

12.503
Trevelyan, Janet Penrose, **THE LIFE OF MRS. HUMPHREY WARD**. 1923.

12.504
Williams, Judith Blow, "Social-Political Theory and Movements" in **A GUIDE TO THE PRINTED MATERIALS FOR ENGLISH SOCIAL AND ECONOMIC HISTORY 1750-1850.** by Judith Blow Williams. New York, 1926.

12.505
Henry, Alice, **WOMEN AND THE LABOR MOVEMENT.** New York, 1927.

12.506
McMillan, Margaret, **THE LIFE OF RACHEL MCMILLAN.** 1927.

12.507
Strachey, Ray, (pseud. for Rachel Costelloe), **WOMEN'S SUFFRAGE AND WOMEN'S SERVICE. THE HISTORY OF THE LONDON AND NATIONAL SOCIETY FOR WOMEN'S SERVICE.** 1927.

12.508
Bryher, Samson, **AN ACCOUNT OF THE LABOUR AND SOCIALIST MOVEMENT IN BRISTOL.** 1929.

12.509
National Council of Women in Great Britain, **THE FIRST SIXTY YEARS.** 1933.

12.510
Women's Service Library, **THE FIRST SEVEN YEARS.** 1933.

12.511
Christie, Octavius Francis, **THE TRANSITION TO DEMOCRACY 1867-1914.** 1934.

12.512
Chamberlain, Austen, **POLITICS FROM THE INSIDE.** 1936.

12.513
Mannin, Ethel, **WOMAN AND THE REVOLUTION.** 1938; New York, 1939.

12.514
Pollit, Harry, **SERVING MY TIME: AN APPRENTICESHIP TO POLITICS.** 1940.

12.515
Adam, H. Pearl, ed., **WOMEN IN COUNCIL: THE JUBILEE BOOK OF THE NATIONAL COUNCIL OF WOMEN OF GREAT BRITAIN.** 1945.

12.516
Cole, Margaret, **GROWING UP IN REVOLUTION.** 1949. See chap. 4 for reminiscences of socialism and feminism, chap. 6 on the Fabians and the Webbs, and chap. 9 on "Recollections of the Webbs"; **THE STORY OF FABIAN SOCIALISM.** 1961.

12.517
Wood, Ethel M., **THE PILGRIMAGE OF PERSEVERANCE.** 1949. See especially: "Government and Women," which traces female political involvement from the fourteenth century to 1914, and "Women and Organizations: Political Organizations."

12.518
PAST AND PRESENT: Adams, W.S., *"Lloyd George and the Labor Movement,"* no. 3 (1953) 55-62; Hart, J., *"Nineteenth-Century Social Reform: A Tory Interpretation of His Tory,"* no. 31 (1965) 39-61; Booth, A., *"Food Riots in the North-West of England 1790-1801,"* no. 77 (1977) 84-107. A large percentage of the rioters were women.

12.519
JOURNAL OF POLITICS: Lewis, G.K., *"Fabian Socialism; Some Aspects of Theory and Practice,"* 3 (1952) 442-470.

12.520
Alford, Muriel Esmee, **DURING SIX REIGNS: LANDMARKS IN THE HISTORY OF THE NATIONAL COUNCIL OF WOMEN OF GREAT BRITAIN.** 1953.

12.521
Pelling, Henry, **THE ORIGINS OF THE LABOUR PARTY 1880-1900.** Oxford, 1954; 2nd ed., 1965.

12.522
Crawford, Floyd Wardlaw, "Some Aspects of the Political and Economic Problems of Woman in English Society, 1884-1901," Ph.D. diss., New York Univ., 1956. Discusses the women's movement for political and economic justice.

12.523
Bealey, Frank and Pelling, Henry, **LABOUR AND POLITICS 1900-1906. A HISTORY OF THE LABOUR REPRESENTATION COMMITTEE.** 1958.

12.524
Roberts, Charles, "Inaugural Address by Lady Carlisle to the Carlisle Women's Association" in **THE RADICAL COUNTESS. THE HISTORY OF THE LIFE OF ROSALIND, COUNTESS OF CARLISLE.** by Charles Roberts. Carlisle, 1962. — *see also:* Henley, Dorothy, **ROSALIND HOWARD, COUNTESS OF CARLISLE.** 1958.

12.525
McBriar, A.M., **FABIAN SOCIALISM AND ENGLISH POLITICS 1884-1918.** 1962. Includes a comprehensive bibliography.

12.526
Butler, D. and Freeman, J., **BRITISH POLITICAL FACTS 1900-1960.** 1963.

12.527
Harrison, Royden John, **BEFORE THE SOCIALISTS: STUDIES IN LABOUR AND POLITICS 1861-1881.** 1965. Working-class politics examined.

12.528
WOMEN IN A CHANGING WORLD. THE DYNAMIC STORY OF THE INTERNATIONAL COUNCIL OF WOMEN SINCE 1888. foreword by Marie-Helene Lefaucheux. 1966. Documents the evolution of the council, provides biographical information concerning its presidents, and lists Committees and their activities.

12.529
Thompson, Paul, **SOCIALISTS, LIBERALS AND LABOUR: THE STRUGGLE FOR LONDON 1885-1914**. 1967.

12.530
HISTORICAL JOURNAL: Blewett, N., *"Freefooders, Balfourites, Whole-hoggers, Factionalism Within the Unionist Party 1906-1910,"* 11 (1968) 95-124.

12.531
MARXISM TODAY: Frow, E. and Frow, R., *"Women in the Early Radical and Labour Movement,"* 12 (1968) 105-112. "The impetus of the economic and social movements which led to the formation of a working-class party agitating for political demands of the charter, developed women thinkers and leaders as well as men" (p. 105).

12.532
Thomas, Donald, "Political Censorship: A Fight to the Finish" in **A LONG TIME BURNING: THE HISTORY OF LITERARY CENSORSHIP IN ENGLAND**. by Donald Thomas. 1969.

12.533
Millett, Kate, **SEXUAL POLITICS**. New York, 1970; *reviewed in:* **MONTHLY REVIEW:** Gough, K., 2 (1971) 47-56. "Although mainly a comparative study of sexual themes in some modern literature, Millett's scope ranges beyond this into trenchant criticisms of the treatment of sex-roles" (p. 47).

12.534
Dangerfield, George, **THE STRANGE DEATH OF LIBERAL ENGLAND**. 1971.

12.535
INTERNATIONAL SOCIALIST REVIEW: O'Brien, J., *"Writing Women Back Into English History,"* 1 (1971) 18-22. Discusses women in working-class political associations in the 1840s.

12.536
Jenness, Linda, ed., **FEMINISM AND SOCIALISM**. 1972.

12.537
Emy, Hugh Vincent, **LIBERALS, RADICALS AND SOCIAL POLITICS, 1892-1914**. 1973.

12.538
Martin, C.E., "Female Chartism: A Study in Politics," M.A. thesis, Univ. of Wales, 1973.

12.539
Rude, George, **CAPTAIN SWING**. Harmondsworth, 1973. Women participated in "Swing" riots in rural areas. See pp. 202-203 and 208-209.

12.540
SOCIETY FOR THE STUDY OF LABOUR HISTORY BULLETIN: Jones, G.S., *"Working-Class Culture and Working-Class Politics in London, 1870-1900: Notes on the Remaking of a Working Class,"* 27 (1973) 29-30.

12.541
Keppel, Sonia, THE SOVEREIGN LADY: A LIFE OF ELIZABETH VASSAL, THIRD LADY HOLLAND. 1974.

12.542
HORIZON: Aronson, T., *"Empress Victoria,"* 16 (1974) 100-105. Delineates the activities of Queen Victoria and her oldest daughter in the unification of Germany.

12.543
Wooton, Graham, PRESSURE GROUPS IN BRITAIN 1720-1970. 1975. Valuable collection of documents with an interpretive essay by the author.

12.544
BRITISH HISTORY ILLUSTRATED: Keegan, J., *"The Unexpected Queen,"* 1 (1975) 44-55. Discusses the political circumstances which brought Queen Victoria to the throne.

12.545
PRINCETON UNIVERSITY LIBRARY CHRONICLE: Bartrum, B., *"A Victorian Political Hostess: The Engagement Book of Lady Stanley of Alderly,"* 36 (1975) 133-146.

12.546
POLITICS AND SOCIETY: Shover, M., *"Roles and Images of Women in World War I Propaganda,"* 5 (1975) 469-486. Analyzes poster propaganda; includes illustrations.

12.547
QUARTERLY BULLETIN OF THE MARX MEMORIAL LIBRARY: *"Helen McFarlane, Chartist and Marxist,"* 74 (1975) 3-6.

12.548
Tholfsen, Trygve R., WORKING CLASS RADICALISM IN MID-VICTORIAN ENGLAND. 1976; *reviewed in:* HISTORICAL STUDIES: Smith, F.B., 17 (1977) 547-548.

12.549
Thompson, Dorothy, (as editor), "Address of the Female Political Union of Newcastle-upon-Tyne To Their Fellow Countrywomen" in THE EARLY CHARTISTS. ed. by Dorothy Thompson. Columbia, 1971; *also printed in:* NORTHERN STAR: (February 2, 1839) n.p. Exemplifies the Chartist attitude that women's political activism must be for the sake of their husbands' rights rather than their own; "Women and Nineteenth Century Radical Politics: A Lost Dimension" in THE RIGHTS AND WRONGS OF WOMEN. ed. by Juliet Mitchell and Ann Oakley. Harmondsworth, 1976. Contrasts middle-and working-class women's status and the various reforms which affected both. Delineates women's participation in the Chartist movement; *reviewed in:* RADICAL HISTORY REVIEW: Rowbotham, S., *"Women and Radical Politics in Britain 1830-1914,"* 19 (1978-1979) 149-159; THE CHARTISTS: POPULAR POLITICS IN THE INDUSTRIAL REVOLUTION. New York, 1984.

12.550
VICTORIAN STUDIES: Kent, C., *"The Whittington Club: A Bohemian Experiment in Middle Class Social Reform,"* 18 (1974) 31-55. The club catered to shop assistants and clerks and admitted women.

12.551
JOURNAL OF SOCIAL HISTORY: Dawley, A. and Faler, P., *"Working-Class Culture and Politics in the Industrial Revolution. Sources of Loyalism and Rebellion,"* 9 (1976) 466-480.

12.552
Lipshitz, Susan, SEXUAL POLITICS IN BRITAIN. A BIBLIOGRAPHICAL GUIDE WITH HISTORICAL NOTES. Hassocks, 1977.

12.553
ANNALS OF THE NEW YORK ACADEMY OF SCIENCES: Walvin, J., *"The Impact of Slavery on British Radical Politics: 1787-1838,"* 292 (1977) 343-355. "The most notable new groups to side with [slave] emancipation were female. In the 1790s, on the other hand, with the exception of Mary Wollstonecraft's contribution, women played no part in the radical societies. But in the 1820s and 1830s female emancipationists provided certain women with their first organized and coherent political role in modern British Society. A female Anti-Slavery Society, founded in 1825 in Sheffield with a membership of 80, within a year had distributed 1400 pamphlets, printed 2,000 copies of tracts, and published a collection of antislavery poetry" (p. 351).

12.554
Powell, Violet, MARGARET, COUNTESS OF JERSEY: A BIOGRAPHY. 1978. Biography of a political hostess.

12.555
Skolnick, Esther S., "Leading Ladies: A Study of Eight Late Victorian and Edwardian Political Wives," Ph.D. diss., Univ. of Illinois, 1978.

12.556
Weinbaum, Betya, THE CURIOUS COURTSHIP OF WOMEN'S LIBERATION AND SOCIALISM. Boston, 1978.

12.557
INTERNATIONAL JOURNAL OF WOMEN'S STUDIES: Pugh, E.L., *"The First Woman Candidate for Parliament: Helen Taylor and the Election of 1885,"* 1 (1978) 378-390.

12.558
Hollis, Patricia, ed., "Address of the Female Political Union of Newcastle to their Fellow Countrywomen" in WOMEN IN PUBLIC: THE WOMEN'S MOVEMENT, 1850-1900. ed. by Patricia Hollis. 1979. Originally printed in 1839. Illustrates the Chartist attitude which excused female political activism when class interests were at stake.

12.559
Rowbotham, Sheila, "The Women's Movement and Organizing for Socialism" in BEYOND THE FRAGMENTS. ed. by Sheila Rowbotham, Lynne Segal, and Hilary Wainwright. 1979. Examines women's participation in socialist and communist movements.

12.560
Whittick, Arnold, WOMAN INTO CITIZEN. 1979. Examines the world-wide movement for women's political emancipation. Illustrated.

12.561
HISTORICAL STUDIES: Rickard, J., *"The Anti-Sweating Movement in Britain and Victoria: The Politics of Empire and Social Reform,"* 18 (1979) 582-597. Analyzes the interconnection of radicalism, imperialism and social reform in this movement, in which a fair number of middle-class women participated.

12.562
Hollis, Patricia, compiler, **WOMEN IN PUBLIC, 1850-1900: DOCUMENTS OF THE VICTORIAN WOMEN'S MOVEMENT.** 1979.

12.563
POLITICAL STUDIES: Brennan, T. and Pateman, C., *"Mere Auxiliaries to the Commonwealth: Women and the Origins of Liberalism,"* 27 (1979) 183-200. "In the seventeenth century, Liberal theory (which posits the idea of 'natural' individual freedom and equality) broke away from the traditional view of a hierarchy of inequality, and opened the field of social contact theory" (n.p.). Contends that "if women are taken into account in liberal theory, most writers retreat to patriarchal assumptions and assertions. The conflict between liberal and patriarchal theory is far from concluded" (p. 183).

12.564
Middleton, Victoria Sharon, "The Exiled Self: Women Writers and Political Fiction," Ph.D. diss., Univ. of California, Berkeley, 1979.

12.565
HISTORIAN: Skolnick, E.S., *"Petticoat Power: The Political Influence of Mrs. Gladstone,"* 42 (1980) 631-647. Examines the activities of Catherine Gladstone and their effect on her husband, William Gladstone and his stay in political office.

12.566
Tank, Susan Patricia, "Social Change and Social Movements: Working-Class Women and Political Activity in Britain 1880-1921," Ph.D. diss., London School of Economics, 1981.

12.567
Zeigler, Harmon L. and Poole, Keith, **WOMEN AND POLITICAL LIFE.** New York, 1981.

12.568
NORTHHAMPTONSHIRE PAST AND PRESENT: Gordon, P., *"Lady Knightley and the South Northhamptonshire Election of 1885,"* 6 (1981-1982) 265-273. Biographical essay on Lady Knightley and the influence she exerted over her husband, Sir Rainald Knightley, a member of Parliament.

12.569
Pugh, Martin, **THE MAKING OF MODERN BRITISH POLITICS 1867-1939.** 1982. Good background work. Includes information on women with annotated bibliography.

12.570
Randall, Vicky, **WOMEN AND POLITICS.** 1982. Examines the literature relevant to the politics of feminist issues, past and present.

12.571
Thomis, Malcolm I. and Grimmett, Jennifer, **WOMEN IN PROTEST 1800-1850.**

1982. See especially: "Chartist Women." Analyzes peaceful and violent collective action carried out by women which may be regarded as criminal. "If indeed there is no such thing as a specifically female kind of protest, it may be that there is a women's perspective to be observed on particular issues, perhaps a women's slightly different approach to the tactics to be employed in staging a campaign. At all events, it is important to attempt to consider how far women's behaviour in social protest, bread rioting, industrial action, or political activity, derives from the fact that the participants were involved as women and not simply as people" (p. 12); *reviewed in:* VICTORIAN STUDIES: Beddoe, D., 29 (1986) 331-332. "This is a work fundamentally entrenched in a male view of history which sees the particular, usually male-dominated movement as the important factor and women as merely contributing to that factor" (p. 331).

12.572
Walker, Linda, FABIANS ON FEMINISM: WRITINGS FROM THE FABIAN WOMEN'S GROUPS 1896-1946. 1982.

12.573
ALBION: Hirshfield, C., *"Liberal Women's Organizations and the War Against the Boers, 1899-1902,"* 14 (1982) 25-49. Delineates the anti-war activities of the Women's National Liberal Association and Liberal Federation.

12.574
FEMINIST REVIEW: Rowan, C., *"Women in the Labour Party 1906-1920,"* no. 12 (1982) 74-91. "Examine[s] the position of women in the Labour Party in the context of their own political situation.... For members of the Women's Labour League, the constraints and contradictions were numerous over and above the daily burdens of housework and childrearing; they were constantly being torn between their class loyalty to a patriarchal Labour Party and their need to assert their rights as women" (p. 74).

12.575
Chew, Doris Nield, THE LIFE AND WRITINGS OF ADA NIELD CHEW. 1983. A working-class socialist and suffragette, Chew embarked on her political career after exposing abusive conditions in a clothing factory at Crew.

12.576
WOMEN, POLITICS AND INDUSTRY, 1906-1918. MINUTES AND RECORDS OF THE WOMEN'S LABOUR LEAGUE. Brighton, 1983. Microform series from Harvester Press.

12.577
Banks, Olive, THE BIOGRAPHICAL DICTIONARY OF ENGLISH FEMINISTS. VOLUME I: 1800-1930. New York, 1985. Subsequent volumes forthcoming. Individuals are assessed in terms of their contribution to the feminist movement within their time period. Gives equal attention to well-known figures such as Millicent Garrett Fawcett and the less well-known, such as Elizabeth Wolstenholme-Elmy.

12.578
Kestner, Joseph, PROTEST AND REFORM: THE BRITISH SOCIAL NARRATIVE BY WOMEN, 1827-1867. Wisconsin, 1985. Surveys the British social protest fiction by women such as Hannah More, Frances Trollope, Mrs. Craik, Elizabeth Stone, Charlotte Tonna, Camilla Toulmin, Mrs. Gaskell, and George Eliot.

12.579
Young, James, **WOMEN AND POPULAR STRUGGLES: A HISTORY OF SCOTTISH AND ENGLISH WORKING-CLASS WOMEN 1500-1984.** Atlantic Highlands, 1985. "The story of women's unceasing agitation for social change." Contexts include Protestant sects, radical movements, trade unions, and socialist groups.

* * *

3. SUFFRAGE: CAMPAIGNS AND CONTROVERSY

12.580
Mill, James, **ESSAY ON GOVERNMENT.** 1818; 1824; 1828; 1937; New York, 1955. "All... individuals whose interests are indisputably included in those of other individuals may be struck off [from the list of voters] without inconvenience.... In this light... women may be regarded the interest of almost all... involved either in [the interest] of their fathers or in that of their husbands" (pp. 73-74). ——*see also:* Pankhurst, Richard K.P., "The Appeal: A Reply to James Mill" in **WILLIAM THOMPSON: BRITAIN'S PIONEER SOCIALIST, FEMINIST AND CO-OPERATOR.** by Richard K.P. Pankhurst. 1954; **JOURNAL OF POLITICS:** Hamburger, J., *"James Mill on Universal Suffrage and the Middle Class,"* 24 (1962) 167-190. "[Mill] does not say it is desirable to exclude women [from universal suffrage, but he wanted to] take away any surface impression of extremism.... Mill was willing to restrict the size of the electoral to the necessity of having informed and reasonable voters" (p. 176); **HISTORY OF POLITICAL THOUGHT:** Ball, T., *"Utilitarianism, Feminism and the Franchise: James Mill and His Critics,"* 1 (1980) 91-116. Argues that Mill's condemnation of Hindu practices toward women reveals a defense of women's rights that contradicts his critics' claims that he was a male supremacist. Also concludes that Jeremy Bentham's Constitutional Code manifests a prejudicial view of female suffrage and a woman's ability to make political judgments.

12.581
NEW MORAL WORLD: *"Is Universal Suffrage Necessary to the Establishment or Perpetuity of Communities?"* no. 198 (1838) 329-330. "As soon as we acquire property, we acquire political rights" (p. 330).

12.582
Richardson, R.J., **THE RIGHTS OF WOMAN; EXHIBITING HER NATURAL, CIVIL AND POLITICAL CLAIMS TO A SHARE IN THE LEGISLATIVE AND EXECUTIVE POWER OF THE STATE.** Edinburgh, 1840.

12.583
Thompson, Thomas Perronet, **EQUAL RIGHT OF WOMEN TO VOTE.** 1841.

12.584
Knight, Anne, **LEAFLET ON WOMEN'S SUFFRAGE.** 1847.

12.585
WOMEN'S RIGHT OF SUFFRAGE. 1849.

12.586
WESTMINSTER REVIEW: Mill, H.T., *"The Enfranchisement of Women,"* 55 (1851) 289-301; *"The Emancipation of Women,"* 102 (1874) 137-174. Review of four books related to women's suffrage; *"Women Ratepayers' Right to Vote,"* 122 (1884) 375-381; McLaren, W.S.B., *"The Political Emancipation of Women,"* 128 (1887) 165-173; *"Results of the Non-Enfranchisement of Women,"* 133 (1890) 231-239; Dietrick, E.B., *"Woman and Negro Suffrage,"* 135 (1891) 364-372; Matters, C.H., *"Woman Suffrage,"* 143 (1895) 534-537; Ignota (pseud. for Wolstenholme-Elmy, E.C.), *"Women's Suffrage,"* 148 (1897) 357-372; Ignota (pseud. for Wolstenholme-Elmy, E.C.), *"Administration Reform and Women's Suffrage,"* 156 (1901) 68-76; Ignota (pseud. for Wolstenholme-Elmy, E.C.), *"Women's Lost Citizenship,"* 159 (1903) 512-522; McIlquham, H., *"Women's Suffrage in the Early Nineteenth Century,"* 160 (1903) 539-551; Ignota (pseud. for Wolstenholme-Elmy, E.C.), *"Enfranchisement of Women,"* 164 (1905) 21-25; *"The Case for the Immediate Enfranchisement of Women of the United Kingdom,"* 166 (1906) 508-521. Discusses the reasons for female suffrage "on the same terms as men" (p. 508). Also gives a summary of the movement's history; Thoresby, F., *"Woman and Woman's Suffrage,"* 166 (1906) 522-530; *"Mr. Asquith and the Women's Liberation Federation,"* 174 (1910) 508-513.

12.587
Justitia (pseud. for Pochin, Mrs. Henry Davis), **THE RIGHT OF WOMEN TO THE EXERCISE OF THE ELECTIVE FRANCHISE.** 2nd ed., 1855; published by the Manchester Women's Suffrage Society, 1873. "The happiness of woman lies not in possession [of masculine physical attributes], but in activity; for it is activity and not possession [that] strengthens and elevates the faculties" (p. 21).

12.588
CURRENT LITERATURE; A CLASSIFIED LIST: 1858 to 1908; *continued as:* **MONTHLY GAZETTE OF CURRENT LITERATURE:** 1908 to 1909; *continued as:* **CURRENT LITERATURE OF THE MONTH:** 1909 to 1926; *"The Hero and the Heroine of the Suffragist Militants,"* n.v. (1912) 162-164; *"Brick Batts for Windows and Votes for Women,"* n.v. (1912) 390-394.

12.589
MACMILLAN'S MAGAZINE: Maurice, F.D., *"The Suffrage Considered in Reference to the Working Class and to the Professional Class,"* 2 (1860) 89-97; Smith, G., *"Female Suffrage,"* 30 (1874) 139-150; Cairries, J.E., *"Woman Suffrage in Reply to Goldwin Smith,"* 30 (1874) 377-388; Zincke, F.B., *"The Labourer and the Franchise,"* 49 (1883) 20-27.

12.590
Cobbe, Frances Power, **THE RED FLAG IN JOHN BULL'S EYES.** 1863; **WHY WOMEN DESIRE THE FRANCHISE.** 1869; "Introduction" in **THE WOMAN QUESTION IN EUROPE: A SERIES OF ORIGINAL ESSAYS.** ed. by Theodore Stanton. New York, 1884. Calls suffrage "the crown and completion of the progress" of women gaining their political rights. "Never was there such a case of such pure and simple Moral Pressure" (p. xvii); **OUR POLICY: AN ADDRESS TO WOMEN CONCERNING THE SUFFRAGE, ETC.** 1888.

12.591
JOURNAL OF SOCIAL SCIENCE: B., *"The Enfranchisement of Female Free-Holders and Householders,"* 1 (1865-1866) 613-620. Propounds contemporary arguments for and against women's suffrage.

12.592
Anstey, T. Chisolm, **ON SOME SUPPOSED CONSTITUTIONAL RESTRAINTS ON THE PARLIAMENTARY FRANCHISE**. 1866; 1867. "The... question... is, whether there be anything in the nature of the office that should make a woman incompetent and we think there is not" (p. 25).

12.593
Bodichon, Barbara Leigh Smith, **OBJECTIONS TO THE ENFRANCHISEMENT OF WOMEN CONSIDERED**. 1866; **REASONS FOR THE ENFRANCHISEMENT OF WOMEN**. 1866; **REASONS FOR AND AGAINST THE ENFRANCHISEMENT OF WOMEN**. 1872. Believes that women's suffrage would inspire a general increase in true public-spiritedness. ——*see also:* ENGLISHWOMAN'S REVIEW: Belloc, B.R.P., *"Barbara Leigh Smith Bodichon,"* 22 (1891) 146; Burton, H., **BARBARA BODICHON 1827-1891**. 1949; Bradbrook, Muriel C., **BARBARA BODICHON, GEORGE ELIOT AND THE LIMITS OF FEMINISM**. Oxford, 1975. Advance in women's emancipation began with educational improvement, representing "social rather than legislative changes" (p. 2); Herstein, Sheila R., "Barbara Leigh Smith Bodichon (1827-1891): A Mid-Victorian Feminist," Ph.D. diss., City Univ., New York, 1980. Examines Bodichon's life, analyzing her contributions to nineteenth-century feminist movements; Mathews, Jacquie, "Barbara Bodichon: Integrity in Diversity (1827-1891)" in **FEMINIST THEORISTS. THREE CENTURIES OF WOMEN'S INTELLECTUAL TRADITIONS**. ed. by Dale Spender. 1983. Biographical essay which explores Bodichon's work as a feminist, law reformer, writer, painter, and advocate of women's education; Herstein, Sheila R., **A MID-VICTORIAN FEMINIST: BARBARA LEIGH SMITH BODICHON**. New Haven, [1986].

12.594
Mill, Harriet Taylor, **THE FIRST PETITION [FOR FEMALE SUFFRAGE]**. 1866. Reprinted by Women's Suffrage Society with 1499 names attached; **ENFRANCHISEMENT OF WOMEN**. 1868; rpt., 1983.

12.595
VICTORIA MAGAZINE: *"Suffrage for Women,"* 7 (1866) 289, 362; 8 (1866-1867) 865; 9 (1867) 236; 17 (1871) 134; 18 (1871-72) 394; 21 (1873) 529; Hoskins, J., *"Suffrage for Women,"* 15 (1870) 227; 18 (1871-1872) 312; *"Campaign of Suffrage for Women,"* 19 (1872) 119; Blair, W.T., *"Suffrage for Women,"* 22 (1873-1874) 535; Cobbe, F.P., *"From a Suffrage Speech by F.P. Cobbe,"* 27 (1876) 274-275; King, Mrs. E.M., *"Suffrage for Women,"* 32 (1878-1879) 265; Lynch, E.M., *"Suffrage for Women,"* 36 (1880) 49.

12.596
Fox, William Johnston, **WOMEN SUFFRAGE**. 1867. Extracts from a speech by a member of Parliament delivered at Oldham on Feb. 4, 1853.

12.597
Kingsford, Ninon, **THE ADMISSION OF WOMEN TO THE PARLIAMENTARY FRANCHISE. AN ESSAY**. 1867.

12.598
Mill, John Stuart, **SPEECH OF MR. JOHN STUART MILL ON THE ADMISSION OF WOMEN TO THE PARLIAMENTARY FRANCHISE. SPOKEN IN THE HOUSE OF COMMONS, MAY 20TH, 1867**. 1867; **ON THE SUBJECTION OF WOMEN**. 1869; rpt., ed. by Sue Mansfield. 1980; Most significant nineteenth-century work on the question of English women's suffrage. A booklength set of

arguments for female public and private equality; **SPEECH IN FAVOR OF WOMEN'S SUFFRAGE JANUARY 12, 1871.** Edinburgh, 1873. ——*see also:* ENGLISH WOMAN'S JOURNAL: *"The Opinions of John Stuart Mill,"* 6 (1860) 1-11; **BLACKWOOD'S MAGAZINE:** Mozley, A., *"Mr. Mill on THE SUBJECTION OF WOMEN,"* 106 (1869) 309-321; **CHRISTIAN OBSERVER AND ADVOCATE:** *"Mill on the Condition of Women,"* 68 (1869) 618-624. Negative review of THE SUBJECTION OF WOMEN; **CONTEMPORARY REVIEW:** Rands, W.B., 14 (1870) 63-89. Review of THE SUBJECTION OF WOMEN; **EDINBURGH REVIEW:** Oliphant, M., *"Mill's THE SUBJECTION OF WOMEN,"* 130 (1869) 572-602. "It is strange to find so profound a mind taking so superficial a view" (p. 578); **FRIENDS QUARTERLY EXAMINER:** Westlake R., *"The Social Position of Woman [with reference to THE SUBJECTION OF WOMEN by J.S. Mill and THE MISSING LAW; OR WOMAN'S BIRTHRIGHT by Mrs. J. Stewart],"* 3 (1869) 432-444. Prefers the style and argumentation of Stewart to Mill, and exhorts readers "whose mental training should fit them to be in advance of public opinion on this matter" to get involved in its solution; Grosvenor Papers, **AN ANSWER TO MR. JOHN STUART MILL'S "SUBJECTION OF WOMEN."** 1869; LANCET: *"J.S. Mill, 'The Subjection of Women,'"* 1 (1869) 510-512. "We cannot help asking ourselves whether women would be really benefited by exercising the suffrage, by obtaining a place in Parliament, or by competing for several employments now followed almost exclusively by the male sex" (p. 510); **SATURDAY REVIEW:** 27 (1869) 813. Review of THE SUBJECTION OF WOMEN; Clayland's Debating Society, **MR. MILL'S "SUBJECTION OF WOMEN" FROM A WOMAN'S POINT OF VIEW.** Manchester, 1870; MacCaig, Donald, **A REPLY TO JOHN STUART MILL ON THE SUBJECTION OF WOMEN.** Philadelphia, 1870; **FRASER'S MAGAZINE:** Taylor, H., *"Mr. Mill on the Subjection of Women,"* 81 (1870) 143-165; Christie, W.D., **JOHN STUART MILL AND MR. ABRAHAM HAYWARD, Q.C. A REPLY ABOUT MILL TO A LETTER TO THE REVEREND STOPFORD BROOKE, PRIVATELY CIRCULATED AND ACTUALLY PUBLISHED.** 1873. Author attempts to clarify information written about Mill at the time of his death; Stephen, James Fitzjames, **LIBERTY, EQUALITY, FRATERNITY.** 1873. Fitzjames disagrees with SUBJECTION OF WOMEN from "the first sentence to the last" and finds Mill's discussion of marriage "distasteful"; **ENGLISHWOMAN'S REVIEW:** *"John Stuart Mill,"* 5 (1873) 173-176; **WOMAN'S SUFFRAGE JOURNAL:** Becker, L.E., *"John Stuart Mill,"* 4 (1873) 82-83; Becker, Lydia Ernestine, **LIBERTY, EQUALITY, FRATERNITY. A REPLY TO MR. FITZJAMES STEPHEN'S STRICTURES ON MR. J.S. MILL'S "SUBJECTION OF WOMEN."** Manchester, 1873; 1874; Fawcett, Millicent Garrett, **MR. FITZJAMES STEPHEN ON THE POSITION OF WOMEN. BEING A REPLY TO MR. STEPHEN ON LIBERTY, EQUALITY, FRATERNITY.** 1873; Fawcett, Millicent Garrett, "Introduction" in **ON LIBERTY, REPRESENTATIVE GOVERNMENT, THE SUBJECTION OF WOMEN. THREE ESSAYS.** by John Stuart Mill. 1912. In an attempt to generate interest in his works, Fawcett gives a brief biographical essay of Mill's writings and beliefs; Carr, Wendell Robert, "Introduction" in **THE SUBJECTION OF WOMEN.** by John Stuart Mill. 1970. Analyzes Mill's work in the political and philosophical context of his time; **REVIEW OF POLITICS:** Kern, P.B., *"Universal Suffrage Without Democracy: Thomas Hare and John Stuart Mill,"* 34 (1972) 306-322.

12.599
Newman, Francis William, **OLD ENGLAND——WOMEN'S RIGHT OF SUFFRAGE.** 1867; **A LECTURE ON WOMEN'S SUFFRAGE DELIVERED IN BRISTOL ATHENAEUM. FEBRUARY 24, 1869.** Bristol, 1869; **A LECTURE ON WOMEN'S SUFFRAGE, DELIVERED AT GUILDHALL BATH ON JANUARY 28, 1870.** Bristol, 1870; **SIXTEEN REASONS.** 1870. Leaflet.

12.600

Taylor, Helen, THE CLAIM OF ENGLISHWOMEN TO THE SUFFRAGE CONSTITUTIONALLY CONSIDERED. 1867.

12.601

National Society for Women's Suffrage (later incorporated with National Union of Women's Suffrage Societies), ANNUAL REPORT[S] OF THE EXECUTIVE COMMITTEE, [MANCHESTER BRANCH]. 1867-1880; FIRST TO SIXTEENTH ANNUAL REPORTS. Manchester, 1868-1883; FIRST TO NINTH REPORTS OF THE EDINBURGH BRANCH. 1868-1877; REPORT OF THE COMMITTEE TO THE COUNCIL [BRISTOL AND CLIFTON BRANCH], NOVEMBER 14, 1868. [1868]; REPORT [BRISTOL AND WEST OF ENGLAND BRANCH]. 1870. 1870; REPORT OF THE MEETING OF THE LONDON NATIONAL SOCIETY FOR WOMEN'S SUFFRAGE HELD MARCH 25, 1870. 1870; WOMEN'S SUFFRAGE. PUBLIC MEETING IN EDINBURGH... UNDER THE AUSPICES OF THE EDINBURGH BRANCH OF THE N.S.W.S. Edinburgh, 1870; REPORT OF THE BRISTOL AND WEST OF ENGLAND BRANCH OF THE N.S.W.S., 1870-1876. Bristol, 1870-76; REPORT OF A MEETING OF THE LONDON NATIONAL SOCIETY FOR WOMEN'S SUFFRAGE HELD... MARCH 26, 1870. 1870; WOMEN'S SUFFRAGE. GREAT MEETING HELD IN EDINBURGH IN THE MUSIC HALL, ON THE 12TH JANUARY, 1871, UNDER THE AUSPICES OF THE EDINBURGH BRANCH OF THE N.S.W.S. Edinburgh, 1871; REPORT OF A PUBLIC MEETING HELD IN THE HANOVER SQUARE ROOMS, LONDON. 1873; OPINIONS OF WOMEN ON WOMEN'S SUFFRAGE. 1877; PAPERS PUBLISHED BY THE SOCIETY. 1877, etc.; OPINIONS OF WOMEN ON WOMEN'S SUFFRAGE. 1879; reviewed in: ENGLISHWOMAN'S REVIEW: 10 (1879) 116-119; OUGHT WOMEN TO HAVE VOTES FOR MEMBERS OF PARLIAMENT? [1879]; REPORT OF THE ANNUAL MEETING. Westminster, 1889-1916; ANNUAL REPORT OF THE COMMITTEE [CENTRAL BRANCH]. 1884; REPORT OF THE EXECUTIVE COMMITTEE PRESENTED AT THE ANNUAL GENERAL MEETING HELD IN THE WESTMINSTER TOWN HALL, JULY 9, 1889. [1889]; DECLARATION IN FAVOUR OF WOMEN'S SUFFRAGE, BEING THE SIGNATURES RECEIVED AT THE OFFICE OF THE CENTRAL COMMITTEE OF THE NATIONAL SOCIETY FOR WOMEN'S SUFFRAGE. 1889; ANNUAL REPORTS [CENTRAL BRANCH]. 1889-1897; WOMEN'S SUFFRAGE. REASONS FOR SUPPORTING THE PROPOSED EXTENSION OF THE PARLIAMENTARY FRANCHISE. 1889; OCCASIONAL PAPERS, 1 TO 11 [CENTRAL AND EAST OF ENGLAND BRANCH]. 1891-1900; LIST OF CANDIDATES IN FAVOR OF THE SUFFRAGE. 1891; LIST OF M.P.S IN FAVOR OF WOMEN'S SUFFRAGE. 1891; THE WORK OF THE CENTRAL COMMITTEE. A SKETCH. Westminster, 1893; REPORT OF THE EXECUTIVE COMMITTEE PRESENTED AT THE ANNUAL GENERAL MEETING... 1893. [1893]; OPINIONS OF LEADERS OF RELIGIOUS THOUGHT ON WOMEN'S SUFFRAGE. 2nd. ed., 1896; PARLIAMENTARY ECHOES. EXTRACTS FROM SPEECHES ON WOMEN'S SUFFRAGE, IN THE HOUSE OF COMMONS. 1896; SPEECHES AT NATIONAL CONFERENCE OF DELEGATES OF WOMEN'S SUFFRAGE SOCIETIES AT BIRMINGHAM, OCTOBER 16. 1896; SOME SUPPORTERS OF THE WOMEN'S SUFFRAGE MOVEMENT. 1897. School board members; ANNUAL REPORTS [CENTRAL AND EAST OF ENGLAND BRANCH]. 1898-1900; ANNUAL REPORTS [NORTH OF ENGLAND BRANCH]. 1898-1911; ANNUAL REPORTS [CENTRAL AND WESTERN BRANCH]. 1898-1900; ANNUAL REPORT [BRISTOL AND WEST OF ENGLAND BRANCH]. 1899-1900; REPORTS OF THE EXECUTIVE COMMITTEE PRESENTED AT THE ANNUAL GENERAL MEETINGS. 1904-1910; ANNUAL REPORT [NORTH HERTFORDSHIRE BRANCH]. 1909-1910; ANNUAL REPORTS [HITCHIN,

STEVENAGE AND DISTRICT BRANCH]. 1912-1914; ANNUAL REPORT [LEICESTER AND LEICESTERSHIRE BRANCH]. 1912; ANNUAL REPORT [PETERSFIELD BRANCH]. 1912. ——*see also:* Infant Protection Life Society, REPLY OF THE INFANT LIFE PROTECTION SOCIETY TO A MEMORIAL OF THE NATIONAL SOCIETY FOR WOMEN'S SUFFRAGE OBJECTING TO THE PROPOSED MEASURES. 1871.

12.602
CONTEMPORARY REVIEW: Becker, L., *"Female Suffrage,"* 4 (1867) 307-316; Wedgewood, J., *"Female Suffrage in its Influence on Married Life,"* 20 (1872) 360-370; Pfeiffer, E., *"Woman's Claim,"* 39 (1881) 265-277; *"The Suffrage for Women in England,"* 47 (1885) 418-435; Haldane, R.B., *"On Some Economic Aspects of Women's Suffrage,"* 58 (1890) 830-838; Fawcett, M.G., *"The Women's Suffrage Question,"* 61 (1892) 763-768; Courtney, L., *"The Woman's Suffrage Question,"* 61 (1892) 768-773; Amos, S.M.S., *"The Woman's Suffrage Question,"* 61 (1892) 773-778; Lyttelton, E., *"Women's Suffrage and the Teachings of St. Paul,"* 69 (1896) 680-691; Billington-Grieg, T., *"The Rebellion of Women,"* 94 (1908) 1-10; Russell, B., *"Liberalism and Women's Suffrage,"* 94 (1908) 11-16.

12.603
FEMALE FRANCHISE. HAVE WOMEN IMMORTAL SOULS? THE POPULAR BELIEF DISPUTED. BY A CLERK IN HOLY ORDERS. 1868.

12.604
FORTNIGHTLY REVIEW: Pankhurst, R.M., *"The Right of Women to Vote Under the Reform Act, 1867,"* 10 (1868) 250-254; Fawcett, M.G., *"The Electoral Disabilities of Women,"* 13 (1870) 622-632; Fawcett, M.G., *"Proportional Representation,"* 22 (1870) 376-382; Russell, K.L., *"The Claims of Women,"* 15 (1871) 95-110; Arnold, A., *"The Political Enfranchisement of Women,"* 17 (1872) 204-214; Fawcett, M.G., *"The Women's Suffrage Bill. I. The Enfranchisement of Women,"* 51 (1889) 555-567; Glennie, J.S.S., *"The Women's Suffrage Bill (No. II): The Proposed Subjection of Men,"* 51 (1889) 568-578; *"Women's Suffrage: A Reply,"* 52 (1889) 123-139; Bury, J.B., *"The Insurrection of Women: A Criticism,"* 58 (1892) 651-666; Jeune, S.M.E., *"The Revolt of the Daughters,"* 61 (1894) 267-276; Billington-Grieg, T., *"The Government and Women's Suffrage,"* 94 (1910) 890-902.

12.605
FRASER'S MAGAZINE: *"Women's Votes: A Dialogue,"* 77 (1868) 577-590.

12.606
ST. JAMES MAGAZINE: *"Womanhood Suffrage,"* 22 (1868) 288-296.

12.607
Becker, Lydia, DIRECTIONS FOR PREPARING A PETITION TO THE HOUSE OF COMMONS. 1869; A REPLY TO THE PROTEST [AGAINST "THE EXTENSION OF THE PARLIAMENTARY FRANCHISE TO WOMEN"] WHICH APPEARED IN THE NINETEENTH CENTURY REVIEW. 1889; WORDS OF A LEADER. BEING EXTRACTS FROM THE WRITINGS OF THE LATE MISS LYDIA BECKER. 2nd ed., 1897. ——*see also:* Holmes, Marion, LYDIA BECKER: A CAMEO LIFE SKETCH. 1913.

12.608
Stewart, Mrs. J., THE MISSING LAW; OR WOMAN'S BIRTHRIGHT. 1869.

12.609

Wedgewood, Julia, "Female Suffrage, Considered Chiefly with Regard to its Indirect Results" in WOMAN'S WORK AND WOMAN'S CULTURE. ed. by Josephine Butler. 1869.

12.610

Amberley, Katherine, THE CLAIMS OF WOMEN TO THE SUFFRAGE. Bristol, 1870.

12.611

Bright, Jacob, SPEECH OF JACOB BRIGHT ON THE ELECTIONAL DISABILITIES OF WOMEN DELIVERED IN EDINBURGH, JANUARY 17, 1870. 1870; SPEECH OF MR. JACOB BRIGHT AT THE ANNUAL MEETING OF THE MANCHESTER SOCIETY FOR WOMEN'S SUFFRAGE. 1872. ——see also: Shore, Arabella, AN ANSWER TO MR. JOHN BRIGHT'S SPEECH ON WOMEN'S SUFFRAGE. 1870; A LETTER TO THE RT. HON. JOHN BRIGHT, M.P., FROM A LADY IN "THE GALLERY." 1876.

12.612

Grosvenor Papers, FEMALE SUFFRAGE: AN ANSWER TO MRS. H. FAWCETT ON THE ELECTORAL DISABILITIES OF WOMEN. 1870.

12.613

Hoskins, James Thorton, A FEW WORDS ON THE WOMAN'S FRANCHISE QUESTION. 1870.

12.614

Howard, J.E., ESSAY ON WOMAN SUFFRAGE. 1870.

12.615

Grey, Maria Georgina, IS THE EXERCISE OF THE SUFFRAGE UNFEMININE? 1870; THE PHYSICAL FORCE TO WOMEN'S SUFFRAGE. 1877.

12.616

ENGLISHWOMAN'S REVIEW: Bodichon, B.L., "Some Probable Consequences of Extending the Franchise to Female Householders," 1 (1866) 26-34. Favors suffrage for female heads of households. Working class-women and women entrepreneurs would probably not contribute much to the public good through their vote, "but not a little indirect good would arise from the increased respect which men of their own class would feel for them" (p. 30); "Authorities and Precedents for Giving the Suffrage to Qualified Women," 1 (1867) 63-75; "Women's Suffrage," 1 (1870) 18-26; "New Objections to Women's Suffrage," 1 (1870) 55-78; "Petition for Extension of Elective Franchise to Women; And For the Women's Disabilities Bill," 1 (1870) 198-210; Fawcett, M.G., "The Electoral Disabilities of Women," 2 (1871) n.p.; "Events of the Quarter: Suffrage," 4 (1873) 32-36; "Public Opinion in the Press on Women's Suffrage," 4 (1873) 29-32; "Suffrage," 4 (1873) 212-231; "Events of the Quarter: The General Election," 5 (1874) 115-117; Ramsey, Miss, "Mildred's Career, a Tale of the Woman's Suffrage Movement," 5 (1874) n.p.; Williams, C., "Union Among Women," 6 (1875) 55-57; "Suffrage," 6 (1875) 79-81; "The Forthcoming Debate on the Women's Disabilities Bill," 7 (1876) n.p.; "Suffrage," 9 (1878) 413-415. Contains information on contemporary suffrage petitions, the behavior of suffrage advocates at election meetings, the election of women School Board members and a Lady Adjutant to the Corps of Commissionaires; "Pegging Away," 9 (1878) 529-537; "The Issue of Two Debates: Suffrage and Married Women's Property," 10 (1879) 97-103; "Three Decades of Progress," 10 (1879) 337-344; "Literature of the Women's

Suffrage Movement in Great Britain," 20 (1889) 529-532.

12.617
Anthony, Charles, THE SOCIAL AND POLITICAL DEPENDENCE OF WOMEN.
1867; 5th ed., 1880.

12.618
FRIENDS QUARTERLY EXAMINER: Bottomly, J.F., *"The Position of Women,"* 4
(1870) 560-571. Responds to feminist claims, arguing that women are equal yet
complementary partners of men; Tanner, S.J., *"Women's Suffrage,"* 42 (1908) 401-
409. Article emphasizes that women should use the vote to improve laws, education,
and working women's conditions.

12.619
WOMAN'S JOURNAL: 1870 to May 1917; vols. 1-48. Publication of the National
American Suffrage Association; Diggs, A.L., *"Mrs. Diggs in England. A Letter to
the Woman's Journal,"* 33 (1903) 2; *"Mrs. Cobden-Sanderson's Address,"* 35 (1907)
205-206.

12.620
WOMEN'S SUFFRAGE JOURNAL: 1870 to 1890; vols. 1-21. Edited by Lydia
Becker; Becker, L., *"The Conservative Party and Women's Suffrage,"* 4 (1873) 2;
"The Future of the Suffrage Movement," 4 (1873) 3-4; Becker, L., *"Progress of the
Movement,"* 4 (1873) 13-14; *"The Liberal Party and Women's Suffrage,"* 4 (1873) 15;
Becker, L., *"Municipal and Parliamentary Elections,"* 4 (1873) 29-30; Becker, L.,
"The Ballot Bill and Women's Suffrage," 4 (1873) 49-50; Becker, L., *"Debate on the
Women's Disabilities Bill,"* 4 (1873) 65-66; Becker, L., *"The County Franchise Bill,"*
4 (1873) 81-82; Becker, L., *"Review of the Session,"* 4 (1873) 117-118; Becker, L.,
"Reconstruction of the Ministry," 4 (1873) 129-131; Becker, L., *"Women's Suffrage
and the General Election,"* 4 (1873) 131-132; Becker, L., *"Women's Suffrage in
Victoria,"* 4 (1873) 141; Becker, L., *"The Bath, Taunton and Hull Elections,"* 4 (1873)
153-155; Becker, L., *"Household Franchise in Counties,"* 4 (1873) 165-166; Becker,
L., *"Review of Progress,"* 5 (1874) 1-2; Becker, L., *"Lord Arthur Russell's Letter,"* 5
(1874) 2; Becker, L., *"Women's Suffrage and the General Election,"* 5 (1874) 17-19;
Becker, L., *"Results of the General Election,"* 5 (1874) 37-38; Becker, L., *"Mr.
Forsyth's Women's Suffrage Bill,"* 5 (1874) 53-54; Becker, L., *"Progress of the
Movement,"* 5 (1874) 54-55; Becker, L., *"Objections Considered,"* 5 (1874) 69-70;
Babb, C.E., *"Political Outcasts,"* 5 (1874) 70-71; Becker, L., *"Approaching Decision
on The Women's Disabilities Bill,"* 5 (1874) 81-82; Becker, L., *"How Men Protect
Women,"* 5 (1874) 82-83; Becker, L., *"Postponement of Debate,"* 5 (1874) 93-94;
Fawcett, M.G., *"Mr. Goldwin Smith on Women's Suffrage,"* 5 (1874) 99-102; Becker,
L., *"The Bill for Next Session,"* 5 (1874) 105-106; *"National Society for Women's
Suffrage Central Committee Meeting,"* 5 (1874) 107-114; Becker, L., *"The Municipal
Franchise Act,"* 5 (1874) 121-122; *"An Undelivered Speech in the Women's Suffrage
Debate,"* 5 (1874) 124; Becker, L., *"Women's Suffrage in Spiritual Affairs,"* 5 (1874)
133-135. Maintains that women should be able to elect temporal leaders since they
already nominate parish clergy. Refers to the Scotch Church Patronage Bill; Becker,
L., *"The Belfast Strike,"* 5 (1874) 134; Becker, L., *"Supplement to the Report on
Petitions,"* 5 (1874) 135; Becker, L., *"Women's Suffrage Versus Mr. Goldwin Smith,"*
5 (1874) 136-137; Becker, L., *"The Electoral Reform Conference,"* 5 (1874) 145-146;
Becker, L., *"Annual Meeting of the Manchester Society,"* 5 (1874) 157-158; Becker,
L., *"Electoral Reform Conference,"* 5 (1874) 158-159; Becker, L., *"Members of
Parliament on Women's Suffrage,"* 6 (1875) 3-4; Becker, L., *"Lord Arthur Russell,
M.P., On Women's Suffrage,"* 6 (1875) 8-9; *"The Right Hon. W.N. Massey, M.P., on
Women's Suffrage,"* 6 (1875) 9; Becker, L., *"Parliamentary Prospects,"* 6 (1875) 13-

14; Becker, L., *"The Approaching Division,"* 6 (1875) 25; *"The Right Hon. E. Horsman on Women's Suffrage,"* 6 (1875) 28; Becker, L., *"Antiquities of Parliament,"* 6 (1875) 38; Becker, L., *"The Movement for Enfranchisement,"* 6 (1875) 38-39; Becker, L., *"Mr. Cowper-Temple's Bill,"* 6 (1875) 39; Becker, L., *"The Approaching Debate,"* 6 (1875) 37-38; Becker, L., *"The Division of 1875,"* 6 (1875) 49-50; Becker, L., *"Articles in the London Papers,"* 6 (1875) 50; Becker, L., *"Review of Debate,"* 6 (1875) 51-52; Becker, L., *"The National Society for Women's Suffrage,"* 6 (1875) 77-79; Becker, L., *"The Meeting in St. George's Hall,"* 6 (1875) 89-91; Becker, L., *"The Debate on the Household Franchise (Counties) Bill,"* 6 (1875) 105-107; Becker, L.E., *"The Anti-Women's Suffrage Committee,"* 6 (1875) 107-108; Becker, L., *"Review of the Session,"* 6 (1875) 117-120; Becker, L., *"The Association for Maintaining the Integrity of the Franchise,"* 6 (1875) 120-122; Becker, L., *"To Him That Hath Shall Be Given,"* 6 (1875) 130; Becker, L., *"There is a Time to Speak,"* 6 (1875) 131-133; Becker, L., *"Mr. Forster and Lord F. Cavendish at Bradford,"* 6 (1875) 141-143; Becker, L., *"Mr. Leatham at Huddersfield,"* 6 (1875) 143; Becker, L., *"Annual General Meeting, Manchester,"* 6 (1875) 153-155; Becker, L., *"Huddersfield Demonstration,"* 6 (1875) 155; Becker, L., *"Man and The Macropod,"* 6 (1875) 157.

12.621
THE DEBATE IN THE HOUSE OF COMMONS ON THE WOMEN'S DISABILITIES BILL, MAY 3. 1871.

12.622
BLACK AND WHITE SLAVES, BEING A REPRINT FROM THE EXAMINER OF OCTOBER 19. 1872.

12.623
Garrett, Rhoda, **THE ELECTORAL DISABILITIES OF WOMEN.** Cheltenham, 1872.

12.624
Haddock, Eliza, **AN ESSAY ON WOMEN'S SUFFRAGE, IS IT DESIRABLE OR OTHERWISE?** 1872.

12.625
Janus (pseud.), **WHY WOMEN CANNOT BE TURNED INTO MEN.** Edinburgh, 1872.

12.626
Robertson, A.J., **WOMEN'S NEED OF REPRESENTATION.** 1872. Lecture in Dublin on February 21st.

12.627
Fawcett, Henry, **DEBATE ON THE WOMEN'S DISABILITIES BILL. HOUSE OF COMMONS,... APRIL 30TH, 1873. SPEECH OF PROFESSOR FAWCETT.** 1873.

12.628
M., E.L., **A FEW WORDS ON WOMEN'S SUFFRAGE.** Dublin, 1873.

12.629
LATEST INTELLIGENCE FROM THE PLANET VENUS. 1874; *rpt. from:* **FRASER'S MAGAZINE:** n.v. (Dec. 1874) n.p.

12.630
Maxse, Frederick Augustus, **OBJECTIONS TO WOMEN'S SUFFRAGE. A SPEECH**

BY ADMIRAL MAXSE, R.N. AT THE ELECTORAL REFORM CONFERENCE.
FREEMASON'S TAVERN, NOV. 19, 1874. 1874; WOMAN'S SUFFRAGE, THE
COUNTERFEIT AND THE TRUE; REASONS FOR OPPOSING BOTH. 1877;
OBJECTIONS TO WOMEN'S SUFFRAGE. 1884.

12.631
Cairnes, John Elliot, WOMEN'S SUFFRAGE: A REPLY [TO J. SMITH]. 1874.

12.632
Shore, Louisa, THE CITIZENSHIP OF WOMEN SOCIALLY CONSIDERED. 1874.

12.633
Burns, Mrs. Dawson [Cecile], A FEW WORDS TO TEMPERANCE WOMEN ON
THE WOMAN'S SUFFRAGE QUESTION. 1876.

12.634
SUFFRAGE FOR WOMEN HOUSEHOLDERS. 1877.

12.635
WOMAN SUFFRAGE. Edinburgh, [1877].

12.636
Gladstone, William Ewart, GLEANINGS OF THE PAST YEARS, 1843-78. New
York, 1878; GLADSTONE ON WOMEN SUFFRAGE. 1892. Women are fit for
legislative duty but not what goes with it, participation; FEMALE SUFFRAGE. A
LETTER TO SAMUEL SMITH. 1892.   —see also: N.S.W.S., TO THE RIGHT
HONOURABLE W.E. GLADSTONE... THE MEMORIAL OF MEMBERS AND
FRIENDS OF THE N.S.W.S. IN CONFERENCE ASSEMBLED AT BIRMINGHAM,
JANUARY 22, 1874, SHEWETH, ETC. [SIGNED C.M. TAYLOR]. 1874;
SPECTATOR: "Mr. Gladstone on Female Suffrage," 68 (1892) 550-551; Winternitz,
M., MR. GLADSTONE AND MADAME CREPZ ON THE EMANCIPATION OF
WOMEN. 1893; Morley, John, LIFE OF WILLIAM EWART GLADSTONE. 1903.

12.637
Webster, Augusta, PARLIAMENTARY FRANCHISE FOR WOMEN RATEPAYERS.
1878.

12.638
Blackburn, Helen, SOME OF THE FACTS OF THE WOMEN'S SUFFRAGE
QUESTION. 1878; COMMENTS ON THE OPPOSITION TO WOMEN'S
SUFFRAGE. 1878; (as editor), BECAUSE. 1888; IN A NUTSHELL. Bristol, 1890;
"Woman Suffrage in England" in THE ENCYCLOPEDIA OF SOCIAL REFORM. ed.
by William Bliss, et al. 1897. Maintains that suffragists are undaunted by their
history of unbroken failure because they are sure that they are winning over public
opinion to their position; WOMEN'S SUFFRAGE IN THE LIGHT OF THE
SECOND READING OF 1867. 1898; WOMEN'S SUFFRAGE: A RECORD OF THE
WOMEN'S SUFFRAGE MOVEMENT IN THE BRITISH ISLES WITH
BIOGRAPHICAL SKETCHES OF MRS. BECKER. 1902. Historical account from
pre-1867 to 1902.   —see also: Fawcett, Millicent Garrett, HELEN BLACKBURN:
MEMOIR AND NOTICES. 1903.

12.639
Potter, George, HOUSEHOLD SUFFRAGE IN COUNTIES. 1878.

12.640
NINETEENTH CENTURY: Arch, J., *"The Labourers and the Vote,"* 3 (1878) 48-52;
Potter, G., *"The Labourers and the Vote (no. 2),"* 3 (1878) 53-70; Gladstone, W.E.,
"Last Words on the County Franchise," 3 (1878) 196-208; Fawcett, M.G., *"Women
and Representative Government,"* 14 (1883) 285-291; Chapman, T.S.R., (Mrs. E.W.),
"The Women's Suffrage," 19 (1886) 561-569; Fawcett, M.G., *"Women's Suffrage: A
Reply,"* 19 (1886) 740-748; Dowager Lady Stanley of Alderly, et al., *"An Appeal
Against Female Suffrage,"* 25 (1889) 781-788; Fawcett, M.G., *"The Appeal Against
Female Suffrage: A Reply. I.,"* 26 (1889) 86-96; Dilke, M., *"The Appeal Against
Female Suffrage: A Reply,"* 26 (1889) 97-103; *"The Appeal Against Female
Suffrage,"* 26 (1889) 104-105; Creighton, L., *"The Appeal Against Female Suffrage:
A Rejoinder,"* 26 (1889) 347-384; Crackanthorpe, B., *"The Revolt of the Daughters,"*
35 (1894) 23-31; Haweis, M.E., *"The Revolt of the Daughters (II). Daughters and
Mothers,"* 35 (1894) 430-436; Cuffe, K., *"A Reply from the Daughters no. 1,"* 35
(1894) 437-442; Russell, A.W.P.S., *"A Reply from the Daughters no. 2,"* 35 (1894)
443-450; Bakewell, R.H., *"New Zealand Under Female Franchise,"* 35 (1894) 268-
275; Chapman, T., *"Women's Suffrage Again!"* 42 (1897) 169-172; Selbourne, M., *"A
Note on Women's Suffrage from the Common Sense Point of View,"* 58 (1905) 306-
307. Cites Queen Victoria as an example that women are as able governors as men
and should therefore have the vote; Massie, E.M., *"A Woman's Plea Against Woman
Suffrage,"* 63 (1908) 381-385; Conway, M., *"Suffragists, Peers and the Crowd,"* 63
(1908) 825-834; Lovat, A.M.F., *"Women and the Suffrage,"* 63 (1908) 64-78; Gore-
Booth, E., *"Women and the Suffrage; A Reply to Lady Lovat and Mrs. Humphrey
Ward,"* 64 (1908) 495-506. "The people who want to restrict women because they
are inferior mentally are really those who believe no such comfortable doctrine, but
are, in simple English, afraid of their competition" (p. 496); Margoliouth, J.P., *"The
Protection of Women: A Reply to Mrs. John Massie,"* 63 (1908) 819-824; Stephen,
C.E., *"The Representation of Women: I. A Conservative Chamber of Women,"* 64
(1908) 1018-1024; Cox, H., *"Possibilities of Compromise,"* 67 (1910) 786-792;
Sellers, E., *"Cassandra on Votes for Women,"* 69 (1911) 487-498; Mallett, C.E.,
"Woman Suffrage and the Liberal Party," 71 (1912) 599-608; Mitra, S.M., *"Voice for
Women—Without Votes,"* 74 (1913) 988-1007.

12.641
Bigg, Louisa, **SHOULD THE PARLIAMENTARY FRANCHISE BE GRANTED TO
WOMEN HOUSEHOLDERS?** 1879.

12.642
Count, William, **ELECTORAL REFORM.** 3rd ed., 1881.

12.643
Higginson, Thomas Wentworth, **COMMON SENSE ABOUT WOMEN.** 1881. ——*see
also:* SPECTATOR: *"Higginson's Common Sense About Women,"* 55 (1882) 1287.

12.644
PROS AND CONS OF WOMAN SUFFRAGE... BY ONE OF THE SEX. Boston,
1882.

12.645
Harberton, Viscount, **OBSERVATIONS ON WOMEN'S SUFFRAGE.** 1882.

12.646
Craigen, Jessie, **LETTER TO THE LADIES OF THE WOMEN'S SUFFRAGE
MOVEMENT.** 1883.

12.647
TWENTY-FIVE REASONS FOR SUPPORTING WOMEN'S SUFFRAGE. 1884.

12.648
Lindsay, Anna, CHRISTIAN WOMEN AS CITIZENS. 1884.

12.649
Miller, Florence Fenwick, WORK OF THE FRANCHISE GUILD. Chicago, 1884;
ON THE PROGRAM OF THE WOMEN'S FRANCHISE LEAGUE. AN ADDRESS
DELIVERED AT THE NATIONAL LIBERAL CLUB, ETC. 1890. —*see also:*
Van Arsdel, Rosemary, "Women's Periodicals and the New Journalism: The Personal
Interview" in PAPERS FOR THE MILLIONS: THE NEW JOURNALISM IN
BRITAIN, 1850S TO 1914. ed. by Joel Wiener. New York, 1988. Through a study
of Florence Fenwick Miller's career in journalism, Van Arsdel shows that by the
1880s, women had become public figures. There is Fenwick Miller herself as an
elected member of the London School Board for Hackney, becoming known for her
controversial opinions. Then there are the female public figures she interviewed for
newspapers and magazines, some of them suffragists.

12.650
Tod, Isabella M.S., WOMEN OF THE NEW FRANCHISE BILL: A LETTER TO
AN ULSTER MEMBER OF PARLIAMENT. Belfast, 1884.

12.651
SATURDAY REVIEW: *"Women's Suffrage,"* 57 (1884) 698-699; *"The Amazonian
Basis,"* 83 (1897) 136-137. Poses the question: With 1,200,000 more women than
men—how many would vote under a suffrage bill?

12.652
Lynch, Mrs. E.M., THE CLAIMS OF WOMEN RATEPAYERS TO THE
PARLIAMENTARY VOTE. 1882.

12.653
Cook, Margaret Mary, WOMEN'S SUFFRAGE. 1885.

12.654
Dilke, [Mrs. Mary Ashton], WOMEN'S SUFFRAGE. introduction by William
Woodall. 1885. Includes appendices of statements on women's suffrage by leading
politicians. Dilke was a prominent labor leader.

12.655
LIST OF PARLIAMENTARY FRIENDS OF WOMEN'S SUFFRAGE. 1886; 1888;
1889.

12.656
Cheetham, Mrs., SPEECH DELIVERED AT A MEETING OF THE SOUTHPORT
WOMEN'S LIBERAL ASSOCIATION NOVEMBER 8, 1886. Bristol, 1886.

12.657
NATIONAL REVIEW: Raikes, H.C., *"Women's Suffrage,"* 4 (1885) 631-641; Smith,
P.V., *"Women's Suffrage,"* 5 (1885) 60-70; Blackburn, H., *"Relation of Women to the
State in Past Time,"* 8 (1886) 392-399. Since women have held positions of power in
the past, they should be entitled to vote. "Many instances of the responsibilities of
women, whether as landed proprietors or as burgesses, testify to their relatively
more influential relations to the State in earlier times of our history" (p. 392);

Smith, G., *"Conservatism and Female Suffrage,"* 10 (1888) 735-752; Fawcett, M.G., *"Women's Suffrage,"* 11 (1888) 44-61; *"Principle Subscribers to the Women's Social and Political Union,"* 63 (1914) 881-884. Listed among the subscribers are Dr. Elizabeth Garrett-Anderson, Christabel Pankhurst, and musician Ethel Smythe.

12.658
WOMEN'S SUFFRAGE CALENDAR: 1886 to 1899; vols. 1-14. Edited by Helen Blackburn.

12.659
Stanton, Elizabeth Cady, Anthony, Susan B., Gage, Matilda Joslyn and Harper, Ida A., **HISTORY OF WOMAN SUFFRAGE.** 6 vols. Rochester, 1887-1922; 1969. See especially: vol. 3 (1876-1887), Chap. 56, "Great Britain" and Chap. 57, "Continental Europe."

12.660
OPINIONS OF CONSERVATIVE LEADERS ON WOMEN'S SUFFRAGE. 1889.

12.661
Hart, Heber L., **WOMEN'S SUFFRAGE AND NATIONAL DANGER: A PLEA FOR THE ASCENDANCY OF MAN.** 1889; 1900; 1909; 1912. Presents the contemporary arguments concerning suffrage, focusing on the opposition.

12.662
Women's Franchise League of Great Britain and Ireland, **REPORT OF PROCEEDINGS AT THE INAUGURAL MEETING.** 1889; **REPORT OF THE EXECUTIVE COMMITTEE.** 1890-[1896]. ——*see also:* Miller, Florence Fenwick, **ON THE PROGRAMME OF THE WOMEN'S FRANCHISE LEAGUE.** 1890.

12.663
National Union of Women's Suffrage Societies, **REPORT OF THE ANNUAL MEETING.** 1889; **PAMPHLETS AND LEAFLETS.** 1909; **WOMEN'S SUFFRAGE: A SURVEY 1908-1912.** [1912]; **LORD HALDANE AND WOMEN'S SUFFRAGE.** [1912]; **THE VITAL CLAIM. AN APPEAL FROM LIBERAL WOMEN TO WOMEN LIBERALS.** [1912]; **THE NEW DEVELOPMENT IN THE POLICY OF THE N.U.W.S.S.** [1912]; **THE LABOUR PARTY AND THE REFORM BILL.** 1912; **THE ACCOUNT OF THE DEPUTATION TO THE PRIME MINISTER.** 1913; **THE POSITION OF THE N.U.W.S.S.** 1913; **A BRIEF REVIEW OF THE WOMEN'S SUFFRAGE MOVEMENT SINCE ITS BEGINNING IN 1832.** 1913; **WOMAN'S SUFFRAGE IN PRACTICE.** 1913; **WHAT IS THE ACTIVE SERVICE LEAGUE?.** 1914; **THE FRIEND OF WOMEN'S SUFFRAGE.** 1914; **UNFULFILLED PLEDGES. OUR CASE AGAINST MR. ASQUITH.** Birmingham, 1914; **THE ALL-BRITISH LIGHTENING CAMPAIGN.** 1914; **ORGANIZATION OF SUFFRAGE WORK.** [1917]. ——*see also:* Hume, Leslie Parker, **THE NATIONAL UNION OF WOMEN'S SUFFRAGE SOCIETIES 1897-1914.** 1982.

12.664
WOMAN'S WORLD: Fawcett, M.G., *"Women's Suffrage,"* 2 (1889) 9-12; Garnett, L.M.J., *"Reasons for Opposing Women's Suffrage,"* 2 (1889) 306-310.

12.665
Pankhurst, Christabel, **THE PARLIAMENTARY VOTE FOR WOMEN.** Manchester, [189?]; **THE MILITANT METHODS OF THE N.W.S.P.U.** [1908]. Cites precedence relating militant methods to enacted reforms; **THE COMMONS DEBATE ON WOMAN SUFFRAGE WITH A REPLY BY CHRISTABEL PANKHURST.** 1908;

"What Woman Suffrage Means" in **THE GIRL'S REALM ANNUAL FOR 1911**. 1911; **WHY WE ARE MILITANT**. 1913; **NO PEACE WITHOUT VICTORY**. 1917; **UNSHACKLED; THE STORY OF HOW WE WON THE VOTE**. ed. by Lord Pethick-Lawrence. 1959. Autobiographical account of Christabel's activities in the suffrage campaign. Includes photographs. ——*see also:* Nevinson, Henry, **MORE CHANGES, MORE CHANGES**. 1925. Comments on Christabel Pankhurst; Mitchell, David, **QUEEN CHRISTABEL**. 1977. Hostile biography; *reviewed in:* **NEW SOCIETY**: Walters, M., *"Camped Up,"* 42 (1977) 588-589. "Mitchell's condescending cleverness spoils what could have been a fascinating book" (p. 589); Sarah, Elizabeth, "Christabel Pankhurst: Reclaiming Her Power (1880-1958)" in **FEMINIST THEORISTS. THREE CENTURIES OF WOMEN'S INTELLECTUAL TRADITIONS**. ed. by Dale Spender. 1983. Criticizes the analyses of socialist feminists concerning Christabel Pankhurst which, according to Sarah, do not emphasize her feminism, devaluing her work for suffrage on the grounds of her upper-class "reactionary" status.

12.666
Allan, J. MacGrigor, **WOMAN SUFFRAGE WRONG IN PRINCIPLE AND PRACTICE**. 1890; 1891.

12.667
Dunkley, Henry, **SHOULD WOMEN HAVE THE VOTE?** Manchester, 1890.

12.668
WOMEN'S PENNY PAPER: Blackburn, H., *"Married Women and the Vote,"* 2 (1890) n.p.

12.669
McIlquham, Harriet, **THE ENFRANCHISEMENT OF WOMEN; AN ANCIENT RIGHT, A MODERN NEED. A PAPER READ... ON THE 11TH DECEMBER 1891**. Bristol, [1891].

12.670
Gay, Susan Elizabeth, **A REPLY TO MR. GLADSTONE'S LETTER ON WOMAN SUFFRAGE, ADDRESSED TO HIM BY A MEMBER OF THE WOMEN'S LIBERAL FEDERATION**. 1892.

12.671
Levy, Joseph Hiam, **THE ENFRANCHISEMENT OF WOMEN**. 1892.

12.672
Women's Emancipation Union, **REPORTS... PRESENTED AT THE... MEETING(S), 1892-1899**. 1892-1899.

12.673
Ellis, Ethelmer (pseud. for Wolstenholme-Elmy, Elizabeth C.), **THE ENFRANCHISEMENT OF WOMEN**. 1892; **THE WOMEN'S EMANCIPATION UNION**. 1899; **WOMEN'S FRANCHISE THE NEED OF THE HOUR**. [ca. 1908]. Author may also be cataloged as Elmy, Elizabeth C. Wolstenholme.

12.674
HUMANITARIAN: 1892 to 1901; vols. 1-9; Fawcett, M.G., *"Politics in the Home,"* 2 (1893) 43-49; Cozens, M., *"The Political Freedom of Women,"* 5 (1896) 285-291; Grove, A., *"Objections to Woman Suffrage Considered,"* 8 (1899) 90-100.

12.675

Fawcett, Millicent Garrett, "The Woman's Suffrage Movement" in **THE WOMAN QUESTION IN EUROPE: A SERIES OF ORIGINAL ESSAYS.** ed. by Theodore Stanton. New York, 1884. Good exposition of Fawcett's conservative suffragist view that women cannot demand the vote as an inalienable right, but only as an expedient measure. "That is to say, on the ground that the good resulting from it would far outweigh any evils that might possibly attend it" (p. 5); **THE WOMEN'S SUFFRAGE QUESTION.** 1893; **WOMAN'S SUFFRAGE: AN ADDRESS DELIVERED AT THE JUNIOR CONSTITUTIONAL CLUB, PICCADILLY ON THURSDAY EVENING, NOVEMBER 11, 1897.** printed for private circulation, 1897; **WOMEN'S SUFFRAGE: A SPEECH DELIVERED TO THE WOMEN'S DEBATING SOCIETY, THE OWENS COLLEGE, MANCHESTER... 1899.** 1899; (and Cooke, W. Radcliffe), **WOMEN'S SUFFRAGE IN PARLIAMENT.** 1899; **EXTRACTS FROM VARIOUS ARTICLES AND SPEECHES BY MRS. HENRY FAWCETT, ON WOMEN'S SUFFRAGE.** [1909]; **WOMEN'S SUFFRAGE: A SHORT HISTORY OF A GREAT MOVEMENT.** 1911; **THE WOMEN'S VICTORY AND AFTER: PERSONAL REMINISCENCES, 1911-1918.** 1920. Discusses how the vote for women was achieved and the difference it made; **WHAT I REMEMBER.** 1924. —*see also:* **FEMALE SUFFRAGE: AN ANSWER TO MRS. H. FAWCETT ON THE ELECTION DISABILITIES OF WOMEN.** 1870; Strachey, Ray, **MILLICENT GARRETT FAWCETT.** 1931; Oakley, Ann, "Millicent Garrett Fawcett: Duty and Determination (1847-1929)" in **FEMINIST THEORISTS. THREE CENTURIES OF WOMEN'S INTELLECTUAL TRADITIONS.** ed. by Dale Spender. 1983. Biographical essay which focuses on Fawcett as a conservative suffrage leader.

12.676

Jones, John Viriam, **THE ENFRANCHISEMENT OF WOMEN: A SPEECH DELIVERED AT A MEETING OF THE CENTRAL NATIONAL SOCIETY FOR WOMEN'S SUFFRAGE ON APRIL 8TH, 1893.** 1893.

12.677

Ostrogorski, Moisei Iakovlevich, **THE RIGHTS OF WOMEN; A COMPARATIVE STUDY IN HISTORY AND LEGISLATION.** trans. ed., 1893; 2nd ed., New York, 1908. Examines constitutional foundations of the suffrage question.

12.678

Women's Liberal Federation, **SUMMARY OF FEDERATION NEWS, NUMBERS 2-76.** 1893-1899.

12.679

Bright, Ursula, "The Origin and Objects of the Women's Franchise League of Great Britain and Ireland" in **THE WORLD'S CONGRESS OF REPRESENTATIVE WOMEN.** ed. by May Wright Sewall. Chicago, 1894.

12.680

Grey, Sir George, **SPEECH AT THE ANNUAL MEETING OF THE CENTRAL COMMITTEE OF THE NATIONAL SOCIETY FOR WOMEN'S SUFFRAGE.** Westminster, 1894.

12.681

Jacobi, Mary Putnam, **"COMMON SENSE" APPLIED TO WOMEN'S SUFFRAGE.** 1894.

12.682

Stopes, Charlotte Carmichael, **BRITISH FREEWOMEN: THEIR HISTORICAL**

PRIVILEGE [OF EXERCISING THE FRANCHISE]. 1894; 1907; **THE CONSTITUTIONAL BASIS OF WOMAN'S SUFFRAGE.** Edinburgh, 1908. Polemical but good example of case statement. *——see also:* Boas, Frederick Samuel, **CHARLOTTE CARMICHAEL STOPES: SOME ASPECTS OF HER LIFE AND WORK.** 1931.

12.683
NEW AGE; A DEMOCRATIC REVIEW OF POLITICS, RELIGION AND LITERATURE: 1894 to 1907; vols. 1-19; 1907 to 1938; vols. 1-62; Gawthorpe, M.E., *"To Any 'Leader Writer,'"* 4 (1908) 204; 205; Taylor, G.R.S., *"Women vs. Prehistoric Man,"* 4 (1909) 495; Tina, B., *"Are Women Anarchists,"* 4 (1909) 398; *"Teachers of Tactics,"* 5 (1909) 459-460; George, W.L., *"Woman's Suffrage——A Lost Cause,"* 5 (1909) 347; Nelson, M., *"Is the Vote Lost?"* 5 (1909) 383; Onslow, Lady, *"Is the Vote Lost?"* 5 (1909) 394; Wells, B.B., *"Suffrage Picketing,"* 5 (1909) 393; *"A Symposium on Women's Suffrage,"* 8 (1911) Supplement.

12.684
SPECTATOR: *"The Average Woman,"* 72 (1894) 819-820; *"Women in the Elections,"* 75 (1895) 109-110.

12.685
WOMEN'S SUFFRAGE NEWS: 1894; vols. 1-6; *superseded by:* **WOMEN'S SUFFRAGE RECORD:** 1903 to 1906.

12.686
Howard, Rosalind Frances (Countess of Carlisle), **APPEAL TO THE WOMEN'S LIBERAL FEDERATION.** 1895.

12.687
Women's National Cooperative Self-Help Society, **[PROGRAMME].** 1895.

12.688
IDLER: Warden, F., et al., *"Should Man Be Woman's God?"* 8 (1895-1896) 187-200.

12.689
Swiney, Rosa Frances Emily (Biggs), **THE PLEA OF DISENFRANCHISED WOMEN.** Cheltenham, 1896.

12.690
Davies, M.L. and Martin, A.L., **WHY WORKING WOMEN NEED THE VOTE.** 1897.

12.691
Robertson, John Mackinnon, **THE VOTE FOR WOMEN.** Bradford, [1897].

12.692
Bright, Ursula, **A REPLY TO "A CRITICISM OF THE TEST QUESTION POLICY."** 1898; **ONE MORE WORD.** 1899.

12.693
Leeds, Hester, **ORIGIN AND GROWTH OF THE UNION OF PRACTICAL SUFFRAGISTS.** 1898.

12.694
Montefiore, Dora B., **WOMEN VITLANDERS.** 1899; (as editor), **THE WOMAN'S**

CALENDAR. 1906. Quotations from various authors.

12.695
Women's Emancipation Union, **REPORTS, 1870-1899.** 1899.

12.696
Hardie, James Keir, **THE LABOUR PARTY AND WOMEN'S SUFFRAGE.** [1900].
Reviews the pattern of women's expectation of suffrage from the date of Lord
Brougham's Act of 1851 and calls for continued agitation; **THE CITIZENSHIP OF
WOMEN: A PLEA FOR WOMEN'S SUFFRAGE.** 1905. Surveys the history of
political reform and how it affected women. Exhorts women to concentrate on
removing sex disqualifications in legislation. —*see also:* Stewart, William, **J.
KEIR HARDIE.** 1921; Morgan, Kenneth Owen, **KEIR HARDIE.** 1967. Brief
biography; Morgan, Kenneth Owen, **KEIR HARDIE. RADICAL AND SOCIALIST.**
1975. Examines "the nature of his influence on the formation and the ideas of the
Labour Movement" (preface).

12.697
Pankhurst, Emmeline, **THE TRIAL OF THE SUFFRAGETTE LEADERS.** [190?].
An account of Mrs. Pankhurst, Christabel Pankhurst and Mrs. Drummond; **THE
IMPORTANCE OF THE VOTE.** 1908; 8th ed., 1913; **SUFFRAGE SPEECHES
FROM THE DOCK: MADE AT THE CONSPIRACY TRIAL, OLD BAILEY, MAY
15-22, 1912.** 1912; **VERBATIM REPORT OF MRS. PANKHURST'S SPEECH,
DELIVERED NOV. 13, 1913, AT PARSON'S THEATRE, HARTFORD CONNECT-
ICUT.** Hartford, 1913; **MY OWN STORY.** 1914; rpt., 1979. Written in collaboration
with an American journalist. Claims that suffrage militancy was inspired by the
violent reaction against women's suffrage. Her crusade for the vote is the organizing
theme of her autobiography; **WHY WE ARE MILITANT.** 1914. —*see also:* West,
Rebecca, "Mrs. Pankhurst" in **THE POST VICTORIANS.** 1933. Biographical essay
illustrated by Pankhurst's political works; Pankhurst, Estelle Sylvia, **THE LIFE OF
EMMELINE PANKHURST: THE SUFFRAGETTE STRUGGLE FOR WOMEN'S
CITIZENSHIP.** 1935; **I KNEW MRS. PANKHURST.** 1945; Kamm, Josephine, **THE
STORY OF EMMELINE PANKHURST.** 1961; **AS THEY SAW HER... EMMELINE
PANKHURST. PORTRAIT OF A WIFE, MOTHER AND SUFFRAGETTE.** 1970;
SIGNS: Marcus, J., *"Transatlantic Sisterhood: Labor and Suffrage Links in the
Letters of Elizabeth Robins and Emmeline Pankhurst [Note],"* 3 (1978) 744-755;
Brendon, Piers, "Mrs. Pankhurst" in **EMINENT EDWARDIANS.** by Piers Brendon.
1979. "Mrs. Emmeline Pankhurst became the most famous... woman of her day by
means of violence" (p. 133).

12.698
Pethick-Lawrence, Frederick William, **THE BYE-ELECTION POLICY OF THE
WOMEN'S SOCIAL AND POLITICAL UNION.** 1908; **WOMEN'S FIGHT FOR THE
VOTE.** 2nd ed., 1911. Comprehensive discussion of why women should have the
vote. Presents arguments against women's suffrage and summarizes the policies of
both the radical and conservative political groups. —*see also:* **CONTEMPORARY
REVIEW:** Hale, T.F., *"F.W. Pethick-Lawrence and the Suffragettes,"* 225 (1974) 83-
89. Celebrates Pethick-Lawrence's role as a major yet frequently unacknowledged
contributor to women's suffrage. Author may be cataloged as Lawrence, Frederick
William Pethick.

12.699
CORNHILL MAGAZINE: Grove, A., *"Women's Suffrage in Times of War,"* 82
(1900) 210-222.

12.700
Union of Practical Suffragists, **THE SPIRIT AND THE LETTER: WOMEN'S SUFFRAGE AND LIBERALISM.** 1901.

12.701
GUNTON'S MAGAZINE: Sedgwick, M.K., *"Some Scientific Aspects of the Woman Suffrage Question,"* 20 (1901) 333-344. "The old notion of 'woman's sphere' narrowed to the round of domestic duties, is obsolete, and a woman may unchallenged do anything right and suited to her capacities. We differ from the suffragists more in methods than in ideals of usefulness, regarding them as radicals who would risk dangerous experiments and endanger the true proportions of life" (p. 333).

12.702
Leppington, Blanche, **SPEECH AT A PUBLIC MEETING IN FAVOUR OF WOMEN'S SUFFRAGE HELD IN CAXTON HALL, WESTMINSTER, NOVEMBER 24, 1902.** 1902.

12.703
Bamford-Slack, Alice Maud Mary, **THE CONSERVATIVE PARTY AND WOMEN SUFFRAGE.** 1903; **LIBERAL REASONS FOR A LIBERAL REFORM. A PLEA FOR EXTENDING THE SUFFRAGE TO WOMEN.** 1909. Author may be cataloged as Slack, Alice Bamford.

12.704
McLaren, Mrs. Eva, **THE HISTORY OF THE WOMEN'S SUFFRAGE MOVEMENT IN THE WOMEN'S LIBERAL FEDERATION.** 1903.

12.705
Gore-Booth, Eva, **WOMEN WORKERS AND PARLIAMENTARY REPRESENTATION.** [1904]; **WOMEN'S WAGES AND THE FRANCHISE AND CERTAIN LEGISLATIVE PROPOSALS.** Manchester, [1906]; "The Women's Suffrage Movement Among Trade Unionists" in **THE CASE FOR WOMEN'S SUFFRAGE.** ed. by Brougham Villiers (pseud.). 1907; **THE TRIBUNAL.** [1916]. Author may be cataloged as Booth, Eva Gore.

12.706
Davies, Emily, **THE WOMEN'S SUFFRAGE MOVEMENT: 1) WHY SHOULD WE CARE FOR IT? 2) HOW CAN WE HELP TO FURTHER IT?** 1905; "Letters to THE TIMES and THE SPECTATOR on Women's Suffrage" and "The Women's Suffrage Movement" in **THOUGHTS ON SOME QUESTIONS RELATING TO WOMEN.** by Emily Davies. Cambridge, 1910. Although Davies believed that women's suffrage would not bring about extensive legislative reform, she supported enfranchisement on the grounds that laws unjust to women would gradually be removed and that women's status would be generally raised with the acquisition of the vote. One of the few educational reformers who supported female suffrage, Davies examines the effect of suffrage on women's economic and educational position. ——*see also:* Stephen, B., **EMILY DAVIES AND GIRTON COLLEGE.** 1927.

12.707
Dicey, Albert Venn, **LECTURES ON THE RELATION BETWEEN LAW AND PUBLIC OPINION IN ENGLAND DURING THE 19TH CENTURY.** 1905; **LETTERS TO A FRIEND ON VOTES FOR WOMEN.** 1909. Woman's first "national" duty is to the home and to give her suffrage would be "exposing an

ancient commonwealth to the risks of a dangerous experiment" (p. 78). ——*see also:* SPECTATOR: *"Professor Dicey's Letters on Woman Suffrage,"* 102 (1909) 979-980; NINETEENTH CENTURY: *"On the Brink of an Abyss,"* 67 (1910) 779-785; Blease, W. Lyon, VOTES FOR WOMEN. AGAINST PREJUDICE: A REPLY TO PROFESSOR DICEY. 1912.

12.708
A LETTER FROM FLORENCE TO M.G. FAWCETT. 1906.

12.709
Lancashire and Cheshire Women's Suffrage Society, Lancashire and Cheshire Women Textile Workers' Committee, Manchester and Salford Women's Trade and Labour Council, JOINT REPORT OF WOMEN'S SUFFRAGE WORK, 1905-1906. [1906].

12.710
Women's Social and Political Union, ANNUAL CONFERENCE REPORTS 1905-1907; ANNUAL REPORT 1907-1914; LEAFLETS. 1908, etc.

12.711
Budgett, Annie P., FACTS BEHIND THE PRESS. 1906. Discusses the biases in newspaper reporting of feminist issues.

12.712
Haslam, Thomas J., THE RIGHT CLAIMS OF WOMEN: AN ADDRESS. Dublin, 1906; WOMEN'S SUFFRAGE FROM A MASCULINE STANDPOINT. Dublin, 1906; SOME LAST WORDS ON WOMEN'S SUFFRAGE. Dublin, 1916.

12.713
Leeds Woman's Suffrage Association, REPORT ON THE CONFERENCE OF THE INTERNATIONAL WOMAN'S SUFFRAGE ALLIANCE HELD AT COPEN-HAGEN, AUGUST 1906. [1906].

12.714
INDEPENDENT: Abbott, E., *"Woman Suffrage Militant: The New Movement in England,"* 61 (1906) 1276-1278. Describes the militant movement as "a phase that bids fair to become triumphant as it has been misrepresented and misunderstood" (p. 1276).

12.715
JUS SUFFRAGII: 1906 to 1916; vols. 1-11. A monthly organ of the International Women's Suffrage Alliance; *superseded by:* INTERNATIONAL WOMEN'S SUFFRAGE NEWS: 1923 to 1930; vols. 11-20.

12.716
Briggs, Annie S., MY PRISON LIFE AND WHY I AM A SUFFRAGETTE. 1907.

12.717
Campbell, R.J., WOMEN'S SUFFRAGE AND THE SOCIAL EVIL. 1907. Claims prostitution is a result of women being excluded from the vote.

12.718
Corelli, Marie (Mary Mackay), WOMAN, OR SUFFRAGE? A QUESTION OF NATIONAL CHOICE. 1907.

12.719
Billington-Grieg, Teresa, **TOWARDS WOMEN'S LIBERTY**. Garden City, 1907; 1910. Illuminates the legal and social problems faced by suffragists and includes a table of legislation concerning enfranchisement; **VERBATIM REPORT OF DEBATE ON DECEMBER 3RD, 1907. SEX EQUALITY (TERESA BILLINGTON-GRIEG) VERSUS ADULT SUFFRAGE (MARGARET G. BONDFIELD)**. 1908; **THE MILITANT SUFFRAGE MOVEMENT: EMANCIPATION IN A HURRY**. Palmer, 1911. Criticizes the militant suffrage movement (after participating in it for five years), but does not condemn it. Exposes the tactics of the W.S.P.U.; **TOWARDS WOMEN'S LIBERTY**. 1913; Garden City, 1917. "The institution of adult suffrage involves two separate principles—the equality of sex and the equality of class" (pp. 79-80); **SUFFRAGIST TACTICS, PAST AND PRESENT**. 1913; *rpt. from:* **FORTNIGHTLY REVIEW**. Author also cataloged as Grieg, Teresa Billington.

12.720
Matthew, Arnold Harris, **WOMAN SUFFRAGE**. 1907.

12.721
Pethick-Lawrence, Emmeline, **THE MEANING OF THE WOMEN'S MOVEMENT**. [1907-1912]. Delineates the objectives of the women's movement with an emphasis on suffrage; **MY PART IN A CHANGING WORLD**. 1938; rpt., 1976. Began her public career as a Sister at the West London Mission. Refused to marry her husband until his political beliefs aligned more closely with her own. After they married, he took her maiden name (Pethick) and made it a part of his own; **THE NEW CRUSADE**. 1907; **THE FAITH THAT IS IN US**. 1909; **A CALL TO WOMEN**. 1911; **IN WOMEN'S SHOES. MRS. PETHICK-LAWRENCE'S SPEECH BEFORE MR. JUSTICE DARLING, AT THE LAW COURTS...** 1913. **SUFFRAGE SPEECHES FROM THE DOCK**. 1913; Author may be cataloged as Lawrence, Emmeline Pethick.

12.722
Robins, Elizabeth, **THE CONVERT**. 1907; rpt., Old Westbury, 1980. A novel depicting women of all classes involved in the suffrage movement. Contains a biography of Robins in the 1980 edition; **WHY?** 1910; **ANCILLA'S SHARE: AN INDICTMENT OF SEX ANTAGONISM**. 1924.

12.723
Villiers, Brougham, (pseud. for Shaw, Frederick John), ed., **THE CASE FOR WOMEN'S SUFFRAGE**. 1907.

12.724
Zangwill, Israel, **TALKED OUT; BEING A VERBATIM REPORT OF THE SPEECH AT EXETER HALL MARCH 8, 1907**. 1907; **ONE AND ONE ARE TWO**. 1907.

12.725
Women's Freedom League, **VERBATIM REPORT OF THE DEBATE ON DEC. 3, 1907: SEX EQUALITY (TERESA BILLINGTON-GRIEG) VERSUS ADULT SUFFRAGE (MARGARET G. BONDFIELD)**. Manchester, 1908; **WHAT TO DO AND HOW TO DO IT**. 1907-1910; **REPORT FOR THE YEAR 1908, AND OF THE FOURTH ANNUAL CONFERENCE**. 1909. A collection of pamphlets, press cuttings, etc.; **MISCELLANEOUS PAMPHLETS AND LEAFLETS [ON THE SUFFRAGE QUESTION]**. 1909. British Museum Library has a good collection; **WOMEN'S FREEDOM LEAGUE OCCASIONAL PAPERS**. ed. by Teresa Billington-Grieg and Maude Fitzherbert. 1909; **THE COMMONS ON THE WOMEN'S BILL...**

[1910 or 1912]. ——*see also:* Newsome, Stella, **WOMEN'S FREEDOM LEAGUE 1907-1957**. 1958; 1960. The Women's Freedom League was the only society that organized public protests in public courts for women being tried by "man-made" laws.

12.726

VOTES FOR WOMEN: Oct. 1907 to Sept. 1918; 9 vols. Edited by Frederick and Emmeline Pethick-Lawrence; Pankhurst, C., *"Objections to Women Suffrage. A Reply to the Principal Arguments of Opponents in the House of Commons on February 28,"* 1 (1907) n.p. Response to thirteen major fallacies about enfranchisement and suffragettes; Pethick-Lawrence, E., *"What the Vote Means,"* 1 (1907) n.p. Addresses mothers and housewives unsupportive of the suffrage movement who have "unspoken ideals" that would be facilitated by the vote; Churchill, W.L.S., *"Mr. Churchill on Votes For Women,"* 2 (1908) 153; 154; Drummond, F., *"The Story of My Third Imprisonment,"* 2 (1908) 108-109; Forbes-Robertson, J., *"A Declaration of Faith. Verbatim Report of a Speech... February 1, 1909,"* 3 (1909) 326-327; Spong, F., *"My Mutiny and Hunger Strike,"* 3 (1909) 1055; *"Stories of the Hunger Strike,"* 3 (1909) 1080-1081.

12.727

WOMEN'S FRANCHISE: 1906 to 1911; vols. 1-3; 1907-1911. Published by the Woman Citizen Publishing Society.

12.728

Simon, Emily Maud, **WOMEN'S SUFFRAGE; SOME SOCIOLOGICAL REASONS FOR OPPOSING THE MOVEMENT.** Birmingham, 1907; **POSITIVE PRINCIPLES FOR ANTI-SUFFRAGISTS.** Birmingham, 1908; **SHALL THE FRANCHISE BE GIVEN TO WOMEN AT TWENTY-ONE.** 1926.

12.729

NATION: *"The Enfranchisement of Women,"* 1 (1907) 63-64; *"The Enfranchisement of Women,"* 1 (1907) 114, 152, 188. Letters to the Editor; *"A Compromise on the Suffrage,"* 7 (1910) 303-304; *"The Evasion of Woman Suffrage,"* 10 (1910) 647-648; *"Parliament and the Women's Bill,"* 9 (1911) 190-191; *"The Government's Three-Fold Task,"* 10 (1911) 538-539; *"Manhood or Adult Suffrage,"* 10 (1911) 225-226; *"Towards Adult Suffrage,"* 10 (1911) 367-369; *"The Prospect of Woman Suffrage,"* 10 (1912) 875-876; *"The Reform Bill and Woman Suffrage,"* 11 (1912) 424-425; *"The Chances for Woman Suffrage,"* 12 (1913) 626-627; *"A Proposal for Woman Suffrage,"* 12 (1913) 876-887; *"Social Order and the Suffrage,"* 13 (1913) 218-219; *"Mr. Asquith and Woman Suffrage,"* 13 (1913) 738-739.

12.730

Aberconway, Laura Elizabeth, **"BETTER AND HAPPIER" AN ANSWER FROM THE LADIES' GALLERY TO THE SPEECHES IN OPPOSITION TO THE WOMEN'S SUFFRAGE BILL, FEBRUARY 28, 1908.** 1908; **THE PRIME MINISTER AND WOMEN'S SUFFRAGE: A CRITICISM OF MRS. ASQUITH'S SPEECH IN THE DEBATE OF MAY 6TH, 1913 ON MR. DICKINSON'S BILL TO CONFER THE PARLIAMENTARY FRANCHISE UPON WOMEN.** 1913.

12.731

Bax, Ernest Belfort, **THE LEGAL SUBJECTION OF MEN: REPLY TO THE SUFFRAGETTES.** 1908; **THE FRAUD OF FEMINISM.** 1913. Anti-suffrage tract.

12.732

Brown, Hubert Morgan, **THE SUFFRAGETTES AND THE GOVERNMENT. (A**

LETTER TO MRS. HERBERT GLADSTONE PROTESTING AGAINST THE TREATMENT IN PRISON OF MRS. PANKHURST AND OTHERS). 1908.

12.733
Campbell, Reginald John, WOMEN'S SUFFRAGE AND THE SOCIAL EVIL: SPEECH DELIVERED ON DECEMBER 17, 1907... UNDER THE AUSPICES OF THE MEN'S LEAGUE FOR WOMEN'S SUFFRAGE. [1908].

12.734
Chomeley, Robert F., THE WOMEN'S ANTI-SUFFRAGE MOVEMENT. 1908.

12.735
Despard, Charlotte, WOMEN'S FRANCHISE AND INDUSTRY. 1908; 1913; WOMAN IN THE NATION. 1913. ——*see also:* WOMAN CITIZEN: Ford, D.M., *"Charlotte Despard, Pioneer,"* 8 (1923) 11; 27. Despard was founder and president of the Women's Freedom League. She retained office for ten years; Linklater, Andro, AN UNHUSBANDED LIFE. CHARLOTTE DESPARD. SUFFRAGETTE, SOCIALIST AND SINN FEINER. 1980.

12.736
Fox, A., A LOP-SIDED KINGDOM: A DIALOGUE. 1908.

12.737
Harrison, Ethbel B., THE FREEDOM OF WOMEN: AN ARRANGEMENT AGAINST THE PROPOSED EXTENSION OF THE SUFFRAGE TO WOMEN. 1908.

12.738
Harrison, Jane Ellen, HOMO SUM: BEING A LETTER TO AN ANTI-SUFFRAGIST FROM AN ANTHROPOLOGIST. 2nd ed., [1908-1910].

12.739
Lloyd-George, David, WOMEN'S SUFFRAGE. 1908. Supportive of female enfranchisement; LLOYD GEORGE ON WOMEN'S SUFFRAGE AT THE ALBERT HALL. 1909.

12.740
Simkins, Maud Ellen, MIXED HERBS: A WORKING WOMAN'S REMONSTRANCE AGAINST THE SUFFRAGE AGITATION. 1908.

12.741
Women's National Anti-Suffrage League, (WNASL), IS THE PARLIAMENTARY SUFFRAGE THE BEST WAY? [1908]; MARRIED WOMEN AND THE FACTORY LAW. [1908]; THE FRANCHISE FOR WOMEN OF PROPERTY. [1908]; TO THE WOMEN OF GREAT BRITAIN. [1908]; WHAT WOMAN SUFFRAGE MEANS. [1908]; WHY THE WOMEN'S ENFRANCHISEMENT... 1908, WOULD BE UNFAIR TO WOMEN IF IT BECAME LAW. [1908]; WOMEN'S SUFFRAGE AND THE NATIONAL WELFARE. [1908]; WOMEN'S SUFFRAGE AND WOMEN'S WAGES. [1908]; PLEASE, ALL WOMEN, READ AND CONSIDER THIS: VOTES FOR WOMEN? [1909]; WHY WOMEN SHOULD NOT VOTE. [1912]; WOMEN'S SUFFRAGE AND AFTER. [1912]; WOMAN'S POSITION UNDER LAWS MADE BY MAN. [1912].

12.742
ANTI-SUFFRAGE REVIEW: 1908 to 1918; nos. 1-112. Published by the National

League for Opposing Women's Suffrage.

12.743
ATLANTIC MONTHLY: Abbott, E., *"The English Working-Woman and the Franchise,"* 102 (1908) 343-346. "A neglected feature of England's spectacular suffrage movement... is the campaign conducted by the working women of the northern textiles districts" (p. 343).

12.744
NEW AGE: Bax, E.B., *"Feminism and Female Suffrage,"* 3 (1908) 88-89; 129; 130; Pethick-Lawrence, E., *"The Symposium on Woman Suffrage: A Reply,"* 8 (1911) 344; Pethick-Lawrence, E., *"Motherhood At Bay,"* n.v. (1913) 90. Billington-Grieg, T., *"Emancipation in a Hurry,"* 8 (1914) 246-248; 270-271; 292-294.

12.745
Bell, Maurice F. (Vicar of St. Marks), **THE CHURCH AND WOMEN'S SUFFRAGE. A SERMON BEFORE THE INAUGURAL MEETING OF THE CHURCH LEAGUE FOR WOMEN'S SUFFRAGE.** 1909.

12.746
Conservative and Unionist Women's Franchise Association, **A REPLY TO THE ANTI-SUFFRAGE MANIFESTO BY "AN OLD-FASHIONED CONSERVATIVE."** [1909].

12.747
Lytton, Constance Georgina, **"NO VOTES FOR WOMEN"; A REPLY TO SOME RECENT ANTI-SUFFRAGISTS.** 1909; (and Wharton, Jane), **PRISONS AND PRISONERS: SOME PERSONAL EXPERIENCES.** 1914; 1976; **LETTERS OF CONSTANCE LYTTON.** ed. by Betty Balfour. 1925. Lytton was a public speaker and agitator for suffrage who was imprisoned four times. Her public career ended when she suffered a stroke in 1912. As an invalid she wrote a book exposing what she saw as the inhumanity of the prison system, drawn from her personal experiences.

12.748
Lytton, Victor Alexander George Robert Bulwer (Earl of Lytton), **THE EARL OF LYTTON ON VOTES FOR WOMEN. A SPEECH DELIVERED AT ST. JAMES'S THEATRE, JUNE 15, 1909.** 1909; **THE HOUSE OF LORDS AND WOMEN'S SUFFRAGE. SPEECH... IN THE DEBATE IN THE HOUSE OF LORDS. MAY 6, 1914.** 1914.

12.749
Hamilton, Cicely, **HOW THE VOTE WAS WON.** 1909; **LIFE ERRANT.** 1935. Hamilton was an actress and playwright who worked for suffrage. Her autobiography provides interesting observations on the "militant" and "constitutional" wings of the movement. From childhood she showed a strong aversion to what she perceived as the Victorian ideal of motherhood. "My personal revolt was feminist rather than suffragist; what I rebelled at chiefly was the dependence implied in the idea of a 'destined' marriage, 'destined' motherhood" (p. 2).

12.750
Healy, Timothy Michael, **VOTES FOR WOMEN.** 1909. Speech in defense of members of Women's Freedom League at Bow Street Police Court August 19, 1909.

12.751
Peterson, H. Frances, **THE BELIEF IN INMATE RIGHTS**. [1909].

12.752
Solomon, Daisy Dorothea, **MY PRISON EXPERIENCES**. 1909.

12.753
Zimmern, Alice, **WOMEN'S SUFFRAGE IN MANY LANDS**. 1909; **DEMAND AND ACHIEVEMENT. THE INTERNATIONAL WOMEN'S SUFFRAGE MOVEMENT**. 1912.

12.754
TIMES: Dicey, A.V., (March 23, 1909) n.p. Letter to the editor cautioning that to grant suffrage to the female majority would "confide to that body" the government of England and the destiny of the Empire.

12.755
WOMAN'S LEADER AND THE COMMON CAUSE: 1909 to 1933; vols. 1-25. Published by the National Union of Women's Suffrage Societies.

12.756
CONSERVATIVE AND UNIONIST WOMEN'S FRANCHISE REVIEW: 1909 to 1916; vols. 1-[27]. Organ of the Conservative and Unionist Women's Franchise Association [Conservative Women's Reform Association]; *superseded by:* **MONTHLY NEWS**: 1914 to 1918; *superseded by:* **MONTHLY NEWS OF THE CONSERVATIVE WOMEN'S REFORM ASSOCIATION**: 1919 to 1924; vols. 1-etc.

12.757
ENGLISHWOMAN: Feb. 1909 to Jan. 1921; vols. 1-49. A Journal for the Enfranchisement of Women. "THE ENGLISHWOMAN is intended to reach the cultured public, and bring before it, in a convincing and moderated form, the case for the enfranchisement of women" (vol. 1, 1909, p. 1). Signed by the editorial committee: Frances Balfour, J.M. Strachey, Cicely Hamilton, Mary Lowndes, and Elisina Grant Richards; Fawcett, M.G., *"Men are Men and Women are Women,"* 1 (1909) 17-30. Addresses criticisms of women's physical force agitation; Shaw, G.B., *"The Unmentionable Case for Women's Suffrage,"* 1 (1909) 112-121; Showden, P., *"The Present Position of Woman Suffrage,"* 20 (1913) 241-248; Wilson, P.W., *"Women's Suffrage and Party Politics,"* 21 (1914) 1-10; Mitchell, K.M., *"Women's Suffrage and the New Liberalism,"* 22 (1914) 241-248.

12.758
MEN'S LEAGUE FOR WOMEN'S SUFFRAGE MONTHLY PAPER: 1909 to 1914. Organ of the Men's League for Women's Suffrage.

12.759
VOTE: 1909 to 1931; vols. 1-34. Organ of the Women's Freedom League; H., M., *"What We Think,"* 1 (1909) 1. Women's suffrage is a "subject of great... national importance... bound to increase in urgency until it is settled" (p. 1).

12.760
Taylor, Robert S., **WOMAN'S SUFFRAGE. AN ARGUMENT AGAINST IT**. [191?].

12.761
Brailsford, Henry Noel, **THE "CONCILIATION" BILL, AN EXPLANATION AND DEFENCE**. [1910]; **WOMEN AND THE REFORM BILL**. 1911; 1912.

12.762
Carter, Huntley, ed., **WOMEN'S SUFFRAGE AND MILITANCY**. 1910-1911.
Responds to an inquiry among "distinguishable persons" on woman's suffrage.

12.763
Church League for Women's Suffrage, **FIRST ANNUAL REPORT TO DECEMBER 31ST 1910**. [1910]. Contains suggestions for helping the League, such as praying for women's suffrage, getting clerical and parochial support, and responding in the press to hostile critics; **LEAFLETS**. [1910-1919]; **MONTHLY REPORTS. MAY-NOVEMBER 1912**. [1912]; **LEAFLET NO. 2**. [1913]; **REPORTS. 1910-1914**. [1914]. **CONSTITUTION. REVISED JANUARY 24, 1914**. 1914.

12.764
England House of Commons, **THE MAN'S CASE FOR GIVING VOTES TO WOMEN. EDITED FROM THE SPEECHES DELIVERED IN THE HOUSE OF COMMONS ON THE SECOND READING OF THE PARLIAMENTARY FRANCHISE (WOMEN) BILL**. 1910.

12.765
Masefield, John, **MY FAITH IN WOMAN SUFFRAGE**. [1910].

12.766
Men's Political Union for Women's Enfranchisement, **ANNUAL REPORT. 1910-1911**. [1910-1911].

12.767
New Constitutional Society for Women's Suffrage, **ANNUAL REPORTS. 1910-1912**. [1910-1912]; **[LEAFLETS]**. [1913].

12.768
North-Western Federation, **ANNUAL REPORT. 1910-1911**. [1910-1911].

12.769
Roberts, Katherine, **PAGES FROM THE DIARY OF A MILITANT SUFFRAGETTE**. Garden City, 1910. First-person account of a woman's involvement in the W.S.P.U., her reactions to prison and public opinion.

12.770
Taylor, I.E. Stillwell, **THE SUFFRAGE MOVEMENT FROM ITS EVOLUTIONARY ASPECT**. 1910.

12.771
Conservative and Unionist Women's Franchise Association, **LEAFLETS**. [1910-1915].

12.772
Sennet, Mrs. Arncliffe, **WOMEN'S SUFFRAGE AND PARLIAMENTARY MORALS**. 1910; **MAKE WAY FOR THE PRIME MINISTER**. 1912.

12.773
COSMOPOLITAN MAGAZINE: Black, W., *"The Case of Mrs. John Smith of London: A Simple Story of the Suffrage Question in England,"* 49 (1910) 381-390.

12.774
FORUM: Henderson, A., *"Votes for Women in England,"* 44 (1910) 569-583. Surveys the English suffragist movement and especially the issue of the Conciliation Bill that was intended to unite "all the varying political sects in support of Woman Suffrage and had successfully met the objections raised to former bills" (p. 582). Defeat of that measure was considered "treachery" by its advocates, among "all classes and both sexes." Article forecasts another wave of militancy.

12.775
LITERARY DIGEST: *"Setback to British Suffragettes,"* 41 (1910) 229-230. "The debate on the [Woman's Franchise] bill shows that the most powerful arguments put forth on either side were not those in favor of, but those in opposition to, the measure" (p. 229). Popular English newspapers are quoted; *"Confessions of a Suffragette,"* 5 (1912) 229-230.

12.776
THE TREATMENT OF THE WOMEN'S DEPUTATIONS BY THE METROPOLI-TAN POLICE. 1911. On the treatment of suffragettes by law-enforcing agents.

12.777
WOMEN MUNICIPAL ELECTORS AND THE PARLIAMENTARY VOTE. [1911].

12.778
WOMEN'S CLAIM TO VOTE AND THE RELATION OF THE SEXES. 1911.

12.779
Bondfield, Margaret, **THE SHOP WORKER AND THE VOTE.** 1911; **A LIFE'S WORK.** 1949. ——*see also:* Hamilton, M.A., **MARGARET BONDFIELD.** 1924; Tracey, Herbert, "Miss Margaret Bondfield: The First Woman in the Ministry" in **THE BOOK OF THE LABOUR PARTY, ITS HISTORY, GROWTH, POLICY AND LEADERS.** ed. by Herbert Tracey. 1925; Clynes, J.R., "The Rt. Hon. Margaret Bondfield, C.H." in **THE BRITISH LABOUR PARTY.** ed. by Herbert Tracey. 1948; **DICTIONARY OF LABOUR BIOGRAPHY:** Miliband, M., *"Bondfield, Margaret Grace (1873-1953) Trade Unionist, Feminist and First Woman Cabinet Minister,"* 2 (1974) 39-45.

12.780
Catholic Women's Suffrage Society (afterwards St. Joan's Social and Political Alliance), **MINUTE BOOKS.** July 14, 1911 to March 4, 1952; **FIRST [-FOURTH 33RD., ETC.] ANNUAL REPORT 1912, ETC.** 1912. The sixth to thirty-second reports were published in the March issues of **CATHOLIC SUFFRAGIST,** afterwards **CATHOLIC CITIZEN:** 1917 to 1943. First annual report discusses formation and early activities of the society.

12.781
Schreiner, Olive, **WOMAN AND LABOUR.** 1911. Schreiner observed an increasing removal of women of her time from the meaningful type of labor that women performed in earlier societies, leading to the feminine consciousness of being superfluous to the needs of society. She refers to "the disco-ordination in woman's present position." ——*see also:* First, Ruth and Scott, Ann, **OLIVE SCHREINER.** 1980. WOMAN AND LABOUR is discussed at length in Chap. 4.

12.782
De Alberti, Leonora, **WOMEN'S SUFFRAGE AND PIOUS OPPONENTS.** 1911. Written by a Catholic suffragist and sponsored by the Catholic Women's

Association, Oxford.

12.783
East Midland Association, **ANNUAL REPORTS.** 1911-1913.

12.784
Fabian Women's Group, **THREE YEARS' WORK, 1908-1911.** 1911; **TO ADULT SUFFRAGISTS. THE PRESENT SUFFRAGE POSITION, ITS ADVANTAGES AND DANGERS.** 1911. "The one burning injustice in our present franchise laws which calls for immediate redress is the degradation inflicted on women by the assumption that they are incapable, merely by reason of their sex, of exercising the elementary rights and duties of citizenship" (n.p.).

12.785
International Woman Suffrage Alliance, **CONGRESS REPORT OF THE SIXTH CONGRESS. STOCKHOLM, SWEDEN... 1911.** 1911; **WOMAN SUFFRAGE IN PRACTICE.** 1913.

12.786
Liddle, Gordon, **THE PRISONER: A SKETCH.** Letchworth, 1911. On force feeding and humiliation of suffragettes in prison.

12.787
Nevinson, Henry W., **WOMEN'S VOTE AND MAN.** 1911.

12.788
North and East Ridings Federation, **ANNUAL REPORT. 1911-1912.** [1911-1912].

12.789
Pankhurst, Estelle Sylvia, **THE SUFFRAGETTE: THE HISTORY OF THE WOMEN'S MILITANT SUFFRAGE MOVEMENT, 1905-1910.** New York, 1911; 1970; **SYLVIA THE SUFFRAGETTE: THE LAST OF THE WOMEN'S MILITANT SUFFRAGIST MOVEMENT, 1905-1910.** 1911; **THE SUFFRAGETTE MOVEMENT: AN INTIMATE ACCOUNT OF PERSONS AND IDEALS.** 1931; 1977. Personal and factual account; "Sylvia Pankhurst" in **MYSELF WHEN YOUNG BY FAMOUS WOMEN OF TODAY.** ed. by Margot Asquith. 1938. *——see also:* Courtney, Janet Elizabeth, "Suffragists and Suffragettes" in **THE WOMEN OF MY TIME.** by Janet Elizabeth Courtney. 1934; Pankhurst, Richard K.P., **SYLVIA PANKHURST. ARTIST AND CRUSADER. AN INTIMATE PORTRAIT.** 1979; Rover, Constance, "The Pankhursts, Purity and the Sex War" in **LOVE, MORALS AND THE FEMINISTS.** by Constance Rover. 1970; Romero, Patricia W., **E. SYLVIA PANKHURST: PORTRAIT OF A RADICAL.** New Haven, 1987.

12.790
Selborne, Earl of, **WHY I BELIEVE IN WOMAN SUFFRAGE.** 1911; **EARL OF SELBORNE'S ADDRESS AT THE HOTEL CECIL MARCH 9, 1911.** [1911].

12.791
Snowden, Philip (Viscount Snowden of Ickonshaw), **IN DEFENSE OF THE CONCILIATION BILL.** 1911; **THE DOMINANT ISSUE.** 1913; **THE PRESENT POSITION OF WOMAN SUFFRAGE;** *rpt. from:* **ENGLISHWOMAN:** 20 (1913) 241-248; **AN AUTOBIOGRAPHY.** 2 vols. 1934.

12.792
Surrey, Sussex and Hants Federation, **ANNUAL REPORTS 1911-1913.** [1911-1913].

12.793
West Midland Federation, **ANNUAL REPORTS. 1911-1913.** [1911-1913].

12.794
FRIEND: Fry, M., *"Friends and Women's Suffrage,"* 52 (1911) 111-112. Dissociates the Friends' Organization from the suffragettes; *"Friends' Council for Women's Suffrage,"* 51 (1911) 80. Record of speeches given at the meeting; *"Friends' Council for Women's Suffrage,"* 51 (1911) 175-176. Speeches concerning the need to alleviate women's working and domestic conditions through suffrage; Neale, J., *"Friends and Women's Suffrage,"* 51 (1911) 311. Views women's suffrage as an intermediate stage of political evolution which will eventually result in political emancipation; Thompson, J., *"Friends' Council for Women's Suffrage,"* 51 (1911) 312; 51 (1911) 326; *"Friends' Council for Women's Suffrage,"* 51 (1911) 379. Arguments in favor of women's suffrage.

12.795
FREEWOMAN: A WEEKLY HUMANIST REVIEW: 1911 to 1912; vols. 1-2; Bickley, F., *"The Present State Of the Suffrage Question, Male Reflections,"* 2 (1912) 409; 410; Sinclair, U.B., *"Impressions of English Suffragism,"* 2 (1912) 125; 126.

12.796
LIFE AND LABOUR: Wayl, B.P., *"Winning the Vote in England,"* 11 (1911) 206-211.

12.797
Carter, Huntley, ed., **WOMEN'S SUFFRAGE AND MILITANCY.** 1912.

12.798
Chapman, Hugh B., **AN APPEAL TO CHURCHMEN.** [1912].

12.799
Christich, Elizabeth, **A WORD ON WOMAN SUFFRAGE.** 1912; **CATHOLIC WOMEN AND THE VOTE.** 1914.

12.800
Curzon, George Nathaniel, **DEPUTATION TO MR. ASQUITH ON WOMAN'S SUFFRAGE.** [1912].

12.801
Drysdale, Charles Vickery, **WHY MEN SHOULD WORK FOR WOMEN'S SUFFRAGE. THE WAGES AND EMPLOYMENT QUESTION.** Birmingham, 1912.

12.802
Graduates' Union for Women's Suffrage, **LIST OF MEMBERS: MARCH 1912.** [1912].

12.803
Grant, John Cameron, **MAN, WOMAN AND THE MACHINE. AN ADDRESS GIVEN BEFORE THE NEW CONSTITUTIONAL SOCIETY FOR WOMEN'S SUFFRAGE.** 1912; **WORKING WOMEN AND THE VOTE: FROM A MAN'S POINT OF VIEW.** 1912.

12.804
Guest, Leslie Haden, **VOTES FOR WOMEN AND THE PUBLIC HEALTH.** 1912.

12.805
Housman, Lawrence, **THE SEX WAR AND WOMEN'S SUFFRAGE.** 1912; **THE UNEXPECTED YEARS.** 1937.

12.806
Kensington, Bishop of, **THE MORAL ISSUES INVOLVED IN THE WOMEN'S MOVEMENT.** [1912]. Urges that women stay out of politics after they obtain the vote since they can get no benefit for themselves.

12.807
Mason, Bertha, **THE STORY OF THE WOMEN'S SUFFRAGE MOVEMENT.** 1912.

12.808
Mitchell, John Malcolm, **COLONIAL STATESMEN AND VOTES FOR WOMEN. LORD CURZON ANSWERED.** [1912].

12.809
Men's League for Women's Suffrage, **REPORT OF SPEECHES DELIVERED AT A GREAT DEMONSTRATION HELD IN QUEEN'S HALL, ON TUESDAY DECEMBER 17, 1907.** [1906]; **THE MEN'S LEAGUE HANDBOOK ON WOMEN'S SUFFRAGE.** 1912. Compilation of essays by various political figures (several of them women) that delineates the reasons for female enfranchisement and explains the controversies surrounding the issue. Includes an appendix of various bills and resolutions.

12.810
National League for Opposing Women's Suffrage, **THE ANTI-SUFFRAGE HANDBOOK.** 1912; **THE RECENT HISTORY OF WOMAN SUFFRAGE.** 1917.

12.811
Nevinson, Margaret W., **FIVE YEARS STRUGGLE FOR FREEDOM: A HISTORY OF THE SUFFRAGE MOVEMENT FROM 1908 TO 1912.** 1912; **ANCIENT SUFFRAGETTES.** 1913.

12.812
North-Eastern Federation of Women's Suffrage Societies, **ANNUAL REPORT.** 1912.

12.813
Oliver, H.E., **CHRISTIAN CITIZENSHIP.** [1912]; **THE PLACE OF WOMEN IN THE COUNCILS OF THE CHURCH.** 1913.

12.814
Owen, Harold, **WOMAN ADRIFT. THE MENACE OF SUFFRAGISM.** New York [1912]; *also titled:* **WOMAN ADRIFT. A STATEMENT OF THE CASE AGAINST SUFFRAGISM.**

12.815
Porritt, Annie G., **THE MILITANT SUFFRAGE MOVEMENT IN ENGLAND.** 1912. Justification for the WSPU's most violent demonstration against Asquith's government.

12.816

Preelooker, Jeakoff, **MORE LIGHT ON THE WOMAN QUESTION: A RECORD OF THE FIRST CONGRESS OF THE MEN'S INTERNATIONAL ALLIANCE FOR WOMEN'S SUFFRAGE HELD IN LONDON.** 1912.

12.817

Richmond, Kenneth, **WHAT'S WRONG WITH THE WORLD—A SUFFRAGIST'S CRITICISM.** 1912.

12.818

Roberts, Ursula, **THE CAUSE OF PURITY AND WOMEN'S SUFFRAGE.** 1912. The vote should be used to curb prostitution by establishing institutions and raising wages.

12.819

Royden, Agnes Maude, **HOW WOMEN USE THE VOTE.** 1912; **PHYSICAL FORCE AND DEMOCRACY.** 1912; **PLAIN ANSWERS TO TANGLED STATEMENTS.** 1912; **"VOTES AND WAGES." HOW WOMEN'S SUFFRAGE WILL IMPROVE THE ECONOMIC POSITION OF WOMEN.** 1912; **EXTRACTS FROM THE MAY MISSION. SPEECHES DELIVERED IN LONDON.** [1913]; **THE TRUE END OF GOVERNMENT, AN APPEAL TO THE UNITED KINGDOM OF GREAT BRITAIN AND IRELAND.** 1913; **SPEECH OF MISS ROYDEN AT THE ALBERT HALL.** 1914; "The Woman's Suffrage Movement 1895-1918" in **WOMEN IN COUNCIL: THE JUBILEE BOOK OF THE NATIONAL COUNCIL OF WOMEN OF GREAT BRITAIN.** ed. by H. Pearl Adams. 1945. Historical outline of the suffrage campaign.

12.820

Scott, Alexander MacCallum, **EQUAL PAY FOR EQUAL WORK, A WOMAN SUFFRAGE FALLACY.** 1912; **THE PHYSICAL FORCE ARGUMENT AGAINST WOMAN SUFFRAGE.** 1912.

12.821

Simms, Albert Ernest Nicholas, **ST. PAUL AND THE WOMAN MOVEMENT.** [1912]. "Those whose aim is to stop rather than understand the controversy [over women's suffrage] will no doubt get from the apostle what they want.... The real grounds upon which they base their opposition... lies in their own temperament" (p. 1).

12.822

Simon, John, **SPEECH BY SIR JOHN SIMON AT THE NATIONAL DELEGATES MEETING OF WOMEN'S LIBERAL FEDERATION.** 1912.

12.823

Spencer, Frederick A.M., **THE MORAL AND RELIGIOUS GROUND FOR WOMEN'S ENFRANCHISEMENT.** [1912]. "The demand for women's suffrage... arises out of the profound moral needs and wants. The Church should... encourage and ennoble these; and also bring them into relation with religion" (p. 1).

12.824

West Lancashire, West Cheshire, and North Wales Federation, **ANNUAL REPORTS. 1912-1913.** [1912-1913].

12.825

West Riding Federation, **ANNUAL REPORTS. 1912-1913.** [1912-1913].

12.826
CHURCH LEAGUE FOR WOMEN'S SUFFRAGE MONTHLY PAPER: 1912 to 1917; vols. 1-6; *superseded by:* **CHURCH MILITANT:** 1918 to 1928; vols. 7-etc. Published by the Church League For Women's Suffrage.

12.827
ENGLISH REVIEW: Nevinson, H.W., *"Women's Vote and Men,"* 3 (1909) 687-696; Kenney, R., *"Women's Suffrage—The Militant Movement in Ruins,"* 13 (1912) 98-108; Fawcett, M.G., *"War and Reconstruction—Women and their Use of the Vote,"* 26 (1918) 260-315; Zangwill, I., *"The Militant Suffragists,"* 15 (1913) 561-577.

12.828
EYE OPENER: 1912 to 1914; vols. 1-2; *superseded by:* **AWAKENER:** Published by the Men's Society for Women's Rights.

12.829
LANCET: Savill, A.F., Moullin, C.W.M. and Horsley, V., *"The Forcible Feeding of Suffrage Prisoners,"* 24 (1912) 549-551.

12.830
SUFFRAGETTE: 1912 to 1915; vols. 1-4. Organ of the Women's Social and Political Union. Edited by Christabel Pankhurst; *continued as:* **BRITANNIA:** 1915 to 1918; vols. 4-7; Kenny, A., *"The Only Remedy: Speech Delivered July 24, 1913,"* 2 (1913) 721; Kenny, A., *"A Real Fraternity. Speech Delivered August 11, 1913,"* 2 (1913) 763.

12.831
Actresses' Franchise League, **ANNUAL REPORT 1912-13**. 1913.

12.832
Chance, Julia Charlotte (Lady), **WOMEN'S SUFFRAGE AND MORALITY**. 1913.

12.833
Chance, Mana (Lady), **THE PREDOMINANCE OF MEN IN THE ANTI-SUFFRAGE FINANCE AND ORGANIZATION**. 1913.

12.834
Clapham Women's Social and Political Union, **ANNUAL REPORT**. 1913.

12.835
Franklin, Margaret Ladd, **THE CASE FOR WOMEN'S SUFFRAGE**. New York, 1913.

12.836
Hanson, Helen B., **FROM EAST TO WEST: WOMEN'S SUFFRAGE IN RELATION TO FOREIGN MISSIONS**. 1913. Hanson believes that the Church's opposition or indifference to the development of the women's movement "is a real stumbling-block in the way of its evangelisation of the world" (p. 1).

12.837
Holmes, Marion, **A.B.C. OF VOTES FOR WOMEN**. 1913. Discusses the importance of gaining the vote to rectify the second-class legal and domestic status of women.

12.838
Jewish League for Women's Suffrage, **LEAFLETS**. [1913, etc.]; **ANNUAL REPORT. 1913-1914**. [1913-1914]; **"THE JEWISH WOMAN IN RELIGIOUS LIFE." A PAPER READ AT THE WOMEN'S CONGRESS IN MUNICH 1912**. 1913. Describes inequality in the Jewish community.

12.839
Kentish Federation, **ANNUAL REPORT**. 1913.

12.840
Moran, Patrick Francis and Cardinal, Archbishop of Sydney, **THE OPINIONS OF TWO CARDINALS (MORAN AND VAUGHAN) ON WOMEN'S SUFFRAGE**. 1913.

12.841
Northern Men's Federation for Women's Suffrage, **DEPUTATION AT BERWICK TO SIR EDWARD GREY OCTOBER 22, 1913**. 1913.

12.842
R., A.J., **THE SUFFRAGE ANNUAL AND WOMEN'S WHO'S WHO**. 1913. Lists suffrage societies and prominent suffragettes. Especially valuable guide.

12.843
Ring, F.C., **WOMEN'S SUFFRAGE AND TEMPERANCE**. 1913.

12.844
Robertson, Margaret, **WORKING MEN AND WOMEN'S SUFFRAGE**. 1913. Working men "do not know that... the 'window smashers' are a mere handful compared to the thousands upon thousands of quiet and orderly women who are working for the Parliamentary vote in constitutional ways" (p. 3).

12.845
Smith, Sybil Mary (Baroness Bicester), **FOR AND AGAINST: A CONVERSATION ON THE SUBJECT OF WOMAN'S SUFFRAGE**. 1913.

12.846
Swanwick, Helena Maria, **THE FUTURE OF THE WOMEN'S MOVEMENT**. 1913.
—*see also:* Swanwick, Helena Maria, **I HAVE BEEN YOUNG**. 1935. Swanwick's autobiography; **DICTIONARY OF LABOUR BIOGRAPHY**: Espinasse, M., *"Swanwick, Helena Maria Lucy (1864-1939) Author, Pacifist, and Suffragist,"* 4 (1974) 168-171.

12.847
Women's Liberal Federation, **WHY MUST THE WOMEN'S LIBERAL FEDERA-TION WORK FOR SUFFRAGE?** 1913; **WHAT SHALL WE DO NEXT?** 1914.

12.848
Women Teachers' Franchise Union, **LEAFLETS**. 1913.

12.849
Wright, Sir Almroth, **THE UNEXPURGATED CASE AGAINST WOMAN SUFFRAGE**. 1913. Claims that immorality and mental disorder are rampant in the suffrage movement, especially among militants.

12.850
AMERICAN POLITICAL SCIENCE REVIEW: Turner, E.R., *"The Woman Suffrage*

Movement in England," 8 (1913) 588-609.

12.851
FRANCISCAN ANNALS AND TERTIARY RECORD: Christich, E., *"Catholic Women and the Vote,"* 38 (1914) 129. "The word 'Catholic' in itself precludes restriction of thought or narrow conception of duty. The Church... is the broadest in intellectual scope, the most insistent on the need for true cultural development, the most tolerant in permission to its members to extend their sphere of action wherever it may be useful or beneficial" (p. 129).

12.852
FREE CHURCH SUFFRAGE TIMES: 1913 to 1915; vols. 1-etc.; *superseded by:* **COMING DAY: THE OFFICIAL ORGAN OF THE FREE CHURCH LEAGUE FOR WOMEN'S SUFFRAGE:** 1916 to 1920; vols. 1-6; *"From the Branches,"* 1 (1914) 75; *"Speech by Rev. R.J. Campbell, M.A., on Woman Suffrage,"* 1 (1914) 71. Expresses disapproval toward violence done in the name of women's suffrage.

12.853
NEW STATESMAN: Fawcett, M.G., *"The Remedy of Political Emancipation,"* Special Supplement (1913) 8-10. The remedy is the vote for women; Pankhurst, C., *"Militancy,"* Special Supplement (1913) 10-11. "The only reason why militancy has not long ago resulted in the conquest of votes for women is that not enough women have been militant" (p. 10); Fawcett, M.G., *"Letter to the Editor Re: Woman Suffrage: The Plea for a Truce,"* 2 (1913) 111. Fawcett pledges support for "truce and amnesty... between the militant suffragists and the government" (p. 111) from the conservative N.U.W.S.S.; Webb, B., *"Voteless Women and Social Revolution,"* 2 (1914) 584-585. Discusses alliance between classes in the women's movement and the need for the press to cover the suffrage issue; Brown, I.J.C., *"Letter to the Editor Re: Voteless Women and the Social Revolution,"* 2 (1914) 687. Questions the validity of Webb's statement that "the votelessness of women is tantamount to a rapidly spreading socialism" (p. 687). Argues that, though socialism includes suffragism, the reverse is not true; Schwimmer, R., *"The British Suffrage Movement as Seen from Abroad,"* 2 (1914) 749-750. A Hungarian woman writes to call an end to militant tactics.

12.854
REVIEW OF REVIEWS: *"The Woman's 'War' in England,"* 43 (1913) 271-272; *"The Woman's Reign of Terror,"* 43 (1913) 537; *"The Commons Vote Against Woman-Suffrage,"* 43 (1913) 661-662; *"Campaign of the 'Wild Women' in England,"* 44 (1914) 25-26.

12.855
SOCIALIST REVIEW: Bensen, T.D., *"Woman, the Vote and the Industrial System,"* 11 (1913) 347-353. Examines the "effect of the enfranchisement of women on the economic relation of the sexes" by juxtaposing capitalist and socialist theories (p. 351); Phillips, M., *"Suffrage and Militancy,"* 11 (1913) 257-262. Questions militant strategies and their effectiveness, concluding that more attention is being given to sensationalized violence by the media and less to the crucial issue of suffrage.

12.856
Lewisham Women's Franchise Club, **PAMPHLETS.** [1914, etc.].

12.857
MacMillan, Chrystal, **FACT VERSUS FANCIES ON WOMAN SUFFRAGE.** 1914.

12.858
South Western Federation, **ANNUAL REPORT**. 1914.

12.859
TORTURE UNDER THE GUISE OF FORCIBLE FEEDING. Glasgow, 1914.

12.860
ANNALS OF THE AMERICAN ACADEMY OF POLITICAL AND SOCIAL SCIENCE: Winsor, M., *"The Militant Suffrage Movement,"* 61 (1914) 134-142.

12.861
CURRENT OPINION: *"The Suffragette Reign of Terror in London,"* 57 (1914) 15-16. Discusses Emmeline Pankhurst's militant crusade for the franchise. "It is imperative to stop the spread of the epidemic of criminal lunacy.... It is having a most detrimental effect on... health. It is a scandal and disgrace to our civilization" (p. 16).

12.862
LIBERAL WOMEN'S REVIEW: 1914. Edited by Mary Somerville. Published by Liberal Women's Suffrage Union. Intended to incite Liberal women to take all possible constitutional means to secure the adoption of Liberal candidates in favor of women's suffrage, and to abstain from working for any anti-suffrage candidates; Cox, V., *"Parliamentary History of Women's Suffrage Movement 1832-1914,"* 3 (1914) 29-33.

12.863
WOMAN'S DREADNOUGHT: 1914 to 1917; vols. 1-4; *superseded by:* **WORKERS' DREADNOUGHT**: 1917 to 1924; vols. 4-11. Published by the East London Federation of Suffragettes and then by the Workers Socialist Federation.

12.864
Knightley, Louisa Mary (Bowater), **THE JOURNALS OF LADY KNIGHTLEY OF FAWSLEY, 1856-1884.** ed. by Julia Cartwright Ady. 1915. Knightley was the first president of the Conservative and Unionist Association for the Franchise of Women, and founder of the Girls' Friendly Society and Working Ladies' Club.

12.865
Seymour, Charles, **ELECTORAL REFORM IN ENGLAND AND WALES: THE DEVELOPMENT OF THE PARLIAMENTARY FRANCHISE, 1832-1885.** New Haven, 1915.

12.866
CATHOLIC SUFFRAGIST: 1915 to 1918; *continued as:* **CATHOLIC CITIZEN**: 1918 to 1943. Organ of St. Joan's Social and Political Alliance; Meynell, A., *"The Catholic Suffragist,"* 1 (1915) 1-2. "The difficult and arduous work of reformers is essentially and fundamentally a moral work. A Catholic suffragist woman is a suffragist on graver grounds and with weightier reasons than any other suffragist in England" (p. 1).

12.867
SKETCH: Pankhurst, E., *"Why Women Should Be Mobilized,"* (March 23, 1915).

12.868
INDEPENDENT SUFFRAGETTE: 1916 to 1917. The Organ of the Independent Women's Social and Political Union.

12.869
THE REPRESENTATION OF THE PEOPLE BILL, 1917. BY A SUFFRAGETTE. 1917.

12.870
Metcalfe, Agnes Edith, WOMAN'S EFFORT. A CHRONICLE OF BRITISH WOMEN'S FIFTY YEARS' STRUGGLE FOR CITIZENSHIP (1865-1914). Oxford, 1917. Comprehensive record that includes a Women's Suffrage Directory and copies of Parliamentary bills. Illustrated with reproductions of cartoons from PUNCH.

12.871
Rooper, Ralph, "Women Enfranchised" in THE MAKING OF WOMEN. OXFORD ESSAYS IN FEMINISM. ed. by Victor Gollancz. 1917.

12.872
Davies, Margaret Llewelyn, THE VOTE AT LAST. 1918. Ramifications of the enfranchisement of qualified women for the working class membership of the Women's Co-operative Guild. ——see also: Gaffin, Jean and Thoms, David, CARING AND SHARING: THE CENTENARY HISTORY OF THE WOMEN'S COOPERATIVE GUILD. 1983.

12.873
Smyth, Ethel Mary, IMPRESSIONS THAT REMAINED: MEMOIRS. 1919; STREAKS OF LIFE. 1921; FEMALE PIPINGS IN EDEN. Edinburgh, 1933; AS TIME WENT ON. 1936; WHAT HAPPENED NEXT. 1940. All autobiographical works that reflect on the suffrage campaign and those who participated in it. Smyth was a prolific composer who also wrote suffrage anthems. ——see also: St. John, Christopher, ETHEL SMYTH: A BIOGRAPHY. 1959.

12.874
Morris, Homer L., PARLIAMENTARY FRANCHISE REFORM IN ENGLAND FROM 1855 TO 1918. New York, 1921. See especially: "Women's Suffrage Becomes a Practical Issue," "Attempts to Enfranchise Women in 1913 and 1914," and "Representation of the People Act 1918."

12.875
Jersey, Lady, FIFTY-ONE YEARS OF VICTORIAN LIFE. 1922. Anti-suffragist.

12.876
Trevelyan, Janet Penrose, THE LIFE OF MRS. HUMPHREY WARD. 1923. See chap. 12 for a discussion of Ward's presidency of the Women's National Anti-Suffrage League, established in 1908.

12.877
Kenney, Annie, MEMOIRS OF A MILITANT. 1924. Kenney was a working-class suffragette. ——see also: Pethick-Lawrence, Frederick William, ...ANNIE KENNEY. CHARACTER SKETCH AND ARTICLE ON "PRISON FACES." [1907].

12.878
Lowther, James William (Viscount Ullswater), A SPEAKER'S COMMENTARIES. 2 vols. 1925.

12.879
Strachey, Ray (pseud. for Rachel Costelloe), WOMEN'S SUFFRAGE AND

WOMEN'S SERVICE. THE HISTORY OF THE LONDON AND NATIONAL SOCIETY FOR WOMEN'S SERVICE. 1927.

12.880
Stephen, Barbara, "Women's Suffrage and the London School Board 1865-1873" in EMILY DAVIES AND GIRTON COLLEGE. by Barbara Stephen. 1927.

12.881
Lang, Elsie M., BRITISH WOMEN IN THE TWENTIETH CENTURY. 1929. See especially: "The Fight for the Franchise."

12.882
Balfour, Frances, NE OBLIVISCARIS. DINNA FORGET. 1930. See vol. 1, chaps. 23 and 24 on women's suffrage. Discusses historical incidents and political victories.

12.883
Fyfe, Henry Hamilton, REVOLT OF WOMEN. 1933.

12.884
Haig, Margaret (Viscountess Rhondda), "On the Outskirts of the Suffrage Movement" in THIS WAS MY WORLD. by Margaret Haig. 1933.

12.885
Sharp, Evelyn, UNFINISHED ADVENTURE. 1933.

12.886
Courtney, Janet, "Suffragists and Suffragettes" in THE WOMEN OF MY TIME. by Janet Courtney. 1934. On Mrs. Humphrey Ward and the Antis.

12.887
Hammond, John L., C.P. SCOTT OF THE MANCHESTER GUARDIAN. New York, 1934. See especially: "Women's Suffrage." "[Scott] was often in sharp controversy with the militant leaders... [but] he was ready to welcome women's suffrage in any form" (p. 102).

12.888
Roper, Esther, ed., PRISON LETTERS OF COUNTESS MARKIEVICZ. 1934.

12.889
Dangerfield, George, "The Women's Rebellion" in THE STRANGE DEATH OF LIBERAL ENGLAND 1910-1914. by George Dangerfield. New York, 1935.

12.890
Chamberlain, Austen, POLITICS FROM THE INSIDE. 1936. Includes letters Chamberlain wrote expressing his anti-suffrage ideas and work.

12.891
NEWSLETTER: 1936; 1938; 1939-1940; 1944; *continued as:* CALLING ALL WOMEN: 1947 to 1949. Organ of the Suffragette Fellowship.

12.892
Oman, Charles, MEMORIES OF VICTORIAN OXFORD. 1941.

12.893
Markham, Violet, RETURN PASSAGE. 1953. Converted from the anti-suffrage

camp because she believed that "Lincoln's principle 'a country cannot be part serf and part free' applied to the relation of men and women as well as to those of black and white" (p. 99).

12.894
Richardson, Mary, **LAUGH A DEFIANCE**. 1953. Richardson's vehemence on the issue of suffrage once led her to slash a Velasquez painting in the National Library. She discusses hostile treatment to the suffragettes.

12.895
Suffragette Fellowship, **IN MEMORIAM. EDYTH HOW-MARTYN**. 1955; **ROLL OF HONOUR: SUFFRAGETTE PRISONERS: 1905-1914**. [c. 1960].

12.896
MANCHESTER REVIEW: Mitchell, H., *"Suffragette Years,"* 7 (1955) 249-260.

12.897
Battiscombe, G., **MRS. GLADSTONE. THE PORTRAIT OF A MARRIAGE**. 1956.

12.898
Bromhead, Peter A., **PRIVATE MEMBERS' BILLS IN THE BRITISH PARLIAMENT**. 1956.

12.899
Fulford, Roger, **VOTES FOR WOMEN. THE STORY OF A STRUGGLE**. 1957. Discusses both militant and conservative activities. See appendix for biographical sketches.

12.900
Phillips, Mary, **THE MILITANT SUFFRAGE CAMPAIGN IN PERSPECTIVE**. 1957.

12.901
Roberts, Charles, "Achievement of Women's Suffrage" in **THE RADICAL COUNTESS. THE HISTORY OF THE LIFE OF ROSALIND COUNTESS OF CARLISLE**. by Charles Roberts. Carlisle, 1962.

12.902
Cross, Colin, **THE LIBERALS IN POINER, 1905-1914**. 1963. General account of policies of the Liberal Party Administration, including those on women's suffrage.

12.903
Coxhead, Eileen Elizabeth, **DAUGHTERS OF ERIN. FIVE WOMEN OF THE IRISH RENASCENCE**. 1965. See pp. 81-122 for an account of Constance Markievicz, an Irish suffragette and political agitator.

12.904
PAST AND PRESENT: Blewett, N., *"The Franchise in the United Kingdom,"* no. 32 (1965) 27-56.

12.905
Dowse, Robert Edward, **LEFT IN THE CENTER: THE INDEPENDENT LABOUR PARTY, 1893-1940**. 1966.

12.906
Hesketh, Phoebe, MY AUNT EDITH. 1966. Story of a militant suffragette.

12.907
Mitchell, David, WOMEN ON THE WARPATH. 1966; THE FIGHTING PANKHURSTS: A STUDY IN TENACITY. New York, 1967.

12.908
Rover, Constance, "The Women's Suffrage Movement in Britain, 1866-1914," Ph.D. diss., Univ. of London, 1966; WOMEN'S SUFFRAGE AND PARTY POLITICS IN BRITAIN 1866-1914. 1967.

12.909
Greenwood, W., THERE WAS A TIME. 1967.

12.910
Marreco, Anne, THE REBEL COUNTESS, THE LIFE AND TIMES OF CONSTANCE MARKIEVICZ. 1967.

12.911
Ramelson, Marion, THE PETTICOAT REBELLION: A CENTURY OF STRUGGLE FOR WOMEN'S RIGHTS. 1967.

12.912
Thompson, Paul, SOCIALISTS, LIBERALS AND LABOUR. 1967.

12.913
Kpzantizis, Judith, compiler, WOMEN IN REVOLT. THE FIGHT FOR EMANCIPATION; A COLLECTION OF CONTEMPORARY DOCUMENTS. 1968.

12.914
Martin, Hazel T., PETTICOAT REBELS. New York, 1968.

12.915
Mitchell, Hannah, THE HARD WAY UP: THE AUTOBIOGRAPHY OF HANNAH MITCHELL, SUFFRAGETTE AND REBEL. ed. by Geoffrey Mitchell. 1968; 1977. Mitchell was a working-class suffrage leader involved in the labor movement in North England.

12.916
HISTORY TODAY: Arnstein, W.L., *"Votes for Women: Myths and Reality. A Study of the Movement for 'Female Emancipation' from the 1860s until 1918,"* 18 (1968) 531-539. Discusses variant politics within the movement.

12.917
Rose, Kenneth, SUPERIOR PERSON. A PORTRAIT OF CURZON AND HIS CIRCLE IN LATE VICTORIAN ENGLAND. 1969.

12.918
Izzard, Molly, A HEROINE IN HER TIME. A LIFE OF DAME GWYNNE-VAUGHAN. 1879-1967. 1970. Izzard founded a Suffrage Society at the University of London.

12.919
Bonney, Nancy, ESSEX WOMEN AND THE CAMPAIGN FOR FEMALE

SUFFRAGE, 1850-1914. 1971.

12.920
Lloyd, Trevor, **SUFFRAGETTES INTERNATIONAL: THE WORLD-WIDE CAMPAIGN FOR WOMEN'S RIGHTS.** 1971.

12.921
Jones, Donald J., "The Asquith Cabinet and Women's Suffrage, 1908-1914," M.A. thesis, Memorial Univ., Canada, 1972. In-depth investigation into the roles played by individual ministers when women suffrage bills were presented. Stress is placed on the growing importance of female enfranchisement as a political problem which eventually threatened the stability of the government.

12.922
Neale, R.S., "Working-Class Women and Women's Suffrage" in **CLASS AND IDEOLOGY IN THE NINETEENTH CENTURY.** by R.S. Neale. 1972. "Militancy was an error but not because it was militant. It was an error because it was militancy directed to obtain objectives too narrowly defined" (p. 144). Neale also discusses class consciousness among the suffragists.

12.923
BULLETIN OF THE SOCIETY FOR THE STUDY OF LABOUR HISTORY: Holmes, C., *"H.M. Hyndman and R.D. Blumenfield: Correspondence in 1913,"* 24 (1972) 27-29. Some of the letters explore the question of women's suffrage.

12.924
Independent Labour Party, **WOMEN IN REBELLION——1900. TWO VIEWS ON CLASS, SOCIALISM AND LIBERATION.** introduction by Suzie Fleming. 1973. This is a reprint of two popular pamphlets, WORKING WOMEN AND THE SUFFRAGE, by Mrs. Wilbaut and WOMAN'S FREEDOM, by Lily Gair Wilkinson. While Wilbaut argued for the vote as a means to emancipate the unpaid housewife, "Wilkinson argued... that the vote wouldn't amount to power" (p. 2). Instead, the latter examined class division, calling for communism as a path towards female emancipation.

12.925
Malmgreen, Gail K., "The Intellectual and Social Origins of the Women's Suffrage Movement in England, 1792-1851," M.A. thesis, Univ. of Rhode Island, 1973; "Women's Suffrage in England: Origins and Alternatives, 1792-1851," M.A. thesis, Hull Univ., 1975.

12.926
Wilson, Alexander, "The Suffrage Movement" in **PRESSURE FROM WITHOUT.** ed. by Patricia Hollis. 1973-1974. Why didn't the NUWSS women lobby more aggressively? As a pressure group, they were perhaps more deferential and less critical of the House of Commons than other groups.

12.927
Raeburn, Antonia, **THE MILITANT SUFFRAGETTES AND THE SUFFRAGETTE VIEW.** 1973; 1975; *reviewed in:* **ORAL HISTORY:** Harrison, B., 2 (1973) 73-76.

12.928
CANADIAN JOURNAL OF HISTORY: Robson, A.P.W., *"The Founding of the National Society for Women's Suffrage, 1866-1867,"* 8 (1973) 1-22. "The painstaking labours of the pioneers of the nineteenth century, if they did not gain women the

vote, achieved for woman the educational, professional, and legal advances which changed her from an inentity to an identity" (p. 1).

12.929
Morgan, David, **SUFFRAGISTS AND LIBERALS: THE POLITICS OF WOMEN SUFFRAGE IN ENGLAND.** Oxford, 1974; 1975.

12.930
Pugh, Martin, "The Background to the Representation of the People Act," Ph.D. diss., Univ. of Bristol, 1974; "Women's Suffrage 1906-1914: The Fruits of Moderation" in **ELECTORAL REFORM IN WAR AND PEACE 1906-1918.** by Martin Pugh. 1978; 1980. Dispels the myth that militant suffragettes had won their campaign by the first world war; **WOMEN'S SUFFRAGE IN BRITAIN 1867-1928.** 1980. "Analyzes the fears... about [women's suffrage]... by both men and women in the Victorian period, and considers how far the social and political obstacles to enfranchisement were overcome before 1914.... Evaluates the contribution made by the militant campaign" (n.p.). ——*see also:* HISTORY: Pugh, M., *"Politics and the Woman's Vote,"* 59 (1974) 358-374.

12.931
Rosen, Andrew, **RISE UP WOMEN! THE MILITANT CAMPAIGN OF THE WOMEN'S SOCIAL AND POLITICAL UNION, 1903-1914.** 1974; 1976. Best work available on the subject.

12.932
Claus, Ruth Freeman, "Militancy in the Suffrage Movement: A Comparison of the English and American Experience," Ph.D. diss., Yale Univ., 1975.

12.933
Harrison, Brian, **SEPARATE SPHERES: THE OPPOSITION TO WOMEN'S SUFFRAGE IN BRITAIN.** 1978; "The Act of Militancy: Violence and the Suffragettes, 1904-1914" in **PEACEABLE KINGDOM: STABILITY AND CHANGE IN MODERN BRITAIN.** Oxford, 1982; "Women's Suffrage at Westminster 1866-1928" in **HIGH AND LOW POLITICS IN MODERN BRITAIN.** ed. by Michael Bentley and John Stevenson. Oxford, 1983. ——*see also:* TIMES LITERARY SUPPLEMENT: *"Men on Women's Side,"* n.v. (Jan. 27, 1978) n.p.

12.934
VICTORIAN PERIODICALS REVIEW: Bostick, T., *"The Press and the Launching of the Women's Suffrage Movement, 1866-1867,"* 13 (1980) 125-131. Examines the enormous influence of women journalists in establishing the women's suffrage movement.

12.935
Davis, Tricia, Durham, Martin, Hall, Catherine, Langan, Mary, and Sutton, David, "'The Public Face of Feminism': Early Twentieth-Century Writings on Women's Suffrage" in **MAKING HISTORIES: STUDIES IN HISTORY WRITING AND POLITICS.** ed. by Richard Johnson, et al. 1982. Considers the past-present relationship between the suffragette struggles of the pre-First World War period and the modern Women's Movement through reading suffragette autobiographies: Emmeline Pankhurst, MY OWN STORY (1914; 1979); Christabel Pankhurst, UNSHACKLED (1959); E. Sylvia Pankhurst, THE SUFFRAGETTE MOVEMENT (1931; 1977); Emmeline Pethick-Lawrence, MY PART IN A CHANGING WORLD (1938); Annie Kenny, MEMORIES OF A MILITANT (1924); Hannah Mitchell, THE HARD WAY UP (1977); Mary R. Richardson, LAUGH A DEFIANCE (1953);

Teresa Billington-Grieg, THE MILITANT SUFFRAGE MOVEMENT (1911); Margaret Bondfield, A LIFE'S WORK (1949); Vera Brittain, TESTAMENT OF EXPERIENCE (1957; 1979). "Modern feminists felt they had little in common with an earlier generation whose work had focused on the entry of women into the public sphere. A second reason is linked to the changing emphasis of the feminist struggle. The struggles of the early twentieth century were centered on the vote; in the past decade the emphasis has shifted... to a recognition of the inadequacy of the analysis of women's oppression which remained at the institutional level, insisting instead on tackling the personal and informal dimensions of a thoroughly patriarchal society" (p. 304).

12.936
WOMEN'S STUDIES INTERNATIONAL FORUM: Caine, B., *"Feminism, Suffrage and the Nineteenth-Century English Women's Movement,"* 5 (1982) 537-550. Explores the relationship between the anti-Contagious Diseases Acts agitation and the development of the suffrage campaign within the women's movement; Jeffreys, S., *"'Free From all Uninvited Touch of Men': Women's Campaigns Around Sexuality, 1880-1914,"* 5 (1982) 629-645. Includes a section, "Sexuality and the Suffrage, 1906-1914." Some of the suffragist organizations, (the Conservative and Unionist Women's Franchise Association, Women's Freedom League, the Men's League for Women's Suffrage, the National Union of Women's Suffrage Societies, the Church League for Women's Suffrage and the Women's Social and Political Union) "were issuing statements on the double standard and prostitution which were practically identical in tone.... the vote was presented as a cure-all for women's grievances" (p. 640); *rpt. as:* REASSESSMENT OF 'FIRST-WAVE' FEMINISM. ed. by Elizabeth Sarah. 1982; Billington, R., *"Ideology and Feminism: Why the Suffragettes were 'Wild Women,'"* 5 (1982) 663-674; Byles, J.M., *"Women's Experience of World War One: Suffragists, Pacifists and Poets,"* 8 (1985) 473-387.

12.937
Spender, Dale, ed., **FEMINIST THEORIES: THREE CENTURIES OF WOMEN'S INTELLECTUAL TRADITIONS.** 1983. Wollstonecraft, Martineau, Bodichon, Butler, Fawcett, Schreiner, Pankhurst (Christabel), and Brittain are included as subjects.

12.938
Garner, Les, **STEPPING STONES TO WOMEN'S LIBERTY: FEMINIST IDEAS IN THE WOMEN'S SUFFRAGE MOVEMENT 1900-1918.** 1984.

12.939
Pugh, Patricia, **EDUCATE, AGITATE, ORGANIZE: 100 YEARS OF FABIAN SOCIALISM.** 1984.

12.940
Durham, Martin, "Suffrage and After: Feminism in the Early Twentieth Century" in **CRISES IN THE BRITISH STATE 1880-1930.** ed. by Mary Langan and Bill Schwarz. 1985.

12.941
Holton, Sandra, **FEMINISM AND DEMOCRACY: WOMEN'S SUFFRAGE AND REFORM POLITICS IN BRITAIN, 1900-1918.** 1986. ——*see also:* Holton, Sandra, "Feminism and Democracy: the NUWSS, 1897-1918," Ph.D. diss., Univ. of Stirling, 1980.

12.942
Delmar, Rosalind, "What's Feminism" in **WHAT IS FEMINISM.** ed. by Juliet Mitchell and Ann Oakley. New York and Toronto, 1986. "Histories of feminism which treat feminism as a social movement tend to concentrate on chronicling the vicissitudes of that movement and subordinate any exploration of the intellectual content of feminism to that main purpose.... To accept, with all its implications, that feminism has not only existed in movements of and for women, but has also been able to exist as an intellectual tendency without a movement, or as a strand within very different movements, is to accept the existence of various forms of feminism (pp. 17-18).... [Problems can derive] from an overstrict identification of feminism with a women's movement, and of the history of feminism with the history of the achievement of the aims of that movement. Such an identification of feminism depends on a definition of feminism as *activity*, whether diffuse or directed to a given end (p. 23).... Instead of a progressive and cumulative history of feminism, it is an historical examination of the dynamics of persistence and change within feminism which is needed.... This inheritance is not simply a part of the past but lives in the present, both as part of the conditions of existence of contemporary feminism, and as a part of that very feminism" (p. 24).... In what form, forms or combinations feminism will survive is not a question which can yet be answered" (p. 29).

12.943
Jalland, Pat, **WOMEN, MARRIAGE AND POLITICS, 1860-1914.** 1986. See her chapter on "Political Wives." "Women's auxiliary political association created in the 1880s played an important role in politicizing women and served as a training ground in the political parties and organization. The original function of the Women's Liberal Federation, the Women's Liberal Unionist Association and the Women's Council of the Primrose League was to organize women as an unpaid party of workers.... Evidence suggests a different interpretation.... From the 1880s the women's political associations encouraged women to debate the female suffrage question.... These auxiliary organizations helped to win for the suffrage cause the sympathy of those women with perhaps the least to gain by the vote but the most to contribute in terms of leadership and influence.... the main suffragist target was the huge Women's Liberal Federation" (p. 216).

12.944
Pugh, Martin, **THE TORIES AND THE PEOPLE 1880-1985.** Oxford, 1986. A major focus is the relationship of the Primrose League to the Tory party. Pugh elaborates his earlier work on the Tories and suffrage, and he also incorporates the pioneer study of Janet Robb, THE PRIMROSE LEAGUE, 1883-1906 (1942); *reviewed in:* **HISTORY WORKSHOP JOURNAL:** Campbell, B., 23 (1987) 198-199. Important review.

12.945
Rubinstein, David, "Introduction" and "Women's Suffrage" in **BEFORE THE SUFFRAGETTES: WOMEN'S EMANCIPATION IN THE 1890'S.** by David Rubinstein. New York, 1986. "I feel that [Andrew] Rosen and [Leslie] Hume... have too lightly dismissed the suffragists of the 1890s. It was in this decade that women first took an important role in party political activity, through the agency of political organizations established in the 1880s. A petition in favour of votes for women secured over a quarter of a million women's signatures by 1896; meetings to support the same end filled the largest halls and crowded into overflow gatherings.... In these respects, and also in terms of a stronger organizational structure, the 1890s marked the start of a new era" (pp. xii-xiii). Compare with Brian Harrison, "Women's Suffrage at Westminster, 1866-1928" in HIGH AND LOW

POLITICS IN MODERN BRITAIN (1983): "The growth-pattern of feminist organizations shows that, after initial success between 1866 and 1871, a long period of decline sets in; this is slow at first, but rapid after the major setback of Gladstone's Reform Bill. Revival begins about 1900 and peaks between 1910 and 1913; thereafter the long period of decline continues up to the Second World War" (p. 87).

12.946
Stevens, Carolyn, "A Suffragette and a Man: Sylvia Pankhurst's Personal and Political Relationship with Keir Harding 1892-1915," Ph.D. diss., Univ. of Rochester, 1986.

12.947
Kent, Susan Kingsley, **SEX AND SUFFRAGE IN BRITAIN 1860-1914.** Princeton, 1987. Discusses the issues and concerns about sexuality that permeated the women's suffrage movement.

12.948
Lacey, Candida Ann, ed., **BARBARA LEIGH SMITH BODICHON AND THE LANGHAM PLACE GROUP.** 1987. Excerpts from writings by Bodichon, Parkes, Bouherett, Faithfull, Craig, Maria Susan Rye, Frances Power Cobbe, Margaret Llewelyn Davies, Elizabeth Garrett, and Elizabeth Blackwell.

12.949
Pierson, Ruth Roach, et al., eds., **WOMEN AND PEACE: THEORETICAL, HISTORICAL AND PRACTICAL PERSPECTIVES.** 1987.

12.950
Kent, Susan Kingsley, **SEX AND SUFFRAGE IN BRITAIN 1860-1914.** Princeton, 1987.